D1201910

THE

WAR OF THE REBELLION:

A COMPILATION OF THE

OFFICIAL RECORDS

OF THE

UNION AND CONFEDERATE ARMIES.

PREPARED, UNDER THE DIRECTION OF THE SECRETARY OF WAR, BY

The late Lieut. Col. **ROBERT N. SCOTT**, Third U. S. Artillery,

PURSUANT TO ACTS OF CONGRESS.

SERIES I—VOLUME XXVII—IN THREE PARTS.
PART I—REPORTS.

WASHINGTON:
GOVERNMENT PRINTING OFFICE.
1889.

Reprinted 1993

Morningside Bookshop

300 sets of Vol. XXVII,
Parts, I, II, III, only
reprinted

This book printed on Glatfelter Acid-Free paper.

MORNINGSIDE HOUSE, INC.
260 Oak Street
Dayton, Ohio 45410

PREFACE.

By an act approved June 23, 1874, Congress made an appropriation "to enable the Secretary of War to begin the publication of the Official Records of the War of the Rebellion, both of the Union and Confederate Armies," and directed him "to have copied for the Public Printer all reports, letters, telegrams, and general orders not heretofore copied or printed, and properly arranged in chronological order."

Appropriations for continuing such preparation have been made from time to time, and the act approved June 16, 1880, has provided "for the printing and binding, under direction of the Secretary of War, of 10,000 copies of a compilation of the Official Records (Union and Confederate) of the War of the Rebellion, so far as the same may be ready for publication, during the fiscal year"; and that "of said number, 7,000 copies shall be for the use of the House of Representatives, 2,000 copies for the use of the Senate, and 1,000 copies for the use of the Executive Departments."*

This compilation will be the first general publication of the military records of the war, and will embrace all official documents that can be obtained by the compiler, and that appear to be of any historical value.

---

* Volumes I to V distributed under act approved June 16, 1880. The act approved August 7, 1882, provides that—

"The volumes of the Official Records of the War of the Rebellion shall be distributed as follows: One thousand copies to the Executive Departments, as now provided by law. One thousand copies for distribution by the Secretary of War among officers of the Army and contributors to the work. Eight thousand three hundred copies shall be sent by the Secretary of War to such libraries, organizations, and individuals as may be designated by the Senators, Representatives, and Delegates of the Forty-seventh Congress. Each Senator shall designate not exceeding twenty-six, and each Representative and Delegate not exceeding twenty-one of such addresses, and the volumes shall be sent thereto from time to time as they are published, until the publication is completed. Senators, Representatives, and Delegates shall inform the Secretary of War in each case how many volumes of those heretofore published they have forwarded to such addresses. The remaining copies of the eleven thousand to be published, and all sets that may not be ordered to be distributed as provided herein, shall be sold by the Secretary of War for cost of publication with ten per cent. added thereto, and the proceeds of such sale shall be covered into the Treasury. If two or more sets of said volumes are ordered to the same address the Secretary of War shall inform the Senators, Representatives, or Delegates, who have designated the same, who thereupon may designate other libraries, organizations, or individuals. The Secretary of War shall report to the first session of the Forty-eighth Congress what volumes of the series heretofore published have not been furnished to such libraries, organizations, and individuals. He shall also inform distributees at whose instance the volumes are sent."

The publication will present the records in the following order of arrangement:

The **1st Series** will embrace the formal reports, both Union and Confederate, of the first seizures of United States property in the Southern States, and of all military operations in the field, with the correspondence, orders, and returns relating specially thereto, and, as proposed is to be accompanied by an Atlas.

In this series the reports will be arranged according to the campaigns and several theaters of operations (in the chronological order of the events), and the Union reports of any event will, as a rule, be immediately followed by the Confederate accounts. The correspondence, &c., not embraced in the "reports" proper will follow (first Union and next Confederate) in chronological order.

The **2d Series** will contain the correspondence, orders, reports, and returns, Union and Confederate, relating to prisoners of war, and (so far as the military authorities were concerned) to State or political prisoners.

The **3d Series** will contain the correspondence, orders, reports, and returns of the Union authorities (embracing their correspondence with the Confederate officials) not relating specially to the subjects of the *first* and *second* series. It will set forth the annual and special reports of the Secretary of War, of the General-in-Chief, and of the chiefs of the several staff corps and departments; the calls for troops, and the correspondence between the national and the several State authorities·

The **4th Series** will exhibit the correspondence, orders, reports, and returns of the Confederate authorities, similar to that indicated for the Union officials, as of the *third* series, but excluding the correspondence between the Union and Confederate authorities given in that series.

ROBERT N. SCOTT,
Major Third Art., and Bvt. Lieut. Col.

WAR DEPARTMENT, *August* 23, 1880.

Approved:

ALEX. RAMSEY,
Secretary of War.

CONTENTS.

CHAPTER XXXIX.

(v)

CONTENTS OF PRECEDING VOLUMES.

VOLUME I.

VOLUME II.

VOLUME III.

VOLUME IV.

VOLUME V.

VOLUME VI.

VOLUME VII.

1863.

	Sunday.	Monday.	Tuesday.	Wednesday.	Thursday.	Friday.	Saturday.		Sunday.	Monday.	Tuesday.	Wednesday.	Thursday.	Friday.	Saturday.
Jan...	....	....	....	....	1	2	3	**July**...	....	....	....	1	2	3	4
	4	5	6	7	8	9	10		5	6	7	8	9	10	11
	11	12	13	14	15	16	17		12	13	14	15	16	17	18
	18	19	20	21	22	23	24		19	20	21	22	23	24	25
	25	26	27	28	29	30	31		26	27	28	29	30	31	....
	....	....	....	....	....	....	....	**Aug**...	....	....	....	....	....	....	1
Feb...	1	2	3	4	5	6	7		2	3	4	5	6	7	8
	8	9	10	11	12	13	14		9	10	11	12	13	14	15
	15	16	17	18	19	20	21		16	17	18	19	20	21	22
	22	23	24	25	26	27	28		23	24	25	26	27	28	29
	....	....	....	....	....	....	....		30	31	....	....	....	....	....
Mar...	1	2	3	4	5	6	7	**Sept**...	....	....	1	2	3	4	5
	8	9	10	11	12	13	14		6	7	8	9	10	11	12
	15	16	17	18	19	20	21		13	14	15	16	17	18	19
	22	23	24	25	26	27	28		20	21	22	23	24	25	26
	29	30	31	....	....	....	....		27	28	29	30	....	....	....
Apr...	....	....	....	1	2	3	4	**Oct**...	....	....	....	....	1	2	3
	5	6	7	8	9	10	11		4	5	6	7	8	9	10
	12	13	14	15	16	17	18		11	12	13	14	15	16	17
	19	20	21	22	23	24	25		18	19	20	21	22	23	24
	26	27	28	29	30	....	....		25	26	27	28	29	30	31
May...	....	....	....	....	....	1	2		....	....	....	....	....	....	....
	3	4	5	6	7	8	9	**Nov**...	1	2	3	4	5	6	7
	10	11	12	13	14	15	16		8	9	10	11	12	13	14
	17	18	19	20	21	22	23		15	16	17	18	19	20	21
	24	25	26	27	28	29	30		22	23	24	25	26	27	28
	31	....	....	....	....	....	....		29	30	....	....	....	....	....
June...	....	1	2	3	4	5	6	**Dec**...	....	....	1	2	3	4	5
	7	8	9	10	11	12	13		6	7	8	9	10	11	12
	14	15	16	17	18	19	20		13	14	15	16	17	18	19
	21	22	23	24	25	26	27		20	21	22	23	24	25	26
	28	29	30	....	....	....	....		27	28	29	30	31	....	....

CHAPTER XXXIX.

OPERATIONS IN NORTH CAROLINA, VIRGINIA, WEST VIRGINIA, MARYLAND, PENNSYLVANIA, AND DEPARTMENT OF THE EAST.

June 3–August 3, 1863.

PART I.

The Gettysburg Campaign.*

SUMMARY OF THE PRINCIPAL EVENTS.†

June 3–Aug. 1, 1863.—The Gettysburg Campaign.

4, 1863.—Skirmish on the Lawyers' road, near Fairfax Court-House, Va.
Skirmish at Frying Pan, Va.

4– 5, 1863.—Expedition from Yorktown to Walkerton and Aylett's, Va.

5– 7, 1863.—Reconnaissance through Gates County, N. C., and down the Chowan River.

6, 1863.—Skirmish near Berryville, Va.

7– 8, 1863.—Expedition from Gainesville, Va.

8, 1863.—Scout from Suffolk, Va., to South Mills, N. C.

9, 1863.—The Departments of the Monongahela and the Susquehanna constituted.

10, 1863.—Capture of the steamer Maple Leaf off Cape Henry, Va.

10, 1863.—Skirmish at Seneca Mills, Md.

Maj. Gen. W. T. H. Brooks, U. S. Army, assumes command of the Department of the Monongahela.

Maj. Gen. Darius N. Couch, U. S. Army, assumes command of the Department of the Susquehanna.

---

*Part I embraces the reports from the Army of the Potomac and Department of Washington relating to the Gettysburg Campaign. Part II embraces the reports relating to that campaign from the Middle Department, Departments of the Susquehanna and West Virginia, and Army of Northern Virginia, together with all reports relating to the other events noted in the Summary.

†Of some of the minor conflicts noted, no circumstantial reports are on file.

June   11, 1863.—Skirmish at Diascund Bridge, Va.
                    Skirmish near Suffolk, Va.
          11–13, 1863.—Expedition from Brightwood, D. C., via Seneca Mills and Pooles-
                    ville, Md., to Leesburg, Aldie, and Chantilly, Va.
          12–18, 1863.—Expedition from Suffolk to the Blackwater, Va.
          14, 1863.—Skirmish at Nine-Mile Ordinary, Va.
          17–18, 1863.—Scout from Rocky Run to Dover and Core Creek, N. C.
          18, 1863.—Scout on the Peninsula, Va.
          18–19, 1863.—Scout from Camp Piatt, on the Big and Little Coal Rivers, W. Va.
          20, 1863.—Skirmish at Diascund Bridge, Va.
          23–28, 1863.—Expedition from Yorktown to the South Anna Bridge, Va., and
                    skirmish.
          24, 1863.—The Department of West Virginia constituted.
          26, 1863.—Skirmish on Loup Creek, W. Va.
          26–27, 1863.—Descent on Portland Harbor, Me.
          28, 1863.—Brig. Gen. Benjamin F. Kelley, U. S. Army, assumes command
                    of the Department of West Virginia.
                    Reconnaissance from Plymouth to Nichol's Mills, N. C.
          29–July 4, 1863.—Confederate expedition to Beverly, W. Va.
July   1, 1863.—Maj. Gen. Daniel H. Hill, C. S. Army, assigned temporarily to
                    command of troops in the Department of Richmond.
          1– 7, 1863.—Expeditions from White House to South Anna River and Bot-
                    tom's Bridge, Va.
          3, 1863.—Suffolk, Va., evacuated by the Union forces.*
          3– 7, 1863.—Raid on the Wilmington and Weldon Railroad, N. C.
          4, 1863.—Skirmish at Fayetteville, W. Va.
          5– 7, 1863.—Expedition from Plymouth to Gardner's Bridge and Williams-
                    ton, N. C.
          8, 1863.—Maj. Gen. Andrew A. Humphreys, U. S. Army, announced as
                    Chief of Staff, Army of the Potomac.
          9, 1863.—Explosion at Fort Lyon, Va.
          —, 1863.—Expedition from Richmond to Mathias Point, Va.
          13–16, 1863.—Reconnaissance from Newport Barracks to Cedar Point and
                    White Oak River, N. C.
                    Draft riots in New York City, Troy, and Boston.
          13–25, 1863.—Expedition from Fayetteville, W. Va., to Wytheville, Va.
          14, 1863.—Maj. Gen. William H. C. Whiting, C. S. Army, assigned to com-
                    mand of the Department of North Carolina.
          15, 1863.—The Departments of North Carolina and of Virginia consolidated.
          17–20, 1863.—Expedition from New Berne to Swift Creek Village, N. C., and
                    skirmish.
          18, 1863.—Maj. Gen. John G. Foster, U. S. Army, assumes command of the
                    Department of Virginia and North Carolina.
                    Maj. Gen. John A. Dix, U. S. Army, assumes command of the
                    Department of the East.
          18–24, 1863.—Expedition from New Berne to Tarborough and Rocky Mount,
                    N. C.
          20, 1863.—Brig. Gen. George W. Getty, U. S. Army, assumes command of
                    the Seventh Army Corps, Department of Virginia and North
                    Carolina.
          21, 1863.—Brig. Gen. John D. Imboden, C. S. Army, assigned to command
                    of the Valley District, Va.
          25, 1863.—Expedition to Gloucester Court-House, Va.

---

*For orders, etc., in relation to, see Series I, Vol. XVIII, pp. 711, 712, 717, 718.

July 25–27, 1863.—Scout to Goose Creek, Va.
      25–31, 1863.—Expedition from New Berne to Winton, and skirmish at Potecasi
              Creek, N. C.
      25–Aug. 3, 1863.—Expedition from Portsmouth, Va., to Jackson, N. C.
      26–29, 1863.—Expedition from Plymouth to Foster's Mills, N. C.
         28, 1863.—Skirmish at Fayetteville, W. Va.
      28–Aug. 3, 1863.—Mosby's operations about Fairfax Court-House, and skirmish
              near Aldie, Va.
         29, 1863.—Brig. Gen. Innis N. Palmer, U. S. Army, assumes command of
              the Eighteenth Army Corps, Department of Virginia and North
              Carolina.
         31, 1863.—Skirmish at Morris' Mills, W. Va.
Aug.   1, 1863.—The Fourth and Seventh Army Corps discontinued.
       1– 8, 1863.—Expedition from Warrenton Junction toward the Blue Ridge
              Mountains, Va.
          2, 1863.—Skirmish at Newtown, Va.

JUNE 3–AUGUST 1, 1863.—The Gettysburg Campaign.

SUMMARY OF THE PRINCIPAL EVENTS.

June   3, 1863.—Skirmish near Fayetteville, Va.
       5–13, 1863.—Skirmishes at Franklin's Crossing (or Deep Run), on the Rappa-
              hannock, Va.
          9, 1863.—Engagements at Brandy Station (or Fleetwood) and Beverly Ford,
              Va.
              Skirmish at Stevensburg, Va.
         12, 1863.—Skirmishes at Newtown, Cedarville, and Middletown, Va.
         13, 1863.—Skirmish at White Post, Va.
              Skirmish at Berryville, Va.
              Skirmish at Opequon Creek, near Winchester, Va.
              Skirmish at Bunker Hill, W. Va.
      13–15, 1863.—Engagement at Winchester, Va.
         14, 1863.—Skirmish at Berryville, Va.
              Skirmish at Martinsburg, W. Va.
         15, 1863.—Skirmish near Williamsport, Md.
         17, 1863.—Skirmishes at Catoctin Creek and Point of Rocks, Md.
              Skirmish at Thoroughfare Gap, Va.
              Action at Aldie, Va.
      17–18, 1863.—Skirmishes at and near Middleburg, Va.
         18, 1863.—Skirmish near Aldie, Va.
         19, 1863.—Action at Middleburg, Va.
         20, 1863.—Skirmish at Middletown, Md.
         21, 1863.—Skirmish near Gainesville, Va.
              Skirmish at Frederick, Md.
              Engagement at Upperville, Va.
      21–25, 1863.—Skirmishes at and about Thoroughfare Gap and Hay Market, Va.
         22, 1863.—Skirmish near Dover, Va.
              Skirmish at Greencastle, Pa.
              Skirmish near Aldie, Va.
         24, 1863.—Skirmish at Sharpsburg, Md.
         25, 1863.—Skirmish near McConnellsburg, Pa.
         26, 1863.—Skirmish near Gettysburg, Pa.

June   27, 1863.—Skirmish near Fairfax Court-House, Va.
          28, 1863.—Maj. Gen. George G. Meade relieves Maj. Gen. Joseph Hooker
                    in command of the Army of the Potomac.
                    Skirmish between Offutt's Cross-Roads and Seneca, Md.
                    Skirmish near Rockville, Md.
                    Skirmish at Fountain Dale, Pa.
                    Skirmish at Wrightsville, Pa.
       28–29, 1863.—Skirmish near Oyster Point, Pa.
                    Affair on the Little River Turnpike, Va.
          29, 1863.—Skirmish at McConnellsburg, Pa.
                    Affairs at Lisbon and Poplar Springs, Md.
                    Skirmish at Westminster, Md.
                    Skirmish at Muddy Branch, Md.
          30, 1863.—Skirmish at Sporting Hill, near Harrisburg, Pa.
                    Skirmish at Fairfield, Pa.
                    Skirmish at Westminster, Md.
                    Action at Hanover, Pa.
                    Evacuation of Maryland Heights, Md.
July   1, 1863.—Skirmish at Carlisle, Pa.
          1–3, 1863.—Battle of Gettysburg, Pa.
            2, 1863.—Skirmish near Chambersburg, Pa.
                    Skirmish at Hunterstown, Pa.
            3, 1863.—Action at Fairfield, Pa.
            4, 1863.—Action at Monterey Gap, Pa.
                    Skirmish at Fairfield Gap, Pa.
                    Skirmish near Emmitsburg, Md.
            5, 1863.—Skirmish at Smithsburg, Md.
                    Skirmish near Green Oak, Pa.
                    Skirmish near Mercersburg, Pa.
                    Skirmish near Fairfield, Pa.
                    Skirmish near Greencastle, Pa.
                    Skirmish at Cunningham's Cross-Roads, Pa.
                    Skirmish at Stevens' Furnace (or Caledonia Iron Works), Pa.
            6, 1863.—Action at Hagerstown, Md.
                    Action at Williamsport, Md.
            7, 1863.—Skirmish at Downsville, Md.
                    Skirmish at Harper's Ferry, W. Va.
                    Reoccupation of Maryland Heights, Md.
                    Skirmish at Funkstown, Md.
            8, 1863.—Action at Boonsborough, Md.
                    Skirmish near Williamsport, Md.
            9, 1863.—Skirmish at Benevola (or Beaver Creek), Md.
           10, 1863.—Skirmish at Old Antietam Forge, near Leitersburg, Md.
                    Skirmish near Clear Spring, Md.
       10–13, 1863.—Skirmishes at and near Hagerstown, Md.
                    Skirmishes at Jones' Cross-Roads, near Williamsport, Md.
                    Skirmishes at and near Funkstown, Md.
       11–14, 1863.—Reconnaissance to, and skirmish (12th) at, Ashby's Gap, Va.
           14, 1863.—Skirmish near Williamsport, Md.
                    Skirmish near Harper's Ferry, W. Va.
                    Action at Falling Waters, Md.
           15, 1863.—Skirmish at Halltown, W. Va.
                    Skirmish at Shepherdstown, W. Va.
           16, 1863.—Skirmish at Shanghai, W. Va.

July   16, 1863.—Action at Shepherdstown, W. Va.
          17, 1863.—Skirmish near North Mountain Station, W. Va.
                   Skirmish at Snicker's Gap, Va.
       18-19, 1863.—Skirmishes at and near Hedgesville and Martinsburg, W. Va.
          20, 1863.—Skirmish near Berry's Ferry, Va.
                   Skirmish at Ashby's Gap, Va.
       21-22, 1863.—Skirmishes at Manassas Gap, Va.
                   Skirmishes at Chester Gap, Va.
          23 1863.—Action at Wapping Heights, Manassas Gap, Va.
                   Skirmish near Gaines' Cross-Roads, Va.
                   Skirmish near Snicker's Gap, Va.
                   Skirmish near Chester Gap, Va.
          24, 1863.—Skirmish at Battle Mountain, near Newby's Cross-Roads, Va.
          25, 1863.—Skirmish at Barbee's Cross-Roads, Va.
       31-Aug. 1, 1863.—Skirmishes at Kelly's Ford, Va.
Aug.   1, 1863.—Action at Brandy Station, Va.

REPORTS.

GENERAL REPORTS.

No. 1.—Maj. Gen. Henry W. Halleck, General-in-Chief, U. S. Army, including operations in Southeastern Virginia and West Virginia.
No. 2.—Brig. Gen. Hermann Haupt, U. S. Army, in charge of Military Railway Department.
No. 3.—Medical Inspector John M. Cuyler, U. S. Army.
No. 4.—Medical Inspector Edward P. Vollum, U. S. Army.

ARMY OF THE POTOMAC.

No. 5.—Maj. Gen. Joseph Hooker, U. S. Army, commanding Army of the Potomac, of operations June 3-27, and correspondence with the authorities in Washington.
No. 6.—Maj. Gen. George G. Meade, U. S. Army, commanding Army of the Potomac, of operations June 28-August 3, and correspondence with the authorities in Washington, etc.
No. 7.—Itinerary of the Army of the Potomac and co-operating forces, June 5-July 31.
No. 8.—Abstract from returns of the Army of the Potomac, June 10-July 31.
No. 9.—Organization of the Army of the Potomac at the battle of Gettysburg, July 1-3.
No. 10.—Return of Casualties in the Union forces at Brandy Station (Fleetwood), Beverly Ford, and Stevensburg, Va., June 9.
No. 11.—Return of Casualties in the Union forces at Aldie, Va., June 17.
No. 12.—Return of Casualties in the Union forces at Upperville, Va., June 21.
No. 13.—Return of Casualties in the Union forces at Gettysburg, Pa., July 1-3.
No. 14.—Return of Casualties in the Union forces at Wapping Heights, Manassas Gap, Va., July 23.
No. 15.—General Return of Casualties in the Union forces during the Gettysburg Campaign, June 3-August 1.
No. 16.—Surg. Jonathan Letterman, U. S. Army, Medical Director, Army of the Potomac.
No. 17.—Capt. Lemuel B. Norton, Chief Signal Officer.
No. 18.—Capt. William J. L. Nicodemus, Signal Officer.
No. 19.—Capt. Nahum Daniels, Signal Officer.

No. 20.—Capt. William G. McCreary, Signal Officer.

No. 21.—Lieut. George A. Fisher, Acting Signal Officer.

No. 22.—Lieut. Ephraim A. Briggs, Acting Signal Officer.

No. 23.—Lieut. Julius M. Swain, Acting Signal Officer.

No. 24.—Brig. Gen. Rufus Ingalls, U. S. Army, Chief Quartermaster.

No. 25.—Brig. Gen. Marsena R. Patrick, U. S. Army, Provost-Marshal-General.

No. 26.—Lieut. John R. Edie, U. S. Ordnance Department, Acting Chief Ordnance Officer.

No. 27.—Brig. Gen. Henry W. Benham, U. S. Army, commanding Engineer Brigade.

No. 28.—Brig. Gen. Henry J. Hunt, U. S. Army, Chief of Artillery.

No. 29.—Maj. Gen. Abner Doubleday, U. S. Army, commanding Third Division of, and First Army Corps.

No. 30.—Maj. Gen. John Newton, U. S. Army, commanding First Army Corps.

No. 31.—Lieut. Joseph G. Rosengarten, One hundred and twenty-first Pennsylvania Infantry, Ordnance Officer.

No. 32.—Brig. Gen. James S. Wadsworth, U. S. Army, commanding First Division.

No. 33.—Col. Henry A. Morrow, Twenty-fourth Michigan Infantry, First Brigade.

No. 34.—Maj. John Mansfield, Second Wisconsin Infantry.

No. 35.—Lieut. Col. Rufus R. Dawes, Sixth Wisconsin Infantry.

No. 36.—Col. William W. Robinson, Seventh Wisconsin Infantry.

No. 37.—Brig. Gen. Lysander Cutler, U. S. Army, commanding Second Brigade.

No. 38.—Col. Ira G. Grover, Seventh Indiana Infantry.

No. 39.—Capt. John E. Cook, Seventy-sixth New York Infantry.

No. 40.—Col. Edward B. Fowler, Eighty-fourth New York Infantry (Fourteenth Militia).

No. 41.—Maj. Edward Pye, Ninety-fifth New York Infantry.

No. 42.—Col. J. William Hofmann, Fifty-sixth Pennsylvania Infantry.

No. 43.—Brig. Gen. John C. Robinson, U. S. Army, commanding Second Division.

No. 44.—Col. Richard Coulter, Eleventh Pennsylvania Infantry, commanding regiment and First Brigade.

No. 45.—Lieut. Col. Augustus B. Farnham, Sixteenth Maine Infantry.

No. 46.—Lieut. Col. N. Walter Batchelder, Thirteenth Massachusetts Infantry.

No. 47.—Maj. Samuel A. Moffett, Ninety-fourth New York Infantry.

No. 48.—Col. Gilbert G. Prey, One hundred and fourth New York Infantry.

No. 49.—Capt. Jacob J. Bierer, Eleventh Pennsylvania Infantry.

No. 50.—Lieut. Col. James MacThomson, One hundred and seventh Pennsylvania Infantry.

No. 51.—Capt. Emanuel D. Roath, One hundred and seventh Pennsylvania Infantry.

No. 52.—Brig. Gen. Henry Baxter, U. S. Army, commanding Second Brigade.

No. 53.—Col. Charles Wheelock, Ninety-seventh New York Infantry.

No. 54.—Capt. Edmund Y. Patterson, Eighty-eighth Pennsylvania Infantry.

No. 55.—Brig. Gen. Thomas A. Rowley, U. S. Army, commanding Third Division.

No. 56.—Col. Chapman Biddle, One hundred and twenty-first Pennsylvania Infantry, commanding regiment and First Brigade.

No. 57.—Col. Theodore B. Gates, Eightieth New York Infantry (Twentieth Militia).

No. 58.—Lieut. Col. Alexander Biddle, One hundred and twenty-first Pennsylvania Infantry.

No. 59.—Lieut. Col. Alfred B. McCalmont, One hundred and forty-second Pennsylvania Infantry.

No. 60.—Lieut. Col. George F. McFarland, One hundred and fifty-first Pennsylvania Infantry.

No. 61.—Col. Roy Stone, One hundred and forty-ninth Pennsylvania Infantry, commanding Second Brigade.

No. 62.—Col. Langhorne Wister, One hundred and fiftieth Pennsylvania Infantry, commanding Second Brigade.

No. 63.—Col. Edmund L. Dana, One hundred and forty-third Pennsylvania Infantry, commanding Second Brigade.

No. 64.—Lieut. Col. John D. Musser, One hundred and forty-third Pennsylvania Infantry.

No. 65.—Lieut. Col. Walton Dwight, One hundred and forty-ninth Pennsylvania Infantry.

No. 66.—Capt. John Irvin, One hundred and forty-ninth Pennsylvania Infantry.

No. 67.—Lieut. Col. Henry S. Huidekoper, One hundred and fiftieth Pennsylvania Infantry.

No. 68.—Capt. George W. Jones, One hundred and fiftieth Pennsylvania Infantry.

No. 69.—Brig. Gen. George J. Stannard, U. S. Army, commanding Third Brigade.

No. 70.—Col. Francis V. Randall, Thirteenth Vermont Infantry.

No. 71.—Col. Charles S. Wainwright, First New York Light Artillery, commanding Artillery Brigade, First Army Corps.

No. 72.—Capt. James A. Hall, Second Maine Battery.

No. 73.—Lieut. Edward N. Whittier, Fifth Maine Battery.

No. 74.—Lieut. George Breck, Battery L, First New York Light Artillery.

No. 75.—Capt. James H. Cooper, Battery B, First Pennsylvania Light Artillery.

No. 76.—Maj. Gen. Winfield S. Hancock, U. S. Army, commanding Second Army Corps.

No. 77.—Brig. Gen. John C. Caldwell, U. S. Army, commanding First Division.

No. 78.—Col. H. Boyd McKeen, Eighty-first Pennsylvania Infantry, commanding First Brigade.

No. 79.—Maj. Richard E. Cross, Fifth New Hampshire Infantry.

No. 80.—Lieut. Col. K. Oscar Broady, Sixty-first New York Infantry.

No. 81.—Lieut. Col. Amos Stroh, Eighty-first Pennsylvania Infantry.

No. 82.—Col. Patrick Kelly, Eighty-eighth New York Infantry, commanding Second Brigade.

No. 83.—Col. Richard Byrnes, Twenty-eighth Massachusetts Infantry.

No. 84.—Capt. Thomas Touhy, Sixty-third New York Infantry.

No. 85.—Lieut. James J. Smith, Sixty-ninth New York Infantry.

No. 86.—Capt. Denis F. Burke, Eighty-eighth New York Infantry.

No. 87.—Maj. St. Clair A. Mulholland, One hundred and sixteenth Pennsylvania Infantry.

No. 88.—Lieut. Col. John Fraser, One hundred and fortieth Pennsylvania Infantry, commanding regiment and Third Brigade.

No. 89.—Capt. William Scherrer, Fifty-second New York Infantry.

No. 90.—Lieut. Col. Alford B. Chapman, Fifty-seventh New York Infantry.

No. 91.—Maj. Peter Nelson, Sixty-sixth New York Infantry.

No. 92.—Col. John R. Brooke, Fifty-third Pennsylvania Infantry, commanding Fourth Brigade.

No. 93.—Col. William P. Baily, Second Delaware Infantry.

No. 94.—Maj. Leman W. Bradley, Sixty-fourth New York Infantry.

No. 95.—Lieut. Col. Richards McMichael, Fifty-third Pennsylvania Infantry.

No. 96.—Capt. John W. Reynolds, One hundred and forty-fifth Pennsylvania Infantry.

No. 97.—Capt. Moses W. Oliver, One hundred and forty-fifth Pennsylvania Infantry.

No. 98.—Brig. Gen. John Gibbon, U. S. Army, commanding Second Division of, and Second Army Corps.

No. 99.—Brig. Gen. William Harrow, U. S. Army, commanding Second Division.

No. 100.—Col. Francis E. Heath, Nineteenth Maine Infantry.

No. 101.—Lieut. Col. George C. Joslin, Fifteenth Massachusetts Infantry.

No. 102.—Capt. Henry C. Coates, First Minnesota Infantry.

No. 103.—Capt. John Darrow, Eighty-second New York Infantry (Second Militia).

No. 104.—Brig. Gen. Alexander S. Webb, U. S. Army, commanding Second Brigade.

No. 105.—Capt. William Davis, Sixty-ninth Pennsylvania Infantry.

No. 106.—Col. R. Penn Smith, Seventy-first Pennsylvania Infantry.

No. 107.—Lieut. Col. Theodore Hesser, Seventy-second Pennsylvania Infantry.

No. 108.—Lieut. Col. William L. Curry, One hundred and sixth Pennsylvania Infantry.

No. 109.—Col. Norman J. Hall, Seventh Michigan Infantry, commanding Third Brigade.

No. 110.—Col. Arthur F. Devereux, Nineteenth Massachusetts Infantry.

No. 111.—Capt. Henry L. Abbott, Twentieth Massachusetts Infantry.

No. 112.—Maj. Sylvanus W. Curtis, Seventh Michigan Infantry.

No. 113.—Col. James E. Mallon, Forty-second New York Infantry.

No. 114.—Capt. William McFadden, Fifty-ninth New York Infantry.

No. 115.—Brig. Gen. Alexander Hays, U. S. Army, commanding Third Division.

No. 116.—Col. Samuel S. Carroll, Eighth Ohio Infantry, commanding First Brigade.

No. 117.—Col. John Coons, Fourteenth Indiana Infantry.

No. 118.—Capt. Nathan Willard, Fourteenth Indiana Infantry, commanding Pioneer Corps.

No. 119.—Lieut. Col. Leonard W. Carpenter, Fourth Ohio Infantry.

No. 120.—Lieut. Col. Franklin Sawyer, Eighth Ohio Infantry.

No. 121.—Capt. Alfred T. Craig, Eighth Ohio Infantry, commanding Provost Guard.

No. 122.—Lieut. Col. Jonathan H. Lockwood, Seventh West Virginia Infantry.

No. 123.—Col. Thomas A. Smyth, First Delaware Infantry, commanding Second Brigade.

No. 124.—Maj. Theodore G. Ellis, Fourteenth Connecticut Infantry.

No. 125.—Lieut. John T. Dent, First Delaware Infantry.

No. 126.—Maj. John T. Hill, Twelfth New Jersey Infantry.

No. 127.—Maj. George F. Hopper, Tenth New York Infantry.

No. 128.—Lieut. Col. James M. Bull, One hundred and twenty-sixth New York Infantry, commanding Third Brigade.

No. 129.—Col. Clinton D. MacDougall, One hundred and Eleventh New York Infantry.

No. 130.—Capt. Aaron P. Seeley, One hundred and Eleventh New York Infantry.

No. 131.—Lieut. Harry L. Haskell, One hundred and twenty-fifth New York Infantry.

No. 132.—Capt. John G. Hazard, First Rhode Island Light Artillery, commanding Artillery Brigade, Second Army Corps.

No. 133.—Maj. Gen. David B. Birney, U. S. Army, commanding First Division of, and Third Army Corps.

No. 134.—Maj. Gen. William H. French, U. S. Army, commanding Third Army Corps.

No. 135.—Brig. Gen. J. H. Hobart Ward, U. S. Army, commanding Second Brigade and First Division.

No. 136.—Capt. Alanson H. Nelson, Fifty-seventh Pennsylvania Infantry, First Brigade.

No. 137.—Maj. John A. Danks, Sixty-third Pennsylvania Infantry.

No. 138.—Col. Andrew H. Tippin, Sixty-eighth Pennsylvania Infantry.

No. 139.—Col. Calvin A. Craig, One hundred and fifth Pennsylvania Infantry.

No. 140.—Capt. Edward R. Bowen, One hundred and fourteenth Pennsylvania Infantry.

No. 141.—Col. Henry J. Madill, One hundred and forty-first Pennsylvania Infantry.
No. 142.—Lieut. Col. William C. L. Taylor, Twentieth Indiana Infantry, Second Brigade.
No. 143.—Col. Moses B. Lakeman, Third Maine Infantry.
No. 144.—Lieut. Charles F. Sawyer, Fourth Maine Infantry.
No. 145.—Capt. Edwin Libby, Fourth Maine Infantry.
No. 146.—Lieut. Col. Benjamin L. Higgins, Eighty-sixth New York Infantry.
No. 147.—Lieut. Col. Francis M. Cummins, One hundred and twenty-fourth New York Infantry.
No. 148.—Maj. John W. Moore, Ninety-ninth Pennsylvania Infantry.
No. 149.—Col. Hiram Berdan, First U. S. Sharpshooters, commanding First and Second U. S. Sharpshooters.
No. 150.—Lieut. Col. Casper Trepp, First U. S. Sharpshooters.
No. 151.—Maj. Homer R. Stoughton, Second U. S. Sharpshooters.
No. 152.—Col. P. Regis de Trobriand, Fifty-fifth New York Infantry, commanding Third Brigade.
No. 153.—Lieut. Col. Charles B. Merrill, Seventeenth Maine Infantry.
No. 154.—Lieut. Col. Edwin S. Pierce, Third Michigan Infantry.
No. 155.—Lieut. Col. John Pulford, Fifth Michigan Infantry.
No. 156.—Col. Thomas W. Egan, Fortieth New York Infantry.
No. 157.—Maj. Isaac Rogers, One hundred and tenth Pennsylvania Infantry.
No. 158.—Brig. Gen. Andrew A. Humphreys, U. S. Army, commanding Second Division.
No. 159.—Brig. Gen. Henry Prince, U. S. Army, commanding Second Division.
No. 160.—Brig. Gen. Joseph B. Carr, U. S. Army, commanding First Brigade.
No. 161.—Lieut. Col. Clark B. Baldwin, First Massachusetts Infantry.
No. 162.—Lieut. Col. Porter D. Tripp, Eleventh Massachusetts Infantry.
No. 163.—Capt. Matthew Donovan, Sixteenth Massachusetts Infantry.
No. 164.—Col. Robert McAllister, Eleventh New Jersey Infantry.
No. 165.—Lieut. John Schoonover, Eleventh New Jersey Infantry.
No. 166.—Capt. William B. Dunning, Eleventh New Jersey Infantry.
No. 167.—Maj. Robert L. Bodine, Twenty-sixth Pennsylvania Infantry.
No. 168.—Lieut. Col. Milton Opp, Eighty-fourth Pennsylvania Infantry.
No. 169.—Col. William R. Brewster, Seventy-third New York Infantry commanding Second Brigade.
No. 170.—Maj. William H. Hugo, Seventieth New York Infantry.
No. 171.—Col. Henry L. Potter, Seventy-first New York Infantry.
No. 172.—Col. John S. Austin, Seventy-second New York Infantry.
No. 173.—Capt. Abram L. Lockwood, One hundred and twentieth New York Infantry.
No. 174.—Col. George C. Burling, Sixth New Jersey Infantry, commanding Third Brigade.
No. 175.—Col. Edward L. Bailey, Second New Hampshire Infantry.
No. 176.—Capt. Henry H. Woolsey and Col. William J. Sewell, Fifth New Jersey Infantry.
No. 177.—Lieut. Col. Stephen R Gilkyson, Sixth New Jersey Infantry.
No. 178.—Maj. Frederick Cooper, Seventh New Jersey Infantry.
No. 179.—Brig. Gen. Washington L. Elliott, U. S. Army, commanding Third Division.
No. 180.—Col. Benjamin F. Smith, One hundred and twenty-sixth Ohio Infantry, commanding Third Brigade.
No. 181.—Capt. George E. Randolph, First Rhode Island Light Artillery, commanding Artillery Brigade, Third Army Corps.
No. 182.—Capt. A. Judson Clark, Battery B, First New Jersey Light Artillery.
No. 183.—Capt. George B. Winslow, Battery D, First New York Light Artillery.

No. 184.—Capt. James E. Smith, Fourth New York Battery.

No. 185.—Lieut. Benjamin Freeborn, Battery E, First Rhode Island Light Artillery.

No. 186.—Lieut. Robert James, Battery K, Fourth U. S. Artillery.

No. 187.—Maj. Gen. George Sykes, U. S. Army, commanding Fifth Army Corps.

No. 188.—Capt. James A. Bates, Chief Ambulance Officer.

No. 189.—Brig. Gen. James Barnes, U. S. Army, commanding First Division.

No. 190.—Brig. Gen. Charles Griffin, U. S. Army, commanding First Division.

No. 191.—Lieut. Joseph C. Ayer, Chief Ambulance Officer, First Division.

No. 192.—Col. William S. Tilton, Twenty-second Massachusetts Infantry, commanding First Brigade.

No. 193.—Col. Jacob B. Sweitzer, Sixty-second Pennsylvania Infantry, commanding Second Brigade.

No. 194.—Col. Strong Vincent, Eighty-third Pennsylvania Infantry, commanding Third Brigade.

No. 195.—Col. James C. Rice, Forty-fourth New York Infantry, commanding regiment and Third Brigade.

No. 196.—Col. Joshua L. Chamberlain, Twentieth Maine Infantry.

No. 197.—Capt. Atherton W. Clark, Twentieth Maine Infantry.

No. 198.—Lieut. Col. Norval E. Welch, Sixteenth Michigan Infantry.

No. 199.—Maj. Robert T. Elliott, Sixteenth Michigan Infantry.

No. 200.—Lieut. Col. Freeman Conner, Forty-fourth New York Infantry.

No. 201.—Capt. Orpheus S. Woodward, Eighty-third Pennsylvania Infantry.

No. 202.—Maj. William H. Lamont, Eighty-third Pennsylvania Infantry.

No. 203.—Brig. Gen. Romeyn B. Ayres, U. S. Army, commanding Second Division.

No. 204.—Col. Hannibal Day, Sixth U. S. Infantry, commanding First Brigade.

No. 205.—Capt. Andrew Sheridan, Third U. S. Infantry

No. 206.—Capt. Julius W. Adams, jr., Fourth U. S. Infantry.

No. 207.—Capt. Levi C. Bootes, Sixth U. S. Infantry.

No. 208.—Capt. Thomas S. Dunn, Twelfth U. S. Infantry.

No. 209.—Capt. W. Harvey Brown, Fourteenth U. S. Infantry.

No. 210.—Maj. Grotius R. Giddings, Fourteenth U. S. Infantry.

No. 211.—Col. Sidney Burbank, Second U. S. Infantry, commanding Second Brigade.

No. 212.—Maj. Arthur T. Lee, Second U. S. Infantry.

No. 213.—Capt. David P. Hancock, Seventh U. S. Infantry.

No. 214.—Capt. William Clinton, Tenth U. S. Infantry.

No. 215.—Maj. De Lancey Floyd-Jones, Eleventh U. S. Infantry.

No. 216.—Lieut. Col. J. Durell Greene, Seventeenth U. S. Infantry.

No. 217.—Col. Kenner Garrard, One hundred and forty-sixth New York Infantry, commanding Third Brigade.

No. 218.—Brig. Gen. Samuel W. Crawford, U. S. Army, commanding Third Division.

No. 219.—Col. William McCandless, Second Pennsylvania Reserves, commanding First Brigade.

No. 220.—Col. Joseph W. Fisher, Fifth Pennsylvania Reserves, commanding Third Brigade.

No. 221.—Capt. Augustus P. Martin, Third Massachusetts Battery, commanding Artillery Brigade, Fifth Army Corps.

No. 222.—Capt. Frank C. Gibbs, Battery L, First Ohio Light Artillery.

No. 223.—Maj. Gen. John Sedgwick, U. S. Army, commanding Sixth Army Corps.

No. 224.—Brig. Gen. Horatio G. Wright, U. S. Army, commanding First Division.

No. 225.—Brig. Gen. Alfred T. A. Torbert, U. S. Army, commanding First Brigade.

No. 226.—Brig. Gen. Joseph J. Bartlett, U. S. Army, commanding Second Brigade, First Division, and Third Division.

No. 227.—Col. Emory Upton, One hundred and twenty-first New York Infantry.

No. 228.—Brig. Gen. David A. Russell, U. S. Army, commanding Third Brigade.

No. 229.—Brig. Gen. Albion P. Howe, U. S. Army, commanding Second Division.

No. 230.—Col. Lewis A. Grant, Fifth Vermont Infantry, commanding Second Brigade.

No. 231.—Brig. Gen. Thomas H. Neill, U. S. Army, commanding Third Brigade and Light Division.

No. 232.—Brig. Gen. Alexander Shaler, U. S. Army, commanding First Brigade, Third Division.

No. 233.—Col. Horatio Rogers, jr., Second Rhode Island Infantry, Second Brigade.

No. 234.—Col. David J. Nevin, Sixty-second New York Infantry, commanding Third Brigade.

No. 235.—Maj. John B. Kohler, Ninety-eighth Pennsylvania Infantry.

No. 236.—Col. John W. Patterson, One hundred and second Pennsylvania Infantry.

No. 237.—Lieut. Col. William H. Moody, One hundred and thirty-ninth Pennsylvania Infantry.

No. 238.—Capt. William H. McCartney, First Massachusetts Battery, Artillery Brigade, Sixth Army Corps.

No. 239.—Capt. Andrew Cowan, First New York Battery.

No. 240.—Capt. William A. Harn, Third New York Battery.

No. 241.—Capt. Richard Waterman, Battery C, First Rhode Island Light Artillery.

No. 242.—Capt. George W. Adams, Battery G, First Rhode Island Light Artillery.

No. 243.—Maj. Gen. Oliver O. Howard, U. S. Army, commanding Eleventh Army Corps, with congratulatory order.

No. 244.—Brig. Gen. Adelbert Ames, U. S. Army, commanding Second Brigade and First Division.

No. 245.—Lieut. Col. Detleo von Einsiedel, Forty-first New York Infantry, First Brigade.

No. 246.—Col. Andrew L. Harris, Seventy-fifth Ohio Infantry, commanding regiment and Second Brigade.

No. 247.—Maj. Allen G. Brady, Seventeenth Connecticut Infantry.

No. 248.—Lieut. Israel White, Twenty-fifth Ohio Infantry.

No. 249.—Capt. John M. Lutz, One hundred and seventh Ohio Infantry.

No. 250.—Brig. Gen. Adolph von Steinwehr, U. S. Army, commanding Second Division.

No. 251.—Col. Orland Smith, Seventy-third Ohio Infantry, commanding Second Brigade.

No. 252.—Col. James Wood, jr., One hundred and thirty-sixth New York Infantry.

No. 253.—Maj. Gen. Carl Schurz, U. S. Army, commanding Third Division.

No. 254.—Brig. Gen. Hector Tyndale, U. S. Army, commanding First Brigade.

No. 255.—Col. Frederick Hecker, Eighty-second Illinois Infantry.

No. 256.—Lieut. Col. Adolphus Dobke, Forty-fifth New York Infantry.

No. 257.—Col. Horace Boughton, One hundred and forty-third New York Infantry.

No. 258.—Lieut. Col. William H. H. Bown, Sixty-first Ohio Infantry.

No. 259.—Capt. Emil Koenig, Fifty-eighth New York Infantry, Second Brigade.

No. 260.—Maj. Benjamin A. Willis, One hundred and nineteenth New York Infantry.

No. 261.—Lieut. Col. David Thomson, Eighty-second Ohio Infantry.

No. 262.—Maj. August Ledig, Seventy-fifth Pennsylvania Infantry.

No. 263.—Col. William H. Jacobs, Twenty-sixth Wisconsin Infantry.

No. 264.—Maj. Thomas W. Osborn, First New York Light Artillery, commanding Artillery Brigade, Eleventh Army Corps.

No. 265.—Capt. Michael Wiedrich, Battery I, First New York Light Artillery.

No. 266.—Lieut. William Wheeler, Thirteenth New York Battery.

No. 354.—Capt. William A. Corrie, Eighth Pennsylvania Cavalry.
No. 355.—Col. J. Irvin Gregg, Sixteenth Pennsylvania Cavalry, commanding Second and Third Brigades.
No. 356.—Col. Charles H. Smith, First Maine Cavalry.
No. 357.—Maj. M. Henry Avery, Tenth New York Cavalry.
No. 358.—Lieut. Col. William E. Doster, Fourth Pennsylvania Cavalry.
No. 359.—Brig. Gen. Judson Kilpatrick, U. S. Army, commanding First Brigade of, and Third Division.
No. 360.—Lieut. Col. Henry E. Davies, jr., Second New York Cavalry, First Brigade.
No. 361.—Brig. Gen. George A. Custer, U. S. Army, commanding Second Brigade of, and Third Division.
No. 362.—Col. Nathaniel P. Richmond, First West Virginia Cavalry, commanding First Brigade, Third Division.
No. 363.—Maj. John Hammond, Fifth New York Cavalry.
No. 364.—Maj. William B. Darlington, Eighteenth Pennsylvania Cavalry.
No. 365.—Lieut. Col. Addison W. Preston, First Vermont Cavalry.
No. 366.—Col. Edward B. Sawyer, First Vermont Cavalry.
No. 367.—Maj. Charles E. Capehart, First West Virginia Cavalry.
No. 368.—Capt. James M. Robertson, Second U. S. Artillery, commanding First Brigade, Horse Artillery.
No. 369.—Capt. Jabez J. Daniels, Ninth Michigan Battery.
No. 370.—Capt. Joseph W. Martin, Sixth New York Battery.
No. 371.—Lieut. J. Wade Wilson, Sixth New York Battery.
No. 372.—Capt. John C. Tidball, Second U. S. Artillery, commanding Second Brigade, Horse Artillery.
No. 373.—Capt. William M. Graham, Battery K, First U. S. Artillery.
No. 374.—Lieut. John H. Calef, Battery A, Second U. S. Artillery.
No. 375.—Lieut. William D. Fuller, Battery C, Third U. S. Artillery.

DEPARTMENT OF WASHINGTON.

No. 376.—Col. James B. Swain, Eleventh New York Cavalry, of skirmish near Fairfax Court-House, Va.
No. 377.—Col. Henry L. Abbot, First Connecticut Heavy Artillery, of affair on Little River Turnpike.
No. 378.—Col. Charles R. Lowell, jr., Second Massachusetts Cavalry, of reconnaissance, July 11–14.

No. 1.

Report of Maj. Gen. Henry W. Halleck, General-in-Chief, U. S. Army, including operations in Southeastern Virginia and West Virginia.

HEADQUARTERS OF THE ARMY,
Washington, D. C., November 15, 1863.

SIR: In compliance with your orders I submit the following summary of military operations since my last annual report:

*   *   *   *   *   *   *

In the early part of June, Lee's army moved up the south bank of the Rappahannock, occupied the gaps of the Blue Ridge, and threatened the Valley of the Shenandoah. General Hooker followed on an interior line by Warrenton Junction, Thoroughfare Gap, and

Leesburg; but the operations of both armies were so masked by the intervening mountains that neither could obtain positive information of the force and movements of the other. Winchester and Martinsburg were at this time occupied by us simply as outposts. Neither place was susceptible of a good defense.

Directions were, therefore, given on June 11 to withdraw these garrisons to Harper's Ferry. But these orders were not obeyed, and, on the 13th, Winchester was attacked and its armament and a part of its garrison captured. Lee now crossed the Potomac near Williamsport, and directed his march upon Harrisburg. General Hooker followed upon his right flank, covering Washington and Baltimore.

On reaching Frederick, Md., June 28, he was, at his own request, relieved from the command, and Major-General Meade appointed in his place.

During these movements, cavalry skirmishes took place at Beverly Ford, Brandy Station, Berryville, and Aldie, some of which were quite severe, but, in the absence of detailed reports, I am unable to give the losses on either side.

When General Meade, under the orders of the President, took command of the Army of the Potomac on June 28, it was mainly concentrated at Frederick, Md. Lee's army was supposed to be advancing against Harrisburg, which was garrisoned by raw militia, upon which little reliance could be placed. Ewell's corps was on the west side of the Susquehanna, between that place and Columbia. Longstreet's corps was near Chambersburg, and Hill's corps between that place and Cashtown. Stuart's cavalry was making a raid between Washington and Frederick, cutting Meade's line of supplies and capturing his trains.

Our force at Harper's Ferry at this time was supposed to be about 11,000. It was incorrectly represented to General Meade to be destitute of provisions, and that he must immediately supply it, or order the abandonment of the place.* Accordingly, a few hours after he assumed the command, he assented to an order, drawn up by an officer of General Hooker's staff, directing General French to send 7,000 men of the garrison to Frederick, and with the remainder, estimated at 4,000, to remove and escort the public property to Washington. This order, based on erroneous representations, was not known in Washington until too late to be countermanded. It was, however, not entirely executed when General Meade very judiciously directed the reoccupation of that important point.

On the 29th, General Meade's army was put in motion, and at night was in position; its left at Emmitsburg, and right at New Windsor. The advance of Buford's cavalry was at Gettysburg, and Kilpatrick's division at Hanover, where it encountered Stuart's cavalry, which had passed around the rear and right of our army without meeting any serious opposition.

On the 30th, the First, Third, and Eleventh Corps were concentrated at Emmitsburg, under General Reynolds, while the right wing moved up to Manchester. Buford reported the enemy in force on the Cashtown road, near Gettysburg, and Reynolds moved up to that place on July 1. He found our cavalry warmly engaged with the enemy, and holding him in check on the Cashtown road. Reynolds immediately deployed the advanced division of the First

---

* See Butterfield to Meade, January 23, 1864, p. 20, and Meade to Butterfield, February 4, 1864, p. 21.

Corps, and ordered the Eleventh Corps to move promptly to its support. Wadsworth's division had driven back the enemy some distance and captured a large number of prisoners, when General Reynolds fell, mortally wounded. The arrival of Ewell's corps about this time by the York and Harrisburg roads compelled General Howard, upon whom the command devolved, to withdraw his force, the First and Eleventh Corps, to the Cemetery Ridge, on the south side of Gettysburg.

About 7 p. m. Generals Sickles and Slocum arrived on the field with the Third and Twelfth Corps, which took position, one on the left and the other on the right of the new line. The battle for the day, however, was over. General Meade arrived on the field during the night with the reserves, and posted his troops in line of battle, the First Corps on the right, the Eleventh Corps next; then the Twelfth Corps, which crossed the Baltimore pike; the Second and Third Corps on the Cemetery Ridge, on the left of the Eleventh Corps. The Fifth Corps, pending the arrival of the Sixth, formed the reserve.

On the arrival of the latter, about 2 p. m., it took the place of the Fifth, which was ordered to take position on the extreme left. The enemy massed his troops on an exterior ridge, about a mile and a half in front of that occupied by us. General Sickles, misinterpreting his orders, instead of placing the Third Corps on the prolongation of the Second, had moved it nearly three-quarters of a mile in advance—an error which nearly proved fatal in the battle.

The enemy attacked this corps on the 2d with great fury, and it was likely to be utterly annihilated, when the Fifth Corps moved up on the left, and enabled it to reform behind the line it was originally ordered to hold. The Sixth Corps and a part of the First were also opportunely thrown into this gap, and succeeded in checking the enemy's advance. About sunset the rebels retired in confusion and disorder.

At 8 p. m. an assault was made from the left of the town, which was gallantly repelled by the First, Second, and Eleventh Corps.

On the morning of the 3d we regained, after a spirited contest, a part of our line on the right, which had been yielded to sustain other points on the 2d. About 1 p. m. the enemy opened an artillery fire of one hundred and twenty-five guns on our center and left. This was followed by an assault of a heavy infantry column on our left and left center, which was successfully repulsed, with a terrible loss to the enemy. This terminated the battle, and the rebels retired, defeated, from the field.

The opposing forces in this sanguinary contest were nearly equal in numbers, and both fought with the most desperate courage. The commanders were also brave, skillful, and experienced, and they handled their troops on the field with distinguished ability; but to General Meade belongs the honor of a well-earned victory in one of the greatest and best-fought battles of the war.

On the morning of the 4th, the enemy apparently occupied a new line in front of our left, but in reality his army had commenced its retreat, carrying off a part of his wounded. His lines, however, were not entirely evacuated until the morning of the 5th, when the cavalry and the Sixth Corps were sent in pursuit.

The days of the 5th and 6th were employed by General Meade in succoring the wounded and burying the dead left on the battle-field. He then started in pursuit of Lee by a flank movement upon Middletown. In the meantime General French had reoccupied Harper's Ferry, destroyed the enemy's pontoon train at Williamsport and Falling Waters, and captured its guards.

Halting a day at Middletown, General Meade crossed South Mountain, and on the 12th found the enemy occupying a strong position on the heights of Marsh Run, in front of Williamsport. Not being attacked in this position, with the swollen waters of the Potomac in his rear, without any means of crossing his artillery, and where a defeat must have caused the surrender of his entire army, Lee had time to construct a pontoon bridge with lumber collected from canal-boats and the ruins of wooden houses, and on the morning of the 14th his army had crossed to the south side of the river. His rear guard, however, was attacked by our cavalry and suffered considerable loss. Thus ended the rebel campaign north of the Potomac, from which important political and military results had been expected.

Our own loss in this short campaign had been very severe, viz: Killed, 2,834; wounded, 13,709; missing, 6,643; total, 23,186.* We captured 3 guns, 41 standards, 13,621 prisoners, and 28,178 small-arms. The entire loss of the enemy is not known, but judging from the numbers of his dead and wounded left on the field, it must have been much greater than ours.

After crossing the Potomac, Lee continued his retreat up the Valley of the Shenandoah and through the gaps of the Blue Ridge until he reached the south bank of the Rapidan, near Orange Court-House, where he took a defensive position to dispute the crossing of the river. General Meade continued his flank pursuit by Harper's Ferry, Berlin, and Warrenton, until he reached Culpeper Court-House, where he halted his army, not deeming it prudent to cross the river and attack the enemy, who was now intrenched on the south bank, which completely commanded the approaches on the north side. During this advance, several cavalry skirmishes took place, but without serious loss on either side.

*   *   *   *   *   *   *

The operations of our troops in West Virginia are referred to here as being intimately connected with those of the Army of the Potomac. The force, being too small to attempt any important campaign by itself, has acted mostly upon the defensive, in repelling raids and breaking up guerrilla bands.

When Lee's army retreated across the Potomac in July last, Brigadier-General Kelley concentrated all his available force on the enemy's flank, near Clear Spring, ready to co-operate in the proposed attack by General Meade. They [the troops in West Virginia] also rendered valuable services in the pursuit, after Lee had effected his passage of the river.

*   *   *   *   *   *   *

When the rebel army was moving north upon Maryland and Pennsylvania, General Dix sent all his available force from Norfolk and Fort Monroe up the York River, for the purpose of cutting off Lee's communications with Richmond, and of attacking that place, which was then defended by only a handful of militia. The expedition, however, failed to accomplish a single object for which it had been fitted out, the failure resulting, it was alleged, from the inefficiency

---

* But see revised statement, p. 187.

of one of the generals in command.* General Dix therefore ordered its return, and sent the troops of which it was composed to re-enforce the army of General Meade north of the Potomac.

* * * * * * *

All of which is respectfully submitted.

H. W. HALLECK,
General-in-Chief.

Hon. E. M. STANTON,
Secretary of War.

ADDENDA.

(No. 1.)

HEADQUARTERS DEPARTMENT OF THE EAST,
New York City, December 15, 1863.

Maj. Gen. H. W. HALLECK,
General-in-Chief:

GENERAL: In your report of the 15th November, to the Secretary of War, I find the following paragraph:

When the rebel army was moving north upon Maryland and Pennsylvania, General Dix sent all of his available force from Norfolk and Fort Monroe up the York River, for the purpose of cutting off Lee's communications with Richmond, and of attacking that place, which was then defended by only a handful of militia. The expedition, however, failed to accomplish a single object for which it had been fitted out, the failure resulting, it was alleged, from the inefficiency of one of the generals commanding. General Dix therefore ordered its return, and sent the troops of which it was composed to re-enforce the army of General Meade north of the Potomac.

As there seems to be a misapprehension on your part in regard to two or three of the most essential particulars, I desire to call your attention to them in connection with the subjoined statement of facts.

1. That I sent all my "available force * * * up the York River, for the purpose of cutting off Lee's communications with Richmond, and of attacking that place."

The following is your order, under which I acted:

Lee's army is in motion toward the Shenandoah Valley. All your available force should be concentrated to threaten Richmond by seizing and destroying their railroad bridges over the South and North Anna Rivers, and do them all the damage possible. If you cannot accomplish this, you can at least occupy a large force of the enemy. There can be no serious danger of an attack on Norfolk now.

It will be perceived that an attack on Richmond was not a part of the plan. That city is understood to be nearly as strongly fortified as Vicksburg, and only to be taken by regular siege.

2. That Richmond "was then defended by only a handful of militia."

An intercepted letter from Jefferson Davis to General Lee, dated the 28th of June, the day the last of my troops arrived at the White House, states that there were three brigades in Richmond, and part of Hill's division, besides Wise's brigade on the east side of the city. These were all regular troops and not militia; there was, in addition, a body of trained artillerists in the intrenchments, the Home Guards, and a convalescent brigade.

---

*See Dix to Halleck, December 15, and reply of December 20, Addenda, Nos. 1 and 2, following; and see, in Part II, expeditions from the White House to South Anna River and Bottom's Bridge, July 1–7.

3. That the "expedition failed to accomplish the object for which it had been fitted out."

The objects of the expedition, as stated in your order, were three-fold: (1) To threaten Richmond; (2) to destroy the railroad bridges over the South and North Anna Rivers, and do the enemy as much damage as possible; and (3) to occupy a large force of the enemy. The first and last of these objects were effectually accomplished, the second partially, and, I may say, substantially. One of the bridges over the South Anna was destroyed. Although the other was not destroyed, the railroad track between it and Richmond was torn up for a considerable distance, and the bridge at Ashland, on the same road, 11 miles out of Richmond, was completely demolished and burned, as well as the depot at that station.

Colonel Spear's expedition, sent out under written instructions, was a most successful and creditable one. He destroyed the first-mentioned bridge and the quartermaster's depot at Hanover Station, bringing back 35 army wagons, 700 horses and mules, and General Fitzhugh [W. H. F.] Lee, the son of the rebel general-in-chief, now in confinement at Fort Lafayette as a hostage, and over 100 prisoners.

I had only been three days at the White House when my forces were ordered back to re-enforce General Meade. At that time I had completely cut off General Lee's communications with Richmond by way of the two railroads crossing the South Anna, and had control of the whole country from the Pamunkey to the Rappahannock.

To myself, this correction of a statement, which I am sure is inadvertent, is of less consequence than to the gallant troops under my command. For their sake I ask permission to give publicity to this letter, or to my report of the expedition, dated the 16th of July last.

I am, very respectfully, your obedient servant,

JOHN A. DIX,
Major-General.

(No. 2.)

WASHINGTON, *December* 20, 1863.

Maj. Gen. JOHN A. DIX,
    New York City:

GENERAL: Your letter (without date) [December 15], in regard to my official report of November 15, is received. I have not been able to give it an earlier answer. I cannot authorize the publication of this letter, nor of your report, but I presume the latter will be officially published, with other reports, by Congress, as I understand they have all been submitted by the War Department.

I very much regret, general, that my report contains anything to which you take exception. I certainly had no intention to reflect upon you, or to find any fault with you as the commanding general of the department. In my opinion, the expedition up the York River did not accomplish the two objects in view, or either of them. You speak of three objects. I think a third was suggested only in case the others failed.

Perhaps I erred in using the word attack instead of threaten; to threaten is not necessarily to attack, but it may imply an attack, if the point to be threatened is found open to one.

I have no time at present to examine the reports or to discuss the matter. I can only add that, while much disappointment was felt here at what was considered a failure of the expedition, no blame whatever was attached to you. Perhaps no blame should have been attributed to any one, but I inferred differently from your own reports and dispatches.

In regard to the force then in Richmond, I derived my information from spies and prisoners of war.

Very respectfully, your obedient servant,

H. W. HALLECK.

(No. 3.)

HDQRS. ELEVENTH AND TWELFTH ARMY CORPS,
Lookout Valley, Tenn., January 23, 1864.

Maj. Gen. GEORGE G. MEADE,
Commanding Army of the Potomac:

GENERAL: I find the following most extraordinary statement in the annual report of the General-in-Chief:

Our force at Harper's Ferry at this time was supposed to be about 11,000. It was incorrectly represented to General Meade to be destitute of provisions, and that he must immediately supply it, or order the abandonment of the place. Accordingly, a few hours after he assumed the command, he assented to an order, drawn up by an officer of General Hooker's staff, directing General French to send 7,000 men of the garrison to Frederick, and with the remainder, estimated at 4,000, to remove and escort the public property to Washington. This order, based on erroneous representations, was not known in Washington until too late to be countermanded. It was, however, not entirely executed when General Meade very judiciously directed the reoccupation of that important point.

Although it does not mention me by name, it will be considered by the public that I was the officer alluded to, as I was, before your assuming command, serving as chief of staff to the army under General Hooker, and am now temporarily serving in that capacity with him, although at the time alluded to I was no more an officer of General Hooker's staff than was Generals Williams, Hunt, Ingalls, or any of the officers serving on the general staff of that army.

Under the presumption that he may allude to me, it is proper, before taking the steps I propose to in the matter, that I should ascertain whether the entirely erroneous statement made by the General-in-Chief in the premises is based upon anything he may have received from you officially or otherwise.

You will certainly well remember that the garrison had an abundance of supplies, and it was so stated by me to you. You will also remember that no order was drawn up until after we had conversed upon the subject, and you had directed the order to be drawn; also that the grounds upon which I advised it were generally, first, that Lee's army, to our then certain knowledge, numbered 91,000 infantry, 12,000 cavalry, and about 275 pieces of artillery; that without this garrison, and taking into consideration our rapid marches, we should be likely to fall short of that number of infantry; that your having an order which gave you control of that garrison would make you responsible, in the event of failure, for not making use of them; that in such an event they would in all probability be required to leave that post; that in the event of success they could be returned at once.

You will also doubtless remember that the bringing on of the general battle at Gettysburg sooner than you expected, by Reynolds' collision with Hill, and the events that followed, prevented French reaching us in time, and it being determined that he could not reach us, orders were given him for his movements contingent upon our success or failure, as the battle would be decided before he could reach us. The telegraphic and other correspondence will show this.

I recall these facts to your recollection, knowing that the duties suddenly imposed upon you at the time may have caused you, while giving attention to other and more pressing duties, to fail to fix decidedly in your mind these points. I shall be glad to know, if such is the case, that some other person than myself is alluded to.

In conclusion, I would repeat the purpose of this communication, and respectfully and earnestly request a reply at your earliest convenience as to whether the statement given above, of the General-in-Chief, is based upon anything he may have received from you officially or otherwise.

Very respectfully, your obedient servant,

DANL. BUTTERFIELD,
Major-General.

(No. 4.)

PHILADELPHIA, *February* 4, 1864.

Maj. Gen. D. BUTTERFIELD,
U. S. Vols., Hdqrs. Eleventh and Twelfth Corps,
Lookout Valley, Tenn.:

GENERAL: I am in receipt of your letter of the 23d ultimo.

I have never made any official communications to the General-in-Chief upon the subject of the withdrawal of the troops from Harper's Ferry, excepting such as were made at the time.

Some time after the battle of Gettysburg, the first time I saw the General-in-Chief, I did in private conversation say to him that my own judgment was in favor of leaving the garrison at Harper's Ferry intact, although I agreed with General Hooker that it was of no importance as a crossing-place of the Potomac River, but I did think it of importance to hold it as a *débouché* into the Cumberland Valley; that after much discussion I yielded to your arguments, and directed 4,000 men to be left to garrison Maryland Heights, and the balance, 7,000, to be brought to Frederick to guard the Baltimore and Ohio Railroad; that late in the night of the 28th, understanding from you that the supply of subsistence stores with the garrison was limited, and that, owing to the difficulty of protecting the canal and railroad, the communications with the place would be precarious, I ordered the abandonment of the place, and detailed the 4,000 men to escort the public property to Washington.

This conversation was private, and was made in explanation of my course, but with no expectation that it would be officially used by the General-in-Chief.

You will see from it that I did not repudiate the responsibility of the act, but that I did state that it was based on arguments used by you and information derived from you.

I shall greatly regret if my recollection of the facts differ from yours, but it is proper I should state that my recollection is clear and distinct as given above.

Respectfully, yours,

GEO. G. MEADE,
Major-General.

No. 2.

*Report of Brig. Gen. Hermann Haupt, U. S. Army, in charge of Military Railway Department.**

WASHINGTON, D. C., *July* 7, 1863.

SIR: I submit herewith a brief report of operations in the Military Railway Department for the last week.

On Monday, June 29, acting under Special Orders, No. 286, a copy of which is inclosed, I repaired to Baltimore, intending to join General Meade at Frederick, and ascertain the condition and requirements of the Army of the Potomac.

Finding the communications broken, both by rail and telegraph, and the road near Sykesville in the possession of the enemy, I concluded to proceed to Harrisburg, ascertain the precise condition of affairs, then work my way by some means to General Meade, and inform him what degree of assistance and co-operation he might expect from the Pennsylvania forces.

Owing to the interruptions of travel, I proceeded to Harrisburg via Reading, arrived in that city Tuesday evening, spent several hours with Governor Curtin and Col. T. A. Scott, and learned the position of affairs. I had written to the Governor from Falmouth soon after the battle of Chancellorsville, informing him that the enemy would soon be in Pennsylvania, and made suggestions of means proper to be resorted to to impede his progress and protect the Pennsylvania Railroad. I found that Colonel Scott had been very active and efficient, and that the Pennsylvania Railroad had been as well protected as the short time would permit.

Very extensive arrangements had been made to procure information from scouts, and I saw clearly that, instead of attacking Harrisburg, an exceedingly rapid concentration of the enemy's forces had been going on that day, tending toward Gettysburg, evidently designed to fall upon and crush in detail the Army of the Potomac before it could fully concentrate or its new commander get it full in hand.

I at once telegraphed to General Halleck and to General Schenck, and suggested that an engine be run from Baltimore to Westminster with express, and a mounted courier dispatched to General Meade. The dispatch was received, and it helped to confirm the correctness of information derived from other sources. It came from the rear of the enemy, while other information could only be derived from the front.

Wednesday I returned to Baltimore, and proceeded to the Relay House, on Northern Central Railroad. I found the Western Maryland Railroad entirely without equipment or facilities for the business to be thrown immediately upon it. It had no experienced officers, no water stations, sidings, turn-tables, or wood sufficient for a business of exceeding three or four trains per day, while the necessities of the service required thirty trains per day to be passed over it. I had engines and cars sent from Alexandria, with full sets of hands. A train-load of sawed and split wood and a supply of buckets were also forwarded. Tanks were filled by dipping water from the streams, and, with other arrangements required by the circumstances of the case, we were enabled to provide for a transportation of 1,500 tons per day each way. In two days the army was supplied not only with

---

*See also report, September 9, 1863, in Series III.

everything required, but with an excess, which has been left for the use of hospitals.

The chief quartermaster of the Army of the Potomac informed me that their supplies had at no time become so low that they could not have been stretched over three days, and on Sunday, when the pursuit of the enemy commenced, they had more than they wished to carry with them.

After organizing the transportation on the Western Maryland Railroad, and leaving it in charge of Adna Anderson, esq., the efficient chief engineer of construction, I proceeded to Hanover with a construction train; passed over the Littlestown Branch; reconstructed a bridge that had been broken down; found General Sickles without means of transportation; arranged to have him sent immediately to Washington; returned to Hanover, and switched off on Gettysburg Branch; proceeded to Oxford, where a large bridge across the Conewago had been burned; decided on mode of repair; set the gangs at work; returned to Oxford, and dispatched train to Junction for more men and materials.

The next morning I left instructions with foreman, after finishing the Conewago Bridge, to proceed to the next bridge, repair it, and work on to Gettysburg, unless he received word from me that the enemy, who were on the road near Gettysburg the previous afternoon, were still there. I then procured a buggy, and proceeded over the turnpike to Gettysburg, finding no enemy except wounded at the farm-houses, the last having retreated the previous evening.

After about three hours with General Meade and other officers at headquarters, I returned to Oxford, and, after completing the railroad to Gettysburg, returned to Baltimore Sunday night, after a very active week, in which my corps, both in construction and transportation, performed services of very great importance. I am particularly indebted to A. Anderson, esq., chief engineer, for his sound judgment and efficiency; also to J. N. Du Barry, superintendent of Northern Central Railroad, for his active co-operation. I have presented to him, as you directed, the thanks of your Department

The construction corps is still at work on the bridges of the Northern Central Railroad, of which nineteen were destroyed, and in two days more I expect that communication with Harrisburg will be re-established.

I cannot speak in terms of too strong commendation of the corps for construction and transportation. No department of the military service is of more importance than that which is charged with constructing, re-opening, and maintaining communications and forwarding supplies. Volunteers have always been ready for any service, however dangerous. At the second battle of Manassas, General Kearny desired me to run a pilot engine over the road, in advance of his troop trains, after a train had been fired upon by a large force of the enemy, and men were found to perform the services without hesitation. Employés of the transportation department have remained at stations long after they had been evacuated by the military in retreat, and have brought away stores to save them from the enemy. At the battle of Fredericksburg, a small force of carpenters, under E. C. Smeed and G. W. Nagle, superintendents of bridge construction, worked for nearly half a day under fire until their ropes were cut, the pulleys smashed, and the timbers knocked about with shells. A military force of 200 men, which had been detailed to assist, straggled off soon after the action commenced, not leaving a single man.

These men are not in a position to acquire military distinction or rewards, but I would fail in my duty if I omitted to signify to you my high appreciation of the labors, services, courage, and fidelity of the corps for construction and transportation in the department of U. S. Military Railroads, and suggest that some recognition of their services would be a great encouragement to men who so richly deserve it.

Very respectfully submitted.

H. HAUPT,
In charge of U. S. Military Railroads.

Hon. E. M. STANTON,
    Secretary of War.

[Inclosure.]

SPECIAL ORDERS, ⎰   HDQRS. OF ARMY, ADJT. GEN.'S OFFICE,
    No. 286. ⎱   *Washington, June 27,* 1863.

Brig. Gen. H. Haupt, U. S. Volunteers, is hereby authorized and directed to do whatever he may deem expedient to facilitate the transportation of troops and supplies to aid the armies in the field in Virginia, Maryland, and Pennsylvania.

By command of Major-General Halleck:

E. D. TOWNSEND,
Assistant Adjutant-General.

No. 3.

Report of Medical Inspector John M. Cuyler, U. S. Army.

WASHINGTON, D. C., *July 27,* 1863.

SIR: I arrived at Gettysburg on the morning of the 10th of July, forty hours later than I had hoped to do, in consequence of the irregularities and interruptions on the railways leading to that place.

Medical Inspector Vollum reached Gettysburg some two or three days in advance of me, and immediately on his arrival made arrangements for sending away such of the wounded as were in a condition to be moved in ambulances or on the railroad. Lieutenant-Colonel Vollum had the immediate charge of forwarding the wounded to the general hospitals designated by yourself. In this he was assisted by Dr. Osborne, of the Army of the Potomac, a very active and energetic officer. Both of these officers performed the duty assigned them with very great faithfulness and efficiency.

I believe the wounded were received at the railroad depot and placed on the cars with as much care, attention, and comfort as was possible under the circumstances.

Before the arrival of the fifty ambulances sent from Washington by yourself, our means of conveying the wounded from the field hospitals to the railroad depot were inadequate, although I am satisfied that as many ambulances were left by the Army of the Potomac as could possibly be spared. The number of medical officers detailed by Medical Director Letterman to remain with the wounded was thought to be sufficient, and probably might have been had not thousands of the enemy's wounded been thrown unexpectedly on our hands. For some days after the battle, many of the rebel wounded were in a most deplorable condition, being without shelter of any sort, and with an insufficient number of medical officers and nurses of their own army.

Every effort was made to alleviate the sufferings of these unfortunate men, and as soon as it could be done they were placed under cover or sent away to some general hospital.

Our wounded, with some few exceptions, were sheltered within a day or two after the battle, and made as comfortable as circumstances would permit. The scarcity of straw for bedding was seriously felt, and it was not until eight or ten days after the conflict that a sufficient quantity could be obtained. As far as my observation extends, the medical officers of the army, and the citizen surgeons who were employed during the emergency, discharged their arduous duties with fidelity and ability. I never saw men work harder and complain less of the difficulties that surrounded them.

Through the efficiency of the medical purveyor, Assistant Surgeon [Jeremiah B.] Brinton, his storehouse was rapidly filled with supplies suitable for the occasion, and, by an arrangement of your own, a liberal supply of ale and porter is daily furnished to such of the wounded as need them.

Up to the 25th instant (the day I left Gettysburg), 15,875 of the wounded had been sent away, and since that time 250 more have been forwarded, amounting in all to 16,125, leaving still at Gettysburg about 3,500, 3,000 of whom, it is believed, are not in a condition to be moved at present. Those who are obliged to remain will be quartered in a large field hospital established at a suitable place near the town, where I hope they will have all the comfort and receive all the attention and kindness to which they are so justly entitled.

I cannot close this brief report without acknowledging the immense aid afforded by the Sanitary and Christian Commissions. The promptness, energy, and great kindness uniformly exhibited by these benevolent associations doubtless helped to save the lives of many, and gladdened the hearts of thousands, who, with their friends scattered throughout our land, will hold their good and noble deeds in grateful remembrance.

To Adams Express we are also greatly indebted for much liberality and kindness extended to the wounded at a time when they were most in need.

JOHN M. CUYLER,
Medical Inspector, U. S. Army.

Brig. Gen. WILLIAM A. HAMMOND,
    Surgeon-General, U. S. Army.

No. 4.

Report of Medical Inspector Edward P. Vollum, U. S. Army.

WASHINGTON, D. C., *July* 25, 1863.

GENERAL : I have the honor to report that, pursuant to your orders of the 7th July, I proceeded on the same day to Gettysburg, Pa., for the purpose of reporting to Medical Inspector Cuyler, U. S. Army, for duty in connection with the transportation of the wounded at that place. I was detained a few hours, on the 8th, at Hanover, Pa., where I found about 150 wounded, chiefly from Kilpatrick's cavalry, under charge of Assistant Surgeon [Perin] Gardner, First [West] Virginia Cavalry. They were comfortably situated in a school-house and in dwellings. The inhabitants had furnished them with bunks, bedding, dressings, utensils, and food in sufficient quantity, the people in each street in the town furnishing food, delicacies, nurses, &c., two days at a time.

I arrived at Gettysburg about 7 p. m. on the 8th, and in consequence of some irregularity or delay in the railroad trains, there were about 2,000 slightly wounded men collected at a point a mile from town, where the trains stopped, without food, shelter, or attendance for the night. Fortunately, through the agents of the Sanitary Commission, these men were all fed, and some 300 sheltered that night. No system had as yet been adopted for the transportation of the wounded, nor had this been possible in the deranged condition of the railroad, though Surg. J. D. Osborne, Fourth New Jersey, detailed for this purpose by Surg. H. Janes, U. S. Volunteers, in charge of the hospitals at Gettysburg, was using his best endeavors to work through the confusion and crowds of wounded with which he was surrounded, and I have to acknowledge the important services of this gentleman until the time of my departure. The railroad authorities were perplexed, and deficient in motive power and rolling stock. The bridges put up since the rebel raids proved too weak excepting for the lightest engines, and for a second time some were carried away by the floods. The telegraph wires were down, and the obstruction to transportation seemed insurmountable until General Haupt arrived and assumed military control of the road to Hanover Junction. We then experienced no further delays till the 18th, when an important bridge on the road to Harrisburg gave way under a cattle train, thus diverting, for the following five days, the trains that were intended for New York to Baltimore and York, Pa.

Medical Inspector Cuyler arrived on the 11th, when I reported to him for duty, and, by mutual arrangement, I continued in immediate charge of the transportation of the wounded, which confined me to the railroad depot and city of Gettysburg. Every train of wounded was placed in charge of a medical officer detailed by Surg. H. Janes. Instruments, dressings, stimulants, &c., were furnished him, and he was instructed to announce his coming by telegraph, if possible, and to report in person to the medical director at the place of his destination. Each car was filled with a sufficient quantity of hay, and, on the longer routes, water-coolers, tin cups, bed-pans, and urinals were placed in them, and guarded on the route by some agents of the Sanitary Commission. In some instances, these conveniencies were furnished by the medical department, but the demand for them by the hospitals often exhausted the supplies at the purveyors. Before leaving, the wounded were fed and watered by the Sanitary Commission, and often hundreds of wounded, laid over for a night or a part of a day, were attended and fed by the Commission, whose agents placed them in the cars. At Hanover Junction they were again refreshed and fed by the Christian Commission. At Baltimore, the agents of several benevolent societies distributed food bountifully to the wounded in the cars immediately on their arrival; and at Harrisburg the Commissary Department had made arrangements for feeding any number likely to pass that way.

The following are the numbers and destination of Union and Confederate wounded sent from Gettysburg up to the 23d; the first 1,462 had left before my arrival:

Date.	Train.	No.	Description.	Destination.	Total per diem.
1863. July 7	5 p. m	164	Union	Baltimore	
7	7 p. m	258	.....do	..do	
7	7.10 p. m	400	.....do	..do	822
8	1.40 p. m	640	.....do	..do	640
9	10.35 a. m	1,012	.....do	..do	
9	5.30 p. m	1,061	.....do	..do	2,073
10	11 a. m	186	.....do	..do	
10	5.15 p. m	620	.....do	..do	806
11	11 a. m	204	.....do	..do	
11	5 p. m	338	.....do	..do	
11	5 p. m	76	Confederate	..do	618
12	10 a. m	327	.....do	..do	
12		28	Union	..do	
12	12.15 p. m	142	.....do	..do	
12		184	Confederate	..do	
12	5 p. m	105	Union	..do	
12		433	Confederate	..do	1,219
13	9 a. m	96	Union	..do	
13		133	Confederate	..do	
13	3 p. m	259	Union	..do	
13		16	Confederate	..do	504
14	9 a. m	130	Union	..do	
14	3 p. m	176	.....do	..do	
14		394	Confederate	..do	700
15	9 a. m	182	Union	..do	
15		37	Confederate	..do	
15	3 p. m	380	Union	..do	
15		6	Confederate	..do	605
16	9 a. m	60	Union	..do	
16	3 p. m	36	.....do	..do	
16		262	Confederate	..do	358
17	9 a. m	20	Union	New York	
17		225	Confederate	..do	
17		204	.....do	..do	
17		80	Union	York, Pa	529
18	9 a. m	47	.....do	..do	
18		183	Confederate	Baltimore	
18	3 p. m	125	Union	York, Pa	
18		350	Confederate	Baltimore	705
19	9 a. m	107	Union	York, Pa	
19		25	Confederate	..do	
19	3 p. m	198	Union	..do	
19		125	Confederate	Baltimore	455
20	9 a. m	257	Union	York, Pa	
20	3 p. m	141	.....do	..do	398
21	11.30 a. m	467	Confederate	New York	
21		33	Union	..do	
21	4 p. m	158	Confederate	..do	
21		54	Union	York, Pa	712
22	11.30 a. m	47	.....do	Harrisburg	
22		154	Confederate	New York	
22	4 p. m	22	Union	Harrisburg	
22		58	Confederate	New York	281
		11,425			11,425

Wounded sent from Gettysburg to 22d instant :
Union 7,608
Confederate.. 3,817

Total 11,425
Union wounded sent to Baltimore, in addition to above :
From Westminister 2,000
From Littleton 2,000
4,000

Total sent off.. 15,425
Deduct Confederate wounded... 3,817

Total Union wounded sent off... 11,608
Union wounded remaining on 22d instant... 1,995

Total Union wounded.. 13,603
Confederate wounded sent off 3,817
Confederate wounded remaining on 22d instant... 2,922

Total Confederate wounded.. 6,739

Grand total in our hands... 20,342

To obtain the whole number of wounded of both sides, there must be added those of Chambersburg, Carlisle, Williamsport, and Hagerstown. * * * Before the arrival of Medical Inspector Cuyler, as far as my time and opportunities admitted, I endeavored to make up the deficiencies in medical supplies at Gettysburg by telegraphing to Surgeon [Josiah] Simpson, U. S. Army, at Baltimore. In reply, he ordered liberal supplies of alcohol, solution chloride of soda, tincture of iron, creosote, nitric acid, permanganate of potassa, buckets, tin cups, stretchers, bed-sacks, and stationery of all kinds for 10,000 men in field hospitals. On the day after my arrival, the demand for stationery, disinfectants, iodine, tincture of iron, and some other articles was so great and immediate, that I purchased them in Gettysburg, and sent the bills to the quartermaster there for payment.

Very respectfully, your obedient servant,

EDW. P. VOLLUM,
Medical Inspector, U. S. Army.

The SURGEON-GENERAL U. S. ARMY.

P. S.—I neglected to comment in the proper place upon the utter indifference manifested by the railroad companies toward the sufferings and wants of our wounded at Gettysburg, Pa. I allude to those over whose roads our mangled soldiers traveled to various points from Gettysburg. The period of ten days following the battle of Gettysburg was the occasion of the greatest amount of human suffering known to this nation since its birth, and, as was natural and unavoidable among a Christian people, benevolent societies, Sanitary and Christian Commissions, express companies, fire organizations, bands of generous people of all denominations, and individuals from great distances, all came forward with their offerings, sympathy, and personal services, forming a spectacle at once touching and magnificent, exceeding any similar outburst of sympathy and sacrifice ever witnessed. The railroad companies, who got the only profit of the battle, and who had the greatest opportunities of ameliorating the sufferings of the wounded, alone stood aloof and rendered no aid. Their trains were allowed to go off without a single individual attached to them in any way authorized to minister to the wounded. There was no check-line or means of stopping the train in case of necessity; no way provided for passing from car to car. The cars—ordinary stock and freight cars—were always unclean; no one connected with the companies to clean them; the dung of cattle and litter from freight often remaining to be removed by any extemporized means at hand. There was no water, or vessels to contain it, no lanterns, no straw—absolutely nothing but the bare cars, filthy from the business of transporting freight and cattle. The only agents of the railroad companies that appeared upon this memorable scene were those sent especially to look after their pecuniary interests, and I can testify to their zeal in getting the actual numbers transported and securing the proper certificates therefor, but beyond this they did nothing.

No. 5.

Reports of Maj. Gen. Joseph Hooker, U. S. Army, commanding Army of the Potomac, of operations June 3–27, and correspondence with the authorities in Washington, etc.

HEADQUARTERS ARMY OF THE POTOMAC,
June 4, 1863.   (Received 9.50 a. m.)

Hon. E. M. STANTON,
    Secretary of War:

It has this moment been reported to me that several of the enemy's camps were removed during last night.   Shall be able to determine the direction shortly if this should be found to be the case.

JOSEPH HOOKER,
Major-General.

—

JUNE 4, 1863.   (Received 12 m.)

Maj. Gen. H. W. HALLECK, &c.,
    Washington:

Following received from General Buford, June 4:

Nothing noteworthy to report.   Yesterday Colonel Duffié's pickets reported enemy crossing in considerable force at Sulphur Springs.   Preparations made to welcome them, but they did not come.   Country and river, as high up as Orleans, New Baltimore, and Thoroughfare Gap, visited yesterday and last night.   Nothing was seen or heard.

JNO. BUFORD.

The movements of the enemy in our front do not indicate what their purpose or object may be.   Has General Dix's force moved to White House or beyond there?   His position, strength, and movements may govern or influence the enemy somewhat.   I should like to be fully advised.

JOSEPH HOOKER,
Major-General, Commanding.

—

HEADQUARTERS ARMY OF THE POTOMAC,
June 4, 1863.   (Received 6.20 p. m.)

Maj. Gen. H. W. HALLECK,
    General-in-Chief:

Following from one of our scouts :

I heard from at least three different parties, who I know had the means of obtaining the correct information, that General Jones had come from the Shenandoah Valley; that his headquarters were either in Rappahannock or Culpeper, and not very far distant from Culpeper Court-House, and that this information was obtained from some of his cavalry whose homes were in Fauquier, and who had been over to see their friends.

DANL. BUTTERFIELD,
Major-General.

(Copy to Secretary of War.)

JUNE 5, 1863—11.30 a. m.

His Excellency THE PRESIDENT OF THE UNITED STATES:

Yesterday morning appearances indicated that during the night the enemy had broken up a few of his camps and abandoned them. These changes were observed on the right of his line, in the vicinity of Hamilton's Crossing. So far as I was enabled to judge, from all my means of information, it was impossible for me to determine satisfactorily whether this movement had merely been a change of camps—the enemy had moved in the direction of Richmond or up the river—but, taken in connection with the fact that some deserters came in from the divisions of Hood and Pickett, I concluded that those divisions had been brought to the front from their late positions at Gordonsville and Taylorsville, and that this could be for no other purpose but to enable the enemy to move up the river, with a view to the execution of a movement similar to that of Lee's last year. He must either have it in mind to cross the Upper Potomac, or to throw his army between mine and Washington, in case I am correct in my conjecture. To accomplish either, he must have been greatly re-enforced, and if making this movement, the fair presumption is that he has been by the troops from Charleston. Of this I have no evidence further than that furnished me by Major-General Dix, that they had come to Richmond.

This morning some more of their camps have disappeared. The picket line along the river is preserved, and as strong as ever.

General Buford, with three divisions of cavalry and ten pieces of artillery, is on the Orange and Alexandria Railroad, and yesterday was along the river beyond Sulphur Springs, and reports no enemy.

As I am liable to be called on to make a movement with the utmost promptitude, I desire that I may be informed as early as practicable of the views of the Government concerning this army.

Under instructions from the major-general commanding the army, dated January 31, I am instructed to keep "in view always the importance of covering Washington and Harper's Ferry, either directly or by so operating as to be able to punish any force of the enemy sent against them." In the event the enemy should move, as I almost anticipate he will, the head of his column will probably be headed toward the Potomac, via Gordonsville or Culpeper, while the rear will rest on Fredericksburg.

After giving the subject my best reflection, I am of opinion that it is my duty to pitch into his rear, although in so doing the head of his column may reach Warrenton before I can return. Will it be within the spirit of my instructions to do so?

In view of these contemplated movements of the enemy, I cannot too forcibly impress upon the mind of His Excellency the President the necessity of having one commander for all of the troops whose operations can have an influence on those of Lee's army. Under the present system, all independent commanders are in ignorance of the movements of the others; at least such is my situation. I trust that I may not be considered in the way to this arrangement, as it is a position I do not desire, and only suggest it, as I feel the necessity for concert as well as vigorous action.

It is necessary for me to say this much that my motives may not be misunderstood.

JOSEPH HOOKER,
Major-General.

WAR DEPARTMENT,
Washington, June 5, 1863—3 p. m.

Major-General HOOKER,
Falmouth, Va.:

Prisoners and deserters brought in here state that Stuart is preparing a column of from 15,000 to 20,000 men, cavalry and artillery, for a raid. They say it will be ready in two or three days.

H. W. HALLECK,
General-in-Chief.

—

WASHINGTON, *June* 5, 1863—4 p. m.

Major-General HOOKER:

Yours of to-day was received an hour ago. So much of professional military skill is requisite to answer it, that I have turned the task over to General Halleck. He promises to perform it with his utmost care. I have but one idea which I think worth suggesting to you, and that is, in case you find Lee coming to the north of the Rappahannock, I would by no means cross to the south of it. If he should leave a rear force at Fredericksburg, tempting you to fall upon it, it would fight in intrenchments and have you at disadvantage, and so, man for man, worst you at that point, while his main force would in some way be getting an advantage of you northward. In one word, I would not take any risk of being entangled upon the river, like an ox jumped half over a fence and liable to be torn by dogs front and rear, without a fair chance to gore one way or kick the other. If Lee would come to my side of the river, I would keep on the same side, and fight him or act on the defense, according as might be my estimate of his strength relatively to my own. But these are mere suggestions, which I desire to be controlled by the judgment of yourself and General Halleck.

A. LINCOLN.

—

WASHINGTON, D. C., *June* 5, 1863—4.40 p. m.

Major-General HOOKER,
Falmouth, Va.:

The President has directed me to reply to your telegram to him of 10 a. m. to-day. My instructions of January 31,* which were then shown to the President, left you entirely free to act as circumstances, in your judgment, might require, with the simple injunction to keep in view the safety of Washington and Harper's Ferry. In regard to the contingency which you suppose may arise of General Lee's leaving a part of his forces in Fredericksburg, while, with the head of his column, he moves by Gordonsville or Culpeper toward the Potomac, it seems to me that such an operation would give you great advantages upon his flank to cut him in two, and fight his divided forces. Would it not be more advantageous to fight his movable column first, instead of first attacking his intrenchments, with your own forces separated by the Rappahannock? Moreover, you are aware that the troops under General Heintzelman are much less than the number recommended by all the boards for the defenses of Wash-

---

*See Series I, Vol. XXV, Part II, p. 12.

ington. Neither this capital nor Harper's Ferry could long hold out against a large force. They must depend for their security very much upon the co-operation of your army. It would, therefore, seem perilous to permit Lee's main force to move upon the Potomac while your army is attacking an intrenched position on the other side of the Rappahannock. Of course your movements must depend in a great measure upon those made by Lee. There is another contingency not altogether improbable—that Lee will seek to hold you in check with his main force, while a strong force will be detached for a raid into Maryland and Pennsylvania. The main force of the enemy in North Carolina have probably come north, but I think all available troops in South Carolina and Georgia have been sent to re-enforce Johnston in Mississippi. Such is the information here. General Heintzelman and General Dix are instructed to telegraph directly to you all the movements which they may ascertain or make. Directions have also been given to forward military information which may be received from General Schenck's command. Any movements you may suggest of troops in these commands will be ordered, if deemed practicable. Lee will probably move light and rapidly. Your movable force should be prepared to do the same.

The foregoing views are approved by the President.

H. W. HALLECK,
General-in-Chief.

—

HEADQUARTERS ARMY OF THE POTOMAC,
June 5, 1863. (Received 6.45 p. m.)

Hon. E. M. STANTON,
  Secretary of War:

The following is a dispatch which has been received from Brigadier-General Buford, commanding at Warrenton Junction :

WARRENTON JUNCTION, June 5, 1863.

Col. A. J. ALEXANDER,
 Assistant Adjutant-General :

I have just received information, which I consider reliable, that all the available cavalry force of the Confederacy is in Culpeper County. Stuart, the two Lees, [B. H.] Robertson, [A. G.] Jenkins, and [W. E.] Jones are all there. Robertson came from North Carolina, Jenkins from Kanawha, and Jones from the Valley. Jones arrived at Culpeper after the others, on the 3d. Since the Chancellorsville fight, their cavalry has been very much increased from the infantry ; 800 Texans, from Hood's command, have been recently mounted on horses from Richmond. My informant, a refugee from Madison County, says that Stuart has 20,000. Can't tell his intentions, but thinks he is going to make a raid.

JNO. BUFORD,
Brigadier-General.

JOSEPH HOOKER,
Major-General.

—

JUNE 5, 1863—9.15 p. m. (Received 9.45.)

His Excellency THE PRESIDENT OF THE UNITED STATES :

Mr. PRESIDENT : I should very much like to have Captain [Tredwell] Moore ordered to this army.

Since writing this morning, I concluded to make a demonstration on the enemy by throwing a couple of bridges across the river at Franklin's Crossing, and to learn, if possible, what the enemy are about.   As soon as we got to work, they began to assemble in great numbers from all quarters, and the more remote are still arriving.

I took about 50 prisoners, and they report that the changes remarked in their camps proceeded from the reorganization of their army, and the assignments of them to new camps.   All of Longstreet's command are now with Lee, but no part of the Charleston forces.   They have no infantry force higher up the Rappahannock than its junction with the Rapidan.   Their cavalry is assembled around Culpeper, but the threat to make a crossing may cause them to return.   I shall keep my bridges down a few days.

> JOSEPH HOOKER,
> *Major-General.*

—

HEADQUARTERS ARMY OF THE POTOMAC,
June 6, 1863—3 p. m.   (Received 3.30 p. m.)
Major-General HALLECK:

As the accumulation of the heavy rebel force of cavalry about Culpeper may mean mischief, I am determined, if practicable, to break it up in its incipiency.   I shall send all my cavalry against them, stiffened by about 3,000 infantry.   It will require until the morning of the 9th for my forces to gain their positions, and at daylight on that day it is my intention to attack them in their camps.   As many of my cavalry are still unserviceable from the effects of Stoneman's raid, I am too weak to cope with the numbers of the enemy if as large as represented.   It would add much to my efficiency if some of Stahel's forces could advance, and hold the fords at Beverly and Sulphur Springs some time during the forenoon of the 9th.   If this should be done, I desire that the officer in command should not be informed of the object of his march, but merely to hold these fords. It is next to impossible to confine information to its proper limits.

I have 2,500 sabers on a reconnaissance to-day in the vicinity of Jefferson.   Jones' brigade, which has been hovering about Milroy all winter, numbering 1,600, is among them; also an additional brigade from North Carolina.

> JOSEPH HOOKER,
> *Major-General.*

—

June 6, 1863—8 p. m.   (Received 8.45 p. m.)
Major-General HALLECK:

I request that I may be informed whether or not I am to receive assistance in my attack on the rebel forces at Culpeper from any portion of Major-General Heintzelman's forces, and, if so, what?

> JOSEPH HOOKER,
> *Major-General.*

—

June 9, 1863—12 m.   (Received o p. m.)
Major-General HALLECK:

Brigadier-General Pleasonton reports that, after a severe encounter with the rebel cavalry over the Beverly Ford, he has not been able to make head against it.   He reports that his movement was anticipated.

> JOSEPH HOOKER,
> *Major-General.*

HEADQUARTERS ARMY OF THE POTOMAC,
June 9, 1863—1 p. m.

Maj. Gen. JOHN A. DIX,
Fort Monroe, Va.:

We have reliable information that Pickett's division, which was lately at Taylorsville, near Hanover Junction, has come up this way and gone toward the Rapidan. Hood's division preceded it in the same direction. We have also reason to believe that the available troops have been withdrawn from Richmond this way, leaving it nearly if not wholly unoccupied.

The country between Fredericksburg and Richmond and below the right flank of Lee's army, which extends only 5 miles below the city, is open and unoccupied, excepting by small bodies and a force which has just gone down on account of a false alarm made by us in that direction. The Thirtieth Virginia alone is left near Hanover Junction. It is a weak regiment.

Our scouts penetrate to Hanover Junction, and we believe the above reliable from previously reported information confirming it, and the character of the scouts. The movements in your direction have been countermanded, probably by my demonstrations.

JOSEPH HOOKER,
Major-General.

(Copy to Major-General Halleck.   Received 6.40 p. m.)

—

JUNE 10, 1863—2.30 p. m.   (Received 5.10 p. m.)

His Excellency the PRESIDENT OF THE UNITED STATES:

Mr. PRESIDENT: General Pleasonton, by telegram forwarded to the major-general commanding the army this morning, reports that he had an affair with the rebel cavalry yesterday near Brandy Station, which resulted in crippling him so much that he will have to abandon his contemplated raid into Maryland, which was to have started this morning.

I am not so certain that the raid will be abandoned from this cause. It may delay the departure a few days. I shall leave the cavalry, which is all that I have mounted, where they are, near Bealeton, with instructions to resist the passage of the river by the enemy's forces. If to effect this he should bring up a considerable force of infantry, that will so much weaken him in my front that I have good reason to believe that I can throw a sufficient force over the river to compel the enemy to abandon his present position. If it should be the intention to send a heavy column of infantry to accompany the cavalry on the proposed raid, he can leave nothing behind to interpose any serious obstacle to my rapid advance on Richmond. I am not satisfied of his intention in this respect, but from certain movements in their corps I cannot regard it as altogether improbable. If it should be found to be the case, will it not promote the true interest of the cause for me to march to Richmond at once? From there all the disposable part of this army can be thrown to any threatened point north of the Potomac at short notice, and, until they can reach their destination, a sufficiency of troops can be collected to check, if not to stop, his invasion. If left to operate from my own judgment, with my present information, I do not hesitate to say that I should adopt this course as being the most speedy and certain mode of giving the rebellion a mortal blow. I desire that you will give it your reflection.   At present the enemy has one corps of infantry at Gordonsville, with the advance at Culpeper, with the manifest tendency of other corps to drift in that direction.   I now have two bridges across the Rappahannock, ready to spring over the river below Fredericksburg, and it is this, I believe, that causes the enemy to hesitate in moving forward.

Major-General Dix informs me that he intends moving two columns up James River to-morrow; but if organized to correspond in numbers to the troops as they have of late been posted, neither column will be successful.   The one on the north side of the river will be too small, and on the south side, with his whole column, I question if Richmond can be taken at all, provided 2,000 or 3,000 men could be assembled to defend it.   The columns should unite at City Point, or below, and move on the north bank of that river.

From information, which I deem reliable, the only troops remaining in Richmond is the provost-guard, 1,500, and all the troops between here and there are brought well to the front.

It would be of incalculable service to this army to be transferred to some more remote point from Washington and Alexandria.   The stampedes in those towns, gotten up, no doubt, by people in the rebel interest, have their influence on my men, for many of them have no means of knowing whether they are with or without cause.   They think there must be some fire where there is so much smoke.

JOSEPH HOOKER,
Major-General.

WASHINGTON, June 10, 1863—6.40 p. m.

Major-General HOOKER:

Your long dispatch of to-day is just received.   If left to me, I would not go south of Rappahannock upon Lee's moving north of it. If you had Richmond invested to-day, you would not be able to take it in twenty days; meanwhile your communications, and with them your army, would be ruined.   I think Lee's army, and not Richmond, is your sure objective point.   If he comes toward the Upper Potomac, follow on his flank and on his inside track, shortening your lines while he lengthens his.   Fight him, too, when opportunity offers.   If he stays where he is, fret him and fret him.

A. LINCOLN.

WASHINGTON, D. C., June 11, 1863—12.40 p. m.

Major-General HOOKER,
        Army of the Potomac:

The President has just referred to me your telegram and his reply of yesterday, with directions to say to you whether or not I agree with him.   I do so fully.

H. W. HALLECK,
General-in-Chief.

HEADQUARTERS ARMY OF THE POTOMAC,
June 11, 1863—9 p. m.   (Received 10.30 p. m.)

Maj. Gen. H. W. HALLECK:

I have just been reliably informed that Pettigrew's and Darnell's [Davis'] brigades from North Carolina are in Heth's division, near

Hamilton's Crossing. I have no information concerning the residue of the forces drawn from North Carolina.

A. P. Hill's corps is on the right, opposite to Franklin's Crossing; Ewell's is in rear of Fredericksburg, and Longstreet's corps and the cavalry are at Culpeper.

I have to-day dispatched the Third Corps to picket the river from Meade's right, at Kelly's Ford, to Beverly Ford, in order to relieve the cavalry in aid of Pleasonton, who is looking after the district of country from Beverly to Sulphur Springs. Pleasonton is weak in cavalry compared with the enemy.

JOSEPH HOOKER,
Major-General.

—

JUNE 12, 1863—7 a. m.   (Received 8.40 a. m.)
Maj. Gen. H. W. HALLECK:

It is reported to me from the balloon that several new rebel camps have made their appearance this morning. There can be no doubt but that the enemy has been greatly re-enforced.

JOSEPH HOOKER,
Major-General.

—

HEADQUARTERS ARMY OF THE POTOMAC,
June 12, 1863—8.30 a. m.   (Received 8.45 a. m.)
Major-General HALLECK,
General-in-Chief:

General Pleasonton, without additional cavalry, I fear will not be able to prevent the rebel cavalry from turning his right. I have not been able to ascertain his precise strength, but know that it is near 7,500, while that of the enemy is certainly not less than 10,000. He now pickets beyond Sulphur Springs. He will, however, do the best he can. If he should be turned, you will perceive that I shall be constrained to abandon the Aquia Creek line of operations.

JOSEPH HOOKER,
Major-General.

———

HEADQUARTERS ARMY OF THE POTOMAC,
June 12, 1863—1.15 p. m.   (Received 1.40 p. m.)
Maj. Gen. H. W. HALLECK,
General-in-Chief:

Learning that the enemy had massed his cavalry near Culpeper for the purpose of a raid, I dispatched General Pleasonton to attack him on his own ground. General Pleasonton crossed the Rappahannock on the 9th, at Beverly and Kelly's Fords, attacked the enemy, and drove him 3 miles, capturing over 200 prisoners and one battle-flag. This, in the face of vastly superior numbers, was only accomplished by hard and desperate fighting by our cavalry, for which they deserve much credit. Their *morale* is splendid. They made many hand-to-hand combats, always driving the enemy before them.

JOSEPH HOOKER,
Major-General.

WASHINGTON, D. C., *June* 12, 1863—1.30 p. m.

Major-General HOOKER,
    Army of the Potomac:

There is no possibility of sending you more cavalry. Horses will be sent as fast as they can be procured.

H. W. HALLECK,
General-in-Chief.

—

EXECUTIVE MANSION,
June 12, 1863—2 p. m.

Major-General HOOKER :

If you can show me a trial of the incendiary shells on Saturday night, I will try to join you at 5 p. m. that day. Answer.

A. LINCOLN.

—

HEADQUARTERS ARMY OF THE POTOMAC,
June 12, 1863—6.20 p. m.   (Received 7 p. m.)

ABRAHAM LINCOLN,
    President of the United States:

If I am not very much mistaken, I shall be constrained to move my army on to the Orange and Alexandria Railroad before that time. I have three corps near there at this time.

I presume that General Halleck showed you my dispatch of this morning; also please see copy of my dispatch to General Dix of to-day.

JOSEPH HOOKER,
Major-General.

—

JUNE 12—9 p. m.

His Excellency the PRESIDENT :

At the time of my reply to your telegram of to-day, I supposed that this was Thursday and not Friday. It will give me great pleasure to have the gun on exhibition at 5 p. m. to-morrow. I have some good targets in the shape of rebel camps which the gun will enfilade.

JOSEPH HOOKER,
Major-General.

—

WASHINGTON, *June* 13, 1863—11.30 a. m.

Major-General HOOKER :

I was coming down this afternoon, but if you prefer I should not, I shall blame you if you do not tell me so.

A. LINCOLN,
President.

—

JUNE 13, 1863.

The PRESIDENT :

Mr. PRESIDENT : It may be well not to come.

JOSEPH HOOKER,
Major-General

JUNE 13, 1863—7 p. m.   (Received 7.45 p. m.)

Maj. Gen. H. W. HALLECK:

All my sources of information confirm the statement that Longstreet's and Ewell's corps have passed through Culpeper and Sperryville, toward the Valley. The instructions of the President, approved by yourself, and your original letter of instructions, compel me, in view of this movement of the enemy, to transfer the operations of this army from the line of the Aquia to the Orange and Alexandria Railroad. Accordingly, directions have been given for the First, Third, Fifth, and Eleventh Corps to rendezvous at Manassas Junction with the cavalry. The Second, Sixth, and Twelfth, with the Reserve Artillery, after covering the withdrawal of Government property from depots, have been directed to march to Dumfries, and from thence to be governed by the movements of the enemy, the object being to bring the two wings together as far in advance on that line as the movements of the enemy will justify.

The corps will be withdrawn from their positions on the river to-night, the line being held by pickets until the proper time arrives for their withdrawal. To-morrow p. m. my headquarters will be at Dumfries.

JOSEPH HOOKER,
Major-General.

—

WASHINGTON, *June* 14, 1863—1.14 p. m.

Major-General HOOKER:

Do you consider it possible that 15,000 of Ewell's men can now be at Winchester?

A. LINCOLN.

—

DUMFRIES, *June* 14, 1863—5 p. m.

Major-General HALLECK:

At 3 p. m. Major-General Hancock informs me that the rebel troops opposite Franklin's Crossing are moving up the river, on the Plank road, in a continuous column. Major-General Hancock covers the withdrawal of the forces and property at that point. No effort has been made to force the passage of the Rappahannock, excepting at Banks' Ford.

JOSEPH HOOKER,
Major-General.

—

DUMFRIES, *June* 14, 1863—5.30 p. m.
(Received 5.40 p. m.)

Hon. E. M. STANTON,
Secretary of War:

Have received dispatch from General Milroy, dated yesterday. Will act on it as soon as I can hear from the column on the Orange and Alexandria Railroad. Instructions were given for Thoroughfare Gap to be taken possession of and held by my cavalry last night. If the enemy should be making for Maryland, I will make the best dispositions in my power to come up with him.

You may rely upon his being in great force wherever he is.

JOSEPH HOOKER,
Major-General.

WASHINGTON, *June* 14, 1863—5.50 p. m.

Major-General HOOKER:

So far as we can make out here, the enemy have Milroy surrounded at Winchester and Tyler at Martinsburg. If they could hold out a few days, could you help them? If the head of Lee's army is at Martinsburg and the tail of it on the Plank road between Fredericksburg and Chancellorsville, the animal must be very slim somewhere. Could you not break him?

A. LINCOLN.

———

ARMY OF THE POTOMAC,
June 14, 1863—7.10 p. m.

The PRESIDENT:

In answer to your dispatch concerning General Ewell, I must refer you to that of General Pleasonton, dated 6.05 p. m. to-day.*

JOSEPH HOOKER,
Major-General.

———

DUMFRIES, *June* 14, 1863—8.30 p. m.   (Received 9 p. m.)

Mr. PRESIDENT: I have reason to believe that Longstreet's and the greater part of Ewell's corps marched from Culpeper, on the Sperryville road, on Sunday last [7th], and that a column, which occupied four hours in passing, followed on Thursday. If this was the case, the head of the column has had time to reach Winchester, and if it is a movement for invasion, it is a fair presumption to conclude that the bulk of his cavalry is with him. The enemy has in this column not less than between 70,000 and 80,000 men. A. P. Hill's corps, of about 30,000, is still on the south side of the Rappahannock, and General Hancock has just informed me that present appearances indicate that he intends to force the passage of the river in the morning. His troops have all been halted at and below Banks' Ford. My trains are all this side of Stafford Court-House, and the public property, I am informed, will be removed from Aquia to-morrow—the sick to-night.

The First Corps is at Kettle Run; the Second on the Rappahannock; the Third and Fifth at Catlett's Station; the Sixth at Potomac Creek; the Eleventh at Centreville; and the Twelfth at Dumfries to-night.

The Second will probably withdraw, the First march to Manassas, and the Sixth to Stafford Court-House during the night.

JOSEPH HOOKER,
Major-General.

———

DUMFRIES, *June* 14, 1863—11.15 p. m.
(Received 11.30 p. m.)

His Excellency the PRESIDENT:

Has anything further been heard from Winchester? Will the President allow me to inquire if it is his opinion that Winchester is surrounded by the rebel forces? I make this inquiry for the reason that General [I. R.] Trimble was recently assigned, in orders, to the

———

*See Pleasonton to Hooker, June 14, Part III, p. 101.

command of that district, and it is not known what command he had, unless his old one, which had Louisiana regiments in it, and it was in Jackson's, now Ewell's, corps. I do not feel like making a move for an enemy until I am satisfied as to his whereabouts. To proceed to Winchester and have him make his appearance elsewhere, would subject me to ridicule. With this feeling, unless otherwise directed, I feel it my duty to proceed to execute the movement indicated on yesterday. I will not, however, issue my order of march until the last moment, in the hope that further information may be received.

JOSEPH HOOKER,
Major-General.

WASHINGTON, *June* 14, 1863—11.55 p. m.
(Received June 15, 12.35 a. m.)

Major-General HOOKER:

Yours of 11.30 [11.15] just received. You have nearly all the elements for forming an opinion whether Winchester is surrounded that I have. I really fear, almost believe, it is. No communication has been had with it during the day, either at Martinsburg or Harper's Ferry. At 7 p. m. we also lost communication with Martinsburg. The enemy had also appeared there some hours before. At 9 p. m. Harper's Ferry said the enemy was reported at Berryville and Smithfield. If I could know that Longstreet and Ewell moved in that direction so long ago as you stated in your last, then I should feel sure that Winchester is strongly invested. It is quite certain that a considerable force of the enemy is thereabout, and I fear it is an overwhelming one compared with Milroy's. I am unable to give you any more certain opinions.

A. LINCOLN.

WASHINGTON, *June* 14, 1863—12 midnight.
Major-General HOOKER,
Dumfries:

No doubt is entertained here that Milroy is surrounded at Winchester, and so closely invested that no scout or other information has been had from him later than 11 o'clock Saturday night. Tyler was also surrounded to-day at Martinsburg. Jenkins was there, and demanded the surrender of the place. Heavy firing was heard in that vicinity until 7 o'clock, and then ceased. The telegraphic communication was broken at the same time, and nothing is known here of the result. The report here is that Ewell's force is at Winchester; this comes from Milroy by the last dispatch sent by him, Saturday night, to General Schenck. Your dispatch has been sent to the President, who will probably reply soon.

EDWIN M. STANTON.

DUMFRIES. *June* 15, 1863—9.15 a. m.
Major-General HALLECK :

The First, Third, Sixth, and Eleventh Corps, with the cavalry, will be assembled at Manassas and Centreville to-night. They have instructions to replenish their forage and rations, which I trust they will be able to do to-day.   The Second Corps will be at Dumfries, the Sixth at Wolf Run Shoals, and the Twelfth at Fairfax Court-House to-night.

Major-General Hancock reports that the rebel forces about Fredericksburg have moved in the direction of Culpeper this morning.

To-night my headquarters will be at Fairfax Station.   If your information from the Upper Potomac should be of a character to justify a movement in that direction, I request that I may be informed of it at the earliest practicable moment.

JOSEPH HOOKER,
Major-General.

—

DUMFRIES, *June* 15, 1863—10.20 a. m.

General HALLECK :

Two of our best scouts returned from the interior, above Fredericksburg, yesterday (Sunday) morning.   They report A. P. Hill, with sixty guns and 20,000 men, left on the heights about Fredericksburg.   On Saturday p. m. 4,000 of this force moved toward Culpeper.   On the same day, General Lee's headquarters were on the Lacy farm, between Brandy Station and Culpeper Court-House. Citizens say that the cavalry expedition was intended for Alexandria, while Lee was to go up the Valley.   They believe that a great cavalry raid is now given up, as the cavalry is divided, a considerable part being still near Brandy Station.   The passage of the infantry is traced across the Hazel River.

The Richmond papers of the 13th blame Stuart much for allowing himself to be surprised in his camp by Pleasonton, and call upon him to do something to retrieve his reputation.   Anxiety expressed concerning the movements on the Peninsula.   Will send the papers to you.

DANL. BUTTERFIELD,
Major-General, Chief of Staff.

—

WASHINGTON, D. C., *June* 15, 1863—12.50 p. m.

Major-General HOOKER,
        Army of the Potomac:

No information of enemy in direction of Winchester and Harper's Ferry as late as that from General Pleasonton.*   The forces at Martinsburg are arriving at Harper's Ferry.

H. W. HALLECK,
General-in-Chief.

—

WASHINGTON, D. C., *June* 15, 1863—2 p. m.

Major-General HOOKER,
        Army of the Potomac:

Garrison of Martinsburg has arrived at Harper's Ferry.   Milroy did not obey orders given on the 11th to abandon Winchester, and

---

* See Pleasonton to Stanton, June 15, Part III, p. 115.

probably has or will be captured.   Harper's Ferry ought to hold out some time.   Pleasonton's telegrams to you contain all the information we have of the enemy's movements.   They are very contradictory.   Your army is entirely free to operate as you desire against Lee's army, so long as you keep his main army from Washington. It is believed that Longstreet and Stuart are crossing the Potomac above and below Harper's Ferry.   They certainly should be pursued. The force used for that purpose must depend upon your information of the movements or position of the remainder of Lee's army.   Leesburg seems about the best point to move on first.   The information sent here by General Pleasonton is very unsatisfactory.   His suggestions to send batteries from here to the mouth of the Monocacy cannot be adopted.*   If we had them to send, they would only be lost.

H. W. HALLECK,
General-in-Chief.

—

WASHINGTON, D. C., *June* 15, 1863—4.05 p. m.

Major-General HOOKER,
Army of the Potomac:

General Meigs is apprehensive that you have not allowed time enough to withdraw material from Aquia Creek.   Please prevent such wanton and wasteful destruction of public property as took place when Burnside withdrew from there last year.

H. W. HALLECK,
General-in-Chief.

—

JUNE 15, 1863.

His Excellency the PRESIDENT OF THE UNITED STATES:

Only two Louisiana brigades in rebel army here.   [H. T.] Hays' brigade, in Early's division, has the Fifth, Sixth, Seventh, Eighth, and Ninth Louisiana.   Prisoners from them would indicate the presence of Ewell's whole corps.   [F. T.] Nicholls' brigade, in Trimble's division, has the First, Second, Tenth, Fourteenth, and Fifteenth Louisiana.   Prisoners from them would not indicate as above, as Trimble has lately been appointed to command the Valley District. Jenkins and Imboden have been in the Valley some time, and their forces are inconsiderable.   Trimble's division is under 8,000.

JOSEPH HOOKER,
Major-General, Commanding.

—

HEADQUARTERS ARMY OF THE POTOMAC,
Fairfax Station, June 15, 1863—6.30 p. m.
(Received 7.30 p. m.)

Major-General HALLECK:

I have left a brigade at Aquia, and ordered them to hold it until further orders.   I apprehend no danger there.

JOSEPH HOOKER,
Major-General.

---

*See Pleasonton to Stanton, Part III, p. 115.

WASHINGTON, *June* 15, 1863—8.30 p. m.
(Received 9.15 p. m.)

Major-General HOOKER,
   Fairfax Station:

The facts are now known here that Winchester and Martinsburg were both besieged yesterday. The troops from Martinsburg have got into Harper's Ferry without loss. Those from Winchester are also in, having lost in killed, wounded, and missing about one-third of their number. Of course, the enemy holds both places, and I think the report is authentic that he is crossing the Potomac at Williamsport. We have not heard of his yet appearing at Harper's Ferry or on the river anywhere below. I would like to hear from you.

          A. LINCOLN.

—

       FAIRFAX STATION, *June* 15, 1863.

His Excellency the PRESIDENT,
   Washington:

Your telegram of 8.30 p. m. received. It seems to disclose the intentions of the enemy to make an invasion, and, if so, it is not in my power to prevent it. I can, however, make an effort to check him until he has concentrated all his forces. I may possibly be able to prevent the junction, and commence the movement during to-morrow. On so short reflection, I am not prepared to say this is the wisest move, nor do I know that my opinion on this subject is wanted. A. P. Hill moved up toward Culpeper this morning, indicating his intention to re-enforce their forces on the Upper Potomac.

       JOSEPH HOOKER,
      Major-General, Commanding.

—

        JUNE 15, 1863—10 p. m.

His Excellency the PRESIDENT OF THE UNITED STATES:

Your dispatch, 8.30, received. My dispatch to General Halleck this morning shows my position to-night With regard to the enemy, your dispatch is more conclusive than any I have received. I now feel that invasion is his settled purpose. If so, he has more to accomplish, but with more hazard, by striking an easterly direction after crossing than a northerly one. It seems to me that he will be more likely to go north, and to incline to the west. He can have no design to look after his rear. It is an act of desperation on his part, no matter in what force he moves. It will kill copperheadism in the North. I do not know that my opinion as to the duty of this army in the case is wanted; if it should be, you know that I will be happy to give it. I have heard nothing of the movements of the enemy to-day, excepting that he has not attempted to follow me across the Rappahannock. I have only heard that all of A. P. Hill's forces moved up the river this morning, in the direction of Culpeper. If it should be determined for me to make a movement in pursuit, which I am not prepared to recommend at this time, I may possibly be able to move some corps to-morrow, and can reach the point of the enemy's crossing in advance of A. P. Hill. If I should move at once, he would **probably** wait until his forces are concentrated. If they are moving toward Maryland, I can better fight them there than make a running fight. If they come up in front of Washington, I can threaten and cut their communications, and Dix can be re-enforced from the south to act on their rear. I could not sit still and have them turn my right. My sources of information could not successfully cover such an extent of country as their movements indicate. I add these as suggestions for your consideration.

JOSEPH HOOKER,
Major-General, Commanding.

—

HEADQUARTERS ARMY OF THE POTOMAC,
Fairfax Station, June 15, 1863—Midnight.
(Received June 16, 1.15 a. m.)

His Excellency the PRESIDENT:

I have received your dispatch of this evening. The Army of the Potomac is in this vicinity, excepting the Second and Sixth Corps, and, as they are marching in rear of all the trains, they will not be up before some time to-morrow.

Perhaps the Second Corps will not be here until some time during to-morrow night. The First and Eleventh Corps were first to arrive on this line, but I have not yet learned whether they have drawn their supplies in readiness to march to-morrow morning or not. As soon as they are provided, they, as well as the others, will be put *en route.*

I have been informed that the enemy nowhere crossed the Rappahannock on our withdrawal from it, but General Hill's troops moved up the river in the direction of Culpeper this morning, for the purpose, I conclude, of re-enforcing Longstreet and Ewell, wherever they may be.

I request that I may be informed what troops there are at Harper's Ferry, and who is in command of them, and also who is in command in this district.

JOSEPH HOOKER,
Major-General.

—

FAIRFAX STATION, June 16, 1863—7 a. m.
(Received 8.35 a. m.)

His Excellency President LINCOLN:

It appears to me from General Couch's dispatch of last night,* received this a. m., that nearly all the cavalry of the Army of the Potomac should at once be sent into Maryland by the most direct route. General Stahel has an abundance to perform all cavalry duty that will be required south of the Potomac. I merely make the suggestion. If any considerable body of enemy's infantry should be thrown across the Potomac, they will probably take the direction of his advance pickets, and in that event it seems to me that a heavy column of ours should be thrown as speedily as possible across the river at Harper's Ferry, while another should be thrown over the most direct line covering Baltimore and Philadelphia. I only speak with reference to this army, as I know nothing of the location or numbers of troops at the disposal of the Government elsewhere.

JOSEPH HOOKER,
Major-General.

---

*See Part III, p. 131.

HEADQUARTERS ARMY OF THE POTOMAC,
Fairfax Station, June 16, 1863—11 a. m.

His Excellency ABRAHAM LINCOLN,
President, &c.:

Please accept my suggestions in regard to what should be done in the spirit with which they were given. They were suggestions merely, for I have not the data necessary to form an enlightened opinion on the case. Upon general principles, I thought those were the movements to make.

You have long been aware, Mr. President, that I have not enjoyed the confidence of the major-general commanding the army, and I can assure you so long as this continues we may look in vain for success, especially as future operations will require our relations to be more dependent upon each other than heretofore.

It may be possible now to move to prevent a junction of A. P. Hill's corps with those of Ewell and Longstreet. If so, please let instructions to that effect be given me. As will appear to you, the chances for my doing this are much smaller than when I was on the Rappahannock, for, if he should hold the passes stoutly, he can cause me delay. You may depend upon it, we can never discover the whereabouts of the enemy, or divine his intentions, so long as he fills the country with a cloud of cavalry. We must break through that to find him.

JOSEPH HOOKER,
Major-General.

—

WASHINGTON, D. C., *June* 16, 1863—11.30 a. m.

Major-General HOOKER,
Fairfax Station:

I do not think there is reliable information that the enemy has crossed the Potomac in any force. Where his main corps are, is still uncertain, and I know of no way to ascertain, excepting through your cavalry, which should be kept near enough to the enemy to at least be able to tell where he is. My suggestion of yesterday, to follow the enemy's advance, by moving a considerable force first to Leesburg, and thence as circumstances may require, is the best one I can make. Unless your army is kept near enough to the enemy to ascertain his movements, yours must be in the dark or on mere conjecture. Tyler is in command at Harper's Ferry, with, it is said, only 9,000 men, but, according to returns of the 11th, he should have at least 13,600. Heintzelman, as you must be aware, commands this department. Besides the divisions of Abercrombie and Stahel, near you, he has little or no movable troops. Telegraph direct to him in all matters connected with the use of his troops.

H. W. HALLECK,
General-in-Chief.

—

WASHINGTON, D. C., *June* 16, 1863—3.50 p. m.

Major-General HOOKER,
Army of the Potomac:

There is now no doubt that the enemy is surrounding Harper's Ferry, but in what force I have no information. General Schenck says our force there is much less than before reported, and cannot hold out very long. He wished to know whether he may expect relief. He can hope for none, excepting from your army.

H. W. HALLECK,
General-in-Chief.

—

HEADQUARTERS ARMY OF THE POTOMAC,
Fairfax Station, June 16, 1863—4. p. m.
(Received 4.50 p. m.)

Maj. Gen. H. W. HALLECK,
General-in-Chief :

Just received your telegram. Please inform me whether our forces at Harper's Ferry are in the town or on the heights, and, if the latter, whether we hold Bolivar, Loudoun, or Maryland Heights, and which, if any ; what bridges at Harper's Ferry, and where ; from what direction is the enemy making his attack ? I suppose it is a couple of long marches from here for troops without trains, but this, of course, will depend upon the position of the enemy.

JOSEPH HOOKER,
Major-General.

—

HEADQUARTERS ARMY OF THE POTOMAC,
Fairfax Station, June 16, 1863—7.30 p. m.

H. W. HALLECK,
General-in-Chief :

In compliance with your directions, I shall march to the relief of Harper's Ferry. I put my column again in motion at 3 a. m. to-morrow. I expect to reach there in two days, and, if possible, earlier. The partial rest of to-day was not lost, being necessary to recruit from forced and heavy marches and fill up supplies.

My headquarters at Farrall [?] Station to-morrow night.

JOSEPH HOOKER,
Major-General.

(Copy to the President.)

—

WASHINGTON, D. C., *June* 16, 1863—8.20 p. m.

Major-General HOOKER,
Army of the Potomac :

Information of enemy's actual position and force in front of Harper's Ferry is as indefinite as that in your front. Nearly everything is conjecture. The only position of the enemy mentioned is Hall-town. The bridges across both rivers at Harper's Ferry are believed to be intact, and most of Tyler's troops on Maryland Heights. Loudoun Heights are not fortified, but swept by Maryland batteries. Your questions have been sent to Tyler, and his answer will be forwarded as soon as received. Any troops you can send to his relief should be in motion. A few of the enemy have shown themselves at Poolesville and Point of Rocks. No definite information of his movements from any place.

H. W. HALLECK,
General-in-Chief.

HEADQUARTERS ARMY OF THE POTOMAC,
June 16, 1863—9.40 p. m.   (Received 9.50 p. m.)

His Excellency the PRESIDENT :

My orders are out to march at 3 o'clock to-morrow morning. It will be likely to be one of vigor and power. I am prepared to move without communications with any place for ten days. I hope to reach my objective point before the arrival of Hill's corps, should it be moving in that direction. If I do not know this fact, I will shortly, but of information to the north of the Potomac I really have nothing.

I wish that it might be made the duty of some person in the telegraph office in Washington to keep me informed of the enemy's movements in Maryland.

JOSEPH HOOKER,
Major-General.

—

WASHINGTON, *June* 16, 1863—10 p. m.

Major-General HOOKER :

To remove all misunderstanding, I now place you in the strict military relation to General Halleck of a commander of one of the armies to the general-in-chief of all the armies. I have not intended differently, but as it seems to be differently understood, I shall direct him to give you orders and you to obey them.

A. LINCOLN.

—

WASHINGTON, D. C., *June* 16, 1863—10.15 p. m.

Major-General HOOKER,
Army of the Potomac:

I have given no directions for your army to move to Harper's Ferry. I have advised the movement of a force, sufficiently strong to meet Longstreet, on Leesburg, to ascertain where the enemy is, and then move to the relief of Harper's Ferry, or elsewhere, as circumstances might require. With the remainder of your force in proper position to support this, I want you to push out your cavalry, to ascertain something definite about the enemy. You are in command of the Army of the Potomac, and will make the particular dispositions as you deem proper. I shall only indicate the objects to be aimed at. We have no positive information of any large force against Harper's Ferry, and it cannot be known whether it will be necessary to go there until you can feel the enemy and ascertain his whereabouts.

H. W. HALLECK,
General-in-Chief.

—

HEADQUARTERS ARMY OF THE POTOMAC,
June 16, 1863. (Received 10.45 p. m.)

Hon. E. M. STANTON,
Secretary of War:

If General Cadwalader has gone to Pennsylvania, please request him to send me information of the rebel movements to the south of there.   Also please have the newspapers announce that I am moving on to the James River line.   I will mask my real movements in these parts.

JOSEPH HOOKER,
Major-General.

WASHINGTON, *June* 16, 1863.
Major-General HOOKER, *Fairfax:*

General Cadwalader has not gone to Pennsylvania, but is here waiting for orders.   You shall be kept posted upon all information received here as to enemy's movements, but must exercise your own judgment as to its credibility.   The very demon of lying seems to be about these times, and generals will have to be broken for ignorance before they will take the trouble to find out the truth of reports.

EDWIN M. STANTON.

WASHINGTON, *June* 17, 1863—9.30 a. m.
Major-General HOOKER:

Mr. Eckert, superintendent of the telegraph office, answers me that he has sent, and will send you, everything that comes to the office.

A. LINCOLN.

HEADQUARTERS ARMY OF THE POTOMAC,
Fairfax Station, June 17, 1863.
Major-General HALLECK,
Commanding, &c.:

Your dispatch of 10 p. m. received by me at 1 a. m.   Will make the dispositions of my forces to comply with the objects aimed at in your dispatch.

The advices heretofore received by telegraph from Washington have stated successively that Martinsburg and Winchester were invested and surrounded; that Harper's Ferry was closely invested, with urgent calls upon me for relief; that the enemy were advancing in three columns through Pennsylvania, and had driven in General Couch's pickets.   Now I am informed, in substance, that General Schenck thinks it all arises from one of his wagon trains; that General Tyler, at Harper's Ferry, whose urgent calls, as represented to me, required under my instructions rapid movements in this direction, seems to think that he is in no danger.

Telegraph operator just reports to me that Harper's Ferry is abandoned by our forces.   Is this true?

Directions have been given for my cavalry to make a reconnaissance in the direction of Winchester and Harper's Ferry, for the purpose of ascertaining the whereabouts and strength of the enemy, and while this is being done, some of the infantry corps will be advanced by easy marches.   As soon as the intentions of the enemy are known to me, I shall be able to advance with rapidity.

My headquarters will be at Fairfax Station to-night.

I should very much like to have reliable and correct information concerning the enemy on the north side of the Potomac.

Very respectfully, your obedient servant,
JOSEPH HOOKER,
Major-General, Commanding.

WASHINGTON, D. C., *June* 17, 1863—11.40 a. m.

Major-General HOOKER,
          Headquarters Army of the Potomac:

No reliable information of rebel movements in Maryland. All telegrams of importance received here are immediately sent to you. All telegrams from you or to you are subject to the hourly inspection of the Secretary of War and the President. No important instructions have or will be sent to you without their knowledge. It is important that the Department be kept advised of all your movements; not in detail, but their general character. Also send all the information you get of the enemy's movements and position.

H. W. HALLECK,
General-in-Chief.

—

JUNE 17, 1863—2 p. m.   (Received 4 p. m.)

Major-General HALLECK:

Advice of the abandonment of Harper's Ferry renders forced marches unnecessary to relieve it. This army will be in position as follows to-night: One corps at Dranesville; one corps at Guilford Station; one corps on Goose Creek, near Trappe Rock; one corps at Gum Springs; one corps at Centreville; one corps at Sangster's Station; one corps at Fairfax Station. Headquarters at Fairfax Station to-night. Cavalry feeling up through Aldie toward Winchester.

JOSEPH HOOKER,
Major-General.

—

WASHINGTON, D. C., *June* 17, 1863—2.10 p. m.

Major-General HOOKER,
          Headquarters Army of the Potomac:

I regret equally with you that reports from north side of the Potomac are so unreliable and contradictory, but they are given to you as received. What is meant by abandoning Harper's Ferry is merely that General Tyler has concentrated his force in the fortifications on Maryland Heights. No enemy in any force has been seen below Harper's Ferry, north of the river, and it is hoped that Tyler's cavalry may get something reliable above. So far, we have had only the wild rumors of panic-stricken people.

H. W. HALLECK,
General-in-Chief.

—

WASHINGTON, D. C., *June* 17, 1863—7.45 p. m.

Major-General HOOKER,
          Army of the Potomac:

My telegram of this morning [afternoon] has informed you what is meant by the abandonment of Harper's Ferry—a mere change of position. It changes in no respect the objects you are to keep in view.

H. W. HALLECK,
General-in-Chief.

FAIRFAX STATION, *June* 17, 1863—9.20 p. m.
(Received 10.40 p. m.)

Major-General HALLECK,
Washington:

I am in constant receipt of copies of dispatches from General Couch with regard to enemy at Chambersburg. Is there, in your opinion, any foundation for the reports? All my cavalry are out, and I have deemed it prudent to suspend any farther advance of the infantry until I have information that the enemy are in force in the Shenandoah Valley. I have just received dispatches from Pleasonton, dated 4.15 p. m. He ran against Fitzhugh Lee's brigade of cavalry near Aldie, and from prisoners learned that Stuart is at Middleburg; and it is further reported that there is no infantry on this side of the Blue Ridge. When the orderly left, Pleasonton had charged and driven Lee out of Aldie. All my cavalry are out.

Has it ever suggested itself to you that this cavalry raid may be a cover to Lee's re-enforcing Bragg or moving troops to the West?

JOSEPH HOOKER,
Major-General.

—

HEADQUARTERS ARMY OF THE POTOMAC,
June 18, 1863. (Received 7.50 a. m.)

Major-General HALLECK,
General-in-Chief:

At my last advices from Pleasonton, he had captured 8 officers and the greater portion of two squadrons of Fitz Lee's brigade of Stuart's cavalry, and driven them out of Aldie.

My instructions to him were to find out what was behind them. At 1 a. m. we received advices that looked as though White, with 400 cavalry, was at Point of Rocks. The Twelfth Corps was immediately ordered to Leesburg, and to hold it and the fords of the Potomac in that vicinity. I ought to have had a large cavalry force and two regiments of infantry at the mouth of the Monocacy last night. Having no means of telegraphic communication there, I am unadvised as to their arrival, and unable to give them orders by telegraph.

A bridge sufficient to cross the Potomac is also to be at that point at noon to-day.

JOSEPH HOOKER,
Major-General.

—

WASHINGTON, D. C., *June* 18, 1863—11 a. m.

Major-General HOOKER,
Army of the Potomac:

I can get no information of the enemy other than that sent to you. Rumors from Pennsylvania are too confused and contradictory to be relied on. Officers and citizens are on a big stampede. They are asking me why does not General Hooker tell where Lee's army is; he is nearest to it. There are numerous suppositions and theories, but all is yet mere conjecture. I only hope for positive information from your front. General Heintzelman has a signal line to Sugar Loaf Mountain, and is directed to send you all the information he obtains. General Kelley is observing the passes west of the Shenandoah, and will give you, through General Schenck, all information he can get. He is very reliable.

H. W. HALLECK,
General-in-Chief..

—

HEADQUARTERS ARMY OF THE POTOMAC,
June 18, 1863—9 a.m. (Received 10 a. m.)

H. W. HALLECK,
General-in-Chief:

Prisoners from Pleasonton's fight—9 officers and 66 men—now on the way to this camp.

Advices received of the arrival of my cavalry force and pontoons at mouth of Monocacy. Sixth Corps moved up to Germantown.

I would request that signal officers be established at Crampton's Pass and South Mountain. They can see the whole country north of the Potomac, and telegraph movements of any column. If my advices of to-day make it advisable, I shall seize and hold those passes. It may be necessary to use General Schenck's troops for that purpose.

JOSEPH HOOKER,
Major-General.

—

JUNE 18, 1863—10.07 a. m.   (Received 10.15 a. m.)

Major-General HALLECK:

GENERAL: I have to request that Brigadier-General Pleasonton, for his gallant conduct at Chancellorsville, his services there, and his attack and surprise of Stuart's force, superior in numbers, on the Rappahannock, June 9, may be made major-general, and assigned to command the cavalry corps.

JOSEPH HOOKER,
Major-General.

(Copy to the President and Secretary of War.)

—

WASHINGTON, D. C., *June* 18, 1863—1 p. m.

Major-General HOOKER,
Army of the Potomac:

Your telegram for a signal station at Crampton's Pass and South Mountain has been sent to Colonel Myer, with directions to carry out your wishes, if he has the means. General Schenck has been notified that you will have control of any of his forces that are within the sphere of your operations. If you want anything of General Schenck or General Heintzelman, telegraph to them direct. Copies of each telegram are always retained at the War Department for the information of the Government.   *   *   *

H. W. HALLECK,
General-in-Chief.

—

JUNE 19, 1863—12 noon.

Major-General HALLECK:

I have asked Generals Schenck and Heintzelman for information as to the location, character, and number of their commands. ' Please direct it to be furnished. I have directed General Stahel to concentrate his cavalry for movement. Please inform General Heintzelman. Are orders for these commands to be given by me where I deem it necessary? The nature of the control to be exercised by me I would like to have distinctly and clearly fixed and understood by Generals Heintzelman and Schenck, that I may not seem to avoid proper channels or to act discourteously toward them.

JOSEPH HOOKER,
Major-General, Commanding.

—

HEADQUARTERS ARMY OF THE POTOMAC,
June 19, 1863. (Received 12 m.)

Major-General HALLECK:

I have just been furnished with an extract from the New York Herald of yesterday concerning the late movements of this army. So long as the newspapers continue to give publicity to our movements, we must not expect to gain any advantage over our adversaries. Is there no way of stopping it? I can suppress the circulation of this paper within my lines, but I cannot prevent their reaching it to the enemy. We could well afford to give millions of money for like information of the enemy.

JOSEPH HOOKER,
Major-General.

—

WASHINGTON, D. C., *June* 19, 1863—1.55 p. m.

Major-General HOOKER,
    Army of the Potomac:

I appreciate as fully as yourself the injury resulting from newspaper publication of the movements, numbers, and position of our troops, but I see no way of preventing it as long as reporters are permitted in our camps. I expelled them all from our lines in Mississippi. Every general must decide for himself what persons he will permit in his camps.

H. W. HALLECK,
General-in-Chief.

—

HEADQUARTERS ARMY OF THE POTOMAC,
June 19, 1863—2 p. m. (Received 2.10 p. m.)

H. W. HALLECK, *General-in-Chief:*

Do you give credit to the reported movements of the enemy as stated in the Chronicle, of this morning?

JOSEPH HOOKER,
Major-General.

—

WASHINGTON, D. C., *June* 19, 1863—3.55 p. m.

Major-General HOOKER,
    Army of the Potomac:

I do not know to what particular statement in the Chronicle you refer. There are several which are contradictory. It now looks very much as if Lee had been trying to draw your right across the Potomac, so as to attack your left. But of that it is impossible to judge until we know where Lee's army is. No large body has appeared either in Maryland or Western Virginia.

H. W. HALLECK,
General-in-Chief.

—

JUNE 19, 1863—7.30 p. m.

Major-General HALLECK :

Reports just received from General Pleasonton, at Aldie, state General [D. McM.] Gregg has been fighting nearly all day—driven the enemy through Middleburg, in direction of Upperville ; has already sent in between 50 and 60 prisoners, one a lieutenant-colonel, and a number of officers of less rank, all from North Carolina. The force encountered was [B. H.] Robertson's brigade, North Carolina troops, supported by two other brigades, all under command of Stuart. Considerable loss inflicted upon the enemy.

My corps are to-night as follows :

Twelfth, Slocum, Leesburg.

Eleventh, Howard, on Goose Creek, 4 miles from Leesburg, toward Aldie.

Fifth, Meade, at Aldie.

First, Reynolds, at Herndon Station and vicinity, on Loudoun and Hampshire Railroad.

Third, Birney, at Gum Spring.

Second, Hancock, at Centreville.

Sixth, Sedgwick, at Germantown.

Pleasonton rests his cavalry at Aldie to-night.

Notwithstanding dispatch sent me by General Tyler, at Williamsport, his [Lee's] delay in my front has caused me to doubt his intention of throwing over any considerable force on Maryland shore. It is the impression of General Pleasonton that his infantry are still on opposite side of Blue Ridge, and that it is his intention to attack in this direction.

JOSEPH HOOKER,
Major-General.

—

JUNE 20, 1863—5.30 p. m.

Major-General HALLECK :

I have moved up Second Corps to Thoroughfare Gap ; a division of Second Corps at Gainesville ; a division of Sixth Corps at Bristoe ; other forces unchanged.

Pleasonton reports Stuart's force in front of him, beyond Middleburg. He will attack him with all his available command early to-morrow. Their cavalry have mounted infantry with them. Infantry soldiers captured report to Pleasonton that Longstreet's rear passed through the Blue Ridge yesterday. I have directed a bridge to be laid at Edwards Ferry to-night.

JOSEPH HOOKER,
Major-General.

—

WASHINGTON, *June* 21, 1863—9 a. m.

Major-General HOOKER :

Operator at Leesburg just now tells us that firing commenced about 7 this morning in direction from here of Aldie's Gap and Middleburg ; has continued all day, and has receded from him, and is apparently now about White Plains ; was very heavy this morning, but lighter now.

A. LINCOLN.

—

CAMP, *June* 21, 1863—5 p. m.   (Received 5.30 p. m.)
The PRESIDENT :

Pleasonton's cavalry and two brigades of Meade's infantry were directed to attack Stuart's cavalry this morning.   The fight commenced about 7 o'clock, and for several hours raged with great violence.   As the sound receded from us, I conclude that the enemy were whipped, and I feel confident that our forces are now driving them across the Blue Ridge, perhaps at Snicker's Gap.   All of the passes in the Blue Ridge, so far as I know, are stoutly held by the enemy, but I was in hopes that Pleasonton would be able to push his adversary so closely as to cross the mountain in their company.

This cavalry force has hitherto prevented me from obtaining satisfactory information as to the whereabouts of the enemy.   They have masked all of their movements.   I have not yet received a word from the front since the beginning of the fight ; from this I conclude the space between me and them has been lengthened since morning.

The cavalry and all the troops are in glorious spirits, and the former have achieved wonders in the last few days.

JOSEPH HOOKER,
Major-General.

—

HEADQUARTERS ARMY OF THE POTOMAC,
June 22, 1863—9.30 a. m.   (Received 10.50 a. m.)
The PRESIDENT :

Mr. PRESIDENT : My latest advices from General Pleasonton dated 4.30 p. m., the 21st.   At that time he had driven the rebel cavalry through Upperville, capturing some of his artillery, and still pursuing.   Appearances favorable.

JOSEPH HOOKER,
Major-General.

—

HEADQUARTERS OF THE ARMY,
Washington, D. C., June 22, 1863.
Major-General HOOKER,
Army of the Potomac :

Orders will be issued placing all that part of the Eighth Corps and of the Middle Department east of Cumberland under your immediate orders.   The Department of Washington will continue as heretofore, your orders being given direct to General Heintzelman, he reporting them to headquarters before executing them, where they conflict with his special instructions.   Affairs in Middle Department are represented as unsatisfactory.   I go immediately to Baltimore to ascertain their condition.

H. W. HALLECK,
General-in-Chief.

WASHINGTON, *June* 22, 1863.

Major-General HOOKER:

Operator at Leesburg just now says:

I heard very little firing this a. m. about daylight, but it seems to have stopped now. It was in about same direction as yesterday, but farther off.

A. LINCOLN,

—

WASHINGTON, D. C., *June* 22, 1863—3.15 p. m.

Major-General HOOKER,
    Army of the Potomac:

In order to give compactness to the command of troops in the field covering Washington and Baltimore, it is proposed to place that part of the Middle Department east of Cumberland, now commanded by General Schenck, under your direct orders. The President directs me to ask you if that arrangement would be agreeable. Please answer as early as possible.

H. W. HALLECK,
    General-in-Chief.

—

JUNE 22, 1863—4.30 p. m.   (Received 4.45 p. m.)

Major-General HALLECK:

Your telegram of 3.15 p. m. to-day is received. In reply, I have to state yes, provided that the same authority is continued to me that I now have, which is to give orders direct to the troops in the departments of Generals Schenck and Heintzelman.

JOSEPH HOOKER,
    Major-General.

—

HEADQUARTERS ARMY OF THE POTOMAC,
    June 24, 1863.

Major-General HALLECK,
    General-in-Chief:

The aspect of the enemy is not much changed from yesterday. Ewell, I conclude, is over the river, and is now up the country, I suppose, for purposes of plunder. The yeomanry of that district should be able to check any extended advance of that column, and protect themselves from their aggression.

Of the troops that marched to the river at Shepherdstown yesterday, I cannot learn that any have crossed, and as soon as I do I shall commence moving, myself, and, indeed, am preparing my new acquisitions for that event; the others are ready. General French is now on his way to Harper's Ferry, and I have given directions for the force at Poolesville to march and report to him, and also for all of Stahel's cavalry, and, if I can do it without attracting observation, I shall send over a corps or two from here, in order, if possible, to sever Ewell from the balance of the rebel army, in case he should make a protracted sojourn with his Pennsylvania neighbors.

If the enemy should conclude not to throw any additional force over the river, I desire to make Washington secure, and, with all the force I can muster, strike for his line of retreat in the direction of Richmond.

I cannot learn the strength of Heintzelman's and Schenck's commands, nor where they are stationed, and hence I send my chief of staff to Washington and Baltimore to ascertain, and also to start out a column of about 15,000 men on the National road as far as Frederick City. In any contingency, whether of an advance or retreat of the enemy, the defense of Washington or Baltimore, this amount of force should be there, and they should be held in readiness to march, which fact I will not be able to know until I put them on the road. I will send the best officers I have to command this body. I desire that instructions may be given Generals Heintzelman and Schenck to direct their commands to obey promptly any orders they may receive from me.

Last evening the colonel commanding at Poolesville responded to his orders to march that he did not belong to my command, but would refer his orders to General Heintzelman. Such delays may bring us reverses. When these instructions are given, I shall not be necessitated to repeat orders to any part of my command to march on the enemy.

Allow me to suggest that the new troops arriving in Baltimore and Washington be at once put in the defenses, and the old ones, excepting those serving with the artillery, be put in marching condition. If this should be done quickly, I think that we may anticipate glorious results from the recent movement of the enemy, whether he should determine to advance or retreat.

I request that my orders be sent me to-day, for outside of the Army of the Potomac I don't know whether I am standing on my head or feet.

I am, very respectfully, your obedient servant,

JOSEPH HOOKER,
Major-General, Commanding.

—

WASHINGTON, D. C., *June* 24, 1863—2.30 p. m.

Major-General HOOKER,
Army of the Potomac:

General Schenck has been notified that the troops of his department in Harper's Ferry and vicinity would obey all orders direct from you, and that he would obey your orders in regard to the other troops of his command. They, however, are nearly all militia.

H. W. HALLECK,
General-in-Chief.

—

HEADQUARTERS ARMY OF THE POTOMAC,
June 25, 1863. (Received 11 a. m.)

Major-General HALLECK:

Subjoined is a dispatch this moment received. It speaks for itself. I request that General Slough be arrested at once, and charges will be forwarded as soon as I have time to prepare them. You will find, I fear, when it is too late, that the effort to preserve department lines will be fatal to the cause of the country.

JOSEPH HOOKER,
Major-General.

[Inclosure.]

UPTON'S HILL, *June* 25, 1863.

Major-General BUTTERFIELD :

A dispatch has been received during the night from General Slough, military governor of Alexandria, informing me that the commanding officer of the Second Brigade, Pennsylvania Reserve Corps, has been instructed by him not to recognize the orders sent to him to prepare to join the division, as directed in your dispatch of June 23.

S. W. CRAWFORD,
Brigadier-General, Commanding.

—

WASHINGTON, D. C., *June* 25, 1863—2 p. m.

Major-General HOOKER,
    Army of the Potomac:

The Second Brigade, to which you refer in your telegram, forms no part of General Crawford's command, which was placed at your orders.   No other troops can be withdrawn from the Defenses of Washington.

H. W. HALLECK,
General-in-Chief.

—

WASHINGTON, D. C., *June* 25, 1863.

Major-General HOOKER,
    Army of the Potomac:

The immense loss and destruction of horses in your army, and the difficulty of supplying this loss, render it necessary that you should impress every serviceable animal likely to fall into the hands of the enemy.   There are many animals in Loudoun County and the adjacent parts of Maryland.   These should be seized, to save them from the enemy, as well as to supply yourself.

H. W. HALLECK,
General-in-Chief.

—

WASHINGTON, *June* 25, 1863.

General HOOKER:

The President has assigned General Hancock to the command of the Second Corps.

E. D. TOWNSEND,
Assistant Adjutant-General.

—

POOLESVILLE, *June* 26, 1863.
(Received 8.15 p. m.)

Major-General HALLECK,
    Washington :

I desire every facility to be in readiness for supplies to be thrown to Frederick by rail.

JOSEPH HOOKER,
Major-General.

HEADQUARTERS ARMY OF THE POTOMAC,
June 26, 1863—7 p. m.   (Received 7.30 p. m.)
Major-General HALLECK:

Is there any reason why Maryland Heights should not be abandoned after the public stores and property are removed?

I propose to visit the place to-morrow, on my way to Frederick,
to satisfy myself on that point.   It must be borne in mind that I am
here with a force inferior in numbers to that of the enemy, and must
have every available man to use on the field.

JOSEPH HOOKER,
Major-General, Commanding.

—

JUNE 26, 1863—8 p. m.   (Received 9.15 p. m.)
Hon. E. M. STANTON,
Secretary of War:

I would respectfully request that Major-General Stahel may be
ordered by telegraph to report to General Couch, with a view to organizing and putting in an efficient condition any mounted troops
that can be raised for service there.   His presence here as senior
major-general will much embarrass me and retard my movements.

JOSEPH HOOKER,
Major-General.

—

POOLESVILLE, *June* 26, 1863—6 p. m.
Maj. T. T. ECKERT:

Dispatch* received.   My compliments to the President, and inform
him that I had not that honor.

JOSEPH HOOKER,
Major-General.

—

JUNE 26, 1863—8 p. m.   (Received 9.10 p. m.)
His Excellency President LINCOLN:

You need not believe any more than you choose of what is published in the Associated Press dispatches concerning this army to-
morrow.   Was it from the newspapers that you received a report, or
an idea, that I was in Washington last night?

JOSEPH HOOKER,
Major-General.

—

WASHINGTON, *June* 27, 1863—8 a. m.
Major-General HOOKER:

It did not come from the newspapers, nor did I believe it, but I
wished to be entirely sure it was a falsehood.

A. LINCOLN.

---

* Not found.   Probably this refers to a report that General Hooker was in Washington on the night of the 25th.   See dispatch, following, from Hooker to the President, June 26, 1863, 8 p. m.

HEADQUARTERS ARMY OF THE POTOMAC,
Poolesville, Md., June 27, 1863.   (Received 9 a. m.)

Maj. Gen. H. W. HALLECK,
General-in-Chief:

That there may be no misunderstanding as to my force, I would respectfully state that, including the portions of General Heintzelman's command, and General Schenck's, now with me, my whole force of enlisted men for duty will not exceed 105,000.   Fourteen batteries of the Artillery Reserve have been sent to Washington.   Of General Abercrombie's force, one brigade has just been sent home from expiration of service, and the others go shortly.   One brigade of General Crawford's force has not reported with it.   I state these facts that there may not be expected of me more than I have material to do with.

My headquarters at Frederick to-night.   Three corps at Middletown, one corps at Knoxville, two at Frederick, and the remaining infantry corps very near there to-night.

JOSEPH HOOKER,
Major-General.

(Copy for President.)

—

HEADQUARTERS ARMY OF THE POTOMAC,
June 27, 1863.

GENERAL-IN-CHIEF AND WAR DEPARTMENT,
Washington:

General Hooker personally has just left here for Harper's Ferry, where he will be about 11 o'clock, Point of Rocks about 10 a. m., and at Frederick to-night.   Copies of all dispatches should be sent to Frederick and Harper's Ferry up to 11 a. m., and after that to Frederick.   The staff are just leaving here for Frederick.

DANL. BUTTERFIELD,
Major-General, Chief of Staff.

—

WASHINGTON, D. C., *June 27,* 1863—10.30 a. m.

General HOOKER,
Army of the Potomac:

Major [James C.] Duane and Captain [George H.] Mendell were ordered to your army, and it is presumed that they are *en route.*   I do not know where they now are, unless in your army.   Maryland Heights have always been regarded as an important point to be held by us, and much expense and labor incurred in fortifying them.   I cannot approve their abandonment, except in case of absolute necessity.

H. W. HALLECK,
General-in-Chief.

—

WASHINGTON, D. C., *June 27,* 1863—12 m.

Major-General HOOKER,
Army of the Potomac:

Major-General Stahel is relieved from duty in the Army of the Potomac, and will report to General Couch, at Harrisburg, to organize and command the cavalry in the Department of the Susquehanna. Lowell's cavalry is the only force for scouts in this department, and cannot be taken from General Heintzelman's command.

H. W. HALLECK,
General-in-Chief.

SANDY HOOK, *June* 27, 1863.
(Received 2.55 p. m.)

Major-General HALLECK,
General-in-Chief:

I have received your telegram in regard to Harper's Ferry. I find 10,000 men here, in condition to take the field. Here they are of no earthly account. They cannot defend a ford of the river, and, as far as Harper's Ferry is concerned, there is nothing of it. As for the fortifications, the work of the troops, they remain when the troops are withdrawn. No enemy will ever take possession of them for them. This is my opinion. All the public property could have been secured to-night, and the troops marched to where they could have been of some service. Now they are but a bait for the rebels, should they return.

I beg that this may be presented to the Secretary of War and His Excellency the President.

JOSEPH HOOKER,
Major-General.

SANDY HOOK, *June* 27, 1863—1 p. m.
(Received 3 p. m.)

Maj. Gen. H. W. HALLECK,
General-in-Chief:

My original instructions require me to cover Harper's Ferry and Washington. I have now imposed upon me, in addition, an enemy in my front of more than my number. I beg to be understood, respectfully, but firmly, that I am unable to comply with this condition with the means at my disposal, and earnestly request that I may at once be relieved from the position I occupy.

JOSEPH HOOKER,
Major-General.

WASHINGTON, D. C.,
June 27, 1863—8 p. m.

Major-General HOOKER,
Army of the Potomac:

Your application to be relieved from your present command is received.

As you were appointed to this command by the President, I have no power to relieve you. Your dispatch has been duly referred for Executive action.

H. W. HALLECK,
General-in-Chief.

No. 6.

Reports of Maj. Gen. George G. Meade, U. S. Army, commanding Army of the Potomac, of operations June 28–August 3, and correspondence with the authorities in Washington, &c.

HEADQUARTERS OF THE ARMY,
Washington, D. C., June 27, 1863.

Maj. Gen. GEORGE G. MEADE,
    Army of the Potomac:

GENERAL : You will receive with this the order of the President placing you in command of the Army of the Potomac. Considering the circumstances, no one ever received a more important command; and I cannot doubt that you will fully justify the confidence which the Government has reposed in you.

You will not be hampered by any minute instructions from these headquarters. Your army is free to act as you may deem proper under the circumstances as they arise. You will, however, keep in view the important fact that the Army of the Potomac is the covering army of Washington as well as the army of operation against the invading forces of the rebels. You will, therefore, maneuver and fight in such a manner as to cover the capital and also Baltimore, as far as circumstances will admit. Should General Lee move upon either of these places, it is expected that you will either anticipate him or arrive with him so as to give him battle.

All forces within the sphere of your operations will be held subject to your orders.

Harper's Ferry and its garrison are under your direct orders.

You are authorized to remove from command, and to send from your army, any officer or other person you may deem proper, and to appoint to command as you may deem expedient.

In fine, general, you are intrusted with all the power and authority which the President, the Secretary of War, or the General-in-Chief can confer on you, and you may rely upon our full support.

You will keep me fully informed of all your movements, and the positions of your own troops and those of the enemy, so far as known.

I shall always be ready to advise and assist you to the utmost of my ability.

Very respectfully, your obedient servant,
H. W. HALLECK,
General-in-Chief.

——

FREDERICK, MD., *June* 28, 1863—7 a. m.
(Received 10 a. m.)

General H. W. HALLECK,
    General-in-Chief:

The order placing me in command of this army is received. As a soldier, I obey it, and to the utmost of my ability will execute it. Totally unexpected as it has been, and in ignorance of the exact condition of the troops and position of the enemy, I can only now say that it appears to me I must move toward the Susquehanna, keeping Washington and Baltimore well covered, and if the enemy is checked in his attempt to cross the Susquehanna, or if he turns toward Baltimore, to give him battle. I would say that I trust every available man that can be spared will be sent to me, as from all accounts the enemy is in strong force.   So soon as I can post myself up, I will communicate more in detail.

GEO. G. MEADE,
Major-General.

—

WASHINGTON, D. C., *June* 28, 1863—1 p. m.

Maj. Gen. GEORGE G. MEADE,
Army of the Potomac:

I fully concur in your general views as to the movements of your army.   All available assistance will be given you.   General Schenck's troops outside the line of defenses will move as you may direct. General Couch is also directed to co-operate with you, and to move his forces as you may order.   It is most probable that Lee will concentrate his forces this side of the Susquehanna.   In regard to supplies of horses, &c., I send herewith a copy of a telegram to General Schenck on the 23d.*

H. W. HALLECK,
General-in-Chief.

—

WASHINGTON, D. C., *June* 28, 1863—12.30 p. m.

Major-General MEADE,
Frederick, Md.:

A brigade of Fitzhugh Lee's cavalry has crossed the Potomac near Seneca Falls, and is making for the railroad to cut off your supplies. There is another brigade of rebel cavalry south of the Potomac, which may follow.   We have no cavalry here to operate against them. General Hooker carried away all of General Heintzelman's cavalry.

H. W. HALLECK,
General-in-Chief.

—

HEADQUARTERS ARMY OF THE POTOMAC,
June 28, 1863—2 p. m.

General HALLECK:

Dispatch received in relation to crossing of enemy's cavalry at Seneca Creek.   Have ordered two brigades and battery to proceed at once in search and pursuit.

GEO. G. MEADE,
Major-General.

—

HEADQUARTERS ARMY OF THE POTOMAC,
Frederick, June 28, 1863—1 p. m.
(Received 2.20 p. m.)

Major-General HALLECK:

Am I permitted, under existing circumstances, to withdraw a portion of the garrison of Harper's Ferry, providing I leave sufficient force to hold Maryland Heights against a *coup de main?*

Reliable intelligence leads to the belief that Stuart has crossed at Williamsport, and is moving toward Hagerstown, in rear of Lee's

---

*See Halleck to Schenck, June 23, Part III, p. 275.

army, and all accounts agree in giving Lee so large a force that I cannot believe he has left any considerable body on the south side of the Potomac.   Please give me your views fully.

GEO. G. MEADE,
Major-General, Commanding.

—

WASHINGTON, D. C., *June* 28, 1863—3.30 p. m.
Major-General MEADE,
Frederick, Md.:
The garrison at Harper's Ferry is under your orders.   You can diminish or increase it as you think the circumstances justify.

H. W. HALLECK,
General-in-Chief.

—

WASHINGTON, D. C., *June* 28, 1863—2 p. m.
Major-General MEADE,
Frederick, Md.:
It is reported here that the supplies at Edwards Ferry and return-ing by the canal are left unprotected.   If so, Lee's cavalry will prob-ably destroy them.   It is reported that Lowell's battalion of cavalry, left at Poolesville, was sent to Sandy Hook, contrary to my orders. If so, there is not a cavalry picket on the line of the Potomac below Edwards Ferry, and we have none here to send out.

H. W. HALLECK,
General-in-Chief.

—

FREDERICK, MD., *June* 28, 1863—2.45 p. m.
(Received 4 p. m.)
Major-General HALLECK:
I would recommend that General Schenck increase the force at Ellicott's Mills, with orders to hold that bridge, and also the Relay Junction, at all hazards.

The Sixth New York State Militia were ordered to be returned to General Schenck from Monocacy Bridge; also a section of artillery there.   They should have started to-day.

GEO. G. MEADE,
Major-General, Commanding.

(Copy to General Schenck.)

—

WASHINGTON, D. C., *June* 28, 1863—3 p. m.
Major-General MEADE,
Frederick, Md.:
It is just reported that your train of one hundred and fifty wagons has been captured by Fitzhugh Lee, near Rockville.   Unless cavalry is sent to guard your communications with Washington, they will be cut off.   It is reported here that there is still a considerable rebel force south of the Potomac.

H. W. HALLECK,
General-in-Chief.

June 28, 1863—3 p. m.   (Received 4.55 p. m.)

Maj. Gen. H. W. Halleck:

Your dispatch concerning capture of one hundred and fifty wagons received. Two brigades of cavalry, with artillery, had already been sent in pursuit of Lee. Colonel Lowell has been directed to return to Poolesville. Do you consider the information at all to be depended upon concerning a force of the enemy south of the Potomac? All our information here tends to show that Lee's entire army passed through Hagerstown, the rear passing yesterday a. m.

> GEO. G. MEADE,
> *Major-General.*

—

June 28, 1863.

Major Eckert,
    Telegraph Superintendent, Washington:

The major-general commanding desires to know if any reliable information can be given as to the direction taken by the cavalry force that   ere at Rockville, the hour they left, the names of any generals or colonels, and the designation of any regiments. Did they return to recross the river, or proceed north, by what road, and when?

> DANL. BUTTERFIELD,
> *Major-General.*

—

Washington, D. C., *June* 28, 1863—7.20 p. m.

Major-General Meade,
    Frederick, Md.:

I doubt if there is any large force south of the Potomac; probably a few thousand cavalry, enough to render it necessary to have a strong rear guard, to protect the trains and picket the river. Lowell's command was ordered on the latter duty, but removed contrary to my positive order, which exposed your trains. We have no cavalry here excepting what we have picked up from Pleasonton's command.

> H. W. HALLECK,
> *General-in-Chief.*

—

Frederick, *June* 28, 1863—8.15 p. m.
(Received 10.20 p. m.)

Major-General Halleck:

Your dispatch received. Colonel Lowell, as soon as your wishes were known, was ordered and will be left, and I shall intrust to him, through you, the guarding of the river. There seems to be no doubt that 3,000 of the enemy's cavalry have been on our right, between us and Washington, to-day. My intention is now to move to-morrow on three lines to Emmitsburg and Westminster, having the army on the road from Emmitsburg through Westminster, or as near there as we can march. This movement is based upon what information we have here of the enemy's movement. The army to-night is as follows: First, Second, Fifth, Eleventh, and Twelfth Corps, with Artillery Reserve, within a few miles of Frederick; the Third Corps, 6 miles out toward Middleburg; the Sixth Corps, toward New Market, and expecting to reach there to-night. I have not decided yet as to the Harper's Ferry garrison. I should like to have your views as to the movement proposed.

GEO. G. MEADE,

Major-General.

—

HEADQUARTERS ARMY OF THE POTOMAC,
June 28, 1863—4.45 p. m.   (Received 6.05 p. m.)

Maj. Gen. H. W. HALLECK, *General-in-Chief:*

The following statement has been furnished me. It is confirmed by information gathered from various other sources regarded as reliable.

I propose to move this army to-morrow in the direction of York.

GEO. G. MEADE,

Major-General.

[Statement.]

Thomas McCammon, blacksmith, a good man, from Hagerstown, left there on horseback at 11 a. m. to-day. Rebel cavalry came first a week ago last Monday. General [A. G.] Jenkins having 1,200 mounted infantry, said to be picked men from Jackson's men, and 300 or 400 cavalry of his own. The cavalry went back and forth out of Pennsylvania, driving horses and cattle, and the first infantry came yesterday a week ago—General Ewell's men. He came personally last Saturday, and was at the Catholic church Sunday, with General Rodes and two other generals. On Monday he left in the direction of Greencastle, in the afternoon, Rodes having left the same morning. Rebel troops have passed every day, more or less, since; some days only three or four regiments or a brigade, and some days, yesterday, for instance, all of Longstreet's command passed through excepting two brigades. Saw Longstreet yesterday. He and Lee had their headquarters at Mr. [James H.] Grove's, just beyond town limits, toward Greencastle, last night, and left there this a. m. at 8 o'clock. Think A. P. Hill went through last Tuesday. Heard from James D. Roman, prominent lawyer and leading Confederate sympathizer, who was talking in the clerk's office last night; said that their officers reported their whole army, 100,000 strong, now in Maryland or Pennsylvania, excepting the cavalry. Mr. [William] Logan, register of wills, and Mr. [William H.] Protzman, very fine men in Hagerstown, have taken pains to count the rebels, and could not make them over 80,000. They counted the artillery; made it two hundred and seventy-five guns. Some of the regiments have only 175 men—two that I saw, 150 men. Largest regiment that I saw was a Maryland regiment, and that was about 700. Don't think their regiments would range 400. Great amount of transportation; great many wagons captured at Winchester. Horses in good condition. Ewell rides in a wagon. Two thousand comprise the mounted infantry and cavalry. Saw Wilcox's brigade wagons yesterday or day before. Saw Kershaw's wagons in town yesterday. Kershaw's brigade is in McLaws' division, Longstreet's corps. Know Hood and Armistead. Have passed through Hood's division and Armistead's brigade. Pickett's division is in Longstreet's corps. The Union men in Hagerstown would count them, and meet at night. Officers and men in good condition; say they are going to Philadelphia. Lots of Confederate money; carry it in flour barrels, and give $5 for cleaning a horse; $5 for two shoes on a horse rather than 50 cents United States money.

HEADQUARTERS ARMY OF THE POTOMAC,
June 28, 1863—7.25 p. m.

General H. W. HALLECK,
          Washington:

General Steinwehr, from the Mountain House, South Mountain, reports that his scouts inform him that 5,000 of Stuart's cavalry passed through Williamsport yesterday afternoon. General Sedgwick, on the march up from Poolesville, reports that 3,000 of the enemy's cavalry, with some artillery, are in his rear. This is communicated to you for your information. My impression is that Stuart has divided his force, with a view of harassing our right and left flanks.

GEO. G. MEADE,
Major-General, Commanding.

—

WASHINGTON, D. C., *June* 29, 1863—10.35 a. m.

Major-General MEADE,
          Frederick, Md.:

I have delayed answering your telegram of 9 p. m., received after midnight, in hopes of ascertaining something more of rebel forces on the Potomac; but there is nothing further that is reliable. The cavalry force in our front is said by some to be two, and by others three, brigades, with seven pieces of artillery. So far as I can judge, without a better knowledge of the enemy's positions, your proposed movement seems good.

H. W. HALLECK,
General-in-Chief.

—

WASHINGTON, D. C., *June* 29, 1863—11 a. m.

Major-General MEADE,
          Frederick, Md.:

Since my last telegram, I have heard from Lowell's cavalry, at Rockville. The rebel cavalry which destroyed the train left Brookville early this morning, apparently for the Relay Junction or Ellicott's Mills. They have with them the captured mules and part of the wagons. Your cavalry may be able to cut them off. [Maj. William H.] Fry's cavalry* will be added to Lowell's, but they are too weak to do much.

H. W. HALLECK,
General-in-Chief.

—

Dispatch found on the body of a soldier, killed June 30, 4½ miles from Glen Rock.

HEADQUARTERS ARMY OF THE POTOMAC,
June 29, 1863—11 a. m.

Maj. Gen. H. W. HALLECK,
          General-in-Chief:

Upon assuming command of the army, and after carefully considering the position of affairs and the movements of the enemy, I have

—

* From dismounted camp.

concluded as follows: To move to-day toward Westminster and Emmitsburg, and the army is now in motion for that line, placing two corps, First and Eleventh, at Emmitsburg; two corps, Third and Twelfth, at Taneytown; one corps, Second, at Frizellburg, and one corps, Fifth, at Union; Sixth Corps at New Windsor; my cavalry guarding my flanks and rear. If Lee is moving for Baltimore, I expect to get between his main army and that place. If he is crossing the Susquehanna, I shall rely upon General Couch, with his force, holding him until I can fall upon his rear and give him battle, which I shall endeavor to do. I have ordered the abandonment of Harper's Ferry, a detachment of not more than 3,000 to proceed with the property, by canal, to Washington, and strengthen your forces there against any cavalry raid; the remainder to move up and join me. The line from Frederick to Baltimore by rail will necessarily be abandoned. While I move forward, I shall incline to the right, toward the Baltimore and Harrisburg road, to cover that, and draw supplies from there, if circumstances permit it, my main objective point being, of course, Lee's army, which I am satisfied has all passed on through Hagerstown toward Chambersburg. My endeavor will be in my movements to hold my force well together, with the hope of falling upon some portion of Lee's army in detail. The cavalry force between me and Washington, as soon as I can learn sufficiently of their movement to pursue and fight without wasting the necessary force by useless movements, will be engaged by my cavalry. Stuart's cavalry, from my best information, have divided into two columns, one on my right, between me and Baltimore, one on my left, through Hagerstown, to join their army. My main point being to find and fight the enemy, I shall have to submit to the cavalry raid around me in some measure. The sections of artillery and small force of cavalry sent from here to Baltimore have been ordered to fall back from Poplar Springs and join General Pleasonton's force, on my right, their route having been intercepted by the enemy's cavalry. I have hastily made up this dispatch to give you the information. Telegraphic communications have been cut off. I have no opportunity to receive a reply to mine asking your advice as to these movements, and upon my best judgment proceed to execute them. I can at present give no orders as to General Schenck's department in Baltimore, or the Potomac in my rear; neither can I, in the absence of telegraphic communication, and on account of the great distance of Couch, exercise any influence, by advice or otherwise, concerning the co-operation of that force. These circumstances are beyond my control. I send this by courier, with the hope and expectation that it will reach you safely. Headquarters to-night are at Middleburg, 3 miles from Uniontown and 13 from Westminster. There is rail communication from Baltimore to Westminster

GEO. G. MEADE,
Major-General

—

HEADQUARTERS ARMY OF THE POTOMAC,
June 30, 1863—10.45 a. m.

Major-General COUCH:

I am in position between Emmitsburg and Westminster, advancing upon the enemy. The enemy (A. P. Hill) holds Cashtown Pass, between Gettysburg and Chambersburg. Their cavalry, three to five brigades, are on my right, between me and the Northern Central.

My force is tolerably well concentrated, moving with all the speed that the trains, roads, and physique of the men will bear.

I am without definite and positive information as to the where-abouts of Longstreet and Ewell. The latter I presume to be in front of you. The army is in good spirits, and we shall push to your relief or the engagement of the enemy as circumstances and the information we receive during the day and on the marches may indicate as most prudent and most likely to lead to ultimate success. I am anxious to hear from you, and get information of the dispositions of the enemy and his movements, so far as you know them. If you are in telegraphic communication or otherwise with Philadelphia, Baltimore, and Washington, I should like supplies and shoes accumulated, to be thrown to me on the line of the Northern Central or the Susquehanna, as circumstances may require or my movements may make most desirable. Please communicate my dispatch to the General-in-Chief; my communications with him are intercepted by the cavalry of the enemy on my right. Can you keep the enemy from crossing the river?

Very respectfully, &c.,

GEO. G. MEADE,
Major-General, Commanding.

—

WASHINGTON, *June* 30, 1863.

Major-General MEADE,
Commanding Army of the Potomac:

GENERAL: Your plan of operations is approved. I have just received your second dispatch by the hands of an orderly.

I write no fuller for obvious reasons.

H. W. HALLECK,
General-in-Chief.

—

WASHINGTON, D. C., *June* 30, 1863—1.30 p. m.

Major-General MEADE,
Army of the Potomac:

If you abandon Harper's Ferry, ordnance stores must not be destroyed. Such destruction can be justified only by absolute necessity. Forces have been sent up the canal to ascertain its condition. It is reported that all your stores and pontoons on the canal have been destroyed and the canal much injured.

H. W. HALLECK,
General-in-Chief.

—

HEADQUARTERS ARMY OF THE POTOMAC,
June 30, 1863—4.30 p. m. (Received July 1, 4 a. m.)

Maj. Gen. H. W. HALLECK,
General-in-Chief:

Headquarters, Taneytown. Two corps between Emmitsburg and Gettysburg, one at Littlestown, one at Manchester, one at Union Mills, one between here and Emmitsburg, one at Frizellburg. Pennsylvania Reserves can't keep up—still in rear. General Lockwood, with the troops from Schenck, still behind; these troops cannot keep up with the marches made by the army.   Our reports seem to place Ewell in the vicinity of York and Harrisburg.   The cavalry that crossed at Seneca Ford have passed on up through Westminster and Hanover, some 6,000 to 8,000 strong.   The people are all so frightened that accurate information is not to be obtained.   I shall push on to-morrow in the direction of Hanover Junction and Hanover, when I hope by July 2 to open communication with Baltimore by telegraph and rail, to renew supplies.   I fear that I shall break down the troops by pushing on much faster, and may have to rest a day.   My move-ment, of course, will be governed much by what I learn of the enemy. The information seems to place Longstreet at Chambersburg, and A. P. Hill moving between Chambersburg and York.   Our cavalry drove a regiment out of Gettysburg this a. m.   Our cavalry engaged with Stuart at Hanover this a. m.   Result not yet known.

GEO. G. MEADE,
Major-General, Commanding.

(Similar telegram sent to General Couch at 5.30 p. m. same date.)

—

WASHINGTON, D. C.,
June 30, 1863—11.30 p. m.

Major-General MEADE:

The following dispatch has just been received, which, although you may be informed on the subject, I have ordered to be sent to you by express:

HARRISBURG, PA.,
June 30, 1863.

Major-General HALLECK.

Lee is falling back suddenly from the vicinity of Harrisburg, and concentrating all his forces.   York has been evacuated.   Carlisle is being evacuated.   The concen-tration appears to be at or near Chambersburg.   The object apparently a sudden movement against Meade, of which he should be advised by courier immediately. A courier might reach Frederick by way of Western Maryland Railroad to West-minster.   This information comes from T. A. Scott, and I think it reliable.

H. HAUPT,
Brigadier-General.

It is proper you should know that General French this morning evacuated Maryland Heights, blowing up his magazine, spiking the large cannon, and destroying surplus stores.   A tele gram from him, received this evening, indicates that he is still at Sandy Hook, wait-ing orders, and doubtful what he should do with his force.   Please instruct him what you wish him to do.

EDWIN M. STANTON,
Secretary of War.

—

SANDY HOOK, MD., *June* 30, 1863—3.30 p. m.
(Received 6 p. m.)

H. W. HALLECK,
General-in-Chief:

I have no orders except from General Butterfield, which urge the movement of these troops within a few days as a necessity for the Army of the Potomac.   The removal of this property must be cov-ered by a large force, as the road is perfectly commanded.   As for defending the property, all that is required is an order not to aban-don, or something definite from some source.   My instructions have placed me on the road for the army with 5,000 untried men. I leave over 3,000 men, who came from Winchester, ready to take the rear at the first alarm.

If I am to be held responsible for evacuation of Maryland Heights, it should be given me reasonable time. I cannot communicate with headquarters Army of the Potomac.

WM. H. FRENCH,
Major-General.

—

HEADQUARTERS ARMY OF THE POTOMAC,
Nine Miles east of Middleburg, July 1, 1863—7 a. m.
(Received 4 p. m.)

Maj. Gen. H. W. HALLECK,
General-in-Chief:

Dispatches of General Couch and General Haupt received. My positions to-day are, one corps at Emmitsburg, two at Gettysburg, one at Taneytown, one at Two Taverns, one at Manchester, one at Hanover. These movements were ordered yesterday, before the receipt of advices of Lee's movements. Our cavalry, under Kilpatrick, had a handsome fight yesterday at Hanover. He reports the capture of 1 battle-flag, a lieutenant-colonel, 1 captain, with 15 or 20 of the enemy killed. The point of Lee's concentration and the nature of the country, when ascertained, will determine whether I attack him or not. Shall advise you further to-day, when satisfied that the enemy are fully withdrawn from the Susquehanna. If General Couch has any reliable force, I shall call upon him to move it to aid me.

GEO. G. MEADE,
Major-General, Commanding.

—

HEADQUARTERS ARMY OF THE POTOMAC,
July 1, 1863—7 a. m.   (Received 3.40 p. m.)

Hon. E. M. STANTON,
Secretary of War:

Dispatch of June 30, 11.30 p. m., received. French was ordered to send 3,000 of his force to Washington, with all his property, then to move up and join me with the balance.

GEO. G. MEADE,
Major-General.

—

TANEYTOWN, *July* 1, 1863—12 m.

General HALLECK:

Dispatch sent last night giving my position at Emmitsburg, Gettysburg, and Hanover.

Ewell is massing at Heidlersburg. A. P. Hill is massed behind the mountains at Cashtown. Longstreet somewhere between Chambersburg and the mountains.

The news proves my advance has answered its purpose. I shall not advance any, but prepare to receive an attack in case Lee makes one. A battle-field is being selected to the rear, on which the army can be rapidly concentrated, on Pike Creek, between Middleburg and Manchester, covering my depot at Westminster.

If I am not attacked, and I can from reliable intelligence have reason to believe I can attack with reasonable degree of success, I will do so; but at present, having relieved the pressure on the Susquehanna, I am now looking to the protection of Washington, and fighting my army to the best advantage.

1 P. M.

The enemy are advancing in force on Gettysburg, and I expect the battle will begin to-day.

GEO. G. MEADE.

—

WASHINGTON, D. C., July 1, 1863—9.15 p. m.

Major-General MEADE,
        Army of the Potomac:

Yours of 12 m. received. Your tactical arrangements for battle seem good, so far as I can judge from my knowledge of the character of the country; but in a strategic view are you not too far east, and may not Lee attempt to turn your left and cut you off from Frederick? Please give your full attention to this suggestion. Lowell's cavalry was sent this morning to escort the stores from Harper's Ferry. This will relieve General French to obey your orders. The destruction of unguarded property on the canal along the Potomac has been terrible. Will not Frederick become a better base of supplies than Westminster? In anticipation of this, I have directed General Schenck to guard that road as well as he can. I have ordered General Couch to co-operate with you as far as possible; but I fear very little reliance can be placed on his troops in an emergency.

H. W. HALLECK,
General-in-Chief.

—

WASHINGTON, D. C., July 1, 1863—10.45 a. m.

Major-General MEADE,
        Army of the Potomac:

The movements of the enemy yesterday indicate his intention to either turn your left, or to come himself by the South Mountain and occupy Cumberland Valley. Do not let him draw you too far to the east.

H. W. HALLECK,
General-in-Chief.

—

HEADQUARTERS ARMY OF THE POTOMAC,
July 1, 1863—6 p. m.
(Received 10.20 p. m., via Frederick City.)

Maj. Gen. H. W. HALLECK,
        General-in-Chief:

The First and Eleventh Corps have been engaged all day in front of Gettysburg. The Twelfth, Third, and Fifth have been moving up, and all, I hope, by this time on the field. This leaves only the Sixth, which will move up to-night. General Reynolds was killed this morning early in the action. I immediately sent up General

Hancock to assume command. A. P. Hill and Ewell are certainly concentrating ; Longstreet's whereabouts I do not know. If he is not up to-morrow, I hope with the force I have concentrated to defeat Hill and Ewell. At any rate, I see no other course than to hazard a general battle. Circumstances during the night may alter this decision, of which I will try to advise you. I have telegraphed Couch that if he can threaten Ewell's rear from Harrisburg without endangering himself, to do so.

GEO. G. MEADE,
Major-General.

—

HEADQUARTERS NEAR GETTYSBURG, PA.,
July 2, 1863—3 p. m.   (Received July 3, 10.20 a. m.)

Maj. Gen. H. W. HALLECK,
General-in-Chief :

I have concentrated my army at this place to-day. The Sixth Corps is just coming in, very much worn out, having been marching since 9 p. m. last night. The army is fatigued. I have to-day, up to this hour, awaited the attack of the enemy, I having a strong position for defensive. I am not determined, as yet, on attacking him till his position is more developed. He has been moving on both my flanks, apparently, but it is difficult to tell exactly his movements. I have delayed attacking, to allow the Sixth Corps and parts of other corps to reach this place and to rest the men. Expecting a battle, I ordered all my trains to the rear. If not attacked, and I can get any positive information of the position of the enemy which will justify me in so doing, I shall attack. If I find it hazardous to do so, or am satisfied the enemy is endeavoring to move to my rear and interpose between me and Washington, I shall fall back to my supplies at Westminster. I will endeavor to advise you as often as possible. In the engagement yesterday the enemy concentrated more rapidly than we could, and toward evening, owing to the superiority of numbers, compelled the Eleventh and First Corps to fall back from the town to the heights this side, on which I am now posted. I feel fully the responsibility resting upon me, but will endeavor to act with caution.

GEO. G. MEADE,
Major-General.

—

HEADQUARTERS ARMY OF THE POTOMAC,
July 2, 1863—8 p. m.   (Received July 3, 5.15 p. m.)

Maj. Gen. H. W. HALLECK,
General-in-Chief :

The enemy attacked me about 4 p. m. this day, and, after one of the severest contests of the war, was repulsed at all points. We have suffered considerably in killed and wounded. Among the former are Brigadier-Generals Paul and Zook, and among the wounded, Generals Sickles, Barlow, Graham, and Warren, slightly. We have taken a large number of prisoners. I shall remain in my present position to-morrow, but am not prepared to say, until better advised of the condition of the army, whether my operations will be of an offensive or defensive character.

GEO. G. MEADE,
Major-General.

*Minutes of council, July 2, 1863.**

QUESTIONS ASKED.

1. Under existing circumstances, is it advisable for this army to remain in its present position, or to retire to another nearer its base of supplies ?

2. It being determined to remain in present position, shall the army attack or wait the attack of the enemy ?

3. If we wait attack, how long ?

REPLIES.

GIBBON :
1. Correct position of the army, but would not retreat.
2. In no condition to attack, in his opinion.
3. Until he moves; until enemy moves.

WILLIAMS :
1. Stay.
2. Wait attack.
3. One day.

BIRNEY :
Same as General Williams.

SYKES :
Same as General Williams.

NEWTON :
1. Correct position of the army, but would not retreat.
2. By all means not attack.
3. If we wait, it will give them a chance to cut our line.

HOWARD :
1. Remain.
2. Wait attack until 4 p. m. to-morrow.
3. If don't attack, attack them.

HANCOCK :
1. Rectify position without moving so as to give up field.
2. Not attack unless our communications are cut.
3. Can't wait long; can't be idle.

SEDGWICK :
1. Remain, and wait attack at least one day.

SLOCUM :
Stay and fight it out.

[Memorandum.]†

SLOCUM :
Stay and fight it out.

NEWTON :
Thinks it is a bad position.

HANCOCK :
Puzzled about practicability of retiring; thinks by holding on ——‡ to mass forces and attack.

---

* Original in pencil, and found among General Meade's papers. See circular of March 10, 1864, from Headquarters Army of the Potomac, and replies thereto, pp. 123 *et seq.;* and Butterfield to Williams, and reply, of March 23, 1864, p. 138.
† This memorandum is without a heading in the original.
‡ Illegible word.

HOWARD:
    Favor of not retiring.
BIRNEY:
    Don't know; Third Corps used up, and not in good condition to fight.
SEDGWICK:
    Doubtful*
Effective strength about 9,000, 12,500, 9,000, 6,000, 8,500, 6,000, 7,000; total, 58,000.

[Indorsement.]

Minutes of council, held Thursday p. m., July 2.

D. B.,
—   M. G., C. of S.

HEADQUARTERS ARMY OF THE POTOMAC,
July 3, 1863—8 a. m.   (Received 5.10 p. m.)

Maj. Gen. H. W. HALLECK,
    General-in-Chief:

The action commenced again at early daylight upon various parts of the line.   The enemy thus far have made no impression upon my position.   All accounts agree in placing the whole army here.   Prisoners report Longstreet's and A. P. Hill's forces much injured yesterday and many general officers killed.   General Barksdale's (Mississippi) dead body is within our lines.   We have thus far sent off about 1,600 prisoners, and a small number yet to be started.   I have given certain instructions to General French, which he will telegraph you.   The dispatches from you yesterday, owing to the disappearance of Caldwell, telegraph operator, are here in cipher, unintelligible.

GEO. G. MEADE,
—   Major-General.

JULY 3, 1863—12.30 p. m.

Major-General HALLECK,   (Received 11 p. m.)
    General-in-Chief:

At the present moment all is quiet.   Considerable firing, both infantry and artillery, has taken place in various parts of our line, but no development of the enemy's intentions.   My cavalry are pushing the enemy on both my flanks, and keeping me advised of any effort to outflank me.   We have taken several hundred prisoners since morning.

GEO. G. MEADE.

—

HEADQUARTERS ARMY OF THE POTOMAC,
Near Gettysburg, July 3, 1863—8.35 p. m.
(Received July 4, 6.10 a. m.)

Major-General HALLECK,
    General-in-Chief:

The enemy opened at 1 p. m. from about 150 guns, concentrated upon my left and center, continuing without intermission for about three hours, at the expiration of which time he assaulted my left center twice, being upon both occasions handsomely repulsed, with severe loss to him, leaving in our hands nearly 3,000 prisoners; among the prisoners, Brigadier-General Armistead and many colonels and officers of lesser rank.   The enemy left many dead upon the field and a large number of wounded in our hands.

---

* Remainder of sentence illegible.

The loss upon our side has been considerable. Major-General Hancock and Brigadier-General Gibbon were wounded. After the repelling of the assault, indications leading to the belief that the enemy might be withdrawing, an armed reconnaissance was pushed forward from the left, and the enemy found to be in force. At the present hour all is quiet. My cavalry have been engaged all day on both flanks of the enemy, harassing and vigorously attacking him with great success, notwithstanding they encountered superior numbers, both of cavalry and infantry. The army is in fine spirits.

> GEO. G. MEADE,
> *Major-General, Commanding.*

—

> NEAR GETTYSBURG, PA., *July* 3, 1863.
> (Received July 4, 4.10 a. m.)

Major-General HALLECK,
      General-in-Chief:

The following dispatches have been intercepted by our scouts.

> DANL. BUTTERFIELD,
> *Major-General, Chief of Staff.*

[Inclosure No. 1.]

> ADJUTANT-GENERAL'S OFFICE,
> *Richmond, Va., June* 29, 1863.

General R. E. LEE,
      Comdg. Army Northern Virginia, Winchester, Va.:

GENERAL: While with the President last night, I received your letter of the 23d instant. After reading it, the President was embarrassed to understand that part of it which refers to the plan of assembling an army at Culpeper Court-House under General Beauregard. This is the first intimation that he has had that such a plan was ever in contemplation, and, taking all things into consideration, he cannot see how it can by any possibility be carried into effect. You will doubtless learn before this reaches you that the enemy has again assembled in force on the Peninsula, estimated between 20,000 and 30,000 men, from 6,000 to 10,000 of whom are reported to be in the vicinity of White House and the remainder at Yorktown. It is impossible to say whether the estimated number is correct, as the several accounts vary and are not deemed altogether reliable; but the estimate, making due allowance for errors, is quite near enough to satisfy the most incredulous that the enemy is in this vicinity in sufficient force in cavalry, artillery, and infantry to do much harm, whether his purpose be to make a demonstration on Richmond or to confine himself to raids in breaking your communications and devastating the country. His efforts in the last case may prove more successful than in the first, if we may judge by what took place at Hanover only two days ago, when about 1,000 or 1,200 of his cavalry suddenly appeared there, and did some execution in breaking the railroad and burning a bridge, some buildings, public stores, &c. It was unfortunate that this raid took place only about two days after General Corse's brigade had left there for Gordonsville. Had it remained at Hanover Junction, it is reasonable to suppose that most of the enemy's cavalry would have been either destroyed or captured and the property saved from injury. Every effort is being made here to be prepared for the enemy at all points, but we must look chiefly to the protection of the capital. In doing this, we may be obliged to hazard something at other points. You can easily estimate your strength here, and I would suggest for your consideration whether, in this state of things, you might not be able to spare a portion of your force to protect your line of communication against attempted raids by the enemy.

Very respectfully, your obedient servant,

S. COOPER,
Adjutant-General.

[Inclosure No. 2.]

RICHMOND, VA., *June 28*, 1863.

General R. E. LEE,
  Commanding, &c.

GENERAL: Yours of the 23d* received this evening, and hasten to reply to the point presented in relation to the forces on the coast of South Carolina and Georgia. The hopes indulged as to our operations at the time which would intervene between the discharge of the enemy's trained troops and the substitution of them by others, have been disappointed by the very error against which it was sought by warning to guard.

Grant reached the river, got re-enforcements, made intrenchments, and General Johnston continues to call for re-enforcements, though his first requisition was more than filled by withdrawing troops from Generals Beauregard and Bragg. General Bragg is threatened with attack, has fallen back to his intrenched position at Tullahoma, and called on Buckner for aid. General Beauregard says † that no troops have been withdrawn by the enemy from his point [front] since those returned to New Berne, and that his whole force is necessary to cover his line, this being in answer to a proposition to him to follow the movement of the enemy, said to be to the west, with all his disposable force, pointing him at the same time to the vital importance of holding the Mississippi, and communicating the fear that Vicksburg would fall unless Johnston was strongly and promptly re-enforced. D. H. Hill has a small force, part of which has been brought here. Clingman's brigade is near Wilmington; Colquitt's, Kinston; Martin's, nominally on railroad (Weldon, &c.). Cooke's, Ransom's, and Jenkins' have been brought here, the last two temporarily from the defense of Petersburg and country thereabouts. Wise's brigade is, as you left it, engaged in the defense of Richmond, and serving in the country to the east of the city. The enemy have been reported in large force at White House, with indications of an advance on Richmond. We are organizing companies for home defense, and the spirit of resistance is increasing. Corse's brigade, in accordance with your orders, left Hanover Junction. All the artillery, I am informed, was taken away, and the single regiment of infantry which constituted the guard for the bridges proved unequal to the duty, as you have no doubt learned. Re-enforcements were ordered to go up, but some delay occurred, and they arrived too late to save the bridge or the brave guard which had unsuccessfully defended it. The Yankees, reported to be three regiments of cavalry, returned from the Central road in the direction of Hanover (Old Town), and nothing has been heard of them since.

It was stated that General W. H. F. Lee was captured at the house

---

* See Addenda, p. 77.
† See Davis to Beauregard, and reply, June 25, 1863, Series I, Vol. XXVIII, Part II, pp. 162, 163.

of Mr. Wickham, but I trust it will prove to be one of the many startling rumors which the newsmongers invent.

The advance of your army increases our want of cavalry on the north and east of the city, but, excepting one regiment from North Carolina, I do not know of any which we can expect soon to be available to us.

In yours of the 20th, you say, "if any of the brigades that I have left behind for the protection of Richmond can, in your opinion, be spared, I should like them to be sent to me." It has been an effort with me to answer the clamor to have troops stopped or recalled, to protect the city and the railroads communicating with your army. Corse's brigade has gone, and Wise's is the only other left by you. Cooke's was in North Carolina, and Davis' brigade was sent to complete Heth's division in place of Cooke's. Ransom's and Jenkins' constitute the defense of the south side as far as Weldon, and are relied on for service elsewhere, from Wilmington to Richmond. General Elzey is positive that the enemy intend to attack here, and his scouts bring intelligence which, if I believed it, would render me no more anxious for the city than at any former time. I do not believe the Yankees have such force as is stated, but that they have enough to render it necessary to keep some troops within reach, and some at Petersburg, at least, until Suffolk is truly evacuated.

Do not understand me as balancing accounts in the matter of brigades; I only repeat that I have not many to send you, and enough to form an army to threaten, if not capture, Washington as soon as it is uncovered by Hooker's army. My purpose was to show you that the force here and in North Carolina is very small, and I may add that the brigades are claimed as properly of their command. Our information as to the enemy may be more full and reliable hereafter. It now is materially greater than when you were here.

Very respectfully and truly, yours,

JEFFERSON DAVIS.

ADDENDA.

HDQRS. ARMY OF NORTHERN VIRGINIA, *June 23, 1863.*

General S. COOPER,
　　Adjutant and Inspector General, Richmond, Va.:

GENERAL: Upon leaving Fredericksburg, a regiment of General Pettigrew's brigade was sent to relieve General Corse's brigade at Hanover Junction, to enable the latter to rejoin his division.

General Corse was subsequently ordered to remain at the Junction, and I have not heard whether he has yet been sent forward or not. If not, I think the regiment will suffice for a guard at that point, and wish Corse's brigade to be ordered to rejoin its division, under General Pickett, as soon as possible.

He will march by Culpeper Court-House, and thence through Chester Gap to Winchester, where he will be instructed by what route to proceed. I wish to have every man that can be spared, and desire that Cooke's brigade may be sent forward by the same route, if it is not needed at Richmond. I think there will be no necessity for keeping a large number of troops at that place, especially if the plan of assembling an army at Culpeper Court-House, under General Beauregard, be adopted.

Very respectfully, your obedient servant,

R. E. LEE,
General.

HEADQUARTERS ARMY OF THE POTOMAC,
July 4, 1863—7 a. m.   (Received 7.20 p. m.)

Major-General HALLECK:

This morning the enemy has withdrawn his pickets from the positions of yesterday.   My own pickets are moving out to ascertain the nature and extent of the enemy's movement.   My information is not sufficient for me to decide its character yet—whether a retreat or maneuver for other purposes.

GEO. G. MEADE,
Major-General.

OPERATOR AT FREDERICK :

Please show copy of this to General French.

———

JULY 4, 1863—12 noon.   (Received July 5, 3.50 p. m.)

Major-General HALLECK,
Washington :

The position of affairs is not materially changed from my last dispatch, 7 a. m.   The enemy apparently has thrown back his left, and placed guns and troops in position in rear of Gettysburg, which we now hold.   The enemy has abandoned large numbers of his killed and wounded on the field.   I shall require some time to get up supplies, ammunition, &c., rest the army, worn out by long marches and three days' hard fighting.   I shall probably be able to give you a return of our captures and losses before night, and return of the enemy's killed and wounded in our hands.

GEO. G. MEADE,
Major-General.

———

JULY 4, 1863.

Major ECKERT:

General Meade desires to know under whose orders and authority the telegraph operators possessing the cipher are appointed and controlled.   The operator, Mr. Caldwell, at these headquarters presumes to act in an independent manner, and has left headquarters for Westminster, selecting his own location, without authority or permission.   The commanding general is unable to send dispatches from these headquarters in cipher in consequence thereof, or to understand those he receives.

DANL. BUTTERFIELD,
Major-General, and Chief of Staff.

———

JULY 4—10 p. m.   (Received July 6, 6.10 a. m.)

Major-General HALLECK :

No change of affairs since dispatch of 12 noon.

I make a reconnaissance to-morrow, to ascertain what the intention of the enemy is.

My cavalry are now moving toward the South Mountain Pass, and, should the enemy retreat, I shall pursue him on his flanks.

GEO. G. MEADE,
Major-General.

[P. S.]—A proposition made by General Lee, under flag of truce, to exchange prisoners, was declined by me.

HDQRS. ARMY OF THE POTOMAC, *July* 5, 1863—8.30 a. m.
                              (Received 8.40 p. m.)
Maj. Gen. H. W. HALLECK:

The enemy retired, under cover of the night and heavy rain, in
the direction of Fairfield and Cashtown. All my available cavalry
are in pursuit, on the enemy's left and rear. My movement will be
made at once on his flank, via Middletown and South Mountain Pass.
I cannot give you the details of our captures in prisoners, colors, and
arms. Upward of twenty battle-flags will be turned in from one
corps. I cannot delay to pick up the *débris* of the battle-field, and
request that all those arrangements may be made by the departments.
My wounded, with those of the enemy in our hands, will be left at
Gettysburg. After burying our own, I am compelled to employ
citizens to bury the enemy's dead. My headquarters will be to-night
at Creagerstown. Communication received from General [W. F.]
Smith, in command of 3,000 men, on the march from Carlisle toward
Cashtown.

Field return last evening gives me about 55,000 effective in the
ranks, exclusive of cavalry, baggage guards, ambulances, attendants,
&c. Every available re-enforcement is required, and should be sent
to Frederick without delay.

                                    GEO. G. MEADE,
                                         Major-General.

———

HDQRS. ARMY OF THE POTOMAC, *July* 5, 1863—6 p. m.
                              (Received 11.30 p. m.)
Maj. Gen. H. W. HALLECK,
            General-in-Chief:

I send copies of all my dispatches since yesterday morning. My
army is all in motion. I shall be at Frederick to-morrow night. I
desire the forces mentioned in your dispatch to Major-General French
to be thrown to Harper's Ferry by rail as soon as possible. I shall
so instruct Major-General French. It is of importance to get possession of South Mountain passes and Maryland Heights.

                                    GEO. G. MEADE,
                                Major-General, Commanding.

———

                              WASHINGTON, D. C., *July* 5, 1863.
Major-General MEADE,
            Army of the Potomac:

Your movements are perfectly satisfactory. Your call for re-
enforcements to Frederick has been anticipated. Call to you all of
Couch's force.

                                    H. W. HALLECK,
                                      General-in-Chief.

———

                              WASHINGTON, D. C., *July* 5, 1863.
Major-General MEADE,
            Army of the Potomac:

You will assume the general command of such of General Couch's
forces as are operating in the field, and direct their movements as you

may deem best. It seems to me that they should connect with your right flank. I think that the troops sent here from Harper's Ferry and a part of the forces now in Baltimore could join General French, and be available for your operations. Four small regiments from North Carolina have reached Baltimore. I am awaiting an answer from my dispatch, sent through General French this morning, in regard to re-enforcing him as above indicated. So long as your movements cover Baltimore and Washington from Lee's main army, they are in no danger from any force the enemy may detach for a raid. We have heard nothing from you since yesterday morning, and are anxious to learn more of the results of your brilliant fighting.

H. W. HALLECK,
General-in-Chief.

—

HEADQUARTERS ARMY OF THE POTOMAC,
Gettysburg, July 6, 1863—2 p. m.   (Received 9.20 p. m.)
Maj. Gen. H. W. HALLECK,
General-in-Chief:

Yesterday I sent General Sedgwick with the Sixth Corps in pursuit of the enemy toward Fairfield, and a brigade of cavalry toward Cashtown. General Sedgwick's report indicating a large force of the enemy in the mountains, I deemed it prudent to suspend the movement to Middletown until I could be certain the enemy were evacuating the Cumberland Valley. I find great difficulty in getting reliable information, but from all I can learn I have reason to believe the enemy is retreating, very much crippled, and hampered with his trains.

General Sedgwick reported that the gap at Fairfield was very formidable, and would enable a small force to hold my column in check for a long time. I have accordingly resumed the movement to Middletown, and I expect by to-morrow night to assemble the army in that vicinity. Supplies will be then provided, and as soon as possible I will cross South Mountain, and proceed in search of the enemy.

Your dispatch requiring me to assume the general command of the forces in the field under General Couch has been received. I know nothing of the position or strength of his command, excepting the advance under General Smith, which I have ordered here, and which I desire should furnish a necessary force to guard this place while the enemy is in the vicinity. A brigade of infantry and one of cavalry, with two batteries, will be left to watch the enemy at Fairfield, and follow them whenever they evacuate the gap. I shall send general instructions to General Couch to move down the Cumberland Valley as far as the enemy evacuates it, and keep up communications with me; but from all the information I can obtain, I do not rely on any active co-operation in battle with this force. If I can get the Army of the Potomac in hand in the Valley, and the enemy have not crossed the river, I shall give him battle, trusting, should misfortune overtake me, that a sufficient number of my force, in connection with what you have in Washington, would reach that place so as to render it secure.

General Trimble, of the Confederate army, was to-day found wounded just outside of Gettysburg. General [J. L.] Kemper was found mortally wounded on the road to Fairfield, and a large number of wounded, estimated as several thousand. Generals Heth, Wade Hampton, Jenkins, and Pender are reported wounded. The losses of the enemy were no doubt very great, and he must be proportionately crippled.

My headquarters will be here to-night, and to-morrow I expect to be at Frederick. My cavalry have been attacking the enemy on both flanks, inflicting as much injury as possible.

GEO. G. MEADE,
Major-General.

—

HEADQUARTERS ARMY OF THE POTOMAC,
July 6, 1863—8 p. m.
(Received July 7, 1.30 a. m.)

General HALLECK:

I shall be very glad to have the four regiments from North Carolina, now at Baltimore, which you propose to add to General French's command. They should be put in marching order, with shelter tents.

GEO. G. MEADE,
Major-General, Commanding.

—

WASHINGTON, D. C., *July* 6, 1863.

Major-General MEADE and
Major-General FRENCH,
     Frederick, Md. :

Fifteen hundred cavalry left here this forenoon on Rockville and Frederick turnpike. They are detachments from the Army of the Potomac, remounted. You can send orders to them on the road to move as you deem best. Elliott's command, with two new batteries. left by railroad this morning.

H. W. HALLECK,
General-in-Chief.

—

WASHINGTON, D. C., *July* 6, 1863—12.30 p. m.

Major-General MEADE and
Major-General FRENCH :

It is just reported here that the bridge at Harper's Ferry was left intact when General French's command abandoned that place. If so, it gives Lee a good crossing, unless it be occupied by us in strong force. No time should be lost in throwing troops on to Maryland Heights.

H. W. HALLECK,
General-in-Chief.

—

HEADQUARTERS ARMY OF THE POTOMAC,
Frederick, July 7, 1863—3.10 p. m.
(Received 4.45 p. m.)

Maj. Gen. H. W. HALLECK:

General Buford reports that he attacked Williamsport yesterday, but found it guarded by a large force of infantry and artillery. Heavy forces were coming into Williamsport all night. French having destroyed their bridges, and the river being unfordable, they are crossing in country flat-boats—a slow operation. My army will be assembling to-day and to-morrow at Middletown. I will imme-

diately move on Williamsport. Should the enemy succeed in crossing the river before I can reach him, I should like to have your
views of subsequent operations—whether to follow up the army in
the Valley, or cross below and nearer Washington.

                                        GEO. G. MEADE,
                                                  Major-General.

                                                  4 P. M.

[P. S.]—An officer of the cavalry from the front reports the enemy's
army as occupying Hagerstown and Williamsport, and guarding their
artillery and trains, which they cannot cross. So soon as my command is supplied and their trains up, I shall move.

———

                    WASHINGTON, D. C., *July* 7, 1863—3 p. m.
Maj. Gen. GEORGE G. MEADE,
              Army of the Potomac:

It gives me great pleasure to inform you that you have been appointed a brigadier-general in the Regular Army, to rank from July
3, the date of your brilliant victory at Gettysburg.

                                        H. W. HALLECK,
                                                  General-in-Chief.

———

                    FREDERICK, MD., *July* 7, 1863—4 p. m.
                                        (Received 5 p. m.)
Maj. Gen. H. W. HALLECK:
              General-in-Chief:

I have received your dispatch announcing my appointment as
brigadier-general in the Regular Army.

Please convey to the President my grateful thanks for this honor,
and receive for yourself my thanks for the kind manner you have
conveyed the notification.

                                        GEO. G. MEADE,
                                                  Major-General.

———

                    FREDERICK, MD., *July* 7, 1863—4 p. m.
                                        (Received 5.25 p. m.)
Maj. Gen. H. W. HALLECK,
              General-in-Chief:

Maryland Heights are at present occupied by Kenly's brigade, 1,700
men. Three thousand additional men and two batteries of artillery
left here this morning for that place. No indications of the enemy
this side of Williamsport and Hagerstown.

The bridge at Harper's Ferry was rendered impassable at both
sides by General French.

                                        GEO. G. MEADE,
                                                  Major-General.

———

                    WASHINGTON, D. C., *July* 7, 1863—8.45 p. m.
Major-General MEADE,
              Frederick, Md.:

You have given the enemy a stunning blow at Gettysburg. Follow it up, and give him another before he can reach the Potomac.

When he crosses, circumstances will determine whether it will be best to pursue him by the Shenandoah Valley or this side of Blue Ridge. There is strong evidence that he is short of artillery ammunition, and, if vigorously pressed, he must suffer.

H. W. HALLECK,
General-in-Chief.

—

WASHINGTON, D. C., *July* 7, 1863.
Major-General MEADE or
Major-General FRENCH,
Frederick, Md.:

What force has been sent to Maryland Heights, and how many have reached there? It seems to me, at the present, to be a most important point, and should be held with forces sufficient to prevent its occupation by the enemy. Should his crossing above be impossible, he will probably attempt to take and hold that position until he can make the passage.

H. W. HALLECK,
General-in-Chief.

—

WASHINGTON, D. C., *July* 7, 1863.
Major-General MEADE,
Frederick, Md.:

I have seen your dispatch to General Couch of 4.40 p. m. You are perfectly right. Push forward, and fight Lee before he can cross the Potomac.

H. W. HALLECK,
General-in-Chief.

—

WASHINGTON, D. C., *July* 7, 1863.
Major-General MEADE,
Army of the Potomac:

I have received from the President the following note, which I respectfully communicate:

Major-General HALLECK:

We have certain information that Vicksburg surrendered to General Grant on the 4th of July. Now, if General Meade can complete his work, so gloriously prosecuted thus far, by the literal or substantial destruction of Lee's army, the rebellion will be over.

Yours, truly,

A. LINCOLN.

H. W. HALLECK,
General-in-Chief.

—

HEADQUARTERS ARMY OF THE POTOMAC,
July 8, 1863—10.30 a. m.
(Received 10.45 p. m.)
Maj. Gen. H. W. HALLECK:

I have ordered General Naglee, with the eight regiments of his command, to Harper's Ferry, to re-enforce General Kenly and to assume command. This will make a force of between 6,000 and 7,000 men. He is directed to hold his command in readiness to move forward to

my support, if required. I have also sent a bridge train there, with
an engineer party, the bridge to be thrown over only when any command, cavalry or other, should arrive there to cross. I leave the
Seventh New York Regiment and a battery of six pieces to defend
this depot against raids.

> GEO. G. MEADE,
> *Major-General, Commanding.*

—

> HEADQUARTERS ARMY OF THE POTOMAC,
> *July* 8, 1863—2 p. m. (Received 2.55 p. m.)

Maj. Gen. H. W. HALLECK,
> *General-in-Chief:*

General Couch learns from scouts that the train at Williamsport
is crossing very slowly. So long as the river is unfordable, the enemy cannot cross. My cavalry report that they had a fight near
Funkstown, through which they drove the enemy to Hagerstown,
where a large infantry force was seen. From all I can gather, the
enemy extends from Hagerstown to Williamsport, covering the march
of their train. Their cavalry and infantry pickets are advanced to
the Hagerstown and Sharpsburg pike, on the general line of the Antietam. We hold Boonsborough, and our pickets, 4 miles in front,
toward Hagerstown, are in contact with the enemy's pickets. My
army is assembling slowly. The rains of yesterday and last night
have made all roads but pikes almost impassable. Artillery and
wagons are stalled; it will take time to collect them together. A
large portion of the men are barefooted. Shoes will arrive at Frederick to-day, and will be issued as soon as possible. The spirit of the
army is high; the men are ready and willing to make every exertion
to push forward. The very first moment I can get the different commands, the artillery and cavalry, properly supplied and in hand, I
will move forward. Be assured I most earnestly desire to try the
fortunes of war with the enemy on this side of the river, hoping
through Providence and the bravery of my men to settle the question, but I should do wrong not to frankly tell you of the difficulties
encountered. I expect to find the enemy in a strong position, well
covered with artillery, and I do not desire to imitate his example at
Gettysburg, and assault a position where the chances were so greatly
against success. I wish in advance to moderate the expectations of
those who, in ignorance of the difficulties to be encountered, may expect too much. All that I can do under the circumstances I pledge
this army to do.

> GEO. G. MEADE,
> *Major-General.*

—

> WASHINGTON, D. C., *July* 8, 1863.

Major-General MEADE,
> *Frederick, Md.:*

There is reliable information that the enemy is crossing at Williamsport. The opportunity to attack his divided forces should not
be lost. The President is urgent and anxious that your army should
move against him by forced marches.

> H. W. HALLECK,
> *General-in-Chief.*

HEADQUARTERS ARMY OF THE POTOMAC,
July 8, 1863—3 p. m.   (Received 3.20 p. m.)

Maj. Gen. H. W. HALLECK,
General-in-Chief :

My information as to the crossing of the enemy does not agree with that just received in your dispatch. His whole force is in position between Funkstown and Williamsport. I have just received information that he has driven my cavalry force in front of Boonsborough. My army is and has been making forced marches, short of rations, and barefooted. One corps marched yesterday and last night over 30 miles. I take occasion to repeat that I will use my utmost efforts to push forward this army.

GEO. G. MEADE,
Major-General.

—

WASHINGTON, D. C., *July* 8, 1863.

Major-General MEADE,
Army of the Potomac :

Do not understand me as expressing any dissatisfaction ; on the contrary, your army has done most nobly. I only wish to give you opinions formed from information received here. It is telegraphed from near Harper's Ferry that the enemy have been crossing for the last two days. It is also reported that they have a bridge across. If Lee's army is so divided by the river, the importance of attacking the part on this side is incalculable. Such an opportunity may never occur again. If, on the contrary, he has massed his whole force on the Antietam, time must be taken to also concentrate your forces. Your opportunities for information are better than mine. General Kelley was ordered some days ago to concentrate at Hancock and attack the enemy's right. General Brooks is also moving from Pittsburgh to re-enforce Kelley. All troops arriving from New York and Fort Monroe are sent directly to Harper's Ferry, unless you order differently. You will have forces sufficient to render your victory certain. My only fear now is that the enemy may escape by crossing the river.

H. W. HALLECK,
General-in-Chief.

—

HEADQUARTERS ARMY OF THE POTOMAC,
July 8, 1863.

Brig. Gen. LORENZO THOMAS,
Adjutant-General, Washington :

GENERAL : I have the honor herewith to transmit thirty-one battle-flags, captured from the enemy in the recent battle at Gettysburg. Several other flags were captured on that occasion, but those sent embrace all thus far sent in by corps commanders.

Very respectfully, your obedient servant,
GEO. G. MEADE,
Major-General, Commanding.

General Barksdale's sword was given in my charge to bring with the above flags.

ED. SCHRIVER.

WASHINGTON, *July* 9, 1863—9.40 a. m.

Major-General MEADE:

If no arrangement was made between you and General Lee for the exchange and parole of prisoners of war, by designating places of delivery, as provided for in seventh article of cartel, no parole given by the troops of either army is valid. Please answer if any such agreement was made.

H. W. HALLECK.

—

HEADQUARTERS ARMY OF THE POTOMAC,
Middletown, July 9, 1863—11 a. m.
(Received 12.10 p. m.)

Maj. Gen. H. W. HALLECK, *General-in-Chief:*

The army is moving in three columns, the right column having in it three corps. The line occupied to-day with the advance will be on the other side of the mountains, from Boonsborough to Rohrersville. Two corps will march without their artillery, the animals being completely exhausted, many falling on the road. The enemy's infantry were driven back yesterday evening from Boonsborough, or, rather,· they retired on being pressed toward Hagerstown. I am still under the impression that Lee's whole army is between Hagerstown and Williamsport, with an advance at Middleburg, on the road to Greencastle, observing Couch. The state of the river and the difficulty of crossing has rendered it imperative on him to have his army, artillery, and trains ready to receive my attack. I propose to move on a line from Boonsborough toward the center of the line from Hagerstown to Williamsport, my left flank looking to the river and my right toward the mountains, keeping the road to Frederick in my rear and center. I shall try to keep as concentrated as the roads by which I can move will admit, so that, should the enemy attack, I can move to meet him, and, if he assumes the defensive, I can deploy as I think proper. I transmit a copy of dispatch, sent to General Smith, at Waynesborough.* One of like tenor was sent to General Couch. The operations of both those officers should be made to conform to mine. They can readily ascertain my progress from scouts and by the movements of the enemy, and, if the forces under them are of any practical value, they could join my right flank and assist in the attack. My cavalry will be pushed to-day well to the front, on the right and left, and I hope will collect information. It is with the greatest difficulty that I can obtain any reliable intelligence of the enemy. I send a dispatch, received this morning from General Neill, in command of a brigade of infantry and cavalry, who followed the retreat of the enemy through Fairfield, and effected a junction with General Smith at Waynesborough. A copy of my dispatch to General Smith is also sent you.* When I spoke of two corps having to leave their batteries behind, I should have stated that they remained at Frederick to get new horses and shoe the others, and that they will rejoin their corps this p. m. The object of the remark was to show the delay. I think the decisive battle of the war will be fought in a few days. In view of its momentous consequences, I desire to adopt such measures as in my judgment will tend to insure success, even though these may be deemed tardy.

GEO. G. MEADE.

---

* See Part III, p. 621.

11.30 A. M.

[P. S.]—A deserter has just been brought within our lines who reports the enemy's army all between Hagerstown and Williamsport; that they have brought up a bridge from Winchester, which is now thrown across at Williamsport; that they are using this bridge, not to cross their forces, but to bring over supplies; that the men are in fine spirits, and the talk among them is they must try it again. This deserter says he belongs to the artillery of Stuart's command. I send the information for what it is worth.

[Inclosure.]

HDQRS. LIGHT DIV., ARMY OF THE POTOMAC, *July* 9, 1863.
General S. WILLIAMS:

SIR: Baldy [W. F.] Smith is here with his command. Colonel [J. I.] Gregg, with brigade of cavalry, who leaves for Boonsborough to-night, will send this.

A scout brings information that Lee has one corps intrenched on the Williamsport pike from Hagerstown; another on Boonsborough pike; and Early is said to be up toward Middleburg (*quien sabe?*), between Newcastle [Greencastle?] and Hagerstown. The news of the capture of Vicksburg is confirmed. Have sent a cavalry reconnaissance toward Hagerstown this morning; it has not returned.

Since writing the above, have felt the enemy's pickets with a regiment of cavalry at a bridge 4 or 5 miles from Hagerstown. They are stubborn. We drove them away, but they returned as we retired. General Smith is in with his mixed command. Am delighted to have the benefit of his counsel and advice. We are all right, but watch Early's division on my right toward Middleburg.

THOS. H. NEILL,
Brigadier-General, Commanding.

——

HEADQUARTERS ARMY OF THE POTOMAC,
July 9, 1863—5.20 p. m.
(Received 7.10 p. m.)
Maj. Gen. H. W. HALLECK,
General-in-Chief:

I transmit herewith a copy of instructions this moment sent to General Naglee at Harper's Ferry.
Very respectfully,

GEO. G. MEADE,
Major-General.

[Inclosure.]

HEADQUARTERS ARMY OF THE POTOMAC,
July 9, 1863—5.20 p. m

Brigadier-General NAGLEE,
Commanding Harper's Ferry:

Organize the re-enforcements in brigades as fast as they arrive, and send them, through Rohrersville, to join the left of the army, seeing that they have haversacks and three days' rations. First secure a garrison of 3,000 or 4,000 men to garrison Maryland Heights against a *coup de main.*

A. A. HUMPHREYS,
Chief of Staff.

WASHINGTON, D. C., *July* 9, 1863—3 p. m.
Maj. Gen. GEORGE G. MEADE,
> *Army of the Potomac:*

The evidence that Lee's army will fight north of the Potomac seems reliable. In that case you will want all your forces in hand. Kelley is collecting at Hancock. I have directed him to push forward, so as to take part in the coming battle. Brooks' militia refused to cross the Pennsylvania line. Everything I can get here will be pushed on to Harper's Ferry, from which place you can call them in to your left. Do not be influenced by any dispatch from here against your own judgment. Regard them as suggestions only. Our information here is not always correct. Take any horses or supplies you can find in the country. They can be settled for afterward. Would it not be well to fortify the Hagerstown Gap, through the South Mountain, as a part of the support?

> H. W. HALLECK,
> *General-in-Chief.*

—

WASHINGTON, D. C., *July* 9, 1863—4.30 p. m.
Major-General MEADE:
> *Army of the Potomac:*

Two full regiments and two complete batteries are ordered to leave here to-night. Three brigades are on their way, and may be expected to-morrow or the day after. They will be sent to Harper's Ferry, unless you wish otherwise. I shall do everything in my power to re-enforce you. I fully appreciate the importance of the coming battle.

> H. W. HALLECK,
> *General-in-Chief.*

—

HEADQUARTERS ARMY OF THE POTOMAC,
> *July* 10, 1863—9 a. m.
> (Received 9.45 a. m.)
Maj. Gen. H. W. HALLECK,
> *General-in-Chief:*

Means of transportation and supplies required by the re-enforcements for this army being at Frederick, it would facilitate their junction with the army if the re-enforcements were sent to Frederick instead of Harper's Ferry.

> GEO. G. MEADE,
> *Major-General.*

—

WASHINGTON, D. C., *July* 10, 1863—11.20 a. m.
Major-General MEADE,
> *Army of the Potomac:*

You can stop at Frederick the re-enforcements ordered to Harper's Ferry. Those ordered hereafter will be directed to Frederick, at your request. I fear the three additional brigades may not reach here before to-morrow night.

> H. W. HALLECK,
> *General-in-Chief.*

HEADQUARTERS ARMY OF THE POTOMAC,
July 10, 1863—1 p. m.
(Received 3.10 p. m.)

Maj. Gen. H. W. HALLECK,
General-in-Chief:

The information received to-day indicates that the enemy occupy positions extending from the Potomac, near Falling Waters, through Downsville to Funkstown, and to the northeast of Hagerstown, Ewell's corps being to the northeast of Hagerstown, Longstreet at Funkstown, and A. P. Hill on their right. These positions they are said to be intrenching. I am advancing on a line perpendicular to the line from Hagerstown to Williamsport, and the army will this evening occupy a position extending from the Boonsborough and Hagerstown road, at a point 1 mile beyond Beaver Creek, to Bakersville, near the Potomac. Our cavalry advanced this morning, drove in the enemy's cavalry on the Boonsborough pike to within a mile of Funkstown, when the enemy displayed a large force, and opened a fire from heavy guns, 20-pounders. I shall advance cautiously on the same line to-morrow until I can develop more fully the enemy's force and position, upon which my future operations will depend. General Smith is still at Waynesborough. A dispatch was received from him at that place this morning. Instructions similar to those of yesterday were sent to him.

GEO. G. MEADE,
Major-General, Commanding.

—

WASHINGTON, D. C.,
July 10, 1863—9 p. m.

Major-General MEADE,
Army of the Potomac:

I think it will be best for you to postpone a general battle till you can concentrate all your forces and get up your reserves and re-enforcements. I will push on the troops as fast as they arrive. It would be well to have staff officers at the Monocacy, to direct the troops arriving where to go, and to see that they are properly fitted out. They should join you by forced marches. Beware of partial combats. Bring up and hurl upon the enemy all your forces, good and bad.

H. W. HALLECK.

—

HEADQUARTERS ARMY OF THE POTOMAC,
July 10, 1863.

The ADJUTANT-GENERAL OF THE ARMY,
Washington:

SIR: I have the honor herewith to transmit five additional battle-flags captured from the enemy by the Second Army Corps in the recent engagement at Gettysburg. I also send a battle-flag captured at Chancellorsville, which has been sent in here.

I am, sir, very respectfully, your obedient servant,

GEO. G. MEADE,
Major-General, Commanding.

HEADQUARTERS ARMY OF THE POTOMAC,
Near Mountain House, July 10, 1863.
(Received 2.55 p. m.)
Maj. Gen. H. W. HALLECK:

In consequence of the very efficient service and the material aid
rendered to me by the cavalry during my recent operations, I would
esteem it a personal favor if the President would assign Major-General Pleasonton to the command of the Cavalry Corps, the position I
found him in when I assumed command.

GEO. G. MEADE,
Major-General, Commanding.

—

WASHINGTON, D. C., *July* 11, 1863—12 m.
Major-General MEADE, *Army of the Potomac:*

Your telegram in relation to General Pleasonton has been shown to
the Secretary of War.   There is no intention to supersede him in command of the cavalry.   General Stoneman remains here.   There is,
however, an objection to any formal order at present.   The three
brigades are arriving.   Assign them and their officers as you may
deem best, without regard to present or former organizations.

H. W. HALLECK,
General-in-Chief.

—

HEADQUARTERS ARMY OF THE POTOMAC,
Antietam Creek, July 11, 1863—4 p. m.
(Received 5.30 p. m.)
Maj. Gen. H. W. HALLECK,
General-in-Chief:

The line of this army was advanced cautiously this morning in the
direction stated in yesterday's dispatch, and at this time its right
rests on the road from Smoketown to Funkstown, about 2 miles from
the latter, the line crossing the Antietam, passing through Jones'
Cross-Roads, the left being near Marsh Run.   Strong reconnaissances
of infantry are being pushed out toward Funkstown, on the left bank
of the Antietam, toward the same point on the right bank, and on the
road from Sharpsburg to Funkstown.   At the same time, cavalry
force is pushing out on the left, on the Boonsborough and Williamsport road, and on the right toward Hagerstown from Chewsville and
Leitersburg.   The cavalry on the Chewsville road advanced without
opposition to within a short distance, about 1½ miles, of Hagerstown.
The cavalry in the direction of Leitersburg and that advancing toward Williamsport have not yet been heard from.   Everything indicates that the enemy is massing between Hagerstown and Williamsport, and from various sources it is stated they are intrenching.
From the representations of General Spinola that the nine months'
men of his command could not be relied upon, as their time had
nearly expired, and my own experience of troops under such circumstances, I have directed the regiments of his brigade to be posted in
the rear.   Troops of this character can be of little service unless they
are pledged to serve beyond their terms of enlistment; and the supplies they consume and the space they occupy on the lines of communication can be illy spared; besides, their presence may have an
injurious effect upon other troops.   I do not, therefore, desire to be

re-enforced by such troops unless they have pledged themselves to remain beyond their terms of service and until I can dispense with their services.

GEO. G. MEADE,
Major-General, Commanding.

—

WASHINGTON, D. C., *July* 11, 1863—9 p. m.

Major-General MEADE,
Army of the Potomac:

The nine months' men told me that they were willing to serve through this crisis under any one but General Spinola, but would not serve under him, as they regarded him as worthless. You are authorized to relieve him and send him away.

H. W. HALLECK,
General-in-Chief.

—

HEADQUARTERS ARMY OF THE POTOMAC,
July 12, 1863—4.30 p. m. (Received 8 p. m.)

Maj. Gen. H. W. HALLECK,
General-in-Chief:

Upon advancing my right flank across the Antietam this morning, the enemy abandoned Funkstown and Hagerstown, and my line now extends from the latter place to Fair Play. The advance of the cavalry on the right showed the enemy to be strongly posted on the Hagerstown and Williamsport road, about 1½ miles from Hagerstown. On the left, the cavalry advance showed them to be in position back of Saint James' College and at Downsville. Their position runs along the high ground from Downsville to near Hagerstown. This position they are intrenching. Batteries are established on it. It is my intention to attack them to-morrow, unless something intervenes to prevent it, for the reason that delay will strengthen the enemy and will not increase my force.

GEO. G. MEADE,
Major-General.

—

HEADQUARTERS ARMY OF THE POTOMAC,
July 13, 1863—5 p. m. (Received 6.40 p. m.)

Maj. Gen. H. W. HALLECK,
General-in-Chief:

In my dispatch of yesterday I stated that it was my intention to attack the enemy to-day, unless something intervened to prevent it. Upon calling my corps commanders together and submitting the question to them, five out of six were unqualifiedly opposed to it. Under these circumstances, in view of the momentous consequences attendant upon a failure to succeed, I did not feel myself authorized to attack until after I had made more careful examination of the enemy's position, strength, and defensive works. These examinations are now being made. So far as completed, they show the enemy to be strongly intrenched on a ridge running from the rear of Hagerstown past Downsville to the Potomac. I shall continue these reconnaissances with the expectation of finding some weak point, upon which, if I succeed, I shall hazard an attack. General W. F. Smith, of the advanced division of General Couch's forces, has arrived here to-day, but from the organization and condition of these troops, and the short time they have to serve, I cannot place much reliance upon them. Difficulties arising with the troops sent me whose terms of service are about expiring, respecting the dates at which they expire, I beg to be informed by the Department upon that head respecting each such regiment sent to me.

GEO. G. MEADE,
Major-General.

—

WASHINGTON, D. C., July 13, 1863—9.30 p. m.

Maj. Gen. GEORGE G. MEADE,
 Army of the Potomac:

Yours of 5 p. m. is received. You are strong enough to attack and defeat the enemy before he can effect a crossing. Act upon your own judgment and make your generals execute your orders. Call no council of war. It is proverbial that councils of war never fight. Re-enforcements are pushed on as rapidly as possible. Do not let the enemy escape.

H. W. HALLECK,
General-in-Chief.

—

HEADQUARTERS ARMY OF THE POTOMAC,
July 14, 1863—11 a. m.   (Received 12.10 p. m.)

Maj. Gen. H. W. HALLECK,
 General-in-Chief:

On advancing my army this morning, with a view of ascertaining the exact position of the enemy and attacking him if the result of the examination should justify me, I found, on reaching his lines, that they were evacuated. I immediately put my army in pursuit, the cavalry in advance. At this period my forces occupy Williamsport, but I have not yet heard from the advance on Falling Waters, where it is reported he crossed his infantry on a bridge. Your instructions as to further movements, in case the enemy are entirely across the river, are desired.

GEO. G. MEADE,
Major-General.

—

WASHINGTON, D. C., July 14, 1863—1 p. m.

Major-General MEADE,
 Army of the Potomac:

The enemy should be pursued and cut up, wherever he may have gone. This pursuit may or may not be upon the rear or flank, as circumstances may require. The inner flank toward Washington presents the greatest advantages. Supply yourself from the country as far as possible. I cannot advise details, as I do not know where Lee's army is, nor where your pontoon bridges are. I need hardly say to you that the escape of Lee's army without another battle has created great dissatisfaction in the mind of the President, and it will require an active and energetic pursuit on your part to remove the impression that it has not been sufficiently active heretofore.

H. W. HALLECK,
General-in-Chief.

WASHINGTON, D. C., *July* 14, 1863—2.30 p. m.

Major-General MEADE,
    Army of the Potomac:

Should you cross at Berlin, or below Harper's Ferry, your supplies for the time can be sent by the Baltimore and Ohio Railroad.   General Meigs will, therefore, recall General Haupt and the Railroad Brigade to repair the Manassas road, so that supplies can meet you by Thoroughfare Gap or Warrenton, should you require them there. Telegraph condition of things.

                    H. W. HALLECK,
                        General-in-Chief.

—

HEADQUARTERS ARMY OF THE POTOMAC,
    July 14, 1863—2.30 p. m.   (Received 3.10 p. m.)

Maj. Gen. H. W. HALLECK,
        General-in-Chief:

Having performed my duty conscientiously and to the best of my ability, the censure of the President conveyed in your dispatch of 1 p. m. this day, is, in my judgment, so undeserved that I feel compelled most respectfully to ask to be immediately relieved from the command of this army.

                    GEO. G. MEADE,
                Major-General, Commanding.

—

HEADQUARTERS ARMY OF THE POTOMAC,
    July 14, 1863—3 p. m.   (Received 3.15 p. m.)

Maj. Gen. H. W. HALLECK,
        General-in-Chief:

My cavalry now occupy Falling Waters, having overtaken and captured a brigade of infantry 1,500 strong, 2 guns, 2 caissons, 2 battle-flags, and a large number of small-arms.   The enemy are all across the Potomac.

                    GEO. G. MEADE,
                        Major-General.

—

HEADQUARTERS ARMY OF THE POTOMAC,
    July 14, 1863—3.30 p. m.   (Received 4 p. m.)

Major-General HALLECK,
        General-in-Chief:

The difficulty of supplying the army in the Valley of the Shenandoah, owing to the destruction of railroad, has decided me to move by Berlin.   I shall pursue and harass the retreat of the enemy with my cavalry.

                    GEO. G. MEADE,
                        Major-General.

—

WASHINGTON, D. C., *July* 14, 1863—4.30 p. m.

Major-General MEADE,
    Army of the Potomac:

My telegram, stating the disappointment of the President at the escape of Lee's army, was not intended as a censure, but as a stimulus to an active pursuit. It is not deemed a sufficient cause for your application to be relieved.

H. W. HALLECK,
General-in-Chief.

HEADQUARTERS ARMY OF THE POTOMAC,
July 14, 1863—8.30 p. m.
(Received 9.30 p. m.)

Maj. Gen. H. W. HALLECK,
General-in-Chief:

My cavalry have captured 500 prisoners, in addition to those previously reported. General Pettigrew, of the Confederate army, was killed this morning in the attack on the enemy's rear guard. His body is in our hands. A division of my cavalry crossed the river at Harper's Ferry to-day, who will pursue and harass the retreat of the enemy and give me information of his movements. General Kelley, with an infantry force, and Averell's cavalry, have reached Williamsport. Am I authorized to detain him here to watch the Potomac while I move to Berlin?

GEO. G. MEADE,
Major-General, Commanding.

WASHINGTON, D. C., *July* 15, 1863—3.30 p. m.
Major-General MEADE,
Army of the Potomac:

General Kelley has been ordered to cross the Potomac and act on Lee's right flank, in order to prevent raids into West Virginia. It is hoped that he may be able to do the enemy some harm there.

H. W. HALLECK,
General-in-Chief.

HEADQUARTERS ARMY OF THE POTOMAC,
Berlin, Md., July 15, 1863—7 p. m.
(Received 8.40 p. m.)

Maj. Gen. H. W. HALLECK,
General-in-Chief:

The army was set in motion this morning at daylight, four corps being directed to this place and three to Harper's Ferry. The bridge at Harper's Ferry was finished yesterday over the Shenandoah, at its mouth. Will be planked by daylight to-morrow. A break in the canal at the mouth of the Monocacy delays the transfer of pontoons from Harper's Ferry to this point; but every effort is being made to repair the canal, which it is expected will be in order to-morrow.

GEO. G. MEADE,
Major-General, Commanding.

HEADQUARTERS ARMY OF THE POTOMAC,
July 15, 1863—8.30 p. m.
(Received 9 p. m.)

Maj. Gen. H. W. HALLECK,
General-in-Chief:

I have ordered General Couch to cover the river from Harper's Ferry upward. Colonel [A. T.] McReynolds is picketing it with his cavalry from Harper's Ferry to Williamsport. General [D. McM.] Gregg overtook and engaged the enemy's cavalry near Charlestown this morning, taking 100 prisoners. He informs me that the enemy's infantry are moving to Winchester.

GEO. G. MEADE,
Major-General.

HEADQUARTERS ARMY OF THE POTOMAC,
July 16, 1863—10 p. m.
(Received 11.30 p. m.)

Maj. Gen. H. W. HALLECK,
General-in-Chief:

The army is concentrated at this place and Harper's Ferry, and are supplying themselves as rapidly as possible with subsistence stores, forage, and certain indispensable articles of clothing. One bridge is completed at Harper's Ferry, and one will be completed at this point by 8 a. m. to-morrow. I shall immediately cross a division of cavalry to push forward and occupy the nearest gaps to Snicker's Gap.

The infantry corps will be moved as soon as their commanders report them ready. I shall push the army forward as rapidly as possible to Warrenton and beyond to Culpeper. I deem it proper, however, to advise you that the army is greatly exhausted by previous service, both men and animals, particularly the latter. My cavalry force, from the casualties of battle and the fatigue of service, is greatly reduced.

The number of men is reported below 10,000; the number of horses below 7,000; of these many barely able to get along. General Pleasonton reports that a considerable number of his officers and men sent to Washington to be remounted have never returned, and that a large number sent to Frederick for the same purpose have not been able to procure horses. It is of the greatest importance that the cavalry should be placed in an efficient condition, as it is only by their prompt movements that I can obtain reliable information of the position of the enemy, and it is only by them I can guard my trains and rear. I beg leave, therefore, to urge that every exertion may be made to procure horses to remount the dismounted men and meet future contingencies.

GEO. G. MEADE,
Major-General.

HEADQUARTERS ARMY OF THE POTOMAC,
July 16, 1863.

ADJUTANT-GENERAL OF THE ARMY,
Washington:

SIR: I have the honor herewith to transmit three battle-flags, captured from the enemy by Brigadier-General Kilpatrick's division of cavalry.

I am, very respectfully, your obedient servant,

GEO. G. MEADE,
Major-General, Commanding.

HEADQUARTERS ARMY OF THE POTOMAC,
Lovettsville, July 18, 1863—7 p. m.
(Received 8.45 p. m.)

Major-General HALLECK,
General-in-Chief:

Four infantry corps, the Reserve Artillery, and two divisions of cavalry have crossed the Potomac at Berlin and Harper's Ferry last evening and to-day. The rest of the army will cross to-morrow.

The division of cavalry which was sent forward yesterday have reported the occupation of Snicker's Gap after a brisk skirmish with the enemy, taking a few prisoners, who reported themselves belonging to White's guerrillas. I send forward to-day another division, to take possession of the gaps as far as Chester Gap.

A cavalry force, two brigades, will be sent to-morrow through Aldie to cover and guard the Orange and Alexandria Railroad to Warrenton Junction and Warrenton. I would be glad to be advised how much of the road can be protected by the troops from Washington.

I have left Brigadier-General Lockwood, with the Maryland troops recently under his command, added to the force previously under General Naglee, making over 4,000 men in all, to hold Harper's Ferry, and directed him to report to General Couch, whom I have directed to assume command of the defense of the Upper Potomac until more definite intelligence is obtained of the movements of the enemy. I have received no intelligence of any kind of the enemy beyond the fact reported by the cavalry sent in pursuit, that he was moving on Winchester. Scouts have been sent in all directions, but none have as yet reported.

I see by the public journals it is intimated that a part of Bragg's army has been sent to Virginia. I presume if any reliable intelligence of this fact reaches you, I shall be fully advised. My present plan is to move rapidly to Warrenton, open my communication by the Orange and Alexandria Railroad, and then be governed by the position and movements of the enemy.

GEO. G. MEADE,
Major-General.

—

WASHINGTON, D. C., July 18, 1863.

Major-General MEADE,
Army of the Potomac:

You need have no fear of Bragg, Johnston, or Beauregard. Not a man will join Lee. His forces can only be re-enforced by a part of D. H. Hill's command, and even then they will be far inferior in numbers to your army.

H. W. HALLECK,
General-in-Chief.

—

HEADQUARTERS ARMY OF THE POTOMAC,
Lovettsville, July 19, 1863—10 a. m.
(Received 10.15 a. m.)

Maj. Gen. H. W. HALLECK,
General-in-Chief:

I am very anxious to have a competent commander for the Second Corps, made vacant by the wounding of Hancock. The very valuable services and most efficient assistance rendered me by Brigadier-General Warren induce me to nominate him for the commission of major-general, to be assigned to the Second Corps. I consider the efficiency and spirit of this army will be greatly promoted by making this appointment, and have therefore to earnestly urge it. I would also be greatly gratified if the commission of brigadier-general could be bestowed on Col. Kenner Garrard, One hundred and forty-sixth New York Volunteers, and Col. Sidney Burbank, Second Infantry.

GEO. G. MEADE,
Major-General.

HEADQUARTERS ARMY OF THE POTOMAC,
July 19, 1863—9.30 p. m.
(Received July 20, 12.50 a. m.)

Maj. Gen. H. W. HALLECK,
General-in-Chief:

The Twelfth, Eleventh, and Sixth Corps crossed the river to-day. The position of the army to-night is as follows, viz:

The Third Corps in the vicinity of Wood Grove, the Second Corps in rear of it, and the Twelfth Corps nearly abreast of Hillsborough; the Fifth Corps in the vicinity of Purcellville, the Reserve Artillery in rear of the Fifth Corps, and the Sixth Corps at the crossing of the Lovettsville and Purcellville pike, by the Waterford and Hillsborough road. The First Corps is in the vicinity of Hamilton, and the Eleventh Corps between Waterford and Hamilton.

It will be seen from this that the army is moving in three columns. Two divisions of cavalry are in front and on the right flank, those in front moving rapidly to overtake the enemy; a brigade in rear, and two brigades moving to protect the Orange and Alexandria Railroad.

The information derived from our scouts represents infantry of the enemy at Front Royal on the 16th, and indicates that his army is moving up the Valley and on Culpeper. After to-day I shall not be in communication with the telegraph until I reach Warrenton.

GEO. G. MEADE,
Major-General, Commanding.

WASHINGTON, D. C., *July* 21, 1863—10 a. m.

Major-General MEADE,
Army of the Potomac:

It is reported that Hill's corps has moved back to Martinsburg, compelling Kelley to recross the Potomac at Cherry Run. General Foster applies for Brig. Gen. H. M. Naglee. He will be ordered to return to Fort Monroe and report to General Foster.

H. W. HALLECK,
General-in-Chief.

HEADQUARTERS AT LINDEN,
Crest of Manassas Gap, July 23, 1863—10 p. m.
(Received, via Harper's Ferry, Va., July 25, 8.40 a. m.)

Maj. Gen. H. W. HALLECK,
General-in-Chief:

On the evening of the 20th, this army was posted on the two pikes from Aldie to Winchester, the cavalry occupying Snicker's and Ashby's Gaps with slight opposition. All the information respecting the enemy indicated that he was still in position from Winchester to Martinsburg. Lest the continuance of my march should enable him to get into my rear and interrupt or interfere with my communications, I halted during the 21st, throwing forward my cavalry to Manassas and Chester Gaps. Manassas Gap my cavalry occupied, but they were driven back from Chester Gap. On the morning of the 22d, being satisfied that the enemy's army was in full movement southward toward Culpeper Court-House or Orange Court-House, I directed two corps to cover my depots at Warrenton and White Plains, and threw forward the other five corps to Manassas Gap. At daylight this morning, the Third Corps entered Manassas Gap, and, advancing beyond the crest, has been skirmishing with and driving back the enemy. At dark the enemy held a position covering the entrance to Chester Gap from Front Royal. The information respecting his army is somewhat contradictory. It is reported to me by signal officers and my cavalry to have been moving with its trains yesterday and to-day up the Valley of the Shenandoah, through Front Royal and Strasburg, and through Chester Gap toward Culpeper, though there are reasons for my considering it probable that but a small portion of his army has passed on. I shall attack his position covering Chester Gap to-morrow at daylight.

GEO. G. MEADE,
Major-General.

WASHINGTON, D. C., *July 23, 1863.*

Maj. Gen. GEORGE G. MEADE,
Army of the Potomac:

GENERAL: Brig. Gen. G. Marston has been assigned by the Secretary of War to the command of Saint Mary's District, Maryland, where he is to establish a camp for prisoners of war. You will assign to him a guard of about 300 men from New Hampshire regiments. It is reported that there are only about that number in the Second, Fifth, and Twelfth New Hampshire Volunteers. If more convenient, any other New Hampshire troops may be taken. It is intended to return these regiments to the Army of the Potomac as soon as they can be filled up with drafted men from that State.

Any prisoners of war you may have will be turned over to General Marston, who is directed to show you his instructions.

Very respectfully, your obedient servant,

H. W. HALLECK,
General-in-Chief.

HEADQUARTERS ARMY OF THE POTOMAC,
July 24, 1863—8 p. m.
(Received, via Warrenton, July 25, 4.10 p. m.)

Major-General HALLECK,
General-in-Chief:

I last night telegraphed you that, after driving the enemy through Manassas Gap, the head of the army, consisting of the Third Corps, had reached within a few miles of Front Royal at sunset, and was in the presence of a considerable force of the enemy, with batteries in position. Prisoners taken belonged to the three several corps of the

Confederate Army, and reliable intelligence was obtained of the arrival of Ewell's corps from Winchester at the close of the engagement. It was not until late in the evening that the army debouched from the pass sufficiently to deploy any larger force than the Third Corps, though this corps was followed immediately by the Fifth and Second. During the night, the Twelfth and two divisions of the Sixth were ordered up, and it was my intention, as reported to you, to attack with my whole force, in the hope of separating the force of the enemy and capturing such portions as had not reached the passes. I regret to inform you that, on advancing this morning at daylight, the enemy had again disappeared, declining battle, and though an immediate advance was made and Front Royal occupied, nothing was seen of him but a rear guard of cavalry with a battery of artillery. I then ascertained that for two days he had been retreating with great celerity, principally through Strasburg and Luray, sending through Chester Gap sufficient force to cover his flank and hold me in check in my advance through Manassas Gap. As evidence of the hurried manner in which the enemy's retreat was conducted, is the fact of his abandoning some 80 wounded in Front Royal without any supplies.

My cavalry have been employed in harassing the enemy, having captured numerous prisoners and several herds of cattle and sheep. Finding the enemy entirely beyond my reach, I have withdrawn the army from Front Royal, through Manassas Gap, and shall concentrate it in the vicinity of Warrenton and Warrenton Junction for supplies and to establish a base of communication.

The losses in yesterday's engagement are reported to amount to some 200 killed and wounded,[*] among the latter General Spinola. The enemy is believed to have gone to Culpeper, and probably beyond.

GEO. G. MEADE,
Major-General.

WASHINGTON, D. C., *July* 25, 1863—12.30 p. m.
Major-General MEADE,
    Army of the Potomac:

Your telegram of 10 p. m., 23d, is just received—the first communication from you for four or five days. The Quartermaster's and Commissary Departments have been prepared to send forward supplies, but were uncertain of the position of your army. Every possible effort has been made to send remounts to your cavalry, but the destruction of horses is enormous. Every serviceable horse in the country occupied should be impressed. They only serve for guerrillas.

H. W. HALLECK,
General-in-Chief.

HEADQUARTERS ARMY OF THE POTOMAC,
    July 25, 1863—2 p. m. (Received 3.50 p. m.)
Maj. Gen. H. W. HALLECK,
    General-in-Chief:

I have just reached Warrenton. The detachments of the Thirteenth and Sixteenth Regiments New York Cavalry, alluded to in

---

* But see revised statement, p. 192.

your dispatch of the 21st, will be ordered to return at once to their regiments in the vicinity of Warrenton.   I take this occasion to request that the detachments of cavalry now about Washington belonging to my command may be immediately ordered to their regiments, more especially those belonging to the First Rhode Island and Twelfth Illinois Regiments.

GEO. G. MEADE,
Major-General. Commanding.

—

HEADQUARTERS ARMY OF THE POTOMAC,
Warrenton, July 25, 1863—7 p. m.
(Received July 26, 12.30 a. m.)

Maj. Gen. H. W. HALLECK,
General-in-Chief:

Your telegram of 12.30 p. m. is received.   I telegraphed you on the 19th instant.   After that date, being away from telegraphic communication, and the guerrillas rendering the transmission of dispatches insecure, I did not telegraph till the 23d, as there was nothing particular to communicate, and nothing definite known of the enemy.   When I left the Potomac River, I requested the quartermaster's and commissary departments to throw supplies to Warrenton and Warrenton Junction.

After I found the movements of the enemy might detain me from reaching Warrenton as soon as originally expected, I requested the chief and acting chief of those departments to have a limited amount of supplies sent to White Plains, to meet contingencies.   The chiefs of these departments with me were fully apprised of my views and plans as soon as they were formed.   As soon as I had crossed the river, I sent two brigades of cavalry to guard the Orange and Alexandria road and its branch to Warrenton, and the very moment my army was within reach of those places, two corps were sent to guard Warrenton, Warrenton Junction, and White Plains.   The service the cavalry have had to perform has been trying on horses, and the rocky character of the roads very destructive of shoes.   Four corps are to-night in this vicinity; the remaining three will be in position to-morrow.   My cavalry are on the Rappahannock.   One division is at Amissville, beyond the Rappahannock, annoying the rear of the enemy; another at Orleans, covering the movements of the infantry. No positive intelligence has been received of the movements of the enemy.

GEO. G. MEADE,
Major-General, Commanding.

—

HEADQUARTERS ARMY OF THE POTOMAC,
Warrenton, July 25, 1863—7 p. m.
(Received 10 p. m.)

Maj. Gen. H. W. HALLECK,
General-in-Chief:

I beg leave to call your attention to my telegram of the 19th instant, making certain nominations of general officers, particularly nominating a commander for the Second Corps, and to ask whether any action has been had on the same.

GEO. G. MEADE,
Major-General.

WASHINGTON, D. C., *July* 26, 1863.

Major-General MEADE,
    Warrenton, Va:

It is impossible to promote General Warren at present. There is no vacancy. I have recommended the discharge of certain useless major-generals, but it has not been acted on. The delay in sending back detachments of cavalry results from want of horse equipments, all on hand having been sent to your army and to General Couch. Others are expected daily.

        H. W. HALLECK,
          General-in-Chief.

—

HEADQUARTERS ARMY OF THE POTOMAC,
    July 26, 1863—8 p. m.   (Received 8.30 p. m.)

Maj. Gen. H. W. HALLECK,
    General-in-Chief:

How far from Alexandria can the troops from Washington guard the Orange and Alexandria Railroad ? I ask, that I may direct my troops to connect with them. Do you desire or expect I should take any steps for the reoccupation of the Shenandoah Valley, now abandoned by the enemy ?

        GEO. G. MEADE,
          Major-General.

—

WASHINGTON, D. C., *July* 27, 1863.

Major-General MEADE,
    Army of the Potomac:

I see no advantage in the reoccupation of the Shenandoah Valley. Lee's army is the objective point. General Heintzelman will reply in regard to his guarding the railroad.

        H. W. HALLECK,
          General-in-Chief.

—

WASHINGTON, D. C., *July* 27, 1863.

Major-General MEADE,
    Warrenton, Va.:

General Heintzelman says that with his present force he cannot guard the road beyond Manassas Junction.

        H. W. HALLECK,
          General-in-Chief.

—

HEADQUARTERS ARMY OF THE POTOMAC,
    Warrenton, July 27, 1863.   (Received 12.15 p. m.)

Maj. Gen. H.. W. HALLECK,
    General-in-Chief:

From Warrenton Junction it is reported that artillery firing is heard in the direction of Aquia Creek and at Fredericksburg. I have sent no force in that direction. Have any been sent from Washington?

        GEO. G. MEADE,
          Major-General.

WASHINGTON, D. C., *July 27*, 1863.
Major-General MEADE, *Warrenton, Va.:*

No troops have been sent in the direction of Aquia Creek or Fredericksburg. The firing is probably from gunboats in that vicinity.

H. W. HALLECK,
General-in-Chief.

—

HEADQUARTERS ARMY OF THE POTOMAC,
Warrenton, July 27, 1863—4 p. m.   (Received 5.45 p. m.)

Maj. Gen. H. W. HALLECK, *General-in-Chief:*

The only object in reoccupying the Valley of the Shenandoah would be to prevent the enemy from having the benefit of the incoming crops, which last year, I understand, he employed his army in gathering, and sent to the rear for winter use. If the Valley is not occupied, would it not be well to direct the forces under General Couch to come here, and occupy and guard the railroad forming my line of communication, which, if the enemy does not make any defense of the Rapidan, will be a very long line, and will require for its security a large detachment from this army? I make this suggestion because I understood the forces under General Couch were under my general command only while my operations were in Maryland and Pennsylvania, and since crossing the Potomac I have exercised no control over them. The condition of my cavalry is such that it will, perhaps, be a day or two before I can throw a large force across the Rappahannock to ascertain the exact position of the enemy.

Scouts report a force at Culpeper and one near Cedar Mountain, though the general impression seems to be that the main body has gone to Gordonsville.

The Rappahannock at Sulphur Springs and below is not fordable at present, having over 4 feet of water.

GEO. G. MEADE,
Major-General.

—

WASHINGTON, D. C., *July 27*, 1863.
Major-General MEADE, *Army of the Potomac:*

The occupation of the Shenandoah is now a matter of very little importance. It is supposed that General Couch's forces, being militia, are about melted away. They would be worthless if ordered forward. General [Charles] Griffin's resignation is accepted.* You will supply his place.

H. W. HALLECK,
General-in-Chief.

—

HEADQUARTERS OF THE ARMY,
Washington, D. C., July 27, 1863.
Maj. Gen. GEORGE G. MEADE,
Commanding Army of the Potomac;
Major-General HEINTZELMAN,
Commanding Department of Washington:

GENERALS: The numerous depredations committed by citizens or rebel soldiers in disguise, harbored and concealed by citizens, along

---

* Acceptance annulled July 28, 1863.—COMPILER.

the Orange and Alexandria Railroad, and within our lines, call for prompt and exemplary punishment.   You will, therefore, arrest and confine for punishment, or put beyond our lines, every citizen against whom there is sufficient evidence of his having engaged in these practices.   You will also notify the people within 10 miles of the railroad that they will be held responsible in their persons and property for any injury done to the road, trains, depots, or stations, by citizens, guerrillas, or persons in disguise, and, in case of such injury, they will be impressed as laborers to repair all damages.

If these measures should not stop such depredations, the entire inhabitants of the district of country along the railroad will be put across the lines and their property taken for Government uses.

Very respectfully, your obedient servant,

H. W. HALLECK,
General-in-Chief.

—

HEADQUARTERS ARMY OF THE POTOMAC,
July 28, 1863.

Brig. Gen. LORENZO THOMAS,
Adjutant-General of the Army:

GENERAL: I have the honor herewith to transmit two additional battle-flags captured from the enemy at the battle of Gettysburg, on which are the following inscriptions, viz: First, "Captured from Eighth Florida Regiment by Sergt. Thomas Horan, Seventy-second New York (Third Excelsior) Volunteers."   Second, "Taken by Capt. Hugo Siedlitz, Company A, Twenty-seventh Pennsylvania Volunteers, from a regiment of Rodes' division, Early's [Ewell's] corps."

I am, general, very respectfully, your obedient servant,

GEO. G. MEADE,
Major-General, Commanding.

—

HEADQUARTERS ARMY OF THE POTOMAC,
July 28, 1863—3 p. m.   (Received 7.35 p. m.)

Maj. Gen. H. W. HALLECK,
General-in-Chief:

I am making every effort to prepare this army for an advance. The principal difficulties encountered are the passage of the Rappahannock (at present unfordable, but which will probably be bridged to-night), also the want of animals for the batteries and cavalry, to supply which the quartermaster's department is doing everything possible.   The recent marches in the mountain passes and the excessive heat of the weather caused a great loss of animals and the exhaustion of many others.   A large proportion of the animals require shoeing. It is also necessary to accumulate subsistence stores to load the trains before starting.   I am in hopes to commence the movement to-morrow, when I shall first throw over a cavalry force to feel for the enemy, and cross the infantry as fast as possible.   My plan is to advance on the railroad to Culpeper and as far beyond as the enemy's position will permit, to detach sufficient force to hold and guard the railroad from Manassas Junction, and thus test the question which has been raised of the capacity of the Orange and Alexandria Railroad to supply the army and the practicability of maintaining open such a long line of communication.

No reliable intelligence of the position of the enemy has been obtained. He pickets the Rappahannock from Fredericksburg to Rappahannock Station. These pickets, however, seem to be mere "lookouts," to warn him of my approach. Some camps can be seen at Pony Mountain, near Culpeper, and in the vicinity of Cedar Mountain.

Contradictory reports from citizens and scouts place the main body, some at Gordonsville, others say at Staunton and Charlottesville, and some assert the retreat has been extended to Richmond. My own expectation is that he will be found behind the line of the Rapidan, which, from all I can learn, presents a favorable line of defense, most of the fords being commanded by the southern bank, where his artillery can be used to advantage. If I can hold the railroad without too great a weakening of my force, and it proves to have the capacity to afford all the supplies needed, I shall advance until the enemy is encountered or definite information obtained of his movements.

By holding the road, I do not refer to the force necessary to prevent the injuries caused by guerrillas, but against large bodies of cavalry or other forces placed on my flank and rear for the purpose of destroying my communications.

GEO. G. MEADE,
Major-General.

P. S.—4 P. M.—A scout just returned from across the river reports the enemy have repaired the railroad bridge across the Rapidan, and are using the road to Culpeper Court-House; that Lee has been re-enforced by D. H. Hill, reported with 10,000 men, and that he intends to make a stand at Culpeper or in its vicinity.

—

UNOFFICIAL.]   HEADQUARTERS OF THE ARMY,
                            Washington, July 28, 1863.
Major-General MEADE,
    Army of the Potomac, Warrenton, Va.:

GENERAL: I take this method of writing you a few words which I could not well communicate in any other way.

Your fight at Gettysburg met with the universal approbation of all military men here. You handled your troops in that battle as well, if not better, than any general has handled his army during the war. You brought all your forces into action at the right time and place, which no commander of the Army of the Potomac has done before. You may well be proud of that battle. The President's order, or proclamation, of July 4, showed how much he appreciated your success.

And now a few words in regard to subsequent events. You should not have been surprised or vexed at the President's disappointment at the escape of Lee's army. He had examined into all the details of sending you re-enforcements, to satisfy himself that every man who could possibly be spared from other places had been sent to your army. He thought that Lee's defeat was so certain that he felt no little impatience at his unexpected escape. I have no doubt, general, that you felt the disappointment as keenly as any one else. Such things sometimes occur to us without any fault of our own. Take it altogether, your short campaign has proved your superior generalship, and you merit, as you will receive, the confidence of the

Government and the gratitude of the country. I need not assure you, general, that I have lost none of the confidence which I felt in you when I recommended you for the command.

Very respectfully, your obedient servant,

H. W. HALLECK.

—

WASHINGTON, D. C., *July* 29, 1863—10 a. m.

Major-General MEADE,
Warrenton, Va.:

The following note of the President is communicated for your information. I will write you more fully to-day:

EXECUTIVE MANSION,
July 29, 1863.

Major-General HALLECK :

Seeing General Meade's dispatch of yesterday to yourself, causes me to fear that he supposes the Government here is demanding of him to bring on a general engagement with Lee as soon as possible. I am claiming no such thing of him. In fact, my judgment is against it; which judgment, of course, I will yield if yours and his are the contrary. If he could not safely, engage Lee at Williamsport, it seems absurd to suppose he can safely engage him now, when he has scarcely more than two-thirds of the force he had at Williamsport, while it must be that Lee has been re-enforced. True, I desired General Meade to pursue Lee across the Potomac, hoping, as has proved true, that he would thereby clear the Baltimore and Ohio Railroad, and get some advantage by harassing him on his retreat. These being past, I am unwilling he should now get into a general engagement on the impression that we here are pressing him, and I shall be glad for you to so inform him, unless your own judgment is against it.

Yours, truly,

A. LINCOLN.

H. W. HALLECK,
General-in-Chief.

—

HEADQUARTERS ARMY OF THE POTOMAC,
July 29, 1863—11 a. m. (Received 11.45 a. m.)

H. W. HALLECK,
General-in-Chief:

Much feeling exists in this army in regard to the Eleventh Corps. This consideration, in addition to my own judgment that the other corps should be increased, induces me to submit to you for approval the propriety of breaking up the organization of this corps by sending General Howard with one division to the Second Corps, which he will then command, another division to the Twelfth Corps, and leaving the third division, under General Schurz, with a brigade of cavalry, to guard my rear from the Rappahannock to Manassas Junction. Please reply as soon as convenient.

GEO. G. MEADE,
Major-General.

—

WASHINGTON, D. C., *July* 29, 1863—2.30 p. m.

Major-General MEADE,
Army of the Potomac:

As it is quite possible that we may be obliged to detach some of your troops, to enforce the draft and to bring on the drafted men, I think it would be best to hold for the present the upper line of the Rappahannock without farther pursuit of Lee.   I will telegraph you as soon as I can get a decision in regard to the Eleventh Corps.

H. W. HALLECK,
General-in-Chief.

—

HEADQUARTERS ARMY OF THE POTOMAC,
July 29, 1863.

Major-General HALLECK,
      General-in-Chief:

GENERAL : Since my dispatch of this morning, I have had a consultation with Major-General Schurz, who has presented views to me which may in some measure modify your action.   I have, therefore, authorized General Schurz to see you on the manner of effecting the change proposed in such way as to be least offensive to the officers and men concerned, and I shall be very glad if the propositions of General Schurz should meet with your approval, as it is my desire to render this change as agreeable to this officer and those under his command as the interests of the public service will permit.

Respectfully, yours,

GEO. G. MEADE,
Major-General.

—

HEADQUARTERS ARMY OF THE POTOMAC,
July 30, 1863—1 p. m.   (Received 3 p. m.)

Major-General HALLECK,
      General-in-Chief:

Your telegrams of yesterday of 10.30 a. m. and 2 p. m. were duly received.   The impression of the President is correct.   I have been acting under the belief, from your telegrams, that it was his and your wish that I should pursue Lee and bring him to a general engagement, if practicable.   The President, however, labors under two misapprehensions: First, I did not fail to attack Lee at Williamsport because I could not do so safely; I simply delayed the attack until, by examination of his position, I could do so with some reasonable degree of probability that the attack would be successful.   He withdrew before that information could be obtained.   Secondly, my army at this moment is about equal in strength to what it was at Williamsport, the re-enforcements, principally Gordon's division, from the Peninsula, which reached me at Berlin, being about equal to the losses sustained by the discharge of the nine months' men.   By nine months' men, I mean those who were with the army at Gettysburg and before, and do not refer to several regiments that reported at Hagerstown, but from their disorganization were never brought to the front.

With this preliminary explanation, and the fact that my army is now in a condition to move, it becomes necessary that the question of an advance should be definitely settled at the earliest possible moment.   The solution of this question will depend in a measure on data not in my possession, such, for instance, as is referred to by you in your telegram of 2.30 p. m., viz, the withdrawal of a part of this army.   So far as the question is a military one, dependent on the relative condition of the two armies, I am of the opinion that, even if Lee has been re-enforced by 10,000 men, owing to the losses sustained by him in his recent campaign, I ought still to be able to cope with him, provided he is not found in a very strong position, where the natural and artificial obstacles to be overcome are such that, with inferior or equal numbers on his part, the advantages referred to in reality make him my superior. This, of course, can only be tested or settled by an advance and coming in contact with him.

The information as to the enemy's position and movements, as previously reported, is very meager and contradictory. I have still to rely on my own judgment and reasoning, which is, as before stated, that he will be found prepared to dispute the passage of the Rapidan, represented to be a very strong line for defense. With my pontoon bridges, the probabilities are, that, avoiding the fords, where, of course, he will be prepared to receive me, I shall be able to find some point where the commanding heights being on my side, with my artillery in position, I can force a passage; and the river once passed, his line becomes untenable. To do this, however, will require the whole force I have at present. Indeed, if it were practicable, I should desire an increase, as I shall have to leave in my rear a large detachment to guard my depots and communications.

To conclude, therefore, in my judgment, if there were no other considerations than the relative strength and position of the two armies, I should favor an advance. Of course, you and the President will be governed by such other considerations as may exist, and your decision, when communicated, will be promptly and strictly complied with.

Presuming, for the purposes of this paper, that it is decided not to advance, the question then arises what course is to be pursued. In your telegram of 2.30 p. m. of yesterday, you indicate holding the line of the Upper Rappahannock. I have to say, in regard to this line, that I do not consider it as offering any particular advantage, as at low stages of water the river is fordable in so many places, and with pontoon trains, which the enemy are known to possess, he can cross where it is not fordable. Hence, it will be impossible, supposing he assumes the offensive, to prevent his turning my flanks, or, as I propose to do at the Rapidan, forcing a passage at some point where he can get the command for his artillery on his side. This will, however, in a measure depend on my strength, which can only be known after you have decided how much of my force you will withdraw.

There is one consideration to which your attention is called, and that is, in case I do not advance, what probability there is that you will be enabled to re-enforce this army more rapidly than the enemy will be his. Our past experience has shown a fertility of resource and a power over his people in bringing out men which leads me to fear that in this respect a delay will be more advantageous to him than to us, notwithstanding the exhaustion and discontent which it is known the war has produced in his country. I shall not make any movement under existing circumstances till your views and wishes are sent to me.

GEO. G. MEADE,
Major-General.

—

WASHINGTON, D. C., *July* 30, 1863.

Major-General MEADE,
Warrenton, Va.:

Four regiments of infantry (not New York or Pennsylvania) will be immediately sent from the Army of the Potomac to New York

Harbor, to report to General Canby. The officer in command will telegraph to the Quartermaster-General the numbers for transportation.

H. W. HALLECK,
General-in-Chief.

—

WASHINGTON, D. C., *July* 30, 1863.
Major-General MEADE,
Warrenton, Va. :

The troops to be sent east should number from 1,500 to 2,000. This detachment is all that it is proposed at present to take from your army; but under no circumstances can we now give you any re-enforcements. Every place has been stripped to the bare poles. Keep up a threatening attitude, but do not advance.

H. W. HALLECK,
General-in-Chief.

—

HEADQUARTERS ARMY OF THE POTOMAC,
July 31, 1863—10.30 a. m. (Received 10.40 a. m.)
H. W. HALLECK,
General-in-Chief:

In compliance with your instructions of yesterday, the following regiments have been ordered to New York Harbor, to report to Brigadier-General Canby: First and Thirty-seventh Massachusetts, Fifth Wisconsin, and Twentieth Indiana; aggregate pr sent for duty, 1,643.

The regiments left here early this morning for Warrenton Junction, there to take railroad transportation to Washington. Owing to the large number of trains now run over the road, I presume the regiments will not reach Washington before to-night.

Col. Oliver Edwards, Thirty-seventh Massachusetts Regiment, commands the troops, and he has been instructed to acquaint the Quartermaster-General, by telegraph, with the strength of his command.

GEO. G. MEADE,
Major-General.

—

WASHINGTON, D. C., *July* 31, 1863—8.45 p. m.
Major-General MEADE,
Warrenton, Va. :

Capt. [S. C.] Means reports that about 500 of the enemy's cavalry have appeared at Point of Rocks. The present time should be availed of to drive out every guerrilla and disloyal man between the Potomac, Rappahannock, and Blue Ridge.

H. W. HALLECK,
General-in-Chief.

—

UNOFFICIAL.]   HEADQUARTERS ARMY OF THE POTOMAC,
July 31, 1863.
Major-General HALLECK,
General-in-Chief :

MY DEAR GENERAL: I thank you most sincerely and heartily for your kind and generous letter of the 28th instant, received last evening. It would be wrong in me to deny that I feared there existed in the minds of both the President and yourself an idea that I had failed to do what another would and could have done in the withdrawal of Lee's army. The expression you have been pleased to use in your letter, to wit, "a feeling of disappointment," is one that I cheerfully accept and readily admit was as keenly felt by myself as any one. But permit me, dear general, to call your attention to the distinction between disappointment and dissatisfaction. The one was a natural feeling, in view of the momentous consequences that would have resulted from a successful attack, but does not necessarily convey with it any censure. I could not view the use of the latter expression in any other light than as intending to convey an expression of opinion on the part of the President that I had failed to do what I might and should have done. Now, let me say, in the frankness which characterizes your letter, that perhaps the President was right; if such was the case, it was my duty to give him an opportunity to replace me by one better fitted for the command of the army. It was, I assure you, with such feelings that I applied to be relieved. It was not from any personal considerations, for I have tried in this whole war to forget all personal considerations, and have always maintained they should not for an instant influence any one's actions.

Of course you will understand that I do not agree that the President was right, and I feel sure when the true state of the case comes to be known, that however natural and great may be the feeling of disappointment, no blame will be attached to any one.

Had I attacked Lee the day I proposed to do so, and in the ignorance that then existed of his position, I have every reason to believe the attack would have been unsuccessful, and would have resulted disastrously. This opinion is founded on the judgment of numerous distinguished officers, after inspecting Lee's vacated works and position. Among these officers I could name Generals Sedgwick, Wright, Slocum, Hays, Sykes, and others.

The idea that Lee had abandoned his lines early in the day that he withdrew, I have positive intelligence is not correct, and that not a man was withdrawn till after dark. I mention these facts to remove the impression, which newspaper correspondents have given the public, that it was only necessary to advance to secure an easy victory. I had great responsibility thrown on me. On one side were the known and important fruits of victory, and, on the other, the equally important and terrible consequences of a defeat. I considered my position at Williamsport very different from that at Gettysburg. When I left Frederick, it was with the firm determination to attack and fight Lee, without regard to time or place, as soon as I could come in contact with him; but after defeating him, and requiring him to abandon his schemes of invasion, I did not think myself justified in making a blind attack simply to prevent his escape, and running all the risks attending such a venture. Now, as I said before, in this, perhaps, I erred in judgment, for I take this occasion to say to you, and through you to the President, that I have no pretensions to any superior capacity for the post he has assigned me to; that all I can do is to exert my utmost efforts and do the best I can; but that the moment those who have a right to judge my actions think, or feel satisfied, either that I am wanting or that another would do better, that moment I earnestly desire to be relieved, not on my own account, but on account of the country and the cause.

You must excuse so much egotism, but your kind letter in a measure renders it necessary. I feel, general, very proud of your good opinion, and assure you I shall endeavor in the future to continue to merit it.

Reciprocating the kind feeling you have expressed, I remain, general, most truly and respectfully, yours,

GEO. G. MEADE,
Major-General.

—

WASHINGTON, D. C., *August* 1, 1863.
Major-General MEADE,
        Warrenton, Va. :

To avoid all misunderstanding on the subject, when in the exercise of the authority conferred on you you assume command of any post or troops belonging to another department, and when you relinquish the command of any such place or troops, please notify the commanding general of that department of your action in the matter.

H. W. HALLECK,
General-in-Chief.

—

HEADQUARTERS ARMY OF THE POTOMAC,
August 1, 1863—4.30 p. m.
(Received 7.15 p. m.)
Maj. Gen. H. W. HALLECK,
        General-in-Chief :

On leaving the Potomac, in view of the probability of the return of Lee or a part of his army into Maryland, I directed General Couch to assume the defense of the river from Williamsport to Harper's Ferry, and placed under his command the garrison at Harper's Ferry, under General Lockwood. My position being now so remote, and the enemy having evacuated the Valley, I have relinquished all control over General Couch, and directed General Lockwood to report to General Schenck.

GEO. G. MEADE,
Major-General.

—

HEADQUARTERS ARMY OF THE POTOMAC,
August 1, 1863—10 p. m.
(Received 11.45 p. m.)
Maj. Gen. H. W. HALLECK,
        General-in-Chief :

In compliance with your instructions to occupy the line of the Upper Rappahannock, this army has to-day been placed in position from Waterloo Crossing on the right to Ellis' Ford on the left. Warrenton, New Baltimore, Brentsville, and Morrisville are all occupied, and connected with the forces on the river by pickets and patrols. The cavalry on the right flank at Amissville, picketing to the mountains; on the left, from Ellis' to United States Ford on the river, thence to Aquia Creek. A brigade of cavalry is at White Plains, scouting between the Bull Run Mountains and the Blue Ridge, in our rear; another brigade scouts on my left, between the Rappahannock and

Occoquan.   Last night and this morning bridges were thrown over the river at the railroad crossing and at Kelly's Ford.   Infantry was crossed at each place, and the necessary works to protect the bridges will be constructed.   The railroad bridge will be immediately repaired.   At 10 a. m. this morning, Buford's cavalry division crossed at the railroad crossing, and soon encountered the enemy's cavalry. The latest report from him, just received, dated 4.30 p. m., he had driven Jones' and Hampton's brigades to within 1½ miles of Culpeper, where he reports A. P. Hill's corps to be in position.   He has been ordered to fall back, and hold as advanced a position in front of the Rappahannock as he can do with security.

GEO. G. MEADE,
Major-General.

—

HEADQUARTERS ARMY OF THE POTOMAC,
August 3, 1863—8 p. m.   (Received 8.50 p. m.)

Maj. Gen. H. W. HALLECK,
General-in-Chief:

No telegram was sent yesterday, being Sunday.   Late Saturday night (August 1), Buford's command of cavalry reported that, after driving the enemy's cavalry to within 1½ miles of Culpeper Court-House, he was met by 5,000 infantry and three batteries of artillery, who compelled him to retire this side of Brandy Station, at which point they ceased their pursuit.   Buford took up a position between the Rappahannock and Brandy Station, which he has held undisturbed yesterday and to-day, though at times to-day the enemy's cavalry assumed a menacing attitude, believed by General Buford an attempt to examine our position.

The position of the army is as last reported, excepting that there are two divisions of the First Corps on the right bank of the Rappahannock, at the railroad crossing, and one brigade of cavalry posted in front of Kelly's Ford, picketing toward Stevensburg and the fords on the Lower Rapidan.   The signal officer on Watery Mountain, near Warrenton, reports the disappearance of camps near Culpeper, and a movement of wagon trains from that point toward Orange Court-House.

The cavalry on the left report no force on this side near Falmouth; but a prisoner states that Cooke's brigade, 3,000 strong, had arrived at Fredericksburg from Richmond.

The railroad bridge over the Rappahannock was repaired to-day.

GEO. G. MEADE,
Major-General.

—

HEADQUARTERS ARMY OF THE POTOMAC,
August 3, 1863.

THE ADJUTANT-GENERAL OF THE ARMY,
Washington, D. C.:

SIR : I have the honor herewith to transmit a tabular statement of the casualties in the Army of the Potomac at the battle of Gettysburg, July 1, 2, and 3, 1863.*

Very respectfully, your obedient servant,

GEO. G. MEADE,
Major-General, Commanding.

---

*But see revised statement, pp. 173-187.

[Inclosure.]

List of killed, wounded, and missing in the Army of the Potomac at the battle of Gettysburg, Pa., July 1, 2, and 3, 1863.

Command.	Killed.		Wounded.		Missing.		Total.		Aggregate.
	Officers.	Enlisted men.	Officers.	Enlisted men.	Officers.	Enlisted men.	Officers.	Enlisted men.	
General headquarters			2	2			2	2	4
FIRST CORPS.									
First Division	12	183	103	1,008	18	972	133	2,163	2,296
Second Division	7	77	56	471	53	876	116	1,424	1,540
Third Division	8	81	41	429	8	446	57	956	1,013
Artillery Brigade		9	4	79		4	4	92	96
Total	27	350	204	1,987	79	2,298	310	4,635	4,945
SECOND CORPS.									
General staff			2				2		2
First Division	18	161	85	776	6	268	109	1,205	1,314
Second Division	29	312	100	1,114	7	89	136	1,515	1,651
Third Division	20	189	67	831	1	154	88	1,174	1,262
Artillery Brigade	2	26	6	113		3	8	142	150
Cavalry Squadron		1		3				4	4
Total	69	689	260	2,837	14	514	343	4,040	4,383
THIRD CORPS.									
General staff			2				2		2
First Division	24	241	102	1,356	12	330	138	1,927	2,065
Second Division	29	284	130	1,385	2	205	161	1,874	2,035
Artillery Brigade		8	3	76		21	3	105	108
Total	53	533	237	2,817	14	556	304	3,906	4,210
FIFTH CORPS.									
First Division	15	146	49	520	1	143	65	809	874
Second Division	10	153	57	736		57	67	946	1,013
Third Division	3	23	17	164		3	20	190	210
Artillery Brigade	1	8	1	32			2	40	42
Total	29	330	124	1,452	1	203	154	1,985	2,139
SIXTH CORPS.									
First Division		2	3	34			3	36	39
Second Division	1	11	5	71		2	6	84	90
Third Division	1	17	11	145		29	12	191	203
Artillery Brigade		4	2	6			2	10	12
Total*	2	34	21	256		31	23	321	344
ELEVENTH CORPS.†									
First Division	12	126	59	820	20	649	91	1,595	1,686
Second Division	3	100	16	460	18	378	37	938	975
Third Division	15	76	49	527	30	490	94	1,093	1,187
Artillery Brigade	1	6	3	53		13	4	72	76
Total	31	308	127	1,860	68	1,530	226	3,698	3,924
TWELFTH CORPS.									
First Division	7	91	25	374	1	28	33	493	526
Second Division	13	100	15	384	2	32	30	516	546
Artillery Brigade				8				8	8
Total	20	191	40	766	3	60	63	1,017	1,080

*All losses in the campaign are included in this table. For casualties in the battle, see pp. 180–182.—COMPILER.

†The reorganization of brigades and divisions after the battle caused the discrepancies between this and the revised statement on pp. 182, 183.—COMPILER.

List of killed, wounded, and missing in the Army of the Potomac at the battle of Gettysburg, Pa., July 1, 2, and 3, 1863—Continued.

Command.	Killed.		Wounded.		Missing.		Total.		Aggregate.
	Officers.	Enlisted men.	Officers.	Enlisted men.	Officers.	Enlisted men.	Officers.	Enlisted men.	
CAVALRY CORPS.									
First Division	1	42	12	164	8	387	21	598	614
Second Division	....	7	6	29	1	108	7	144	151
Third Division	9	68	28	285	27	726	64	1,079	1,143
Total	10	117	46	478	36	1,221	92	1,816	1,908
Artillery Reserve	2	39	15	182	......	15	17	236	253

RECAPITULATION.

Officers and men.	Killed.	Wounded.	Missing.
Officers	243	1,076	215
Enlisted men	2,591	12,637	6,428
Total	2,834	13,713	6,643
Aggregate*	....	....	23,190

HEADQUARTERS ARMY OF THE POTOMAC,
August 4, 1863—9 p. m.   (Received 11 p. m.)
Maj. Gen. H. W. HALLECK, *General-in-Chief:*

Matters remain much the same as reported yesterday. A reconnaissance by the cavalry on the right proves the abandonment of the line of the Hedgman's River, hitherto held by the enemy's pickets, our cavalry crossing without opposition at Rixeyville, and meeting no enemy until within 2 miles of Culpeper, when they encountered a superior cavalry force about 4 p. m. The enemy attacked Buford in front of Rappahannock railroad crossing with cavalry and artillery. They were readily repulsed by Buford, and driven for some distance, until, being without orders to advance, he saw no object in continuing the pursuit. Two deserters who came in to-day from Longstreet's corps, who left their regiment yesterday, report that their corps was on the march from Orange Court-House, and that Hill's corps followed Longstreet. Ewell is understood to be in the vicinity of Madison Court-House. This information confirms the cavalry reports and the signals from Watery Mountain. I am of the opinion that the movement of Buford on Saturday was considered an advance, and that Lee has withdrawn his infantry behind the Rapidan. I shall make no further movements without your instructions, except to occupy as much of the ground between the Rappahannock and Rapidan by my cavalry as I can without requiring too great and unnecessary loss on my part.

GEO. G. MEADE,
Major-General.

* But see revised statement, p. 187.

HEADQUARTERS ARMY OF THE POTOMAC,
October 1, 1863.

GENERAL : I have the honor to submit herewith a report of the operations of this army during the month of July last, including the details of the battle of Gettysburg, delayed by the failure to receive until now the reports of several corps and division commanders, who were severely wounded in the battle.

On June 28, I received the orders of the President of the United States placing me in command of the Army of the Potomac. The situation of affairs at that time was briefly as follows:

The Confederate army, commanded by General R. E. Lee, estimated at over 100,000 strong, of all arms, had crossed the Potomac River and advanced up the Cumberland Valley. Reliable intelligence placed his advance (Ewell's corps) on the Susquehanna, at Harrisburg and Columbia ; Longstreet's corps at Chambersburg, and Hill's corps between that place and Cashtown. My own army, of which the most recent return showed an aggregate of a little over 100,000, was situated in and around Frederick, Md., extending from Harper's Ferry to the mouth of the Monocacy, and from Middletown to Frederick.

June 28 was spent in ascertaining the position and strength of the different corps of the army, but principally in bringing up the cavalry, which had been covering the rear of the army in its passage over the Potomac, and to which a large increase had just been made from the forces previously attached to the Defenses of Washington. Orders were given on that day to Major-General French, commanding at Harper's Ferry, to move with 7,000 men of his command to occupy Frederick and the line of the Baltimore and Ohio Railroad, and, with the balance of his force, estimated at 4,000, to remove and escort the public property to Washington.

On the 29th, the army was put in motion, and on the evening of that day was in position, the left at Emmitsburg and the right at New Windsor. Buford's division of cavalry was on the left flank, with the advance at Gettysburg. Kilpatrick's division was in the front at Hanover, where he encountered this day General Stuart's Confederate cavalry, which had crossed the Potomac at Seneca Creek, and, passing our right flank, was making its way toward Carlisle, having escaped Gregg's division, delayed in taking position on the right flank by the occupation of the roads by columns of infantry.

On the 30th, the right flank of the army was moved up to Manchester, the left still being at Emmitsburg, in the vicinity of which place three corps (the First, Eleventh, and Third) were collected, under the orders of Major-General Reynolds. General Buford having reported from Gettysburg the appearance of the enemy on the Cashtown road in some force, General Reynolds was directed to occupy Gettysburg.

On reaching that place on July 1, General Reynolds found Buford's cavalry warmly engaged with the enemy, who had debouched his infantry through the mountains on the Cashtown road, but was being held in check in the most gallant manner by Buford's cavalry. Major-General Reynolds immediately moved around the town of Gettysburg, and advanced on the Cashtown road, and without a moment's hesitation deployed his advanced division and attacked the enemy, at the same time sending orders for the Eleventh Corps (General Howard) to advance as promptly as possible. Soon after making his dispositions for the attack, Major-General Reynolds fell, mortally wounded, the command of the First Corps devolving on Major-General Doubleday, and the command of the field on Major-General Howard, who arrived about this time, 11.30 a. m., with the Eleventh Corps, then commanded by Major-General Schurz. Major-General Howard pushed forward two divisions of the Eleventh Corps to the support of the First Corps, now warmly engaged with the enemy on the ridge to the north of the town, and posted his Third Division, with three batteries of artillery, on the Cemetery Ridge, on the south side of the town.

Up to this time the battle had been with the forces of the enemy debouching from the mountains on the Cashtown road, known to be Hill's corps. In the early part of the action, success was on our side, Wadsworth's division, of the First Corps, having driven the enemy back some distance, capturing numerous prisoners, among them General Archer, of the Confederate army. The arrival of re-enforcements for the enemy on the Cashtown road, and the junction of Ewell's corps, coming on the York and Harrisburg roads, which occurred between 1 and 2 p. m., enabled the enemy to bring vastly superior forces against both the First and Eleventh Corps, outflanking our line of battle, and pressing it so severely that about 4 p. m. Major-General Howard deemed it prudent to withdraw these two corps to the Cemetery Ridge, on the south side of the town, which operation was successfully accomplished; not, however, without considerable loss in prisoners, arising from the confusion incident to portions of both corps passing through the town, and the men getting confused in the streets.

About the time of this withdrawal, Major-General Hancock arrived, whom I had dispatched to represent me on the field, on hearing of the death of General Reynolds. In conjunction with Major-General Howard, General Hancock proceeded to post the troops on the Cemetery Ridge, and to repel an attack that the enemy made on our right flank. This attack was not, however, very vigorous, and the enemy, seeing the strength of the position occupied, seemed to be satisfied with the success he had accomplished, desisting from any further attack this day.

About 7 p. m., Major-Generals Slocum and Sickles, with the Twelfth Corps and part of the Third, reached the ground, and took post on the right and left of the troops previously posted. Being satisfied from the reports received from the field that it was the intention of the enemy to support with his whole army the attack already made, and the reports from Major-Generals Hancock and Howard on the character of the position being favorable, I determined to give battle at this point; and, early in the evening of the 1st, issued orders to all the corps to concentrate at Gettysburg, directing all trains to be sent to the rear, at Westminster.

At 10 p. m. of the 1st, I broke up my headquarters, which until then had been at Taneytown, and proceeded to the field, arriving there at 1 a. m. of the 2d. So soon as it was light, I proceeded to inspect the position occupied, and to make arrangements for posting the several corps as they should reach the ground.

By 7 a. m. the Second and Fifth Corps, with the rest of the Third, had reached the ground, and were posted as follows: The Eleventh Corps retained its position on the Cemetery Ridge, just opposite the town; the First Corps was posted on the right of the Eleventh, on an elevated knoll, connecting with a ridge extending to the south and east, on which the Twelfth Corps was placed, the right of the

Twelfth Corps resting on a small stream at a point where it crossed the Baltimore pike, and which formed, on the right flank of the Twelfth, something of an obstacle. The Cemetery Ridge extended in a westerly and southerly direction, gradually diminishing in elevation until it came to a very prominent ridge called Round Top, running east and west. The Second and Third Corps were directed to occupy the continuation of the Cemetery Ridge on the left of the Eleventh Corps. The Fifth Corps, pending the arrival of the Sixth, was held in reserve.

While these dispositions were being made, the enemy was massing his troops on an exterior ridge, distant from the line occupied by us from 1 mile to 1½ miles.

At 2 p. m. the Sixth Corps arrived, after a march of 32 miles, accomplished from 9 p. m. the day previous. On its arrival being reported, I immediately directed the Fifth Corps to move over to our extreme left, and the Sixth to occupy its place as a reserve for the right.

About 3 p. m. I rode out to the extreme left, to await the arrival of the Fifth Corps and to post it, when I found that Major-General Sickles, commanding the Third Corps, not fully apprehending the instructions in regard to the position to be occupied, had advanced, or rather was in the act of advancing, his corps some half a mile or three-quarters of a mile in front of the line of the Second Corps, on the prolongation of which it was designed his corps should rest. Having found Major-General Sickles, I was explaining to him that he was too far in advance, and discussing with him the propriety of withdrawing, when the enemy opened on him with several batteries in his front and on his flank, and immediately brought forward columns of infantry and made a most vigorous assault. The Third Corps sustained the shock most heroically. Troops from the Second Corps were immediately sent by Major-General Hancock to cover the right flank of the Third Corps, and soon after the assault commenced the Fifth Corps most fortunately arrived and took position on the left of the Third, Major-General Sykes, commanding, immediately sending a force to occupy the Round Top Ridge, where a most furious contest was maintained, the enemy making desperate but unsuccessful efforts to secure it.

Notwithstanding the stubborn resistance of the Third Corps, under Major-General Birney (Major-General Sickles having been wounded early in the action), the superiority of numbers of the enemy enabling him to outflank the corps in its advanced position, General Birney was compelled to fall back and reform behind the line originally designed to be held.

In the meantime, perceiving the great exertions of the enemy, the Sixth Corps, Major-General Sedgwick, and part of the First Corps (to the command of which I had assigned Major-General Newton), particularly Lockwood's Maryland brigade,* together with detachments from the Second Corps, were all brought up at different periods, and succeeded, together with the gallant resistance of the Fifth Corps, in checking and finally repulsing the assault of the enemy, who retired in confusion and disorder about sunset, and ceased any further efforts on the extreme left.† An assault was, however, made about 8 p. m. on the Eleventh Corps from the left of the town, which

---

* See Williams to Slocum, December 26, 1863, p. 765.
† See Meade to Halleck, February 25, 1864, p. 120.

was repelled, with the assistance of troops from the Second and First Corps.

During the heavy assault upon our extreme left, portions of the Twelfth Corps were sent as re-enforcements. During their absence, the line on the extreme right was held by a very much reduced force. This was taken advantage of by the enemy, who, during the absence of Geary's division of the Twelfth Corps, advanced and occupied a part of his line.*

On the morning of the 3d, General Geary (having returned during the night) attacked at early dawn the enemy, and succeeded in driving him back and reoccupying his former position. A spirited contest was, however, maintained all the morning along this part of the line, General Geary, re-enforced by Wheaton's brigade, Sixth Corps, maintaining his position, and inflicting very severe losses on the enemy.*

With this exception, the quiet of the lines remained undisturbed till 1 p. m. on the 3d, when the enemy opened from over one hundred and twenty-five guns, playing upon our center and left. This cannonade continued for over two hours, when our guns, in obedience to my orders, failing to make any reply, the enemy ceased firing, and soon his masses of infantry became visible, forming for an assault on our left and left center. The assault was made with great firmness, directed principally against the point occupied by the Second Corps, and was repelled with equal firmness by the troops of that corps, supported by Doubleday's division and Stannard's brigade of the First Corps. During the assault, both Major-General Hancock, commanding the left center, and Brigadier-General Gibbon, commanding Second Corps, were severely wounded. This terminated the battle, the enemy retiring to his lines, leaving the field strewn with his dead and wounded, and numerous prisoners in our hands.

Buford's division of cavalry, after its arduous service at Gettysburg on the 1st, was on the 2d sent to Westminster to refit and guard our trains. Kilpatrick's division, that on the 29th, 30th, and 1st had been successfully engaging the enemy's cavalry, was on the 3d sent on our extreme left, on the Emmitsburg road, where good service was rendered in assaulting the enemy's line and occupying his attention. At the same time, General Gregg was engaged with the enemy on our extreme right, having passed across the Baltimore pike and Bonaughtown road, and boldly attacked the enemy's left and rear.

On the morning of the 4th, reconnaissances developed that the enemy had drawn back his left flank, but maintained his position in front of our left, apparently assuming a new line parallel to the mountains.

On the morning of the 5th, it was ascertained the enemy was in full retreat by the Fairfield and Cashtown roads. The Sixth Corps was immediately sent in pursuit on the Fairfield road, and the cavalry on the Cashtown road and by the Emmitsburg and Monterey Passes.

July 5 and 6 were employed in succoring the wounded and burying the dead. Major-General Sedgwick, commanding the Sixth Corps, having pushed the pursuit of the enemy as far as the Fairfield Pass, in the mountains, and reporting that the pass was a very strong one, in which a small force of the enemy could hold in check and delay for a considerable time any pursuing force, I determined to follow the enemy by a flank movement, and, accordingly, leaving McIn-

* See Meade to Halleck, February 25, 1864, p. 120.

tosh's brigade of cavalry and Neill's brigade of infantry to continue harassing the enemy, put the army in motion for Middletown, Md. Orders were immediately sent to Major-General French at Frederick to reoccupy Harper's Ferry and send a force to occupy Turner's Pass, in South Mountain. I subsequently ascertained Major-General French had not only anticipated these orders in part, but had pushed a cavalry force to Williamsport and Falling Waters, where they destroyed the enemy's pontoon bridge and captured its guard. Buford was at the same time sent to Williamsport and Hagerstown.

The duty above assigned to the cavalry was most successfully accomplished, the enemy being greatly harassed, his trains destroyed, and many captures of guns and prisoners made.

After halting a day at Middletown to procure necessary supplies and bring up the trains, the army moved through the South Mountain, and by July 12 was in front of the enemy, who occupied a strong position on the heights of Marsh Run, in advance of Williamsport. In taking this position, several skirmishes and affairs had been had with the enemy, principally by the cavalry and the Eleventh and Sixth Corps.

The 13th was occupied in reconnaissances of the enemy's position and preparations for attack, but, on advancing on the morning of the 14th, it was ascertained he had retired the night previous by a bridge at Falling Waters and the ford at Williamsport. The cavalry in pursuit overtook the rear guard at Falling Waters, capturing two guns and numerous prisoners.

Previous to the retreat of the enemy, Gregg's division of cavalry was crossed at Harper's Ferry, and, coming up with the rear of the enemy at Charlestown and Shepherdstown, had a spirited contest, in which the enemy was driven to Martinsburg and Winchester and pressed and harassed in his retreat.

The pursuit was resumed by a flank movement, the army crossing the Potomac at Berlin and moving down the Loudoun Valley. The cavalry were immediately pushed into the several passes of the Blue Ridge, and, having learned from scouts the withdrawal of the Confederate army from the lower valley of the Shenandoah, the army, the Third Corps, Major-General French, in advance, was moved into the Manassas Gap, in the hope of being able to intercept a portion of the enemy.

The possession of the gap was disputed so successfully as to enable the rear guard to withdraw by way of Strasburg, the Confederate army retiring to the Rapidan. A position was taken with this army on the line of the Rappahannock, and the campaign terminated about the close of July.

The result of the campaign may be briefly stated in the defeat of the enemy at Gettysburg, his compulsory evacuation of Pennsylvania and Maryland, and withdrawal from the upper valley of the Shenandoah, and in the capture of 3 guns, 41 standards, and 13,621 prisoners ; 24,978 small-arms were collected on the battle-field.

Our own losses were very severe, amounting, as will be seen by the accompanying return, to 2,834 killed, 13,709 [13,713] wounded, and 6,643 missing ; in all, 23,186 [23,190].*

It is impossible in a report of this nature to enumerate all the instances of gallantry and good conduct which distinguished such a hard-fought field as Gettysburg. The reports of corps commanders

---

*Reference is to table on p. 112 ; but see revised statement, p. 187.

and their subordinates, herewith submitted, will furnish all information upon this subject. I will only add my tribute to the heroic bravery of the whole army, officers and men, which, under the blessing of Divine Providence, enabled a crowning victory to be obtained, which I feel confident the country will never cease to bear in grateful remembrance.

It is my duty, as well as my pleasure, to call attention to the earnest efforts of co-operation on the part of Maj. Gen. D. N. Couch, commanding Department of the Susquehanna, and particularly to his advance, 4,000 men, under Brig. Gen. W. F. Smith, who joined me at Boonsborough just prior to the withdrawal of the Confederate army.

In conclusion, I desire to return my thanks to my staff, general and personal, to each and all of whom I was indebted for unremitting activity and most efficient assistance.

Very respectfully, your obedient servant,

GEO. G. MEADE,
Major-General, Commanding.

Brig. Gen. LORENZO THOMAS,
Adjutant-General, U. S. Army, Washington, D. C.

—

WASHINGTON, D. C., *October* 2, 1863.

Brigadier-General WILLIAMS,
Assistant Adjutant-General, Army of the Potomac:

How many Confederate dead were buried after the battle of Gettysburg—officers, privates?

J. C. KELTON,
Assistant Adjutant-General.

—

HEADQUARTERS ARMY OF THE POTOMAC,
October 3, 1863—8.20 p. m.   (Received 8.50 p. m.)

Maj. Gen. H. W. HALLECK,
General-in-Chief:

So far as can be stated from any information now at my command, 126 Confederate officers and 2,764 men were buried by our troops at Gettysburg. This does not, however, include those buried by the Eleventh and Twelfth Corps, and it is known that quite a large number were buried by the latter corps. The commanders of those corps can doubtless give you the numbers buried by their commands. When this army left the vicinity of Gettysburg, a considerable number of dead remained unburied, and the provost-marshal-general contracted with a Mr. [Samuel] Herbst, of Gettysburg, to bury them. He can state the number buried by him. Captain [William G.] Rankin, assistant quartermaster, who paid Mr. Herbst, can also supply this information. It may be added that the enemy buried a large number of his dead before leaving the field. The reports of the number of Confederate dead buried by the Eleventh and Twelfth Corps, although called for July 4, had not been sent in when those corps were detached from this army.

GEO. G. MEADE,
Major-General.

HEADQUARTERS ARMY OF THE POTOMAC,
October 5, 1863.   (Received 3.30 p. m.)

Maj. Gen. H. W. HALLECK,
General-in-Chief:

In addition to the number of Confederate dead buried at Gettysburg, stated in my dispatch of the 3d instant, I have now to report 2 officers and 62 men buried by the Fifth Corps.

GEO. G. MEADE,
Major-General.

—

HEADQUARTERS ARMY OF THE POTOMAC,
February 25, 1864.

GENERAL: I transmit herewith the report of Brig. Gen. T. H. Ruger, commanding First Division, Twelfth Army Corps, and those of his brigade and regimental commanders, of the operations of his division at the battle of Gettysburg. These reports were only recently received by me, owing to General Ruger being detached with a large portion of his command not long after the battle, and soon after his return the corps was ordered to Tennessee. I beg these reports may be placed on file as part of my official report of that battle.

I embrace this opportunity to make certain corrections and alterations in my report, to which my attention has been called by Major-General Slocum.* These alterations are as follows:

1. In relating the occurrences of July 2, I state:

In the meantime, perceiving the great exertions on the part of the enemy, the Sixth Corps (Major-General Sedgwick), and part of the First Corps (to the command of which I had assigned Major-General Newton), particularly Lockwood's Maryland brigade, together with detachments from the Second Corps, were all brought up, &c.

This should read:

In the meantime, perceiving the great exertions on the part of the enemy, the Sixth Corps (Major-General Sedgwick), and part of the First Corps (to the command of which corps I had assigned Major-General Newton), together with detachments from the Second Corps, were all brought up. Subsequently the First Division and Lockwood's brigade, of the Twelfth Corps, under the immediate command of Brig. Gen. A. S. Williams, then temporarily commanding the corps, arrived at the scene of action, the services of Lockwood's brigade being particularly mentioned.

2. In relating the occurrences of July 3:

During the heavy assaults upon our extreme left, portions of the Twelfth Corps were sent as re-enforcements. During their absence, the line of the extreme right was held by a much-reduced force, and was taken advantage of by the enemy, who, during the absence of Geary's division, Twelfth Corps, advanced and occupied a part of the line.

On the morning of the 3d, General Geary, having returned during the night, was attacked at early dawn by the enemy, but succeeded in driving him back and occupying his former position. A spirited contest was maintained all the morning along this part of the line. General Geary, re-enforced by Wheaton's brigade, Sixth Corps, maintained his position, inflicting severe losses on the enemy.

This should read:

During the heavy assaults upon our extreme left, the First Division and Lockwood's brigade, of the Twelfth Corps, were sent as re-enforcements, as already reported. Two brigades of Geary's division (Second, of this corps) were also detached for the same purpose, but did not arrive at the scene of action, owing to having mistaken the road. The detachment of so large a portion of the Twelfth Corps, with

—

* See Slocum's report of December 30, 1863, p. 763, and Meade's reply of February 25, 1864, p. 769.

its temporary commander, Brig. Gen. A. S. Williams, left the defense of the line previously held to the remaining brigade of the Second Division, commanded by Brigadier-General Greene, who held the left of the Twelfth Corps, now become the extreme right of the army. The enemy, perceiving the withdrawal of our troops, advanced and attacked General Greene with great vigor, who, making a gallant defense, and being soon re-enforced by portions of the First and Eleventh Corps, contiguous to him, succeeded in repulsing all the efforts of the enemy to dislodge him.

After night, on the return of the detachments sent to the left, it was found the enemy was occupying portions of the line of breastworks thrown up by the Twelfth Corps. Brigadier-General Williams, in command, immediately made arrangements, by the disposition of his artillery and instructions to both divisions, commanded, respectively, by Brigadier-Generals Geary and Ruger, to attack the enemy at daylight, and regain the position formerly occupied by the corps. In the meantime, the enemy brought up strong re-enforcements, and at early daylight a spirited contest commenced, which continued until after 10 a. m., the result of which was the repulse of the enemy in all his attempts to advance and his final abandonment of the position he had taken the evening before. During this contest, Shaler's brigade, Sixth Corps, was sent to re-enforce the Twelfth Corps. With this exception, the lines remained undisturbed, &c.

I should be glad, as an act of justice, if this communication could be published.

Respectfully, your obedient servant,

GEO. G. MEADE,
Major-General, Commanding.

Maj. Gen. H. W. HALLECK,
General-in-Chief, Washington, D. C.

[Indorsements.]

FEBRUARY 29, 1864.

Respectfully referred to the Secretary of War, with the recommendation that this be published with General Meade's former report.

H. W. HALLECK,
General-in-Chief.

ADJUTANT-GENERAL'S OFFICE, *March* 2, 1864.

Respectfully submitted to the Secretary of War.

W. A. NICHOLS,
Assistant Adjutant-General.

WAR DEPARTMENT, *March* 2, 1864.

Approved.
By order of the Secretary of War:

JAS. A. HARDIE,
Assistant Adjutant-General.

—

WAR DEPARTMENT, *Washington, March* 9, 1864.

Maj. Gen. GEORGE G. MEADE,
Commanding Army of the Potomac:

GENERAL : I am instructed by the Secretary of War to direct your attention to the inclosed slip, taken from the Washington Daily Chronicle of to-day, and to inquire if it be the fact that you have addressed a communication with regard to military operations to a member of the Senate. If such be the case, the Secretary desires to be informed what authority for the proceeding was previously obtained by you.

I have the honor to be, general, very respectfully, your obedient servant,

JAS. A. HARDIE,
Assistant Adjutant-General.

[Inclosure.]

Major-General Meade has addressed a letter to Senator Johnson, of Maryland, in which he explains the allegations in the speech of Senator Wilkinson on Friday last, based upon certain information communicated to the latter by one or two officers of the army. As the subject is likely to give rise to discussion, and we believe to a satisfactory solution, we will only add that the letter to 'Senator Johnson is accepted as a full vindication of General Meade by all who have read it.

—

HDQRS. ARMY OF THE POTOMAC, *March* 9, 1864.

Maj. Gen. D. B. BIRNEY,
    Commanding [*First*] *Division, Third Army Corps:*

GENERAL : I beg leave to call your attention to articles in the New York journals of the 8th instant, purporting to give portions of your testimony recently given before the Committee on the Conduct of the War.

The character of those articles, in my judgment, authorizes me, as your superior officer, before taking action on them, that I should ask you whether you have any objection to give to me (as it appears has been given to others) a succinct statement of your evidence.

Very respectfully, &c.,

GEO. G. MEADE,
Major-General, Commanding.

—

HEADQUARTERS FIRST DIVISION, THIRD ARMY CORPS,
March 10, 1864.

Maj. Gen. GEORGE G. MEADE,
    Commanding Army of the Potomac:

GENERAL : I have the honor to acknowledge the receipt of your favor of the 9th instant.

The articles in the New York Times and Herald of the 8th instant are the only ones that I have seen referring to my testimony before the Congressional Committee on the Conduct of the War. These articles do great injustice to the character of my testimony, and were penned by some person ignorant of it.

My testimony was from the time Major-General Hooker assumed command of the army to the present time, and was a continuation of my testimony given a year since before the same committee, and was confined almost entirely to the operations of the division and corps whilst under my command. My opinion as to the movements of the army and its conduct was given only in reply to direct questions, and, I presume, carried with it only the weight of my military standing. In my opinion, there is nothing in my testimony that should alter the personal and official relations existing between us.

As I was ordered by the War Department before the committee, and have the impression that my testimony is beyond my control, I must respectfully decline to give it in detail or more succinctly without referring to the authority that called it forth.

I will with pleasure give you, at any time you may desire, my recollections, reports, and views on the same points.

I am, general, your obedient servant,

D. B. BIRNEY,
Major-General Volunteers.

MARCH 10, 1864.

Col. J. A. HARDIE,
  Assistant Adjutant-General:

I have the honor to acknowledge the receipt of your letter of the 9th instant, inquiring, on the part of the honorable Secretary of War, whether I had written, as is asserted in the Washington Chronicle, a letter to the Hon. Reverdy Johnson on military operations, and, if so, by what authority.

In reply, I beg to state that on my return from my recent visit to Washington, I found a note from the Hon. Reverdy Johnson, accompanied by a copy of the Congressional Globe, to which Mr. Johnson invited my attention as containing a defense which he (a perfect stranger to me) had made in reply to certain allegations in a speech of the Hon. Mr. Wilkinson, of Minnesota, touching my operations at the battle of Gettysburg, and inquiring of me whether he was not right in denying these allegations.

In reply to this note, after thanking Mr. Johnson for his defense, I explained to him how the allegations had arisen and the plausible foundation for them. This letter was a private one, not in the slightest degree intended for publication or circulation, and I was not aware that I required any authority before writing it, particularly as it touched upon operations that occurred nearly nine months since, the official reports of which have for some time been made public. It is true, when in Washington I mentioned to the honorable Secretary my disposition to reply to Mr. Wilkinson, that he suggested my sending any communication I might write through the Department; but I understood this to be a friendly suggestion, inasmuch as had I written such a letter, it would have been designed for the public, and its passing through the Department would have given it the form of an official document. I did not understand the honorable Secretary's suggestion to imply I should be violating any orders, or etiquette, if I had not so sent this letter through the Department; much less did I consider his remark as intended to prohibit private correspondence on my part to friends, explaining the false and slanderous charges with which the press of the whole country has been filled for the last week. I regret I did not retain a copy of Mr. Johnson's note and my reply; the latter I will endeavor to obtain, and transmit to the honorable Secretary, and I trust this explanation will be by him deemed satisfactory.

Very respectfully, &c.,

GEO. G. MEADE,
  Major-General, Commanding.

—

CIRCULAR.*]   HEADQUARTERS ARMY OF THE POTOMAC,
  March 10, 1864.

SIR : Your attention is respectfully invited to the articles which have recently appeared in the newspapers, charging the commanding general with favoring a retreat of the army from Gettysburg on the 2d July last.

These articles are supposed to be based upon the transactions of a council, or meeting of corps commanders, held on the evening of the

* Sent to Generals Gibbon, Newton, Sedgwick, Slocum, Sykes, and A. S. Williams.

2d July ; and, if you have no objection to so doing, the commanding general desires that you will furnish him, in the course of to-day, with a short statement, giving your recollection of what transpired at the council, and mentioning whether he at any time insisted on the withdrawal of the army from before Gettysburg.

By command of Major-General Meade :

S. WILLIAMS,
Assistant Adjutant-General.

—

HDQRS. FIFTH CORPS, ARMY OF THE POTOMAC,
March 10, 1864.

Major-General MEADE,
Commanding Army of the Potomac :

GENERAL : I have seen in late papers, and in the speech of a member of the United States Senate, statements charging you with having ordered a retreat of the army at the battle of Gettysburg.

I commanded a corps in that battle ; was present at a meeting on the night of the 2d and 3d of July, when yourself and corps commanders discussed the events then taking place ; remember distinctly the number of soldiers we thought we could take into action after the fight on the 2d ; remember more distinctly the expressed determination of each commander present to fight that battle out then and there, and never received or heard of any order directing a retreat of the army.

I am, general, very respectfully, your obedient servant,

GEO. SYKES,
Major-General, Commanding Fifth Corps.

—

HDQRS. FIRST ARMY CORPS, ARMY OF THE POTOMAC,
March 10, 1864.

Brig. Gen. S. WILLIAMS,
Asst. Adjt. Gen., Hdqrs. Army of the Potomac :

GENERAL : Your circular note of this date, in relation to reports to the effect that the commanding general advocated a retreat of the army on the 2d day of July last, and particularly in reference to the proceedings of a council of war, held on the night of the 2d, has been received.

In reply, I have to state that I was frequently with the commanding general on that day, and was likewise present at the council, and nothing that I heard him say has ever given me the impression that he insisted on the withdrawal of the army from before Gettysburg.

There was a discussion in the council, not concerning a retreat, but concerning the dispositions proper to make should the enemy endeavor to turn our position, by getting between us and Emmitsburg, by passing entirely around our left flank, and I imagine this to have been the exclusive foundation of such report to the prejudice of the commanding general.

Respectfully, your most obedient servant,

JOHN NEWTON,
Major-General, Commanding.

HEADQUARTERS SIXTH CORPS,
March 10, 1864.

Brig. Gen. S. WILLIAMS,
 Assistant Adjutant-General:

GENERAL: My attention has been called to several articles which have recently appeared in the papers, insinuating or charging the general commanding the Army of the Potomac with ordering or favoring a retreat of the army on the evening of July 2, at Gettysburg.

I took no minutes of the council of corps commanders held on the evening of that day, but my present recollection is that three questions, viz, of attacking the enemy, of sustaining an attack, or taking up a new position, were submitted. The council was unanimous—with, I think, one exception—to sustain the attack in our then present position.

At no time in my presence did the general commanding insist or advise a withdrawal of the army, for such advice would have great weight with me, and I know the matter did not engage my serious attention.

I am positive that the general commanding could not have insisted, much less have given the order, to withdraw the army from its position. In a council on the evening of the 3d, the two questions of following the enemy or moving on parallel lines were submitted, and I think the council were unanimous, and their decision adopted by the general, of moving parallel to the enemy, and attacking him when possible.

 I am, very respectfully, your obedient servant,
   JOHN SEDGWICK,
   Major-General, Commanding.

——

HDQRS. CAVALRY CORPS, ARMY OF THE POTOMAC,
March 10, 1864.

Brig. Gen. S. WILLIAMS,
 Assistant Adjutant-General, Army of the Potomac:

GENERAL: I have the honor to acknowledge the receipt of a communication, of yesterday's date, from the major-general commanding the Army of the Potomac.

This communication has just been received. It calls my attention to articles in the New York journals of the 8th instant, purporting to give portions of your testimony recently given before the Committee on the Conduct of the War.

It further states—

The character of these articles, in my judgment, justifies me, as your superior officer, before taking action on them, that I should ask you whether you have any objection to give me (as it appears has been given to others) a succinct statement of your evidence.

In reply, I desire to inform the major-general commanding that he is mistaken in supposing I have given a succinct statement of my evidence before the war committee to anybody. The evidence was taken down by a stenographer, and I was informed as soon as it was translated I would have an opportunity of correcting it. I have not seen the evidence, as witten, up to this time, and having been on the stand nearly two hours and a half, I could not transcribe it from

memory. I am perfectly willing that the major-general commanding should have a copy of my evidence, but as I consider it is now
the property of the Government, I will forward a copy of his letter
to the chairman of the Committee on the Conduct of the War, with
the request that it may be furnished him.

I am, general, very respectfully, your obedient servant,

A. PLEASONTON,
Major-General, Commanding.

HEADQUARTERS ARMY OF THE POTOMAC,
March 10, 1864.

Major-General MEADE,
Commanding Army of the Potomac:

GENERAL: I have the honor to make the following statement in
regard to orders carried by me on the 1st day of July, 1863:

Early on the afternoon of the 1st of July, 1863, I was sent from
headquarters, at Taneytown, with sealed orders to General Slocum,
commanding Twelfth Corps, who was then on the road to Gettysburg, via Littlestown and Two Taverns. These orders I delivered to
Lieutenant-Colonel [Hiram C.] Rodgers, assistant adjutant-general
of the Twelfth Corps, at Two Taverns, between 3 and 4 p. m. of that
day, and was requested by him to say that the corps was on the move,
and advancing as rapidly as possible.

I also had a communication addressed to Generals Slocum and
Sykes. This I delivered to General Slocum, who was somewhat in
advance of his corps, near Gettysburg. After reading it, he returned
it to me, to take to General Sykes at Hanover.

My recollection of this communication now is, that it was a circular notifying corps commanders of the fall of General Reynolds, and
that General Hancock had been sent to take his place, and urging
them to push forward with all possible dispatch.

I am, general, very respectfully, your obedient servant,

A. G. MASON,
Captain, and Aide-de-Camp.

HEADQUARTERS RENDEZVOUS FOR DRAFTED MEN,
Philadelphia, Pa., March 14, 1864.

Brig. Gen. S. WILLIAMS,
Assistant Adjutant-General, Army of the Potomac:

GENERAL: I have the honor to acknowledge the receipt of your
circular of the 10th instant, in regard to the council of war held at
General Meade's headquarters on the evening of the 2d July last,
and in reply to state:

1. I was a member of that council, having been placed by General
Hancock in command of the Second Corps when he was detached to
take command of the Third Corps, after its defeat, on the afternoon
of the 2d.

2. The result of the day's fight was then, I believe, for the first time
fully known. It, together with our military situation, were fully
discussed and commented upon by the members. It thus appeared
that the Third Corps had been badly defeated, and rendered for the
time comparatively useless; that the enemy, taking advantage of the

absence of a portion of the Twelfth Corps sent over to the assistance of our left center after the defeat of the Third Corps, had obtained a footing in a portion of our line on the right, and that to the right of Cemetery Hill he had driven a portion of the Eleventh Corps out of the line, taken possession of some of our batteries there, and had been himself driven out by the timely arrival of Carroll's brigade, sent by me, according to General Hancock's direction, over to the right, "to the sound of the firing." Otherwise our line remained intact.

3. One of the corps commanders, Newton, urged some objections against the military position of our line, and when the council came to decide upon a number of points which were written out by General Butterfield, chief of staff, and submitted to its vote, one of the questions was to this effect: "Should the army remain in its present position, or retire to a better one?" Being the youngest member of the council, I was required to vote first, and on this particular point I voted—having General Newton's objection in my mind, and having confidence in his judgment as a military engineer—that we should as far as possible correct our position, but on no account to change it so much that any one could construe it into a retreat. My recollection is that General Newton voted substantially the same way, and that every other member voted simply to remain and offer battle. So that the decision of the council to remain in position was unanimous.

4. I never heard General Meade say one word in favor of a retreat, nor do I believe that he did so, being confident I should have heard it, the council meeting in a room not to exceed 10 feet square.

I recollect there was great good feeling amongst the corps commanders at their agreeing so unanimously, and General Meade's announcement, in a decided manner, "Such, then, is the decision."

There were a number of other questions of minor importance put and decided which I do not deem it necessary to refer to.

It may not be out of place here to state that during a portion of the sitting of the council, which continued up to nearly 12 o'clock, fighting was going on on the right of our line, where the portion of the Twelfth Corps, returning to its position from the left center, was attempting to dislodge the enemy from the footing he had gained in our line.

I am, general, very respectfully, your obedient servant,
JOHN GIBBON,
Brigadier-General of Volunteers, Commanding.

———

MARCH 15, 1864.

Col. E. D. TOWNSEND,
Assistant Adjutant-General:

I inclose herewith a slip from the New York Herald of the 12th instant, containing a communication signed "Historicus," purporting to give an account of the battle of Gettysburg, to which I desire to call the attention of the War Department, and ask such action thereon as may be deemed proper and suitable. For the past fortnight the public press of the whole country has been teeming with articles, all having for their object assaults upon my reputation as an officer, and tending to throw discredit upon my operations at Gettysburg and my official report of the same.

I have not noticed any of these attacks, and should not now take action, but that the character of the communication inclosed bears such manifest proofs that it was written either by some one present at the battle, or dictated by some one present, and having access not only to official documents but to confidential papers that were never issued to the army, much less made public.

I cannot resist the belief that this letter was either written or dictated by Maj. Gen. D. E. Sickles.

An issue has been raised between that officer and myself in regard to the judgment displayed by him in the position he took with his corps at Gettysburg. In my official report I deemed it proper to state that this position was a false and untenable one, but I did General Sickles the justice to express the opinion that, although he had committed an error of judgment, it was done through a misapprehension of orders, and not from any intention to act contrary to my wishes. The prominence given to General Sickles' operations in the inclosed communication, the labored argument to prove his good judgment and my failings, all lead me to the conclusion he is directly or indirectly the author.

As the communication contains so many statements prejudicial to my reputation, I feel called upon to ask the interposition of the Department, as I desire to consider the questions raised purely official. I have to ask, therefore, that the Department will take steps to ascertain whether Major-General Sickles has authorized or indorses this communication, and, in the event of his replying in the affirmative, I have to request of the President of the United States a court of inquiry, that the whole subject may be thoroughly investigated and the truth made known. Should this course not be deemed advisable, any other action the Department may deem proper I desire should be taken; and should the Department decline any action, then I desire authority to make use of and publish such official documents as in my judgment are necessary for my defense.

Very respectfully,

GEO. G. MEADE,
Major-General, Commanding.

[Inclosure.]

THE BATTLE OF GETTYSBURG—IMPORTANT COMMUNICATION FROM AN EYE-WITNESS—HOW THE VICTORY WAS WON AND HOW ITS ADVANTAGES WERE LOST—GENERALS HALLECK'S AND MEADE'S OFFICIAL REPORTS REFUTED, ETC.

To the Editor of the Herald:

The battle of Gettysburg is the decisive battle of this war. It not only saved the North from invasion, but turned the tide of victory in our favor. The opinion of Europe on the failure of the rebellion dates from this great conflict. How essential, then, that its real history should be known. Up to this moment no clear narrative has appeared. The sketches of the press, the reports of Generals Halleck and Meade, and the oration of Mr. Everett, give only phases of this terrible struggle, and that not very correctly. To supply this *hiatus*, I send you a connected, and, I hope, lucid review of its main features. I have not ventured to touch on the thrilling incidents and affecting details of such a strife, but have confined myself to a succinct relation of its principal events and the actors therein. My only motive is to vindicate history, do honor to the fallen, and justice to the suvivors when unfairly impeached.

General Meade took command of the Army of the Potomac on

Sunday, the 28th of June, at Frederick, Md. On Monday, as he states, the army was put in motion, and by Tuesday night the right flank had reached Manchester and the left occupied Emmitsburg. General Buford's cavalry had advanced as far as Gettysburg, and reported that the Confederate army was debouching from the mountains, on the Cashtown road. Upon this intelligence, General Reynolds was ordered to advance on Gettysburg with the First and Eleventh Corps, which he reached early on the 1st of July, and found Buford's cavalry already engaged with the enemy—the corps of General Hill. Rapidly making his dispositions, General Reynolds joined in the conflict, and soon fell, mortally wounded. The command of the field then devolved on General Howard, of the Eleventh Corps, who maintained his position till about 2 p. m., when the enemy was heavily re-enforced by the arrival of Ewell's corps. The battle now raged fearfully, between Hill's and Ewell's corps on one side and the First and Eleventh Corps on the other, till about 4 p. m., when General Howard was compelled to yield to the superior numbers of the enemy, and fall back (losing many prisoners—nearly 4,000) to the south side of Gettysburg. His position was eminently critical, when, to the great relief of both the general and our valiant troops, a division of the Third Corps, under the immediate command of General Sickles, arrived, and the fighting for that day was at an end.

It should be mentioned that the Third Corps was stationed at Emmitsburg, by order of General Meade, with a view to protect that important point ; but information continuing to reach General Sickles that the First and Eleventh Corps were in great danger,* he decided to assume the grave responsibility of moving to their relief without• orders. Leaving two brigades at Emmitsburg, he made a forced march of 10 miles, in spite of the heat and dust, in three hours, and had the satisfaction to be hailed by General Howard, on his reaching the field, with the flattering phrase, "Here you are, general, always reliable, always first," a generous tribute from one soldier to another.

General Slocum, of the Twelfth Corps, had arrived a short time before, but his corps was then some 4 miles distant. In the early part of the evening (Wednesday), a conference of the leading generals took place, when some insisted on falling back toward Taneytown, while others urged the expediency of maintaining their present position as offering rare advantages for the inevitable and decisive contest that must occur on the following day. It appears that General Meade had issued a circular (of which I saw several copies) on the morning of Wednesday, July 1, to all his corps commanders, stating that his advance had accomplished all the objects contemplated, namely, the relief of Harrisburg and Philadelphia, and that he would now desist altogether from the offensive. He proposed to post the whole army in line of battle on Pipe Creek, the right flank resting on Manchester and the left on Middleburg, in-

---

* Besides numerous reports, the following brief communication reached him which accidentally fell into my hands:

"GETTYSBURG, *July* 1.

"General SICKLES :

"General Doubleday (First Corps) says for God's sake come up with all speed They are pressing us hard.

"H. T. LEE,
"*Lieutenant, A. D. C.*"

volving an entire change of front, and there await the movements of the enemy. The position which General Meade had selected for the final struggle between the two armies was some 15 miles distant from Gettysburg, where fate willed that it should occur. Whether this important circular ordering him to fall back reached the lamented Reynolds before he became engaged at Gettysburg, it is difficult to say. It could not have failed to reach General Sickles ; but he happily determined to push on to the rescue of the First and Eleventh Corps, already engaged. It is strange that General Meade should make no mention in his report of this singular and most important fact : that he issued a plan of campaign on Wednesday, July 1, directing his whole army to retire and take up the defensive on Pipe Creek almost at the moment that his left flank was fiercely struggling with the right wing of the enemy. This proves how often the plans of a general are frustrated by unlooked-for contingencies.

General Meade broke up his quarters at Taneytown, as he states, at 11 p. m. on Wednesday, and reached Gettysburg at 1 a. m. Thursday, July 2. Early in the morning he set to work examining the position of the various army corps. It is hardly true to say that he imitated the example of all prudent commanders on the eve of a battle, and made a complete survey of the ground he occupied.

It was on these occasions that the genius of the first Napoleon revealed itself ; for at a glance he saw the advantages of his own position and the assailable point of the enemy. It seems that General Lee was somewhat more astute than Meade in this, for in his report he states what he deemed " the most favorable point " for his attack. " In front of General Longstreet " (opposite our left wing), Lee remarks, " the enemy held a position from which, if he could be driven, it was thought our army could be used to advantage in assailing the more elevated ground beyond, and thus enable us to reach the crest of the ridge. That officer, then, was directed to carry this position." It is plain enough that Lee regarded the point where our left was posted as the key to our position, and if that could be taken from us our defeat was inevitable. It is not to be supposed that General Meade refused to see this ; but as he makes no mention of it in his report, I propose, for the sake of the future historian of the battle, to tell what I know about it.

Near this important ground was posted the valiant Third Corps, and its commander, General Sickles, saw at once how necessary it was to occupy the elevated ground in his front toward the Emmitsburg road, and to extend his lines to the commanding eminence known as the Round Top, or Sugar Loaf hill. Unless this were done, the left and rear of our army would be in the greatest danger. Sickles concluded that no time was to be lost, as he observed the enemy massing large bodies of troops on their right (our left). Receiving no orders, and filled with anxiety, he reported in person to General Meade, and urged the advance he deemed so essential. "O," said Meade, "generals are all apt to look for the attack to be made where they are." Whether this was a jest or a sneer Sickles did not stop to consider, but begged Meade to go over the ground with him instantly ; but the commander-in-chief declined this on account of other duties. Yielding, however, to the prolonged solicitations of Sickles, General Meade desired General Hunt, chief of artillery, to accompany Sickles, and report the result of their reconnaissance. Hunt concurred with Sickles as to the line to be occupied—the advance line from the left of the Second Corps to the Round Top hill—but he declined to give any orders until he had reported to General Meade, remarking, however, that he (General Sickles) would doubtless receive orders immediately.

Two p. m. came, and yet no orders. Why was this? Other orders than those expected by General Sickles were, it appears, in preparation at headquarters. It has since been stated, upon unquestionable authority, that General Meade had decided upon a retreat, and that an order to withdraw from the position held by our army was penned by his chief of staff, General Butterfield, though happily its promulgation never took place. This order is probably on record in the Adjutant-General's Office.

Meanwhile the enemy's columns were moving rapidly around to our left and rear. These facts were again reported to headquarters, but brought no response. Buford's cavalry had been massed on the left, covering that flank with outposts, and videttes were thrown forward on the Emmitsburg road. While awaiting the expected orders, Sickles made good use of his time in leveling all the fences and stone walls, so as to facilitate the movements of his troops and to favor the operations of the cavalry. What, then, was the surprise of Sickles to see of a sudden all the cavalry withdrawn, leaving his flank entirely exposed! He sent an earnest remonstrance to General Meade, whose reply was that he did not intend to withdraw the cavalry, and that a part of this division (Buford's) should be sent back. It never returned. Under these circumstances, Sickles threw forward three regiments of light troops as skirmishers and for outpost duty.

The critical moment had now arrived. The enemy's movements indicated their purpose to seize the Round Top hill; and this in their possession, General Longstreet would have had easy work in cutting up our left wing. To prevent this disaster, Sickles waited no longer for orders from General Meade, but directed General Hobart Ward's brigade and Smith's battery (Fourth New York) to secure that vital position, and at the same time advancing his line of battle about 300 yards, so as to hold the crest in his front, he extended his left to support Ward and cover the threatened rear of the army.

These dispositions were made in the very face of the enemy, who were advancing in columns of attack, and Sickles dreaded lest the conflict should open before his dispositions were completed. At this juncture he was summoned to report in person at headquarters, to attend a council of corps commanders. His preparations were of such moment and the attack so near, that General Sickles delayed attending the council, while giving all his attention to the carrying out of his orders.

A second peremptory summons came from General Meade, and, leaving his unfinished task to the active supervision of General Birney and General Humphreys, Sickles rode off to the rear to headquarters. Before he had reached there, the sound of cannon announced that the battle had begun. Hastening rapidly on, he was met by General Meade at the door of his quarters, who said, "General, I will not ask you to dismount; the enemy are engaging your front; the council is over." It was an unfortunate moment, as it proved, for a council of war. Sickles, putting spurs to his horse, flew back to his command, and, finding that Graham's brigade was not advanced as far as he desired, he was pushing that brigade and a battery forward about 100 yards, when General Meade at length arrived on the field. The following colloquy ensued, which I gathered from several officers present: "Are you not too much extended,

general?" said Meade. "Can you hold this front?" "Yes," replied
Sickles, "until more troops are brought up; the enemy are attacking
in force, and I shall need support." General Meade then let drop some
remark showing that his mind was still wavering as to the extent of
ground covered by the Third Corps. Sickles replied,· "General, I
have received no orders. I have made these dispositions to the best
of my judgment. Of course, I shall be happy to modify them according to your views." "No," said Meade, "I will send you the Fifth
Corps, and you may send for support from the Second Corps." "I
shall need more artillery," added Sickles. "Send to the Artillery
Reserve for all you want," replied Meade; "I will direct General
Hunt to send you all you ask for." The conference was then abruptly terminated by a heavy shower of shells, probably directed at
the group, and General Meade rode off. Sickles received no further
orders that day.

There is no doubt, I may venture to add, that Sickles' line was
too much extended for the number of troops under his command; but
his great aim was to prevent the enemy getting between his flank and
the Round Top alluded to. This was worth the risk, in his opinion,
of momentarily weakening his lines. The contest now going on was
of the most fierce and sanguinary description. The entire right wing
of the enemy was concentrated on the devoted Third Corps; for the
object of Lee, as he states, was "to carry" the ground which Sickles
occupied, and which both generals evidently regarded as of the highest importance. While this terrific combat was raging on our left,
Lee ordered Ewell "to attack" our right wing and Hill "to threaten"
our center, both with the object, as he says in his report, to divert
re-enforcements from reaching our left, which, as we have seen, Longstreet was "directed to carry." Well may General Meade in his report say, "the Third Corps sustained the shock most heroically;" for
they fought like lions, against tremendous odds, for nearly an hour
before the Fifth Corps, under Sykes, came up, who was immediately
put in position by General Sickles to the left of the Third Corps, and
General Sykes was desired to relieve Ward's brigade and Smith's
battery on the Round Top, and hold the line from thence to Birney's
left (First Division, Third Corps). Strange to say, this movement
was not promptly carried out, and there was imminent danger of
losing the Round Top, for Longstreet was making desperate exertions
to "carry it."

Fearing this result, Sickles sent orders to General Crawford, of
the Fifth Corps, to re-enforce Ward's brigade; but he declined to
move without orders from his own corps commander, Sykes; but
Captain [Alexander] Moore, of Sickles' staff, at length overcame his
scruples, and he reached the disputed point just in time to prevent its
falling into the enemy's hands. Considering our force unequal to the
exigency, Sickles called on the heroic troops of the Second Corps for
support, and they gave it with a will. The struggle now became
deadly. The columns of Longstreet charged with reckless fury upon
our troops; but they were met with a valor and stern fortitude that
defied their utmost efforts. An alarming incident, however, occurred.
Barnes' division, of the Fifth Corps, suddenly gave way; and Sickles,
seeing this, put a battery in position to check the enemy if he broke
through this gap on our front, and General Birney was sent to order
Barnes back into line. "No," he said; "impossible. It is too hot.
My men cannot stand it."

Remonstrance was unavailing, and Sickles dispatched his aides to bring up any troops they met to fill this blank. Major [Henry E.] Tremain, of his staff, fell in with General Zook, at the head of his brigade (Second Corps), and this gallant officer instantly vol-unteered to take Barnes' place. When they reached the ground, Barnes' disordered troops impeded the advance of the brigade. "If you can't get out of the way," cried Zook, "lie down, and I will march over you." Barnes ordered his men to lie down, and the chivalric Zook and his splendid brigade, under the personal direction of General Birney, did march over them and right into the breach. Alas! poor Zook soon fell, mortally wounded, and half of his brigade perished with him. It was about this time—near 7 p. m.—that Sickles was struck by a cannon-ball that tore off his right leg, and he was borne from the field.

It was now pretty clear that General Meade had awakened to the fact which he treated with such indifference when pressed on him by Sickles in the morning—that our left was the assailable point, if not the key to our position, for he began to pour in re-enforcements whose presence in the beginning of the action would have saved thousands of lives. "Perceiving great exertions on the part of the enemy," says Meade's report, "the Sixth Corps (Sedgwick's) and part of the First Corps (Newton's), Lockwood's Maryland brigade, together with detachments from the Second Corps, were all brought up at different periods, and succeeded, together with the gallant resistance of the Fifth Corps, in checking and finally repulsing the assault of the enemy, who retired in confusion and disorder about sunset, and ceased any further efforts."

If this remarkable concentration of troops was necessary, at last, to save the left of our army, it is almost incredible that the single corps of General Sickles was able to withstand the impetuous onset of Longstreet's legions for nearly an hour before any succor reached it.

On Friday, July 3, the enemy renewed their efforts to carry out the original design of Lee by overthrowing our left wing, and Longstreet was re-enforced by Pickett's three brigades, and further supported by one division and two brigades from Hill's corps.

In addition to this heavy mass of infantry, the entire artillery of the rebel army was concentrated against our left. After his oversight of the day before, it may be supposed that General Meade was better prepared to defend his left, and had made adequate preparations. About 1 p. m. the enemy opened a furious cannonade upon our left and left center, which continued some two hours, with occasional responses from us. At about 3 p. m. the enemy moved forward in column, and once more essayed to carry our position on the left. It was during this conflict that General Hancock, commander of the Second Corps, a gallant soldier and accomplished officer, was wounded by a musket-ball and obliged to retire. He contributed greatly by his energy and valor to the success of the day. Meanwhile our artillery opened with vigor, and inflicted great damage. After a severe and prolonged struggle, the enemy at length fell back, and abandoned the contest. "Owing to the strength of the enemy's position," says Lee's report, "and the reduction of our ammunition, a renewal of the engagement could not be hazarded." Hence it is plain that our good fortune in preserving our position on the left gave us the victory at Gettysburg; and yet General Meade, not having sufficiently examined the ground before the battle, disregarded the repeated warnings of that sagacious officer, General Sickles, as well as the report of his own chief of artillery, General Hunt, who concurred in all the suggestions of the commander of the Third Corps.

Without meaning to do injustice to General Meade, it must be admitted that his report of this great battle is at such variance with all the statements which have appeared in the press, that it is due not only to history, but to the indomitable prowess of our heroic army, that every fact sustained by concurrent testimony should be given in order to fully establish the truth. I reserve for any suitable occasion abundant documentary evidence to support the facts furnished.

On Saturday, July 4, both armies continued to face each other during the entire day, without either manifesting a disposition to attack. "The enemy," says Meade, "drew back his left flank, but maintained his position in front of our left," as if always conscious that our vulnerable point was there, and they were loth to retire from it. On the night of the 4th, Lee, finding his ammunition exhausted and his subsistence imperiled, decided to withdraw, and he began his retreat toward Williamsport, with 4,000 of our prisoners and all his immense trains. On the morning of the 5th, this event became known, and General Meade dispatched the Sixth Corps in pursuit, together with some squadrons of cavalry. "The 5th and 6th of July were employed," says Meade's report, "in succoring the wounded and burying the dead." The enemy made good use of all this precious time in pushing on toward Williamsport as rapidly as possible; and it was fortunate for them that detachments were not detailed for these solemn and affecting duties and that our whole army was not launched in prompt and eager pursuit. They were burdened with heavy trains filled with plunder, without ammunition, and wofully demoralized. Had the half of our army, flushed with success, fallen on them in flank or rear, or anywhere or anyhow, General Lee might have got across the Potomac, but his army never. "The trains, with the wounded and prisoners," says Lee's report, "were compelled to await at Williamsport (about the 8th of July) the subsiding of the river and the construction of boats. * * * The enemy had not yet made his appearance." The rebel army must have trembled with anxiety lest the dreaded Yankees should heave in sight before they could escape over the swollen Potomac, which Providence seemed to have destined as the place of their surrender.

It was not till the 12th of July that our army, too long delayed, came up; but, unfortunately, the enemy had nearly finished their preparations for flight. "An attack," says Lee, "was awaited during that and the succeeding day. This did not take place, though the two armies were in close proximity." Why it did not take place the country has never yet understood. General Meade in his report gives no explanation. The press of the day stated that General Meade again held councils of war at this supreme moment, and that several of his generals opposed falling on the crippled enemy. All we know is that Lee, having completed his preparations, slipped quietly over the river on the morning of the 14th. "The crossing was not completed until 1 p. m.," says Lee, "when the bridge was removed. The enemy offered no serious interruption, and the movement was attended with no loss of *matériel* excepting a few disabled wagons and two pieces of artillery, which the horses were unable to drag through the deep mud."

It seems that General Meade and the recalcitrant members of the council of war finally made up their minds to attack. "But on advancing on the morning of the 14th," reports General Meade, "it was ascertained he [the enemy] had retired the night previous by the bridge at Falling Waters and the ford at Williamsport."

In striking confirmation of the sketch now given of this important battle, it may be interesting to quote a few brief extracts from the diary of a British officer who was a guest of General Lee during the campaign in Pennsylvania, and which was published in Blackwood's Magazine in September last. The writer was an eye-witness of the battle of Gettysburg, and the hearty praise he lavishes upon the Confederate troops and their generals shows that all his sympathies were with the South, and he takes no pains to conceal his prejudices against the North. Speaking of the moment when the columns of Longstreet had been finally repulsed by our left on Friday afternoon, July 3, he says: "It is difficult to exaggerate the critical state of affairs as they appeared about this time. If the enemy or his general had shown any enterprise, there is no saying what might have happened. General Longstreet talked to me," he narrates, "for a long time about the battle. The general said the mistake Lee had made was in not concentrating the army more and making the attack with 30,000 men instead of 15,000. It is impossible to avoid seeing," adds the English officer, "that the cause of this check to the Confederates lies in their utter contempt for the enemy." He continues: "Wagons, horses, mules, and cattle captured in Pennsylvania—the solid advantages of this campaign—have been passing slowly along this road (Fairfield) all day (July 4). So interminable was this train that it soon became evident that we should not be able to start. As soon as it became dark, we all lay around a big fire, and I heard reports coming in from the different generals that the enemy was retiring, and had been doing so all day long. But this, of course, could make no difference to General Lee's plans. Ammunition he must have, as he had failed to capture it from the enemy according to precedent. Our progress," he continues, "was naturally very slow, indeed, and we took eight hours to go as many miles."

I will close these extracts with the following graphic sketch of a "stampede" which occurred on Monday, July 6, about 7 p. m., and which demonstrates most unequivocally the utter demoralization of the Confederate army. The writer states:

About 7 p. m. we rode through Hagerstown, in the streets of which were several dead horses and a few dead men. After proceeding about a mile beyond the town, we halted, and General Longstreet sent four cavalrymen up a lane, with directions to report everything they saw. We then dismounted and lay down. About ten minutes later (being nearly dark) we heard a sudden rush—a panic—and then a regular stampede commenced, in the midst of which I descried our four cavalry heroes crossing a field as fast as they could gallop. All was now complete confusion, officers mounting their horses and pursuing those which had got loose, and soldiers climbing over fences for protection against the supposed advancing Yankees. In the midst of the din, I heard an artillery officer shouting to his cannoneers to stand by him, and plant the guns in a proper position for enfilading the lane. I also distinguished Longstreet walking about, hustled by the excited crowd, and remarking in angry tones, which could scarcely be heard, and to which no attention was paid, "Now, you don't know what it is; you don't know what it is." While the row and confusion were at their height, the object of all this alarm at length emerged from the dark lane, in the shape of a domestic four-wheeled carriage, with a harmless load of females. The stampede had, however, spread, increased in the rear, and caused much harm and delay.

It is to be hoped that the above narrative will be regarded as dispassionate, as it is meant to be impartial. Some slight errors may have crept in; but this may possibly stimulate others to come forward with a rectification. Had General Meade been more copious in his report and less reserved as to his own important acts, the necessity for this communication would not have existed.

HISTORICUS.

—

HDQRS. CAVALRY CORPS, ARMY OF THE POTOMAC,
March 18, 1864.

Brig. Gen. S. WILLIAMS,
 Assistant Adjutant-General, Army of the Potomac:

GENERAL: I have the honor to inclose, for the information of the major-general commanding, a copy of my letter to Senator Wade, chairman of the Joint Committee on the Conduct of the War, expressing my willingness for Major-General Meade to be furnished my testimony before said committee; also a copy of Senator Wade's reply to the same.

 I am, general, very respectfully, your obedient servant,
A. PLEASONTON,
Major-General, Commanding.

[Inclosure No. 1.]

HDQRS. CAVALRY CORPS, ARMY OF THE POTOMAC,
March 11, 1864.

Hon. B. F. WADE,
 Chairman of the Committee on the Conduct of the War:

SIR: I have the honor to inclose a copy of a communication received yesterday from Maj. Gen. George G. Meade, commanding the Army of the Potomac; also a copy of my answer to the same.

I desire to state that, should the Committee on the Conduct of the War consider it proper, I am willing Major-General Meade be furnished a succinct statement of my testimony before it.

 I remain, sir, very respectfully, your obedient servant,
A. PLEASONTON,
Major-General, Commanding.

[Inclosure No. 2.]

WASHINGTON, D. C., *March* 15, 1864.

Maj. Gen. A. PLEASONTON,
 Army of the Potomac:

SIR: Your communication, inclosing copy of one from General Meade to yourself in relation to your testimony before the Joint Committee on the Conduct of the War, has been received.

The committee for more than three years past have acted, and continue to act, upon the rule that the testimony taken by them shall be made known to no one until such time as they shall authorize it to be done. So careful have they been in this respect, that they have usually requested of their witnesses to inform no one of the character of their testimony. They have not done so this session, supposing that their desire was sufficiently well understood to render it unnecessary.

In one instance only has any witness been permitted to see and examine the testimony before the committee themselves made it public. General Charles P. Stone made application to the committee, not to the witnesses themselves, for permission to examine the testimony in relation to his administration, basing his application upon the ground that he had reason to believe that his long imprisonment in Fort Lafayette was, to some extent, caused by that testimony. The permission was accordingly granted to him.

The committee do not now see any good reason to induce them to depart from a rule so long established and hitherto so strictly adhered to. Should satisfactory reasons hereafter be presented, they would undoubtedly grant such a privilege to others. Until then they deem it expedient to adhere to the rule here indicated.

The committee cannot suppose that any person would for a moment seriously entertain the idea of calling any witness they may think proper to examine to account for the testimony he may give. Being clothed by Congress with all its powers in the premises, their own self-respect and dignity will not permit them to acknowledge the right of any person to question their authority to examine any one upon any subject which they have been authorized and directed to investigate. In order to do that, every witness must feel himself perfectly free to answer any interrogations the committee may ask, or to give any testimony which may relate to the subject upon which he may be examined.

I remain, very respectfully,

B. F. WADE,
Chairman, &c.

—

PRIVATE AND CONFIDENTIAL.]   HDQRS. OF THE ARMY,

Washington, March 20, 1864.

Maj. Gen. GEORGE G. MEADE,
Army of the Potomac:

GENERAL: The Secretary of War has shown me your letter in regard to the communication in the Herald signed "Historicus." I have no doubt that and other articles of the same kind in the New York papers were written or dictated by General Sickles; nevertheless, you will not be able to fix on him the authorship, and nothing would suit him better than to get you into a personal or newspaper controversy. He would there be perfectly at home, and, with his facilities for controlling or giving color to the New York press, would have greatly the advantage. My advice would be to ignore him entirely in this controversy, unless he makes himself officially amenable, which I think he is too shrewd to do. He cannot by these newspaper articles injure your military reputation in the slightest degree. Indeed, I think that any attacks from him will have the contrary effect.

Yours, truly,

H. W. HALLECK.

—

CONFIDENTIAL.]   HDQRS. ARMY OF THE POTOMAC,

March 22, 1864.

Maj. Gen. H. W. HALLECK,
Washington, D. C.:

GENERAL: I have received and thank you for your friendly letter of the 20th instant. I have no intention of entering into a personal or newspaper controversy with General Sickles. I hardly expected he would acknowledge writing, or being a party to the writing, of the letter by Historicus; but I did expect he would have the manliness to say, though he was not a party to its publication, that its contents were, in his judgment and belief, correct and true.   As these statements are in direct conflict with my official report, I thought this might be considered sufficiently official by the Department to justify an investigation.   Of course, if he denies having had anything to do with the matter, why that is an end of it.

I am not as philosophical as you are, nor do I consider it good policy to permit such slanders as have been circulated to pass entirely unnoticed.   They have an influence with many people to whom I am a stranger; indeed, even my friends, believing me innocent, have still been puzzled to account for and understand these charges.

I had no intention of annoying the Department, and if you and the Secretary think it better policy for me to keep quiet, I will withdraw the letter I have written, or remain satisfied with an official reply that the Department cannot interfere or take action on an anonymous communication.

Truly, yours,

GEO. G. MEADE.

—

BRANDY STATION, VA., *March* 22, 1864.

Major-General MEADE:

SIR: I have the honor to submit the following statement of facts relative to the battle of July 2, at Gettysburg:

At the opening of the battle of July 2, there were no troops belonging to General Sickles' corps on Round Top ridge.

General Sickles, when called upon by General Warren, through me, to furnish troops for the defense of that position, refused to do so, stating that his whole command was necessary to defend his front, or words to that effect.

General Sykes furnished troops for the object stated above as soon as called upon to do so.

I have the honor to be, very respectfully, your obedient servant,

RANALD S. MACKENZIE,

First Lieutenant, Corps of Engineers.

—

WASHINGTON, D. C., *March* 23, 1864.

Brig. Gen. S. WILLIAMS,

    Assistant Adjutant-General, Army of the Potomac:

The Congressional Committee on the Conduct of the War have summoned me before them.   I desire, before testifying, to have the rough minutes of the council of July 2, which I mailed to you; also the manifold writer which I used and left with you; also the originals of all dispatches, orders, &c., prepared by me.   Should General Meade consent, will you please send them to me, by special messenger, at Willard's?   Please answer.

DANL. BUTTERFIELD,

Major-General.

—

MARCH 23, 1864—5.40 p. m.

Maj. Gen. D. BUTTERFIELD,

    Willard's Hotel, Washington:

Your dispatch received.   As you are not now connected with the Army of the Potomac, the major-general commanding declines furnishing you with the records of said army. Any papers appertaining to this army that the Committee on the Conduct of the War may call for, will, of course, be promptly and cheerfully furnished. I have no recollection of ever having received the rough minutes of the council of July 2, which you say you mailed to me. The records have recently been thoroughly examined, and no such paper has been found.

S. WILLIAMS,
Assistant Adjutant-General.

—

HDQRS. 1ST DIV., 12TH CORPS, ARMY OF THE CUMBERLAND,
Tullahoma, Tenn., March 23, 1864.

Brig. Gen. S. WILLIAMS,
Assistant Adjutant-General, Army of the Potomac:

GENERAL : I have the honor to acknowledge the receipt of your circular communication of the 10th instant.

My recollections of the council or meeting of corps commanders, held on the evening of the 2d July last, are briefly these :

After some desultory conversation, having reference mainly to the amount of supplies and the strength of each corps, and, incidentally, to the results of the afternoon attack upon our left, and to the defensible character of the position around Gettysburg compared with others named, three questions were read by the chief of staff for the opinion of the general officers present. In substance they were :

1. Shall the army remain in its present position ?
2. If so, how long ?
3. Shall it act on the defensive or offensive ?

The vote was, I think, unanimous to remain, and to act on the defensive, and the commanding general announced that his orders would be in accordance with this opinion.

I heard no expression from him which led me to think he was in favor of withdrawing the army from before Gettysburg.

I have the honor to be, general, very respectfully, your obedient servant,

A. S. WILLIAMS,
Brigadier-General of Volunteers.

—

EXECUTIVE MANSION,
Washington, March 29, 1864.

Major-General MEADE:

MY DEAR SIR : Your letter to Colonel Townsend,* inclosing a slip from the Herald, and asking a court of inquiry, has been laid before me by the Secretary of War, with the request that I would consider it. It is quite natural that you should feel some sensibility on the subject ; yet I am not impressed, nor do I think the country is impressed, with the belief that your honor demands, or the public interest demands, such an inquiry. The country knows that at all events you have done good service ; and I believe it agrees with me that it is much better for you to be engaged in trying to do more than to be diverted, as you necessarily would be, by a court of inquiry.

Yours, truly,

A. LINCOLN.

---

*Of March 15, 1864, p. 127.

ADDENDA.

III.—PUBLIC RESOLUTION—No. 9.

A RESOLUTION expressive of the thanks of Congress to Maj. Gen. Joseph Hooker, Maj. Gen. George G. Meade, Maj. Gen. Oliver O. Howard, and the officers and soldiers of the Army of the Potomac.

Resolved by the Senate and House of Representatives of the United States of America, in Congress assembled, That the gratitude of the American people, and the thanks of their Representatives in Congress, are due, and are hereby tendered, to Maj. Gen. Joseph Hooker, and the officers and soldiers of the Army of the Potomac, for the skill, energy, and endurance which first covered Washington and Baltimore from the meditated blow of the advancing and powerful army of rebels led by General Robert E. Lee ; and to Maj. Gen. George G. Meade, Maj. Gen. Oliver O. Howard, and the officers and soldiers of that army, for the skill and heroic valor which, at Gettysburg, repulsed, defeated, and drove back, broken and dispirited, beyond the Rappahannock, the veteran army of the rebellion.

Approved January 28, 1864.

No. 7.

Itinerary of the Army of the Potomac and co-operating forces, June 5–July 31, 1863. *

June 5.—The Army of the Potomac, commanded by Maj. Gen. Joseph Hooker, with headquarters near Falmouth, was posted on the north bank of the Rappahannock River, confronting the Confederate Army of Northern Virginia, under General Robert E. Lee, mainly concentrated about the town of Fredericksburg, on the south bank of the river. The several commands of the Army of the Potomac were distributed as follows : First Corps (Reynolds'), in the vicinity of White Oak Church; Second Corps (Couch's), near Falmouth; Third Corps (Birney's), at Boscobel, near Falmouth; Fifth Corps (Meade's), in the vicinity of Banks', United States, and adjacent fords on the Rappahannock; Sixth Corps (Sedgwick's), near White Oak Church, with the Second Division (Howe's) thrown forward to Franklin's Crossing of the Rappahannock, a little below Fredericksburg, near the mouth of Deep Run; Eleventh Corps (Howard's), near Brooke's Station, on the Aquia Creek Railroad; and the Twelfth Corps (Slocum's), near Stafford Court-House and Aquia Landing. The Cavalry Corps (Pleasonton's, with headquarters at Manassas Junction) had two divisions (Duffié's and Gregg's) and the Cavalry Reserve Brigade, all under Buford, in the vicinity of Warrenton Junction, and one division (B. F. Davis') in the neighborhood of Brooke's Station. The Artillery Reserve (R. O. Tyler's) was near Falmouth.

June 6.—Howe's (Second) division, Sixth Army Corps, crossed the Rappahannock at Franklin's Crossing, and, after a skirmish, occupied the enemy's rifle-pits. Wright's (First) and Newton's (Third) divisions of the same corps moved to the same point from White Oak Church, taking position on the north bank of the river.

---

* Compiled by Mr. Joseph W. Kirkley, of the Adjutant-General's Office, under direction of Adjutant-General Richard C. Drum, U. S. Army.

June 7.—Wright's (First) division, Sixth Corps, was sent across the Rappahannock at Franklin's Crossing, relieving Howe's (Second) division, which returned to the north side.

June 8.—The Cavalry Corps (Pleasonton's), consisting of Buford's (First), D. McM. Gregg's (Third), and Duffié's (Second) divisions, and the Regular Reserve Brigade, supported by detachments of infantry, under Generals Adelbert Ames and David A. Russell, moved to Kelly's and Beverly Fords, preparatory to crossing the Rappahannock on a reconnaissance toward Culpeper.

June 9.—Newton's (Third) division, Sixth Corps, relieved Wright's (First) division on the south bank of the Rappahannock at Franklin's Crossing. The Cavalry Corps, supported by Generals Ames' and Russell's infantry, crossed the Rappahannock at Kelly's and Beverly Fords, fought the enemy at or near Beverly Ford, Brandy Station, and Stevensburg, and recrossed the river at Rappahannock Station and Beverly Ford.

June 10.—The Cavalry Corps took position in the neighborhood of Warrenton Junction.. Its infantry supports in the reconnaissance of the day previous rejoined their respective commands. Howe's (Second) division, Sixth Corps, moved from Franklin's Crossing to Aquia Creek.

June 11.—The Third Corps marched from Boscobel, near Falmouth, to Hartwood Church.

June 12.—The First Corps marched from Fitzhugh's plantation and White Oak Church to Deep Run; the Third Corps from Hartwood Church to Bealeton, with Humphreys' (Third) division, advanced to the Rappahannock; the Eleventh Corps from the vicinity of Brooke's Station to Hartwood Church; and Headquarters Cavalry Corps from Manassas Junction to Warrenton Junction.

The advance of the Confederate army skirmished with the Union troops at Newtown, Cedarville, and Middletown, in the Shenandoah Valley.

June 13.—The First Corps marched from Deep Run to Bealeton; the Fifth Corps from the vicinity of Banks' Ford, via Grove Church, toward Morrisville; Wright's (First) and Newton's (Third) divisions, Sixth Corps, from Franklin's Crossing to Potomac Creek; the Eleventh Corps, from Hartwood Church to Catlett's Station; the Twelfth Corps from near Stafford Court-House and Aquia Creek Landing *en route* to Dumfries; Wyndham's brigade of Gregg's cavalry division from Warrenton Junction to Warrenton; and the Artillery Reserve from near Falmouth to Stafford Court-House. McReynolds' (Third) brigade, of Milroy's division, Eighth Army Corps, marched from Berryville to Winchester.

June 14.—Headquarters Army of the Potomac moved from near Falmouth to Dumfries; the First and Third Corps marched from Bealeton to Manassas Junction; the Fifth Corps arrived at Morrisville, and marched thence, via Bristersburg, to Catlett's Station; Wright's (First) and Newton's (Third) divisions, Sixth Corps, moved from Potomac Creek to Stafford Court-House; the Eleventh Corps from Catlett's Station to Manassas Junction, and thence toward Centreville; the Twelfth Corps reached Dumfries; and the Artillery Reserve moved from Stafford Court-House to Wolf Run Shoals. Daniel Tyler's command, of the Eighth Army Corps, fell back from Martinsburg to Maryland Heights.

June 15.—Headquarters Army of the Potomac moved from Dumfries to Fairfax Station; the Second Corps (Hancock's*) moved from Falmouth to near Aquia; the Fifth Corps from Catlett's Station, via Bristoe Station, to Manassas Junction; the Sixth Corps from Aquia Creek and Stafford Court-House to Dumfries; the Twelfth Corps from Dumfries to Fairfax Court-House; the Cavalry Corps † (except Wyndham's brigade, which marched from Warrenton to Manassas Junction, and thence on the 16th to Union Mills) from Warrenton Junction to Union Mills and Bristoe Station; the Artillery Reserve from Wolf Run Shoals to Fairfax Court-House; and the Eleventh Corps arrived at Centreville. Milroy's (Second) division, of the Eighth Army Corps, evacuated Winchester, and fell back to Maryland Heights and Hancock, Md.

June 16.—The Second Corps marched from near Aquia, via Dumfries, to Wolf Run Shoals, on the Occoquan; the Sixth Corps from Dumfries to Fairfax Station; and the Cavalry Corps from Union Mills and Bristoe Station to Manassas Junction and Bull Run.

June 17.—The First Corps marched from Manassas Junction to Herndon Station; the Second Corps from Wolf Run Shoals to Sangster's Station; the Third Corps from Manassas Junction to Centreville; the Fifth Corps from Manassas Junction to Gum Springs; the Eleventh Corps from Centreville to Cow-Horn Ford, or Trappe Rock, on Goose Creek; and the Twelfth Corps from Fairfax Court-House to near Dranesville. The Cavalry Corps moved from Manassas Junction and Bull Run to Aldie.

June 18.—Headquarters Army of the Potomac moved from Fairfax Station to Fairfax Court-House; the Sixth Corps from Fairfax Station to Germantown; and the Twelfth Corps from near Dranesville to Leesburg. J. I. Gregg's cavalry brigade advanced from Aldie to Middleburg, and returned to a point midway between the two places.

June 19.—The First Corps marched from Herndon Station to Guilford Station; the Third Corps from Centreville to Gum Springs; and the Fifth Corps from Gum Springs to Aldie. Gregg's cavalry division, except McIntosh's (late Wyndham's) brigade, advanced to Middleburg. McIntosh's brigade moved from Aldie to Hay Market.

June 20.—The Second Corps moved from Sangster's Station to Centreville, and thence toward Thoroughfare Gap; the Second Division (Howe's), Sixth Corps, from Germantown to Bristoe Station.

June 21.—The Second Corps arrived at Gainesville and Thoroughfare Gap. The Cavalry Corps (except McIntosh's brigade, of Gregg's division), supported by Barnes' (First) division, Fifth Corps, marched from Aldie and Middleburg to Upperville. McIntosh's cavalry brigade marched from Hay Market to Aldie, and thence to Upperville. Stahel's division of cavalry, from the Defenses of Washington, moved from Fairfax Court-House, via Centreville and Gainesville, to Buckland Mills.

June 22.—The Cavalry Corps and Barnes' (First) division, of the Fifth Corps, returned from Upperville to Aldie. Stahel's cavalry division moved from Buckland Mills, via New Baltimore, to Warrenton.

---

*General Hancock assumed command of the Second Corps June 9, 1863, succeeding General Couch, who was assigned to the command of the Department of the Susquehanna.

† By orders of June 13, 1863, this corps was reduced from three to two divisions, commanded by Brig. Gens. John Buford and D. McM. Gregg.

June 23.—Stahel's cavalry division moved from Warrenton, via Gainesville, to Fairfax Court-House.

June 24.—Newton's (Third) division, Sixth Corps, moved from Germantown to Centreville, and the Eleventh Corps from Cow-Horn Ford, or Trappe Rock, on Goose Creek, to the south bank of the Potomac, at Edwards Ferry. Stahel's cavalry division moved from Fairfax Court-House to near Dranesville.

June 25.—The First Corps marched from Guilford Station, Va., to Barnesville, Md.; the Third Corps from Gum Springs, Va., to the north side of the Potomac, at Edwards Ferry and the mouth of the Monocacy; the Eleventh Corps from Edwards Ferry, Va., to Jefferson, Md.; and the Artillery Reserve from Fairfax Court-House, Va., to near Poolesville, Md. These commands crossed the Potomac at Edwards Ferry. The Second Corps marched from Thoroughfare Gap and Gainesville to Gum Springs. Howe's (Second) division, Sixth Corps, moved from Bristoe Station to Centreville; Crawford's division (two brigades) of Pennsylvania Reserves, from the Defenses of Washington, marched from Fairfax Station and Upton's Hill to Vienna. Stannard's Vermont Brigade, from the Defenses of Washington, left the mouth of the Occoquan *en route* to join the Army of the Potomac. Stahel's cavalry division moved from near Dranesville, Va., via Young's Island Ford, on the Potomac, *en route* to Frederick, Md.

June 26.—Headquarters Army of the Potomac moved from Fairfax Court-House, Va., via Dranesville and Edwards Ferry, to Poolesville, Md.; the First Corps from Barnesville to Jefferson, Md.; the Second Corps from Gum Springs, Va., to the north side of the Potomac, at Edwards Ferry; the Third Corps from the mouth of the Monocacy to Point of Rocks, Md.; the Fifth Corps from Aldie, Va., via Carter's Mills, Leesburg, and Edwards Ferry, to within 4 miles of the mouth of the Monocacy, Md.; the Sixth Corps from Germantown and Centreville to Dranesville, Va.; the Eleventh Corps from Jefferson to Middletown, Md.; the Twelfth Corps from Leesburg, Va., via Edwards Ferry, to the mouth of the Monocacy, Md.; and the Cavalry Corps (Buford's and Gregg's divisions) from Aldie to Leesburg, Va. Stahel's cavalry division was *en route* between the Potomac and Frederick, Md. Crawford's Pennsylvania Reserves moved from Vienna to Goose Creek, Va.

June 27.—Headquarters Army of the Potomac moved from Poolesville to Frederick, Md.; the First Corps from Jefferson to Middletown, Md.; the Second Corps from near Edwards Ferry, via Poolesville, to Barnesville, Md.; the Third Corps from Point of Rocks, via Jefferson, to Middletown, Md.; the Fifth Corps from a point between Edwards Ferry and the mouth of the Monocacy to Ballinger's Creek, near Frederick, Md.; the Sixth Corps from Dranesville, Va., via Edwards Ferry, to near Poolesville, Md.; the Twelfth Corps from near the mouth of the Monocacy, via Point of Rocks, to Knoxville, Md.; Buford's cavalry division from Leesburg, Va., via Edwards Ferry, to near Jefferson, Md.; Gregg's cavalry division from Leesburg, Va., via Edwards Ferry, toward Frederick, Md.; and the Artillery Reserve from Poolesville to Frederick, Md. Stahel's cavalry division reached Frederick, Md. Crawford's Pennsylvania Reserves moved from Goose Creek, Va., via Edwards Ferry, to the mouth of the Monocacy, Md.

June 28.—The First Corps marched from Middletown to Frederick; the Second Corps from Barnesville to Monocacy Junction; the

Third Corps* from Middletown to near Woodsborough; the Sixth Corps from near Poolesville to Hyattstown; the Eleventh Corps from Middletown to near Frederick, and the Twelfth Corps from Knoxville to Frederick. Buford's cavalry division moved from near Jefferson to Middletown; Gregg's cavalry division reached Frederick, and marched thence to New Market and Ridgeville. Crawford's Pennsylvania Reserves marched from the mouth of the Monocacy, and joined the Fifth Corps† at Ballinger's Creek. Stahel's cavalry division was assigned to the Cavalry Corps, as the Third Division, under Brig. Gen. Judson Kilpatrick, with Brig. Gen. Elon J. Farnsworth commanding the First Brigade and Brig. Gen. George A. Custer commanding the Second Brigade.

June 29.—Headquarters Army of the Potomac moved from Frederick to Middleburg; the First and Eleventh Corps from Frederick to Emmitsburg; the Second Corps from Monocacy Junction, via Liberty and Johnsville, to Uniontown; the Third Corps from near Woodsborough to Taneytown; the Fifth Corps from Ballinger's Creek, via Frederick and Mount Pleasant, to Liberty; the Sixth Corps from Hyattstown, via New Market and Ridgeville, to New Windsor; the Twelfth Corps from Frederick to Taneytown and Bruceville; Gamble's (First) and Devin's (Second) brigades, of Buford's (First) cavalry division, from Middletown, via Boonsborough, Cavetown, and Monterey Springs, to near Fairfield; Merritt's reserve cavalry brigade, of the same division, from Middletown to Mechanicstown; Gregg's (Second) cavalry division from New Market and Ridgeville to New Windsor; Kilpatrick's (Third) cavalry division from Frederick to Littlestown; and the Artillery Reserve from Frederick to Bruceville.

June 30.—Headquarters Army of the Potomac moved from Middleburg to Taneytown; the First Corps from Emmitsburg to Marsh Run; the Third Corps from Taneytown to Bridgeport; the Fifth Corps from Liberty, via Johnsville, Union Bridge, and Union, to Union Mills; the Sixth Corps from New Windsor to Manchester; the Twelfth Corps from Taneytown and Bruceville to Littlestown; Gamble's and Devin's brigades, of Buford's cavalry division, from near Fairfield, via Emmitsburg, to Gettysburg; Gregg's cavalry division from New Windsor to Westminster, and thence to Manchester; Kilpatrick's cavalry division from Littlestown to Hanover; and the Artillery Reserve from Bruceville to Taneytown. Kenly's and Morris' brigades, of French's division, left Maryland Heights for Frederick, and Elliott's and Smith's brigades, of the same division, moved from the Heights, by way of the Chesapeake and Ohio Canal, for Washington.

July 1.—The First Corps moved from Marsh Run and the Eleventh Corps from Emmitsburg to Gettysburg; the Second Corps from Uniontown, via Taneytown, to near Gettysburg; the Third Corps from Bridgeport, via Emmitsburg, to the field of Gettysburg; the Fifth Corps from Union Mills, via Hanover and McSherrystown, to Bonaughtown; the Sixth Corps from Manchester *en route* to Gettysburg; and the Twelfth Corps from Littlestown, via Two Taverns, to the field of Gettysburg. Gregg's cavalry division marched from Man-

---

* Maj. Gen. D. E. Sickles resumed command of the Third Corps, relieving Maj. Gen. D. B. Birney, who had been temporarily in command.

† Maj. Gen. George G. Meade relinquished command of the Fifth Corps to Maj. Gen. George Sykes, and assumed command of the Army of the Potomac, relieving Maj. Gen. Joseph Hooker.

chester to Hanover Junction, whence McIntosh's and J. I. Gregg's brigades proceeded to Hanover, while Huey's brigade returned to Manchester. Kilpatrick's cavalry division moved from Hanover, via Abbottsville, to Berlin; and the Artillery Reserve (Ransom's and Fitzhugh's brigades) from Taneytown to near Gettysburg. Stannard's Vermont Brigade, from the Defenses of Washington, joined the First Corps on the field of Gettysburg. W. F. Smith's (First) division, of the Department of the Susquehanna, marched from the vicinity of Harrisburg to Carlisle. Kenly's and Morris' brigades of French's division reached Frederick.

July 2.—The Second, Fifth, and Sixth Corps, Lockwood's brigade, from the Middle Department, McIntosh's and J. I. Gregg's brigades, of D. McM. Gregg's cavalry division, Kilpatrick's cavalry division, and the Artillery Reserve, reached the field of Gettysburg. Gamble's and Devin's brigades, of Buford's cavalry division, marched from Gettysburg to Taneytown, and Merritt's reserve brigade from Mechanicstown to Emmitsburg.

July 3.—Gamble's and Devin's brigades, of Buford's cavalry division, moved from Taneytown to Westminster; Merritt's reserve brigade from Emmitsburg to the field of Gettysburg; and Huey's brigade, of Gregg's cavalry division, from Manchester to Westminster.

July 4.—Gamble's and Devin's brigades, of Buford's cavalry division, marched from Westminster, and Merritt's reserve brigade from Gettysburg, *en route* to Frederick; Huey's brigade, of Gregg's cavalry division, from Westminster, via Emmitsburg, to Monterey; J. I. Gregg's cavalry brigade from Gettysburg to Hunterstown; and Kilpatrick's cavalry division from Gettysburg, via Emmitsburg, to Monterey. Smith's division, of Couch's command, moved from Carlisle, via Mount Holly, to Pine Grove, and the remainder of Couch's troops from the vicinity of Harrisburg toward Shippensburg and Chambersburg. Elliott's and Smith's brigades, of French's division, arrived at Washington from Maryland Heights, and moved to Tennallytown. Morris' brigade, of French's division, marched from Frederick to Turner's Gap, in South Mountain.

July 5.—Leaving Gettysburg, the Second Corps marched to Two Taverns; the Fifth Corps to Marsh Run; the Sixth Corps to Fairfield; the Eleventh Corps to Rock Creek; the Twelfth Corps to Littlestown; McIntosh's brigade, of Gregg's cavalry division, to Emmitsburg; and the Artillery Reserve to Littlestown. Buford's cavalry division reached Frederick. J. I. Gregg's cavalry brigade moved from Hunterstown to Greenwood. Kilpatrick's cavalry division and Huey's brigade, of Gregg's cavalry division, marched from Monterey, via Smithsburg, to Boonsborough.

July 6.—The First Corps marched from Gettysburg to Emmitsburg; the Fifth Corps from Marsh Run to Moritz's Cross-Roads; the Sixth Corps from Fairfield to Emmitsburg, except Neill's (Third) brigade, of Howe's (Second) division, which, in conjunction with McIntosh's brigade of cavalry, was left at Fairfield to pursue the enemy; the Eleventh Corps from Rock Creek to Emmitsburg; Buford's cavalry division from Frederick to Williamsport and thence back to Jones' Cross-Roads; Kilpatrick's cavalry division and Huey's brigade, of Gregg's cavalry division, from Boonsborough, via Hagerstown* and Williamsport, to Jones' Cross-Roads; McIntosh's brigade,

---

* Richmond's brigade, of Kilpatrick's division, remained at Hagerstown, whence it retired toward Boonsborough.

of Gregg's cavalry division, from Emmitsburg to Fairfield; and J. I. Gregg's brigade, of Gregg's cavalry division, from Greenwood to Marion. Smith's division, of Couch's command, moved from Pine Grove to Newman's Pass. Kenly's brigade, of French's division, marched from Frederick *en route* to Maryland Heights. Elliott's and Smith's brigades, of French's division, left Tennallytown, via Washington and the Baltimore and Ohio Railroad, *en route* to Frederick.

July 7.—Headquarters Army of the Potomac moved from Get-tysburg to Frederick; the First Corps from Emmitsburg to Ham-burg; the Second Corps from Two Taverns to Taneytown; the Third Corps from Gettysburg, via Emmitsburg, to Mechanicstown; the Fifth Corps from Moritz's Cross-Roads, via Emmitsburg, to Utica; the Sixth Corps from Emmitsburg to Mountain Pass, near Ham-burg; the Eleventh Corps from Emmitsburg to Middletown; the Twelfth Corps from Littlestown to Walkersville; and the Artillery Reserve from Littlestown to Woodsborough. Buford's and Kilpat-rick's cavalry divisions and Huey's brigade, of Gregg's cavalry di-vision, moved from Jones' Cross-Roads to Boonsborough. J. I. Gregg's cavalry brigade was moving *en route* from Chambersburg to Middletown. McIntosh's brigade of cavalry and Neill's brigade, of the Sixth Corps, moved from Fairfield to Waynesborough. Smith's division, of Couch's command, marched from Newman's Pass to Alto-dale. Kenly's brigade, of French's division, with other troops for-warded by Schenck from Baltimore, reoccupied Maryland Heights. Elliott's and Smith's brigades, of French's division, reached Fred-erick from Washington.

July 8.—Headquarters Army of the Potomac moved from Fred-erick to Middletown; the First Corps from Hamburg to Turner's Gap, in South Mountain; the Second Corps from Taneytown to Fred-erick; the Third Corps from Mechanicstown to a point 3 miles south-west of Frederick; the Fifth Corps from Utica to Middletown; the Sixth Corps from near Hamburg to Middletown; the Eleventh Corps from Middletown to Turner's Gap, in South Mountain, Schurz's (Third) division being advanced to Boonsborough; the Twelfth Corps from Walkersville to Jefferson ; and the Artillery Reserve from Woodsborough to Frederick. J. I. Gregg's cavalry brigade was moving *en route* from Chambersburg to Middletown. Smith's divis-ion, of Couch's command, moved from Altodale to Waynesborough. Campbell's and Mulligan's brigades, of Kelley's command, Depart-ment of West Virginia, were concentrated at Hancock, whence they moved to Fairview, on North Mountain.

July 9.—Headquarters Army of the Potomac moved from Middle-town to Turner's Gap ; the Second Corps from Frederick to Roh-rersville ; the Third Corps from near Frederick to Fox's Gap, in South Mountain ; the Fifth Corps from Middletown, via Fox's Gap, to near Boonsborough ; the Sixth Corps from Middletown to Boonsborough ; the Twelfth Corps from Jefferson to Rohrersville; and the Artillery Reserve from Frederick to Boonsborough. J. I. Gregg's cavalry brigade reached Middletown from Chambersburg. Elliott's and Smith's brigades, of French's division, marched from Frederick to Middletown.

July 10.—Headquarters Army of the Potomac moved from Turn-er's Gap to Beaver Creek, beyond Boonsborough ; the First Corps from Turner's Gap to Beaver Creek, where it was joined by Kenly's brigade, of French's division, from Maryland Heights ; the Second

Corps from Rohrersville to near Tilghmanton; the Third Corps from Fox's Gap, through Boonsborough, to Antietam Creek, in the vicinity of Jones' Cross-Roads, where it was joined by Elliott's and Smith's brigades, of French's division, which marched from Middletown, and Morris' brigade, of the same division, which marched from Turner's Gap; the Fifth Corps from near Boonsborough to Delaware Mills, on Antietam Creek; the Sixth Corps from Boonsborough to Beaver Creek; the Eleventh Corps from Turner's Gap to Beaver Creek; and the Twelfth Corps from Rohrersville to Bakersville. Buford's and Kilpatrick's cavalry divisions moved from Boonsborough to Funkstown; Huey's brigade, of Gregg's cavalry division, from Boonsborough to Jones' Cross-Roads, and McIntosh's cavalry brigade from Waynesborough, via Smithsburg and Leitersburg, to Old Antietam Forge, and back to Waynesborough.

July 11.—The Second Corps moved from near Tilghmanton to the neighborhood of Jones' Cross-Roads; the Twelfth Corps from Bakersville to Fair Play and Jones' Cross-Roads; Gamble's and Devin's brigades, of Buford's cavalry division, from Funkstown to Bakersville; J. I. Gregg's cavalry brigade from Middletown to Boonsborough; Kilpatrick's cavalry division from Funkstown to near Hagerstown; the Artillery Reserve from Boonsborough to Benevola; Neill's brigade, of the Sixth Corps, and Smith's division, of Couch's command, from Waynesborough to Leitersburg.

July 12.—The First, Sixth, and Eleventh Corps moved from Beaver Creek to Funkstown; McIntosh's cavalry brigade from Waynesborough, via Leitersburg, to Boonsborough; Kilpatrick's cavalry division and Ames' (First) division, Eleventh Corps, occupied Hagerstown; Neill's brigade, of the Sixth Corps, moved from Leitersburg to Funkstown, where it rejoined its corps; Smith's division (except one brigade, left at Waynesborough) from Leitersburg to Cavetown; Dana's (Second) division, of Couch's command, from Chambersburg to Greencastle; and Averell's cavalry brigade, Department of West Virginia, from Cumberland *en route* to Fairview.

July 13.—The Sixth Corps moved from Funkstown to the vicinity of Hagerstown; the Artillery Reserve from Benevola to Jones' Cross-Roads, two brigades remaining at the latter place and the others returning to Benevola; Smith's division, of Couch's command, from Waynesborough and Cavetown to Hagerstown and Beaver Creek. Averell's cavalry brigade joined Kelley's infantry at Fairview.

July 14.—The First Corps marched from Funkstown to Williamsport; the Second Corps from near Jones' Cross-Roads to near Falling Waters; the Third Corps from Antietam Creek, near Jones' Cross-Roads, across Marsh Creek; the Fifth Corps from the vicinity of Roxbury Mills, on Antietam Creek, to near Williamsport; the Sixth Corps from the neighborhood of Hagerstown to Williamsport; the Eleventh Corps from Funkstown, via Hagerstown, to Williamsport; and Williams' (First) division, of the Twelfth Corps, from Jones' Cross-Roads to near Falling Waters, and thence to near Williamsport. Buford's cavalry division moved from Bakersville to Falling Waters; McIntosh's and J. I. Gregg's brigades, of D. McM. Gregg's cavalry division, from Boonsborough to Harper's Ferry; Huey's brigade, of same division, from Jones' Cross-Roads, via Williamsport, to Falling Waters; and Kilpatrick's cavalry division from Hagerstown, via Williamsport, to Falling Waters. Kelley's command, Department of West Virginia, marched from Fairview to Williamsport.

July 15.—Headquarters Army of the Potomac moved from Beaver

Creek to Berlin; the First Corps from Williamsport to Rohrersville; the Second Corps from near Falling Waters to near Sandy Hook; the Third Corps from Marsh Creek to near Burnside's bridge, on the Antietam; the Fifth Corps from near Williamsport to Burkittsville; the Sixth Corps from Williamsport to Boonsborough; the Eleventh Corps from Williamsport, via Hagerstown, to Middletown; and the Twelfth Corps from Fair Play and near Williamsport to Sandy Hook. Two brigades of the Artillery Reserve moved from Jones' Cross-Roads, and, joining the remainder of the reserve at Benevola, the whole command marched thence, via Middletown, to Berlin. Buford's cavalry division moved from Falling Waters to Berlin; McIntosh's and J. I. Gregg's brigades, of D. McM. Gregg's cavalry division, from Harper's Ferry, via Halltown, to Shepherdstown; Huey's brigade, of same division, from Falling Waters to Boonsborough; and Kilpatrick's cavalry division from Falling Waters, via Williamsport and Hagerstown, to Boonsborough. Kelley's command, Department of West Virginia, marched from Williamsport to Indian Springs.

July 16.—The First Corps marched from Rohrersville to near Berlin ; the Third Corps from Burnside's bridge to Pleasant Valley, near Sandy Hook ; the Fifth Corps from Burkittsville, via Petersville, to near Berlin ; the Sixth Corps from Boonsborough to near Berlin; the Eleventh Corps from Middletown, via Jefferson, to Berlin; and the Twelfth Corps from Sandy Hook to Pleasant Valley. Buford's cavalry division moved from Berlin to Petersville; Huey's brigade, of Gregg's cavalry division, from Boonsborough, via Harper's Ferry, to Shepherdstown ; and Kilpatrick's division from Boonsborough to Berlin, whence De Forest's (First) brigade proceeded to Harper's Ferry.

July 17.—The Third Corps moved from near Sandy Hook, crossed the Potomac at Harper's Ferry, and proceeded to a point 3 miles south of the Ferry; the Fifth Corps moved from near Berlin to Lovettsville, crossing the Potomac at Berlin. Gregg's cavalry division marched from Shepherdstown to Harper's Ferry; Kilpatrick's cavalry division from Berlin and Harper's Ferry to Purcellville, Custer's brigade crossing the Potomac at Berlin, and De Forest's brigade the Shenandoah at Harper's Ferry. Kelley's command, Department of West Virginia, moved from Indian Springs, Md., to Hedgesville, W. Va., crossing the Potomac at Cherry Run.

July 18.—Headquarters Army of the Potomac moved from Berlin, Md., to Lovettsville, Va.; the First Corps from near Berlin to Waterford, crossing the Potomac at Berlin ; the Second Corps from near Sandy Hook to Hillsborough, crossing the Potomac and Shenandoah Rivers at Harper's Ferry; the Third Corps from near Harper's Ferry to Hillsborough; the Fifth Corps from Lovettsville to near Purcellville ; the Artillery Reserve from Berlin to Wheatland; and Buford's cavalry division from Petersville to Purcellville, crossing the Potomac at Berlin.

July 19.—Headquarters Army of the Potomac moved from Lovettsville to Wheatland; the First Corps from Waterford to Hamilton; the Second and Third Corps from Hillsborough to Wood Grove; the Fifth Corps from near Purcellville to a point on the road to Philomont; the Sixth Corps from near Berlin to Wheatland, and the Eleventh Corps from Berlin to near Hamilton, both corps crossing the Potomac at Berlin; the Artillery Reserve from Wheatland to Purcellville; and the Twelfth Corps from Pleasant Valley to near Hillsborough, crossing the Potomac and Shenandoah Rivers at Harper's Ferry. Buford's cavalry division moved from Purcellville, via Philomont, to near Rector's Cross-Roads. McIntosh's brigade, of Gregg's cavalry division, moved from Harper's Ferry toward Hillsborough, and Huey's and J. I. Gregg's brigades, of the same division, from Harper's Ferry to Lovettsville. Kilpatrick's division of cavalry marched from Purcellville to Upperville. Kelley's command, Department of West Virginia, fell back from Hedgesville to the Maryland side of the Potomac at Cherry Run.

July 20.—Headquarters Army of the Potomac moved from Wheatland to Union; the First Corps from Hamilton to Middleburg; the Second and Third Corps from Wood Grove, the former going to Bloomfield and the latter to Upperville; the Fifth Corps from a point on the Purcellville and Philomont road, via Union, to Panther Skin Creek ; the Sixth Corps from Wheatland to near Beaver Dam; the Eleventh Corps from near Hamilton, via Mount Gilead, to Mountville; the Twelfth Corps from near Hillsborough, via Wood Grove, to Snickersville; and the Artillery Reserve from Purcellville to Union. Buford's cavalry division moved from near Rector's Cross-Roads to Rectortown, Gamble's brigade going thence to Chester Gap, Devin's brigade to Salem, and Merritt's brigade to Manassas Gap. McIntosh's brigade, of Gregg's cavalry division, reached Hillsborough, and marched thence toward Purcellville. Huey's and J. I. Gregg's brigades, of same division, moved from Lovettsville to Goose Creek.

July 21.—Huey's and J. I. Gregg's brigades, of D. McM. Gregg's cavalry division, moved from Goose Creek to Bull Run; McIntosh's brigade returned to Hillsborough; Kelley's command, Department of West Virginia, recrossed the Potomac from Maryland into Virginia at Cherry Run.

July 22.—Headquarters Army of the Potomac moved from Union to Upperville; the First Corps from Middleburg to White Plains; the Second Corps from Bloomfield to Paris; the Third Corps from Upperville, via Piedmont, to Linden; the Fifth Corps from Panther Skin Creek to Rectortown; and the Sixth Corps from near Beaver Dam to Rectortown. Devin's brigade, of Buford's cavalry division, moved from Salem to Barbee's Cross-Roads; Huey's and J. I. Gregg's brigades, of D. McM. Gregg's cavalry division, from Bull Run to Broad Run; and Kilpatrick's cavalry division from Upperville to Piedmont.

July 23.—Headquarters Army of the Potomac moved from Upperville to Linden; the First Corps from White Plains to Warrenton; the Second Corps from Paris to Linden; the Third Corps from Linden to Manassas Gap; the Fifth Corps from Rectortown, via Markham Station, Farrowsville, and Linden, to Manassas Gap ; the Sixth Corps from Rectortown to White Plains and Barbee's Cross-Roads; the Eleventh Corps from Mountville to New Baltimore; the Twelfth Corps from Snickersville to Ashby's Gap and thence to Markham Station; and the Artillery Reserve from Union to near Rock Creek. Buford's cavalry division concentrated at Barbee's Cross-Roads; McIntosh's brigade, of Gregg's cavalry division, moved from Hillsborough to Snickersville; and Kilpatrick's cavalry division from Piedmont to Amissville.

July 24.—Headquarters Army of the Potomac moved from Linden to Salem; the Second Corps from Linden to Markham Station; the First Division (Wright's), Sixth Corps, from White Plains to New Baltimore; the Second Division (Howe's), Sixth Corps, from Barbee's Cross-Roads to Markham Station and thence to Orleans; the Third Division (Bartlett's), Sixth Corps, from Barbee's Cross-Roads to Thumb Run; and the Twelfth Corps from Markham Station to Linden, countermarching, via Markham Station, to Piedmont. Huey's and J. I. Gregg's brigades, of D. McM. Gregg's cavalry division, moved from Broad Run to Warrenton Junction. Kelley's command, Department of West Virginia, advanced from Cherry Run to Hedgesville.

July 25.—Headquarters Army of the Potomac moved from Salem to Warrenton; the First Corps from Warrenton to Warrenton Junction, the Second Division (Robinson's) going on to Bealeton; the Second Corps from Markham Station to White Plains; the Third Corps from Manassas Gap to near Salem; the Fifth Corps from Manassas Gap, via Farrowsville and Barbee's Cross-Roads, to Thumb Run; the Sixth Corps concentrated at Warrenton, Wright's (First) division moving from New Baltimore, Howe's (Second) division from Orleans, and Bartlett's (Third) division from Thumb Run; the Eleventh Corps moved from New Baltimore to Warrenton Junction; and the Twelfth Corps from Piedmont, via Rectortown and White Plains, to Thoroughfare Gap. The Artillery Reserve reached Warrenton. Kelley's command, Department of West Virginia, occupied Martinsburg.

July 26.—The Second Corps marched from White Plains to near Germantown; the Third Corps from near Salem to vicinity of Warrenton; the Fifth Corps from Thumb Run to vicinity of Warrenton, Crawford's (Third) division taking position at Fayetteville; and the Twelfth Corps from Thoroughfare Gap, via Greenwich and Catlett's Station, to Warrenton Junction. Buford's cavalry division took position at Warrenton and Fayetteville. McIntosh's brigade, of Gregg's cavalry division, marched from Snickersville, via Upperville, to Middleburg. Kelley's command, Department of West Virginia, occupied Winchester.

July 27.—The Fifth Corps encamped between Warrenton and Fayetteville. McIntosh's brigade, of Gregg's cavalry division, marched from Middleburg, via White Plains, New Baltimore, and Warrenton. toward Warrenton Junction.

July 28.—McIntosh's brigade, of Gregg's cavalry division. moved, via Warrenton Junction, to Catlett's Station.

July 29.—D. McM. Gregg's cavalry division moved from Warrenton Junction and Catlett's Station to Warrenton.

July 30.—Kenly's (Third) division, First Corps, moved from Warrenton Junction to Rappahannock Station; the Second Corps from near Germantown to Elk Run; D. McM. Gregg's cavalry division from Warrenton to Amissville; and Kilpatrick's cavalry division from Amissville to Warrenton.

July 31.—The Second Corps marched from Elk Run to Morrisville; Howe's (Second) division, Sixth Corps, from Warrenton to near Waterloo; the Twelfth Corps from Warrenton Junction to Kelly's Ford; and Kilpatrick's cavalry division from Warrenton to Warrenton Junction.

No. 8.

Abstract from returns of the Army of the Potomac, June 10–July 31, 1863.

JUNE 10, 1863.

Command	Present for duty.		Aggregate present.	Present for duty equipped.*						Pieces of artillery.
				Infantry.		Cavalry.		Artillery.		
	Officers.	Men.		Officers.	Men.	Officers.	Men.	Officers.	Men.	
General headquarters	56		56							
Provost-guard (Patrick)	107	1,720	2,096							
Engineer Brigade (Benham)	57	1,383	1,706							
Guards and orderlies (Ingalls)	2	46	55			2	50			
Signal Corps (Norton)	7	29	40							
First Army Corps (Reynolds)	772	11,340	14,603	723	10,540			21	599	28
Second Army Corps (Couch)	874	11,361	14,058	728	9,096	2	82	12	544	24
Third Army Corps (Sickles)	700	11,898	13,967	592	9,129			15	664	30
Fifth Army Corps (Meade)	630	10,136	12,623	592	9,229			23	896	42
Sixth Army Corps (Sedgwick)	979	15,408	18,774	1,034	14,238	5	120	29	988	48
Eleventh Army Corps (Howard)	527	10,177	12,867	482	9,294	4	43	16	694	24
Twelfth Army Corps (Slocum)	439	7,925	9,904	417	7,752			16	570	32
Cavalry Corps† (Pleasonton)	566	9,626	12,162							22
Artillery Reserve (Tyler)	106	2,864	3,189	21	325			85	2,589	160
Total	5,822	93,913	116,100	4,589	69,603	13	295	217	7,494	410

* Or actually available for the line of battle at the date of the regimental reports.
† From returns for May 31, the latest received when above return was prepared. But see p. 906.

JUNE 20, 1863.

Command	Officers.	Men.	Aggregate present.	Officers.	Men.	Officers.	Men.	Officers.	Men.	Pieces.
General headquarters	52		52							
Provost-guard (Patrick)	106	1,659	2,088							
Engineer Brigade (Benham)	35	731	864							
Guards and orderlies (Ingalls)	2	48	56			2	52			
Signal Corps (Norton)	5	29	38							
First Army Corps (Reynolds)	718	9,175	11,719	650	8,317			20	593	28
Second Army Corps (Hancock)	856	10,519	12,744	819	9,631	3	79	13	538	24
Third Army Corps (Birney)	803	11,849	13,984	750	10,504			17	651	30
Fifth Army Corps (Meade)	615	9,688	11,868	538	8,582					26
Sixth Army Corps (Sedgwick)	994	14,430	17,418	953	13,102	5	119	30	1,008	48
Eleventh Army Corps (Howard)	585	9,949	12,063	542	9,078	4	55	15	630	26
Twelfth Army Corps (Slocum)	520	8,188	9,961	496	7,802			11	377	20
Cavalry Corps* (Pleasonton)	566	9,626	12,162							22
Artillery Reserve (Tyler)	118	3,108	3,466	22	321			96	2,787	145
Total	5,975	88,999	108,433	4,770	67,337	14	305	202	6,584	369

* Taken from return for May 31, the last received, and does not account for Tidball's brigade of horse artillery.

JUNE 30, 1863.

Command	Officers.	Men.	Aggregate present.	Officers.	Men.	Officers.	Men.	Officers.	Men.	Pieces.
General headquarters	50		50							
Provost-guard (Patrick)	84	1,445	1,787							
Engineer Brigade (Benham)	40	906	1,131							
Guards and orderlies (Ingalls)	2	47	57							
Signal Corps (Norton)	6		6							
First Army Corps (Reynolds)	759	9,596	12,157	687	8,716			21	598	28
Second Army Corps (Hancock)	968	12,088	14,373	927	11,436	3	79	14	537	24
Third Army Corps (Sickles)	831	11,799	13,881	796	10,451			19	658	30
Fifth Army Corps (Sykes)	837	12,374	15,102	797	11,157			8	547	26
Sixth Army Corps (Sedgwick)	1,031	14,679	17,625	986	13,530	5	119	33	1,006	48
Eleventh Army Corps (Howard)	603	9,973	12,096	549	8,648	6	46	15	629	26
Twelfth Army Corps (Slocum)	541	8,056	9,816	521	7,672			12	384	20
Cavalry Corps* (Pleasonton)	773	14,200	17,104							50
Artillery Reserve (Tyler)	104	2,464	2,745	23	312			72	2,139	†110
Total	6,629	97,627	117,930	5,286	71,922	14	244	194	6,498	362

* From monthly return of the corps. The "present for duty equipped" not reported in original.
† The original reports 150 guns in Artillery Reserve, and a grand total of 402; but return of the Artillery Reserve gives only 110 guns.

Abstract from returns of the Army of the Potomac, &c.—Continued.

JULY 10, 1863.

Command.	Present for duty.		Aggregate present.	Present for duty equipped.						Pieces of artillery.
				Infantry.		Cavalry.		Artillery.		
	Officers.	Men.		Officers.	Men.	Officers.	Men.	Officers.	Men.	
General headquarters	39		39							
Provost-guard (Patrick)	82	1,419	1,734							
Engineer Brigade (Benham)	21	341	459							
Engineer Battalion (Mendell)	7	300	353							
Guards and orderlies (Ingalls)	2	51	57							
Signal Corps (Norton)	6		6							
First Army Corps (Newton)	429	4,363	6,091	372	3,509			18	515	24
Second Army Corps (Hays)	620	7,625	9,389	583	6,899	2	79	10	503	16
Third Army Corps (French)	896	13,506	15,779	779	11,543			35	1,079	51
Fifth Army Corps (Sykes)	668	9,401	11,835	636	8,241			8	432	22
Sixth Army Corps (Sedgwick)	991	13,654	16,351	926	12,320			27	955	48
Eleventh Army Corps (Howard)	412	6,483	8,206			5	110	11	570	24
Twelfth Army Corps (Slocum)	576	8,503	10,400	545	8,022	5	35	12	385	20
Cavalry Corps (Pleasonton)	612	11,230	13,717			567	10,242	20	672	50
Artillery Reserve (Tyler)	112	2,882	3,148	37	219			67	2,161	94
Total	5,473	79,758	97,564	3,878	50,753	579	10,466	208	7,272	349

JULY 20, 1863.

Command.	Present for duty.		Aggregate present.	Infantry.		Cavalry.		Artillery.		Pieces of artillery.
	Officers.	Men.		Officers.	Men.	Officers.	Men.	Officers.	Men.	
General headquarters	37		37							
Provost-guard (Patrick)	102	1,661	1,982							
Engineer Brigade (Benham)	22	301	426							
Engineer Battalion (Mendell)	9	291	354							
Guards and orderlies (Ingalls)	2	47	57							
Signal Corps (Norton)	6		6							
First Army Corps (Newton)	708	9,122	11,457	651	8,227			15	514	24
Second Army Corps (Hays)	625	7,731	9,546	598	6,872	2	76	14	622	26
Third Army Corps (French)	893	13,540	15,772	786	11,489			30	984	48
Fifth Army Corps (Sykes)	662	9,322	11,727	621	8,191			9	423	28
Sixth Army Corps (Sedgwick)	983	13,269	15,964	928	12,156			22	798	42
Eleventh Army Corps (Howard)	646	10,543	12,741	604	9,677	5	110			
Twelfth Army Corps (Slocum)	499	7,619	9,244	471	7,197	4	42	13	379	20
Cavalry Corps (Pleasonton)	596	10,896	13,409			537	9,591	25	903	64
Artillery Reserve (Tyler)	108	2,607	2,901	36	697	2	47	62	1,861	78
Total	5,898	86,949	105,623	4,695	64,506	550	9,866	190	6,484	330

JULY 31, 1863.

Command.	Present for duty.		Aggregate present.	Infantry.		Cavalry.		Artillery.		Pieces of artillery.
	Officers.	Men.		Officers.	Men.	Officers.	Men.	Officers.	Men.	
General headquarters	40		40							
Provost-guard (Patrick)	102	1,693	2,003							
Engineer Brigade (Benham)	23	320	452							
Engineer Battalion (Mendell)	7	310	379							
Guards and orderlies (Ingalls)	2	45	57							
Signal Corps (Norton)	6		6							
First Army Corps (Newton)	530	6,910	9,032	472	6,128			16	515	23
Second Army Corps (Hays)	525	7,151	8,933	516	6,426		60	13	527	22
Third Army Corps (French)	764	12,731	15,129	716	10,761			27	929	48
Fifth Army Corps (Sykes)	603	9,016	11,430	585	8,041			10	257	28
Sixth Army Corps (Sedgwick)	867	12,833	15,513	825	11,787	5	110	21	755	42
Eleventh Army Corps (Howard)	542	9,711	11,857	497	8,793	4	37	9	548	25
Twelfth Army Corps (Slocum)	445	7,328	8,950	412	6,925			12	370	20
Cavalry Corps (Pleasonton)	598	10,715	13,934			508	8,138	20	754	48
Artillery Reserve (Tyler)	91	2,160	2,437	18	265	2	47	60	1,750	80
Total	5,145	80,923	100,152	4,041	59,126	519	8,392	188	6,405	336

Consolidated field return of the Army of the Potomac.

JULY 4, 1863.

Command.	Strength.*				
	Infantry.		Artillery.		
	Officers.	Men.	Officers.	Men.	Aggregate.
First Army Corps:					
First Division	144	1,458			1,602
Second Division	124	906			1,030
Third Division	144	2,125			2,269
Artillery Brigade			12	517	529
Total First Army Corps†	412	4,489	12	517	5,430
Second Army Corps:					
First Division	152	1,694			1,846
Second Division	170	1,807			1,977
Third Division	209	2,422			2,631
Artillery Brigade				475	475
Total Second Army Corps	531	5,923		475	6,924
Third Army Corps:					
First Division	225	2,765			2,990
Second Division	213	2,367			2,580
Artillery Brigade			16	544	560
Total Third Army Corps	438	5,132	16	544	6,130
Fifth Army Corps:					
First Division	237	3,235			3,472
Second Division	188	2,834			3,022
Third Division	201	2,414			2,615
Artillery Brigade			14	430	444
Total Fifth Army Corps	626	8,483	14	430	9,553
Sixth Army Corps:					
First Division	287	3,886			4,173
Second Division	215	3,209			3,424
Third Division	281	3,947			4,228
Artillery Brigade			29	978	1,007
Total Sixth Army Corps	783	11,042	29	978	12,832
Eleventh Army Corps:					
First Division	66	1,116			1,182
Second Division	127	1,982			2,109
Third Division	108	1,620			1,728
Artillery Brigade‡			10	484	494
Total Eleventh Army Corps	301	4,718	10	484	5,513
Twelfth Army Corps;					
First Division	275	4,088			4,363
Second Division	167	3,287			3,454
Lockwood's brigade	83	1,379			1,462
10th Maine Infantry	6	164			170
Artillery Brigade§			9	299	308
Total Twelfth Army Corps	531	8,918	9	299	9,757
Grand total ‖	3,622	48,705	90	3,727	56,139

* Reported by the First, Second, Fifth, and Eleventh Corps as "present for duty;" by the Third Corps as "effective strength," and by the Twelfth Corps as "for duty equipped."
† One regiment detailed as wagon guard not reported.
‡ Does not include Battery K, First Ohio Light Artillery.
§ Does not include Battery M, First New York Light Artillery.
‖ General headquarters, the Cavalry Corps and Artillery Reserve not reported.

Consolidated field return of the Army of the Potomac—Continued.

JULY 14, 1863.

Command.	Strength.						Aggregate.
	Infantry.		Cavalry.		Artillery.		
	Officers.	Men.	Officers.	Men.	Officers.	Men.	
First Army Corps (Newton)	651	7,852	...	...	16	535	9,054
Second Army Corps (Hays)	575	6,973	3	12	17	725	8,305
Third Army Corps (French)	744	12,232	...	...	25	756	13,757
Fifth Army Corps (Sykes)	604	7,995	...	...	19	516	9,134
Sixth Army Corps (Sedgwick)	900	12,169	5	110	29	952	14,165
Eleventh Army Corps (Howard)	475	7,811	...	...	11	589	8,886
Twelfth Army Corps (Slocum)	546	8,118	...	...	12	385	9,061
Cavalry Corps (Pleasonton)	...	...	696	11,957	7	484	13,144
Artillery Reserve (Tyler)	...	...	...	...	88	2,409	2,497
Engineer Brigade (Benham)	21	341	...	...	...	...	362
Harper's Ferry, W. Va. (Naglee)	...	...	...	...	...	...	3,383
Frederick, Md	...	...	...	...	...	...	1,500
Maryland Heights, Md. (Briggs)	...	...	...	...	...	...	1,777
South Mountain, Md. (Spinola)	...	...	...	...	...	...	1,723
McReynolds' cavalry	...	...	...	...	...	...	2,184
Total	...	...	...	...	...	...	98,932

Field report of the Cavalry Corps, Army of the Potomac.

JUNE 28, 1863.

Command.	Officers.	Enlisted men.	Horses of officers.	Horses of enlisted men.	Officers sick.	Enlisted men sick.	Horses serviceable.	Horses unserviceable.
Corps headquarters	20	300	60	275	...	...	355	...
First Division	179	4,019	...	...	3	113	4,570	590
Second Division	266	4,347	...	...	7	156	4,534	834
Stahel's division	231	3,291	...	...	8	331	(*)	(*)
Brigade Horse Artillery	7	484	...	...	2	20	736	...
Total	708	12,441	60	275	20	620	10,195	1,424

* Major-General Stahel does not report the number of his horses.

A. J. ALEXANDER,
Assistant Adjutant-General.

Artillery in the Army of the Potomac, Brig. Gen. H. J. Hunt, U. S. Army, comdg.

JUNE 30, 1863.

Command.	Present for duty equipped.			Guns.						
				Rifled.				Smooth-bore.		
	Batteries.	Officers.	Enlisted men.	4½-inch.	20-pounder Parrotts.	3-inch.	10-pounder Parrotts.	12-pounders.	6-pounders.	Total.
First Army Corps	5	21	598	...	...	16	...	12	...	28
Second Army Corps	4	14	537	...	...	12	...	12	...	24
Third Army Corps	5	19	658	...	...	...	12	18	...	30
Fifth Army Corps	5	8	547	...	...	8	6	12	...	26
Sixth Army Corps	8	33	1,006	...	...	12	18	18	...	48
Eleventh Army Corps	5	15	629	...	...	10	...	16	...	26
Twelfth Army Corps	4	12	384	...	...	...	10	10	...	20
Cavalry Corps*	10	23	831	...	...	50	...	...	...	50
Artillery Reserve†	23	72	2,139	8	6	40	14	38	4	110
Total	69	217	7,329	8	6	148	60	136	4	362

* The "present for duty" given. No report of "present for duty equipped."
† The infantry train and headquarters' guards excluded. The 4½-inch guns were not at Gettysburg.

No. 9.

Organization of the Army of the Potomac, Maj. Gen. George G. Meade, U. S. Army, commanding, at the battle of Gettysburg, July 1–3, 1863.

GENERAL HEADQUARTERS.

COMMAND OF THE PROVOST-MARSHAL-GENERAL.

Brig. Gen. MARSENA R. PATRICK.

93d New York,* Col. John S. Crocker.
8th United States (eight companies),* Capt. Edwin W. H. Read.
2d Pennsylvania Cavalry, Col. R. Butler Price.
6th Pennsylvania Cavalry, Companies E and I, Capt. James Starr.
Regular cavalry (detachments from 1st, 2d, 5th, and 6th Regiments).

SIGNAL CORPS.

Capt. LEMUEL B. NORTON.

GUARDS AND ORDERLIES.

Oneida (New York) Cavalry, Capt. Daniel P. Mann.

ARTILLERY.†

Brig. Gen. HENRY J. HUNT.

ENGINEER BRIGADE.‡

Brig. Gen. HENRY W. BENHAM.

15th New York (three companies), Maj. Walter L. Cassin.
50th New York, Col. William H. Pettes.
United States Battalion, Capt. George H. Mendell.

FIRST ARMY CORPS.§

Maj. Gen. ABNER DOUBLEDAY.
Maj. Gen. JOHN NEWTON.

GENERAL HEADQUARTERS.

1st Maine Cavalry, Company L, Capt. Constantine Taylor.

FIRST DIVISION.

Brig. Gen. JAMES S. WADSWORTH.

First Brigade.

Brig. Gen. SOLOMON MEREDITH.
Col. WILLIAM W. ROBINSON.

19th Indiana, Col. Samuel J. Williams.
24th Michigan:
    Col. Henry A. Morrow.
    Capt. Albert M. Edwards.
2d Wisconsin:
    Col. Lucius Fairchild.
    Maj. John Mansfield.
    Capt. George H. Otis.
6th Wisconsin, Lieut. Col. Rufus R. Dawes.
7th Wisconsin:
    Col. William W. Robinson.
    Maj. Mark Finnicum.

Second Brigade.

Brig. Gen. LYSANDER CUTLER.

7th Indiana, Col. Ira G. Grover.
76th New York:
    Maj. Andrew J. Grover.
    Capt. John E. Cook.
84th New York (14th Militia), Col. Edward B. Fowler.
95th New York:
    Col. George H. Biddle.
    Maj. Edward Pye.
147th New York:
    Lieut. Col. Francis C. Miller.
    Maj. George Harney.
56th Pennsylvania (nine companies), Col. J. William Hofmann.

---

* Not engaged.
† See artillery brigades attached to army corps and the reserve.
‡ Not engaged.   With exception of the regular battalion, it was, July 1, and while at Beaver Dam Creek, Md., ordered to Washington, D. C., where it arrived July 3.
§ Maj. Gen. John F. Reynolds, of this corps, was killed July 1, while in command of the left wing of the army; General Doubleday commanded the corps July 1, and General Newton, who was assigned to that command on the 1st, superseded him July 2.

SECOND DIVISION.

Brig. Gen. JOHN C. ROBINSON.

First Brigade.	*Second Brigade.*
Brig. Gen. GABRIEL R. PAUL.	Brig. Gen. HENRY BAXTER.
Col. SAMUEL H. LEONARD.	
Col. ADRIAN R. ROOT.	12th Massachusetts:
Col. RICHARD COULTER.	Col. James L. Bates.
Col. PETER LYLE.	Lieut. Col. David Allen, jr.
Col. RICHARD COULTER.	83d New York (9th Militia), Lieut. Col.
	Joseph A. Moesch.
16th Maine:	97th New York:
Col. Charles W. Tilden.	Col. Charles Wheelock.
Maj. Archibald D. Leavitt.	Maj. Charles Northrup.
13th Massachusetts:	11th Pennsylvania:*
Col. Samuel H. Leonard.	Col. Richard Coulter.
Lieut. Col. N. Walter Batchel-	Capt. Benjamin F. Haines.
der.	Capt. John B. Overmyer.
94th New York:	88th Pennsylvania:
Col. Adrian R. Root.	Maj. Benezet F. Foust.
Maj. Samuel A. Moffett.	Capt. Henry Whiteside.
104th New York, Col. Gilbert G. Prey.	90th Pennsylvania:
107th Pennsylvania:	Col. Peter Lyle.
Lieut. Col. James MacThomson.	Maj. Alfred J. Sellers.
Capt. Emanuel D. Roath.	Col. Peter Lyle.

THIRD DIVISION.

Brig. Gen. THOMAS A. ROWLEY.
Maj. Gen. ABNER DOUBLEDAY.

First Brigade.	*Second Brigade.*
Col. CHAPMAN BIDDLE.	Col. ROY STONE.
Brig. Gen. THOMAS A. ROWLEY.	Col. LANGHORNE WISTER.
Col. CHAPMAN BIDDLE.	Col. EDMUND L. DANA.
80th New York (20th Militia), Col. Theo-	143d Pennsylvania:
dore B. Gates.	Col. Edmund L. Dana.
121st Pennsylvania:	Lieut. Col. John D. Musser.
Maj. Alexander Biddle.	149th Pennsylvania:
Col. Chapman Biddle.	Lieut. Col. Walton Dwight
Maj. Alexander Biddle.	Capt. James Glenn.
142d Pennsylvania:	150th Pennsylvania:
Col. Robert P. Cummins.	Col. Langhorne Wister.
Lieut. Col. A. B. McCalmont.	Lieut. Col. H. S. Huidekoper.
151st Pennsylvania:	Capt. Cornelius C. Widdis.
Lieut. Col. George F. McFarland.	
Capt. Walter L. Owens.	
Col. Harrison Allen.	

Third Brigade.

Brig. Gen. GEORGE J. STANNARD.
Col. FRANCIS V. RANDALL.

12th Vermont,† Col. Asa P. Blunt.
13th Vermont:
   Col. Francis V. Randall,
   Maj. Joseph J. Boynton.
   Lieut. Col. William D. Munson.
14th Vermont, Col. William T. Nichols.
15th Vermont,† Col. Redfield Proctor.
16th Vermont, Col. Wheelock G. Veazey.

---

* Transferred, in afternoon of July 1, to the First Brigade.
† Guarding trains, and not engaged in the battle.

ARTILLERY BRIGADE.

Col. CHARLES S. WAINWRIGHT.

Maine Light, 2d Battery (B), Capt. James A. Hall.
Maine Light, 5th Battery (E):
    Capt. Greenleaf T. Stevens.
    Lieut. Edward N. Whittier.
1st New York Light, Battery L:*
    Capt. Gilbert H. Reynolds.
    Lieut. George Breck.
1st Pennsylvania Light, Battery B, Capt. James H. Cooper.
4th United States, Battery B, Lieut. James Stewart.

SECOND ARMY CORPS.†

Maj. Gen. WINFIELD S. HANCOCK.
Brig. Gen. JOHN GIBBON.

GENERAL HEADQUARTERS.

6th New York Cavalry, Companies D and K, Capt. Riley Johnson.

FIRST DIVISION.

Brig. Gen. JOHN C. CALDWELL.

First Brigade.

Col. EDWARD E. CROSS.
Col. H. BOYD MCKEEN.

5th New Hampshire, Lieut. Col. Charles E. Hapgood.
61st New York, Lieut. Col. K. Oscar Broady.
81st Pennsylvania:
    Col. H. Boyd McKeen.
    Lieut. Col. Amos Stroh.
148th Pennsylvania, Lieut. Col. Robert McFarlane.

Second Brigade.

Col. PATRICK KELLY.

28th Massachusetts, Col. R. Byrnes.
63d New York (two companies):
    Lieut. Col. Richard C. Bentley.
    Capt. Thomas Touhy.
69th New York (two companies):
    Capt. Richard Moroney.
    Lieut. James J. Smith.
88th New York (two companies), Capt. Denis F. Burke.
116th Pennsylvania (four companies), Maj. St. Clair A. Mulholland.

Third Brigade.

Brig. Gen. SAMUEL K. ZOOK.
Lieut. Col. JOHN FRASER.

52d New York:
    Lieut. Col. C. G. Freudenberg.
    Capt. William Scherrer.
57th New York, Lieut. Col. Alford B. Chapman.
66th New York:
    Col. Orlando H. Morris.
    Lieut. Col. John S. Hammell.
    Maj. Peter Nelson.
140th Pennsylvania:
    Col. Richard P. Roberts.
    Lieut. Col. John Fraser.

Fourth Brigade.

Col. JOHN R. BROOKE.

27th Connecticut (two companies):
    Lieut. Col. Henry C. Merwin.
    Maj. James H. Coburn.
2d Delaware:
    Col. William P. Baily.
    Capt. Charles H. Christman.
64th New York:
    Col. Daniel G. Bingham.
    Maj. Leman W. Bradley.
53d Pennsylvania, Lieut. Col. Richards McMichael.
145th Pennsylvania (seven companies):
    Col. Hiram L. Brown.
    Capt. John W. Reynolds.
    Capt. Moses W. Oliver.

---

* Battery E, 1st New York Light Artillery, attached.
† After the death of General Reynolds, General Hancock was assigned to the command of all the troops on the field of battle, relieving General Howard, who had succeeded General Reynolds. General Gibbon, of the Second Division, assumed command of the corps. These assignments terminated on the evening of July 1. Similar changes in commanders occurred during the battle of the 2d, when General Hancock was put in command of the Third Corps, in addition to that of his own. He was wounded on the 3d, and Brig. Gen. William Hays was assigned to the command of the corps.

SECOND DIVISION.

Brig. Gen. JOHN GIBBON,
Brig. Gen. WILLIAM HARROW.

First Brigade.

Brig. Gen. WILLIAM HARROW.
Col. FRANCIS E. HEATH.

19th Maine:
    Col. Francis E. Heath.
    Lieut. Col. Henry W. Cunning-
      ham.
15th Massachusetts:
    Col. George H. Ward.
    Lieut. Col. George C. Joslin.
1st Minnesota:*
    Col. William Colvill, jr.
    Capt. Nathan S. Messick.
    Capt. Henry C. Coates.
82d New York (2d Militia):
    Lieut. Col. James Huston.
    Capt. John Darrow.

Second Brigade.

Brig. Gen. ALEXANDER S. WEBB.

69th Pennsylvania:
    Col. Dennis O'Kane.
    Capt. William Davis.
71st Pennsylvania, Col. Richard Penn
    Smith.
72d Pennsylvania:
    Col. De Witt C. Baxter.
    Lieut. Col. Theodore Hesser.
106th Pennsylvania, Lieut. Col. William
    L. Curry.

Third Brigade.

Col. NORMAN J. HALL.

19th Massachusetts, Col. Arthur F. Dev-
    ereux.
20th Massachusetts:
    Col. Paul J. Revere.
    Lieut. Col. George N. Macy.
    Capt. Henry L. Abbott.
7th Michigan:
    Lieut. Col. Amos E. Steele, jr.
    Maj. Sylvanus W. Curtis.
42d New York, Col. James E. Mallon.
59th New York (four companies):
    Lieut. Col. Max A. Thoman.
    Capt. William McFadden.

Unattached.

Massachusetts Sharpshooters, 1st Com-
    pany:
    Capt. William Plumer.
    Lieut. Emerson L. Bicknell.

THIRD DIVISION.

Brig. Gen. ALEXANDER HAYS.

First Brigade.

Col. SAMUEL S. CARROLL.

14th Indiana, Col. John Coons.
4th Ohio, Lieut. Col. Leonard W. Car-
    penter.
8th Ohio, Lieut. Col. Franklin Sawyer.
7th West Virginia, Lieut. Col. Jonathan
    H. Lockwood.

Second Brigade.

Col. THOMAS A. SMYTH.
Lieut. Col. FRANCIS E. PIERCE.

14th Connecticut, Maj. Theodore G.
    Ellis.
1st Delaware:
    Lieut. Col. Edward P. Harris.
    Capt. Thomas B. Hizar.
    Lieut. William Smith.
    Lieut. John T. Dent.
12th New Jersey, Maj. John T. Hill.
10th New York (battalion), Maj. George
    F. Hopper.
108th New York, Lieut. Col. Francis E.
    Pierce.

---

*2d Company Minnesota Sharpshooters attached.

Third Brigade.

Col. GEORGE L. WILLARD.
Col. ELIAKIM SHERRILL.
Lieut. Col. JAMES M. BULL.

39th New York (four companies), Maj. Hugo Hildebrandt.
111th New York:
 Col. Clinton D. MacDougall.
 Lieut. Col. Isaac M. Lusk.
 Capt. Aaron P. Seeley.
125th New York, Lieut. Col. Levin Crandell.
126th New York:
 Col. Eliakim Sherrill.
 Lieut. Col. James M. Bull.

ARTILLERY BRIGADE.

Capt. JOHN G. HAZARD.

1st New York Light, Battery B:*
 Lieut. Albert S. Sheldon.
 Capt. James McKay Rorty.
 Lieut. Robert E. Rogers.
1st Rhode Island Light, Battery A, Capt. William A. Arnold.
1st Rhode Island Light, Battery B:
 Lieut. T. Fred. Brown.
 Lieut. Walter S. Perrin.
1st United States, Battery I:
 Lieut. George A. Woodruff.
 Lieut. Tully McCrea.
4th United States, Battery A:
 Lieut. Alonzo H. Cushing.
 Sergt. Frederick Fuger.

THIRD ARMY CORPS.

Maj. Gen. DANIEL E. SICKLES.
Maj. Gen. DAVID B. BIRNEY.

FIRST DIVISION.

Maj. Gen. DAVID B. BIRNEY.
Brig. Gen. J. H. HOBART WARD.

First Brigade.

Brig. Gen. CHARLES K. GRAHAM.
Col. ANDREW H. TIPPIN.

57th Pennsylvania (eight companies):
 Col. Peter Sides.
 Capt. Alanson H. Nelson.
63d Pennsylvania, Maj. John A. Danks.
68th Pennsylvania:
 Col. Andrew H. Tippin.
 Capt. Milton S. Davis.[?]
105th Pennsylvania, Col. Calvin A. Craig.
114th Pennsylvania:
 Lieut. Col. Frederick F. Cavada.
 Capt. Edward R. Bowen.
141st Pennsylvania, Col. Henry J. Madill.

Second Brigade.

Brig. Gen. J. H. HOBART WARD.
Col. HIRAM BERDAN.

20th Indiana:
 Col. John Wheeler.
 Lieut. Col. William C. L. Taylor.
3d Maine, Col. Moses B. Lakeman.
4th Maine:
 Col. Elijah Walker.
 Capt. Edwin Libby.
86th New York, Lieut. Col. Benjamin L.
 Higgins.
124th New York:
 Col. A. Van Horne Ellis.
 Lieut. Col. Francis M. Cummins.
99th Pennsylvania, Maj. John W.
 Moore.
1st United States Sharpshooters:
 Col. Hiram Berdan.
 Lieut. Col. Casper Trepp.
2d United States Sharpshooters (eight
 companies), Maj. Homer R.
 Stoughton.

*Transferred from Artillery Reserve, July 1; 14th New York Battery attached.

Third Brigade.

Col. P. REGIS DE TROBRIAND.

17th Maine, Lieut. Col. Charles B. Merrill.
3d Michigan:
    Col. Byron R. Pierce.
    Lieut. Col. Edwin S. Pierce.
5th Michigan, Lieut. Col. John Pulford.
40th New York, Col. Thomas W. Egan.
110th Pennsylvania (six companies):
    Lieut. Col. David M. Jones.
    Maj. Isaac Rogers.

SECOND DIVISION.

Brig. Gen. ANDREW A. HUMPHREYS.

First Brigade.

Brig. Gen. JOSEPH B. CARR.

1st Massachusetts, Lieut. Col. Clark B.
    Baldwin.
11th Massachusetts, Lieut. Col. Porter D.
    Tripp.
16th Massachusetts:
    Lieut. Col. Waldo Merriam.
    Capt. Matthew Donovan.
12th New Hampshire, Capt. John F.
    Langley.
11th New Jersey:
    Col. Robert McAllister.
    Capt. Luther Martin.
    Lieut. John Schoonover.
    Capt. William H. Lloyd.
    Capt. Samuel T. Sleeper.
    Lieut. John Schoonover.
26th Pennsylvania, Maj. Robert L. Bo-
    dine.
84th Pennsylvania,* Lieut. Col. Milton
    Opp.

Second Brigade.

Col. WILLIAM R. BREWSTER.

70th New York, Col. J. Egbert Farnum.
71st New York, Col. Henry L. Potter.
72d New York:
    Col. John S. Austin.
    Lieut. Col. John Leonard.
73d New York, Maj. Michael W. Burns.
74th New York, Lieut. Col. Thomas
    Holt.
120th New York:
    Lieut. Col. Cornelius D. West-
    brook.
    Maj. John R. Tappen.

Third Brigade.

Col. GEORGE C. BURLING.

2d New Hampshire, Col. Edward L. Bailey.
5th New Jersey:
    Col. William J. Sewell.
    Capt. Thomas C. Godfrey.
    Capt. Henry H. Woolsey.
6th New Jersey, Lieut. Col. Stephen R. Gilkyson.
7th New Jersey:
    Col. Louis R. Francine.
    Maj. Frederick Cooper.
8th New Jersey:
    Col. John Ramsey.
    Capt. John G. Langston.
115th Pennsylvania, Maj. John P. Dunne.

---

*Guarding corps trains, and not engaged in the battle.

ARTILLERY BRIGADE.

Capt. GEORGE E. RANDOLPH.
Capt. A. JUDSON CLARK.

New Jersey Light, 2d Battery:
   Capt. A. Judson Clark.
   Lieut. Robert Sims.
1st New York Light, Battery D, Capt. George B. Winslow.
New York Light, 4th Battery, Capt. James E. Smith.
1st Rhode Island Light, Battery E:
   Lieut. John K. Bucklyn.
   Lieut. Benjamin Freeborn.
4th United States, Battery K:
   Lieut. Francis W. Seeley.
   Lieut. Robert James.

FIFTH ARMY CORPS.

Maj. Gen. GEORGE SYKES.

GENERAL HEADQUARTERS.

12th New York Infantry, Companies D and E, Capt. Henry W. Rider.
17th Pennsylvania Cavalry, Companies D and H, Capt. William Thompson.

FIRST DIVISION.

Brig. Gen. JAMES BARNES.

First Brigade.	*Second Brigade.*
Col. WILLIAM S. TILTON.	Col. JACOB B. SWEITZER.
18th Massachusetts, Col. Joseph Hayes.	9th Massachusetts, Col. Patrick R.
22d Massachusetts, Lieut. Col. Thomas	Guiney.
Sherwin, jr.	32d Massachusetts, Col. G. L. Prescott.
1st Michigan:	4th Michigan :
Col. Ira C. Abbott.	Col. Harrison H. Jeffords.
Lieut. Col. William A. Throop.	Lieut. Col. George W. Lumbard.
118th Pennsylvania, Lieut. Col. James	62d Pennsylvania, Lieut. Col. James C.
Gwyn.	Hull.

Third Brigade.

Col. STRONG VINCENT.
Col. JAMES C. RICE.

20th Maine, Col. Joshua L. Chamberlain.
16th Michigan, Lieut. Col. Norval E. Welch.
44th New York :
   Col. James C. Rice.
   Lieut. Col. Freeman Conner.
83d Pennsylvania, Capt. Orpheus S. Woodward.

SECOND DIVISION.

Brig. Gen. ROMEYN B. AYRES.

First Brigade.	*Second Brigade.*
Col. HANNIBAL DAY.	Col. SIDNEY BURBANK.
3d United States (six companies):	2d United States (six companies):
Capt. Henry W. Freedley.	Maj. Arthur T. Lee.
Capt. Richard G. Lay.	Capt. Samuel A. McKee.
4th United States (four companies),	7th United States (four companies),
Capt. Julius W. Adams, jr.	Capt. David P. Hancock.
6th United States (five companies),	10th United States (three companies),
Capt. Levi C. Bootes.	Capt. William Clinton.
12th United States (eight companies),	11th United States (six companies), Maj.
Capt. Thomas S. Dunn.	De Lancey Floyd-Jones.
14th United States (eight companies),	17th United States (seven companies),
Maj. Grotius R. Giddings.	Lieut. Col. J. Durell Greene.

Third Brigade.

Brig. Gen. STEPHEN H. WEED.
Col. KENNER GARRARD.

140th New York:
  Col. Patrick H. O'Rorke.
  Lieut. Col. Louis Ernst.
146th New York:
  Col. Kenner Garrard.
  Lieut. Col. David T. Jenkins.
91st Pennsylvania, Lieut. Col. Joseph H. Sinex.
155th Pennsylvania, Lieut. Col. John H. Cain.

THIRD DIVISION.*

Brig. Gen. SAMUEL W. CRAWFORD.

First Brigade.	*Third Brigade.*
Col. WILLIAM McCANDLESS.	Col. JOSEPH W. FISHER.
1st Pennsylvania Reserves (nine companies), Col. William C. Talley.	5th Pennsylvania Reserves, Lieut. Col. George Dare.
2d Pennsylvania Reserves, Lieut. Col. George A. Woodward.	9th Pennsylvania Reserves, Lieut. Col. James McK. Snodgrass.
6th Pennsylvania Reserves, Lieut. Col. Wellington H. Ent.	10th Pennsylvania Reserves, Col. Adoniram J. Warner.
13th Pennsylvania Reserves:	11th Pennsylvania Reserves, Col. Samuel M. Jackson.
Col. Charles F. Taylor.	12th Pennsylvania Reserves (nine companies), Col. Martin D. Hardin.
Maj. William R. Hartshorne.	

ARTILLERY BRIGADE.

Capt. AUGUSTUS P. MARTIN.

Massachusetts Light, 3d Battery (C), Lieut. Aaron F. Walcott.
1st New York Light, Battery C, Capt. Almont Barnes.
1st Ohio Light, Battery L, Capt. Frank C. Gibbs.
5th United States, Battery D:
  Lieut. Charles E. Hazlett.
  Lieut. Benjamin F. Rittenhouse.
5th United States, Battery I:
  Lieut. Malbone F. Watson.
  Lieut. Charles C. MacConnell.

SIXTH ARMY CORPS.

Maj. Gen. JOHN SEDGWICK.

GENERAL HEADQUARTERS.

1st New Jersey Cavalry, Company L, ⎰ Capt. William S. Craft.
1st Pennsylvania Cavalry, Company H, ⎱

FIRST DIVISION.

Brig. Gen. HORATIO G. WRIGHT.

Provost Guard.

4th New Jersey (three companies), Capt. William R. Maxwell.

First Brigade.	*Second Brigade.*
Brig. Gen. A. T. A. TORBERT.	Brig. Gen. JOSEPH J. BARTLETT.†
1st New Jersey, Lieut. Col. William Henry, jr.	5th Maine, Col. Clark S. Edwards.
2d New Jersey, Lieut. Col. Charles Wiebecke.	121st New York, Col. Emory Upton.
3d New Jersey, Lieut. Col. Edward L. Campbell.	95th Pennsylvania, Lieut. Col. Edward Carroll.
15th New Jersey, Col. William H. Penrose.	96th Pennsylvania, Maj. William H. Lessig.

---

*Joined corps June 28. The Second Brigade left in the Department of Washington.
†Also in command of the Third Brigade, Third Division, on July 3.

Third Brigade.

Brig. Gen. DAVID A. RUSSELL.

6th Maine, Col. Hiram Burnham.
49th Pennsylvania (four companies), Lieut. Col. Thomas M. Hulings.
119th Pennsylvania, Col. Peter C. Ellmaker.
5th Wisconsin, Col. Thomas S. Allen.

SECOND DIVISION.*

Brig. Gen. ALBION P. HOWE.

<table>
<tr><td>

Second Brigade.

Col. LEWIS A. GRANT.

2d Vermont, Col. James H. Walbridge.
3d Vermont, Col. Thomas O. Seaver.
4th Vermont, Col. Charles B. Stoughton.
5th Vermont, Lieut. Col. John R. Lewis.
6th Vermont, Col. Elisha L. Barney.

</td><td>

Third Brigade.

Brig. Gen. THOMAS H. NEILL.

7th Maine (six companies), Lieut. Col. Selden Connor.
33d New York (detachment), Capt. Henry J. Gifford.
43d New York, Lieut. Col. John Wilson.
49th New York, Col. Daniel D. Bidwell.
77th New York, Lieut. Col. Winsor B. French.
61st Pennsylvania, Lieut. Col. George F. Smith.

</td></tr>
</table>

THIRD DIVISION.

Maj. Gen. JOHN NEWTON.†
Brig. Gen. FRANK WHEATON.

<table>
<tr><td>

First Brigade.

Brig. Gen. ALEXANDER SHALER.

65th New York, Col. Joseph E. Hamblin.
67th New York, Col. Nelson Cross.
122d New York, Col. Silas Titus.
23d Pennsylvania, Lieut. Col. John F. Glenn.
82d Pennsylvania, Col. Isaac C. Bassett.

</td><td>

Second Brigade.

Col. HENRY L. EUSTIS.

7th Massachusetts, Lieut. Col. Franklin P. Harlow.
10th Massachusetts, Lieut. Col. Joseph B. Parsons.
37th Massachusetts, Col. Oliver Edwards.
2d Rhode Island, Col. Horatio Rogers, jr.

</td></tr>
</table>

Third Brigade.

Brig. Gen. FRANK WHEATON.
Col. DAVID J. NEVIN.

62d New York :
    Col. David J. Nevin.
    Lieut. Col. Theodore B. Hamilton.
93d Pennsylvania, Maj. John I. Nevin.
98th Pennsylvania, Maj. John B. Kohler.
102d Pennsylvania,‡ Col. John W. Patterson.
139th Pennsylvania:
    Col. Frederick H. Collier.
    Lieut. Col. William H. Moody.

ARTILLERY BRIGADE.

Col. CHARLES H. TOMPKINS.

Massachusetts Light, 1st Battery (A), Capt. William H. McCartney.
New York Light, 1st Battery, Capt. Andrew Cowan.
New York Light, 3d Battery, Capt. William A. Harn.
1st Rhode Island Light, Battery C, Capt. Richard Waterman.
1st Rhode Island Light, Battery G, Capt. George W. Adams.
2d United States, Battery D, Lieut. Edward B. Williston,
2d United States, Battery G, Lieut. John H. Butler.
5th United States, Battery F, Lieut. Leonard Martin.

---

* No First Brigade in division.
† See foot note (§), p. 155.
‡ Guarding wagon train at Westminster, and not engaged in the battle.

ELEVENTH ARMY CORPS.*

Maj. Gen. OLIVER O. HOWARD.

GENERAL HEADQUARTERS.

1st Indiana Cavalry, Companies I and K, Capt. Abram Sharra.
8th New York Infantry (one company), Lieut. Hermann Foerster.

FIRST DIVISION.

Brig. Gen. FRANCIS C. BARLOW.
Brig. Gen. ADELBERT AMES.

First Brigade.	*Second Brigade.*
Col. LEOPOLD VON GILSA.	Brig. Gen. ADELBERT AMES.
	Col. ANDREW L. HARRIS.
41st New York (nine companies), Lieut. Col. Detleo von Einsiedel.	17th Connecticut:
	Lieut. Col. Douglas Fowler.
54th New York:	Maj. Allen G. Brady.
Maj. Stephen Kovacs.	25th Ohio:
Lieut. Ernst Both [?].	Lieut. Col. Jeremiah Williams.
68th New York, Col. Gotthilf Bourry.	Capt. Nathaniel J. Manning.
153d Pennsylvania, Maj. John F. Frueauff.	Lieut. William Maloney.
	Lieut. Israel White.
	75th Ohio:
	Col. 'Andrew L. Harris.
	Capt. George B. Fox.
	107th Ohio:
	Col. Seraphim Meyer.
	Capt. John M. Lutz.

SECOND DIVISION.

Brig. Gen. ADOLPH VON STEINWEHR.

First Brigade.	*Second Brigade.*
Col. CHARLES R. COSTER.	Col. ORLAND SMITH.
134th New York, Lieut. Col. Allan H. Jackson.	33d Massachusetts, Col. Adin B. Underwood.
154th New York, Lieut. Col. D. B. Allen.	136th New York, Col. James Wood, jr.
27th Pennsylvania, Lieut. Col. Lorenz Cantador.	55th Ohio, Col. Charles B. Gambee.
73d Pennsylvania, Capt. D. F. Kelley.	73d Ohio, Lieut. Col. Richard Long.

THIRD DIVISION.

Maj. Gen. CARL SCHURZ.

First Brigade.	*Second Brigade.*
Brig. Gen. ALEX. SCHIMMELFENNIG.	Col. W. KRZYZANOWSKI.
Col. GEORGE VON AMSBERG.	
82d Illinois, Lieut. Col. Edward S. Salomon.	58th New York:
	Lieut. Col. August Otto.
45th New York :	Capt. Emil Koenig.
Col. George von Amsberg.	119th New York:
Lieut. Col. Adolphus Dobke.	Col. John T. Lockman.
157th New York, Col. Philip P. Brown, jr.	Lieut. Col. Edward F. Lloyd.
61st Ohio, Col. Stephen J. McGroarty.	82d Ohio:
74th Pennsylvania:	Col. James S. Robinson.
Col. Adolph von Hartung.	Lieut. Col. David Thomson.
Lieut. Col. Alexander von Mitzel.	75th Pennsylvania:
Capt. Gustav Schleiter.	Col. Francis Mahler.
Capt. Henry Krauseneck.	Maj. August Ledig.
	26th Wisconsin:
	Lieut. Col. Hans Boebel.
	Capt. John W. Fuchs.

---

* During the interval between the death of General Reynolds and the arrival of General Hancock, on the afternoon of July 1, all the troops on the field of battle were commanded by General Howard, General Schurz taking command of the Eleventh Corps, and General Schimmelfennig of the Third Division.

ARTILLERY BRIGADE.

Maj. Tʜᴏᴍᴀꜱ W. Oꜱʙᴏʀɴ.

1st New York Light, Battery I, Capt. Michael Wiedrich.
New York Light, 13th Battery, Lieut. William Wheeler.
1st Ohio Light, Battery I, Capt. Hubert Dilger.
1st Ohio Light, Battery K, Capt. Lewis Heckman.
4th United States, Battery G:
    Lieut. Bayard Wilkeson.
    Lieut. Eugene A. Bancroft.

TWELFTH ARMY CORPS.

Maj. Gen. Hᴇɴʀʏ W. Sʟᴏᴄᴜᴍ.*
Brig. Gen. Aʟᴘʜᴇᴜꜱ S. Wɪʟʟɪᴀᴍꜱ.

PROVOST GUARD.

10th Maine (four companies), Capt John D. Beardsley.

FIRST DIVISION.

Brig. Gen. Aʟᴘʜᴇᴜꜱ S. Wɪʟʟɪᴀᴍꜱ.
Brig. Gen. Tʜᴏᴍᴀꜱ H. Rᴜɢᴇʀ.

First Brigade.	*Second Brigade.†*
Col. Aʀᴄʜɪʙᴀʟᴅ L. McDᴏᴜɢᴀʟʟ.	Brig. Gen. Hᴇɴʀʏ H. Lᴏᴄᴋᴡᴏᴏᴅ,
5th Connecticut, Col. W. W. Packer.	1st Maryland, Potomac Home ⎱ ri-
20th Connecticut, Lieut. Col. William	gade, Col. William P. Maulsby.
B. Wooster.	1st Maryland, Eastern Shore, Col.
3d Maryland, Col. Jos. M. Sudsburg.	James Wallace.
123d New York:	150th New York, Col. John H. Ketcham.
Lieut. Col. James C. Rogers.	
Capt. Adolphus H. Tanner.	
145th New York, Col. E. L. Price.	
46th Pennsylvania, Col. James L. Sel-	
fridge.	

Third Brigade.

Brig. Gen. Tʜᴏᴍᴀꜱ H. Rᴜɢᴇʀ.
Col. Sɪʟᴀꜱ Cᴏʟɢʀᴏᴠᴇ.

27th Indiana:
    Col. Silas Colgrove.
    Lieut. Col. John R. Fesler.
2d Massachusetts:
    Lieut. Col. Charles R. Mudge.
    Maj. Charles F. Morse.
13th New Jersey, Col. Ezra A. Carman.
107th New York, Col. Nirom M. Crane.
3d Wisconsin, Col. William Hawley.

SECOND DIVISION.

Brig. Gen. Jᴏʜɴ W. Gᴇᴀʀʏ.

First Brigade.	*Second Brigade.*
Col. Cʜᴀʀʟᴇꜱ Cᴀɴᴅʏ.	Col. Gᴇᴏʀɢᴇ A. Cᴏʙʜᴀᴍ, Jr.
5th Ohio, Col. John H. Patrick.	Brig. Gᴇɴ. Tʜᴏᴍᴀꜱ L. Kᴀɴᴇ.
7th Ohio, Col. William R. Creighton.	Col. Gᴇᴏʀɢᴇ A. Cᴏʙʜᴀᴍ, Jr.
29th Ohio:	29th Pennsylvania, Col. William Rick-
Capt. Wilbur F. Stevens.	ards, jr.
Capt. Edward Hayes.	109th Pennsylvania, Capt. F. L. Gimber.
66th Ohio, Lieut. Col. Eugene Powell.	111th Pennsylvania:
28th Pennsylvania, Capt. John Flynn.	Lieut. Col. Thomas M. Walker.
147th Pennsylvania (eight companies),	Col. George A. Cobham, jr.
Lieut. Col. Ario Pardee, jr.	Lieut. Col. Thomas M. Walker.

---

* Exercised command of the right wing of the army during a part of the battle.
But see Slocum to Meade, December 30, 1863, p. 763, and Meade to Slocum, Febru-
ary 25, 1864, p. 769.
† Unassigned during progress of battle; afterward attached to First Division, as
Second Brigade. The command theretofore known as the Second (or Jackson's)
Brigade had previously been consolidated with the First Brigade.

Third Brigade.

Brig. Gen. GEORGE S. GREENE.

60th New York, Col. Abel Godard.
78th New York, Lieut. Col. Herbert von Hammerstein.
102d New York:
　　Col. James C. Lane.
　　Capt. Lewis R. Stegman.
137th New York, Col. David Ireland.
149th New York:
　　Col. Henry A. Barnum.
　　Lieut. Col. Charles B. Randall.

ARTILLERY BRIGADE.

Lieut. EDWARD D. MUHLENBERG.

1st New York Light, Battery M, Lieut. Charles E. Winegar.
Pennsylvania Light, Battery E, Lieut. Charles A. Atwell.
4th United States, Battery F, Lieut. Sylvanus T. Rugg.
5th United States, Battery K, Lieut. David H. Kinzie.

CAVALRY CORPS.

Maj. Gen. ALFRED PLEASONTON.

FIRST DIVISION.

Brig. Gen. JOHN BUFORD.

First Brigade.	*Second Brigade.*
Col. WILLIAM GAMBLE.	Col. THOMAS C. DEVIN.
8th Illinois, Maj. John L. Beveridge. 12th Illinois (four cos.),) Col. George H. 3d Indiana (six cos.),) Chapman. 8th New York, Lieut. Col. William L. Markell.	6th New York, Maj. Wm. E. Beardsley. 9th New York, Col. William Sackett. 17th Pennsylvania, Col. J. H. Kellogg. 3d West Virginia (two companies), Capt. Seymour B. Conger.

Reserve Brigade.

Brig. Gen. WESLEY MERRITT.

6th Pennsylvania, Maj. James H. Haseltine.
1st United States, Capt. Richard S. C. Lord.
2d United States, Capt. T. F. Rodenbough.
5th United States, Capt. Julius W. Mason.
6th United States:
　　Maj. Samuel H. Starr.
　　Lieut. Louis H. Carpenter.
　　Lieut. Nicholas Nolan.
　　Capt. Ira W. Claflin.

SECOND DIVISION.

Brig. Gen. DAVID McM. GREGG.

Headquarters Guard.

1st Ohio, Company A, Capt. Noah Jones.

First Brigade.	*Second Brigade.‡*
Col. JOHN B. McINTOSH.	Col. PENNOCK HUEY.
1st Maryland (eleven companies), Lieut. Col. James M. Deems. Purnell (Maryland) Legion, Company A, Capt. Robert E. Duvall. 1st Massachusetts,* Lieut. Col. Greely S. Curtis. 1st New Jersey, Maj. M. H. Beaumont. 1st Pennsylvania, Col. John P. Taylor. 3d Pennsylvania, Lieut. Col. E. S. Jones. 3d Pennsylvania Heavy Artillery, Section Battery H,† Capt. W. D. Rank.	2d New York, Lieut. Col. Otto Harhaus. 4th New York, Lieut. Col. Augustus Pruyn. 6th Ohio (ten companies), Maj. William Stedman. 8th Pennsylvania, Capt. William A. Corrie.

---

*Served with the Sixth Army Corps, and on the right flank.
†Serving as light artillery.
‡At Westminster, etc., and not engaged in the battle.

Third Brigade.

Col. J. IRVIN GREGG.

1st Maine (ten companies), Lieut. Col. Charles H. Smith.
10th New York, Maj. M. Henry Avery.
4th Pennsylvania, Lieut. Col. William E. Doster.
16th Pennsylvania, Lieut. Col. John K. Robison.

THIRD DIVISION.

Brig. Gen. JUDSON KILPATRICK.

Headquarters Guard.

1st Ohio, Company C, Capt. Samuel N. Stanford.

First Brigade.	*Second Brigade.*
Brig. Gen. ELON J. FARNSWORTH. Col. NATHANIEL P. RICHMOND.	Brig. Gen. GEORGE A. CUSTER.
5th New York, Maj. John Hammond. 18th Pennsylvania, Lieut. Col. William P. Brinton. 1st Vermont, Lieut. Col. Addison W. Preston. 1st West Virginia (ten companies): Col. Nathaniel P. Richmond. Maj. Charles E. Capehart.	1st Michigan, Col. Charles H. Town. 5th Michigan, Col. Russell A. Alger. 6th Michigan, Col. George Gray. 7th Michigan (ten companies), Col. William D. Mann.

HORSE ARTILLERY.

First Brigade.	*Second Brigade.*
Capt. JAMES M. ROBERTSON.	Capt. JOHN C. TIDBALL.
9th Michigan Battery, Capt. Jabez J. Daniels. 6th New York Battery, Capt. Joseph W. Martin. 2d United States, Batteries B and L, Lieut. Edward Heaton. 2d United States, Battery M, Lieut. A. C. M. Pennington, jr. 4th United States, Battery E, Lieut. Samuel S. Elder.	1st United States, Batteries E and G, Capt. Alanson M. Randol. 1st United States, Battery K, Capt. William M. Graham. 2d United States, Battery A, Lieut. John H. Calef. 3d United States, Battery C, Lieut. William D. Fuller.*

ARTILLERY RESERVE.

Brig. Gen. ROBERT O. TYLER.
Capt. JAMES M. ROBERTSON.

Headquarters Guard.

32d Massachusetts Infantry, Company C, Capt. Josiah C. Fuller.

First Regular Brigade.	*First Volunteer Brigade.*
Capt. DUNBAR R. RANSOM.	Lieut. Col. FREEMAN McGILVERY.
1st United States, Battery H: Lieut. Chandler P. Eakin. Lieut. Philip D. Mason. 3d United States, Batteries F and K, Lieut. John G. Turnbull. 4th United States, Battery C, Lieut. Evan Thomas. 5th United States, Battery C, Lieut. Gulian V. Weir.	Massachusetts Light, 5th Battery (E),† Capt. Charles A. Phillips. Massachusetts Light, 9th Battery: Capt. John Bigelow. Lieut. Richard S. Milton. New York Light, 15th Battery, Capt. Patrick Hart. Pennsylvania Light, Batteries C and F, Capt. James Thompson.

---

* With Huey's Cavalry Brigade, and not engaged in the battle.
† 10th New York Battery attached.

Second Volunteer Brigade.

Capt. ELIJAH D. TAFT.

1st Connecticut Heavy, Battery B,* Capt.
   Albert F. Brooker.
1st Connecticut Heavy, Battery M,* Capt.
   Franklin A. Pratt.
Connecticut Light, 2d Battery, Capt.
   John W. Sterling.
New York Light, 5th Battery, Capt.
   Elijah D. Taft.

Third Volunteer Brigade.

Capt. JAMES F. HUNTINGTON.

New Hampshire Light, 1st Battery, Capt.
   Frederick M. Edgell.
1st Ohio Light, Battery H, Lieut. George
   W. Norton.
1st Pennsylvania Light, Batteries F and
   G, Capt. R. Bruce Ricketts.
West Virginia Light, Battery C, Capt.
   Wallace Hill.

Fourth Volunteer Brigade.

Capt. ROBERT H. FITZHUGH.

Maine Light, 6th Battery (F), Lieut. Edwin B. Dow.
Maryland Light, Battery A, Capt. James H. Rigby.
New Jersey Light, 1st Battery, Lieut. Augustin N. Parsons.
1st New York Light, Battery G, Capt. Nelson Ames.
1st New York Light, Battery K,† Capt. Robert H. Fitzhugh.

Train Guard.

4th New Jersey Infantry (seven companies), Maj. Charles Ewing.

No. 10.

Return of Casualties in the Union forces at Brandy Station (Fleet-wood), Beverly Ford, and Stevensburg, Va., June 9, 1863.

[Compiled from nominal list of casualties, returns, &c.]

Command.	Killed.		Wounded.		Captured or missing.		Aggregate.
	Officers.	Enlisted men.	Officers.	Enlisted men.	Officers.	Enlisted men.	
CAVALRY CORPS.							
Brig. Gen. ALFRED PLEASONTON.							
FIRST DIVISION.							
Brig. Gen. JOHN BUFORD.‡							
Staff..	.. ..	.. ..	......	....	1	....	1
First Brigade.							
Col. BENJAMIN F. DAVIS.							
8th Illinois...................................	......	1	4	42	......	3	50
3d Indiana..................................	......	1	1	22	......	......	24
8th New York................................	3	9	2	29	......	7	50
2d U. S. Artillery, Batteries B and L......	......	....	......	3	......	....	3
Total First Brigade	3	11	7	96	......	10	127
Second Brigade.							
Col. THOMAS C. DEVIN.							
6th New York................................	......	....	1	3	......	....	4
9th New York................................	......	....	2	13	......	1	16
7th Pennsylvania............................	......	....	1	2	......	....	3
3d West Virginia	......	....	......	3	......	....	3
Total Second Brigade	......	....	4	21	......	1	26
Total First Division.......................	3	11	11	117	1	11	154

* Not engaged.
† 11th New York Battery attached.
‡ Had command of the right wing, consisting of the First Cavalry Division and the Cavalry Reserve Brigade, and a brigade of infantry under Brig. Gen. Adelbert Ames.

Return of Casualties in the Union forces, &c.—Continued.

Command.	Killed.		Wounded.		Captured or missing.		Aggregate.
	Officers.	Enlisted men.	Officers.	Enlisted men.	Officers.	Enlisted men.	
RESERVE BRIGADE.							
Maj. CHARLES J. WHITING.							
6th Pensylvania	1	4	2	23	3	75	108
1st United States		1		1		.....	2
2d United States	1	10	4	25	3	23	66
5th United States		6	2	15	.....	15	38
6th United States	1	7	1	25	2	30	66
4th U. S. Artillery, Battery E							
Total Reserve Brigade	3	28	9	89	8	143	280
SECOND DIVISION.*							
Col. ALFRED N. DUFFIÉ.							
First Brigade.							
Col. LOUIS P. DI CESNOLA.							
1st Massachusetts		2		9		5	16
6th Ohio				2		1	3
1st Rhode Island		2				3	5
Total First Brigade		4		11		9	24
Second Brigade.							
Col. J. IRVIN GREGG.							
3d Pennsylvania							
4th Pennsylvania				1		4	5
16th Pennsylvania							
Total Second Brigade				1		4	5
Artillery.							
2d United States, Battery M							
Total Second Division		4		12		13	29
THIRD DIVISION.							
Brig. Gen. DAVID McM. GREGG.†							
Staff					1		1
First Brigade.							
Col. JUDSON KILPATRICK.							
1st Maine				10		25	35
2d New York		4	1	13		21	39
10th New York	1	2	3	15	1	60	82
Orton's Company District of Columbia							
Total First Brigade	1	6	4	38	1	106	156
Second Brigade.							
Col. PERCY WYNDHAM.							
1st Maryland	1	5	3	10	2	42	63
1st New Jersey	2	5	4	17		24	52
1st Pennsylvania		5	3	15		12	35
Total Second Brigade	3	15	10	42	2	78	150

* The losses of this division occurred in skirmish at Stevensburg.
† Had command of the left wing, consisting of the Second and Third Cavalry Divisions, and a brigade of infantry under Brig. Gen. David A. Russell.

Return of Casualties in the Union forces, &c.—Continued.

Command.	Killed.		Wounded.		Captured or missing.		Aggregate.
	Officers.	Enlisted men.	Officers.	Enlisted men.	Officers.	Enlisted men.	
Artillery.							
New York Light, 6th Battery...........	......	......	......	8	......	13	21
Total Third Division...............	4	21	14	88	4	197	328
ATTACHED TROOPS.*							
Brig. Gen. ADELBERT AMES.							
2d Massachusetts...............	......	1	......	3	......	2	6
33d Massachusetts...............	......	......	......	3	......	......	3
86th New York..................	......	2	......	24	......	......	26
124th New York.................	......	2	1	11	......	......	14
3d Wisconsin..................	......	1	......	14	......	......	15
1st U. S. Artillery, Battery K......	......	......	......	2	......	......	2
Total...................	......	6	1	57	......	2	66
ATTACHED TROOPS.†							
Brig. Gen. DAVID A. RUSSELL.							
2d Wisconsin..................	......	......	......	......	......	......	......
7th Wisconsin..................	......	......	......	......	......	......	......
56th Pennsylvania...............	......	1	......	5	......	3	9
Total...................	......	1	......	5	......	3	9
Grand total...............	10	71	35	368	13	369	866

OFFICERS KILLED.

MARYLAND.

Capt. Francis M. Kreager, 1st Cavalry.

NEW JERSEY.

Lieut. Col. Virgil Brodrick, 1st Cavalry. | Maj. John H. Shelmire, 1st Cavalry.

NEW YORK.

Col. Benjamin F. Davis, 8th Cavalry. | Lieut. Henry C. Cutler, 8th Cavalry.
Capt. Benjamin F. Foote, 8th Cavalry. | Lieut. William J. Robb, 10th Cavalry.

PENNSYLVANIA.

Capt. Charles B. Davis, 6th Cavalry.

UNITED STATES ARMY.

Capt. Charles W. Canfield, 2d Cavalry. | Lieut. Isaac M. Ward, 6th Cavalry.

OFFICERS MORTALLY WOUNDED.

ILLINOIS.

Maj. Alpheus Clark, 8th Cavalry. | Capt. John G. Smith, 8th Cavalry.

NEW YORK.

Lieut. William W. Phillips, 6th Cavalry. | Lieut. James E. Reeves, 8th Cavalry.
Lieut. Benjamin C. Efner, 8th Cavalry. | Lieut. John B. King, 10th Cavalry.

* With right wing.   † With left wing.

No. 11.

Return of Casualties in the Union forces at Aldie, Va., June 17, 1863.

[Compiled from nominal list of casualties, returns, &c.]

Command.	Killed.		Wounded.		Captured or missing.		Aggregate.
	Officers.	Enlisted men.	Officers.	Enlisted men.	Officers.	Enlisted men.	
1st Maine Cavalry	2	4	......	19	......	4	29
1st Massachusetts Cavalry	......	20	4	53	4	86	167
2d New York Cavalry	2	14	3	16	......	15	50
4th New York Cavalry	......	5	......	22	2	13	42
6th Ohio Cavalry	......	3	2	12	......	......	17
Total	4	46	9	122	6	118	305

OFFICERS KILLED.

MAINE.

Lieut. Calvin S. Douty, 1st Cavalry. | Capt. George J. Summat, 1st Cavalry.

NEW YORK.

Lieut. A. F. Martenson, 2d Cavalry. | Lieut. Daniel Whittaker, 2d Cavalry.

OFFICERS MORTALLY WOUNDED.

OHIO.

Maj. Benjamin C. Stanhope, 6th Cavalry.

No. 12.

Return of Casualties in the Union forces at Upperville, Va., June 21, 1863.

[Compiled from nominal list of casualties, returns, &c.]

Command.	Killed.		Wounded.		Captured or missing.		Aggregate.
	Officers.	Enlisted men.	Officers.	Enlisted men.	Officers.	Enlisted men.	
CAVALRY CORPS.							
Brig. Gen. ALFRED PLEASONTON.							
FIRST DIVISION.							
Brig. Gen. JOHN BUFORD.							
First Brigade.							
Col. WILLIAM GAMBLE.							
8th Illinois	......	2	......	17	......	......	19
12th Illinois	......	2	1	13	......	4	20
3d Indiana	......	......	......	4	......	1	5
8th New York	......	......	......	......	......	......	......
Total First Brigade	......	4	1	34	......	5	44

Return of Casualties in the Union forces at Upperville, Va. &c.—Continued.

Command.	Killed.		Wounded.		Captured or missing.		Aggregate.
	Officers.	Enlisted men.	Officers.	Enlisted men.	Officers.	Enlisted men.	
Second Brigade.							
Col. THOMAS C. DEVIN.							
6th New York							
9th New York							
17th Pennsylvania			1	7			8
3d West Virginia							
Total Second Brigade........			1	7			8
Reserve Brigade.							
Maj. SAMUEL H. STARR.							
6th Pennsylvania							
1st United States		1	2	11		39	53
2d United States							
5th United States		1					1
6th United States...........			1	5		3	9
Total Reserve Brigade.......		2	3	16		42	63
Artillery.							
1st United States, Battery K							
Total First Division		6	5	57		47	115
SECOND DIVISION.							
Brig. Gen. DAVID McM. GREGG.							
Second Brigade.							
Brig. Gen. JUDSON KILPATRICK.							
1st Massachusetts							
2d New York................		1	1	4			6
4th New York...............			1	17	1	8	27
6th Ohio		1	3	13		7	24
Total Second Brigade.....		2	5	34	1	15	57
Third Brigade.							
Col. J. IRVIN GREGG.							
1st Maine...................			1	6		2	9
4th Pennsylvania............		1		3		2	6
3d U. S. Artillery, Battery C		1					1
Total Third Brigade		2	1	9		4	16
Total Second Division		4	6	43	1	19	73
ATTACHED INFANTRY.							
Col. STRONG VINCENT.							
20th Maine..................		1		7			8
16th Michigan...............			2	7			9
44th New York..............		1		2			3
83d Pennsylvania............				1			1
Total Attached Infantry......		2	2	17			21
Grand total		12	13	117	1	66	209

OFFICERS MORTALLY WOUNDED.

ILLINOIS.

Lieut. John G. Smith, 8th Cavalry.

MICHIGAN.

Capt. Judd M. Mott, 16th Infantry.

No. 13.

Return of Casualties in the Union forces, commanded by Maj. Gen. George G. Meade, U. S. Army, at the battle of Gettysburg, Pa., July 1–3, 1863. *

Command.	Killed.		Wounded.		Captured or missing.		Aggregate.
	Officers.	Enlisted men.	Officers.	Enlisted men.	Officers.	Enlisted men.	
GENERAL HEADQUARTERS.							
Staff..			2	2			4
FIRST ARMY CORPS.							
Maj. Gen. JOHN F. REYNOLDS.†							
Maj. Gen. ABNER DOUBLEDAY.							
Maj. Gen. JOHN NEWTON.							
GENERAL HEADQUARTERS.							
Staff..	1		1				2
1st Maine Cavalry, Company L....................		1		2			3
FIRST DIVISION.							
Brig. Gen. JAMES S. WADSWORTH.							
First Brigade.							
Brig. Gen. SOLOMON MEREDITH.							
Col. WILLIAM W. ROBINSON.							
Staff			1				1
19th Indiana...................................	2	25	12	121	4	46	210
24th Michigan..................................	8	59	13	197	3	83	363
2d Wisconsin...................................	1	25	11	144	5	47	233
6th Wisconsin..................................	2	28	7	109		22	168
7th Wisconsin..................................		21	10	95	1	51	178
Total First Brigade......................	13	158	54	666	13	249	1,153
Second Brigade.							
Brig. Gen. LYSANDER CUTLER.							
7th Indiana....................................		2		5		3	10
76th New York	2	30	16	116		70	234
84th New York (14th Militia)....................		13	6	99		99	217
95th New York		7	8	54	1	45	115
147th New York	3	57	9	135		92	296
56th Pennsylvania..............................	1	13	5	56	1	54	130
Total Second Brigade	6	122	44	465	2	363	1,002
Total First Division............	19	280	98	1,131	15	612	2,155
SECOND DIVISION.							
Brig. Gen. JOHN C. ROBINSON.							
Staff...			1				1
First Brigade.							
Brig. Gen. GABRIEL R. PAUL.							
Col. SAMUEL H. LEONARD.							
Col. ADRIAN R. ROOT.							
Col. RICHARD COULTER.							
Col. PETER LYLE.							
Col. RICHARD COULTER.							
Staff...			1	1	2	1	5
16th Maine.....................................	2	7	5	54	11	153	232
13th Massachusetts.............................		7	4	73	3	98	185
94th New York		12	6	52	8	167	245
104th New York		11	10	81	10	82	194
11th Pennsylvania‡.............................		1	2	12			15
107th Pennsylvania.............................		11	8	48	6	92	165
Total First Brigade......................	2	49	36	321	40	593	1,041

* Also includes losses in skirmishes, July 4.
† See foot-note (§) on p. 155.
‡ Transferred, on afternoon of July 1, from the Second to the First Brigade. Its losses after July 1 are reported with the latter brigade.

Return of Casualties in the Union forces, &c.—Continued.

Command.	Killed. Officers.	Killed. Enlisted men.	Wounded. Officers.	Wounded. Enlisted men.	Captured or missing. Officers.	Captured or missing. Enlisted men.	Aggregate.
Second Brigade.							
Brig. Gen. HENRY BAXTER.							
Staff					1		1
12th Massachusetts	2	3	7	45	3	59	119
83d New York (9th Militia)	2	4	3	15	.....	58	82
97th New York	2	10	9	27	3	75	126
11th Pennsylvania*	.....	5	6	46	.....	60	117
88th Pennsylvania	.....	4	3	52	4	47	110
90th Pennsylvania	1	7	3	42	1	39	93
Total Second Brigade	7	33	31	227	12	338	648
Total Second Division	9	82	68	548	52	931	1,690
THIRD DIVISION.							
Brig. Gen. THOMAS A. ROWLEY.							
Maj. Gen. ABNER DOUBLEDAY.							
Staff			1				1
First Brigade.							
Col. CHAPMAN BIDDLE.							
Brig. Gen. THOMAS A. ROWLEY.							
Col. CHAPMAN BIDDLE.							
Staff			1				1
80th New York (20th Militia)	3	32	15	96	1	23	170
121st Pennsylvania	.....	12	5	101	1	60	179
142d Pennsylvania	3	10	11	117	2	68	211
151st Pennsylvania	2	49	9	202	4	71	337
Total First Brigade	8	103	41	516	8	222	898
Second Brigade.							
Col. ROY STONE.							
Col. LANGHORNE WISTER.							
Col. EDMUND L. DANA.							
143d Pennsylvania	1	20	11	130	.....	91	253
149th Pennsylvania	1	52	14	158	4	107	336
150th Pennsylvania	2	33	10	142	4	73	264
Total Second Brigade	4	105	35	430	8	271	853
Third Brigade.							
Brig. Gen. GEORGE J. STANNARD.							
Col. FRANCIS V. RANDALL.							
Staff			2				2
13th Vermont	.....	10	4	99	.....	10	123
14th Vermont	1	18	1	66	.....	21	107
16th Vermont	.....	16	5	97	.....	1	119
Total Third Brigade	1	44	12	262	.....	32	351
Total Third Division	13	252	89	1,208	16	525	2,103
ARTILLERY BRIGADE.							
Col. CHARLES S. WAINWRIGHT.							
Maine Light, 2d Battery (B)	.....	.....	.....	18	.....	.....	18
Maine Light, 5th Battery (E)	.....	3	2	11	.....	7	23
1st New York Light, Battery L†	.....	1	1	14	.....	1	17
1st Pennsylvania Light, Battery B	.....	3	1	8	.....		12
4th United States, Battery B	.....	2	2	29	.....	3	36
Total Artillery Brigade	.....	9	6	80	.....	11	106
Total First Army Corps	42	624	162	2,969	83	2,079	6,059

*Transferred, on afternoon of July 1, from the Second to the First Brigade. Its losses after July 1 are reported with the latter brigade.
†Battery E, 1st New York Light Artillery, attached.

Return of Casualties in the Union forces, &c.—Continued.

Command.	Killed.		Wounded.		Captured or missing.		Aggregate.
	Officers.	Enlisted men.	Officers.	Enlisted men.	Officers.	Enlisted men.	
SECOND ARMY CORPS.							
Maj. Gen. WINFIELD S. HANCOCK.* Brig. Gen. JOHN GIBBON.							
GENERAL HEADQUARTERS.							
Staff..	......	......	3	......	......	......	3
6th New York Cavalry, Companies D and K	......	1	......	3	......	......	4
FIRST DIVISION.							
Brig. Gen. JOHN C. CALDWELL.							
First Brigade.							
Col. EDWARD E. CROSS. Col. H. BOYD McKEEN.							
Staff..	......	......	1	......	......	......	1
5th New Hampshire............................	1	26	4	49	......	......	80
61st New York	......	6	6	50	......	......	62
81st Pennsylvania..............................	......	5	5	44	......	8	62
148th Pennsylvania.............................	1	18	6	95	......	5	125
Total First Brigade	2	55	22	238	......	13	330
Second Brigade.							
Col. PATRICK KELLY.							
28th Massachusetts..	......	8	1	56	......	35	100
62d New York	......	5	1	9	1	7	23
69th New York	......	5	1	13	......	6	25
88th New York	1	6	1	16	......	4	28
116th Pennsylvania	......	2	......	11	1	8	22
Total Second Brigade	1	26	4	105	2	60	198
Third Brigade.							
Brig. Gen. SAMUEL K. ZOOK. Lieut. Col. JOHN FRASER.							
Staff..	1	......	......	......	......	......	1
52d New York	1	1	3	23	......	10	38
57th New York ....:...................	......	4	2	26	......	2	34
66th New York	2	3	5	24	1	9	44
140th Pennsylvania	3	34	8	136	3	57	241
Total Third Brigade	7	42	18	209	4	78	358
Fourth Brigade.							
Col. JOHN R. BROOKE.							
27th Connecticut	2	8	4	19	......	4	37
2d Delaware..................................	2	9	7	54	......	12	84
64th New York	4	11	7	57	......	19	98
53d Pennsylvania..............................	......	7	11	56	......	6	80
145th Pennsylvania...	......	11	9	60	......	10	90
Total Fourth Brigade	8	46	38	246	......	51	389
Total First Division	18	169	82	798	6	202	1,275
SECOND DIVISION.							
Brig. Gen. JOHN GIBBON. Brig. Gen. WILLIAM HARROW.							
Staff..	......	......	3	......	......	......	3

*See foot-note (†) on p. 157.

Return of Casualties in the Union forces, &c.—Continued.

Command.	Killed.		Wounded.		Captured or missing.		Aggregate.
	Officers.	Enlisted men.	Officers.	Enlisted men.	Officers.	Enlisted men.	
First Brigade.							
Brig. Gen. WILLIAM HARROW. Col. FRANCIS E. HEATH.							
Staff			1				1
19th Maine	1	28	11	159		4	203
15th Massachusetts	3	20	8	89		28	148
1st Minnesota*	3	47	14	159		1	224
82d New York (2d Militia)	3	42	12	120	1	14	192
Total First Brigade	10	137	46	527	1	47	765
Second Brigade.							
Brig. Gen. ALEXANDER S. WEBB.							
69th Pennsylvania	4	36	8	72	2	15	137
71st Pennsylvania	2	19	3	55	3	16	98
72d Pennsylvania	2	42	7	139		2	192
106th Pennsylvania	1	8	9	45		1	64
Total Second Brigade	9	105	27	311	5	34	491
Third Brigade.							
Col. NORMAN J. HALL.							
19th Massachusetts	2	7	9	52		7	77
20th Massachusetts	2	28	8	86		3	127
7th Michigan	2	19	3	41			65
42d New York		15	6	49		4	74
59th New York		6	3	25			34
Total Third Brigade	6	75	29	253		14	377
Unattached.							
1st Company Massachusetts Sharpshooters		2		6			8
Total Second Division	25	319	105	1,097	6	95	1,647
THIRD DIVISION.							
Brig. Gen. ALEXANDER HAYS.							
First Brigade.							
Col. SAMUEL S. CARROLL.							
14th Indiana		6	3	22			31
4th Ohio	2	7	1	16		5	31
8th Ohio	1	17	10	73		1	102
7th West Virginia		5	1	40		1	47
Total First Brigade	3	35	15	151		7	211
Second Brigade.							
Col. THOMAS A. SMYTH. Lieut. Col. FRANCIS E. PIERCE.							
14th Connecticut		10	10	42		4	66
1st Delaware	1	9	10	44	1	12	77
12th New Jersey	2	21	4	79		9	115
10th New York (battalion)		2		4			6
108th New York	3	13	10	76			102
Total Second Brigade	6	55	34	245	1	25	366

*2d Company Minnesota Sharpshooters attached.

Return of Casualties in the Union forces, &c.—Continued.

Command.	Killed.		Wounded.		Captured or missing.		Aggregate.
	Officers.	Enlisted men.	Officers.	Enlisted men.	Officers.	Enlisted men.	
Third Brigade.							
Col. GEORGE L. WILLARD.							
Col. ELIAKIM SHERRILL.							
Lieut. Col. JAMES M. BULL.							
39th New York	1	14	3	77	......	....	95
111th New York	3	55	8	169	......	14	249
125th New York	2	24	6	98	......	9	139
126th New York	5	35	9	172	......	10	231
Total Third Brigade	11	128	26	516	......	33	714
Total Third Division	20	218	75	912	1	65	1,291
ARTILLERY BRIGADE.							
Capt. JOHN G. HAZARD.							
1st New York Light, Battery B*	1	9	1	15	......	....	26
1st Rhode Island Light, Battery A	......	3	1	27	......	1	32
1st Rhode Island Light, Battery B	1	6	1	18	......	2	28
1st United States, Battery I	......	1	1	23	......	....	25
4th United States, Battery A	1	5	1	31	......	....	38
Total Artillery Brigade	3	24	5	114	......	3	149
Total Second Army Corps	66	731	270	2,924	13	365	4,369
THIRD ARMY CORPS.							
Maj. Gen. DANIEL E. SICKLES.							
Maj. Gen. DAVID B. BIRNEY.							
Staff	......	....	2	....	......	....	2
FIRST DIVISION.							
Maj. Gen. DAVID B. BIRNEY.							
Brig. Gen. J. H. HOBART WARD.							
First Brigade.							
Brig. Gen. CHARLES K. GRAHAM.							
Col. ANDREW H. TIPPIN.							
Staff	......	....	3	....	......	....	3
57th Pennsylvania	2	9	9	37	3	55	115
63d Pennsylvania	......	1	3	26	......	4	34
68th Pennsylvania	3	10	9	117	......	13	152
105th Pennsylvania	1	7	14	101	......	9	132
114th Pennsylvania	......	9	1	85	3	57	155
141st Pennsylvania	......	25	6	97	......	21	149
Total First Brigade	6	61	45	463	6	159	740
Second Brigade.							
Brig. Gen. J. H. HOBART WARD.							
Col. HIRAM BERDAN.							
Staff	......	....	1	....	......	....	1
20th Indiana	2	30	9	105	......	10	156
3d Maine	1	17	2	57	......	45	122
4th Maine	2	9	3	56	4	70	144
86th New York	1	10	3	48	1	3	66
124th New York	4	24	3	54	......	5	90
99th Pennsylvania	1	17	4	77	......	•11	110
1st United States Sharpshooters	1	5	4	33	......	6	49
2d United States Sharpshooters	......	5	4	19	1	14	43
Total Second Brigade	12	117	33	449	6	164	781

* Transcribed from Artillery Reserve, July 1; 14th New York Battery attached.

Return of Casualties in the Union forces, &c.—Continued.

Command.	Killed.		Wounded.		Captured or missing.		Aggregate.
	Officers.	Enlisted men.	Officers.	Enlisted men.	Officers.	Enlisted men.	
Third Brigade.							
Col. P. Regis de Trobriand.							
17th Maine	1	17	7	105	......	3	133
3d Michigan	......	7	3	28	......	7	45
5th Michigan	2	17	8	78	......	4	109
40th New York	1	22	4	116	......	7	150
110th Pennsylvania	......	8	6	39	......		53
Total Third Brigade	4	71	28	366	......	21	490
Total First Division	22	249	106	1,278	12	344	2,011
SECOND DIVISION.							
Brig. Gen. Andrew A. Humphreys.							
Staff	......	2	2	7	......	......	11
First Brigade.							
Brig. Gen. Joseph B. Carr.							
Staff			2				2
1st Massachusetts	1	15	8	75	......	21	120
11th Massachusetts	1	22	7	89	2	8	129
16th Massachusetts	3	12	4	49	......	13	81
12th New Hampshire	1	19	5	65	......	2	92
11th New Jersey	3	14	9	115	......	12	153
26th Pennsylvania	1	29	10	166	......	7	213
Total First Brigade	10	111	45	559	2	63	790
Second Brigade.							
Col. William R. Brewster.							
Staff			2				2
70th New York		20	8	85	......	4	117
71st New York	1	9	6	62	......	13	91
72d New York		7	7	72	......	28	114
73d New York	4	47	11	92	......	8	162
74th New York		12	6	68	......	3	89
120th New York	7	25	10	144	......	17	203
Total Second Brigade	12	120	50	523	......	73	778
Third Brigade.							
Col. George C. Burling.							
2d New Hampshire	3	17	18	119	......	36	193
5th New Jersey	2	11	5	60	......	16	94
6th New Jersey	......	1	3	29	......	8	41
7th New Jersey	1	14	10	76	......	13	114
8th New Jersey	......	7	7	31	......	2	47
115th Pennsylvania	......	3	......	18	......	3	24
Total Third Brigade	6	53	43	333	......	78	513
Total Second Division	28	256	140	1,422	2	214	2,092
ARTILLERY BRIGADE.							
Capt. George E. Randolph.							
Capt. A. Judson Clark.							
New Jersey Light, 2d Battery	......	1	......	16	......	3	20
1st New York Light, Battery D	......		......	10	......	8	18
New York Light, 4th Battery	......	2	......	10	......	1	13
1st Rhode Island Light, Battery E	......	3	2	24	......	1	30
4th United States, Battery K	......	2	1	18	......	4	25
Total Artillery Brigade	......	8	3	78	......	17	106
Total Third Army Corps	50	543	251	2,778	14	575	4,211

Return of Casualties in the Union forces, &c.—Continued.

Command.	Killed.		Wounded.		Captured or missing.		Aggregate.
	Officers.	Enlisted men.	Officers.	Enlisted men.	Officers.	Enlisted men.	
FIFTH ARMY CORPS.							
Maj. Gen. GEORGE SYKES.							
FIRST DIVISION.							
Brig. Gen. JAMES BARNES.							
First Brigade.							
Col. WILLIAM S. TILTON.							
18th Massachusetts	.....	1	.....	23	.....	3	27
22d Massachusetts	.....	3	3	24	.....	1	31
1st Michigan	1	4	6	27	.....	4	42
118th Pennsylvania	1	2	3	16	.....	3	25
Total First Brigade	2	10	12	90	.....	11	125
Second Brigade.							
Col. JACOB B. SWEITZER.							
9th Massachusetts	.....	1	.....	6	.....	.....	7
32d Massachusetts	1	12	7	55	.....	5	80
4th Michigan	1	24	9	55	1	75	165
62d Pennsylvania	4	24	10	97	.....	40	175
Total Second Brigade	6	61	26	213	1	120	427
Third Brigade.							
Col. STRONG VINCENT. Col. JAMES C. RICE.							
Staff	.....	.....	1	.....	.....	.....	1
20th Maine	.....	29	6	85	.....	5	125
16th Michigan	3	20	2	32	.....	3	60
44th New York	2	24	5	77	.....	3	111
83d Pennsylvania	1	9	3	42	.....	.....	55
Total Third Brigade	6	82	17	236	.....	11	352
Total First Division	14	153	55	539	1	142	904
SECOND DIVISION.							
Brig. Gen. ROMEYN B. AYRES.							
First Brigade.							
Col. HANNIBAL DAY.							
Staff	.....	.....	.....	1	.....	.....	1
3d United States	.....	6	4	62	.....	1	73
4th United States	.....	10	2	28	.....	.....	40
6th United States	.....	4	1	39	.....	.....	44
12th United States	1	7	4	67	.....	13	92
14th United States	.....	18	2	108	.....	4	132
Total First Brigade	1	45	13	305	.....	18	382
Second Brigade.							
Col. SIDNEY BURBANK.							
2d United States	1	5	4	51	.....	6	67
7th United States	1	11	3	42	.....	2	59
10th United States	1	15	5	27	.....	3	51
11th United States	3	16	7	85	.....	9	120
17th United States	1	24	13	105	.....	7	150
Total Second Brigade	7	71	32	310	.....	27	447

Return of Casualties in the Union forces, &c.—Continued.

Command.	Killed. Officers.	Killed. Enlisted men.	Wounded. Officers.	Wounded. Enlisted men.	Captured or missing. Officers.	Captured or missing. Enlisted men.	Aggregate.
Third Brigade.							
Brig. Gen. STEPHEN H. WEED. Col. KENNER GARRARD.							
Staff	1						1
140th New York	1	25	5	84		18	133
146th New York		4	2	22			28
91st Pennsylvania		3	2	14			19
155th Pennsylvania		6	2	11			19
Total Third Brigade	2	38	11	131		18	200
Total Second Division	10	154	56	746		63	1,029
THIRD DIVISION.							
Brig. Gen. SAMUEL W. CRAWFORD.							
First Brigade.							
Col. WILLIAM MCCANDLESS.							
1st Pennsylvania Reserves		8	3	35			46
2d Pennsylvania Reserves		3	2	31		1	37
6th Pennsylvania Reserves		2	1	21			24
13th Pennsylvania Reserves (1st Rifles)	2	5	8	31		2	48
Total First Brigade	2	18	14	118		3	155
Third Brigade.							
Col. JOSEPH W. FISHER.							
5th Pennsylvania Reserves				2			2
9th Pennsylvania Reserves				5			5
10th Pennsylvania Reserves		2		3			5
11th Pennsylvania Reserves	1	2	3	35			41
12th Pennsylvania Reserves		1		1			2
Total Third Brigade	1	5	3	46			55
Total Third Division	3	23	17	164		3	210
ARTILLERY BRIGADE.							
Capt. AUGUSTUS P. MARTIN.							
Massachusetts Light, 3d Battery (C)				6			6
1st Ohio Light, Battery L				2			2
5th United States, Battery D	1	6		6			13
5th United States, Battery I		1	1	18		2	22
Total Artillery Brigade	1	7	1	32		2	43
Ambulance Corps				1			1
Total Fifth Army Corps	28	337	129	1,482	1	210	2,187
SIXTH ARMY CORPS.							
Maj. Gen. JOHN SEDGWICK.							
FIRST DIVISION.							
Brig. Gen. HORATIO G. WRIGHT.							
First Brigade.							
Brig. Gen. ALFRED T. A. TORBERT.							
2d New Jersey				6			6
3d New Jersey				2			2
15th New Jersey				3			3
Total First Brigade				11			11

Return of Casualties in the Union forces, &c.—Continued.

Command.	Killed.		Wounded.		Captured or missing.		Aggregate.
	Officers.	Enlisted men.	Officers.	Enlisted men.	Officers.	Enlisted men.	
Second Brigade.							
Brig. Gen. JOSEPH J. BARTLETT.							
121st New York	......	......	......	2	......	......	2
95th Pennsylvania	......	1	......	1	......	......	2
96th Pennsylvania	......	......	......	1	......	......	1
Total Second Brigade	......	1	......	4	......	......	5
Third Brigade.							
Brig. Gen. DAVID A. RUSSELL.							
119th Pennsylvania	......	......	......	2	......	......	2
Total Third Brigade	......	......	......	2	......	......	2
Total First Division	......	1	......	17	......	......	18
SECOND DIVISION.							
Brig. Gen. ALBION P. HOWE.							
Second Brigade.							
Col. LEWIS A. GRANT.							
4th Vermont	......	......	......	1	......	......	1
Total Second Brigade	......	......	......	1	......	......	1
Third Brigade.							
Brig. Gen. THOMAS H. NEILL.							
7th Maine	......	......	......	6	......	......	6
43d New York	1	1	......	2	......	1	5
49th New York	......	......	......	2	......	......	2
61st Pennsylvania	......	......	......	1	......	1	2
Total Third Brigade	1	1	.....	11	......	2	15
Total Second Division	1	1	......	12	......	2	16
THIRD DIVISION.							
Maj. Gen. JOHN NEWTON.							
Brig. Gen. FRANK WHEATON.							
First Brigade.							
Brig. Gen. ALEXANDER SHALER.							
65th New York	......	4	......	5	......	......	9
67th New York	......	......	......	......	......	1	1
122d New York	......	10	2	30	......	2	44
23d Pennsylvania	1	......	1	12	......	......	14
82d Pennsylvania	......	......	......	6	......	......	6
Total First Brigade	1	14	3	53	......	3	74
Second Brigade.							
Col. HENRY L. EUSTIS.							
7th Massachusetts	......	......	...	6	......	......	6
10th Massachusetts	......	......	1	3	......	5	9
37th Massachusetts	......	2	1	25	......	19	47
2d Rhode Island	......	......	1	5	......	1	7
Total Second Brigade	......	3	2	39	......	25	69

Return of Casualties in the Union forces, &c.—Continued.

Command.	Killed.		Wounded.		Captured or missing.		Aggregate
	Officers.	Enlisted men.	Officers.	Enlisted men.	Officers.	Enlisted men.	
Third Brigade.							
Brig. Gen. FRANK WHEATON. Col. DAVID J. NEVIN.							
62d New York		1	1	10			12
93d Pennsylvania			1	9			10
98th Pennsylvania			2	9			11
139th Pennsylvania		1	3	16			20
Total Third Brigade		2	7	44			53
Total Third Division	1	19	12	136		28	196
ARTILLERY BRIGADE.							
Col. CHARLES H. TOMPKINS.							
New York Light, 1st Battery		4	2	6			12
Total Artillery Brigade		4	2	6			12
Total Sixth Army Corps	2	25	14	171		30	242
ELEVENTH ARMY CORPS.							
Maj. Gen. OLIVER O. HOWARD.							
GENERAL HEADQUARTERS.							
Staff			1				1
1st Indiana Cavalry, Companies I and K						3	3
FIRST DIVISION.							
Brig. Gen. FRANCIS C. BARLOW. Brig. Gen. ADELBERT AMES.							
Staff			1				1
First Brigade.							
Col. LEOPOLD VON GILSA.							
Staff	1						1
41st New York	1	14	8	50		2	75
54th New York		7	2	45	4	44	102
68th New York	1	7	4	59	2	65	138
153d Pennsylvania	1	22	7	135		46	211
Total First Brigade	4	50	21	289	6	157	527
Second Brigade.							
Brig. Gen. ADELBERT AMES. Col. ANDREW L. HARRIS.							
17th Connecticut	2	18	4	77	2	94	197
25th Ohio	1	8	5	95	3	72	184
75th Ohio	2	14	7	67	4	92	186
107th Ohio		23	8	103		77	211
Total Second Brigade	5	63	24	342	9	335	778
Total First Division	9	113	46	631	15	492	1,306
SECOND DIVISION.							
Brig. Gen. ADOLPH VON STEINWEHR.							
Staff			1				1

Return of Casualties in the Union forces, &c.—Continued.

Command.	Killed.		Wounded.		Captured or missing.		Aggregate.
	Officers.	Enlisted men.	Officers.	Enlisted men.	Officers.	Enlisted men.	
First Brigade.							
Col. CHARLES R. COSTER.							
134th New York	1	41	4	147	2	57	252
154th New York		1	1	20	9	169	200
27th Pennsylvania	2	4	3	26	1	75	111
73d Pennsylvania		7		27			34
Total First Brigade	3	53	8	220	12	301	597
Second Brigade.							
Col. ORLAND SMITH.							
33d Massachusetts		7		38			45
136th New York		17	1	88	1	2	109
55th Ohio		6	1	30	1	11	49
73d Ohio		21	3	117		4	145
Total Second Brigade		51	5	273	2	17	348
Total Second Division	3	10	14	493	14	318	946
THIRD DIVISION.							
Maj. Gen. CARL SCHURZ.							
First Brigade.							
Brig. Gen. A. SCHIMMELFENNIG.							
Col. GEORGE VON AMSBERG.							
82d Illinois		4	1	18	4	85	112
45th New York		11	1	34	14	164	224
157th New York	4	23	8	158	6	108	307
61st Ohio	2	4	6	30	2	10	54
74th Pennsylvania	2	8	4	36	2	58	110
Total First Brigade	8	50	20	276	28	425	807
Second Brigade.							
Col. W. KRZYZANOWSKI.							
58th New York	1	1	2	13		3	20
119th New York	•2	9	4	66	1	58	140
82d Ohio	4	13	14	71	2	77	181
75th Pennsylvania	3	16	5	84		3	111
26th Wisconsin	2	24	11	118	2	60	217
Total Second Brigade	12	63	36	352	5	201	669
Total Third Division	20	113	56	628	33	626	1,476
ARTILLERY BRIGADE.							
Maj. THOMAS W. OSBORN.							
1st New York Light, Battery I		3	2	8			13
New York Light, 13th Battery				8		3	11
1st Ohio Light, Battery I				13			13
1st Ohio Light, Battery K		2	1	10		2	15
4th United States, Battery G	1	1		11		4	17
Total Artillery Brigade	1	6	3	50		9	69
Total Eleventh Army Corps	33	336	120	1,802	62	1,448	3,801

Return of Casualties in the Union forces, &c.—Continued.

Command.	Killed.		Wounded.		Captured or missing.		Aggregate.
	Officers.	Enlisted men.	Officers.	Enlisted men.	Officers.	Enlisted men.	
TWELFTH ARMY CORPS.							
Maj. Gen. HENRY W. SLOCUM.*							
Brig. Gen. ALPHEUS S. WILLIAMS.							
FIRST DIVISION.							
Brig. Gen. ALPHEUS S. WILLIAMS.							
Brig. Gen. THOMAS H. RUGER.							
First Brigade.							
Col. ARCHIBALD L. McDOUGALL.							
5th Connecticut				2		5	7
20th Connecticut		5		22		1	28
3d Maryland	1			6			8
123d New York		3	1	9	1		14
145th New York		1	1	8			10
46th Pennsylvania		2	1	9		1	13
Total First Brigade	1	11	4	56	1	7	80
Second Brigade.							
Brig. Gen. HENRY H. LOCKWOOD.							
1st Maryland, Potomac Home Brigade	3	20	3	77		1	104
1st Maryland, Eastern Shore		5		18		2	25
150th New York		7		23		15	45
Total Second Brigade	3	32	3	118		18	174
Third Brigade.							
Brig. Gen. THOMAS H. RUGER.							
Col. SILAS COLGROVE.							
27th Indiana		23	8	78		1	110
2d Massachusetts	2	21	8	101		4	136
13th New Jersey		1	3	17			21
107th New York				2			2
3d Wisconsin		2	1	7			10
Total Third Brigade	2	47	20	205		5	279
Total First Division	6	90	27	379	1	30	533
SECOND DIVISION.							
Brig. Gen. JOHN W. GEARY.							
First Brigade.							
Col. CHARLES CANDY.							
5th Ohio	1	1	1	15			18
7th Ohio		1		17			18
29th Ohio	2	5		31			38
66th Ohio			3	14			17
28th Pennsylvania		3	1	22		2	28
147th Pennsylvania	1	4		15			20
Total First Brigade	4	14	5	114		2	130
Second Brigade.							
Col. GEORGE A. COBHAM, Jr.							
Brig. Gen. THOMAS L. KANE.							
Col. GEORGE A. COBHAM, Jr.							
29th Pennsylvania	2	13		43		8	66
109th Pennsylvania		3		6		1	10
111th Pennsylvania		5	1	16			22
Total Second Brigade	2	21	1	65		9	98

*See foot-note (*) on p. 165.

Return of Casualties in the Union forces, &c.—Continued.

Command.	Killed.		Wounded.		Captured or missing.		Aggregate.
	Officers.	Enlisted men.	Officers.	Enlisted men.	Officers.	Enlisted men.	
Third Brigade.							
Brig. Gen. GEORGE S. GREENE.							
60th New York		11	2	39			52
78th New York		6	1	20	1	2	30
102d New York	2	2	1	16		8	29
137th New York	4	36	3	84		10	137
149th New York		6	3	43		3	55
Total Third Brigade	6	61	10	202	1	23	303
Total Second Division	12	96	16	381	1	34	540
ARTILLERY BRIGADE.							
Lieut. EDWARD D. MUHLENBERG.							
Pennsylvania Light, Battery E				3			3
4th United States, Battery F				1			1
5th United States, Battery K				5			5
Total Artillery Brigade				9			9
Total Twelfth Army Corps	18	186	43	769	2	64	1,082
CAVALRY CORPS.							
Maj. Gen. ALFRED PLEASONTON.							
FIRST DIVISION.							
Brig. Gen. JOHN BUFORD.							
First Brigade.							
Col. WILLIAM GAMBLE.							
8th Illinois		1	1	4		1	7
12th Illinois (four companies)		4	3	7		6	20
3d Indiana (six companies)	1	5	1	20		5	32
8th New York		2	1	21		16	40
Total First Brigade	1	12	6	52		28	99
Second Brigade.							
Col. THOMAS C. DEVIN.							
6th New York				1		8	9
9th New York		2		2		7	11
17th Pennsylvania						4	4
3d West Virginia (two companies)						4	4
Total Second Brigade		2		3		23	28
Reserve Brigade.							
Brig. Gen. WESLEY MERRITT.							
6th Pennsylvania		3		7		2	12
1st United States		1		9		5	15
2d United States		3	1	6	1	6	17
5th United States				4		1	5
6th United States*		6	5	23	5	203	242
Total Reserve Brigade		13	6	49	6	217	291
Total First Division	1	27	12	104	6	268	418

*Losses occurred at Fairfield, Pa.

Return of Casualties in the Union forces, &c.—Continued.

Command.	Killed. Officers.	Killed. Enlisted men.	Wounded. Officers.	Wounded. Enlisted men.	Captured or missing. Officers.	Captured or missing. Enlisted men.	Aggregate.
SECOND DIVISION.							
Brig. Gen. DAVID McM. GREGG.							
First Brigade.							
Col. JOHN B. McINTOSH.							
1st Maryland				2		1	3
1st New Jersey			2	7			9
1st Pennsylvania						2	2
3d Pennsylvania			5	10		6	21
Total First Brigade			7	19		9	35
Third Brigade.							
Col. J. IRVIN GREGG.							
1st Maine		1		4			5
10th New York		2		4	1	2	9
4th Pennsylvania		1					1
16th Pennsylvania		2		4			6
Total Third Brigade		6		12	1	2	21
Total Second Division		6	7	31	1	11	56
THIRD DIVISION.							
Brig. Gen. JUDSON KILPATRICK.							
First Brigade.							
Brig. Gen. ELON J. FARNSWORTH. Col. NATHANIEL P. RICHMOND.							
Staff	1						1
5th New York		1		1		4	6
18th Pennsylvania		2		4		8	14
1st Vermont		13	3	22		27	65
1st West Virginia	2	2	3	1	1	3	12
Total First Brigade	3	18	6	28	1	42	98
Second Brigade.							
Brig. Gen. GEORGE A. CUSTER.							
1st Michigan		10	6	37		20	73
5th Michigan	1	7	1	29		18	56
6th Michigan		1	2	24		1	28
7th Michigan		13	4	44		39	100
Total Second Brigade	1	31	13	134		78	257
Total Third Division	4	49	19	162	1	120	355
HORSE ARTILLERY.							
First Brigade.							
Capt. JAMES M. ROBERTSON.							
9th Michigan		1		4			5
6th New York				1			1
2d United States, Battery M			1				1
4th United States, Battery E		1					1
Total First Brigade		2	1	5			8
Second Brigade.							
Capt. JOHN C. TIDBALL.							
1st United States, Battery K		2		1			3
2d United States, Battery A				12			12
Total Second Brigade		2		13			15
Total Cavalry Corps	5	86	39	315	8	399	852

Return of Casualties in the Union forces, &c.—Continued.

Command.	Killed.		Wounded.		Captured or missing.		Aggregate.
	Officers.	Enlisted men.	Officers.	Enlisted men.	Officers.	Enlisted men.	
ARTILLERY RESERVE.							
Brig. Gen. ROBERT O. TYLER. Capt. JAMES M. ROBERTSON.							
First Regular Brigade.							
Capt. DUNBAR R. RANSOM.							
1st United States, Battery H..................	.....	1	1	7	......	1	10
3d United States, Batteries F and K..............	1	8	.....	14	......	1	24
4th United States, Battery C....................	.....	1	1	16	......	....	18
5th United States, Battery C....................	.....	2	2	12	......	....	16
Total First Regular Brigade.................	1	12	4	49	......	2	68
First Volunteer Brigade.							
Lieut. Col. FREEMAN McGILVERY.							
Massachusetts Light, 5th Battery (E)*............	.....	4	1	16	......	....	21
Massachusetts Light, 9th Battery.............	1	7	2	16	......	2	28
New York Light, 15th Battery................	.....	3	2	11	......	....	16
Pennsylvania Light, Batteries C and F..........	.....	2	5	18	......	3	28
Total First Volunteer Brigade.............	1	16	10	61	......	5	93
Second Volunteer Brigade.							
Capt. ELIJAH D. TAFT.							
Connecticut Light, 2d Battery....................	......	....	......	3	......	2	5
New York Light, 5th Battery	......	1	......	2	......	....	3
Total Second Volunteer Brigade	......	1	......	5	......	2	8
Third Volunteer Brigade.							
Capt. JAMES F. HUNTINGTON.							
New Hampshire Light, 1st Battery................	......	....	......	3	......	....	3
1st Ohio Light, Battery H.......................	......	2	......	5	......	....	7
1st Pennsylvania Light, Batteries F and G.........	......	6	1	13	......	3	23
West Virginia Light, Battery C	......	2	......	2	......	....	4
Total Third Volunteer Brigade	......	10	1	23	......	3	37
Fourth Volunteer Brigade.							
Capt. ROBERT H. FITZHUGH.							
Maine Light, 6th Battery (F)....................	......	....	......	13	......	....	13
New Jersey Light, 1st Battery	......	2	......	7	......	....	9
1st New York Light, Battery G	......	....	......	7	......	....	7
1st New York Light, Battery K †	......	....	......	7	......	....	7
Total Fourth Volunteer Brigade	......	2	......	34	......	....	36
Total Artillery Reserve......................	2	41	15	172	......	12	242

RECAPITULATION.

	Killed.		Wounded.		Captured or missing.		Aggregate.
	Officers.	Enlisted men.	Officers.	Enlisted men.	Officers.	Enlisted men.	
General headquarters	......	.....	2	2	......	......	4
First Army Corps	42	624	262	2,969	83	2,079	6,059
Second Army Corps	66	731	270	2,924	13	365	4,369
Third Army Corps.........................	50	543	251	2,778	14	575	4,211
Fifth Army Corps................................	28	337	129	1,482	1	210	2,187
Sixth Army Corps................................	2	25	14	171	......	30	242
Eleventh Army Corps	33	336	120	1,802	62	1,448	3,801
Twelfth Army Corps	18	186	43	769	2	64	1,082
Cavalry Corps...................................	5	86	39	315	8	399	852
Artillery Reserve................................	2	41	15	172	......	12	242
Total Army of the Potomac.................	246	2,909	1,145	13,384	183	5,182	23,049

*10th New York Battery attached, whose loss, here included, was 2 men killed and 3 men wounded.

†11th New York Battery attached.

OFFICERS KILLED.

CONNECTICUT.

Lieut. Colonel Douglas Fowler, 17th Infantry.
Capt. James E. Moore, 17th Infantry.

Lieut. Col. Henry C. Merwin, 27th Infantry.
Lieut. Jedediah Chapman, jr., 27th Infantry.

DELAWARE.

Lieut. William Smith, 1st Infantry.
Lieut. Hamill W. Ottey, 2d Infantry.

Lieut. George G. Plank, 2d Infantry.

INDIANA.

Maj. Charles Lemmon, 3d Cavalry.
Lieut. Crockett T. East, 19th Infantry.
Lieut. Richard Jones, 19th Infantry.

Col. John Wheeler, 20th Infantry.
Lieut. Ezra B. Robbins, 20th Infantry.

MAINE.

Capt. John C. Keene, 3d Infantry.
Lieut. Charles S. McCobb, 4th Infantry.
Lieut. Orpheus Roberts, 4th Infantry.
Capt. Oliver H. Lowell, 16th Infantry.

Capt. Stephen C. Whitehouse, 16th Infantry.
Lieut. Hiram R. Dyer, 17th Infantry.
Capt. George D. Smith, 19th Infantry.

MARYLAND.

Lieut. Charles E. Eader, 1st Infantry, Potomac Home Brigade.
Lieut. James T. Smith, 1st Infantry, Potomac Home Brigade.

Lieut. John L. Willman, 1st Infantry, Potomac Home Brigade.
Capt. Henry Fenton, 3d Infantry.

MASSACHUSETTS.

Lieut. Christopher Erickson, 9th Battery, Light Artillery.
Lieut. Henry Hartley, 1st Infantry.
Lieut. Col. Charles R. Mudge, 2d Infantry.
Lieut. Henry V. D. Stone, 2d Infantry.
Capt. Edwin Humphrey, 11th Infantry.
Lieut. Charles G. Russell, 12th Infantry.
Lieut. Francis Thomas, 12th Infantry.
Col. George H. Ward, 15th Infantry.
Capt. Hans P. Jorgenson, 15th Infantry.

Capt. John Murkland, 15th Infantry.
Capt. Leander G. King, 16th Infantry.
Capt. David W. Roche, 16th Infantry.
Lieut. George F. Brown, 16th Infantry.
Lieut. Herman Donath, 19th Infantry.
Lieut. Sherman S. Robinson, 19th Infantry.
Lieut. Sumner Paine, 20th Infantry.
Lieut. Henry Ropes, 20th Infantry.
Lieut. William H. Barrows, 32d Infantry.

MICHIGAN.

Maj. Noah H. Ferry, 5th Cavalry.
Lieut. Amos M. Ladd, 1st Infantry.
Col. Harrison H. Jeffords, 4th Infantry.
Capt. Peter Generous, 5th Infantry.
Lieut. John P. Thelen, 5th Infantry.
Lieut. Col. Amos E. Steele, jr., 7th Infantry.
Lieut. Albert Slafter, 7th Infantry.
Lieut. William H. Borden, 16th Infantry.
Lieut. Butler Browne, 16th Infantry.
Lieut. Wallace Jewett, 16th Infantry.

Capt. Malachi J. O'Donnell, 24th Infantry.
Capt. William J. Speed, 24th Infantry.
Lieut. Gilbert A. Dickey, 24th Infantry.
Lieut. Newell Grace, 24th Infantry.
Lieut. Reuben H. Humphreville, 24th Infantry.
Lieut. Winfield S. Safford, 24th Infantry.
Lieut. Lucius L. Shattuck, 24th Infantry.
Lieut. Walter H. Wallace, 24th Infantry.

MINNESOTA.

Capt. Nathan S. Messick, 1st Infantry.
Capt. Louis Muller, 1st Infantry.

Lieut. Waldo Farrar, 1st Infantry.

NEW HAMPSHIRE.

Capt. Joseph A. Hubbard, 2d Infantry.
Capt. Henry N. Metcalf, 2d Infantry.
Lieut. George W. Roberts, 2d Infantry.

Col. Edward E. Cross, 5th Infantry.
Lieut. Henry A. L. French, 12th Infantry.

NEW JERSEY.

Capt. Thomas Kelly, 5th Infantry.
Lieut. Henry R. Clark, 5th Infantry.
Lieut. Charles F. Walker, 7th Infantry.
Capt. Andrew H. Ackerman, 11th Infantry.

Capt. Doraster B. Logan, 11th Infantry.
Capt. Luther Martin, 11th Infantry.
Capt. Charles K. Horsfall, 12th Infantry.
Lieut. Richard Townsend, 12th Infantry.

NEW YORK.

Capt. James McKay Rorty, 14th Battery, Light Artillery.
Lieut. F. J. T. Blume, 2d Battery, Light Artillery.
Lieut. Theodore Paush, 39th Infantry.
Lieut. William H. H. Johnson, 40th Infantry.
Lieut. Reinhold Winzer, 41st Infantry.
Capt. William H. Gilfillan, 43d Infantry.
Capt. Lucius S. Larrabee, 44th Infantry.
Lieut. Eugene L. Dunham, 44th Infantry.
Maj. Edward Venuti, 52d Infantry.
Lieut. Louis Deitrich, 58th Infantry.
Capt. Henry V. Fuller, 64th Infantry.
Lieut. Willis G. Babcock, 64th Infantry.
Lieut. Alfred H. Lewis, 64th Infantry.
Lieut. Ira S. Thurber, 64th Infantry.
Capt. George H. Ince, 66th Infantry.
Capt. Elijah F. Munn, 66th Infantry.
Capt. Otto Friedrich, 68th Infantry.
Lieut. Andrew W. Estes, 71st Infantry.
Capt. Eugene C. Shine, 73d Infantry.
Lieut. William L. Herbert, 73d Infantry.
Lieut. James Marksman, 73d Infantry.
Lieut. George P. Dennen, 73d Infantry.
Maj. Andrew J. Grover, 76th Infantry.
Capt. Robert B. Everett, 76th Infantry.
Capt. Ambrose N. Baldwin, 80th Infantry.
Capt. Joseph S. Corbin, 80th Infantry.
Lieut. George W. Brankstone, 80th Infantry.
Lieut. Col. James Huston, 82d Infantry.
Capt. Jonah C. Hoyt, 82d Infantry.
Lieut. John H. McDonald, 82d Infantry.
Capt. Thomas W. Quirk, 83d Infantry.
Lieut. Charles A. Clark, 83d Infantry.
Capt. John N. Warner, 86th Infantry.
Lieut. William McClelland, 88th Infantry.
Lieut. William J. Morrin, 97th Infantry.
Lieut. James H. Stiles, 97th Infantry.
Capt. John Mead, 102d Infantry.
Lieut. Josiah V. Upham, 102d Infantry.
Lieut. Carl V. Amiet, 108th Infantry.
Lieut. Dayton T. Card, 108th Infantry.
Lieut. Robert Evans, 108th Infantry.

Lieut. John H. Drake, 111th Infantry.
Lieut. Erastus M. Granger, 111th Infantry.
Lieut. Augustus W. Proseus, 111th Infantry.
Lieut. Emil Frost, 119th Infantry.
Lieut. Matthias Rosemann, 119th Infantry.
Capt. Ayres G. Barker, 120th Infantry.
Capt. Lansing Hollister, 120th Infantry.
Lieut. John R. Burhans, 120th Infantry.
Lieut. Jason Carle, 120th Infantry.
Lieut. Michael E. Creighton, 120th Infantry.
Lieut. Frederick Freelewick, 120th Infantry.
Lieut. Edward H. Ketchum, 120th Infantry.
Col. A. Van Horne Ellis, 124th Infantry.
Maj. James Cromwell, 124th Infantry.
Capt. Isaac Nichols, 124th Infantry.
Lieut. Milnor Brown, 124th Infantry.
Col. George L. Willard, 125th Infantry.
Capt. Ephraim Wood, 125th Infantry.
Col. Eliakim Sherrill, 126th Infantry.
Capt. Orin J. Herendeen, 126th Infantry.
Capt. Isaac Shimer, 126th Infantry.
Capt. Charles M. Wheeler, 126th Infantry.
Lieut. Rufus P. Holmes, 126th Infantry.
Lieut. Henry I. Palmer, 134th Infantry.
Capt. Oscar C. Williams, 137th Infantry.
Capt. Joseph H. Gregg, 137th Infantry.
Lieut. Henry G. Hallett, 137th Infantry.
Lieut. John H. Van Emburgh, 137th Infantry.
Col. Patrick H. O'Rorke, 140th Infantry.
Lieut. Guilford D. Mace, 147th Infantry.
Lieut. Sylvester J. Taylor, 147th Infantry.
Lieut. David G. Van Dusen, 147th Infantry.
Lieut. Col. George Arrowsmith, 157th Infantry.
Capt. Jason K. Backus, 157th Infantry.
Capt. Harrison Frank, 157th Infantry.
Lieut. Randall D. Lower, 157th Infantry.

OHIO.

Lieut. Addison H. Edgar, 4th Infantry.
Lieut. Samuel J. Shoub, 4th Infantry.
Lieut. Henry C. Brinkman, 5th Infantry.
Lieut. Elijah Hayden, 8th Infantry.
Lieut. Lewis E. Wilson, 25th Infantry.
Lieut. George Hayward, 29th Infantry.
Lieut. John G. Marsh, 29th Infantry.
Capt. James M. Reynolds, 61st Infantry.

Asst. Surg. William S. Moore, 61st Infantry.
Capt. James C. Mulharen, 75th Infantry.
Capt. Mahlon B. Briggs, 75th Infantry.
Lieut. Stowell L. Burnham, 82d Infantry.
Lieut. Henry Jacoby, 82d Infantry.
Lieut. George W. McGary, 82d Infantry.
Lieut. Philander C. Meredith, 82d Infantry.

PENNSYLVANIA.

Lieut. John O. H. Woods, 11th Reserves.
Col. Charles F. Taylor, 13th Reserves.
Lieut Robert Hall, 13th Reserves.
Lieut. Joshua S. Garsed, 23d Infantry.
Lieut. Benjamin R. Wright, 26th Infantry.
Lieut. Walter S. Briggs, 27th Infantry.
Lieut. John Kuempel, 27th Infantry.
Lieut. Edward J. Harvey, 29th Infantry.
Lieut. John J. McKeever, 29th Infantry.
Lieut. John D. Gordon, 56th Infantry.
Lieut. John F. Cox, 57th Infantry.
Lieut. Henry Mitchell, 57th Infantry.
Maj. William G. Lowry, 62d Infantry.
Capt. Edwin H. Little, 62d Infantry.
Lieut. Scott C. McDowell, 62d Infantry.
Lieut. Josiah C. Mouck, 62d Infantry.
Capt. George W. McLearn, 68th Infantry.
Lieut. Andrew Black, 68th Infantry.
Lieut. John Reynolds, 68th Infantry.
Lieut. Col. Martin Tschudy, 69th Infantry.
Capt. Michael Duffy, 69th Infantry.
Capt. George C. Thompson, 69th Infantry.
Lieut. Charles F. Kelly, 69th Infantry.
Capt. William H. Dull, 71st Infantry.
Capt. John M. Steffan, 71st Infantry.
Capt. Andrew McBride, 72d Infantry.
Lieut. Sutton Jones, 72d Infantry.
Capt. Anton Heilig, 74th Infantry.

Lieut. William Roth, 74th Infantry.
Col. Francis Mahler, 75th Infantry.
Lieut. Henry Hauschild, 75th Infantry.
Lieut. Louis Mahler, 75th Infantry.
Capt. John M. Sell, 83d Infantry.
Chaplain Horatio S. Howell, 90th Infantry.
Lieut. John R. Nice, 99th Infantry.
Lieut. George W. Crossley, 105th Infantry.
Lieut. William H. Smith, 106th Infantry.
Capt. Richard W. Davids, 118th Infantry.
Col. Richard P. Roberts, 140th Infantry.
Capt. David Acheson, 140th Infantry.
Lieut. Alexander M. Wilson, 140th Infantry.
Col. Robert P. Cummins, 142d Infantry.
Capt. Charles H. Flagg, 142d Infantry.
Lieut. Edward B. Hurst, 142d Infantry.
Lieut. Charles W. Betzenberger, 143d Infantry.
Lieut. Horatio F. Lewis, 145th Infantry.
Lieut. William H. Tourison, 147th Infantry.
Capt. Robert M. Forster, 148th Infantry.
Capt. Alfred J. Sofield, 149th Infantry.
Lieut. Charles P. Keyser, 150th Infantry.
Lieut. Elias D. Weidensaul, 150th Infantry.
Lieut. Aaron S. Seaman, 151st Infantry.
Lieut. George A. Trexler, 151st Infantry.
Lieut. William H. Beaver, 153d Infantry.

RHODE ISLAND.

Lieut. Joseph S. Milne, Battery B, 1st Light Artillery.

UNITED STATES ARMY.

Lieut. Manning Livingston, 3d Artillery.
Lieut. Alonzo H. Cushing, 4th Artillery.
Lieut. Bayard Wilkeson, 4th Artillery.
Lieut. Charles E. Hazlett, 5th Artillery.
Lieut. Frank C. Goodrich, 2d Infantry.
Lieut. Wesley F. Miller, 7th Infantry.
Lieut. William J. Fisher, 10th Infantry.

Capt. Thomas O. Barri, 11th Infantry.
Lieut. Herbert Kenaston, 11th Infantry.
Lieut. Henry Rochford, 11th Infantry.
Lieut. Silas A. Miller, 12th Infantry.
Lieut. William H. Chamberlin, 17th Infantry.

UNITED STATES SHARPSHOOTERS.

Lieut. George W. Sheldon, 1st Regiment.

UNITED STATES VOLUNTEERS.

Maj. Gen. John F. Reynolds.
Brig. Gen. Elon J. Farnsworth.

Brig. Gen. Stephen H. Weed.
Brig. Gen. Samuel K. Zook.

VERMONT.

Lieut. William H. Hamilton, 14th Infantry.

WEST VIRGINIA.

Capt. William N. Harris, 1st Cavalry. | Lieut. Sidnier W. Knowles, 1st Cavalry.

WISCONSIN.

Lieut. William S. Winegar, 2d Infantry.
Capt. John Ticknor, 6th Infantry.
Lieut. Orrin D. Chapman, 6th Infantry.

Capt. William Smith, 26th Infantry.
Lieut. Martin Young, 26th Infantry.

OFFICERS MORTALLY WOUNDED.

DELAWARE.

Capt. Martin W. B. Ellegood, 1st Infantry.

MAINE.

Maj. Ebenezer Whitcomb, 4th Infantry.
Lieut. George M. Bragg, 4th Infantry.
Capt. Almon L. Fogg, 17th Infantry.
Capt. Milton M. Young, 17th Infantry.

Lieut. Leroy S. Scott, 19th Infantry.
Capt. Charles W. Billings, 20th Infantry.
Lieut. Warren L. Kendall, 20th Infantry.
Lieut. Arad H. Linscott, 20th Infantry.

MASSACHUSETTS.

Capt. Thomas. B. Fox, jr., 2d Infantry.
Capt. Thomas R. Robeson, 2d Infantry.
Lieut. William B. Mitchell, 11th Infantry.

Lieut. Elisha G. Buss, 15th Infantry.
Capt. Charles R. Johnson, 16th Infantry.
Col. Paul J. Revere, 20th Infantry.
Lieut. Charles K. Knowles, 22d Infantry.

MINNESOTA.

Capt. Wilson B. Farrell, 1st Infantry.
Capt. Joseph Periam, 1st Infantry.

Lieut. David B. Demarest, 1st Infantry.
Lieut. Charles H. Mason, 1st Infantry.

NEW HAMPSHIRE.

Lieut. William W. Ballard, 2d Infantry.
Lieut. Edmund Dascomb, 2d Infantry.
Lieut. Charles W. Patch, 2d Infantry.

Lieut. Charles Vickery, 2d Infantry.
Lieut. Ruel G. Austin, 5th Infantry.

NEW JERSEY.

Capt. Edward P. Berry, 5th Infantry.
Col. Louis R. Francine, 7th Infantry.

Capt. Andrew S. Davis, 8th Infantry.
Maj. Philip J. Kearny, 11th Infantry.

NEW YORK.

Capt. Charles D. Follett, 8th Cavalry.
Lieut. Adolph Wagner, 39th Infantry.
Lieut. Benjamin N. Thomas, 44th Infantry.
Capt. Edward Antonieski, 58th Infantry.
Capt. Gustave Stoldt, 58th Infantry.
Lieut. Col. Max A. Thoman, 59th Infantry.
Lieut. William H. Pohlman, 59th Infantry.
Lieut. Myron D. Stanley, 60th Infantry.
Lieut. Franklin K. Garland, 61st Infantry.
Lieut. Charles A. Foss, 72d Infantry.
Lieut. Martin E. Higgins, 73d Infantry.
Capt. William H. Chester, 74th Infantry.
Capt. Robert Story, 76th Infantry.

Lieut. Philip Keeler, 76th Infantry.
Lieut. Robert G. Noxon, 76th Infantry.
Lieut. John Cranston, 82d Infantry.
Lieut. Rush P. Cady, 97th Infantry.
Lieut. Thomas Johnston, 104th Infantry.
Capt. Otto Trumpelman, 119th Infantry.
Lieut. William J. Cockburn, 120th Infantry.
Capt. Norman F. Weer, 123d Infantry.
Lieut. Jacob Sherman, 126th Infantry.
Lieut. Charles P. Klein, 140th Infantry.
Lieut. Hugh McGraw, 140th Infantry.
Lieut. William P. Schenck, 147th Infantry.
Lieut. Daniel McAssy, 147th Infantry.
Capt. George A. Adams, 157th Infantry.
Lieut. Joseph F. Henery, 157th Infantry.

OHIO.

Lieut. Daniel W. Williams, 61st Infantry.
Maj. Joshua G. Palmer, 66th Infantry.
Capt. George M. Doherty, 73d Infantry.
Lieut. Thomas Wheeler, 75th Infantry.

Capt. John Costen, 82d Infantry.
Capt. William D. W. Mitchell, 82d Infantry.
Capt. Barnet T. Steiner, 107th Infantry.

PENNSYLVANIA.

Lieut. Joseph H. Miller, 16th Cavalry.
Lieut. Frank B. Bird, 26th Infantry.
Capt. James Brown, 62d Infantry.
Lieut. Patrick Morris, 62d Infantry.
Lieut. Lewis W. Ealer, 68th Infantry.
Col. Dennis O'Kane, 69th Infantry.
Lieut. William J. Sill, 75th Infantry.
Lieut. Isaac A. Dunsten, 105th Infantry.
Lieut. Ferdinand M. Pleis, 106th Infantry.
Capt. Jeremiah M. Sample, 139th Infantry.

Maj. Israel P. Spalding, 141st Infantry.
Lieut. Andrew G. Tucker, 142d Infantry.
Lieut. Lyman R. Nicholson, 143d Infantry.
Capt. George G. Griswold, 145th Infantry.
Lieut. George H. Finch, 145th Infantry.
Lieut. John A. Bayard, 148th Infantry.
Lieut. Henry Chancellor, jr., 150th Infantry.

UNITED STATES ARMY.

Lieut. George de V. Selden, 2d Cavalry.
Lieut. Christian Balder, 6th Cavalry.
Lieut. George A. Woodruff, 1st Artillery.
Lieut. Richard R. Crawford, 7th Infantry.

Lieut. Michael C. Boyce, 10th Infantry.
Lieut. Amaziah J. Barber, 11th Infantry.
Lieut. Edward S. Abbot, 17th Infantry.

UNITED STATES VOLUNTEERS.

Brig. Gen. Strong Vincent.
Capt. John P. Blinn, Assistant Adjutant-General.

Capt. James J. Griffiths, Aide-de-Camp.

VERMONT.

Lieut. John T. Sennott, 13th Infantry.   Lieut. Cyrus B. Lawton, 16th Infantry.

WISCONSIN.

Lieut. Col. George H. Stevens, 2d Infantry.

No. 14.

Return of Casualties in the Union forces at Wapping Heights, Manasas Gap, Va., July 23, 1863.

[Compiled from nominal list of casualties, returns, &c.]

Command.	Killed.		Wounded.		Captured or missing.		Aggregate.
	Officers.	Enlisted men.	Officers.	Enlisted men.	Officers.	Enlisted men.	
General staff			1				1
20th Indiana				4			4
3d Maine				3			3
4th Maine				1			1
17th Maine				1			1
6th Maryland				1			1
2d New Hampshire				1			1
5th New Jersey				1			1
70th New York	1	10		21			32
71st New York		2		13			15
72d New York				8			8
73d New York		1		7			8
74th New York	2	2		7			11
124th New York		1		1			2
63d Pennsylvania				5			5
84th Pennsylvania				1			1
1st U. S. Sharpshooters		1	1	6			8
Total	3	17	2	81			103

OFFICERS KILLED.

NEW YORK.

Capt. Benjamin Price, 70th Infantry.
Lieut. Charles S. Preston, 74th Infantry.

Lieut. James Short, 74th Infantry.

No. 15.

General Return of Casualties in the Union forces during the Gettysburg Campaign, June 3–August 1, 1863.

[Compiled from nominal list of casualties, returns, &c.]

Location.	Killed. Officers.	Killed. Enlisted men.	Wounded. Officers.	Wounded. Enlisted men.	Captured or missing. Officers.	Captured or missing. Enlisted men.	Aggregate.
Near Fayetteville, Va., June 3			1			3	4
Franklin's Crossing, or Deep Run, Va., June 5–13		9	3	45			57
Brandy Station (Fleetwood) and Beverly Ford, Va., June 9.*	10	67	35	356	13	356	837
Stevensburg, Va., June 9*		4		12		13	29
Berryville, Va., June 13				2		2	4
Opequon Creek, Va., June 13		2		15			17
Bunker Hill, W. Va., June 13	1	6	2	33	1	54	97
Winchester, Va., June 13–15†	7	88	12	336	144	3,856	4,443
Berryville, Va., June 14				1		2	3
Martinsburg, W. Va., June 14		4	1	8	6	140	159
Williamsport, Md., June 15	1					2	3
Aldie, Va., June 17*	4	46	9	122	6	118	305
Catoctin Creek and Point of Rocks, Md., June 17.		1		3		26	30
Middleburg, Va., June 17–18	1	3	5	24	12	225	270
Middleburg, Va., June 19	4	12	4	42		37	99
Upperville, Va., June 21*		12	13	117	1	66	209
Near Gainesville, Va., June 21						9	9
Thoroughfare Gap and Hay Market, Va., June 21–25.		1		6		41	48
Near Aldie, Va., June 22		1		2		2	5
Greencastle, Pa., June 22		1					1
McConnellsburg, Pa., June 25						10	10
Near Gettysburg, Pa., June 26						176	176
Near Fairfax Court-House, Va., June 27		3	1	14	3	52	73
Near Rockville, Md., June 28				3		16	19
Wrightsville, Pa., June 28				12		11	23
Muddy Branch, Md., June 29				7			7
Westminster, Md., June 29		2		8	3	36	49
Hanover, Pa., June 30	2	17	6	67	5	118	215
Sporting Hill, near Harrisburg, Pa., June 30			2	7			9
Carlisle, Pa., July 1				12			12
Gettysburg, Pa., July 1–4*	246	2,909	1,145	13,384	183	5,182	23,049
Fairfield Gap, Pa., July 4	1		1	2	4	13	21
Monterey Gap, Pa., July 4		1	3	9	1	29	43
Emmitsburg, Md., July 4					1	67	68
Cunningham's Cross-Roads, Pa., July 5		2				1	3
Near Greencastle, Pa., July 5				1		18	19
Near Fairfield, Pa., July 5		2		5			7
Smithsburg, Md., July 5			1	5		4	10
Hagerstown, Md., July 6	3	16	5	45	10	184	263
Williamsport, Md., July 6	1	13	3	34	3	66	120
Downsville, Md., July 7		1		1			2
Funkstown, Md., July 7		6	1	8		50	65
Boonsborough, Md., July 8		8	5	49		18	80
Near Williamsport, Md., July 8				4			4
Benevola or Beaver Creek, Md., July 9		3		17		5	25
Funkstown, Md., July 10–13		14	7	70	1	5	97
Hagerstown, Md., July 10–13		5	4	27	1	12	49
Jones' Cross-Roads, Md., July 10–13		2		7		2	11
Ashby's Gap, Va., July 12		2		6	2	7	17
Near Williamsport, Md., July 14				2		5	7
Falling Waters, Md., July 14	3	28	2	56	2	30	121
Near Harper's Ferry, W. Va., July 14					1	24	25
Halltown, W. Va., July 15			1	2		2	5
Shepherdstown, W. Va., July 15				1			1
Shepherdstown, W. Va., July 16		8	8	64		24	104
Snicker's Gap, Va., July 17				3		1	4
Hedgesville and Martinsburg, W. Va., July 18–19		1		4			5

* For detailed statement, see pp. 168–173.
† For detailed statement, see Part II, p. —.

General Return of Casualties in the Union forces, &c.—Continued.

Location.	Killed.		Wounded.		Captured or missing.		Aggregate.
	Officers.	Enlisted men.	Officers.	Enlisted men.	Officers.	Enlisted men.	
Ashby's Gap, Va., July 20				3		3	6
Berry's Ferry, Va., July 20				3		3	6
Manassas Gap, Va., July 21–22		9		12		8	29
Chester Gap, Va., July 21–22		1		8		16	25
Wapping Heights, Manassas Gap., Va., July 23*	3	17	2	81			103
Near Gaines' Cross-Roads, Va., July 23				1		5	6
Near Snicker's Gap, Va., July 23				1		3	4
Battle Mountain, near Newby's Cross-Roads, Va, July 24.		4	1	11		14	30
Brandy Station, Va., August 1		21	10	94		20	145
Miscellaneous affairs *en route*		2		6	8	226	242
Total	287	3,355	1,294	15,282	407	11,418	32,043

Supplemental list of officers killed, or who died of wounds received in action.

KILLED.

Lieut. Michael S. Slothower, 87th Pennsylvania Infantry, at Bunker Hill, W. Va., June 13.

Lieut. Jacob A. Metz, 1st Maryland (Potomac Home Brigade) Cavalry, near Williamsport, Md., June 15.

Lieut. Joseph A. Chedel, jr., 1st Rhode Island Cavalry, near Middleburg, Va., June 18.

Lieuts. George S. Kimball, Mark Neville, and Ephriam H. Taylor, 1st Maine Cavalry, and Lieut. Horatio H. Boyd, 10th New York Cavalry, at Middleburg, Va., June 19.

Lieuts. Alexander Gall and Elam S. Dye, 5th New York Cavalry, at Hanover, Pa., June 30.

Lieut. James S. McElhenny, 1st Michigan Cavalry, at Fairfield Gap, Pa., July 4.

Capt. William C. Lindsey, 18th Pennsylvania Cavalry; Capt. John W. Woodward, 1st Vermont Cavalry; and Lieut. Irvin C. Swentzel, 1st West Virginia Cavalry, at Hagerstown, Md., July 6.

Lieut. Aaron C. Jewett, 6th Michigan Cavalry, at Williamsport, Md., July 6.

Capts. Peter A. Weber and David G. Royce, and Lieut. Charles E. Bolza, 6th Michigan Cavalry, at Falling Waters, Md., July 14.

DIED OF WOUNDS.

Lieuts. Bronson Beardsley and Edward S. Hawes, 10th New York Cavalry, wounded at Middleburg, Va., June 19.

Capt. William R. Elliott, 1st Michigan Cavalry, wounded at Fairfield Gap, Pa., July 4.

Lieut. Henry W. Clark, 1st West Virginia Cavalry, wounded at Monterey Gap, Pa., July 4.

Lieut. William W. Williams, 5th U. S. Artillery, wounded at Smithsburg, Md., July 5.

Capt. Charles J. Snyder, 1st Michigan Cavalry, wounded at Hagerstown, Md., July 6.

Maj. William H. Medill, 8th Illinois Cavalry, wounded at Williamsport, Md., July 6.

*For detailed statement, see p. 192.

No. 16.

Report of Surg. Jonathan Letterman, U. S. Army, Medical Director,
Army of the Potomac.

HEADQUARTERS ARMY OF THE POTOMAC,
MEDICAL DIRECTOR'S OFFICE,
Camp near Culpeper Court-House, Va., October 3, 1863.

GENERAL: I have the honor to submit the following report on the operations of the medical department of this army at the battle of Gettysburg, July 1, 2, and 3:

As the subject of transportation has an important bearing upon the manner in which the wounded are attended to after a battle, it is necessary to make some allusion to the manner in which this department was supplied. It is scarcely necessary to say that if the transportation is not sufficient to enable the officers of the department to conduct it properly, the effect must fall upon the wounded.

In the autumn of 1862, I investigated the subject very carefully, with the view to the adoption of some system instead of the irregular method and want of system which prior to that time was in vogue, to limit the amount necessary, and to have that amount always available. The transportation was one wagon to each regiment and one to each brigade. This gave all that was required, and it was not too much; and, it may be remarked, was a reduction of nearly one-half of that which had been in use prior to that time. This system worked well. At the battle of Chancellorsville, the department had upon the left bank of the Rappahannock means sufficient, had it been allowed to use them, for taking care of many more wounded than there came under its control.

On June 19, while the army was on the march, as it were, from before Fredericksburg to some unknown point north of the Potomac River, the headquarters being near Fairfax Court-House, Va., the transportation of the department was cut down by Major-General Hooker on an average of two wagons in a brigade, in opposition to my opinion, expressed verbally and in writing. This reduction necessitated the turning in of a large portion of the supplies, tents, &c., which were necessary for the proper care of the wounded in the event of a battle. Three wagons were assigned to a brigade of 1,500 men, doing away with regimental wagons. This method in its practical working is no system at all, as it is liable to constant changes, and proved to be, what I supposed at the time it would be, a failure to give the department the means necessary to conduct its operations.

The headquarters left Fairfax Court-House on June 26 ultimo, for some point as yet unknown in Maryland or Pennsylvania.

On the 25th of that month, I directed Assistant Surgeon [Jeremiah B.] Brinton, U. S. Army, to proceed to Washington, and obtain the supplies I had ordered the medical purveyor to have put up, and there await orders.

On the 26th, he was ordered to proceed with them to Frederick. This step was taken to obviate the want of supplies consequent upon the reduction of transportation. At this date it was not known that the army would be near Frederick; still, the risk had to be run, and the event justified the order, Dr. Brinton arriving at Frederick on June 28, the day after the arrival of headquarters there, with twenty-five army wagon loads of such supplies as would be most required in case of a battle. The train with these supplies followed that of head-quarters until we reached Taneytown.

On July 1, the trains were not permitted to go farther, and, on the 2d, were ordered farther to the rear, near Westminster.

On the 1st, it was ordered that "corps commanders and the commander of the Artillery Reserve will at once send to the rear all their trains (excepting ammunition wagons and ambulances), parking them between Union Mills and Westminster."

On the 2d, these trains were ordered still farther to the rear, and parked near Westminster, nearly 25 miles distant from the battle-field. The effect of this order was to deprive the department almost wholly of the means for taking care of the wounded until the result of the engagement of the 2d and 3d was fully known. I do not instance the effect of this order, excepting to show the influence of it upon the department. The expediency of the order I, of course, do not pretend to question, but its effect was to deprive this department of the appliances necessary for the proper care of the wounded, without which it is as impossible to have them properly attended to as it is to fight a battle without ammunition. In most of the corps the wagons exclusively used for medicines moved with the ambulances, so that the medical officers had a sufficient supply of dressings, chloroform, and such articles until the supplies came up, but the tents and other appliances, which are as necessary, were not available until July 5.

The supply of Dr. Brinton reached the field on the evening of July 4. This supply, together with the supplies ordered by me on July 5 and 6, gave more than was required. The reports of Dr. Brinton and Dr. [John H.] Taylor show that I ordered more supplies than were used up to the 18th of July, when the hospitals were taken from under my control. Surgeon Taylor, medical inspector of this army, who was ordered on July 29 to Gettysburg, to examine into the state of affairs there, reports to me that he made "the question of supplies a subject of special inquiry among the medical officers who had remained with the wounded during and for a month subsequent to the battle. The testimony in every instance was conclusive that at no time had there been any deficiency, but, on the contrary, that the supply furnished by the medical purveyor had been and still continued to be abundant." This is, perhaps, sufficient to show that not only were supplies ordered in advance, but that they were on hand when required, notwithstanding the difficulty in consequence of the inability of the railroad to meet the requirements made upon it, until after General Haupt took charge of it on July 9. I have not deemed it necessary to present any tables showing the amounts ordered and issued, considering what I have just given as ample enough to show the action of this department. The chief want was tents and other appliances for the better care of the wounded. I had an interview with the commanding general on the evening of July 3, after the battle was over, to obtain permission to order up the wagons containing the tents, &c. This request he did not think expedient to grant but in part, allowing one-half the wagons to come to the front; the remainder were brought up as soon as it was considered by him proper to permit it. To show the result of the system adopted upon my recommendation regarding transportation, and the effect of the system of field hospitals, I may here instance the hospital of the Twelfth Corps, in which the transportation was not reduced nor the wagons sent to the rear at Gettysburg.

Surgeon [John] McNulty, medical director of that corps, reports that "it is with extreme satisfaction that I can assure you that it enabled me to remove the wounded from the field, shelter, feed them, and dress their wounds within six hours after the battle ended, and to have every capital operation performed within twenty-four hours after the injury was received." I can, I think, safely say that such would have been the result in other corps had the same facilities been allowed—a result not to have been surpassed, if equaled, in any battle of magnitude that has ever taken place.

A great difficulty always exists in having food for the wounded. By the exertions of Colonel [Henry F.] Clarke, chief commissary, 30,000 rations were brought up on July 4 and distributed to the hospitals. Some of the hospitals were supplied by the commissaries of the corps to which they belonged. Arrangements were made by him to have supplies in abundance brought to Gettysburg for the wounded; he ordered them, and if the railroad could have transported them they would have been on hand.

Over 650 medical officers are reported as present for duty at that battle. These officers were engaged assiduously, day and night, with little rest, until the 6th, and in the Second Corps until July 7, in attendance upon the wounded. The labor performed by these officers was immense. Some of them fainted from exhaustion, induced by over-exertion, and others became ill from the same cause. The skill and devotion shown by the medical officers of this army were worthy of all commendation ; they could not be surpassed. Their conduct as officers and as professional men was admirable. Thirteen of them were wounded, one of whom (Asst. Surg. W. S. Moore, Sixty-first Ohio Volunteers, Eleventh Corps) died on July 6 from the effects of his wounds, received on the 3d. The idea, very prevalent, that medical officers are not exposed to fire, is thus shown to be wholly erroneous. The greater portion of the surgical labor was performed before the army left. The time for primary operations had passed, and what remained to be done was to attend to making the men comfortable, dress their wounds, and perform such secondary operations as from time to time might be necessary. One hundred and six medical officers were left behind when the army left ; no more could be left, as it was expected that another battle would within three or four days take place, and in all probability as many wounded thrown upon our hands as at the battle of the 2d and 3d, which had just occurred. No reliance can be placed on surgeons from civil life during or after a battle. They cannot or will not submit to the privations and discomforts which are necessary, and the great majority think more of their own personal comfort than they do of the wounded. Little more can be said of those officers who have for a long period been in hospitals. I regret to make such a statement, but it is a fact and often a practical one. Dr. [Henry] Janes, who was left in charge of the hospitals at Gettysburg, reports that quite a number of surgeons came and volunteered their services, but "they were of little use." This fact is so well known in this army that medical officers prefer to do the work rather than have them present, and the wounded men, too, are much better satisfied to be attended by their own surgeons. I, however, asked the Surgeon-General, July 7, to send 20 medical officers to report to Dr. Janes, hoping they might prove of some benefit, under the direction of the medical officers of this army who had been left behind. I cannot learn that they were ever sent.

Dr. Janes was left in general charge of the hospitals, and, to provide against contingencies, was directed, if he could not communicate with me, to do so directly with the Surgeon-General, so that he had full power to call directly upon the Surgeon-General to supply any want that might arise.

The ambulance corps throughout the army acted in the most commendable manner during those days of severe labor. Notwithstanding the great number of wounded, amounting to 14,193, I have it from the most reliable authority and from my own observation that not one wounded man of all that number was left on the field within our lines early on the morning of July 4. A few were found after daylight beyond our farthest pickets, and these were brought in, although the ambulance men were fired upon when engaged in this duty by the enemy, who were within easy range. In addition to this duty, the line of battle was of such a character, resembling somewhat that of a horseshoe, that it became necessary to remove most of the hospitals farther to the rear as the enemy's fire drew nearer.

This corps did not escape unhurt; 1 officer and 4 privates were killed and 17 wounded while in the discharge of their duties. A number of horses were killed and wounded, and some ambulances injured. These facts will show the commendable and efficient manner in which the duties devolving upon this corps were performed, and great credit is deservedly due to the officers and men for their praiseworthy conduct. I know of no battle-field from which wounded men have been so speedily and so carefully removed, and I have every reason to feel satisfied that their duties could not have been performed better or more fearlessly.

Before the army left Gettysburg, and knowing that the wounded had been brought in from the field, six ambulances and four wagons were ordered to be left from each corps, to convey the wounded from their hospitals to the railroad depot, for transportation to the other hospitals. From the Cavalry Corps but four ambulances were ordered, as this corps had a number captured by the enemy at or near Hanover a few days previous. I was informed by General Ingalls that the railroad to Gettysburg would be in operation on the 6th, and upon this based my action. Had such been the case, this number would have been sufficient. As it proved that this was not in good running order for some time after that date, it would have been better to have left more ambulances. I acted on the best information that could be obtained.

The number of our wounded, from the most reliable information at my command, amounted to 14,193.* The number of Confederate wounded who fell into our hands was 6,802, making the total number of wounded thrown by that battle upon this department 20,995. The wounded of July 1 fell into the hands of the enemy, and came under our control on the 4th of that month. Instruments and medical supplies belonging to the First and Eleventh Corps were in some instances taken from the medical officers of those corps by the enemy.

Previous to leaving Gettysburg, I, on July 5 and 6, ordered supplies to be sent to Frederick from Washington and Philadelphia, to meet the wants of the department in the event of another battle, which there was every reason to suppose would occur shortly after the army left Gettysburg. While at the latter place, I asked the Surgeon-General to have 50 medical officers ready to meet me at such a point as I should thereafter indicate.

---

*But see revised statement, p. 187.

On July 7, I desired them to be sent to Frederick. Late in the night of July 9, 47 reported. These officers were designed to make up, as far as possible, the deficiency of medical officers existing in consequence of the large detail from this army left at Gettysburg.

Tents were ordered by my request, and the corps supplied as far as their transportation would permit, and the remainder kept in reserve. It is not necessary to enter into a detailed list of the articles ordered and on hand ready for the anticipated battle. I have the orders in my office, and it is with pleasure I can state for the information of the commanding general that, notwithstanding the short time in which I had to make the necessary preparations, this department was, when near Boonsborough, fully prepared to take care of the wounded of another battle of as great magnitude as that which this army had just passed through at Gettysburg.

It is unnecessary to do more than make an allusion to the difficulties which surrounded this department at the engagement at Gettysburg. The inadequate amount of transportation; the impossibility of having that allowed brought to the front; the cutting off our communication with Baltimore, first by way of Frederick and then by way of Westminster; the uncertainty, even as late as the morning of July 1, as to a battle taking place at all, and, if it did, at what point it would occur; the total inadequacy of the railroad to Gettysburg to meet the demands made upon it after the battle was over; the excessive rains which fell at that time—all conspired to render the management of the department one of exceeding difficulty, and yet abundance of medical supplies were on hand at all times; rations were provided, shelter obtained, as soon as the wagons were allowed to come to the front, although not as abundant as necessary on account of the reduced transportation. Medical officers, attendants, ambulances, and wagons left when the army started for Maryland, and the wounded were well taken care of, and especially so when we consider the circumstances under which the battle was fought and the length and severity of the engagement.

The conduct of the medical officers was admirable. Their labors not only began with the beginning of the battle, but lasted long after the battle had ended. When other officers had time to rest, they were busily at work—and not merely at work, but working earnestly and devotedly.

I have not considered it necessary to give in this report other than a very general outline of the operations of this department at that time. To enter into a detailed account of them would, I presume, be more than the commanding general would desire.

I am, general, very respectfully, your obedient servant,

JONA. LETTERMAN,
Medical Director.

Brig. Gen. S. WILLIAMS, *A. A. G., Army of the Potomac.*

No. 17.

Report of Capt. Lemuel B. Norton, Chief Signal Officer.

SIGNAL DEPT., HDQRS. ARMY OF THE POTOMAC,
September 18, 1863.

GENERAL: I have the honor to submit the following report of the operations of the signal corps of the Army of the Potomac, from June 14 to August 1, including the late Maryland Campaign:

In view of the contemplated movement of this army from the line of the Rappahannock, in June last the following detail of signal officers was made by direction of the commanding general, viz: The right wing was supplied with 6, the left wing with 4, and the center with 4, 8 officers being held as a reserve, to be used wherever the changes in the position of the army might render them of the greatest service.

On June 14, the headquarters of this army moved from the vicinity of Falmouth to Dumfries. The signal officers detailed for the three subdivisions of the army moved with the commander of each, while the party in reserve remained near the headquarters of the general commanding. Early on this day, by order of the chief of staff, two signal officers reported to Brig. Gen. G. K. Warren, who was to assume command of the troops in charge of the Government property about to be removed from Aquia Creek. A station of observation was established upon Fort No. 2, at that place, communicating with the gunboats Mahaska and Freeborn (lying off the creek, for the purpose of covering the withdrawal of stores and troops), upon which vessels signal parties had been previously stationed. Many messages were sent between these stations, and communication successfully kept up until the night of the 16th, when, the object of the flotilla having been attained, the officers rejoined the reserve. The party on station of observation at the Phillips House, opposite Fredericksburg, remained on duty all this day, and reported to General W. S. Hancock the frequent changes made by the enemy on the other side of the river.

On the 15th, two reconnaissances were made toward Centreville by the officers attached to the First Corps, and reports sent to Maj. Gen. J. F. Reynolds.

On the 16th, a loop of signal telegraph wire was run out, connecting general headquarters at Fairfax Station with the Morse telegraph office at the depot.

On the 17th, Capt. B. F. Fisher, chief acting signal officer, went out upon a reconnaissance, and in the evening was captured by the enemy near Aldie.

On the 18th, communication by signal telegraph was established, by the direction of the chief of staff, between general headquarters, near Fairfax Court-House, and the headquarters of Maj. Gen. J. F. Reynolds, near Herndon Station.

On the 19th, a signal telegraph line was extended from Herndon to Guilford Station, to which point General Reynolds had moved his headquarters.

On the 20th, by direction of the chief of staff, two signal officers were assigned to each army corps. Communication was opened by flag signals between the First Corps headquarters, at Guilford Station, the Eleventh Corps, at Trappe Rock, and the Twelfth Corps, at Leesburg. The officers at the last-named point worked successfully also with the signal station at Poolesville, Md., and through it with those at Sugar Loaf Mountain, Point of Rocks, and Maryland Heights. Thus, conjointly by flag signals and the signal telegraph, a complete line was established from a reliable station of observation on Maryland Heights direct to the commanding general at Fairfax Court-House, giving to him at the same time a rapid means of communication with all the corps above named. A reconnaissance was made for General H. W. Slocum by the signal officers attached to his command.

On the 21st and 22d, the stations occupied on the 19th and 20th worked successfully, and two reconnaissances as far as the Bull Run Mountains were made for General W. S. Hancock.

On the 23d, the lines already in operation were made still more perfect by the establishment of a station near the headquarters of the Fifth and Cavalry Corps, at Aldie, which, communicating with the Eleventh Corps, furnished a safe means of transmitting messages between the commanding general and Maj. Gens. A. Pleasonton, G. G. Meade, and other corps commanders.

On the 24th, the lines previously established worked uninterruptedly. Intelligence of the crossing of the Potomac by the enemy was received this day from the following message:-

> MARYLAND HEIGHTS SIGNAL STATION,
> *June 24—10.40 a. m.*
>
> General SLOCUM:
>
> Large trains are crossing at Sharpsburg. Artillery and general trains are passing near Charlestown toward Shepherdstown.
>
> FISHER,
> *Lieutenant, Signal Officer.*

A message confirming the above was received, via Washington, late in the afternoon by the commanding general from General Tyler, at Maryland Heights.

On the 25th, all signal communication was discontinued upon the removal of the army corps, and the signal telegraph line withdrawn. Two officers made separate reconnaissances for General W. S. Hancock, while two others performed the same duties for General J. F. Reynolds.

On the 26th, general headquarters moved to Poolesville. By direction of the general commanding, three signal officers were ordered to report for duty to Maj. Gen. A. Pleasonton, commanding Cavalry Corps.

On the 27th, the headquarters of this army moved to Frederick, and an attempt was made to open communication between this point and the station on Sugar Loaf Mountain, which proved unsuccessful, on account of the unfavorable condition of the atmosphere. A station of observation was established at Middletown, and communication opened from that place to another point of observation at South Mountain Pass, and the results reported to Generals J. F. Reynolds and O. O. Howard.

On the 28th and 29th, no signal operations were found necessary.

On the 30th, general headquarters removed to Taneytown. A signal station was placed in the church steeple at that place, and a party sent to Emmitsburg for the purpose of opening a line between General J. F. Reynolds and headquarters. Communication was not opened this day on account of the haziness of the atmosphere. The signal officer with General John Buford, who occupied the town of Gettysburg, took position in the steeple of the college, and reported to General Buford the whereabouts and movements of the enemy. The officers attached to the First Corps, from a station of observation on the mountain back of Emmitsburg, made a telescopic reconnaissance toward Gettysburg, reporting the results to the general commanding that corps.

On July 1, general headquarters remained near Taneytown. A station of observation was established, first on the college and subsequently on the court-house in Gettysburg, and reports of the position, numbers, and movements of the enemy sent by signals to General Howard, on Cemetery Hill, southeast of the town. In the afternoon of this day two reconnaissances were made from Gettysburg, for the information of General W. S. Hancock, by the signal officer temporarily attached to his staff.

In the evening I was made acquainted by the general commanding with the line of defense to be occupied by the army in case the enemy made an irresistible attack upon our position, and directed by him to " examine the line thoroughly, and at once upon the commencement of the movement extend telegraphic communication from each of the following points, viz, general headquarters, near Frizellburg, Manchester, Union Mills, Middleburg, and the Taneytown road."

In order that these instructions might be promptly and successfully fulfilled, signal telegraph trains were sent to Frizellburg, and everything held in readiness to extend the wire at a moment's notice to the points desired by the commanding general. During the whole of this day, endeavors were made to open the signal line between general headquarters, Emmitsburg, and Round Top Mountain, but, on account of the smokiness of the atmosphere, the desired result was not obtained until 11 p. m., when the first message was received. These lines were kept open during the subsequent battle at Gettysburg and until July 6. In the event of the repulse and retirement of our army, they must have been eminently useful.

Late in the evening of this day, I was directed by the chief of staff to start at daylight the next morning with the signal officers held in reserve, and rejoin the commanding general on the field at Gettysburg.

On July 2, I reported at an early hour at the point selected for headquarters of the army for that day, but found the signal officers, who had been previously assigned to the different army corps, already on the field, and that through their exertions the general commanding had been placed in communication with nearly all the corps commanders.

Before 11 a. m. every desirable point of observation was occupied by a signal officer, and communication opened from General Meade's headquarters to those of every corps commander.

A station was established upon Round Top Mountain, on the left of our line, and from this point the greater part of the enemy's forces could be seen and their movements reported. From this position, at 3.30 p. m., the signal officer discovered the enemy massing upon General Sickles' left, and reported the fact to General Sickles and to the general commanding.

At 5.30 p. m. the enemy opened a terrific fire, but our left was fully prepared for them, and the fight gradually extended to the whole front, so that every signal flag was kept almost constantly working. The station at Round Top was once, and that at General Meade's headquarters twice, broken up by the rapid advance of the enemy and the severity of the fire, but were immediately reoccupied when the positions became tenable. An important station of observation was also opened on the right of our center, near Cemetery Hill, from which the whole of the left of the rebel army was closely watched. A short time before the action opened, two officers were sent to reconnoiter the enemy's extréme left, and their reports were given to the commanding general. The stations established during the day were held at night.

On July 3, the same positions were occupied by the signal officers as on the day previous, and the reports of movements, &c., unfailingly sent to the commanding general. The station at General Meade's headquarters and that at General Howard's were rendered inoperative for a couple of hours by the furious attack of the rebels upon our center, but both were again actively employed as soon as the tremendous fire moderated sufficiently to permit of messages being read and transmitted with accuracy. The station on Round Top continued to report throughout the day discoveries in regard to the enemy's position. In the evening, the commanding general removed his headquarters to a strip of woods on the Taneytown road, and another station was established at this point, still maintaining communication with those previously opened.

On July 4, at 5.40 a. m., the signal officer from a station on the college in Gettysburg reported to the general commanding "that the enemy had evacuated the position they held yesterday," and at 9.30 a. m. reported the new line occupied by them, and that they were retreating toward Hagerstown. This station was kept open all day, and information in regard to the movements of the enemy sent in by orderly. General Meade's headquarters were removed to the Baltimore pike, and this was made the terminus of all signal lines.

July 5.—All signal stations were this day discontinued, excepting those on Round Top Mountain, Cemetery Hill, court-house, and General Meade's headquarters. The officers previously assigned to army corps moved with them. A signal officer accompanied General G. K. Warren with the advance of the Sixth Corps, and communication was kept up by him with Round Top Mountain, thus enabling the party at the latter place to make known his discoveries in regard to the enemy to General Warren.

On July 6, the lines between Round Top and Taneytown and Emmitsburg and Taneytown were discontinued. The two officers attached to the First Corps made a telescopic reconnaissance from the hill back of Emmitsburg, and sent the information obtained to Maj. Gen. John Newton. The same officers subsequently occupied signal stations at Turner's Gap and Washington Monument, and reported the result of their observations of Hagerstown and vicinity to Generals Sedgwick and Newton.

July 7, the headquarters of the army moved to Frederick. The signal officer who had been previously assigned to duty with the detached command under General Neill made a reconnaissance near Waynesborough, Pa., discovering the whereabouts and movements of the enemy.

On July 8, in the afternoon, general headquarters moved to Middletown. A party of signal officers, under charge of Capt. W. J. L. Nicodemus, arrived from Washington, for the purpose of working in conjunction with the signal corps of this army. Captain Nicodemus opened a line of communication between Frederick and South Mountain Pass.

On July 9, headquarters of the army moved to Turner's Gap. A station was occupied near this place, communicating, through others at Middletown and Crampton's Pass, with Maryland Heights. This line, appearing of little importance on account of telegraphic facilities, was abandoned the same day, and its officers ordered to more active duty in the front. A station of observation was established on Washington Monument, near South Mountain Pass, from which Hagerstown and the whole valley could be seen.

On July 10, the general commanding and his staff removed to a bivouac near Beaver Creek crossing, west of Boonsborough. In the evening, communication was opened from general headquarters, through Washington Monument station, with headquarters of the Second and Twelfth Corps, near Bakersville; Third and Fifth Corps near Antietam Bridge, and the First and Sixth Corps near Beaver Creek crossing, on the Hagerstown pike. On this day the officer who accompanied General Neill on his expedition from a point selected by him on Franklin's Cliff, South Mountain Range, near Leitersburg, discovered the numbers and position of the enemy in and around Hagerstown, and sent the information to General Neill, and by orderly to General Meade.

On July 11, by direction of the assistant adjutant-general, a signal telegraph line was run out between general headquarters and those of General John Sedgwick, on the Hagerstown pike, 5 miles distant. No communication was had by flag signals this day on account of the thick haze. Two reconnaissances were made toward Hagerstown for Generals Howard and Kilpatrick by the officers attached to their respective commands.

On July 12, a party was sent to open a line of signals between general headquarters and the brigade of General Neill, near Leitersburg, but the attempt failed by reason of the thickness of the atmosphere. The signal telegraph wire was this day extended to General Sedgwick's new headquarters at Funkstown, and another run out between general headquarters and those of General Slocum, 2½ miles distant and near Four Corners. Both lines worked with but slight interruptions until the night of the 14th, when they were withdrawn. Flag signals were worked between the headquarters of the Fifth Corps and others in the vicinity; also between General Howard's headquarters, at Funkstown, and a station of observation in Hagerstown.

On July 13, all signal communication previously established was still kept up. Two officers were sent to make a telescopic reconnaissance from Elk Mountain.

On July 14, the enemy were discovered to have crossed the river during the night before. At the close of this day all signal stations and lines were discontinued.

On July 15, the headquarters of the army moved to Berlin. A signal station was opened at that place, communicating with a lookout station on Maryland Heights. This line remained in operation until the 18th.

On July 16, the signal telegraph line was run from general headquarters to the Eleventh Corps headquarters, 1½ miles distant. Two officers were sent to make a telescopic reconnaissance from Loudoun Heights. Their reports were transmitted to the general commanding by orderly.

On July 17, communication was opened by flag signals between headquarters at Berlin and an outpost station at Point of Rocks. An officer was sent to occupy a point of observation on Short Mountain.

On July 18, general headquarters moved to Lovettsville, Va. A line of flag signals was worked between the Third and Fifth Corps.

On July 19, headquarters of the army were moved to Wheatland, and communication established from thence to the lookout station on Short Mountain, and also between that mountain and the Fifth Corps headquarters.

On July 20, the general headquarters moved to Union, and in the evening signals by torch were worked between that place and a station of observation at Snicker's Gap, on the Blue Ridge. The whereabouts and movements of the enemy in the Shenandoah Valley were discovered and correctly reported to the commanding general by the officers on this station. A party was ordered to open station and make a reconnaissance at Ashby's Gap. They arrived at that point at 8 p. m., but for some undiscovered reason failed to open communication with general headquarters during the night.

On July 21, the officers at Ashby's Gap made known the numbers, movements, and position of the enemy in the Valley to General G. A. Custer, and through General W. H. French to the general commanding. At 8 p. m. two officers were ordered on a reconnaissance to Manassas Gap. The party at Snicker's Gap station reported frequently during the day to the general commanding their observations of the enemy.

On July 22, communication was opened by flag signals, via Union, with Snicker's and Ashby's Gaps. General headquarters moved to Upperville. Attempts were made to open [communication] between this point and Ashby's Gap station, but failed from difficulty and delay experienced in finding a suitable point near headquarters. The officer at Manassas Gap transmitted by orderly to the general commanding the results of his observations. A line of signals was opened between Ashby's Gap and the Fifth Corps headquarters, near Rectortown. A point at Manassas Gap was selected for telescopic reconnaissances by the officer attached to General Merritt's command, from which he was driven shortly afterward by an attack of the enemy.

On July 23, general headquarters moved to Piedmont at noon, and to Markham Station in the evening, and communication was opened from the latter place to Ashby's Gap, via Piedmont. At 6 p. m. the officer in charge of signals at the front of Manassas Gap established a line between General Meade's headquarters, at Linden Station, General French, with the advance, and General Sykes. This line was discontinued upon the withdrawal of our infantry the next morning. The officer with the Fifth Corps occupied a point overlooking Front Royal, and sent information of the enemy by flag signals to General Sykes.

On July 24, at an early hour, I proceeded with four officers to the extreme advance of our army, but did not succeed in rendering any service before the enemy had evacuated Front Royal and its vicinity. In the afternoon, general headquarters moved to Salem. Signal communication was opened between General Newton's headquarters, at Warrenton, and General Howard's, at New Baltimore. This line was discontinued the next day upon the removal of the Eleventh Corps to Warrenton Junction.

On July 25, headquarters of the army moved to Warrenton. A station of observation was established near Amissville for General Custer.

On July 26, a signal telegraph line was run between general headquarters and General Sedgwick's headquarters, on the Waterloo road, 2½ miles distant. Another line was also extended from headquarters to the office of the Morse telegraph, in Warrenton. A station of observation was put up on Watery Mountain, communicating by flag signals to general headquarters.

On July 29, the line to Watery Mountain was continued to General Custer's headquarters, at Amissville,

On July 30 and 31, the communication opened on the 29th remained intact.

In summing up the operations of the signal corps of this army for the month and a half herein recorded, I find that sixty-seven signal stations of observation and communication were occupied, eight signal telegraph lines established, and seventeen extra reconnaissances made.

I have stated as concisely as possible the amount and character of the work performed. When it failed in a signal point of view it has been noted; but of the real value of the information obtained by the corps and the importance of other services rendered, the commanding general and the corps commanders are best able to judge.

A map is herewith inclosed,* indicating by the signal flags placed upon it the majority of the points at which stations were occupied; by dotted red lines where communication by flag signals was established, and by plain red lines where the signal telegraph was used.

During the late movements of the army, 3 signal officers and 6 flagmen were captured by the enemy. The only reported injuries were those of 2 flagmen slightly wounded at the battle of Gettysburg. The capture of Capt. B. F. Fisher, chief acting signal officer, has been previously mentioned. Capt. C. S. Kendall and Lieut. L. R. Fortescue, acting signal officers, were taken at Emmitsburg, where they had been on station, by Stuart's cavalry upon their retreat from Gettysburg, July 5.

The following officers are entitled to mention for the active part taken by them in the late operations of the corps, and for the prompt and efficient manner in which they discharged every duty, both under the fire of the enemy and on the march: Capts. James S. Hall and P. A. Taylor, serving with Second Army Corps; Capts. P. Babcock, jr., and T. R. Clark, serving with Eleventh Army Corps; Capts. Joseph Gloskoski and Richard Dinsmore, serving with Cavalry Corps; Capt. F. E. Beardslee, in charge signal telegraph train; First Lieuts. J. C. Wiggins and N. H. Camp, serving with First Army Corps; First Lieut. George J. Clarke, serving with Sixth Army Corps; First Lieut. J. E. Holland, serving with Twelfth Army Corps. First Lieuts. William S. Stryker, adjutant, and A. B. Capron, acting assistant quartermaster and acting ordnance officer of Signal Corps, have discharged the duties of their respective positions throughout the campaign with a care and faithfulness which entitles them to commendation. I take pleasure in still further mentioning Capt. D. E. Castle, of this corps, for distinguished gallantry and close attention to duty under most trying circumstances. On July 3, when the enemy made their furious attack upon our center at Gettysburg, Captain Castle occupied a signal station at General Meade's headquarters, near Cemetery Hill, and remained there on duty after all others had been driven away. His flagmen had also left with his signal equipments, under the impression that their officer had gone with the rest. Having occasion to send a couple of important messages to the general commanding, then at General Slocum's headquarters, Captain Castle quickly cut a pole, extemporized a signal flag from a bedsheet procured near by, and sent his dispatches through under a most galling fire. It was to Captain Castle's keensightedness and good judgment that I am indebted for the first information obtained of the enemy's position and movements in the Shenandoah Valley on July

---

* To appear in Atlas.

21. His discoveries were made known to the commanding general at that time.

I have the honor to be, general, very respectfully, your obedient servant,

L. B. NORTON,
Captain, and Chief Signal Officer, Army of the Potomac.

Brig. Gen. S. WILLIAMS,
Assistant Adjutant-General, Army of the Potomac.

No. 18.

Report of Capt. William J. L. Nicodemus, Signal Officer.

GEORGETOWN, D. C., *July* 21, 1863.

CAPTAIN: I have the honor to report that, in obedience to Special Orders, No. 106, dated Office of the Signal Officer, Washington, July 6, 1863, I reported to General French, at Frederick.

July 7.—On the 7th instant, with 12 officers and 27 enlisted men, General French ordered me to report to General Meade, who ordered me to the front, then the South Mountain Pass; ordered Lieutenants [Charles] Herzog and [Thomas P.] Rushby to Maryland Heights; Lieutenant Fisher to Crampton's Pass; Captain Daniels, with Captain Denicke and Lieutenants [William J.] Galbraith, Briggs, Denicke, Swain, and [S. Cary] Tuckerman, to the front, with the following instructions:

You will open communication between Frederick City and South Mountain Pass, and establish observation stations to command the Boonsborough Valley.

July 8.—Left Frederick City on the 8th instant, accompanied by Captain McCreary. Lieutenant [William S.] Andrews being sick, was left at Frederick City, with orders to report to me as soon as able. Broke up stations along the route as fast as Morse's telegraph communication was established. Captain Daniels opened communication at 12 m. between battle-field and South Mountain station. Result of the day's fighting was driving the enemy to Beaver Creek Bridge, on Boonsborough and Hagerstown pike, 3½ miles north of Boonsborough. All movements of the enemy were observed from Washington Monument, on South Mountain, by Captain [Ernst A.] and Lieutenant [C. F. M.] Denicke, and promptly reported to the different headquarters concerned.

July 9.—General Buford on the 9th drove the enemy about 2 miles. A line of signal stations commanded the enemy's front. A timely report of Captain McCreary prevented our left from being flanked this day.

July 10.—Heavy skirmishing on the left; enemy driven to Funkstown; his dispositions accurately reported to the general commanding.

July 11.—Captain McCreary reported:

Enemy falling back, breaking up camps at Hagerstown, and moving toward Williamsport, trains going in direction of Shepherdstown.

Condition of enemy's intrenchments at Funkstown reported by Captain Daniels.

July 12.—Enemy driven to intrenchments west and southwest of Hagerstown, and signal stations established in different parts of the town, 9.30 a. m.

July 13.—Progress of the enemy's earthworks reported. No fighting.

July 14.—Evacuation of the enemy reported at 4 a. m. by Captain Daniels. At 9.30 a. m. reported to General Couch near Chambersburg:

Enemy crossing at Williamsport; Army of Potomac in close pursuit.

This message reached General Couch five hours before General Meade's dispatch to that effect. At 10.30 a. m. reported to General Averell at Chambersburg, who reported at once to General Kelley at Fairview. General Kelley at once threw his whole force in motion for Williamsport. On arriving at Williamsport, found the enemy had succeeded in crossing the river; drew in my party, and returned to the signal camp of instruction on the 17th instant.

I forward reports of the officers of my command, except of Lieutenant Andrews, left sick at Frederick, and Captain and Lieutenant Denicke, ordered to report to General Kelley at Hancock. The reports of the last two will be forwarded as soon as practicable. I transmit herewith a few of the messages sent to the colonel commanding not mentioned in the reports of Captain Daniels and Lieutenant Swain.

In conclusion, I would add that the weather was exceedingly unfavorable for signals; that the party, officers and men, worked cheerfully and hard, and that I am particularly indebted to Captains Daniels and McCreary and Lieutenant Swain for what was accomplished.

Very respectfully, sir, your obedient servant,

WM. J. L. NICODEMUS,
Captain, &c., Commanding.

Capt. H. S. Tafft,
Signal Officer.

No. 19.

Report of Capt. Nahum Daniels, Signal Officer.

Georgetown, D. C., *July* 18, 1863.

Captain: I have the honor to submit the following report:

Agreeably to orders received at Frederick, Md., July 7, at 6 p. m. I started with Captain Denicke, Lieutenants Denicke, Galbraith, Briggs, and Swain to open communication by signals from the advance of our army, then near Boonsborough, to Frederick. I left Lieutenant Galbraith at South Mountain Pass, with instructions to open an intermediate station at that point between Frederick and Washington Monument. On the morning of the 8th instant, I ordered Captain Denicke and Lieutenant Denicke to open a station on Washington Monument; also procured a detail of men to cut away the timber which obstructed the view near the monument. At 8 a. m. I ordered Lieutenant Swain to open a station at Boonsborough, then our extreme advance. Lieutenant Briggs also proceeded to open a station on the Blue [Elk] Ridge, about 4 miles from Boonsborough. At 10 a. m. our forces commenced skirmishing with the enemy. I immediately proceeded to the front, and opened communication with the Washington Monument, about 1 mile from Boonsborough. on the Hagerstown pike. I directed Lieutenant

Swain to take charge of the station at this point.   At 11 a. m. I sent the following message to Captain Nicodemus :

Our advance is engaged with the enemy. Captain Denicke reported no communication yet with Frederick.

It being now quite clear, I ordered Captain Denicke to report by signal to me the movements of the enemy, which I reported to the commanding officer in front. Our forces were now engaged a distance of 3 miles in front. Lieutenant Swain remained at his post receiving messages, subject to a severe fire. I cannot too highly mention his bearing while under fire. At 1 p. m. the engagement became quite warm, Captain Denicke reporting constantly to me the every movement of the enemy, which was immediately reported to General Buford, while he by such reports was enabled to be fully prepared to meet every movement of the enemy, knowing in advance what their force was, and the kind of force. At 3 p. m., finding that communication was not open to Frederick, I ordered Lieutenant Denicke to assist Lieutenant Galbraith in opening through to that place.   The following messages were sent to General Buford:

The enemy are advancing in front and on our right. A large cavalry force in front.

DANIELS,
Captain.

General BUFORD :
Infantry are advancing on our right.

DANIELS,
Captain.

Enemy are advancing; skirmishing on our right.

DANIELS.
Captain.

General BUFORD:
Enemy have just placed a battery on left of road, behind a large barn.

DANIELS,
Captain.

SIGNAL STATION, NEAR BOONSBOROUGH.
Captain NICODEMUS:
Our forces are now hotly engaged with the enemy. Send forage to Captain Denicke, now here.

DANIELS,
Captain.

General BUFORD:
Enemy's skirmishers are advancing on our right.

DANIELS,
Captain.

JULY 9.
Captain NICODEMUS:
Enemy's cavalry pickets are 1 mile in advance.

DANIELS,
Captain.

JULY 10, 1863.
General BUFORD:
Three regiments of infantry are on the right of road, 2 miles above, and two trains.

DANIELS,
Captain.

General BUFORD:

The enemy have cavalry pickets 2 miles to our right. A wagon train is moving from there toward Frederick.

DANIELS,
Captain.

JULY 11, 1863.

General Commanding:

The enemy's cavalry are crossing the creek on our left in force.

DANIELS,
Captain.

General Commanding:

Enemy are advancing infantry across the Antietam, about 1 mile to our left.

DANIELS,
Captain, and Signal Officer.

General Commanding:

The enemy are advancing infantry and cavalry across the Antietam about 1 mile to our left.

DANIELS,
Captain, and Signal Officer.

General SEDGWICK:

GENERAL: The enemy are intrenching on the crest of a hill one-half mile east of Funkstown, and have batteries on the hill north of Funkstown, supported by infantry.

DANIELS,
Captain, and Signal Officer.

JULY 13, 1863.

General Commanding:

GENERAL: The enemy are intrenching on the crest of the hill 1 mile east of Funkstown, and have batteries on the hills north of Funkstown, supported by infantry.

DANIELS,
Captain, and Signal Officer.

SEMINARY STATION—6 a. m.

Generals MEADE and SEDGWICK :

GENERALS: Enemy's skirmishers are advancing on our right—the right of town.

DANIELS,
Captain, and Signal Officer.

JULY 15, 1863.

General SEDGWICK;

The enemy occupy the same position as last night. All quiet.

JULY 15, 1863.

General SEDGWICK:

The enemy are hard at work on breastworks, and placing artillery in position.

SWAIN.

GENERAL: Citizens report siege guns northwest of town on the works.

Major-General MEADE:

GENERAL: I have ascertained upon good authority the position of rebel forces now in front. General Hood's headquarters are 1¼ miles in front of the Female Seminary on the pike; General Longstreet on his right, Generals Heth and Ransom between Longstreet and the river. General Lee's headquarters near Saint James' College. The enemy have a line of rifle-pits extending from the National pike to the river below Williamsport, and in rear of the rifle-pits are circular redoubts, in which are placed their guns, five of which near the town are 32-pounders.

N. DANIELS,
Captain, and Signal Officer.

July 14, 1863.—At 4 a. m. discovered that the enemy had evacuated their works; tried to communicate the facts through Lieutenant

Tuckerman by signals to Generals Meade and Sedgwick, but was unable to call him; but immediately communicated the fact by telegraph to Col. A. J. Myer, to the generals commanding, and to Captain Nicodemus by signals at 6 a. m. I immediately ordered Lieutenants Swain and Galbraith to take their stations on the enemy's works, which they did, Lieutenant Galbraith being the first to enter them. He immediately communicated to me the fact, by signals, that the enemy had left at 2 a. m. I then proceeded to Williamsport with Lieutenants Swain, Tuckerman, and Galbraith, and opened a station on the magazine at that place; also directed Lieutenants Swain, Galbraith, and Tuckerman to open communication by signals with Falling Waters, which they nearly accomplished that night. I at the same time was trying to open with Captain Denicke at Fairview, but was unable to do so.

I would most respectfully call your attention to the uniform good conduct and gallantry while under fire of Privates A. V. Richards and Edward H. Haskell, both doing their duty manfully under fire; would also state that several important messages were not taken down at the time when sent, and were forgotten.

All of which I most respectfully submit.

I have the honor to remain, your obedient servant,

N. DANIELS,
Captain, and Signal Officer.

Capt. WILLIAM J. L. NICODEMUS,
Signal Officer.

No. 20.

Report of Capt. William G. McCreary, Signal Officer.

SIGNAL CAMP OF INSTRUCTION,
July 20, 1863.

CAPTAIN: I have the honor to submit the following report of operations from July 6 to July 16, 1863, during the retreat of the rebel forces under General Lee from Maryland:

I received my orders July 6, and same evening started for Frederick; arrived there on the evening of the 7th instant. On the 8th, the Army of the Potomac being on the move, I started for South Mountain, where our advance line rested. Was ordered back to Middletown by you, to open a station there. Upon my arrival there, I found General Meade had established his headquarters, and Captain Norton agreeing to relieve me with one of his officers, I returned to report to you at the pass. Early next morning, with the advance of our troops, in company with yourself, advanced beyond Boonsborough, when I was directed by you to report to the right, with the right brigade of General Buford's cavalry division, General Merritt commanding, Captain Daniels being in the center and Lieutenant Tuckerman on the left of same division, to keep open communication along the line.

Soon after taking our positions, an advance was made along the line, and we advanced with them. At the crossing of Beaver Creek, the enemy were established with infantry, cavalry, and artillery, to dispute our advance, but after a severe skirmish were driven back.

Early next morning, July 10, moved forward, and drove them to Antietam, a distance of 4 miles. During this movement, I was in communication with Captain Daniels, but the rapid movements of our forces prevented sending many messages; but from our points of observation much valuable information was furnished the commanding officers, for which we received their personal thanks.

On the 11th instant, I was requested by you to proceed to Black Rock, an elevated and naked rock on South Mountain Range, but on my arrival found the valley so covered with fog that I was unable to see anything, and returned to the valley.

On the 12th, again went to Black Rock, and on that day and the 13th endeavored to get communication, but in vain. On the evening of the 13th, left and went to Funkstown.

Early on the morning of the 14th, received communication from Captain Daniels that the enemy had vacated their works. This communication you furnished General Howard. About 5.15 a. m., with yourself, rode forward to their works, where Lieutenant Galbraith opened a station. At this point met some citizens who had been impressed by the rebels on the previous night and compelled to act as guides, and when within 2 miles of Williamsport had been permitted to return. Their report that there were no rebels on this side of Williamsport was transmitted to General Meade by you. After consulting you, concluded our best course was to proceed and try to get the same information to General Kelley, at Fairview. On arriving at the junction of the Fairview and Greencastle turnpike, an orderly, Private Voohees, of the Sixth New York Cavalry, who had been assigned me, was sent with dispatches to meet the Pennsylvania troops, said to be coming from Chambersburg. Near Greencastle he met the column under General Dana, who, considering the dispatches important, sent him to General Couch, at Chambersburg. General Couch thanked the signal officer for the timely information (these arrived five hours in advance of the dispatches from General Meade), and caused a rapid movement of these forces.

At the Conococheague Bridge a Union paroled soldier and a rebel of the Sixth North Carolina Infantry were picked up. The former had been across the Potomac, and reported that the enemy were almost entirely across. The rebel was sent to General Kelley.

On approaching Clear Spring, met the advance of General Averell's cavalry brigade, cautiously feeling their way. On being informed there was no enemy in their front, they halted until we could inform Generals Averell and Kelley ; upon doing so, General Kelley immediately moved his whole division rapidly in the direction of Williamsport. After resting our horses, we followed, overtaking the column, and arrived at Williamsport to find the enemy gone, as we had reported. Although the weather was such that but comparatively little could be accomplished by signals, yet I received the personal thanks of Generals Merritt, Kelley, and Averell for much valuable and reliable information furnished them. From this point returned to camp.

The following are some of the communications sent and received:

JULY 9.

General MERRITT :

A battery of the enemy is visible on the crest of the hill. I can also see bayonets, indicating that it is supported by infantry. No cavalry visible except pickets.

McCREARY,
Signal Officer.

JULY 10.

General MERRITT:

Three squadrons of rebel cavalry have passed to our right, and are concealed behind the woods. We have not any skirmishers in that direction.

McCREARY,
Signal Officer.

To Commander of the Right:

Cease firing in your front. Captain McCreary, signal officer, reports three squadrons of cavalry passing to your right. Throw out skirmishers, and keep a sharp lookout to prevent being flanked.

MERRITT,
General.

General Howard wishes to know anything relative to the enemy's movements in front.

T. R. CLARK.

All quiet. Enemy are throwing up earthworks near Antietam Creek.

McCREARY.

Our cavalry are retiring from the right. The enemy's cavalry and infantry are advancing on the left.

DANIELS.

JULY 13.

Captain NICODEMUS:

The enemy are reported by a citizen from within their lines to have broken up their camps, and to be moving all their wagon trains toward Falling Waters.

Respectfully, your obedient servant,

W. G. McCREARY,
Captain, Signal Corps, U. S. Army.

Capt. WILLIAM J. L. NICODEMUS,
Signal Officer.

No. 21.

Report of Lieut. George A. Fisher, Acting Signal Officer.

GEORGETOWN, D. C., *July* 18, 1863.

CAPTAIN : I have the honor to submit the following report of duty performed since July 6, 1863:

On the evening of the 6th, was ordered to precede the main party, with Lieutenants Herzog and Rushby, and with our men accompany and guard the wagon train to Frederick, Md., where we arrived on the 8th instant, and immediately reported to you at your headquarters.

About an hour afterward I received orders from you to proceed without delay to Crampton's Gap, in the South Mountain Range, and open communication with Middletown, Maryland Heights, and South Mountain, if possible, and take observations of the movements of the enemy. I endeavored that evening to open communication, but was unable to find a point where I could see more than one of the stations, and, after calling Maryland Heights for some time, was obliged to give it up for the night.

Early next morning I moved across the gap, and proceeded along the ridge about 3 miles, and selected a station from which, with some labor, I was enabled to communicate with both Middletown and Maryland Heights, thus completing the line of stations between Maryland Heights and Hagerstown.

On the 12th instant, Captains [Joseph] Gloskoski and [Richard] Dinsmore received orders from Captain Norton to close up the station at Middletown and rejoin his command. I was then obliged to find some other station with which to keep up the line of communication, and was enabled to do so with Lieutenant Briggs, who was at Elk Ridge, in communication with South Mountain. Owing to the state of the weather, for the most of the time we were unable to take many observations, but embraced every opportunity that presented itself. I submit a few of the messages transmitted :

MARYLAND HEIGHTS, *July* 14, 1863.

Captain NICODEMUS :

Our troops crossed and reoccupied Harper's Ferry and Bolivar Heights to-day. Can see no indication or movement of any troops in or near Martinsburg.

HERZOG,
Lieutenant.

JULY 15, 1863.

Captain NICODEMUS :

All quiet at Maryland Heights ; very few troops here.

HERZOG.

July 15, I was ordered to close up station and report to you at Frederick without delay.

Very respectfully, your obedient servant,

GEO. A. FISHER,
Lieutenant, Acting Signal Officer.

No. 22.

Report of Lieut. Ephraim A. Briggs, Acting Signal Officer.

INSTRUCTION CAMP, U. S. SIGNAL CORPS,
July 19, 1863.

CAPTAIN: In compliance with an order received this morning to make an official report of all duty performed by me as acting signal officer of the Washington Reserve Signal Corps since the 6th instant, I submit the following:

At 5 p. m. of the 6th instant, I received orders to be prepared to leave camp with the party going to the front for active duty in the field.

At 8 p. m. the 6th instant, said party left camp, Georgetown, D. C., proceeding toward Frederick, riding all night, arriving at Frederick, Md., 5 p. m. of the 7th instant, when I was ordered to proceed toward South Mountain without delay, in company with Capt. N. Daniels. We proceeded to South Mountain, opening signal station on the Washington Monument at 9 a. m. of the 8th instant, the heavy rain falling all night preventing its being sooner accomplished.

By order of Captain Daniels, I proceeded to Elk Mountain to open signal station communication with one on Washington Monument. Arriving at Elk Mountain 11 a. m., I opened station, and called Monument until 1 p. m.; had no reply; atmosphere was clear. I saw the enemy's pickets within 2 miles of this point. At 2.30 p. m., commenced and called Monument all the afternoon, excepting from 4 p. m. until

5.30 p. m., without receiving reply; 4 p. m. received following message by orderly:

To Signal Officer:
    Ascertain and send immediate report whether the rebels are in Sharpsburg or Keedysville. Their evident intention is to take Sharpsburg. Make report in writing, and send by orderly.

                            A. B. JEROME,
            First Lieutenant, and Acting Assistant Signal Officer.

At 4.15 p. m. sent following answer:

Lieutenant JEROME:
    I can see no signs of enemy occupying Sharpsburg or Keedysville. Their cavalry were in both places this morning, I am informed by reliable citizens.
    If you can communicate with Washington Monument, tell them to answer my call.

                            E. A. BRIGGS,
                First Lieutenant, and Acting Signal Officer.

At 9 p. m. returned to Boonsborough, and procured rations and forage for my men and animals, oil, &c.
    At 10.30 a. m., received following by orderly:

Lieutenant BRIGGS:
    Proceed to station on Elk Ridge, which you occupied last night, and communicate with station one-half mile northeast of Boonsborough. If you cannot see that station, communicate with the Monument.

                            NICODEMUS,
                    Captain, Signal Officer.

July 9.—The day smoky; not ab.   do anything.
    July 10.—Called the Monument from 8.30 a. m. an hour and thirty minutes before any reply.
    At 3 p. m. received from Monument signal station:

To ELK MOUNTAIN:
    You will go to the gap, and open with Bakersville and the white flag at the foot of the Monument.
    By order of—

                            NORTON,
                                Captain.

In obedience to above, I spent from that time till 6 p. m. answering and swinging, as I saw three or four white flags swinging in vicinity of Bakersville, though facing too much to my right. Swung torch during the evening without any success.
    Called the Monument to report I was not able to communicate with Bakersville; after an hour's work, gave them up.
    July 11.—The morning thick and hazy. Clear at 10.30 a. m.
    At 1 p. m. received from Washington Monument:

Lieutenant BRIGGS:
    I want communication with Maryland Heights, through Boonsborough and Lieutenant Fisher.

                            NICODEMUS,
                                Captain.

5 p. m.—Sent from Elk Mountain:

Captain NICODEMUS:
    I have seen Fisher, at Crampton's Pass, and have communication open with Maryland Heights when atmosphere permits.

                            E. A. BRIGGS,
                    Lieutenant, Acting Signal Officer.

10 *p. m.*—Sent from Elk Mountain:

Captain NICODEMUS:

Maryland Heights are in full view of this point, or at Crampton's house. On this range, both Maryland Heights and Monument are to be seen, and commanding miles of the river and fords at the same time; the latter not to be seen from this point excepting at Dam No. 4.

E. A. BRIGGS,
Lieutenant, Acting Signal Officer.

Through messenger, I called Monument till 12 a. m. and got no reply, and sent it by an orderly.

July 12.—Thick and excessively smoky all day; not able to see anything.

12 *m.*—Received by Orderly Knapp:

Lieutenant BRIGGS:

You will open signal station on Elk Mountain, beyond Keedysville, communicating with Maryland Heights, Crampton's Pass, Washington Monument, and, when Downsville station is open, with Fairview. You will report to me through Washington Monument station, or in any way possible. My headquarters are with the right wing. Answer all flags. You will be relieved when station is not needed.

NICODEMUS,
Captain, Signal Officer.

Sent the following at 1 p. m.:

Captain NICODEMUS:

My men are in need of rations and my animals of forage. Please light a fire at 9 p. m., that I may find your locality. In order to run this station successfully, requires more men.

Your obedient servant,

BRIGGS,
Lieutenant, and Acting Signal Officer.

3.30 *p. m.*—Heavy shower until 5.30 p. m. Worked until 12 m. Could not get the Monument. Went to bed.

July 13.—Day rainy and thick. Cut the timber and bushes from top of mountain, so as to command all points. Built a tower. Had calls from several signal officers of Army of the Potomac viewing the country and Antietam battle-ground.

ELK MOUNTAIN, 12 m.

Captain NICODEMUS:

The weather has prevented my getting Bakersville or Downsville. Communication to Maryland Heights is perfect. I tried to communicate with you via the Monument yesterday without any success.

E. A. BRIGGS,
Lieutenant, and Acting Signal Officer.

July 14, 8 a. m.—Sent from Elk Mountain:

Captain NICODEMUS:

Captain Norton orders me to Crampton's house, on this range of mountains. I await your order.

BRIGGS,
Lieutenant, and Acting Signal Officer.

Kept a close watch all day for flags, and till 1 a. m. July 15 for lights near Mount Moriah or Donnellies Hill.

8.30 *p. m.*—Received from Fisher, at Crampton's Pass:

Captain NICODEMUS:

Our troops crossed and reoccupied Harper's Ferry and Bolivar Heights. Saw Martinsburg to-day; no movement to indicate troops there.

HERZOG,
Lieutenant, and Acting Signal Officer.

Called Monument one hour, and closed up, unable to forward the message.

July 15.—Smoky all morning and afternoon. Orderly brought following message:

Lieutenants Herzog, Rushby, Briggs, and Fisher, with parties, will report to me at Frederick without delay.

NICODEMUS,

Captain, Signal Officer Comdg. Washington Reserve Signal Party.

Sent same to Lieutenant Fisher without any delay, and immediately repaired to Frederick and awaited further orders.

July 17, 12 *m.*—Party left Frederick, proceeding toward Rockville; at Nielsville, by order of Captain Nicodemus, I remained there until the wagon train came up and took charge of them, not going in camp until next morning. Arose at 3 a. m.; prepared for an early start on the road at 5 a. m.; moved moderately, reaching George-town, D. C., at 12.30 p. m. of 18th instant.

I would most respectfully mention Private Temple for his untiring attention to duties on station and uniform good behavior. Private Boynton seems to be a most willing man, ever ready, but lacking experience. I would also say I never have been found absent from post.

I am, yours, respectfully,

E. A. BRIGGS,

Lieutenant, and Acting Signal Officer.

Capt. WILLIAM J. L. NICODEMUS,
Signal Officer.

No. 23.

Report of Lieut. Julius M. Swain, Acting Signal Officer.

GEORGETOWN, D. C., *July* 18, 1863.

CAPTAIN: I beg leave to submit the following report, which I regret contains but an imperfect record of the messages sent while with the signal party recently under your command in Maryland:

I had the misfortune to lose my memorandum book containing a copy of the messages sent to General Buford from station near Boonsborough during the engagement on the afternoon of the 8th instant, as well as some others of later date.

In accordance, with your orders, I left Frederick on the evening of the 7th instant, and proceeded to South Mountain Gap, in company with Captain Denicke, at which point we were ordered to report to Captain Daniels, July 8. We arrived at 3 a. m., and as it was raining very hard and Captain Daniels could not be found, we lay by till daylight.

Captain Daniels arrived at the Mountain House at 8 o'clock, and as soon as the weather would permit, about 9 a. m., I was ordered to Boonsborough, where I arrived at 10 o'clock, and reported to General Kilpatrick, after which I opened station on hill in rear of town, which commanded a good view of our front.

Saw the enemy's battery open on us at 10.30 a. m., and shortly afterward, when they changed position and advanced toward Boonsborough by the pike, reported fact to commanding officer.

At 12 m. Captain Daniels opened station near the Hagerstown pike, about 1 mile beyond Boonsborough, and ordered me to join him, which I did at once.

I remained there during the day in communication with Captain Denicke, on Washington Monument, whose station overlooked the enemy, and sent frequent messages from him to General Buford, then in command.

At 3 p. m. sent the following :

Captain DENICKE:

Lieutenant Denicke will open communication between you and Frederick.

DANIELS,
Captain.

July 9.—Enemy retreated last evening about 2 miles toward Funkstown, and Captain Daniels went to front this morning, leaving me on the station opened yesterday.

On your arrival, about noon, you ordered me to send frequent dispatches to Colonel Myer at Washington, apprising him of all movements of interest.

Sent following:

BOONSBOROUGH, *July* 9—7.30 p. m.

Heavy skirmishing has just opened about 3 miles from here, on Hagerstown road.

NICODEMUS,
Captain.

July 10.—Removed station to hill near Boonsborough, and opened communication with Lieutenant Tuckerman on left of our line, with Captain Denicke on Monument, and Captain Stone on Sharpsburg pike, near General French's headquarters.

Received orders to report all important messages by telegraph to General Meade and Colonel Myer.

During the day sent the following telegrams:

BOONSBOROUGH, *July* 10—7 a. m.

Col. ALBERT J. MYER:

Heavy skirmishing has just commenced about 4 miles from here, toward Williamsport.   The Sixth Army Corps is in advance, on way to front.

NICODEMUS,
Captain.

SIGNAL STATION NEAR BOONSBOROUGH,
July 10—8 a. m.

Col. ALBERT J. MYER:

The skirmishing has become quite general, with heavy artillery firing. The First Corps just passed here, on way to front.

NICODEMUS,
Captain.

BOONSBOROUGH, *July* 10—10 a. m.

Col. ALBERT J. MYER:

Heavy firing still continues near Funkstown.   In my dispatch of this morning, I should have said Hagerstown instead of Williamsport.

NICODEMUS,
Captain.

BOONSBOROUGH, *July* 10—11.30 a. m.

Colonel MYER:

Has been no firing for an hour. Eleventh Corps, General Howard, just passed, and have taken the Williamsport road.   The men are in excellent spirits.

NICODEMUS,
Captain.

BOONSBOROUGH—1 p. m.
Col. ALBERT J. MYER:

Our right has driven the enemy to Funkstown, 2 miles from Hagerstown.
NICODEMUS,
Captain

3.30 p. m.
Col. ALBERT J MYER:

The infantry relieved the cavalry at 2 p. m.   Sharp firing since.   The enemy still occupies Funkstown and the crossing of the Big Antietam.
NICODEMUS,
Captain.

SIGNAL STATION, *Boonsborough*—6 p. m.
Major-General MEADE:

I have been informed by the citizens that it is reported a large amount of ammunition is expected by the rebs to-day from Richmond.
By order of Major-General French:
C. F. STONE,
Captain, and Signal Officer.

July 11, agreeably to your order, I reported to you at station 1 mile east of Funkstown with party this noon.   Remained on your station during afternoon and night.   I had communication with Lieutenant Galbraith, and with Captain [William H.] Hill and Lieutenant [Isaac S.] Lyon, of Fifth Corps.

STATION NEAR FUNKSTOWN, *July* 12, 1863—8.30 p. m.
Colonel MYER:

Our line has crossed the creek beyond Funkstown.
NICODEMUS,
Captain.

Sent copy of above to General Meade.   Remained on station till 9.30 a. m., when you ordered me to follow you to Hagerstown.

Arrived there at 10 o'clock, just as the enemy was shelling our battery near seminary, after their rear had passed out of town. Opened station nearly 1 mile beyond seminary, at right of Greencastle pike, but, not having a good situation, I moved by your permission to the northwest of Hagerstown, near Catholic cemetery, where I had an excellent view of all movements on our right.

At 12 m. I sent you the following by orderly:

STATION NEAR HAGERSTOWN.
Captain NICODEMUS:

I made a circuit after I left you till I came in sight of enemy's left; then I placed my party in the hollow, and watched them over the hill.

Their left is advancing slowly but surely, and now occupies ground which I left within half an hour.   I sent note to Captain Oliphant, commanding Fifth Michigan Cavalry, who are the outer vedettes.

From what I can see I think the rebels are in considerable force over the crest of the hill.   We can see them here with the naked eye.   My flag is behind the hill, though in plain sight of you at left of Catholic cemetery.

Very respectfully, your obedient servant,
JULIUS M. SWAIN,
Lieutenant, and Acting Signal Officer.

At 3 p. m. I notified you that about 500 cavalry had come down the hill toward me, a portion of whom were in line of battle; also that I saw 20 mounted men, with axes, ride rapidly to right of our line.   At 5.30 p. m. I sent you the following:

SIGNAL STATION—5.30 p. m.
Captain NICODEMUS:

For two hours before the rain I saw a commanding officer, with low black hat and heavy black beard, with his staff and orderlies, 24 in number.   He was evidently making a reconnaissance, and now I see his headquarters are pitched on crest of the hill, in plain sight. About 500 cavalry are massed in front, and their picket line is very strong. Commanding officers are now evidently directing their movements, and I see three squads on the hill, where the officers are pointing to our right and making various gestures. It looks as if the cavalry were preparing to make a charge into town.

The "graybacks" are getting very impudent, and are firing on our skirmishers in all directions, especially on extreme right, where they have been quiet all day.

Since I commenced to write, the cavalry I spoke of have mounted, and seem to be in readiness for a move. A citizen, whom I saw a mile from here, tells me that the enemy has a line of intrenchments just over the hill, as he was there yesterday and saw the works.

Very respectfully,

JULIUS M. SWAIN,
Lieutenant, and Acting Signal Officer.

July 13.—Notified you at 6 a. m. that the enemy was hard at work throwing up breastworks, and later in the forenoon sent you a message that they had placed three sections of battery in position, bearing about 30 degrees east of north, in a direction to repel an attack from our right. Notified you several times during the day of the progress of the enemy's work.

At 7.30 p. m. sent the following message:

Our cavalry, under General Kilpatrick, who were massed in the hollow on our right, were forced to retire when about to charge on the enemy.

Rained nearly all night, and on the morning of the 14th was hazy till 6 o'clock, when we discovered that the enemy had abandoned his works. Sent you message to that effect, and was ordered to open station on the hill recently occupied by them. Proceeded there at once, and in half an hour was ordered to report to you at Williamsport, in company with Lieutenant Galbraith. On my arrival, was ordered to Falling Waters, and at 3.30 opened station there, and communicated with Captain Daniels at Williamsport.

Sent following message :

Captain DANIELS :

No signs of the enemy. They all crossed here before noon. Remained on station till 7.30 p. m., when I found that I could not communicate with any one, as the station at Williamsport had been broken up.

July 15.—Reported to camp near Funkstown, and was ordered by Captain McCreary to return to Hagerstown, to rest the horses and remain till party came up.

July 16.—Came to Frederick, where we spent the night.

July 17.—Returned to signal camp, Georgetown, D. C.

Before closing this report, I wish to call your attention to Private Ezra M. Chaffee, Sixth Michigan Cavalry, Company F, who acted as orderly eight days, and by his promptness, strict attention to duty, and cheerful disposition rendered me much assistance. I respectfully recommend that he be detailed for duty in this corps, as I feel that he would make an excellent flagman.

Very respectfully, your obedient servant,

JULIUS M. SWAIN,
Second Lieut. Thirty-ninth Massachusetts Vols.,
Acting Signal Officer.

Capt. WILLIAM J. L. NICODEMUS,
Signal Officer.

No. 24.

*Reports of Brig. Gen. Rufus Ingalls, U. S. Army, Chief Quarter-
master.* *

HEADQUARTERS ARMY OF THE POTOMAC,
Camp near Culpeper, Va., September 29, 1863.

GENERAL: In compliance with your General Orders, No. 13, of July
22 last, I have the honor to submit the following report on the operations of the quartermaster's department of the Army of the Potomac
during the fiscal year ending June 30:

*   *   *   *   *   *   *

On June 14, we broke up our headquarters camp near Falmouth,
and pursued the route by Dumfries, Fairfax, Leesburg, Edwards
Ferry, and Poolesville, to Frederick City, on our second Maryland
Campaign. The army was in excellent condition, and transportation
was perfect, and our sources of supply same as in first campaign.
The officers in our department were thoroughly trained in their
duties. It was almost as easy to maneuver the trains as the troops.
It is, therefore, unnecessary to go further into the details of the
march.

The rebel army had again invaded Maryland, and had even advanced as far as Carlisle and York, in Pennsylvania. The Army of
the Potomac was again in pursuit of its inveterate foe, and finally
met him in pitched battle of three days' fighting, and compelled him
to again recross the Potomac.

General Meade, justly the conqueror and hero of Gettysburg, assumed command of the army on June 28.

On the last day of the fiscal year, two days later, I was at Taneytown, with headquarters of the army.

*   *   *   *   *   *

RUFUS INGALLS,
Chief Quartermaster.

The QUARTERMASTER-GENERAL OF THE ARMY.

———

OFFICE OF CHIEF QUARTERMASTER,
ARMIES OPERATING AGAINST RICHMOND,
City Point, Va., August 28, 1864.

GENERAL: In compliance with your General Orders, No. 29, of the
6th ultimo, calling for an annual report for the fiscal year ending
June 30, I have the honor to submit the following:

*   *   *   *   *   *   *

On July 1, the headquarters remained at that point [Taneytown,
Md.], while the army was being concentrated at Gettysburg. The
First and Eleventh Corps opened the great battle of Gettysburg on
that day. The wagon trains and all *impedimenta* had been assem.
bled at Westminster, on the pike and railroad leading to Baltimore,
at a distance of about 25 miles in rear of the army. No baggage was
allowed in front. Officers and men went forward without tents and

---

* Extracts from annual reports.

with only a short supply of food. A portion only of the ammunition wagons and ambulances was brought up to the immediate rear of our lines. This arrangement, which is always made in this army on the eve of battle and marches in presence of the enemy, enables experienced and active officers to supply their commands without risking the loss of trains or obstructing roads over which the columns march. Empty wagons can be sent to the rear, and loaded ones, or pack trains, brought up during the night, or at such times and places as will not interfere with the movements of troops.

On this campaign, from the Rappahannock to the James, our trains, large as they were necessarily, being over four thousand heavy wagons, never delayed the march of a column, and, excepting small-ammunition trains, were never seen by our troops. The main trains were conducted on roads to our rear and left without the loss of a wagon.

On the morning of July 2, I arrived at Gettysburg, and was present during the battle which resulted so favorably to our arms. Arrangements were made to issue supplies at Westminster, brought over the branch road from Baltimore, and at Frederick by the Baltimore and Ohio Railroad. Telegraphic communications extended from these points to Baltimore, Washington, &c., and our army communicated every third hour with them by means of relays of cavalry couriers. Ample supplies of forage, clothing, and subsistence were received and issued to fill every necessary want without in any instance retarding military movements. All stores thrown forward over these routes and not issued were returned to the main depot at Washington, and again forwarded on the Orange and Alexandria Railroad after the army had crossed to the south side of the Potomac.

After the retreat of the rebel army from Gettysburg, General Meade on July 6 ordered the concentration of the Army of the Potomac at Middletown on the evening of the 7th. The trains were directed to join their respective corps; all those that were at Westminster to pass through Frederick, to enable them to fill up with supplies. The headquarters were in Frederick the night of the 6th.

The army was moved on the 9th from Middletown to the vicinity of Boonsborough. The order of the day directed that no trains but ammunition wagons, medical wagons, and ambulances should accompany the troops. Supply and baggage wagons were to be parked in the Middletown Valley, on the roads taken by their respective corps. No special guards were to be left with the trains. Every man able to do duty was required to be in the ranks.

It was here known to the general commanding that the enemy had not crossed to the south bank, as had been rumored, but was in force, and intrenched on the north bank, from Williamsport to Shepherdstown; hence the precautions in regard to the trains and preparations for battle.

On the 10th, 11th, 12th, and 13th, the Army of the Potomac was engaged in taking up positions in front of the enemy and in making reconnaissances. During this time the trains remained in Middletown Valley. Our headquarters were on the Antietam, upon the road from Boonsborough to Williamsport. The army was kept supplied with all that was absolutely essential and nothing more. At our headquarters, for example, we only had a few tent flies, blankets, a few small portable paper cases, and two or three days' cooked food.

On the night of the 13th, the rebel army crossed into Virginia. This fact was well established in the mind of the general commanding the

Army of the Potomac by 12 o'clock on the 14th. He issued orders on that day, moving the army on the 15th as follows: The Twelfth and Second Corps to move [by way] of Downsville, Bakersville, Mercersville, Sharpsburg, and the Antietam Iron Works, and encamp in Pleasant Valley, near Harper's Ferry. The Fifth and First Corps by Williamsport and Boonsborough road, via Jones' Cross-Roads; thence to Keedysville by the road between the Sharpsburg pike and the Antietam to Keedysville; thence through Fox's Gap to Burkittsville by the road nearest the mountain (the shortest road), and thence to Berlin. The Sixth and Eleventh Corps, via Funkstown and Boonsborough, through Turner's Gap to Middletown; thence to Petersville and Berlin. The Artillery Reserve to move by way of Boonsborough pike, through Turner's Gap to Middletown, and thence to the vicinity of Berlin by Petersville; to take precedence as far as Middletown, after which to march between the Sixth and Eleventh Corps. The trains to join their respective corps at their camps in the vicinity of Harper's Ferry and Berlin. The corps to move in the order named, and the corps in advance to march at early daylight, and to be followed by the next corps when the road is clear. Headquarters to be at Berlin on the night of the 15th.

I have indicated this movement of the 15th in detail in order to exhibit in this report the usual manner of moving a large army and concentrating it at a particular point.

On the 16th, orders were issued to the army to replenish its supplies from the depots which I had established at Berlin, Sandy Hook, and Harper's Ferry, and to be quickly prepared to continue the march with three days' cooked rations in haversacks, three days' hard bread and small rations in the regimental wagons, and, in addition, two days' salt meat and seven days' hard bread and small rations in the wagons of the supply trains. The army was supplied with clothing, fresh horses, and mules. Our lines of supply were the Chesapeake and Ohio Canal and Baltimore and Ohio Railroad. The supplies furnished here were expected to answer until we could reach the Manassas Gap road at Gainesville and White Plains, and the Warrenton branch at Warrenton.

The Third and Fifth Corps having crossed into the Piney Run Valley near Lovettsville, the rest of the army followed on the 18th and 19th.

The Second and Twelfth Corps crossed at Harper's Ferry, and the First, Sixth, and Eleventh Corps, Artillery Reserve, and headquarters at Berlin, each command followed by its own trains. The rear guard of the cavalry crossed at both points after the Sixth and Twelfth Corps. It will be seen by reference to my last annual report that General McClellan made the passage of this river at the same points with the same army, marching in the same direction, in pursuit of the same enemy, on the last of October and first of November the preceding year. General Meade pursued the same routes as far as Warrenton as were taken by the army in November, 1862. Some of his corps deviated somewhat and made demonstrations at Manassas Gap, &c., but not materially different in results from the year before.

I left the army at Berlin, and went to Washington to make arrangements for supplies over the Orange and Alexandria Railroad. Having perfected the arrangements and submitted requisitions, I proceeded by rail to White Plains, on the Manassas Gap Railroad, on the 24th, and rejoined headquarters at Warrenton on the evening of the 25th.

The campaign ended here, and our army shortly took up a line across the Orange and Alexandria Railroad, near the Rappahannock, the right of our infantry resting at the Waterloo Crossing, the left at Ellis' Ford. Cavalry was on both flanks and in rear. Our lines of communications were protected by the Department of Washington to the Bull Run Bridge, and by the Eleventh Corps from that point to Catlett's.

The headquarters were at Germantown, on the railroad, about 3½ miles south of Warrenton Junction. The depots were established at Warrenton Junction, Warrenton, and Bealeton.

The army remained in this position quietly until the middle of September.

*   *   *   *   *   *   *

I am, very respectfully, your most obedient servant,

RUFUS INGALLS,
Brigadier-General, and Chief Quartermaster,
Armies operating against Richmond.

Bvt. Maj. Gen. M. C. MEIGS,
Quartermaster-General, U. S. Army, Washington, D. C.

No. 25.

Report of Brig. Gen. Marsena R. Patrick, U. S. Army, Provost-Marshal-General.

OFFICE PROVOST-MARSHAL,
October 4, 1863.

Estimate of captures from the enemy during their raid into Pennsylvania, in June and July, 1863.

Where confined.	Officers.	Enlisted men.
Fort Delaware	417	7,244
De Camp General Hospital, David's Island, N. Y	65	2,472
West's buildings, Baltimore, Md	51	632
United States hospital, Chester, Pa	83	1,049
United States hospital, Gettysburg, Pa	112	1,235
United States hospital, Harrisburg, Pa	14	111
United States hospital, Frederick, Md	12	124
Total	754	12,867

I have consulted Colonel Hoffman, commissary-general of prisoners, who makes up the above as the closest estimate that can be made of captures on the north side of the Potomac. Of those at Fort Delaware, many were sick and wounded, but in general able to travel. Colonel Hoffman thinks these might amount to 700.

Respectfully submitted.

M. R. PATRICK,
Provost-Marshal-General.

No. 26.

Report of Lieut. John R. Edie, Acting Chief Ordnance Officer, Army of the Potomac.

REPORT OF ORDNANCE AND ORDNANCE STORES COLLECTED ON THE BATTLE-FIELD OF GETTYSBURG, AND SHIPPED TO THE WASHINGTON ARSENAL.

Collected by—

Lieut. Morris Schaff, Ordnance Department:

Muskets	19,664
Bayonets	9,250
Small-arms ammunition ....rounds..	14,000
Cartridge-boxes	1,200
Sabers	300
Artillery wheels	26

Lieut. William J. Augustine, First Division, Twelfth Army Corps:

Muskets	804
Cartridge-boxes	390
Cartridge-box belts	250
Cartridge-box plates	400
Waist-belts	187
Waist-belt plates	100
Cap-pouches	136
Bayonet-scabbards	100

Lieut. Edward H. Newcomb, Third Division, Eleventh Army Corps:

Muskets	1,142
Bayonets	581
Accouterments	441

Capt. George A. Batchelder, First Division, Fifth Army Corps:

Muskets	800

Capt. James G. Derrickson, First Division, Second Army Corps:

Muskets	425
Cartridge-boxes	50
Sabers	2
Cartridge-box belts	50

Lieut. W. E. Potter, Third Division, Second Army Corps:

Muskets	339
Bayonets	110
Cartridge-boxes	110
Cap-pouches	110
Bayonet-scabbards	110

Capt. G. M. Elliott, Second Division, Twelfth Army Corps:

Muskets	1,680
Bayonets	639
Accouterments	200
Sabers	13

Capt. W. E. Graves, Tenth New York Cavalry:

Cartridge-boxes	84
Carbines	114
Revolvers	5
Swivels	82
Sabers	51
Saber-belts	10
Gun-slings	76

Capt. John Dessauer:

Bayonets 11
Rifles 10
Accouterments 2
Saber-belts 10
Caissons and limbers.. 2

Captain Hall, Second Maine Battery:

Guns—rifled.. 2
Gun-carriages 1
Limbers... 2

JNO. R. EDIE,
Lieut. Acting Chief Ordnance Officer, Army Potomac.

No. 27.

*Report of Brig. Gen. Henry W. Benham, U. S. Army, commanding
Engineer Brigade.*

HEADQUARTERS ENGINEER BRIGADE,
NEAR NAVY YARD, WASHINGTON,
Engineer Depot, June 18, 1863—8 a. m.

I have the honor to make the following brief report of my operations since the receipt of the order to take up the bridges on the
Rappahannock on the 13th instant:

I was down at the crossing with my men and teams about 9 p. m.,
when I had been notified that all would be across. The crossing
commenced, however, only at about 10 p. m., and at about 11.10 I
was notified by General Newton that one bridge could be taken up,
and at about 12.10 that the second could be removed. The troops,
however, continued to straggle down for nearly three hours after,
boats being sent over for them. Although the night was a part of
the time intensely dark, the two bridges were taken up, and I saw
the last chess loaded at about 4 a. m. The last pontoon was specially
reported to me to be on its truck, and every truck with its pontoon,
some delay being caused by hunting up the pontoons, which the men
of the crossing force, as reported to me, had left adrift after crossing
their commands.

The bridge train closed upon our old camp-ground about 5 a. m.,
and, after the necessary feeding of the teams, started at once for
Aquia Creek, I myself preceding them, reaching that station about
8 a. m., in time to obtain a boat and go with the regular battalion to
Occoquan to see the bridge laid there, which was completed at about
5 p. m. of the 14th, or one hour earlier than the order required. The
fact being reported through General Slocum, I at once returned to
Aquia Creek, and found that the pontoons, having been delayed by
the blocking of the road by the teams of the Sixth Corps, which had
started before the bridges were up, had only been able to reach
Aquia Creek late in the afternoon, and I learned from General Warren that General Butterfield, fearing they would obstruct or be too
late to join the other trains of the army on the left [right] bank, had
ordered they should be crossed to Liverpool Point, on the right [left]
bank of the Potomac, for passage to Alexandria. As I found the
road very bad at Occoquan Bridge, and thought it much better 2
miles below, I telegraphed to you about 9 p. m. that I would hold a

long bridge ready until 8 o'clock the next morning. Between 11 and 12 p. m. General Warren informed me that this bridge was desired, and I had it started with a proper working force, to reach the bar of the Occoquan about daylight.

I then remained at Aquia until 11 a. m. of the 15th, until several hours after the mass of the pontoons had left for Washington, and until about one-half of the land transportation had been crossed to Liverpool Point, when I proceeded to Alexandria, to arrange for the arrival and proper disposition of the command. The regulars and the Fiftieth Regiment arrived about noon of the 16th with the Occoquan bridges.

About 8 p. m. of the 16th, I received an order to have a bridge of 1,200 feet in the Georgetown Canal by daylight on the 17th, which I at once directed the whole command to prepare, it requiring much time to unload trucks and rearrange the boats for passing the locks. The regular engineers were assigned to the duty of laying this bridge.

About 2 a. m. of the 17th, I received a dispatch directing the bridge to be laid at Noland's Ford by noon of the 18th, and, it appearing necessary by this dispatch, I ordered 250 more men of the Fiftieth to accompany the bridge. The wording of the dispatch left me to believe I was to go up also, leaving my trains here until otherwise advised, since by the time I could prepare the orders for the additional men, &c., the last of the boats had started for Georgetown, so that I was not able to send the last information to Captain [Charles N.] Turnbull. The men of the Fiftieth, however, though delayed some two hours by the fault or misunderstanding of a steamer captain, were started at about 8 a. m.

Captain Turnbull was fortunately up with his boats, all in the canal, about 6 a. m., and he wrote me that he was putting them through the set of locks then above, which was what I expected and desired. Between 5 and 6 a. m. I sent to the quartermaster to have teams arranged to tow them up the canal, but was told I must send to Washington for them, and the delay of the boats, as above, made it necessary to send a staff officer by land to Washington; and about 10 a. m. he was able to arrange for the teams, which reached the upper locks about 12.30 o'clock.

Captain Turnbull, as he states, as no direct order had been given (in fact, though it was sent, it had not been pressed forward to him because he reported he was doing it), and because his men were fatigued, stopped the passing of his boats through the locks, so they did not all get through till 1 to 2 p. m., when the teams were connected as fast as possible, and the boats moved off rapidly before 3 p. m., and with every prospect of being at Noland's Ford by the hour originally ordered. No delay on the part of any of this command has occurred, unless possibly one or two hours were lost by stopping the passage of the boats through the locks, which had been reported to me as going on, as above stated.

On returning to this depot, about 5 p. m., I found the trains from Liverpool Point coming in, having made, as reported, fully 60 miles since 10 a. m. of the preceding day, the 15th, and the ambulance train of sick and wounded had just arrived. The delay at Liverpool Point was occasioned by the large quantity of material that had to be taken from the steamers and reloaded after Aquia Creek had been actually abandoned.

I am now about to bring the bridges from Alexandria to this depot for rearrangement and repairs. We have nearly 200 pontoons to examine and arrange into bridges, and about 1,200 animals of the trains to be cared for, while the total effective force of my brigade (except the company and fractional company at work in the depot and the company at Harper's Ferry) is only about 1,000 to 1,100 men, and of them nearly 600 are now up the Potomac, under Major Spaulding and Captain Turnbull, and the balance of the command, some 200 of the Fiftieth, now at Alexandria, under Colonel Pettes, and the three years' men of the Fifteenth, now being reorganized under Major Cassin, and just in here with the trains, should, as I would respectfully recommend, all be concentrated at this depot, when the services of all will be required for the care and guarding of this large number of animals and the speedy restoration of the bridges to a serviceable condition, which will be immediately reported to headquarters.

I am, very respectfully, your obedient servant,
H. W. BENHAM,
Brigadier-General, Commanding.

General S. WILLIAMS,
Assistant Adjutant-General, Army of the Potomac.

[Indorsement.]

Direct the corps of engineers now at Harper's Ferry to report to Captain Turnbull, and for General Benham to concentrate the remaining part of command, now in Washington and Alexandria, to hold them at his depot, in readiness to march at the shortest notice.

J. H.

Telegraph this to Generals Benham and Tyler, at Sandy Hook.

SEPTEMBER. 29—6.15 p. m.

Done.

D. B.

No. 28.

Reports of Brig. Gen. Henry J. Hunt, U. S. Army, Chief of Artillery, Army of the Potomac.

ARTILLERY HEADQUARTERS, ARMY OF THE POTOMAC,
September 27, 1863.

GENERAL: I have the honor to submit the following report of the operations of the artillery of this army in the battle of Gettysburg, July 1, 2, and 3:

On July 1, Reynolds' (First) and Howard's (Eleventh) corps and Buford's division of cavalry, the whole under the command of Maj. Gen. J. F. Reynolds, engaged the enemy on the west and northwest of the town of Gettysburg. On the west of Gettysburg, about a third of a mile distant, there is a ridge running nearly north and south, parallel to the Emmitsburg pike. This ridge, on which the seminary is situated, is crossed by the Cashtown pike about 100 or 150 yards north of the seminary, and some 50 yards farther on it is cut by a railroad. On the west of the seminary is a grove of large trees, and the summit of the ridge and the upper part of both its slopes are more or less covered with open woods through its entire length. The ground slopes gradually to the west, and again rising, forms a second ridge, parallel to and about 500 yards distant from the Seminary Ridge. This second ridge is wider and smoother than that upon which the seminary stands, and terminates about 200 yards north of the point at which the Cashtown road crosses it. Near this point, and to the south of it, are a house and barn, with some five or six acres of orchard and wooded grounds, the rest of the ridge being cleared. It was in the skirmish near this house that General Reynolds fell, and over the country covered by the ridge that the First Corps fought. To the north and east, beyond where the Seminary Ridge terminates, the country is more flat, and this ground was occupied by the Eleventh Corps, the front of which was in a nearly perpendicular position to that of the First Corps, and faced the north.

About 10.15 a. m. Hall's battery (Second Maine, six 3-inch) was ordered into action by General Reynolds on the right of the Cashtown road, on the second ridge, and some 500 yards beyond the seminary. The enemy had previously opened fire from a battery of six guns at a distance of about 1,300 yards, and directly in front of this position, on Reynolds' troops, and Hall, on coming into action, replied with effect. In the course of half an hour, a body of the enemy's infantry approached the right of Hall's battery under cover of a ravine, and opened upon him at a distance of 60 or 80 yards, killing and wounding a number of his men and horses. The right and center sections replied with canister, while the left section continued its fire on the enemy's battery. The supports now falling back, Captain Hall found it necessary to retire, which he did by sections.

Soon after, the Third Division (Rowley's), First Corps, occupied the open ground on this ridge with Cooper's battery (B, First Pennsylvania, four 3-inch), which took post in an oat-field, about 380 yards south of the Cashtown road.

The Second Division (Robinson's) occupied a road on the west slope of the Seminary Ridge, north of the railroad, and the Eleventh Corps came into position on the flat ground farther north, and in a position nearly perpendicular to that of the First Corps. Colonel Wainwright, commanding the artillery of the First Corps, sent Stewart's battery (B, Fourth United States, six 12-pounders) to report to General Robinson, and ordered Reynolds to move with his battery to the support of Calef's horse battery (A, Second United States, six 3-inch), which had been placed in position by General Wadsworth on the spot just occupied by Hall's (Second Maine, six 3-inch), and was sharply engaged with the enemy's battery in its front. Reynolds had hardly taken position when the enemy opened a severe fire from a second battery immediately on his right. The cross-fire of the enemy's two batteries caused both Calef's and Reynolds' to retire, Reynolds taking up a new position at right angles to the ridge, with his left covered by the woods, near the house and barn referred to. While executing this movement, Captain Reynolds was severely wounded in the right eye, but refused to quit the field. The enemy's battery soon after ceased its fire. At the request of General Wadsworth, Colonel Wainwright posted Wilber's section of Reynolds' battery in the orchard on the south side of the Cashtown road, where he was sheltered from the fire of the enemy's battery on his right flank by the intervening house and barn, and moved the other two sections to the south side of the wood, on the open crest.

In the meantime the Eleventh Corps had taken position, and Dilger's battery (I, First Ohio, six 12-pounders), attached to Schurz's division, soon became engaged with one of the enemy's batteries at 1,000 yards distance, which was soon re-enforced by another. Dilger maintained his position until re-enforced by Wheeler (Thirteenth New York Independent, four 3-inch), sent to his assistance by Major Osborn, commanding the artillery of the corps, when a sharp contest ensued, the result of which was one piece of Wheeler's dismounted and five of the enemy's, which Major Osborn states they left on the ground. The enemy suffered the most loss. During this action, Captain Dilger several times changed the positions of his batteries with excellent effect, selecting his ground with judgment.

About 11 a. m. Wilkeson's battery (G, Fourth United States, four 12-pounders) came up, and reported to General Barlow, who posted it close to the enemy's line of infantry, with which it immediately became engaged, sustaining at the same time the fire of two of his batteries.

In the commencement of this unequal contest, Lieut. Bayard Wilkeson (Fourth U. S. Artillery), commanding the battery, a young officer of great gallantry, fell, mortally wounded, and was carried from the field. Lieutenant Bancroft succeeded to the command, and by changing position and distributing his sections, in order to meet the different movements of the enemy, succeeded in maintaining himself handsomely until the division fell back to the town, when he withdrew to Cemetery Hill.

About 4 p. m. the troops were withdrawn to Cemetery Hill, and Schurz's division, with Heckman's (K, First Ohio, four 12-pounders) and Wiedrich's (I, First New York, six 3-inch) batteries, were posted so as to cover the movement of the corps, Wiedrich's being placed on the hill in front of the cemetery entrance. Heckman worked his guns well, and held his ground until the enemy entered his battery. He then retired with the loss of one gun, the battery being so much crippled that it was sent to the rear, and was not again called into action.

Wiedrich's battery was actively engaged, and about 4.30 p. m. the enemy made an attempt to turn our right, but his line was very soon broken by the fire of this battery, and the attempt failed.

The First Corps was withdrawn about the same time as the Eleventh. Colonel Wainwright, commanding the artillery of this corps, understanding the order to hold Cemetery Hill to apply to Seminary Hill, posted Cooper's battery (B, First Pennsylvania, four 3-inch) in front of the professor's house. Captain Stevens (Fifth Maine, six 12-pounders) was soon after posted by General Doubleday on Cooper's right. Soon after, the enemy emerged in two strong columns from the woods in front, about 500 yards distant, outflanked our line nearly a third of a mile, then formed in two lines of battle, and advanced directly up the crest. During this movement, Reynolds battery (L, First New York, six 3-inch) opened on the columns, but the fire of his sections was much interfered with by the movements of our own infantry in their front. Colonel Wainwright therefore moved these two sections, under Lieutenant Breck, to a strong stone wall on the seminary crest, near Stevens' position. The movement was not ordered until the enemy, outnumbering our troops 5 to 1, were within 200 yards of the battery. Lieutenant Wilber's section of the same battery soon after fell back with his supports (L, First New York, six 3-inch; Fifth Maine, six 12-pounders, and Cooper's, B, First Pennsylvania, four 3-inch) to the same position, thus concentrating sixteen guns. Stewart's battery (B, Fourth United States, six 12-pounders) was also on the same line, half of the battery between the Cashtown pike and the railroad, the other half across the railroad, in the corner of a wood. The enemy's lines continued to advance across the space between the two crests, but when the first line was within about 100 yards of the seminary, Lieutenant Davison, Fourth U. S. Artillery, commanding the left half of Stewart's battery, placed his guns on the Cashtown pike, so as to enfilade the whole line. This movement, well sustained by the other batteries, brought the first line to a halt, but the second, supported by a column deployed from the Cashtown road, pushed on. An order was now received by Captain Stevens from General Wadsworth, directing his battery to withdraw, but Colonel Wainwright, not knowing this, and still under the'mistaken impression as to the importance of holding Seminary Hill, directed all the batteries to maintain their positions.

In a few minutes, however, all our infantry were seen rapidly retreating toward the town, and the batteries were all limbered to the rear, and moved off down the Cashtown pike, maintaining a walk until the infantry had left it. By this time our retreating columns were lapped by the enemy's skirmishers, who opened a severe fire from behind a fence within 50 yards of the road. As soon as the road was clear, the batteries moved at a trot, but it was too late to save all the material. Lieutenant Wilber's last piece (L, First New York, six 3-inch) had 1 of its wheel-horses shot, and, by the time this could be disengaged, 3 others were shot and Lieutenant Wilbur's own horse killed. It was impossible to move the piece off, and it was lost. No blame apparently can be attached to the officers of this or of Heckman's battery (K, First Ohio, four 12-pounders) for the loss of the two guns in the retiring of the two corps. It was the necessary result of the obstinate resistance made to the enemy, so as to cover the withdrawal of their respective corps. Three of the caisson bodies of Stewart's battery were broken down, 1 of his caissons exploded, 2 of his guns had been disabled by the breaking of their pointing rings, and 3 of Hall's guns dismounted.

The losses of the batteries of the First Corps in these operations were heavy ; 83 officers and men killed and wounded, including 6 officers wounded (Capt. G. T. Stevens and Lieut. C. O. Hunt, Fifth Maine, severely; Capt. G. H. Reynolds, L, First New York, severely; Lieut. J. Stewart, Fourth Artillery, slightly; Lieut. J. Davison, Fourth Artillery, severely ; Lieut. W. C. Miller, B, First Pennsylvania, slightly), and about 80 horses, a large proportion of the latter between the Seminary Ridge and the town, the enemy having at that time a fire upon them from both flanks and the rear, and no infantry replying. The batteries passed immediately through the town, and were placed with those of the Eleventh Corps in position on Cemetery Hill, so as to command the town and the approaches from the northwest. The batteries north of the Baltimore pike in front of the cemetery gate, under the command of Colonel Wainwright, chief of artillery, First Corps, were posted as follows: Stewart's battery (B, Fourth United States, four light 12-pounders) across the road, so as to command the approaches from town ; then Wiedrich's (I, First New York Artillery, four 3-inch), Cooper's (B, First Pennsylvania Artillery, four 3-inch), and Reynolds' (L, First New York Artillery, five 3-inch), in all thirteen 3-inch guns, along the north front, some of them in such a position that they could be turned to bear upon the town and the field of battle of the 1st. Stevens' battery (Fifth Maine, six 12-pounders) was posted to the right and some 50 yards in front of this line, on a knoll, from whence they could obtain an oblique fire upon the hills in front of our line, and a flanking fire at close quarters upon any attacking columns. Each of the guns in these batteries had a small earthwork thrown up in its front, to afford a partial shelter from the fire of the enemy's sharpshooters. Osborn's batteries (Bancroft's, G, Fourth U. S. Artillery, six 12-pounders; Dilger's, I, First Ohio, six 12-pounders; Wheeler's, Thirteenth New York, three 3-inch), of the Eleventh Corps, with the exception of Wiedrich's, transferred to Colonel Wainright, Heckman's, crippled and sent to the rear, and one gun of Wheeler's dismounted, were placed in the cemetery grounds, to the north of the Baltimore road.

On the night of July 1, the commanding general left Taneytown, and reached Gettysburg about 2 a. m. of the 2d. Soon after his arrival, he directed me to see to the position of the artillery, and make such arrangements respecting it as were necessary. I examined the positions at Cemetery Hill, so far as the darkness would permit, and then accompanied the general and Major-General Howard in an inspection of the west front of the field, occupied by the Second and Third Corps. Cemetery Hill commanded the positions which could be occupied by the enemy to the north and northwest. Toward the south the line occupied the crest of a gentle elevation, which, concealing everything immediately behind it from the observation of the enemy, commanded the ground to the west, which sloped down gradually for a few hundred yards, and then rising, formed another crest, varying from half to three-quarters of a mile distant. The summit of this crest was wooded, and toward the south bent eastwardly and crossed the Emmitsburg road, forming a very favorable position for the enemy's artillery, and affording concealment to his movements in that direction. About half or three-quarters of a mile south of the cemetery our own crest and the ground in front of it were broken by groves of trees, and still farther on by rough and rocky ground. At a distance of about 2 miles from Cemetery Hill, a high, rocky, and broken peak formed the natural termination of our lines. The broken character of the ground in front of the southern half of our line was unfavorable to the use of artillery. From the cemetery, as a center, the right of our line extended toward the east, and lay on the north of the Baltimore pike. The ground is hilly, heavily wooded, and intersected with ravines and small water-courses, very unfavorable to the use of artillery. The First and Eleventh Corps were stationed on and near Cemetery Hill. The Second Corps (Hancock's) stretched along the crest on the left of the Cemetery Hill, with the Third Corps (Sickles') on its left. To the right of the cemetery lay a portion of the First Corps (Newton's), and beyond it the Twelfth (Slocum's).

At or near daylight, Major-General Slocum reported to the commanding general that there was a gap between the left of his line and the right of the First Corps, which he feared would be taken advantage of by the enemy, as he apprehended an immediate attack. The general commanding then gave me directions to make the necessary arrangements to meet the emergency. I considered this, in connection with the order previously given me, as a recognition, for the present, at least, of the position I had held at Antietam and Fredericksburg, as commander of the artillery of the army, and proceeded to make the necessary dispositions and to give all directions I considered necessary during the rest of the battle. In order to cover the gap between the First and Second Corps, the batteries of the Twelfth Corps (Muhlenberg's, F, Fourth United States, six 12-pounders; Kinzie's, K, Fifth United States, four 12-pounders; Winegar's, M,

First New York, four 10-pounders, and Knap's, E, Pennsylvania, six 10-pounders) were placed so as to command the outlet from that interval toward the Baltimore pike, and such of the batteries on Cemetery Hill as commanded the ground and its approaches from the side of the enemy were also placed in position. The interval between the lines was too broken and too heavily wooded to permit the artillery to be placed on the immediate line of battle. These positions were held by the batteries until the infantry line was completed and well strengthened, when the artillery was arranged for any attack the enemy could make.

The batteries at the cemetery, under command of Colonel Wainwright, remained as already described, and Major Osborn, chief of artillery of the Eleventh Corps, was directed to take command on the south of the road. I re-enforced him with half of Hall's battery (Second Maine, three 3-inch) from the First Corps, the other half being disabled, and five batteries (Eakin's, H, First United States, six 12-pounders; Taft's, Fifth New York, six 20-pounders; Hill's, C, First West Virginia, four 10-pounders; Huntington's, H, First Ohio, six 3-inch, and Edgell's, First New Hampshire, six 3-inch) from the Artillery Reserve, thus placing at his disposal, including the three batteries (Bancroft's, G, Fourth United States, six 12-pounders; Dilger's, I, First Ohio, six 12-pounders, and Wheeler's, Thirteenth New York, three 3-inch) of his own corps remaining to him, six 20-pounder Parrotts, twenty-two light rifles, and eighteen light 12-pounders. These were stationed as follows: On the right, resting next the Baltimore road and facing the Emmitsburg, Dilger; on his left, Bancroft; then, in the order named, Eakin, Wheeler, Hill, and Hall. These eighteen light 12-pounders and ten light rifles commanded the enemy's positions to the right of the town. In rear of Bancroft and perpendicular to him were Taft's six 20-pounder Parrotts; on Taft's right and rear were Huntington's 3-inch guns; these batteries facing the north. This arrangement, in connection with that of Wainwright, brought all the positions within range of the cemetery that the enemy could occupy with artillery under a commanding fire. The batteries were all brought into requisition at different periods of the battle.

July 2, during the morning, several moving columns of the enemy, passing toward our right, were shelled, and compelled to make detours, or seek the cover of ravines to make their movements.

At about 3.30 p. m. the enemy established a battery of ten guns (four 20-pounders and six 10-pounder Parrotts) in a wheat-field to the north and a little to the east of the Cemetery Hill, and distant some 1,200 or 1,300 yards, and opened a remarkably accurate fire upon our batteries. We soon gained a decided advantage over them, and at the end of an hour or more compelled them to withdraw, drawing off two of their pieces by hand. Twenty-eight horses were afterward found on the knoll. The enemy suffered severely, and, although we were successful, we had cause to regret that our 4½-inch guns had been left at Westminster, as the position offered great advantages for them.

The enemy endeavored to re-establish his battery farther to his right, but as we could in this position bring a larger number of guns to bear than before, he was soon driven off. Cooper's battery (B, First Pennsylvania, four 3-inch), which had suffered severely in this affair, was now relieved by Ricketts', from the Artillery Reserve.

In this cannonade, Lieut. C. P. Eakin, First U. S. Artillery, was badly wounded and carried off the field, and Lieut. P. D. Mason, First U. S. Artillery, assumed command of the battery.

About the same hour, 3.30 p. m., as the enemy was seriously annoying the left of the Twelfth Corps, three guns of Knap's battery, under command of Lieutenant Geary and Van Reed's section of K, Fifth U. S. Artillery, were placed in an eligible position, about 200 yards from the right of the First Corps. As soon as their presence (Knap's Pennsylvania Battery, 10-pounders, and Kinzie's, K, Fifth U. S. Artillery, light 12-pounders) was noticed, the enemy turned his battery (eight guns) upon them, but after a spirited contest of thirty minutes, in which he had a caisson blown up, his guns were silenced. The conduct of both Lieutenants Geary and Van Reed is highly spoken of by their chiefs of artillery.

When the infantry of the Twelfth Corps crossed over to the support of the Third Corps, on the left of our line, these guns were withdrawn and rejoined their batteries.

About sunset the enemy again opened from a knoll in front of the cemetery, distant about 1,800 yards, and this was soon followed by a powerful infantry attack on the position by General Rodes' Louisiana [?] brigade.* As their columns moved out of the town, they came under the fire of Stevens' battery (Fifth Maine), at 800 yards distance. Wheeling into line, they pushed up the hill. As their line became unmasked, all the guns that could be brought to bear upon them, some twenty, were opened, first with shrapnel and then with canister, with excellent effect. The center and left were beaten back, but their right worked their way up under cover of the houses, and pushed completely through Wiedrich's battery (I, First New York, six 3-inch) into Ricketts' (F and G, First Pennsylvania, six 3-inch). The cannoneers of both batteries stood well to their guns, and when no longer able to hold them, fought with handspikes, rammers, and even stones, joining the infantry in driving them out, and capturing several prisoners. This attack of Rodes was mainly repelled by the artillery alone. The loss of the enemy was reported to be large by their wounded in the affair, who afterward fell under the care of our surgeons in Gettysburg.

About 12 m. a detachment of Berdan's Sharpshooters was sent into the woods near the point where the enemy's crest opposite the left of our army cuts the Emmitsburg road, and reported the enemy as moving in force toward our left flank.

About 2 p. m. General Sickles formed his corps in line to meet an attack from this direction, his right resting on the Emmitsburg road, in a peach orchard, in advance of the center of our left, and his line extending in a general direction toward Sugar Loaf or Round Top, a peak which terminated our line on the left. At this time I reached the ground, and found Captain Randolph, chief of artillery Third Corps, making arrangements to station his battery on the right, those on the left having already been posted as follows : Smith's battery (Fourth New York, six 10-pounders) on the extreme left and on a steep and rocky eminence in advance of Sugar Loaf, and on his right Winslow's (D, First New York, six 12-pounders), in a wheat-field, separated from Smith by a belt of woods. I accompanied Captain Randolph, first sending to General Tyler, commanding the Artillery Reserve, for two batteries, one of light 12-pounders and one of rifles,

---

*Rodes' division comprised only North Carolina, Georgia, and Alabama troops. Reference is probably to Hays' Louisiana brigade.—COMPILER.

and assisted him in posting the other batteries as follows : Clark's battery (B, First New Jersey, six 10-pounders) on the line to the left of the peach orchard ; Ames' (G, First New York, six 12-pounders), from the Artillery Reserve, in the orchard, both facing the south, and perpendicular to the Emmitsburg road ; then along the Emmitsburg road and facing the west, Randolph's (E, First Rhode Island, six 12-pounders), and Seeley's (K, Fourth United States, six 12-pounders) batteries, Seeley's well to the right of Randolph's.   While Ames and Clark were moving up, the enemy opened a brisk fire upon them from a position near the Emmitsburg road and on the opposite side of it.

By this time, about 3.30 p. m., Major McGilvery came up from the Artillery Reserve with three batteries—Bigelow's (Ninth Massachusetts, four 12-pounders) ; Phillips' (Fifth Massachusetts, six 3-inch), and Hart's (Fifteenth New York, four 12-pounders)—which I ordered into position on the left of Clark's.   As I saw that more batteries of the enemy were getting into position on the south of the Emmitsburg road and forming opposite to this line, I sent to the reserve for more rifled guns, and then, as Smith (Fourth New York, six 10-pounders) had not opened, I went to his battery to ascertain the cause.   When I arrived, he had succeeded in getting his guns into position, and just opened fire.   As his position commanded that of the enemy and enfiladed their line, his fire was very effective, and with that of Ames (G, First New York, six 12-pounders) and Clark (B, First New Jersey, six 10-pounders) in front, soon silenced that battery.   In the meantime the enemy had established his new batteries to the north of the road, and Smith turned his guns upon them.   I now moved along the line and examined the condition of the different batteries.   Winslow (D, First New York, six 12-pounders) had not yet been attacked, his position facing a wood at short range that the enemy had not yet occupied.   Bigelow, Phillips, and Hart were hotly engaged, and the battle soon raged along the lines.

In the meantime the additional batteries ordered from the reserve— Thompson's (C and F, Pennsylvania, six 3-inch) and Sterling's (Second Connecticut, four James and two howitzers), and Ransom's brigade, consisting of Thomas' (C, Fourth United States, six 12-pounders), Weir's (C, Fifth United States, six 12-pounders), and Turnbull's (F and K, Third United States, six 12-pounders) batteries —were brought up by General Tyler in person.   Ransom's brigade was formed on the crest, above general headquarters, and soon after Turnbull's, Weir's, and Thomas' batteries were ordered forward to join Humphreys' division, taking position on the right of Seeley.

Some time after, two batteries of the Fifth Corps—Watson's (I, Fifth United States, four 3-inch) and Walcott's (C, Massachusetts Artillery, six 12-pounders)—were brought upon the ground by some staff officer of General Sickles; but for this there seemed to be no necessity, abundant provision having been made to supply all needs from the Artillery Reserve.   The effect was to deprive the Fifth Corps of its batteries, without the knowledge and to the inconvenience of the commander of the corps.   The batteries were exposed to heavy front and enfilading fires, and suffered terribly, but as rapidly as any were disabled they were retired and replaced by others.   Watson (I, Fifth United States, four 3-inch) relieved Ames' battery (G, First New York, six 12-pounders); Thompson's (Pennsylvania, six 3-inch) took position near it, relieving Hart (Fifteenth New York, four 12-pounders).   Turnbull's (F and K, Third United States, six 12-pounders) was posted near the Emmitsburg road. The officers and men performed their duties with great gallantry and success, notwithstanding the unfavorable nature of the ground, which gave the enemy all the advantages of position, driving off several of the enemy's batteries, silencing others, and doing good execution on his infantry, until about 5.30 or 6 p. m., when the line was forced back, and the batteries were compelled to withdraw.

So great had been the loss in men and horses, that many of the carriages had to be withdrawn by hand and others left on the field, which, with the exception of four, were afterward brought off. Three of these belonged to Smith's battery (Fourth New York, six 10-pounders), on our extreme left. The guns were stationed on the brow of a very precipitous and rocky height, beyond a ravine in front of our line. The difficulty of getting these guns up the height had caused the delay in Smith's opening his fire. He fought them to the last moment in hopes of keeping the enemy off, and in the belief that the ground would be in our possession again before the guns could be carried off by the enemy. He got off one of the four guns he had placed on the height, but was compelled to abandon the other three. The fourth of the guns lost belonged to Thompson's battery, the horses being all killed, the men engaged in hauling off the other pieces by hand, and his infantry supports having left him. In withdrawing, many acts of gallantry were performed, the enemy in several instances being driven out from the batteries by the cannoneers and such assistance as they could procure from the infantry near them. The line reformed on the crest, which constituted our original line, and repulsed all further attacks.

The batteries of the Second Corps were posted on the morning of the 2d by its chief of artillery, Captain Hazard, First Rhode Island Artillery, as follows, from left to right, connecting with the batteries of the Third Corps on the left, and those on Cemetery Hill on the right: Rorty's (B, First New York, four 10-pounders), Brown's (B, First Rhode Island, six 12-pounders), Cushing's (A, Fourth United States, six 3-inch), Arnold's (A, First Rhode Island, six 3-inch), and Woodruff's (I, First United States, six 12-pounders). The enemy opened upon them several times during the morning, but were always silenced by their concentrated fire.

When the Third Corps fell back, about 6 p. m., their batteries opened a vigorous fire, and the two left batteries (Rorty's and Brown's) conformed their movements to those of the infantry. When the crest of the hill occupied by our lines was reached, it gave the batteries a commanding position; a rapid fire was opened, and the enemy gradually driven back. Brown's battery suffered so severely in men and horses that it became necessary to send two guns to the rear.

The artillery of the Fifth Corps arrived on the field between 4 and 5 p. m. Hazlett's (D, Fifth United States, six 10-pounders), Walcott's (C, Massachusetts Artillery, six 12-pounders), and Watson's (I, Fifth United States, four 3-inch) batteries, with the First Division of the corps; Gibbs' (L, First Ohio, six 12-pounders), and Barnes' (C, First New York, four 3-inch), with Second Division. I have already stated that Watson's and Walcott's were taken from their positions by order of Major-General Sickles, and noted their services. Walcott's was not engaged, but was under fire; 6 men wounded, and 6 horses killed and wounded.

About 4.30 p. m. Hazlett's battery was moved to the extreme left, placed in position on Round Top, and immediately opened upon that portion of the enemy's force which attacked the First Division, and continued it until night with marked effect, as its fire enfiladed the enemy's line.   Guthrie's section of Gibbs' battery was posted on the same hill on the right of Hazlett, and Walworth's section at the base of the hill, commanding the ravine in front of Round Top, the remaining section being held in reserve.   These sections did excellent service, especially Guthrie's.   On this afternoon, Lieut. Charles E. Hazlett, Fifth U. S. Artillery, a young officer, who had gained an enviable reputation for gallantry, skill, and devotion to his country and the service, received a mortal wound, and died the same evening.

For more detailed reports of the services of the artillery in the action on our left, I respectfully refer to the reports of General Tyler, commanding Artillery Reserve, and to the reports of the chiefs of artillery of the Second, Third, and Fifth Corps, transmitted herewith. It will be perceived that the batteries suffered severely in officers, men, and horses, losing a large proportionate number of officers—3 killed (Lieut. Charles E. Hazlett, Fifth Artillery, commanding Battery B; Lieut. M. Livingston, Third Artillery, commanding Turnbull's battery; Lieut. C. Erickson, Bigelow's battery); and 12 wounded (Capt. D. R. Ransom, Third Artillery, commanding Regular Brigade, Artillery Reserve; Capt. J. Thompson, C, Pennsylvania Artillery; Capt. N. Irish, D, Pennsylvania Artillery; Capt. Patrick Hart, Fifteenth New York Battery; Lieut. T. F. Brown, Hazard's battery; Lieut. Samuel Canby, Fourth Artillery, Cushing's battery; Lieut. J. K. Bucklyn, First Rhode Island, Randolph's battery; Lieut. F. W. Seeley, Fourth U. S. Artillery, commanding Battery K; Lieut. M. F. Watson, Fifth U. S. Artillery, commanding Battery I; Lieut. J. L. Miller, Thompson's battery, mortally; Lieut. E. M. Knox, Fifteenth New York Battery; Lieut. E. Spence, Ricketts' battery).

The night of the 2d was devoted in great part to repairing damages, replenishing the ammunition chests, and reducing and reorganizing such batteries as had lost so many men and horses as to be unable efficiently to work the full number of guns.

By daylight next morning this duty had been performed so far as possible, and, when it was found impossible to reorganize in time, the batteries were withdrawn, replaced by others from the Artillery Reserve, and finished their work during the next morning.

On the evening of July 2, a portion of Slocum's corps (the Second) [Twelfth], which formed the right of our line, was sent to re-enforce the left.   During its absence, the enemy took possession of a portion of the line in the woods, and it was resolved to drive him out at daylight.   Knap's battery (E, Pennsylvania, six 10-pounders) was placed on the hill known as Slocum's headquarters, and near the Baltimore pike, and Winegar's battery (M, First New York, four 10-pounders) at a short distance east of it.   These batteries overlooked and commanded the ground vacated by the corps.

At 1 a. m. of the 3d, Muhlenberg's (F, Fourth United States, six 12-pounders) and Kinzie's (K, Fifth United States, four 12-pounders) batteries were posted opposite the center of the line of the Twelfth Corps, so as to command the ravine formed by Rock Creek.

At 4.30 a. m. these batteries opened, and fired without intermission for fifteen minutes into the wood, at a range of from 600 to 800 yards. Soon after daylight, Rigby's battery (A, Maryland, six 3-inch) was also placed on the hill, and at 5.30 a. m. all the batteries opened, and continued firing at intervals until 10 a. m., when the infantry succeeded in driving out the enemy and reoccupied their position of the day before. In this work the artillery rendered good servce.

At our center, on and near Cemetery Hill, the batteries were in position very nearly the same as on the previous day. Those outside of the cemetery gate and north of the Baltimore pike, under the command of Colonel Wainwright, First New York Artillery, were, from right to left: Stevens' (Fifth Maine, six 12-pounders), Reynolds' (L, First New York, four 3-inch), Ricketts' (F, First Pennsylvania, six 3-inch)—which had relieved Cooper's (B, First Pennsylvania, four 3-inch) the night before—Wiedrich's (I, First New York, four 3-inch), and Stewart's (B, Fourth United States, four 12-pounders). The batteries south of the pike, and under command of Major Osborn, First New York Artillery, were: Dilger's (I, First Ohio, six 12-pounders), Bancroft's (G, Fourth United States, six 12-pounders), Eakin's (H, First United States, six 12-pounders), Wheeler's (Thirteenth New York, three 3-inch), Hill's (C, First West Virginia, four 10-pounders), and Taft's (Fifth New York, six 20-pounders).

On the left of the cemetery the batteries of the Second Corps were in line on the crest occupied by their corps in the following order, from right to left: Woodruff's (I, First United States, six 12-pounders), Arnold's (A, First Rhode Island, six 3-inch), Cushing's (A, Fourth United States, six 3-inch), Brown's (B, First Rhode Island, four 12-pounders), and Rorty's (B, First New York, four 10-pounders), all under command of Captain Hazard, chief of artillery.

Next on the left of the artillery of the Second Corps were stationed Thomas' battery (C, Fourth United States, six 12-pounders), and on his left Major McGilvery's command, consisting of Thompson's (C and F, Pennsylvania, five 3-inch), Phillips' (Fifth Massachusetts, six 3-inch), Hart's (Fifteenth New York, four 12-pounders), Sterling's (Second Connecticut, four James and two howitzers), Rank's section (two 3-inch), Dow's (Sixth Maine, four 12-pounders), and Ames' (G, First New York, six 12-pounders), all of the Artillery Reserve, to which was added, soon after the cannonade commenced, Cooper's battery (B, First Pennsylvania, four 3-inch), of the First Corps.

On our extreme left, occupying the position of the day before, were Gibbs' (L, First Ohio, six 12-pounders) and Rittenhouse's (late Hazlett's, D, Fifth United States, six 10-pounders) batteries. Gibbs' was, however, too distant from the enemy's position for 12-pounders, and was not used during the day, although under fire. Rittenhouse was in an excellent position for the service of his rifled guns, on the top of Round Top. We had thus on the western crest line seventy-five guns, which could be aided by a few of those on Cemetery Hill. There was but little firing during the morning.

At 10 a. m. I made an inspection of the whole line, ascertaining that all the batteries—only those of our right serving with the Twelfth Corps being engaged at the time—were in good condition and well supplied with ammunition. As the enemy was evidently increasing his artillery force in front of our left, I gave instructions to the batteries and to the chiefs of artillery not to fire at small bodies, nor to allow their fire to be drawn without promise of adequate results; to watch the enemy closely, and when he opened to concentrate the fire of their guns on one battery at a time until it was silenced; under all circumstances to fire deliberately, and to husband their ammunition as much as possible.

I had just finished my inspection, and was with Lieutenant Rittenhouse on the top of Round Top, when the enemy opened, at about 1 p. m., along his whole right, a furious cannonade on the left of our line. I estimated the number of his guns bearing on our west front at from one hundred to one hundred and twenty. I have since seen it stated by the enemy's correspondents that there were sixty guns from Longstreet's, and fifty-five from Hill's corps, making one hundred and fifteen in all. To oppose these we could not, from our restricted position, bring more than eighty to reply effectively. Our fire was well withheld until the first burst was over, excepting from the extreme right and left of our positions. It was then opened deliberately and with excellent effect. As soon as the nature of the enemy's attack was made clear, and I could form an opinion as to the number of his guns, for which my position afforded great facility, I went to the park of the Artillery Reserve, and ordered all the batteries to be ready to move at a moment's notice, and hastened to report to the commanding general, but found he had left his headquarters. I then proceeded along the line, to observe the effects of the cannonade and to replace such batteries as should become disabled.

About 2.30 p. m., finding our ammunition running low and that it was very unsafe to bring up loads of it, a number of caissons and limbers having been exploded, I directed that the fire should be gradually stopped, which was done, and the enemy soon slackened his fire also. I then sent orders for such batteries as were necessary to replace exhausted ones, and all that were disposable were sent me.

About 3 p. m., and soon after the enemy's fire had ceased, he formed a column of attack in the edge of the woods in front of the Second Corps. At this time Fitzhugh's (K, First New York, six 3-inch), Parsons' (A, First New Jersey, six 10-pounders), Weir's (C, Fifth United States, six 12-pounders), and Cowan's (First New York Independent, six 3-inch) batteries reached this point, and were put in position in front of the advancing enemy. I rode down to McGilvery's batteries, and directed them to take the enemy in flank as they approached. The enemy advanced magnificently, unshaken by the shot and shell which tore through his ranks from his front and from our left. The batteries of the Second Corps on our right, having nearly exhausted their supply of ammunition, except canister, were compelled to withhold their fire until the enemy, who approached in three lines, came within its range. When our canister fire and musketry were opened upon them, it occasioned disorder, but still they advanced gallantly until they reached the stone wall behind which our troops lay. Here ensued a desperate conflict, the enemy succeeding in passing the wall and entering our lines, causing great destruction of life, especially among the batteries. Infantry troops were, however, advanced from our right; the rear line of the enemy broke, and the others, who had fought with a gallantry that excited the admiration of our troops, found themselves cut off and compelled to surrender. As soon as their fate was evident, the enemy opened his batteries upon the masses of our troops at this point without regard to the presence of his own. Toward the close of this struggle, Rorty's (B, First New York, four 10-pounders), Arnold's (A, First Rhode Island, six 3-inch), and Cushing's (A, Fourth United States, six 3-inch) batteries, which had lost heavily in men and horses, were withdrawn, and as soon as the affair was over their places were filled with fresh ones.

Soon the necessary measures had been taken to restore this portion of the line to an efficient condition. It required but a few minutes, as the batteries, as fast as withdrawn from any point, were sent to the Artillery Reserve, replenished with ammunition, reorganized, returned to the rear of the lines, and there awaited assignment. I then went to the left, to see that proper measures had been taken there for the same object. On my way, I saw that the enemy was forming a second column of attack to his right of the point where the first was formed, and in front of the position of the First Corps (Newton's). I gave instructions to the artillery, under command of Major McGilvery, to be ready to meet the first movements of the enemy in front, and, returning to the position of the Second Corps, directed the batteries there, mostly belonging to the Artillery Reserve, to take the enemy in flank as he advanced. When the enemy moved, these orders were well executed, and before he reached our line he was brought to a stand. The appearance of a body of our infantry moving down in front of our lines from the direction of the Second Corps caused the enemy to move off by his right flank, under cover of the woods and undergrowth, and, a few minutes after, the column had broken up, and in the utmost confusion the men of which it was composed fled across the ground over which they had just before advanced, and took refuge behind their batteries. The attacks on the part of the enemy were not well managed. Their artillery fire was too much dispersed, and failed to produce the intended effect. It was, however, so severe and so well sustained that it put to the test, and fully proved, the discipline and excellence of our troops. The two assaults, had they been simultaneous, would have divided our artillery fire. As it was, each attack was met by a heavy front and flank fire of our artillery, the batteries which met the enemy directly in front in one assault taking him in flank in the other.

The losses of the artillery on this day, and especially in the assault on the Second Corps, were very large. The loss in officers was 3 killed, 2 mortally and 9 severely wounded. Killed: Capt. J. M. Rorty, B, First New York; Lieut. A. H. Cushing, Fourth United States; Lieut. G. A. Woodruff, First United States (mortally wounded); Lieut. J. S. Milne, First Rhode Island; Lieut. A. H. Whitaker, Ninth Massachusetts (wounded severely); Capt. J. Bigelow, Ninth Massachusetts; Lieut. A. S. Sheldon, B, First New York; Lieut. H. H. Baldwin, Fifth United States; Lieut. J. McGilvray, Fourth United States; Lieut. R. C. Hazlett, Fourth Pennsylvania Battery; Lieut. J. Stephenson, Fourth Pennsylvania Battery; Lieut. H. D. Scott, Battery E, Massachusetts; Lieut. W. P. Wright, First New York Battery; Lieut. W. H. Johnson, First New York Battery. Captain Rorty, who had taken command of his battery but three days before, fell, fighting, at his guns. Lieutenants Cushing and Woodruff belonged to a class of young officers who, although of the lowest commissioned rank, have gained distinguished army reputation. The destruction of *matériel* was large. The enemy's cannonade, in which he must have almost exhausted his ammunition, was well sustained, and cost us a great many horses and the explosion of an unusually large number of caissons and limbers. The whole slope behind our crest, although concealed from the enemy, was swept by his shot, and offered no protection to horses or carriages. The enemy's superiority in the number of guns was fully matched by the superior accuracy of ours, and a personal inspection of the line he occupied, made on the 5th, enables me to state with certainty that his losses in *matériel* in this artillery combat were equal to ours, while the marks of the shot in the trees on both crests bear conclusive evidence of the superiority of our practice.

This struggle closed the battle, and the night of the 3d, like the previous one, was devoted to repairs and reorganization. A large number of batteries had been so reduced in men and horses that many guns and carriages, after completing the outfit of those which remained with the army, were sent to the rear and turned in to the ordnance department.

Our losses in the three days' operations, as reported, were as follows:

Casualties, July 1, 2, and 3.

Organizations.	Number of guns.	Killed.		Wounded.		Missing.	Horses.
		Officers.	Men.	Officers.	Men.		
In the corps	212	5	57	18	361	52	565
Artillery Reserve..	108	2	41	15	171	15	316
Total ..:...	320	7	98	33	532	67	881

Of these 320 guns, 142 were light 12-pounders, 106 3-inch guns, 6 20-pounders, 60 10-pounder Parrott guns, and a battery of 4 James rifles and 2 12-pounder howitzers, which joined the army on the march to Gettysburg. This table excludes the Horse Artillery, 44 3-inch guns, serving with the cavalry. It will be seen that the Artillery Reserve, every gun of which was brought into requisition, bore, as in all the campaigns of the Army of the Potomac, its full share, and more, of the losses.

The expenditure of ammunition in the three days amounted to 32,781 rounds, averaging over 100 rounds per gun. Many rounds were lost in the caissons and limbers by explosions and otherwise. The supply carried with the army being 270 rounds per gun, left sufficient to fill the ammunition chests and enable the army to fight another battle. There was for a short time during the battle a fear that the ammunition would give out. This fear was caused by the large and unreasonable demands made by corps commanders who had left their own trains or a portion of them behind, contrary to the orders of the commanding general. In this emergency, the train of the Artillery Reserve, as on so many other occasions, supplied all demands, and proved its great usefulness to the army.

For a more particular account of the operations of the artillery and of their relations to those of the other arms of service, I respectfully refer to the report of the commander of the Artillery Reserve, and to those of the chiefs of artillery of the army corps, transmitted herewith, to which reports I also refer for the names of those who distinguished themselves by their conduct and courage.

I have to acknowledge my indebtedness to these officers: Brig. Gen. R. O. Tyler, commanding Artillery Reserve; Col. C. S. Wainwright, First New York Artillery, First Corps; Capt. J. G. Hazard, First Rhode Island Artillery, Second Corps; Capt. G. E. Randolph, First Rhode Island Artillery, Third Corps; Capt. A. P. Martin, Third Massachusetts Battery, Fifth Corps; Col. C. H. Tompkins, First Rhode Island Artillery, Sixth Corps; Maj. T. W. Osborn, First New York Artillery, Eleventh Corps; Lieut. E. D. Muhlenberg,

Fourth U. S. Artillery, Twelfth Corps, for their zealous co-opera-tion in all the administrative labors that devolved upon me, and for the efficiency with which they discharged their duties in the field.

My staff—Lieut. Col. E. R. Warner, First New York Artillery, inspector of artillery ; Capt. J. N. Craig, assistant adjutant-general, and Lieut. C. E. Bissell, aide-de-camp—performed the duties devolv-ing upon them with intelligence and gallantry.

Upon Lieutenant-Colonel Warner fell much of the labor required in the reorganization of batteries withdrawn from the field and in replacing them. These duties and others which devolved upon him were discharged with his accustomed energy and thoroughness. Lieutenant Bissell was my only aide, and was, therefore, busily em-ployed. He was much exposed, his duties keeping him more or less under fire at every point at which attacks were made.

In my report of the battle of Chancellorsville, I took occasion to call attention to the great evils arising from the want of field officers for the artillery. The operations of this campaign, and especially the battle of Gettysburg, afford further proofs, if such were neces-sary, of the mistaken policy of depriving so important an arm of the officers necessary for managing it. In this campaign, for the command of 67 batteries (372 guns), with over 8,000 men and 7,000 horses, and all the *matériel*, and large ammunition trains, I had one general officer commanding the reserve, and but four field officers (Brig. Gen. R. O. Tyler, U. S. Volunteers, commanding Artillery Reserve; Lieut. Col. F. McGilvery, First Maine Artillery, command-ing brigade Artillery Reserve ; Col. C. H. Tompkins, First Rhode Island Artillery, Sixth Corps ; Col. C. S. Wainwright, First New York Artillery, First Corps ; Maj. T. W. Osborn, First New York Artillery, Eleventh Corps ; Capt. J. M. Robertson, Second U. S. Artillery, commanding First Brigade Horse Artillery; Capt. J. C. Tidball, Second U. S. Artillery, commanding Second Brigade Horse Artillery).

In the seven corps, the artillery of two were commanded by colonels, of one by a major, of three by captains, and of one by a lieutenant, taken from their batteries for the purpose. The two brigades of horse artillery attached to the cavalry were commanded by captains, and there was one field officer in the reserve. The most of these commands in any other army would have been considered proper ones for a general officer. In no army would the command of the artillery of a corps be considered of less importance, to say the least, than that of a brigade of infantry. In none of our corps ought the artillery commander to have been of less rank than a colonel, and in all there should have been a proper proportion of field officers, with the necessary staffs. The defects of our organization were made palpable at Gettysburg, not only on the field, but in the necessary and important duties of reorganizing the batteries, repairing dam-ages, and getting the artillery in condition to renew the battle, or take the road in efficient condition on the morning after a conflict.

I respectfully and urgently call the attention of the commanding general, and through him of the War Department, to this subject.

Not only does the service suffer, necessarily, from the great de-ficiency of officers of rank, but a policy which closes the door of promotion to battery officers, and places them and the arm itself under a ban, and degrades them in comparison with other arms of service, induces discontent, and has caused many of our best officers to seek positions, wherever they can find them, which will remove them from this branch of the service. We have lost many such officers, and unless something is done to cure the evil we will lose more.

The reports of the horse artillery were rendered to the cavalry officers under whose orders they served, and I have not yet received all of them. As their operations were detached from those of the main body of the army, and do not naturally connect with them, I reserve them as the subject of a separate report.

Very respectfully, your obedient servant,

HENRY J. HUNT,
Brigadier-General and Chief of Artillery, Commanding.

Brig. Gen. S. WILLIAMS,
Assistant Adjutant-General, Army of the Potomac.

ARTILLERY HDQRS. ARMY OF THE POTOMAC,
October 4, 1863.

GENERAL : In compliance with your directions, I have the honor to state that the following were the captures from the army in the recent operations:

First Corps lost one gun, 3-inch, from Reynolds' battery (L, First New York), July 1; Eleventh Corps, one light 12-pounder, Heckman's battery (K, First Ohio), July 1; Third Corps, three 10-pounder Parrotts, Smith's Fourth Independent New York Battery, July 2; Artillery Reserve, one 3-inch, Thompson's battery, Third and Fourth Pennsylvania, July 2; six lost.

I received no report of captures from the enemy in an official form, although I heard that the cavalry had picked up several on the road, and that two were taken at Falling Waters.

Respectfully, your obedient servant,

HENRY J. HUNT,
Major-General, Chief of Artillery.

Brig. Gen. S. WILLIAMS,
Assistant Adjutant-General.

No. 29.

Reports of Maj. Gen. Abner Doubleday, U. S. Army, commanding Third Division of, and First Army Corps.

WASHINGTON, D. C., *December 14, 1863.*

GENERAL: I have the honor to report that, on the morning of June 28, the First Corps left Middletown, Md., for Frederick, and encamped in the western suburbs of that town, picketing the roads toward the northwest.

On the 29th, it left Frederick, and after a long and toilsome march arrived at Emmitsburg; passed through that place, and bivouacked for the night on the heights to the north. This position had been carefully selected by General Reynolds as a defensive line, the rebels having been reported in some strength at Fairfield.

On the 30th, we made a short march of 3 or 4 miles to Marsh Creek, where we again took up a defensive position, Wadsworth's division, with Hall's (Second Maine) battery, covering the Gettysburg road; my own division, with Cooper's (First Pennsylvania Reserve Volunteer) battery, covering the Fairfield road, and Robinson's division, with the remaining three batteries, some miles in rear as a reserve. It was General Reynolds' intention to dispute the enemy's advance at this point, falling back, however, in case of a serious attack, to the ground already chosen at Emmitsburg. Here he received orders to reassume the command of the right wing, consisting of his own (First), Howard's (Eleventh), and Sickles' (Third) corps. In consequence of this order, he directed me to take command of the First Corps.

On the eventful morning of July 1, between 7 and 8 o'clock, General Reynolds sent for me for the purpose of explaining the telegrams received by him in relation to the movements of the rebels and the latest position of our own troops. This information showed that the enemy was reported in force at Cashtown and Mummasburg, and that our cavalry was skirmishing with them on the roads leading from Gettysburg to those places. He told me he had already given orders to Wadsworth's division, with Hall's battery, to move forward, and that he would accompany these troops in person, while I remained to bring up the balance of the corps. Owing to the intervals between the divisions and the necessity of calling in the pickets, from an hour and a half to two hours elapsed before the remaining troops were *en route*. Wadsworth's division was, therefore, obliged to sustain the brunt of the action alone for this length of time. As soon as I saw that Robinson's and Rowley's divisions, with the remaining batteries, had commenced the march, I rode on in advance of the column.

The sound of rapid cannon firing convinced me that our cavalry was warmly engaged. I pushed forward at full speed, and soon overtook Wadsworth's division, which had left the main road and was filing rapidly through woods and fields toward a ridge which ran north and south, about 400 yards to the west of the seminary, which is itself about a quarter of a mile to the west of Gettysburg, and located on a similar ridge parallel to the first. About 200 yards farther on, the former range of heights sloped down, and ended in a ravine called Willoughby's Run. On the most westerly of these ridges, General Reynolds had directed his line of battle to be formed, and was himself superintending the placing of Cutler's brigade as I rode up. I had previously sent an aide (Lieutenant Marten) to the general for instructions. He returned with orders for me to attend to the Millerstown road, on the left of our line. A small piece of woods cut the line of battle in about two equal parts. These woods possessed all the advantages of a redoubt, strengthening the center of our line, and enfilading the enemy's columns should they advance in the open spaces on either side. I deemed the extremity of the woods, which extended to the summit of the ridge, to be the key of the position, and urged that portion of Meredith's brigade, the Western men assigned to its defense, to hold it to the last extremity. Full of the memory of their past achievements, they replied cheerfully and proudly, "If we can't hold it, where will you find men who can?" General Reynolds' intention appeared to be simply to defend the two roads entering the town from the northwest and southwest, and to occupy and hold the woods between them. The principal effort of the enemy was made on the Cashtown road from the northwest, and was opposed at first by Cutler's brigade and Hall's battery, the former stretching across, the latter posted on, the right of the road.

Immediately on my arrival at the ridge, I rode to the left to examine the ground in that direction, and then was engaged in overseeing the operations of Meredith's brigade, commonly known as the Iron Brigade. These troops were formed in the following order, from right to left: The Second Wisconsin, Seventh Wisconsin, Nineteenth Indiana, and Twenty-fourth Michigan Volunteers. The Sixth Wisconsin, together with the brigade guard, under Lieutenants Harris, of the Sixth Wisconsin, and Showalter, of the Second Wisconsin, had been detached by my order, to remain with me as a reserve. There was no time to be lost, as the enemy was already in the woods, and advancing at double-quick to seize this important central position and hold the ridge. The Iron Brigade, led by the Second Wisconsin in line, and followed by the other regiments, deployed *en échelon* without a moment's hesitation, charged with the utmost steadiness and fury, hurled the enemy back into the run, captured, after a sharp and desperate conflict, nearly 1,000 prisoners—all from Archer's brigade—and reformed their lines on the high ground beyond the ravine.

The Second Wisconsin, in this contest, under the gallant Colonel Fairchild, was particularly distinguished. It accomplished the difficult task of driving superior numbers of rebel infantry from the shelter of the woods, and to it also belongs the honor of capturing General Archer himself. He was brought in by Private Patrick Maloney, of Company G. It is to be lamented that this brave Irishman was subsequently killed in the action.

The troops were now withdrawn to the eastern side of the run by my order, and reformed on a line with the Second Wisconsin, the Seventh Wisconsin taking the right of the new line and the Nineteenth Indiana the left. Immediately after this, I took my position behind the left wing. I had hardly done so when I learned, with deep sorrow, that our brave and lamented commander, Major-General Reynolds, had just been shot, and was no more. This melancholy event occurred in the beginning of the attack referred to, about 10.15 a. m. The whole burden of the battle was thus suddenly thrown upon me.

The death of General Reynolds was followed by other disasters. A column of the enemy's infantry had succeeded in approaching Hall's battery to within a distance of 60 yards by charging up the ravine on his right, and had poured in a terrible and destructive fire at that short range. At the same time a vastly superior force advanced in two lines against Cutler, in front and on his right flank. General Wadsworth directed this brigade to fall back to the shelter of the woods on Seminary Ridge. This left Captain Hall without any supports to his battery, and, as he received no orders to withdraw, his situation soon became a precarious one.

The One hundred and forty-seventh New York Volunteers, of Cutler's brigade, did not receive the order to retire; Lieutenant-Colonel Miller, its commander, having been wounded, was unable to communicate his instructions to his successor, Major Harney. The latter bravely held the regiment to its position until the enemy was in possession of the railroad cut on his left, thus intercepting his line of retreat. During the half hour which elapsed before he could be relieved, his loss was 207 killed and wounded out of 380.

The dispositions made by Captain Hall to meet the emergency and save his battery were both able and resolute. He broke the force of the charge against him by firing canister, and then ordered his battery to retire by sections. The right section, while falling back, was charged upon by the enemy's skirmishers, and 4 of the horses of one piece shot. The cannoneers, however, drew off the piece by hand. In reference to this period of the action, Captain Hall says, in his official report:

As the last piece of the battery was coming away, all of its horses were shot, and I was about to return for it myself, when General Wadsworth gave me a peremptory order to lose no time, but get my battery in position near the barn on the heights, to cover the retiring of the troops. I sent a sergeant and 5 men after the piece, all of whom were wounded or taken prisoners.

Captain Hall was now withdrawn behind Seminary Ridge by way of the railroad grading, which runs nearly parallel to the Cashtown road, and is about 100 yards from it—an unfortunate route to take, as it was swept by the enemy's guns. He was soon afterward assigned to a new and more advanced position by an aide-de-camp of the division commander, but, in attempting to occupy it, he was fired upon by the rebel advance, who already held possession of the ground, and he again withdrew.

The whole of these events had occurred on the right so soon after my arrival, that there was no opportunity for me to interpose, issue orders, or regulate the retreat. The moment was a critical one, involving the defeat, perhaps the utter rout, of our forces. I immediately sent for one of Meredith's regiments (the Sixth Wisconsin), a gallant body of men, whom I knew could be relied upon. Forming them rapidly perpendicular to the line of battle on the enemy's flank, I directed them to attack immediately. Lieutenant-Colonel Dawes, their commander, ordered a charge, which was gallantly executed. The enemy made a hurried attempt to change front to meet the attack, and flung his troops into the railroad cut for safety. The Ninety-fifth New York Volunteers, Colonel Biddle, and the Fourteenth Brooklyn, under Colonel Fowler, joined in the charge; the cut was carried at the point of the bayonet, and two regiments of Davis' (rebel) brigade were taken prisoners.

The results of this maneuver were the capture of the two rebel regiments referred to, with their battle-flags, the release of the One hundred and forty-seventh New York Volunteers, which had been cut off, and the recapture of one of Hall's pieces, which had been left, in consequence of all the horses having been shot down and men wounded or killed. I immediately directed the original line of battle to be resumed, which was done. All this was accomplished in less than half an hour, and before General Howard had arrived on the field or assumed command. Tidball's horse battery was now ordered up by General Wadsworth, to replace Hall's battery, which had been very much cut up. Tidball was soon hotly engaged with a battery in his front. Soon after, Captain Reynolds was sent to relieve him.

Upon taking a retrospect of the field, it might seem, in view of the fact that we were finally forced to retreat, that this would have been a proper time to retire; but to fall back without orders from the commanding general might have inflicted lasting disgrace upon the corps, and as General Reynolds, who was high in the confidence of General Meade, had formed his lines to resist the entrance of the enemy into Gettysburg, I naturally supposed that it was the intention to defend the place.

There were abundant reasons for holding it, for it is the junction of seven great roads leading to Hagerstown, Chambersburg, Carlisle, York, Baltimore, Taneytown, and Washington, and is also an important railroad terminus. The places above mentioned are on the circumference of a circle of which it is the center. It was, therefore, a strategic point of no ordinary importance. Its possession would have been invaluable to Lee, shortening and strengthening his line to Williamsport, and serving as a base of maneuvers for future operations. I knew that Slocum's and Sickles' corps were within striking distance when we left Marsh Creek; that Howard's corps was already passing through the streets of the town, and that the remaining divisions of the First Corps were almost up. A retreat without hard fighting has a tendency to demoralize the troops who retire, and would, in the present instance, in my opinion, have dispirited the whole army and injured its *morale*, while it encouraged the enemy in the same proportion. There never was an occasion in which the result could have been more momentous upon our national destiny. Final success in this war can only be attained by desperate fighting, and the infliction of heavy loss upon the enemy; nor could I have retreated without the full knowledge and approbation of General Howard, who was my superior officer, and who had now arrived on the field. Had I done so, it would have uncovered the left flank of his corps. If circumstances required it, it was his place, not mine, to issue the order. General Howard, from his commanding position on Cemetery Hill, could overlook all the enemy's movements as well as our own, and I therefore relied much upon his superior facilities for observation to give me timely warning of any unusual danger.

I sent word to him shortly after this that, in addition to the forces opposed to me, Ewell's corps was coming down on my right flank, and requested him to protect that portion of the line with the Eleventh Corps. Almost at the same time he sent me the same information, together with instructions to hold Seminary Hill at all hazards, if driven back. Just previous to this, the remainder of the First Corps, consisting of Robinson's and Rowley's divisions, came up. I immediately directed General Robinson to station his division in reserve at the seminary, and to throw up some slight intrenchments, to aid me in holding that point in case I should be driven back. I divided Rowley's division, sending Stone's brigade to the open space on the right of the wood, to close the interval between Cutler and Meredith. The other brigade, under Colonel Biddle, One hundred and twenty-first Pennsylvania Volunteers, was posted on the left and rear of the Iron Brigade, toward the Millerstown road. General Rowley had charge of this part of the line. Later in the day he intrusted the extreme left to Colonel Gates, Twentieth New York State Militia, who, with his own regiment and the One hundred and fifty-first Pennsylvania Volunteers, under Lieutenant-Colonel McFarland, stubbornly maintained it to the last. He was greatly aided in this by two companies of skirmishers from his regiment, who occupied a house and barn in advance of our left, on the other side of the ravine. I relied greatly on Stone's brigade to hold the post assigned them, as I soon saw I would be obliged to change front with a portion of my line to face the northwest, and his brigade held the pivot of the movement. My confidence in this noble body of men was not misplaced, as will be shown hereafter. They repulsed the repeated attacks of vastly superior numbers at close quarters, and maintained their position until the final retreat of the whole line. Stone himself was shot down, battling to the last. The gallant Colonel Wister, who succeeded him in command, was also wounded, and the command devolved upon Colonel Dana, of the One hundred and forty-third Pennsylvania Volunteers. This brigade, in common with almost every regiment in the Third Division, were Pennsylvanians, and were actuated by a heroic desire to avenge the invasion of their native State.

General Howard now formed his lines to resist the advance of Ewell's corps, which came from the northeast. The corps of A. P. Hill, opposite us, at once made a junction with the new-comers. This compelled me also to change front, with Wadsworth's division on Stone's brigade as a pivot, so that the two branches of my line of battle were facing, the one west, the other northwest. I relied upon the woods and ridges to partially shield the troops from an enfilading fire. In consequence of Ewell's new line of battle, Wadsworth threw back Cutler's brigade to Seminary Ridge, to avoid a battery upon his flank. Both Tidball's and Reynolds' batteries were obliged to retire, as they were exposed to a cross-fire from two directions. Captain Reynolds was badly wounded in the eye, but for a long time refused to leave the field.

Colonel Stone, who had been contending with very little shelter against the rebel infantry and two batteries on the other side of the run, suffered some loss from the same enfilading battery which had rendered a change of front necessary on the part of Wadsworth. Leaving Colonel Wister's regiment, the One hundred and fiftieth Pennsylvania Volunteers, still facing the west, he threw successively Lieutenant-Colonel Dwight, with the One hundred and forty-ninth Pennsylvania, and Colonel Dana, with the One hundred and forty-third Pennsylvania, into the Cashtown road, facing a little east of north. As this left an open space of some 200 yards between the right of Stone and the left of Cutler, and as the rebels at this time were not making any strong demonstrations against our left, Cooper's battery fired through the interval, and Biddle's brigade changed front to support it.

Shortly after this, Lieutenant Wilber, of Battery L, First New York Artillery, was sent, in answer to a request from General Wadsworth for a battery, and posted in an orchard on the south side of the Cashtown road, where the right flank was sheltered by a house and barn. The remaining two sections were posted on the open crest, also to the south of the road.

I had hoped General Howard would have been able to connect with the right of my line, but after General Schurz had formed his division, there was a wide interval between the two corps. This gap might have been filled by my falling back to the Seminary Ridge, but unfortunately that ridge is open ground, and could have been, as it was afterward, enfiladed by Ewell's batteries throughout its whole extent. Finding it necessary to stop this gap at all hazards, I directed General Robinson, whose division I had kept in reserve, to send one of his brigades there. He detailed General Baxter for that purpose. This brigade moved forward and formed on the right of Wadsworth's division, but an interval still existed of nearly 400 yards between Baxter's right and the Eleventh Corps. The enemy attacked in this interval, and were driven back by a change of front. They then assailed the left flank of the brigade, obliging Baxter again to change front. He drove the rebels before him in handsome style, but was constantly outflanked and enfiladed. Nevertheless, the brigade behaved nobly, capturing a great number of prisoners, the Eighty-eighth Pennsylvania taking two battle-flags and the Ninety-seventh New York one.   They were greatly aided in this by a galling fire poured in on the flanks of the enemy by the Twelfth Massachusetts.

Finding Baxter was in danger of being overpowered, I directed General Robinson to go in person to his assistance with the remainder of his division (Paul's brigade).   Stewart's battery, of the Fourth U. S. Artillery, was also sent to report to General Robinson.   Part of Paul's brigade was posted by General Robinson as a support to Baxter against an enemy advancing on our front, and part was posted perpendicular to our line to protect the right flank.   General Robinson says:

The enemy now made repeated attacks on the division, in all of which he was handsomely repulsed, with the loss of three flags and about 1,000 prisoners.   In one of these attacks I was deprived of the services of the veteran commander of the First Brigade, Brigadier-General Paul, who fell, severely wounded, while gallantly directing and encouraging his command.   The division held this position on the right, receiving and repelling the fierce attacks of a greatly superior number, not only in front, but on the flanks, and, when the enemy's ranks were broken, charging upon him, and capturing his colors and his men, from about noon until nearly 5 p. m., when I received orders to withdraw.   These orders not being received until all the other troops, except Stewart's battery, had commenced moving to the rear, the division held its ground until outflanked right and left, and retired, fighting. From the nature of the enemy's attacks, frequent changes were rendered necessary, and they were made promptly, under a galling fire.   Soldiers never fought better or inflicted severer blows upon the enemy.   When out of ammunition, their boxes were replenished from those of their killed or wounded comrades.

Ewell's forces advanced about 1.30 p. m. in two deployed lines, supported by a third line of battalions *en masse*.   A portion of these made the attack already referred to against Baxter's left, in which they were repulsed.   Their defeat was partly owing to the fact that they became separated from their main line, and swung around in such a manner as to expose their flank to Colonel Stone's troops in the road, who took advantage of the opportunity to pour in a destructive fire at long range.

Having thus failed in their assault upon Robinson's division, they next made a determined advance against the two regiments in the road. To meet this, Colonel Stone sent one of these regiments, the One hundred and forty-ninth Pennsylvania, under Lieutenant-Colonel Dwight, forward to the railroad cut.   This formed *en échelon* about 100 yards to the front and left of Colonel Dana's regiment (One hundred and forty-third Pennsylvania Volunteers).   In spite of two most effective volleys of musketry, the enemy struggled on to within 30 yards of the cut.   Here, however, they were driven back in confusion by a spirited bayonet charge ordered by Lieutenant-Colonel Dwight. Dana was at the same time warmly engaged in protecting the flank of the advanced regiment.   The enemy, immediately after this, brought a battery to enfilade the cut, and Dwight was forced to fall back to his first position, on Dana's left.

It was in this affair that Colonel Stone was severely wounded, and Colonel Wister assumed command of the brigade.

The rebels now advanced from the northwest to flank the two regiments in the road, but the One hundred and fiftieth Regiment, under Lieutenant-Colonel Huidekoper, changed front forward and met the enemy precisely as Dwight had met them, with two volleys of musketry and a gallant bayonet charge, led by Colonel Wister in person; this dispersed them.   Another desperate onslaught came from the north, passed the railroad cut, and almost reached the road, only, however, to encounter another defeat from the irresistible bayonets of our men. The next attack came from the west, but was again repulsed by the indomitable One hundred and fiftieth Regiment.

Colonel Wister was now severely wounded in the face. Colonel Dana, who assumed command, contested the position with varying fortunes until the close of the battle. Just previous to this, the brave and resolute Lieutenant-Colonel Huidekoper had faced four companies of his regiment to contend with the opposing forces from the west, while six companies kept off an entire brigade from the north. Lieutenant-Colonel Huidekoper lost his arm at this point, and as Major Chamberlain was also wounded, the command devolved upon Captain Widdis.

Lieutenant-Colonel Dwight was left upon the field wounded in three places, and fell temporarily into the hands of the enemy. Every regiment of Stone's brigade changed front forward, and two regiments changed front to the rear while closely engaged. The most eminent military writers regard the first movement as difficult, and the last as almost impossible, to be executed under fire.

About 4 p. m. the enemy, having been strongly re-enforced, advanced in large numbers, everywhere deploying into double and triple lines, overlapping our left for a third of a mile, pressing heavily upon our right, and overwhelming our center. It was evident Lee's whole army was approaching. Our tired troops had been fighting desperately, some of them for six hours. They were thoroughly exhausted, and General Howard had no re-enforcements to give me. It became necessary to retreat. All my reserves had been thrown in, and the First Corps was now fighting in a single line.

It is stated by General Wadsworth in his official report that the portion of the Eleventh Corps nearest to us, unable to stand the pressure, had fallen back some time before this, and that our right flank was thus uncovered, so far as that corps was concerned. Biddle's brigade about this time again changed front to meet the strong lines advancing from the west. I now gave orders to fall back, this and Meredith's brigades covering the movement by occupying the intrenchments in front of the seminary, which I had directed to be thrown up as a precautionary measure to assist in holding the new position. Cooper's battery was assigned by the chief of artillery on the north, and Stevens' battery (Fifth Maine) on the south of the seminary, and the shattered remnants of the Iron Brigade also fell into line. From behind the feeble barricade of rails these brave men stemmed the fierce tide which pressed upon them incessantly, and held the rebel lines, which encircled them on three sides, at bay until the greater portion of the corps had retired. The One hundred and fifty-first, One hundred and forty-second, One hundred and twenty-first Pennsylvania Volunteers, and Twentieth New York State Militia, of Biddle's command (the last two under Colonel Gates, of the Twentieth New York State Militia), and the Second and Seventh Wisconsin and Nineteenth Indiana, of the Iron Brigade, here made their final stand. Captain [Hollon] Richardson, acting assistant inspector-general, of Meredith's staff, rode up and down the lines, waving a regimental flag and encouraging the men to do their duty.

The troops, with the assistance of part of Stewart's battery, under Lieutenant Davison, poured in so deadly a fire as to wholly break up and disable the first line of the enemy approaching from the west; but the other lines pressed on, and soon commenced a flank attack, which it was no longer possible to answer.   When all the troops at this point were overpowered, Captain Glenn, of the One hundred and forty-ninth Pennsylvania Volunteers, in command of my head-quarters guard, defended the building for fully twenty minutes against a whole brigade of the enemy, enabling the few remaining troops, the ambulances, artillery, &c., to retreat in comparative safety.

The batteries had all been brought back from their advanced positions and posted on Seminary Hill.   They greatly assisted the orderly retreat, retarding the enemy by their fire.   They lost heavily in men and horses at this point, and, as they retired to the town, were subjected to so heavy a fire that the last gun was left, the horses being all shot down by the enemy's skirmishers, who had formed line within 50 yards of the road by which the artillery was obliged to pass.

The First Corps only consisted of about 8,200 men when it entered the battle.   It was reduced at the close of the engagement to about 2,450.   It must be remembered that A. P. Hill's corps alone, which fought us on the west, was estimated at 35,000 men, of which 25,000, under Heth and Pender, were in line opposed to us, and that Ewell's corps, which attacked us on the north, was said to amount to 30,000 more.   Its two divisions with which we contended, under Rodes and Early, contained about 20,000 men.   Reserves amounting to 20,000 additional men, belonging to the two corps, and backed by the whole rebel army, were within a few hours' march.   When that part of the Eleventh Corps adjacent to us fell back, a force of 30,000 men was thrown upon the First Corps, which in the beginning only contained about 8,200.

I remained at the seminary superintending the final movement until thousands of hostile bayonets made their appearance around the sides of the building.   I then rode back and rejoined my command, nearly all of whom were filing through the town.   As we passed through the streets, the pale and frightened inhabitants came out of their houses, offering us food and drink and the expression of their deep sorrow and sympathy.   The written statements of the division commanders in regard to the details of this p riod are slightly conflicting.   I therefore present extracts from the reports themselves. General Robinson has already been quoted.

General Wadsworth says:

I received orders direct from Major-General Howard to hold Seminary Ridge as long as possible.   Tidball's battery had been driven back, but about 3 p. m. Battery B, Fourth Regular Artillery, commanded by Lieutenant Stewart, came to our assistance, and rendered effective service, demolishing a brigade of the enemy by a destructive fire of canister and shell.   Battery L, First New York Artillery, and the Fifth Maine Battery, were likewise engaged in position near the seminary.

At about 2.30 p. m. Major-General Schurz, who had been advanced on our right, fell back after partially engaging the enemy, and left our right exposed.   The enemy advanced in large force from that direction, and on our left the Third Division of this corps was driven back.   Finding myself outflanked on both right and left, heavily pressed in front, and my ammunition nearly exhausted, I ordered the command to retire at 3.45 o'clock.   The movement was effected in good order, and all the artillery brought off safely, excepting one caisson, the Seventh Wisconsin bringing up the rear and suffering heavily with the whole of the command from the fire from our front and both flanks.   The severity of the contest during the day will be indicated by the painful fact that at least half of the officers and men who went into the engagement were killed or wounded.

General Rowley says :

A general advance of the enemy's infantry was now made in two very strong lines, the right of which outflanked the First Brigade, at that time consisting only of three small regiments, numbering together not over 830 men and officers, the

One hundred and fifty-first Pennsylvania Volunteers having been previously detached from that brigade to support the part of our line on the right of the wood. When the enemy was first observed advancing on their extreme right, they issued from a piece of woods extending north and south, a mile distant from the First Brigade, the brigade being then faced to the north, and almost at right angles to its original position. A change of front of this part of the division was ordered, and executed under a heavy fire. After the change, the One hundred and forty-second Pennsylvania Volunteers and Twentieth New York State Militia were on the right and center of the brigade, and the One hundred and twenty-first Pennsylvania Volunteers on the left, with the battery between the One hundred and forty-second Pennsylvania Volunteers and Twentieth New York State Militia. Notwithstanding the murderous fire with which the enemy was received by my left, the disparity between the contending forces was too great to render it possible for our line to hold its position. The First Brigade gradually fell back, firing, until it reached a cover of rails, hastily thrown up by some of the other troops, in front of the seminary. Here it remained, together with some men of the First Division, fighting desperately, and until time was afforded to most of our other troops, to the artillery, and to the ambulances to withdraw in an orderly manner from the town in the direction of Cemetery Hill, and until the advancing lines of the enemy were gaining on our flanks. At the breastworks, Colonel Biddle, commanding the First Brigade, was wounded in the head by a shot, but he still remained on the field, and retired with his men, and reformed them on arriving in rear of Cemetery Hill, behind which Colonel Dana, with the Second Brigade, with reformed lines, was also again ready for service. The Second Brigade, on first falling back, halted in a peach orchard, where it renewed its fire, giving time for the removal of a battery which had been established there.

Arrived at the cemetery, our lines, with those of the Eleventh Corps, were reformed under the direction of Major-General Howard. Our batteries were placed upon the summit of the hill, the First Corps having been directed to occupy the ground to the west of the road, the Eleventh Corps being on its right. A portion of the troops was placed behind the hill in reserve.

Major-General Hancock now rode up, and informed me he had been placed in command of both corps. He at once directed me to send a force to support a battery which had been established on a lower range of hills, some 100 yards to the east of our position, protecting our flank in that direction. I complied with the order, and sent the remainder of Wadsworth's division there. Immediately afterward orders came from Major-General Howard, who ranked Hancock, to send the troops in another direction. This occasioned at the time some little delay and confusion. No very serious demonstrations were made against our new position, and the hours passed away until sundown in comparative quiet.

The operations of the day were of necessity accompanied by severe losses in killed, wounded, and missing, on account of the great disparity in numbers and the prolonged nature of the contest. This preliminary battle, however, had the most important bearing on the results of the next two days, as it enabled the whole army to come up and re-enforce the admirable position to which we had retreated. Had we retired earlier in the day, without co-operation with the other parts of the army, the enemy by a vigorous pursuit might have penetrated between the corps of Sickles and Slocum, and have either crushed them in detail or flung them off in eccentric directions. The whole retreat from the commencement was most creditable to the troops engaged. There was no hurry and no confusion, but the regiments fell back calmly, turning from time to time to check the enemy's advance by volleys of musketry, and again retreating. From the admixture of so many different regiments at the seminary, it became impossible to reorganize them in good order without a delay which would have exposed the men to certain destruction. I saw, however, no running or undue haste. All the troops passed tranquilly on, although the enemy was firing into them from the side streets, and all reformed promptly on their arrival at Cemetery Hill, and in a very short time were again ready for service. The Sixth Wisconsin marched through the streets in a body, stopping from time to time to return the fire of the enemy, and giving hearty cheers for the good old cause and the Sixth Wisconsin Volunteers.

I have said the losses were exceedingly heavy. More than half of those who went into the battle were killed or wounded. In the Second Wisconsin, 69 came back out of 302 ; in the Nineteenth Indiana, 78 returned out of 288 ; the One hundred and fiftieth Pennsylvania Volunteers, Colonel Wister's regiment, out of about 400 men and 17 officers, lost, in killed, wounded, and missing, 16 officers and about 316 men ; the One hundred and and forty-ninth Pennsylvania Volunteers lost in the same proportion.

That portion of the Eleventh Corps posted beyond the almshouse had fought with great obstinacy until its right flank was turned by Early's division, and further resistance had become hopeless. It then fell back to the town, and choked up the main street at the very time Paul's brigade was attempting to pass. This resulted in heavy loss to the brigade.

It gives me great pleasure to state that my division commanders used unwearied efforts to hold the portions of the line assigned them. General Robinson guarded the right flank with great courage and skill when it was left exposed toward the close of the day. General Wadsworth's division opened the combat, and defended the center of the line to the very last, while General Rowley held the left wing under the most adverse circumstances, and, with a portion of Wadsworth's men, covered the retreat of the main body by successive *échelons* of resistance.

I concur with the division commanders in their estimate of the good conduct and valuable services of the following-named officers and men.

General Wadsworth says of the First Division :

The officers of my staff and of my command performed their whole duty without an exception. Under these circumstances, I cannot particularly commend any of them without doing injustice to others equally meritorious.

General Cutler, commanding the Second Brigade, First Division, whose coolness and self-possession were remarkable, and who had two horses shot under him, says :

Colonel Hofmann, Fifty-sixth Pennsylvania Volunteers; Major Harney, One hundred and forty-seventh New York Volunteers ; Major Pye, Ninety-fifth New York Volunteers, and Captain Cook, Seventy-sixth New York Volunteers, deserve special mention for gallantry and coolness. Colonel Fowler, Fourteenth Brooklyn, for charging the enemy at the railroad cut, in connection with the Ninety-fifth New York and Sixth Wisconsin, by which the One hundred and forty-seventh New York was relieved from its perilous position. Major Grover, commanding the Seventy-sixth New York Volunteers, a brave and efficient officer, was killed early in the action of the 1st instant, and the command devolved upon Capt. John E. Cook, and most ably and faithfully did he perform his duty. Lieutenant-Colonel Miller, commanding the One hundred and forty-seventh New York Volunteers, was severely wounded at the head of his regiment on the 1st instant. Colonel Biddle, Ninety-fifth New York, was wounded in the breast. Major Harney, of the One hundred and forty-seventh New York Volunteers, and Major Pye, of the Ninety-fifth New York, on assuming command of their respective regiments, did all that brave men and good soldiers could do, and deserve well for their services. Sergt. Henry H. Hubbard, Company C, One hundred and forty-seventh New York, was in command of the provost-guard of the brigade on the morning of the 1st instant. He formed the guard, consisting of 18 men, on the right of the Seventy-sixth New York, and fought until the battle was over, losing 12 of his men. He deserves promotion. The color-sergeant of the One hundred and forty-seventh New York was killed, and the colors were caught by Sergt. William A. Wybourn, of Company I, One hundred and forty-seventh New York, and brought off the battle-field by him, notwithstanding he was himself severely wounded.

In closing, I beg leave to acknowledge my great obligations to Capt. J. A. Kellogg, acting assistant adjutant-general; Capt. William Bloodgood, acting aide; Lieut. S. W. Woodrow, of the Ninety-fifth New York, and Lieut. T. W. Miller, volunteer aide on my staff. These officers all acted with the most perfect coolness and bravery throughout the whole action. Every one of my staff and orderlies were dismounted by having their horses shot; Lieutenant Miller and Captain Bloodgood twice each, and Lieutenant Woodrow three times.

The report of General Meredith, commanding the First Brigade, First Division, has not been received, he having sustained severe internal injuries by the falling of his wounded horse. Copies of several of the regimental reports, however, having been laid before me, I take pleasure in calling attention to the following-named officers and men mentioned by regimental commanders:

The Seventh Wisconsin Volunteers was commanded by Col. W. W Robinson, whose conduct was everything that could be desired. He speaks of Lieutenant-Colonel Callis, who was wounded, and of Major Finnicum; also of Sergt. Daniel McDermott, color-bearer, who had his flag-staff shattered by canister shot during the retreat, and who was himself severely wounded. While in this condition, he was placed upon a caisson, and rode off waving his tattered flag in defiance of the enemy.

No report has been obtained from the commanding officer of the Twenty-fourth Michigan or Second Wisconsin Regiments, excepting a brief statement from Lieutenant-Colonel Mansfield, of the latter regiment, giving the number of killed, wounded, and missing.

In the Nineteenth Indiana, Private James Stickley, of Company C, deserves special mention for refusing to leave the field when badly wounded. He was killed late in the action. Lieutenant Jones, of Company B, and Lieutenant East, of Company C, fell while cheering on their men. Sergeants [James] Ferguson and [Andrew] Beshears, of Company H; [Thomas] Winset and [Thomas J.] Daugherty, of Company K; [Thomas K.] Michener, of Company E, and [Allen W.] Ogborn, of Company B, were among the killed who are worthy of special notice. The active and fearless Lieutenant-Colonel Dudley lost a leg; Major Lindley, always cool and courageous, was wounded in the hand; Captains Holloway, Ives, and Shafer, and Lieutenants Wilson, Schlagle, Campbell, Witemyre, Macy, Branson, Patrick, Gisse, and Nash were also wounded while doing all that men could do to insure success. The two last-mentioned officers refused to leave the field. Captains Hart, Makepeace, and Greene, and Lieutenant Richardson, fell into the enemy's hands. This regiment was commanded by Col. Samuel J. Williams, and to his promptness, courage, and skill it is in a great measure indebted for increasing the high reputation it already enjoyed.

In the Sixth Wisconsin, Adjt. Edward P. Brooks is mentioned for greatly aiding the successful capture of the two regiments in the railroad cut, by throwing a body of men into the cut so as to enfilade the rebel line. Corpl. F. Asbury Waller, of Company I, captured the colors of the Second Mississippi previous to the surrender of that regiment. Major Hauser was particularly brave and efficient. Capt. John Ticknor and Lieut. Orrin D. Chapman, who were killed in the charge, were a great loss to the service. Capt. Rollin P. Converse and Lieut. Charles P. Hyatt, of Company B, and Lieutenant Gol-termann, of Company F, were also among the highly distinguished. The commander of the regiment, Lieut. Col. R. R. Dawes, proved himself to be one of the ablest officers on the field.

General Robinson, commanding the Second Division, thus com-mends the officers and men of his command:

The instances of distinguished gallantry are too numerous to be embodied in this report, and I leave it to the brigade and regimental commanders to do justice to those under their immediate commands. When all did so well it is difficult to dis-criminate. As, however, they came under my personal observation, I cheerfully indorse the remarks of General Baxter in commendation of Colonel Coulter, Eleventh Pennsylvania Volunteers; Colonel Wheelock, Ninety-seventh New York; Colonel Lyle, Ninetieth Pennsylvania; Colonel Bates and Lieutenant-Colonel Allen, Twelfth Massachusetts; Lieutenant-Colonel Moesch, Eighty-third New York, and Major Foust, Eighty-eighth Pennsylvania. After the fall of General Paul, the command of the First Brigade devolved successively upon Colonel Leonard, Thirteenth Massa-chusetts, Colonel Root, Ninety-fourth New York, and Colonel Coulter, Eleventh Pennsylvania, all of whom were wounded while exercising command. My thanks are due to Brigadier-Generals Paul and Baxter for the able and zealous manner in which they handled their brigades. The officers of my staff were actively engaged during the whole of the three days' engagements. Lieutenant Morgan, acting assist-ant adjutant-general, Lieutenant Hallock, aide-de-camp, and Lieutenants Bratton and Mead, acting aides, were at all times distinguished for their gallantry and good conduct. Captain Hovey, acting assistant inspector-general, was wounded and taken from the field early in the day. Lieutenant Smith, ordnance officer, was diligent in the performance of his duty. It affords me pleasure to call special at-tention to the gallant conduct of one of my orderlies, Sergt. Ebenezer S. Johnson, First Maine Cavalry, whose chevrons should be exchanged for the epaulette. When we make officers of such men, the soldier receives his true reward and the service great benefit.

General Rowley, commanding the Third Division, says:

I take pleasure in calling to the notice of the commanding general, Col. Chapman Biddle, commanding the First Brigade, and Colonel Dana, commanding the Second Brigade, and also the following officers, recommended by brigade commanders: Colonel Gates, Twentieth New York State Militia; Lieutenant-Colonel McFarland, One hundred and fifty-first Pennsylvania Volunteers (severely wounded); Lieuten-ant-Colonel McCalmont and Major Biddle, One hundred and forty-second Pennsyl-vania Volunteers; Major Musser, One hundred and forty-third Pennsylvania Vol-unteers; Lieutenant-Colonel Dwight and Captains Irvin and Glenn, One hundred and forty-ninth Pennsylvania Volunteers, and Colonel Wister, Lieutenant-Colonel Huidekoper, Major Chamberlain, and Adjutant Ashurst, One hundred and fiftieth Pennsylvania Volunteers, as being distinguished for bravery. The members of the brigade staff are likewise favorably noticed. I would also call to the notice of the commanding general, Lieut. William L. Wilson (slightly wounded), acting assistant adjutant-general; Captain Flagg (killed July 3), acting assistant inspector-general, and Lieutenant Moore, One hundred and forty-third Pennsylvania Volunteers, aide-de-camp—all acting on my staff July 1—for gallant conduct. The death of Colonel Cummins, One hundred and forty-second Pennsylvania Volunteers, a brave and efficient officer, has occasioned feelings of regret throughout the command.

My thanks are specially due to a citizen of Gettysburg named John Burns, who, although over seventy years of age, shouldered his musket, and offered his services to Colonel Wister, One hundred and fiftieth Pennsylvania Volunteers. Colonel Wister advised him to fight in the woods, as there was more shelter there, but he preferred to join our line of skirmishers in the open fields. When the troops retired, he fought with the Iron Brigade. He was wounded in three places. Private Dennis Buckley, of Company H, Sixth Michigan Cavalry, having had his horse shot under him, also joined the One hundred and fiftieth Pennsylvania Volunteers, and fought through-out the day. Shortly after he came up, a shell from a rebel battery exploded in the midst of Company C, killing 2 men and dangerously wounding 3 others.   Buckley joined this company, saying, "This is the company for me," and remained throughout the entire engagement, doing excellent service with his carbine.   He escaped unhurt.

General Rowley himself displayed great bravery.   He was several times struck by spent shot and pieces of shell, and on the third day his horse was killed by a cannon-shot while he was holding him by the bridle and conversing with me.

Colonel Wainwright, chief of artillery, mentions in terms of commendation Captain Reynolds, whose heroism was conspicuous; Captain Tidball, Captain Cooper, Captain Stevens, the oft-distinguished Lieutenant Stewart, Lieutenant Davison, Lieutenant Breck.   Lieutenant Wilbur's gallantry is also the subject of much praise.

In conclusion, I desire to speak of the officers of my own staff. Colonel Wainwright, chief of artillery, was unremitting in the discharge of his duties; Lieutenant-Colonel [Henry C.] Bankhead, inspector-general, rendered most valuable services in carrying orders and reconnoitering the enemy's movements; Surgeons Heard and [Thomas H.] Bache refused to leave our wounded, and remained with them as prisoners at Gettysburg until the retreat of the enemy released and restored them to duty.   Lieutenant-Colonel [Charles E.] Livingston, acting assistant inspector-general; Captain [Edward C.] Baird, assistant adjutant-general; Captain [Eminel P.] Halstead, assistant adjutant-general; Lieutenants [Henry T.] Lee and [Benjamin T.] Marten, aides-de-camp; Lieutenant [Harry C.] Egbert, commissary of musters; Lieutenant [Frank H.] Cowdrey, assistant commissary of musters; Lieutenant [Harrison] Lambdin, acting aide-de-camp, all distinguished on other fields of battle, were equally distinguished on the present occasion.   Lieutenant [Meredith L.] Jones, acting aide-de-camp, behaved with great coolness and courage.   Lieutenant [Jacob F.] Slagle, acting judge-advocate-general, was active in carrying orders to exposed parts of the field.

General Wadsworth has furnished me the following list of his staff, all of whom were distinguished for intrepidity and intelligent action : Lieutenant-Colonel [John A.] Kress, assistant inspector-general ; Major [Clinton H.] Meneely, aide-de-camp ; Lieutenant [Earl M.] Rogers, provost-marshal; Lieutenant [Edward] Carrington, aide-de-camp; Captain [Charles H.] Ford, acting aide-de-camp; Captain [Timothy E.] Ellsworth, aide-de-camp, and Captain [Charles] McClure, commissary of subsistence.

Colonel [John G.] Stephenson, Librarian of Congress, acted as volunteer aide to General Meredith.   He exposed himself freely on all occasions, and rendered many valuable services.

I am much indebted, too, to Major [William] Riddle and Captains [Craig W.] Wadsworth and [Robert W.] Mitchell (General Reynolds' aides), who kindly volunteered their services and were of great assistance; Captain [William H.] Wilcox, aide-de-camp, also brought me some orders from General Howard, and rendered himself useful; Captain Taylor, commanding General Reynolds' escort, also reported to me, and was well employed in various duties, particularly in driving back stragglers at the close of the day.

Lieutenant-Colonel [James J.] Dana, assistant quartermaster, and Lieutenant-Colonel [James M.] Sanderson, commissary of subsistence, deserve mention for services rendered in their respective departments.

Colonel Fairchild, Second Wisconsin, who lost an arm, is universally spoken of in the highest terms.

Colonel Morrow, Twenty-fourth Michigan, who was wounded while bringing off a regimental flag he had saved, fell into the hands of the enemy, but escaped afterward when they retreated from Gettysburg. Colonel Morrow had some interesting conversations with General Ewell, of the rebel army, in relation to the battle and its incidents, and I obtained a statement from him on this subject, showing how the fight was regarded from a rebel point of view, and the unwilling admiration it excited.*

I have the honor to be, very respectfully, your obedient servant,

A. DOUBLEDAY,
Major-General of Volunteers.

Brig. Gen. S. WILLIAMS,
  Asst. Adjutant-General, Hdqrs. Army of the Potomac.

—

JANUARY 2, 1864.

Major-General DOUBLEDAY,
  Washington:

In answer to your letter of the 30th ultimo to Major-General Meade, I am instructed by him to say that he has no objection, provided the War Department consent thereto, to the publication of the report heretofore presented by you of the operations of your command at Gettysburg, which accompanied the commanding general's report of that battle, and is now among the records of the Adjutant-General's office. But the commanding general declines sanctioning the publication of the more detailed report you state you have prepared until he shall have had an opportunity of examining it, and he considers that if you have a report designed to take the place of that formerly rendered by you, the same should be transmitted to him, to be forwarded to the War Department, with such observations, if any, as he may desire to offer in connection with it.

Very respectfully, &c.,

A. A. HUMPHREYS.
Major-General and Chief of Staff.

—

HEADQUARTERS ARMY OF THE POTOMAC,
January 5, 1864.

Major-General DOUBLEDAY,
  Washington:

I am directed by Major-General Meade to inform you that your revised report of the part taken by your command at the battle of Gettysburg has been transmitted to the Adjutant-General of the Army, with the request that it be substituted for the report heretofore rendered by you.

I am instructed to add that the commanding general has no objection to the publication of your revised report, if the same be sanctioned by the War Department.

Very respectfully, &c.,

S. WILLIAMS,
Assistant Adjutant-General.

---

* See Colonel Morrow's report, p. 272.

NEW YORK, *September* 19, 1863.

GENERAL: I have the honor to report that, on the evening of July 1, I resumed command of the Third Division of the First Corps, consisting of Rowley's and Dana's brigades. A third brigade of Vermont troops, under General Stannard, also reported to me about twilight of the same day. It consisted of the Twelfth, Thirteenth, Fourteenth, Fifteenth, and Sixteenth Regiments. The Twelfth and Fifteenth had been directed to act as a guard to the wagon train. The Fifteenth came up the next morning, but was again ordered back for the same purpose. The remaining regiments, having marched with General Sickles' troops through some mistake, were placed in the same line with them on the night of the 1st. They joined me the next morning, and were posted with my other brigades principally in reserve behind the western part of Cemetery Hill, to assist in the defense of that important position.

On the 2d, the left wing of the Thirteenth Vermont Regiment, under Lieutenant-Colonel Munson, was ordered forward to support a battery, and a company of the Sixteenth Vermont was sent out as a support to the skirmishers in front.

Toward twilight on the evening of the 2d, I received orders from the corps commander to form my men at once, and go to the assistance of Hancock's corps, which had been driven in by a desperate charge of the enemy. I marched my command as rapidly as possible to the place indicated, which was about a quarter of a mile west of the cemetery, and formed them on several lines by regiments for a charge. It was now discovered that the enemy had retired, and we were ordered to halt. My advance, however, consisting of five companies of the Thirteenth Vermont, under Colonel Randall, met Major-General Hancock, and asked permission of him to keep on and endeavor to rescue the guns of a regular battery, which had just been captured. The request was granted. Colonel Randall charged the retreating enemy in handsome style, retook the four guns that had just been lost, and also took two rebel guns, making six in all.

My division bivouacked for the night on the ground occupied by us. The Sixteenth Vermont, under Colonel Veazey, was thrown out to the front on picket. The Vermonters, with the Twentieth New York and One hundred and fifty-first Pennsylvania Volunteers, held the front line during the remainder of the action, and the troops of Rowley's and Dana's brigades, with the exceptions I have named, held the second and third lines.

About 2 p. m. a terrific artillery fire opened on us from more than 100 guns. The firing was accurate and incessant, and lasted for several hours, blowing up caissons from time to time, and sweeping away artillery and staff horses, as well as men, in every direction. I told the brigade commanders to shelter men and officers as much as possible, and, when the fire slackened, to be prepared to spring to their feet and meet the enemy with the bayonet, if necessary.

Toward 5 o'clock I received notice from General Hancock and others that the final charge of the enemy had commenced. Shortly afterward several batteries and divisions from other corps reported to me as re-enforcements. I posted them, with the approbation of the corps commander, along the crest, at the points most threatened by the enemy's advance.

With reference to this period of the action, I desire to quote the reports of General Stannard and Colonel Gates, of the Twentieth New

York, the parties who were most actively engaged in my own division in repelling the charge.

General Stannard says:

The front line thus established was held by my brigade for twenty-six hours. At about 4 o'clock on the morning of the 3d, the enemy commenced a vigorous artillery attack, which continued for a short time, upon my position. During its continuance I moved the Fourteenth, under command of Colonel Nichols, to the front of the main line about 75 yards, which was done at double-quick in good order. I then, with permission from my immediate commander, selected a position to occupy, if attacked with infantry, some distance in front of the main line.

At about 2 p. m. the enemy again commenced a vigorous attack upon my position. After subjecting us for an hour and a half to the severest cannonade of the whole battle, from 100 guns or more, the enemy charged with a heavy column of infantry, at least one division in close column by regiments. The charge was aimed directly upon my command, but, owing apparently to the firm front shown them, the enemy diverged midway, and came upon the line upon my right. But they did not thus escape the warm reception prepared for them by the Vermonters. During this charge, the enemy suffered from the fire of the Thirteenth and Fourteenth, the range being short. At the commencement of the attack, I called in the Sixteenth Regiment from the skirmish line, and placed it in close column by division in my immediate rear. As soon as the change in the point of attack became evident, I ordered a flank attack upon the enemy's column. Forming in the open meadow in front of our lines, the Thirteenth changed front forward on the first company; the Sixteenth, after deploying, performed the same, and formed on the left of the Thirteenth, at right angles to the main line of our army, bringing them in line of battle upon the flank of the charging divisions of the enemy, and opened a destructive fire at short range, which the enemy sustained but a very few moments before the larger portion of them surrendered and marched in—not as conquerors, but as captives. I then ordered the two regiments into their former position. The order was not filled when I saw another rebel column charging immediately upon our left. Colonel Veazey, of the Sixteenth, was at once ordered to attack it in its turn upon the flank. This was done as successfully as before. The rebel forces, already decimated by the fire of the Fourteenth Regiment, Colonel Nichols commanding, were scooped almost *en masse into our* lines. The Sixteenth in this charge took the regimental colors of the Second Florida and Eighth Virginia Regiments, and the battle-flag of another rebel regiment. The Sixteenth was supported in this new and advanced position by four companies of the Fourteenth, under command of Lieutenant-Colonel Rose.

*   *   *   *   *   *   *

The movements I have briefly described were executed in the open field under a very heavy fire of shell, grape, and musketry, and they were performed with the promptness and precision of battalion drill. They ended the contest in the center and substantially closed the battle. Officers and men behaved like veterans, although it was for most of them their first battle.

To this splendid record I have nothing to add.

Colonel Gates, of the Twentieth New York Volunteers, says:

At 12.30 p. m. on the 3d, the enemy opened a furious cannonade upon our left center, which continued about two hours. At the end of that time his infantry advanced in two lines upon my position. When his first line received our fire, he faced to his left, and moved in the new direction until nearly opposite the hill on our left center, when he faced to the right, and moved rapidly in line of battle toward the hill. The second line followed the movements of the first. Perceiving that his intention was to get possession of the hill and the batteries upon it, which would have cut our line and greatly endangered our army, I moved my two regiments by the right flank quickly up to the hillside, which he had already commenced ascending. Here some very sharp fighting took place. The enemy had got possession of the fence at the foot of the hill and of the slashing on the hillside caused by felling trees to clear the range for our guns. The fighting was now at quarter pistol range, and the fence and fallen trees gave the enemy considerable protection. I therefore ordered my men forward, and they sprang through and over the slashing and up to the fence, the enemy generally dropping their arms and surrendering themselves. Very few of the force that advanced to this attack got back to their own lines again. A great many prisoners were taken, whom I sent to the provost-marshal without guard or escort, as I had no men to spare.

I think these extracts show that it is to General Stannard and Colonel Gates the country is mainly indebted for the repulse of the enemy's charge and the final victory of July 3.

The troops in the second and third lines also deserve special commendation, as they were equally exposed to the enemy's missiles. Although the artillery fire was very severe, I did not see a man desert his post.

After the retreat of the enemy, we remained where we were, and bivouacked upon the field. The Vermont regiment, on picket, was relieved, through the kindness of General Birney, by a division of the Third Corps.

On the 4th, my troops still retained the same position on the field of battle.

On the 5th, they retired a few hundred yards to obtain a more pleasant encampment.

On the 6th, they remained in the same place.

On the 7th, I left very early under orders for Washington.

Among the circumstances worthy of mention which occurred on the third day was the death of the rebel General Barksdale. He was brought into my lines by my acting assistant inspector-general, Lieutenant-Colonel [C. E.] Livingston. His dying speech and last messages for his family, together with the valuables about his person, were intrusted by him to Lieutenant-Colonel Livingston.

I have already mentioned my staff in my report of the operations of the corps on the 1st. They did their whole duty without exception. Several had their horses shot. Lieutenant Cowdrey, assistant commissary of musters, was wounded.

I was myself struck toward the close of the day by a piece of shell, but was not seriously injured.

Dr. [George M.] Ramsay, chief surgeon of the division, is entitled to my thanks for his valuable services. Captain [Chandler] Hall, assistant quartermaster; Captain [John D.] Adair, commissary of subsistence; Lieutenant [Charles T.] Shaw, ordnance officer, and Lieutenant [George R.] Snowden, of the ambulance corps, were all zealous and efficient in the discharge of their duties.

I have the honor to be, very respectfully, your obedient servant,

A. DOUBLEDAY,
Major-General of Volunteers.

Brig. Gen. S. WILLIAMS,
Asst. Adjt. Gen., Headquarters Army of the Potomac.

No. 30.

Reports of Maj. Gen. John Newton, U. S. Army, commanding First Army Corps.

HEADQUARTERS FIRST ARMY CORPS,
September 30, 1863.

GENERAL : I have the honor to submit the following report of the operations of this corps at the battle of Gettysburg and subsequently, until its arrival at Warrenton Junction :

July 1.—The operations of this day are fully set forth in Maj. Gen. Abner Doubleday's report, who commanded the corps in the bloody and important battle which inaugurated the three days' fighting at Gettysburg.

July 2.—In obedience to an order from Headquarters Army of the Potomac, dated July 1, I reported in person to the general commanding, at the cemetery gate, early in the morning of this day, and assumed command of the First Corps. I found the First Division (Brigadier-General Wadsworth) occupying the high wooded hill and slopes immediately on the right of General Howard's position on Cemetery Hill, an important position, from which it was not detached during the subsequent operations at Gettysburg. Major-General Doubleday's (Third) division was in reserve behind the Eleventh Corps on Cemetery Hill. Brigadier-General Robinson's (Second) division was likewise posted on the Cemetery Hill, but on the left of the Eleventh Corps, and facing to the left in the position afterward occupied by the Second Corps. The artillery of the corps, except one battery with the First Division, was posted on Cemetery Hill, and was not detached from this position during all the subsequent fighting. Beyond an occasional shot at the moving columns of the enemy, everything remained quiet until the afternoon, when the enemy opened a brisk cannonade on my position, which was vigorously and effectively returned.

Near sundown I was summoned to move my troops in haste to fill a gap in the line on the left of the Second Corps, into which the enemy was on the point of entering. Notwithstanding the inconvenient positions of the Second and Third Divisions, these were quickly filed into the new position in time to stay the progress of the enemy, who relinquished their attempt on our appearance. I was deeply gratified at the promptitude with which these divisions moved at this critical period, their movement not consuming one-half the time it would have taken on drill. During this movement, the right wing of the Thirteenth Vermont, under Colonel Randall, charged upon the enemy, retook four of our guns, and captured two guns and 80 prisoners from them. Two more of our guns were retaken by the Second Brigade, Third Division.

Night coming on, and active operations closing here for the day, parties were sent to the front to bring in such guns as had been left. They were successful to some extent, but the number thus reclaimed has never been reported. The Second Division was sent back to Cemetery Hill, to support the Eleventh Corps, which was threatened by the enemy. The First Division was vigorously attacked about sundown by the enemy, who were handsomely repulsed. One brigade of the Twelfth Corps, on their right, participated in this action. The position of the Eleventh Corps was attacked about the same time, the enemy succeeding in some instances in getting into the batteries, from which they were driven by the cannoneers themselves.

July 3.—The dawn of day found the position of the First Corps as follows: The First Division as before reported; the Second Division on Cemetery Hill, ready to support the Eleventh Corps or the Second Corps; the Third Division on the left center and adjoining the left of General Hancock's position. Between the left of the Third Division and General Sykes' position on the left (an interval by my estimate of over half a mile), there were no troops in position. I reported this fact immediately to the general commanding, who authorized me to go to General Sedgwick, on the extreme left, and obtain troops from him to fill this gap. While proceeding on this mission, I encountered Caldwell's division, of the Second Corps, not then forming part of General Hancock's line of battle, and with this officer's consent I put it in position on the left of the Third Division,

First Corps.   General Sedgwick could only spare me the First New Jersey brigade (General Torbert), which was placed in position on the left of General Caldwell.   My own batteries, occupying important positions in the center and right center, might not with propriety be removed, and I therefore applied and obtained permission to call upon the Artillery Reserve for batteries.

By about 12 o'clock I considered my line between the left of General Hancock's and the right of General Sykes' as very secure, having in position the infantry above mentioned, batteries from the Artillery Reserve, from the Third Corps, and one battery from the Sixth Corps.

I must mention that the Third Corps, under Major-General Birney, which had suffered severely in the previous day's fight, I found posted directly in rear of my line of battle, and I made arrangements with General Birney to draw upon him for such support as might be needed; and I take advantage of this opportunity to express my obligations for the cheerful and handsome manner in which he responded to every call made upon him.

Near 1 p. m. the enemy opened with about one hundred and twenty guns upon the position of the army, and kept up an incessant fire for a long period.   This was intended to demoralize our troops and to cover the onset of their assaulting columns.   They failed in their first object, our troops sustaining this terrific fire with admirable equanimity.   At length their columns of attack began to move; one heavy column, a division, by General Stannard's report, marching by battalion front, directed itself upon the front of the Third (Doubleday's) Division, First Corps, but meeting with a warm fire from his front line of battle, composed of the Thirteenth, Fourteenth, and Sixteenth Vermont Regiments, the Twentieth New York State Militia, and the One hundred and fifty-first Pennsylvania Volunteers, swerved to the right to attack General Hancock.   General Stannard immediately changed front forward, and, falling upon their flank, routed them, taking a large number of prisoners.   This had hardly been done, when another column, attempting the left of General Doubleday's front, was attacked in flank in a similar way and nearly the whole column killed, wounded, or captured.   For these brilliant episodes of the battle, I respectfully call the attention of the general commanding to the reports of Major-General Doubleday and Brigadier-General Stannard.

I wish to call particular attention to the conduct of the regiments above mentioned, and to the skillful manner in which they were handled on this day, as being greatly instrumental in overthrowing the enemy's grand attack and in gaining for us a glorious victory. Brigadier-General Stannard, who was wounded the day before, refused to quit the field, and highly distinguished himself by his coolness and skill.   Major-General Doubleday narrowly escaped with his life, having suffered a severe contusion from a fragment of a shell.

With the first movement of the assaulting column of the enemy, I called upon General Birney for troops to form a reserve, first for one and subsequently for another division, which were promptly sent. With a portion of these troops I re-enforced General Hancock, who was severely pressed by heavy masses of the enemy, holding the remainder in readiness to fall upon the enemy should they succeed in penetrating our lines—a contingency which fortunately did not occur.   The Second Division, under General Robinson, was moved to sustain General Hancock's right, but did not become engaged.   The First Division was also not engaged.   The batteries of the corps, in common with the other batteries in position, vigorously and effectively replied to the enemy's cannonading on this day. After the repulse of the enemy's attack (General Hancock having been wounded), I was placed in command of the line connecting General Sykes with General Howard.

I conclude this report of the battle of Gettysburg by paying my tribute to the gallant and efficient conduct of the staff : Capt. Craig W. Wadsworth, additional aide-de-camp; Capt. John S. Bliss, Sixty-seventh New York Volunteers, aide-de-camp, severely wounded; Lieut. H. W. Jackson, Fourth New Jersey Volunteers, aide-de-camp; Lieut. Col. H. C. Bankhead, assistant inspector-general; Lieutenant-Colonel Sanderson, commissary of subsistence, and First Lieut. H. C. Egbert, Twelfth U. S. Infantry, commissary of musters.

Colonel Wainwright, the chief of artillery of the corps; Captain Stevens, Fifth Maine Battery; Captain Reynolds, Battery L, First New York Artillery; Captain Cooper, Battery B, First Pennsylvania; Captain Hall, Second Maine Battery, and Lieutenant Stewart, Battery B, Fourth U. S. Artillery, all displayed the greatest gallantry throughout the engagements of the three days.

Surg. J. Theodore Heard, medical director, and Surg. T. H. Bache, medical inspector, remained in the town of Gettysburg during its occupation by the enemy, and deserve the highest praise for their zealous and unremitting attention to the wounded.

July 4, the troops maintained the same position. The day was devoted to collecting and caring for the wounded.

On the 5th, the corps was concentrated, and attention was also given to the collecting of arms, the burial of the dead, and the care of the wounded.

On the 6th, the corps marched to Emmitsburg.

On the 7th, marched to Hamburg.

On the 8th, marched to Turner's Gap, where it took up position against a threatened attack of the enemy.

On the 10th, it took position beyond Beaver Creek.

On the 12th, it marched to Funkstown heights, and was posted in line of battle in presence of the enemy.

On the 14th, it marched to Williamsport.

On the 15th, to near Crampton's Pass.

On the 16th, to near Berlin.

On the 18th, it crossed the Potomac, and marched thence to Waterford, Va.

On the 19th, to Hamilton.

On the 20th, to Middleburg.

On the 22d, to White Plains.

On the 23d, to Warrenton.

On the 25th, to Warrenton Junction.

Very respectfully, your obedient servant,

JOHN NEWTON,
Major-General, Commanding.

Brig. Gen. S. WILLIAMS, *Assistant Adjutant-General.*

—

HEADQUARTERS FIRST ARMY CORPS,
Near Gettysburg, Pa., July 5, 1863.

GENERAL: In compliance with circular of yesterday, I have the honor to forward you the following information:

The number of colors ascertained to have been captured by this command in the late action was seven. Two, however, of the seven were again lost—one by the party capturing the colors being again captured, and one taken from the private who captured it by some unknown colonel.

There have been buried, in front of this command, up to this date, but 4 officers and 103 enlisted men of the enemy's dead. This arises from the want of tools, which were all taken from the corps in the action of the 1st instant.

The entire command is supplied with 60 rounds of ammunition per man, and three days' rations from this a. m. Artillery ammunition report inclosed.*

I am, general, very respectfully, &c.,

JOHN NEWTON,
Major-General, Commanding.

Brig. Gen. S. WILLIAMS, *Assistant Adjutant-General.*

HEADQUARTERS FIRST ARMY CORPS,
September 11, 1863.

SIR: I have the honor to report, in compliance with circular of this date, that no guns were lost by this corps during the recent campaign. Two guns are reported captured from the enemy by General Stannard on the evening of the 2d July.

Very respectfully, your obedient servant,

JOHN NEWTON,
Major-General, Commanding.

Brig. Gen. S. WILLIAMS, *Assistant Adjutant-General.*

HDQRS. FIRST ARMY CORPS, *October* 3, 1863.

The number of rebel dead buried by this corps at Gettysburg, as reported by divisions, is 7 officers and 404 men.

JOHN NEWTON,
Major-General.

Brig. Gen. S. WILLIAMS, *Assistant Adjutant-General.*

No. 31.

Report of Lieut. Joseph G. Rosengarten, One hundred and twenty-first Pennsylvania Infantry, Ordnance Officer.

HDQRS. FIRST ARMY CORPS, ARMY OF THE POTOMAC,
Hamilton, Loudoun County, Va., July 19, 1863.

GENERAL : I have the honor to report that the following arms and equipments were captured from the enemy in the recent engagements near Gettysburg :

Springfield rifled muskets	174
Enfield rifled muskets	2,402
Austrian rifled muskets	64
English rifled muskets	26
Harper's Ferry smooth-bore	212
Various	80
Total	2,958

---

* Omitted.

Of these, a large part were turned in by the division ordnance officer to Lieutenant Edie at Frederick, and the balance were left at Gettysburg or used in arming returned convalescents, escaped prisoners, &c.

Turned in to post ordnance officer at Frederick, Md. :

Cartridge boxes	1,246
Cap-pouches	848
Cartridge-boxes, waist-belts, and plates	500
Bayonet scabbards	1,156

Issued to the troops of the Third Division :

Gun-slings	125
Ramrods	40
Small-arms ammunition rounds	5,000

And that the following amount of small-arms ammunition was expended, viz:

	Caliber.	Rounds.
First Division	.58	60,000
	.54	4,000
	.57	16,000
Second Division		34,000
Issued from First Division train to Third Division	.57	8,000
	.57	90,000
	.58	7,000
	.54	5,000
	.57	3,000
	.69	1,000
Issued from First Division train to Third Division, Eleventh Army	.54	8,000
Corps	.54	5,000
Total		241,000

Very respectfully,

J. G. ROSENGARTEN,
Ordnance Officer, First Army Corps.

General S. WILLIAMS,
Asst. Adjt. Gen., Hdqrs. Army of the Potomac.

No. 32.

Report of Brig. Gen. James S. Wadsworth, U. S. Army, commanding First Division.

HEADQUARTERS FIRST DIVISION, FIRST ARMY CORPS,
In the Field, near Gettysburg, Pa., July 4, 1863.

SIR: I have the honor to report to the major-general commanding the movements of this division during the last three days.

On the morning of July 1, at 8 a. m., the division moved from Marsh Creek on Gettysburg, under the immediate direction of our deeply lamented commander, Major-General Reynolds. I understand that the general received information when we were within about a mile of the town that the enemy were approaching from the direction of Cashtown. He immediately turned the head of the column to the left, across the fields, and struck the Cashtown road about three-quarters of a mile west of Gettysburg at about 10 a. m. The Second Brigade, Brigadier-General Cutler, led the column, followed by the Second Maine Battery, Captain Hall, the First Brigade, Brigadier-

General Meredith, bringing up the rear.   Here we met the advance guard of the enemy.   Three regiments of the Second Brigade were ordered to deploy on the right of the road, the battery was placed in position near the road, and the balance of the division ordered up to the left of the road.

The right became sharply engaged before the line was formed, and at this time (about 10.15 a. m.) our gallant leader fell, mortally wounded.   The right encountered a heavy force, were outnumbered, outflanked, and after a resolute contest, bravely conducted by Brigadier-General Cutler, fell back in good order to Seminary Ridge, near the town, and a portion of the command to a point still nearer the town.   As they fell back, followed by the enemy, the Fourteenth New York State Militia, Colonel Fowler; Sixth Wisconsin Volunteers, Lieutenant-Colonel Dawes, and Ninety-fifth New York Volunteers, Colonel Biddle, gallantly charged on the advance of the enemy, and captured a large number of prisoners, including two entire regiments with their flags..   The other regiments of the First Brigade advanced farther on the left, and captured several hundred prisoners, including Brigadier-General Archer.   The enemy fell back.   I reformed the line, the Second Brigade on the right, on a ridge, the First in a piece of woodland on the left.   The battery had fallen to the rear, disabled by the loss of horses.   I found Tidball's battery on Seminary Ridge, and advanced it to the front line, where it engaged a battery of the enemy in front of us.   Major-General Doubleday, commanding the corps at that time, arrived on the ground about the time, or very soon after, General Reynolds fell, with the Second and Third Divisions.

The enemy advanced in heavy force on our right, and placed a battery in position to enfilade the line, and I was obliged to order the right to fall back to Seminary Ridge, forming the line northwesterly and diagonal to the Cashtown road.   Two brigades of the Second Division were sent to our right, and gallantly held the enemy in check for an hour, capturing a large number of prisoners.   I received orders direct from Major-General Howard to hold Seminary Ridge as long as possible.

Tidball's battery had been driven back, but about 3 p. m. Battery B, Fourth Regular Artillery, commanded by Lieutenant Stewart, came to our assistance, and rendered effective service, demolishing a brigade of the enemy by a destructive fire of canister and shell.   Battery L, First New York Artillery, and the Fifth Maine Battery were likewise engaged in position near the seminary.

At about 2.30 p. m. Major-General Schurz, who had been advanced on our right, fell back after partially engaging the enemy, and left our right exposed.   The enemy advanced in large force from that direction, and on our left the Third Division of this corps was driven back.   Finding myself outflanked on both right and left, heavily pressed in front, and my ammunition nearly exhausted, at 3.45 o'clock I ordered the command to retire.   The movement was effected in good order, and all the artillery brought off safely, excepting one caisson, the Seventh Wisconsin bringing up the rear, and suffering heavily, with the whole of the command, from the fire from our front and both flanks.

The severity of the contest during the day will be indicated by the painful fact that at least half of the officers and men who went into the engagement were killed or wounded.

On the evening of the 1st, we were ordered to occupy a hill on the right of the cemetery, which we held on the 2d and 3d against a sharp attack of the enemy on the evening of the 2d and morning of the 3d, with small loss to us.

The officers of my staff and of my command performed their whole duty without an exception. Under these circumstances I cannot particularly commend any of them without doing injustice to others equally meritorious.

I have the honor to be, very respectfully, your obedient servant,
JAS. S. WADSWORTH,
Brigadier-General of Volunteers.

The ASSISTANT-ADJUTANT GENERAL,
First Army Corps.

No. 33.

Report of Col. Henry A. Morrow, Twenty-fourth Michigan Infantry, First Brigade.

HDQRS. FIRST BRIG., FIRST DIV., FIRST ARMY CORPS,
Culpeper, Va., February 22, 1864.

CAPTAIN: I have the honor to submit the following report of the part taken by the Twenty-fourth Michigan Volunteers in the battle of Gettysburg, July 1, 1863, and the events immediately preceding:

On June 28, we marched from Middletown, Md., to near Frederick City, and on the 29th we marched to Emmitsburg. The latter was a long march, in which the troops suffered much from fatigue.

On June 30, we marched 3 or 4 miles, and bivouacked near Marsh Creek.

At an early hour on July 1, we marched in the direction of Gettysburg, distant 6 or 7 miles. The report of artillery was soon heard in the direction of this place, which indicated that our cavalry had already engaged the enemy. Our pace was considerably quickened, and about 9 a. m. we came near the town of Gettysburg, and filed off to the left, leaving it on our right. We crossed an insignificant branch, and were moved forward into line of battle on the double-quick. The cavalry immediately in our front was hotly engaged with the enemy, and the brigade was ordered to advance at once, no order being given or time allowed for loading our guns. I halted my regiment for this purpose, but was directed by a staff officer—I think he belonged to the staff of General Wadsworth—to move forward immediately without loading, which I did. The order to charge was now given, and the brigade dashed up and over the hill and down into the ravine, through which flows Willoughby's Run, where we captured a large number of prisoners, being a part of General Archer's brigade. The cavalry in the meantime had taken position on our left flank. In this affair the Twenty-fourth Michigan occupied the extreme left of the brigade, the Nineteenth Indiana being on our right.

I here lost my color-bearer, Abel G. Peck (a brave and faithful soldier), several of my color-guard, and many of my men.

After advancing to the crest of the hill beyond the run, we were halted, and threw out skirmishers to the front and also to the left, near a brick house.

We now received orders to withdraw to the east bank of the

stream, which was done. The brigade changed front forward on first battalion, and marched into the woods known as McPherson's woods, and formed in line of battle, the Nineteenth Indiana being on the left of the Twenty-fourth Michigan and the Seventh Wisconsin on its right. In executing this movement, my lieutenant-colonel and adjutant were severely wounded, and did not afterward rejoin the regiment, the former having lost a leg, and the latter being severely wounded in the groin. The line of the Twenty-fourth Michigan curved a little backward on the right, that wing being thrown back, so as to connect with the Seventh Wisconsin. Skirmishers were immediately deployed in front, and became at once engaged with the enemy.

The woods were shelled, but I have no casualties to report as occurring at this time. I sent officers several times to the general commanding to report the condition of the line, and suggesting a change of position, as it was, in my judgment, untenable. To these reports of the condition of our line, I received answer that the position was ordered to be held, and must be held at all hazards.

The enemy advanced in two lines of battle, their right extending beyond and overlapping our left. I gave direction to the men to withhold their fire until the enemy should come within short range of our guns. This was done, but the nature of the ground was such that I am inclined to think we inflicted but little injury on the enemy at this time. Their advance was not checked, and they came on with rapid strides, yelling like demons. The Nineteenth Indiana, on our left, fought most gallantly, but was overpowered by superior numbers, the enemy having also the advantage of position, and, after a severe loss, was forced back. The left of my regiment was now exposed to an enfilading fire, and orders were given for this portion of the line to swing back, so as to face the enemy, now on this flank. Pending the execution of this movement, the enemy advanced in such force as to compel me to fall back and take a new position a short distance in the rear.

In the meantime I had lost in killed and wounded several of my best officers and many of my men. Among the former were Capt. William J. Speed, acting major, and Lieutenant Dickey, a young officer of great promise. Charles Ballare, my second color-bearer, was killed here.

The second line was promptly formed, and we made a desperate resistance, but the enemy accumulating in our front, and our losses being very great, we were forced to fall back and take up a third position beyond a slight ravine. My third color-bearer, Augustus Ernest, of Company K, was killed on this line. Maj. E. B. Wight, acting lieutenant-colonel, was wounded at this time and compelled to leave the field.

By this time the ranks were so diminished that scarcely a fourth of the forces taken into action could be rallied. Corpl. Andrew Wagner, Company F, one of the color guard, took the colors, and was ordered by me to plant them in a position to which I designed to rally the men. He was wounded in the breast and left on the field. I now took the flag from the ground, where it had fallen, and was rallying the remnant of my regiment, when Private William Kelly, of Company E, took the colors from my hands, remarking, as he did so, "The colonel of the Twenty-fourth shall never carry the flag while I am alive." He was killed instantly. Private Lilburn A. Spaulding, of Company K, seized the colors and bore them for a time.

Subsequently I took them from him to rally the men, and kept them until I was wounded.

We had inflicted severe loss on the enemy, but their numbers were so overpowering and our own losses had been so great that we were unable to maintain our position, and were forced back, step by step, contesting every foot of ground, to the barricade. I was wounded just before reaching the barricade, west of the seminary building, and left the field. Previous to abandoning our last position, orders were received to fall back, given, I believe, by Major-General Doubleday.

The command of the regiment now devolved upon Capt. Albert M. Edwards, who collected the remnant of it, and fell back with the brigade to Culp's Hill, which it held for the two succeeding days.

Shortly after I was wounded, Captain Edwards found the colors in the hands of a wounded soldier, who had fallen on the east side of the barricade. He was reclining on his right side, and was holding the colors in his left hand. I have not been able to ascertain the name of this brave soldier in whose paralyzed hands Captain Edwards found the flag. Captain Edwards describes him as being severely wounded, and he is, therefore, probably among our dead. His name may forever be unknown, but his bravery will never die.

Captain Edwards behaved very gallantly at this time in rallying the men under a murderous fire.

The field over which we fought, from our first line of battle in McPherson's woods to the barricade near the seminary, was strewn with the killed and wounded. Our losses were very large, exceeding, perhaps, the losses sustained by any one regiment of equal size in a single engagement of this or any other war.

The strength of the regiment on July 1 was as follows:

Field officers	3
Staff officers	1
Line officers	24
Non-commissioned officers and privates	468
Total	496

The losses sustained by the regiment were as follows:

Officers and men.	Killed.	Wounded.	Total.
Field officers		3	3
Staff officers		1	1
Line officers	8	10	18
Non-commissioned officers	22	41	63
Privates	49	182	231
Total*	79	237	316

About 80 of the enlisted men and 3 officers were reported as missing in action. Many of the men have never been heard from, and are known not to be in the hands of the enemy. They were undoubtedly killed, but, not having been so reported, are not included in the above. Capt. George C. Gordon and First Lieut. Asa W. Sprague and Second Lieut. H. Rees Whiting were captured, and are still prisoners at Richmond.

* But see revised statement, p. 173.

Nearly all our wounded, myself among them, fell into the hands of the enemy when he took possession of the town of Gettysburg. When the enemy evacuated the place, on the night of the 3d instant, most of the wounded were left behind.

The regiment occupied Culp's Hill during the battles of July 3 and 4, but sustained little or no loss. During the battle of the 1st instant, the regiment lost in killed four color-bearers—Abel G. Peck, Charles Ballare, Augustus Ernest, and William Kelly. During the engagement of the 1st, the flag was carried by no less than nine persons, four of the number having been killed and three wounded. All of the color guard were killed or wounded. The officers wounded were: Col. Henry A. Morrow, scalp wound; Lieut. Col. Mark Flanigan, lost leg; Maj. Edwin B. Wight, lost an eye; Capt. William H. Rexford, severely in leg; Capt. William W. Wight, slightly in leg; Capt. William Hutchinson, contusion on leg; Capt. Richard S. Dillon, severely in leg; Capt. Charles A. Hoyt, severely in leg; Lieut. John M. Farland, wounded by fall; Lieut. William R. Dodsley, slightly wounded; Lieut. Abraham Earnshaw, wounded in side; Lieut. Frederick A. Buhl, severely in thigh; Lieut. Edwin E. Norton, slightly; Lieut. Michael Dempsey, slightly. The officers killed were: Capts. William J. Speed and Malachi J. O'Donnell; Lieuts. Walter H. Wallace, Winfield S. Safford, Newell Grace, Reuben H. Humphreville, Gilbert A. Dickey, and Lucius L. Shattuck.

Of the killed nothing less can be said than that their conduct in this memorable battle was brave and daring, and was creditable alike to themselves and the service. It will not be disparaging to his brave comrades who fell on this terrible but glorious day to say that Captain Speed's death was a severe loss to the service and an almost irreparable one to his regiment. He was amiable, intelligent, honorable, and brave, and was universally respected and esteemed by all who knew him.

Captain O'Donnell was a young officer who had given strong proofs of courage and capacity, and whose death was deeply deplored in the regiment.

Lieutenant Wallace served in the Peninsular Campaign under General McClellan, and lost an eye at the battle of Fair Oaks. He was a brave officer, an honorable man, and a good disciplinarian.

Lieutenant Dickey joined the regiment in the capacity of commissary sergeant, and for his integrity, capacity, and attention to business was promoted to the rank of sergeant-major, and thence to a second lieutenancy. He had given great promise for future usefulness and distinction. He was the first commissioned officer of the regiment killed at Gettysburg.

Lieutenants Grace, Humphreville, Safford, and Shattuck were distinguished in the regiment for their attention to duty, for the amiability of their manners, and for their unflinching courage in battle. Lieutenant Grace was one of the bravest men I ever knew. The remains of Captain Speed and Lieutenants Wallace and Safford were conveyed to Michigan by their friends, for interment, but the remains of the other officers sleep, with the brave non-commissioned officers and privates who fell that day, in the cemetery in which a grateful nation will, at no distant period, erect a mausoleum to perpetuate the memories of its defenders.

Lieutenant-Colonel Flanigan lost his leg in this battle. His conduct here, as everywhere in battle, was gallant and daring. Major Wight acquitted himself in the most creditable manner, and remained at his post until forced by his wound to leave the field. Both of these officers have since been discharged from service on account of their wounds. They were universally esteemed and respected.

Captain Hutchinson received a severe contusion in the groin early in the day, but remained with his company and behaved very gallantly.

Captain Rexford was wounded in the change of front already referred to. His conduct here, as everywhere, was gallant and conspicuous.

Captain Edwards displayed great coolness and courage, and deserves honorable mention.

Captain Dillon commanded his company with skill, and behaved very handsomely in skirmishing in front of McPherson's woods.

Capt. William W. Wight exhibited much coolness and courage.

Lieutenant Dempsey was conspicuous for his gallantry in the charge across Willoughby's Run.

Lieutenant Hutton was near me when I was wounded, and it was mainly through his assistance that I got off the field. His conduct in the engagement was all that could be desired, and confirmed my former opinion of his value as an officer.

Captains Hoyt and Gordon, Lieutenants Farland, Dodsley, Sprague, Witherspoon, Norton, Buhl, Earnshaw, and Whiting, all acquitted themselves honorably. Their conduct was such as to win the confidence and respect of their men, and deserves the commendation of their commanding officer.

In justice to the memory of the brave non-commissioned officers who were killed at Gettysburg, and whose conduct is highly praised by their superiors, I give their names below: Sergts. Andrew J. Price and George Cline, Company B; Joseph Eberle, Company D; Charles Bucklin, Company F; George Colburn, Company C; John Powell, Company H; and Corpls. William Ziegler, Company A; Joseph Carroll and John H. Pardington, Company B; Otis Southworth, Company C; David E. Rounds and James Stirling, Company D; John Walls, Company E; I. W. Evans, Company F; William H. Luce, Jerome F. Failes, and Thomas Suggett, Company G; George N. Bentley and James B. Myers, Company I; and Jerome J. Le Fevre, Company K.

It would be impossible within the limits of a report like this to do more than give the names of these brave sergeants and corporals. Their history is a part of the history of the regiment, and its future historian will narrate their heroic conduct on the ever-memorable field of Gettysburg.

Sergt. Maj. Andrew J. Connor was conspicuous for his bravery, and was severely wounded. Long before his wound was healed he returned to duty in the regiment. First Sergt. George W. Haight was suffering from a wound received at Fitzhugh's Crossing, but went into battle on July 1, and was severely wounded in the leg. He deserves mention for his bravery.

In response to a circular addressed by me to my company officers, asking for the names of such non-commissioned officers and privates as particularly distinguished themselves at Gettysburg, I have received the following : Private Augustus Sink, Company A, is spoken of by Captain Dillon in very high terms of praise for his gallantry on the skirmish line in front of McPherson's woods.

Capt. Albert M. Edwards says of First Sergt. Bucklin and Corpl. I. W. Evans : " They were both killed on the field. Both were particularly distinguished in camp for their excellent moral character and the purity of their lives and example, and in the field for their unflinching courage and devotion." This is high praise, and well bestowed.

Corpls. Edward Dwyer and William Carroll, of Company B, died in hospital of the wounds received in this day's fight. Captain Burchell says : " They were efficient and brave men, and sacrificed their lives in the discharge of their duties."

Captain Witherspoon, himself a brave soldier, writes that Sergt. Augustus Pomeroy, of Company C, particularly distinguished himself by his gallantry and devotion. Being too severely wounded to handle his musket, he tore cartridges for his more fortunate comrades, and subsequently rendered valuable services in taking care of the wounded. Such conduct in officer or soldier deserves to be recorded.

First Sergt. William J. Nagle, of Company A, came under my own eye, and was wounded very near me. His conduct was brave almost to temerity. He died in hospital from the wound received in this battle. He was a brave, worthy, and intelligent soldier.

Captain Farland, of Company D, speaks in high terms of praise of Sergt. Joseph Eberle and Corpls. David E. Rounds, James Stirling, and Andrew Strong. Corporal Strong came under my eye, and it affords me great pleasure to bear witness to his bravery. Sergt. Eberle continued in the fight after being twice wounded. Private John George Klink, of Company F, acquitted himself finely, and deserves notice.

Surgeon Beach and Assistant Surgeons Collar and Towar were devoted and untiring in their attention to the wounded. Of Dr. Beach it may be truly said that no surgeon in the Army of the Potomac rendered more valuable services at Gettysburg than he. Chaplain William C. Way was early in attendance at the hospital, and rendered valuable services. He remained in attendance on the wounded several weeks after the battle, and both officers and men speak in the highest terms of praise of his kindness and efficiency. This report would have been imperfect without this reference to the surgeons and chaplain, whose conduct elicited universal remark.

During the time I was a prisoner I conversed freely with distinguished rebel officers in relation to the battle on the 1st instant, and, without exception, they spoke in terms of admiration of the conduct of our troops, and especially of that of the troops composing the First Army Corps. One of them informed me that Lieut. Gen. A. P. Hill said that he had never known the Federals to fight so well. At first the officers seemed very sanguine of their ability to dislodge the Army of the Potomac from its position, and the capture of Washington and Baltimore was considered a thing almost accomplished, and this feeling was fully shared by the private soldiers; but the admirable means taken by General Meade to meet every attack, and the successful manner in which he repulsed them, seemed to have a powerful influence in abating their confidence before the final order was received for the evacuation of the town.

From the cupola in the steeple of the court-house at Gettysburg I was an eye-witness of the movements of the rebel army and of the dispositions made of the troops for the famous attacks on the left, right, and center of our position. The preparations for the final attack on our left center on Friday afternoon came directly under my eye.

From an officer of the rank of major, on the staff of Lieut. Gen. A. P. Hill, I was informed that the rebel army present at Gettysburg was about 90,000 strong, and that their line of battle was estimated to be 8 miles long.

The death of Major-General Reynolds was well known to the enemy, and the highest opinions of his skill and bravery were freely expressed.

It did not seem to be well understood by the enemy that there had been a change in the commanders of the Army of the Potomac, and I was frequently asked if such was the case.

The name of Capt. George W. Burchell does not appear in connection with the battle of Gettysburg, for the reason that he was prevented by sickness from being there. He was wounded at Fitzhugh's Crossing in April, and at the time of the battle of Gettysburg was confined to quarters at Emmitsburg.

I have the honor to be, captain, your obedient servant,
                              HENRY A. MORROW,
                    Colonel Twenty-fourth Michigan Volunteers.

Capt. J. D. Wood, *Assistant Adjutant-General.*

No. 34.

Report of Maj. John Mansfield, Second Wisconsin Infantry.

BEVERLY FORD, VA., *November* 15, 1863.

SIR: In reporting the part taken by this regiment in the battle of Gettysburg, I have the honor to state:

The regiment formed a part of the First Brigade of Wadsworth's division of the First Army Corps, Army of the Potomac, and on the morning of July 1, 1863, it had the right, and approached Gettysburg from the Emmitsburg pike. About 10 a. m., when near the town of Gettysburg, the brigade was filed into the field on the left and west of Gettysburg, in the direction of and left of Seminary Ridge. Here the Federal cavalry were in line with a battery, actively engaged with the enemy's advancing infantry. By order of the division commander, through Colonel Kress, his acting aide-de-camp, this regiment was thrown forward into line of battle in front of the cavalry, and ordered to advance, to repel an assault of the enemy's infantry upon the battery.

The field officers, Colonel Fairchild, Lieutenant-Colonel Stevens, and Maj. John Mansfield, immediately dismounted, and, taking their proper places in line, advanced the regiment up a gentle slope, and when on its crest we received a volley of musketry from the enemy's line, from which many officers and men fell, among them Lieutenant-Colonel Stevens, mortally wounded. The advance of the regiment was steadily kept up under the direction of Colonel Fairchild, slightly obliquing to the right into a piece of timber skirting the ridge and extending several hundred yards to the right and front of our position.

After pushing the advance for about 50 yards into this timber, in the face of a most terrific fire of musketry, Colonel Fairchild received a severe wound in the left arm, shattering his elbow. Being so completely disabled, and suffering from loss of blood, he was taken to the rear, when Major Mansfield assumed command of the regiment.

Mansfield continued to advance the regiment to near close quarters, when the line of the enemy in our immediate front yielded, a portion seeking cover in a deep excavation, the balance seeking refuge behind trees and a slight elevation of the ground, from which they attempted to reform their broken lines. I ordered a charge upon this last position of the enemy, which was gallantly made at the double-quick, the enemy breaking in confusion to the rear, escaping from the timber into the open fields beyond. In this charge we captured a large number of prisoners, including several officers, among them General Archer, who was taken by Private Patrick Maloney, of Company G, of our regiment, and brought to me, to whom he surrendered his sword, which I passed over with the prisoners to Lieut. D. B. Dailey, acting aide-de-camp on the brigade staff. I regret to say that this gallant soldier (Private Maloney) was killed in action later in the day.

After this disposition of the prisoners, the regiment was formed in line in the open field beyond the timber. Here the balance of the brigade was formed on our left. We were soon faced to the rear, and retired about midway through the timber, where we were ordered to lie down. We remained in position some two hours or more, when the enemy were discovered emerging from the timber beyond the field we had just left, in two lines, with a heavy line of skirmishers.

The front line of the enemy, with skirmishers, advanced directly to the front, while the second line advanced obliquely to the left. In a short time the enemy's skirmishers and our own became actively engaged, which continued with great spirit for a time, when it was discovered an attempt was being made to flank our position by the second line. An order was given to fall back toward Seminary Ridge, then directly in our rear, and in which was placed and at work the Fifth Maine Battery.

This movement was made in good order, firing as we retired. About half the distance from where we commenced to retire to this new position, I faced the regiment to the front, and again moved to meet the advancing columns of the enemy, when I discovered the enemy closing in upon our left. I again faced to the rear, and took up a position on the ridge referred to, on the right of the brigade already in position. At this time and point the battle raged with great fury, near the close of which I received a severe gun-shot wound·in my left leg, near the knee-joint. Being unable to remain standing, I was taken to temporary shelter, when almost immediately the brigade and regiment fell back to Cemetery Hill.

The casualties to the regiment resulting from this day's fight, for the numbers engaged, are believed to be unparalleled in the history of the war, and are here given as follows :

Casualties.	Officers.	Men.	Total.
Engaged	29	273	302
Killed	2	25	27
Wounded	11	142	153
Missing	6	47	53
Total	19	214	233
Left for duty			69

From such a record I may be spared from making what seems the usual commonplace remark, "that both officers and men behaved well." No such record as here made can be shown excepting by a cool indifference to danger and long continued and stubborn resistance, resulting from hard-earned experience and thorough discipline.

I desire to call the attention of the general commanding to Lieut. Henry B. Harshaw, acting adjutant, for his ready and active assistance on several occasions during the trials of the day. Also to Corporal [Rasselas] Davidson, of Company H, and Corpl. Paul V. Brisbois, of Company G, for gallantly seizing (one the State, the other the National) colors of the regiment, after their respective bearers had been shot down in a storm of bullets, and carrying them undismayed throughout the remainder of the battle, and bearing them in safety and in triumph off the field.

JNO. MANSFIELD,
Major, Commanding Regiment.

Capt. J. D. WOOD,
 Asst. Adjt. Gen., First Brig., First Div., First Corps.

No. 35.

Reports of Lieut. Col. Rufus R. Dawes, Sixth Wisconsin Infantry.

HDQRS. SIXTH WISCONSIN VOLUNTEERS,
July 17, 1863.

CAPTAIN: I have the honor to report as follows of the operations of the regiment under my command during the action of July 1, near Gettysburg, Pa.:

On the morning of July 1, as the brigade moved forward, in support of the Second Brigade of this division, to engage the enemy, I received an order to move my command forward rapidly and form it on the left of the line of the brigade. Without checking from a double-quick, the regiment formed into line, the men loading as they marched, and moved forward rapidly and steadily toward the position assigned.

Before reaching my position in the line of battle, I was ordered to halt, and hold my men in reserve. At this juncture, the brigade guard (2 officers and 100 men, under command of First Lieut. Lloyd G. Harris, of the Sixth Wisconsin), by direction of General Solomon Meredith, reported to me for duty in the impending battle. I divided the guard into two companies, placing the first on the right flank of the regiment, under command of Second Lieut. Levi Showalter, of the Second Wisconsin; the second on the left, under command of Lieutenant Harris. I now received a second order to advance, which I was proceeding to execute when, by command of Maj. Gen. A. Doubleday, commanding the corps, the regiment was again halted (my left resting on the Fairfield road), and detached from the brigade as a general reserve to the line of the division, now hotly engaged throughout. In a very few moments I received an order from Major-General Doubleday to move at once to the support of the right of the line of the division (Seventy-sixth New York, Fifty-sixth Pennsylvania, and One hundred and forty-seventh New York), which was being forced back and outflanked by the enemy. I marched by the right flank double-quick toward the point indicated. Before reaching a position where I could be of service, the enemy had succeeded in turning the flank, and, flushed with victory, was pressing rapidly in pursuit of our retreating line, threatening the rear of the First Brigade (Meredith's Iron Brigade), engaged in the woods on the left. I filed to the right and rear, to throw my line in front of the enemy, and moved by the left flank forward in line of battle upon his advancing line. My men kept up a steady double-quick, never faltering or breaking under the fire, which had become very galling. When my line had reached a fence on the Chambersburg turnpike, about 40 rods from the line of the enemy, I ordered a fire by file. This checked the advance of the rebels, who took refuge in a railroad cut (an unfinished railroad cut through the ridge west of the seminary), from which they opened a murderous fire upon us. I immediately ordered the men over the fence, with a view to charging the cut. The Ninety-fifth New York and Fourteenth Brooklyn here joined on my left.

My men continued firing and advancing steadily. I ran to Major Pye, of the Ninety-fifth New York Volunteers, commanding, as I supposed, the line on my left, and, requesting him to move forward with me, immediately gave the order to charge. The men of the whole line moved forward upon a double-quick, well closed, in face of a terribly destructive fire from the enemy. When our line reached the edge of the cut, the rebels began throwing down their arms in token of surrender.

Adjt. Ed. P. Brooks, with promptness and foresight, moved a detachment of 20 men in position to enfilade the cut from the right, when the entire regiment in my front, after some murderous skirmishing by the more desperate, threw down their arms.

Maj. John A. Blair, commanding the regiment (Second Mississippi Volunteers), upon my demand, surrendered his sword and regiment to me. I directed him to have his men fall in without arms, and move to the rear, in charge of Maj. John F. Hauser, of this regiment. Major Hauser informs me that by direction of General James S. Wadsworth, commanding division, he placed in charge of a cavalry guard 7 officers and about 225 men. The battle-flag of the regiment was captured before the surrender by Corpl. F. Asbury Waller, of Company I,* and has been forwarded, in obedience to orders, to army headquarters.

The loss sustained by my command in this charge was not less than 160 men killed or wounded.

After this capture of prisoners, by direction of General Wadsworth, I took position in a piece of woods on the right of the railroad cut near the seminary, where I remained about thirty minutes and reorganized my shattered regiment. I was then ordered forward to occupy the next crest in front, in support of a battery on the left of the cut I had previously charged. The enemy opened fire on my advancing line from a battery of six guns, killing and wounding several men. I took possession of the crest, where I remained until the battery had retired and the enemy had pressed back our line on my right and left, when I moved back under cover of the railroad cut, and, by direction of General Wadsworth, took position again in the wood, in support of four pieces of Stewart's battery (B, Fourth U. S. Artillery), where I remained until ordered by General Wadsworth to retire in good order beyond this city (Gettysburg). Faced

---

* A medal of honor was awarded to Corporal Waller for this service.—COMPILER.

by the rear rank, and moved (my right near railroad embankment) steadily back in line of battle over the open field to the city, almost directly toward the lines of the enemy, who had completely out flanked us on the Eleventh Corps front, and already gained posses sion of a portion of the city.   There was much confusion; the streets were crowded with retiring troops, batteries, and ambulance trains. The men were almost prostrated with over-exertion and heat.   The rebel sharpshooters (Ewell's troops) occupied the streets on our left, and their lines of battle almost completely encircled the city; but by great exertion on the part of the officers the regiment preserved its integrity, and the men, assembling around their colors, gave in the streets hearty cheers for the old Sixth and the good cause.   I moved to Cemetery Hill, and by direction of General Wadsworth, in open field on Culp's Hill, reported for duty to Col. W. W. Robinson, now commanding the brigade.

The loss of the regiment on July 1 was: Officers, 2 killed and 5 wounded; enlisted men, 27 killed, 106 wounded, and 24 missing.

The loss sustained by the brigade guard in the charge upon the railroad cut I cannot give.   Both officers commanding, Lieutenants Harris and Showalter, were disabled by wounds received in the charge.

I can only say that the men of the Sixth most nobly sustained their history in this desperate struggle.

Capt. John Ticknor, of Company K, was instantly killed while cheering his men on to the charge.   This officer rose from the ranks, winning his captaincy for coolness and efficiency in command of skirmishers at South Mountain, and was distinguished for bravery upon every battle-field of the regiment.   A good officer, a brave man, a genial, whole-souled companion, Ticknor will be sadly missed*from our circle.

Second Lieut. Orrin D. Chapman was also killed at the railroad cut.   He was in command of Company C.   He had but lately been commissioned.   He was always a faithful, obedient soldier, and as an officer brave and efficient.

The officers, without exception, behaved, as on many battle-fields before, with devoted courage, each holding his own life and safety of less account than the good conduct of his men and regiment.

To Major Hauser and Adjutant Brooks I am much indebted for assistance in maneuvering the regiment throughout the battle.   I cannot speak too highly of the bravery and efficiency in action of each of these officers.

Without reflection upon other officers of the line, I feel it due to their conspicuous bravery and good conduct that I should mention Capt. Rollin P. Converse and Lieut. Charles P. Hyatt, of Company B, and Lieutenant Goltermann, of Company F.   Captain Converse commanded the party who brought safely from the field and saved from capture the gun of the Second Maine Battery that had been abandoned to the enemy.   We recaptured this piece in a charge at the railroad cut.

I have the honor to be, very respectfully, your obedient servant,

R. R. DAWES,

Lieutenant-Colonel, Comdg. Sixth Wisconsin Volunteers.

Capt. J. D. WOOD,
    Asst. Adjt. Gen., First Brig., First Div., First Corps.

HEADQUARTERS SIXTH WISCONSIN VOLUNTEERS,
July 4, 1863.

SIR: I have the honor to report that the accompanying battle-flag of the Second Mississippi Volunteers was captured by the regiment under my command under the following circumstances:

Shortly after the opening of the action on the morning of July 1, the regiment was, by command of Major-General Doubleday, detached from the brigade, and ordered to the support of the right of the line of the division, which was being forced back and outflanked by the enemy. I moved as rapidly as possible on the advancing lines of the enemy, joining with the Ninety-fifth New York and Fourteenth Brooklyn on my left. A brisk fire was opened throughout the line, which soon checked the enemy and forced him to take refuge in a railroad cut. I ordered a charge upon the cut. The men moved forward, well closed and upon a run. When our line reached the edge of the cut, the rebels ceased firing and threw down their arms. At my demand, Major [J. A.] Blair, commanding the regiment in my front, the Second Mississippi, surrendered his sword and regiment.

The battle-flag was taken before the surrender by Corpl. F. Asbury Waller, of Company I, and sent to the rear in charge of Sergt. William Evans, of Company H, who was badly wounded. The sergeant was taken prisoner by the enemy and held for two days in Gettysburg; but with the assistance of some ladies of the city, whose names I have not learned, he successfully concealed the colors, and, finally, when the enemy retired, brought it safely to the regiment.

R. R. DAWES,
Lieutenant-Colonel, Comdg. Sixth Wisconsin Volunteers.

Capt. T. E. ELLSWORTH,
Actg. Asst. Adjutant-General, First Division, First Corps.

No. 36.

Report of Col. William W. Robinson, Seventh Wisconsin Infantry.

HEADQUARTERS SEVENTH WISCONSIN VOLUNTEERS,
November 18, 1863.

SIR: I have the honor to submit the following report of the part taken by the Seventh Regiment Wisconsin Volunteer Infantry, under my command, in the engagement at Gettysburg on July 1:

We left our camp, on the road running from Emmitsburg to Gettysburg, about 5 miles from the latter place, early on the morning of the 1st, with the brigade, the Second Wisconsin leading, the Seventh next in column. Arrived in the vicinity of Gettysburg about 10 a. m., when we heard firing to the left of the town, and were informed that our cavalry were engaged with the enemy's advance. The brigade was immediately moved across the field to the left, to the point where the cavalry were engaged, where we formed them in position behind a grove of timber and slight elevation of land, their position being behind and parallel to this ridge, with their skirmishers dismounted and thrown forward of the ridge. Just at the time we came up, a brigade of the enemy's infantry was advancing upon the position. We were ordered to take position on the ridge in front of the cavalry as quickly as possible. I immediately formed companies, and threw the battalion forward into line in bouble-quick, and advanced to the top of the ridge. We had not halted to load, and no orders had been received to do so, for the reason, I suppose, that no one expected we were to be engaged so suddenly. I, however, gave the order to load during the movement, which was executed by the men while on the double-quick, so that no time was lost by this omission. I halted the battalion on the summit of the ridge until the Nineteenth Indiana and Twenty-fourth Michigan, which were in my rear in column, had formed on my left.

In the meantime the Second Wisconsin—which was next in front of me in column, in its evolution into line was formed to my right and the length of the battalion in advance; this threw them behind the grove before mentioned, into which they advanced without halting—had engaged the enemy. My right was now resting near this grove, with the Nineteenth and Twenty-fourth on my left. Immediately in [front], and running parallel to and about 200 yards from my front, was a ravine, through which runs a small rivulet; from this ravine a heavy fire was opened. I was at first uncertain, in the dense smoke and from the near proximity of the fire, whether it was the enemy or the left wing of the Second Wisconsin.

At this moment Captain Wadsworth, of the division staff, rode up from the right. I asked could he tell what troops those were firing in the ravine. He pointed a little farther to the left up the ravine (where I saw the rebel battle-flag), and said it was the enemy, and that the general directed that we should drive them out. I moved the line forward to the crest of the ridge, delivered a volley, and gave the order to charge. The three regiments—Seventh Wisconsin, Nineteenth Indiana, and Twenty-fourth Michigan—rushed into the ravine with a yell. The enemy—what was left of them able to walk—threw down their arms, ducked through between our files, and passed to the rear. We moved up the opposite bank to the top of the hill, where I halted the line. In this charge we passed by and beyond the position occupied by the Second Wisconsin in the grove. We had occupied our new position but a few minutes when Captain Richardson, of the brigade staff, brought an order to change front to the rear on the left battalion. While this evolution was being executed, General Meredith came up, and directed me to place my regiment in the grove on the right of the Second. I took the position indicated, my right resting on the open fields, and threw out skirmishers to the front. In this position we lay some hours under a severe artillery fire. From my position I could see the movements of the enemy in our front.

Early in the afternoon columns of infantry were seen moving to our left, evidently with the intention of turning our left. Also heavy columns were being massed in our front. This information I sent to the general, and the order I received was to hold the position at all hazards. In a short time the enemy advanced into the wood in our front, lay down behind the crest of the hill and behind the trees, and opened a galling fire. About the same time I discovered he had gained our left and rear, and soon after a small detachment was brought from some other division to attack this latter force of the enemy; but this detachment was too small, and was soon repulsed. The troops on our right had fallen back; the Twenty-fourth and Nineteenth, on the left of the brigade, were being badly cut up by superior numbers; the Second and Seventh were keeping up a rapid fire upon the enemy in front, but, I think, without doing him much injury, as he was pro·

tected by the hill and timber. He was rapidly gaining ground on our left; still, no order came to change our position. The Seventh was receiving a galling fire and the Second was being badly cut up, when Captain Richardson brought me the order to retire to Seminary Ridge. I retired by the right of companies to the rear some 150 or 200 yards, halted, and wheeled into line again to support the other regiments in retiring. Then again retired about the same distance, and again wheeled into line, and so on until I reached the foot of Seminary Ridge. On this ridge, directly in my rear, a battery had been placed, and opened upon the advancing foe. Down the slope, some 40 yards in front of this battery, I found a slight breastwork of loose rails, which, I suppose, had been thrown together by some of our troops in the earlier part of the day, behind which I threw the regiment.

During this movement we were exposed not only to the fire of the advancing enemy in front, but also to that from the brigade which had turned our left flank, and was now advancing from that direction in line obliquely to our new position. It was with some difficulty I restrained the men from firing until the enemy got as near as I wanted them. When they were within easy range, the order was given, and their ranks went down like grass before the scythe from the united fire of our regiments and the battery. There were very few, if any, of that brigade escaped death or wounds. The regiment held this position until all the troops on our right and left had retired. The battery had limbered up and retired. The enemy, in overwhelming numbers, had again turned both our flanks, with a line formed on each perpendicular to ours, and reaching a considerable distance to our rear, forming three sides of a square around us, with the open side to our rear and toward the town.

At this time Captain Richardson, of the brigade staff, again brought me the order to retire through the town. I again retired, by the right of companies to the rear, through the orchard over the ridge, and then by the right flank by file left into column, and moved on to the turnpike and through the town to Cemetery Hill, being the rear of the troops from that part of the field.

Immediately upon my arrival at the cemetery, I was ordered by General Wadsworth to take command of the brigade. In retiring from our last position on Seminary Ridge, as I came out of the orchard, I found the enemy advancing in line perpendicular to the left and to the rear of our late position, and within 300 yards of me. They immediately opened fire upon us. To the right of our position and on the opposite side of the turnpike, some little distance from it, was another line of theirs, with their left reaching near the town. This line was stationary and was supported by artillery. In passing out, we were exposed to this enfilading fire from both these lines, as well as from their artillery. It was here I met with the heaviest losses from the regiment during the day.

Throughout the whole engagement—the morning charge, where the regiment captured one of General Archer's regiments; under the severe artillery fire of the midday, and in the unequal combat of the afternoon; in the steadiness exhibited in retiring and promptness in reforming line, time and time again, under a most galling fire; in the firmness with which they held the last position, and kept up a rapid and well-directed fire upon the advancing enemy until left alone and the order was received to retire—the regiment displayed all the coolness, bravery, and prowess that has won for it honorable distinction in previous battles.   Every officer and enlisted man performed his whole duty.*

I may mention, without the notice being invidious to others, the conduct of Lieut. Col. John B. Callis and Maj. Mark Finnicum. From both these officers I received able assistance.   Their conduct was a repetition of their gallantry on previous battle-fields. Lieutenant-Colonel Callis was severely wounded late in the day. Also, Sergt. Daniel McDermott, color-bearer, who was severely wounded just as we were entering the town, retiring, by a charge of grape and canister, the same charge shivering the flag-staff into a number of pieces.   McDermott was placed upon a caisson that was moving ahead of us, still hanging to the tattered banner, which he waved in defiance at the foe as he rode off.   He has carried this color through every battle in which the regiment has been engaged.

Our casualties were:

Officers and men.	Killed.	Wounded.	Missing.	Total.
Officers...........	......	10	1	11
Enlisted men......	26	99	42	167
Total...........	26	109	43	178

Respectfully, your obedient servant,

W. W. ROBINSON,
Colonel, Commanding Seventh Wisconsin Volunteers.

Capt. J. D. WOOD,
Assistant Adjutant-General, First Brigade.

No. 37.

Report of Brig. Gen. Lysander Cutler, U. S. Army, commanding Second Brigade.

HDQRS. SECOND BRIG., FIRST DIV., FIRST ARMY CORPS,
In the Field, July 9, 1863.

SIR: I have the honor to make the following report of the part performed by this brigade in the actions of the 1st, 2d, and 3d days of the month, near Gettysburg, Pa.:

The brigade—excepting the Seventh Indiana, which was on duty in the rear—moved from camp early on the 1st instant (being the leading brigade of the corps) on toward Gettysburg.   As we approached, and when within about 2 miles of the town, I was ordered to move obliquely to the left across the fields to the ridge near the seminary, west of the town, where the enemy were already engaging our cavalry.   I moved forward across the railroad with the Seventy-sixth New York Volunteers, One hundred and forty-seventh New York Volunteers, and the Fifty-sixth Pennsylvania Volunteers, immediately formed in line of battle, and found myself engaged with a vastly superior force of the enemy, advancing in two lines, at short

---

* A medal of honor was awarded to Sergt. Jefferson Coates for gallantry in this engagement.—COMPILER.

range, in front and on my right flank. The Ninety-fifth New York Volunteers and the Fourteenth Brooklyn had been detached to the left, by order of General Reynolds, to support the Second Maine Battery and to hold the enemy in check until other troops could arrive. The three regiments under my immediate command fought as only brave men can fight, and held their ground until ordered to fall back, by General Wadsworth, to the woods on the next ridge. The Fifty-sixth Pennsylvania and Seventy-sixth New York fell back. The One hundred and forty-seventh did not receive the order, in consequence of Lieutenant-Colonel Miller being wounded at the moment of receiving it. Major Harney held the regiment to its position until the enemy were in possession of the railroad cut on his left, when it was impossible for him to retire until relieved by a charge on the enemy from the left by the Sixth Wisconsin, Ninety-fifth New York, and Fourteenth Brooklyn, which resulted in capturing a large body of the enemy and enabling Major Harney to bring off the remainder of his regiment.

The loss of this gallant regiment was fearful at this point, being 2 officers killed and 10 wounded, 42 men killed and 153 wounded—207 out of 380 men and officers within half an hour.

The Seventy-sixth New York fared no better. They went in with 348 men and 27 officers; their loss during the same time was 2 officers killed, 16 wounded, 27 men killed, and 124 wounded within thirty minutes.

The loss of the Fifty-sixth Pennsylvania was also severe. They went into action with 17 officers and 235 men, and lost 6 officers wounded, 1 mortally, and 8 men killed and 64 wounded at that point.

After falling back to the woods, and subsequently farther back, I received orders again to advance and occupy the crest of the ridge. Although reduced by a loss of half their numbers, the men bravely and cheerfully moved back to renew the fight. On my way back, I was joined by the Ninety-fifth New York, Fourteenth Brooklyn, and Sixth Wisconsin. After occupying the old ground from half to three-quarters of an hour, I discovered the enemy putting a battery in position on my right flank and moving forward large bodies of infantry in the same direction. This being reported to General Wadsworth, he directed me to take such a position as I judged proper. I left the Fourteenth Brooklyn to assist the Sixth Wisconsin in supporting the battery, and with the balance of the brigade present changed front to the right, and endeavored to hold the enemy in check as best I could, having no support on either my right or left until 2 o'clock, when a brigade from the Second Division formed on my right, and the Eleventh Corps came in on the right of them. Immediately after, a column of the enemy moved on the Second Division. I at once pushed my brigade through the woods, came in on their flank, and opened so hot a fire on them that one regiment threw down their arms and surrendered. By this time the enemy was so close on my left flank that I again changed front, and came into line on Robinson's left, where I remained until out of ammunition, and was relieved by other troops, when I fell back under the hill, and sent for ammunition.

The Eleventh Corps was already moving into town, and soon the enemy appeared, advancing in line of battle. After waiting about twenty minutes, I moved the brigade to the railroad, with a view to forming under cover of its bank and trying to hold him in check there, when I received an order through Colonel Bankhead to send three regiments to aid in repelling the enemy near the seminary. I immediately sent the Fourteenth Brooklyn and the One hundred and forty-seventh and Seventy-sixth New York, where they remained until I received orders to move my brigade to the rear in the best order I could. I moved off on the railroad embankment, and, although exposed to the enemy's fire on both flanks, the men marched with perfect steadiness and no excitement. Their steadiness had the effect to bring the enemy to a halt, when he threw out skirmishers, thus relieving me from the fire of his main line on the left. The brigade completely covered the troops who were retiring on my right from the fire of the enemy on my left. I suffered severely while retiring, having myself a horse killed on the railroad and another wounded going through town. After passing through town to Cemetery Hill, I was joined by the Seventh Indiana, which had come up. The Seventh was sent, by order of General Wadsworth, to hold the crest of a hill to the right, and the balance of the brigade, having been in action from 10 a. m. until 4 p. m., were allowed to rest for the night.

Early on the morning of the 2d instant, the brigade was moved to the hill, and took a position between the First Brigade and General Greene's brigade of the Twelfth Corps. I consider it unnecessary to particularize as to the operations of the 2d and 3d instant, as most of the time we were immediately under the eye of the division commander. Sufficient to say that the fighting on those days was mostly in the trenches, with small loss to us and great loss to the enemy.

It affords me the highest satisfaction to bear testimony to the good conduct of all the officers and men of the brigade, with but one or two exceptions. Colonel Hofmann, Fifty-sixth Pennsylvania Volunteers; Major Harney, One hundred and forty-seventh New York Volunteers; Major Pye, Ninety-fifth New York Volunteers; Captain Cook, Seventy-sixth New York Volunteers, deserve special mention for gallantry and coolness. Colonel Fowler, Fourteenth Brooklyn, for charging the enemy at the railroad cut in connection with the Ninety-fifth New York and Sixth Wisconsin, by which the One hundred and forty-seventh New York was relieved from its perilous position.

Major Grover, commanding Seventy-sixth New York Volunteers, a brave and efficient officer, was killed early in the action of the 1st instant, and the command devolved upon Capt. John E. Cook, and most ably and faithfully did he perform the duty.

Lieutenant-Colonel Miller, commanding the One. hundred and forty-seventh New York Volunteers, was severely wounded at the head of his regiment on the 1st instant.

Colonel Biddle, Ninety-fifth New York Volunteers, was wounded in the breast.

Major Harney, of the One hundred and forty-seventh New York, and Major Pye, of the Ninety-fifth New York, on assuming command of their respective regiments, did all that brave men and good soldiers could do, and deserve well for their services.

Sergt. Henry H. Hubbard, Company D, One hundred and forty-seventh New York Volunteers, was in command of the provost guard of the brigade on the morning of the 1st instant. He formed the guard, consisting of 18 men, on the right of the Seventy-sixth New York, and fought until the battle was over, losing 12 of his men. He deserves promotion.

The color-sergeant of the One hundred and forty-seventh New York was killed, and the colors were caught by Sergt. William

A. Wybourn, of Company I, One hundred and forty-seventh New York, and brought off the battle-field by him, notwithstanding he was himself severely wounded.

For amount of losses in the several regiments, I refer to separate reports on that subject.* The loss is fearful, and I can only hope that the country may not again require that these brave men shall go through so severe an ordeal.

In closing, I beg to acknowledge my great obligations to Capt. John A. Kellogg, acting assistant adjutant-general; Capt. William Bloodgood, acting aide; Lieut. S. W. Woodrow, of the Ninety-fifth New York Volunteers, and Lieut. T. W. Miller, volunteer aide on my staff.

On the 1st instant, Captain Bloodgood and Lieutenant Woodrow were severely wounded. These officers all acted with the most perfect coolness and bravery during the whole action. Every one of my staff and orderlies was dismounted by having their horses shot; Lieutenant Miller and Captain Bloodgood twice each, and Lieutenant Woodrow three times. Lieutenant [Homer] Chisman, acting assistant inspector-general, came up from the rear, and joined me at 3 o'clock on the 1st instant; Lieutenant Burritt, of the Fifty-sixth Pennsylvania Volunteers, was detailed on my staff on the 2d instant, and both behaved admirably.

Captain Kellogg not only behaved admirably on the whole, but deserves special notice for his exertions in rallying the men when repulsed on the 1st; for his efficiency in moving and placing re-enforcements to the right on the night of the 2d, when the enemy were making strenuous efforts to turn our right flank, and for having cut down with his saber a cowardly field officer of another corps who was endeavoring to march his men out of the trenches, and for keeping the men in their position.

I am, sir, very respectfully, your obedient servant,

L. CUTLER,
Brig. Gen., Comdg. 2d Brig., 1st Div., 1st Army Corps.

Capt. T. E. ELLSWORTH,
Aide-de-Camp, and Acting Assistant Adjutant-General.

No. 38.

Report of Col. Ira G. Grover, Seventh Indiana Infantry.

HDQRS. SEVENTH REGIMENT INDIANA VOLUNTEERS,
July 9, 1863.

SIR: In accordance with circular from brigade headquarters, I have the honor to submit the following report of the action of the regiment under my command from the 1st instant to the present date:

On the afternoon of July 1, I joined the brigade at Gettysburg, having been previously detached at Emmitsburg by order of General Reynolds. By command of General Wadsworth, we took up a position on the hill east of Gettysburg, forming at that time the extreme right of our lines. We immediately commenced the construction of a temporary breastwork. During the succeeding night a force of the enemy attempted to penetrate our lines, but were easily driven off,

---

*Embodied in revised statement, p. 173.

supposing themselves confronted by a heavy force. This position we continued to occupy until the evening of the 3d instant, the fire of the enemy being more or less severe during the entire time, when we were ordered, with two other regiments of the brigade, to the support of a portion of the Eleventh Corps on Cemetery Hill.

On the following morning we were ordered to advance through the town, under command of Colonel Hofmann, of the Fifty-sixth Pennsylvania Volunteers. Having arrived near the farther extremity of the village, the order was countermanded, and we returned to the position taken on the 1st instant.

On the morning of July 5, we took up position on the battle-field south of town, in connection with the brigade.

On the following day, marched to Emmitsburg, and the next day crossed the Catoctin Mountain.

The day following we marched through Middletown, crossing South Mountain, and took up position in our present camp.

The officers of my command, without exception, were unfaltering in the discharge of their duties and behaved with commendable bravery. The men are equally deserving of credit.

I deem it proper to make special mention of Sergeant [William] Hussey, Company B. On the night of the 1st instant, unassisted, he captured a lieutenant of the Twenty-fifth Virginia Regiment and drove off a squad of 20 men.

Accompanying this report I send you a list of the casualties.*

Very respectfully, your obedient servant,

IRA G. GROVER,
Colonel, Commanding Seventh Indiana Volunteers.

Capt. J. A. KELLOGG,
Actg. Asst. Adjt. Gen., 2d Brig., 1st. Div., 1st Army Corps.

No. 39.

Report of Capt. John E. Cook, Seventy-sixth New York Infantry.

CAMP NEAR BOONSBOROUGH, MD.,
July 11, 1863.

CAPTAIN: I have the honor to report that on July 1, at about 10.30 a. m., being the extreme advance regiment of the First Corps, we reached the battle-field near the seminary at Gettysburg, and while marching by the flank were opened upon by the enemy, stationed in large force at a distance of about 30 rods, where they were lying down concealed from view in a wheat-field. We were exposed to their fire several minutes before replying. The men were cautioned to hold their fire until the enemy appeared, when orders were given to commence firing. At this juncture, a large force of the enemy deployed upon our right flank, subjecting us to a galling cross-fire. Major Grover then ordered the right wing to change front to the rear to oppose the new force. Simultaneously with this he fell, mortally wounded, and the brigade commander ordered the regiment to fall back. This was done in good order and the line reformed on the railroad track near the seminary. We again advanced and took our old ground, which we held for some time; then fell back to the woods

---

* Embodied in revised statement. p. 173.

on the brow of the hill; thence advanced right-oblique a short distance, obtained a good position, and silenced the fire of the enemy, who lay behind a fence in the hollow. Here we shot down their colors (having done so twice in the first engagement), and a portion of our regiment charged with the Ninety-fourth New York, and took a large body of the enemy and a stand of colors. Being out of ammunition, the Ninety-fourth New York relieved us, and we were not again under infantry fire until we passed through Gettysburg. Here we lost 8 or 10 men by falling bricks and infantry fire in the streets; since which time the history of the regiment is that of the brigade. After this we had a few men slightly wounded on the hill in the rear of the town. The whole regiment behaved admirably, with one or two exceptions. Each man came up to the mark without flinching, and remained there, taking careful aim and displaying great coolness.

I desire to mention particularly the following officers for distinguished bravery and coolness on the field: Capts. J. L. Goddard, Company F; H. W. Pierce, Company A; and S. M. Byram, Company D; First Lieuts. C. A. Watkins, Company G; J. C. Hatch, Company C; and N. G. Bartholomew, Company K; First Sergts. Ira C. Potter, Company A; Silas Smith, Company I; and Homer D. Call; and Sergts. George W. Steele, Company G; and B. I. D. Fox, Company H.

The casualties were as follows: Killed, 32; wounded, 132; missing, 70. Total, 234.

I have the honor to remain, your obedient servant,

JOHN E. COOK,
Captain, Comdg. Seventy-sixth New York Volunteers.

Capt. J. A. KELLOGG,
Acting Assistant Adjutant-General, Second Brigade.

No. 40.

Report of Col. Edward B. Fowler, Eighty-fourth New York Infantry (Fourteenth Militia).

HDQRS. FOURTEENTH NEW YORK STATE MILITIA,
July 9, 1863.

GENERAL: I have the honor to transmit the following report of the three days' battle, July 1, 2, and 3, 1863:

On entering the field, the Ninety-fifth New York Volunteers and Fourteenth Regiment New York State Militia were formed on the left of the brigade, a house and garden intervening between them and the right wing. We were at once engaged by the enemy's skirmishers from woods to our left and front. We drove the enemy back, and I then found that the enemy were advancing on our right, and were then to our rear, and in possession of one of our pieces of artillery. I immediately ordered my command, Ninety-fifth New York Volunteers and Fourteenth New York State Militia, to march in retreat until on a line with the enemy, and then changed front perpendicular to face them, the enemy also changing front to meet us. At this time the Sixth Wisconsin Regiment gallantly advanced to our assistance. The enemy then took possession of a railroad cut, and I gave the order to charge them, which order was carried out gallantly by all the regiments, by which the piece of artillery was recaptured. The advance was continued until near the cut, when I directed the Sixth Wisconsin to flank it by throwing forward their right, which being done, all the enemy within our reach surrendered—officers, battle-flag, and men. Those in line on the left of my line escaped by following through the railroad cut. I held this position until ordered to the rear to join the brigade.

The conduct of both officers and men in the whole command deserves the highest praise. The loss was very severe on our side, but I think much greater on the part of the enemy. The Fourteenth participated in the action of the brigade during the remainder of the day, and the retreat through Gettysburg to near position on Cemetery Heights. On the 2d instant this regiment remained in the second line of the position of the brigade until near dark, when it was ordered to re-enforce General Greene on the right, and became engaged partially with a regiment of the enemy, supposed to be the Tenth Virginia, who had penetrated inside our lines. As I was in doubt whether they were friends or enemies, I hesitated in opening fire upon them, but at length gave them a volley, which drove them from their position on our flank. The regiment remained with General Greene all night, part of the time in the trenches, and was relieved shortly after sunrise, and returned to the brigade. On the morning of the 3d instant, we were ordered again to the right, to re-enforce General Geary. Fought in the trenches, and lay in reserve until 5 p. m., when the regiment was relieved and ordered to join the brigade.

The loss of the regiment for the three days' fight amounts to nearly 50 per cent. of the force engaged, as shown by list already forwarded. I cannot praise too highly the gallantry of the whole command, both officers and men ; all doing so well that I would be unjust to particularize individual cases.

Respectfully, &c.,

E. B. FOWLER,
Colonel, Comdg. Fourteenth New York State Militia.

General LYSANDER CUTLER,
Comdg. Second Brig., First Div., First Army Corps.

No. 41.

Report of Maj. Edward Pye, Ninety-fifth New York Infantry.

IN THE FIELD, *July* 11, 1863.

SIR : In compliance with circular from brigade headquarters, I have the honor to report:

The Ninety-fifth Regiment, under command of Col. George H. Biddle, was marched in front of the enemy on the 1st instant and engaged them. The left wing of your brigade, comprising the Fourteenth New York State Militia and the Ninety-fifth New York Volunteers, under the command of Colonel Fowler, seeing the right wing of the brigade give way, retired a short distance, and then formed line of battle in connection with the Sixth Wisconsin Volunteers, and together charged upon and took as prisoners a large number of the enemy, being part of the same force which had previously driven back the right wing of the brigade.

At this time Colonel Biddle was wounded and retired from the field. I then took command of the regiment, in which I was ably assisted by Capt. James Creney, senior captain of the regiment. We were ordered to retire to a new position, in doing which we assisted in dragging off by hand a piece of artillery left on the field. We again advanced to near the ground where the right wing had been engaged in the morning. Being outflanked, we again retired, after which we changed direction to the right and again engaged the enemy. From this position we were also compelled to retire by reason of being flanked by the enemy.

We were next ordered to a position on the right of the Theological Seminary, and again engaged the enemy. From this position we retired along with the whole First Army Corps.

My regiment behaved very well, and gave me just cause to be proud of it. All the officers, with one or two exceptions, behaved well.

This regiment lost, in killed, 7; wounded, 8 officers and 54 men, and missing (mostly prisoners), 1 officer and 45 men.

On the 2d instant, we occupied the intrenchments on the right, and aided in repelling the enemy. No casualties occurred.

On the 3d instant, we continued in the same intrenchments until about 3 p. m., when we were ordered, with the Fifty-sixth Pennsylvania Volunteers and Seventh Indiana Volunteers, to support the left at a point near the cemetery. Our aid was not needed. We remained here during the night, and returned to our former position on the right on the morning of the 4th instant.

I will take occasion to recommend for promotion several non-commissioned officers who deserve special mention.

I have the honor to remain, very respectfully, your obedient servant,

E. PYE,
Major, Comdg. Ninety-fifth New York Volunteer Regiment.

Capt. J. A. KELLOGG,
    A. A. A. G., 2d Brig., 1st Div., 1st Army Corps.

No. 42.

Report of Col. J. William Hofmann, Fifty-sixth Pennsylvania Infantry.

IN THE FIELD, *July* 11, 1863.

CAPTAIN: I have the honor to report the operations of my regiment from the morning of the 1st instant to date.

On the morning of the 1st instant, the regiment, under my command, left camp on the Emmitsburg and Gettysburg road, near Marsh Creek. We numbered 17 officers and 235 enlisted men for duty.

We marched to Gettysburg, and engaged the enemy at 11 a. m. We suffered severely. In twenty minutes our loss in killed and wounded was over 70.

On the 2d instant, we engaged the enemy on the ridge in rear of the town. Our loss here was 2 enlisted men killed and 3 wounded. Total loss: Killed, enlisted men, 10; wounded, 6 officers and 64 enlisted men; prisoners, 2 officers, enlisted men unknown; missing, 38 enlisted men.

My officers and men did all that could be asked of brave men. Of the enlisted men it is but just to mention Corporal [Patrick] Burns. of Company D, acting color-bearer, who was wounded while gallantly waving the flag in the face of the enemy on the evening of the 2d instant. Private [George] Nolter, of Company D, was successful in capturing a major of the rebel army on the morning of the 4th instant.

Of the officers wounded, Lieutenant Gordon, Company B, has since died. A list of names of the killed and wounded is herewith submitted.*

I am, very respectfully, your obedient servant,

J. W. HOFMANN,
Colonel, Comdg. Fifty-sixth Pennsylvania Volunteers.

Captain KELLOGG,
A. A. A. G., 2d Brig., 1st Div., 1st Army Corps.

No. 43.

Report of Brig. Gen. John C. Robinson, U. S. Army, commanding Second Division.

HDQRS. SECOND DIVISION, FIRST ARMY CORPS,
July 18, 1863.

SIR : I have the honor to submit the following report of the operations of this division in the engagements of the 1st, 2d, and 3d instant :

On the morning of Wednesday, the 1st, the division marched from Emmitsburg, bringing up the rear of the column, and when about 3 miles from Gettysburg, hearing firing in front, it was pushed rapidly forward, and, arriving on the field, was placed, by order of the major-general commanding First Corps, in reserve, near the seminary. Almost immediately after taking this position, I received notice that the enemy was advancing a heavy column of infantry on the right of our line of battle, when I sent the Second Brigade, under Brigadier-General Baxter, to meet it. Orders being received at this time to hold the seminary, the First Brigade, under Brigadier-General Paul, was set at work to intrench the ridge on which it is situated. I then rode to the right of the line, to superintend the operations there. On my arrival, I found my Second Brigade so placed as to cover our right flank, but with too great an interval between it and the line of the First Division. I at once directed General Baxter to change front forward on his left battalion, and to close this interval, toward which the enemy was making his way. By the time this change was effected, the whole front of the brigade became hotly engaged, but succeeded in repulsing the attack. The enemy, however, soon after brought up fresh forces in increased masses, when, finding the position so seriously threatened, I sent for and brought up the First Brigade, and placed part of it in the position first occupied by Baxter's brigade, and the remaining battalions as a support to his second position. The enemy now made repeated attacks on the division, in all of which he was handsomely repulsed, with the loss of three flags and about 1,000 prisoners.

---

* Embodied in revised statement, p. 173.

In one of these attacks I was deprived of the services of the veteran commander of the First Brigade, Brigadier-General Paul, who fell, severely wounded, while gallantly directing and encouraging his command.

The division held this position on the right—receiving and repelling the fierce attacks of a greatly superior force, not only in front, but on the flank, and, when the enemy's ranks were broken, charging upon him and capturing his colors and men—from about noon until nearly 5 p. m., when I received orders to withdraw. These orders not being received until all other troops (except Stewart's battery) had commenced moving to the rear, the division held its ground until outflanked right and left, and retired fighting.

From the nature of the enemy's attacks, frequent changes were rendered necessary, and they were made promptly under a galling fire. No soldiers ever fought better, or inflicted severer blows upon the enemy. When out of ammunition, their boxes were replenished from those of their killed and wounded comrades.

The instances of distinguished gallantry are too numerous to be embodied in this report, and I leave it to the brigade and regimental commanders to do justice to those under their immediate command. Where all did so well, it is difficult to discriminate. As, however, they came under my personal observation, I cheerfully indorse the remarks of General Baxter in commendation of Colonel Coulter, Eleventh Pennsylvania; Colonel Wheelock, Ninety-seventh New York; Colonel Lyle, Ninetieth Pennsylvania; Colonel Bates and Lieutenant-Colonel Allen, Twelfth Massachusetts; Lieutenant-Colonel Moesch, Eighty-third New York, and Major Foust, Eighty-eighth Pennsylvania.

After the fall of General Paul, the command of the First Brigade devolved successively upon Colonel Leonard, Thirteenth Massachusetts, Colonel Root, Ninety-fourth New York, and Colonel Coulter, Eleventh Pennsylvania, all of whom were wounded while exercising the command.

After withdrawing from this contest, I took up a position on a ridge to the left of the cemetery, facing the Emmitsburg road, and remained there until afternoon of the next day, when I was relieved by a division of the Second Corps, and ordered to the support of the Eleventh Corps. In the evening, I was ordered to the left of our line, but was soon after directed to return.

On Friday morning, 3d instant, the division was massed, and held ready to push forward to the support of the Twelfth Corps, then engaged with the enemy on our right.

About noon, I was informed by the major-general commanding the army that he anticipated an attack on the cemetery by the enemy's forces massed in the town, and was directed to so place my command that if our line gave way I could attack the enemy on his flank. I proceeded to make this change of position at the moment the enemy commenced the terrific artillery fire of that day. Never before were troops so exposed to such a fire of shot and shell, and yet the movement was made in perfect order and with little loss.

Later in the day, the enemy having made his attack on our left instead of the center, I was ordered to the right of the Second Corps, which position I held until Sunday, when the line was withdrawn.

My thanks are due to Brigadier-Generals Baxter and Paul for the able and zealous manner in which they handled their brigades. The officers of my staff were actively engaged during the whole of the three days' engagements. Lieutenant [Samuel M.] Morgan, acting assistant adjutant-general; Lieutenant [Frederick M.] Hallock, aide-de-camp, and Lieutenants Bratton and Mead, acting aides, were at all times distinguished for their gallantry and good conduct. Captain [John G.] Hovey, acting assistant inspector-general, was wounded and taken from the field early in the fight. Lieutenant Smith, ordnance officer, was diligent in the performance of his duty, and collected and turned in 2,251 muskets and a large number of equipments.

It affords me pleasure to call special attention to the gallant conduct of one of my orderlies, Sergt. Ebenezer S. Johnson, First Maine Cavalry, whose chevrons should be exchanged for the epaulette. When we m ke officers of such men, the soldier receives his true reward and the service great benefit.

This division went into battle with less than 2,500 officers and men, and sustained a loss of 1,667, of which 124 were commissioned officers.

I transmit herewith a nominal and tabular statement of casualties, showing the loss of each regiment.*

Very respectfully, your obedient servant,

JNO. C. ROBINSON,
Brigadier-General, Commanding Division.

The ASSISTANT ADJUTANT-GENERAL,
First Army Corps.

ADDENDA.

HDQRS. SECOND DIVISION, FIRST ARMY CORPS,
November 15, 1863.

Maj. Gen. GEORGE G. MEADE,
Commanding Army of the Potomac:

GENERAL: I feel it is my duty to inform you of the intense mortification and disappointment felt by my division in reading your report of the battle of Gettysburg.

For nearly four hours on July 1 we were hotly engaged against overwhelming numbers, repulsed repeated attacks of the enemy, captured three flags and a very large number of prisoners, and were the last to leave the field.

The division formed the right of the line of battle of the First Corps, and during the whole time had to fight the enemy in front and protect our right flank (the division of the Eleventh Corps being at no time less than half a mile in rear). We went into action with less than 2,500 men and lost considerably more than half our number.

We have been proud of our efforts on that day, and hoped that they would be recognized. It is but natural we should feel disappointed that we are not once referred to in the report of the commanding general.

Trusting that you will investigate this matter and give us due credit, I am, general, very respectfully, your obedient servant,

JNO. C. ROBINSON,
Brigadier-General, Commanding Division.

---

*Embodied in revised statement, pp. 173, 174.

HDQRS. SECOND DIVISION, FIRST ARMY CORPS,
July 5, 1863.

General WILLIAMS,
    Assistant Adjutant-General, Army of the Potomac:

I have the honor to send by bearer two stand of colors captured by this division in the action of July 1. One taken besides was retained by Colonel Wheelock, who was afterward taken prisoner.

Very respectfully, your obedient servant,

JNO. C. ROBINSON,
Brigadier-General, Commanding Division.

No. 44.

Reports of Col. Richard Coulter, Eleventh Pennsylvania Infantry, commanding regiment and First Brigade.

GETTYSBURG, PA., *July 6, 1863.*

SIR: I report the following as the part taken by my command in the action with the enemy on July 1, near Gettysburg, Pa.:

The First Division had been for some time engaged when this brigade, about 11 a. m., was massed on the west side and near the embankment of the railroad. At this point I was directed by the general commanding the brigade to proceed with the Ninety-seventh New York Volunteers, Colonel Wheelock, and my own, Eleventh Regiment Pennsylvania Volunteers, which I did, deploying both regiments, and moved with skirmishers about a quarter of a mile beyond the railroad track. Discovering that the enemy's movement was being directed against the left flank, I changed front to the left, and took position on the ridge (where the fighting subsequently took place), connecting the left of my command upon the right of General Cutler's brigade, of the First Division. I was here joined on the right by General Baxter, who resumed command of the entire line.

The skirmishers had been a short time engaged, and about 12.30 p. m. the firing became general along the entire line. The enemy, after several attempts, finding it impossible to force our position, commenced moving his troops toward the left, under a galling and effective fire from our line. While this was being done, a sally was made by part of the brigade (the Ninety-seventh New York Volunteers and my own regiment engaging in it), which resulted in the capture of about 500 of the enemy.

The line was steadily maintained under a brisk fire until after 3 p. m., at which time, the ammunition being exhausted, we were relieved by a portion of the First Brigade. Upon being so relieved, the regiment was moved to the railroad embankment on the left, and there remained in support of a battery until ordered to fall back to the town of Gettysburg, the enemy having in the meantime turned both flanks; then retired with the brigade along the railroad, suffering most severely from a galling fire of musketry and artillery. The division immediately assumed another position in the rear of the town, on Cemetery Hill. Here my regiment was transferred to the First Brigade, and I assumed the command of the brigade. At this point, therefore, my report ceases as connected with the Second Brigade.

The loss in my regiment during this period was: Killed—enlisted men, 5; wounded—commissioned officers, 6; enlisted men, 44; missing—commissioned officers, 3; enlisted men, 63; of which a report has heretofore been furnished. Some of those reported missing, it has since been ascertained, were wounded; others were secured upon the retaking of the town, the residue having been taken by the enemy. An additional and detailed report of the losses will be made so soon as the necessary information can be had.*

The conduct of both officers and men as they came under my observation during this trying engagement was most creditable, so much so as to secure even the encomiums of the enemy. Not a single case of faltering came under my notice.

I desire to mention the gallantry of Colonel Wheelock and Lieutenant-Colonel Spofford, of the Ninety-seventh New York Volunteers, the first for the manner in which he brought his regiment into action and sustained it, the second on account of his moving forward and fighting the skirmishers of the two regiments as he did. Both subsequently fell into the hands of the enemy.

I wish also to call attention to the conduct of one of General Robinson's mounted orderlies, Sergeant Johnson, of the First Maine Cavalry. The promptitude with which he conveyed orders and communicated information was highly creditable. He has proved himself on this as well as on other fields to be a brave soldier.

I have the honor to remain, yours, respectfully,

R. COULTER,
Colonel Eleventh Regiment Pennsylvania Volunteers.

The ACTING ASSISTANT ADJUTANT-GENERAL,
Second Brigade, Second Division, First Army Corps.

—

BALTIMORE, MD., *July* 9, 1863.

SIR: The following is a report of the part taken by the First Brigade in the engagements with the enemy, from the 1st to the 4th instant, at Gettysburg, Pa.:

My regiment was transferred from the Second to the First Brigade about 5 p. m. on the 1st instant, when the division was formed in the cemetery. I was directed to assume command on account of the disability of General Paul and loss of other field officers. I can, therefore, state but little of the part taken in the engagement of the earlier part of the day on the west side of the town, excepting what is contained in the reports of the several regimental commanders, which accompany and are made part of this report.

In the action, this brigade was formed on the left of the Second Brigade and right of the First Division, and was engaged until 3 p. m., when a part was moved to the right, to relieve the Second Brigade, their ammunition being exhausted. Both flanks of the corps in the meantime having been turned by the enemy, this brigade retired, with the residue of the division, under a very destructive fire, along the railroad embankment and through the town to the cemetery, where the division was reformed about 5 p. m. Here, as before stated, I assumed command.

Later in the evening, moved toward the left, and took position on the left of the Eleventh Corps, and, having built breastworks of such materials as were at hand, remained there in support of the batteries at that point until relieved by the Third Division, Second Corps, about noon next day.

---

* See revised statement, p. 173.

About 7 o'clock in the evening were moved farther to the left, to support the operations of the Third Corps, in which we were subjected to a considerable artillery fire, with some loss; which duty being accomplished, we returned.

. About 10 p. m. were placed in position on the Emmitsburg and Gettysburg road and in front of the cemetery, to support a portion of the Eleventh Corps, from which duty we were relieved at daylight on the 3d.

About 2 p. m. of the 3d, the artillery fire becoming heavy and general along the line, the brigade was moved quickly to the right, to the support of Captain Ricketts' and other batteries operating on the right of the cemetery. Here we remained about an hour, and were exposed to both the front and rear fire of artillery and the enemy's skirmishers. When about to move on return to the left, I was wounded and temporarily disabled, and the command was transferred to Colonel Lyle, of the Ninetieth Pennsylvania Volunteer Regiment. I remained with the brigade, however, and soon after resumed the command.

About 3 p. m. moved rapidly to the left, under a severe fire, to the support of the Second Corps, upon which the enemy appeared to have concentrated their attack, and took position in support of a battery on the right of the Third Division, Second Corps. Brisk skirmishing was kept up with considerable loss on both sides until 9 p. m. About 11 p. m., it being ascertained that the enemy were removing the fences within reach, either for the purpose of making defense against attack or of opening the way, the breastworks in our front were much strengthened by the addition of stone and timber, the brigade working almost the entire night.

No change was made on the 4th. The skirmishing was continued with some loss.

The following table gives the loss each day:

Date.	Killed.		Wounded.		Missing.		Total.		
	Officers.	Enlisted men.	Officers.	Enlisted men.	Officers.	Enlisted men.	Officers.	Enlisted men.	Aggregate.
July 1	1	35	35	68	39	598	75	701	776
July 2	......	5	1	9	1	12	2	26	28
July 3	......	1	7	4	......	2	7	7	14
July 4	......	1	......	2	......	......	......	3	3
Total*	1	42	43	83	40	612	84	737	821

This table does not include the loss of the Eleventh Pennsylvania Volunteers on the 1st instant, it being then attached to the Second Brigade, and its loss being accounted for with that brigade. Many reported missing, it has been since ascertained, were killed or wounded. Some were recovered on re-entering the town, and the residue are in the hands of the enemy.

The conduct of officers and men, so far as they came under my observation, was in every way creditable.

Three officers of General Paul's staff being reported among the missing, I selected Adjt. A. R. Small, Sixteenth Maine, as acting as-

---

* But see revised statement, p. 173.

sistant adjutant-general, and Lieutenant Howe, of the Thirteenth Massachusetts, as aide-de-camp, of whom I desire to make special mention for assistance rendered me.

This report is made under unfavorable circumstances, away from the brigade, and without means of obtaining full information, which facts will account for any deficiencies.

I have the honor to remain, your obedient servant,

R. COULTER,
Colonel, Commanding Brigade.

Lieut. S. M. MORGAN,
Acting Assistant Adjutant-General, Second Division.

No. 45.

Report of Lieut. Col. Augustus B. Farnham, Sixteenth Maine Infantry.

HEADQUARTERS SIXTEENTH MAINE VOLUNTEERS,
August 19, 1863.

Report of the part taken by the Sixteenth Maine Volunteers in the recent operations of the army, from June 28 to July 24, 1863.

June 28, 1863.—On picket 5 miles to the north of Middletown, Md. At 3 p. m. received orders to be ready for a move, and at 4 p. m. the regiment moved by the old road over the mountains to Frederick City, arriving there at 3 a. m. on the morning of the 29th. Resumed our line of march at 5 a. m., and marched a distance of 26 miles, passing through Emmitsburg at 6 p. m., and camped near the town. Distance marched from 4 p. m. June 28 till 6 p. m. June 29, 40 miles.

June 30.—Marched at 8 a. m., and, after proceeding about 4 miles, crossed the Pennsylvania line, and camped for the night.

July 1.—Marched at 6 a. m. After proceeding a short distance, heard cannonading to the front. After reaching the battle-ground, we were ordered with the rest of the brigade forward toward the right and in rear of a large house and ridge, where we halted for a few moments. We were then ordered, with the Ninety-fourth New York Volunteers, to the left and front, and threw up a barricade of rails, &c. In fifteen minutes we were ordered to the right, to engage the enemy at the top of the ridge, and which being done we changed front, our right resting on the top of the ridge and running parallel with the fence and woods and in front of our original lines. Here we engaged the enemy, and drove him from his position, after which we were ordered to the rear in the woods, where we lay skirmishing with the enemy a few moments. We were then ordered, alone, by General Robinson, to take possession of a hill which commanded the road, and hold the same as long as there was a man left. We took the position as ordered, and held the same until, finding the enemy in such force, and rapidly advancing on us, and seeing no support coming to our aid, we fell back into the hollow, and formed again, but could not hold our position, and finally fell back into the woods, where we engaged the enemy until, finding that we were again left without support, and the enemy engaging us both front and flank, ordered a retreat, but not in time to reach the main body of the brigade.

Our loss in killed, wounded, and missing for the day was: Officers killed, 1; enlisted men killed, 8; officers wounded, 5; enlisted men wounded, 47; officers missing, 11; enlisted men missing, 151; total, 223.

July 2.—Supported a battery on Cemetery Hill until nearly dark, when we were ordered to the left, and ran the gauntlet of a very heavy artillery fire, reaching the point of attack just as the enemy were being driven back. We returned to our position on the right, and about 9 p. m. moved on the hill in front of the batteries and near the town, where we were much annoyed by the enemy's sharpshooters firing from the windows and houses.

July 3.—Soon after daylight we were ordered to the rear of the batteries. As we rode up from behind the stone wall, we received a volley from the enemy's pickets, but fortunately did us no damage. We held a position in support of a battery until the enemy making a desperate attack on the center, our division was sent to re-enforce the Second Corps. Reached the point of attack as the enemy were being driven back broken and defeated. We relieved the Second Corps, built breastworks on the edge of the woods, and, after sending out a strong picket, bivouacked for the night.

July 4.—Our pickets skirmished with the enemy's during the day.

July 5.—The regiment was relieved at 12 m., and moved to the left and rear, and bivouacked in a small piece of woods for the night.

Our loss in killed and wounded during the 2d, 3d, 4th, and 5th, was as follows: Officers killed, none; enlisted men killed, none; officers wounded, 1; enlisted men wounded, 3; total, 4.

July 6.—Moved at 7 a. m. and camped near Emmitsburg. Length of march, 8 miles.

July 7.—Marched through Emmitsburg, Mechanicstown, over the Catoctin Mountains, and camped on the western slope, 4 miles north of Middletown. Length of march, 25 miles.

July 8.—Marched at daylight in a heavy rain. Passed through Middletown, and halted 1 mile west of the town at 11 a. m. Marched again at 4 p. m., and bivouacked on the western slope of South Mountain.

July 9.—Remained in line of battle on South Mountain.

July 10.—Marched at 5 a. m. through Boonsborough, and halted 3 miles west of the town and threw up breastworks. Moved about 80 rods to the rear, and threw up more breastworks at right angles with the first, the former running north and south. Length of march, 7 miles.

July 11.—Remained in line near Beaver Creek till 3 p. m., when we went on picket.

July 12.—Were called in at 10 a. m. Moved through Funkstown, and formed a line of battle on north side of Antietam Creek, facing Hagerstown, at 4 p. m. Remained in line two hours, and then moved by the left flank about 40 rods, and formed on the left by file into line; then by the left flank about 30 rods, and built breastworks; then bivouacked for the night.

July 13.—Remained in line ; some skirmishing in front.

July 14.—Moved at 1 o'clock toward Williamsport, and camped 1 mile this side of the town.

July 15.—Marched at 5.30 a. m., and passed through Smoketown, Keedysville, and Knoxville, and camped at the base of the Catoctin Mountains, on the west side, near Crampton's Gap.

July 16.—Marched at 6 a. m., and passed through Crampton's Gap past Burkittsville, and camped near Berlin.

July 17.—Remained in camp.

July 18.—Marched at 6 a. m., and crossed the Potomac at Berlin. Passed east of Lovettsville, and bivouacked near Waterford.   Length of march, 10 miles.

July 19.—Marched at 6 a. m. through Waterford, by Harmony Church, through Hamilton, and camped half a mile west of the town. Length of march, 6 miles.

July 20.—Marched to Middleburg; distance, 15 miles.

July 21.—Remained in camp.

July 22.—Marched at 7 p. m. toward White Plains.   Until about 11 p. m. the marching was very slow and tedious, being in the rear of the train.   At 12 o'clock men still on the march.

July 23.—Marched until 4 a. m., and bivouacked at White Plains. At 7 a. m. marched toward Warrenton.   Reached Warrenton at 5 p. m., and formed a line of battle on the southwest side of the town. Bivouacked for the night.

A. B. FARNHAM,
Lieutenant-Colonel, Commanding Sixteenth Maine Volunteers.

[Capt. BYRON PORTER,
　　Assistant Adjutant-General.]

No. 46.

*Report of Lieut. Col. N. Walter Batchelder, Thirteenth Massa-
chusetts Infantry.*

HDQRS. THIRTEENTH MASSACHUSETTS VOLUNTEERS,
August 21, 1863.

SIR: In compliance with circular received August 18, 1863, I have the honor to submit the following report of the part taken by my regiment in the movements of the army, from June 28 till its arrival at Warrenton, Va. :

June 28.—Broke camp at Middletown, Md. at 3.30 p. m., and marched over the old mountain road to near Frederick City, arriving in camp at 8 p. m.   Distance marched was 9 miles.

June 29.—Marched at 5 a. m., passing through Emmitsburg at 5.30 p. m.; camped near the town.   Distance marched was 26 miles, the greater part of the march being over mud roads in very bad condition, owing to continued rains.

June 30.—Marched at 8 a. m., and, after proceeding about 6 miles, crossing the Pennsylvania line, halted and formed line of battle, the First Division having encountered the pickets of the enemy.

July 1.—Marched at 6 a. m.   After proceeding about 4 miles, heard cannonading in front, our cavalry and flying artillery having engaged the advance of the enemy.   We rapidly neared the firing, and General Paul notified the brigade that they were immediately going into an engagement.

We left the road, and moved out to the front of Gettysburg, and soon came under the fire of the enemy.   The enemy so far outnumbering us, our brigade was sent into action by regiments, and with so great an interval between my regiment and the one on my left that we were not able to properly support each other.   My regiment was on the extreme right flank of the division and the edge of the woods in which the action commenced.

Colonel Leonard was wounded early in the fight, and the command devolved upon me.

A steady fire was kept up by the men for upward of an hour. At last, being seriously annoyed by the fire of a regiment of the enemy sheltered behind the banks of Chambersburg pike road, I ordered a charge on the road, which resulted in driving the enemy from their position, leaving in our hands 132 prisoners, 7 of whom were commissioned officers. They were safely sent to the rear and turned over to the provost guard.

A division of the Eleventh Corps on our right giving way before a charge of the enemy, left our flank exposed, and, no support coming up, a retreat was ordered, and we fell back through the town to the heights in the rear, where the command was reorganized. About 100 were taken prisoners on the way to the rear. The regiment went into action with 260 muskets. The total loss in killed, wounded, and prisoners in the day's battle was 189.

July 2.—Supported batteries on Cemetery Hill until nearly dark, when we were ordered to the left. Reached the point of attack too late to participate in the action. Returned to our position on the right, and were ordered to the front of the batteries and near the town.

July 3.—At daylight were ordered to the rear of the batteries. Remained there until afternoon, when we were sent to support the center, which the enemy were making desperate efforts to break.

Reached the point of attack as the enemy were handsomely forced back by the Second Corps. Relieved the troops that had been engaged, built earthworks in the edge of the woods, and, after detailing a strong picket, bivouacked.

July 4.—Picket skirmishing was kept up all day, with very few casualties. Rain fell nearly all day.

July 5.—At daylight discovered that the enemy had retreated. At 9 a. m. moved to the left, and occupied part of the ground on which the Third Corps had fought.

July 6.—Formed line at 6 a. m., and marched toward Emmitsburg. After marching 6 miles, were halted and marched back 2 miles, resting in a piece of woods until afternoon. Again formed and marched to within 2 miles of Emmitsburg, and went into camp.

July 7.—Marched by the rough mountain road to Belleville; distance, 20 miles.

July 8.—Marched through Middletown and South Mountain Gap, and threw up earthworks on the west side of the ridge. Distance marched, 18 miles.

July 10.—Marched through Boonsborough to Beaver Creek and built more earthworks. After completing the works, were ordered to change front to rear, and to build another line of works.

July 11.—Late in the afternoon went on picket.

July 12.—Withdrawn from picket early in the morning, marched to Funkstown and on the Hagerstown road. Formed line of battle on the left of the road, and again intrenched.

July 14.—At daylight it was evident the enemy had left our front. Marched at 2 p. m., and reached Williamsport before night. Went into camp.

July 15.—Marched early, and camped at night near Crampton's Gap.

July 16.—Marched through Crampton's Gap and Burkittsville, camping near Berlin.

July 18.—Crossed the Potomac on pontoons, and camped near Waterford.

July 19.—Marched to Hamilton.

July 20.—Marched to Middleburg.

July 22.—Marched as rear guard to the supply train. Arrived at White Plains at 3 a. m. of the 23d.

July 23.—Marched at 10 a. m., and reached Warrenton at 4 p. m., and went into camp.

Very respectfully, your obedient servant,

N. W. BATCHELDER,
Lieutenant-Colonel, Comdg. Thirteenth Massachusetts Vols.

Capt. BYRON PORTER,
Assistant Adjutant-General.

No. 47.

Report of Maj. Samuel A. Moffett, Ninety-fourth New York Infantry.

RAPPAHANNOCK STATION, VA.,
August 20, 1863.

CAPTAIN: I beg leave respectfully to submit the following report of the part taken by the Ninety-fourth Regiment New York Volunteers, commanded by Col. A. R. Root, from June 28 until its arrival at Warrenton on July 23, 1863:

On the afternoon of June 28, we marched 7 miles, to near Frederick City. On the 29th, we marched a little beyond Emmitsburg, near which place the Ninety-fourth picketed during the night. The next morning marched about 3 miles out of the village, where we remained during the day.

July 1, marched to near Gettysburg, and, after moving forward to near the brick seminary, we were ordered to throw up breastworks. After remaining here a short time, we were ordered forward. We advanced through the woods to a fence, beyond which was the enemy. After dislodging and driving them from their position, we commenced to charge across the field, but after proceeding a part of the way were met by a large opposing force, and at the same time became aware of their advance on our left flank, threatening to cut off our retreat. We immediately fell back in good order to the woods. At this period, Colonel Root being wounded, the command of the regiment devolved upon me. We remained in the woods about half an hour, slightly changing our position several times. I was then ordered by General Robinson to take my command to the crest of the hill near by, which I immediately did. I remained in this position until we fell back to the hill on the south side of the town, losing heavily in wounded and prisoners.

The report of this day is necessarily meager, as Colonel Root, who had command of the regiment during the hottest of the engagement, is absent a prisoner, and, no doubt, is possessed of much valuable information concerning the battle which I had not the means of ascertaining.

We remained in the vicinity of Cemetery Hill during July 2 and 3, occasionally changing our position in obedience to orders. We were constantly under fire, either from the batteries of the enemy or from their sharpshooters, but, fortunately, no one was killed and but few were wounded. Late in the afternoon of the 3d, in the midst of a heavy fire, we moved a short distance to the left of the hill, where we immediately threw up breastworks. Our skirmishers, which were at once sent forward, remained out during the night and the day following.

On the morning of the 5th, we marched to the left about 1 mile, and here remained during the day and night.

The next morning we commenced a march which was continued during the two following days, passing on our way the villages of Emmitsburg and Middletown. On the 8th, we halted on the western slope of South Mountain range, and immediately threw up breastworks. Here we remained until the 10th, when we moved forward to near Little Beavertown, on Beaver Creek, and again threw up intrenchments. At this place the Ninety-fourth New York was ordered out on picket duty, which we performed until the following day. On the morning of the 12th, we again moved forward, and marched to near Hagerstown, where we immediately proceeded to intrench ourselves in close proximity to the intrenchments of the enemy. Our skirmishers were engaged during the night and the next day, but no casualties occurred. Early on the morning of the 14th, it was discovered that the skirmishers of the enemy had been withdrawn, and that their line of intrenchments had been abandoned. Soon after, we received orders to advance, which we did without opposition, arriving near Williamsport late in the afternoon of the same day, and learning that the entire force of the enemy had recrossed the river.

The next day, in compliance with orders, we faced about and marched toward Berlin, which place we reached about noon, July 16. Here we encamped until the morning of the 18th, when we crossed the Potomac River, marching in a southerly direction. Continuing our march, we passed the villages of Waterford, Middleburg, and White Plains, and reached Warrenton on the 23d day of July, 1863.

S. A. MOFFETT,
Major, Commanding Ninety-fourth Regiment.

Capt. BYRON PORTER,
    Assistant Adjutant-General.

No. 48.

Report of Col. Gilbert G. Prey, One hundred and fourth New York Infantry.

HDQRS. 104TH REGIMENT NEW YORK VOLUNTEERS,
August 18, 1863.

CAPTAIN : In accordance with circular from headquarters Army of the Potomac, August 12, 1863, I have the honor to report that on the 28th of June last the One hundred and fourth Regiment New York Volunteers marched from Middletown, Md., to Frederick City, Md.; bivouacked for the night. On the 29th, marched to Emmitsburg, Md.; bivouacked for the night about 1 mile west of the town. On the morning of the 30th, marched across the State line into Pennsylvania, north of Emmitsburg; bivouacked until the next morning, when we resumed the march to Gettysburg, where we arrived about 1 o'clock.

When the brigade was first formed in line of battle, my regiment was placed on the right center, and ordered to throw up a breast-work of such material as they could find. In a few minutes the order was countermanded, and we marched by the right flank in rear of the Thirteenth Massachusetts Regiment across the railroad embankment, passing through a piece of woods some distance into an open field. I was ordered to form line by Brigadier-General Paul on the right of the Thirteenth Massachusetts Regiment, and, while doing so, was ordered by Brigadier-General Robinson, commanding division, to form on the left, and did so, my left resting near the Ninety-seventh Regiment (New York), my line running obliquely with the crest of the hill, where the enemy was strongly posted behind a stone wall covered with thick underbrush, the fire from the wall taking us on the flank as the line advanced. I ordered my three left companies to gain the wall and dislodge the enemy, which they did in gallant style. The enemy retired in confusion before them. I then advanced my line to the road on which the enemy had been posted. Here some 35 or 40 prisoners were taken, but having neither officers nor men to spare to take charge of them, I directed them to pass to the rear and join some already taken by the Thirteenth Massachusetts, which they did. Fifteen or 20 more prisoners were afterward taken by my regiment and sent to the rear. Shortly after gaining the road, the enemy began to move to our left in considerable force, and, as that was entirely unsupported, I caused my regiment to change front and take position behind the stone wall from which we had previously driven the enemy.

As they still continued to advance on our front and right flank, I moved to the left, to connect with the Ninety-seventh New York. There we remained, firing, and held our position until ordered to retire. A list of the casualties has already been forwarded.

We retired, and formed line behind a stone wall some 300 or 400 yards to the left of the cemetery, nearly parallel to the pike leading to Emmitsburg; remained there until the next morning, when we were moved to the right, to support a battery on Cemetery Hill. Remained there until about sundown of that day (July 2), when we were marched to the left, where the battle was raging at the time; formed line in rear of a portion of the Second Corps. When the battle closed, we were again marched to the right, and formed in line behind a stone wall on the west of the cemetery, and nearly down to the town; lay on our arms during the night. The next morning (July 3), we marched, under the fire of the enemy's sharpshooters, to the rear of the cemetery, to support a battery, as on the day before. About 2 o'clock of that day we were marched to the right of the cemetery, to screen us from the shot and shell that were playing into the place where we were; lay there about two hours, when we were marched, through a galling fire of shot, shell, and bullets, across the cemetery and to the left, and formed line in front of a brass battery in the woods immediately to the left of the cemetery. Sent out skirmishers. Continued in that position and capacity until about noon of the 5th, when we were marched to the left, and bivouacked near Round Top Mountain, so called. The next day (July 6) we marched to the State line near Emmitsburg; from thence (July 7) over the mountain to near Middletown; bivouacked for the night, and the next morning (July 8) passed through Middletown and bivouacked about 1 mile out toward South Mountain. Toward night marched to the western slope of the

South Mountain, near and to the north of Turner's Gap, formed line, and were ordered to throw up a breastwork of stones, of which there was an abundance. Remained there until the 10th, and then marched on the pike toward Hagerstown, through Boonsborough, to within 3 miles of Funkstown, and filed to the right some three-fourths of a mile from the pike, and formed line nearly parallel to the pike, and were ordered to throw up breastworks, which we did, and remained there until the 12th July; then marched to Funkstown, formed line nearly parallel with Antietam Creek; was ordered to throw up breastworks. Remained there until the 14th July; thence to near Williamsport; bivouacked over night. The next morning (July 15) marched to near Crampton's Gap; bivouacked on the west side of the mountain. Thence (July 16) to Berlin; remained there until July 18, when we marched to Waterford, Va. Thence (July 19) to Hamilton. Thence to Middleburg July 20; remained there until July 22, when we marched to White Plains, arriving there at day-light July 23. Thence the same day to Warrenton.

GILBERT G. PREY,
Colonel One hundred and fourth New York Volunteers.

Capt. Byron Porter,
Assistant Adjutant-General.

No. 49.

Report of Capt. Jacob J. Bierer, Eleventh Pennsylvania Infantry.

HDQRS. ELEVENTH PENNSYLVANIA VOL. REGIMENT,
August 22, 1863.

SIR: In reply to circular from Headquarters Army of the Potomac, August 12, 1863, I respectfully make the following report:

About 2 p. m. June 28, the regiment marched from Middletown, Md., to the left of Frederick City, and encamped about 2 miles from said city.

June 29.—Early we left camp and marched through Mechanics-town, and encamped near Emmitsburg, Md.

June 30.—Marched through Emmitsburg on the Gettysburg road, and encamped 2 miles east of town and about one-fourth of a mile north of the Maryland and Pennsylvania line; there mustered for pay.

July 1.—The regiment marched to Gettysburg and were engaged with the enemy, Colonel Coulter being in command, whose report has already been made.

July 2.—The regiment, on the evening of July 1, having taken position in rear of breastworks on the south side of the town, was early this morning relieved by troops of the Second Corps, and marched about one-fourth of a mile to Cemetery Hill, in rear of which, with the division, it was formed to support a battery stationed on the hill. It remained here until 8 p. m., when it was marched to the left.

At 9.30 p. m. it resumed its former position, and was subsequently formed in rear of a stone wall between the hill and town, along the road, where it remained until the morning of the 3d, at daylight, when it was moved to the position it formerly occupied in the rear of the cemetery. It remained until noon, when it was moved to the right.

About 2 p. m. the enemy commenced shelling so heavily as to make it necessary to move to the north side of the hill, where it remained about an hour, when it was marched across the cemetery to the right of the position occupied on the 2d, where it was formed in line, and remained during the balance of the day and until the 5th.

July 5.—Early in the morning the regiment, together with the brigade, was withdrawn from the rifle-pits and moved to the left, where we remained during the day and night.

July 6.—Early in the morning we left this position and moved to the State line of Pennsylvania, in Adams County, a distance of 6 miles, toward Emmitsburg, Md., and was there detailed for picket duty.

July 7.—At 3 a. m. the pickets were called in and the regiment rejoined the brigade ; marched through Emmitsburg and Mechanicstown, and encamped in the evening on a range of the South Mountain, about 5 miles from Middletown, Md.

July 8.—Started at daylight and marched through Middletown, Md., and bivouacked on the north side of South Mountain, and remained there during the night and next day, having thrown up intrenchments.

July 10.—At 8 a. m. moved from this position, marching through Boonsborough. Was halted at Beaver Creek, and threw up breastworks, expecting to be attacked by the enemy, and lay in this position during Saturday, the 11th.

July 12, Sunday.—At 12 m. left encampment ; moved to Funkstown, crossing Antietam Creek ; formed line of battle, and intrenched in the evening, having marched about 7 miles.

July 13.—Remained in the intrenchments thrown up on the previous day.

July 14.—The enemy having left our front, marched to within 1½ miles of Williamsport.

July 15.—Marched through Keedysville, Md., and Petersville, and encamped at the foot of South Mountain.

July 16.—At 5.30 a. m. marched across South Mountain, passing through Burkittsville, and encamped near Berlin early in the day, and remained there during the day and night and next day until the morning of the 18th.

July 18.—Passed through Berlin, and, crossing the river on pontoon bridge, marched to Waterford. On this day the regiment, temporarily assigned to the First Brigade, was, in accordance with new orders from headquarters Second Division, of July 18, transferred to the Second Brigade.

July 19.—At 8 a. m. left Waterford and marched to Hamilton.

July 20.—Crossing Goose Creek ; came to Middleburg, where we encamped, and remained on the 20th and 21st.

July 22.—Left camp at 6 p. m., and, marching through the night, arrived at White Plains at 3 o'clock in the morning.

July 23.—Left camp at 8 a. m. and marched toward Warrenton, Va., where we arrived at 3 p. m.

I have the honor to be, yours, respectfully,

J. J. BIERER,
Captain, Comdg. Eleventh Pennsylvania Volunteers.

Lieut. J. H. SMITH,
Acting Assistant Adjutant-General.

No. 50.

Report of Lieut. Col. James MacThomson, One hundred and seventh Pennsylvania Infantry.

HEADQUARTERS 107TH PENNSYLVANIA VOLUNTEERS,
July 10, 1863.

LIEUTENANT: I have the honor to submit the following necessarily short report of the part the regiment under my command took in the engagement of July 1:

Went into the fight at about 1 p. m., with 230 guns and 25 commissioned officers, the men loading as they walked. Were in action about two hours. Captured more prisoners than the regiment numbered. I regret to report the loss of large numbers of most excellent soldiers.

The casualties are, as far as ascertained, as follows: Field officers, lieutenant-colonel slightly, major severely, wounded; 3 commissioned officers known to be wounded, and 6 commissioned officers missing; 11 enlisted men known to be killed, 48 known to be wounded, and 93 missing.

Men could not have fought better than these men, and I am gratified to say that not a single exhibition of cowardice of either officers or men was observed during the whole engagement.

Respectfully submitted.

With much respect, I am, lieutenant, your most obedient servant,

JAMES MacTHOMSON,
Lieutenant-Colonel, Comdg. 107th Pennsylvania Volunteers.

Lieutenant SMALL,
A. A. A. G., First Brig., Second Div., First Army Corps.

No. 51.

Report of Capt. Emanuel D. Roath, One hundred and seventh Pennsylvania Infantry.

RAPPAHANNOCK, VA.,
August 15, 1863.

CAPTAIN: I have the honor to submit the following report, as per orders from brigade headquarters, from June 28 to July 22, inclusive, viz:

June 28.—Left camp near Middletown, Md., and marched to Frederick City, Md.

June 29.—We marched from Frederick City to Emmitsburg, passing on the way through Lewistown, Mechanicstown, and Catoctin Furnace settlement; also passing those famous Catholic institutions of learning, viz, the college and sisterhood near Emmitsburg. Having marched all day in rain and mud, reaching our destination of 23 miles at 5.30 p. m., the men were much fatigued on the march, but all answered and were accounted for at roll-call. We bivouacked about 1 mile west of Emmitsburg.

June 30.—We marched toward Gettysburg, and bivouacked about

3 miles north of Emmitsburg for the remainder of the day and night on Pennsylvania soil.

The following is the report of Lieut. Col. J. MacThomson, of the One hundred and seventh Pennsylvania Volunteers, during the action of July 1, at Gettysburg, he being in command up to that time, viz:*

July 1.—After the engagement, we fell back to the left of Cemetery Hill, and threw up strong breastworks, which we occupied until next morning.

July 2.—During the forenoon we were relieved by the Third Division, Second Corps, and taken a few hundred yards in the rear to support a battery. We lay on our arms until about 6.30 p. m., when we were marched to the left, toward the Round Top, under a heavy and effective fire, to assist in driving the rebel hordes back in the famous charge of the second day of the fight. After the charge, we marched back to near the cemetery, and were ordered to lay in rear of a stone fence, being a protection for the men from the enemy's sharpshooters in our front.

Our casualties during the second day were 1 commissioned officer and several men wounded. Our strength was about 78 guns and 12 commissioned officers.

July 3.—At 4.30 a. m. we were posted in the rear of Cemetery Hill, in support of the batteries stationed on that point, remaining in that position until 1.30 p. m., when the enemy opened upon us with a heavy and furious artillery fire. Our division was moved to the right of Cemetery Hill, at the same time lying under two direct fires of the enemy's sharpshooters and one battery. The strife became terrific and the artillery firing terrible. At this crisis our services were required to support the batteries, when the regiment was marched with others along the crest or brow of the hill in rear of the batteries, through the most deadly fire ever man passed through, it appearing as though every portion of the atmosphere contained a deadly missile.

After our services were no longer needed to support the batteries, the division to which my regiment was attached was moved to the left of Cemetery Hill, to participate in crowning our arms with the glorious victory achieved that day.

My strength was about 72 guns and 11 commissioned officers. Casualties, 2 commissioned officers wounded; 1 private killed and several slightly wounded. The day being very hot, 3 of my men were carried insensible from the field on account of the intense heat.

After resting a few hours, we sent out a line of skirmishers to the front, and threw up breastworks to protect the men in our position, where we remained for the night.

July 4.—We lay all day in the position of the previous night and strengthened it; did some skirmishing with the enemy's sharpshooters; had no casualties.

It is proper here for me to state that the officers and men displayed great gallantry and determination throughout all the engagements of the previous days, and are entitled to the praise and gratitude of a free and loyal people.

July 5.—After the skirmish line was relieved, we fell back some distance, and encamped for the night.

July 6.—Left camp on or near the battle-field, and marched and

---

*See preceding report.

counter-marched a short distance; halted until 4 p. m., when we were ordered forward again some distance, and encamped about 3 miles north of Emmitsburg, on Pennsylvania soil.

July 7.—Brigade ordered into line, and took up its line of march toward Middletown, Md., passing through Franklin Mills and Mechanicstown; also crossed the Catoctin Mountains, and encamped near Beallsville, Md.

July 8.—Left camp near Beallsville, marched through the place to Middletown, and encamped a few hours south of the town in a heavy rain, it having also rained all the previous night. At 4 p. m. we again took up our line of march to South Mountain. Bivouacked there until the 10th, in line of preparation. Our cavalry had quite a sharp and successful encounter with the enemy on the 9th.

July 10.—Moved forward, passing through Boonsborough and Benevola to near Beaver Creek, and intrenched; lay in that position until the 12th.

July 11.—My regiment was detailed for picket, and was stationed at Beaver Creek, a fine, thriving settlement; the enemy in large numbers in the neighborhood.

July 12, Sunday.—Marched through Funkstown and bivouacked near Hagerstown, Md., throwing up strong breastworks, and remained there until the 14th.

July 14.—Left the breastworks and moved toward Williamsport, passing through and over the strong and abandoned works of the enemy, and bivouacked about 1 mile east of Williamsport for the night. The last of the enemy had recrossed the Potomac during the day, our cavalry capturing about 700 of them on their retreat and destroying a great portion of their train.

July 15.—Took up the line of march toward Berlin, passing through Jones' Cross-Roads, Smoketown, Marsh, Keedysville, Locust Street, and Rohrersville, and bivouacked for the night near Crampton's Gap.

July 16.—Marched through the gap (while passing through the gap from the most elevated positions we had a fine view of Pleasant Valley, Md., and it was a grand scene, for nature had just clothed it in the richest garb to welcome, as it were, the loyal and victorious army of the Union), leaving Burkittsville to our left, which is a fine, pleasant town, and bivouacked about 3 miles from Berlin, and remained there until the 18th.

July 18.—Marched to Berlin, crossed the Potomac into Loudoun County, Va., leaving Lovettsville to our right, and encamped near Waterford.

July 19.—Marched through Waterford to Hamilton, and bivouacked in a fine woods (Sunday).

July 20.—Marched to Middleburg, and lay encamped near the town along the Aldie pike until 6 p. m. of the 21st. Marched to White Plains during the night, arriving there at 4 a. m. on the morning of the 22d. After a few hours' rest and breakfast, we moved to Warrenton same day. Had no casualties during the march.

Respectfully submitted.

I am, captain, with much respect, your most obedient servant,

E. D. ROATH,
Captain, Comdg. One hundred and seventh Pa. Vols.

Capt. Byron Porter,
Asst. Adjt. Gen., First Brig., Second Div., First Army Corps.

No. 52.

Report of Brig. Gen. Henry Baxter, U. S. Army, commanding Second Brigade.

HDQRS. SECOND BRIG., SECOND DIV., FIRST ARMY CORPS,
Camp near Berlin, Md., July 17, 1863.

SIR: I have the honor to report the following as the part taken by the Second Brigade in the battle of Gettysburg:

On Wednesday, July 1, we were early under arms and on the march from our bivouac, near Emmitsburg, for Gettysburg. We heard cannonading as we approached, and marched as rapidly as possible, arriving near the front where the battle was raging at 11 a. m., halting here a few moments. An order arriving from General Robinson, commanding division, before the brigade had halted, to send forward two regiments at once, the Eleventh Pennsylvania Volunteers, Colonel Coulter, and the Ninety-seventh New York, Colonel Wheelock, continued their march, moving to the front. The remaining four regiments were ordered forward in a very few moments, and formed on the right of the two regiments already sent forward, which were on the right of the First Division (General Wadsworth). Indications being that we should be attacked on our right flank, I at once changed front by filing to the right and forming forward on first battalion, a division of the Eleventh Corps being on our right at least 400 yards. I immediately sent skirmishers forward, but the enemy now appearing on our left flank, I had again to change front to the left, and moved forward to the crest of the hill, bringing us before the enemy, when the brigade opened on the advancing foes a most deadly fire, soon causing them to recoil and give way. Another line immediately took the place of that repulsed, and at this time they appeared on our right flank, making it necessary for the Ninetieth Pennsylvania Volunteer Regiment, Colonel Lyle, to change front to meet them, which they did in perfect order, receiving meanwhile a very severe fire. Again their lines were repulsed and again re-enforced. The Ninety-seventh New York Volunteers, Colonel Wheelock, Eighty-third New York Volunteers, Lieutenant-Colonel Moesch, and Eighty-eighth Pennsylvania Volunteers, Major Foust, made a charge, capturing many prisoners, the Eighty-eighth Pennsylvania Volunteers taking two battle-flags and the Ninety-seventh New York Volunteers one from the enemy. The Twelfth Massachusetts Volunteers had a galling fire on the flank of this brigade at this time, which I think had a great influence upon its surrender.

We were relieved by the First Brigade of the Second Division, having been engaged over two hours, and having suffered severely and expended our ammunition. We were then ordered to the support of Captain Stewart's battery, where we remained until ordered from the field by General Robinson, having been outflanked on our right and left, and retired, under a galling fire, through Gettysburg to Cemetery Hill.

I cannot speak in too high praise of the regimental commanders— Colonel Coulter, of the Eleventh Pennsylvania Volunteers; Colonel Wheelock, of the Ninety-seventh New York Volunteers; Colonel Lyle, of the Ninetieth Pennsylvania Volunteers; and Colonel Bates, of the Twelfth Massachusetts Volunteers, who was wounded during the action, but remained until struck a second time and forced to retire, leaving the command with Lieutenant-Colonel Allen, who acquitted himself nobly; Lieutenant-Colonel Moesch, Eighty-third New York Volunteers, and Major Foust, of the Eighty-eighth Pennsylvania Volunteers—who could all be seen in the thickest of the fight, cheering on their men, and giving system and efficiency to their work. Indeed, officers and men of the command behaved nobly.

Colonel Wheelock, being in the rear, was taken prisoner while passing through Gettysburg, but I have the extreme satisfaction of reporting his escape and return to his regiment, where he was received with cheer upon cheer.

It is with pleasure I make favorable mention of the members of my staff: Lieutenant [David P.] Weaver, acting assistant adjutant-general, who exhibited a coolness and bravery seldom excelled, until he was struck in the foot by a bullet, making it necessary for him to retire. Lieutenant [Francis] Thomas, acting assistant inspector-general, and Lieutenant [Robert C.] Knaggs, aide-de-camp, rendered me every assistance possible. Lieutenant Thomas passed through the battle nobly and with honor to himself, but while passing through the streets of Gettysburg was struck by a shell, killing him instantly. Lieutenant Knaggs was taken prisoner in Gettysburg while executing one of my orders.

Just before we moved from this point, Colonel Coulter was assigned to the command of the First Brigade, taking his regiment (Eleventh Pennsylvania Volunteers) with him.

About 5 o'clock the brigade moved, with the division, from Cemetery Hill to the left and forward, near and parallel with the Emmitsburg road, where we formed in line of battle and made temporary breastworks, and remained in this position until about 10 o'clock on the morning of the 2d, when we were relieved by General Webb's brigade, of the Second Corps, moving to the rear a short distance, where we remained until about 4 p. m. We were then ordered to the right a short distance, to support a battery of the Eleventh Corps, remaining in this position until about 6 o'clock, being exposed to the enemy's shells and sharpshooters, and losing some men. We were now ordered to the left, to the assistance of a division of the Third Corps, which was hard pressed, and, while moving into position, some of the enemy's shells struck in our ranks, killing and wounding a few men. When we arrived in position, we were ordered by General Robinson to at once send skirmishers to the front, which was done, but no enemy was found, they having been driven. It was now dark, and we were ordered to the right, to the support of a line of the Eleventh Corps, near the position we last left, where we remained until the morning of the 3d instant, when we were again ordered to the support of the batteries of the Eleventh Corps, where we had been the evening previous.

About 9 a. m. we were ordered to the right and rear of Cemetery Hill, in support of the Twelfth Corps, which was then heavily engaged, remaining until about 1 p. m. We were now ordered to the right and front of Cemetery Hill, in support of the batteries, sustaining a heavy fire from the enemy's batteries for nearly two hours. We were then ordered to the left and rear of Cemetery Hill, where we had but just formed line of battle when we were ordered to the left, and on the right of General Hays' division, of the Second Corps, where we at once formed line of battle, throwing up breastworks.

In taking this position, we passed under one of the most galling fires of artillery ever witnessed. The main attack had been repulsed, but we were sorely annoyed by the enemy's skirmishers and sharpshooters, and, by order of General Robinson, I at once threw out skirmishers to meet them. The Twelfth Massachusetts Volunteers and a detachment of the Ninetieth Pennsylvania Volunteers were ordered forward to drive them back, which was done promptly and with deserved credit to those engaged, moving steadily forward to a point where the ground sloped toward the enemy, though not without considerable loss, and there holding their position.

Here it becomes my duty to report one officer of this command unfavorably—Major Northrup, commmanding the Ninety-seventh New York Volunteers, who relieved the picket about 1 o'clock on the morning of the 4th, dropped his line back from the crest of the slope already mentioned some 15 rods (more or less) without being pressed, where I found his line just after daylight in the morning, he having left it and come in to inquire if it was not time for him to be relieved. I refused to relieve him until he re-established his line, which was done, but not without some work. I think it due to the men to say I do not believe they were at fault.

We remained in our present position until the morning of the 5th, when it was found the enemy had disappeared, and we shortly moved out of the intrenchments to the left, where we bivouacked for the night.

A list, by name, of casualties has been previously forwarded.*

The brigade went into the battle of the 1st instant with a few less than 1,200, and lost, to the time of withdrawing from our last position taken, 645, the heavy loss being on the 1st instant.

Very respectfully, your obedient servant,

H. BAXTER,
Brigadier-General, Commanding Brigade.

Lieut. S. M. MORGAN,
Acting Asst. Adjutant-General, Second Division.

No. 53.

Report of Col. Charles Wheelock, Ninety-seventh New York Infantry.

————, —— —, 1863.

CAPTAIN: In accordance with orders from brigade headquarters, I would respectfully report the part taken by the Ninety-seventh Regiment New York Volunteers in the battle of July 1, 2, and 3, at Gettysburg, Pa., to wit:

On the morning of July 1, at 7 a. m., we left Emmitsburg, Md., reaching Gettysburg, Pa., at 1 p. m. same day, and immediately formed line of battle north of the town, on the flat, our line being parallel with the railroad. We soon changed our front, and took a position on the crest of the hill between the railroad and the road north of the town, about three-quarters of a mile from the town. I immediately sent out Companies A and F as skirmishers, and, within 30 yards of our front, receiving the enemy's fire, finding it proceeding from a stone wall and the embankment of the road, our skirmishers soon drove them from their position, but they soon returned with a full force, our skirmishers falling back to our line of battle, which

---

* Embodied in revised statement, p. 174.

was a strong one. Our whole line became engaged, and the enemy fell back out of sight. Soon their second line appeared on our front. After firing several rounds, and finding them, as I thought, crippled, the order was given to charge. The Ninety-seventh New York Volunteers succeeded in charging over the ground without having any killed and but few wounded. We brought out as prisoners 213 officers and men of the Twentieth North Carolina Regiment, with their colors. We took more prisoners than we had men in our regiment at the time. Soon after returning, we made a second charge, bringing in over 80 prisoners. At this time the third line of the enemy appeared, and the force on our right flank (part of the Eleventh Corps) giving way, and also our left flank, we fell back, as ordered, to the second line. Being hard pressed by superior numbers, the whole brigade fell back to the third line. After keeping our line against a superior force, a heavy line of the enemy coming on our flank and almost in our rear, the whole line fell back and through the village, many being taken prisoners, myself included.

I cannot give a detailed account of the second and third days, as I was not present, but learn from the officers of the regiment that they were on duty all the time, either skirmishing or supporting batteries. The regiment was under command of Maj. Charles Northrup after my capture.

I cannot name officers and men for bravery, as I should do injustice to others. All did their duty, and seemed to vie with each other.

Lieut. Col. J. P. Spofford had his horse shot, and I consider acted most bravely; in fact, all did their duty to my entire satisfaction.

I wish to say one word outside of my regiment in regard to Generals Baxter and Robinson. They were on every part of the field, encouraging and stimulating the men by their presence and bravery.*

Yours, respectfully,

CHARLES WHEELOCK,
Colonel, Comdg. Ninety-seventh New York Volunteers.

Capt. FREDERICK GUYER,
  A. A. A. G., Second Brig., Second Div., First Army Corps.

No. 54.

Report of Capt. Edmund Y. Patterson, Eighty-eighth Pennsylvania Infantry.

NEAR RAPPAHANNOCK STATION, VA.,
  August 22, 1863.

SIR: In obedience to circular from headquarters Army of the Potomac, August 12, 1863, I make the following report of operations from June 28 to July 23, date of arrival at Warrenton, Va.:

June 28.—Having been in camp with the brigade, we received orders to march about 4 p. m., and about 9 p. m. halted outside of Frederick City, Md., and encamped for the night.

June 29.—Left camp at Frederick, and marched to Emmitsburg and encamped.

---

*Nominal list of casualties, here omitted, embodied in revised statement, p. 174.

June 30.—Lay at Emmitsburg in camp until p. m., when the regiment was ordered on picket, and remained on duty until July 1, when we were ordered, about 7 a. m., to rejoin the brigade, which was then on the march to Gettysburg.

About 11 a. m., while marching along, we heard cannonading, and after marching in quick and double-quick time some 2 miles, we were drawn up in line of battle along a stone fence. We then changed our position by left flank, file left, which brought us on a slight hill, and we immediately engaged the enemy, who were advancing on us. Having expended nearly all our ammunition, we charged upon the enemy, capturing a number of prisoners and the colors of the Twenty-third North Carolina and Sixteenth Alabama Regiments. Returning to the line of battle, we continued to fire the few remaining cartridges on hand until we found that the enemy were flanking us, when we fell back through the town, the enemy rapidly following and firing upon us. A new line of battle was formed and cartridges distributed. We then took a position on the left of the hill, which was afterward the center of the line of battle, and threw up breastworks made of rails and earth.

July 2.—Were moved about to different parts of the battle-field, but were not engaged in musketry.

July 3.—At daybreak, were behind a stone wall on Cemetery Hill, behind part of the Eleventh Corps. Batteries soon became engaged, and a few of our men were wounded.

About 2 p. m. the enemy opened upon us from all sides. We were then at the foot of Cemetery Hill, and were compelled to change our position for safety during the heaviest of the fire.

About 6 p. m. we were run double-quick to the center, where we found hard fighting had been progressing. We immediately threw up breastworks of rails, and part of the regiment was ordered out on picket, where the enemy's sharpstooters annoyed us and wounded several.

July 4.—Everything in our front unusually quiet. We lay all day behind the breastworks.

July 5.—At daybreak we found the enemy had retreated, but remained behind our breastworks.

July 6.—Changed our position about one-half mile to the left, behind breastworks, and then marched to Emmitsburg, about 10 miles.

July 7.—Marched from Emmitsburg to Middletown.

July 8.—About 4 p. m. marched to South Mountain, by way of Antietam battle-field, and immediately threw up breastworks along the foot of the mountain with the rest of the brigade.

July 9.—Lay behind the breastworks.

July 10.—Left South Mountain about 9 a. m.; marched about 5 miles, formed line of battle, and threw up fortifications near Boonsborough, Md.

July 11.—Lay all day behind breastworks.

July 12.—Left breastworks and marched within 1 mile of Hagerstown, Md., and about 5 p. m. commenced to throw up breastworks.

July 13.—Lay behind breastworks.

July 14.—Left breastworks about 1 p. m., and marched to Williamsport, Md., and encamped about 1 mile from the town.

July 15.—Left camp near Williamsport about 5 a. m., and halted near Rohrersville.

July 16.—Left camp near Rohrersville, and marched to Berlin, Md.

July 17.—Lay in camp at Berlin, Md.

July 18.—Left camp near Berlin, Md.; crossed the Potomac upon a pontoon bridge, and reached Waterford.

July 19.—Left Waterford, and marched some 5 miles to Harmony Church, Va.

July 20.—Marched to Middleburg and encamped.

July 21.—Remained in camp.

July 22.—Left Middleburg about 6.30 p. m., marched all night, and halted at White Plains, Va., three hours.

July 23.—Continued our march to Warrenton, Va., arriving about 5 p. m.

I append a list of killed, wounded, and missing during July 1, 2, and 3.*

I have the honor to be, very respectfully, your obedient servant,

E. Y. PATTERSON,
Captain, Commanding Regiment.

Lieutenant-Colonel LEECH,
Commanding Brigade.

No. 55.

Report of Brig. Gen. Thomas A. Rowley, U. S. Army, commanding Third Division.

HEADQUARTERS THIRD DIVISION, FIRST ARMY CORPS,
July 28, 1863.

COLONEL: I have the honor to submit the following report of the operations of the division under my command at Gettysburg, Pa., on July 1:

The command itself had devolved upon me the day previous. The division was composed of two brigades : The First, commanded by Col. Chapman Biddle, of the One hundred and twenty-first Pennsylvania Volunteers, consisted of the One hundred and twenty-first, One hundred and forty-second, and One hundred and fifty-first Pennsylvania Volunteers, and the Twentieth New York State Militia; the Second, commanded by Col. Roy Stone, of the One hundred and forty-ninth Pennsylvania Volunteers, consisted of the One hundred and forty-third, One hundred and forty-ninth, and One hundred and fiftieth Pennsylvania Volunteers.

On the morning of July 1, these two brigades were marched in the direction of Gettysburg from different points within 5 or 6 miles of that town, the First Brigade being detached, and directed to take the advance with a battery of four pieces.

Toward 11 o'clock these two portions of my division reached the battle-field from the south, and occupied the several positions assigned them on the right and left of the Lutheran Theological Seminary, at the distance of a half mile or more to the west of it. The brigades were separated then by an interval of from 150 to 200 yards. That portion of the field on which the troops of the Third Division were engaged was undulating, here and there covered with grain, and a small woods extended across it in a westerly direction, nearly dividing the ground into two equal parts. The First Brigade occupied the southern half, and, facing west, formed on the ground

---

*Embodied in revised statement, p. 174.

chosen by our late distinguished corps commander, Major-General Reynolds, to whose skillful selection of the position much of the ultimate success of our army may be attributed. The Second Brigade, facing in the same direction as the First, threw forward its skirmishers, as did also the First, to cover the general line.

During the day the whole division was exposed to a severe direct and enfilading fire, the Second Brigade in the earlier part of the engagement being the principal object of attack. A determined effort of the enemy later to turn my right flank was met by an immediate change of front and so destructive a fire from the Second Brigade that the advancing lines of the rebels, though well covered by artillery, were compelled to fall back with broken ranks to a shelter where they could be reformed.

Colonel Stone having been severely wounded, the command of the Second Brigade was then assumed by Colonel Wister, who, in the repulse of a renewed effort of the enemy, was also disabled, when the command devolved upon Colonel Dana, of the One hundred and forty-third Pennsylvania Volunteers. The position selected by General Reynolds had been steadily and determinedly maintained until nearly 4 o'clock in the afternoon against very greatly superior numbers of the enemy, in order that the other corps of our army, then on the march, might be enabled to reach and occupy the ground selected for future operations.

A general advance of the enemy's infantry was now made in two very strong lines, the right of which greatly outflanked the First Brigade, at that time consisting only of three small regiments, numbering together not over 830 men and officers, the One hundred and fifty-first Pennsylvania Volunteer Regiment having been previously detached from that brigade to support the part of our line on the right of the woods. When the enemy were first observed advancing on their extreme right, they issued from a piece of woods extending north and south, a mile distant from the First Brigade, the brigade being then faced to the north, and almost at right angles with its original position. A change of front of this part of the division was ordered and executed under a heavy fire.

After the change, the One hundred and forty-second Pennsylvania Volunteers and Twentieth New York State Militia were on the right and center of the brigade, and the One hundred and twenty-first Pennsylvania Volunteers on the left, with the battery between the One hundred and forty-second and Twentieth New York State Militia. Notwithstanding the murderous fire with which the enemy were received by my left, the disparity between the contending forces was too great to render it possible for our line to hold its position. The First Brigade gradually fell back, firing, until it reached a cover of rails hastily thrown up by some of the other troops in front of the seminary. Here it remained, together with some men of the First Division, fighting desperately and until time was afforded to most of our other troops, to the artillery, and to the ambulances to withdraw in an orderly manner from the town in the direction of the cemetery, and until the advancing lines of the enemy were gaining our flanks.

At the breastworks, Colonel Biddle, commanding the First Brigade, was wounded in the head by a shot, but he still remained on the field, and retired with his command and reformed it on arriving in the rear of Cemetery Hill, behind which Colonel Dana, with the Second Brigade, with reformed lines, was also again in readiness for service. The Second Brigade on first falling back halted in a peach orchard, where it renewed its fire, giving time for the removal of a battery which had been established there.

The general good conduct of the division renders it difficult to par-ticularize individual acts of gallantry.

I take pleasure in. calling to the notice of the commanding general Col. Chapman Biddle, commanding First Brigade, and Colonel Dana, commanding Second Brigade, and also the following officers, recom-mended by brigade commanders : Colonel Gates, Twentieth New York State Militia; Lieutenant-Colonel McFarland, commanding One hundred and fifty-first Pennsylvania Volunteers (severely wounded); Lieutenant-Colonel McCalmont, of the One hundred and forty-second Pennsylvania Volunteers; Maj. Alexander Biddle, One hundred and Twenty-first Pennsylvania Volunteers; Major Musser, One hun-dred and forty-third Pennsylvania Volunteers; Lieutenant-Colonel Dwight, Captains Irvin and Glenn, One hundred and forty-ninth Pennsylvania Volunteers; Colonel Wister and Lieutenant-Colonel Huidekoper, One hundred and fiftieth Pennsylvania Volunteers; Major Chamberlain, One hundred and forty-ninth Pennsylvania Vol-unteers,* and Adjutant Ashurst, One hundred and fiftieth Pennsyl-vania Volunteers, as being distinguished for bravery. The mem-bers of the Second Brigade staff are likewise favorably noticed.

I would also call to the notice of the commanding general Lieut. William L. Wilson (slightly wounded), acting assistant adjutant-gen-eral; Captain Flagg, assistant inspector-general (killed on July 3), and Lieutenant Moore, One hundred and forty-third Pennsylvania Volunteers, aide-de-camp (all acting on staff July 1), for gallant con-duct.

The death of Colonel Cummins, One hundred and forty-second Pennsylvania Volunteers, a brave and efficient officer, has occasioned feelings of regret throughout the command.

An official list of killed, wounded, and missing has already been returned to headquarters. †

  Yours, &c.,

      THOMAS A. ROWLEY,
 Brig. Gen., Comdg. Third Div., First Corps, Army of Potomac.

Lieutenant-Colonel KINGSBURY,
  Assistant Adjutant-General, First Army Corps.

No. 56.

Reports of Col. Chapman Biddle, One hundred and twenty-first Penn-sylvania Infantry, commanding regiment and First Brigade.

HDQRS. FIRST BRIG., THIRD DIV., FIRST ARMY CORPS,
  In the Field, near Gettysburg, Pa., July 2, 1863.

LIEUTENANT: I have the honor to submit, for the information of the general commanding the division, the following sketch of the operations of the brigade in the action of Wednesday, the 1st instant, near Gettysburg, Pa.:

Early in the morning of the 1st, I was directed to move with the brigade and a battery of four pieces of artillery about 1½ miles in

---
 *One hundred and fiftieth Pennsylvania Volunteers.
 † Embodied in revised statement, p. 174.

advance of the other divisions of the corps toward Gettysburg, where it was supposed the enemy were in considerable force. The route taken by the brigade brought us, about 11 a. m., to within 1 mile of the town, in a westerly direction from it. The heavy firing then heard indicated that a portion of our forces were engaged with the enemy. The brigade was accordingly pushed forward and formed in line as soon as possible on the extreme left, in a field one-third of a mile in front of the seminary and facing west. The battery was also placed in position, and its fire directed toward the northwest, on the left of a piece of woods in which the First Division of the corps was then engaged with the enemy. In front of our line, and at the distance of three-quarters of a mile or more, were woods running nearly parallel with it, and between these woods and our line and toward our left were a brick house and a large stone barn. The barn affording cover to the enemy's sharpshooters, who were then skirmishing in front of us, a company of skirmishers was sent from the Twentieth New York Regiment for the purpose of protecting the battery. The position of the brigade was varied two or three times in order to shelter the men from the heavy artillery fire of the enemy, which at one time enfiladed them from the north. During the morning, rebel infantry were observed on the edge of the woods first referred to, and between 2 and 3 p. m. a large body of them, amounting to a division or more, advanced in two lines toward us. Of the four small regiments constituting the brigade, one (One hundred and fifty-first) had been previously detached to support a portion of the corps to our right and rear. The remaining three were drawn up in the following order: The One hundred and forty-second on the right, Twentieth New York in the center, and the One hundred and twenty-first on the left, the battery occupying a space between the One hundred and forty-second and the Twentieth. Notwithstanding the great disparity of the contending forces, and the left of our line being outflanked by at least one and probably two regiments, and the enemy's fire, direct and oblique, being very severe, the men of the brigade continued to hold their position for some time, until, being without any support, they were compelled about 4 p. m. to retire to a cover on the edge of the town, immediately in front of the seminary. Here they remained, doing good service, checking the farther advance of the enemy, till the batteries and many of the troops in the town had withdrawn in the direction of Belleview Cemetery, when they retired to that point.

The total number of officers and men who went into the action was 1,287; out of this, 440 were either killed or wounded, and 457 are missing,* leaving as the present effective force only 390 officers and men.

As during the greater part of the time the general witnessed the behavior of the troops, it might seem scarcely necessary to make any reference to it, but I would be doing injustice to the officers and men were I not to say that their gallant conduct was even more than could have been expected from men under the trying circumstances of their situation, and in this opinion I think he will heartily concur. I respectfully refer to the list (herewith sent) of those who are reported by their regimental commanders as having particularly distinguished themselves.

It gives me pleasure to make mention of the excellent conduct of Colonel Gates, of the Twentieth New York; Lieutenant-Colonel

---

* But see revised statement, p. 174.

McCalmont, of the One hundred and forty-second Pennsylvania Volunteers, and of Major Biddle, commanding the One hundred and twenty-first Pennsylvania Volunteers. I desire also to call attention to the valuable services rendered me by Captain Warren (One hundred and forty-second Pennsylvania Volunteers), acting brigade inspector, and Lieut. T. M. Hall (One hundred and twenty-first Pennsylvania Volunteers), acting assistant adjutant-general, during the action.

I regret to add that Lieutenant-Colonel McFarland (One hundred and fifty-first Pennsylvania Volunteers) was badly wounded while faithfully discharging his duties. The death of Colonel Cummins, of the One hundred and forty-second [Pennsylvania], a brave and efficient officer, has occasioned feelings of deep regret throughout the command.

I am, very respectfully, your obedient servant,

CHAPMAN BIDDLE,
Colonel 121st Pennsylvania Volunteers, Comdg. Brigade.

Lieut. W. L. Wilson,
Actg. Asst. Adjt. Gen., Third Div., First Army Corps.

—

HEADQUARTERS 121ST PENNSYLVANIA VOL. REGT.,
Near Gettysburg, Pa., July 4, 1863.

LIEUTENANT: I have the honor to report that the command of the First Brigade, which had devolved upon me on the night of June 30 and during July 1, was resumed on the 2d instant by General Rowley. The report of the operations of the brigade on the first day's fight has already been furnished, including that of the One hundred and twenty-first Regiment Pennsylvania Volunteers. I have now to add a few words in reference to the part taken by the regiment on the 2d and 3d instant.

On the morning of the 2d, the regiment was moved into a field to the south of and near the cemetery, and placed under cover of a stone wall by the roadside, where it remained during the forenoon. Toward 12 m. it was exposed to a severe shelling, which reached it from both the front and the rear during a sharp attack made by the enemy on our extreme right. The peculiar shape of the general line of battle, resembling somewhat a flattened horseshoe, will account for this effect. In the afternoon the fire slackened, when the regiment was moved behind a wall on the other side of the road, in which position its defenses were reached by the enemy's musketry. The attack on this part of our line ceased toward evening, when the regiment changed its position to a field in front, and subsequently to the road, where the night was passed.

On the morning of the 3d, the regiment was moved to the left, to a field nearly opposite to our left center, where it remained during the morning, exposed somewhat to the enemy's fire. Toward 1 p. m. a violent cannonading from a very large number of pieces of artillery was concentrated on our position, which continued for upward of two hours and a half without intermission, destroying much of the breastwork sheltering the men, and wounding 3 of them. During the hottest part of this fire the regiment was moved in good order to an adjoining field to the left, and placed behind a breastwork of rails near the crest of a hill, where it remained throughout the attack on the center. This attack, of a most determined character, was finally and successfully repulsed toward sundown by the troops in the first line, supported by our artillery. The steadiness of the men during the fury of the unparalleled artillery fire of the enemy cannot be too highly commended, and to it in some measure may be attributed the brilliant results of this day's operations.

I have the honor to be, very respectfully, your obedient servant,

CHAPMAN BIDDLE,
Colonel One hundred and twenty-first Pennsylvania Vols.

Lieutenant WILSON, *Acting Assistant Adjutant-General.*

No. 57.

Reports of Col. Theodore B. Gates, Eightieth New York Infantry (Twentieth Militia).

HDQRS. TWENTIETH REGT. NEW YORK STATE MILITIA,
In Field, near Gettysburg, Pa., July 2, 1863.

COLONEL: I have the honor to submit the following report of the recent operations of this command:

My regiment joined the brigade near Emmitsburg on the afternoon of the 30th ultimo, and on the following morning at 8 o'clock I marched with the brigade and reached a position near the enemy, about 1½ miles west of Gettysburg, where the brigade was immediately formed in line of battle, faced due north, my battalion holding the left. The brigade was soon afterward moved by the right flank some half a mile to the southeast, and a new line of battle formed, faced to the west. In this position the brigade advanced through the open fields into a valley and to the edge of a piece of woods, where for a time the fire of the enemy's musketry and artillery was quite heavy. We were shortly after ordered to retire over the crest of the hill in the cleared field, where the men were somewhat protected. When in this position, I was ordered to advance a company of skirmishers to a brick house and stone barn opposite our left flank and some eighth of a mile in front, just across the valley before referred to. I detached Captain Baldwin, Company K, for this duty.

About 1 p. m. we moved by the left flank into the Gettysburg road, when this regiment and the One hundred and fifty-first Pennsylvania Volunteers formed line of battle, faced to the north, the other two regiments of the brigade being drawn up in line in front. During this change of front, the artillery fire of the enemy was severe.

At 2.30 p. m. the lines were advanced across the fields and front changed to the left until we resumed the third position of the forenoon. This movement was made under a warm artillery fire. The enemy soon afterward advanced two very strong lines of infantry, and, driving in our skirmishers (I had some time before, at the request of Captain Baldwin and by permission of Colonel Biddle, reenforced Captain Baldwin with Company G, Captain Cunningham), moved rapidly on our lines. Their line extended the front of two regiments beyond our left flank, completely enfilading our line, and pouring a terrible fire into our front and left flank. We held the position until the artillery was removed, and then fell back slowly behind a barricade of rails, some eighth of a mile in our rear and in front of Gettysburg College, the enemy following rapidly in great force. Here the men were rallied and formed behind the barricade, and checked the enemy's advance, and finally compelled him to retire.   He soon advanced again, however, and prolonged his line to our left, again turned our flank, and compelled us to retire.   We fell back through Gettysburg to the high ground south of the town, and formed along the road west of the cemetery, where we were relieved at about 11 o'clock this a. m.   In retiring from the barricade, and until we had reached the interior of the city, we were under the fire of the enemy's infantry upon our rear and both flanks.

I cannot speak in too high terms of the conduct of the officers and men under my command.   It would be unjust to attempt any discrimination when all did their duty so well.

My loss in this action was very heavy, as you will perceive from the report made to you last evening.*

I have the honor to be, colonel, very respectfully.

THEODORE B. GATES,
Colonel, Commanding.

Colonel BIDDLE,
Comdg. First Brig., Third Div., First Army Corps.

—

HDQRS. TWENTIETH REGT. NEW YORK STATE MILITIA,
Near Gettysburg, Pa., July 4, 1863.

GENERAL: I have the honor to submit the following report of the part taken by my regiment and the One hundred and fifty-first Pennsylvania Volunteers, under Captain Owens, in the battle of the 3d instant at this place :

These two regiments had been thrown forward on the afternoon of the 2d as a part of the support of the troops at that time engaged on the left of our line, and when the fighting ceased they were assigned to the front line, a little to the left of the center of our line of battle. The two regiments were put in position behind a rail fence, which they converted into a barricade that afforded some security against the enemy's sharpshooters, and proved of especial service the next day during the artillery and musketry fire.   The two regiments were posted with the Twentieth New York State Militia on the right.   We occupied this line during the night.

Nothing of particular note occurred until 12.30 p. m. of the 3d, when the enemy opened from his right-center battery, which was soon followed by all his guns on his right and center, and the position occupied by my command was swept by a tempest of shot and shell, which continued for nearly three hours, and surpassed, in rapidity of firing and in the number of guns employed, anything I had before witnessed during the war.   As the cannonading subsided, the enemy's infantry began to debouch from the orchard and woods on his right center, and moved in line of battle across the open fields between my position and the highway from Gettysburg to Emmitsburg.   His troops were formed in two lines, the second line, however, not covering the left battalion of the first.   They advanced rapidly, firing as they came, our skirmishers falling back before them.   My men opened upon them when they reached the farther edge of the valley in front of us, and the first line immediately flanked to the left and moved rapidly in the new direction.   As the second line received our fire, it began to oblique to the left, and finally closed its left upon the right of the first line, when all flanked to the

---

* Embodied in revised statement, p. 174.

right and moved forward in one line of battle, firing rapidly. Perceiving that the design was to break through our left center, and gain the heights and batteries covering them, between the road sweeping around the left of the cemetery and the open fields between the enemy's line and ours, I moved my command by the right flank toward our center, corresponding with the enemy's movements, and pouring a continuous fire into his ranks as we advanced. The enemy came forward with unusual determination, and, although his ranks were momentarily thinned, he continued to advance until he reached the fence at the foot of the hill immediately beneath our left-center battery, this affording him considerable protection, and he threw some of his force over the fence and into the slashing on the hillside made to clear the range for our guns. The contest for the possession of this hillside and fence was especially obstinate, and for a considerable time the chances of success appeared to favor first one side and then the other. Each seemed to appreciate the fact that the possession of the heights was all-important, and each fought with the utmost desperation. The men were now within quarter pistol range, and the fence and fallen trees gave the enemy considerable cover. I then ordered an advance, and the two regiments pushed briskly through the slashing to the fence, cheering as they went, and the enemy broke and hastily retreated in great disorder, while we poured into their broken line a heavy and continuous fire. This concluded the fighting at this point, and left us in undisputed possession of the contested ground.

We took a large number of prisoners, and the ground in front was strewn with the dead and wounded of the enemy.

It may not be improper to remark that during this almost hand-to-hand contest the enemy's batteries played upon friend and foe alike, doing quite as much damage in their own ranks as in ours.

Both regiments behaved with great gallantry, and I believe I do them but simple justice when I attest that to their persistent efforts the Army of the Potomac owes very much of its success of the day.

I learned from prisoners that the troops engaged with us were Pickett's division, of Longstreet's corps, and more than six times outnumbered my command.

Among the killed and wounded in my immediate front was one colonel and several line officers. Two colors were left upon the ground by the enemy, and were picked up by some troops who came upon the field from our right after the fighting was over.

The lists of killed and wounded will be speedily submitted.*

I am, yours, &c.,

THEODORE B. GATES,
Colonel, Commanding.

Brigadier-General ROWLEY,
Commanding Brigade.

—

HDQRS. TWENTIETH NEW YORK STATE MILITIA,
Brandy Station, Va., January 30, 1864.

GENERAL: I beg leave to submit the following condensed report of the movements and operations of my command during the three days' battle at Gettysburg:

Marched with brigade at 8 a. m., July 1, and between 10 and 11

* See p. 174.

o'clock that morning encountered the enemy's skirmishers 1½ miles west of Gettysburg, Pa. Line of battle by brigade was immediately formed in the Hagerstown road, my regiment on the left, and the brigade advanced 200 or 300 yards, where it was faced by the right flank and moved through the fields toward Gettysburg, crossing Willoughby's Run between the road and a house and outbuildings, around which our dismounted cavalry were skirmishing.

Reaching the low ground between the seminary and the first ridge west of it, the brigade filed to the left and took position in line of battle on the easterly slope of the ridge and nearly opposite the seminary, facing west. Remaining here a few minutes only, we moved forward over the ridge and down into the ravine through which Willoughby's Run flows, the right of the brigade passing near the grove where General Reynolds fell. Here we first received the enemy's infantry fire, but did not reply to it, and were shortly moved back on to the ridge, all the regiments of the brigade passing over and taking cover under the ridge save mine, which was ordered to halt on the crest, and was faced toward the enemy; but an occasional shot reached us in the position.

Having remained here some twenty minutes, I was ordered to throw out a company of skirmishers to occupy the house and buildings already spoken of, and now on our left and some 30 rods in advance of us. Captain Baldwin, Company K, was detailed for that duty, and soon gained possession of the buildings.

Some two hours afterward he sent me word that he was severely pressed, and asked for re-enforcements. I detached to his aid Captain Cunningham, Company G. These two companies held these buildings until the enemy actually surrounded them on three sides, and had fired the outbuildings and attempted to fire the house, when, to avoid being captured, the men were withdrawn, and, moving through the ravine southerly, and covered in a measure by a small party of our cavalry, they escaped and rejoined the regiment that evening on Cemetery Hill. The regiment was soon afterward moved back into the brigade line.

About 2 p. m. the enemy opened an enfilading fire upon us with two or three Rodman guns planted upon an elevation a mile or more to our right, and upon what seemed to be the shoulder of the ridge under which we were then lying. The brigade was then ordered up, and moved by the left flank partly across the Hagerstown road, when it was halted, and after some ten minutes, during which the enemy obtained a very accurate range of us, the brigade was posted in the road, faced to the north, and partially covered by the fence and bank at the roadside.

Some thirty minutes afterward the brigade was formed in two lines, Colonel Biddle, of the One hundred and forty-second Pennsylvania Volunteers, commanding the first line, and Colonel Gates, of the Twentieth New York State Militia, commanding the second. In this formation the brigade moved across the field at the foot of and parallel with the ridge until we reached a point opposite the seminary, when they changed direction to the left, and while the first line moved toward and nearly opposite the woods where General Reynolds fell, the second moved up to the top of the ridge to support a battery. The enemy were now advancing toward our position in line of battle, and the infantry fire became very severe. The battery was compelled to retire after firing a few rounds, and, finding that our line was rapidly retiring on my right, and the enemy were moving down the Hagerstown road on my left, to cut me off from Gettysburg, I gave the order to fall back, and the troops slowly retired in the direction of the seminary, fighting so obstinately as they moved off that the enemy's pursuit was cautious and tardy.

Reaching the barricade near the seminary, the two regiments were immediately formed in rear of it and on the left of the other regiments of the brigade. The enemy advanced in heavy lines across the field in front, and when they got within short range, we opened on them with such effect that they retired over the ridge. They soon, however, advanced again in greater force, the right of their lines extending across the Hagerstown road and sweeping entirely around our left. The fighting for some time was most desperate.

Colonel Biddle received a wound in the head, and turned over the command of the brigade to Colonel Gates, whose horse was shot under him five times during this brief contest. Colonel Biddle (who but temporarily left the field), after consultation with Colonel Gates, ordered a retreat. At this time nearly, if not quite, all our troops were in full retreat upon Gettysburg, and our brigade was exposed to a murderous fire in front and on both flanks. It was impossible to hold the position longer without sacrificing the brigade. The troops moved off in tolerable order, passing the seminary and taking the railroad into Gettysburg. The Twentieth New York State Militia marched in rear of the brigade, covering the movement, which was executed under heavy fire.

Reaching Cemetery Hill, the brigade was posted in line along the Taneytown road, where it remained until 11 a. m. the next day, when it was relieved.

About 5 p. m. on July 2, the brigade was ordered to the left center, to support the Second Corps, which had been advanced to the relief of the Third. Two regiments only of the brigade—the Twentieth New York State Militia and the One hundred and fifty-first Pennsylvania Volunteers, the latter under command of Captain Owens—reached the front line, where they were halted on the last and lowest of the ridges running nearly north and south between the Taneytown and Emmitsburg roads. Some 300 yards on our right was a bluff, on which were standing a few trees and a battery. The trees on the westerly face of the bluff had been felled to clear a range for the guns. A rail fence stood at the foot of the bluff and extended along the ridge southerly. A little in advance and to our left was a small grove. The ground in front descended gradually to a little valley, wet and marshy, and then by a corresponding ascent reached the Emmitsburg road and the position occupied by the enemy. Some 300 yards in rear of me was a ridge, running parallel to the one I was on, but much higher. On my right was one regiment of Stannard's brigade; on my left two others, and one in rear and partly to my left. Receiving no orders, and finding myself the senior officer of the brigade present, I assumed command of the two regiments, and in the course of the evening constructed a breastwork of the fence heretofore mentioned and of such other material as could be procured.

About 5 a. m. on the 3d, the enemy opened with artillery, and for some time kept up a brisk fire upon our position. This finally ceased, and until about 1 p. m. no further firing took place on this part of the line.

During this interval, the Vermont troops threw up a breastwork to my left and about 100 feet in advance of my line, masked by the small grove before mentioned. The regiment of that brigade on my right took position in rear of this new work, leaving open the space between my right and the bluff, on which was the nearest battery.

At 1 o'clock the enemy opened from his right-center battery, which was soon followed by all his guns on his right and center, and the position occupied by my command was swept by a tempest of shot and shell from upward of one hundred guns for nearly three hours. When the cannonading subsided, the enemy's infantry debouched from the orchard and woods on his right center, and moved in two lines of battle across the fields toward the position I have described. Our skirmishers (from the Vermont brigade) fell back before them, and sought cover behind the breastworks on my left. The enemy came forward rapidly, and began firing as soon as they were within range of our men. When they had approached within about 200 feet of the bottom of the valley heretofore mentioned, the troops of my command opened a warm fire upon them. Almost immediately the first line faced by the left flank, and moved at a double-quick up the valley and toward Gettysburg. The second line followed the movement. Reaching a position opposite the bluff, they faced to the right, and moved forward rapidly in line of battle. Perceiving that their purpose was to gain the bluff, I moved my command by the right flank up to the foot of the bluff, delivering our fire as we marched, and keeping between the enemy and the object of his enterprise. He succeeded in reaching the fence at the foot of the bluff, but with ranks broken and his men evidently disheartened. Some succeeded in getting over the fence into the slashing, from which and behind the fence they kept up a murderous fire. The men were now within quarter pistol-range, and, as the fence and fallen trees gave the enemy considerable cover, I ordered the Twentieth New York State Militia and the One hundred and fifty-first Pennsylvania Volunteers to advance to the fence, which they did, cheering, and in gallant style, and poured a volley into the enemy at very short range, who now completely broke, and those who did not seek to escape by flight threw down their arms. Very few of those who fled reached their own lines. Many turned after having run several rods and surrendered themselves. We took a large number of prisoners, and the ground in front of us was strewn with their dead and wounded. During the latter part of this struggle, and after it ceased, the enemy's batteries played upon friend and foe alike. The troops engaged with us were Pickett's division, of Longstreet's Corps.

Among the killed and wounded in my immediate front was Colonel [J. G.] Hodges, Fourteenth Virginia, and several line officers. Two colors were left upon the ground by the enemy. Thus terminated the final and main attack upon our left center.

It was now nearly 6 p. m., and my command was relieved by a portion of the Second Corps, and withdrawn to the Taneytown road, where it remained through the night. It will thus be perceived that the two regiments I had the honor to command were either actually engaged with the enemy or occupying a position in the front line from the beginning of the battle on the morning of July 1 until its close on the evening of the 3d, excepting only about six hours on the 2d.

I went into action on the 1st with 28 officers and 259 men. I lost during the three days 3 officers killed, 15 wounded, and 1 taken prisoner; enlisted men, 32 killed, 96 wounded, and 23 taken prisoners. Total, 170. My loss in killed and wounded was two-thirds of my officers and half of my men.

I have no report of the casualties in the One hundred and fifty-first Pennsylvania Volunteers. They behaved with the utmost gallantry, and their loss was very severe.

I have the honor to be, general, very respectfully, your obedient servant,

THEODORE B. GATES,
Colonel, Commanding.

A. DOUBLEDAY,
    Major-General of Volunteers.

No. 58.

Reports of Lieut. Col. Alexander Biddle, One hundred and twenty-first Pennsylvania Infantry.

BIVOUAC IN THE FIELD,
Thursday, July 2, 1863.

COLONEL : The One hundred and twenty-first Pennsylvania Volunteer Regiment, under my command, marched from W. R. White's house, in Freedom Township, yesterday morning, Wednesday, July 1. On arriving at the top of the hill bordering the valley in which Gettysburg lies, we were marched into a field on the left of a wood, through which we saw the First Division driving the enemy. We remained in this field, exposed at all times to an enfilading or direct fire, sometimes facing northwardly and sometimes westwardly, as the attack of the enemy varied. A large body of the enemy's troops had been seen to the west of our position throughout the day. While we were taking up a position facing to the north, to support a battery at the corner of a wood, the troops were seen advancing. We were ordered to form to meet them, and changed front to effect it. As the proper position assigned to the One hundred and twenty-first Regiment was immediately in front of the battery, we were moved to the extreme left, with the Twentieth New York on our right. I saw the line of the enemy slowly approaching up the hill, extending far beyond our left flank, for which we had no defense. As the enemy's faces appeared over the crest of the hill, we fired effectually into them, and, soon after, received a crushing fire from their right, under which our ranks were broken and became massed together as we endeavored to change front to the left to meet them. The immediate attack on our front was destroyed by our first fire. The officers made every possible effort to form their men, and Captains Ashworth and Sterling and Lieutenants Ruth and Funk were all wounded. The regiment, broken and scattered, retreated to the wood around the hospital and maintained a scattering fire. Here, with the broken remnants of other regiments, they defended the fence of the hospital grounds with great determination. Finding the enemy were moving out on our left flank, with the intention of closing in on the only opening into the barricade, I reported the fact to the division commander, and by his directions returned to the fence barricade. The rebels, advancing on our left flank, soon turned the position, and our regimental colors, with the few men left with them, moved out of the hospital grounds through the town to our present position, where we now have almost exactly one-fourth of our force and one commissioned officer besides myself.

I beg particularly to call attention to the meritorious conduct of Sergeant [William] Hardy, color-bearer, who carried off the regimental colors, the staff shot to pieces in his hands; also to the gallantry of Captain Ashworth and Lieutenant Ruth, both wounded; also to Lieutenants Funk and Dorr and Captain Sterling. Acting Sergeant-Major [Henry M.] Cowpland, Sergeant [Henry H.] Herpst, in command of Company A, and Sergeant [Charles] Winkworth, are all deserving of high commendation; also Corporal [John M.] Bingham, of Company A.

The constant changes of position which the regiment was ordered to make, and the seeming uncertainty of which way we were to expect an attack, or what position we were to defend, was exceedingly trying to the discipline of the regiment. Their conduct was, in my opinion, far beyond praise.

I also wish to call attention to those whom the men speak of as deserving of high commendation—Sergeants [Robert F.] Bates, [William A.] McCoy, [Joshua L.] Childs (wounded, who insisted on remaining with his company), [John] McTaggart, James Allen, and Charles Barlow, Corporals Daniel H. Weikel and [Edward D.] Knight, and Privates T. B. H. McPherson and William Branson.

Respectfully submitted.

A. BIDDLE,
Major 121st Pennsylvania Volunteer Regiment.

[Col. CHAPMAN BIDDLE,
Comdg. First Brig., Third Div., First Army Corps.]

—

CAMP AT RAPPAHANNOCK STATION, VA.,
August 20, 1863.

LIEUTENANT: In obedience to orders requiring a report of the movement of this command from June 28 to the time of its arrival at Warrenton, I respectfully submit the following statement, in addition to the report already presented of its action on July 1, 2, and 3, on the battle-field of Gettysburg, viz:

July 4.—Remained in position under arms on the battle-field of Gettysburg.

July 5.—Encamped on a slight elevation near by, to avoid the ground, saturated by an exceedingly heavy rain.

July 6.—Marched to near Emmitsburg, and encamped northeast of the town.

July 7.—Marched toward Middletown, and encamped, after crossing a range of hills, about 5 miles from the town.

July 8.—Marched through South Mountain Pass, and bivouacked in position on its western side.

July 9.—Marched to near Boonsborough, on Beaver Dam Creek.

July 10.—Changed position, and constructed a slight breastwork to cover the right flank of the army.

July 11.—Remained in position.

July 12.—Marched through Funkstown, crossed the Antietam, and came under the fire of the enemy's skirmishers. Formed line of battle, and threw up timber and earth defenses.

July 13.—Same position.

July 14.—Moved toward Williamsport, and encamped; no opposition.

July 15.—Retraced our previous day's march, and thence through Keedysville to foot of South Mountain, near Crampton's Gap and farm.

July 16.—Crossed the mountain, and marched through Burkittsville to a point near Petersville and Berlin, and encamped.

July 17.—In camp.

July 18.—Marched through Berlin across Potomac to near Waterford.

July 19.—Marched through Hamilton (Harmony), and encamped.

July 20.—Marched to Middleburg.

July 21.—Remained in camp.

July 22.—At 5.30 p. m., marched, escorting train to White Plains.

July 23.—Marched to Warrenton.

The above concludes the movements of the regiment since the battle of Gettysburg, in which it lost two-thirds of its strength.

June 28.—The regiment marched from Middletown to Frederick, Md.

June 29.—The regiment marched to Emmitsburg.

June 30.—Moved forward about 5 miles, and was sent forward to picket east and west from Marsh to Middle Creek, the center of the line being the cross-roads near to Ross White's house, where the Millerstown (Fairfield and Bull Frog) road and Gettysburg road intersect each other. There is no incident of moment to mention that I am aware of.

Respectfully submitted.

ALEXANDER BIDDLE,
Lieutenant-Colonel, Comdg. 121st Penn. Vol. Regt.

Lieut. W. L. WILSON,
Acting Assistant Adjutant-General.

No. 59.

Report of Lieut. Col. Alfred B. McCalmont, One hundred and forty-second Pennsylvania Infantry.

NEAR GETTYSBURG, PA.,
July 4, 1863.

SIR: I have the honor to submit the following report of the participation of this regiment in the battle of Gettysburg after the close of the operations of July 1:

On the night of the 1st, the men under my command, numbering 80 for duty, lay on their arms in the rear of batteries at the cemetery, and under orders to support them in the event of an attack. We remained in the same position until the evening of the 2d, when, with the regiment of Colonel Biddle (One hundred and twenty-first Pennsylvania Volunteers), we were required to remove to the opposite side of the road. The men lay on their arms during the night but a few rods from their previous resting-place.

Early in the forenoon of the 3d, my command was formed in line with the One hundred and twenty-first Pennsylvania Volunteers on the western side of the road, about 50 rods to the left of the former position. About 2 p. m. the enemy opened a very severe artillery fire on our front and along the whole line. This was followed by a general advance of their infantry. When the latter movement took place, my regiment, with the approval of General Rowley, was advanced to a rude breastwork of rails on the right of the Second Brigade. Another line of our forces lay in front of us. The advance of the enemy at this point was met so promptly and gallantly by the troops in the first line, that the men of my command had neither occasion nor opportunity to do more than fire an occasional shot at a few sharpshooters, who, from covered positions, were trying to pick off the artillerymen in a battery immediately in our rear. The attacking column was completly destroyed or captured, without having materially disturbed the line of our forces in front of this position, and without having made it necessary for the second line, in which we were placed, to participate in the fight. We remained in the same position until 9 p. m., when we were relieved by other troops, and the regiment was withdrawn to a point near the road to rest during the night.

Although my small command was exposed, in common with the rest of the brigade, to a severe artillery fire during the afternoon of the 3d, in addition to an occasional fire of less intensity during the whole of the previous day, we have no serious casualties to report. Two men only were slightly wounded by the explosion of a shell on the afternoon of the 3d.

The fall of Capt. C. H. Flagg, of this regiment, who was a member of General Rowley's staff, and who was killed by a shell on the evening of the 3d, does not come properly within the scope of this report; but I cannot refrain from saying that his loss is deeply deplored by the company which he had long ably led, and by all others who knew him.

While it is true that my remnant of a regiment had but little part in the great results of July 2 and 3, I am glad to say that the officers and men exhibited commendable firmness, and were ready cheerfully to undergo greater trials than fell to their lot.

With great respect, I have the honor to be, your obedient servant,

ALFRED B. McCALMONT,
Lieutenant-Colonel, Commanding.

Lieut. W. L. WILSON,
A. A. A. G., First Brig., Third Div., First Corps.

No. 60.

Report of Lieut. Col. George F. McFarland, One hundred and fifty-first Pennsylvania Infantry.

McALISTERVILLE, JUNIATA COUNTY, PA.,
March 15, 1864.

GENERAL: On the morning of July 1, 1863, at 8 a. m., the One hundred and fifty-first Regiment Pennsylvania Volunteers, under my command, moved from its bivouac on George Spangler's farm, about 6 miles from Emmitsburg, Md., and the same distance from Gettysburg, Pa. The First Brigade, Third Division, First Army Corps, to which it belonged, taking a northeasterly course, crossed Marsh Creek and marched up the left bank of a small stream (Willoughby's Run), debouching about a mile southwest of Gettysburg on the Hagerstown road, where it formed in line of battle, at 10.30 a. m., on the left flank of the First Corps. The One hundred and fifty-first Pennsylvania, being on the left of the brigade, formed the extreme left of the corps.

Our arrival at this point was greeted by the booming of cannon, Buford's cavalry, dismounted, with some artillery having engaged the enemy—the advance of Pender's division of A. P. Hill's corps— a short time previous. Without delay the brigade advanced obliquely to the right, over a small open hollow, to the edge of a ridge west of the Theological Seminary. Here, by the order of General Rowley, knapsacks were unslung, after which we advanced to the top of the ridge. About the same time, General Reynolds having been killed, General Doubleday, our division commander, took command of the corps, General Rowley of the division, and Colonel Biddle, of the One hundred and twenty-first Regiment Pennsylvania Volunteers, of the brigade.

All firing now ceased for perhaps an hour, when, about noon, the enemy opened on our right. As this was a flank fire, we were soon ordered back into the hollow. Here, guarding the batteries, we were subject to a constant fire of shot and shell for two hours and a half, frequently changing our position.

About 2 p. m. the One hundred and fifty-first Pennsylvania Volunteers was detached from the brigade by General Rowley, and ordered to take a position behind a fence running along the south end of the seminary grove.

Shortly after this it occupied a temporary breastwork made of rails, stumps, &c., by the Second Brigade, Second Division, through the west edge of the grove, and parallel with the seminary.

By this time a line of battle was forming in our front, which soon after advanced to the ridge west of the seminary, occupied earlier in the day. In this line there was a gap or interval left immediately in our front between the balance of our own brigade and General Meredith's brigade, of the First Division, on the right. Into this interval the One hundred and fifty-first Pennsylvania Volunteers was ordered by General Rowley in person, and, crossing the breastwork behind which it lay, it advanced and closed the interval. The position of the regiment was now such that a little more than one-half of its left wing extended beyond the strip of woods on the ridge directly west of the seminary. The enemy greeted me with a volley which brought several of my men down, ere I had halted in position. Having previously cautioned the men against excitement and firing at random, and the enemy being partly concealed in the woods on lower ground than we occupied, I did not order them to fire a regular volley, but each man to fire as he saw an enemy on which to take a steady aim. This was strictly observed, and during the next hour's terrific fighting many of the enemy were brought low.

I know not how men could have fought more desperately, exhibited more coolness, or contested the field with more determined courage than did those of the One hundred and fifty-first Pennsylvania Volunteers on that ever-memorable day. But the fire of the enemy, at least two to one, was very severe and destructive, and my gallant officers and men fell thick and fast. This was especially true after he, while moving to outflank the forces on my left, suffered very heavily from our deliberate oblique fire; for exasperated, no doubt, by this, his fire was now concentrated upon us. Notwithstanding this, the regiment held its ground and maintained the unequal contest until the forces both on my right and left had fallen back and gained a considerable distance to the rear. Then, finding that I was entirely unsupported, exposed to a rapidly increasing fire in front, and in danger of being surrounded, I ordered the regiment to fall back, which it did in good order, to the temporary breastwork from which it had advanced, the enemy following closely, but cautiously. Here I halted, with fragments of Meredith's brigade on my right and portions of the Twentieth New York State Militia, One hundred and twenty-first Pennsylvania Volunteers, and One hundred and forty-second Pennsylvania Volunteers, on my left. An unknown mounted officer brought me the flag of this latter regiment to know whether it was mine. The colonel having already fallen, I ordered it to be placed on my left, and portions of the regiment rallied around it and fought bravely.

We now quickly checked the advance of the enemy. In fact, having the advantage of breastworks and woods, our fire was so destructive that the enemy's lines in front were broken, and his first attempt to flank us greeted with such an accurate oblique fire that it failed. But in a second attempt, made soon after, he gained our left flank, moving in single file and at double-quick. Up to this time the officers and men under my command had fought with the determined courage of veterans, and an effectiveness which the enemy himself respected and afterward acknowledged (to me in conversation while a prisoner in their hands). Not a man had left the ranks, even to carry a wounded comrade to the rear. But the regiment had lost terribly, and now did not number one-fourth of what it did two hours earlier in the day. The enemy, on the contrary, had increased, and was now rapidly forming on my left. All support had left both flanks and were already well to the rear. Hence I ordered the shattered remnants of as brave a regiment as ever entered the field to fall back, and accompanied it a few paces. Then stopping, perhaps 20 paces from the seminary, I turned, and, stooping down, examined the condition of the enemy in front.

At this instant, 4.20 p. m., I was hit by a flank fire in both legs at the same instant, which caused the amputation of my right leg, and so shattered my left that it is now, at the end of eight and a half months, still unhealed and unserviceable. I was carried into the seminary by Private [Lyman D.] Wilson, of Company F, the only man near me, and who narrowly escaped, a ball carrying away the middle button on my coat-sleeve while my arm was around his neck.

The regiment, passing on, had gained the north end of the seminary, and was fortunately covered from the flank fire (volley) which wounded me. It moved through the town to Cemetery Hill, where 8 officers and 113 men answered to roll-call next morning, though 21 officers and 446 men had gone into the fight. Two captains remained, one of whom (Captain Owens, of Company D) commanded the regiment during the second and third days of the battle. It participated in the glorious repulse of the enemy's final charge on the left center on the evening of the third day, and was complimented in an order you (General Doubleday) issued the next day. Adjutant Allen and several men were wounded, and Lieutenant Trexler, of Company K, killed. It is with pleasure that I refer to the bravery and efficiency of the officers and the heroic, self-sacrificing spirit manifested by the men of the One hundred and fifty-first Pennsylvania Volunteers.

I regret the loss of the many gallant patriots who lost their lives or received honorable scars in its ranks ; but I rejoice it was in the battle of Gettysburg and in defense of human freedom and republican institutions.

Of course, you have a detailed statement of the losses of my regiment.* I will add, however, that by the 6th of July 173 wounded officers and men were collected in the seminary hospital, where I lay, from it alone, while many others were in other hospitals or had perished on the field.

As you doubtless have an official report, and this is prepared for your own gratification, I have written freely and more at length than otherwise. I have stated nothing, however, but what I know or have good reason to believe to be correct, and consequently hope this report may correspond to or agree with other reports and observations you may have collected.

Respectfully submitted.

GEO. F. McFARLAND.

Maj. Gen. A. DOUBLEDAY.

No. 61.

Report of Col. Roy Stone, One hundred and forty-ninth Pennsylvania Infantry, commanding Second Brigade.

———, —— —, 1863.

GENERAL: I have the honor to report that, in accordance with orders received directly from yourself, at 11 o'clock a. m., July 1, I posted my brigade (One hundred and forty-third, One hundred and forty-ninth, and One hundred and fiftieth Pennsylvania Volunteers) between the two brigades of Wadsworth's division, upon the ridge in advance of Seminary Ridge, my right resting upon the Chambersburg or Cashtown road and left extending nearly to the wood occupied by General Meredith's brigade, with a strong force of skirmishers thrown well down the next slope, and the road held by a platoon of sharpshooters.

The skirmishers having to advance over an open field, without the slightest shelter, and under a hot fire from the enemy's skirmishers concealed behind a fence, did not stop to fire a shot, but, dashing forward at a full run, drove the rebel line from the fence, and held it throughout the day. As we came upon the field, the enemy opened fire upon us from two batteries on the opposite ridge, and continued it, with some intermissions, during the action. Our low ridge afforded slight shelter from this fire, but no better was attainable, and our first disposition was unchanged until between 12 and 1 o'clock, when a new battery upon a hill on the extreme right opened a most destructive enfilade of our line, and at the same time all the troops upon my right fell back nearly a half mile to the Seminary Ridge.

This made my position hazardous and difficult in the extreme, but rendered its maintenance all the more important. I threw one regiment (One hundred and forty-ninth, Lieutenant-Colonel Dwight commanding) into the road, and disposed the others on the left of the stone building, to conceal them from the enfilading battery. My line thus formed a right angle facing north and west. Soon after, as the enemy's infantry was developed in heavy force upon the right, I sent another regiment (One hundred and forty-third, Colonel Dana) to the right of the One hundred and forty-ninth. At about 1.30 p. m. the

* See p. 174.

grand advance of the enemy's infantry began. From my position I was enabled to trace their formation for at least 2 miles. It appeared to be a nearly continuous line of deployed battalions, with other battalions in mass or reserve. Their line being formed not parallel but obliquely to ours, their left first became engaged with the troops on the northern prolongation of Seminary Ridge. The battalions engaged soon took a direction parallel to those opposed to them, thus causing a break in their line and exposing the flank of those engaged to the fire of my two regiments in the Chambersburg road. Though at the longest range of our pieces, we poured a most destructive fire upon their flanks, and, together with the fire in their front, scattered them over the fields.

A heavy force was then formed in two lines parallel to the Chambersburg road, and pressed forward to the attack of my position. Anticipating this, I had sent Colonel Dwight (One hundred and forty-ninth) forward to occupy a deep railroad cutting about 100 yards from the road, and when they came to a fence within pistol-shot of his line he gave them a staggering volley; reloading as they climbed the fence, and waiting till they came within 30 yards, gave them another volley, and charged, driving them back over the fence in utter confusion.

Returning to the cut, he found that the enemy had planted a battery which perfectly enfiladed and made it untenable, and he was obliged to fall back to the road. Colonel Dana meanwhile had been engaged with the enemy directly in his front and preventing them from outflanking Colonel Dwight on the right, and Colonel Wister had been holding our original line, now the left front. Being wounded about this time and carried from the field, I cannot speak so definitely of the remainder of the action.

Colonel Wister (One hundred and fiftieth) assumed command of the brigade, and finding the enemy were advancing from the northwest, brought up his own regiment, and, making a new disposition, drove back that force. Again they advanced from the north, and, struggling over the railroad cut, came nearly to the road, but a vigorous bayonet charge drove them back. Another attack from the west was met by another change of front and repulsed. Colonel Wister being wounded, the command devolved on Colonel Dana, who continued to contest the position with varying fortunes until it was reported that the enemy had turned his left flank as well as his right. An officer who was sent to learn the truth of the report found the wood occupied by the enemy; this made a retreat necessary to prevent being completely surrounded, and the command fell back, making an occasional stand and fighting all the way to Seminary Ridge. There a firm stand was made and a battery brought off; thence the retreat was continued through the town, in which the troops suffered heavily from the fire of the enemy, who already occupied the streets on both their flanks. Of the part taken by the remnant of my brigade in the battle of the 2d and 3d, report was made by Colonel Dana, commanding.

No language can do justice to the conduct of my officers and men on the bloody "first day;" to the coolness with which they watched and awaited, under a fierce storm of shot and shell, the approach of the enemy's overwhelming masses; their ready obedience to orders, and the prompt and perfect execution, under fire, of all the tactics of the battle-field; to the fierceness of their repeated attacks, or to the desperate tenacity of their resistance.

They fought as if each man felt that upon his own arm hung the fate of the day and the nation. Nearly two-thirds of my command fell on the field. Every field officer save one was wounded and disabled. Their names are to be found already in your general report. Not one of them left the field until completely disabled. Colonel Wister, while commanding the brigade, though badly wounded in the mouth and unable to speak, remained in the front of the battle, as did also Lieutenant-Colonel Huidekoper, commanding One hundred and fiftieth, with his right arm shattered and a wound in the leg, and Lieutenant-Colonel Dwight, commanding One hundred and forty-ninth, with a dangerous gun-shot wound through the thigh. Not being in possession of the regimental reports, I regret that I cannot do justice to the line officers who were particularly distinguished, and for the same reason I have been unable to give as complete an account of the action as I could have wished. To the courage and skill of regimental commanders is due in great measure the successful maintenance of the position.

The officers of my own staff present, and to whose bravery and intelligence high praise is due, were Lieutenant [John E.] Parsons, acting assistant adjutant-general, and Lieutenants Dalgliesh and Walters, aides-de-camp. The two latter served also under Colonel Wister and Colonel Dana while those officers commanded the brigade, and received from them the highest commendation.

Lieutenant Walters is especially praised for his gallantry in rallying and leading in repeated charges such portions of the troops as had become detached from their commands.

I have the honor to be, general, very respectfully, your obedient servant,

ROY STONE,
Colonel 149th Pennsylvania Volunteers.

Maj. Gen. A. Doubleday.

No. 62.

Report of Col. Langhorne Wister, One hundred and fiftieth Pennsylvania Infantry, commanding Second Brigade.

Hdqrs. Second Brig., Third Div., First Army Corps,
Rappahannock, Va., September 12, 1863.

Colonel: I have the honor, in accordance with orders received from headquarters Third Division, to report the action taken by this brigade in the battle of Gettysburg on July 1, 2, and 3.

Before proceeding with the report, I would state that the brigade was commanded first by Col. Roy Stone, then by the undersigned, and lastly by Col. E. L. Dana, of the One hundred and forty-third Pennsylvania Volunteer Regiment.

This brigade encamped on the evening of June 30 at a point about 6 miles from Gettysburg and on the north side of Marsh Creek. On the morning of July 1, at about 9.30 o'clock, it took up its line of march for Gettysburg. After marching about 3 miles very slowly, cannonading was heard in our front, and an order was received to march the men as fast as possible, which was done, the brigade arriving at or near the Gettysburg Seminary at about 12 m. Colonel

Stone there ordered the men to unsling and pile knapsacks and to load, which having been done he moved the command in column by battalion toward a house and barn on the Chambersburg pike. The One hundred and fiftieth Regiment occupied the ground to the left of the house, its right resting near the One hundred and forty-third and left about 300 yards from General S. Meredith's command (of First Division). The One hundred and forty-third occupied the space between the barn and house, the One hundred and forty-ninth being on the right of the barn, with no support in sight upon its right flank. The whole line faced to the west. From unslinging knapsacks to this time a heavy cannonading was directed upon us by the enemy, killing and wounding a number of men, under which the brigade behaved with the utmost coolness. After being in the position above mentioned for some time, Colonel Stone ordered a change to be made, as the range of the enemy's guns was so exact. This change was effected also with the greatest coolness. The ground or line now occupied by the brigade was in the form of a right angle, the right of the One hundred and fiftieth and left of the One hundred and forty-ninth Regiments being within 100 yards of the barn, respectively, the One hundred and forty-third regiment accompanying the right of the line.

In the meantime one company from each regiment had been detached as skirmishers (these companies were, of the One hundred and fiftieth, Capt. G. W. Jones; One hundred and forty-third, Capt. C. M. Conyngham; One hundred and forty-ninth, Capt. J. C. Johnson), and were engaged with the skirmishers of the enemy. These companies fought splendidly, and retarded the advance of the enemy greatly, they being, however, at last driven in. The enemy advanced in column by battalion slowly but steadily until they came to about 150 yards from our line, when a well-directed fire was delivered upon them from our whole front, killing and wounding many and driving the remainder of their first line almost entirely to the rear of the second line, with the exception of some who succeeded in getting into the railroad cut, which was in front of the One hundred and forty-third and One hundred and forty-ninth Regiments. Upon these, Colonel Stone ordered a charge to be made by the One hundred and forty-ninth, which was entirely successful in driving them out. The One hundred and forty-ninth then took up its original position on the Chambersburg turnpike, and awaited the advance of the second rebel line, and the first one, now reformed.

About this time Colonel Stone was wounded severely, and was carried into the barn before spoken of. The command then devolved upon me. By this time a furious musketry fire was again going on along the whole line, and soon the enemy began another advance, in the greatest force, on the front of the One hundred and forty-ninth and One hundred and forty-third Regiments. I accordingly divided the One hundred and fiftieth into two wings—the right under Lieutenant-Colonel Huidekoper, the left under Maj. T. Chamberlain. That under Lieutenant-Colonel Huidekoper I ordered to change front forward, so as to occupy the same line as the One hundred and forty-third and One hundred and forty-ninth Regiments. This it did in good order, though under a very severe musketry fire. The left wing of the One hundred and fiftieth was kept in its former position, to keep in check three times its number. The gradual advance of the enemy had by this time brought many of them into the railroad cut again; consequently I ordered a charge to be made by the One hundred and forty-ninth and right wing of the One hundred and fiftieth Regiment, which was as successful in driving the enemy out as the former one.

About this time, Lieut. Col. W. Dwight, commanding One hundred and forty-ninth Regiment, was wounded in the thigh; Maj. T. Chamberlain, commanding left wing One hundred and fiftieth Regiment, through left breast and shoulder; Lieutenant-Colonel Huidekoper, commanding right wing One hundred and fiftieth Regiment, through the upper bone of right arm; also Adjt. R. L. Ashurst, One hundred and fiftieth Regiment, through the arm. Five minutes after, I was wounded in the mouth, which made it impossible for me longer to command; consequently I sent word to Col. E. L. Dana to take command of the brigade. In five minutes after, the advance of overpowering numbers of the enemy compelled the brigade to fall back gradually, which they did, fighting all the way. Colonel Dana being at this time in command, I extract from his report:

Facing to the rear, our lines were withdrawn in good order to a point midway between the barn and the spot designated as the peach orchard. The brigade was again halted in the rear of and as a support to a battery of artillery, and again renewed its fire. The supply of ammunition, 60 rounds per man, becoming exhausted, was here renewed. On the withdrawal of the artillery, this command moved on toward and through the town, falling in with the rear of other divisions, sustaining with them a destructive fire in its passage through the streets, and at length reached and was halted upon Cemetery Hill.

Formed in line in the rear of a battery, the men here bivouacked for the night. With the exception of skirmishing between ours and the advance posts, and the occasional interchange of artillery fire, the morning of Thursday, July 2, in this immediate part of the line, passed in comparative quiet.

In the afternoon, a severe engagement occurred upon our left, and simultaneously a cannonade opened between our batteries on Cemetery Hill and the enemy.

Later in the afternoon, this brigade, together with the First, was moved at double-quick and under a sharp fire about half a mile toward the left, to re-enforce that portion of the line. The One hundred and forty-ninth and One hundred and fiftieth Regiments were advanced, under Captains Glenn and Jones, some 600 yards to the front, until they encountered and engaged the pickets of the enemy. Remaining in position until morning, this detachment succeeded in bringing off the field two pieces of artillery and caissons, and rejoined the brigade.

On the morning of July 3, during the interval between the firing, this command threw up a rude breastwork of rails and stone in front of its position, which was in the second line, and held and occupied the same during the terrific cannonade and the final and decisive infantry struggle which have rendered this day historical.

The conduct of both officers and men during this tremendous struggle was all that could be desired from the most exacting. On the first day the brigade was in the most imminent danger of being cut off, as no order had been received to retire, and the enemy occupied the ground on our left flank, which was left vacant by the withdrawal of the Iron Brigade (General Meredith). The Eleventh Corps, which, in a measure, supported our right, had withdrawn some time before. The determined resistance of this command alone saved it, the enemy supposing a much larger force in their front.

Having first taken position about 12 m., the brigade did not retire until after 3 p. m., when all other troops had left the field, and only left the seminary at about 3.40 o'clock. Taking into consideration that the force opposed to it was more than twice as large, the result is wonderful. The enemy had, to my certain knowledge, six regiments, any one of which contained 500 men, all of which were in full view, opposed entirely to this small brigade. Col. Roy Stone, during the time he was in command, displayed the utmost coolness and skill, and deserves much credit for the position taken up, which had not to be materially changed during the action (until the retreat commenced), and for the movements made upon the field. Col. E. L. Dana conducted the retreat from the barn to Cemetery Hill, and was during that time distinguished for his coolness and judgment.

Lieutenant-Colonel Huidekoper, One hundred and fiftieth Regiment, kept the field for a long time after his right arm was shattered, as did also Lieutenant-Colonel Dwight, commanding One hundred and forty-ninth Regiment.

Maj. T. Chamberlain and Adjutant Ashurst, of the One hundred and fiftieth Regiment, behaved in the most gallant manner. The line officers of the whole brigade also behaved, with scarcely an exception, splendidly.

Colonel Dana mentions Captains Jones and Glenn, of the One hundred and fiftieth and One hundred and forty-ninth Regiments, respectively, who commanded after their field officers were wounded, as being of great service to him.

Lieuts. William M. Dalgliesh and B. Walters, of the personal staff of Colonel Stone, and afterward of myself and Colonel Dana, behaved during the whole fight brilliantly, riding into the hottest of the fire. Each had a horse killed, the former under him, the latter while standing near him.

I herewith submit the following report of casualties in this brigade : Killed, 115; wounded, 429; missing, 284.   Total, 828.*

The brigade went into action with 1,300 men.

I am, very respectfully, your obedient servant,

LANGHORNE WISTER,
Col. 150th Pennsylvania Volunteers, Comdg. Second Brig.

No. 63.

Report of Col. Edmund L. Dana, One hundred and forty-third Pennsylvania Infantry, commanding Second Brigade.

HDQRS. SECOND BRIG., THIRD DIV., FIRST ARMY CORPS,
Camp near Warrenton Junction, Va., July 29, 1863.

SIR : The command of the brigade devolved upon me early in the action of July 1, in the midst of a severe fire, and after the preliminary dispositions of the several regiments to receive the enemy had been made.   Up to this time my attention had been chiefly occupied with my own regiment—One hundred and forty-third Pennsylvania Volunteers.   All the field officers of the One hundred and forty-ninth and One hundred and fiftieth Pennsylvania Volunteer Regiments are absent by reason of wounds received in the first day's engagement, and it is possible, therefore, that omissions may occur in the following report.

On the morning of July 1, the brigade, comprising the One hundred and forty-third, One hundred and forty-ninth, and One hundred and fiftieth Pennsylvania Volunteers, marched from Marsh Creek, where it had halted the previous evening, and, when within some 2 miles of Gettysburg, a heavy firing at the front indicated that the advance had become engaged with the enemy.   Hurrying forward to a point a short distance west or northwest of the town, the brigade formed in column of regiments, and, leaving knapsacks and blankets behind, agreeably to orders, advanced at a double-quick

---

*But see revised statement, p. 174.

through fields and up a gentle ascent toward the enemy. Attaining the crest of the hill or slope, a line was formed to the right and somewhat in advance of the First Brigade, with the One hundred and fiftieth Regiment on the left, the One hundred and forty-third in the center, and the One hundred and forty-ninth upon the right. The One hundred and fiftieth and One hundred and forty-third occupied the interval between a grove of woods on the left (in or near which General Reynolds was killed) and a barn and stone dwelling on the right, while the One hundred and forty-ninth was formed on an extension of the line to the right of the barn and between it and the railroad cut. The troops occupied this position for a short time under a fire of round shot and shell, when the enemy's advance, preceded by skirmishers, was discovered, and at the same time an artillery fire was opened on our right, enfilading our line. Company B, of the One hundred and fiftieth Pennsylvania Volunteers, under Capt. G. W. Jones; Company A, of the One hundred and forty-third Pennsylvania Volunteers, under Capt. C. M. Conyngham, and Company K, of the One hundred and forty-ninth, under Capt. John C. Johnson, were deployed to the front as skirmishers, and soon after became warmly engaged. Later in the day, Company E, of the One hundred and forty-ninth, under Capt. Z. C. McCulloch, was detached for like duty, and these four companies, under their gallant officers, were employed in this service during the early part of the engagement, and until forced back by overwhelming numbers upon the main line.

The attack upon our right became so severe that a partial change of front was necessary, and the One hundred and forty-third and One hundred and forty-ninth Regiments, under a severe fire, were formed in a line, facing the right and at a right angle with the first line, along a road which runs parallel with and distant about 100 yards from the railroad cut. The One hundred and forty-third Regiment took position to the right of the One hundred and forty-ninth, while the One hundred and fiftieth retained its original position, being merely deployed to occupy the space between the grove and barn, and fill up the interval exposed by the removal of the One hundred and forty-third to its new position. This movement had scarcely been completed when the enemy advanced against our entire front in large numbers, and, when within easy range, were received with an effective fire from our whole line, which threw them into confusion, and a charge by the One hundred and forty-ninth forward to the railroad cut being made, they fell back to a sheltered position, where they were re-enforced and their broken ranks reformed.

At about this point in the action, Colonels Stone, of the One hundred and forty-ninth, and Wister, of the One hundred and fiftieth, having been wounded, I took command of the brigade. The contest soon became severe and close. Three successive assaults upon our line were repulsed, in which we sustained heavy losses in killed and wounded, but the enemy evidently, from the numbers left upon the ground at each repulse, suffered still more severely.

The brigade went into position at about 11 a. m.; became engaged about noon. The conflict had continued until about 4 p. m., when a more heavy advance by the enemy was made and again checked by a well-directed fire, but the support both upon our right and left having been withdrawn, his superior numbers enabled the enemy to extend his lines, so as to threaten both our flanks and rear.

In addition to Colonels Stone and Wister, Lieutenant-Colonel

Dwight, commanding the One hundred and forty-ninth, Lieutenant-Colonel Huidekoper, Major Chamberlain, and Adjutant Ashurst, of the One hundred and fiftieth, with most of the commissioned officers of three regiments, had been wounded. These casualties, with the heavy loss of enlisted men, made it necessary, in order to save the command from capture or entire destruction, to move to some point of support. Facing to the rear, the line was withdrawn in good order some distance toward the town, where it was halted, and several volleys were fired at the advancing enemy. Moving thence nearer the town to a peach orchard, not far from where the railroad embankment begins, the brigade was again halted, and, together with a portion of a battery of artillery and parties that had become separated from their regiments, renewed the fire. The supply of ammunition—60 rounds per man—having been exhausted, was here replaced and expended.

On the withdrawal of the artillery, this command moved along the embankment toward and through the town, the last organized body of troops, I believe, to leave the field, and, falling in with numbers of the First Division, First Army Corps, and some of the Eleventh Corps, passed through the streets under a destructive fire, and between 5 and 6 p. m. reached and was halted on Cemetery Hill. A line was formed near a low wall facing the town, and the arrival and position of what remained of the brigade were reported to the division and corps commanders.

With the exception of some skirmishing between the advanced posts and occasional artillery firing, the morning of Thursday, July 2, on this part of the field passed in comparative quiet.

In the afternoon, a severe engagement occurred on our left, and simultaneously a cannonade opened between our batteries on Cemetery Hill and those of the enemy. Later in the day this brigade, with the First, moved at a double-quick and under a sharp fire about half a mile to the left and front, to re-enforce that portion of the line. The One hundred and forty-ninth and One hundred and fiftieth Regiments, under Captains Glenn and Jones, were here advanced some 600 yards, until they encountered the enemy's pickets, and in the morning rejoined the brigade, bringing with them two pieces of artillery and caissons recovered from the field.

On the morning of Friday, July 3, during intervals between the artillery firing, this command threw up a slight breastwork of rails and stones in front of its position, which was in the second line, and held it during the terrific cannonade in the afternoon and the decisive and final infantry charge of General Longstreet, which have rendered this day historical.

The conduct of both officers and men during this protracted contest, with few exceptions, merits the highest commendation. The lines were formed, changes of front made, under heavy fire, with steadiness and precision; and the final withdrawal from the field, on the first day, under the pressure of overwhelming numbers upon flank and rear, was effected without panic or confusion.

Where all behaved so well, it seems unjust to particularize, yet I cannot withhold my acknowledgment of the coolness and ability of Maj. John D. Musser, commanding the One hundred and forty-third; of Captain Glenn, commanding the One hundred and forty-ninth after Lieutenant-Colonel Dwight and Acting Maj. John Irvin, in the fearless discharge of their duties, had been wounded, and of Capt. G. W. Jones, both upon the skirmish line and in command of the

One hundred and fiftieth after the field officers of that regiment had been disabled.   Lieuts. William M. Dalgliesh and B. Walters, acting aides, rendered efficient services during the first and also the second and third days' engagement.   The horse of the former was shot under him; that of the latter while temporarily dismounted.

Brigade Surgeon Reamer, One hundred and forty-third Pennsylvania Volunteers ; Surgeon Quinan, of the One hundred and fiftieth; Assistant Surgeons Fulton, of the One hundred and forty-third, and Hunter, of the One hundred and forty-ninth Regiments, detailed for hospital duty at the beginning of the action of July 1, were taken prisoners in the town, but continued their care of the wounded until it was reoccupied by our troops.   Assistant Surgeon Scott, of the One hundred and forty-third Regiment, remained with the regiment and was faithful in his attention to the wounded of July 2 and 3.

This command marched from Gettysburg on the morning of July 6, following up with other troops the retreat of General Lee.

On the afternoon of the 10th, coming up with his rear at or near Funkstown, Md., preparations were made for an attack.   My brigade being in the front line, skirmishers were thrown out, and a brisk fire opened.   Night came on, and the enemy withdrew.   Our troops advanced to the Potomac, crossed into Virginia, and by easy marches came on to this place.   The following is a statement of the casualties sustained by this brigade :

The One hundred and forty-third Pennsylvania Volunteers went into action July 1 with 465 men.

Officers and men.	Killed.	Wounded.	Prisoners.	Missing.	Total.
Commissioned officers	1	10	....	....	11
Enlisted men	20	130	65	26	241
Total	21	140	65	26	252

The One hundred and forty-ninth went into action with 450 men.

Officers and men.	Killed.	Wounded.	Prisoners and missing.	Total.
Commissioned officers	1	*12	4	17
Enlisted men	33	159	127	319
Total	34	171	131	336

The One hundred and fiftieth Pennsylvania Volunteers went into action with 400 men.

Officers and men.	Killed.	Wounded.	Prisoners and missing.	Total.
Commissioned officers	1	†10	4	15
Enlisted men	28	141	80	249
Total	29	151	84	264

*2 field and 10 line.   † 4 field and 6 line.

The brigade went into action July 1 with 1,315 men.

Officers and men.	Killed.	Wounded.	Prisoners and missing.	Total.
Commissioned officers	3	32	8	43
Enlisted men	81	430	298	809
Total	84	462	306	852

By far the larger portion of this loss was sustained July 1. Very respectfully submitted.

EDMUND L. DANA,
Colonel, Comdg. Second Brig., Third Div., First Army Corps.

Maj. E. C. BAIRD,
Asst. Adjt. Gen., Third Div., First Army Corps.

No. 64.

Reports of Lieut. Col. John D. Musser, One hundred and forty-third Pennsylvania Infantry.

CAMP NEAR GETTYSBURG, PA.,
July 4, 1863.

COLONEL: I have the honor to make a report of the participation of the One hundred and forty-third Pennsylvania Volunteer Regiment in the battle of Gettysburg, July 1, after the command was turned over to me, which occurred while holding the road west of the town, where the One hundred and forty-ninth and One hundred and forty-third had been ordered by command of Colonel Stone.

It was in the hottest of the fire that I assumed the command, and had simply to hold the position, which we did as long as it could be held without being all captured, as the enemy were rapidly falling back on our left and flanking us on the right.

Up to this time but few had been killed or wounded. Capts. G. N. Reichard, Plotz, and Conyngham, among the officers, were wounded early in the action; Captain Reichard alone left on the field.

After the enemy had driven the One hundred and forty-ninth from our left, I gave the command to move back. After crossing the crest of a hill, which lay a quarter of a mile in our rear and toward the town, we halted, faced about, and fired several volleys, checking their advance in front but not on our flanks. We then fell back to a peach orchard, where our battery was stationed. We again halted, and, with others, saved the battery, leaving the men (not ours) to pull it out of range by hand. It was with great difficulty I could get all the men to fall back from this point, which was a good one, and in front of which the enemy fell thick and fast. Still they moved in columns on our right and left, and superior numbers compelled us to fall back to the town, which, I might say, was done in good order, and only when peremptorily ordered to do so. The road from this hill (Battery Hill) to town was 10 to 12 feet high, and crossed over a stream and low meadow. Before leaving, the enemy had come out of the

woods on our right (as we faced the enemy at the battery), and it was
while going through the meadow my men fell so rapidly that I concluded to take them on the other side of this high road. But the
balls and shell were as thick, if not thicker, on the right as on the
left side.

While making the observation, I received a ball through my pants,
slightly wounding the skin near the knee. I rejoined the regiment,
knowing this to be the safest side. I felt like making another stand,
but utter destruction would have been inevitable, as the enemy deployed as soon as they left the woods, making intervals between their
men, which gave them a decided advantage over us. I am pleased
to say my men behaved nobly, and fought under great disadvantage
and against greatly superior numbers.

Among the officers killed I have to record that of Lieut. Charles
W. Betzenberger, who was wounded in the hand early in the action,
but nobly stood at the head of his company while supporting the
battery in the peach orchard. He moved back only when ordered,
and fell, mortally wounded, near the town.

Among the wounded I have the honor to report the name of Capt.
Charles M. Conyngham, of Company A, who was wounded while
out skirmishing, but remained with his company, and remained at
the peach orchard until the order was given to move back. I saw
him, after we had passed through the town, seemingly exhausted, and
ordered my horse back to help him up the hill, but, just as he was
mounting, he was again shot in the hip, after which I did not see him,
but am happy to report his wounds are not of a dangerous character.
Lieut. C. C. Plotz was wounded early in the action, and also afterward again on the road into town. Capt. George N. Reichard, of
Company C, was wounded in the shoulder while holding the road,
and afterward taken prisoner. Capt. Asher Gaylord, of Company
D, was wounded in both legs while in the peach orchard, and left
on the field. Lieut. William Lafrance, of Company E, was shot
through the arm while passing through the town. Capt. William
A. Tubbs, slight wound in head and taken prisoner. Lieut. H. M.
Gordon, shot through the leg, and taken prisoner while crawling
after the regiment. Lieut. Lyman R. Nicholson, wounded through
the shoulder after leaving the peach orchard; supposed to be of a serious character, but refused to have any one remain with him on the field.
Lieut. O. E. Vaughan, of Company K, received a slight bruise on
the head from a ball, although not close enough to cut the skin, yet
may properly be called a wound.

I am happy to say that among those not killed or wounded, all,
with one exception, stood at their posts and acted in the most becoming and commendable manner, deserving of the highest praise
and commendation.

John Jones, jr., adjutant, reported himself wounded, although I
have not been able to learn where, or whether sufficiently serious to
have prevented him rejoining his regiment after passing through
the town, and therefore report him among the doubtful.

Lieut. Benjamin F. Walters, of the One hundred and forty-third
Regiment, but on your staff, showed great bravery, and distinguished
himself, being conspicuous on all parts of the field; but I suppose he
will come more properly under the head of your report.

In summing up my report of the casualties of the day, I have to
report as follows: Killed, 1 officer and 19 non-commissioned officers
and privates; wounded, 10 officers and 116 non-commissioned officers

and men; prisoners, 65, and missing 25—most of the latter supposed to be either killed, wounded, or prisoners. Entered the battle with 465.

It was our first engagement, and if any censure be attached to our regiment, it must be for not falling back sooner.

I have the honor to remain, yours, very respectfully,

JNO. D. MUSSER,
Major, Comdg. 143d Regt. Pennsylvania Volunteers.

—

CAMP NEAR HARPER'S FERRY, VA.,
——, —— —, 1863.

COLONEL: In continuing my report of the three days' fight at Gettysburg, I must begin with the position occupied by the One hundred and forty-third Pennsylvania Volunteer Regiment on the morning of July 2.

We were ordered first to occupy a position in the rear of a battery a little south of Cemetery Hill, and upon which a most determined and incessant fire was kept up the greater part of the afternoon, but without effect, owing to the enemy's shot being too high. The failure to silence the battery at this point compelled the enemy to make an attack farther to our left, to which part of the line our brigade was double-quicked, to assist in driving back the enemy and recapturing some guns.

We lay upon our arms all night in line of battle. I am happy to be able to say that both officers and men behaved nobly, notwithstanding the severity of our loss on the previous day.

No casualties occurred to my command during the day.

July 3.—This morning at daylight we commenced throwing up such breastworks as could be made, in the absence of tools of any kind, with rails and stones. In the course of the forenoon, we succeeded in getting together quite a number of both, proving a tolerable shelter for my men, who were placed directly in the rear of a battery which had been captured, but retaken again, the day before.

In the afternoon the enemy opened upon us. We had not taken our position yet, but lay some distance in the rear. While doing so, a shell struck in Company D, instantly killing 1 and wounding others. I then ordered my men up to the breastwork, after which no shell struck among the men, but a number were wounded with pieces. We remained under the concentrated fire of several batteries, but all proved useless; they could not silence our batteries, and made the attack with infantry, farther to our right. The column in front swung round upon the flank of the enemy. Our line did not move from the support of the battery.

I have the honor to report that all of my command stood at their posts amid all the iron that filled the air.

Early in the action, Capt. C. K. Hughes received a slight wound from a piece of shell, and left the field.

The casualties of the day are as follows: 1 commissioned officer and 14 non-commissioned officers and privates wounded, 1 missing, and 1 man out of Company D killed.

I have the honor to be, your obedient servant,

JNO. D. MUSSER,
Lieut. Col., Comdg. 143d Regt. Pennsylvania Vols.

No. 65.

Report of Lieut. Col. Walton Dwight, One hundred and forty-ninth Pennsylvania Infantry.

HDQRS. 149TH REGIMENT PENNSYLVANIA VOLUNTEERS,
September 12, 1863.

COLONEL: Relative to the part enacted by the One hundred and forty-ninth Regiment Pennsylvania Volunteers at the late battle of Gettysburg, I have the honor to submit the following report of the first day :

Wednesday, July 1, as we were moving on Gettysburg from the Emmitsburg direction, and within 1½ miles of the town, an order came back to quicken pace to a double-quick, which was immediately done, when we also broke to the left of the town, passing in rear of the First and Second Divisions of the corps, which were then in position and engaging the enemy about 1½ miles in front of Gettysburg, in the Chambersburg direction, line of battle of the First Corps being at right angles with the Chambersburg pike and to the left. My regiment was ordered into position on the right flank of the corps line of battle, and at right angles with same, being in parallel line with the Chambersburg pike; the One hundred and fiftieth Regiment on my left and at right angles with me; the One hundred and forty-third Pennsylvania Volunteers on my right and in parallel line. During all this time we were subjected to a heavy artillery fire from both front and right flank, the one proceeding from A. P. Hill's (rebel) line, 1 mile distant on the Chambersburg pike, the other from Ewell's (rebel) line to our right, and about three-quarters of a mile distant. We suffered severely from the latter. Previous to my getting into position on the pike, Col. Roy Stone, commanding the brigade, ordered me to throw out companies as skirmishers—one to deploy in front of the One hundred and fiftieth Regiment, and proper front of the corps, the other on the right flank and in my front. I ordered Captain Johnson, Company K, to the front of the One hundred and fiftieth Regiment. The order was promptly executed, the men moving out on double-quick, and immediately engaging the enemy on the skirmish line, a short distance in advance of the One hundred and fiftieth Regiment's line of battle. They were soon compelled to retire to the line of the One hundred and fiftieth Regiment, where they remained during the balance of the engagement. The skirmishing of Johnson was lively. Loss, severe; conduct, excellent.

In the meantime I had ordered Captain McCullough, of Company E, to my front 100 paces, to rail fence, where he engaged the enemy's advance, which was then moving on us from the right. This order was also promptly obeyed, and reflects much credit on Captain McCullough and his command for the gallant manner it was executed. During this time, and after getting in position on the pike, in accordance with orders from Colonel Stone, I directed my regiment to fire over the heads of my skirmishers at the enemy, about one-third of a mile distant on the brow of a hill, who were then massing in large force preparatory to a general advance on our right and on the Eleventh Corps, which was stationed across the roads to our right and rear. At this time the One hundred and fiftieth Regiment was hotly engaged with a brigade of the enemy from A. P. Hill's corps, the One hundred and forty-third Regiment not yet engaged, but lying down in line of battle to my right.

In the meantime the enemy, who had been massing on our right, made a furious advance on the Eleventh Corps in large force, and at the same time moved on my front with one brigade of three regiments, whereupon Colonel Stone ordered me to move my regiment forward and take possession of the railroad cut, about 50 paces to my front ; also to plant my colors 20 paces on the left flank of the regiment; all of which was accomplished in good order and while the enemy were moving over the low ground between the two positions; consequently our change of position was unknown to the enemy.

My skirmishers were gradually driven in, when I ordered them to take position on the right of the regiment, my men being deployed in single line in the cut, their arms resting on the bank, with orders to take deliberate aim at the knees of the front rank of the enemy as he came up. My position was undiscovered by the enemy until he reached a rail fence, 22 paces in my front, when he saw my colors flying, and immediately ordered the first battalion of his brigade to fire, my regiment not suffering therefrom, as it was directed at the colors. I now ordered my regiment to fire by battalion. Its effect on the enemy was terrible, he being at the time brigade *en masse*, at 9-pace interval. He now broke to the rear in great confusion. In the meantime I had ordered my regiment to load, when the enemy advanced the second time, and made a most desperate effort to carry my position by assault, in which we handsomely repulsed him by reserving our fire until we could almost reach him with the muzzles of our pieces. Again he fell back. This fight was of the most desperate character, we losing heavily, the enemy's dead and wounded completely covering the ground in our front.

At this stage of the contest, and during the heat of the fight in our front, the enemy had planted three or four pieces of artillery in an orchard on our left, about half a mile distant, commanding the cut I occupied, and had also, under cover of the hill we were fighting over, succeeded in moving up on my left flank part of a brigade, all of which was discovered in time to save my regiment by moving it rapidly back to my first position on the pike, but, I regret to inform you, not in time to save our colors, which were still where I first planted them, 20 paces on the left flank of the regiment, the color-guard all being killed or wounded while defending them. To have saved my colors would have been to advance between two forces of the enemy, both my superiors in numbers ; also to have put my command under an enfilade battery fire. It would have been certain surrender or destruction. I saved the regiment and lost the colors.

The One hundred and forty-third Pennsylvania Volunteers during all this time had remained in their original position on the pike, but now poured in on the enemy, who were advancing on their front, a vigorous fire, the One hundred and fiftieth still holding stubbornly its first line, although fighting desperate odds. Colonel Stone, commanding brigade, was wounded and carried from the field immediately after ordering me forward to the railroad cut. However, the first disposition of the brigade was not changed during the entire day, although we were actually fighting three of the enemy's brigades with our three regiments—a sufficient comment upon the excellent disposition of the command by Colonel Stone in the beginning of the engagement.

Col. Langhorne Wister, of the One hundred and fiftieth Regiment, now commanded the brigade. The enemy in the meantime broke over the hill, partially to our front and flank, in large force, whereupon they received such a reception at the hands of the right wing of the One hundred and fiftieth and my regiment that they soon retired with heavy loss. The enemy had also, under face of a heavy fire from the One hundred and forty-third, succeeded in occupying the railroad cut I had just vacated, and were giving us much trouble. Whereupon Colonel Wister ordered me to charge them out, which our boys and the right wing of the One hundred and fiftieth did in gallant style, completely clearing them out. We again occupied our original position, but were fearfully decimated in both officers and men, not having at this time one-half the number we went into the engagement with. The One hundred and fiftieth were as badly off as ourselves, all its field officers being compelled to leave the field from severe wounds, although they had up to this time gallantly remained, cheering their men on to noble deeds by their actions, although wounded.

Early in the engagement my acting major was also compelled to leave the field on account of wounds received in the head. Having no other field officers, and myself suffering severely from a wound through the thigh, received at the railroad cut early in the action, the enemy slowly closing up on our rear in large force, also working in rapidly on our flanks, owing to the withdrawal of the First and Second Divisions and the breaking way of the Eleventh Corps on our right flank, we had no other resort left but to retire in the direction of the town, which we did slowly, contesting the ground inch by inch back to the Gettysburg Seminary, where we made a most desperate stand with the fragments of the brigade, and succeeded in holding the ground against vastly superior numbers until one of our batteries stationed here could limber to the rear, when the brigade was taken from the field by Colonel Dana, who did most gallant work on the retreat from McPherson's barn to the seminary, he protecting the flank resting on the railroad cut against great odds by the hardest fighting.

I was compelled, from exhaustion and loss of blood, to drop down at this latter point.

I would here mention Captain Glenn, of my regiment, commanding provost guard, Third Division, as having conducted his command very gallantly, he after the first day commanding the regiment until the return of Captain Irvin, acting major, wounded in the head the first day.

The regiment, although under fire the remaining three days' fight, lost but slightly. Their actions—everywhere commendable, knowing, as every man did from the beginning of the engagement, that we were fighting vastly superior numbers, with no reserve, the contest being hand to hand, and in the face of all this every man obeying every order cheerfully, and in every instance every man performing his whole duty—certainly must challenge the admiration of all. Where all did so well it is impossible for me to discriminate in favor of any single individual. However, of the line officers, I would particularly speak of Capt. A. J. Sofield, Company A, who fell while gallantly leading his command on the railroad cut in the second charge. As a gentleman and man possessed of true courage and coolness he had no superior. We deeply regret his loss. I would also mention Capt. Brice H. Blair, of Company I, as having particularly distinguished himself for bravery and coolness, he gallantly keeping the field after losing an arm, until loss of blood compelled him to retire. Also Capt. John H. Bassler, of Company C, severely wounded early in the fight. His coolness and bravery are unquestionable. I would also mention in the same category Captains Soult and Jones, of Companies H and G. Their conduct was splendid; both severely wounded. Captain Johnson, of Company K, captured by the enemy at the Gettysburg Seminary, is worthy of particular mention, he having distinguished himself throughout the entire day.

I would also in this connection bear evidence of the excellent conduct of Colonel Stone's staff, I having been particularly aided, after losing nearly all of my own officers, by Lieutenants Dalgliesh and Walters, the latter more especially under my attention and at my assistance, and for gallantry not excelled by any man in the command.

Please find below a list of killed, wounded, and missing ;* and here allow me to remark that the missing are nearly all wounded and prisoners, we being compelled to leave all our severely wounded behind. Having no official notification of their whereabouts, I have to report them missing.

We entered the engagement with about 450 men, and came out with about 100, leaving our casualties about 350, or a loss of a little over three out of four.

I am, colonel, very respectfully, your most obedient servant,

WALTON DWIGHT,
Lieutenant-Colonel, Comdg. 149th Pennsylvania Volunteers.

Col. LANGHORNE WISTER,
    Comdg. Second Brig., Third Div., First Army Corps.

No. 66.

Report of Capt. John Irvin, One hundred and forty-ninth Pennsylvania Infantry.

HEADQUARTERS 149TH REGT. PENNSYLVANIA VOLS.,
July 17, 1863.

SIR : I have the honor to submit the following report of the part taken by the One hundred and forty-ninth Regiment Pennsylvania Volunteers in the late engagement near Gettysburg, Pa. :

On the morning of July 1, our regiment, under command of Lieutenant-Colonel Dwight, forming a part of the Second Brigade (commanded by Colonel Roy Stone), Third Division, First Army Corps, marched from a point about 4 miles north of Emmitsburg, Md. When we arrived within about 2 miles of Gettysburg, Pa., we heard the fire of artillery in the direction of the town, when we received orders to double-quick and come up under the fire of the enemy's guns. We formed into line, marched forward in a direction northwest of the town, and, arriving at a barn near by, we received orders from Colonel Stone to lie down and shelter ourselves from the fire of the enemy.

---

*Embodied in revised statement, p. 174.

We remained in this position for a period of fifteen or twenty minutes, when our regiment was ordered to take a position on a road leading from the town, crossing our line at right angles, we occupying the right of the brigade.   After we had been there some time, the One hundred and forty-third Regiment Pennsylvania Volunteers, commanded by Colonel Dana, took their position on our right, which left us in the center, the One hundred and fiftieth Regiment Pennsylvania Volunteers being on our left.   These dispositions were made under a very heavy fire from the enemy's batteries on our front and left flank.   We remained in this position until a line of the enemy's infantry made its appearance on our front.   Company E was then ordered out as skirmishers, Company K having been ordered out as skirmishers before we had changed our front to the road, which now placed them upon our left.   When the enemy came up to the proper distance, we received orders to fire, which was done very briskly and with good effect, breaking the first line of the enemy.   We were then ordered forward by Colonel Stone, and advanced in line to a deep railroad cut, which ran parallel with our line and about 100 yards in front.   Our regiment went into this and lay along the opposite side, pouring in a sharp fire over the top of the bank.   After remaining here a few minutes, a second line of the enemy came up, and we were compelled to fall back to our former position on the road, where we remained firing on the advancing line.   They were finally repulsed, falling back in disorder.

Colonel Stone received a severe wound while making the charge, and was carried off the field.

Colonel Wister, now commanding the brigade, ordered us forward on a second charge.   When near the railroad cut, a third line of the enemy made its appearance, compelling us to fall back again to the road.   During this time we were receiving a galling fire on our left, which prevented the left wing of the regiment from making a stand on the road, which changed front, faced to the left, where the One hundred and fiftieth Regiment was then engaged.

I received a slight wound in the head at this time, and went to the hospital to have it dressed ; was there but a short time when I was taken prisoner; consequently cannot give you a report of the part this regiment subsequently took.

Colonel Wister was wounded early in the engagement, and Colonel Dana assumed command of the brigade.   Lieutenant-Colonel Dwight, commanding the regiment, was wounded in the leg about the time I left the field.

The brigade fell back to a position on Cemetery Hill, where the command of the regiment devolved upon Captain Glenn.   He commanded from the evening of the 1st to the morning of the 6th instant, when I reported to the regiment for duty, and have commanded since.

We marched from near Gettysburg, leaving there the morning of the 6th instant, to near Funkstown, Md., where we encountered the enemy.   We were placed in the front line, and built a rifle-pit under a sharp fire from the enemy's skirmishers.   This was Sunday, the 10th instant.   The regiment suffered none at this place.

In the engagement of the 1st instant, both officers and men behaved with great gallantry, not leaving the field until they were completely overwhelmed by the enemy's advancing columns, when they received orders to fall back.   I believe our brigade was the last to leave the field.

The following are the casualties of the regiment:

Officers and men.	Killed.	Wounded.	Missing.	Total.
Officers........	1	12	4	17
Enlisted men........	33	159	127	319
Total.......	34	171	131	336

The regiment went into action with about 450.

I am, very respectfully, your obedient servant,

JOHN IRVIN,
Captain, Comdg. 149th Regt. Pennsylvania Vols.

Lieut. WILLIAM M. DALGLIESH,
Acting Assistant Adjutant-General.

No. 67.

Report of Lieut. Col. Henry S. Huidekoper, One hundred and fiftieth Pennsylvania Infantry.

————, ————, 1863.

SIR : Report of the action of the One hundred and fiftieth Regiment Pennsylvania Volunteers at Gettysburg, Pa., on July 1:

On the morning of July 1, the One hundred and fiftieth Regiment Pennsylvania Volunteers left camp near Emmitsburg, and about noon arrived on the battle-field at Gettysburg. Rapidly throwing off their knapsacks, the regiment moved up on the ground between the Iron Brigade and the other regiments of Colonel Stone's brigade, which reached to the Chambersburg road. After lying under shelling for an hour, the command of the regiment fell to me, Colonel Wister taking command of the brigade. Almost immediately, by order of Colonel Wister, a change of front forward on first company was made with regularity and promptness, and in that new position, protected by a fence, our men awaited the charge of a rebel regiment which was attempting to flank the One hundred and forty-third and One hundred and forty-ninth Regiments, which had gallantly repulsed an attack in their front. At the distance of 50 yards, a volley was poured into the rebels, which staggered them so completely that a second one was fired before an attempt was made to advance or retreat. At this juncture, Colonel Wister ordered the regiment to charge, and led it in person. The rebels were utterly routed, and the colors of the One hundred and forty-ninth Pennsylvania Volunteers, which had been lost, were recaptured and restored to that regiment.

The One hundred and fiftieth then fell back to the position from which it had advanced. The firing of the enemy, who was approaching in front of the corps, now became fearful, and the regiment changed front to rear to meet this new attack. The movement was made in perfect order, and then bravely did the men move to the front, following the color-sergeant, who rushed to place his standard on the small rise of ground in advance. Four companies again changed **front to resist the flank attack, while the remainder of the regiment** fought one entire brigade, which was prevented from advancing by a high fence. The severe loss attending fighting at such odds soon compelled our men to give way, but a battery coming up on our left, another stand was necessary, and again was the regiment moved forward until the battery had wheeled around and moved to the rear. At this moment a wound compelled me to relinquish the command to Captain Widdis, Major Chamberlain having been severely wounded some time before.

I cannot praise too highly the conduct of both officers and men. It was all that could have been desired. Among the many brave, I would especially commend for coolness and courage Major Chamberlain, Adjutant Ashurst, Lieutenants Sears, Chancellor (who lost his leg and has since died), Bell, Kilgore, Color-bearer [John] Pieffer, Sergeant [Duffy B.] Torbett, and Corporal [Roe] Reisinger.

The regiment numbered, including 17 officers, before the battle nearly 400 at roll-call; in the evening but 2 officers, 1 of those wounded, and 84 men were present. As far as I can learn, the number killed was about 60; the rest were wounded or captured.

I am, your obedient servant,

H. S. HUIDEKOPER,
Lieut. Col. One hundred and fiftieth Pennsylvania Vols.

Lieutenant DALGLIESH,
A. A. A. G., Second Brig., Third Div., First Corps.

No. 68.

Report of Capt. George W. Jones, One hundred and fiftieth Pennsylvania Infantry.

CAMP NEAR BERLIN, MD., *July* 17, 1863.

SIR: I have the honor to report that, on the 1st instant, this regiment was drawn into line of battle on the west side of Gettysburg, Pa., in front of the enemy, and ordered to divest themselves of everything but their guns, accouterments, haversacks, and canteens. This being done, Company B was detailed as skirmishers, who advanced about one-half mile, and engaged the enemy for three-quarters of an hour, when the main body of the regiment became engaged, and did not retire until compelled to do so by the advance of a line of battle of the enemy, when they fell back to the main line of the regiment.

After the skirmishers were sent out, the regiment advanced a short distance, and took advantage of a slight rise in the ground as a protection against the enemy's shells. Here the regiment lay for nearly three hours under a heavy fire of artillery, when the enemy's line of battle advanced from the woods into the open field, and we were ordered to advance to a fence on the highest ground in our front. The enemy's line of infantry opened fire upon us as soon as we made our appearance, and we became hotly engaged for some time, when the enemy's line was compelled to give way, and they fled in confusion. A second line advanced and met with the same fate. A third and much stronger line appeared in our front and on both flanks, which forced our flanks to retire, and we were ordered by you to fall back, which was done in good order, to a battery in our rear. Here we rallied, and engaged the enemy for a short time, when we again received the order to fall back, which was done through the second line of defenses on Cemetery Hill, and formed into line. Our ammunition being entirely exhausted, we were here supplied with 60 rounds of cartridges.

On the 2d, we supported a battery until about 6 p. m., when we were ordered to the front and on the left of the Fifth Corps as pickets. We were ordered to advance our line until we encountered the enemy's line of pickets, which was done, and we exchanged a few shots and were ordered to fall back, bringing with us two guns and caissons.

Our line of pickets was stationed about 600 yards in front of the defenses, and remained here until the morning of the 3d, when we were relieved by a line of skirmishers, and retired to the second line of defenses, under a heavy fire of shell from the enemy's batteries. This command lay all day and night of the 3d under all the heavy cannonading of that memorable day.

Inclosed is a statement of the casualties in this command.

Officers and men.	Killed.	Wounded.	Missing.	Total.
Commissioned officers	1	6	4	11
Enlisted men	28	141	80	249
Total*	29	147	84	260

Most respectfully, yours,

G. W. JONES,
Captain Company B, Comdg. 150th Pennsylvania Vols.

Colonel DANA,
Comdg. Second Brig., Third Div., First Army Corps.

No. 69.

Report of Brig. Gen. George J. Stannard, U. S. Army, commanding Third Brigade.

HDQRS. THIRD BRIG., THIRD DIV., FIRST ARMY CORPS,
Gettysburg, Pa., July 4, 1863.

SIR: I have the honor to report that the Second Vermont Brigade, under my command, marched from the line of the Defenses of Washington, upon the Occoquan, on the 25th ultimo, under orders to report to Major-General Reynolds, commanding the First Army Corps. The brigade joined that corps at this place on the evening of July 1, after an exhausting march of seven days' duration. The distance marched averaged about 18 miles per day. The men marched well, with no straggling. Rain fell on every day of the seven, and considering the condition of the roads, the distance traveled (from the mouth of Occoquan to Gettysburg) could not have been accomplished in less time.

---

* But see revised statement, p. 174.

We reached the battle-ground in front of Gettysburg too late in the day to take part in the hard-contested battle of July 1, and my tired troops upon their arrival were placed in position in column by regiments on the front line, in connection with the Third Army Corps. Before reaching the ground, the Twelfth Regiment, under command of Colonel Blunt, and Fifteenth Regiment, under command of Colonel Proctor, were detailed, by order of General Reynolds, as guard to the wagon train of the corps in the rear. I was detailed, per order of Major-General Slocum, as general field officer, and met Major-General Meade, in company with Major-General Howard, near my command about 3 a. m. of the 2d instant. The Fifteenth Regiment rejoined the brigade in the morning, but was again ordered back on the same duty about noon.

On the morning of the 2d instant, we were allowed to join the First Army Corps, and reported to Major-General Doubleday, agreeably to previous orders, and were placed in the rear of the left of Cemetery Hill. After the opening of the battle of July 2, the left wing of the Thirteenth Regiment, under command of Lieutenant-Colonel Munson, was ordered forward as support to a battery, and a company of the Sixteenth Regiment was sent as a support to the skirmishers in our front. While stationing them, Capt. A. G. Foster, assistant inspector-general of my staff, was seriously wounded by a ball through both legs, depriving me of his valuable services for the remainder of the battle.

Just before dark of the same day, the lines of our army on the left center having become broken under a desperate charge of the enemy, my brigade was ordered up. The right wing of the Thirteenth Regiment, under Colonel Randall, was in the advance, and, upon reaching the break in the line, was granted by Major-General Hancock, commanding upon the spot, the privilege of making the effort to retake the guns of Company C, regular battery, which had just been captured by the enemy. This they performed in a gallant charge, in which Colonel Randall's horse was shot under him. Four guns of the battery were retaken, and two rebel field pieces, with about 80 prisoners, were captured by five companies of the Thirteenth Regiment in this single charge. I placed the Sixteenth, under command of Colonel Veazey, on picket, agreeably to orders, extending to the left of our immediate front. The front thus established was held by my brigade for twenty-six hours.

At about 4 o'clock on the morning of the 3d, the enemy commenced a vigorous artillery attack, which continued for a short time upon my position. During its continuance, I moved the Fourteenth, under command of Colonel Nichols, to the front of the main line about 75 yards, which was done at double-quick in good order. I then, with permission from my immediate commander, selected a position to occupy, if attacked with infantry, some distance in front of the main line.

At about 2 p. m. the enemy again commenced a vigorous attack upon my position. After subjecting us for one and one-half hours to the severest cannonade of the whole battle, from one hundred guns or more, the enemy charged with a heavy column of infantry, at least one division, in close column by regiments. The charge was aimed directly upon my command, but owing apparently to the firm front shown them, the enemy diverged midway, and came upon the line on my right. But they did not thus escape the warm reception prepared for them by the Vermonters. During this charge the enemy suffered from the fire of the Thirteenth and Fourteenth, the range being short. At the commencement of the attack, I called the Sixteenth from the skirmish line, and placed them in close column by division in my immediate rear. As soon as the change of the point of attack became evident, I ordered a flank attack upon the enemy's column. Forming in the open meadow in front of our lines, the Thirteenth changed front forward on first company; the Sixteenth, after deploying, performed the same, and formed on the left of the Thirteenth, at right angles to the main line of our army, bringing them in line of battle upon the flank of the charging division of the enemy, and opened a destructive fire at short range, which the enemy sustained but a very few moments before the larger portion of them surrendered and marched in—not as conquerors, but as captives. I then ordered the two regiments into their former position. The order was not filled when I saw another rebel column charging immediately upon our left. Colonel Veazey, of the Sixteenth, was at once ordered to attack it in its turn upon the flank. This was done as successfully as before. The rebel forces, already decimated by the fire of the Fourteenth Regiment, Colonel Nichols, were scooped almost *en masse* into our lines. The Sixteenth took in this charge the regimental colors of the Second Florida and Eighth Virginia Regiments, and the battle-flag of another regiment. The Sixteenth was supported in this new and advanced position by four companies of the Fourteenth, under command of Lieutenant-Colonel Rose.

The movements I have briefly described were executed in the open field, under a very heavy fire of shell, grape, and musketry, and they were performed with the promptness and precision of battalion drill. They ended the contest in the center and substantially closed the battle. Officers and men behaved like veterans, although it was for most of them their first battle, and I am content to leave it to the witnesses of the fight whether or not they have sustained the credit of the service and the honor of our Green Mountain State.

The members of my staff—Capt. William H. Hill, assistant adjutant-general; Lieuts. George W. Hooker and G. G. Benedict, aides-de-camp; Lieutenant [Francis G.] Clark, provost-marshal, and Lieut. S. F. Prentiss, ordnance officer—executed all my orders with the utmost promptness, and by their coolness under fire and good example contributed essentially to the success of the day.

There were 350 killed, wounded, and missing from my three regiments engaged; of the missing, only 1 is known to have been taken prisoner.

I am, with much respect, your obedient servant,

GEO. J. STANNARD,
Brig. Gen. of Vols., Comdg. 3d Brig., 3d Div., 1st A. C.

Lieut. Col. C. KINGSBURY, Jr.,
Assistant Adjutant-General.

ADDENDA.

GENERAL ORDERS, } HDQRS. THIRD DIV., FIRST ARMY CORPS,
No. —.   }   *July* 4, 1863.

The major-general commanding the division desires to return his thanks to the Vermont Brigade, the One hundred and fifty-first Pennsylvania Volunteers, and the Twentieth New York State Militia, for their gallant conduct in resisting, in the front line, the main attack of the enemy upon this position, after sustaining a terrific fire from seventy-five to one hundred pieces of artillery. He congratulates them upon contributing so essentially to the glorious and, it is to be hoped, the final victory of yesterday.

By command of Major-General Doubleday:

EDWARD C. BAIRD,
Captain, and Assistant Adjutant-General.

No. 70.

Report of Col. Francis V. Randall, Thirteenth Vermont Infantry.

CAMP NEAR MIDDLETOWN, MD.,
July 10, 1863.

GENERAL: In compliance with your request, I make the following report of the part taken by my regiment (Thirteenth Vermont) July 1, 2, and 3 instant:

Prior to June 24, my regiment was doing picket duty on the Occoquan River, from Occoquan Bay to near Wolf Run Shoals, headquarters near the village of Occoquan. The balance of our brigade (Second Vermont Brigade) was stationed at or near Union Mills.

On the evening of June 24, I received orders to call in my pickets and join the brigade at Centreville, which I did on June 25. The brigade consisted of the Twelfth, Thirteenth, Fourteenth, Fifteenth, and Sixteenth Vermont Regiments, commanded by Brig. Gen. George J. Stannard. The brigade then marched to Gettysburg, arriving there on July 1, at about 5 p. m. My regiment, with the Fourteenth and Sixteenth, took position on Cemetery Hill, in rear of our line of battle, made up of the First and Eleventh Corps.

On the morning of the 2d, we occupied substantially the same position until about 2 p. m., when I was ordered to advance five of my companies, under Lieutenant-Colonel Munson, to support a battery in our front. Soon after this, I was ordered to advance the balance of my regiment a little to the front and to the left of our former position, which brought us nearly in rear of the right of the Second Corps. This took me entirely out of the line occupied by the rest of our brigade, and I received no further orders from our brigade headquarters during the remainder of that day. A heavy fight was going on in our front, in which the Second and Third Corps were engaged, and we received some injury from the artillery fire of the rebels without being able to engage in the fight. At this time an officer, whom I did not know at the moment, but who proved to be General Doubleday, came galloping over the hill from General Hancock's position, and approached my regiment. After having found what regiment we were, and making a few inspiriting remarks to my men, he directed me to take my regiment in the direction from which he had come, and report to General Hancock, whom I would find there, and hard pressed, and he said he feared he would lose his artillery or some of it before I could get there. I started, riding in advance of my regiment to meet General Hancock and find where I was needed, so as to be able to place my men in position without exposing them too long under fire. As I reached the ridge or highest ground between the cemetery and Little Round Top Mountain, I met General Hancock, who was encouraging and rallying his men to hold on to the position. He told me the rebels had captured a battery he had had there, and pointed out to me the way they had gone with it, and asked me if I could retake it. I told him I thought I could, and that I was willing to try. He said it would be a hazardous job, and he would not order it, but, if I thought I could do it, I might try. By this time my regiment had come up, and I moved them to the front far enough so that when I deployed them in line of battle they would leave Hancock's men in their rear. They were now in column by divisions, and I gave the order to deploy in line, instructing each captain as to what we were to do as they came on to the line, and, taking my position to lead them, gave the order to advance.

At this time my horse was killed, and I fell to the ground with him. While on the ground, I discovered a rebel line debouching from the woods on our left, and forming substantially across our track about 40 rods in our front. We received one volley from them, which did us very little injury, when my men sprang forward with the bayonet with so much precipitancy that they appeared to be taken wholly by surprise, and threw themselves in the grass, surrendering, and we passed over them. General Hancock followed up the movement, and told me to press on for the guns and he would take care of the prisoners, which he did, and we continued our pursuit of the guns, which we overtook about half way to the Emmitsburg road, and recaptured them, with some prisoners. These guns, as I am told, belong to the Fifth U. S. Regulars, Lieutenant Weir. There were four of them.

We were now very near the Emmitsburg road, and I advanced my line to the road, and sent my adjutant (James S. Peck) back to inform General Hancock of our position. While he was gone, the rebels advanced two pieces of artillery into the road about 100 rods to the south of us, and commenced to shell us down the road, whereupon I detached one company, and advanced them under cover of the road, dug way, and fences, with instructions to charge upon and seize those guns, which they did most gallantly. We also captured the rebel picket reserve, consisting of 3 officers and 80 men, who had concealed themselves in a house near by.

In pursuance of orders from General Hancock, we now slowly fell back to the main line of battle. It was dark, and no further operations took place on our part that night.

In the morning of the third day of the battle, we were placed in the front line, to the left of Cemetery Hill. In this position we remained, sustaining the same against the heavy assaults which were made on our position during the day.

During the heavy artillery fire on the afternoon of that day, preceding Longstreet's great charge, my regiment being badly exposed, I asked permission to advance it a little to the front, about 15 rods, so as to take advantage of some rocky points that emerged from the ground, and also the more favorable conformation of the ground. This was granted me, and I immediately advanced my regiment to the more favorable position, and the Fourteenth Vermont, which occupied the position next to my left, also advanced, so as to conform to my line. This placed us that much farther to the front than the regiments to the right and left of us, but gave us a very favorable position, which we immediately strengthened with loose stones and rails that we found in the vicinity. Before we had fairly completed our little arrangements, the great charge commenced, and the course they took brought them directly on these two regiments. Our general officers were quite solicitous for this position, General Hancock repeatedly coming to me and giving us the benefit of his advice and encouragement, and offered us supports, but my men, as well as those of the Fourteenth Regiment, expressed a desire to hold the place alone if they could. The heavy rebel column, which I need not describe, bore down steadily upon us until about half way from the Emmitsburg road to our position. Our men were directed to withhold their fire up to this time, when the two regiments rose up and poured in a volley that seemed to level their front rank and all mounted officers. We continued to pour in our fire as best we could, and very soon the charging column seemed to slacken and nearly halt. In this way they staggered for a moment, and commenced to move by their left flank toward a position more nearly in front of the cemetery. As our front became uncovered, I moved my regiment a little by the flank, so as to extricate my left from some shrubbery that partially surrounded and hid them, when I changed front forward on my right company, throwing my left flank toward the rebel main line of battle. The Fourteenth Regiment remained in their position. The Sixteenth Regiment, or a portion of it, were on the skirmish line, and were driven in by this charge.

General Doubleday at this time rode up to me, and assured me that my movement would be a success, and he ordered the regiments to my right to cease firing and allow me to pass in front of their line, which we did, following the rebel column so close that when they faced to charge up Cemetery Hill we were within 15 rods of them, and they passed directly in review before us, my men at the same time pouring one of the most withering fires I had ever beheld into their exposed flank. We had fired about 10 rounds per man when they seemed to be in utter confusion, and large numbers came in in rear of my regiment for shelter. I do not know how many prisoners my regiment captured, but I had apparently more than there were men in my regiment.

While this was going on, the Sixteenth Regiment, Colonel Veazey, came up in my rear (having gathered up his regiment as far as he could after having been driven in with the skirmish line), and formed his regiment in rear and partially to my left, where he succeeded in capturing some prisoners. He had been in this position but a few moments when we discovered a small rebel column approaching over nearly the same ground the main rebel column had passed over, and for the moment it seemed as though we should be squeezed between the two, but Colonel Veazey promptly faced his regiment about, and advanced to meet this new danger, and I very quickly followed. When I got nearly opposite my original position, General Stannard sent orders to me to bring my regiment back to the main line, and he sent a portion of the Fourteenth Regiment to support Colonel Veazey. This rebel column, however, about that time commenced to diverge in the opposite direction, and entered the woods to the south of us, where they were pursued by the Sixteenth and Fourteenth Regiments. This substantially ended our part in the battle.

General Hancock was wounded while sitting on his horse giving me some directions. I was standing very near him, and assisted him from his horse. General Stannard was also wounded soon after, and compelled reluctantly to leave the field, since which time I have been in command of the brigade.

The casualties in my regiment, as near as I can now ascertain, were 8 killed, 89 wounded, and 26 missing.* As we know of none captured,

---

* But see revised statement, p. 174.

probably many of the 26 may prove to have been killed, or severely wounded, and cared for in some private house.

FRANCIS V. RANDALL,
Colonel Thirteenth Regiment Vermont Volunteers.

Major-General NEWTON,
Commanding First Army Corps.

No. 71.

Report of Col. Charles S. Wainwright, First New York Light Artillery, commanding Artillery Brigade, First Army Corps.

HEADQUARTERS ARTILLERY BRIGADE, FIRST CORPS,
July 17, 1863.

GENERAL . I have the honor to submit the following report of the part taken by my command in the battle of Gettysburg on the 1st, 2d, and 3d instant:

On the night of June 30, the main body of the command lay about 2 miles from Emmitsburg, while the Second Maine Battery, Captain Hall, was in position a couple of miles farther on, commanding the bridge on the Gettysburg turnpike over Marsh Creek, having been ordered to report to Brigadier-General Wadsworth, commanding the advance division.

About 8 o'clock on the morning of the 1st, we received orders to march to Gettysburg, no intimation, however, being given that we were likely to fall in with the enemy near that place, which had been occupied by our cavalry twenty-four hours before.

The corps marched in the following order: First Division, General Wadsworth, Hall's battery; Third Division, General Rowley, Artillery Brigade; Second Division, General Robinson; Major-General Doubleday temporarily in command of the corps. About 4 miles this side of Gettysburg, the Third Division took a by-road to the left, Captain Cooper's battery of four 3-inch guns following them.

The first intimation I received of the proximity of the enemy was the sound of firing when we arrived within some 2 miles of Gettysburg and at about 10.30 a. m. I immediately joined General Doubleday, and by his order moved the three batteries remaining with me across the fields toward the seminary or college. On our arrival at this point, we learned that a portion of the advance division had been engaged with the enemy and had been drawn in; also the death of our commanding officer, Maj. Gen. J. F. Reynolds. Captain Hall's battery (Second Maine) had been in action at this point. Having seen nothing of it myself, I insert his own report, as follows:

My battery was ordered into position by General Reynolds on the right of the Cashtown road, some 400 yards beyond Seminary Hill, on the south and west of the town. The enemy had previously opened a battery of six guns directly in our front, at 1,300 yards distance, which they concentrated upon me as I went into position, but with very little effect.

We opened upon this battery with shot and shell at 10.45 a. m., our first six shots causing the enemy to change position of two of his guns and place them under cover behind a barn. In twenty-five minutes from the time we opened fire, a column of the enemy's infantry charged up a ravine on our right flank, within 60 yards of my right piece, when they commenced shooting down my horses and wounding my men. I ordered the right and center sections to open upon this column with canister, and kept the left firing upon the enemy's artillery. This canister fire was very effective. and broke the charge of the enemy, when, just at this moment, to my surprise, I saw my support falling back without any orders having been given me to retire.   Feeling that if the position was too advanced for infantry it was equally so for artillery, I ordered the battery to retire by sections, although having no order to do so.   The support falling back rapidly, the right section of the battery, which I ordered to take position some 75 yards to the rear, to cover the retiring of the other four pieces, was charged upon by the enemy's skirmishers and 4 of the horses from one of the guns shot.   The men of the section dragged this gun off by hand. As the last piece of the battery was coming away, all its horses were shot, and I was about to return for it myself when General Wadsworth gave me a peremptory order to lose no time, but get my battery in position near the town, on the heights, to cover the retiring of the troops.   I sent a sergeant with 5 men after the piece, all, of whom were wounded or taken prisoners.

I had got near to the position I had been ordered to take, when I received another order from General Wadsworth to bring my guns immediately back; the officer bringing the order saying he would show me the road to take, which was the railroad grading leading out from town, which was swept at the time by two of the enemy's guns from the hills beyond, through the excavations at Seminary Hill. Having gotten on to this road, from its construction I could not turn from it on either side, and was obliged to advance 1,200 yards under this raking fire.   Arriving at Seminary Hill, I found no one to show me the position I was to occupy, and placed my battery in park under cover of the hill, and went forward to see where to take position, when I again met an aide of General Wadsworth, who ordered me to go to the right along the woods, pass over the crest and over a ravine, and there take position.   Obeying this order, I moved toward the right until met by an orderly, who informed me I was going directly into the enemy's lines, which were advancing from this direction.   I halted my command, and rode forwar , but before reaching the described position was fired upon by the enemy's skirmishers.   I then countermarched my battery, and moved to near the seminary.

Gettysburg Seminary is situated on a ridge about a quarter of a mile from the town, the ridge running nearly north and south and parallel with the Emmitsburg pike.   It is crossed by the Cashtown turnpike about 100 yards north of the seminary, and cut through by the railroad some 40 yards farther on.   The west front of the seminary is shaded by a grove of large trees, and the whole top of the ridge on both sides is more or less crowned with open woods through its entire length.   Beyond this ridge the ground falls gradually to the west, and rises again into a parallel ridge at a distance of about 400 yards.   This second ridge is wider and smoother than that on which the seminary stands, but ends about 200 yards north of where the Cashtown pike crosses it.

On the south side of this point is a house and large barn, with an apple orchard and some 5 acres of wood to the south of it; the rest of the ridge is cleared.   It was around this house and wood that the first skirmish, in which General Reynolds fell, took place.

Having massed the batteries immediately in rear of the first ridge, I rode forward to examine the ground in front, and was met by a member of General Doubleday's staff, with an order to post a battery on the outer ridge, if possible.   Directing Captain Reynolds to move his battery of six 3-inch guns forward, I rode up on to the ridge, but finding that the battery would be exposed and totally without support, I withdrew it before it reached the crest.   Soon afterward the Third Division, with Cooper's battery, arrived and took position along the open part of the crest, the battery being posted in an oat-field some 350 yards south of the Cashtown road.

One brigade of the First Division had meantime reoccupied the wood where the first engagement took place, and General Wadsworth sent to ask for a battery, but as there was no infantry to protect its right flank, and Captain Hall had previously come so near to losing his battery in the same position, I did not consider it safe to place a battery in that position until our Second Division, which was just arriving, had taken position and I had examined the ground on the flank, the enemy being quiet at this time.

Finding General Robinson's division and the Second Brigade of the First Division occupying a wood on the west slope of Seminary Ridge north of the railroad, and the Eleventh Corps coming into position across the flat at right angles to our front, I returned to the Cashtown road, and directed Lieutenant Stewart to report to General Robinson with his battery, which had previously been posted some 200 yards south of the seminary, but not engaged.

Meantime General Wadsworth had ordered Captain Tidball's horse battery into position on the right of his First Brigade, where Captain Hall's battery had been, and it had just commenced a sharp engagement with the enemy's battery directly in front. As soon as possible, I moved Reynolds' battery up to relieve Tidball's, but it had not fairly gotten into position before the enemy opened a severe fire from a second battery immediately on our right. By this cross-fire both batteries were obliged to withdraw, Reynolds taking position again at right angles to the ridge, so that his left was covered by the woods. While removing his battery, Captain Reynolds received a severe wound in the right eye, but refused for some time to leave the field. The enemy's battery soon after ceased firing. Receiving another request from General Wadsworth for some guns on his front, I posted Lieutenant Wilber, with a section of Company L, First New York, in the orchard on the south side of the Cashtown road, where he was sheltered from the fire of the enemy's battery on his right flank by the intervening house and barn, and moved the remaining four pieces around to the south side of the wood on the open crest.

Having heard incidentally some directions given to General Doubleday about holding Cemetery Hill, and not knowing that there was such a place, while the seminary was called indiscriminately cemetery and seminary, I supposed the latter was meant. I therefore directed Captain Cooper to take a good position in front of the professor's house on this ridge, and sent an order to Captain Stevens, of the Fifth Maine Battery, to occupy the position first assigned to Lieutenant Stewart. Soon after this, the enemy filed in two strong columns out of the woods, about 500 yards to our front, and marched steadily down to our left until they outflanked us nearly a third of a mile. They then formed in double line of battle, and came directly up the crest. During this movement, Battery L opened on the columns, but the firing of Lieutenant Breck's four guns was much interfered with by our own infantry moving in front of his pieces. As we had no regular line of battle on this crest, and the enemy outnumbered us five to one, I withdrew Lieutenant Breck's two sections when their first line was within about 200 yards, and ordered him behind a strong stone wall on the seminary crest.

Meantime General Doubleday had removed Captain Stevens' battery to the right of Captain Cooper's, and Lieutenant Wilber's section falling back with its support came into position at the same point, thus concentrating twelve guns in so small a space that they were hardly 5 yards apart. Lieutenant Stewart's battery was also in position on the same line, half the battery between the Cashtown pike and the railroad, the other half across the railroad in the corner of a wood.

The enemy's lines continued to advance steadily across the space between the two crests, but when the first line was within about 100 yards of the seminary, Lieutenant Davison, commanding the left half of Stewart's battery, swung his guns around on the Cashtown pike, so as to enfilade the whole line. This, with the fire of the other batteries, checked them for a moment at this point, but it was only for a moment, as their second line did not halt, but pushed on, strongly re-enforced by a third column deploying from the Cashtown road. An order was now received by Captain Stevens from General Wadsworth to withdraw his battery. Not knowing that he had received such an order, and still under the false impression as to the importance attached to holding Seminary Hill, I directed all the batteries to remain in position. A few minutes, however, showed me our infantry rapidly retreating to the town. All the batteries were at once limbered to the rear, and moved at a walk down the Cashtown pike until the infantry had all left it and passed under cover of the railroad embankment. By this time the enemy's skirmishers had lapped our retreating columns and opened a severe fire from behind a paling fence running parallel to and within 50 yards of the road. The pike being clear, the batteries now broke into a trot, but it was too late to save everything. Lieutenant Wilber's (Battery L, First New York) last piece had the off wheel-horse shot, and just as he had disengaged it, 3 more of the horses were shot down and his own horse killed, so that it was impossible for him to bring it off. It affords me pleasure to say that not the slightest blame can be attributed to Lieutenant Wilber in the loss of this gun.

Three caissons belonging to Battery B, Fourth U. S. Artillery, also broke down before we entered the town, and the bodies had to be abandoned. Another caisson of the same battery was struck by a shell and destroyed. Four officers were struck while in position on Seminary Hill, two of them severely wounded.

The loss of the batteries during the day's engagement was heavy, amounting in all to 83 officers and men and about 80 horses. A large proportion of the last were hit while passing over the short open space between Seminary Ridge and the town, the enemy having at that time a fire upon us from three sides, and our infantry not replying.

The batteries passed immediately through the town along with the other troops, and were placed in position again on reaching Cemetery Hill along with several of the Eleventh Corps batteries, so as to command the town and the approach from the northwest in case the enemy should attempt to follow us through the town.

At dusk, no attack having been made, the batteries on the hill outside the cemetery gate were posted as follows, and light earthworks thrown up in front of each gun to protect the men from the fire of the enemy's sharpshooters: Four guns of Battery B, Fourth U. S. Artillery, across the road so as to command the approaches from the town (two guns of this battery had been disabled by loss of pointing rings) along the north front of the hill; four guns of Battery I, First New York Artillery (Captain Wiedrich's, Eleventh Corps), on the left; next Cooper's battery, and then Reynolds', giving thirteen 3-inch guns on this front, some of which could also be turned upon the town and our old position of the morning. The Fifth Maine battery was posted to the right and some 50 yards in front of this line, on a small knoll, from whence they could obtain an oblique fire upon the hills in front of our line as well as a flanking fire at close quarters upon any attacking columns. Captain Hall's (Second Maine) remaining three guns (the others had been dismounted) were in position on the left of the cemetery—by order of Major-General Howard—where he remained during the next day's engagement, after which he reported to General Tyler for repairs.

July 2.—During the morning several moving columns of the enemy were shelled at intervals, but no engagements occurred until about 4 p. m., when they planted a battery of four 20-pounders and six 10-pounder Parrotts in a wheat-field on our immediate front, at about 1,300 yards, and opened the most accurate fire I have ever yet seen from their artillery. We replied with our thirteen 3-inch guns with good effect. It was an hour and a half, however, before we were able to compel them to withdraw, and then they hauled off their two right pieces by hand. Twenty-eight dead horses were found on the knoll occupied by this battery. A portion of the guns again took position farther to the right, but were soon silenced, as we could bring an additional number of pieces to bear on them there. Soon after, Captain Cooper's battery, which had suffered considerably, was relieved by Captain Ricketts' battery of six 3-inch guns.

About dusk they again opened from a knoll on our left and front, distant 1,800 yards, which fire was followed by a strong attack upon our position by General Rodes' Louisiana [?] brigade. As their column filed out of the town they came under the fire of the Fifth Maine Battery at about 800 yards. Wheeling into line, they swung around, their right resting on the town, and pushed up the hill, which is quite steep at this corner. As their line became fully unmasked, all the guns which could be brought to bear were opened on them, at first with shrapnel and afterward with canister, making a total of fifteen guns in their front and six on their left flank. Their center and left never mounted the hill at all, but their right worked its way up under cover of the houses, and pushed completely through Wiedrich's battery into Ricketts'. The cannoneers of both these batteries stood well to their guns, driving the enemy off with fence-rails and stones and capturing a few prisoners. I believe it may be claimed that this attack was almost entirely repelled by the artillery. My surgeon, who was in the town and dressed many of their wounded that night, tells me that they reported their loss in this attack as very great.

July 3.—There was no serious attack upon the position we held during this day's fight. The batteries fired occasional shots at bodies of the enemy's troops in the distance during the morning, and joined in the general artillery engagement in the afternoon. The fire of the enemy's batteries was noticed to be much less accurate than on the previous day, owing, I think, in a measure to their keeping their guns too much under cover of the hills on which they were posted.

With regard to the behavior of the batteries during this three days' fight, I have only to say that all the officers and men performed their duty to my perfect satisfaction. I would mention the case of a shell exploding immediately under one of Captain Cooper's guns in the heat of the second day's engagement, killing or wounding all the detachment around the gun, yet fire from that piece was reopened before all the wounded men were removed. I do not know that I can mention any officer or man in the batteries as particularly prominent above the others, but would respectfully call attention to First Sergt. John Mitchell, of Battery B, Fourth U. S. Artillery, who took command of the left half battery after Lieutenant Davison was wounded, and showed himself as efficient as an officer during an engagement as I have noticed him to be in his drill and the general routine of the battery.

I remain, general, very respectfully, your obedient servant,
C. S. WAINWRIGHT,
Col. First N. Y. Art., Comdg. Art. Brig., First Army Corps.

Brig. Gen. HENRY J. HUNT,
Chief of Artillery, Army of the Potomac.

No. 72.

Report of Capt. James A. Hall, Second Maine Battery.

NEAR BERLIN, MD.,
July 16, 1863.

COLONEL: I have the honor to submit the following as my report of the part taken by my battery at the battle of Gettysburg, on July 1, 2, and 3:

We were in camp on the morning of July 1, at Marsh Creek, 4 miles from Gettysburg. At 9 a. m. marched, following the advance brigade of the First Division, First Army Corps, to the battle-field, about a half mile south and west of town, where we were ordered into position by General Reynolds on the right of the Cashtown road, some 400 yards beyond Seminary Hill. The enemy had previously opened a battery of six guns directly in our front at 1,300 yards distance, which they concentrated upon me as I went into position, but with very little effect.

We opened upon this battery with shot and shell at 10.45 a. m., our first six shots causing the enemy to change the position of two of his guns and place them under cover behind a barn. In twenty-five minutes from the time we opened fire, a column of the enemy's infantry charged up a ravine on our right flank within 60 yards of my right piece, when they commenced shooting down my horses and wounding my men. I ordered the right and center sections to open upon this column with canister, and kept the left firing upon the enemy's artillery. This canister fire was very effective, and broke the charge of the enemy, when, just at this moment, to my surprise I saw my support falling back without any order having been given me to retire. Feeling that if the position was too advanced for infantry it was equally so for artillery, I ordered the battery to retire by sections, although having no order to do so. The support falling back rapidly, the right section of the battery, which I ordered to take position some 75 yards to the rear, to cover the retiring of the other four pieces, was charged upon by the enemy's skirmishers and 4 of the horses from one of the guns shot. The men of the section dragged this gun off by hand.

As the last piece of the battery was coming away, all its horses were shot, and I was about to return for it myself, when General Wadsworth gave me a peremptory order to lose no time, but get my battery in position near the town, on the heights, to cover the retiring of the troops.

I sent a sergeant with 5 men after the piece, all of whom were wounded or taken prisoners. I had got near to the position I had been ordered to take, when I received another order from General Wadsworth to bring my guns immediately back; the officer bringing the order saying he would show me the road to take, which was the railroad grading leading out from town, which was swept at the time by two of the enemy's guns from the hills beyond, through the excavations at Seminary Hill.

Having gotten on to this road, from its construction I could not turn from it on either side, and was obliged to advance 1,200 yards under this raking fire. Arriving at Seminary Hill, I found no one to show me the position I was to occupy, and placed my battery in park under cover of the hill, and went forward to see where to take position, when I again met an aide of General Wadsworth, who ordered me to go to the right along the woods, pass over the crest and over a ravine, and there take position.

Obeying this order, I moved toward the right until met by an orderly, who informed me I was going directly into the enemy's lines, which were advancing from this direction. I halted my command, and rode forward, but before reaching the described position was fired upon by the enemy's skirmishers. I then countermarched my battery, and moved to near the seminary, and was going forward to ascertain, if possible, where to go, when I met Colonel Wainwright, who informed me my abandoned gun was still on the field, and that he had refused to put the battery into the position desired by General Wadsworth. I then took a limber, and went back upon the field with 1 sergeant, and recovered the abandoned gun with parts of all the harness, and immediately moved back through the town, putting my only three guns which were not disabled in position, by order of General Howard, on the left of the cemetery.

On the 2d, we opened fire in reply to the enemy's guns at 4.15 p. m., and continued in action until the enemy's artillery ceased for the day, during which time another gun was disabled by its axle breaking by the recoil, when I was relieved by a battery from the Reserve Artillery, and, by order of General Newton, went to the rear to repair damages, and the battery took no further part in the engagement.

Casualties first day, 18 men wounded and 4 taken prisoners; 28 horses killed and 6 wounded; one gun-carriage rendered useless; two axles broken. Second day, one axle broken. Fired during engagement, 635 rounds of ammunition.

Very respectfully, your obedient servant,

> JAMES A. HALL,
> *Captain, Commanding Second Maine Battery.*

Col. C. S. WAINWRIGHT,
    Comdg. Artillery Brigade, First Army Corps.

No. 73.

Report of Lieut. Edward N. Whittier, Fifth Maine Battery.

HDQRS. FIFTH BATTERY MAINE VOLS.,
    July 16, 1863.

ADJUTANT: I have the honor to submit the following report of the part taken by the battery in the battle at Gettysburg, Pa., on the 1st, 2d, and 3d of the present month:

At a few minutes past 2, July 1, the battery being in position on the left of the seminary, orders were received by Captain Stevens to relieve Stewart's battery, and we took position on his left, one piece thrown forward to the front of the building, and opened with spherical case and shell on the enemy, rapidly advancing on our direct front.

After they were repulsed, when within range of our canister, the guns were turned to the right on the columns advancing across the turnpike, marching to our left, using solid shot and canister. When the enemy had driven our infantry from the woods protecting our left flank, by order of General Wadsworth, commanding First Division, the battery was limbered up and passed through the town, and was placed in position on the knoll to the right and rear of Cemetery Hill, and opened on bodies of infantry crossing the fields to our right.

During the night, temporary earthworks were thrown up covering the pieces.

On the morning of the 2d instant, on advice received from General Ames, the battery opened at 1,500 yards on columns of the enemy's infantry passing within range, and inflicted some considerable damage.

In the afternoon, engaged at extreme range the enemy's battery. At dusk opened with the whole battery at 1,200 yards on the enemy's line advancing from the edge of the town, and, by changing front and firing to the left, enfiladed their lines, at a distance of 800 yards, with spherical case and shell, and later with solid shot and canister, expending the entire contents of the limber chests, which contained upward of 46 rounds of canister repacked from caissons. The enemy having been driven back and the ammunition exhausted, the battery was withdrawn, the caissons and limbers refilled, and the same position reoccupied at 10.30 p. m.

Early on the morning of the 3d instant, engaged the enemy's battery, and, after firing for an hour, ceased firing by order of the colonel commanding, no damage being inflicted by us other than with solid shot at 1,800 yards.

I have the honor to acknowledge the timely services of the officers and men of the Twenty-fourth Michigan, my cannoneers becoming temporarily exhausted by the difficult service of the pieces, and the hearty and gallant co-operation of Colonel Underwood, Thirty-third Massachusetts Regiment, Eleventh Corps, in sending men to assist in serving ammunition and in the reconstruction of the works which protected us.

It is with much pain that I have to announce the temporary loss to the battery of Captain Stevens and Lieutenant Hunt, both wounded in the active discharge of their duties; Lieutenant Hunt at the seminary during the enemy's charge on our position, and Captain Stevens on the morning of the 2d by a bullet from the town; and among the killed, Sullivan Luce, acting corporal, who had on several occasions won the commendation of his commanding officer for soldierly and gallant qualities.

List of killed, wounded, and prisoners:* Six enlisted men missing; since reported as prisoners, paroled, and sent to West Chester, Pa.

---

* Embodied in revised statement, p. 174.

	Rounds.
Expenditure of ammunition:	
Solid shot	384
Spherical case	380
Shell	112
Canister	103
Total	979
Horses killed	7
Horses wounded	10
Total	17

I am, with due respect, your most obedient servant,

E. N. WHITTIER,
First Lieut., Comdg. Fifth Battery Maine Vols.

Lieut. A. MATTHEWSON,
A. A. A., Artillery Brig., First Army Corps.

No. 74.

Report of Lieut. George Breck, Battery L, First New York Light Artillery.

IN CAMP NEAR PETERSVILLE, MD., *July* 16, 1863.

SIR: I have the honor to submit the following report of the action of Bat ery L, First New York Artillery, during the three days' engagement at Gettysburg, on the 1st, 2d, and 3d instant:

At about 11 a. m. of the 1st instant, my battery, then in command of Capt. Gilbert H. Reynolds, arrived at the scene of action, after a hurried march from Emmitsburg. The battery was immediately moved into the field west of the town, where several positions were taken and abandoned without opening fire. About 1 p. m. the battery was ordered by Col. C. S. Wainwright to advance to the support of Tidball's battery, which occupied a knoll across a road to the front and extreme left of our line as then engaged. One section of the battery had hardly come into position when, in addition to the galling fire in front, an enfilading fire was opened from the left, which completely swept the position and forced both batteries to retire. At this point, Captain Reynolds was severely wounded, and the command of the battery devolved upon me.

I brought the pieces again into position about 500 yards in rear of the first position, and in a line nearly west of the brick seminary.

After an engagement of nearly an hour's duration in the last-named position, I moved my battery to the crest of a hill to the left and front, and fired about 6 rounds at the lines of the enemy, which were very steadily extended around our left.

The right section of the battery, under command of Lieut. B. W. Wilber, was ordered to go still farther to the left, where a few rounds only were fired, when the section was forced to retire with our troops, who were rapidly falling back, closely pressed by the enemy. The other four pieces, under command of Lieut. William H. Bower and the immediate supervision of Colonel Wainwright, returned to the second position above named. As the infantry were falling back close upon the guns, no fire was opened, and the four pieces again retired, and took position upon the ridge running south from the brick seminary and in rear of the belt of timber to the left of that building. After firing a number of rounds in this position, including some canister, and with great effect, the enemy charging upon the guns, the four pieces again retired under cover of the line of cavalry already formed to cover the withdrawal of our troops. These pieces, the supply of ammunition being exhausted, were then conducted from here by Lieutenant Bower to a position of security on the Taneytown road. I accompanied the right section, which, continuing to retire, took its third position on the ridge running south from the seminary, near a small house and orchard. Here, after expending a few rounds, including canister, the section was ordered to again retire, which it did by a road leading through the town.

Soon after getting into the road, the 6 horses of the rear piece were shot down, the enemy close to the right and front. Lieutenant Wilber's horse was at the same time shot under him, and, as the enemy was rapidly advancing, the piece disabled was obliged to be abandoned, and fell into the enemy's possession. The other piece Lieutenant Wilber succeeded in conducting through the town, and took position on the right slope of Cemetery Hill and in front of the cemetery gate. At the time the piece in question was lost, I had run the remaining part of the battery safely from the field to the Taneytown road, and was hastening to remove the caissons in the same direction, as the enemy was rapidly advancing his right toward the Emmitsburg road, where said caissons were in park. I finally succeeded in joining the caissons with the four pieces, and, after replenishing with ammunition, I took position with the five remaining pieces of the battery to the front and right of the cemetery gate, as before mentioned, which position, by order of Colonel Wainwright, I caused to be intrenched, and held during the two following days of the battle. In the position last assumed, my command was the third battery to the right of the right angle formed by our line of artillery near the town and ranged upon by the enemy's center. With the exception of picket firing, a general quiet was maintained along the lines on the 2d instant, until about 4 p. m., when the enemy attempted to break our lines on the left. At the same time, a line of batteries directly in my front opened a simultaneous and very severe fire, to which we replied steadily, and before dusk succeeded in silencing most of their fire. This action continued about four hours, almost without intermission. The battery to the right of our front, and situated on a knoll in a wheat-field about 1,800 yards distant, upon which I principally directed my fire, was silenced and forced to retire in the early part of the engagement. After our forces obtained possession of the ground occupied by this battery, three guns were found disabled and abandoned, furnishing very good proof of the accuracy and skill of my gunners.

A considerable fire of infantry followed the cannonade, and terminated in an unsuccessful charge upon my battery and the two upon my left. This charge was mostly repelled by the infantry in support, whose presence in front prevented the use of canister. The enemy being driven back, the engagement closed for the day. In this action the axle of one of my guns was broken, disabling the piece, in consequence of which it was sent to the Artillery Reserve, by order of Colonel Wainwright, to be repaired. During the cannonade, an ammunition chest of one of my caisson limbers was struck by a shell, exploding a few rounds of ammunition which it contained, and completely destroying it.

At about 2 p. m. a battery nearly 2,500 yards distant on my front opened and delivered at intervals an irregular and inaccurate fire, to which at first my gunners replied, but shortly after were forbidden to return the fire.

I sustained in the three days' engagement the following losses: One man killed, a private, and 16 wounded, including Captain Reynolds and 2 non-commissioned officers. One of the wounded men has since died. I had 22 horses killed and disabled. Two horses were wounded by fragments of shells from a battery of 20-pounder Parrotts in the cemetery in my rear, which seemed too often to explode prematurely.

The amount of ammunition expended during the three days' battle was 1,290 rounds, consisting of Schenkl percussion, 523 rounds; Schenkl compound, 715 rounds; and canister, 52 rounds. Two chests of ammunition, 100 rounds, were issued to Captain Wiedrich's battery by order of Colonel Wainwright.

The officers and men acted with much bravery, coolness, and collectedness. Though greatly fatigued and exhausted by almost constant labor and watchfulness for three days, the men performed their duties cheerfully and quite enthusiastically. I would mention in a particular manner, Bugler R. Mastin Smith, who, when one of the cannoneers was wounded, dismounted from his horse and bravely filled the part of the wounded man.

I remain, respectfully, your obedient servant,

GEORGE BRECK,
First Lieut., Comdg. Battery L, First New York Artillery.

Lieut. A. MATTHEWSON,
Actg. Asst. Adjt. Gen., Artillery Brig., First Army Corps.

No. 75.

Report of Capt. James H. Cooper, Battery B, First Pennsylvania Light Artillery.

HDQRS. BATTERY B, FIRST PA. ART., *July* 17, 1863.

ADJUTANT: I have the honor to herewith transmit a report of the action of Battery B, First Pennsylvania Artillery, in the battle of Gettysburg, Pa.

On the morning of the 1st of July, the battery marched from camp near Emmitsburg, Md., to the vicinity of Gettysburg, Pa. Here it was placed in position by Colonel Wainwright, about 12 m., on the left of the Third Division, First Army Corps, and fired about twenty-five shots at a battery in front, which was firing upon the infantry of the corps and Captain Hall's battery. This battery soon ceased firing, and another directly on the right opened, when we changed front to the right, by order of Colonel Wainwright, and engaged it for a few minutes, when the colonel ordered the battery to be placed in position near the Gettysburg Seminary. Here it remained unengaged for a few minutes, when a battery in front again opened and fired a few minutes, when the enemy's infantry made its appearance along the woods and crest in our front. The fire of the battery was then concentrated upon them, case shot and shell being used until canister range was obtained, and this, with the assistance of Lieutenant Stewart's and Captain Stevens' batteries, reduced the enemy's lines very much. At about 5 p. m., all infantry support having been driven back, the battery was compelled to retire through Gettysburg to Cemetery Hill.

In this day's engagement about 400 rounds of ammunition were expended, but three guns being engaged, one axle having broken from recoil at the first few shots. The following are the casualties of this day's engagement, viz: Lieutenant Miller, wounded slightly; Private A. P. Alcorn, wounded severely and taken prisoner; Private John Pauly, wounded severely; Private John W. Phillips, wounded severely; Private Asahel Shaffer, wounded slightly; 2 horses killed.

At about sunset in the evening, having refilled the ammunition chests, the battery was placed in position, by order of Colonel Wainwright, on the crest of the hill in rear of Gettysburg, and fronting to the northeast. The battery remained in this position without firing until 9.30 a. m., July 2, when occasional shots were fired at small bodies of the enemy's infantry and cavalry which were maneuvering in the skirts of timber from 1 mile to 1¼ miles distant until 4 p. m., when the enemy brought a number of 10 and 20 pounder Parrott guns into position in the open field about 1,400 and 2,000 yards distant, and opened a vigorous fire upon the position. To this fire the battery replied, and, with the assistance of a battery on its left, Reynolds' and Stevens' batteries on the right, the enemy's guns were silenced in about two and a half hours' firing. The battery fired occasional shots into the position of these batteries until about 7 p. m., when it was relieved by Captain Ricketts' battery, and ordered by Colonel Wainwright to report to General Tyler, commanding Artillery Reserve, to refit and fill ammunition chests, one gun having been dismounted late in this day's engagement. I was again ready for action by 11 a. m., but, receiving no orders, the battery remained in General Tyler's camp until the 3d instant.

The casualties of this day's engagement were: Private J. H. McCleary, killed; Private P. G. Hoagland, killed; Private Jesse Temple, wounded severely; Private J. C. Cornelius, wounded slightly; Private D. W. Taylor, wounded slightly; Corpl. Joseph Reed, wounded slightly; 1 horse killed, 2 horses disabled. About 500 rounds of ammunition were expended. On the afternoon of the 3d instant, about 3 p. m., during a heavy cannonade, the battery was ordered into position among the batteries in the Second Corps front, and immediately opened upon a shattered battery of the enemy which was firing on our front. This battery soon ceased or withdrew. The battery ceased firing for one-half hour, when a line of the enemy's infantry appeared, approaching over the crest of a hill about 1,000 yards distant. Into this line this battery, in connection with the adjacent batteries, fired case shot until they reached canister range, when a few charges were fired into them, completely routing them, without any infantry assistance.

The casualties of this day's engagement were: Private Frederick Workman, wounded slightly. About 150 rounds of ammunition were expended in this day's engagement. The battery remained in this position until the afternoon of July 5, when, by order of Colonel Wainwright, it rejoined the Artillery Brigade. The total of ammunition expended in these three days' engagements was 1,050 rounds.

J. H. COOPER,

Captain, Comdg. Battery B, Pennsylvania Artillery.

Lieut. A. Matthewson,

　Actg. Asst. Adjt. Gen., Artillery Brig., First Army Corps,

No. 76.

Reports of Maj. Gen. Winfield S. Hancock, U. S. Army, command-
ing Second Army Corps.

5.25 [P. M., JULY 1, 1863.]

GENERAL: When I arrived here an hour since, I found that our troops had given up the front of Gettysburg and the town. ˙We have now taken up a position in the cemetery, and cannot well be taken. It is a position, however, easily turned. Slocum is now coming on the ground, and is taking position on the right, which will protect the right. But we have, as yet, no troops on the left, the Third Corps not having yet reported; but I suppose that it is marching up. If so, its flank march will in a degree protect our left flank. In the meantime Gibbon had better march on so as to take position on our right or left, to our rear, as may be necessary, in some commanding position. General G. will see this dispatch. The battle is quiet now. I think we will be all right until night. I have sent all the trains back. When night comes, it can be told better what had best be done. I think we can retire; if not, we can fight here, as the ground appears not unfavorable with good troops. I will communicate in a few moments with General Slocum, and transfer the command to him.

Howard says that Doubleday's command gave way.

General Warren is here.

Your obedient servant,

WINF'D S. HANCOCK,
Major-General, Commanding Corps.

General BUTTERFIELD, *Chief of Staff.*

—

HEADQUARTERS SECOND CORPS, *July* 3, 1863.

Although I repulsed a tremendous attack, yet on seeing it from my left and advancing to the right, I, much to my sorrow, found that the twelve guns on my salient had been removed by some one, whom I call upon you to hold accountable, as without them, with worse troops, I should certainly have lost the day. I arrived just in time to put a small battalion of infantry in the place occupied by those two batteries.

I have never seen a more formidable attack, and if the Sixth and Fifth Corps have pressed up, the enemy will be destroyed. The enemy must be short of ammunition, as I was shot with a tenpenny nail. I did not leave the field till the victory was entirely secured and the enemy no longer in sight. I am badly wounded, though I trust not seriously. I had to break the line to attack the enemy in flank on my right, where the enemy was most persistent after the front attack was repelled. Not a rebel was in sight upright when I left. The line should be immediately restored and perfected. General Caldwell is in command of the corps, and I have directed him to restore the line.

Your obedient servant,

WINF'D S. HANCOCK,
Major-General,
By A. N. DOUGHERTY,
Surgeon, and Medical Director Second Corps.

General MEADE,

TWELFTH CORPS HOSPITAL, *July* 3, 1863.

GENERAL: A great many colors were taken by our troops to-day—one brigade took ten. In order to collect them, it would be well to send a circular for each regimental commander to report the number taken. I have seen several on the road to-day.

Very respectfully, your obedient servant,

WINF'D S. HANCOCK,
Major-General.

[General MEADE.]

—

HEADQUARTERS SECOND CORPS, *July* 5, 1863.

I have the honor to transmit herewith twenty-two flags captured by this corps in the last battle at Gettysburg.

Very respectfully, your obedient servant,

E. P. BROWNSON,
Captain, and Aide-de-Camp.

General WILLIAMS,
Assistant Adjutant-General.

—

———, —— —, 1863.

GENERAL: I have the honor to submit the following report of the operations of my command from June 28 until July 5, inclusive:

On the morning of June 28, the Second Corps marched from near Sugar Loaf Mountain, Md., with orders from Major-General Hooker to encamp at Frederick. When near Monocacy Junction, the corps was ordered into camp near that place by Major-General Meade, who had that day assumed command of the army.

On the morning of the 29th, orders were received for the corps to march at 4 a. m. and move to Frizellburg. An accident delaying the delivery of the order, the command was not in motion until 8 a. m.

At 10 p. m. the command was halted for the night 1 mile beyond Uniontown, having accomplished with its entire train a march of over 30 miles. Frizellburg was not reached, owing to its being considerably farther from Monocacy Junction than indicated by the maps.

At Uniontown I ascertained that Stuart was at Westminster with a heavy force of cavalry and a number of guns, which information I communicated to the major-general commanding.

The corps remained in camp at Uniontown on the 30th.

On the morning of July 1, the command marched to Taneytown, going into bivouac about 11 a. m. I then proceeded in person to General Meade's headquarters, and, on reporting to him, was informed as to his intention with reference to giving battle to the enemy, the orders for preparatory movements being then ready for issue.

A few minutes before 1 p. m., I received orders to proceed in person to the front, and assume command of the First, Third, and Eleventh Corps, in consequence of the death of Major-General Reynolds. Having been fully informed by the major-general commanding as to his intentions, I was instructed by him to give the necessary directions upon my arrival at the front for the movement of troops and trains to the rear toward the line of battle he had selected, should I deem it expedient to do so. If the ground was suitable, and circumstances made it wise, I was directed to establish the line of battle at Gettysburg.

Turning over the command of the Second Corps to Brigadier-General Gibbon, under instructions from General Meade, at 1.10 o'clock I was on the road to Gettysburg, accompanied by my personal aides, Lieutenant-Colonel Morgan, chief of staff, Second Corps, and the signal party of the corps, under command of Captain Hall.

At 3 p. m. I arrived at Gettysburg and assumed the command. At this time the First and Eleventh Corps were retiring through the town, closely pursued by the enemy. The cavalry of General Buford was occupying a firm position on the plain to the left of Gettysburg, covering the rear of the retreating corps. The Third Corps had not yet arrived from Emmitsburg. Orders were at once given to establish a line of battle on Cemetery Hill, with skirmishers occupying that part of the town immediately in our front. The position just on the southern edge of Gettysburg, overlooking the town and commanding the Emmitsburg and Taneytown roads and the Baltimore turnpike, was already partially occupied by direction of Major-General Howard. Some difficulty was experienced in forming the troops of the Eleventh Corps, but by vigorous efforts a sufficiently formidable line was established to deter the enemy from any serious assault on the position. They pushed forward a line of battle for a short distance east of the Baltimore turnpike, but it was easily checked by the fire of our artillery. In forming the lines, I received material assistance from Major-General Howard, Brigadier-Generals Warren and Buford, and officers of General Howard's command.

As soon as the line of battle mentioned above was shown by the enemy, Wadsworth's division, First Corps, and a battery (thought to be the Fifth Maine) were placed on the eminence just across the turnpike, and commanding completely this approach. This important position was held by the division during the remainder of the operations near Gettysburg. The rest of the First Corps, under Major-General Doubleday, was on the right and left of the Taneytown road, and connected with the left of the Eleventh Corps, which occupied that part of Cemetery Hill immediately to the right and left of the Baltimore turnpike. A division of the Twelfth Corps, under Brigadier-General Williams, arrived as these arrangements were being completed, and was established, by order of Major-General Slocum, some distance to the right and rear of Wadsworth's division. Brigadier-General Geary's division, of the Twelfth Corps, arriving on the ground subsequently, and not being able to communicate with Major-General Slocum, I ordered the division to the high ground to the right of and near Round Top Mountain, commanding the Gettysburg and Emmitsburg road, as well as the Gettysburg and Taneytown road to our rear.

The trains of all the troops under my command were ordered to the rear, that they might not interfere with any movement of troops that might be directed by the major-general commanding.

My aide, Major Mitchell, was then sent to General Meade to inform him of the state of affairs, and to say that I would hold the position until night. Shortly after, I addressed a communication to the major-general commanding, sending it by Captain Parker, of my staff, giving in detail the information in my possession, and informing him that the position at Gettysburg was a very strong one, having for its disadvantage that it might be easily turned, and leaving to him the responsibility whether the battle should be fought at Gettysburg or at a place first selected by him.

Between 5 and 6 o'clock, my dispositions having been completed, Major-General Slocum arrived on the field, and, considering that my functions had ceased, I transferred the command to him   The head of the Third Corps appeared in sight shortly afterward, on the Emmitsburg road.

About dark I started for the headquarters of the army, still at Taneytown, 13 miles distant, and reported in person to General Meade.   I then ascertained that he had already given orders for the corps in the rear to advance at once to Gettysburg, and was about proceeding there in person.

The Second Army Corps had marched from Taneytown toward Gettysburg at 1.30 p. m., and bivouacked for the night about 3 miles in rear of the town.   The march was resumed at daylight, and I rejoined the corps before its arrival on the field, which took place about 7 a. m. of the 2d.   The troops were soon placed in position, the right resting near the Emmitsburg road, to the west of Cemetery Hill, connecting there on the right with the Eleventh Corps and on the left with the Third Corps, the line of battle extending along the crest from the left of Cemetery Hill to Round Top Mountain, the ground being less elevated, as near Round Top.   The Third Division, Brigadier-General Hays commanding, was placed on the right; the Second Division, Brigadier-General Gibbon commanding, was placed in the center, and the First Division, Brigadier-General Caldwell commanding, was on the left.   The batteries of the corps were disposed from right to left as follows: Woodruff's (I, First U. S. Artillery), Arnold's (A, First Rhode Island), Cushing's (A, Fourth U. S. Artillery), Brown's (B, First Rhode Island), and Rorty's (B, First New York). Each division had one of its brigades in rear as a reserve.

Sharp skirmishing occurred at intervals during the morning, particularly in front of Hays' division, where quite a number of prisoners were taken from the enemy.   The artillery was also frequently engaged, but no severe fighting took place until about 3 p. m., when the Third Corps advanced from its position toward the Emmitsburg road and became heavily engaged.   Subsequently the Fifth Corps became engaged in the vicinity of Round Top, in support of and some distance to the rear of the Third Corps.

Having been directed by General Meade to send a division to the assistance of the Third Corps, with orders to report to General Sykes, commanding Fifth Corps, the First Division, under Brigadier-General Caldwell, was dispatched to the scene of conflict.   The division was assigned to its position by one of Major-General Sykes' staff officers.   As soon as it could form line of battle, the division advanced, the left along the foot of Round Top Mountain, and drove the enemy steadily before it until, from the want of any connection on its right, the right flank of the division was turned by a column of the enemy, which had passed unobserved at a considerable distance to its right and almost to its rear, where it formed line of battle and soon forced the division to retire, with a loss of nearly half its numbers.   Three out of four of the brigade commanders were disabled, Brigadier-General Zook, a gallant officer, being killed early in the action; Col. E. E. Cross, Fifth New Hampshire Volunteers, commanding First Brigade, whose intrepid bearing had been so often exhibited on the battle-field, was mortally, and Col. J. R. Brooke, Fifty-third Pennsylvania, commanding Fourth Brigade, slightly, wounded.

The orders of General Meade were that this division should return to its original position after being relieved by the Fifth Corps.   It was reformed some distance in rear of the line of battle, but did not return until after dark, when I ordered it to the position it held in the morning.

The Third Corps having advanced far beyond the original line of battle, and Caldwell's division having been detached, a large interval remained on the left of the Second Division without troops. To remedy this in part, General Gibbon extended his line to the left by adding to it his reserve brigade. The right of the Third Corps rested near the brick house, near the Emmitsburg road, a considerable distance in front of Gibbon's division, the general direction of the line being parallel to that road. To strengthen the point between the right of the Third Corps and his left, General Gibbon sent two regiments of General Harrow's brigade (the Fifteenth Massachusetts, Col. G. H. Ward, and the Eighty-second New York Volunteers, Colonel Huston) to occupy a crest on the right of the brick house, which position was considerably strengthened by a slight breastwork of such materials as the adjoining fences afforded. Brown's battery (B, First Rhode Island) occupied a position in rear and somewhat to the left of these two regiments.

Owing to the advanced position of the Third Corps, a very considerable gap was made between its left and the right of the Fifth Corps, through which the column of the enemy which turned the right flank of Caldwell's division appears to have passed.

About this time, General Meade informed me that General Sickles had been wounded, and directed me to assume command of the Third Corps in addition to that of my own. By this arrangement, the immediate command of the Second Corps devolved again upon General Gibbon, and that of the Third upon General Birney. I had just before received an order from General Meade to send a brigade to the assistance of General Birney (whose division had occupied the extreme left of Sickles' corps), and to send two regiments to General Humphreys, who commanded the right of that corps. I immediately led the brigade (Third Brigade, Third Division, under Colonel Willard) intended for General Birney toward the left of the original line of battle of the Third Corps, and was about proceeding with it to the front, when I encountered General Birney, who informed me that his troops had all been driven to the rear, and had left the position to which I was moving. General Birney proceeded to the rear to collect his command. General Humphreys' small command yet remained in position. The force which had turned General Caldwell's right and driven the left of the Third Corps now approached the line of battle as originally established. Humphreys' command was forced back, contesting the ground stubbornly. The two regiments sent from the Second Division to General Humphreys' assistance (Nineteenth Massachusetts, Colonel Devereux, and Forty-second New York, Colonel Mallon, both under command of Colonel Mallon) had not arrived on the ground, though under musketry fire, when, observing that General Humphreys' command was rapidly retiring, they formed line of battle, delivered a few volleys at the advancing enemy, and themselves retired in good order to their position in line in the Second Corps, having suffered a heavy loss. The enemy pushed them so closely that a number of prisoners were captured by these regiments. The two regiments and battery referred to above as having been advanced by General Gibbon to the vicinity of the brick house did excellent service in protecting the flank of General Humphreys' command and in preventing it from being cut off from the line of battle. The enemy's attack being on their flank, the two regiments were, however, forced to retire, having met with heavy losses, Colonels Ward and Huston both being killed. One gun of the battery they had supported, and which was served to the last by the cannoneers, fell into the hands of the enemy temporarily.

I directed General Humphreys to form his command on the ground from which General Caldwell had moved to the support of the Third Corps, which was promptly done. The number of his troops collected was, however, very small, scarcely equal to an ordinary battalion, but with many colors, this small command being composed of the fragments of many shattered regiments. Three guns of one of its batteries had been left on the field, owing to the losses of horses and men. I established Colonel Willard's brigade at the point through which General Birney's division had retired, and fronting the approach of the enemy, who were pressing vigorously on. There were no other troops on its right or left, and the brigade soon became engaged, losing its commander, Colonel Willard, and many officers and men,

At this juncture, re-enforcements, for which I had previously sent to General Meade by a staff officer, consisting of a part of General Newton's corps (Doubleday's division and the remnant of Robinson's), arrived, established themselves on the line, meeting the enemy at once, and doing good execution.

Proceeding along the line, I met a regiment of the enemy, the head of whose column was about passing through an unprotected interval in our line. A fringe of undergrowth in front of the line offered facilities for it to approach very close to our lines without being observed. It was advancing firing, and had already twice wounded my aide, Captain Miller. The First Minnesota Regiment coming up at this moment, charged the rebel regiment in handsome style, capturing its colors, and driving it back in disorder.

I cannot speak too highly of this regiment and its commander in its attack, as well as in its subsequent advance against the enemy, in which it lost three-fourths of the officers and men engaged. One of the regiments of the Vermont Brigade afterward advanced upon its right, and retook the guns of one of the reserve batteries, from which the cannoneers and supports had been driven.

The enemy was now attacking our whole front at different points. On the right advancing from the direction of the brick house on the Emmitsburg road toward Gibbon's division, where he was promptly checked and driven from that portion of Brown's battery temporarily captured. In this last operation the Nineteenth Maine, Col. F. E. Heath commanding, bore a conspicuous part.

On the left of the Second Corps, the line being still incomplete, and intervals existing through which the enemy approached our line of battle, General Meade brought up in person a part of the Twelfth Corps, consisting of two regiments of Lockwood's brigade, under Brig. Gen. H. H. Lockwood, which formed line, and advanced against the enemy, then closely engaged with us, and he was soon driven from the field. By the advance of these regiments, the artillery which had been left on the field in the Third Corps line was recaptured from the enemy. Humphreys' division participated in this advance and in the recapture of its guns.

Brigadier-General Barksdale, of the rebel service, was left on the field, mortally wounded.

The Third Brigade of the Third Division, commanded by Colonel Sherrill, after Colonel Willard's death, made a gallant advance on the enemy's batteries to the right of the brick house, in which the One hundred and eleventh New York Volunteers, under Colonel Mac-Dougall, bore a distinguished part. This brigade lost nearly one-half its numbers.

It was nearly dark. Proceeding to the right of the Second Corps, near Cemetery Hill, and hearing a heavy engagement on General Howard's front, the firing seeming to come nearer and nearer, I directed General Gibbon to send Colonel Carroll's brigade, Third Division, to that point, to report to General Howard at once. I was gratified to hear subsequently, from General Howard in person, that it arrived at a very critical time, and that this unexpected re-enforcement materially assisted him in driving the enemy from his front. Hearing firing farther to the right, and believing it to be on General Slocum's front, and fearing that the troops he had sent to me had left him without sufficient force, I directed General Gibbon to send two regiments to that point. The Seventy-first Pennsylvania, Col. R. Penn Smith, and the One hundred and sixth Pennsylvania, Lieut. Col. W. L. Curry, were dispatched, but they also reported to Major-General Howard. The One hundred and sixth Pennsylvania Volunteers remained until relieved next day, doing good service. The Seventy-first returned to its command about midnight, without having received orders to do so, after suffering some loss.

In addition to the troops specially mentioned heretofore as being on the line of the Second Corps on July 2, I would mention Battery C, Fourth U. S. Artillery, commanded by Lieut. Evan Thomas. This officer is particularly mentioned for bravery and good conduct. A battery of the Artillery Reserve, commanded by ——, was also on the line during this action.

During the night of the 2d, the batteries were supplied with ammunition as far as practicable. Having brought but half the ammunition train of the corps, we were dependent somewhat on others. The battery ammunition was supplied by the train of the Artillery Reserve, though not to the full extent required.

For details of the important service rendered by the First Division of the Second Corps, during the time it was detached in the afternoon of the 2d instant, I refer you to the clear and concise report of its commander, Brigadier-General Caldwell, which is herewith transmitted. Between 500 and 600 prisoners were captured by this division on that occasion.

The corps had been so weakened by its losses on the 2d, that on the 3d instant it required every available man in the line of battle to cover the ground held the previous day. Colonel Carroll's brigade, of General Hays' division, was retained by General Howard, and, with the exception of the Eighth Ohio, was not engaged with the Second Corps during the day.

The early morning passed in comparative quiet along our front, but the heavy and continued firing on the right indicated that the efforts of the enemy were being directed on the Twelfth Corps. Trifling affairs occurred at intervals between the enemy's skirmishers and our own, and the artillery of the corps was frequently and successfully engaged with that of the enemy.

From 11 a. m. until 1 p. m. there was an ominous stillness. About 1 o'clock, apparently by a given signal, the enemy opened upon our front with the heaviest artillery fire I have ever known. Their guns were in position at an average distance of about 1,400 yards from my line, and ran in a semicircle from the town of Gettysburg to a point

opposite Round Top Mountain. Their number is variously estimated at from one hundred and fifteen to one hundred and fifty.
The air was filled with projectiles, there being scarcely an instant
but that several were seen bursting at once. No irregularity of
ground afforded much protection, and the plain in rear of the line
of battle was soon swept of everything movable. The infantry
troops maintained their position with great steadiness, covering
themselves as best they might by the temporary but trifling defenses they had erected and the accidents of the ground. Scarcely a
straggler was seen, but all waited the cessation of the fierce cannonade, knowing well what it foreshadowed. The artillery of the corps,
imperfectly supplied with ammunition, replied to the enemy most
gallantly, maintaining the unequal contest in a manner that reflected
the highest honor on this arm of the service. Brown's battery (B,
First Rhode Island), which had suffered severely on the 2d, and expended all of its canister on that day, retired before the cannonading
ceased, not being effective for further service. The remaining batteries continued their fire until only canister remained to them, and
then ceased.

After an hour and forty-five minutes, the fire of the enemy became
less furious, and immediately their infantry was seen in the woods
beyond the Emmitsburg road, preparing for the assault. A strong
line of skirmishers soon advanced (followed by two deployed lines of
battle), supported at different points by small columns of infantry.
Their lines were formed with a precision and steadiness that extorted
the admiration of the witnesses of that memorable scene. The left of
the enemy extended slightly beyond the right of General Alexander
Hays' division, the right being about opposite the left of General
Gibbon's. Their line of battle thus covered a front of not more than
two of the small and incomplete divisions of the corps. The whole
attacking force is estimated to have exceeded 15,000 men.

No attempt was made to check the advance of the enemy until the
first line had arrived within about 700 yards of our position, when
a feeble fire of artillery was opened upon it, but with no material
effect, and without delaying for a moment its determined advance.
The column pressed on, coming within musketry range without receiving immediately our fire, our men evincing a striking disposition
to withhold it until it could be delivered with deadly effect.

Two regiments of Stannard's Vermont Brigade (of the First Corps),
which had been posted in a little grove in front of and at a considerable angle with the main line, first opened with an oblique fire upon
the right of the enemy's column, which had the effect to make the
troops on that flank double in a little toward their left. They still
pressed on, however, without halting to return the fire. The rifled
guns of our artillery, having fired away all their canister, were now
withdrawn, or left on the ground inactive, to await the issue of the
struggle between the opposing infantry. Arrived at between 200 and
300 yards, the troops of the enemy were met by a destructive fire from
the divisions of Gibbon and Hays, which they promptly returned,
and the fight at once became fierce and general. In front of Hays'
division it was not of very long duration. Mowed down by canister
from Woodruff's battery, and by the fire from two regiments judiciously posted by General Hays in his extreme front and right, and
by the fire of different lines in the rear, the enemy broke in great disorder, leaving fifteen colors and nearly 2,000 prisoners in the hands of
this division. Those of the enemy's troops who did not fall into

disorder in front of the Third Division were moved to the right, and re-enforced the line attacking Gibbon's division. The right of the attacking line having been repulsed by Hall's and Harrow's brigades, of the latter division, assisted by the fire of the Vermont regiments before referred to, doubled to its left and also re-enforced the center, and thus the attack was in its fullest strength opposite the brigade of General Webb. This brigade was disposed in two lines. Two regiments of the brigade, the Sixty-ninth and Seventy-first Pennsylvania Volunteers, were behind a low stone wall and a slight breastwork hastily constructed by them, the remainder of the brigade being behind the crest some 60 paces to the rear, and so disposed as to fire over the heads of those in front. When the enemy's line had nearly reached the stone wall, led by General Armistead, the most of that part of Webb's brigade posted here abandoned their position, but fortunately did not retreat entirely. They were, by the personal bravery of General Webb and his officers, immediately formed behind the crest before referred to, which was occupied by the remnant of the brigade.

Emboldened by seeing this indication of weakness, the enemy pushed forward more pertinaciously, numbers of them crossing over the breastwork abandoned by the troops. The fight here became very close and deadly. The enemy's battle-flags were soon seen waving on the stone wall. Passing at this time, Colonel Devereux, commanding the Nineteenth Massachusetts Volunteers, anxious to be in the right place, applied to me for permission to move his regiment to the right and to the front, where the line had been broken. I granted it, and his regiment and Colonel Mallon's (Forty-second New York Volunteers, on his right) proceeded there at once; but the enemy having left Colonel Hall's front, as described before, this officer promptly moved his command by the right flank to still further re-enforce the position of General Webb, and was immediately followed by Harrow's brigade. The movement was executed, but not without confusion, owing to many men leaving their ranks to fire at the enemy from the breastwork. The situation was now very peculiar. The men of all the brigades had in some measure lost their regimental organization, but individually they were firm. The ambition of individual commanders to promptly cover the point penetrated by the enemy, the smoke of battle, and the intensity of the close engagement, caused this confusion. The point, however, was now covered. In regular formation our line would have stood four ranks deep.

The colors of the different regiments were now advanced, waving in defiance of the long line of battle-flags presented by the enemy. The men pressed firmly after them, under the energetic commands and example of their officers, and after a few moments of desperate fighting the enemy's troops were repulsed, threw down their arms, and sought safety in flight or by throwing themselves on the ground to escape our fire. The battle-flags were ours and the victory was won.

Gibbon's division secured 12 stand of colors and prisoners enough to swell the number captured by the corps to about 4,500.

While the enemy was still in front of Gibbon's division, I directed Colonel [General] Stannard to send two regiments of his Vermont Brigade, First Corps, to a point which would strike the enemy on the right flank. I cannot report on the execution of this order, as Colonel [General] Stannard's report has not passed through my hands; but from the good conduct of these troops during the action

I have no doubt the service was promptly performed. Just in time to increase the panic of the fleeing fugitives, Battery K, Fifth U. S. Artillery, Lieutenant Kinzie commanding, and Fitzhugh's New York battery arrived, and opened on them. The enemy's attack was feebly renewed immediately after his first repulse. A single line of battle, with its left running nearly along the line followed by the right of the preceding lines, and numbering about 3,000 men, advanced, but it was utterly broken by the fire of the batteries on my left before it arrived within musketry range. A large number of the enemy came in and gave themselves up as soon as their line was broken, and 2 stand of colors fell into our hands.

This great victory was not gained without irreparable losses. In addition to those previously mentioned, the following regimental commanders were killed: Col. Dennis O'Kane, Sixty-ninth Pennsylvania Volunteers; Lieut. Col. Max A. Thoman, Fifty-ninth New York Volunteers; Col. Richard P. Roberts, One hundred and fortieth Pennsylvania Volunteers (on the 2d); Col. P. J. Revere, Twentieth Massachusetts Volunteers, and Lieutenant-Colonel Steele, Seventh Michigan Volunteers. The number of casualties among the field officers was very great, many of the regiments losing them all.

Toward the close of the main contest, I had the misfortune to lose the valuable services of a distinguished officer, Brig. Gen. John Gibbon, commanding Second Division, who was severely wounded. A short time afterward I was myself wounded, but was enabled to remain on the field until the action was entirely over, when I transferred the command to Brigadier-General Caldwell.

The services of the artillery during this engagement are particularly spoken of in the report of the commander of the artillery. Its losses in officers, men, and *matériel* will sufficiently attest the severity of the ordeal to which it was subjected. Three of the battery commanders, Captain Rorty and Lieuts. A. H. Cushing and G. A. Woodruff, all able, experienced, and distinguished officers, were killed, and another battery commander, Lieut. T. F. Brown, First Rhode Island Artillery, severely wounded.

The losses of the corps during the action at Gettysburg amounted to 4,323 officers and men killed, wounded, and missing. The strength of the corps in the action was about 10,000 officers and men. A statement of the losses in detail is herewith inclosed.*

To speak of the conduct of the troops would seem to be unnecessary, but still it may be justly remarked that this corps sustained its well-earned reputation on many fields, and that the boast of its gallant first commander, the late Maj. Gen. E. V. Sumner, that the Second Corps had "never given to the enemy a gun or color," holds good now as it did under the command of my predecessor, Major-General Couch. To attest to its good conduct and the perils through which it has passed, it may be stated that its losses in battle have been greater than those of any other corps in the Army of the Potomac, or probably in the service, notwithstanding it has usually been numerically weakest.

For the services of the commanders of divisions, Brig. Gens. John Gibbon, Alexander Hays, and John C. Caldwell, I need only to refer to the history of the deeds of their commands.

Brig. Gens. John Gibbon and Alexander Hays, being more particularly under my eye in the crisis of the battle, it is but just that I

---

*Embodied in revised statement. pp. 175-177.

should state that their conduct was all that could be desired in division commanders.

Capt. J. G. Hazard, commander of artillery of the corps, performed his duty in a commendable manner, behaving in the field with gallantry and directing his artillery with skill and judgment.

I desire particularly to refer to the services of a gallant young officer, First Lieut. F. A. Haskell, aide-de-camp to Brigadier-General Gibbon, who, at a critical period of the battle, when the contending forces were but 50 or 60 yards apart, believing that an example was necessary, and ready to sacrifice his life, rode between the contending lines with the view of giving encouragement to ours and leading it forward, he being at that moment the only mounted officer in a similar position. He was slightly wounded and his horse was shot in several places.

Brigadier-General Webb; Col. N. J. Hall, commanding brigade; Colonel Devereux, Nineteenth Massachusetts; Colonel Mallon, Forty-second New York; Col. R. Penn Smith, Seventy-first Pennsylvania, and others, whom I regret I am unable to name, performed in like manner most distinguished services in leading their men forward at a critical period in the contest.

Captain Hall, Fifty-third Pennsylvania Volunteers, and Lieutenant Taylor, both of the signal corps, are entitled to mention at my hands for their energy and usefulness displayed during the entire battle.

For the services of other officers who distinguished themselves, not heretofore mentioned in this report (there are many of them), I respectfully refer to the reports of division, brigade, and regimental commanders, and to the report of the commander of artillery, herewith transmitted.

Lieut. Col. C. H. Morgan, inspector-general and chief of staff, performed highly important services during the entire campaign. His intelligence on all occasions, his forethought, and fine conduct on the field of battle, entitled him to high praise.

Lieutenant-Colonel Batchelder, chief quartermaster, and Lieut. Col. J. S. Smith, chief commissary, ably conducted the services of their departments. Their duties were such as to cause them not to be present on the field of battle.

Surg. A. N. Dougherty, medical director of the corps, in the performance of his duties gave me entire satisfaction. No matter whether under the fire of the enemy or not, he was always at his post.

Maj. S. O. Bull, Fifty-third Pennsylvania Volunteers, provost-marshal of the corps, was actively engaged during the action in taking charge of the prisoners captured from the enemy. During the time of the engagement, he was under the orders of the provost-marshal-general of the army.

Maj. W. G. Mitchell, my senior aide-de-camp and acting assistant adjutant-general, who distinguished himself on several perilous occasions during this battle; Capt. I. B. Parker, aide-de-camp, and Capt. W. D. W. Miller, aide-de-camp, twice severely wounded on the 2d, behaved with their usual gallantry, and added to the esteem their fine conduct has gained for them on many fields.

Capt. H. H. Bingham, judge-advocate, slightly wounded, and Captain Brownson, commissary of musters, acting as aides for me on the occasion, behaved with great gallantry, and shared all the dangers of the field.

My personal orderlies—Sergeant [Owen] McKenzie, Private James

Wells, color-bearer Sixth New York Cavalry, and Privates [Alvin] Stearns and [David] Smith, Company D, Sixth New York Cavalry— behaved with their usual bravery, and always faithfully remained at their posts, no matter how dangerous their position.

I desire to bring particularly to the notice of the major-general commanding the case of Sergt. Frederick Fuger, first sergeant of Battery A, Fourth U. S. Artillery. During the action of the 3d, his conduct was such as to entitle him to promotion, and his character is such as to make this a proper method of rewarding his services. In this connection I refer to the report of Brigadier-General Webb.

Attached hereto is a tabular statement of casualties.*

With reference to the number of colors taken from the enemy, it is proper to say that each division has been credited with the number actually turned in, and for which receipts are held, making the aggregate of twenty-seven. There were undoubtedly thirty-three colors captured, the balance having been secreted as individual trophies.

I have the honor to be, very respectfully, your obedient servant,

WINF'D S. HANCOCK,
Major-General, Commanding Second Corps.

Brig. Gen. S. WILLIAMS,
Assistant Adjutant-General, Army of the Potomac.

ADDENDA.

HEADQUARTERS SECOND ARMY CORPS,
October 24, 1863.

Brig. Gen. S. WILLIAMS,
Assistant Adjutant-General, Army of the Potomac:

GENERAL : At the request of Major-General Hancock, I submit the following corrections in his official report of the operations of the Second Corps at Gettysburg. The general wishes the changes made in the copy of his report understood to have been already forwarded to the War Department:

In the description of the fight of July 2, the sentence, "The force which had turned General Caldwell's right and driven the left of the Third Corps now approached the line of battle as originally established, driving Humphreys' command rapidly back," to be changed to read as follows: "The force, &c., * * * approached the line of battle as originally established. Humphreys' command was forced back, contesting the ground stubbornly."

Again, on next page, for "Their artillery had been left on the field," read, "Three guns of one of its batteries had been left on the field, owing to the losses of horses and men."

Again, after the sentence, "By the advance of these regiments the artillery which had been left on the field in the Third Corps line was recaptured from the enemy," insert the following sentence: "Humphreys' division participated in this advance and in the recapture of its guns."

The report forwarded to general headquarters not being accessible, I am not able to refer to pages and lines when indicating the corrections desired by Major-General Hancock.

I am, general, very respectfully,

C. H. MORGAN,
Lieutenant-Colonel, and Assistant Inspector-General.

---

* Embodied in revised statement, pp. 175–177.

[Indorsement.]

HDQRS. ARMY OF THE POTOMAC, *October 28, 1863.*

Respectfully forwarded to the Adjutant-General, with request that General Hancock's report of the battle of Gettysburg, forwarded some time since, may be altered as suggested within.

GEO. G. MEADE,
Major-General, Commanding.

—

HEADQUARTERS SECOND ARMY CORPS,
Sandy Hook, Md., July 17, 1863.

Brig. Gen. S. WILLIAMS,
Assistant Adjutant-General, Army of the Potomac:

SIR: I have the honor to report the following number of dead buried at Gettysburg, Pa., by my command, from July 2 to 5, inclusive:

Forces.	Officers.	Enlisted men.	Total.
Union	18	369	387
Rebel	60	1,182	1,242
Total	78	1,551	1,629

REMARKS.—One female (private), in rebel uniform.

I am, general, very respectfully, your obedient servant,
WILLIAM HAYS,
Brigadier-General, Commanding Corps.

—

HEADQUARTERS SECOND ARMY CORPS,
Sandy Hook, Md., July 17, 1863.

Brig. Gen. S. WILLIAMS,
Assistant Adjutant-General, Army of the Potomac:

GENERAL: I have the honor to report the following as being the number of arms collected by my command from the battle-field of Gettysburg: 5,976 stand of small-arms.

I am, general, very respectfully, your obedient servant,
WILLIAM HAYS,
Brigadier-General, Commanding Second Corps.

—

HEADQUARTERS SECOND ARMY CORPS,
Morrisville, Va., August 26, 1863.

Brig. Gen. S. WILLIAMS,
Asst. Adjt. Gen., Hdqrs. Army of the Potomac:

GENERAL: I have the honor to report, in pursuance of Special Orders, No. 227, of the 24th instant, headquarters Army of the Potomac, that no guns were taken by the enemy from this command during the recent campaign in Pennsylvania and Maryland, and that no guns were taken from the enemy by this command during the same period.

I am, general, very respectfully, your obedient servant,
G. K. WARREN,
Major-General, Commanding.

No. 77.

Report of Brig. Gen. John C. Caldwell, U. S. Army, commanding First Division.

HEADQUARTERS FIRST DIVISION, SECOND CORPS,
September 5, 1863.

COLONEL: I have the honor to transmit the following report of the part taken by my division in the battle of Gettysburg, July 2 and 3:

My command arrived on the field of battle on the morning of July 2, and was placed in position by General Hancock on the left of the Second Division, in columns of regiments by brigades. Early in the afternoon the Second Corps, which had moved forward some distance toward the Emmitsburg road, engaged the enemy, and I was ordered to its support. I had moved but part of the distance required, when a column of the Fifth Corps appeared, coming to the assistance of the Second, and by order I resumed my former position. The battle was raging with considerable fury at the left, where, between 4 and 5 o'clock, I received orders to report with my command to General Sykes. I moved off immediately by the left flank, and sent forward my aide (Lieutenant Cross) to find General Sykes, but he did not succeed in finding him. Before reaching the position designated for me, I met a staff officer (I think the adjutant-general of General Sykes), who told me he had orders where to place me. I moved forward rapidly, a portion of the time at double-quick, as the Third Corps was said to be hard pressed. The position assigned me was on the right of the Fifth and the left of the Third Corps, and I was ordered to check and drive back the enemy who were advancing at that point. I ordered Colonel Cross, commanding the First Brigade, to advance in line of battle through a wheat-field, his left resting on the woods which skirted the field. He had advanced but a short distance when he encountered the enemy, and opened upon him a terrific fire, driving him steadily to the farther end of the wheat-field.

In the meantime I had put the Second Brigade in on the right of the First, and they advanced in like manner, driving the enemy before them. The Third Brigade I ordered still farther to the right, to connect with the Third Corps, while I held the Fourth Brigade in reserve. The First, Second, and Third Brigades advanced with the utmost gallantry, driving the enemy before them over difficult and rocky ground, which was desperately contested by the slowly retreating foe. The First Brigade, which had been longest engaged, had expended all its ammunition, when I ordered Colonel Brooke to relieve it. He advanced with his usual gallantry, and drove the enemy until he gained the crest of the hill, which was afterward gained by the whole of my line. In this advantageous position I halted, and called upon General Barnes, who was some distance in the rear, to send a brigade to the support of my line. He readily complied, and ordered the brigade of Colonel [Sweitzer] forward into the wheat-field. I then galloped to the left to make a connection with General Ayres, and found that I had advanced some distance beyond him. He, however, gave the order to his line to move forward and connect with my left. Thus far everything had progressed favorably. I had gained a position which, if properly supported on the flanks, I thought impregnable from the front. General Ayres was moving forward to connect with my left, but I found on going to the right that all the troops on my right had broken and were fleeing to the rear in great confusion. As soon as they broke, and before I could change front, the enemy in great numbers came in upon my right flank and even my rear, compelling me to fall back or have my command taken prisoners. My men fell back under a very heavy cross-fire, generally in good order, but necessarily with some confusion. I reformed them behind a stone wall until relieved by the Twelfth Corps.

By direction of Major-General Hancock, I marched my command back to the ground it had occupied in the earlier part of the day, where we lay on our arms until the morning of the 3d. I then formed what was left of the division in one line on a slight crest, and began to throw up breastworks. Before noon we had a work which served to protect the men during the artillery fire which followed.

About noon the enemy opened upon us with all his artillery the most fearful fire I have ever witnessed. Although this lasted an hour, but one of my men was killed and very few wounded.

Nearly at the same time with the grand assault which, following the artillery fire, was made upon our center, a single line, I should think a small brigade, advanced in our immediate front, but did not succeed in getting beyond our picket, being broken by the fire of our artillery. A large portion of this force came in and gave themselves up as prisoners.

The division on the afternoon of the 2d fought with its accustomed gallantry, and performed everything that could be expected of either officers or men. The large number of its killed and wounded attest its desperate valor. That it fell back was owing entirely to the breaking of the troops on the right, permitting the enemy to get on its flank and its rear.

While driving the enemy triumphantly before them, two of my brigade commanders, Brigadier-General Zook and Colonel Cross, of the Fifth New Hampshire Volunteers, fell, mortally wounded. They were both old and tried soldiers, and the country can illy spare their services. They both fell in the front of battle while driving back the invader, and lived long enough to know that their blood had not been shed in vain, but that the enemy had been driven back with terrible repulse. A grateful country will remember their virtues and hold them up to the admiration of posterity.

Colonel Roberts, One hundred and fortieth Pennsylvania Volunteers, and Lieutenant-Colonel Merwin, Twenty-seventh Connecticut Volunteers, were instantly killed; both gallant officers and brave men.

Colonel McKeen, Eighty-first Pennsylvania Volunteers, who, after the fall of Colonel Cross, succeeded to the command of the First Brigade, behaved, as he always has on every battle-field, with the most distinguished gallantry, and brought off his command in perfect order.

Lieutenant-Colonel Hapgood, Fifth New Hampshire Volunteers, and Lieutenant-Colonel Broady, Sixty-first New York Volunteers, behaved with the utmost coolness and bravery, and added to their already high reputation.

Colonel Kelly behaved with his wonted gallantry.

The conduct of Lieutenant-Colonel Fraser, One hundred and fortieth Pennsylvania Volunteers, and Lieutenant-Colonel Chapman, Fifty-seventh New York Volunteers, was worthy of all praise.

Of the merit of Colonel Brooke, commanding Fourth Brigade,

too much can scarcely be said.   His services on this as well as many other fields have fairly earned him promotion.

Colonels Brown and Baily are deserving of high praise.

The members of my staff rendered most efficient service.   I would mention as worthy of particular commendation Lieutenants [Daniel K.] Cross and [William P.] Wilson and Majors [George W.] Scott and [John] Hancock.

I have before had occasion to mention the bravery and good conduct of my orderly, Corpl. Uriah N. Parmelee, Company D, Sixth New York Cavalry.   On this occasion he not only behaved with great bravery, but was of great assistance to me in checking fugitives.   I respectfully recommend his promotion.

The lists of killed, wounded, and missing have already been forwarded.*

I am, sir, very respectfully, your obedient servant,

JOHN C. CALDWELL,
Brigadier-General, Commanding Division.

Lieut. Col. FRANCIS A. WALKER,
Assistant Adjutant-General, Second Corps.

No. 78.

Report of Col. H. Boyd McKeen, Eighty-first Pennsylvania Infantry, commanding First Brigade.

CAMP ON THE FIELD, *August* 11, 1863.

MAJOR: I have the honor to submit the following report of the First Brigade in the action at Gettysburg, Pa., July 2 and 3:

Early in the morning of the 2d, the brigade was massed in the woods to the left and rear of the position occupied by the corps when in line.

At 10 a. m. the brigade massed in column of regiments on the left of the division and the left center of the general line of battle.   Here we remained until 4 p. m., when the division was detached from the corps and marched to the left of the line, to check the advance of the enemy.   The brigade moved by the left flank from the position on the left of the center, until it reached the foot of Sugar Loaf Hill, and then formed line of battle in rear of a stone wall, over which we advanced and engaged the enemy.   At this time I was in command of the One hundred and forty-eighth Pennsylvania Volunteers.   The brigade was formed in the following order: The Sixty-first New York Volunteers, Eighty-first and One hundred and forty-eighth Pennsylvania Volunteers, and Fifth New Hampshire Volunteers, and the Sixty-first and Eighty-first and a portion of the One hundred and forty-eighth advanced in a wheat-field; the remainder of the One hundred and forty-eighth and Fifth New Hampshire Volunteers in a thick woods.   The brigade steadily drove the enemy back to the far end of the wheat-field, a distance of over 400 yards.   So quickly was this done that prisoners were taken by the brigade before the enemy had time to spring from their hiding-places to retreat.   A brigade of the Fifth Corps relieved the Sixty-first, Eighty-first, and a portion of the One hundred and forty-eighth.   Perceiving that if the balance of the brigade should retire it would expose the left flank of this bri-

---
* Embodied in revised statement, p. 175.

gade, I kept the balance of the One hundred and forty-eighth in position. At this time I was informed that Colonel Cross, who commanded the brigade, was mortally wounded, and that the command of the brigade devolved upon me.

The Fifth and One hundred and forty-eighth remained in position, steadily holding the enemy in check, until every round of cartridge in this portion of the brigade was expended, and even then held their position until relieved by a brigade of General Barnes' division, of the Fifth Corps. Passing the relieving brigade by file, they retired in splendid order, as they were enfiladed by a galling fire from our left flank (faced to the rear). Joining the balance of the brigade at the stone wall first spoken of, the brigade rejoined the division, and again moved to their old position on the left center.

Early on the morning of the 3d, breastworks were thrown up by the brigade. Unmolested we remained in this position until 4 p. m., when the enemy opened upon our position a terrible fire (artillery), which, however, did the brigade but little injury, owing to the breastworks thrown up in the morning.

About 5 p. m. three columns of attack debouched from an orchard in our immediate front, moving by their left flank, traversed the field in our front, and vigorously attacked the center of our line and to our immediate right. Almost simultaneously a single brigade of Florida troops advanced upon our position, but were broken by the artillery just as they were getting within musket-range. A large portion of this brigade ran into our lines and delivered themselves up as prisoners. This was the last effort of the enemy.

I have only to state that the brigade fought with its usual gallantry, and that the regiment I had the honor to command in the early part of the engagement, comparatively a new one, equaled in coolness and gallantry the balance of the brigade, old veterans of the Peninsula.

That gallant officer, Col. E. E. Cross, Fifth New Hampshire Volunteers, who led the brigade into action, fell, while bravely cheering his troops.

Great credit is due to the brigade staff for their gallantry upon the field, of which number Captain [George H.] Caldwell, assistant adjutant-general, and Lieutenant [John H.] Root, assistant inspector-general, were wounded severely in the discharge of their duties.

The following are the casualties in the brigade:

Officers and men.	Killed.	Wounded.	Missing.	Total.
Commissioned officers	3	21	......	24
Enlisted men	56	238	12	306
Total	59	259	12	330

Total strength of the brigade going into action, 780 muskets.

At 4 o'clock on the afternoon of July 5, the brigade was ordered out of its position, and from this date, by a series of marches, reached a position near Tilghmanton, Md., on the 10th instant. While lying here, the brigade supported Carroll's brigade, Third Division, Second Corps, on a reconnaissance, and drove the enemy to within 3 miles of

Hagerstown, on the Hagerstown turnpike, falling back, however, to Jones' Cross-Roads, near which point the brigade threw up works, in anticipation of a general engagement with the enemy.

On the 14th instant, my command held the advance in pursuit of the enemy's rear guard, capturing some 50 prisoners, and giving up the pursuit near Falling Waters. From this place the First Brigade, with the balance of the division, moved by rapid marches to Harper's Ferry, W. Va., halting for supplies a few days on the southern side of Maryland Heights, near Sandy Hook, and crossing the Potomac on the 18th. Shortly after crossing the river, on the same day, I received an order to report to the surgeon-in-chief of the general hospital in Philadelphia, and I immediately turned the command over to Lieutenant-Colonel **McFarlane, One** hundred and forty-eighth Pennsylvania Volunteers.

Up to this time, after leaving Gettysburg, the brigade met with no loss whatever in killed or wounded.

Respectfully,

H. BOYD McKEEN,
Colonel, Commanding First Brigade.

Maj. JOHN HANCOCK,
A. A. G., First Division, Second Army Corps.

No. 79.

Report of Maj. Richard E. Cross, Fifth New Hampshire Infantry.

CAMP NEAR HARPER'S FERRY, W. VA.,
July 16, 1863.

COLONEL: I have the honor to transmit the following report of the part taken by the Fifth New Hampshire Volunteers in the actions of July 2 and 3, and the pursuit of the 14th instant:

The regiment went into action, July 2, with 14 commissioned officers and 165 men; were under a heavy fire for two hours, every officer and man doing his duty. At the end of that time, having expended all of our ammunition, we were relieved by the Fifth Army Corps. The regiment fell back, firing, in good order.

The loss of the regiment was 1 commissioned officer killed and 4 wounded; 25 enlisted men killed and 49 wounded.

On the morning of the 3d instant, the regiment occupied the same ground which it held on the morning of the 2d. The forenoon was spent in throwing up intrenchments, which proved of great benefit to the regiment, as the enemy opened a tremendous cannonade on our line at about 2 p. m. During all this heavy fire we lost but 1 man, who was killed on the picket line.

On the 14th instant, the regiment was attached to Colonel Brooke's brigade, and acted as skirmishers, following up the enemy to within a short distance of Falling Waters, capturing some 50 prisoners, all of whom were turned over to the provost guard.

During all the fourteen days of fighting, marching, and skirmishing, the regiment has behaved in the most gallant and satisfactory manner, enduring all their hardships without a murmur.

Among the officers who particularly distinguished themselves on July 2, I would mention the names of Capt. J. S. Ricker, Company

C; Capt. G. F. Goodwin, Company D; Lieut. William McGee, Company E, and Sergt. Maj. E. H. Marston.

Col. E. E. Cross being in command of the brigade, the command of the regiment devolved upon Lieut. Col. C. E. Hapgood, who behaved in the most gallant manner, but who, I am sorry to say, we were compelled to leave behind at Frederick, Md., on account of sickness, which prevented him from sharing the victory and hardships of the 14th instant.

I am, colonel, very respectfully,

R. E. CROSS,
Major, Commanding Fifth New Hampshire Volunteers.

Col. H. B. McKEEN, *Commanding Brigade.*

No. 80.

Report of Lieut. Col. K. Oscar Broady, Sixty-first New York Infantry.

CAMP NEAR SANDY HOOK, MD.,
July 16, 1863.

SIR: I have the honor to submit the following report:

In the forenoon of the 2d instant, my regiment, together with the rest of the brigade, arrived on the field near Gettysburg, Pa., and was halted near and to the left of Cemetery Hill. The brigade was formed in close column by battalion, the Sixty-first New York Volunteers being the second in column, with the Fifth New Hampshire Volunteers in front and the One hundred and forty-eighth Pennsylvania Volunteers in the rear. While here, and at a halt, we were occasionally exposed to the enemy's artillery fire, but without sustaining any loss to our number. About 4 p. m. the Fifth New Hampshire Volunteers were removed from the column, leaving the Sixty-first New York in the front.

About 6 p. m. we were marched by the left flank for about half a mile to the front and left of our previous position, when the brigade was formed in line of battle by inversion and faced by the rear rank, thus leaving my command still on the right of the line. We then advanced to the front for about 200 yards, and engaged the enemy, who was mostly sheltered behind a stone-wall fence, used as a breastwork. The enemy's fire was particularly severe on that part of the line where the Sixty-first New York was posted.

The loss sustained here was 6 commissioned officers wounded, of whom 1 has since died; 6 enlisted men killed and 50 wounded. Being able to bring into action only 90 muskets, it will be seen I sustained a loss of almost two-thirds of the whole strength.

The wounds received by my men seemed to be of an unusually severe character, and it is to be feared that the greater portion of the wounded will never be fit for active service again.

The engagement lasted about half an hour, when we were relieved by a brigade of the Fifth Corps. Soon after being relieved, I received orders from Lieut. D. K. Cross, on General Caldwell's staff, to form my command into a guard, and take to the rear 100 prisoners, just brought in by another brigade. Not finding any provost guard anywhere on the road, I had to conduct these prisoners for about 2 miles to the rear, and kept guard over them for the night.

On the morning of the 3d, I left them with 1 lieutenant of my regiment and 16 men as provost guard, and returned with the rest of my command to the front, and joined the brigade, which was then occupying almost the same ground as on the day previous. Having thrown up earthworks in front, we remained here, exposed to a very heavy artillery fire from the enemy during the day, but without any loss to our number.

We continued in this position until the forenoon of the 5th instant, when it was fully ascertained that the enemy had fallen back, and we again resumed the march.

During the whole engagement my command, officers and men, behaved with the utmost coolness and valor. They performed all that could be expected or demanded of true and good soldiers. To particularize would not be just where every man is worthy of praise.

Very respectfully, your obedient servant,

K. O. BROADY,
Lieutenant-Colonel, Comdg. Sixty-first New York Volunteers.

Lieut. J. B. HALLENBECK,
Acting Assistant Adjutant-General, First Brigade.

No. 81.

Report of Lieut. Col. Amos Stroh, Eighty-first Pennsylvania Infantry.

NEAR GETTYSBURG, PA., *July* 5, 1863.

SIR: I have the honor to make the following report of the part taken by the Eighty-first Pennsylvania Volunteers during the recent engagement:

About 5 o'clock on the evening of the 2d instant, we were moved to the left, where we found a heavy infantry fight going on. We took our position on a knoll in an open field, on the edge of which the enemy lay, under cover of a stone wall and partly concealed by a dense wood. Here we opened fire, and expended nearly all our ammunition, when we were relieved by another regiment taking our place. We lay on the field a short time, and then marched still farther to the rear, and took position with the One hundred and forty-eighth Pennsylvania Volunteers behind a stone fence, where we were joined by the balance of the brigade, and marched back to the position we occupied in the early part of the day, and which we still occupy.

Our loss during the day was 5 men killed, 5 officers and 44 men wounded, and 8 men missing. Compared to the number we took into action, our loss was nearly as great as in any former engagement.

On the morning of the 5th instant, we threw up breastworks, which have been of great protection to the men. During the artillery firing of the 3d and 4th instant, the regiment was not actively engaged, and suffered no loss during the attacks made by the enemy on this front.

Respectfully,

AMOS STROH,
Lieut. Col., Comdg. Eighty-first Pennsylvania Volunteers.

ACTING ASSISTANT ADJUTANT-GENERAL,
First Brigade.

No. 82.

Report of Col. Patrick Kelly, Eighty-eighth New York Infantry,
commanding Second Brigade.

HEADQUARTERS SECOND BRIGADE, FIRST DIVISION,
Near Morrisville, Va., August 9, 1863.

MAJOR: I have the honor to forward the following report of the part taken by this brigade in the battle of Gettysburg, Pa., on July 2 and 3:

About 10 p. m. on the 1st, we arrived within 2 or 3 miles of Gettysburg; bivouacked in an adjacent field; threw out our pickets, and at 4.30 o'clock next morning (2d), marched toward Gettysburg. Arriving on the heights near the village, and in view of the enemy's pickets, we took a position in two lines on the right of the First Brigade, stacked arms, and allowed the men to rest.

About 3 p. m. the brigade, with the rest of the division, moved about half a mile to the left and forward. Were then ordered to take our original position, which we did.

About 5 p. m. received orders to march by the left flank, which we did, preceded by the First Brigade. Both brigades advanced in line of battle through a wheat-field into a wood, in which was a considerable quantity of very large rocks, behind which they poured into us a brisk fire while advancing. We, however, drove them a considerable distance, and sent a great many prisoners to the rear. After being, I should think, about three-quarters of an hour engaged, the troops on our left had retired, and the enemy pressing hard on that point, on going to the right of the brigade I found the enemy forming line faced to our right along the edge of the wood. Finding myself in this very disagreeable position, I ordered the brigade to fall back, firing. We here encountered a most terrific fire, and narrowly escaped being captured. We, however, got out, reformed the brigade, and joined the division near the Second Division hospital. It was now after nightfall, and, soon after, we were moved to the front, and slept on our arms all night.

Early next morning (3d), we were ordered to throw up breastworks, behind which we remained all day, under probably the heaviest artillery fire ever heard, with a loss of only 1 man wounded.

The 4th and a portion of the 5th were spent in burying the dead, attending to the wounded, and collecting arms and equipments.

About 4.30 p. m. on the 5th, marched off the battle-field to a place called Two Taverns.

Before closing this report, it gives me pleasure to say that both officers and men of this command have acted to my entire satisfaction during the engagement. Mentioning the names of a few would be doing injustice to the rest. The command took into action an aggregate of 530 men. The casualties are as follows:

Officers and men.	Killed.	Wounded.	Missing.	Total.
Commissioned officers	1	4	2	7
Enlisted men	29	108	58	195
Total*	30	112	60	202

* But see revised statement, p. 175.

Accompanying this, I forward the report of each regimental commander.

Very respectfully,

P. KELLY,
Colonel, Commanding Brigade.

Maj. JOHN HANCOCK, *Assistant Adjutant-General.*

No. 83.

Report of Col. Richard Byrnes, Twenty-eighth Massachusetts Infantry.

NEAR BEALETON, VA., *August 2*, 1863.

SIR: I have the honor to transmit the following report of the part taken by this regiment during the battle of Gettysburg, Pa., July 2 and 3:

At 3 p. m., July 2, the order was given to advance, and the regiment proceeded a short distance forward and to the left, and then was ordered back to its original position. Soon after was ordered to move to the left, and about 5.30 o'clock became engaged with the enemy, who were posted in an advantageous position on the crest of a rocky hill. We forced them to retire from this eminence, and advanced over the top and almost to the bottom of the other side of the hill, being all the time exposed to a very severe fire of musketry, and losing many men in killed and wounded.

About 7 p. m., finding all save this regiment were retiring from the hill, and that the enemy were on both our flanks, as well as in front, I brought my command from the field, losing many men from the concentrated fire of the rebels. Our loss in this action was 100 in killed, wounded, and missing, out of 224 taken into the engagement.

I reformed the regiment, and rejoined the brigade near the Second Division hospital about dark, and soon after were moved to the front, where we remained all night, and in the morning erected breastworks of rails and earth, behind which we remained throughout the entire day, during the greater portion of which the enemy kept up an extremely heavy fire of artillery, and made two attempts to force our lines, but were repulsed on each occasion with great loss. On account of being sheltered by our earthworks, which we erected on the 3d instant, we suffered no casualties from the enemy's fire.

I have the honor to be, sir, your obedient servant,

RICHARD BYRNES,
Colonel, Comdg. Twenty-eighth Massachusetts Vols.

Lieut. W. S. BAILEY, *Acting Assistant Adjutant-General.*

No. 84.

Report of Capt. Thomas Touhy, Sixty-third New York Infantry.

HDQRS. SIXTY-THIRD BATTALION NEW YORK VOLS.,
August 2, 1863.

LIEUTENANT: I have the honor to most respectfully make the following report of the part the Sixty-third Battalion New York Volunteers took in the battle of Gettysburg, July 2:

For more effective duty in action, the Sixty-third was consolidated with the Sixty-ninth and Eighty-eighth Battalions New York Volunteers. The three battalions, composed of two companies each, were commanded by Lieut. Col. R. C. Bentley, of the Sixty-third, forming a part of the Second Brigade, First Division, Second Corps, and were with the division when it advanced to the front line on the morning of July 2, where we lay in line of battle until about 4 p. m., and were then ordered to advance with the brigade into the woods on the left of our position, where we engaged the enemy's infantry and fought them over an hour, driving them a distance of over three-quarters of a mile, and capturing many prisoners, among whom were some officers. The battalion was armed with smooth-bore Springfield muskets, caliber .69, and each man before going into action was provided with 60 rounds of buck-and-ball cartridges, caliber .69. Our aggregate strength was 75 men, out of which we lost the following:

Officers and men.	Killed.	Wounded.	Missing.	Prisoners.	Total.
Commissioned officers	......	1	......	1	2
Enlisted men.	6	9	7	......	22
Total	6	10	7	1	24

Among the wounded was Lieut. Col. R. C. Bentley, who was struck in the left leg with a piece of shell. Second Lieut. Dominick I. Connally was taken prisoner, and is now at Richmond, Va.

I take pleasure in stating that both officers and men behaved in the most creditable manner, showing great coolness and bravery while under fire.

The battalion after being relieved returned to the position they at first occupied, threw up breastworks, and were under heavy fire from the enemy's batteries all the succeeding day (July 3), having 1 man wounded by explosion of a shell.

All of which is most respectfully submitted.

THOMAS TOUHY,
Captain Company A, Commanding Battalion.

Lieut. W. S. BAILEY,
Acting Assistant Adjutant-General, Second Brigade.

No. 85.

Report of Lieut. James J. Smith, Sixty-ninth New York Infantry.

HDQRS. SIXTY-NINTH REGIMENT, NEW YORK VOLS.,
August 5, 1863.

LIEUTENANT: In compliance with notice from brigade headquarters, I beg leave to submit the following report of the part this regiment took in the action near Gettysburg, Pa.:

We arrived near Gettysburg on the evening of July 1, having marched from Uniontown, Md.

About 10 a. m. July 2 we were placed in position in line of battle, forming at the time part of the second line, the Twenty-eighth Massachusetts Volunteers, of our own brigade, being immediately in our front. The regiment was engaged during the morning and up to 5 p. m. in taking down fences, &c., sometimes under a heavy artillery fire.

At 5 p. m. we received orders to move rapidly to the left, to a point about 2 miles distant, and at the base of a rocky and precipitous hill, occupied by our troops, then attacked by the enemy in strong force. Marching by the flank, we moved up to and across a corn-field and entered a wood, on each side of which was an open corn-field, that on the left occupied by our troops (I think some of the Fifth Corps), one regiment of which I recognized as the Fourth U. S. Infantry. After the line was formed, we moved forward until we met the enemy, who were posted behind large bowlders of rock, with which the place abounded; but after our line delivered one or two volleys, the enemy were noticed to waver, and upon the advance of our line (firing) the enemy fell back, contesting the ground doggedly. One charge to the front brought us in a lot of prisoners, who were immediately sent to the rear. Our line moved forward (still firing), I should judge, not less than 200 yards, all the time preserving a good line and occupying the most advanced part of the line of battle, when we came suddenly under a very severe fire from the front, most probably another line of battle of the enemy; we also about this time got orders to fall back. We had scarcely got this order when we were attacked by the enemy on our right flank in strong force, and extending some distance to the rear, evidently with the intention of surrounding us. It was impossible after falling back to rally the men, as the enemy's line extended down to the corn-field that we had to cross; also there was no line immediately in rear of us to rally on; also in consequence of the small number of men in our regiment falling back in double-quick time, and the great confusion that prevailed at the time we crossed the corn-field. I collected about one dozen of our men together, and was informed that the division was reforming on the ground that we occupied in the morning. Arriving on the ground where the division was forming, I reported to Colonel Brooke, Fifty-third Pennsylvania Volunteers, then commanding division.

It was here I was informed for the first time of the wounding of Capt. Richard Moroney, who commanded the regiment on entering the field, and I take great pleasure in saying that I can testify to the able manner in which he managed our little battalion as our commanding officer during the engagement and up to the time of receiving his wounds. After most of the division were collected together, we got orders to move to the right, to occupy a certain part of the field, near where we were posted previous to going into action. We reached the said place about 10 p. m., and got into position for the night.

Next morning the line was advanced to the front and left under a heavy artillery fire. Most of the day engaged in throwing up earthworks and strengthening our position..

About 1 p. m. the enemy advanced a strong column against the line, but were repulsed with great loss, many of the men throwing down their arms and coming in as prisoners.

On the morning of July 4, Lieutenant O'Neil reported to me, he having been absent without leave, keeping with him 7 or 8 enlisted men, since July 2, the time of the engagement. Charges have been preferred against him.

I beg leave to report that this regiment entered the field with 6 officers and 69 enlisted men, and that we lost during the action 5 men killed, 1 officer and 13 men wounded, and 6 men missing.

In conclusion, I will state that, with the single exception that I have made above, I feel proud to say that all the officers and men engaged in the action acted as good soldiers and brave men.

I have the honor to be, lieutenant, very respectfully, yours, &c.,

JAMES J. SMITH,
1st Lieut. and Adjt., Comdg. Sixty-ninth Regt. New York Vols.

Lieut. W. S. BAILEY,
Actg. Asst. Adjt. Gen., Second Brig., First Div., Second Corps.

No. 86.

Report of Capt. Denis F. Burke, Eighty-eighth New York Infantry.

CAMP NEAR MORRISVILLE, VA.,
August 3, 1863.

LIEUTENANT: I have the honor to forward the following report of the Eighty-eighth New York Volunteers during the action at Gettysburg, Pa., on July 2 and 3:

On the morning of the 2d, this regiment advanced in line, and took up position on the left of the town of Gettysburg, in conjunction with the other regiments of this brigade. We held this position until about 5 p. m., when, the enemy having massed his forces on the left of our position, we were ordered to advance, and support the troops already in position there. We made our advance in brigade line of battle, being exposed during this time to a heavy fire of musketry and artillery. We steadily drove the enemy, charging repeatedly, and finally caused them to retreat in utter confusion, though we were opposed by a greatly superior force.

Both officers and men displayed the greatest gallantry and bravery, cheering and encouraging their comrades during the thickest of the fight. We drove the enemy for over half a mile through a thickly wooded and rocky country, and held our position until relieved by the Third Brigade.

The strength of the regiment entering the fight was 90 men, all told. Out of this number we lost 1 officer and 7 enlisted men killed, 1 officer and 16 men wounded, and 3 enlisted men missing, supposed killed.

I would beg to recommend to your notice for bravery and excellent conduct on the field the following-named officers: Capt. Patrick Ryder, First Lieuts. Charles M. Granger and Thomas H. O'Brien, and Second Lieut. Patrick J. McCabe; but the conduct of Adjt. William McClelland—severely wounded, since dead—deserves particular notice. At all times in the hottest part of the fight, he kept encouraging the men and inciting them to still greater deeds of valor —a brave soldier and a good man, whom we can illy afford to spare.

Our division being outflanked on our right, we were ordered to fall back, which we did, and formed again to the left of the position we held in the morning and on the prolongation of our line.

We rested on our arms all night, and assisted, with the other regiments of the brigade, in throwing up breastworks, which we completed early on the morning of the 3d, and held until the close of the battle. The enemy shelled us at intervals during the morning, and at 10 a. m. opened with a severity which good military judges have pronounced to be the severest artillery fire of the war. Under cover of his artillery, the enemy advanced and charged upon our lines, but was everywhere repulsed with terrific slaughter, and finally compelled to retire dismayed and routed. Numbers of the enemy threw down their arms, and, rushing into our lines, surrendered as prisoners of war.

We were engaged in perfecting and repairing the breeches made in our breastworks on the evening of the 3d, and on the 4th in collecting arms and equipments left on the battle-field.

On the morning of the 5th, our pickets having discovered that the enemy was falling back, a reconnaissance was made, and found that the enemy was in full retreat toward the Potomac.

We held our position until the evening of the 5th, details in the meantime being engaged in burying the dead and attending to the wants of the wounded left on the battle-field. We then moved in the direction of Frederick, Md., under orders from headquarters.

In conclusion, I am proud to say that the Eighty-eighth acted in this fight as it has always done on former occasions when it has met the enemy.

DENIS F. BURKE,
Captain, Comdg. Eighty-eighth New York Volunteers.

Lieut. W. S. BAILEY,
Acting Assistant Adjutant-General, Second Brigade.

No. 87.

Report of Maj. St. Clair A. Mulholland, One hundred and sixteenth Pennsylvania Infantry.

IN CAMP, SANDY HOOK, MD.,
July 17, 1863.

SIR: In accordance with section 742, paragraph 36, page 107, Revised Army Regulations, I have the honor to submit the following report of the part taken by my command in the action at Gettysburg, Pa., July 2 and 3:

After a long and fatiguing march, we arrived on the evening of the 1st instant within about 3 miles of Gettysburg, and by order of General Caldwell, our division commander, encamped for the night in a neighboring field. Shortly after daybreak on the morning of the 2d, in compliance with orders received, the brigade of which my regiment has the honor of being a part moved up to a field within sight of the enemy's pickets. Our division was ployed in mass in column of regiments, my regiment being placed in the front line. Here we stacked arms, and ordered the men to rest. We remained in this position during the forenoon of the 2d instant. Heavy firing was heard at intervals on our right during the day, although everything remained quiet in the vicinity of my command until about 3 p. m.

About this time firing commenced on our left, I think about three-fourths of a mile distant. The firing had continued about an hour when orders came for us to fall in. We at once took arms, and were marched by the left flank toward the scene of action. After marching nearly 1 mile, and the division being in line of battle, we advanced to support (I think) a portion of the Third Army Corps, which was then engaged. The brigade to which we are attached advanced in line of battle, left in front, gallantly led by Col. P. Kelly, of the Eighty-eighth New York Volunteers. As we advanced, portions of the Third Corps retired, passing through the intervals of our line. Having entered a dense woods, we began to ascend a hill, where large bowlders of rocks impeded our progress, notwithstanding which we advanced in good order. We soon came within sight of the enemy, who occupied the crest of the hill, and who immediately opened fire at our approach. Our brigade returned the fire with good effect. After firing for about ten minutes, the order was given to advance, which the brigade did in excellent style, driving the enemy from their position, which we at once occupied. We took many prisoners at this point, hundreds of the enemy laying down their arms and passing to the rear. We found the position which our foes had occupied but a few moments before thickly strewn with the dead and wounded. Here we again opened fire, the enemy having rallied to oppose our farther advance. After being engaged for about twenty minutes and the enemy having been re-enforced, the division began to retire in good order. At this time the division was completely outflanked by the enemy, who had formed a line facing the right flank of our brigade. This line was formed along the edge of a wheat-field, about a quarter of a mile in rear of our brigade. This field we had to cross to get to the rear. In doing so, we encountered the full sweep of the enemy's fire, which at this point was most destructive. Many of the division fell before this terrible fire.

After passing to the rear, I found Colonel Brooke, Fourth Brigade, forming the division in a field adjoining the Second Division hospital; he told me he had orders from General Caldwell to that effect. I then halted what remained of my command, and rendered all the assistance I could in gathering together members of the Second Brigade.

Shortly after dark we were again marched to the front, and placed in the same position that we had occupied in the morning. Here we lay on our arms all night, and were awakened at daybreak by the sound of the enemy's cannon. Major-General Hancock passed along early in the day, and moved our line a little forward, in order that we might have a better range and our fire be more effective, should the enemy attack us. We immediately commenced to intrench our new position, and by 11 a. m. had quite a formidable breastwork thrown up. All this forenoon we could see the enemy preparing to attack us. Several batteries were placed in position opposite our line, and everything indicated that an attack was intended.

About noon the attack commenced by a most terrific shelling of our lines by the enemy, but, thanks to our earthworks and the inaccurate aim of the gunners, none of my command were injured. After shelling our position for about two hours, the fire of the artillery somewhat slackened, and a heavy force of rebel infantry was seen advancing upon our works. At this moment our artillery, which up to this time had remained almost silent, opened with terrible effect upon the advancing lines, tearing great gaps in their ranks and strewing the field with dead and wounded. Notwithstanding the destructive fire under which they were placed, the enemy continued to advance with a degree of ardor, coolness, and bravery worthy of a better cause, until, reaching a ravine which ran parallel with our line, about midway between us and their artillery, they halted, being under cover and no longer exposed to our fire. They halted but to surrender. Finding, I presume, that their ranks were too much thinned to think of charging our works, knowing the heavy loss they would sustain in attempting to reach their own lines again, and thinking discretion the better part of valor, they laid down their arms and surrendered almost to a man. Perceiving the failure of their infantry to carry our position, the enemy again opened their batteries, but, after another hour's fire, withdrew, leaving us victors of the field.

During the day's fighting the heat was very great, and the men, being exposed and having neither shelter nor water, suffered intensely. Soon after sunset the same evening the rain commenced to descend in torrents, wetting every one, filling the rifle-pits, and making us most uncomfortable. But my command was ever hopeful, and bore the fatigue and suffering incidental to a great battle with the cheerfulness that ever characterizes the true soldier.

The sun rose on the morning of the 4th instant and found us victors of every part of the field. We remained in the same position until the afternoon of this day, when my command, with the division, formed line, and marched to the village of Two Taverns, where we encamped for the night.

In closing my report, I cannot refrain from mentioning the cool and gallant bearing of my command. Of the officers it is almost useless for me to speak. Every one did his duty in a manner that excited my warmest admiration and gratitude. Were I to mention any one in particular it would be but showing injustice to the rest, as each one tried to excel the other in deeds of gallantry and daring. Of the enlisted men, I feel happy in mentioning the names of Color Sergt. Abraham T. Detweiler, Sergt. Thomas Detweiler, Company A, and Private Jefferson Carl, Company C, as having especially distinguished themselves in the action of the 2d instant.

Our casualties during the three days' continuance of the fight were 2 men killed, 12 wounded, and 1 officer (Capt. John Teed) and 7 enlisted men missing.

Respectfully submitted.

Your obedient servant,

ST. CLAIR A. MULHOLLAND,
Major, Comdg. 116th Pennsylvania Volunteers.

Capt. Theo. W. Greig,
Acting Assistant Adjutant-General.

No. 88.

Reports of Lieut. Col. John Fraser, One hundred and fortieth Pennsylvania Infantry, commanding regiment and Third Brigade.

Hdqrs. 140th Regiment Pennsylvania Volunteers,
August 8, 1863.

Major: I have the honor to submit the following report of the part taken by the Third Brigade in the recent engagement with the enemy at Gettysburg, Pa. :

On the morning of July 2, this brigade arrived on the battle-field, under the command of Brigadier-General Zook, and was placed in order of column in rear of the Second Brigade.

About 4 p. m. on same day, the brigade was marched rapidly toward the left, to assist the Third Corps, which was at the time engaged with the enemy. When the brigade arrived nearly opposite the position assigned to it, it was formed in order of battle, having the One hundred and fortieth Pennsylvania Volunteers on the extreme right, the Sixty-sixth New York Volunteers in the center, the Fifty-second New York Volunteers on the left, and the Fifty-seventh New York Volunteers a short distance in the rear as a reserve, and was moved rapidly forward to engage the enemy. The brigade advanced steadily, driving the enemy before it, until it reached its most advanced position on the crest of a small hill. It held this position until it became necessary to retreat, the enemy having brought forward fresh troops, who succeeded in flanking us on the right and left. The retreat, however, did not commence before it had become general on other parts of the line.

Shortly after the close of this action, July 2, the brigade assembled, and was formed in line of battle in the position assigned to it, on the left center of the battle-field, about 50 paces in rear of the Second Brigade.

The severe and long-continued artillery fire which the enemy opened on us preparatory to their fruitless attack upon the left center, on the afternoon of July 3, inflicted no loss on the brigade. It was unnecessary for the brigade to take an active part in this engagement, the enemy having failed to advance beyond our picket line.

The conduct of officers and men deserves very high commendation.

In the action of July 2, the brigade lost its highly esteemed general, several gallant officers, and a large number of brave men. A list of casualties has been already forwarded.*

I have the honor to be, major, yours, respectfully,

JOHN FRASER,
Lieut. Col. 140th Pennsylvania Vols., Comdg. Third Brig.

Maj. JOHN HANCOCK,
Assistant Adjutant-General, First Division.

HEADQUARTERS 140TH PENNSYLVANIA VOLUNTEERS,
August 7, 1863.

CAPTAIN: I have the honor to submit the following report of the part taken by the One hundred and fortieth Regiment Pennsylvania Volunteers in the recent engagements at Gettysburg, Pa.:

On the morning of July 2, this regiment, under the command of Col. R. P. Roberts, arrived on the battle-ground, where it remained for several hours in order of columns by wings, right wing in front, a few paces in rear of the Second Brigade.

About 4 p. m. the brigade was marched rapidly to the left, to assist the Third Corps, which was then sustaining a fierce attack. When it arrived nearly opposite the place assigned to it, the brigade was formed in line of battle, with the One hundred and fortieth Pennsylvania Volunteers on the extreme right, and was moved rapidly forward to engage the enemy. As soon as the order was given, this

---

*Embodied in revised statement, p. 175.

regiment opened a brisk fire, which it kept up with great firmness and coolness, steadily driving the enemy before it until we reached the crest of a small hill. During the advance to this crest, the four left companies of this regiment, with the regiments to the left, gradually made a considerable wheel to the right. Shortly after reaching the crest, I observed a great many to the left of this brigade moving rapidly to the rear, and the rebels, apparently fresh troops, in large numbers and in good order marching to outflank us on the right. Anxious to know what orders General Zook had to give in the crisis, I sent twice to get instructions from him, but neither the general nor any of his staff could be found. I did not know at the time, nor until after the fight was over, that General Zook had been mortally wounded when leading the brigade into action. Inferring, from the large numbers of men who to the left of my regiment were continuously rushing to the rear, that a large portion of our division was actually retreating, I judged it necessary for the safety of those who had wheeled considerably into the enemy's ground to maintain my position and keep the enemy at bay as long as possible. I therefore held my position until I considered it necessary to order my men to march in retreat, which they did at first in good order, the four right companies halting several times, and firing, to check the pursuit of the enemy.

After this engagement on the 2d, the regiment assembled with the rest of the brigade, and formed in line of battle on the left center of the battle-ground and about 50 paces in rear of the Second Brigade.

On the morning of July 3, the regiment, pursuant to orders, constructed breastworks immediately in front of its line. The severe and long-continued artillery fire which the rebels opened upon us prior to their fruitless attack upon our position in the afternoon of this day, did no harm to any one in the regiment.

Colonel Roberts was killed while bravely leading on his men at the commencement of the action on July 2.

The conduct of officers and men in these engagements at Gettysburg deserves the highest praise.

A list of the heavy casualties of the regiment has been already forwarded.*

I have the honor to be, captain, yours, respectfully,
JOHN FRASER,
Lieutenant-Colonel 140th Pennsylvania Volunteers.

Capt. GEORGE W. JONES,
Acting Assistant Adjutant-General, Third Brigade.

No. 89.

Report of Capt. William Scherrer, Fifty-second New York Infantry.

CAMP NEAR MORRISVILLE, VA., *August 2,* 1863.

CAPTAIN : In compliance with circular from headquarters Second Army Corps, August 2, I have the honor to report that on July 2 this regiment arrived on the field near Gettysburg at about 10 a. m.

At 4 p. m. the regiment, under command of Lieut. Col. Charles G. Freudenberg, was ordered by General Zook, commanding this bri-

---

* Embodied in revised statement, p. 175.

gade, to advance toward our left, which was done in double-quick and in good order. Passing in line of battle through a small wood, the regiment finally arrived at a corn-field, where the battle had been already raging for several hours. Here the regiment, together with the brigade, commenced firing, giving the enemy, who was about 100 yards in front of our line, three or four good volleys. The position being too exposed, the regiment advanced on the enemy, who was then seen fleeing in all directions. Driving them about 1,500 or 2,000 yards through the woods and over the rocks, the regiment arrived on the edge of the woods, and was there ordered to halt.

About twenty-five minutes afterward the regiment was ordered to fall back, as the enemy had flanked us on our right.

During this engagement, which lasted over an hour, the regiment lost as follows: Killed, 1 officer and 1 enlisted man; wounded, 3 officers and 21 enlisted men, and missing, 8 enlisted men. Three enlisted men died since in hospital near Gettysburg.

The regiment then organized again, and rested for the night near the Taneytown road.

On July 3, the regiment occupied a position on the left of the battle-field, and opposite the enemy's batteries, which could plainly be seen. During the shell fire, which commenced soon after 12 o'clock, the regiment was much exposed, but, fortunately, lost but 2 enlisted men, very slightly wounded by a piece of shell.

During the fight on July 2, the officers and men of this regiment performed their duties to their utmost endeavors.

I am, captain, very respectfully, your obedient servant,

WM. SCHERRER,
Captain, Comdg. 52d Regiment New York Vols.

Capt. GEORGE W. JONES,
Actg. Asst. Adjt. Gen., Third Brigade.

No. 90.

Report of Lieut. Col. Alford B. Chapman, Fifty-seventh New York Infantry.

CAMP NEAR MORRISVILLE, VA.,
August 5, 1863.

CAPTAIN: I have the honor to submit the following report of the part taken by this regiment in the recent actions near Gettysburg, Pa.:

This brigade, having been detailed the day previous as guard to the wagon train, did not arrive on the scene of action until the morning of July 2. On the afternoon of that day, the division was moved rapidly to the left, to the support of the Third Corps, then engaged in repelling a severe attack of the enemy on that point. This regiment brought up the rear of the brigade, which was then the rearmost of the division, but in taking position in line was moved to the right. I was directed by General Zook to take a position in supporting distance of the front line. I moved into the position assigned me, within a few rods of the front line. The firing at this time was very severe, and General Zook was soon after mortally wounded and taken from the field. Shortly afterward, a staff officer rode up to me and stated that the right of the line had broken, and that the enemy were coming in rapidly on that flank, advising me to move my regiment to the rear to avoid being taken. I determined and was about to change front forward to the right and endeavor to protect the right flank of the brigade, when the whole line in front of me suddenly gave way, breaking through the ranks of my regiment in considerable disorder. I held my men together until the greater part of the front line had broken through, and then moved to the rear in line and in good order, the enemy following closely.

During this retrograde movement I halted my regiment several times, and endeavored to rally men enough on its flanks to check the advance of the enemy, but without success. Another line of our troops soon after moved into action, and I reported to General Caldwell, and joined other regiments of the division then collecting together.

On the morning of July 3, I was directed to erect slight breastworks in front of my regiment, the division being then in line to the right of the field in which it was engaged the day previous. This was done in a short time, and proved of great service during the day in protecting the men from the fire of artillery. During the day we sustained the most severe and long-continued artillery fire of the war, followed by a most determined infantry attack, which was successfully repulsed. In our immediate front the enemy's infantry did not succeed in advancing beyond our picket line excepting as prisoners of war.

The list of casualties in my regiment has been heretofore forwarded.*

I am, sir, very respectfully, your obedient servant,

A. B. CHAPMAN,
Lieut. Col. Fifty-Seventh New York Vols., Comdg. Regt.

Capt. GEORGE W. JONES,
Acting Assistant Adjutant-General.

No. 91.

Report of Maj. Peter Nelson, Sixty-sixth New York Infantry.

NEAR MORRISVILLE, VA., *August* 3, 1863.

SIR: In compliance with orders from brigade headquarters, I have the honor to submit the following report of the operations of the Sixty-sixth New York Volunteers in the action of Gettysburg, July 2, 3, and 4:

This regiment, under the command of Col. O. H. Morris, arrived on the ground on the morning of the 2d, after a very fatiguing march from Uniontown, Md., which occupied us the whole of the previous day and night. We formed line of battle, with the One hundred and fortieth Pennsylvania Volunteers in our front in two lines, the Fifty-second New York Volunteers on our right, and the Fifty-seventh New York Volunteers in our rear. We here stacked arms, and permitted the men to take that rest they so much required.

About 4 p. m. the rebels opened on us with a severe fire of artillery,

---

* Embodied in revised statement, p. 175.

from which we unfortunately lost Capt. E. F. Munn, commanding Company G, who was instantly killed by almost the first shell that was thrown. We were immediately under arms and moved to the left a short distance, then to the front, and finally back to our first position, the whole division participating in the movement. Soon after halting, we were moved by the left flank, in the direction of which heavy firing was heard, which movement was performed in admirable order, although under a heavy fire of artillery. After moving a distance of about one-quarter of a mile, we were halted, and then moved by battalion successively to the right, in order to bring us into brigade line, right in front. As soon as we had obtained our position we, were ordered by the left flank into the woods in front of us. Very soon we were under fire of musketry, but, nothing daunted, we pressed steadily forward through wheat-fields, woods, over rail fences 10 feet high, stone walls, ditches, deep ravines, rocks, and all sorts of obstructions, every one of which had served as cover for the enemy, and from which a murderous fire was poured upon us as we advanced, but without avail, as nothing could stop the impetuosity of our men, who, without waiting to load or even fix bayonets, rushed eagerly forward at a run, their cry being constantly, "Forward! Charge!" We passed large numbers of rebels in our advance, of whom, however, we took but little notice, so interested were we in our pursuit of the retreating foe. Arrived at a rocky ridge about 300 yards from where we commenced our victorious advance, we halted, taking the movement from the right, and engaged the enemy at short range. Here fell many noble men. Capt. G. H. Ince was killed; Col. O. H. Morris, commanding the regiment, was among the first wounded and went to the rear. Lieutenant-Colonel Hammell soon followed. First Lieutenants Banta, Hardenbrook, and Gosse were also seriously hurt, as well as many enlisted men.

By this time, owing to the distance we had advanced in line of battle at a run, and the irregularity of the ground we had advanced over, we were in a deplorable state of confusion; men from every regiment in the division were intermingled with ours in one confused mass.

While personally engaged in endeavoring to reform the regiment, and obtain something like order, I perceived the right of the line retiring. On inquiring the cause, I learned that the enemy had turned our right flank; also that all the senior officers of the brigade were either killed or wounded.

In accordance with instructions received previous to entering the engagement, to regulate our movement by the right, I gave orders to retire, which movement was executed as well as could be expected under the circumstances.

The colors were brought off the field by Capt. John F. Bartholf, who reported with the remnant of the regiment to General Caldwell and then to Lieutenant-Colonel Chapman, who was assigned to the command of the brigade.

Early on the morning of the 3d, orders were received to intrench ourselves. This we did as well as we could with the means at hand, under a severe fire of artillery, which continued all day, but without serious injury to my command. This embraces about all connected with my command during the engagement.

Of the behavior of officers and men engaged in it, I cannot speak too highly, especially of those enumerated above as killed and wounded. They suffered nobly while doing their duty bravely in behalf of their country and the cause of justice, humanity, and the enforcement of the laws.

I have the honor to remain, very respectfully, &c.,

P. NELSON,
Major, Commanding Sixty-sixth New York Volunteers.

Capt. GEORGE W. JONES,
Aetg. Asst. Adjt. Gen., Third Brigade, First Division.

No. 92.

Reports of Col. John R. Brooke, Fifty-third Pennsylvania Infantry, commanding Fourth Brigade.

HDQRS. FOURTH BRIG., FIRST DIV., SECOND ARMY CORPS,
Bivouac near Thoroughfare Gap, Va., June 23, 1863.

SIR: In accordance with instructions received this day from head-quarters First Division, I have the honor to make the following report of the operations of my command on the 14th and 15th instant:

At about 4 p. m., June 14, having previously received orders therefor from the major-general commanding corps, proceeded to Banks' Ford, arriving there about 6 p. m., the detachment under my command consisting of portions of the Fifty-third Pennsylvania, One hundred and forty-fifth Pennsylvania, Second Delaware, Sixty-fourth New York, Twenty-seventh Connecticut, and two pieces of artillery from Battery A, Fourth U. S. Artillery. The command was halted when near the ford, at a point as near as could be reached without being exposed to view. I at once moved forward with three of my regiments (Second Delaware, One hundred and forty-fifth Pennsylvania, and Sixty-fourth New York), and posted them to support the picket on duty there, consisting of the Fifty-second New York, commanded by Lieutenant-Colonel Freudenberg. In the wood to the rear of the first-mentioned regiment, a battalion of the Eighth Pennsylvania Cavalry was bivouacked, under command of Captain Wickersham.

In accordance with orders furnished me by the major-general commanding the corps, I proceeded when fully dark to withdraw the infantry pickets and post cavalry, with instructions to follow the infantry at the expiration of one and a half hours. The command having been collected, and joined by the Fifty-second New York, took up the line of march, and had reached within a short distance of the main Warrenton road, when Lieut. W. D. W. Miller, aide-de-camp, arrived with orders to replace the infantry pickets at the ford, and move with the rest of the command to Berea Church, and occupy the cross-roads at that point. The Fifty-second New York again took up the picket line at the ford, supported by the Second Delaware, the remainder of the detachment moving on to Berea Church, where the troops were put into position, the artillery being posted to the best advantage to cover the roads. The detachment arrived at the church about 11 p. m.

Having thrown out pickets, the men were permitted to sleep on their arms until, at or about 1.30 a. m., Lieutenant Miller, aide-de-camp, arrived with orders to abandon the ford at once, and to move the whole detachment to Stafford Court-House, the choice of roads being left to my discretion.

At 5.30 a. m. the infantry all assembled at Berea Church. The command was moved at once, taking the shortest road to Stafford Court-House, the whole detachment arriving there safely about 9.30 a. m., June 15.

No casualties occurred to the detachment while under my command, nor were any of the enemy seen, excepting those in their works on the right bank of the river, opposite the ford.

Respectfully, your obedient servant,

JOHN R. BROOKE,
Colonel, Commanding Brigade.

Maj. JOHN HANCOCK,
Assistant Adjutant-General.

—

HDQRS. FOURTH BRIG., FIRST DIV., SECOND A. C.,
August 15, 1863.

SIR: I have the honor to make the following report of the late actions at Gettysburg, Pa., and subsequent movements to Warrenton, Va.:

June 29, at about 6 a. m., marched from Monocacy Bridge, below Frederick City, Md., to Uniontown, a distance of about 31 miles, where the troops remained until July 1, at 6 a. m., when they marched for Taneytown. On reaching the latter, it became evident an engagement was in progress with the enemy at or near Gettysburg, Pa., when the march was continued, and the command arrived at a point about 3 miles from Gettysburg about 9.30 p. m. The brigade then took a position on the right of the road, and, after establishing a picket line on the right flank, extending to the rear, the men were allowed to sleep.

On the morning of July 2, at about 3 a. m., the command moved forward in column for the field of battle, arriving there soon after sunrise, and, forming the right of the division, was formed in mass by columns of regiments on the left of the Second Division. During the day, the enemy were evidently feeling our position from right to left.

At about 5 p. m. a furious attack was made upon our left. In a short time, General Caldwell directed me to move to the left. I immediately marched, following the Irish Brigade, and forming in line in a copse of woods in rear of the Irish Brigade, and, moving forward in supporting distance, I crossed an open field or marsh, when, meeting the general commanding the division, he commanded me to halt my line. He then moved the Irish Brigade to the right, leaving my brigade in rear of and at supporting distance from the First Brigade, Colonel Cross, which was then hotly engaged beyond the crest, behind which I then was. In a short time the general commanding directed me to relieve the First Brigade. I advanced in line, faced by the rear rank (which formation was necessary, from the fact that there was not time to form by the front rank), and, passing the line of Colonel Cross at the edge of a wheat-field, I became at once hotly engaged. Pressing forward, firing as we went, we drove back the first line of the enemy, capturing a great number, and then charging the second line, drove it from its almost impregnable position on a rocky crest.

I now found my flanks threatened by a strong force of the enemy, and immediately sent an officer to the general commanding the division for assistance, and finding also a part of the Third Brigade close at hand, I immediately ordered them in and held my ground.   Both my aides being wounded, and myself severely bruised, I with great difficulty was able to maintain a proper knowledge of the enemy. Being notified about this time that a heavy column of the enemy was coming upon my left, I immediately took measures to meet them, sending word to that effect to the general commanding.   I held them at bay for some time, when word was brought me that my right was being turned, and finding no troops coming to my support, and finding that unless I retired all would be killed or captured, I reluctantly gave the order to retire, and in good order the whole command came off the field slowly, and, firing as they retired, succeeded in bringing off nearly all their wounded.   In passing back over the wheat-field, I found the enemy had nearly closed in my rear, and had the movement not been executed at the time it was, I feel convinced that all would have been lost by death, wounds, or capture.

I cannot speak in too high terms of the bravery and cool, steady bearing of the troops.

The greater part of the command reformed behind some stone walls, ready to fight to the last, but other troops coming up, relieved them, and the brigade reformed in rear of the hill called Round Top.

The loss in officers and non-commissioned officers was very large, leaving companies without officers and first sergeants.

After reforming, the general commanding again took position near the position occupied in the morning, where we bivouacked for the night.

July 3, early, the general commanding directed me to form on the left of the Third Brigade.   The enemy, seeing the movement, immediately commenced a brisk shelling, which killed and wounded several men.   Here we were directed by General Caldwell to throw up rifle-pits.   In the afternoon a terrific cannonade was opened upon our lines, followed by an infantry attack, which did not, however, direct itself against our line.   After the failure of this attack, nothing of importance transpired, the enemy evidently being defeated.

It is with regret that I record the death of the gallant Lieut. Col. H. C. Merwin, of the Twenty-seventh Connecticut, who fell in the thickest of the fight.   His death is a national loss.   All other officers and all the men behaved with extraordinary bravery.

Of my staff, Capt. H. J. Smith and Lieut. C. F. Smith were seriously wounded.   Lieut. Charles P. Hatch, acting assistant adjutant-general, Capt. A. M. Wright, acting assistant inspector-general, and Lieut. J. J. Whitney rendered me efficier' and valuable service.   I would respectfully ask for them the notice of the general commanding.

The list of casualties has already been furnished.*   The proportion of killed and wounded to the number engaged will show how desperately the fight raged.

July 4 passed without much fighting, and on the 5th, at 4 p. m., by order of the general commanding the division, took up line of march, following the Third Brigade; forded Marsh Creek, and marched a short distance beyond Two Taverns, Pa.   Remained at this point until 5 a. m. July 7, when marched for and arrived at Taneytown at 11 a. m.

On July 8, 9, 10, and 11, marched by way of Frederick, Crampton's Pass, Rohrersville, Keedysville, and the old Antietam battlefield to Jones' Cross-Roads, and, forming line parallel to the Hagerstown turnpike, bivouacked.

---

*Embodied in revised statement, p. 175.

On the 12th, moved forward about three-quarters of a mile, and took up an advantageous position on a crest, in heavy timber; threw up strong intrenchments at this point.

On the morning of the 14th, at 5 o'clock, received orders to move my brigade to the front and feel the enemy. The Fifth New Hampshire and Fifty-seventh New York were temporarily attached to my command; the Twenty-seventh Connecticut and One hundred and forty-fifth Pennsylvania were temporarily detached, not being drilled as skirmishers. Advancing, with the brigade deployed as skirmishers, I moved on the enemy's works, but found them evacuated; took many prisoners, and pressed forward to Falling Waters, where slight skirmishing occurred. The enemy having crossed, with the exception of those taken, bivouacked near Falling Waters for the night.

On the 15th, marched for Sandy Hook, by way of Downsville and Sharpsburg, arriving at Sandy Hook on the 16th, a. m.

On the 18th, took up line of march (leaving the Twenty-seventh Connecticut, whose term of service had nearly expired), crossing the Potomac and Shenandoah at Harper's Ferry. Bivouacked near Keys' Pass, in Loudoun Valley.

On July 19 and 20, marched to near Upperville, remaining here until July 22, when the march was resumed via Upperville to Paris. My brigade was ordered to occupy Ashby's Gap and remain until relieved by the Twelfth Corps.

At 2.30 p. m. on the 23d, being relieved by a brigade of the Twelfth Corps, I pushed on after the corps (which had marched to Markham, near Manassas Gap, at an early hour), reaching Markham at dark; and receiving orders to push on and join the corps, which had been ordered to Linden, I marched through the Gap, and joined the division about 1 a. m., this being the hardest march the troops ever made, being over a hilly, rocky, and marshy country, and it being very dark.

On the 24th, at 12 m., took up line of march again, reaching Markham at 6 p. m.

On the 25th and 26th, marched by way of White Plains and Warrenton to within 3 miles of Warrenton Junction.

During the long marches and hard fighting of this campaign, it is but just to say that the men did all that was required of them without a murmur and in a true soldierly spirit.

Respectfully, your obedient servant,

JOHN R. BROOKE,
Colonel, Commanding Brigade.

Maj. JOHN HANCOCK, *Assistant Adjutant-General.*

No. 93.

Report of Col. William P. Baily, Second Delaware Infantry.

CAMP NEAR BEALETON STATION, VA.,
August 15, 1863.

SIR: In obedience to circular from headquarters Army of the Potomac, dated August 12, 1863, I have the honor to submit the following report of this command from June 28 until its arrival in the vicinity of Warrenton, Va.:

At 6 a. m. Monday, June 29, we broke camp, being then within 4 or 5 miles of Frederick City, Md., and took up a line of march across

MAP. XXXIX.]　THE GETTYSBURG CAMPAIGN.　**403**

the Monocacy River Bridge, and successively passed through the villages and towns of Mount Pleasant, Liberty, Union Bridge, Johnsville, and Middletown, reaching a short distance beyond Uniontown, Md., at or about 10 p. m., and bivouacked for the night, having marched a distance, as is usually computed, from 32 to 35 miles. After getting in camp, a detail was taken from this command for picket.

Tuesday, June 30.—The regiment was mustered and inspected for pay.

Wednesday, July 1.—At 8 a. m. we took up a line of march, passing through Taneytown, crossing the Maryland line into Pennsylvania, halting at about 9 p. m. within 5 or 6 miles of Gettysburg, where we threw up a breastwork of rails and dirt, which was completed about midnight. Marched this day about 14 miles.

Thursday, July 2.—At daylight the regiment, by order of Colonel Brooke, commanding brigade, moved toward Gettysburg, and about 6 a. m. the regiment was placed in line of battle, occupying a position on the right of the brigade.

At 4.30 p. m. the regiment moved with the brigade about half a mile to the left, where we deployed by the left flank and faced by the rear rank, and faced the enemy. At this moment, Colonel Brooke ordered the line forward. The regiment moved briskly and with regularity, crossing stone walls, fences, and a morass in face of a heavy fire of musketry. The enemy immediately in our front occupied a most advantageous position behind a ledge of rocks upon the brow of a hill. At the foot of this hill the regiment opened fire upon the enemy, and advanced rapidly up the ascent, driving him from his position, capturing a number of prisoners, among whom were 2 commissioned officers. The enemy at this point attempted to rally and regain the ground he had lost, but was held in check. He then made a strong demonstration on our right flank (now our left). There being no support on this flank, the regiment was in danger of being outflanked, when orders were received from Colonel Brooke, commanding brigade, to fall back. The regiment then withdrew and took position on the right of the woods, about 600 yards in the rear of the position it held. The regiment bivouacked at this place. In this engagement our loss was severe.

At 4 o'clock on the morning of the 3d, we received orders to fall in, and move to the left and front, and form line of battle behind the crest of a hill. The enemy immediately opened his batteries with great vigor upon this position, at a range of about 1,500 yards. The colonel commanding then ordered the line about 60 yards to the front, where we threw up breastworks.

At 9 a. m. Captain Evans, of Company A, was detailed with 30 men to picket in our front. During the day he sent in 64 prisoners, chiefly from North Carolina and Georgia regiments. The enemy kept up a constant and rapid fire of shot and shell upon our position from 5 a. m. until 4 p. m.

I regret to report the loss of Lieut. H. W. Ottey, Company B, and Lieut. George G. Plank, Company E, who were killed in the discharge of their duty in the action of the 2d.

It would be invidious to particularize or make any selections where all had discharged their duty nobly and with so much gallantry.

In the action on July 3, the regiment was commanded by Captain Christman. Total of our casualties was 87.*

---

*But see revised statement, p. 175.

Saturday, July 4.—The regiment still in command of Captain Christman, with no change of position. By command of Colonel Brooke, commanding brigade, details were early made to bury our dead and bring in our wounded. All was quiet in our immediate front, excepting picket firing and an occasional shell from the enemy. Toward noon, lines of our troops, of another corps, were deployed some three-fourths of a mile in our front.

Sunday, July 5.—It was discerned that the enemy had left his position the night previous. At about 3 p. m., by order of Colonel Brooke, commanding brigade, we left the breastworks, and took up a line of march, and at 8 p. m. halted at the Two Taverns, having marched about 8 miles. We bivouacked here for the night.

Monday, July 6.—We remained at the Two Taverns all of this date.

Tuesday, July 7.—We again took up a line of march, and reached within half a mile of Taneytown, where we then halted at noon and bivouacked, marching some 8 miles.

Wednesday, July 8.—We again took up a line of march at 6 a. m. in a heavy storm, which rendered the roads, fields, and runs in a terrible condition. At 5 p. m. we halted, and bivouacked for the night on the banks of the Monocacy River, distant about 6½ miles from Frederick City. Marched nearly 20 miles this date.

Thursday, July 9.—We again took up a line of march at 6 a. m., passing through Frederick City, Jefferson, and Burkittsville, and, passing through Crampton's Gap, Md., bivouacked for the night, having marched 20 miles this date.

Friday, July 10.—Again took up a line of march at 6 a. m., passing through Keedysville, and halted after having made 11 miles, and bivouacked.

Saturday, July 11.—Again took up a line of march, and reached Jones' Cross-Roads, when, at 11 a. m., the enemy's pickets were met. By order of the colonel commanding brigade, we took up a position in a wheat-field, the left of the command resting near the Hagerstown turnpike. A detail of skirmishers was made from this regiment at 3 p. m., who advanced upon the enemy's skirmishers in our front, and drove them about half a mile, occupying at dark their position. At 9 p. m. our position was changed, so as to become parallel with the turnpike road, and we then rested for the night on our arms.

Sunday, July 12.—At 3 p. m., by command of the colonel commanding brigade, this command moved out to the front, occupying the position of our skirmishers of the 11th instant. The skirmishers in our front also moved forward. At dark we were ordered to throw up breastworks, which we did, of rails and dirt. There was an occasional shot between the pickets during the day. It rained very heavily during the night.

Monday, July 13.—At daylight we commenced strengthening our breastworks, expecting an attack from the enemy at any moment during the day.

Tuesday, July 14.—By command of Colonel Brooke, commanding brigade, at daylight the regiment was deployed as skirmishers, and moved forward, passing over the enemy's works down to the Potomac River at Falling Waters without opposition.

Wednesday, July 15.—Took up a line of march at 7 a. m., and arrived at sundown near Maryland Heights; bivouacked for the night.

Thursday, July 16.—Took up a line of march at 9 a. m., and encamped at Sandy Hook.

Friday, July 17.—Lay all day at this place.

Saturday, July 18.—Took up a line of march at 6 a. m., and crossed the Potomac River, passing through Harper's Ferry, across the Shenandoah River, and into Virginia once more. We then struck into Loudoun Valley, and, after marching 6 miles, we halted and bivouacked for the night.

Sunday, July 19.—Took up a line of march, and, after marching 8 miles, halted and bivouacked for the night. This day was very warm and close.

Monday, July 20.—Took up a line of march at 8 a. m., and marched about 5 miles and bivouacked near Snickersville.

Tuesday, July 21.—In the same place we stopped at last night.

Wednesday, July 22.—Took up a line of march at 1 p. m., and marched to Ashby's Gap. Our brigade (the Fourth) went on picket, passing through the village of Paris. The enemy's cavalry was seen during the day.

Thursday, July 23.—The corps started on the march at daylight, our brigade remaining on picket until 1 p. m., when we were relieved by a brigade of the Twelfth Corps. We then started to rejoin our corps at Manassas Gap, reaching that place at midnight. This was, without exception, the hardest march we had ever endured; not that the distance was great, but the roads were so stony, hilly, and so many small streams to cross. The Third Corps had a skirmish with A. P. Hill's corps during the day.

Friday, July 24.—Took up a line of march, and halted near a small village at the mouth of the Gap and bivouacked for the night.

Saturday, July 25.—Took up a line of march; reached White Plains, near Thoroughfare Gap, and bivouacked for the night.

Sunday, July 26.—Took up a line of march at 5 a. m., and passed through White Plains and New Baltimore, and reached Warrenton about noon. After resting about an hour, we marched to Catlett's Station. Distance marched, about 20 miles.

The above is a correct report to the best of my knowledge.

I am, sir, very respectfully, your obedient servant,

WM. P. BAILY,
Colonel Second Delaware Volunteers.

Lieut. CHARLES P. HATCH,
Acting Assistant Adjutant-General.

No. 94.

Reports of Maj. Leman W. Bradley, Sixty-fourth New York Infantry.

PLEASANT VALLEY, MD., *July* 17, 1863.

SIR: I have the honor to report the part taken by the Sixty-fourth Regiment New York Volunteers at the battle of Gettysburg, Pa., July 2 and 3.

The regiment went into the engagement on July 2 under the command of Col. Daniel G. Bingham, numbering 185 enlisted men carrying rifles, and 19 commissioned officers.

The regiment was deployed in line faced by the rear rank on the right of the Fifty-third Pennsylvania Regiment, the left of the Second Delaware Regiment resting on our right. The regiment advanced with the brigade rapidly and steadily under a sharp fire from the enemy, whom we drove before us, killing, wounding, and taking many prisoners.

Our loss on the 2d was:

Officers and men.	Killed.	Wounded.	Missing.	Total.
Commissioned officers	4	7	......	11
Enlisted men	11	54	18	83
Total	15	61	18	94

On the morning of the 3d, the Sixty-fourth was in line on the left of the brigade, and mustered for action 1 field officer, 5 captains, 6 lieutenants, and 85 enlisted men with rifles.

Colonel Bingham being wounded and at division hospital, the command of the regiment devolved upon Major Bradley. Breastworks were built to our front, which proved a defense against the heavy cannonading received from the enemy on that day.

Our only loss this day was 1 man wounded on picket, under the command of Capt. W. W. Wait.

I am happy to say, as far as came to my knowledge, every officer and enlisted man did his duty in such a manner as to honor himself, his regiment, his brigade, and his country.

On the 4th, we buried our dead and held short religious services, conducted by the chaplain of the One hundred and forty-fifth Pennsylvania Regiment.

On Sunday morning, the 5th, we had an inspection of arms. At 4 p. m. the regiment marched with its brigade in the direction of Frederick City, Md.

Most respectfully, yours,

L. W. BRADLEY,
Major, Comdg. Sixty-fourth New York Volunteers.

Lieut. CHARLES P. HATCH,
Acting Assistant Adjutant-General, Brooke's Brigade.

———

NEAR KELLY'S FORD, VA., *August 15, 1863.*

SIR: I have the honor to submit the following report of the proceedings of the Sixty-fourth New York Volunteers from June 28 till the time of going into camp near Warrenton:

Tuesday, June 28, the regiment, under the command of Col. D. G. Bingham, marched with the brigade at 6 a. m. from Barnesville, Md. After a march of 12 miles, bivouacked on the banks of the Monocacy, 3 miles from Frederick City.

On the 29th, we were ordered to be in readiness to move at 6 a. m., at which time the regiment marched with the brigade toward Uniontown, at which place we arrived in the evening, after a march of over 30 miles.

On the 30th, we remained at Uniontown, and the regiment was mustered for pay.

July 1, marched from Uniontown, passing through Taneytown, beyond which we made a halt, and were making arrangements to encamp when we were ordered to march.

At evening we halted about 3 miles from Gettysburg, and were ordered to build breastworks. Before the works were finished, we were ordered to rest.

At 2.30 a. m., July 2, we were ordered to pack up quietly and cook coffee. At 4.10 a. m. we moved about 1 mile to the front, and at 5.45 a. m. halted in a wood. At 6.10 a. m. we marched with the brigade out of the wood across the Taneytown road. At 7 a. m. were formed with the brigade in line, by brigade in mass, fronting west, in a position a half mile southwest of Cemetery Hill. At 5.15 p. m. we moved in mass by brigade nearly a mile to the left. The regiment was deployed into line, faced by the rear rank, on the right of the Fifty-third Pennsylvania Regiment, the left of the Second Delaware resting on our right. The regiment advanced with the brigade rapidly and steadily under a sharp fire from the enemy, whom we drove before us, killing, wounding, and taking many prisoners.

The regiment went into the engagement numbering 202 enlisted men carrying rifles, 2 field, 1 staff, and 16 line officers. Our loss this day was as follows:

Officers and men.	Killed.	Wounded.	Missing.	Total.
Commissioned officers	4	7	......	11
Enlisted men	11	54	18	83
Total	15	61	18	94

The service lost in the killed the brave Capt. Henry V. Fuller, who had distinguished himself for gallantly in every action in which the regiment had been engaged. He was so well known in his brigade and division as to make it unnecessary for me to say anything in his praise.

Capt. A. H. Lewis and Lieutenants Babcock and Thurber, who fell at the same time, were highly esteemed as officers and gentlemen. They died facing the foe.

On the morning of the 3d, the Sixty-fourth was in line on the left of the brigade, and mustered for action 1 field officer, 5 captains, 6 lieutenants, and 85 enlisted men with rifles.

Colonel Bingham being wounded and at the division hospital, the command of the regiment devolved upon Major Bradley. Breastworks were built to our front, which proved a protection against the heavy cannonading from the enemy on that day.

Our loss on the 3d was 1 man, wounded on picket, under the command of Capt. W. W. Wait.

I am happy to say, so far as came to my knowledge, that during the two days' engagement every officer and enlisted man did his duty in such a manner as to honor himself, his regiment, his brigade, and his country.

On the 4th we buried our dead and held short religious services, conducted by Chaplain John H. W. Stuckenberg, of the One hundred and forty-fifth Pennsylvania Volunteers. Afterward I sent out a detail to collect arms and accouterments on the battle-field.

On Sunday morning, the 5th, I had an inspection of arms. At 4 p. m. marched with brigade in the direction of Frederick City; bivouacked at 8 p. m. at Two Taverns.

During the 6th, we remained in bivouac.

On the 7th, marched 9½ miles to near Taneytown; received rations and bivouacked.

On the 8th, marched at 5 a. m. Soon after moving, a hard rain came on, making the roads very muddy. This was a hard day's march for the men; bivouacked for the night near Frederick City.

July 9, marched at 5 a. m., Sixty-fourth leading the brigade; bivouacked near [Crampton's Gap], Md.

On the 10th, moved at 5 a. m.; crossed Antietam River at Keedysville; marched 3½ miles, and formed a line of battle; at night bivouacked.

On the 11th, reveille at 4 a. m.; marched at 6 a. m.; formed line of battle at 11 a. m. at Lapham's [Jones'] Cross-Roads; sent picket detail to brigade headquarters of 1 captain, 1 lieutenant, and 43 enlisted men.

Remained here until the afternoon of the 12th, when we advanced with the brigade to a wood, where we formed line of battle on the crest of a rocky ledge, Sixty-fourth on the right. At dark, commenced throwing up intrenchments.

On the 13th, we finished our breastworks.

On the 14th, at 6 a. m., the brigade advanced toward Falling Waters. The Sixty-fourth were deployed as skirmishers, the left connecting with the right of the Fifth New Hampshire. We moved as skirmishers in this position several miles, when I was ordered to Colonel Brooke, who ordered me to march as support to line of skirmishers on the left of Lieutenant-Colonel Chapman, of the Fifty-seventh New York. I was afterward ordered to take charge of 164 enlisted men and 2 commissioned officers, taken prisoners by the skirmishers of the Fourth Brigade. The provost-marshal coming up, relieved me, when I reported to the brigade, which had halted in a ravine, where we bivouacked for the night.

On the 15th, marched at 5 a. m., Sixty-fourth leading the brigade. Marched to nearly opposite Harper's Ferry, when we bivouacked by the side of the canal for the night.

On the 16th, marched at 9 a. m. to Pleasant Valley, and bivouacked, and issued clothing to the men.

On the 17th, remained at Pleasant Valley. The men, obeying the injunction of the brigade commander, bathed freely.

On the 18th, marched at 6 a. m. Crossed the Potomac on pontoon bridge at Harper's Ferry. Marched south 7 miles, and bivouacked.

At 11 a. m. on the 19th, marched 6 miles farther south, and bivouacked.

On the 20th, marched at 8.30 a. m.; bivouacked near Bloomfield.

On the 21st, did not move.

Wednesday, July 22, marched at 2 p. m. and halted toward evening with the brigade, holding Ashby's Gap.

On the 23d, at 2 p. m., left Ashby's Gap and marched about 8 miles toward Manassas Gap, when we halted at dusk and issued rations. Heard firing in the direction of Manassas Gap. Were soon ordered to pack up, and were very soon on our way with the brigade to Manassas Gap, which we entered and passed through, bivouacking at 1 a. m. of the 24th.

At 1 p. m. marched back through the gap, and bivouacked near Martin's [Markham] Station at 5 p. m.

On the 25th, moved at 5 a. m.; bivouacked near White Plains.

Sunday, 26th, marched at 5 a. m. Passed through White Plains and Warrenton.

At 5 p. m. halted in a large field about 2 miles from Warrenton Junction. Bivouacked, and remained till the afternoon of the 30th, when we moved with the brigade to the vicinity of our present camping place.

Before bringing this report to a close, I would mention Asst. Surg. Charles T. Kelsey as deserving worthy and especial notice in the fight at Gettysburg as at Chancellorsville. He went into battle with his regiment, encouraging the men by words and actions; was with us when we deployed into line, and did not halt until he had wounded men to attend to.

We had 16 commissioned officers and 126 enlisted men for duty in the field. A detail of officers and men has been sent to the State of New York for drafted men. It is hoped our numbers will soon be increased.

Both officers and men are in good spirits, having the utmost confidence in and great attachment for Col. John R. Brooke, their brigade commander. They will cheerfully obey any order he may give, or, as heretofore, follow where he leads.

I am, sir, most respectfully, your obedient servant,

L. W. BRADLEY,
Major, Commanding Regiment.

Lieut. CHARLES P. HATCH,
Actg. Asst. Adjt. Gen., Brooke's Brigade.

No. 95.

Reports of Lieut. Col. Richards McMichael, Fifty-third Pennsylvania Infantry.

NEAR SANDY HOOK, MD., July 17, 1863.

SIR: I have the honor to transmit the following report of the part taken by my command in the late action near Gettysburg, Pa.:

My regiment arrived on the field about 8 a. m. July 2, and was marched to a position in the rear of the left center of the battle-line, where we remained for several hours.

Between the hours of 3 and 4 p. m., in accordance with the orders of Colonel Brooke, commanding brigade, I moved by the left flank to the left, and formed line of battle on the edge of a wood, with the Sixty-fourth New York on my right and the Twenty-seventh Connecticut Volunteers on the left. All this time we were exposed to a severe shelling from the enemy's batteries. My command was then moved forward in order of battle through a wheat-field, about the center of which we commenced firing, continuing for fifteen minutes or more, when orders were received from Colonel Brooke to fix bayonets.

This was done, and, in connection with the brigade, we charged upon the enemy, driving him before us, capturing some prisoners, and finally carrying the crest of the hill. This position was held for a short time, when it was discovered that the enemy was crowding upon our flanks. The brigade, including my command, was ordered by Colonel Brooke to fall back. This was done successfully through a heavy fire from the enemy's infantry and artillery.

About 8 a. m. I marched to a position near the one I held just before the action, where the regiment bivouacked during the night.

During the morning of the 3d, my command was engaged in throwing up earthworks.

In the afternoon, we were under a severe artillery fire for several hours, but there were no casualties.

The loss in my command is proportionately large, the casualties nearly all occurring in the hotly contested engagement in the wheat-field.

All my officers and men did their duty nobly and well.

I herewith forward you a list of casualties.*

I have the honor to be, sir, respectfully, your obedient servant,

R. McMICHAEL,
Lieut. Col., Comdg. Fifty-third Pennsylvania Volunteers.

Lieut. CHARLES P. HATCH,
Actg. Asst. Adjt. Gen., Fourth Brigade.

—

HDQRS. FIFTY-THIRD PENNSYLVANIA VOLUNTEERS,
August 3, 1863.

SIR: As required by circular from brigade headquarters of this date, I have the honor to transmit the following report of the operations of my command at the battle of Gettysburg:

I arrived on the field with my command about 8 a. m. on July 2, and was marched to a position in the rear of the left center of the line.

Remaining here about an hour, I marched with the remainder of the brigade to a position on the front, where I remained until 3 p. m., when the engagement opened. From 3 to 5 p. m. we were under a severe shelling fire, at which hour, in compliance with the orders of Colonel Brooke, commanding brigade, I moved with the brigade by the left flank across a field, finally forming line of battle, with a grain-field in the front. The Sixty-fourth New York Volunteers was on my right and the Twenty-seventh Connecticut Volunteers on my left. I then, as ordered by Colonel Brooke, in conjunction with the brigade, moved forward in line of battle.. When midway in the grain-field, firing commenced, lasting about fifteen minutes, when, in accordance with orders from Colonel Brooke, bayonets were fixed, and I charged upon the enemy, driving him from his strong position on the crest of the hill in our front. The position was held about fifteen minutes, when it was discovered that the enemy in force was getting in the flank and rear; then I fell back, in accordance with orders from Colonel Brooke.

During the night of the 2d, my regiment was engaged in constructing breastworks.

On the 3d, my command lay behind the intrenchments under a heavy artillery fire.

My command went into action with 15 officers and 120 enlisted men.

---

* Embodied in revised statement, p. 175.

The loss in the regiment is as follows:

Officers and men.	Killed.	Wounded.	Missing.	Total.
Officers		8		8
Enlisted men	7	58	6	71
Total*	7	66	6	79

Very respectfully, your obedient servant,
R. McMICHAEL,
Lieutenant-Colonel, Commanding Regiment.

Lieut. CHARLES P. HATCH,
Acting Assistant Adjutant-General.

—

HDQRS. FIFTY-THIRD PENNSYLVANIA VOLUNTEERS,
Near Morrisville, Va., August 14, 1863.

SIR: In compliance with circular orders from headquarters Army of the Potomac, I have the honor to forward the following report of the operations of my command from June 28 to the date of our arrival in the present camp:

At 6 o'clock on the morning of June 28, my regiment, in its proper position in the line of the brigade, moved from bivouac near Barnesville, Md., on the Frederick City road, arriving at Monocacy at 2 p. m., at which place, in compliance with orders, I bivouacked for the night.

The line of march was taken up at 8 a. m. on the 29th. I passed over the Monocacy Creek on the bridge at the railroad station, and marched on the Frederick pike until within a few miles of the city, when the column headed to the right, repassed the Monocacy, and continued marching northward, passing through the towns of Mount Pleasant, Liberty, and Johnsville.

At 12 midnight I bivouacked in a wood near Uniontown. I marched 30 miles during the day, and many of my men were too much exhausted to reach the place of bivouac. All of them rejoined the regiment before morning.

On the 30th, the regiment was mustered for pay.

Early on July 1, I, in my proper position in the line of the brigade, moved on the Gettysburg road.

At 4 p. m. I passed over the Pennsylvania line. There was heavy cannonading in my front.

At nightfall, I received orders to bivouac, and immediately after was ordered to march my regiment on picket. I did so. My line of outposts covered the right flank of the First Division and connected with the picket line of the Twelfth Corps.

At daybreak on the 2d, I withdrew the pickets, in accordance with the orders of Colonel Brooke, commanding brigade, and, falling into my assigned position in line of march, moved toward Gettysburg, arriving on the field about 8 a. m. I was marched to a position in the rear of the left center of the line of battle then forming, where I remained about one hour, when my command was marched to a posi-

* But see revised statement, p. 175.

tion on the front line. I remained in this position until midafternoon, when the action commenced. For several hours I remained inactive under a severe shelling from the guns of the enemy.

About 5 p. m., in compliance with orders from Colonel Brooke, commanding brigade, I, in connection with the brigade, moved by the left flank toward the left of the line, and formed in line of battle near a grain-field. The Sixty-fourth New York was on my right and the Twenty-seventh Connecticut on my left. In accordance with the orders of the brigade commander, I fixed bayonets, and, in line with the rest of the brigade, charged upon the enemy. The rebels gave way; were forced from a strong position on the crest of a hill in our immediate front. The position was held until the enemy commenced to mass heavy columns on our flanks for the purpose of cutting us off; then, in compliance with orders of Colonel Brooke, I retired, halting and reforming near Round Top hill. My command lost heavily in the action—about 70 per cent.

My officers and men exhibited commendable gallantry throughout the action. During the night, my command was engaged in throwing up breastworks.

On the 3d, I was in the intrenchments and under a heavy artillery fire, and also on the 4th.

At noon on the 5th, I, in line with the brigade, marched on the Baltimore pike, and bivouacked for the night at a place called Two Taverns, where we remained until midday of the 7th, when I moved to near Taneytown and bivouacked.

On the 8th, marched over wretched roads and through a heavy rain-storm to near Frederick City.

On the 9th, marched through Frederick; moved on the Harper's Ferry pike through Jefferson, and halted for the night near Burkittsville.

On the 11th, about noon, arrived at Jones' Cross-Roads. I, in accordance with the orders of Colonel Brooke, deployed my regiment as skirmishers, and advanced to near the edge of a wood in which the rebel skirmishers were posted. There was lively firing on my left, but my regiment was not engaged. Toward evening I advanced to the wood. Line of battle was formed with the line of the brigade. During the night my command was actively engaged in throwing up breastworks covering my front.

On the 12th and 13th, I lay inactive behind the earthworks.

On the morning of the 14th, in compliance with the orders of Colonel Brooke, I moved to the front of the fortifications, and deployed my command as skirmishers. The Second Delaware was on my right, and my left joined the line of skirmishers of the Twelfth Corps, and rested on the Williamsport road. According to orders, I advanced cautiously, but had not gone far ere I discovered that the enemy had vacated his outer line of works near Williamsport. I moved to the right of the road, and, leaving the town on my right, advanced the skirmish line toward Falling Waters, near which place, in a ravine, a number of prisoners were captured. Near Falling Waters we bivouacked for the night.

On the 15th, I moved through Sharpsburg to near Harper's Ferry.

On the 16th, moved to Sandy Hook, near which place encamped.

On the 18th, broke camp, and passed over the Potomac into Virginia.

On the 20th, reached Bloomfield, near which place I remained until the 22d, when the column moved to Ashby's Gap, my command, in connection with the brigade, going to the highest point of ascent in the Gap, and remained on picket all night.

My command moved from the Gap about 2 p. m. on the 23d, and marched toward Manassas Gap. Arrived at Markham about sundown, from thence making a difficult forced march in the dark, over a miserable road, when I bivouacked about 4 miles from Front Royal.

On the 24th, I moved back in the Gap, and bivouacked near Markham.

On the 25th, moved to White Plains.

On the 26th, marched through New Baltimore and Warrenton, and went into camp about 2 miles from Warrenton Junction.

On the 30th, again marched, and arrived at the present camp on the 1st of the present month.

I am, sir, very respectfully, your obedient servant,

R. McMICHAEL,
Lieutenant-Colonel, Comdg. Fifty-third Pennsylvania Regt.

Lieut. CHARLES P. HATCH,
Acting Assistant Adjutant-General, Fourth Brigade.

No. 96.

Report of Capt. John W. Reynolds, One hundred and forty-fifth Pennsylvania Infantry.

HEADQUARTERS 145TH PENNSYLVANIA VOLUNTEERS,
August 14, 1863.

DEAR SIR: I have the honor of submitting the following report of the movements of this regiment during the period commencing June 28 and terminating July 26:

The regiment arrived at Monocacy Station, a point on the Baltimore and Ohio Railroad, 3 miles south of Frederick, Md., on Sunday, June 28, about 2 p. m., and encamped for the night in a field with the rest of the brigade.

We started next morning (Monday) at 8 o'clock, Colonel Brown commanding the regiment, and marched to a camp a mile east of Uniontown, Md., having traveled about 30 miles during the day.

Tuesday, June 30, the regiment remained in camp and was mustered for pay.

Wednesday, July 1, the regiment was detached from the brigade, and ordered to act as a guard to the wagon train of the First Division, Second Corps. About noon we started in the rear of the wagon train, and marched a mile toward Taneytown; here we halted for about an hour, and then received an order to rejoin the brigade, several miles in advance. We moved forward and overtook the brigade near Taneytown; thence advanced to a position 3 miles south of Gettysburg, where the brigade was drawn up in line of battle, the One hundred and forty-fifth Regiment being on the right and occupying a wheat-field.

The next morning (July 2), we moved forward at daylight about 2 miles, and turned to the right into the woods, where we halted and formed into column by division. Remaining about an hour, the command "Attention" was given, and the regiment moved out to the road again, which we crossed, and, having advanced a short distance, we formed in line of battle in the rear of the brigade, which was then in column by regiments, holding a position a short distance to the left of Cemetery Hill. Having stacked arms, we remained here until about 4 o'clock in the afternoon, when we moved by the left flank about a quarter of a mile, but soon returned again to our former position. About 5 o'clock we were again ordered to march by the left flank. We moved half a mile to the left and formed in line of battle, faced by the rear rank, the brigade forming a single line of battle; our regiment, on the left, now became the right. We lay down for a short time, and then moved forward into a wheat-field, halted, and commenced firing. Soon Colonel Brown was severely wounded and left the field, and, being the senior officer present, I assumed command of the regiment.

About this time the order was given to move forward, and we advanced rapidly with the rest of the brigade for several hundred yards, the enemy retreating, until we came to a ledge of rocks; here a number of the rebels threw down their arms and surrendered, passing to our rear. We continued firing at this point for twenty minutes, when we received an order to fall back. The enemy was already attempting to turn our flank, and had we remained much longer we would have been taken prisoners.

The regiment retired, and again took the position that it had occupied during the day. Having received a slight wound in the head, I went to the hospital, and the command of the regiment devolved upon Captain Oliver.

In the action of July 2, the regiment lost 1 officer killed and 8 officers wounded; 11 enlisted men killed, 59 enlisted men wounded, and 10 enlisted men missing.

On Friday, the regiment built a line of intrenchments just in front of its position occupied on Thursday, and lay there all day, subject to a severe fire from the enemy's artillery for several hours. At 4 p. m. a detail for picket was sent to the front and deployed as skirmishers; 1 man was wounded.

On Saturday, July 4, the regiment still occupied very nearly the same position, the pickets having rejoined the regiment.

A detail from the regiment went out on Sunday, July 5, to assist in burying the dead. At 4 p. m. the regiment marched along the Baltimore turnpike about 5 miles, and encamped near a place called Two Taverns. The regiment remained here until the morning of July 7, when it marched to Taneytown, and encamped.

Wednesday, July 8.—Moved to a camp near Frederick, Md.

July 9.—Passed through Frederick, thence through South Mountain Pass, and encamped.

Friday, July 10.—Crossed Antietam Creek, and encamped on the Hagerstown turnpike.

July 11.—Moved to Jones' Cross-Roads and encamped, and sent out a detail of skirmishers.

July 12.—Advanced 2 miles, and commenced intrenching.

July 13.—Worked in intrenchments.

July 14.—Moved forward to Falling Waters and encamped.

July 15.—Marched along canal to a point near Harper's Ferry.

July 16.—Moved to Sandy Hook and encamped. Remained in camp until the morning of July 18, when the regiment crossed the Potomac at Harper's Ferry, then crossed the Shenandoah River, and marched to a point near Keys' Pass, Va., where we encamped. Lieutenant-Colonel McCreary here joined the regiment, and assumed command.

July 19, *Sunday.*—Marched 6 miles and encamped.

July 20.—Moved to a camp a mile southwest of Bloomfield, Va. Remained until July 22, when we moved to Ashby's Gap.

July 23.—Marched through Markham Station, and encamped in Manassas Gap.

July 24.—Returned to Markham Station.

July 25.—Moved to White Plains and encamped.

July 26, *Sunday.*—Marched through Warrenton, and encamped near Warrenton Junction.

Very respectfully, your obedient servant,

JOHN W. REYNOLDS,

Capt., Comdg. One hundred and forty-fifth Pennsylvania Vols.

Lieut. CHARLES P. HATCH,

Acting Assistant Adjutant-General, Fourth Brigade.

No. 97.

Report of Capt. Moses W. Oliver, One hundred and forty-fifth Pennsylvania Infantry.

CAMP NEAR SANDY HOOK, MD.,
July 16, 1863.

ADJUTANT: The captain commanding would respectfully submit the following report of the part performed by the One hundred and forty-fifth Regiment Pennsylvania Volunteers in the late engagement near Gettysburg, Pa.:

Arriving at the scene of action at 6 a. m. of the 2d, we were assigned the left of the brigade, where we remained until after 4 p. m., when, by order of Colonel Brooke, we were moved by the left flank; were deployed in line of battle, our regiment changed in line by being thrown to the right of the brigade.

Again moving by the left, in line of battle, we advanced into a wheat-field, where we became engaged with the enemy. Colonel Brown here being wounded, the command devolved on Captain Reynolds.

The regiment gallantly pressed on, driving the enemy before them, until we reached a ledge of rocks in the woods, where it fought bravely until the command to fall back was given, which was executed in as good order as possible.

Captain Reynolds being wounded soon after the order to fall back was given, the command devolved upon myself.

Being again formed in line of battle early in the morning of the 3d to the left of the position occupied by the brigade on the previous day, our regiment still occupying the right, we were engaged the greater part of the forenoon in throwing up intrenchments, in which we remained for the rest of the day.

In the afternoon, a picket detail of 1 commissioned officer and 16 enlisted men was made, who remained on duty until late in the evening of July 4. Until 5 p. m., July 5, we occupied the same position as on the 3d, at which time, by order of Colonel Brooke, we left the field of battle.

On the 2d and 3d, quite a number of prisoners were taken by the regiment, but I have been unable to ascertain the number.

Respectfully,

M. W. OLIVER,
Captain, Commanding Regiment.

Lieut. JOHN D. BLACK,
Adjutant 145th Pennsylvania Volunteers.

No. 98.

Report of Brig. Gen. John Gibbon, U. S. Army, commanding Second Division of, and Second Army Corps.

BALTIMORE, MD.,
August 7, 1863.

SIR: I have the honor to submit the following report of the operations of the Second Division during the battle of Gettysburg, on July 2 and 3:

The report will refer partly to the Second Division and partly to the Second Corps, in command of which I was twice placed, first at Taneytown, and again during the battle of the 2d, when General Hancock was ordered to take command of the Third Corps.

The corps arrived upon the ground on the morning of the 2d, and was placed in position with the right (Third Division, Brig. Gen. A. Hays) resting near the cemetery and extending along the crest of a hill which, turning to the left, ran parallel to the turnpike and toward a prominent hill called Round Top. The Second Division came next, and the First Division (Brigadier-General Caldwell) was upon the left, connecting with the Third Corps, and was afterward detached for service with that corps.

At the advance of the Third Corps at 4 p. m., the division was in the following order: Webb's brigade on the right, partially behind a low stone wall, and protecting Cushing's battery, Fourth U. S. Artillery, which was on its right; Brown's Rhode Island battery was on Webb's left; Hall's brigade prolonged the line to the left, while Harrow's was held in reserve to the rear.

At 4 o'clock the Third Corps advanced, and, swinging round its left flank, took up a position along the Emmitsburg road. To give support to its right flank, I ordered forward two regiments of Harrow's brigade, to occupy a position along that road and to the right of a brick house. Here they tore down the fences and constructed breastworks, behind which they did most excellent service in checking the advance of the enemy, and preventing him from cutting off the Third Corps from our lines. For the same purpose, I sent a 12-pounder battery to the right and rear of these two regiments, to fire across the Emmitsburg road at some of the enemy's batteries established there.

No sooner was the Third Corps in position, with its right resting near the brick house and the left "in the air," than the enemy made a most furious assault with infantry and artillery on that flank, rolling it back and enfilading the whole line. Such a flank attack could not be successfully resisted, and although dispositions were made to check the advance of the enemy, he came on so rapidly as to drive everything before him. I directed solid shot to be thrown from our batteries over the heads of our own men, and, on the application of General Humphreys, sent two of my regiments to his assistance.

About this time the command of the corps was turned over to me by Major-General Hancock. The smoke was at this time so dense that but little could be seen of the battle, and I directed some of the guns to cease firing, fearing they might injure our own men or uselessly waste their ammunition.

The Eighty-second New York and Fifteenth Massachusetts, near the brick house, were overpowered, outflanked by the enemy in pursuit of the Third Corps, and forced back after heavy loss, including both commanding officers. The Nineteenth Massachusetts, Colonel Devereux, and Forty-second New York, Colonel Mallon, sent to the assistance of General Humphreys, finding themselves unable with that small force to stem the triumphant advance of the enemy, retired, after a short struggle, in good order.

The enemy came on with such impetuosity that the head of his column came quite through a vacancy in our line to the left of my division, opened by detaching troops to other points. By the steadiness, however, of the troops in the immediate vicinity, and the timely arrival of the Twelfth Corps, this advance was checked and driven back with considerable loss, the pursuit being continued for some distance beyond our lines, and all the guns overrun by the enemy retaken. Darkness ended the contest here, but it continued for some time on our right, in front of the Eleventh Corps. I sent Carroll's brigade, of the Third Division, and two regiments of Webb's brigade to its assistance.

July 3.—Skirmishing continued all along the line at intervals during the morning, and some little artillery firing occurred, but at 1 o'clock (at which time, General Hancock having resumed command of the corps, I returned to my division) the enemy opened with his artillery all along his line, and for two hours the most terrific shower of shot and shell continued, ably responded to by our batteries. At the end of that time the fire on both sides slackened, and the enemy displayed his first line coming out of the woods, and preceded by a heavy line of skirmishers, which commenced immediately to push ours back. The line moved steadily to the front in a way to excite the admiration of every one, and was followed by a second and third, extending all along our front as far as the eye could reach. Our guns were run well forward, so as to give them a good sweep over the ground, loaded with canister, and the men warned to keep well under cover, and to reserve their fire until the enemy got well within range. As the front line came up, it was met with such a withering fire of canister and musketry as soon melted it away, but still on they came from behind, pressing forward to the wall. By this time most of our artillerymen had fallen, and but an occasional cannon shot along our part of the line interrupted the continuous rattle of musketry. The right of the enemy's line did not extend as far as the left of my division, and, while urging forward some of my left regiments to take his line in flank, I was wounded and left ·the field. The rest is told by the brigade reports.

Webb's line of three small regiments was overwhelmed and driven back by the superior masses of the enemy, but Hall's men, skillfully directed by himself and the gallant Devereux, Mallon, and others, rushed to the rescue, fell upon him in flank, and, with the assistance of some of the First Brigade and of Webb's men, who, under the direction of their brave commander, Colonel Smith, Seventy-first

Pennsylvania, and others, had turned again, drove him back over the wall, capturing a large number of prisoners and many colors.

The repulse of this assault was most gallant, and I desire to call special attention to the great gallantry and conspicuous qualities displayed by Brigadier-General Webb and Colonel Hall. Their services were invaluable, and it is safe to say that, without their presence, the enemy would have succeeded in gaining a foothold at that point.

Attention is also called to the officers and men specially mentioned by the various reports.

I desire to call particular attention to the manner in which several of the subordinate reports mention the services of my gallant aide, Lieut. F. A. Haskell, Sixth Wisconsin, and to add my testimony of his valuable services. This young officer has been through many battles, and distinguished himself alike in all by his conspicuous coolness and bravery, and in this one was slightly wounded, but refused to quit the field. It has always been a source of regret to me that our military system offers no plan for rewarding his merit and services as they deserve.

Major Baird, Eighty-second New York, my division inspector-general, received a severe wound in the foot while gallantly carrying an order for me on the 2d. Such men as these should be promoted on the field, though I regret to say they are frequently overlooked by the State authorities, and incompetent persons (not soldiers) placed over their heads. I have urged Major Baird for the colonelcy of his regiment, now vacant.

Captain [John P.] Wood, assistant adjutant-general, was injured by his horse being shot and falling upon him early on the 3d.

Captain Wessels, One hundred and sixth Pennsylvania, my division judge-advocate, and Lieutenant Moale, Nineteenth U. S. Infantry, aide-de-camp, were with me on the field, and behaved with great coolness and gallantry.

Our batteries were served in the most gallant style, continuing their fire to the last under the most trying circumstances. The heavy loss in officers and men, horses and *matériel*, attest at the same time the severity of the enemy's fire and the noble manner in which it was sustained.

Our loss in killed and wounded was fearful, especially among the field officers, demonstrating how gallantly the men were led. Colonel Ward, Fifteenth Massachusetts; Lieutenant-Colonel Huston, Eighty-Second New York; Colonel O'Kane and Lieutenant-Colonel Tschudy, Sixty-ninth Pennsylvania; Colonel Revere, Twentieth Massachusetts; Lieutenant-Colonel Steele, Seventh Michigan, and Lieutenant-Colonel Thoman, Fifty-ninth New York, were killed; and Colonel Baxter, Seventy-second Pennsylvania; Colonel Colvill, Lieutenant-Colonel Adams, and Major Downie, First Minnesota; Lieutenant-Colonel Macy, Twentieth Massachusetts, and Lieutenant-Colonel Wass and Major Rice, Nineteenth Massachusetts, were wounded.

The division went into action about 3,800 strong; lost in killed and wounded over 1,600, and captured more prisoners than it had men on the ground at the end of the conflict, besides many colors.

I am, sir, very respectfully, your obedient servant,

JOHN GIBBON,
Brigadier-General of Volunteers, Commanding Division.

Maj. W. G. Mitchell,
Acting Assistant Adjutant-General, Second Corps.

No. 99.

*Reports of Brig. Gen. William Harrow, U. S. Army, commanding
Second Division.*

HEADQUARTERS SECOND DIVISION, SECOND ARMY CORPS,
July 16, 1863.

SIR: I have the honor to submit the following in reference to the
part taken by the Second Division, Second Corps, in the late sanguinary engagement of the 2d and 3d instant, near Gettysburg, Pa.:

The division arrived upon the battle-field on the morning of the 2d,
and was ordered into position by Brig. Gen. John Gibbon, as follows:
The Second Brigade, General Webb commanding, occupied the right
of the division, and was stationed on the crest of a ridge, the left
resting nearly opposite a two-story brick house about 300 yards in
front of the line, the right resting upon and covered by a stone fence,
and connecting with the left of the command of Brigadier-General
Hays, commanding Third Division, Second Corps. The Third
Brigade, Colonel Hall, Seventh Michigan Volunteers, commanding,
connected with the left of General Webb's brigade, and continued
the line in the direction of Round Top Mountain to the left, their
two brigades covering a front of 500 yards. The First Brigade, my
own command, was placed in reserve 100 yards in rear of the Second
and Third Brigades and opposite the center of the line. The division
occupied the position indicated when the advance of Major-General
Sickles developed the enemy in force, in rear of a range of hills to
the left and front of his command, sheltered by a dense wood, which
was skirted in front by a smaller growth of thick bushes.

At this time, by direction of General Gibbon, two regiments of
my command (the Fifteenth Massachusetts Volunteers, Colonel
Ward, and Eighty-second New York, Colonel Huston commanding)
advanced to the front of the general line, and were placed on the
Gettysburg and Emmitsburg road, on the right of the brick house
before referred to, the left of Colonel Huston's command resting at
the house, Colonel Ward prolonging the line to the right. The First
Minnesota Volunteers, Colonel Colvill commanding, by the direction
of General Gibbon, were moved from their original position in the
rear, to the left of a battery commanded by Lieutenant Thomas, and
stationed on the high ground a short distance to the left of the division line of battle. The Nineteenth Maine Volunteers, Colonel
Heath commanding, were moved to the left and front of the division
line, and placed in position to the right of a battery commanded by
Lieutenant Brown. These dispositions being made, the division
waited the approach of the enemy. It soon becoming evident that
a general engagement would follow the attack upon Major-General
Sickles, he retired toward the general line, the enemy pushing forward with great impetuosity. As the enemy advanced, the first of
the division to engage them were the Eighty-second New York and
Fifteenth Massachusetts Volunteers, from their position on the Gettysburg and Emmitsburg road. These two regiments, in the aggregate not more than 700 strong, and without support on their line,
but partially protected by the rails of a fence which they had hastily
taken down and piled in their front, gallantly sustained an unequal
contest against greatly superior numbers until the enemy's advance
had reached their left flank, when they retired, but not before suffer-

ing heavy losses and inflicting more than a corresponding punishment upon their assailants. It was in this advanced line that Colonels Ward and Huston both fell, mortally wounded (each since dead), and here also many line officers were killed and wounded. The enemy continued to advance until they attacked with great fury the commands of Colonels Colvill and Heath, endeavoring to take the batteries under their protection. In this assault, Colonel Colvill, Lieutenant-Colonel Adams, and Major Downie were shot down, the two former severely, and I fear mortally, wounded, but the command maintained its position until supported by the arrival of other troops.

It would be unjust to a young and accomplished officer, Lieutenant Thomas, not to bear testimony here to his gallantry, and to credit him with destroying large numbers of the enemy by the very effective fire of his guns. His exertions contributed largely to checking and finally repulsing the enemy at this point.

Colonel Heath, Nineteenth Maine Volunteers, was attacked with equal desperation, the enemy at one time obtaining possession of three of the guns of the battery on his left. These guns he retook and carried from the field, most of the battery horses having been killed and many of the gunners killed and wounded. The officers and men of this command, as also the officers and men of the battery, deserve high commendation for their determination and valor.

The final repulse of the enemy accomplished, dispositions were made for the contest of the succeeding day (July 3) by General Gibbon, as follows: The Second and Third Brigades on this day occupied the position of the day previous, the First Brigade continuing the line to the left. The entire line was strengthened during the night by such means as could be commanded.

At 1 p. m. the enemy opened a fierce cannonade upon the line from a hundred or more guns, which was continued until nearly 3 p. m., when his infantry columns moved from the woods, 1,000 yards in front, and steadily advanced to the assault. After crossing the Emmitsburg and Gettysburg road in two lines, with supports upon the right and left, accommodating their advance to the inequalities of the surface, so as to cover themselves as far as possible by the low grounds in front of the division, this movement brought them first in range of the guns of the First Brigade, but the crest of the hill occupied by the right of Colonel Hall and the left of General Webb seemed to be the point to which their main attack was directed. As this purpose became manifest, the Third and First Brigades, of this division, inclined to the right, engaging the enemy as they moved, the whole command meeting the shock from the enemy's heaviest lines and supports near the crest of the ridge. Here the contest raged with almost unparalleled ferocity for nearly an hour, when the enemy was routed and fled in disorder.

I have no words to express the unwavering courage and daring of the entire command in this the final struggle. Many prisoners, including many officers, were taken here; also many battle-flags were captured.

It would be gross injustice to claim a greater share of this triumph for one brigade of the division to the exclusion of another. It was a common struggle and a common success, as the gallant dead and wounded of each of the brigades of the division there fallen amply testify. The First Brigade carried off the field four of the enemy's battle-flags; each of the other brigades as many or more.

The loss of the First Brigade during the two days was:

Officers and men.	Killed.	Wounded.	Missing.	Total.
Commissioned officers...	12	43	......	55
Non-commissioned officers and privates........................	136	531	......	667
Total*..	148	574	......	722

An official list of the names and rank of each has been forwarded.

For more particular details of the conduct and losses of the Second and Third Brigades, reference is had to the reports of the brigade commanders. This report has been amplified, so far as it applies to the First Brigade, more than would otherwise have been necessary, for the reason that throughout the entire engagement of the 2d instant, and until the day was well-nigh won on the 3d, Brigadier-General Gibbon commanded the division, and only relinquished the command when forced to quit the field, having been severely wounded.

I cannot omit this occasion to say that his sagacity, coolness, and courage on each day won for him the highest admiration, adding to the high character he had previously established as a commander. He merits the consideration of his superiors and his Government, and his services will no doubt be suitably acknowledged. I trust he will make for his division a more elaborate report, in which he can suitably mention his staff officers; it will be a pleasant duty to perform.

I mean not to disparage any other by saying his aide-de-camp, Lieutenant Haskell, greatly distinguished himself by his constant exertion in the most exposed places.

My own assistant adjutant-general, Capt. John P. Blinn, throughout both days manifested himself a thorough soldier and patriot. He fell, mortally wounded, on the 3d, while gallantly cheering on the men of the command to which he was attached. No tribute can now reach him, but a worthier man and soldier has not died for his country.

Captain Cooper, acting assistant inspector-general, First Brigade, and Lieutenants Biggs and White, my aides, severally deserve commendation. The latter was severely injured by the fall of his horse, which was shot under him during the action.

The division took into action 3,773 men, and lost 1,657.*

In conclusion, I hope it is not too much to say that this division contributed very largely to the success of the 3d instant, if, indeed, they did not save the day, as the chief attack of the enemy was directed against the position they occupied.

I have the honor to be, sir, very respectfully, your obedient servant,

WM. HARROW,
Brigadier-General, Comdg. Second Division, Second Corps.

Capt. E. P. BROWNSON,
Acting Assistant Adjutant-General, Second Army Corps.

---

* But see revised statement, p. 176.

———, — —, 1863.

The following is a numerical list of killed, wounded, and missing in the Second Division, Second Corps, during the engagement near Gettysburg, Pa., July 2 and 3.*

The First Brigade estimates that 1,740 guns were picked up by the Fifteenth Massachusetts, Nineteenth Maine, and First Minnesota Volunteers, of that command.

The Second Brigade reports 1,284 rifles and 972 sets of accouterments picked up.

The Third Brigade reports that no account of arms collected by that brigade can be given, as they were removed from the field after collection by details by ordnance officers of the First and Second Divisions.

WM. HARROW,
Brigadier-General, Commanding Division.

———

No. 100.

Report of Col. Francis E. Heath, Nineteenth Maine Infantry.

NEAR GETTYSBURG, PA.,
July 4, 1863.

I have the honor to make the following report of the share taken by my regiment in the late engagements:

On the afternoon of the 2d, my regiment was placed in position, under the eye of the general commanding, to the left, and supporting Brown's Rhode Island battery.

At a little past 6 p. m. the enemy advanced and my regiment became engaged. After firing about 10 rounds, I ordered an advance, and took quite a number of prisoners. I also retook four Napoleon guns that had been abandoned by some of our forces that had been posted to my left and front. The guns were sent immediately to the rear, after which I fell back to our old position.

On the following day my position was on the left of the Eighty-second New York Volunteers, and, when the enemy advanced, I was ordered with the rest of the brigade to the support of the Second Brigade.

While there engaged, I lost very heavily, especially in non-commissioned officers. Two battle-flags of the enemy were taken by men of my regiment, but were torn from the lances by men of other regiments.

Of the conduct of the officers and men of my regiment. I cannot speak too highly. I would gladly particularize, but any distinction would be invidious, for all did nobly.

I have already forwarded a list of casualties.*

Very respectfully, your obedient servant,

F. E. HEATH,
Colonel, Commanding.

ACTING ASSISTANT ADJUTANT-GENERAL,
First Brigade.

---

*Embodied in revised statement, p. 176.

No. 101.

Reports of Lieut. Col. George C. Joslin, Fifteenth Massachusetts Infantry.

IN THE FIELD,
July 11, 1863.

SIR: I have the honor to make the following report of the part taken by the Fifteenth Regiment Massachusetts Volunteers in the action of July 2 and 3, at Gettysburg, Pa.:

Early on the morning of the 2d, we moved from our place of bivouac, immediately in the rear of the First Minnesota, and took our position in close column by regiments near the battle-field, stacked arms, and remained until about 4 o'clock in the afternoon, when the enemy opened fire from their batteries. Colonel Ward, who had been in command of the brigade, was here relieved, and took command of the regiment, and moved by order of General Harrow to the front of our batteries, and took position on the right of the Eighty-second New York, their left resting near a brick house about 200 yards to the front, nothing connecting on our right. Here we built a small breastwork of rails behind the fence, during which time the enemy were being engaged on our left and a rapid picket firing in our front. We remained in this position about half an hour, when the pickets were driven in, and the Eighty-second New York became engaged. Upon the approach of the enemy, their batteries in our rear opened fire with grape and canister, by which we lost a large number killed and wounded.

At this time the Eighty-second New York fell back, exposing our left and rear to a deadly fire from the rebel infantry. Here Colonel Ward received wounds from which he has since died. We now opened a rapid fire, but being left alone could hold the position but a short time, when we retired in some disorder, being pressed so closely that we lost quite a number of prisoners, captured by the enemy. We reformed our line in rear of the batteries, and rejoined the brigade, which was moved after dark to the front line, and took position on the left of the First Minnesota, which was the extreme left of the brigade, where we remained until about 2.30 p. m. of the following day.

About 1 p. m. the enemy opened a heavy fire of artillery upon our lines, during which we lost 1 man killed and 2 wounded. Soon after, an attack of infantry was made by the enemy on the right of our lines, and we moved by the right flank a short distance and became hotly engaged. After about an hour's fighting, the enemy were repulsed, during which engagement the regiment sustained a heavy loss. After about an hour, we were ordered to our former position, and from there deployed to the front as skirmishers, where we remained until relieved, about 8 a. m. the next day, our ammunition being expended. During the skirmish we lost 2 men wounded.

We went into action with 18 officers and 221 men. During the three days, our loss in killed was 3 officers, 19 enlisted men; wounded, 8 officers and 85 enlisted men; missing, 28 enlisted men, supposed to be captured.*

The behavior of the officers and men under my command during the engagements was as good as I could wish. It would do injustice to particularize officers of the line, they all acted with so much cool-

---

* But see revised statement, p. 176.

ness and bravery. I would mention especially Major Hooper and Lieutenant Earle, acting adjutant, they both being with me the whole time and showing the greatest bravery.

Very respectfully, your obedient servant,

GEO. C. JOSLIN,
Lieutenant-Colonel, Commanding Regiment.

Lieut. F. W. HASKELL,
Actg. Asst. Adjt. Gen., First Brigade, Second Division.

—

SANDY HOOK, MD.,
July 16, 1863.

SIR: In compliance with circular orders from brigade headquarters of this date, I submit the following report of casualties during the engagement at Gettysburg, Pa., July 2 and 3:

Officers.
Killed 3
Wounded 8

Total 11

Enlisted men:
Killed 19
Wounded 85
Missing 2

Total 106

Prisoners 26
Buried by regimental detail:
    Officers 1
    Enlisted men 9
Guns brought in by regimental detail 60

I am, very respectfully, your obedient servant,

GEO C. JOSLIN,
Lieutenant-Colonel, Commanding Regiment.

Lieutenant HASKELL,
Acting Assistant Adjutant-General.

—

No. 102:

Report of Capt. Henry C. Coates, First Minnesota Infantry.

NEAR ELLIS' FORD, VA.,
August 3, 1863.

SIR: Pursuant to circular of this date, I respectfully submit the following statement of the part taken by this regiment in the late battle near Gettysburg, Pa.:

About 3 o'clock on the morning of July 2, we were ordered into position near the center of our line of battle, to the left of the town. The battle commenced at daylight, and raged with fury the entire day. We remained under a severe artillery fire, but were not actively engaged until about 5 p. m., when we were moved to support Battery C, Fourth U. S. Artillery. Company F was about this time detached from the regiment as skirmishers, and Company L as sharpshooters.

Our infantry in front of us had advanced upon the enemy and pushed him for a while, but were in turn driven back in some confusion, the enemy following in heavy force. To check the enemy, we were ordered to advance, which we did, moving at double-quick down the slope of the hill right upon the rebel line. The fire we encountered here was terrible, and, although we inflicted severe punishment upon the enemy, and stopped his advance, we there lost in killed and wounded more than two-thirds of our men and officers who were engaged.

Here Captain Muller, of Company E, and Lieutenant Farrar, of Company I, were killed; Captain Periam, of Company K, mortally wounded. Colonel Colvill, Lieutenant-Colonel Adams, Major Downie, Adjutant Peller, and Lieutenants Sinclair, Company B; Demarest, Company E; De Gray, Company G; and Boyd, Company I, were severely wounded.

The command of the regiment now devolved upon Capt. Nathan S. Messick, and we were moved again to the right, near the position first occupied by us, where we slept on our arms during the night.

At daybreak the next morning the enemy renewed the battle with vigor on the right and left of our line with infantry, and about 10 a. m. opened upon the center, where we were posted, a most severe fire of artillery, which continued without intermission until 3 p. m., when heavy columns of the enemy's infantry were thrown suddenly forward against our position. They marched resolutely in the face of a withering fire up to our lines, and succeeded in planting their colors on one of our batteries. The point of attack was to the right of our position, and held by the Second Brigade of our division (Second Division, Second Army Corps). As the enemy approached, we were moved by the right flank to oppose them, firing upon them as we approached, and sustaining their fire, together with the fire of batteries which they had brought up to within short range. The fighting here was desperate for a time. At length the regiment and others closed in upon the enemy, and nearly the whole of the rebel force which remained alive were taken prisoners. About 500 were captured by this regiment; also the colors of the Twenty-eighth Virginia Regiment, taken by Private Marshall Sherman, of Company C.*

The regiment here again lost severely. Capt. Nathan S. Messick, while gallantly leading the regiment, fell early in the action. Capt. W. B. Farrell, Company C, was mortally wounded, and died on the day following. Lieutenants Mason and Heffelfinger, Company D, Harmon, Company C, and May, Company B, were wounded.

The enemy did not recover from this repulse, and the battle was now won. The entire regiment, excepting Company L, was in this last fight. This company had been detached as sharpshooters, to support Kirby's battery, where it did very effective service. Every man in the regiment did his whole duty.

The accompanying list of killed and wounded shows the severity of our loss.†

Your obedient servant,

> **H. C. COATES,**
> *Captain, Commanding Regiment.*

Lieut. F. W. HASKELL,
Acting Assistant Adjutant-General.

---

*A medal of honor awarded to Sherman for this service.
†Embodied in revised statement, p. 176.

No. 103.

Reports of Capt. John Darrow, Eighty-second New York Infantry (Second Militia).

CAMP ON LOGAN'S FARM, VA., *August* 3, 1863.

SIR: In obedience to orders from superior headquarters, I have the honor to report the part this regiment has taken in the engagement before Gettysburg.

We arrived on the field under the command of Lieut. Col. James Huston; were sent to the front as a picket support, with the Fifteenth Massachusetts Volunteers on our right. The ninth and tenth companies were sent to a brick house near the left of our line, and had orders to burn it, if necessary, on the approach of the enemy.

About 6 p. m. the enemy advanced in our front and turned our left flank. We held our position for a short time, but as the enemy was getting in our rear we retired to our first line, where the regiment reformed under a galling fire; then advanced, driving the enemy before us; regained our former position, capturing the battle-flags of the Forty-eighth Georgia Regiment.

In this action we lost 13 officers and 140 men killed and wounded. Our lieutenant-colonel was among the killed, having received two wounds, one in the head and the other in the leg.

In the action of the 3d, we lost a number of men during the cannonade. When the enemy advanced, we were ordered to the right toward a small grove, and charged through it, driving the enemy before us, and captured two flags from the First and Seventh Virginia Regiments, with a loss of 4 officers and 65 men. We then took our former position on the right of our brigade.

To speak in praise of any where all did so well, would be impossible. I take pleasure in mentioning the following officers: Captain Hughes did all a brave officer could; also Captain Maxwell. Adjutant Simms deserves all the praise and honor due a brave and gallant officer. Lieutenants Herbert, Cronin, and Kelly did their duty nobly and fearlessly. Assistant Surgeon Lewis did his duty nobly and with unremitting attention.

JOHN DARROW,
Captain, Commanding Regiment.

Lieutenant HASKELL, *Acting Assistant Adjutant-General.*

———

NEAR KNOXVILLE, MD., *July* 16, 1863.

SIR: In accordance with circular of date July 16, 1863, I would respectfully render the following report:

Officers and men.	Killed.	Wounded.	Missing.	Buried by regimental detail.	Total.
Commissioned officers	3	12	1	37	53
Enlisted men	40	125	14	....	179
Total*	43	137	15	37	232

JOHN DARROW,
Captain, Commanding Regiment.

Lieut. F. W. HASKELL, *Actg. Asst. Adjt. Gen., 1st Brig.*

———

*But see revised statement, p. 176.

No. 104.

*Reports of Brig. Gen. Alexander S. Webb, U. S. Army, command-
ing Second Brigade.*

HDQRS. SECOND BRIG., SECOND DIV., SECOND ARMY CORPS,
Jones' Cross-Roads, Md., July 12, 1863.

CAPTAIN: I would respectfully submit the following report of the
operations of this brigade in the action of July 2 and 3:

By command of Brig. Gen. John Gibbon, commanding division,
this brigade was put in position at 6.30 a. m. on the 2d, on Granite
Ridge, on the right of the division, its right resting on Cushing's
battery (A, Fourth U. S. Artillery), and its left on Battery B, First
Rhode Island Artillery, Lieutenant Brown commanding. The Sixty-
ninth Regiment was placed behind a fence a little in advance of the
ridge; the remaining three regiments of the brigade under cover of
the hill in rear. Brown's battery was, in the course of the day,
moved to the front of the Sixty-ninth Regiment. It remained at
this point until the assault at 6.30 p. m. During the day both of the
batteries on the flanks of the brigade engaged those of the enemy.
The shelling wounded but few.

In the morning, Capt. John J. Sperry, of the One hundred and
Sixth Pennsylvania Volunteers, was sent out with Companies A and
I, of the Seventy-second Pennsylvania Volunteers, and A and B, of
the One hundred and sixth Pennsylvania Volunteers, to skirmish
and to watch the movements of the enemy. He lost a number of men
and had several officers wounded in performing this important duty.

Capts. John J. Sperry and James C. Lynch, of the One hundred
and sixth Pennsylvania Volunteers, and Captains Cook and Suplee,
of the Seventy-second Pennsylvania Volunteers, deserve honorable
mention for their coolness, intelligence, and zeal shown both on the
2d and 3d.

The enemy made the assault of the 2d at about 6.30 p. m. Their
line of battle advanced beyond one gun of Brown's battery, receiving
at that point the fire of the Sixty-ninth Pennsylvania Volunteers and
that of the Seventy-first Pennsylvania Volunteers, advanced to the
support of the Sixty-ninth; also that of the One hundred and sixth
and Seventy-second Pennsylvania Volunteers, which had previously
been moved to the left, by command of Major-General Hancock.
Colonel Baxter, Seventy-second Pennsylvania Volunteers, at this
time was wounded. They halted, wavered, and fell back, pursued
by the One hundred and Sixth, Seventy-second, and part of the Seventy-first Pennsylvania Volunteers. The One hundred and sixth and
Seventy-second Pennsylvania Volunteers followed them to the Emmitsburg road, capturing and sending to the rear about 250 prisoners, among whom were 1 colonel, 5 captains, and 15 lieutenants.
The Seventy-first Pennsylvania Volunteers captured about 20 prisoners at the position previously held by the Rhode Island battery.

The One hundred and sixth Pennsylvania Volunteers were ordered
back from the Emmitsburg road a little before dark, and ordered to
report to Major-General Howard, commanding Eleventh Army Corps,
then near the cemetery. For a report of its operations I refer to
inclosed report of the regimental commander. The Seventy-first
Pennsylvania Volunteers was detached to report at the same place
a little after dark. It returned at about 12 o'clock without orders.
The report of the colonel, annexed, is important.

OPERATIONS OF JULY 3.

About 1 p. m. the enemy opened with more than twenty batteries upon our line. By 2.45 o'clock had silenced the Rhode Island battery and all the guns but one of Cushing's battery, and had plainly shown by his concentration of fire on this and the Third Brigade that an important assault was to be expected.

I had sent, at 2 p. m., Captain Banes, assistant adjutant-general of the brigade, for two batteries to replace Cushing's and Brown's. Just before the assault, Captain Wheeler's [Cowan's] battery, First New York Artillery [First New York Independent Battery], had gotten in position on the left, in the place occupied by the Rhode Island battery, which had retired with a loss of all its officers but one.

At 3 o'clock the enemy's line of battle left the woods in our front; moved in perfect order across the Emmitsburg road; formed in the hollow in our immediate front several lines of battle, under a fire of spherical case from Wheeler's [Cowan's] battery and Cushing's gun, and advanced for the assault.

The Seventy-first Pennsylvania Volunteers were advanced to the wall on the right of the Sixty-ninth Pennsylvania Volunteers. Three of Cushing's guns were run down to the fence, carrying with them their canister. The Seventy-second Pennsylvania Volunteers were held in reserve under the crest of the hill. The enemy advanced steadily to the fence, driving out a portion of the Seventy-first Pennsylvania Volunteers. General Armistead passed over the fence with probably over 100 of his command and with several battle-flags. The Seventy-second Pennsylvania Volunteers were ordered up to hold the crest, and advanced to within 40 paces of the enemy's line. Colonel Smith, commanding the Seventy-first Pennsylvania Volunteers, threw two companies of his command behind the stone wall on the right of Cushing's battery, 50 paces retired from the point of attack. This disposition of his troops was most important. Colonel Smith showed true military intelligence on the field. The Sixty-ninth Pennsylvania Volunteers and most of the Seventy-first Pennsylvania Volunteers, even after the enemy were in their rear, held their position. The Seventy-second Pennsylvania Volunteers fought steadily and persistently, but the enemy would probably have succeeded in piercing our lines had not Colonel Hall advanced with several of his regiments to my support. Defeated, routed, the enemy fled in disorder. General Armistead was left, mortally wounded, within my lines, and 42 of the enemy who crossed the fence lay dead.

This brigade captured nearly 1,000 prisoners, 6 battle-flags (4 have been turned in), and picked up 1,400 stand of arms and 903 sets of accouterments.

The loss of the brigade on the 2d and 3d was 43 commissioned officers and 482 enlisted men.* But 47 enlisted men are missing.

The conduct of this brigade was most satisfactory. Officers and men did their whole duty.

The Sixty-ninth Pennsylvania Volunteers lost all its field officers, but held its ground. The cover in its front was not well built, and it lost many men lying on the ground; still, I saw none retire from the fence.

A portion of the One hundred and sixth Pennsylvania Volunteers, left behind the previous evening under Captain Ford, took part in

---

* But see revised statement, p. 176.

repelling the assault. I lost gallant officers and men. They need no tribute from me. A nominal list has been sent in.

I feel that the general commanding has had abundant proof that as a brigade the Second can be relied upon for the performance of any duty which may be required of it.

Lieut. A. H. Cushing, Fourth U. S. Artillery, fell, mortally wounded, at the fence by the side of his guns. Cool, brave, competent, he fought for an hour and a half after he had reported to me that he was wounded in both thighs.

I desire to call attention to the brave conduct of Lieut. Joseph S. Milne, Battery B, First Rhode Island Artillery, serving with Lieutenant Cushing.

I recommend for promotion Sergts. Frederick Fuger and Edward M. Irving, of that battery; also Acting Gunner Francis Abraham. This battery was nobly served.

Capt. C. H. Banes, assistant adjutant-general of this brigade, assisted at all points in strengthening the line, and encouraging the men and officers by his coolness. I recommend him for honorable mention.

I have the honor to be, captain, very respectfully, your obedient servant,

ALEX. S. WEBB,
Brigadier-General, Commanding.

Capt. A. H. EMBLER,
Acting Assistant Adjutant-General.

—

HDQRS. SECOND BRIG., SECOND DIV., SECOND ARMY CORPS,
Camp near Bealeton, Va., August 14, 1863.

CAPTAIN: I have the honor to submit the following as the report of the operations of this brigade between June 28 and July 26, inclusive, in obedience to circular received yesterday morning from headquarters Army of the Potomac:

June 28.—The brigade went into camp near the left bank of Monocacy River and on the Frederick turnpike. General Webb took command at 5 p. m.

June 29.—Left Monocacy River at 6 a. m. and marched to Uniontown, via Liberty, Johnsville, and Union Bridge, reaching Uniontown at 9 p. m., a distance of 33 miles.

June 30.—Remained in camp all day.

July 1.—Marched to within about 4 miles of Gettysburg. This brigade was put in position with the division, to cover the retreat of the First Army Corps, should that be ordered.

July 2.—Marched to Gettysburg battle-field; took post on Granite Ridge, and repelled assault of the enemy at 5 p. m.

July 3.—Remained on the battle-field; repelled assault at 3 p. m. For official report of these two days' operations, see report of the battle of Gettysburg.

July 4.—Buried dead and collected arms and accouterments.

July 5.—Marched at 12 m. from the battle-field; encamped at Two Taverns.

July 6.—Remained in camp.

July 7.—Marched at 5 a. m. to Taneytown.

July 8.—Marched at 5 a. m. to Walkersville, a distance of 4 miles from Frederick.

July 9.—Left camp at 5 a. m., passed through Frederick, Jefferson, Burkittsville, and Crampton's Pass, and encamped near Rohrersville, a distance of 22 miles.

July 10.—Left camp at 5 a. m., passed through Keedysville and Smoketown, and encamped near Tilghmanton, a distance of 12 miles.

July 11.—Marched 2 miles to cross-roads on Hagerstown turnpike, and took position on the left of the Fifth Army Corps. At 11 p. m. moved on the turnpike toward Hagerstown, and bivouacked in the road until the morning of July 12. Moved on the turnpike; took several positions, and finally took position facing northwest and in front of Saint James' College. After dark, received orders to intrench.

July 13.—Threw forward right wing, and took position facing west, and intrenched.

July 14.—Advanced to near Williamsport; bivouacked for the night.

July 15.—Marched via Sharpsburg to within 3 miles of Sandy Hook, and bivouacked on the canal bank; distance, 19 miles.

July 16.—Marched to Pleasant Valley.

July 17.—Remained in camp.

July 18.—Left camp at 6 a. m.; crossed the Potomac and Shenandoah Rivers, passing southeast of Loudoun Heights, and encamped 9 miles from Harper's Ferry.

July 19.—Moved at 10 a. m., and marched to Woodgrove.

July 20.—Marched to Bloomfield, guarding wagon train; distance, 12 miles.

July 21.—Remained in camp.

July 22.—Left Bloomfield at 1 p. m. and marched to Ashby's Gap; distance, 10 miles.

July 23.—Left at 4.30 a. m.; marched to Manassas Gap; halted at Markham to allow the Third and Fifth Corps to pass; moved in the Gap beyond Linden, and took position in rear of the Third Corps.

July 24.—Moved back to near Markham, and halted for the night.

July 25.—Marched to White Plains, via Rectortown; distance, about 19 miles.

July 26.—Left camp at 5 a. m. and marched to a point west of the Warrenton Branch Railroad, about 2 miles from the Junction, via New Baltimore and Warrenton.

I am, very respectfully, your obedient servant,

ALEX. S. WEBB,
Brig. Gen. of Volunteers, Comdg. Brigade.

Capt. J. P. Wood,
Assistant Adjutant-General.

No. 105.

Report of Capt. William Davis, Sixty-ninth Pennsylvania Infantry.

JONES' CROSS-ROADS, MD., *July* 12, 1863.

CAPTAIN: In compliance with general orders, I herewith send you a brief report of the part our regiment took in the recent engagement with the enemy in the vicinity of Gettysburg, Pa., and the casualties attending the same.

In compliance with an order from Brigadier-General Webb, we took up our line of position behind a temporary breastwork made of fence-rails, strengthened with stone, on the morning of July 2, and remained in that position till the enemy advanced upon us, about 4 o'clock in the afternoon. The battery of the First Rhode Island, being immediately in our front, had kept up a fierce cannonading for two hours before, and doubtless had done great execution on the rebel lines. This fact rendered our position a mark of no insignificance. The capture of the battery became a matter of great importance to the rebels, as future events proved fully. Onward they came, and absolutely seized upon the cannon. To prevent this, all the energy and power that could be brought to bear against such a result was brought into requisition. Our men fought with the bravery and coolness of veterans, and, after fighting with desperation for a period of one hour or more, we had the satisfaction of seeing the rebels turn and flee in a perfect panic.

We lost in this engagement:

Officers and men.	Killed.	Wounded.	Total.
Officers...	2	2	4
Enlisted men...	9	15	24
Total...	11	17	28

The battle commenced on the 3d instant at about 4 p. m. We still held the position assigned us the day previous. At about 1 o'clock a most fierce cannonading took place, and was continued without intermission till about 3 o'clock, when the rebels advanced a large infantry force against our whole line. Onward they came, and it would seem as if no power could hold them in check. Our troops, with few exceptions, met them bravely, but still they came, and, as they advanced to the right of our regiment, turned by the right flank and literally came right on top of our men. But if they succeeded thus far in their advance, they were here held in check, for new ardor seemed to inspire our men to greater exertions. Our whole brigade here became engaged with them, and, with the help of the Tammany Regiment and the Twentieth Massachusetts Regiment, drove them from the front of our line.

We lost very heavily, and among the number killed we have to deplore our colonel, D. O'Kane, and lieutenant-colonel, M. Tschudy. Our major was also wounded at this juncture, and the command fell into my hands.

After the enemy had been completely driven back, I put our men to work to still further strengthen our position in the event of any other advance on the part of the enemy on the following day.

We lost in the engagement:

Officers and men.	Killed.	Wounded.	Missing.	Total.
Officers...	3	7	2	12
Enlisted men...	29	64	16	109
Total...	32	71	18	121

Our killed were all buried together, and their graves marked, so that their friends and connections can easily find them if they wish to have them disinterred. The wounded were taken to hospitals temporarily erected, and cared for as well as circumstances would admit.

Very respectfully, your obedient servant,

WM. DAVIS,
Capt., Comdg. Sixty-ninth Pennsylvania Volunteers.

Capt. C. H. BANES, *Assistant Adjutant-General.*

No. 106.

Report of Col. R. Penn Smith, Seventy-first Pennsylvania Infantry.

JONES' CROSS-ROADS, MD., *July* 12, 1863.

CAPTAIN: I have the honor to report the conduct of the Seventy-first Pennsylvania Volunteers during the late battles at Gettysburg, Pa., July 2 and 3.

In the afternoon of the 2d instant, I went to the support of the Sixty-ninth Pennsylvania Volunteers, then on the front, and became engaged with the enemy, taking some 20 prisoners and retaking a brass cannon and limber which the enemy held.

About dark of this day, by an order through Captain Duffy, I was ordered to the support of a portion of the Eleventh Corps. Having arrived on the ground, I could find no general to report to who had command of any one portion of the troops. An adjutant-general directed me to proceed to the front, assuring me that all was safe on either flank. Arriving at the front, I became engaged with the enemy on the front. At the same time he attacked me on my right and rear. I immediately ordered my command to retire to the road in my rear, when I returned to camp against orders. During the engagement, I lost 3 commissioned officers and 11 enlisted men.

On the 3d instant, some 50 of my men assisted in working Lieutenant Cushing's battery, while the balance were in position, protected by a stone wall from an infantry attack, engaging the enemy and scattering confusion in his ranks, taking some 500 prisoners, as many arms, and 3 stand of rebel colors.* Loss, 22 killed, 59 wounded, and 19 missing.†

Among so many conspicuous acts of valor and daring, it is difficult to particularize individuals. I cannot but speak of my regiment in the highest terms.

I would call attention to the conduct of Captain McMahon and Private Young, of Company C, both of whom are under sentence of court-martial. I pray that the approval or disapproval of the findings of the court in the case of the first may be influenced in a great degree by his noble conduct in the field, and of the latter that the sentence may be revoked.

I am, with great respect, your obedient servant,

R. PENN SMITH,
Colonel, Comdg. Seventy-first Pennsylvania Volunteers.

Capt. C. H. BANES, *Assistant Adjutant-General.*

---

* A medal of honor awarded to Private John E. Clopp for the capture of the flag of the Ninth Virginia Infantry.
† But see revised statement, p. 176.

No. 107.

Report of Lieut. Col. Theodore Hesser, Seventy-second Pennsylvania Infantry.

JONES' CROSS-ROADS, MD., *July* 11, 1863.

CAPTAIN: I have the honor to submit the following report of the operations of my regiment on July 2 and 3, at Gettysburg, Pa.:

On the 2d instant, the regiment supported a battery until 6 p. m., when (the first line of battle giving way) orders were received to advance and assist in reoccupying the ground lost, which orders were executed without, however, becoming directly engaged.

On the 3d instant, the regiment was again assigned the duty of supporting a battery, which position it occupied (under a terrific fire of the enemy's artillery) until 3 p. m., at which time they were ordered to advance upon the stone wall on our immediate front, it being discovered that the enemy were making a demonstration in that direction. At this point the regiment became engaged with Pickett's division of the rebel army, and, after a severe contest, lasting about half an hour, succeeded in routing the enemy and occupying the wall, which position it held until the withdrawal of the brigade on the morning of the 5th. In this engagement the regiment captured two rebel colors and a number of prisoners.

I would especially mention Companies A and I, Captains Suplee and Cook, for the creditable manner in which they performed the skirmishing for the brigade in the engagements of both days.

The aggregate losses of the regiment in the two days' engagements are as follows:

Officers and men.	Killed.	Wounded.	Missing.	Total.
Commissioned officers	2	7	......	9
Enlisted men	34	151	3	188
Total*	36	158	3	197

Respectfully submitted.

THEO. HESSER,
Lieut. Col., Comdg. Seventy-second Pennsylvania Vols.

Capt. C. H. BANES, *Assistant Adjutant-General.*

No. 108.

Report of Lieut. Col. William L. Curry, One hundred and sixth Pennsylvania Infantry.

JONES' CROSS-ROADS, MD., *July* 11, 1863.

CAPTAIN: I beg leave respectfully to report the operations of this regiment during the battles before Gettysburg, Pa., from July 2 to 5, inclusive.

After arriving upon the ground the morning of the 2d instant, by order of General Webb the regiment was placed in position near the

---

* But see revised statement, p. 176.

front and center of the line. Two companies (A and B) were deployed as skirmishers in front of the line. They were warmly engaged until the action became general. The coolness and intrepidity with which they were handled kept the enemy at bay, and reflects great credit upon the officers and men of these two companies. Our left having attacked the enemy, were, after a desperate conflict, compelled to retire.

At this time the enemy opened upon our lines a furious cannonade, wounding one of our officers and several men. Under cover of this fire they advanced their infantry, driving back our first line, and forcing the artillery on my immediate front to withdraw. By order of Brigadier-General Webb, I advanced the regiment by the left flank, and formed in rear of the second line. Shortly after, orders were received to move forward. I advanced the regiment to the crest of the hill, and opened fire upon the enemy. After several volleys, perceiving that we checked his advance, and seeing his lines waver, I ordered bayonets fixed and a charge to be made, which movement resulted in a complete success, the enemy retiring in confusion to his original position in the woods. We pursued the fleeing enemy to the Emmitsburg road, when, perceiving that we were separated from the line on our left by a space of 70 yards, and having no troops on our right, excepting the remnant of the Eighty-second New York Volunteers, I halted the regiment, and sent to the rear for support, having first deployed skirmishers on my front. The officer whom I sent not returning, I left the regiment in charge of Major Stover, and personally applied to General Webb for support, and I was ordered to withdraw the regiment to its original position.

In the charge we made, we recovered three guns which had been abandoned. I sent them to the rear by hand. We also captured and sent to the rear about 250 prisoners, among whom were 1 colonel ([William] Gibson, Forty-eighth Georgia), 5 captains, and 15 lieutenants.

Ten minutes after we returned, the firing not having ceased upon the right, we were ordered to proceed in the direction of the firing, and report to Major-General Howard, commanding the Eleventh Corps, who assigned us to the command of General Ames, by whose order we were placed in the front line, on the right of the Gettysburg road and near the cemetery. We remained there until the morning of July 4, having been exposed to a very severe and concentrated fire from three batteries.

On the morning of the 3d, I detailed a body of sharpshooters, who, under cover of the houses in the vicinity, kept up a continuous fire upon the enemy's sharpshooters, who were picking off the gunners of our batteries. I have reason to believe that the enemy's sharpshooters suffered considerably from this body of men.

Early on the morning of the 4th, a body of skirmishers preceding us, General Ames, commanding First Division, Eleventh Army Corps, marched the regiment through the town of Gettysburg, and placed us in position on a slight eminence on the north of the town. Afterward I was ordered to conduct the regiment to our original position near the cemetery, where we remained until the morning of the 5th, when we were relieved by the following order:

HEADQUARTERS ELEVENTH ARMY CORPS, ARMY OF THE POTOMAC,
Gettysburg, Pa., July 5, 1863.

The Commanding Officer, One hundred and Sixth Pennsylvania Volunteers:

By direction of the commanding general, you are relieved from duty with this corps, and will rejoin your corps. The general commanding directs me to express his thanks for your kind support.

Very respectfully, your obedient servant,

T. A. MEYSENBURG,
Assistant Adjutant-General.

I will add that the two skirmishing companies detailed on the morning of the 2d did not accompany the regiment to the right, but remained in the center, and took an active part in the engagement on the afternoon of the 3d.

I have already furnished you with a list of the killed and wounded.*

I take great pleasure in saying that every officer and man performed his entire duty, and evinced a determination which must soon be crowned with success.

Early in the engagement, Adjt. F. M. Pleis was severely wounded and Lieut. John A. Steel was ordered to act as adjutant. Adjt. F. M. Pleis, while on the field, by his daring courage and example to the men, contributed much to the success which attended us. His successor, Lieut. John A. Steel, by his example and disregard of danger, rendered valuable services on the field, and is entitled to more than a passing notice.

I make especial mention of Maj. John H. Stover, who, by his coolness and daring, rendered me much valuable assistance. I also bear willing testimony to the good conduct of Capts. John J. Sperry, R. H. Ford, and James C. Lynch, and Lieut. C. S. Schwartz. In fact, the same may be said of every officer in my command.

Respectfully submitted.

W. L. CURRY,
Lieut. Col., Comdg. 106th Pennsylvania Volunteers.

Capt. C. H. BANES,
Assistant Adjutant-General.

No. 109.

Reports of Col. Norman J. Hall, Seventh Michigan Infantry, commanding Third Brigade.

HDQRS. THIRD BRIG., SECOND DIV., SECOND CORPS,
Pleasant Valley, Md., July 17, 1863.

CAPTAIN: I have the honor to submit the following report of the operations of the brigade under my command in the recent engagements near Gettysburg, Pa.:

The brigade, composed of the Seventh Michigan Volunteers, Forty-Second New York Volunteers, Twentieth Massachusetts Volunteers, Nineteenth Massachusetts Volunteers, and Fifty-ninth New York Volunteers, had, on the morning of July 2, just completed a march of about 190 miles with scarcely a day's rest. Arriving on the morning of that day upon the ground occupied by the troops who had been engaged with the enemy on the previous day, it was at once placed in column of battalions upon a crest which extended from the cemetery to Round Top. Upon the right of the column was the Second Brigade of this division, and upon the left was Captain Brown's battery. A division of the First Corps was in position on

---

*Embodied in revised statement, p. 176.

the left of the battery, but soon after removed and the ground was occupied by regiments of this brigade. A few rails were disposed in front of the line, to form a slight shelter. Until 4.30 p. m. the firing near this position was confined to artillery and the pickets.

About this time the Third Corps, holding the line on the left of the Second Corps, and but a short distance from this brigade, was advanced, and the engagement became general. Met by a far superior force of the enemy, the Third Corps was forced to retire, closely pursued. An order was received to send two regiments to the left to report to General Humphreys, and a staff officer came to conduct them. Being dispatched accordingly, two regiments moved rapidly forward and were soon lost to sight in the smoke of the battle. Conducted by the flank through the flying lines of our troops, and left by the staff officer—whom they have not seen since—to their own resources, they formed line of battle, delivered several volleys into the enemy in their front, staggering him for an instant, and, under this cover, withdrew in good order with a few prisoners, but with a loss of nearly one-third of their number.

These regiments (the Forty-second New York and Nineteenth Massachusetts) were the last of our troops to fall back at that point, and in their regularity presented a striking contrast with the fugitives. The enemy having an enfilading fire upon the lines of the Third Corps and troops called to its support, his advance was irresistible, its regularity surprising, and its rapidity fearful.

An interval of nearly a quarter of a mile was opened from the left of my position, and though re-enforcements were sent in great numbers to fill the gap, they halted, and formed their lines behind the part of the line which still remained firm. Convinced that they were needed at the undefended point, and seeing no general officer to direct, I felt authorized (as a moment's delay might prove fatal) to move them, and I transferred several regiments. When Major-General Hancock came to this point he approved the order, and himself moved others in the same direction. The enemy being now within 30 or 40 yards of the line of this brigade, the men, lying down, poured into him so well-directed a fire that he halted, fell back, and finally broke in great disorder. The rebel General Barksdale was mortally wounded and two colors left on the ground within 20 yards of the line of the Seventh Michigan Volunteers.

In his advance the enemy drove in some batteries placed before the line. One was driven through the line of the Twentieth Massachusetts Volunteers, which was lying down, and two guns left scarcely 6 feet in rear of that regiment. The one nearer the line was fired in that position, blowing a gap, and severely burning several men. Had not this portion of the line, which was not yet joined on its left by re-enforcements, stood firm, the interval would at least have been greatly increased and the result might have been incalculably disastrous.

For a few moments the enemy held possession of a portion of a disabled battery in front of the line, but was speedily driven from it by the fire from the division. The picket from this brigade made a strong resistance to the advance of the enemy. All its officers were wounded and many men killed or wounded, but few were captured by the enemy.

Colonel Revere, Captain Patten, Lieutenant Cowgill, of the Twentieth Massachusetts Volunteers; Lieutenant Slafter, Seventh Michigan Volunteers; Lieutenant-Colonel Thoman and Lieutenant Pohlman, of the Fifty-ninth New York Volunteers, and about 150 men were killed or wounded at their posts during this day's fight.

No serious attempt was again made by the enemy on the 2d against the position of the Second Corps. During the night the line was strengthened as much as possible with rails, stones, and earth thrown up with sticks and boards, no tools being obtainable.

Nothing more than occasional skirmishing occurred until the afternoon of the 3d. At 1 o'clock the enemy opened with artillery upon that portion of the line between the cemetery and the right of the Fifth Corps, several hundred yards from Round Top. The number of pieces which concentrated their fire upon this line is said to have been about one hundred and fifty. The object was evidently to destroy our batteries and drive the infantry from the slight crest which marked the line of battle, while the concentration of fire upon the hill occupied by the Second and the right of the Third Brigades indicated where the real attack was to be made. The experience of the terrible grandeur of that rain of missiles and that chaos of strange and terror-spreading sounds, unexampled, perhaps, in history, must ever remain undescribed, but can never be forgotten by those who survived it.

I cannot suffer this opportunity to pass without paying just tribute to the noble service of the officers and men of the batteries that were served within my sight. Never before during this war were so many batteries subjected to so terrible a test. Horses, men, and carriages were piled together, but the fire scarcely slackened for an instant so long as the guns were standing.

Lieutenant Cushing, of Battery A, Fourth U. S. Artillery, challenged the admiration of all who saw him. Three of his limbers were blown up and changed with the caisson limbers under fire. Several wheels were shot off his guns and replaced, till at last, severely wounded himself, his officers all killed or wounded, and with but cannoneers enough to man a section, he pushed his gun to the fence in front, and was killed while serving his last canister into the ranks of the advancing enemy.

Knowing that the enemy's infantry would attack soon, I sent Lieutenant [William R.] Driver, acting assistant adjutant-general, to the Artillery Reserve for batteries, with orders to conduct them to the crest, if they were granted, with all possible speed. He arrived with one, which, though too late for service in arresting the advance of the enemy, yet had the opportunity to do him much damage.

At 3 o'clock exactly the fire of the enemy slackened, and his first line of battle advanced from the woods in front in beautiful order. About 100 yards in rear came a second line, and opposite the main point of attack was what appeared to be a column of battalions.

The accompanying diagram will illustrate the disposition of the troops of my own command. This sketch does not pretend to accuracy in distances or angles.

The conformation of the ground enabled the enemy, after advancing near the lines, to obtain cover. Arrived at this point, one battalion continued to move toward the point A, occupied by the Second and Third Brigades of the Second Division. The other battalions moved by the flank until completely masked by the preceding one, when they moved by the flank again, thus forming a column of regiments. The few pieces of artillery still in position were directed upon this column, while the rebel cannon again opened with shell, firing over their own troops.

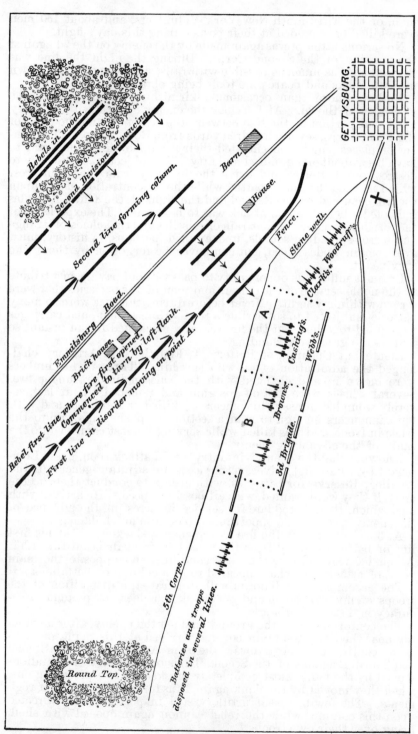

* Should be Arnold's.

The perfect order and steady but rapid advance of the enemy called forth praise from our troops, but gave their line an appearance of being fearfully irresistible.   My line was single, the only support (the Seventy-second Pennsylvania Volunteers) having been called away by General Webb before the action had fairly commenced.   There was a disposition in the men to reserve their fire for close quarters, but when I observed the movement the enemy was endeavoring to execute, I caused the Seventh Michigan and Twentieth Massachusetts Volunteers to open fire at about 200 yards.   The deadly aim of the former regiment was attested by the line of slain within its range. This had a great effect upon the result, for it caused the enemy to move rapidly at one point and consequently to crowd in front—being occasioned at the point where his column was forming, he did not recover from this disorder.   The remainder of our line reserved its fire until within 100 yards, some regiments waiting even until but 50 paces intervened between them and the enemy.

There was but a moment of doubtful contest in front of the position of this brigade.   The enemy halted to deliver his fire, wavered, and fled, while the line of the fallen perfectly marked the limit of his advance.   The troops were pouring into the ranks of the fleeing enemy that rapid and accurate fire, the delivery of which victorious lines always so much enjoy, when I saw that a portion of the line of General Webb on my right had given way, and many men were making to the rear as fast as possible, while the enemy was pouring over the rails that had been a slight cover for the troops.

Having gained this apparent advantage, the enemy seemed to turn again and re-engage my whole line.   Going to the left, I found two regiments that could be spared from some command there, and endeavored to move them by the right flank to the break, but, coming under a warm fire, they crowded to the slight cover of the rail fence, mixing with the troops already there.   Finding it impossible to draw them out and reform, and seeing no unengaged troops within reach, I was forced to order my own brigade back from the line, and move it by the flank under a heavy fire.   The enemy was rapidly gaining a foothold; organization was mostly lost; in the confusion commands were useless, while a disposition on the part of the men to fall back a pace or two each time to load, gave the line a retiring direction. With the officers of my staff and a few others, who seemed to comprehend what was required, the head of the line, still slowly moving by the flank, was crowded closer to the enemy and the men obliged to load in their places.   I did not see any man of my command who appeared disposed to run away, but the confusion first caused by the two regiments above spoken of so destroyed the formation in two ranks that in some places the line was several files deep.

In pressing the line as closely upon the enemy as possible, it took the form here represented:

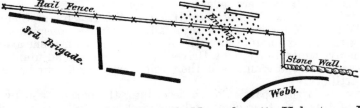

During this time, the Fifteenth Massachusetts Volunteers, First Minnesota, and Nineteenth Maine Volunteers, from the First Brigade of this division, had joined the line, and are entitled to a full share in the credit of the final repulse.

The line remained in this way for about ten minutes, rather giving way than advancing, when, by a simultaneous effort upon the part of all the officers I could instruct, aided by the general advance of many of the colors, the line closed with the enemy, and, after a few minutes of desperate, often hand-to-hand fighting, the crowd—for such had become that part of the enemy's column that had passed the fence—threw down their arms and were taken prisoners of war, while the remainder broke and fled in great disorder. The Second Brigade had again joined the right of my line, which now occupied the position originally held by that command.

Generals Garnett and Armistead were picked up near this point, together with many colonels and officers of other grades.

Twenty battle-flags were captured in a space of 100 yards square. Several colors were stolen or taken with violence by officers of high rank from brave soldiers who had rushed forward and honestly captured them from the enemy, and were probably turned in as taken by commands which were not within 100 yards of the point of attack. Death is too light a punishment for such a dastardly offense.

To the efforts of a few officers and the courage and good discipline of the men is due the great result of the final repulse of the enemy. Conspicuous acts of individual bravery were unusually frequent. Colors were captured with clubbed muskets, and many men of both our own and the enemy had their clothes blown off for a large space around their wounds by the close discharge.

Between 1,500 and 2,000 prisoners were captured at the point of attack, where the First, Second, and Third Brigades were equally present. Piles of dead and thousands of wounded upon both sides attested the desperation of assailants and defenders.

The services of many officers of my command would, under ordinary circumstances, claim particular notice and reward, but so great was the necessity for every possible exertion that all who saw their duty I believe did it, forgetting all question of danger.

I cannot omit speaking in the highest terms of the magnificent conduct of Lieutenant Haskell, of General Gibbon's staff, in bringing forward regiments and in nerving the troops to their work by word and fearless example. Lieutenant-Colonel Steele, of the Seventh Michigan Volunteers, behaved most gallantly, and was killed in the line of his regiment, urging men forward. Every regimental commander did his whole duty nobly. Three of the 5 were killed or have since died of their wounds, viz: Colonel Revere, of the Twentieth Massachusetts Volunteers; Lieutenant-Colonel Thoman, Fifty-ninth New York Volunteers, and Lieutenant-Colonel Steele, Seventh Michigan Volunteers. Lieutenant-Colonel Macy, Twentieth Massachusetts; Lieutenant-Colonel Wass and Major Rice, Nineteenth Massachusetts Volunteers, were severely wounded.

Captains [S. Newell] Smith and [George W.] Leach and Lieutenant [William E.] Barrows, of my staff, were most conspicuous in closing the ranks, maintaining the lines, and pressing them against the enemy, while Lieutenant Driver, acting assistant adjutant-general, twice ran the gauntlet of the terrific artillery fire in bringing fresh artillery.

I have been thus particular in describing the parts taken by the troops of this and other commands near by because I feel bound in justice to the men of my command, and those who assisted them on that day at that point, to claim for them what fortune gave them an opportunity to do and what their arms accomplished. While the attack was general and was repulsed along the whole line, still, the tremendous effort of the rebel chief was against the point which happened to be occupied by the Second and Third Brigades of the Second Division, Second Corps. It was fully repulsed in front of the Third Brigade, which then fell upon the partially successful enemy on the line of the Second Brigade, and, with the assistance before mentioned, drove him back, finishing the day there and completing the destruction of his splendid division and many of its supports. The attack was afterward renewed upon the left of the line, near Round Top, but without the vigor and desperation that characterized the previous effort.

In claiming for my brigade and a few other troops the turning point of the battle of July 3, I do not forget how liable inferior commanders are to regard only what takes place in their own front, or how extended a view it must require to judge of the relative importance of different points of the line of battle. The decision of the rebel commander was upon that point; the concentration of artillery fire was upon that point; the din of battle developed in a column of attack upon that point; the greatest effort and greatest carnage was at that point; and the victory was at that point.

No other inducement than the desire to do justice to troops who so nobly and at so dear a rate accomplished such a result, though their presence was primarily a matter of chance, would make me place myself in a position to defend an assertion generally so difficult to establish.

Very respectfully,

NORMAN J. HALL,
Colonel, Commanding Brigade.

Capt. A. H. EMBLER,
Actg. Asst. Adjt. Gen., Second Div., Second Corps.

NEW YORK, *August* 3, 1863.

COLONEL: I observed some time since in a printed official paper naming the flags captured at Gettysburg, Pa., on the 3d of July, that the Department was not in possession of information regarding who captured several of them. I think it my duty to furnish you the necessary information, as far as concerns my own command.

I attached labels to each one of the flags below named, but they were probably lost in transportation.

Battle-flag of Fourteenth Virginia Infantry, captured by Corpl. J. H. De Castro, Nineteenth Massachusetts Volunteers; Twenty-second North Carolina, by Private Michael McDonough, Forty-second New York Volunteers; Nineteenth Virginia, by Corpl. B. F. Falls, Nineteenth Massachusetts Volunteers; Eighteenth Virginia, by Second Lieut. C. E. Hunt, Fifty-ninth New York Volunteers; Forty-eighth Georgia, by Sergt. James Wiley, Fifty-ninth New York Volunteers; Fifty-seventh Virginia Infantry, by Private B. H. Jellison, Nineteenth Massachusetts Volunteers; one flag, designation unknown, captured by Private John Robinson, Company I, Nineteenth Massachusetts Volunteers; also one captured by Private William Dunning, Seventh Michigan Volunteers. These last two I have not the information to enable me to describe at present. For the others,

I have receipts from General Harrow, commanding division, and they are named as received in the printed paper I saw in Washington.

V ill you have the goodness to cause the six named to be marked and ⁀redited to the men and regiments by whom they were captured? The regiments are all of the Third Brigade, Second Division, Second Corps, which I have had the honor to command till a week or two ago.

Very respectfully,

NORMAN J. HALL,
Colonel 7th Michigan Vols., and 1st Lieut. 5th U. S. Artillery.

Col. E. D. TOWNSEND,
Assistant Adjutant-General, U. S. Army.

No. 110.

Report of Col. Arthur F. Devereux, Nineteenth Massachusetts Infantry.

TANEYTOWN, MD., *July* 7, 1863.

SIR: I have the honor to submit the following report of the part which my regiment took in the late engagement near Gettysburg:

On the evening of July 1, the corps was halted about 2 miles from the battle-ground.

At daybreak of the 2d, were marched to the front, this division forming in columns of regiments by brigade on the right of the road, with its front toward the right of the position held by our army. Remaining there perhaps an hour, it crossed the road, and, by a countermarch of regiments, assumed a front in an opposite direction, the Second Brigade on the right, the Third Brigade on the left, and the First Brigade in the rear as reserve, two regiments, each of the Second and Third Brigades, being thrown in advance of the column in position behind some fences. The division rested there during the day.

About 5 p. m., some time after the Third Corps had been engaged on our left, Colonel Mallon, commanding Forty-second New York, and myself were ordered by the brigade commander to follow a staff officer, whom he pointed out, but whose name and rank I do not know, which was done, my regiment leading. Just before this, our attacking columns of the Third Corps, which had at first advanced, had begun to give way, and when we reached the rear of their position, a distance of perhaps an eighth of a mile from where we started, were completely broken, and running to the rear in great confusion. I asked the officer leading us what was the object intended for us to accomplish and what position to take up. He answered, " In support of Humphreys' division." I pointed out to him how useless to attempt to form a support for a division in the open field with two small regiments, numbering but 290 men together, and when that division was so much broken and fleeing in such confusion. He gave me no satisfactory answer, and at that moment galloped off.

Left to ourselves, I suggested to Colonel Mallon that the two regiments be formed behind the crest of a short knoll some distance in our front, there to lie down, wait until our retreating line, which was right upon us then, had passed, deliver a volley by the rear and front ranks, to check the pursuing enemy, and then make good our retreat. We gained the position without delay, lay down until everything in front and on both flanks had passed us to the rear, then, giving the command to my regiment, I fired two volleys, as, I believe, also did Colonel Mallon. It became necessary then to retreat immediately to avoid capture, the enemy's line outflanking us on the right and left hundreds of yards to each side, and very near—so near, indeed, that both regiments captured several prisoners. The retreat of the two regiments commenced in good order, Colonel Mallon's regiment leading, my regiment marching in his rear.

In a short time we met the second line of our men pressing forward. Passing through them a distance of perhaps 25 yards, we halted, as did also the line we had just met. At this point the two regiments rested on a slope fronting the enemy, exposed to their artillery fire, which was very hot, unable to use our own fire on the columns of the enemy because of the line in front, in consequence of which the two regiments withdrew for shelter behind the crest.

By this time it was quite dark, and in about half an hour Captain Leach, of the brigade staff, brought orders for us to rejoin the brigade in the old position. We rested there all night, and in the morning the two regiments were put in support of a battery at that point, the other regiments in the brigade lying in front under the wall.

Everything remained quiet on our front until 1 p. m., when, at a signal of a gun fired to our left, a most terrific cannonade commenced on the batteries and the troops in the center of our line, a portion of which was held by our brigade. It was the most terrific cannonading of the war. I have been told that one hundred and ten pieces of the enemy were firing upon our center at once. The men lay quiet and steady, and I am sure none of my regiment left the position where I ordered them to lie down. The cannonade lasted two hours.

The battery behind which we lay was disabled in the first hour's cannonading. The captain of it asked me if my men would volunteer to assist in manning his battery. I told him yes, and sent immediately 6 men to carry ammunition, and at a further call shortly after, 20 more to assist in working the pieces.

I desire here to mention the gallant conduct of Second Lieut. Moses Shackley, who insisted on joining the volunteers, walking from piece to piece, encouraging and assisting the men, although I told him that it was not required of him, and advised him to lie down with the regiment for shelter.

Just about 3 o'clock the enemy's cannonade slackened, and columns of attack appeared emerging from the woods across the open field in our front. They advanced gallantly upon our position, which was held firmly excepting immediately upon the right of our brigade line, at which point the left of the next brigade of our line seemed to give way in some confusion. Just then Major-General Hancock appeared on the left of my regiment. I ran to him, and asked permission to advance it to the point needed. Receiving it, I marched my regiment with all speed, obliquing to the right through the battery, and reached the desired point directly behind Colonel Mallon's regiment, which, being on my right when we started, had reached there first.

There was considerable confusion here, from the men running to the rear from the first line, and the two mentioned regiments coming up on a short space closely following each other, joined also by the Twentieth Massachusetts, having repulsed the enemy from their immediate front, but who still strongly pressed the attack at this point where our lines had given way. For an instant it seemed to hang in the balance whether we should drive the enemy out of our works, which they had entered, or they succeed in carrying the position; but I firmly believe that the extraordinary exertions of a few officers, among whom were conspicuous the brigade commander and staff, Lieutenant Haskell, of the division staff, Colonel Mallon, and some officers of my own regiment whom I saw, the line was carried back to the rifle-pits, driving the enemy out.

Just at this moment the enemy, as if actuated by one instinct, threw down their arms in a body, burst into our lines by hundreds, delivering themselves up as prisoners, and the battle was won, very few of the enemy attempting to retreat across the field to their own lines.

We must have killed, wounded, and captured the entire attacking column, with comparatively few exceptions. I might add here that when the enemy first broke our lines, and our men rallied to retrieve the lost ground, the enemy's artillery again opened on our troops collecting at that point, and continued to fire after the position was retaken, seemingly intended for their own troops, who had delivered themselves up in such numbers.

During the obstinate fight at this place, the two lines being actually hand to hand, my regiment captured four regimental colors from the enemy—one by Corpl. Joseph H. De Castro, Company I; another by Private John Robinson, Company I; another by Corpl. Benjamin F. Falls, Company A, and another by Private Benjamin H. Jellison, Company C.

A fifth one was handed to me by a sergeant of my regiment, but on representations from General Webb that he took the colors and gave them to my sergeant for safe-keeping, it has been delivered over to him. Three of the four taken by my regiment were taken from the hands of the rebel color-bearers, the fourth picked up beyond the stone wall. Three of these (the Fourteenth, Nineteenth, and Fifty-seventh Virginia, and marked with the numbers of their regiments, respectively) have been turned over to the brigade commander. The fourth I am unable positively to account for, but have been informed was probably carried off the field by Major Rice when wounded, and by him taken home. That four were taken by my regiment, as above stated, I am sure, as I have minute statements in each case from company commanders whom I called on for a report.*

It would be difficult to distinguish further than I have the individual officers and men under my command. The field and line officers universally and the men under my command behaved as steadily and as gallantly as men could do. I have but one instance of failure to report, that of Corporal [E. Augustus] Nichols, Company C, who was brought back, going to the rear, during the infantry fight.

Respectfully,

A. F. DEVEREUX,
Colonel Nineteenth Massachusetts, Comdg. Regiment.

Lieut. WILLIAM R. DRIVER,
A. A. A. G., Third Brig., Second Div., Second Corps.

---

* Medals of honor awarded to Corporals De Castro and Falls and Privates Jellison and Robinson for the capture of these flags. See also p. 441.

No. 111.

Report of Capt. Henry L. Abbott, Twentieth Massachusetts Infantry.

NEAR SANDY HOOK, MD., *July* 16, 1863.

SIR. I have the honor to make the following report of the part taken by the Twentieth Regiment Massachusetts Volunteers in the battle of Gettysburg, on July 2 and 3:

In the first day's action (July 2), the regiment was in the second line all day, lying down, and, though not firing a shot, met with some losses from the shot and shell which came through the first line when the enemy advanced at the close of the day to the position held by the Second Division of the Second Corps. Col. Paul J. Revere was mortally wounded, and some 10 or 11 men were killed and wounded.

Two companies had been previously sent out as skirmishers, some distance in front of our lines, under Captain Patten. I wish to mention this officer particularly for the most distinguished gallantry with which he held his position after losing a third of his command (10 men), remaining on the field after he himself had been severely wounded, only retiring his command when our own advance had been driven back completely routed and the rebel line was close upon him. Second Lieutenant Cowgill was also wounded on this picket.

After the repulse of the enemy on this night (the 2d), the regiment was moved up into the front line, where, during the night, with a single shovel, they threw up a slight rifle-pit, a foot deep and a foot high.

On the next day the regiment retained the same position.

About 2 p. m. the enemy opened a terrific cannonade, lasting perhaps two hours. The regiment lost only 4 or 5 men by this fire, being sheltered more by the slight depression in the ground where the pit was dug than by the earth thrown up, which was too thin to stop anything more than a spent ball.

After the cessation of the enemy's artillery fire, their infantry advanced in large force. The men were kept lying on their bellies, without firing a shot, until orders to fire came from Colonel Hall, commanding the brigade, the enemy having got within 3 or 4 rods of us, when the regiment rose up and delivered two or three volleys, which broke the rebel regiment opposite us entirely to pieces, leaving only scattered groups. When the enemy's advance was first checked by our fire, they tried to return it, but with little effect, hitting only 4 or 5 men.

We were feeling all the enthusiasm of victory, the men shouting out, "Fredericksburg," imagining the victory as complete everywhere else as it was in front of the Third Brigade, when Colonel Macy drew my attention to a spot some rods to the right of us, near a clump of trees, where the enemy seemed to have broken in. The regiment immediately got orders to face to the right and to file to the right, with the intention of forming a line at right angles with the original one; in other words, changing front to the right. The noise was such, however, that it was impossible to make any order heard. An order having been given, though it could not be heard, was naturally interpreted to be an order to retire and form a new line not outflanked by the enemy. The regiment accordingly retired some 2 rods, but in the most perfect order. Perceiving, however, that an example could be seen, though words could not be heard, all the officers of the regiment rushed to the front, and without further formalities the regiment was hurried to the important spot. When they arrived there, there was a very thin line contending with the enemy, who was behind a rail fence, with the exception of a small number that climbed over, who were speedily dispatched. The enemy poured in a severe musketry fire, and at the clump of trees they burst also several shells, so that our loss was very heavy, more than half the enlisted men of the regiment being killed or disabled, while there remained but 3 out of 13 officers. Moreover, the contest round this important spot was very confused, every man fighting on his own hook, different regiments being mixed together, and half a dozen colors in a bunch, it being impossible to preserve a regimental line.

Notwithstanding these adverse circumstances, the men of this command kept so well together that after the contest near the trees, which lasted half an hour or so, was ended, I was enabled to collect, with the assistance of Lieutenant Summerhayes and Lieutenant Perkins, in an incredibly short period, nearly all the surviving men of the regiment, and returned them to their original place in the pits. At the suggestion of Lieutenant Haskell, on the division staff, I prepared to move back to the trees again, having 100 men collected together. This order was, however, countermanded by Colonel Devereux, commanding the left wing of the brigade, because of the second and last advance of the enemy on our extreme left, which happened only a very short time after the completion of our own success at the clump of trees. Without meaning to reflect on other regiments at all, I think it but fair to this command to state that I observed at the time that very few other regiments had even settled on a rendezvous for their scattered members.

It seems to me that great praise is due the enlisted men of this regiment for the speed with which they reorganized, for the discipline and *esprit de corps* which made them stick together in such a scene of confusion, where organization had been so completely broken up for the time. All the officers of the regiment behaved with the greatest gallantry, but I am enabled to select two, as their position or occupation made them more conspicuous than the rest. One of these (Captain Patten) I have already mentioned. The other is First Lieut. Henry Ropes, who was shot dead. Never before has this regiment, in the death of any officer, received one-half so heavy a blow. His conduct in this action, as in all previous ones, was perfectly brave, but not with the bravery of excitement that nerves common men. He was in battle absolutely cool and collected, apparently unconscious of the existence of such a feeling as personal danger, the slight impetuosity and excitability natural to him at ordinary times being sobered down into the utmost self-possession, giving him an eye that noticed every circumstance, no matter how thick the shot and shell; a judgment that suggested in every case the proper measures, and a decision that made the application instantaneous. It is impossible for me to conceive of a man more perfectly master of himself; more completely noting and remembering every circumstance in times when the ordinary brave man sees nothing but a tumult and remembers after it is over nothing but a whirl of events which he is unable to separate. Lieutenant Ropes' behavior in this battle was more conspicuous for coolness and absolute disregard of personal danger than I have ever witnessed in any other man. He entered the service and remained in it until his death from the purest patriotism; not a single ambitious or selfish motive mingled with it. He would have made the noblest sacrifice where he knew that no man would even hear it as readily as if the eyes of the whole world were fixed upon him. Such perfect purity of sentiment deserves this distinguished mention, which Lieutenant Ropes himself would have been the last to expect.

I find it impossible to discriminate among the enlisted men, as all behaved so well (there being but 4 missing), and particularly as 7 company commanders, the only proper persons to report the behavior of their men, are absent, killed or wounded.

I have the honor to be,

H. L. ABBOTT,
Captain, Comdg. Twentieth Massachusetts Volunteers.

Lieutenant DRIVER,
Acting Assistant Adjutant-General.

No. 112.

Reports of Maj. Sylvanus W. Curtis, Seventh Michigan Infantry.

CAMP IN PLEASANT VALLEY, MD., *July* 16, 1863.

SIR : This regiment left its temporary encampment, about 2 miles south of Gettysburg, on the morning of July 2, pursuant to orders, the regiments of the brigade in the following order: The Forty-second New York, Twentieth and Nineteenth Massachusetts, Seventh Michigan, and Fifty-ninth New York, respectively. Moving across an open field, I was ordered to form line on the left of the Fifty-ninth New York to support a battery, which took a position on our right and left flank, and a few paces in front of our line, our line of battle being partially covered in front by a rail fence. This was converted into a sort of barricade by bringing rails from the adjoining fences. Our front was an open field of considerable extent; the enemy held the woods beyond, about 160 rods distant. Soon after we took our position, some skirmishing took place along our front and on the right.

About 4 p. m. the enemy opened fire from their artillery on the extreme left. This continued about one hour, doing no damage. Soon after, the enemy were seen forming their infantry, preparatory to an advance on our lines. The batteries on our right and left opened their fire, and did considerable execution in their ranks as they advanced. Our skirmishers were soon driven in. As soon as they (the enemy) came within range, a rapid and destructive fire opened on them along our line. The enemy continued to advance boldly until within 30 or 40 yards of our line, where, partially protected by rocks and shrubs, they continued to pour in a galling fire. The artillerymen belonging to the batteries being nearly all killed or wounded, the guns were silenced.

Advancing boldly to the battery on our left, the enemy took possession, planting a battle-flag upon one of them. Their triumph, however, was short. A deadly volley was poured upon them at not more than 30 yards distance. Their color-bearer fell, pierced by a dozen bullets. Many others were killed or wounded, and they were forced to fall back to their cover, and the battery was saved. During the hottest of the firing many of the enemy were seen to throw down their guns, and, creeping along the ground to our lines, surrendered as prisoners. The enemy, failing most completely in their attempt to carry our line by assault, retreated in considerable disorder.

The firing had nearly or quite ceased when two regiments (names unknown) filed past our left flank, and formed in front and to the left of our line. Several officers and men of the regiment saw them pick up two battle-flags and one regimental color from the ground directly in front of our line, which the enemy had left behind in their hasty retreat.

The conduct of both officers and men was in the highest degree commendable, so far as came under my observation. Lieutenant-Colonel Steele (since killed) particularly distinguished himself for coolness while directing the fire of the men to various points along the line.

The engagement lasted from 4 o'clock until dusk, when the firing ceased along the front. Farther to the right it continued much later. A strong picket line was posted in front, a proportionate number being detailed from this regiment for this purpose. The wounded were cared for as far as possible. The men rested on their arms during the night.

The next morning about daylight (July 3), skirmishing commenced along the front. The enemy's artillery also threw shells along the line occasionally, doing little or no injury, however. At 10 o'clock all was quiet, comparatively, along our front.

At 1 p. m. the enemy, having massed their artillery at the edge of the woods, suddenly opened a heavy fire along our line, directed principally at our batteries in position on our right and left; also those on the hill in our rear. We were obliged to lie as close as possible behind our slight breastwork, which afforded but little protection. The cannonade lasted about two hours. Our escape with so slight loss seems little short of miraculous.

The smoke from the enemy's guns had scarcely cleared away when their columns of infantry were seen advancing to the charge. Our line reserved its fire until they had advanced to within short range, when it was opened with deadly effect. The enemy's first line advanced to within 20 rods, when they commenced moving by the left flank, which obliged us to direct our fire to the right oblique, in order to keep them within range as long as possible. Our right flank having been completely turned by the giving way of a portion of the Second Brigade, we were ordered to fall back a short distance, which movement was effected in very good order under the circumstances. Again rallying to the assistance of other regiments which now came up, the enemy were finally driven back, and the regiment again occupied its former position.

Our loss during the two days' engagements was very heavy, the proportion of the killed to the wounded being unusually large. I herewith forward a complete list of killed and wounded, together with nature of wounds so far as known.*

Lieutenant-Colonel Steele fell near the close of the engagement, and while gallantly rallying his command to repel the (for a time) successful advance of the enemy.

I have the honor to be, very respectfully, your obedient servant,

S. W. CURTIS,
Major, Commanding.

Lieut. WILLIAM R. DRIVER, *Actg. Asst. Adjt. Gen.*

----

*Embodied in revised statement, p. 176.

AUGUST 6, 1863.

GENERAL: I have the honor to report to you that, on the evening of July 1, this regiment, under the command of Lieutenant-Colonel Steele, reached a point some 4 miles south of Gettysburg, Pa., and formed a line a short distance to the left of the road, and extending into the woods on the southern slope of a high conical hill.

Immediately after arriving in position, pickets were thrown out on the left flank, and a breastwork made of some rails lying near our line. The men then prepared and ate their suppers and lay on their arms.

At 5 o'clock next day it marched on the Gettysburg road to a point on Cemetery Hill, near the center of our line of battle. Here this regiment, with the Fifty-ninth New York, was ordered to the front to support a battery. We were posted about 150 yards to the left of the summit of the hill, about 2 acres of which were covered with a dense growth of small oaks. Our left rested on the battery. Our right was partially concealed by a cluster of small trees and shrubs. We had then present 14 officers and 151 muskets.

Immediately on getting into position, barricades were made of rails, and partially screened from observation by bushes. Skirmishing commenced in front of us immediately after getting into position, and continued until 4.15 p. m., when the enemy's artillery opened upon us, and a general artillery duel soon commenced, and continued without intermission until 5 p. m., when the fire slackened, and their infantry columns were seen advancing on our line. They succeeded in passing through between the guns of the battery on our left, driving the gunners from their posts. The line on our left gave way and our flank was almost turned, but the enemy's line was fast melting away under the scathing fire of our men, who remained unflinchingly at their posts, and they soon retired in utter confusion, leaving a large number of killed and wounded. They also left in front of us 3 stand of colors, which were picked up by other regiments who followed them up.

A large number of prisoners fell into our hands and were immediately sent to the rear; among them one colonel, slightly wounded in one of his fingers, and several minor officers.

This ended the fight for the day, and the men lay down supperless about 10 o'clock, to obtain what rest they could.

Our loss was 9 killed and 10 wounded.

At daylight on the 3d, the enemy again opened a furious cannonade, but did us no harm, their fire being principally directed to the artillery on either side of us. This continued until 9 o'clock, when all became quiet, except a desultory fire from pickets and sharpshooters on both sides.

About 10.30 all firing ceased until 1 p. m, when the enemy fired a signal gun from the right of their line, which was instantly followed by the roar of all their artillery, which had been massed in the edge of the woods opposite our line in such a manner as to bring this regiment nearly in the center of their fire. Owing to our peculiar situation in regard to their fire, not as much damage was done us as would naturally be expected from such a storm of missiles. Nearly all the shot and shell struck in front and ricochetted over us, or passed over us and burst in our rear.

This continued until 4 p. m., when their infantry columns were seen advancing. Orders were given the men to reserve their fire until the enemy were within short range. They soon came within a very short distance, and our fire was opened upon them with terrible effect, mowing them down by scores. Still they came on till within a few yards of us, when the order was given to fix bayonets. The men expressed a determination to hold their works at all hazards. Many of the enemy at this time crawled on their hands and feet under the sheet of fire, and, coming up to our lines, surrendered themselves prisoners. The enemy, soon finding our fire too hot for them, moved by the left flank, and joined in the assault upon the crest of the hill, driving our line from its position.

At this time Colonel Steele received an order to form the regiment nearly at right angles to its then position, with the intention of attacking the enemy's right flank, which had become exposed. Owing to the great noise, the order was not understood by any excepting those nearest Colonel Steele. The rest of the officers seeing the men, as they supposed, retreating, made all efforts to rally them. A part of them came back; the remainder kept on with Colonel Steele, who advanced with them to the crest of the hill, when he fell, instantly killed by a bullet through his brain. The greater part of the regiment remained in their works and did great execution by a well-directed fire upon the flanks of the enemy. The field was soon won and the enemy fleeing in great disorder. A great number of prisoners were taken, and a large amount of small-arms, ammunition, &c., was left upon the field.

The men by this time had become very much exhausted from previous long marches, constant watchfulness, and having been destitute of food nearly two days; yet all were cheerful, and worked during the night to improve their breastworks in anticipation of an attack next morning. Though but one spade could be obtained, the rails were nearly covered with earth by daylight.

Most of the men worked till late in the night in bringing in and caring for the wounded.

Our loss was 12 killed and 34 wounded, making the loss in both actions 21 killed and 44 wounded. The disproportionate number of killed arose from the fact that the men were partially protected by the breastwork of rails, and the greater part of them were consequently hit in the head and upper part of the body.

The 4th was spent in burying the dead, gathering up the arms left on the field, and taking care of the wounded.

Too much cannot be said in praise of the conduct of both officers and men. Where all did their duty to the fullest extent it would seem invidious to particularize. One instance deserves mention, not only for the bravery of the soldier, but for the dastardly conduct of the officer concerned. Private William Deming, of Company F, during the assault on the crest of the hill, had shot a rebel color-bearer and taken the color from him. While loading his piece, with the flag by his side, a colonel rode up to him, and, menacing him with his saber, forced the color from him; even threatening to cut him down if he did not give it up. I regret to say that it was impossible to identify the officer alluded to. The act was witnessed by several who stood near.

I am, very respectfully, your obedient servant,

S. W. CURTIS,
Major, Commanding Regiment.

Brig. Gen. LORENZO THOMAS,
Adjutant-General, U. S. Army.

No. 113.

Report of Col. James E. Mallon, Forty-second New York Infantry.

CAMP NEAR SANDY HOOK, MD.,
July 16, 1863.

SIR: I have the honor to report the following as the part taken by this regiment during the actions of July 2 and 3, near Gettysburg, Pa.:

On the morning of the 2d instant, this regiment was placed, by order of Colonel Hall, commanding brigade, in position to the left of the clump of trees near which were posted the batteries of the corps.

During the morning I was called upon to furnish two companies for skirmish duty. Company F, Capt. J. W. Tobin, and Company D, Second Lieut. John Maguire, were detailed for this purpose. This small body, numbering in all but 36 enlisted men, did their duty faithfully.

About 5 or 6 p. m. this regiment, with the Nineteenth Massachusetts, was ordered to go forward to the left to the assistance of General Humphreys. The staff officer who conducted us led the commands, they marching by the right flank until they were well brought under musketry fire. At this time all the troops to the front were precipitately retiring in great disorder. To avoid the enfilading effect of the fire, which was now rapidly thinning the ranks; to infuse confidence in the hearts of those who among those retreating might have some manhood left; to present a disciplined, unwavering front toward the rapidly approaching and confident enemy, the two regiments formed line.

From the moment of the commencement of this movement, I saw nothing of the staff officer who conducted us. When the rebels had arrived within 50 yards of the line, Colonel Devereux and myself consulted as to the best course to be pursued. Already we were receiving fire from both flanks. We concluded that the best thing to be done was to retire. After having poured into the rebels several volleys, the regiments, the Nineteenth Massachusetts covering, moved to the rear. When we had retired about 200 yards, we were ordered by Captain Leach, of the brigade staff, to rejoin the brigade. During this engagement the regiment lost 3 killed and 12 wounded.

On the afternoon of the 3d instant, about 1 o'clock, the enemy opened with a destructive artillery fire, which will ever be remembered by those subjected to its fury. After this fire, which lasted about four hours, had considerably slackened, the infantry of the enemy debouched from the woods to our front for the grand attack of the battle. This regiment was posted about 100 yards in rear of the front line. When those of the enemy who approached our brigade front had been successfully disposed of, and when those who had with great energy and persistence penetrated that portion of our line to our right, near the corps batteries, I caused the regiment to be formed in line facing the decisive point.

The line was but fairly established, and but just started in the direction of the contested point, when Colonel Hall, with words of encouragement, cheered us forward. With the impetus conveyed by these words, the regiment vigorously advanced, and in that charge which rescued our batteries from the hands of our foe, which saved our army from disaster and defeat, which gave to us glorious, triumphant success, this regiment was foremost and its flag in the advance.

The color-bearer, Sergt. Michael Cuddy, who established his **great** and superior courage in the first Fredericksburg battle, on this occasion displayed the most heroic bravery. When he fell, mortally wounded, he rose by a convulsive effort, and triumphantly waved in the face of the rebels, not 10 yards distant, that flag he loved so dearly, of which he was so proud, and for which his valuable life, without a murmur, was freely given up.

The next day and the day after were spent in burying the dead. The detail from this regiment buried 84 rebels.

The officers and men of this regiment did their duty fearlessly during the three days it was exposed to fire at Gettysburg. I have heard of no instance of misbehavior, and of none of special excellence excepting in the case of Sergeant Cuddy, the color-bearer, to whom I have already referred. All did well, and all deserve credit.

The regiment lost 15 killed, 55 wounded, and 4 missing; total, 74. I append a correct list of casualties.*

Very respectfully, your obedient servant,

J. E. MALLON,
Colonel Forty-second New York Volunteers.

Lieut. WILLIAM R. DRIVER,
A. A. A. G., Third Brig., Second Div., Second Corps.

No. 114.

Report of Capt. William McFadden, Fifty-ninth New York Infantry.

IN THE FIELD, MD., NEAR HARPER'S FERRY, W. VA.,
July 16, 1863.

SIR: In compliance with circular of this date, I have the honor to submit the following report, viz:

On July 2, the battalion was ordered to move at 5 a. m. on the road leading to Gettysburg, Pa. When we arrived within 1 mile in the rear of said town, we were halted by the brigade commander. We were then ordered to take our position behind a fence.

About 3 p. m. the enemy opened on us, throwing shot and shell, and about an hour later advanced his infantry. As soon as they came within range, we opened fire. Their numbers were much greater than ours. They fled in disorder, we killing, wounding, and taking prisoners to exceed double the number of our men engaged. After carrying off our wounded and bringing in a large number of arms, we lay down to rest on the battle-field.

Our loss was 2 sergeants killed, Lieut. Col. Max A. Thoman and Lieutenant Schneider, and 11 privates wounded.

July 3, in the morning, the enemy opened fire with shell, but soon ceased. The line continued quiet until 1 p. m., when he opened on us with a terrible fire of shot and shell, continuing for nearly two hours; then advanced his infantry (their numbers, as the day before, greatly exceeding ours) within 20 yards of our line. He then broke in disorder, leaving us victors of our position. Our loss, 4 killed; 1 officer and 13 enlisted men wounded. The enemy's loss was very heavy in killed and wounded, and the capture of his men large.

----

* Embodied in revised statement, p. 176.

The behavior of both men and officers during the two battles was excellent, ably sustaining the past reputation of the Third Brigade.*

Respectfully, your obedient servant,

WILLIAM McFADDEN,
Captain, Comdg. Fifty-ninth Regiment New York Vols.

Capt. HORACE P. RUGG,
Commanding Fifty-ninth New York Volunteers.

No. 115.

Reports of Brig. Gen. Alexander Hays, U. S. Army, commanding Third Division.

HEADQUARTERS THIRD DIVISION, SECOND CORPS,
July 8, 1863.

SIR: I have the honor to report through you the part taken by this division in the battle near Gettysburg, Pa.

On July 2, the division, moving on the Taneytown road, arrived within about a mile of the town, where it was assigned a position on a ridge nearly parallel with the road, facing westward. A stone wall just below the crest of the hill gave much strength to the position, and an open space of half a mile in our front afforded the artillery posted on the right and left flanks a fair field for effective service. A strong line of skirmishers was thrown forward to our front, and during the day contended successfully with the enemy. Twice, at least, sorties were made from our position by the Twelfth New Jersey Volunteers, First Delaware, and Fourteenth Connecticut Regiments against a barn and house one-fourth of a mile in advance of our position, returning in each case successfully with prisoners.

Col. G. L. Willard, One hundred and twenty-fifth New York Volunteers, commanding the Third Brigade, was early in the day withdrawn from the division by the major-general commanding, and took a prominent part in the engagement on our left.

The history of this brigade's operations is written in blood. Colonel Willard was killed, and next day, after the brigade had rejoined the division, his successor, Col. Eliakim Sherrill, One hundred and twenty-sixth New York Volunteers, also fell. Col. Clinton Dougall MacDougall, One hundred and eleventh New York Volunteers, and Maj. Hugo Hildebrandt, Thirty-ninth New York Volunteers, were each severely wounded, leaving the brigade in command of a lieutenant-colonel. The loss of this brigade amounts to one-half the casualties in the division. The acts of traitors at Harper's Ferry had not tainted their patriotism.

The operations of the First Brigade, commanded by Col. S. S. Carroll, are fully set forth in his own accompanying report. Too much credit cannot be given him and his command for the gallant manner in which they went to the relief of the troops on our right. The darkness of night was no obstacle, and I have no doubt their timely arrival and merits will be acknowledged by the general commanding in that part of the field.

The Second Brigade, Col. Thomas A. Smyth, First Delaware Vol-

---

* A medal of honor awarded to Sergt. James Wiley for the capture of the flag of the Forty-eighth Georgia Infantry.

unteers, remained continuously in protection of our front along the stone wall and in support of our line of skirmishers.

Throughout the 2d, the enemy kept up a desultory fire from their artillery, posted on the skirts of the distant timber, frequently shifting their batteries and opening suddenly on our line. In no case were they enabled long to retain position, but were relieved or driven off by the effective fire of our artillerists. The ensuing night passed in comparative quietness, our men resting on their arms.

The daylight of the 3d was a signal for renewed hostilities, and during the forenoon was a repetition of the practice of the previous day, excepting that their skirmishers appeared more pertinacious in their assault.

About 11 a. m. an entire lull occurred, which was continued until nearly 2 p. m. Anticipating the movement of the enemy, I caused the house and barn in our front, which interrupted the fire of our artillery, to be burned. At the hour last named, they opened upon our front the most terrific and uninterrupted fire from artillery. I cannot believe there were less than eighty pieces bearing on us within good range. It was continued uninterruptedly until 4.30 o'clock, when a heavy column of the enemy moved forward in three lines, preceded by a strong line of skirmishers, debouched from the wood opposite our line. Their march was as steady as if impelled by machinery, unbroken by our artillery, which played upon them a storm of missiles. When within 100 yards of our line of infantry, the fire of our men could no longer be restrained. Four lines rose from behind our stone wall, and before the smoke of our first volley had cleared away, the enemy, in dismay and consternation, were seeking safety in flight. Every attempt by their officers to rally them was vain. In less time than I can recount it, they were throwing away their arms and appealing most piteously for mercy. The angel of death alone can produce such a field as was presented.

The division captured and turned into corps headquarters fifteen battle-flags or banners. A number of other flags were captured, but had been surreptitiously disposed of, in the subsequent excitement of battle, before they could be collected.

I transmit the report of Lieut. W. E. Potter,* showing a collection by him of 2,500 stand of arms, besides an estimate of 1,000 left upon the ground for want of time to collect them. From my own personal examination of the field, I am satisfied the number estimated is not too great. Of the prisoners which fell into our hands, I regret that no accurate account could be kept but by estimate, which cannot be less than 1,500.

Colonel Smyth, commanding Second Brigade, was severely wounded in the head and face by a shell, which, however, did not prevent his return to duty next day.

I commend to the notice of the general commanding and the War Department the gallant conduct of my commanders of brigades and regiments, trusting that they, in return, will not be forgetful of meritorious subordinates. When all behaved unexceptionably it is difficult to discriminate. The coolness and determination evinced by our officers and men reflect back credit on their former commanders.

I cannot omit the high recommendation of credit which is due Dr. Isaac Scott, medical director of the division, and all his assistants. No case of neglect or evasion of their duties has come to my notice.

---

*Omitted.

Lieutenant [John S.] Sullivan, of the ambulance corps, deserves the highest credit for his courage and the fearless manner he discharged his duties, continually, under the fire of the enemy's skirmishers, bringing off the wounded and assisting in keeping up the stragglers.

Lieut. W. E. Potter, ordnance officer, was indefatigable in the discharge of his duties.

Capt. George P. Corts, assistant adjutant-general, and my aide, Lieut. David Shields, Sixty-third Pennsylvania Volunteers, were constantly by my side, exhibiting, as always heretofore, self-possession and courage of the highest order. Captain Corts lost 2 horses, killed, and Lieutenant Shields 1.

Division quartermaster, Captain [Marshall I.] Ludington, and commissary officer, Captain [Columbus J.] Queen, discharged their duties to my entire satisfaction, and deserve the notice of their respective departments.

Second Lieut. E. J. Hueston, One hundred and eleventh New York Volunteers, attracted my attention by his exemplary conduct in charge of posting and encouraging our pickets. As a present recognition, I have appointed him an acting aide on my staff.

By accompanying report, the entire loss of the division in the two days' action will be seen to be 1,285 men killed, wounded, and missing.

I am, very respectfully, your obedient servant,

ALEX. HAYS,
Brigadier-General of Volunteers, Commanding Division.

Lieut. Col. C. H. MORGAN,
Chief of Staff.

HDQRS. THIRD DIVISION, SECOND ARMY CORPS,
August 15, 1863.

SIR: In compliance with orders, I have the honor to submit a supplement to my report of the part taken by this division in the operations prior to and following the battle of Gettysburg, Pa.

On June 28, broke camp near Barnesville, Md., and marched to the vicinity of Frederick City, Md.

On the 29th, marched at 1 p. m. through Liberty, Johnsville, and Union Bridge, to Uniontown, Md.; distance, over 30 miles. Encamped at 3 a. m. June 30. Same day changed camp to north side of Uniontown.

On July 1, marched through Taneytown to within about 3 miles of Gettysburg, Pa.

On July 2, moved to Gettysburg, and took position in line of battle. (For operations of July 2, 3, and 4, I respectfully refer you to a copy of my official report for those days, herewith inclosed.)

On July 5, moved from vicinity of Gettysburg, Pa., to Two Taverns, remaining in camp at latter place on the 6th.

On July 7, 8, 9, and 10, marched to near Frederick City, Md.

On July 11, marched to Jones' Cross-Roads, and went into line of battle. Toward evening, received orders from general commanding corps directing the sending of the First Brigade, Col. S. S. Carroll commanding, on a reconnaissance toward Funkstown, Md. This brigade encountered the enemy's pickets about 3 miles from Jones' Cross-Roads. Some skirmishing ensued, without loss on our side, save the slight wounding of 1 man. The enemy retired to the cover of his earthworks.

During the night, the remainder of the division, Second and Third Brigades, was ordered forward to the support of the First. Formed line of battle, and on the following day (12th) changed position twice. During the night threw up earthworks, line connecting on the right with the Fifth Corps, and on the left with the Second Division of the Second Corps.

On July 13, moved forward half a mile. Again formed line of battle, supported on the flanks by same troops as the previous day. Employed during the afternoon and evening intrenching our line. Some picket firing, without any loss to my command.

On July 14, advanced toward Williamsport, Md.

On July 15, marched from Williamsport, via Sharpsburg, Md., to Sandy Hook, Md.

July 16 and 17, encamped near Sandy Hook, Md.

On July 18, crossed the Potomac and Shenandoah Rivers; marched to near Hillsborough, Va., and encamped.

On July 19, marched to Woodgrove, Va.

On July 20, marched to Bloomfield, Va., and encamped until 22d, when the march was resumed to Ashby's Gap, Va.

On July 23, marched to Markham Station, on the Manassas Gap Railroad. Same evening, with the corps, moved to the support of the Third Corps, which was engaged with the enemy on Wapping Heights. Took position behind Third Corps.

On July 24, returned to Markham Station.

On July 25, marched to White Plains, Va.

On July 26, resumed the march, arriving near Warrenton Junction, Va., same day, where we remained encamped July 27, 28, and 29.

Respectfully submitted.

ALEX. HAYS,
Brigadier-General of Volunteers, Comdg. Division.

Capt. E. P. Brownson,
    Aide-de-Camp, and Actg. Asst. Adjt. Gen.

No. 116.

Report of Col. Samuel S. Carroll, Eighth Ohio Infantry, commanding First Brigade.

HDQRS. FIRST BRIG., THIRD DIV., SECOND CORPS,
       Two Taverns, Pa., July 5, 1863.

SIR: I have the honor to submit the following report of the part taken by the brigade which I have the honor to command in the battle of Gettysburg:

On the 2d instant, by command of Brigadier-General Hays, commanding division, the brigade was formed in line of regiments, right in front, between Woodruff's battery on the left and the Taneytown road on the right, at about 8 a. m.

An hour afterward an order was received from the same source to send four companies to the front as a support to the skirmishers already there, who seemed to be hard pressed, and four companies from the Fourth Ohio Volunteers were sent out. They kept up a brisk interchange of shots with the enemy's skirmishers. At 12 m. those four companies were relieved by two others from the same regiment.

About 1 p. m. the enemy opened upon our position with shell, and fired a dozen or two rounds. Immediately afterward their skirmishers commenced to advance and ours to retire. At this juncture, an order was received from the brigadier-general commanding division to send my leading regiment to their support, and I immediately took the Eighth Ohio out some 200 yards to the front, directing Lieutenant-Colonel Sawyer, commanding, to advance two companies deployed as skirmishers and relieve those of the Fourth Ohio Volunteers, and to maintain his position at all hazards, as he would be supported by the rest of the brigade.

About 6 p. m. the enemy opened a severe artillery fire upon the Second and Third Brigades, of this division, on the left of Woodruff's battery, advancing their infantry at the same time in their front, when orders were received from the brigadier-general commanding to move three regiments (Fourteenth Indiana, Fourth Ohio, and Seventh West Virginia) by the left flank, and take position on the left of the Second Brigade, which was executed under a heavy discharge of shot, shell, and musketry. This position was retained but a few minutes when orders were received from the same source to return with two regiments to the old position, which was done, leaving the Fourth Ohio on the left of the Second Brigade.

About dark, I received orders through Major Norvell, adjutant-general of the division, to move immediately to the assistance of part of the Eleventh Corps supporting batteries on Cemetery Hill, as they were being driven back, and the enemy were charging those batteries, and that I would be conducted by an aide of General Howard's. Moved immediately with three regiments, the Fourteenth Indiana leading. We found the enemy up to and some of them in among the front guns of the batteries on the road. Owing to the artillery fire from our own guns, it was impossible to advance by a longer front than that of a regiment, and it being perfectly dark, and with no guide, I had to find the enemy's line entirely by their fire. For the first few minutes they had a cross-fire upon us from a stone wall on the right of the road, but, by changing the front of the Seventh West Virginia, they were soon driven from there. The firing continued until about 10.20, when they fell back out of range, and skirmishers were advanced in our front. General Ames' division then made connection with me on our right and left.

This position we maintained until the 5th. We were exposed to a great deal of cross-firing during the heavy cannonading of the 3d, and kept up occasional skirmishing with the enemy up to the evening of that date, besides being annoyed by sharpshooters from the town, who had a flank fire upon us. The Eighth Ohio retained their position in front of the extreme right of the corps until after the severe fighting of the 3d, when they were relieved, after being in front over twenty-four hours, and receiving the first of the attack of the 3d, and maintaining their position until the line of the enemy was up with them, when they changed front, and opened fire on their flank, charging them and inflicting great damage.

Too much credit cannot be given to both the officers and men of that regiment, as well as their gallant leader, Lieut. Col. Franklin Sawyer, and Captain Kenny, acting major. I commend in the same terms the officers and men of the other three regiments, who, throughout the whole time, acted with soldierlike coolness and courage, as they always do. I would mention by name Col. J. Coons, Lieutenant-Colonel Cavins, and Major Houghton, Fourteenth Indiana; Lieutenant-Colonel Carpenter, commanding, and Major Stewart, Fourth Ohio, and Lieutenant-Colonel Lockwood, Seventh West Virginia Volunteers, the only field officers present, for gallant and meritorious conduct on the field.

My thanks are due to my staff, Lieut. J. G. Reid, Eighth Ohio Volunteers, acting assistant adjutant-general; Capt. J. E. Gregg, acting assistant inspector-general; Capt. S. Fiske, Fourteenth Connecticut, aide-de-camp; Lieut. J. H. Carr, Fourth Ohio Volunteers, aide-de-camp, and Lieutenant Van Dyke, Fourteenth Indiana, for their valuable assistance in a trying emergency.

Captain Willard, Fourteenth Indiana Volunteers, with his pioneer corps, worked most untiringly, caring for the wounded, burying the dead, and collecting arms and accouterments from the field, and were under fire while the brigade was. Captain Craig, Eighth Ohio, commanding provost guard, was busied in assisting the pioneer corps, taking charge of and turning over prisoners.

My adjutant, Lieutenant Reid, had his horse shot on the night of the 3d.

The Eighth Ohio took 3 stand of colors and the Fourteenth Indiana 1.

The brigade captured 252 prisoners, among them several field and general officers; also cared for 113 wounded, most of them rebels, and buried 37 rebel dead. The pioneer corps gathered from the field 349 stand of arms and accouterments. All our wounded were moved from the field to the hospital and our own dead buried.

I append herewith a summary of casualties in this brigade,* and inclose reports of commanders of regiments and detachments.

I have the honor to be, very respectfully, your obedient servant,

S. S. CARROLL,
Colonel, Commanding Brigade.

Maj. J. M. NORVELL,
 Assistant Adjutant-General.

No. 117.

Report of Col. John Coons, Fourteenth Indiana Infantry.

NEAR GETTYSBURG, PA., *July* 5, 1863.

SIR: I have the honor to submit the following report of the part taken by this regiment in the action of July 2 and 3:

The regiment was moved forward with our brigade on July 2, to support Woodruff's battery, which was in position near the center of our line of battle. A lively skirmish was kept up all the morning in our front by the skirmishers detailed from the other regiments of our brigade.

At 4.30 p. m. the enemy opened upon our position with artillery; their fire was heavy and continuous.

At 6 o'clock I was ordered to support the Eighth Ohio, which had been detailed as skirmishers. A report then came that General Howard's position, on the right center, was attacked in force by the enemy.

---

* Embodied in revised statement, p. 176.

About dark, under orders from Colonel Carroll, I moved to the right with the brigade, to support the batteries on the right of the cemetery. Arrived at Ricketts' battery and the others, we found their support, belonging to the Eleventh Corps, gone, and one of the guns in possession of the enemy, their advance having reached the crest of the hill. I immediately formed my regiment into line, and advanced upon them with fixed bayonets, driving them from the gun they had taken down the hill over a stone fence 100 yards in front of the battery. At this point we gave them two or three volleys, when they fell back. I formed my line along the stone fence, with the Seventh West Virginia on my left and the Fourth Ohio on my right. My regiment captured 1 stand of colors, 1 lieutenant-colonel, 1 major, 2 lieutenants, and 14 privates.

On the 3d, my line of skirmishers was engaged all day with those of the enemy, with small loss, and the regiment was under a severe cross-fire of artillery for a long time.

My officers and men behaved with their usual gallantry.

Recapitulation of casualties.

Officers and men.	Killed.	Wounded.	Total.
Officers		3	3
Enlisted men	6	22	28
Total	6	25	31

Respectfully submitted.

JOHN COONS,
Colonel, Commanding.

Lieut. J. G. REID,
  Acting Assistant Adjutant-General.

No. 118.

Report of Capt. Nathan Willard, Fourteenth Indiana Infantry, commanding Pioneer Corps.

CAMP NEAR GETTYSBURG, PA.,
July 5, 1863.

SIR: I have the honor to make the following report of the part taken by the pioneers under my command in the recent engagements near Gettysburg, Pa.:

On the 2d instant, after leveling the fences and clearing the field of obstructions, in accordance with the order of Colonel Carroll, commanding brigade, I formed my command immediately in the rear of the brigade, and maintained that position during the engagements.

My command buried 4 officers and 38 enlisted men of our brigade; also 37 rebels, including 2 officers. They assisted 113 of the wounded from the field, many of whom were of the rebel army. We also collected 349 stand of arms immediately in front of the brigade, which were captured by it.

My command consisted of 2 lieutenants and 50 enlisted men, all of whom, with an exception or two, behaved with great coolness, and performed their several duties to my entire satisfaction.

My loss consisted of 2 slightly wounded.

All of which is most respectfully submitted.

N. WILLARD,
Capt., and Chief of Pioneers, 1st Brig., 3d Div., 2d A. C.

Lieut. J. G. REID, *Acting Assistant Adjutant-General.*

No. 119.

Report of Lieut. Col. Leonard W. Carpenter Fourth Ohio Infantry.

CAMP NEAR TWO TAVERNS, PA.,
July 6, 1863.

SIR: I have the honor to submit the following report of the part taken by the Fourth Regiment Ohio Infantry, under my command, in the battle near Gettysburg, on the 2d and 3d instant:

On the 2d, early in the morning, I moved, with the balance of the brigade, from a point about 1½ miles in rear of the cemetery, where we had bivouacked during the night of the 1st, a little in rear of Cemetery Hill, with my right resting on the road leading from Taneytown to Gettysburg, facing toward the latter place.

At 9.30 a. m. I received orders to advance four companies of my regiment to support the line of pickets, which I did, under command of Major Stewart, and at 3 p. m. I relieved them with two companies under Captain Grubb.

At 4 p. m. the enemy opened with his artillery, and for two hours we were exposed to a heavy fire of shot and shell, which, however, did but little damage.

At 6 p. m. I received orders to change my position farther to the left, and formed between two batteries, at right angles to my former line of battle. I remained here for one and a half hours, the whole time exposed to the enemy's artillery and sharpshooters, but being somewhat protected by a fence, the regiment did not suffer greatly.

At 7.30 o'clock I received orders to again change my position, and, under the guidance of Captain Gregg, acting assistant inspector-general, First Brigade, I moved across the Taneytown road, and formed in line of battle to the right of the cemetery, and moved forward, and, finding the enemy in possession of a part of our line, we drove them before us, and captured a number of prisoners. We remained in position during the night, throwing out pickets well to the front.

On the 3d, we retained our position, and awaited patiently, under a terrific fire of artillery, the approach of the enemy, but they did not again attempt that portion of our line that day or subsequently. We captured 34 prisoners and 200 stand of arms.

We were armed on going into the fight with the smooth-bore muskets, but these were exchanged for good Springfield rifles that we captured from the enemy.

The regiment numbered on going into the fight 22 commissioned officers and 277 enlisted men.

The officers and men behaved most handsomely, and the regiment maneuvered on the field as if on drill. I beg leave to make special mention of Captain Grubb, who was in command of the two companies that were on picket when the battle commenced, and was wounded; also of Captain Camp. Lieuts. S. J. Shoub and A. H. Edgar, both young and promising officers, were killed early in the engagement.

The following is a list of the casualties:

Officers and men.	Killed.	Wounded.	Missing.	Total.
Commissioned officers	2	1	......	3
Enlisted men	5	17	5	27
Total *	7	18	5	30

Very respectfully, your obedient servant,

L. W. CARPENTER,
Lieut. Col., Comdg. Fourth Regt. Ohio Vol. Infantry.

Lieut. J. G. REID,
A. A. A. G., First Brig., Third Div., Second Corps.

No. 120.

Report of Lieut. Col. Franklin Sawyer, Eighth Ohio Infantry.

ON THE FIELD, NEAR GETTYSBURG, PA., *July 5*, 1863.

SIR: I have the honor to make the following report of the part taken by the Eighth Regiment Ohio Volunteers during the late battle near this place:

The Eighth Regiment occupied the right of the brigade, and participated in the several maneuvers and changes of position by the brigade until about 4 p. m. of the 2d instant, when I received an order from Col. S. S. Carroll, U. S. Army, commanding brigade, to move my regiment forward to the picket line in front of our position and on the left of the pickets of the Eleventh Corps. This was at once executed, the regiment moving forward gallantly under a smart fire of the enemy's pickets and sharpshooters. I received a further order from Colonel Carroll to throw forward four companies as an advanced line, and to support them with the balance of the regiment, and to hold my line to the last man.

The enemy did not advance upon us in force until about 4 p. m. of the 3d, and our position was maintained during the twenty-four hours without any relief, although we had suffered severely from the enemy's pickets, sharpshooters, and shell, 4 of my men having been killed, and 1 captain, 1 lieutenant, the sergeant-major, and 38 men wounded up to noon of the 3d.

Soon after 2 p. m. the enemy opened a terrific fire from sixty-four pieces of artillery, in a semicircle which inclosed my position. This was replied to by our batteries, and we suffered severely under the fire for nearly two hours.

This artillery duel was followed by an immediate advance of two divisions of the enemy's infantry, which advanced at the first in three long lines of battle, but ployed into close column by division as they advanced, excepting, perhaps, a regiment on each flank. The

* But see revised statement, p. 176.

column directed itself upon our battery to my left, and the line on the left flank of the column directly upon my position. I advanced my reserve to the picket front, and as the rebel line came within about 100 yards, we poured in a well-directed fire, which broke the rebel line, and it soon fled in the wildest confusion.

Being relieved from this direction, I changed front forward on the left company, thus presenting our front to the left flank of the advancing rebel column. Our fire was poured into their flank with terrible effect for a few minutes before the Second Brigade at the battery opened, but almost instantly on the fire from the front, together with the concentrated fire from our batteries, the whole mass gave way, some fleeing to the front, some to the rear, and some through our lines, until the whole plain was covered with unarmed rebels, waving coats, hats, and handkerchiefs in token of a wish to surrender.

The Eighth pressed forward, capturing a large number of prisoners (about 200) and 3 stand of colors; one marked Thirty-fourth North Carolina and one Thirty-eighth Virginia were captured by Sergt. Daniel Miller, of Company G, and have been turned over, by order of Colonel Carroll, to the division commander. One captured by Private James Richmond, of Company F, was taken from him on the field by a staff officer of our army, but whose name is unknown.*

During this time we were under a terrific fire from the rebel batteries and infantry, and my loss in all on both days is 101 killed and wounded and 1 missing, and includes 4 captains wounded, 1 first lieutenant killed and 1 wounded, 4 second lieutenants wounded, the sergeant-major wounded, 2 orderly sergeants killed and 4 wounded, 2 duty sergeants killed and 6 wounded, 2 color corporals wounded, 1 corporal killed and 8 wounded, 9 privates killed on the field (4 since died), 52 wounded, and 1 missing.

My officers and men behaved with the utmost courage and bravery, and have contributed all that could be asked of any men to the glorious results of that day.

I desire to mention especially Capt. William Kenny, who acted as major, and Adjt. John W. De Puy, who behaved with great gallantry, and rendered me every assistance. Captains [John] Reid, Miller, Pierce, and Nickerson were all wounded while gallantly leading their companies, Captain Nickerson, it is feared, mortally, while Captain Lewis, Lieutenants O'Reilly, Farnum, Galwey, Travis, and Hysung, who were in command of companies, deserve the highest praise and credit. I have to lament the death of Lieutenant Hayden, who fell while cheering his men to the conflict.

I would also mention especially the color sergeants, [James] Conlan and [Romeo W.] Foster, who bore our colors (which were often struck) gallantly to the front during the whole of the fierce conflict.

A list of the killed and wounded has already been forwarded, but several have since died, making a revised list necessary, which will be forwarded as soon as possible.

I have the honor to be, sir, your obedient servant,

FRANKLIN SAWYER,
Lieutenant-Colonel, Commanding.

Lieut. J. G. REID,
Actg. Asst. Adjt. Gen., 1st Brig., 3d Div., 2d Corps.

---

* Medals of honor awarded to Sergeant Miller and Private Richmond.

No. 121.

*Report of Capt. Alfred T. Craig, Eighth Ohio Infantry, command-
ing Provost Guard.*

CAMP, PROVOST GUARD, 1ST BRIG., 3D DIV., 2D CORPS,
July 7, 1863.

SIR: Having been detailed as commander of the provost guard of
the First Brigade, I have the honor to submit the following report
of the duties performed and the part taken by my detachment previous to and during the engagement with the enemy at Gettysburg,
and also from that time to the present date:

The detachment consisted of 1 captain, 1 second lieutenant, 1 sergeant, 3 corporals, and 30 privates. Agreeably to order, they entered upon the duty assigned to them, in the rear of the brigade on
the 1st instant, in keeping up stragglers, &c. On the 3d instant, there
was placed in my custody 102 Confederate prisoners, captured by the
First Brigade, Third Division, Second Corps, the whole of whom were
turned over by me to different provost-marshals.

Jacob Sheets, of Company I, Fourth Ohio Volunteer Infantry, was
killed in the engagement on the 2d instant; Simon Main, Company
F, Seventh [West] Virginia, wounded in the leg by a piece of shell,
and Oscar M. Hall, Company H, Fourteenth Indiana, wounded in
the hand by a gunshot.

I have the honor to be, very respectfully,
A. T. CRAIG,
Capt., Comdg. Provost Guard, 1st Brig., 3d Div., 2d Corps.

Lieut. J. G. REID,
Acting Assistant Adjutant-General.

No. 122.

*Report of Lieut. Col. Jonathan H. Lockwood, Seventh West Vir-
ginia Infantry.*

CAMP NEAR GETTYSBURG, PA.,
July 5, 1863.

SIR: In obedience to orders, I have the honor to submit the following report of the part taken by the Seventh West Virginia in the late
engagement near Gettysburg:

About 8 a. m. on the 2d instant, under the command of Colonel
Carroll, the Seventh West Virginia, with the Fourteenth Indiana,
Fourth and Eighth Ohio Volunteers, were massed in front of the
enemy and near their center. About 4 p. m. the Seventh West Virginia and Fourteenth Indiana changed position on the left of the
enemy's right center, where we remained but a short time, when the
Seventh West Virginia was ordered back, and placed to protect the
Fourth U. S. Artillery, where we remained under heavy fire from
the enemy's batteries until about 8 o'clock, at which time, in connection with the Fourteenth Indiana, we were ordered to the right of
Cemetery Hill, in support of Battery L, First New York Artillery,
and on arriving there we found the battery about to be taken charge
of by the enemy, who were in large force; whereupon we immedi-

ately charged upon the enemy, and succeeded in completely routing the entire force and driving them beyond their lines, capturing a number of prisoners, and removing their dead and wounded in order to establish our line on the line previously occupied by the enemy.

Among the prisoners captured was the colonel of the Seventh Virginia Volunteers, and colonel and major of the Twenty-first North Carolina Volunteers.

Having established our lines, we remained at this position during the night and the day and the night of the 3d.

From 6 a. m. until about dusk on the 3d, we lay under heavy fire and cross-fire from the enemy's batteries. We had brisk skirmishing in our front during the time we occupied that position. During the whole engagement the field was contested with a spirit of determination on our side to gain the victory.

Our loss is as follows: Lieutenant-colonel wounded; 5 enlisted men killed; 42 enlisted men wounded, and 13 enlisted men missing*—a list of the same having previously been forwarded.

My officers and men behaved with admirable coolness and undaunted courage, and deserve well of their country.

I have the honor to be, your obedient servant,

J. H. LOCKWOOD,
Lieutenant-Colonel, Commanding.

Lieut. J. G. REID,
Acting Assistant Adjutant-General.

No. 123.

Report of Col. Thomas A. Smyth, First Delaware Infantry, commanding Second Brigade.

HDQRS. SECOND BRIG., TRIRD DIV., SECOND CORPS,
July 17, 1863.

CAPTAIN: I have the honor to make the following report of the part taken by this brigade in the action at Gettysburg, Pa., from July 1 to 4:

Being in camp at Uniontown, Md., on the morning of July 1, I received an order to march at 6.30 a. m.; marched to Taneytown, and halted until 12 m., when the command resumed the march toward Gettysburg, and encamped about 3 miles from the town.

At 4 a. m. on the 2d, the brigade was placed in position on the hills overlooking the town, my command being placed on the left of the First Brigade. This position we occupied until the termination of the action on the night of the 3d.

Skirmishing commenced briskly along our front. At 8 a. m. the First Delaware Volunteers were sent out as skirmishers, and the One hundred and eighth New York Volunteers were assigned to the support of Woodruff's battery.

At 2 p. m. the enemy opened upon us with a severe fire of artillery, accompanied by an advance of infantry, which drove in our skirmishers. They were, however, immediately replaced, and the enemy's

---

* But see revised statement, p. 176.

skirmishers retired to their original position, excepting that a force of them retained possession of a large barn about 400 yards in front of our line.

Four companies of the Twelfth New Jersey Volunteers were sent to retake the barn and to dislodge the enemy's sharpshooters, which they succeeded in doing, capturing 92 prisoners, including 7 commissioned officers. The enemy advanced in turn, and recaptured the barn.

The First Delaware Volunteers and four more companies of the Twelfth New Jersey Volunteers, under the command of Captain Thompson, Twelfth New Jersey, were subsequently sent to again take possession of the barn, which they did, having taken 10 prisoners, one of whom was a major. Observing that the enemy was moving in force along a ravine toward the barn, Captain Thompson thought proper to retire.

Firing ceased about 9 p. m., the remainder of the night being quiet.

Artillery firing from both sides began at 4 a. m. on the morning of the 3d, the heaviest firing being on our right. Skirmishing with artillery and infantry continued all along the line until 10.30 a. m., when a lull ensued, which lasted up to 2 p. m. The barn and house near it being reoccupied by the enemy's sharpshooters, an order was received from General Hays, commanding the division, to take the house and barn at all hazards and hold it. The Fourteenth Connecticut Volunteers was detailed on this service, which it gallantly performed. Soon after, an order came from General Hays to burn the house and barn, and they were accordingly fired.

At 2 p. m. a most terrific cannonading was opened upon our front by the simultaneous discharge of a whole battery. This fire, from an extended line of the enemy's batteries, concentrated on the small space occupied by our troops, and continued without intermission until 5 p. m.

The officers and men behaved with the greatest coolness, and endured this terrible fire with much fortitude. As the fire of the enemy's batteries slackened, their infantry moved upon our position in three lines, preceded by skirmishers.

My men were directed to reserve their fire until the foe was within 50 yards, when so effective and incessant was the fire from my line that the advancing enemy was staggered, thrown into confusion, and finally fled from the field, throwing away their arms in their flight. Many threw themselves on the ground to escape our destructive fire, and raised their hands in token of surrender.

The number of prisoners captured by this brigade is estimated at from 1,200 to 1,500. The number of small-arms collected by them is estimated at 2,000. This command captured 9 battle-flags, as follows: The Fourteenth Connecticut Volunteers, 4; the First Delaware Volunteers, 3, and the Twelfth New Jersey, 2.

The One hundred and eighth New York Volunteers rendered very efficient service while supporting Woodruff's battery, and lost heavily, the casualties being about half of the regiment in action. The men assisted in maneuvering the guns when so many of the horses were killed that the guns, limbers, and caissons could with difficulty be moved.

During the cannonading, having received a wound, I was obliged to quit the field, and surrendered the command to Lieut. Col. Francis E. Pierce, One hundred and eighth New York Volunteers.

The casualties in my command were as follows:

Command.	Officers.			Enlisted men.			
	Killed.	Wounded.	Missing.	Killed.	Wounded.	Missing.	Total.
Brigade staff		2					2
1st Regiment Delaware Volunteers	2	2	1	7	41	10	63
108th New York Volunteers	3	10		13	76		102
14th Connecticut Volunteers		10		10	42	4	66
12th New Jersey Volunteers	2	4		21	75	11	113
1st Battalion 10th New York				2	4		6
Total *	7	28	1	53	238	25	352

I desire to call the attention of the general commanding to the bravery, self-possession, and energy of Lieut. Col. F. E. Pierce, commanding One hundred and eighth New York Volunteers, who, throughout the heaviest of the fire, showed the greatest unconcern, passing along his line and encouraging his men; Maj. John T. Hill, commanding Twelfth New Jersey Volunteers, who directed his men to retain their fire during the charge of the enemy until they were within 20 yards, when, at his command, so tremendous a fire of buck and ball was poured into their ranks as to render it impossible that one of them could reach the breastwork; Maj. Theodore G. Ellis, commanding Fourteenth Connecticut Volunteers, who led the last attack on the house and barn occupied by the enemy's sharpshooters in a very spirited manner, completely routing them, and Lieut. William Smith, who commanded the First Delaware Volunteers during the attack upon our front. He was a brave and efficient officer, and was instantly killed, with one of the enemy's captured flags in his hand.

I would also particularly mention the able and efficient services of the gentlemen composing my staff: Lieut. William P. Seville, acting assistant adjutant-general; Capt. James Parke Postles, acting assistant inspector-general, and Lieut. Charles S. Schaeffer, aide-de-camp, who was wounded, and Lieut. Theron E. Parsons, aide-de-camp. These officers are deserving of much credit for their conduct during the whole action. Lieut. William P. Seville and Capt. J. P. Postles I wish specially to recommend to your notice as really meritorious officers.

THOS. A. SMYTH,
Colonel First Delaware Volunteers, Comdg. Brigade.

Capt. GEORGE P. CORTS, *Assistant Adjutant-General.*

No. 124.

Report of Maj. Theodore G. Ellis, Fourteenth Connecticut Infantry.

CAMP NEAR GETTYSBURG, PA., *July* 6, 1863.

SIR: I have the honor to report the following as the part taken by the Fourteenth Connecticut Volunteers in the late battle at this place :

We arrived on the ground on the morning of the 2d instant, after

---

*But see revised statement, p. 176.

being out the night before on picket some 2 miles back, and rejoined the brigade.   During the forenoon we supported Woodruff's battery, regular artillery, until our position was changed farther to the left, to support Arnold's (First Rhode Island) battery.   Here we remained all night, with a slight change of position, throwing out pickets to the front.

During the day the regiment was at times under a heavy shell fire, but met with no loss, excepting in the case of Captain Coit, who was seriously injured accidentally by a runaway horse.

On the morning of the 3d, two companies were advanced as skirmishers, under the command of Captains Townsend and Lucas, who maintained their ground nobly until the grand attack of the afternoon, when they were driven in by the advancing lines of the enemy. In the forenoon the regiment was ordered to take and hold two buildings, a large barn and house, outside of our lines of skirmishers, a little to the right of our position, from which the enemy were seriously annoying our troops.   The barn was gallantly charged and taken by four companies, under the command of Captain Moore, the remainder of the regiment, commanded by myself, making the attack upon the house.

The whole distance from our lines to these buildings being commanded by the enemy's sharpshooters, we met with some loss in the attack.   It was here that Lieutenants Seward and Seymour were wounded.   While the regiment was within these buildings and firing from them upon the enemy, a case shot entered the upper part of the barn and exploded, killing and wounding some of our men.

Having received orders to destroy these buildings, they were fired in several places, after removing from them our killed and wounded. We then returned to the picket reserve, bringing off all our wounded and arms.

Being again ordered to support Arnold's battery, we formed on its right, where we remained under the terrific shell fire of Friday afternoon, from 1 p. m. until the battery retired, when I moved the regiment forward and to the left, to cover the space previously occupied by the battery.

About this time two lines of battle, extending across the plain for more than a mile, preceded by a line of skirmishers and re-enforced on the right and left by a third line, were observed to emerge from the woods, about one-third of a mile distant and running parallel to our front, and advanced steadily across the intervening plain.   The spectacle was magnificent.   They advanced in perfect order, the line of skirmishers firing.   Our men were formed in a single line along an almost continuous line of low stone wall and fence, which offered considerable protection from the enemy's fire.

When the first line of the enemy had advanced to within about 200 yards, our fire opened almost simultaneously along our whole line. The enemy's first line was broken and hurled back upon the second, throwing that also into confusion.   Detached portions of the line were rallied, and for a short time maintained their ground, but being rapidly mown down by our terribly destructive fire, they commenced falling back.   A portion of this regiment then charged upon the retreating rebels, capturing five regimental battle-flags and over 40 prisoners.   There also came into the lines of this regiment about 100 or more of the enemy, some of whom were wounded, and gave themselves up.

Among the officers who personally surrendered to me were the following: Col. John A. Fite, Seventh Tennessee, and Lieut. Col. N. J.

George, First Tennessee [Provisional Army], not wounded; Lieutenant-Colonel [Marcus A.] Parks, Fifty-second North Carolina, and Maj. John Q. Richardson, wounded. Among those who were taken prisoners or came within our lines wounded were the following line officers: Capts. G. A. Graves, Twenty-second North Carolina; George Gilliam, Fifty-second North Carolina; J. M. Kincaid, Fifty-second North Carolina; First. Lieuts. J. C. Warren, Fifty-second North Carolina, and J. N. Robertson, Fifth Alabama [Battalion]. There were many other field and line officers captured whose names were not ascertained.

The colors captured belonged to the following regiments: Fourteenth Tennessee, First Tennessee [Provisional Army], Sixteenth North Carolina, Fourth Virginia, and Fifty-second North Carolina. The colors of the First [Provisional Army] and Fourteenth Tennessee and Sixteenth North Carolina have each the following inscriptions: "Seven Pines, Mechanicsville, Cold Harbor, Shepherdstown, Fredericksburg, Chancellorsville, Ox Hill, Harper's Ferry, Sharpsburg, Frazier's Farm, Cedar Run, Manassas." The colors of the Fourteenth Tennessee were the first taken, and were captured by Sergt. Maj. William B. Hincks. Those of the Fifty-second North Carolina were new, without number or inscription, and were taken by Corpl. Christopher Flynn, of Company K. Those of the Sixteenth North Carolina were taken by Private E. W. Bacon, of Company F. The colors of the Fourth Virginia were turned over to the provost guard, which took charge of the first lot of prisoners taken.*

The following is a corrected return of the killed, wounded, and missing in the above engagement:

Officers and men.	Killed.	Wounded.	Missing.	Total.
Commissioned officers	......	10	......	10
Enlisted men	10	42	4	56
Total	10	52	4	66

The regiment went into action with about 160 muskets.

Very respectfully, your obedient servant,

THEO. G. ELLIS,

Major, Commanding Fourteenth Connecticut Volunteers.

Lieut. WILLIAM P. SEVILLE,

A. A. A. G., 2d Brig., 3d Div., 2d Army Corps.

No. 125.

Report of Lieut. John T. Dent, First Delaware Infantry.

——, —— —, 1863.

SIR: I have the honor to submit the following as the report of the part taken by the First Regiment Delaware Infantry at the battle of Gettysburg:

On the evening of July 1, the regiment, under command of Lieut.

---

*Medals of honor awarded to Sergeant Hincks, Corporal Flynn, and Private Bacon.

Col. E. P. Harris, bivouacked to the right of the Taneytown road, within 3 miles of Gettysburg.

Early on the morning of July 2, the line of march was resumed. We arrived on the field about 4 a. m., when we were massed in column behind Woodruff's battery, in which position we lay for about an hour. We then moved a short distance to the left, when we were deployed as skirmishers some 500 yards in front of the main line, where we remained actively engaged during the entire day.

About 4 p. m., the ammunition of the men being exhausted, Lieutenant-Colonel Harris withdrew the right wing of the regiment from the skirmish line, for which he was placed under arrest by General Hancock. The command then devolved on Capt. Thomas B. Hizar, of Company I. We were then assigned position in the line of battle, behind a fallen stone wall to the left of Woodruff's and right of Arnold's batteries.

About dark, the left wing of the regiment was driven in off the skirmish line. Captain Hizar, commanding the regiment, was about this time wounded. He remained in command until 11 p. m., when he retired. The command then devolved on Lieut. William Smith, Company A.

During the day the regiment lost in commissioned officers 1 killed (Capt. M. W. B. Ellegood), 3 wounded, and 1 taken prisoner; 4 enlisted men killed, 13 wounded, and 10 prisoners.

During the night of the 2d and the day of the 3d, the regiment remained in the same position, and it was there it received the united attack of the Pickett and Pender columns. These columns overlapped in our immediate front, and made the pressure on our line very heavy, the Pickett column moving on us in an oblique direction from the left, the Pender column moving on us in an oblique direction from the right, both columns converging in our immediate front. The regiment, however, with iron will stubbornly maintained its position, and repulsed the combined attack. As soon as the charge of the enemy was broken, the regiment sprang over the wall and gave them a countercharge, capturing many prisoners and five battle-flags.

It was in this charge that Lieut. William Smith, commanding the regiment, fell, and, when picked up, his sword was found in one hand and a captured rebel flag in the other.

The command then devolved upon John T. Dent, the first lieutenant of Company G.

Late in the afternoon of the third day, the regiment was ordered to charge on the ruins of the burnt barn in our front and dislodge a small body of the enemy, who were occupying the same and annoying our relief parties engaged in bringing in and relieving the wounded. This object accomplished, the command returned to the main line, where they remained during the night.

On the morning of the 4th, Lieutenant-Colonel Harris was restored to command.

Special mention should be made of Capt. M. W. B. Ellegood, Company E, who fell on the skirmish line, and Lieut. William Smith, who commanded the regiment during the charge, and fell, mortally wounded, with a captured flag in his hand; and of First Lieut. Andrew Wall, who, though not on duty, by his coolness and presence gave encouragement to the men. Also, of Color Sergt. John M. Dunn, who, colors in hand, led the regiment across the stone wall in its countercharge; and of Color Sergt. Thomas Seymour, who was cut in two by a shell, and Privates William Williams, of Company

A; B. McCarren, of Company C, and J. B. Mayberry, of Company F, who each captured flags.*

During the two days' fight the regiment lost—

Officers and men.	Killed.	Wounded.	Prisoners.	Total.
Commissioned officers	2	4	1	7
Enlisted men	10	41	10	61
Total †	12	45	11	68

The enemy's loss in our front was very severe; the ground was literally black with killed and wounded.

Your obedient servant,

JOHN T. DENT,
Late Major First Delaware Vol. Inf., and Lieut. Co. G.

[Lieut. WILLIAM P. SEVILLE,
A. A. A. G., 2d Brig., 3d Div., 2d Army Corps.]

No. 126.

Report of Maj. John T. Hill, Twelfth New Jersey Infantry.

HDQRS. TWELFTH REGT. NEW JERSEY VOLUNTEERS,
July 16, 1863.

SIR: I have the honor to report the action of the regiment I have the honor to command during the engagements of the 2d, 3d, and 4th instant to have been as follows:

At 5 p. m. on the 2d instant, four companies (B, H, E, and G) were detailed to take a large barn on our picket line, taken from us and held by the enemy. Under command of Captain Jobes, Company G, they charged gallantly upon the building, surrounding it, and capturing 92 prisoners, including 7 commissioned officers; losing in the attack 2 officers and 40 men killed and wounded.

At 6 p. m. the same day the balance of my command moved to the front line, taking position behind a stone fence to the left of Kirby's battery, remaining in this position until the afternoon of the 5th instant.

At 7.30 a. m. of the 3d instant, five companies (D, C, K, F, and A), under command of Captain Thompson, Company K, again drove the enemy from the shelter of the barn, capturing a major and 1 man, relieving our lines from an annoying fire from the enemy's sharpshooters posted therein.

At 4 p. m. of the 3d instant, the whole line became engaged in repulsing an attack in force made by the enemy, completely routing them, capturing prisoners estimated to number 500 men, and 2 colors.

We collected and turned in 751 small-arms, picked up in our immediate front.

---

* Medals of honor awarded to Privates Mayberry and McCarren.
† But see revised statement, p. 176.

Officers and men behaved with the greatest gallantry. I take pleasure in calling your attention to the meritorious conduct of Captains Thompson, Jobes, and Chew, Adjutant Franklin, Lieutenants McComb, Trimble, Acton, Phipps, Williams, Eastwick, and Dare, Sergeant-Major [Edward M.] Du Bois, and Color Sergeants [Charles E.] Cheeseman and [William H.] Griffin.

Our casualties were—

Officers and men.	Killed.	Wounded.	Missing.	Total.
Commissioned officers	2	4	.....	6
Enlisted men	21	75	11	107
Total*	23	79	11	113

I am, colonel, very respectfully, your obedient servant,
JOHN T. HILL,
Major, Commanding Twelfth New Jersey Volunteers.

Colonel MORRIS,
Comdg. Second Brig., Third Div., Second Army Corps.

No. 127.

Report of Maj. George F. Hopper, Tenth New York Infantry.

NEAR SANDY HOOK, MD.,
July 16, 1863.

SIR: I have the honor to forward to you the following report of the transactions and movements of my command, near Gettysburg, Pa., during the battle of the 2d and 3d instant:

On the afternoon of the 2d instant, I received orders to deploy in the rear of the Third Division, for the purpose of arresting stragglers, which order I immediately carried out.

On the 3d instant, were encamped at division headquarters until the opening of the fight in the afternoon, when I again deployed the battalion pursuant to orders received.

At about 3 p. m. was ordered to assemble my command and take it to the front. While complying with this order, some 1,800 rebel prisoners were turned over to my charge, and I placed guards over them.

About 4 p. m. was ordered to General Patrick's headquarters, in charge of these prisoners. Reached that place about 6 p. m., and encamped all night, under orders from General Patrick.

Lost in the engagement: Killed, 2; wounded, 4.

I have the honor to be, sir, your obedient servant,
GEO. F. HOPPER,
Major, Commanding Battalion.

Lieut. WILLIAM P. SEVILLE,
Acting Assistant Adjutant-General.

---

*But see revised statement, p. 176.

No. 128.

Reports of Lieut. Col. James M. Bull, One hundred and twenty-sixth New York Infantry, commanding Third Brigade.

HDQRS. THIRD BRIG., THIRD DIV., SECOND ARMY CORPS,
Camp near Frederick, Md., July 8, 1863.

SIR: I have the honor to make the following statement in relation to the operations of the Third Brigade, Third Division, Second Army Corps, in the battle of July 2 and 3, near Gettysburg, Pa.:

The brigade, under the command of Col. G. L. Willard, of the One hundred and twenty-fifth New York Volunteer Regiment, first took its position, by direction of the division general, by battalion in mass near a barn a little south of the hill known as Cemetery Hill. The Thirty-ninth New York Volunteers, under the command of Major Hildebrandt, was, by order of the general commanding the division, sent to the front as skirmishers. The regiment deployed, and for some four hours did very effective service against the skirmishers of the enemy.

During this skirmish, the regiment lost 26 enlisted men killed and wounded, and 2 commissioned officers wounded; one of whom, Lieutenant Wagner, has since died.

About noon, the division general ordered the regiment withdrawn, and the brigade soon after changed its position, and was massed by battalion on a hill to the left of Cemetery Hill.

At about 4 p. m., by order of the division general, the brigade moved from its position by the left flank about a quarter of a mile toward the left of the line, where it was formed in line of battle, and ordered by Colonel Willard to charge two rebel batteries, supported by infantry, posted on the hill in front of the position occupied by the brigade. The regiments composing the brigade were then commanded as follows: Colonel Sherrill, One hundred and twenty-sixth New York Volunteers; Colonel MacDougall, One hundred and eleventh New York Volunteers; Lieutenant-Colonel Crandell, One hundred and twenty-fifth New York Volunteers; Major Hildebrandt, Thirty-ninth New York Volunteers. The line advanced over declining ground, through a dense underbrush extending to the base of the hill previously mentioned, in as good order as the circumstances of the case would admit of, at which place (the base of the hill) the alignment, without stopping, was partially rectified.

Contrary, as is evident, to the expectations of the brigade commander, the rebels in considerable force were found in this underbrush. They fired upon the brigade as it advanced, which fire was returned by a portion of the brigade without halting. Many fell in the charge through the woods. Reaching the base of the hill, the brigade advanced at a "charge bayonets" up the hill mentioned, and within a few minutes recaptured part of a battery previously taken from us. After taking the battery, the brigade continued to advance under the fire of a battery higher up the hill on the left and a concentric fire of musketry on the right. The commander, finding his brigade unable to stand so severe a fire, ordered the regiments to retire, which was done in good order down the hill and through the underbrush before mentioned.

After emerging from the underbrush, the line was reformed by direction of Colonel Willard, and immediately afterward he was killed by a shot from a rebel battery on the hill. Colonel Sherrill then assumed command, and conducted the brigade to its original position, pursuant to the order of Colonel Willard, given just before his death.

The coolness, courage, and determination displayed by officers and men throughout this trying occasion reflect great credit on them, and it is believed that the charge aided materially in maintaining our lines during that day. After the cessation of the firing, the brigade reoccupied the position it held in the morning.

During the forenoon and part of the afternoon of the second day, large details were made from the several regiments of the brigade for skirmishing, such details being actively engaged in skirmishing with the enemy on the flat in front of the crest of the hill occupied by our artillery and infantry, extending left from Cemetery Hill. In anticipation of an attack upon the line on the crest of the hill mentioned, the regiments composing this brigade were formed in two lines, nearly parallel, some distance apart, under the slope of the hill occupied by us, being so placed as supports to the artillery.

About 1 p. m. the enemy opened from his batteries planted on the slope of the hill across the flat mentioned, evidently with the intention of silencing our batteries, and a terrific cannonade ensued, which continued about two hours, during which period the regiments remained in the position before stated. Near the close of this severe artillery duel, the regiments were formed on the hill with other regiments of the division, to repel an infantry attack. The enemy, advancing in four lines across the flat, were subjected to a murderous fire of musketry and artillery, and were driven back in confusion, after an engagement of about an hour.*

The regiment behaved well during this engagement, to the best of my knowledge and belief. The brigade was commanded by Colonel Sherrill until his death, about 4 p. m., when the command devolved upon Lieut. Col. James M. Bull, his seniors in the brigade having been killed or disabled.

In this engagement a severe loss was sustained by the brigade in killed and wounded, the precise number of which I am unable to report.

The regiments maintained their positions mentioned on the slope of the hill during the next day, sending out details to skirmish on the flat.

Herewith are inclosed lists of the killed, wounded, and missing of the several regiments of the brigade, which are as accurate as I can now furnish.†

I am, sir, very respectfully, your obedient servant,

JAMES M. BULL,
Lieut. Col. 126th New York Vols., Comdg. Brigade.

Capt. G. P. Corts, *Assistant Adjutant-General.*

———

HDQRS. THIRD BRIG., THIRD DIV., SECOND ARMY CORPS,
Camp near Sandy Hook, Md., July 17, 1863.

SIR : Replying to the circular dated Philadelphia, Pa., July 7, 1863, I beg leave to represent that I have made diligent inquiry as to the subject-matter of said circular.

---

*Medals of honor awarded to Capt. Morris Brown, jr., Sergt. George H. Dore, and Private Jerry Wall, all of the One hundred and twenty-sixth New York, for the capture of Confederate colors.

†See revised statement, p. 177.

During the afternoon of Thursday, the 2d instant, this brigade was formed and marched by the flank toward the left.   During this march the Thirty-ninth New York Volunteers, by order of Colonel Willard, were detached, and ordered about a third of a mile from the point where the residue of the brigade advanced in line of battle. The commanding officer of this regiment claims that, in obedience to such order, at the point designated, he charged on a line of rebel skirmishers, drove them in, and retook four pieces of artillery with caissons belonging to Battery I, Fifth U. S. Artillery, which had been captured by the enemy.   The commanders of the other regiments of the brigade claim that at least two of these guns and caissons were captured in the advance of the brigade.

I am unable to settle the conflict of statement from my personal knowledge, nor am I able to state whether any regiment of this brigade is the one referred to in this circular from my knowledge, or from evidence before me which I deem conclusive.

Very respectfully, your obedient servant,

JAMES M. BULL,
Lieutenant-Colonel, Commanding Third Brigade.

Capt. G. P. CORTS,
Assistant Adjutant-General.

No. 129.

Report of Col. Clinton D. MacDougall, One hundred and Eleventh New York Infantry.

CAMP NEAR ELK RUN, VA.,
August 26, 1863.

COLONEL: After recovering from wounds received at Gettysburg, July 3, and my return to my regiment, upon assuming command of this brigade I found, upon looking over the official report and other papers pertaining to the battle, a circular from Major-General Hancock, of which I insert a copy.   I have every reason to suppose the general referred to my regiment, as will appear from my statement following the circular.

CIRCULAR.]   PHILADELPHIA, PA.,
July 7, 1863.

Major-General Hancock desires to know the designation of a certain regiment, and the name of its commander, belonging to the First, Second, or Twelfth Corps, which, at the instance of General Hancock, charged a rebel regiment which had passed through our lines on Thursday evening, 2d instant.   The conduct of this regiment and its commander were so marked in this as in the subsequent advance in line of battle, that General Hancock desires properly to notice the subject.

By order of Major-General Hancock:

W. G. MITCHELL,
Aide-de-Camp, and Assistant Adjutant-General.

On Thursday evening, July 2, when the Third Brigade, Third Division, Second Corps, marched down from the left of Cemetery Hill to re-enforce the Third Corps (as I was afterward informed), the brigade commander ordered me to remain at the left in reserve about 200 yards in the rear, when General Hancock came riding up shortly, and ordered me with my regiment to the right in great haste, to charge the rebel advance, which had broken through our lines on the right of the Third Brigade, and had advanced between 20 and 30 rods beyond our lines, and was in the act of turning the right flank of our brigade. The rebels were driven back by me beyond our brigade line and almost into the mouth of their own batteries, which they had advanced upon us. I held that position under a murderous fire until I was ordered by our brigade commander to fall back and take a new position, throwing a heavy line of skirmishers forward when my line rested. The rebels did not advance after that to engage the skirmishers that night.

So severe was the fire to which we were subjected, that my loss in that charge was 185 men killed and wounded in less than twenty minutes, out of about 390 taken into the fight.

I wish to make this statement, as I was absent at the time General Hancock's circular was received at brigade headquarters, and have had no chance until now to make my statement of the affair. If my regiment is the one entitled to the credit of the act referred to by General Hancock, I am desirous they should have it. My losses that day were more than double any regiment in the brigade.

I have taken the liberty of inclosing a copy of this to General Hancock at his residence.

Very respectfully, yours,

C. D. MacDOUGALL,
Col. 111th Regt. N. Y. Vols., 3d Brig., 3d Div., 2d A. C.

Lieut. Col. FRANCIS A. WALKER,
Assistant Adjutant-General.

No. 130.

Report of Capt. Aaron P. Seeley, One hundred and eleventh New York Infantry.

——, —— —, 1863.

LIEUTENANT: I have the honor to report to the commandant of the brigade that the One hundred and eleventh New York Volunteers marched at 3 a. m. to the heights south of Gettysburg with the brigade on the morning of July 2, and lay in rear of the One hundred and twenty-sixth and One hundred and twenty-fifth New York Volunteers, with the battalion of the Thirty-ninth New York Volunteers in our rear. We lay in this position until about 5 p. m., most of the afternoon under a furious shelling from the enemy.

About 5 p. m., by order of Colonel Willard, One hundred and twenty-fifth New York Volunteers, commanding brigade, the regiment fell in with the rest of the brigade and moved by the left flank about half a mile to the left; then, by order of the same officer, moved a short distance to the right, and formed a line of battle with the brigade, the One hundred and eleventh holding the right.

During the movement to the right, we were under a heavy fire of shell and canister from the batteries of the enemy, commingled with the bullets of a triumphant horde of rebels who had forced their way up to the position previously held by others of our Union forces, who had been compelled to give way before their attack, with the loss of four of our cannon.

At the command, the regiment with the brigade—not a man in the whole line faltering or hesitating for an instant—hurled themselves upon the advancing foe. The rebel ranks were broken through, and, as they hurriedly retreated, volley after volley was poured into them by our still advancing regiment. The ground over which the first of the charge was made was a sort of swale, covered with rocks, thickly interspersed with bushes, scrub oaks, and trees. Beyond was open ground, ascending toward the west. As we emerged upon the open ground, we were met by a terrible storm of grape and canister. Without an instant's hesitation the regiment still advanced until they had driven the enemy from the possession of the four cannon previously captured by the rebels. The Thirty-ninth New York Volunteers afterward brought in those guns. In obedience to the order of Colonel Willard, the regiment then came to the right-about, and at quick time, the rebel fire of shell and canister continuing, moved back to the position it held before charging. Skirmishers were thrown out to the front, and, after about half an hour, the regiment moved back to its original position.

Some idea of the fire under which the regiment passed during the charge may be formed from the fact that the right company (A) lost 33 men killed and wounded; the next two companies to the left lost 27, killed and wounded. We lost Lieut. A. W. Proseus, of Company E, during this charge, a gallant officer, who was leading his company forward.

The next morning (July 3) the regiment fell in at 3 a. m., the enemy having commenced a furious shelling upon our position at that time, which fire died away at about 9 a. m. The quiet which then succeeded was unbroken until about 1 p. m., when there was opened upon our position a cannonading and shelling unparalleled, it is believed, in warfare. During the hottest of this fire the regiment formed and marched by the right flank up to the crest of the hill, and formed a line of battle in rear of the Twelfth New Jersey, who were lying under the shelter of a low stone wall. We here lay down upon the ground, the shot and shell filling the air above our heads and often striking among us.

We lost a number of men during this shelling, among them Lieut. John H. Drake, of Company F, an officer loved and lamented by the whole regiment.

After this infernal shelling had lasted for about two hours, we rose to our feet to meet the assault of the enemy, who were seen advancing in three heavy compact lines, preceded by a cloud of skirmishers. Not a man flinched, but every brow was knit and lip compressed with stern determination to win or die, and win they did. The number of dead and wounded in front of our position after the battle was over and the rebel mass had been hurled back showed the accuracy of our fire.

Over 400 prisoners were counted by one of our officers as taken by the regiment. A number of stand of colors were also captured, but it is impossible to state the number.

I may add that during the whole of both these days of battle the One hundred and eleventh had skirmishers in front of their position continually.

Owing to the loss and absence of commissioned officers and of the non-commissioned officers having the regimental and company rolls in their charge, it is impossible to give a correct statement of our loss. From the best information I can obtain, we took into the action about 400 men, rank and file. Our loss in killed is 57, and wounded and missing 171.

In the killed are included First Lieut. John H. Drake, Company F; Second Lieutenant Granger, Company D; First Lieutenant Proseus,

Company E, and Sergt. Maj. Irving P. Jaques. Among the seriously wounded are Col. C. D. MacDougall; Acting Adjutant Capron; Captain Holmes, Company D, Captain Mead, Company I, and Captain Smith, Company K.

Lieutenant-Colonel Lusk was thrown from his horse and seriously injured during the first part of July 3, thus leaving no field officer with the regiment.

I am, respectfully, your obedient servant,

A. P. SEELEY,
Capt., Comdg. One hundred and eleventh New York Vols.

Lieutenant SHELDON,
Acting Assistant Adjutant-General.

No. 131.

Report of Lieut. Harry L. Haskell, One hundred and twenty-fifth New York Infantry.

———, —— —, 1863.

SIR : The regiment left Centreville, Va., on June 25, and arrived at Gettysburg on the morning of July 2. Took position on a nameless hill, situated about half a mile from the village. Three companies were immediately after our arrival deployed as skirmishers in front of our position, suffering some considerable loss during the day.

Just before sunset of that day the brigade was ordered to take position on and support the left, where the entire brigade charged the enemy and drove them, after which we were ordered by Colonel Willard, commanding the brigade, to retreat, which was done in excellent order. The loss on that day was heavy.

About 9 p. m. took the position previously occupied, and held it until after the battle.

On the 3d, skirmishers were kept in front of our position. About 2 p. m. the enemy formed line, and made a desperate charge on our position, and was repulsed with heavy loss. All prisoners agree in saying that it was by far the most desperate battle of the war. Nothing further, other than skirmishing, occurred on our front up to the time the enemy fell back.

The regiment left Gettysburg July 5.

HARRY L. HASKELL,
Second Lieutenant, and Acting Adjutant.

[Lieut. ELIAS P. SHELDON,
Acting Assistant Adjutant-General.]

No. 132.

Report of Capt. John G. Hazard, First Rhode Island Light Artillery, commanding Artillery Brigade, Second Army Corps.

HDQRS. ARTILLERY BRIGADE, SECOND ARMY CORPS,
August 1, 1863.

SIR: I have the honor to transmit the following report of the part taken by the batteries of this brigade in the battle of July 2 and 3:

On the morning of July 1, the brigade—composed of Light Company I, First U. S. Artillery, First Lieut. George A. Woodruff commanding; Battery A, Fourth U. S. Artillery, First Lieut. A. H. Cushing commanding; Battery A, First Rhode Island Light Artillery, Capt. W. A. Arnold commanding; Battery B, First Rhode Island Light Artillery, First Lieut. T. Frederick Brown commanding; Battery B, First New York Artillery, Capt. J. M. Rorty commanding—moved from Uniontown, Md., to Taneytown, where a halt of three hours was made.

At 2 p. m. the brigade moved toward Gettysburg, Pa., to the support of the First Corps, then engaged with the enemy, and at 11 p. m. went into position 3 miles southeast of Gettysburg, on the Taneytown road and facing Gettysburg.

The brigade moved with the corps at daylight on July 2 toward Gettysburg, and, upon the establishment of the battle-line of the corps to the left of the Taneytown road, took position in the following order, as shown in diagram: On the right, in a grove, Light Company I (six light 12-pounders); 150 yards to the left, Battery A, First Rhode Island Light Artillery, and Battery A, Fourth U. S. Artillery (both six 3-inch batteries). Upon their left was placed Battery B, First Rhode Island Light Artillery (six light 12-pounders), while to the extreme left, and operating with the First Division of the corps, was placed Battery B, First New York Artillery (four 10-pounder Parrotts).

At 11 a. m. the enemy was seen in force in the woods to the front and right, and shell and case shot were fired till their disappearance. The enemy opened with artillery several times during the day, but was always silenced by the concentrated fire of our own artillery.

About 4 p. m. the Third Corps advanced to the Emmitsburg road, and, upon being repulsed, our lines were opened upon by the enemy with artillery. A vigorous fire was returned.

At 6 p. m. the enemy advanced in force, and, after a sharp contest, our lines were pushed back several hundred yards, the two batteries on the left—Battery B, First New York Artillery, and Battery B, First Rhode Island Light Artillery—conforming their movements to that of the infantry. Upon gaining a more commanding position upon the crest of the hill, a rapid fire was opened upon the enemy, causing great slaughter, and steadily driving them back.

The two batteries on the left, being at the main point of attack on the left and center of the line, suffered most severely. Battery B, First New York Artillery, lost 1 man killed, 8 men wounded, and 13 horses disabled. Battery B, First Rhode Island Light Artillery, lost 1 man killed, 7 men wounded, and 2 missing. This battery was exposed to a most severe infantry fire; 24 horses were killed and 6 disabled, and it became necessary to send two guns to the rear. First Lieut. T. Fred. Brown was severely wounded in the neck by a musket-shot while gallantly commanding the battery, and the command devolved upon First Lieut. W. S. Perrin. First Lieut. Samuel Canby, Battery A, Fourth U. S. Artillery, was severely wounded in the hand.

The morning of July 3 was quiet until about 8 o'clock, when the enemy suddenly opened fire upon our position, exploding three limbers of Battery A, Fourth U. S. Artillery, but otherwise causing little loss. Little reply was made, save by Light Company I, First U. S. Artillery, which battery during the forenoon had eight separate engagements with the enemy.

At 1 p. m. the artillery of the enemy opened along the whole line,

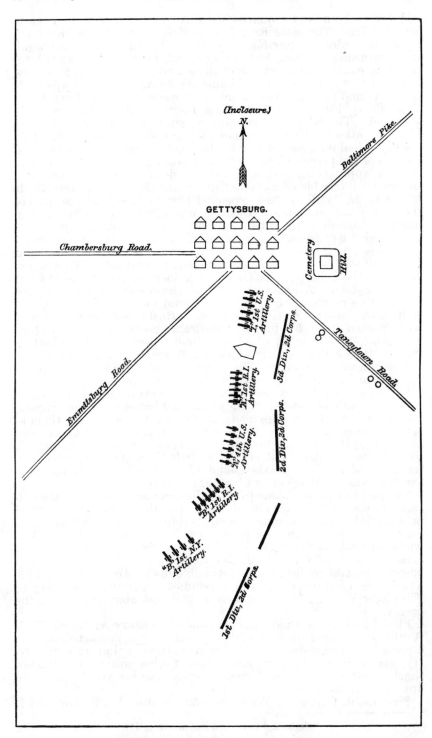

and for an hour and a quarter we were subjected to a very warm artillery fire. The batteries did not at first reply, till the fire of the enemy becoming too terrible, they returned it till all their ammunition, excepting canister, had been expended; they then waited for the anticipated infantry attack of the enemy. Battery B, First New York Artillery, was entirely exhausted; its ammunition expended; its horses and men killed and disabled; the commanding officer, Capt. J. M. Rorty, killed, and senior First Lieut. A. S. Sheldon severely wounded. The other batteries were in similar condition; still, they bided the attack. The rebel lines advanced slowly but surely; half the valley had been passed over by them before the guns dared expend a round of the precious ammunition remaining on hand. The enemy steadily approached, and, when within deadly range, canister was thrown with terrible effect into their ranks. Battery A, First Rhode Island Light Artillery, had expended every round, and the lines of the enemy still advanced. Cushing was killed; Milne had fallen, mortally wounded; their battery was exhausted, their ammunition gone, and it was feared the guns would be lost if not withdrawn.

At this trying moment the two batteries were taken away; but Woodruff still remained in the grove, and poured death and destruction into the rebel lines. They had gained the crest, and but few shots remained. All seemed lost, and the enemy, exultant, rushed on. But on reaching the crest they found our infantry, fresh and waiting on the opposite side. The tide turned; backward and downward rushed the rebel line, shattered and broken, and the victory was gained. Woodruff, who had gallantly commanded the battery through the action of July 2 and 3, fell, mortally wounded, at the very moment of victory. The command of the battery devolved upon Second Lieut. Tully McCrea, First U. S. Artillery.

Batteries from the Artillery Reserve of the army immediately occupied the positions vacated by the exhausted batteries of the brigade, and immediate efforts were made to recuperate and restore them to serviceable condition. So great was the loss in officers, men, and horses, that it was found necessary to consolidate Light Company I, First U. S. Artillery, Battery A, Fourth U. S. Artillery, and Batteries A and B, First Rhode Island Light Artillery, thus reducing the five batteries that entered the fight to three.

The greatest praise is due to the gallantry and courage of the officers and men of the brigade, of whom one-third were either killed or wounded. The fire under which they fought on the afternoon of July 3 was most severe and terrible, as the inclosed list of killed, wounded, and missing* will sufficiently testify.

In the death of Capt. J. M. Rorty the brigade has lost a worthy officer, a gallant soldier, and an estimable man. He had enjoyed his new position but one day, having assumed command of Battery B, First New York Artillery, on July 2, as it was about to engage the enemy.

First Lieut. A. H. Cushing, commanding Battery A, Fourth U. S. Artillery, fell on July 3, mortally wounded by a musket-shot. He especially distinguished himself for his extreme gallantry and bravery, his courage and ability, and his love for his profession. His untimely death and the loss of such a promise as his youth cherished are sincerely mourned.

First Lieut. George A. Woodruff, commanding Light Company I,

---

* Embodied in revised statement, p. 177.

First U. S. Artillery, fell, mortally wounded, on July 3, while the rebel lines, after a most successful and daring advance, were being pushed back in destruction and defeat.   To the manner in which the guns of his battery were served and his unflinching courage and determination may be due the pertinacity with which this part of the line was so gallantly held under a most severe attack.   Lieutenant Woodruff was an able soldier, distinguished for his excellent judgment and firmness in execution, and his loss is one which cannot be easily replaced.   He expired on July 4, and, at his own request, was buried on the field on which he had yielded his life to his country.

Second Lieut. Joseph S. Milne, First Rhode Island Light Artillery, was mortally wounded on the afternoon of July 3 by a musket-shot through the lungs. He survived his wound one week, and breathed his last at Gettysburg on July 10.   In his regiment he was noted for his bravery and willingness to encounter death in any guise, while his modesty and manliness gained for him the ready esteem of his many comrades.   His death is a loss to all, and we cannot but mourn that so bright a life should thus suddenly be veiled in death.   At the time of his decease he was attached to Battery A, Fourth U. S. Artillery, with which battery he had served during the campaign.   Every officer in this battery was either killed or wounded.

First Lieut. T. Fred. Brown, Battery B, First Rhode Island Light Artillery, was severely wounded in the neck on the afternoon of July 2.   This officer deserves great praise for the cool and able manner in which he commanded his battery, although exposed to a most galling infantry fire, in a position to the front of the line of the corps, where his horses were shot down faster than they could be replaced. The guns were served admirably and with precision, driving the rebels with great loss.

Honorable mention should be made of First Lieut. A. S. Sheldon, Battery B, First New York Artillery, wounded on the afternoon of July 3; of Capt. W. A. Arnold, commanding Battery A, First Rhode Island Light Artillery, who, after gallantly fighting his own battery and saving it, also withdrew the battery of A, Fourth U. S. Artillery, Cushing and Milne having fallen; of Second Lieuts. Tully McCrea and John Egan, First U. S. Artillery, for their distinguished coolness and bravery, and of First Lieut. R. E. Rogers, First New York Artillery, upon whom the command of Battery B, First New York Artillery, finally devolved.

Special mention is made of First Sergt. Frederick Fuger, of Battery A, Fourth U. S. Artillery, for his bravery during the battle, especially exhibited when all his officers had fallen, and he, in the heat of the fire, was obliged to assume command of the company. He is most earnestly recommended for promotion, having proved himself a brave soldier and a modest but competent officer.

I beg leave to call particular attention to First Lieut. G. L. Dwight, ordnance officer and acting adjutant of the brigade, for the untiring energy displayed in supplying the brigade with ammunition, and the efficient service rendered in the field.   Reposing the utmost confidence in this officer's abilities, I most respectfully recommend him for promotion.

JNO. G. HAZARD,
Capt. First Rhode Island Light Artillery, Comdg. Brigade.

Lieut. Col. C. H. MORGAN,
Chief of Staff, Second Army Corps.

No. 133.

Reports of Maj. Gen. David B. Birney, U. S. Army, commanding First Division of, and Third Army Corps.

HDQRS. BIRNEY'S DIVISION, THIRD CORPS, *August* 7, 1863.

COLONEL : I have the honor to submit the following report of the movements and actions of this division from June 28 to July 3, during which time it was under my command:

On the morning of June 28, the Third Corps, under my command, marched from Middletown, Md., to Frederick, at which place Major-General Sickles reported for duty and relieved me from the command of the corps. I resumed command of this division, and marched to Walkersville, on the road to Taneytown, and bivouacked beyond the town.

On June 30, it remained in bivouac until 3 p. m., and I then received orders to proceed immediately to Emmitsburg. Under orders from Major-General Sickles, the command bivouacked within 1½ miles of the town.

On the morning of July 1, the division took position beyond Emmitsburg, toward Gettysburg, covering the road from Fairfield and Gettysburg.

During the afternoon of the same day, at 2 o'clock, I was ordered by Major-General Sickles to proceed immediately to Gettysburg with my First and Second Brigades and three batteries, reporting to Major-General Howard, then engaged with the enemy. The Third Brigade, Colonel De Trobriand, was left in position at Emmitsburg, covering the road referred to and as a protection to the corps trains.

My command reached Gettysburg at 5.30 p. m., marching with enthusiasm and alacrity over the road, rendered almost impassable by mud and the passage over it of the First and Eleventh Corps through the rain.

On the morning of July 2, about 9 o'clock, the Third Brigade, Colonel De Trobriand, relieved by orders of the commanding general, rejoined the division.

At 7 a. m., under orders from Major-General Sickles, I relieved Geary's division, and formed a line, resting its left on the Sugar Loaf Mountain and the right thrown in a direct line toward the cemetery, connecting on the right with the Second Division of this corps. My picket line was in the Emmitsburg road, with sharpshooters some 300 yards in advance.

At 12 m., believing from the constant fire of the enemy that a movement was being made toward the left, I received permission from Major-General Sickles to send 100 of Berdan's Sharpshooters, with the Third Maine Regiment as a support, and feel the enemy's right. I sent Capt. J. C. Briscoe, of my staff, with the reconnaissance, which was under Colonel Berdan's command. They advanced from the peach orchard out the Millerstown road, and entered the woods in order to flank the enemy. The skirmishers of the enemy were driven in, but three columns of their forces were found marching to our left. The force sent by me was driven back by overwhelming numbers, with the loss of about 60, killed and wounded.

Communicating this important information to Major-General Sickles, I was ordered by that officer to change my front to meet the attack. I did this by advancing my left 500 yards, and swinging around the right so as to rest on the Emmitsburg road at the peach orchard. He also informed me that a division from the Second and one from the Fifth Corps had been ordered to be in readiness to support me.

My line was formed with Ward on the left, resting on the mountain, De Trobriand in the center, and Graham on my right in the peach orchard, with his right on the Emmitsburg road. Smith's battery of rifled guns was placed so as to command the gorge at the base of the Sugar Loaf Mountain; Winslow's battery on the right of Ward's brigade, and a battery from the Artillery Reserve; also Clark's and Ames' batteries to the right, in rear of the peach orchard, supported by Graham's brigade, and the Third Michigan, from the Third Brigade, and the Third Maine, from the Second Brigade. Randolph's, Seeley's, and Turnbull's batteries were placed near the Emmitsburg road, on the front, parallel with it. I immediately sent an aide to Major-General Sykes asking for the division promised to support my left. I now opened (say at 3.30 p. m.) with Clark's and Smith's batteries upon the columns of the enemy moving toward our left, parallel with the Emmitsburg road.

At 4 o'clock the enemy returned the artillery fire on my entire front, and advanced their infantry *en masse*, covered by a cloud of skirmishers. Major-General Sykes reached my left opportunely, and protected that flank. A portion of his command, under General Barnes, had been placed in rear of the right of De Trobriand's brigade, but during the fight he withdrew his force, and formed some 300 yards farther in the rear.

As the fight was now furious, and my thin line reached from Sugar Loaf Hill to the Emmitsburg road, fully a mile in length, I was obliged to send for more re-enforcements to Major-General Sickles, and Major Tremain, aide-de-camp to the commanding general, soon appeared with a brigade of the Second Corps, which behaved most handsomely, and, leading them forward, it soon restored the center of my line, and we drove the enemy from that point, to fall with redoubled force on Ward's brigade. My thin lines swayed to and fro during the fight, and my regiments were moved constantly on the double-quick from one part of the line to the other, to re-enforce assailed points.

I cannot estimate too highly the services of the regiments from Burling's brigade, Second Division (the Fifth, Sixth, and Seventh New Jersey Volunteers and Second New Hampshire). These regiments were sent to me during the contest, and most gallantly did they sustain the glorious reputation won by them in former battles.

Graham's brigade was subjected at the point of the angle of the line on the Emmitsburg road to a fearful artillery fire, enfilading his line, but this brigade, with the assistance of the Third Maine, from the Second Brigade, and the Third Michigan, from the Third Brigade of this division, held the peach orchard until nearly dusk, when, finding the right unsupported, it fell back to the next ridge.

At 6 o'clock I found Major-General Sickles seriously wounded, and, at his request, took command of the troops. I immediately visited Humphreys' division, and, finding that the enemy, advancing through a gap in the line of my division, would take it in reverse, I ordered a change of front. General Humphreys accomplished this promptly under a most effective artillery and musketry fire, and, advancing his division rapidly, recaptured several batteries that the enemy had temporary possession of.

Major-General Hancock reached me about 7.30 o'clock with a brigade of fresh troops, and, at his request, I assigned them a position. My division was relieved from the front line by the Second and Fifth Corps toward dusk.

The annexed tables of casualties show the nature of the engagement and its terrific character.* Several of my regiments lost more than 50 per cent. of their number and almost every officer engaged. One regiment, the One hundred and forty-first Pennsylvania Volunteers, Colonel Madill, lost, out of 200 taken into the fight, 149 men and officers killed and wounded.

Accompanying this report I send those of the brigade and regimental commanders, which give in detail the movements of their commands. Every regiment of my command did its whole duty, and officers vied with each other in honorable emulation to repel the masses that were hurled on my small division for three hours.

The batteries were well handled, and I have no report of any guns being lost, as, in retiring, we hauled the disabled pieces from the field.

The First Brigade, composed of Pennsylvania regiments, commanded by Brig. Gen. C. K. Graham, tried with its skeleton ranks to even outdo Chancellorsville. General Graham was wounded and fell into the hands of the enemy, with Lieutenant-Colonel Cavada, of the One hundred and fourteenth Pennsylvania Volunteers, and Major Neeper, of the Fifty-seventh Pennsylvania Volunteers. The Fifty-seventh Pennsylvania Volunteers, Colonel Sides; Sixty-third Pennsylvania Volunteers, Major Danks; Sixty-eighth Pennsylvania Volunteers, Colonel Tippin; One hundred and fifth Pennsylvania Volunteers, Colonel Craig; One hundred and fourteenth Pennsylvania Volunteers, Lieutenant-Colonel Cavada, and the One hundred and forty-first Pennsylvania Volunteers, Colonel Madill, composed this brigade, and have made its reputation equal to any in this army. General Graham showed the same coolness, daring, and endurance under the terrible fire that distinguished him at Chancellorsville.

The Second Brigade, Brigadier-General Ward, held also a post of great honor and importance, and fully sustained its old reputation. The First U. S. Sharpshooters, Colonel Berdan, and Second U. S. Sharpshooters, Major Stoughton; Third Maine, Colonel Lakeman; Fourth Maine, Colonel Walker; Twentieth Indiana, Colonel Wheeler; Ninety-ninth Pennsylvania, Major Moore; One hundred and twenty-fourth New York, Colonel Ellis, and Eighty-sixth New York, Lieutenant-Colonel Higgins, composed this brigade.

Colonel Walker, who had so distinguished himself on the Peninsula and at Manassas, Chantilly, Fredericksburg, and Chancellorsville, was seriously wounded; and those gallant officers, Colonels Ellis and Wheeler, fell, dead, with their crowns to the foe, at the head of their regiments. I am indebted to Brigadier-General Ward for his cordial co-operation.

The Third Brigade, Colonel De Trobriand commanding, held the center of my line. The Fortieth New York, Col. T. W. Egan; Third Michigan, Colonel Pierce; Fifth Michigan, Lieutenant-Colonel Pulford; Seventeenth Maine, Lieutenant-Colonel Merrill; and One hundred and tenth Pennsylvania, Lieut. Col. D. M. Jones, composed this brigade.

Colonel De Trobriand deserves my heartiest thanks for his skillful disposition of his command by gallantly holding his advanced position until relieved by other troops. This officer is one of the oldest

---

*Embodied in revised statement, p. 177.

in commission as colonel in the volunteer service; has been distinguished in nearly every engagement of the Army of the Potomac, and certainly deserves the rank of brigadier-general of volunteers, to which he has been recommended.

The Fortieth Regiment New York Volunteers, Colonel Egan, was sent by me, under charge of Captain Briscoe, aide-de-camp, to strengthen General Ward's line, and, led by its gallant, dashing colonel, charged the enemy and drove him back from his advanced point, and poured the most terrific fire into his ranks. This regiment is composed of the old Fortieth, and gallant men from the Eighty-seventh, One hundred and first, Thirty-eighth, and Fifty-fifth New York consolidated with it, making a glorious unit.

The Seventeenth Maine Regiment, Lieutenant-Colonel Merrill, was driven back from its position by overwhelming force, but, responding to my personal appeal, again charged the enemy across the small wheat-field, and retook their position. This regiment behaved most gallantly, and evinced a high state of discipline. Their enthusiasm was cheering, and the assistance rendered by its charge most important.

I have already mentioned the valuable aid rendered to me by the command of Colonel Burling, commanding the Third Brigade of the Second Division. This officer and his gallant old regiments never did better service at a better time.

I annex a map, showing the position of my troops and the batteries supported by us.*

In a special report to be made under paragraph 743, Revised Regulations, I will mention those officers and soldiers deserving special mention.

Colonel Berdan, of the Sharpshooters, and Captain Briscoe, of my staff, deserve mention for their services in leading the reconnaissance before the battle, and for the valuable information derived from it.

The two regiments of sharpshooters, under Colonel Berdan and Major Stoughton, were of the most essential service in covering my front with a cloud of sharpshooters, and pouring a constant and galling fire into the enemy's line of skirmishers.

All of the members of my staff were efficient and ready with their services in the field.

During July 3, this division, under command of General Ward, was held in reserve, and during the heavy artillery fire of that day was brought up under it to support General Newton's line. The enemy were, however, repulsed without its assistance.

Annexed is a list of casualties† and map alluded to in my report.

I am, your obedient servant,

D. B. BIRNEY,
Major-General, U. S. Vols., Comdg. Division.

Lieut. Col. O. H. HART, *A. A. G., Third Corps.*

—

HEADQUARTERS THIRD ARMY CORPS,
In the Field, July 4, 1863.

GENERAL: In compliance with a circular from headquarters Army of Potomac, of this date, I have the honor to report as follows:

A portion of the First Division, with Colonel Eustis' brigade, of the Sixth Corps, is on the front line, on the left of the Second Corps.

---

*See p. 486.   † Embodied in revised statement, p. 177.

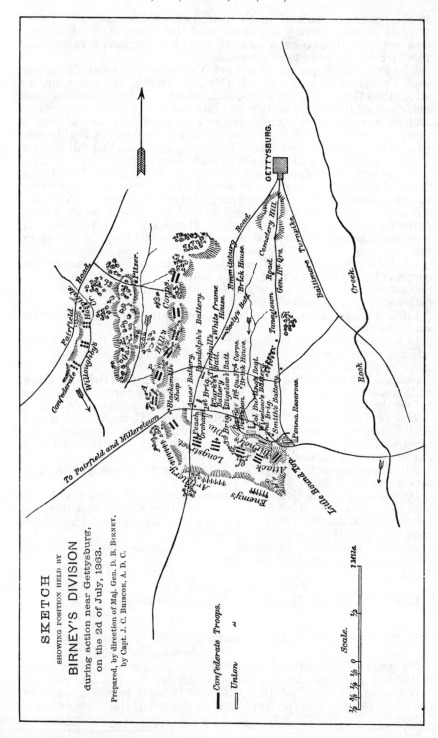

SKETCH

SHOWING POSITION HELD BY

BIRNEY'S DIVISION

during action near Gettysburg,
on the 2d of July, 1863.

Prepared, by direction of Maj. Gen. D. B. Birney,
by Capt. J. C. Briscoe, A. D. C.

Confederate Troops.

Union

Scale.   1 Mile.

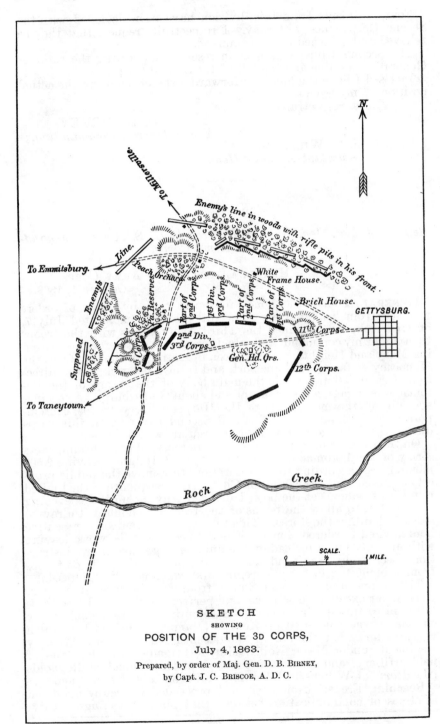

SKETCH
SHOWING
POSITION OF THE 3D CORPS,
July 4, 1863.
Prepared, by order of Maj. Gen. D. B. BIRNEY,
by Capt. J. C. BRISCOE, A. D. C.

Four regiments from this division have been detached with the Second Corps since yesterday. I respectfully request that they be relieved and returned to my command.

The Second Division is held in reserve, supporting the right of General Sykes' line and the left of the Second Corps.

Inclosed I have the honor to forward a sketch showing the actual position of my troops.*

Yours, respectfully,

D. B. BIRNEY,
Major-General, Commanding.

Brig. Gen. S. WILLIAMS,
  Assistant Adjutant-General.

No. 134.

Reports of Maj. Gen. William H. French, U. S. Army, commanding Third Army Corps.

HEADQUARTERS THIRD ARMY CORPS,
October 1, 1863.

GENERAL: I have the honor to report that, by virtue of orders received from headquarters Army of the Potomac, dated July 7, at Frederick, Md., I joined the Third Army Corps with the troops then under my command, and which were part of the force garrisoning Maryland Heights, and had been operating on the line from the Monocacy as far as Williamsport, and from Frederick in the direction of Emmitsburg, while the main body of the Army of the Potomac was engaging the enemy at and about Gettysburg. A succinct account of the movements of the Harper's Ferry troops, contemporary with those of the First and Second Divisions of this corps during the dates called for by your circular, will be given.

On the evening of June 28, orders were received from headquarters Army of the Potomac to evacuate Maryland Heights, leaving 2,500 men, or less, according to my discretion, to remove the public property and escort it to Washington City. In consequence of the limited number of wagons at the post, I delayed leaving until the evening of the 29th, to allow the teams of the troops I should withdraw to assist in hauling the stores. This they did for seventeen consecutive hours, when I ordered General Elliott to continue the work, leaving with him 4,000 men instead of the number suggested in my instructions, because his command (about 2,500, composed chiefly of troops from Winchester, in parts of regiments) was much disorganized.

The troops under Colonel Smith, from Martinsburg, 1,500 men, were under excellent discipline, and perfectly reliable. I left these latter also, anticipating their soon rejoining. Thus detached, my command was composed of Kenly's (Maryland) brigade, to which was attached a battalion of the Fourteenth Massachusetts Artillery Regiment, under Major Rolfe; Morris' brigade, three batteries of field artillery, and about 900 cavalry, under Colonel McReynolds (the *débris* of Winchester), being, of all arms, about 7,000 men.

Reaching Frederick on June 30, I proceeded to occupy points on the lines of communication between that place, Washington City,

*See p. 487.

Baltimore, and the headquarters of the army, with posts of observation toward Williamsport, Emmitsburg, and Harper's Ferry.

As soon as I heard the cannon at Gettysburg on July 3, the dispositions of the troops were changed from a passive to an active state. I directed a detachment of cavalry to be sent by Colonel McReynolds to Falling Waters, to reconnoiter for a pontoon bridge, said to be there, and to destroy it. This expedition, under Major Foley, Fourteenth Pennsylvania Cavalry, was executed with great judgment and perfect success. The report of that officer is appended.* Following on this, I sent Morris' brigade, a battery of artillery, and a detachment of cavalry, in all about 4,000 strong, to advance as far as South Mountain and Crampton's Pass, which to occupy and hold. One regiment of the Maryland Brigade was posted on the Emmitsburg road, with a detachment of cavalry at the latter place.

On July 5, another expedition was sent to Harper's Ferry, where the enemy had floored the railroad bridge, and was crossing the river in small detachments. Under the direction of Major [H. A.] Cole, the trestle-work on each side of the bridge was destroyed; also the bridge over the canal.

On the 6th, I was ordered to reoccupy with a portion of my command Maryland Heights. Kenly's brigade was detached for that purpose, and subsequently Briggs' brigade, and afterward, on the 7th, the brigade of Naglee. The Seventh New York City Guards, under Colonel Lefferts, I directed to garrison the city of Frederick, appointing that officer military governor.

The troops which had been left at Harper's Ferry rejoined my command on this date, under Brigadier-General Elliott. With these and General Morris' brigade, and the three batteries of artillery, I joined the Third Corps, and assumed command on July 9. The cavalry was directed to report to the chief of that arm.

The Third Corps in the movements toward and in the vicinity of Williamsport, on July 10, 11, 12, and 13, was held in reserve, but after the army assembled at Harper's Ferry it took the advance in the passage of the Potomac and in the marches, preceding the entrance of Manassas Gap, through Hillsborough, Woodgrove, Upperville, and Piedmont, at which places it bivouacked after a day's march.

At Upperville, on the evening of July 22, I was ordered to move upon Manassas Gap, to hold two divisions at Piedmont, and send forward a third to re-enforce Brigadier-General Buford, who had been directed to seize the Gap. The First Division, under Brigadier-General Ward, arrived at Linden Station, in the Gap, at 11 p. m., and, in conjunction with the cavalry, took possession of the Gap.

The Second and Third Divisions pushed forward at early daylight on the 23d, the head of column arriving at Linden about 9 a. m. The cavalry had been relieved at that time by General Ward, whom I directed to send out a small battalion of skirmishers to feel the enemy and to compel him to show his pickets on the heights as well as in the ravines.

In the meantime a line of skirmishers was deployed from the right to the left in the Gap, covering the whole front; the ridge roads were covered by artillery and infantry, and my flanks and rear as well guarded as the rugged nature of the country permitted. These dis-

---

* Not found.

positions were followed by the massing of the Second and Third Divisions to follow the First Division, deployed in line of battle, when the advance was ordered of my entire force. The skirmishers met the enemy at various points of its extended line, and steadily drove them until the entire line of heights had been carried, which was done in a most dashing style under the personal direction of Brigadier-General Ward.

The enemy was now reported as forming his line of battle near the Chester Gap road and to the left of the Pass. Continuous columns of cavalry, infantry, artillery, and baggage-wagons were seen during the day moving from the direction of Winchester toward Strasburg, Luray, and Front Royal, the force in front of us being evidently a large flank guard to delay our advance.

The First Division was formed in line of battle, supported by the Second, and the Third Division held in reserve. The enemy had rallied his skirmishers in his front and behind the slopes which descend from Wapping Heights, carried by Ward's division. I sent an order to General Prince by Lieutenant-Colonel Hayden, chief of staff, to send a brigade to penetrate the ravine in front and cut the enemy's line, and to drive them away.

The Excelsior Brigade was selected to carry out my orders, and moved rapidly to execute them. Descending the precipitous slopes of Wapping Heights, they were directed upon the valley which separated the series of knolls in our front, behind the principal of which the enemy, perceiving the object of the movement, concentrated. The brigade was at once deployed at the base of the knoll, and advanced upon the enemy. Halting for a moment upon the crest of the hill, the line rushed upon the enemy with the bayonet, giving cheer after cheer, and driving him back in confusion out of the Gap.

Nothing could be more brilliant than the conduct of the officers and men in this affair, evidencing fighting qualities of the highest order.

Brigadier-General Spinola, who led and commanded the brigade, was twice wounded. After the front had been entirely cleared, the other brigades of the Second Division moved down in rear of the Excelsior, which, being taken for a threat upon the road to Front Royal by the enemy, a few random shots from two rifled guns near the road were sent into our lines at a great range. It was now almost nightfall, and the men, exhausted by a long and arduous march and spirited attack, were permitted to lie on their arms. The list of casualties in this affair is attached to this report.

On the following morning, the Second Division pickets being pushed out, it was discovered that the enemy had withdrawn in the night. That division was sent to Front Royal with a battery, but finding no enemy in force, it was directed to return, and the march was resumed to Warrenton, near which town the corps went into camp. The reports of division and subordinate commanders, herewith inclosed, set forth more in detail the circumstances of the marches and bivouacs of their several commands.

The soldierlike spirit which entered into the performance of the duties of these troops, whether in contact with the enemy or while advancing to meet him, is worthy of the highest commendation.

To my staff (administrative)—Lieut. Col. George H. Wood, chief commissary of subsistence; Capt. A. Judson Clark, acting chief of artillery; Lieut. Col. J. B. Howard, chief quartermaster; Capt. B. W. Hoxie, acting chief ordnance officer, and Capt. Amos Webster, chief ambulance officer—I was indebted for the energy which was displayed in their respective departments.

Acting Medical Director [James T.] Calhoun established his hospital and removed the wounded under the most difficult circumstances, but with great professional ability and success.

To Lieutenant-Colonel [Julius] Hayden, chief of staff, who was untiring in his duties, assisted by Major [Samuel B.] Hayman, commissary of musters, my especial thanks are due. I desire particularly to mention them to the general commanding the Army of the Potomac.

My personal staff was zealous as always. I would also mention Cadet [George G.] Greenough, acting aide-de-camp, who conveyed my orders with precision and exhibited great coolness under fire.

List of casualties at Wapping Heights is herewith inclosed.

The loss of the enemy on that occasion was estimated at 250 killed and wounded, and the same number of prisoners.

I am, general, very respectfully, your obedient servant,

WM. H. FRENCH,
Major-General, Commanding.

Brig. Gen. S. WILLIAMS,
Asst. Adjt. Gen., Hdqrs. Army of the Potomac.

[Inclosure.]

Recapitulation of casualties at Wapping Heights.

Command.	Killed.		Wounded.		Total.		Aggregate.
	Officers.	Enlisted men.	Officers.	Enlisted men.	Officers	Enlisted men.	
General officers			1	......	1	......	1
First Division....................................		2	1	21	1	23	24
Second Division	3	16	1	60	4	76	80
Total	3	18	3	81	6	99	105

HEADQUARTERS THIRD ARMY CORPS,
July 9, 1863.

GENERAL: I have the honor to report that the details from this corps have buried the following number of dead on the battle-field of Gettysburg, July 4 and 5:

Command.	Federal.		Confederate.	
	Officers.	Enlisted men.	Officers.	Enlisted men.
Buried on the 4th:				
First Division....................................	7	275	19	113
Second Division.................................	1	32	3	141
Total.............	8	307	22	254

	Federal.		Confederate.	
Command.	Officers.	Enlisted men.	Officers.	Enlisted men.
Buried on the 5th:				
First Division..	7	285	29	143
Second Division...	6	178	......	235
Total..	13	463	29	378
Grand total...	21	770	51	632

I am, very respectfully, your obedient servant,

WM. H. FRENCH,
Major-General, Commanding.

Brig. Gen. S. WILLIAMS,
Asst. Adjt. Gen., Army of the Potomac.

—

HEADQUARTERS THIRD ARMY CORPS,
August 16, 1863.

GENERAL: I have the honor to report, in compliance with circular from headquarters Army of the Potomac, dated August 14, 1863, the following list of re-enforcements which joined this command between the 7th and 14th of July, which composes the Third Division:

First Brigade.—Fourteenth New Jersey Volunteers, Tenth Vermont Volunteers, Sixth New York Artillery, and One hundred and fifty-first New York Volunteers.

Second Brigade.—One hundred and tenth Ohio Volunteers, One hundred and twenty-second Ohio Volunteers, One hundred and thirty-eighth Pennsylvania Volunteers, and Sixth Maryland Volunteers.

Third Brigade.—One hundred and twenty-sixth Ohio Volunteers, One hundred and sixth New York Volunteers, Eighty-seventh Pennsylvania Volunteers, and Sixty-seventh Pennsylvania Volunteers.

Very respectfully, your obedient servant,

WM. H. FRENCH,
Major-General, Commanding.

Brig. Gen. S. WILLIAMS,
Asst. Adjt. Gen., Army of the Potomac.

—

HEADQUARTERS THIRD ARMY CORPS,
September 13, 1863.

GENERAL: In compliance with Special Orders, No. 227, headquarters Army of the Potomac, dated August 24, 1863, I have the honor to report that no guns were lost in this corps, with the exception of three Parrott guns of the Fourth New York Independent Battery, during the engagement of July 2; also that no guns were taken from the enemy by this command during the recent operations in Pennsylvania and Maryland.

I am, general, very respectfully, your obedient servant,

WM. H. FRENCH,
Major-General, Commanding.

Brig. Gen. S. WILLIAMS,
Asst. Adjt. Gen., Army of the Potomac.

No. 135.

Reports of Brig. Gen. J. H. Hobart Ward, U. S. Army, com-
manding Second Brigade and First Division.

HDQRS. SECOND BRIG., FIRST DIV.; THIRD CORPS,
August 4, 1863.

CAPTAIN: I have the honor to transmit a report of the action and movements of my brigade on July 1, 2, 3, and 4.

This brigade with the other brigades of the division arrived at Emmitsburg, Md., on July 1, at 3 p. m., and, while making dispositions for bivouacking for the night, received orders to proceed to Gettysburg, 10 miles distant, to support the First and Eleventh Corps, then engaged with the enemy. The command arrived at Gettysburg about dark by a forced march over horrible roads, and bivouacked for the night.

On the morning of the 2d, by direction of Major-General Birney, the brigade took a temporary position about 1 mile in rear of the Emmitsburg road, which was subsequently changed to a position at right angles with the Emmitsburg road, the left resting on a rocky eminence near Round Top or Sugar Loaf hill, that being the extreme left of the army. Previous to this the two regiments of sharpshooters and the Third Maine Regiment, all under command of Colonel Berdan, were detached to make a reconnaissance. Colonel Berdan's report is hereto annexed.

After placing my brigade in the position assigned, Major Stoughton, of the Second U. S. Sharpshooters, reported to me with his command. I directed him to advance his command as skirmishers across the field in front of mine for half a mile and await further orders. They had scarcely obtained the position designated before the skirmishers of the enemy issued from a wood in front, followed by heavy lines of infantry. Captain Smith's battery of rifled guns, posted on the eminence on my left, opened on the advancing enemy, as well as Captain Winslow's battery on my right, the enemy replying from a battery near the Emmitsburg road. The supports of the first two lines of the enemy were now coming up in columns *en masse*, while we had but a single line of battle to receive the shock. Our skirmishers were now forced to draw back. My line awaited the clash. To the regiments on the right, who were sheltered in a wood, I gave directions not to fire until they could plainly see the enemy; to those who were on the left, not to fire at a longer distance than 200 yards.

The enemy had now approached to within 200 yards of my position, in line and *en masse*, yelling and shouting. My command did not fire a shot until the enemy came within the distance prescribed, when the whole command fired a volley. This checked the enemy's advance suddenly, which gave our men an opportunity to reload, when another volley was fired into them. The enemy now exhibited much disorder, and, taking advantage of this circumstance, I advanced my right and center with a view of obtaining a position behind a stone wall, about 160 yards in advance, and which the enemy was endeavoring to reach. While advancing, the rear columns of the enemy pressed forward to the support of the advance, who rallied and again advanced. This time our single line was forced back a short distance by the heavy columns of the enemy. In this manner for the space of one and a half hours did we advance and retire, both parties endeavoring to gain possession of the stone wall.

In the meantime I had sent to General Birney for re-enforcements, who directed Colonel Egan, with the Fortieth New York, to report. The enemy now concentrated his force on our extreme left, with the intention to turn our left flank through a gorge between my left and Sugar Loaf hill. The Fortieth New York was dispatched to cover the gorge, which they did most effectually. Our men, now much exhausted and nearly destitute of ammunition, were relieved by a portion of the Second and Fifth Corps, when we retired and bivouacked for the night.

The unfortunate accident to Major-General Sickles placed me in command of the division. The action of the brigade on the succeeding day will be included in the report of Colonel Berdan, who succeeded me in command.

This brigade, with the exception of Antietam, has been engaged in every battle fought by the Army of the Potomac, and has been frequently mentioned for its gallantry, but on this occasion it eclipsed all its former actions. The immense force opposed to them was at one time almost overwhelming. The number of effective men in the brigade when they engaged the enemy was not 1,500, while the loss is nearly 800. Out of 14 field officers, we lost 8.

The Third and Fourth Maine, Twentieth Indiana, and Ninety-ninth Pennsylvania Volunteers, the veterans of this brigade, to their world-wide reputation have added new laurels, and, if possible, excelled themselves. The First and Second U. S. Sharpshooters and the Eighty-sixth and One hundred and twenty-fourth New York Volunteers, recently assigned to this brigade, have richly earned the title to wear the "Kearny patch."

The Twentieth Indiana lost its colonel (shot through the head), than whom a more gallant soldier and efficient officer did not exist. The great State of Indiana may well feel proud of John Wheeler, the hero, the patriot, and the honest man. He was worthy to command the glorious Twentieth, and his command was proud of him.

The One hundred and Twenty-fourth New York lost its colonel and major (both shot through the head). Col. A. Van Horne Ellis was one of those dashing and chivalrous spirits that we frequently read of, but seldom encounter in real life. He fell while gallantly leading his men in a charge. In this he was ably seconded by Lieutenant-Colonel Cummins and Major Cromwell, the major falling within a few seconds of the colonel, and the lieutenant-colonel being severely wounded.

Colonel Walker, of the Fourth Maine, was severely wounded in the leg, but refused to leave the field until his regiment retired.

Lieutenant-Colonel Higgins, Eighty-sixth New York Volunteers, was also severely wounded side by side with the colonel of the One hundred and twenty-fourth New York Volunteers.

Major Lee, Third Maine, and Major Whitcomb, Fourth Maine, were also severely wounded in the various actions of their regiments.

To the officers and men of my command, without exception, my thanks and the thanks of the country are eminently due. For nearly two hours my brigade was opposed to at least 10,000 of the enemy, in line and *en masse*.

Besides the killed and wounded mentioned, I would particularly call the attention of the major-general commanding to the gallant conduct of Colonel Berdan, U. S. Sharpshooters; Colonel Lakeman, Third Maine; Lieutenant-Colonel Taylor, Twentieth Indiana; Major Moore, Ninety-ninth Pennsylvania Volunteers; Major Stoughton,

Second U. S. Sharpshooters, and Major Lansing, Eighty-sixth New York, who vied with each other in doing their whole duty.

It would afford me much gratification to speak of others in the terms they deserve, but space will not permit. I would respectfully refer to the regimental reports for a detailed statement of the particular deeds of many other gallant officers. I cannot omit, however, the names of a few gallant non-commissioned officers, viz: Sergt. Henry O. Ripley, color sergeant, Fourth Maine, Sergt. H. M. Munsell, Ninety-ninth Pennsylvania Volunteers, and Sergt. Maj. William B. Van Houten, One hundred and twenty-fourth New York, who, by their bravery and example, inspired all in their vicinity. It is to be hoped that a suitable reward, by promotion and otherwise, will be awarded these splendid soldiers.

I cannot close this report with justice to myself without mentioning the able, efficient, and gallant services of my staff, who were unremitting in their exertions in forming the men for action, and encouraging by example when engaged: Capt. J. M. Cooney, assistant adjutant-general; Capt. G. W. Meikel, Twentieth Indiana, acting assistant inspector-general, and Lieuts. S. J. Leigh and A. M. Raphall, aides-de-camp. I also regret to say that Lieutenant Raphall was so severely wounded as to require the amputation of his right arm.

The total loss in my brigade was 46 officers and 712 enlisted men.

To Dr. Orpheus Everts, Twentieth Indiana, acting brigade surgeon, the thanks of the many sufferers in this command are tendered for his undivided attention to their wants and comfort.

I herewith transmit official reports of regimental commanders.

The valuable service rendered by Col. T. W. Egan, Lieutenant-Colonel Merrill, and their noble regiments (Fortieth New York and Seventeenth Maine) at an opportune moment cannot be overestimated. Their steadiness and valor were not unknown to me, having had the honor to command them on other occasions. They came to me at the right time, were put in the right place, and well did they perform the duty assigned them.

Respectfully submitted.

J. H. HOBART WARD,
Brigadier-General.

Capt. W. F. A. Torbert,
　Actg. Asst. Adjt. Gen., Third Army Corps.

—

Hdqrs. First Division, Third Army Corps,
July 27, 1863.

Sir: In compliance with circular from headquarters Third Corps, of July 27, 1863, I have the honor to report the operations of this division on July 22, 23, 24, and 25.

On July 22, this division, with Fourth Maine and Keystone Batteries, left Upperville at 2 p. m. in advance of the corps, *en route* for Piedmont. On arriving at that point, instructions were received from Major-General French that this division would proceed to Manassas Gap, and support General Buford, who anticipated an attack.

Putting the troops in motion, I dispatched a staff officer to General Buford to report. On his return, he informed me that General Buford had left, but that General Merritt, with one brigade of cavalry, held the Gap, and was anxious for the arrival of supports, as he expected an attack the next morning. I pushed on to Petersburg, 8 miles from Piedmont, and bivouacked between 11 and 12 p. m. about 1½ miles from the cavalry.

On the morning of the 23d, the command joined the cavalry between 4 and 5 a. m. After an interview with General Merritt, he informed me that he had directions to move to another position. I immediately took measures to relieve his command and outposts, placing the batteries in position to command the Gap, and awaited further orders, in the meantime sending scouts to the front, to ascertain the position of the enemy.

About 10 a. m. General French, with the balance of the corps, arrived. In the meantime the scouts had reported the enemy's pickets on the hills at the entrance of the Gap. General French now ordered my command forward. We advanced to within a short distance of the base of the several hills on which the enemy was established. I immediately sent forward skirmishers with heavy supports, covering in extent the surface of a mile, many regiments of the command being detached on picket and in support of batteries within the Gap.

Dispositions having been made, the whole force now advanced together, steadily but surely driving the enemy from his positions until all the hills were in our possession. The enemy retreated, and took position in the valley beyond, on the road leading from the Gap to Front Royal. I ordered a portion of the First and Third Brigades forward, to support the skirmishers and drive the enemy out. This order was countermanded, and the Second Brigade, Second Division, was ordered to report to me for that purpose, and the First and Third Brigades were dispatched to the extreme left of my position, to cover that flank. The enemy could now plainly be seen in three heavy columns, moving southward by the flank.

General Spinola, commanding Second Brigade, Second Division, reported to me through one of his staff officers. The general being my senior, I did not presume to give him orders, but made such suggestions to the general as I deemed necessary under the circumstances, but which he entirely approved and adopted, forming his troops in a ravine in front of the enemy's position, and charging them in magnificent style, driving them from the field in confusion, the major-general commanding the corps witnessing the whole operation. In this charge General Spinola was twice wounded.

I now received orders, in consequence of the lateness of the hour, to cease operations and make dispositions for the night.

On the morning of the 24th, the Second Division having been ordered forward to Front Royal on a reconnaissance, this division was ordered to its support. The Second Division advancing to the town with but slight opposition, the active service of this division was not required. The division then returned to Piedmont, and, after two days' march, arrived at Warrenton, and is now stationed in advance of the corps.

In conclusion, I have to state that the whole division sustained its already well-earned reputation; no retrograding from commencement to end. I herewith transmit list of casualties in this division.*

I am, captain, very respectfully, your obedient servant,

J. H. HOBART WARD,
Brigadier-General.

Capt. W. F. A. Torbert,
    Actg. Asst. Adjt. Gen., Third Army Corps.

---

*Embodied in revised statement, p. 192.

No. 136.

Report of Capt. Alanson H. Nelson, Fifty-seventh Pennsylvania Infantry, First Brigade.

CAMP IN THE FIELD,
July 10, 1863.

SIR: I have the honor to report the following as the part the Fifty-seventh Pennsylvania Volunteers took in the late engagement at Gettysburg, Pa.:

About 2 p. m. of the 1st instant, we broke camp near Emmitsburg, and marched to a point near Gettysburg; formed in column by regiments about half a mile in rear of the battle-field, where we bivouacked for the night.

The next morning we advanced to the right and rear of the peach orchard, and remained about one hour; then advanced to the front and deployed, taking a position on the right of the One hundred and fourteenth Pennsylvania Volunteers and near the brick house, where we were exposed to a very severe shelling for about two hours, when, at the request of Captain Randolph, we advanced to the brick house and met the enemy in force, who was advancing on us in three lines.

We engaged him about twenty minutes, but, being overpowered by a superior force, we were obliged to fall back, the One hundred and fourteenth Pennsylvania Volunteers having done so already.

We finally reformed in the rear, near the Baltimore pike and a large yellow barn, where we remained until 8 a. m. of the next day (3d instant), when we were ordered to the front as a reserve.

About 3 p. m. on the 3d instant, we were ordered forward with the brigade to support a battery in General Doubleday's division, First Corps, where we remained until dark; then moved to the front, and acted as a picket reserve until the morning of the 4th instant, when we moved to the left and in rear of a line of breastworks, where we remained until ordered on the present march.

We lost in killed, wounded, and missing 115, viz:

Officers and men.	Killed.	Wounded.	Missing.	Total.
Commissioned officers	2	8	3	13
Enlisted men	9	39	54	102
Total	11	47	57	115

All in the command acted well and fought bravely, and where all acted so well it was impossible for one to distinguish himself more than another.

I am, sir, very respectfully, your obedient servant,

A. H. NELSON,
Captain, Commanding Regiment.

ASSISTANT ADJUTANT-GENERAL,
First Brigade, First Division, Third Corps.

No. 137.

Report of Maj. John A. Danks, Sixty-third Pennsylvania Infantry.

HDQRS. SIXTY-THIRD PENNSYLVANIA VOLUNTEERS,
July 10, 1863.

LIEUTENANT: I have the honor to submit the following statement of the actions of the Sixty-third Regiment Pennsylvania Volunteers in the engagement of July 1, 2, and 3:

On Wednesday, July 1, the Sixty-third, with the rest of the brigade, moved from camp in the field near Emmitsburg, Md., to a point near Gettysburg, Pa. From this point the regiment was ordered on picket, and posted on line with the Emmitsburg pike.

On the morning of July 2, the enemy made his appearance in our front, and opened fire on our outposts. Firing was kept up until the general engagement was brought on, between the hours of 3 and 4 p. m.

At 5.30 p. m. the regiment was relieved from the picket line by a regiment of the Second Division, Third Corps. I then withdrew the regiment, our ammunition having been exhausted; fell back in good order, when I met the balance of the brigade, and, after a few minutes' rest, moved forward with the brigade to an open field, where we encamped for the night.

Early on the morning of the 3d, we were again ordered to the front, where we lay in position until 10 a. m., when the enemy attempted to pierce the center of the line. To this point we were ordered to move as rapidly as possible, which the regiment accomplished, and immediately took a position in support of a battery. We were exposed during the day to a severe fire of shot and shell.

Our loss during the 1st, 2d, and 3d was 1 killed, 31 wounded, and 4 missing; total, 36.*

I remain, lieutenant, very respectfully, your obedient servant,

JOHN A. DANKS,
Major, Comdg. Sixty-third Pennsylvania Volunteers.

Lieutenant BENSON,
Acting Assistant Adjutant-General.

No. 138.

Report of Col. Andrew H. Tippin, Sixty-eighth Pennsylvania Infantry.

HDQRS. SIXTY-EIGHTH REGT. PENNSYLVANIA VOLS.,
August 4, 1863.

LIEUTENANT: In compliance with orders from headquarters, of the 27th ultimo, I respectfully submit the following report of the operations of my regiment in the recent engagements at and near Gettysburg:

On the morning of July 2, I moved my regiment with the brigade to the position assigned us in a large open field in the rear of our line of skirmishers, then engaged with the enemy's skirmishers in front. The brigade was deployed in line of battle by battalions, doubled on the center, my regiment being on the left of the line.

After remaining in this position some time, the brigade was moved farther to the front, immediately in rear of Clark's battery, deployed

---

*But see revised statement, p. 177.

in line of battle, and ordered to lie down. We remained in this position nearly two hours, suffering severely from the destructive fire of the enemy's batteries posted on our left and front. I was then ordered to move my regiment forward into a peach orchard, and fronting a road running parallel with the enemy's front. We had been in this position but a short time when significant movements on the part of the enemy made it evident we were about to be attacked. Soon he advanced. I ordered the men to reserve their fire until reaching a certain point, when a destructive fire was opened, the enemy halting and dropping behind a fence. Receiving re-enforcements, and heavy masses of his infantry coming down on our right, I ordered my command to fall back to the position in the rear of the batteries, which was done in good order. Here I met General Graham, who ordered me at once to engage the enemy coming down on our right flank, which was promptly done under his directions.

Here, too, the gallant general was severely wounded and subsequently made prisoner. He declined any assistance, and directed me to take command and fight on. I supposed him able to get to the rear, as, after dismounting, he walked with apparently little difficulty.

We held the position as long as it was possible to hold it. The artillery having retired, and the ranks very much decimated by the fire of the enemy, who was pushing forward in heavy masses, I ordered the command to retire in order, which was done.

I reported to General Ward, now in command of the division, who assigned me a position, with directions to bivouac for the night.

On the morning of the 3d, I was ordered with the brigade to proceed with the division to a field a short distance from the place where we bivouacked, and stack arms. Remaining but a short time, I was ordered to move with the division to the left, where we formed line of battle in the rear, supporting a part of the Fifth Army Corps.

In the afternoon, the brigade again moved with the division to the rear of the center and in support of a battery. We remained here until evening, when I was relieved of the command.

I regret the loss of a great many gallant officers and men of my regiment. The brave Captain McLearn and the no less conspicuous Lieutenants Black and Reynolds all fell close to the enemy while cheering on their men. Lieutenant-Colonel Reynolds, Major Winslow, Captains Funston, Young, and Fulmer, and Lieutenants [John J.] Fenlin, jr., Ealer, Guest, Porter, and Heston, all wounded, bear evidence of their good conduct and gallant behavior. I can also bear testimony to the gallantry of the other officers of the command.

Of the non-commissioned officers and privates of the regiment I cannot speak with too much praise. Their obedience to command and the determined stand made against overwhelming odds, their thinned ranks fully prove. Animated by the glorious cause in which they were engaged, each vied with the other in deeds of gallant daring.

A list of the casualties has already been forwarded. A tabular statement of killed, wounded, and missing is herewith appended.*

Very respectfully, your obedient servant,

A. H. TIPPIN,
Colonel Sixty-eighth Regiment Pennsylvania Volunteers.

Lieut. R. DALE BENSON,
A. A. G., First Brig., First Div., Third Corps.

---

*Embodied in revised statement, p. 177.

No. 139.

Report of Col. Calvin A. Craig, One hundred and fifth Pennsylvania Infantry.

HEADQUARTERS 105TH PENNSYLVANIA VOLUNTEERS,
July 11, 1863.

LIEUTENANT: I have the honor to submit the following report of the part taken by this regiment in the battle of Gettysburg, Pa., from July 1 to 4, inclusive:

On the afternoon of the 1st instant, the regiment moved with the rest of the brigade at 1.15 p. m., with 20 officers and 257 men, from a point about 1 mile east of Emmitsburg, Md., where we had encamped the night previous, and marched to a point about half a mile west of the town and near the Hagerstown road, where we received orders to encamp.

At 4 p. m. the order was countermanded, and we took up the line of march in the direction of Gettysburg, Pa. The march was a very severe one and fatigued the men very much, but the regiment stood the march well, and when the brigade bivouacked for the night 1 mile south of Gettysburg, we had only 3 men who had fallen out of the ranks on the march. These rejoined us during the night.

On the morning of the 2d, we moved with the balance of the brigade a short distance, when line of battle was formed about half a mile east of and parallel with the Emmitsburg road, in which position we remained until 11.15 a. m., when we received orders to move to the front to support the Sixty-third Pennsylvania Volunteers, who were deployed as skirmishers along the Emmitsburg road. My regiment took position immediately in their rear, with Companies A, F, D, I, and C deployed, the other companies in reserve. The fire from the enemy's sharpshooters was severe. One man was killed very soon after we got into position.

At 1 p. m. orders were received from General Graham to rejoin the brigade, and to take position in rear of the Fifty-seventh Pennsylvania Volunteers, and on the right of the One hundred and fourteenth Pennsylvania Volunteers, in column doubled on the center.

The regiment remained in this position until 2 p. m. We then moved forward with the brigade to a point near the brick house on the Emmitsburg road, where we halted and deployed, still maintaining our relative positions, my right resting on a by-road running at right angles with the Emmitsburg road. At this time the enemy opened with his artillery a very destructive fire. My regiment suffered a loss of some 12 men while in this position.

At 4 p. m. we again moved forward near the brick house and immediately in its rear. At this time I noticed the enemy's infantry advancing from the woods on the left of the house and in its rear, and seeing that I could do nothing in the position I then occupied (in the rear of the Fifty-seventh Pennsylvania Volunteers), and that I must necessarily suffer severely, I ordered the regiment forward to fill a vacancy on the right of the Fifty-seventh Pennsylvania Volunteers, in the front line and a little beyond the Emmitsburg road. Having gained this position, the fire from the enemy being very severe, we immediately opened fire.

After occupying this position for a short time, I noticed the regiments on my immediate left (One hundred and fourteenth and Fifty-seventh Pennsylvania Volunteers) cluster in groups behind the brick house and adjacent out-buildings. A few moments later the One hundred and fourteenth fell to the rear, and the Fifty-seventh very soon followed, leaving my left flank entirely unprotected.

The enemy, taking advantage of this, advanced across the Emmitsburg road, in front of the house, and immediately opened fire upon our left flank. Seeing this, I ordered my regiment to retire slowly a short distance, and changed front to the rear on the first company. A small remnant of the Fifty-seventh Pennsylvania Volunteers rallied with us, and formed line along the by-road before mentioned, where we again opened fire, and checked the advancing rebels for a few minutes; but the regiment being so small and both flanks being entirely unprotected, I ordered the regiment to retire slowly, and formed line again a short distance to the rear. The troops in our rear by this time were beginning to be effective, and the brigade having gone to the rear, I formed with these troops, and fought with them, sometimes advancing and sometimes retreating, but do not know whose troops they were.

Soon after, I saw General Humphreys, and formed line with some of his troops. From this point we advanced steadily until we had regained nearly all the ground we had lost. Noticing at this time three pieces of artillery that had been abandoned by our artillerists and turned upon us by the advancing rebels (and who were in turn compelled to abandon them), I sent forward my few remaining men to bring them off the field, but being unable to bring them all off, I got assistance from some men of the Excelsior Brigade with two of the pieces, and brought the third off the field with my own men. I withdrew all my men with this piece, and finally delivered it to Sergt. Daniel A. Whitesell, Battery C, Fifth U. S. Artillery, who identified it as one of the pieces belonging to that battery.

About this time, Captain [Timothy L.] Maynard, of General Graham's staff, came up. I reported to him for orders from General Graham, and was informed that the corps was forming at a certain point. I moved the regiment, but could not find the brigade (it was now quite dark), but formed on the right of the Third Brigade. Soon after, I moved under the direction of Lieutenants Benson and [George W.] Perkins, of General Graham's staff, and joined the brigade, and bivouacked for the night.

The next morning, July 3, we again moved forward with the brigade, and occupied a position in the third line of battle and in the rear of the Fifth Corps, where we remained until about 2 p. m., when we were again ordered with the brigade to the center, our forces there having been attacked, and formed line of battle in the rear of the batteries at that point. We remained in this position until 9 p. m., when the regiment with the brigade moved to the front and formed line of battle on the first line, relieving the Vermont Brigade, of the First Corps. We remained in this position during the night. In the morning, the line was withdrawn and the troops occupying it marched a short distance to the rear. The entire rebel front line had also retired. Several unimportant movements took place during the day, but nothing worthy of note.

The entire loss in the regiment during this time was 1 officer killed, 13 officers wounded, 7 enlisted men killed, 101 enlisted men wounded, and 9 enlisted men missing, making a total of 131 men.*

The regiment never fought better or with more enthusiasm. The

---

* But see revised statement, p. 177.

list of casualties proves with what determination they contested every inch of ground. Fourteen officers out of 17 combatants were either killed or wounded, and 117 men out of 257 were either killed, wounded, or missing, being nearly one-half of the entire number taken into action. No instance of cowardice occurred during the engagements. All seemed to feel that they were fighting on the soil of their native State, and that they would either conquer or yield up their lives in her defense.

I cannot make particular mention of individual bravery. All, both officers and men, seemed imbued with the same spirit, which was one of determination never to yield, but to fight to the bitter end, and until there was not a single rebel in arms to pollute the soil of their native State.

Very respectfully, your obedient servant,

C. A. CRAIG,
Colonel One hundred and fifth Pennsylvania Volunteers.

Lieut. R. Dale Benson,
A. A. A. G., First Brigade, First Division, Third Corps.

No. 140.

Report of Capt. Edward R. Bowen, One hundred and fourteenth Pennsylvania Infantry.

Fox's Gap, South Mountain, Md.,
July 12, 1863.

Sir: I have the honor to submit the following report of the part taken by the One hundred and fourteenth Regiment Pennsylvania Volunteers in the recent operations against the enemy, near Gettysburg, Pa.:

On July 1, the regiment left Emmitsburg, Md., at about 2 p. m., and moved in the direction of Gettysburg, which place we reached at about 7 p. m., and encamped on the south side of the town.

The regiment moved to the front on the morning of the 2d, and at 1 p. m. advanced to the front of the woods and formed with the brigade a line of battle, in columns doubled on the center, to the left and rear of the Fifty-seventh Pennsylvania Volunteers.

Clark's (First New Jersey) battery then took up a position in front, and opened on the enemy. We remained here until ordered to advance with the brigade, maintaining the same position to the Fifty-seventh Pennsylvania Volunteers until we reached an oat-field, where we were ordered to deploy, which we did, the One hundred and fifth Pennsylvania Volunteers being on our right and the Sixty-eighth Pennsylvania Volunteers on our left. At this moment we were ordered to lie down. The enemy then opened on us with his batteries, and for about two and a half hours we lay under a most severe fire, losing, however, but few men, the enemy's range being too high.

Captain Randolph, chief of artillery of the corps, at this moment rode up to the regiment, and ordered us to advance, saying, "If you want to save my battery, move forward. I cannot find the general. I give the order on my own responsibility." We then advanced, passing through his battery, which immediately limbered up and went to the rear, and the regiment, crossing the road, formed a line of battle, our line on the right joining the Fifty-seventh Pennsylvania Volunteers.

Seeing the enemy advancing in force, I ordered the right wing of the regiment to advance to the rear of the brick house, and attempted to form a line with the Fifty-seventh Pennsylvania Volunteers, who were already there. In this I was but partially successful, as the enemy had already advanced so quickly and in such force as to gain the road, and, pouring a murderous fire on our flank, threw the left wing of the regiment on to the right in much confusion. I attempted to rally the regiment across the road, but could not succeed in doing so, the enemy advancing so rapidly and my men falling in such numbers as to prevent my succeeding in doing so. I succeeded, however, in rallying a number around the colors, and brought them off, but, in doing so, got separated from the brigade, and night coming on, I was unable to find them, although I used every effort to do so.

I remained where I was until early daylight of the 3d, when I rejoined the brigade, and we lay all the morning of the 3d in the woods, where we were supplied with rations, and remained until about 3 p. m., when I was ordered to move up to the right by the double-quick, being detached from the brigade to support Cowan's (First New York) battery.

At this time, Colonel Madill, of the One hundred and forty-first Pennsylvania Volunteers, assumed command of the brigade, and I took command of his regiment and my own.

At about 7 p. m. I was ordered to get ready to be relieved, and to send to the front a detail to collect the arms which had been left there. We collected about 300 pieces.

At about 8 p. m. I rejoined the brigade, and went to the extreme front, where we remained until 8 o'clock next morning, the 4th instant, when I again made a detail to gather up arms.

We lay in rear of the batteries all that day and night, and next morning marched to the rear in the woods, where we remained until 4 a. m. of the 6th instant, when we marched toward Emmitsburg, Md.

While falling back from the brick house on to the road, and very hotly pressed by the enemy, I saw Lieutenant-Colonel Cavada, who was then commanding the regiment, stopping at a log house in an orchard on our right. I inquired if he was wounded; he replied that he was not, but utterly exhausted. I begged him to make an effort to come on, as the enemy were only a few yards from him and advancing rapidly. He replied that he could not, and I left him there, and not having heard from him since, I have no doubt he was taken prisoner there. I assumed command of the regiment at this time.

I also report a number of men as missing whom I have no doubt were killed and their bodies burned when the barn was burned down, and some, I have no doubt, were taken prisoners at the brick house, among them 2 second lieutenants.

In closing this report, I beg leave to ask that it may be remembered that I was not in command of the regiment until after Lieutenant-Colonel Cavada's capture, and that consequently the report of all that precedes is compiled solely from my own observations and memory.

It affords me great pleasure to testify to the great gallantry and cool courage of Brigadier-General Graham, commanding the First Brigade, First Division, Third Corps, of which my regiment is a part, and to express my regret, in which I am joined by all the officers of my regiment, at his having been wounded, and trust that, his wound proving slight, he will soon return to again lead us to victory.

I am also happy to be able to mention Captains [Francis] Fix and Eddy, the former of whom received a painful wound, and also Lieutenants Robinson, Newlin, and A. W. Fix, for their bravery and efficient assistance during the engagement.

I am, sir, your most obedient servant,

E. R. BOWEN,
Capt., Comdg. 114th Pennsylvania Vols.

Lieut. R. DALE BENSON,
Acting Assistant Adjutant-General.

No. 141.

Report of Col. Henry J. Madill, One hundred and forty-first Pennsylvania Infantry.

HDQRS. 141ST REGIMENT PENNSYLVANIA VOLUNTEERS,
——, —— —, 1863.

SIR: In compliance with circular from division headquarters, I submit the following statement of the movements of my regiment during the engagement of July 2 and 3, at Gettysburg, Pa.:

During the forenoon of July 2, we moved into a field beyond a small house and to the left of a road leading from the wooden house, near which General Sickles established his headquarters, to the Emmitsburg pike, and here, by command of General Graham, we then formed in line of battle, the Fifty-seventh Pennsylvania Volunteers on the right of the line, the Sixty-eighth Pennsylvania Volunteers on the left, and my regiment in the center, the One hundred and fifth and One hundred and fourteenth Pennsylvania Volunteers supporting.

The line was doubled on the center, Clark's battery in our front. They delivered a few shots, receiving but little response. The battery then moved up the hill and a little to the left, and took a position in the peach orchard, near the Emmitsburg pike. In the meanwhile our line advanced up the slope and deployed in the oat-field, some 15 rods from the pike, and were ordered to lie down. At this point we sustained a severe fire from artillery for some time, the enemy having a good range.

After remaining in this position for some twenty minutes or more, I received an order from General Graham, through the acting assistant adjutant-general (Lieutenant [Charles H.] Graves), to move my regiment out, and place it in front of Clark's battery. This order was in a few minutes countermanded, and I formed my regiment in rear of that battery, and, while supporting that battery, the Second New Hampshire was ordered up to my support. They took position in my rear. Here the fire from the enemy's artillery was very severe, and we sustained a considerable loss in killed and wounded.

At this time it was observed that the enemy was advancing in strong force from across and down the Emmitsburg pike. My regiment, together with two others (the Third Michigan [Colonel Pierce], and Third Maine, Colonel Lakeman), were ordered to the front of the peach orchard, the battery occupying that position having withdrawn and left the field. We advanced, the Third Maine on my right and the Third Michigan (Colonel Pierce) on my left.

The enemy was advancing in two columns, one column crossing the pike beyond the stone barn and advancing in two lines in the direction of the position occupied by the Second and Third Brigades, which were to our left and somewhat to our rear. When they advanced below the stone barn, they endeavored to extend their lines to the left. It was at this time that my regiment, with the two others spoken of, was ordered forward. We engaged the flank of the enemy, and prevented him from extending his lines this side of the small creek that runs through the field near the stone barn.

At this time the other column had advanced up to the pike and deployed, and was marching on the point we were occupying. The battery in position near the road and immediately to the left of the log house withdrew. The Third Maine, after exchanging a few shots with the enemy at this point, withdrew. Colonel Pierce's regiment (Third Michigan) withdrew about the same time, or a few minutes before. I found myself alone, with a small regiment of about 180 men.

I continued to hold my position for a short time, when I withdrew from that position and took a position in rear of the Sixty-eighth Pennsylvania Volunteers, who were engaged with the enemy in front of the barn, near the brick house. When I took this position the Sixty-eighth withdrew, the balance of the brigade having previously withdrawn. I was thus left alone on the hill occupied by the brigade in the afternoon. The enemy, after the falling back of the Sixty-eighth, advanced to the barn. I engaged them at this point, and held them in check for twenty minutes or upward, but being overpowered by the large numbers of the enemy, I was compelled to retire, which I reluctantly did.

It was at this point that my regiment suffered so severely; 25 of my men were killed here and 5 of my officers severely wounded, besides a large number of non-commissioned officers. Among the severely wounded, and who have since died, were the color-bearers and all of the color guard.

In my opinion, had the Second Division maintained its position as persistently as the First did, we would not have been compelled to abandon that position. They gave way some time before the First Brigade was compelled to retire. The retiring of the First Brigade, in my opinion, was caused by the premature abandoning of their position by the Second Division.

I took 200 men into the fight, with 9 officers. Out of that number I lost 145 men and 6 commissioned officers, the largest proportionate loss in the corps in that fight, and, I think, in the army, in this or any other battle.

I would especially call attention to Sergt. Maj. Joseph G. Fell for his good conduct on the field. The part he took in fearlessly exposing himself during the whole of the fight, and especially during the latter part of it, deserves to be particularly noticed; also Corporal Berry, who carried the colors. Though wounded three times, he refused to give up his colors, and did not yield them until helplessly stricken down the fourth time. Such men deserve particular notice.

Of the conduct of my officers and men, I am happy to say that they are all entitled to great credit. Not one of my men failed me under the most trying circumstances, and to my officers I am under great obligations for their coolness and efficiency under the circumstances.

I regret to say that Major Spalding received two severe wounds, one in each leg, and that he was taken prisoner by the enemy. He lost his left leg; it was amputated below the knee by the enemy.

The movements of the regiment on the 3d were unimportant, and do not require a detailed statement. The brigade was gotten together in the morning of the 3d, and during the greater part of that day occupied a position in the second line. In the afternoon, under the command of Colonel Tippin, went to the right and near the cemetery, and my regiment reported to General Webb, and here supported a battery. In the evening we went with the balance of the division to the front and picketed a part of the line. Were withdrawn on the morning of the 4th, and on the 5th left Gettysburg with the corps.

Respectfully submitted.

H. J. MADILL,
Colonel One hundred and Forty-first Pennsylvania Vols.

Acting Assistant Adjutant-General,
First Brigade.

No. 142.

Report of Lieut. Col. William C. L. Taylor, Twentieth Indiana Infantry, Second Brigade.

——, —— —, 1863.

Sir: In compliance with circular from brigade headquarters, I have the honor to submit the following report of the part taken by the Twentieth Indiana Volunteers in the battle of Gettysburg, July 2, 3, and 4:

On the morning of the 2d, the regiment was moved to the extreme left, to support the Ninety-ninth Pennsylvania and other troops then in the advance.

Early in the day the whole brigade moved forward. The Twentieth Indiana moved to the front, and formed line of battle in a grove, its right connecting with the Ninety-ninth Pennsylvania Volunteers and its left with the Eighty-sixth New York Volunteers.

About 4 p. m. our line was attacked by the enemy. The brigade soon after advanced to the brow of a small hill, about 150 yards from the position it occupied when first attacked. At this place the Ninety-ninth Pennsylvania was withdrawn from the right, which left the Twentieth Indiana on the extreme right of the brigade. Two companies (B and H), under command of Capt. Charles A. Bell, were deployed as skirmishers on the right and front of the regiment to protect our right flank, which was, after the withdrawal of the Ninety-ninth Pennsylvania, pressed by a heavy column of the enemy. These two companies held in check the enemy on our right until the regiment retired from the field. The regiment held the position assigned it until the brigade commenced to retire. The regiment fell back in good order.

On the morning of July 3, the regiment was in reserve. About 11 a. m. the Twentieth Indiana with the other regiments of the brigade moved to the support of the batteries near the left center, where it remained until the morning of July 4, at which time it moved to the front and relieved the skirmish line, our right connecting with the Fourth Maine and our left with the U. S. Sharpshooters.

On the morning of the 5th, our skirmish line was relieved, and the regiment rejoined the brigade.

The loss of the Twentieth Indiana during the engagement was 28 killed, also the colonel of the regiment and 1 line officer, 109 wounded, including 8 officers, and 11 missing.*

I have the honor to be, respectfully, your obedient servant,

W. C. L. TAYLOR,
Lieutenant-Colonel, Commanding Twentieth Indiana.

ASSISTANT ADJUTANT-GENERAL,
Second Brigade, First Division, Third Corps.

No. 143.

Reports of Col. Moses B. Lakeman, Third Maine Infantry.

NEAR WARRENTON, VA.,
July 27, 1863.

CAPTAIN: I have the honor to submit the following report of the part taken by my regiment at the battle of Gettysburg, Pa., on the 2d instant:

By order, I formed my regiment in line of battle parallel to and facing the Emmitsburg road, on the right of the brigade, at early morn. Soon after, by order of General Ward, I moved my regiment as a support for a body of sharpshooters, under command of Colonel Berdan, to whom I was ordered to report, by Captain Briscoe, of General Birney's staff.

Advancing to and for some distance on the Emmitsburg road, I approached a dense wood on the west side of the road, and on entering it formed my regiment (as ordered) to support the advancing line of skirmishers, and followed at supporting distance. They soon, however, became hotly engaged, and, by order of Colonel Berdan, I advanced double-quick to the line they occupied, and instantly formed my regiment under a heavy fire from the enemy, which we returned with a good will. Here I labored under a decided disadvantage, which will account for my heavy loss. The skirmishers were well secured behind trees, while my battalion filled the intervals. The enemy showed himself in overwhelming force, but so well did we hold our position that his advance was much checked and very disastrous, and not until ordered by Colonel Berdan to fall back did a single man leave the ranks, with the exception of those slightly wounded, when I retired, giving an occasional volley to check his advance, which now became quicker.

I was obliged to leave my dead and seriously wounded on the field, and on arriving at the road formed my regiment, which had gotten somewhat confused from loss of men and obstructions in our retreat.

This engagement was short but very severe, and serves to give me a renewal of confidence in the men I command. I sustained a loss of 48 in killed, wounded, and missing.

While on the move to join my brigade, I received an order from General Birney to take position in a peach orchard on the right of my previous one, and accordingly moved my regiment there and occupied it. Here I was enabled several times during the day to re-

---

* But see revised statement, p. 177.

pulse the enemy's skirmishers (who seemed very anxious to drive us from it), and also to seriously harass the left flank of their advancing columns to the position which the other regiments of the brigade were holding, changing my front as circumstances required. In this position my regiment lay about midway between our own and the enemy's batteries, and a few of my command were more or less seriously injured from the frequent explosion of shells immediately over us.

I was heavily pressed in front and on my right flank about 4 p. m., but succeeded in repulsing, with considerable loss, the force, which was much greater than mine, and sent them flying back to their covers. An hour later they came forward again with a force much greater than before, but I engaged them and held them for some fifteen minutes, when I received a severe flank fire on my left. I then saw a large force marching round to cut me off, and ordered my regiment to retire, and while doing so we received a most distressing fire, which threw my command into much confusion, and mixing them up with a portion of the First Brigade, which was also falling back.

I regret to report the loss of my national colors, for no men fought harder under it that day than did my regiment, but Captain Keene, of the color company, and his first and only lieutenant, Henry Penniman, fell, the former pierced by four bullets, the latter severely wounded in the leg. The color-bearer fell, wounded; 2 of the guard were killed, and 4 others seriously wounded ; and, as darkness was fast approaching, I did not miss it till the following morning. If I had, they would have had me and my little squad or I would have had my flag.

As soon as I could rally the remains of my shattered regiment, I joined the brigade, and the men lay on their arms during the night.

I am proud to say the conduct of my officers and men throughout the entire day is deserving the highest praise. Their coolness and courage in resisting a force which they could plainly see was four times their number I cannot pass over lightly, but feel somewhat recompensed for my loss by the knowledge that the few I have left are of the same material as the gallant spirits that have fallen.

I entered the engagement of the morning with 14 officers and 196 rifles, and lost during the day 113 killed, wounded, and missing, including Major Lee wounded, Captain Keene killed, &c., a list of which has already been sent to headquarters.

I have the honor to be, captain, very respectfully, your obedient servant,

MOSES B. LAKEMAN,
Colonel, Commanding Third Maine Regiment.

Capt. John M. Cooney,
Asst. Adjt. Gen., Second Brig., First Div., Third Corps.

—

HEADQUARTERS THIRD MAINE REGIMENT,
July 27, 1863.

Colonel : I herewith respectfully report the movements of my regiment under your command at the battle of Gettysburg, on the 3d, 4th, and 5th instant.

On or about noon of the 3d instant, I was, by order from General Ward, sent as support to the Second Division of the Second Corps,

which was being heavily pressed by the enemy, but who had succeeded in repulsing them before my arrival. I reported to General
Webb, and placed my regiment, as ordered by him, in support of a
battery in our front, but our services were not required throughout
the p. m. or night.

Early on the morning of the 4th instant, I, with the Fourth Maine,
Ninety-ninth Pennsylvania, and Twentieth Indiana Regiments, advanced to the front, sending forward the skirmishers of the Second
Corps, and, taking position on the Emmitsburg road, previously the
skirmish line, relieved the skirmishers in my front, thereby being
supported by, instead of supporting, the Second Corps. Quite brisk
skirmishing took place during the day, but without loss, I am happy
to state, to my regiment.

I remained on this line until about 12 m. on the 5th, when I retired
to the position occupied the previous morning, leaving my skirmishers still to the front, when, finding the enemy had gone, my
skirmishers were relieved, and I, with the other regiments, joined the
brigade.

Respectfully submitted.

MOSES B. LAKEMAN,

Colonel, Commanding Third Maine Regiment.

P. S.—Permit me to add that the conduct of my officers and men
throughout the whole of the trying engagement was admirable in
the extreme, and they are highly deserving of special mention.

No. 144.

Report of Lieut. Charles F. Sawyer, Fourth Maine Infantry.

NEAR WARRENTON, VA., *July 27, 1863.*

SIR: I have the honor to submit the following report of the operations of this regiment at Gettysburg the first of the present month.
The colonel commanding the regiment being wounded, much may be
omitted.

July 1, the regiment arrived near Gettysburg, and received orders
to go on picket, connecting on the right with the First Corps and on
the left with the Ninety-ninth Pennsylvania Volunteers.

On the morning of the 2d, some picket firing took place, which was
not responded to.

About 11 a. m. were withdrawn and ordered to rejoin the brigade,
which was done immediately. Were then assigned position on the
left of the brigade, and advanced to a position on a rocky hill, in support of the Fourth New York Battery. The position of the regiment
was changed to the left of the battery on the advance of the enemy,
one company (F) being left on the brow of the hill, the rest of the
regiment being in the ravine, and left of the line extending on to the
side of the hill on the left. A brigade was then advancing over the
hill, apparently with the intention of connecting on our left flank,
our men then engaging the enemy in our front. Scouts were then
sent on our left, the movements of the enemy indicating a flank movement. Some of the Second U. S. Sharpshooters fell back through
our line, and reported the enemy advancing a column on the hill to
flank us, at the same time a few shots of the enemy were fired on
our flank, and the brigade on our left, before mentioned, was seen to
fall back. A column of the enemy was then seen moving rapidly to

our left, not over 50 yards distant, in the woods. The position of the regiment was then changed to engage the enemy on our left, when we engaged them, they paying no attention to our firing, 5 to 8 rounds being expended before they returned the fire, which came on our front and left flank. Our principal loss was in this place, the men expending on an average 25 rounds before falling back.

Had the brigade seen advancing connected on our left, we could have held our position without any doubt. The regiment fell back to the edge of the woods and again engaged the enemy. The regiment was somewhat broken, being mixed with other regiments of our brigade.

Colonel Walker and Major Whitcomb were wounded in the first of the engagement. The colonel retained command of the regiment until it finally fell back. His wounds being very painful, he was taken to the rear. The command then devolved on Capt. Edwin Libby, he being the senior officer present.

On the first intimation of the enemy's advance on the left, the adjutant was immediately sent by the colonel to report that fact to the commanding officer of the brigade.

CHARLES F. SAWYER,
Adjutant Fourth Maine Volunteers.

Capt. JOHN M. COONEY, <i>Assistant Adjutant-General.</i>

No. 145.

Report of Capt. Edwin Libby, Fourth Maine Infantry.

—— , —— —, 1863.

SIR: I have the honor to submit the following report in connection with the above:

Being senior officer present, I assumed command of the regiment after it fell back from its position, and collected it together to rejoin the brigade, which was immediately done, there being but very few stragglers from the regiment.

July 3, about 2 p. m., were ordered under arms, and with the brigade moved to the support of the Second Division, Second Corps, which was then engaging the enemy. On arriving there, were assigned to position in rear of the —— Battery.

July 4, early in the morning, were ordered to the front as skirmishers and support. The casualties were but 2 men wounded.

At night, were ordered to our former position in rear of the battery, leaving sentinels to the front.

On the evening of the 5th, were relieved, and proceeded to the ground occupied on the 3d instant.

The casualties on the 2d instant were as follows:

Officers and men.	Killed.	Wounded.	Missing.	Total.
Commissioned officers	3	2	4	9
Enlisted men	10	53	67	130
Total*	13	55	71	†141

* But see revised statement, p. 177.
† Including 2 wounded on the 4th.

I would also bring to your notice for gallant and meritorious conduct Sergt. Henry O. Ripley, the color-bearer of the regiment, whose daring and gallantry won for him the admiration of all—thirty-one bullet holes being put through the flag and the staff shot off from his hands. His color guard all being killed or wounded, he waved his flag defiantly in the face of the enemy.

I have the honor to be, your obedient servant,

EDWIN LIBBY,
Captain Fourth Maine Volunteers.

Capt. JOHN M. COONEY,
Assistant Adjutant-General.

No. 146.

Report of Lieut. Col. Benjamin L. Higgins, Eighty-sixth New York Infantry.

HDQRS. EIGHTY-SIXTH REGT. NEW YORK VOLS.,
August 5, 1863.

SIR: I have the honor to report that at 6 a. m. July 2 my regiment left camp with 268 men for line of battle, and moved with brigade to take position in line, which position was obtained about 7.30 a. m. behind a stone wall, with the Twentieth Indiana on my right and the One hundred and twenty-fourth New York on my left. After remaining inactive until 10 a. m., I was ordered by General Ward to send forward a sufficient body of men, under charge of a commissioned officer, to demolish all stone walls and fences in our front to the Emmitsburg road. I immediately sent Captain Baker, of Company G, with 35 men on that duty.

At about 11 a. m. Captain Baker returned, and reported his mission accomplished.

About 12 m. I received orders (which I immediately obeyed) to march my regiment to the right by the flank until I cleared the stone wall, then move to the front in line of battle, retaining the same position in reference to other regiments of the brigade as when first formed in line of battle. After advancing about half a mile to the middle of a wheat-field, and halting, we were ordered to march the regiment by the left flank, which we did to the summit of the hill near the extreme left of our line.

The line was formed, the regiment still retaining its relative position with the Twentieth Indiana and the One hundred and twenty-fourth New York. My regiment, excepting the left company, was in the woods, in which position it remained inactive until about 4.30 p. m., when the enemy commenced shelling us, and our skirmishers began to be driven in, followed by a large force of the enemy in line of battle. At this time I was ordered to commence firing. We held our position here, keeping up active firing, for about fifteen minutes, when we were ordered to advance. This was done promptly for about 50 yards, when we were ordered to halt and commence firing. In this position my regiment remained actively engaging the enemy for about half an hour, when, being wounded, I was obliged to leave the line, the major succeeding me in command.

The regiment was then ordered to about-face and march to the rear, which was obeyed, and on arriving at our original position was ordered to halt, about-face, and commence firing, all of which was done with alacrity for about ten or fifteen minutes, when we were relieved and ordered to march to the rear. The regiment was not again engaged during the day.

The casualties in my regiment during the engagement were as follows:

Officers and men.	Killed.	Wounded.	Missing.	Total.
Commissioned officers	1	3	1	5
Enlisted men	11	40	......	51
Total*	12	43	1	56

Early on the morning of the 3d, my regiment was marched to a piece of woods near the center of our line of battle, where it remained during the day, part of the time under the artillery fire of the enemy, until 4 p. m., when it was ordered forward to the support of batteries, in which position it remained until about 8 p. m., when firing ceased. During this time we had 3 men wounded.* The regiment was then moved a short distance by the right flank, say 300 yards, then about 100 yards to the front, where it was halted, and remained under arms during the night.

On the morning of the 4th, in compliance with an order from headquarters, the regiment was engaged in collecting arms and accouterments.

On the 5th, my regiment was ordered to the piece of woods, where it remained until 4 a. m. of the 6th, when it marched from the battle-field.

Respectfully submitted.

B. L. HIGGINS,
Lieut. Col., Comdg. Eighty-sixth New York Vols.

Capt. JOHN M. COONEY,
Captain, and Assistant Adjutant-General.

No. 147.

Report of Lieut. Col. Francis M. Cummins, One hundred and twenty-fourth New York Infantry.

HDQRS. 124TH REGIMENT NEW YORK VOLUNTEERS,
July 28, 1863.

SIR: I have the honor to report that this regiment, being in position on a rocky bluff, near the extreme left of the line, occupied by the Third Corps at Gettysburg on the afternoon of July 2, was attacked between the hours of 3 and 4 o'clock by a heavy force of the enemy. We held this position for over two hours, when, after having lost in killed and wounded our colonel, lieutenant-colonel, and

---

* But see revised statement, p. 177.

major, 4 line officers, and 82 enlisted men, you ordered us to fall back, which we did in good order.

F. M. CUMMINS,
Lieutenant-Colonel, Comdg. 124th New York Volunteers.

Brig. Gen. J. H. HOBART WARD,
Commanding Second Brigade.

No. 148.

Report of Maj. John W. Moore, Ninety-ninth Pennsylvania Infantry.

NEAR WARRENTON, VA., *July 27, 1863.*

SIR: I have the honor to make the following report of the part my command took in the action before Gettysburg, on the 1st, 2d, and 3d instant:

We arrived before Gettysburg, by way of the Emmitsburg road, a short time after sunset of the 1st instant, and bivouacked for the night in a field on the right of the road, distant about 1 mile from the town.

Early on the morning of the 2d instant, I was ordered to place my regiment in line of battle on the right of the brigade, which formed the extreme left of the line. After lying in this position from two to three hours, I was ordered by General Ward to report with my regiment to Major-General Birney, who in turn ordered me to a position as support to the Third Maine Regiment, which was engaged in skirmishing with the enemy on the Emmitsburg road. This position I held for over an hour, when General Ward advanced the balance of the brigade, joined on my right, changed front, and moved farther to the left, as the enemy was massing his forces and moving on our left flank.

During the afternoon my regiment, with the Twentieth Indiana, was ordered forward through the woods to support Berdan's Sharpshooters. At this time the engagement became very general with the enemy, who was throwing a large force against our brigade, in hopes of breaking through our lines. I was now ordered by General Ward to march my regiment double-quick from the right to the left of the brigade. This movement, rapidly executed, placed my command on the brow of a hill, overlooking a deep ravine interspersed with large bowlders of rock.

Here the conflict was fierce. I held this position for over thirty minutes, until the brigade began to retire on the right, when I ordered the regiment to fall back slowly, covering the rear. General Ward moved the brigade in the rear of General Sykes' division, Fifth Corps, and formed in line of battle. Subsequently I moved with the brigade to the rear, and bivouacked for the night.

Early on the morning of the 3d, I moved my regiment with the brigade to the woods, near the ground occupied by us on the morning of the 2d instant. I remained here until about 1 o'clock, when I moved my regiment, with the Third and Fourth Maine and Twentieth Indiana, of our brigade, under command of Colonel Lakeman, of Third Maine, where I took position on the right of the left center, and reported to General Webb, who commanded the Second Brigade, Second Division, Second Army Corps.

Here the fighting just previous to our arrival had been terrrible. My regiment held the front line, when a lieutenant of Battery A, Fourth U. S. Artillery, asked me to draw his pieces to the rear, to prevent them falling into the hands of the enemy, he having only 6 men and 3 horses left that were not disabled. The request was promptly complied with, and the battery removed to the rear, under cover of a hill. Later in the day, another battery was placed in the position of the one removed by my regiment.

We lay in this position during the night of the 3d, and on the morning of the 4th were ordered by Colonel Lakeman to move forward across a field to the Emmitsburg road, where we lay in line of battle, with a line of our skirmishers advanced, during the day and until 10 o'clock at night, when we were ordered by Colonel Lakeman to fall back and bivouac for the night in rear of a line of the Second Army Corps.

On the morning of the 5th, I was ordered to move with the brigade to about the same position we occupied on the morning of the 2d before being engaged with the enemy; there we remained during the day.

In closing my report, it affords me no small degree of pleasure to be able to say that all of my command behaved nobly, standing unmoved under the enemy's fire and resisting superior numbers with spirit and determination.

I cannot speak too highly of the manner in which the officers of my command acted, without exception gallantly and efficiently performing every duty assigned them.

I lament to say that First Lieut. John R. Nice, commanding Company H, a brave, efficient, and gallant officer, was mortally wounded in the action of the 2d, and died a few hours afterward. Three other officers were wounded and 102 enlisted men reported killed, wounded, and missing, whose names have been reported in the list of casualties.*

The courageous conduct of Color Sergt. Harvey M. Munsell, and the manner in which he bore the regimental colors during the conflict, has induced me to make special mention of his case as one worthy of the most decided approval.

Respectfully submitted.

JOHN W. MOORE,
Major, Comdg. Ninety-ninth Pennsylvania Volunteers.

Capt. JOHN M. COONEY,
Assistant Adjutant-General.

No. 149.

Report of Col. Hiram Berdan, First U. S. Sharpshooters, commanding First and Second U. S. Sharpshooters.

HEADQUARTERS FIRST U. S. SHARPSHOOTERS,
July 29, 1863.

CAPTAIN: I have the honor to submit the following report of the operations of the Sharpshooters at the battle near Gettysburg:

On the morning of July 2, I received instructions from the divis-

---

* Embodied in revised statement, p. 177.

ion commander to assume command of the First and Second Regiments of Sharpshooters, and to report direct to division headquarters.   In accordance with instructions received, I posted the Second
Regiment, Major Stoughton commanding, on our left, to act as
flankers, and the First Regiment on our front.

About 7.30 a. m. I received orders to send forward a detachment
of 100 sharpshooters to discover, if possible, what the enemy was
doing.   I went out with the detail, and posted them on the crest of
the hill beyond the Emmitsburg road, and where they kept up a constant fire nearly all day upon the enemy in the woods beyond until
they were driven in, about 5 p. m., by a heavy force of the enemy,
after having expended all their ammunition.

As it was impossible with this force to proceed far enough to discover what was being done by the enemy in the rear of this woods,
I reported the fact to Major-General Birney, and about 11 a. m. I
received an order from him to send out another detachment of 100
sharpshooters farther to the left of our lines, and to take the Third
Maine Volunteers as support, with directions to feel the enemy, and
to discover their movements, if possible.

I moved down the Emmitsburg road some distance beyond our
extreme left and deployed the sharpshooters in a line running nearly
east and west, and moved forward in a northerly direction parallel
with the Emmitsburg road.   We soon came upon the enemy, and
drove them sufficiently to discover three columns in motion in rear
of the woods, changing direction, as it were, by the right flank.   We
attacked them vigorously on the flank, and from our having come
upon them very unexpectedly, and getting close upon them, we were
enabled to do great execution, and threw them for a time into confusion.   They soon rallied, however, and attacked us, when, having
accomplished the object of the reconnaissance, I withdrew under
cover of the woods, bringing off most of our wounded, and reported
about 2 o'clock to Major-General Birney the result of our operations
and discoveries.

The Second Regiment was deployed in front of the Second Brigade
by order of General Ward, and moved forward to a favorable position, where they held the enemy's skirmishers in check and did good
execution, breaking the enemy's front line three times, and finally
fell back as the enemy advanced in heavy force, remaining in action
with the remainder of the brigade during the engagement.   The balance of the First Regiment, under the immediate command of Captain Baker, moved forward to the right of the peach orchard, on the
right of the First Brigade, where they had a splendid chance for
execution, the enemy coming forward in heavy lines.   I relieved
them from time to time as they exhausted their ammunition.

On the 3d, a detachment of about 100 sharpshooters was sent, under
command of Captain Baker, as sharpshooters, to cover the front of
the Sixth Corps.   They remained there all day, constantly firing,
and toward night advanced, driving the enemy's skirmishers some
distance, and capturing 18 prisoners.   The balance of the command
was moved toward the right with the rest of the division, to the support of some batteries, where nothing of importance occurred.

On the morning of the 4th, the Second Regiment was deployed in
the field in front of our position on the 3d, and advanced, driving
the enemy's skirmishers to the edge of the woods, which position they
held until relieved at 7.30 p. m. by a New Jersey regiment, having been under heavy picket firing all day.

The entire command, with very few exceptions, behaved most gallantly.

I desire to make special mention of Colonel Lakeman and Major Lee, of the Third Maine Regiment, for their services on the reconnaissance, in which the Third Maine was used as a support to the detachment of sharpshooters.

I desire to make special mention also of Captain Nash, who rendered invaluable assistance in the reconnaissance referred to, and behaved most gallantly; also of Major Stoughton and Captain Baker, for their judgment and skill in handling their troops under fire; also Lieutenant Norton, acting adjutant of the Second Regiment, who displayed great bravery, and who with a small squad captured and sent to the rear 22 prisoners on Thursday.

We went into action with about 450 rifles. During the three days, we expended 14,400 rounds of ammunition.

Our total loss was:

Officers and men.	Killed.	Wounded.	Missing.	Total.
Commissioned officers	2	7	1	10
Enlisted men	10	52	17	79
Total*	12	59	18	89

I trust that the sharpshooters lost none of their reputation at Gettysburg. Though operating in small detachments, and with other troops, and in such extensive engagements, their deeds may not have been so conspicuous as on some former occasions where the whole force was used together.

I have the honor to be, captain, your obedient servant,

H. BERDAN,
Colonel, Commanding U. S. Sharpshooters.

Capt. F. BIRNEY, *Assistant Adjutant-General.*

No. 150.

Report of Lieut. Col. Casper Trepp, First U. S. Sharpshooters.

HDQRS. FIRST REGIMENT U. S. SHARPSHOOTERS,
July 29, 1863.

CAPTAIN: In accordance with directions received from headquarters Second Brigade, to report the part taken by my command in the action at Gettysburg, Pa., I have the honor to report as follows:

Early in the morning of July 2, this regiment was posted so, and with instructions, to protect the left flank of the Third Corps. Soon thereafter the dispositions were changed, and I received an order to send 100 men on a reconnaissance in front of the right of the Third Army Corps. This detachment I conducted in person, and deployed them. The command was given to Capt. John Wilson, a very efficient officer, and I returned to the regiment. I then received another order for 100 men for a reconnaissance. Following the aide-de-camp, I conducted this second detachment directly to and followed

---

* But see revised statement, p. 177.

the road in plain view of the enemy. This detachment might have been marched from the original position to a point where the engagement took place perfectly concealed from view of the enemy and without loss of time. As we marched, the enemy must have seen every man from the time we reached the road until we entered the woods on the Fairfield road, giving the enemy time enough to counter-maneuver. The enemy gained yet more time by reason of the Third Maine, Colonel Lakeman, who supported us, halting on the Emmitsburg road, according to his instructions.

All this time we were marching or halting in plain view of the enemy. For this violation of rules of secret expeditions we paid dearly, for when we entered the woods, advancing as skirmishers, we met the enemy's skirmishers very soon after crossing the road. The position of the companies of my regiment was, D and E on the left, F and I on the right, Third Maine as reserve. We drove the enemy about 300 yards, when he made a stand behind a rail fence. The firing was very brisk for about ten minutes, during which time we maintained our position. Col. H. Berdan then gave the order to fall back, firing, which was done in good order, the enemy pursuing a short distance.

This command was collected and formed on the Emmitsburg road, having lost 1 commissioned officer killed, 2 officers wounded, and 16 enlisted men killed, wounded, and missing.

With the balance of this command, I was then posted as a support to Capt. J. H. Baker's line of skirmishers from this regiment, in front of the center of the Third Army Corps.

On examining the ammunition of my detachment, I found that we had not more than about 5 rounds per man. At the time the heavy cannonading began, Col. H. Berdan ordered this detachment to fall back to the position of the morning.

As Capt. J. H. Baker is now wounded and absent, I am unable to furnish the details concerning the detachment under his command, but I am informed that he took his position without order, following the instincts of the true soldier, the sound of the firing, and that at one time, when the enemy pushed his skirmish line to and across the road, he charged with part of his command on the enemy, driving them across the field.

I have to call especial attention to the good behavior of this officer in all the engagements, and I would respectfully recommend him for decoration or honorable mention. The same of Privates Martin V. Nichols and William H. Nichols, Company H, who distinguished themselves on this and on former occasions by bravery and intelligence.

This part of the line lost 3 killed and 5 wounded.

The part of the line under Capt. John Wilson maintained its position for nearly the entire day, and until the ammunition was expended, and only after it was repeatedly called to fall back behind Brigadier-General Carr's brigade it did so, the enemy following in line of battle.

This part of the line lost 1 commissioned officer wounded, 2 enlisted men killed, and 11 wounded.

When the brigade was relieved, we joined, and encamped with them.

July 3.—Capt. J. H. Baker was detached with the Fifth Army Corps, with Companies C, I, and K. The service they performed was to protect batteries. On this occasion, Corporal [Wellington]

Fitch, of Company C, distinguished himself by making a bold re-connaissance alone, which resulted in capturing a squad of rebel sharpshooters that greatly annoyed our artillery.

The rest of the regiment was sent to a point more to the right, where the First Army Corps was posted. Nothing occurred to be mentioned.

July 4.—the regiment was sent on picket, but was soon recalled. While so posted, we lost 3 men wounded.

In the afternoon Capt. John Wilson went with 100 men on a re-connaissance. Nothing reported to have happened worthy to be mentioned.

I have the honor to be, very respectfully, your obedient servant,

C. TREPP,
Lieutenant-Colonel, Comdg. First U. S. Sharpshooters.

Capt. JOHN M. COONEY, *Asst. Adjt. Gen., Second Brig.*

No. 151.

Report of Maj. Homer R. Stoughton, Second U. S. Sharpshooters.

HDQRS. SECOND REGIMENT U. S. SHARPSHOOTERS,
July 27, 1863.

CAPTAIN : I have the honor to report the operations of the Second U. S. Sharpshooters at Gettysburg, Pa., as follows :

On the morning of July 2, I was placed in line on the extreme left of the Third Corps, remaining there for nearly one hour, when the colonel commanding instructed me to place my command in a position to cover a ravine near Sugar Loaf hill, which I did by putting Company H on the brow of the hill, with vedettes overlooking the ravine, and Company D in the ravine near the woods, to watch the enemy's movements in that direction. Companies A, E, G, and C formed a line perpendicular to the cross-road that intersects with the Emmitsburg pike. Companies B and F, I held in reserve.

I remained in this position until about 2 p. m., when General Ward directed that I should deploy my regiment across the ravine and through the woods on the right, and advance. I moved forward to a brook some 200 yards beyond a second cross-road running per-pendicular to the Emmitsburg pike, and intersecting with it in front of Sugar Loaf hill. I sent forward scouts to reconnoiter the ground. I then rode out perhaps the distance of half a mile, and discovered the enemy's skirmishers advancing on my right, which, being un-supported by any connection with skirmishers on my right, I was compelled to withdraw to protect my flank. In this position we had but little time to wait. The enemy's skirmishers advanced to the top of the hill in our front, and immediately after they placed a bat-tery directly in our front, and being too far for our range, I sent for-ward a few men under cover of woods on the left, and silenced one piece nearest us.

The enemy then advanced a line of battle covering our entire front and flank. While they were advancing, the Second Regiment did splendid execution, killing and wounding a great many. One regi-ment broke three times, and rallied, before it would advance. I held my position until their line of battle was within 100 yards of me and their skirmishers were pushing my right flank, when I ordered my men to fall back, firing as they retired.   My left wing retreated up the hill and allowed the enemy to pass up the ravine, when they poured a destructive fire into his flank and rear.

Here Adjutant Norton, with about a dozen men, captured and sent to the rear 22 prisoners.   Special mention should be made of this officer for his coolness and bravery during this day's engagement.

The right wing fell back gradually until they mingled with the regiments composing the Second Brigade, and remained till night, when the brigade was relieved.

In this day's action were wounded Capts. E. T. Rowell (acting major), J. McClure, and A. Buxton.   Our loss was 28 killed, wounded, and missing.   Among the missing was Lieut. D. B. Pettijohn, Company A.

On the 3d instant, the Second Regiment was not engaged, with the exception of about a dozen volunteers, who went out to the front of the breastworks of the First Army Corps, to silence one of the enemy's guns, which was accomplished, losing 1 killed and 1 wounded.

On the 4th instant, I was ordered to move forward to the Emmitsburg pike, a few hundred yards to the left of the cemetery, and to deploy four companies to skirmish through the field to the woods in front.   The enemy was driven back to his earthworks, about 150 or 200 yards from his first position.   We held this position through the day, under a sharp fire from his sharpshooters.

The regiment sustained a loss this day of 3 killed and 8 wounded. Among the wounded was Lieutenant Law, Company E.

At 7.30 p. m. I was relieved by a New Jersey regiment, of the Sixth Corps, and rejoined the brigade.

I have the honor to remain, your obedient servant,
HOMER R. STOUGHTON,
Major, Commanding Second U. S. Sharpshooters.

Capt. John M. Cooney,
A. A. G., Second Brig., First Div., Third Army Corps.

No. 152.

Report of Col. P. Regis de Trobriand, Fifty-fifth New York Infantry, commanding Third Brigade.

Headquarters Third Brigade, *July* —, 1863.

Captain: I have the honor of submitting the following report of the part acted by the Third Brigade, First Division, Third Corps, under my command, in the battle of Gettysburg, on the 2d and 3d instant:

On July 1, I had been left with my command, and a battery of artillery from the First New York Artillery at Emmitsburg, to hold the place, in connection with a brigade from the Second Division, while the balance of the Third Corps was moving toward Gettysburg.

But an order having reached me at 2 o'clock on the following morning to join the corps, I started at daybreak, and reported to Major General Birney about 10 o'clock.

About 2 p. m. the same day, a line of battle was formed in expectation of an impending attack from the enemy on our left.   The First Brigade (General Graham's) formed the left end of our front line, and the Second Brigade (General Ward's) was drawn *en potence* to prevent a flank movement, while the Third Brigade occupied the apex of the angle, being in column by regiments, ready to support either of the other two brigades according to circumstances.

In the meantime the enemy had been steadily moving large masses of troops under cover of the woods toward our left, out of range of musketry, and covering himself with a line of skirmishers, the march by the left flank of which was the indication of the direction of the probable attack. Our skirmishers soon after having been hardly pressed, and the fire becoming more brisk, I was ordered to detach a regiment to their support, and while our artillery was opening fire I sent the Third Regiment Michigan Volunteers, which, under the command of Col. Byron R. Pierce, proceeded forward to a peach orchard close to the road to Emmitsburg, and, deploying rapidly, checked any farther advance of the rebel skirmishers on that point.

Still, the forces of the enemy were passing around our left, and when in proper position, their columns rushed forward on General Ward's brigade, drawn in line to receive the shock. The accustomed yells of the Confederates and the intensity of the firing on my left had scarcely announced the precise point and the violence of the attack, when I extended my right by moving the Seventeenth Maine Volunteers, Lieutenant-Colonel Merrill commanding, across a wheat-field, in order to fill a gap open there, thereby re-enforcing General Ward. The Seventeenth Maine took a strong position behind a stone wall, and did good service at this point. Soon after, I was ordered to send a regiment to support General Ward, and I immediately detached for that purpose the Fortieth New York Volunteers, Colonel Egan, which marched forward, and aided efficiently in checking the enemy's advance in the most exposed position on our extreme left.

The battle was raging on my left and right to the rear on both sides, in consequence of my advanced position as already explained, and soon these two attacks came converging on the angle of which I formed the summit, with the Fifth Michigan, Lieutenant-Colonel Pulford, and the One hundred and tenth Pennsylvania, Major Jones, the only two regiments left at that point. Fortunately my position there was a strong one, in a wood commanding a narrow ravine, which the enemy attempted in vain to cross under our fire.

The unflinching bravery of the Fifth Michigan, which sustained the loss of more than one-half of its number without yielding a foot of ground, deserves to be especially mentioned here with due commendation. Had a sufficient force been there under my orders when the enemy gave up forcing our position, I would not have hesitated to try to break his line at that point; but two regiments from the Fifth Corps, sent there to my support, having fallen back without engaging the enemy (by what orders I could never ascertain), and some points of our line yielding under a disproportionate contest for want of timely support, I found myself in danger of being surrounded, and fell back out of the woods, where the enemy did not risk to follow us. I found the Seventeenth Maine in a wheat-field, where it had followed the receding movement of the line.

As the enemy was pressing upon us on that side, I made a *retour offensif* with that regiment, re-enforced by the Fifth Michigan, keeping the enemy at bay in the woods until the arrival of sufficient re-enforcements from the Second Corps allowed us to be relieved when our ammunition was just exhausted.

By order of Major-General Birney, who was present with us in the wheat-field, I then took my command to the adjoining wood in the rear, and then farther off, to avoid unnecessary losses by the fire of the enemy, which disabled some of my men in that position. I was soon joined there by the Third Michigan, and later in the evening by the Fortieth New York.

On July 3, when the last and furious attack of the enemy took place on our right, my brigade was at once brought to form a second line, supporting our batteries, when, without being actually engaged, several officers and men were wounded by the too well directed fire of the enemy's artillery.

At night I was put in command of the advance line across that part of the battle-field, which I occupied until the following day with two brigades, the Third and First, without any special occurrence to mention.

It becomes now my gratifying duty to state how nobly the officers and men of my command have sustained at Gettysburg the glorious reputation won on many other battle-fields by the old Kearny (now Birney's) division.

The regimental commanders have gallantly and efficiently done their duty. Among them Col. B. R. Pierce, Third Michigan, was wounded in the leg, since amputated, as also Maj. D. M. Jones, One hundred and tenth Pennsylvania. Lieut. Col. John Pulford, Fifth Michigan, was slightly wounded in the hand. Col. T. W. Egan had his horse killed under him.

I could not mention here the field or line officers who have distinguished themselves under my eyes without injustice to the others, all of them having behaved in the most gallant manner.

The officers of my staff I must mention as brave and efficient in action. Capt. Ben. M. Piatt, assistant adjutant-general, had his horse shot under him, while he was himself slightly hit. Capt. I. C. Smith, acting assistant inspector-general, was severely wounded in the leg, which will deprive me for a time of the services of that most valuable officer. My two aides, Lieuts. E. B. Houghton and G. W. Waldron, lent me good assistance by their gallant alacrity in the performance of their duties.

Casualties.

Command.	Killed.		Wounded.		Missing.		
	Officers.	Enlisted men.	Officers.	Enlisted men.	Officers.	Enlisted men.	Total.
Headquarters Third Brigade			1				1
40th New York	1	28	6	114		5	154
17th Maine	1	17	7	105		2	132
110th Pennsylvania		8	6	39			53
5th Michigan	2	17	8	74		4	105
3d Michigan		7	2	29		7	45
Total*	4	77	30	361		18	490

Respectfully submitted.

R. DE TROBRIAND,
Colonel, Commanding Brigade.

Capt. F. BIRNEY, *Asst. Adjt. Gen., First Division.*

* But see revised statement, p. 178.

No. 153.

Report of Lieut. Col. Charles B. Merrill, Seventeenth Maine Infantry.

BATTLE-FIELD OF GETTYSBURG, PA.,
July 5, 1863.

SIR: In compliance with orders from brigade headquarters, I have the honor to submit the following report of the part sustained by the Seventeenth Regiment Maine Volunteers under my command in the battle of Gettysburg:

On the morning of July 2, we broke camp at Emmitsburg at 4.30 o'clock, and marched toward Gettysburg, arriving upon the battle-field about 10 o'clock. Already the pickets of both armies were busily engaged, and with our brigade we were at once drawn up in line of battle, facing the pike leading to Gettysburg, where we rested under arms for an hour. Soon after this the line was changed, and we were moved forward and placed in a new position, supporting a line of skirmishers thrown toward the front by this brigade.

About 4 p. m., the brigade of General Ward having become actively engaged with the enemy on our left, I was ordered by Colonel De Trobriand to march my regiment to connect with and support the line of General Ward, on his right. The regiment at once moved by the left flank, and, crossing an interval between the two brigades, our line was formed behind a stone wall, which afforded a strong position. We opened fire upon the enemy, then within 100 yards of us. The contest became very severe, the enemy at times being driven back by our line, and then by superior numbers compelling us in turn to give way. The ground was hotly contested, but we held our position till, finding the right of my regiment outflanked and exposed to a murderous fire from the enemy's re-enforcements, I was obliged to form a new line, changing the right wing of the regiment into position at a right angle with the left. This movement was executed in good order, under a heavy fire from the advancing foe. In this position we continued the fight, checking the enemy till, receiving orders to retire, we fell back across a wheat-field in our rear to the edge of the woods.

At this point, Major-General Birney rode upon the field and directed our line to advance. With cheers for our gallant commander, the regiment moved quickly forward, and pouring into the enemy volley upon volley, their advance was checked. The contest was now of a most deadly character, almost hand to hand, and our loss was very severe. In the color guard of 10, but 3 escaped uninjured.

Our ammunition being exhausted and fresh troops having arrived to take our places, we were ordered to withdraw from the field, which we did in good order. A new line was then formed but a short distance to the rear, where we bivouacked for the night.

At early dawn (July 3) the regiment was drawn up in line of battle in the same position held by us on the previous forenoon. At 1 p. m., the enemy opening upon the whole line of our army a heavy artillery fire, and advancing to break through the position held by the right, we were ordered to proceed to re-enforce General Double-day. Proceeding at the double-quick, we were soon placed in line, supporting the Ninth Michigan Battery. Throughout the terrible attack of the enemy, we were exposed to a severe artillery fire, and suffered heavy loss of officers and men. After dark, the regiment was sent to the front on picket duty, where we remained during the night. Much attention was given by our men to the care of the wounded left upon the field.

On July 4, the regiment was occupied nearly all day in throwing up earthworks, expecting a renewal of the attack by the enemy.

On July 5, we moved into our present position.

It is with sadness that I am compelled to report the loss of several valuable line officers: Lieutenant Dyer, commanding Company G, was instantly killed in the engagement on the 2d, while Captain Fogg, Company H, was carried from the field mortally wounded. Adjt. C. W. Roberts, a gallant soldier, was seriously wounded in the leg, requiring amputation.

Throughout these engagements both officers and men of my command behaved with gallantry, and their conduct was worthy of the cause in which they were engaged and of the noble division to which they belong. Many of the men were without shoes; the whole command had been without rations for nearly twenty-four hours, and, after a long and tedious march from Camp Sickles, were poorly fitted for the labors which they were called upon to perform.

Our gratitude is due to Almighty God for the success with which He has crowned our exertions.

The list of casualties, herewith annexed, shows the severity of the contest in which the regiment participated:

Officers and men.	Killed.	Wounded.	Missing.	Total.
Officers	1	7	.....	8
Enlisted men	17	105	2	124
Total*	18	112	2	132

I have the honor to be, your obedient servant,

CHARLES BENJAMIN MERRILL,
Lieut. Col., Comdg. Seventeenth Regt. Maine Volunteers.

Capt. BEN. M. PIATT, *Assistant Adjutant-General.*

No. 154.

Report of Lieut. Col. Edwin S. Pierce, Third Michigan Infantry.

HDQRS. THIRD REGIMENT MICHIGAN VOLUNTEERS,
August 4, 1863.

CAPTAIN: I have the honor to report the part taken by this regiment in the battle of Gettysburg, on July 2 and 3.

We left Emmitsburg at 3 a. m. on the 2d, and arrived at Gettysburg about 12 m. On our nearing Gettysburg, the enemy appeared in our rear and left flank. We were then marched near and to the left of the Taneytown road, where the brigade was formed in column of regiments, we occupying the right, where we halted for a short time. Then we were moved forward about 1 mile, when the enemy made his appearance in force, and was driving in our pickets. The

---

* But see revised statement, p. 178.

colonel was then ordered to deploy his regiment as skirmishers. He moved his regiment by the right flank to the left of the peach orchard, of which the enemy held a portion, where he deployed Companies I, F, and K, deploying forward on the right of Company F. We drove the enemy's skirmishers back to and beyond the stone house and barn on the left of the Emmitsburg road, our right resting in front of the orchard, near the road.

Upon gaining this position, we discovered that the enemy was massing his forces on our left. I reported the same to General Sickles, and kept him informed of the enemy's movements. During the engagement, the enemy made several attempts to retake the house and barn, but were repulsed with heavy loss, our men fighting with a desperation never before witnessed, and at times at a range of not over 50 yards.

Company A was detached to support a portion of General Graham's line on our right. They advanced to the brick house on the right of the Emmitsburg road, holding their position until overpowered by a superior force. The most of General Graham's force having retired, we held our position until about 7 p. m., when the left had retired so far that we were in danger of being flanked. We retired in good order, and assisted in bringing off a portion of two batteries.

It was at this time that the colonel was wounded, and I assumed command, he having remained mounted during the entire engagement, and constantly on the skirmish line cheering the men on. We rejoined the brigade where it was formed at the commencement, when we were marched across the Taneytown road, and bivouacked for the night.

Our loss was as follows:

Officers and men.	Killed.	Wounded.	Missing.	Total.
Officers		3		3
Men	7	28	7	42
Total	7	31	7	45

On the morning of the 3d, we moved forward to the first position occupied on the 2d, and were formed the same, where we remained till about 3 p. m. Thence we were moved off by the right flank at double-quick to where the enemy was trying to pierce our center. The regiment was here detached, and sent to the support of the Second Division, Second Corps, where we assisted in repulsing the enemy, who had succeeded in breaking through a portion of their line.

The regiment occupied the front line till the morning of the 5th, when we rejoined our brigade. No casualties occurred to the regiment during this day's action.

In closing this report, I cannot particularize any of the officers or men, but I am proud to state that they did their duty without an exception.

I have the honor to be, very respectfully, your obedient servant,

EDWIN S. PIERCE,
Lieut. Col., Comdg. Third Regiment Michigan Volunteers.

Capt. Ben. M. Piatt,
Asst. Adjt. Gen., Third Brig., First Div., Third Corps.

No. 155.

Report of Lieut. Col. John Pulford, Fifth Michigan Infantry.

CAMP NEAR SULPHUR SPRINGS, VA.,
August 2, 1863.

SIR : I have the honor to report to the major-general commanding First Division, Third Corps, through you, the part taken by my regiment in the battle of Gettysburg, on July 2 and 3.

About 1 p. m. on the 2d, I was detached from the brigade and ordered to the front to support Tidball's battery. I formed a line of battle to the right of the battery, and remained in this position about one hour, when I received an order from Major-General Birney to rejoin my brigade, which I did.

I was then ordered to form on the left of the first line of our brigade, which I did.

About 4 p. m. I received orders from Col. R. de Trobriand, commanding brigade, to take my regiment to the front, and deploy three companies as skirmishers.

I executed this order, and, having advanced about 200 rods, I was met by the enemy, who attacked in force and drove in my skirmishers.

I opened fire from the battalion reserve about 4.30 p. m. We continued firing until 6.30 p. m., under the direction of the brigade commander, when I was ordered to rejoin the brigade, and retired with the same to an open field a short distance in the rear, where we bivouacked for the night.

On the morning of the 3d, I advanced with the brigade to a belt of woods, being the same ground occupied the day previous, where I formed a line of battle to the right of the brigade. I remained in this position till about 2 p. m., when I moved with the brigade about 1 mile to the right, where I remained till about 6.30 p. m. under nearly a continuous artillery fire, but without any occurrences worthy of special mention.

I cannot make honorable mention of any particular officer or man, but take much pleasure in reporting that all did their duty most nobly.

All of which is very respectfully submitted.

JOHN PULFORD,
Lieut. Col., Commanding Fifth Michigan Volunteers.

Capt. F. BIRNEY,
Assistant Adjutant-General.

Recapitulation.

Officers and men.	Killed.	Wounded.	Missing.	Total.
Officers	2	8		10
Enlisted men	17	74	4	95
Total*	19	82	4	105

* But see revised statement, p. 178.

No. 156.

Report of Col. Thomas W. Egan, Fortieth New York Infantry.

SULPHUR SPRINGS, VA.,
August 1, 1863.

CAPTAIN: I have the honor to submit the following account of the part taken by the Fortieth Regiment New York Volunteers in the battle of Gettysburg, Pa.:

On the morning of July 2, after a prolonged and tedious march of many days, my command, following the brigade, moved from Emmitsburg, Md., up the pike leading to Gettysburg, Pa., to unite with the remainder of the division, which had been pushed ahead the night previous. Arriving within about 2 miles of Gettysburg, moved to the right, and formed line of battle with the brigade in a wood of oaks and among rocks, about half a mile from the Emmitsburg road, and facing toward it. *

Resting here a few hours, marched by the flank to the left and front across an open field about 200 yards into another woods, taking position in line of battle as before, still facing the Emmitsburg road, which was at this time held by the enemy.

At this point we were subjected to an enfilading fire from the enemy's batteries, which compelled a change of position. Moving across a road leading from the Emmitsburg road to the Baltimore pike, we again formed line of battle, when I was moved, by order of Colonel de Trobriand, with the rest of the brigade, marching in line of battle, about 100 yards to the left and front, to the support of a battery which was stationed near a peach orchard.

At about 4 o'clock were relieved by a portion of the Fifth Corps, when I was ordered by Major-General Birney to move by the left flank through the woods across a field of wheat, in front of Captain Winslow's battery, to a position pointed out to me by Capt. J. C. Briscoe, in a ravine bounded on the left by high hills and upon the right by a gentle ridge.

The enemy had at this time partly succeeded in flanking the Second Brigade upon my right by a movement upon their left. Captain Smith's (Fourth New York) battery was stationed upon the ridge at my right, and was in a very perilous situation. The enemy having already captured two of his pieces, he called upon me in beseeching terms to save his battery. I then moved in line of battle, with my right connecting with the Second Brigade regiments, which were on the right of the battery, under a terrific fire of the enemy's infantry, who were strongly disposed behind the natural defenses of rocks and ridges, encountering also a destructive fire from his artillery. I immediately ordered my men to charge, when with great alacrity they pushed forward at a double-quick, crossing a marsh up to their knees in mud and water.

The enemy fell back upon my advance, but it was attended with no particular advantage to ourselves, for their new position was very much stronger than the first. All attempts to dislodge them from the second line proving unsuccessful, and discovering that they had gained ground upon my right, which threatened a flank movement, the regiments on my right having fallen to the rear and exposed us to a cross-fire, I was compelled to fall back, rallying my men upon the ridge over which I passed.

In moving in, my command suffered terribly, and here I have to regret the loss of one of my bravest and best officers, Lieut. William H. H. Johnson, who was acting adjutant. While nobly and gallantly urging on the men, he was killed instantly by a Minie ball. I sustained also the loss of many of my bravest and most faithful men, who nobly fell in the performance of their sacred duty, facing the enemy of our country.

It becomes my painful duty also to record the loss by wounds of many of my best officers and most worthy men. Among the number was the gallant and brave Lieut. Col. Augustus J. Warner, who received a severe wound in the leg while rendering me the most valuable assistance. Capt. M. M. Cannon and Lieuts. W. H. Gilder and R. M. Boody also received severe wounds while greatly distinguishing themselves at their post of duty.

An overpowering force of the enemy again compelled us to fall back, when I again rallied the scattered remnant of my command, and made a stand near the position occupied by Captain Winslow's battery, when I received orders from Capt. J. C. Briscoe to move my command back to join the brigade, but I was not able to find the brigade, when I was ordered to bivouac for the night in rear of the position first occupied before the battle.

Early upon the following morning, moved to the position first occupied before the battle, to the support of the Fifth Corps, where we remained until the middle of the afternoon, when I received orders to move by the flank, following the brigade, to the right and rear, to the support of the batteries placed in position in an open field, in anticipation of a concentrated movement of the enemy upon this point. Here I sustained the loss of several men from the terrific fire of the enemy's batteries.

We remained in this position until night, when I received orders from Colonel de Trobriand to move my regiment by the flank to the front for picket duty. I established my line, in pursuance of orders, about 200 yards from the Emmitsburg road and parallel with it.

Early next morning was relieved, it being ascertained that the enemy had evacuated, and rejoined the brigade about 400 yards to the rear, when I was again moved with the brigade back to the position occupied in the afternoon of the previous day. Here bivouacked for the night.

The next morning my command was moved with the brigade to the woods first occupied on the morning of the 2d instant, to await orders to follow up the fleeing enemy.

In concluding this report, it becomes my duty, as well as pleasure, to make the highest mention of Capt. B. M. Piatt, assistant adjutant-general, Third Brigade. Too much cannot be said of this brave and gallant officer. Always cool under the most trying circumstances, by his courage and example he afforded services that were of infinite value in restoring order to my command. When his horse was shot under him, he still remained in the van, always by my side, greatly distinguishing himself by noble conduct. The highest praise is also due to Capt. J. C. Briscoe for the valuable services he rendered at a time when most required.

Among the officers of my command who escaped injury, it is difficult to select the most deserving; each nobly performed his duty to my entire satisfaction.

The color guard, under Sergt. Andrew J. Wadleigh, well sustained the former reputation of that corps. They were foremost in the advance, and raised the noble ensign defiantly.

Respectfully submitting the above, I am, captain, your obedient servant,

T. W. EGAN,
Colonel Fortieth New York Volunteers.

Capt. BEN. M. PIATT,
Assistant Adjutant-General, Third Brigade.

Recapitulation.

Officers and men.	Killed.	Wounded.	Missing.	Total.
Officers	1	6	......	7
Enlisted men	28	114	5	147
Total*	29	120	5	154

No. 157.

Report of Maj. Isaac Rogers, One hundred and tenth Pennsylvania Infantry.

NEAR WARRENTON, VA., *August* 4, 1863.

SIR: I have the honor to report to Major-General Birney, through you, the part the One hundred and tenth Regiment Pennsylvania Volunteers took in the battle of Gettysburg, Pa., on July 2 and 3.

After arriving as far to the front as was deemed prudent, the regiment was moved off the road with the brigade in the edge of a woods to the right.

At 1 p. m. Lieutenant-Colonel Jones, commanding regiment, was ordered to move forward to a piece of woods and form a line of battle. After this was done, he was ordered to move within supporting distance of our skirmishers, which was promptly and calmly done under fire of artillery.

After being in this position until 3.30 p. m., the lieutenant-colonel was ordered by a staff officer to advance 50 paces and join the brigade on the right, under a heavy fire of artillery, which was done with much coolness. After getting established in this position, the skirmishers were driven back, when the general engagement commenced at 4 p. m.

Here Lieut. Col. David M. Jones was severely wounded, and the command of the regiment was given over to me.

The battle continued with a determination on both sides to conquer or die until 6 p. m., when the enemy in our front fell back, and the order to cease firing was given. This being done, I was ordered by a staff officer to fall back and give place to fresh troops, which was done, moving through a piece of woods, where the brigade was bivouacked for the night. Here my command was prepared for action on the following day.

Early on the morning of the 3d, I was ordered to move a short distance to the right, behind a piece of woods and near corps head-

---

* But see revised statement, p. 178.

quarters. After being in this position forty minutes, I was ordered to take up a position on the same ground occupied by this regiment the day before, previous to going into action.

At 1.30 p. m. I was ordered to move forward to a stone fence. Soon after being in this position, I was ordered to change position, and was conducted to the right, behind a battery, where I remained during the afternoon. The fire of the artillery was kept up all afternoon. The casualties in my command, though, were trifling, 2 men being slightly wounded.

At 8 p. m. I was ordered to move forward to act as a picket during the night, which was done. Here we remained until morning behind temporary earthworks.

My command behaved well during the two days' battle, and as all did well and deserve praise, I will not particularly speak of any one.

Casualties.

Officers and men.	In action.	Killed.	Wounded.	Total loss.
Officers.........	16	.....	6	6
Enlisted men.........	136	8	39	47
Total	152	8	45	53

Among the officers wounded was Lieut. Col. David M. Jones.

I am, sir, most respectfully, your obedient servant,

ISAAC ROGERS,
Major, Commanding Regiment.

ASSISTANT ADJUTANT-GENERAL,
First Division, Third Army Corps.

No. 158.

Report of Brig. Gen. Andrew A. Humphreys, U. S. Army, commanding Second Division.

CAMP, HEADQUARTERS ARMY OF THE POTOMAC,
August 16, 1863.

COLONEL: I submit, for the information of the major-general commanding Third Corps, the following report of the operations of my division (Second Division, Third Corps) during the recent campaign, up to July 9, on the morning of which day I was relieved from the command of the division, having been appointed chief of staff at the headquarters of this army:

On June 11, about midday, while encamped near Falmouth, Va., orders were received by me from the headquarters of the corps to march at 2 o'clock on the Warrenton road, which order was complied with, the division bivouacking for the night at Hartwood Church.

The march was resumed the next morning at 6 o'clock, my division leading. Upon arriving at Morrisville, I was directed to move to the Rappahannock River, and cover that part of it from Wheatley's Ford, near Kellysville, to Beverly Ford, near the upper forks; to throw up such works and make such defensive arrangements as would render it impracticable for the enemy to cross in my front. It was past midnight of the 12th before my command, after a march of from 22 to 25 miles, was in position at all the fords, it having been posted under my own supervision. Rifle-pits and batteries were thrown up at the crossings, and the railroad bridge was rendered impassable.

On the afternoon of the 13th, the Second Brigade rejoined the division, having been on picket on the 11th, from which it was not relieved until between midnight and morning of the 12th.

On the morning of the 14th, before daylight, it was marched to Kelly's Ford, to relieve the detachments of the Fifth Corps holding that ford.

On the evening of the 14th, in compliance with orders from the corps commander, as soon as it was sufficiently dark to conceal the movement of my troops, the division was concentrated on the railroad, and the march to Manassas Junction was begun.

I reached Cedar Run, near Catlett's Station, between 7 and 8 a. m. of the 15th, where, by authority of the corps commander, the division was halted for rest until 2 p. m., when the march was resumed. It was painful in the extreme, for owing to the long-continued drought, streams, usually of considerable magnitude, were dried up, the dust lay some inches deep on the roadway, and the fields were equally uncomfortable. The suffering from heat, dust, thirst, fatigue, and exhaustion was very great. It was near midnight when the division reached Manassas Junction, after a march varying in the different brigades from 25 to 29 miles.

On the 16th, we remained at Manassas Junction, resting.

On the 17th, marched to Centreville, and on the 19th to Gum Springs, where the division remained until the 25th, when at 10 a. m. it marched to Edwards Ferry, through Fairfarm and Franklinville, and crossing the Potomac on the pontoon bridge about 5 p. m., marched on the tow-path of the canal to the mouth of the Monocacy, reaching that point about midnight, after a march of not less than 25 miles, that portion on the tow-path being rendered very fatiguing and exhausting by a heavy rain that set in at nightfall. The whole command, officers and men, were more exhausted by this march than by that of the 14th and 15th.

On the 26th, the division marched to the vicinity of the Point of Rocks, and bivouacked on the farm of Dr. Duvall, near the summit of the Catoctin Mountain.

On the 27th, marched to the vicinity of Middletown, on the Hagerstown pike, via Jefferson.

On the 28th, marched through Frederick, crossed the Monocacy 3 miles above, and bivouacked for the night 7 miles from that town, on the Woodsborough road.

On the 29th, marched to Taneytown through Woodsborough and Bruceville.

On the 30th, made a short march after midday on the road to Emmitsburg, bivouacking about midway between the two places.

On July 1, marched through Emmitsburg, and halted 1 mile out of the town, on the Waynesborough pike. While I was engaged in a careful examination of the ground in front of Emmitsburg, the division was ordered at 3 p. m. to move up to Gettysburg, 12 miles distant, where an engagement had taken place between the two corps of Generals Reynolds and Howard (the First and Eleventh Corps) and the enemy.

A brigade (the Third) and a battery (Smith's) were left, in accordance with orders, in position on the Waynesborough pike. I overtook the head of the division (the First and Second Brigades, with one battery of artillery, Seeley's) 1 mile from the halting ground, and found Lieutenant-Colonel Hayden, assistant inspector-general, Third Corps, with some guides there, for the purpose of pointing out the route the division was to follow. This was on a road nearly parallel to the main road from Emmitsburg to Gettysburg, and about 2 miles west of it.

When half-way to Gettysburg, a dispatch from General Howard to General Sickles, commanding the Third Corps, was delivered to me by Captain McBlair, of the staff, in which the latter general was warned to look out for his left in coming up to Gettysburg, and about the same time I learned from a citizen, who had guided part of General Reynolds' command, that our troops occupied no ground near Gettysburg west of the road from that town to Emmitsburg.

As we approached the crossing of Marsh Run, I was directed by General Sickles, through a staff officer, to take position on the left of Gettysburg as soon as I came up. For reasons that will be apparent, from this statement I concluded that my division should from this point follow the road leading into the main road to Gettysburg, reaching the latter road in about a mile and a half, and at a distance from Gettysburg of about 2 miles; but Lieutenant-Colonel Hayden was positive that General Sickles had instructed him to guide the division by way of the Black Horse Tavern, on the road from Fairfield to Gettysburg. Accordingly, I moved the division in that direction, but, upon approaching the Black Horse Tavern, I found myself in the immediate vicinity of the enemy, who occupied that road in strong force. He was not aware of my presence, and I might have attacked him at daylight with the certainty of at least temporary success; but I was 3 miles distant from the remainder of the army, and I believed such a course would have been inconsistent with the general plan of operations of the commanding general. I accordingly retraced my steps, and marched by the route I have heretofore indicated, bivouacking at 1 a. m. on July 2 about 1 mile from Gettysburg and eastward of the Emmitsburg road.

At an early hour of the morning, my division was massed in the vicinity of its bivouac, facing the Emmitsburg road, near the crest of the ridge running from the cemetery of Gettysburg, in a southerly direction, to a rugged, conical-shaped hill, which I find goes by the name of Round Top, about 2 miles from Gettysburg.

At 9 a. m. the Third Brigade, with Smith's battery, joined the division, having been ordered up by Major-General Meade, commanding the army. It marched by the main road from Emmitsburg to Gettysburg.

Shortly after midday, I was ordered to form my division in line of battle, my left joining the right of the First Division of the Third Corps, Major-General Birney commanding, and my right resting opposite the left of General Caldwell's division, of the Second Corps, which was massed on the crest near my place of bivouac. The line I was directed to occupy was near the foot of the westerly slope of the ridge I have already mentioned, from which foot-slope the ground rose to the Emmitsburg road, which runs on the crest of a ridge nearly parallel to the Round Top ridge. This second ridge declines again immediately west of the road, at the distance of 200 or 300 yards from which the edge of a wood runs parallel to it. This wood was occupied by the enemy, whose pickets were exchanging shots from an early hour in the morning with our pickets thrown out beyond the road on the westerly slope.

The front allotted to me admitted of my forming the First Brigade, commanded by Brig. Gen. Joseph B. Carr, in line of battle, with one regiment of the Second Brigade on its left, the Seventy-first New York (Second Excelsior), commanded by Col. H. L. Potter. The Second Brigade, commanded by Col. W. R. Brewster, was formed in line of battalions in mass 200 yards in rear of the first line, and the Third Brigade, commanded by Col. George C. Burling, was massed 200 yards in rear of the second line, opposite its center. On the east side of the Emmitsburg road, opposite the middle of my line, was a log house surrounded by an orchard. This I occupied with the Seventy-third New York (Fourth Excelsior), Second Brigade, Maj. M. W. Burns commanding. This regiment was subsequently relieved by the Sixteenth Massachusetts, First Brigade. A series of peach orchards extended to the left along the Emmitsburg road some distance beyond the point where the road from Marsh Run crosses the Emmitsburg road. This Marsh Run road extends over to the Taneytown road and Baltimore pike, crossing the former just north of the Round Top. The ground occupied by my division and in my front was open. Communication with all points of it had been made easy by removing such of the fences as were in the way. Seeley's battery (K, Fourth U. S. Artillery) was placed at my disposal.

Shortly after these dispositions were made, I was directed to move my Third Brigade to the rear of the right of General Birney's division, and make it subject to his order for support, which was accordingly done. I was at the same time authorized to draw support, should I need it, from General Caldwell's division, Second Corps, and by General Hunt, chief of artillery, was authorized to draw from the Artillery Reserve should I require more.

About 4 p. m., in compliance with General Sickles' orders, I moved my division forward, so that the first line ran along the Emmitsburg road a short distance behind the crest upon which that road lies. At the same time I ordered Lieutenant Seeley to place his battery in position on the right of the log house. As the division moved forward in two lines, as heretofore described, the enemy opened with artillery, which enfiladed us from the left, and subsequently with artillery on our front, both with but little effect. In reply to my inquiry whether I should attack, I was directed to remain in position. Lieutenant Seeley's battery was transferred to the left of the log house, and soon silenced the battery in our front. The position he vacated was immediately occupied by a battery (parts of F and K, Third U. S. Artillery) commanded by Lieut. J. G. Turnbull, sent at my request from the Artillery Reserve. Captain Ransom, Third U. S. Artillery, while engaged in supervising the posting of this battery, was severely wounded.

The division on my left was now engaged with the enemy's infantry, which in my front merely made demonstrations, but did not drive in my pickets.

Colonel Sewell, commanding the Fifth New Jersey Volunteers, of my Third Brigade, reported to me at this time and relieved the pickets of General Graham's brigade (on my left), some of which extended over a part of my front. This regiment had been posted but a short time when a most urgent request was made by a staff officer of General Sickles that another regiment should be sent to the support of General Birney (Graham's brigade), leaving it to me, however, to decide whether it could be sent.

At this moment, Colonel Sewell sent me word that the enemy was driving in my pickets, and was about advancing in two lines to the attack. The demand for aid was so urgent, however, that I sent Major Burns' Fourth Excelsior to General Graham's brigade, and at the same time dispatched one of my aides, Lieutenant Christiancy, to General Hancock, commanding Second Corps (General Caldwell's division having been sent to the extreme left), with the request that he would send a brigade, if possible, to my support.

Seeley's battery had now opened upon the enemy's infantry as they began to advance. Turnbull's battery was likewise directed against them, and I was about to throw somewhat forward the left of my infantry and engage the enemy with it, when I received orders from General Birney (General Sickles having been dangerously wounded and carried from the field) to throw back my left, and form a line oblique to and in rear of the one I then held, and was informed that the First Division would complete the line to the Round Top ridge. This I did under a heavy fire of artillery and infantry from the enemy, who now advanced on my whole front.

At this time, Colonel Sewell's regiment returned to the line, having maintained most gallantly its position on picket, with very heavy loss. Seeley's battery remained to the last moment, withdrawing without difficulty, but with severe loss in killed and wounded, including its commander among the latter. His loss was 2 enlisted men killed; 1 commissioned officer and 19 enlisted men wounded; 1 enlisted man missing, and 25 horses killed and disabled.

My infantry now engaged the enemy's, but my left was in air (although I extended it as far as possible with my Second Brigade), and, being the only troops on the field, the enemy's whole attention was directed to my division, which was forced back slowly, firing as they receded. Lieutenant Turnbull fell back with the infantry, suffering severe loss in men and horses, himself wounded. His loss was 1 commissioned officer and 8 enlisted men killed; 14 enlisted men wounded; 1 enlisted man missing, and 44 horses killed.

The two regiments sent me by General Hancock were judiciously posted by Lieut. H. C. Christiancy in support of my right. At this time I received orders through a staff officer from General Birney to withdraw to the Round Top ridge—an order previously conveyed to General Carr, commanding the First Brigade on the right, by General Birney in person. This order I complied with, retiring very slowly, continuing the contest with the enemy, whose fire of artillery and infantry was destructive in the extreme.

Upon arriving at the crest of the ridge mentioned, the remnants of my division formed on the left of General Hancock's troops, whose artillery opened upon the enemy, about 100 yards distant. The infantry joined, and the enemy broke and was driven from the field, rapidly followed by Hancock's troops and the remnants of my two brigades, who took many prisoners and brought off two pieces of our artillery which had been left after all the horses were killed.

Sergt. Thomas Hogan, Third Excelsior, brought to me on the field the flag of the Eighth Florida Regiment, which he had captured. He deserves reward.

It was now near dusk, and the contest for the day was closed. Its severity may be judged by the fact that the loss in killed, wounded, and missing of my division, 5,000 strong, was 2,088, of whom 171 were officers and 1,917 enlisted men. The missing numbered 3 officers and 263 enlisted men, the greater part of whom were probably wounded; some were killed.

I append a tabular list of the loss.*

As I have already stated, my Third Brigade was ordered to the support of Major-General Birney, commanding the First Division. The accompanying report of Col. George C. Burling, commanding that brigade, exhibits the disposition that was made of the regiments of the brigade. In succession they, with the exception of Colonel Sewell's regiment, were sent to aid the brigades of the First Division. The Seventh New Jersey, Col. Louis R. Francine commanding, and the Second New Hampshire, Col. Edward L. Bailey commanding, were sent to the support of General Graham's brigade, and the Eighth New Jersey, Colonel Ramsey commanding, the Sixth New Jersey, Lieut. Col. S. R. Gilkyson commanding, and the One hundred and fifteenth Pennsylvania, Major Dunne commanding, were sent to the support of General Ward's brigade.

For the part taken in the engagement by these regiments, I must refer to the reports of the commanders of these brigades. That they did their duty in a manner comporting with their high reputation is manifest from the severe loss they met with—430 killed and wounded. Colonel Sewell, Colonel Francine, Colonel Ramsey, and Lieutenant-Colonel Price, officers distinguished for their skill and gallantry, were severely wounded. Colonel Francine's wound proved to be mortal. Colonel Bailey and Lieutenant-Colonel Carr, Second New Hampshire, were also wounded.

The fortune of war rarely places troops under more trying circumstances than those in which my division found itself on this day, and it is greatly to their honor that their soldierly bearing sustained the high reputation they had already won in the severest battles of the war. The fine qualities of many officers were brought out conspicuously. In some instances their gallant conduct fell under my own observation. I wish particularly to recommend to notice the cool courage, determination, and skillful handling of their troops by the two brigade commanders, Brigadier-General Carr and Col. William R. Brewster, and to ask attention to the officers mentioned by them as distinguished by their conduct.

My attention was attracted by the gallant bearing of Capt. Le Grand Benedict, assistant adjutant-general, First Brigade, and of Lieut. E. A. Belger, aide, staff of Second Brigade. Lieut. F. W. Seeley's gallantry, skill, good judgment, and effective management of his battery excited my admiration, as well as that of every officer who saw him. I should not omit to mention the bold and determined manner in which Lieutenant Turnbull managed his battery. Lieut. Manning Livingston, of this battery, was killed during the engagement.

Of my own staff, part of whom had gone through hotly contested fields with me before, I might well use the highest terms of commendation that language admits of, though in speaking of their acts I am painfully reminded that as yet I have been powerless to further the advancement they have won while serving with me. Most conspicuous for gallantry and untiring efforts in aiding me in forming, encouraging, and leading the troops were Capt. Carswell McClellan,

---

*See revised statement, p. 178.

of the adjutant-general's department, my special aide; Capt. William Henry Chester, special aide, mortally wounded ; and Lieut. H. H. Humphreys, aide, wounded.

I beg leave also to express my sense of the obligations I am under for valuable services rendered me on the field by Maj. Charles Hamlin, assistant adjutant-general; Capt. A. F. Cavada, assistant inspector-general, and my aide, Lieut. Henry C. Christiancy. The judicious disposition by the latter of the re-enforcements he brought me is particularly deserving of mention.

The officers whose gallant and meritorious conduct General Carr brings to my notice are, using the language of General Carr:

Col. Robert McAllister, commanding Eleventh New Jersey Volunteers, twice wounded; Lieut. Col. Porter D. Tripp, commanding Eleventh Massachusetts Volunteers; Lieut. Col. Waldo Merriam, commanding Sixteenth Massachusetts Volunteers, wounded; Maj. Robert L. Bodine, commanding Twenty-sixth Pennsylvania Volunteers; Maj. Philip J. Kearny, Eleventh New Jersey Volunteers, seriously wounded, since dead; Major McDonald, Eleventh Massachusetts Volunteers, wounded; Captain Tomlinson, Twenty-sixth Pennsylvania Volunteers, acting lieutenant-colonel; Captain Goodfellow, Twenty-sixth Pennsylvania Volunteers, wounded, and Adjt. John Schoonover, Eleventh New Jersey Volunteers, who was twice wounded, but remained in command of his regiment; and to the following officers of my staff, to whom my sincere thanks are due for valuable services rendered: Capt. Le Grand Benedict, assistant adjutant-general; Capt. George E. Henry, First Massachusetts Volunteers, acting aide-de-camp, and Lieut. John Oldershaw, Eleventh New Jersey Volunteers, acting assistant inspector-general.

Colonel Brewster's mention of those of his brigade distinguished for their conduct is as follows:

The conduct and bearing of both officers and men was so good under the fatigues of the long and tiresome marches, and so gallant, brave, and steady in action, that it is almost impossible to particularize individual acts. It is enough to say that every officer and man in the command seemed determined to sustain the reputation of the brigade, earned on many a hard-fought field, and how well they succeeded is best shown by the loss sustained.

The members of my staff—Adjt. Gen. J. P. Finkelmeier, Capt. George Le Fort, acting assistant inspector-general, and Lieuts. J. A. Smith and Belger—were very active in the field, and behaved in the most gallant manner, conveying my orders under the hottest fire. Major Finkelmeier and Captain Le Fort were both wounded, and obliged to leave the field before the action was over. * * * Col. John S. Austin, Third Excelsior, Asst. Surg. Joseph D. Stewart, Fifth Excelsior, and Lieut. Col. C. D. Westbrook, One hundred and twentieth New York Volunteers, were also wounded.

Col. George C. Burling, commanding Third Brigade, expresses himself in relation to the conduct of his brigade in the following terms:

During the two days of fighting, both officers and men behaved with their usual gallantry. I thank Capt. T. W. Eayre, assistant adjutant-general; Capt. J. W. Crawford, acting commissary of subsistence; Lieutenant Bruen, acting aide-de-camp, and Lieutenant Clark, ambulance officer, for their gallantry and promptness in conveying my orders. The last named was mortally wounded, and died on the field.

Colonel Sewell's conspicuous gallantry in the maintenance of his post has been already mentioned by me. He was severely wounded soon after his regiment rejoined the main line.

The enemy having been driven from the field, I formed my division on the left of Hancock's (Second) corps, along the Round Top ridge, where it remained during the night. Parties were at once sent out to bring in the wounded. Lieutenant [William J.] Rusling, ambulance officer, was promptly on the ground.

At daylight on the 3d, the enemy opened a brisk artillery fire upon my division, which, however, soon abated. About sunrise, by order of General Birney, I moved my division to the left and rear, to resupply ammunition, distribute rations, and bring up stragglers. My Third Brigade joined me here. After an hour thus spent, my division was moved to the front again, and massed in rear of the right of the First and left of the Second Corps, a disposition which was soon changed, my division being moved to the left, and massed in rear and support of the Fifth Corps and part of the Sixth Corps, near where the Marsh Run road passes by the Round Top. It remained thus posted until about 4.30 o'clock, when it was moved rapidly to the right, and formed in mass by battalion in rear and support of the left of the Second and right of the First Corps, several batteries being in position in my front. Here it remained until dusk, losing several valuable officers and a large number of men from the enemy's artillery fire. My special aide, Captain McClellan, was wounded.

At dusk, the position was resumed in rear of the Fifth and Sixth Corps, where my division remained during July 4, 5, and 6, engaged in bringing in the wounded, burying the dead, and collecting arms.

My thanks are due to Capt. G. S. Russell, provost-marshal of the division, for the faithful manner in which the duties of his command were performed in the battle. It was judiciously posted, but from the nature of the ground was subjected to constant fire, causing the loss of several men.

The great distance of the hospital from the field and the necessity of my continued presence with the division prevented my making the visits to it which I had been in the habit of doing. My staff officers were sent by me to see to the wounded. Surgeon Calhoun, medical director of my division, was placed in charge of the corps hospital, owing to the absence of the corps medical director, and, aided by Surg. C. K. Irwin, acting medical director of the division, and its medical officers, gave every possible attention and skillful treatment to those whom the fortunes of the combat brought upon his hands.

The enterprise and energy of Captain [B. Weller] Hoxie, ordnance officer of the division, entitle him to my thanks, which are also due, for the faithful performance of duty, to Captain [James D.] Earle, commissary of subsistence, and Captain [Thomas P.] Johnston, assistant quartermaster.

At 3 a. m. of the 7th, my division marched on the Emmitsburg road, and bivouacked for the night at Mechanicsville, 9 miles south of Emmitsburg.

At 6 a. m. of the 8th, the march was resumed for Middletown, on the Frederick and Hagerstown pike, by way of Hamburg and the mountain pass in that vicinity, but in consequence of the heavy rains of the night and morning, the roads being nearly impassable, the route was changed to that through Frederick, and the division bivouacked from 2 to 3 miles beyond Frederick, and about 4 miles from Middletown. At midnight I received directions to join the headquarters of the army at Middletown, having been announced in orders as chief of staff of the Army of the Potomac, directions that I complied with at once, turning over the command of the division to Brigadier-General Carr.

In parting from this celebrated division, after having commanded it for the brief period of fifty days, I trust that I may be excused for expressing my admiration for its high soldierly qualities. It is impossible to pass it in review, even, without perceiving that its ranks are filled with men who are soldiers in the best meaning of the term, and that it possesses in the grade of commissioned officers men whose skill, courage, and accomplishments would grace any service.

Very respectfully, your obedient servant,

A. A. HUMPHREYS,
Major-General of Volunteers, Commanding Division.

Lieut. Col. O. H. HART,
Assistant Adjutant-General, Third Corps.

No. 159.

Report of Brig. Gen. Henry Prince, U. S. Army, commanding Second Division.

HEADQUARTERS SECOND DIVISION, THIRD CORPS,
Camp near Beverly Ford, Va., August 21, 1863.

CAPTAIN: By a circular from headquarters Army of the Potomac, dated August 12, 1863, a report of the operations of this command is required, to extend from June 28 until arriving in the vicinity of Warrenton, July 25. The report thus required for the portion of the time including the battle of Gettysburg and to July 9, is, as I am informed by him, made by Maj. Gen. A. A. Humphreys, U. S. Volunteers, who turned over the command on that date to Brig. Gen. Joseph B. Carr, U. S. Volunteers.

On the evening of July 9, I bivouacked with this division on the top of South Mountain, and I assumed command of it, by orders from corps headquarters, at that place on the morning of the 10th.

The operations of my command from July 9 to the arrival at Warrenton are as follows:

July 9.—General Carr assumed command of the division, which marched at 5 a. m. from Frederick to Middletown, Fox's Pass of the South Mountain, across the mountain, and bivouacked at 7.30 p. m. on its west verge.

July 10.—At 6.30 a. m. General Prince assumed command of the division. The division marched at 9.30 a. m.; passed through Keedysville, where it crossed the Little Antietam on a stone bridge, and bivouacked a mile from the bridge at 7.15 p. m., on top of the hill.

At 10.50 p. m. left bivouac, by orders from corps headquarters, to proceed forthwith to Boole's Mill. Recrossed the Antietam, and turned up stream. Bivouacked at 3 a. m. on the high land, upon the Boonsborough and Williamsport turnpike. The bivouac was necessarily in a wheat-field, the stacks of which the men slept on, which were thus trampled considerably. Some of the wheat was fed to horses, which would otherwise have been without feed, the route by which we marched being choked by teams, keeping ours back. I am particular in stating the circumstances of this injury to wheat, as formal complaint was made in regard to it, reflecting on the division. I myself had nothing but wheat to sleep on.

July 11.—Left bivouac at 6 a. m. Marched to Beaver Creek, and bivouacked there in rear of the First Division of Third Corps.

At 4.30 p. m. returned 1 mile on the road, and, taking left hand at forks, forded Beaver Creek. Crossed the Antietam on a stone bridge at Boole's Mill. Bivouacked three-quarters of a mile below the mill, on the Antietam.

July 12.—Moved forward 2 miles, and occupied the west verge of a copse, where the division bivouacked in line of battle near Jones' Cross-Roads.

July 14.—Left the bivouac last mentioned at 5.30 a. m., with orders from corps headquarters to advance on the Williamsport turnpike, and occupy the position vacated by the First Division, Twelfth Corps, which advanced to reconnoiter the enemy. Occupied this position till 11.20 a. m. Marched at that hour toward Williamsport, crossing Marsh Run, passing through the enemy's evacuated works, which covered their approaches with artillery and infantry fire, and bivouacked at 3.20 p. m. on the pike, 4 miles, as was said, from Williamsport.

July 15.—Left bivouac at 6 a. m. Marched through Fair Play, Tilghmanton, and Sharpsburg, crossing the battle-field of Antietam, which was marked by the trees being battered, without exception, on the side facing us, we going southward. Crossed the Antietam on a stone bridge, and bivouacked half a mile from it, on top of the hill, at 1.30 p. m.

July 16.—Left bivouac at 6 a. m. Passed through Rohrersville, by mistake of the guide, and Brownsville. Bivouacked at the forks of road, 4 miles from Harper's Ferry.

July 17.—Left bivouac at 4.30 p. m. Crossed the Potomac at Harper's Ferry on a pontoon bridge. Crossed the Shenandoah, and bivouacked on Sweet Run, 3 miles from Harper's Ferry, at 7.15 p. m.

July 18.—Marched at 4 a. m. up Sweet Run to Hillsborough, and bivouacked west of the town. The advance guard passed through the town, as I had been informed some of the enemy were there.

July 19.—Marched at 7.45 a. m. Passed near Woodgrove, and bivouacked 1 mile west of the town, on the right of the pike, facing Ashby's Gap. The division was re-enforced in this position by Battery B, First New Jersey Artillery, commanded by Lieut. Robert Sims.

July 22.—Left bivouac near Ashby's Gap at 3.15 p. m., and bivouacked at Piedmont Station, on the Manassas Railroad, at 6.50 p. m.

The account of the 23d, 24th, and 25th is detailed in the following report rendered to headquarters Third Corps on July 29:

HEADQUARTERS SECOND DIVISION, THIRD CORPS,
Camp near Warrenton, Va., July 29, 1863.

CAPTAIN : Pursuant to your circular, I have the honor to report the operations of this division during July 23, 24, and 25:

The division marched from its bivouac at Piedmont early on the morning of the 23d instant, following the road into Manassas Gap. At Linden we came up with the First Division of the corps, and I then formed the three brigades in three columns in mass, and was ordered in this manner to follow and support the First Division, which was deployed to the front. This was done, by orders from headquarters of the corps, until the First Division had carried the high ridge crossing our course, upon which the enemy first made fight. This was a very high and steep ridge, and, being cleared, the whole mechanism of the advance was visible, furnishing a magnificent scene.

When my columns arrived at the top, I found the line of the First Division deployed along the crest, occupying it far to the right and left. Its skirmishers, advanced below on the other side, were stationary, and warmly engaged with those of the enemy, both parties seeking the cover of the ground from each other, but perfectly in view from the top of the ridge.

At this juncture I received permission from corps headquarters to employ my division where I saw best. I then directed Brigadier-General Spinola to march his brigade (the Excelsior) by the flank along the hollow, then in our view, winding to the front and center of the high ridge on which we stood, keeping on the lowest ground within it, and, on debouching from it by the left flank, to advance in line by his proper front up the hill he would find himself at the base of, and take it. This hill was the key of the ground occupied by the enemy's skirmishers. The First and Third Brigades were already in position to support this charge by advancing down the counter-fort of the main ridge, a nearer route to the hill referred to.

The line of the Second Brigade made its appearance at the base of the hill between 5 and 6 p. m., and began to ascend before its right was clear of the hollow or ravine, which did not give it so fair a start as might otherwise have been; but nothing can transcend the gallantry with which it rose to the crest and drove the enemy from it. In the moment of this success, a second crest of the same hill, 200 yards beyond the first and confounded with it until this time, came into their view, behind which the enemy rose from his prone posture as thick as men can stand, opening a furious fire of musketry. At the same time a six-gun battery, still farther beyond, opened with shell. I now advanced the Third Brigade, commanded by Colonel Burling, with orders to occupy the crest just taken. It deployed, advancing, and arrived promptly and in perfect order at its position. The First Brigade, commanded by Brigadier-General Carr, I brought forward in mass to the position of support for the flanks of the Third.

The severest part of the charge of the Excelsior Brigade was before it after taking the first crest, but without hesitation, with the determination of the Union soldier and the fury of the hurricane, it took the second crest, and exposed the enemy (scampering away from it) to fire while descending the one side of a deep cleared hollow and climbing up the other.

Directions had been sent by me to the brigade while charging the second crest to halt upon and maintain that crest, and to restore its line there, and I arrived there with part of my staff in time to assist in doing this. A farther advance without preparation would have been irregular. A very deep and wide hollow now ran down on the left and to the front of our position, and on our right front was a high, wooded mountain, running up to a peak. The woods at the base of this mountain extended to our position, separated from it by a gully. The driven rebels were to be seen pouring into that part of the woods nearest us, evidently to attack the right flank of my advanced line, the Excelsior Brigade.

Accordingly, I extended my second line to the right, so that it would enfilade the woods. This extension was made up of the troops commanded by Colonel de Trobriand, which did not report to me, but, seeing them come at this time to the front, I ordered them into my second line and afterward to move some distance to the right, for the purpose above named. I also brought General Carr's brigade up to the second line, and established it there in mass near the road, which cut the line at right angles and passed through the woods. The enemy threw solid shot and shell at the troops of General Carr and Colonel de Trobriand during their movements without effect. While making these dispositions, darkness settled down and overtook us, and the troops of my division slept on their arms.

The simple narrative of this infantry exploit, unaided by any other arm of the service, is the most just commendation that can be made of those who performed it. It is impossible to mention their names. Brig. Gen. F. B. Spinola, U. S. Volunteers, while leading his brigade toward the second of the crests taken by it, fell, wounded in two places, severely, but not seriously. The command of the brigade devolved from that time upon Col. J. Egbert Farnum, First Excelsior Regiment.

At daylight of the following morning, my pickets and skirmishers explored the ground of the enemy, and found it occupied only by the dead men they in their hasty departure had left behind. The merit of this discovery is due to the vigilance of Colonel Farnum. On this being reported, I received orders from corps headquarters to advance immediately with the division, which was soon re-enforced by the Keystone Battery, Captain Hastings, and a squadron of cavalry under Captain Mason. My orders were to proceed to Front Royal, and on being satisfied that there were only cavalry and artillery in my front, to return.

Nearing Front Royal some irregular cavalry and a piece or two of artillery skirmished with us and threw a few shells without effect, and their dust, as seen from the heights west of the village, showed them to be far beyond our reach when we arrived there. Throughout this advance the Second New Hampshire Volunteers, of the Third Brigade (whose turn came to lead the column this day), were deployed as skirmishers to the front. I captured 203 of the enemy in Front Royal, but as they were, most of them, unfit to march, being the wounded and sick, I left nearly all of them there. Having demonstrated that there was no important force of the enemy in that quarter, I immediately began my return march. At dark, after an arduous day's march and some handsome soldiership, my command bivouacked near Markham Station, in Manassas Gap.

On the 25th instant, the division overtook the corps, resumed its place in column, and bivouacked with it 7 miles from Warrenton, after a hard march.

I transmit herewith a tabular statement of the killed and wounded of the division, and a list of their names,* nearly all of which casualties occurred in the Second Brigade; also the reports of Brig. Gen. Joseph B. Carr, commanding First Brigade;

---

* Embodied in revised statement, p. 192.

Col. J. Egbert Farnum, First Excelsior Regiment, commanding Second Brigade: Col. George C. Burling, Sixth New Jersey Volunteers, commanding Third Brigade; also the report of Capt. John W. Holmes, U. S. Volunteers, provost-marshal of this division, of prisoners taken at Front Royal.

May I be permitted to mention the staff officers to whom I am indebted for correct transmission of my orders in these arduous operations? They were: Capt. George S. Russell, aide-de-camp; Capt. John W. Holmes, division provost-marshal; First Lieut. Albert Ordway, aide-de-camp and acting assistant adjutant-general, and Second Lieut. L. F. Haskell, aide-de-camp and acting assistant inspector-general. Lieutenant Haskell was the only one of my personal staff in the battle of Cedar Mountain who survived the wounds received there. I regret to see that gallantry such as he exhibited there and at Pea Ridge and the first Bull Run receives no notice by brevet or otherwise from the Government. He bore my orders on the 23d into the thickest of the fight.

Very respectfully your obedient servant,

HENRY PRINCE,
Brigadier-General of Volunteers, Comdg. Division.

Capt. W. F. A. TORBERT,
A. D. C. and A. A. A. G., Third Army Corps.

The above report omits to state what is found in the accompanying reports from brigades, viz, that on July 23 the following detachments were made, pursuant to orders received from headquarters of the Third Corps, viz, one regiment (the Sixth New Jersey Volunteers) to guard the train; one regiment (the Seventh New Jersey Volunteers) to support battery on the heights commanding Chester Gap; one regiment (the First Massachusetts Volunteers) to report to General Ward, immediately in our front; one regiment (the Twenty-sixth Pennsylvania Volunteers) to support Winslow's battery, north of the road, and one regiment (the One hundred and twentieth New York Volunteers) to picket the road to Chester Gap.

During the action, while advancing with, close in rear of, and supporting the First Division of this corps, I received orders from the headquarters of the corps to direct General Spinola to report with the Second Brigade to General Ward, commanding the First Division. At the summit of the ridge I learned from General Ward in person that he did not take the command of General Spinola, and that his brigade was returned to my command.

July 26.—Left bivouac at 5.45 a. m.; passed through Warrenton at 9 a. m., and bivouacked 3 miles from Warrenton, on the Sulphur Springs road.

Respectfully submitted.

HENRY PRINCE,
Brigadier-General of Volunteers, Commanding.

Capt. W. H. HILL,
Assistant Adjutant-General, Third Army Corps.

[Inclosure.]

Recapitulation of losses at Manassas Gap, Va., July 23, 1863.

Command.	Killed.			Wounded.			Aggregate.
	Officers.	Enlisted men.	Total killed.	Officers.	Enlisted men.	Total wounded.	
First Brigade					1	1	1
Second Brigade	3	15	18	1	56	59	75
Third Brigade					2	2	2
Total	3	15	18	1	59	62	78

HEADQUARTERS THIRD ARMY CORPS,
August 26, 1863.

GENERAL: In looking over the report of Brigadier-General Prince, commanding Second Division of the corps, in the affair at Wapping Heights, I find the following:

At this juncture I received permission from corps headquarters to employ my division where I saw best. I then directed Brigadier-General Spinola to march his brigade (the Excelsior) by flank along the hollow, then in our view, winding to the front and center of the high ridge on which we stood, keeping on the lowest ground within it, and, on debouching from it by the left flank, to advance in line by his proper front up the hill he would find himself at the base of, and take it, &c.

This latter sentence taken in connection with the one which precedes it would leave the impression that the change of the Excelsior Brigade originated with General Prince. I am satisfied that such could never have been the intention of the general, and consider it nothing more than right that I should say that I conveyed the order to General Prince from General French, directing him to make the attack, and pointed out to him the route to be taken by General Spinola, and then General Prince replied to me that he would head the attack or govern the movement himself, or words to that effect.

I am, general, yours, respectfully,

J. HAYDEN,
Lieutenant-Colonel, and Assistant Inspector-General.

Major-General FRENCH,
Commanding Third Army Corps.

No. 160.

Reports of Brig. Gen. Joseph B. Carr, U. S. Army, commanding First Brigade.

HDQRS. FIRST BRIG., SECOND DIV., THIRD CORPS,
Camp near Beverly Ford, Va., August 1, 1863.

SIR: In compliance with orders from headquarters Second Division, Third Corps, I have the honor to transmit the following report of the operations of my command from the beginning of the campaign up to and including the 8th ultimo:

On Thursday, June 11, by direction of the division commander, I broke camp, marched my command to Hartwood Church, and bivouacked for the night.

At 6 a. m. on Friday, June 12, took up the line of march toward Rappahannock Station, reaching that point at 7.30 p. m. Here, by order of Major Hamlin, assistant adjutant-general of division, I formed my command in a field, in column of regiments, and soon after moved out and advanced to near Beverly Ford, reaching that place at 10 p. m., establishing a picket line along the river and at the ford. During this day's march, nearly 25 miles, many men were compelled to quit the ranks in consequence of exhaustion, consequent upon the excessive heat and unusually dusty roads.

On Saturday, June 13, at 9 p. m., a detail of 200 men reported at brigade headquarters, in accordance with instructions, for the purpose of throwing up intrenchments, but as the tools did not arrive until 2 a. m. on Sunday, June 14, work was not commenced until that hour.

At 9 p. m. moved from Beverly Ford, passing Bealeton at 10 p. m.

Monday, June 15, reached Warrenton Junction at 8 a. m., and halted one-half mile from the station.

At 1 p. m. left the Junction and marched to Manassas. This march was one of the most severe in my experience, the air being almost suffocating, the dust blinding, and the heat intolerable. Many men suffered from *coup de soleil*, and a large number sank by the way-side, utterly helpless and exhausted.

At 2 o'clock on the morning of Tuesday, June 16, my brigade halted and went into bivouac. At noon the location of my camp was changed a short distance to the right and rear, where the men were permitted to rest.

At 10 a. m. on Wednesday, June 17, I moved 2 miles in the direction of Centreville, and halted in a grove by the side of Bull Run Creek, to enable my men to bathe.

At 4 p. m. I pushed on to Centreville, and went into camp at 7 p. m. near a fine stream of water.

On Thursday, June 18, at 6 p. m., changed location of camp 1 mile to the right, and established a picket line, with Colonel McAllister, Eleventh New Jersey Volunteers, as officer of the day.

At 2.45 p. m. on Friday, June 19, we marched to Gum Springs, reaching that place at 7 p. m., and immediately throwing out a picket detail, consisting of the First and Eleventh Massachusetts Volunteers and Twenty-sixth Pennsylvania Volunteers.

On Thursday, June 25, received orders to be in readiness to move at 5.40 a. m.; moved at 10 a. m., passing through Fairfarm and Frank-linville, and crossing the Potomac into Maryland at 5 p. m. Marched along the canal to the Monocacy Aqueduct, halting at 1 o'clock on the morning of Friday, June 26, with about 300 men, the remainder having fallen out during the march, weary and exhausted. Early in the morning I sent back a field officer, who brought up the stragglers at 10 a. m.

At 11 a. m. marched to Point of Rocks, and bivouacked at 5 p. m.

On Saturday, June 27, marched to Jefferson, and halted for two hours.

At 1 p. m. left Jefferson, and marched to Burkittsville, where I relieved a brigade from the —— Corps, and threw out a strong picket force.

At 9.20 a. m. on Sunday, June 28, left Burkittsville, and marched to Middletown, halting an hour for dinner. Pushed on to Frederick, passing through the city at 6 p. m.; halted just outside the city for supper, and then crossed the Monocacy, going into bivouac at 10.30 p. m.

Monday, June 29, left at 5.20 a. m., and marched to Taneytown, passing through Walkersville, Woodsborough, and Ladiesburg.

At 4.20 p. m. on Tuesday, June 30, left Taneytown, and marched to Bridgeport, going into bivouac at 6.30 p. m.

At 8 a. m. on Wednesday, July 1, left Bridgeport, and marched to Emmitsburg, reaching that place at 1.15 p. m. After a halt of two hours, received orders to move with all possible haste to Gettysburg, as General Howard, commanding Eleventh Corps, had attacked the enemy and been repulsed. General Humphreys, commanding the division, being absent by orders from corps headquarters, for the purpose of selecting a position for the corps, and believing the enemy to be near at hand, I immediately ordered the division under arms, and took up the line of march toward Gettysburg, leaving one battery and the Third Brigade (commanded by Col. George C. Burling) at Emmitsburg.

When about 1 mile from that town, General Humphreys joined the division, and resumed command. The column was guided by a civilian (a doctor) from Emmitsburg and Lieutenant-Colonel Hayden, assistant inspector-general of the corps. When about 3 miles from Gettysburg, we crossed Marsh Creek and advanced on the left-hand road about a mile, when we were suddenly halted by General Humphreys as a measure of precaution. Lieutenant-Colonel Hayden, who had been in advance with the guides, soon after rode up to General Humphreys, and stated that we were but 200 yards from the enemy's pickets.

General Humphreys rode forward to the Black Horse Tavern, on the road from Fairfield to Gettysburg, and finding the information to be correct, and that the enemy occupied the road in heavy force, and believing that an engagement with him at the distance of 3 miles from the rest of the army, with the enemy between the army and his division, would be inconsistent with the plan of battle, faced the division about, and marched to the rear until striking the main road, upon which we proceeded to Gettysburg, reaching that place and going into bivouac at 1.30 a. m. on Thursday, July 2.

This position I retained until 12.30 p. m., at which hour I was ordered to move to the front and form line of battle on the prolongation of a line composed of the First Division of the Third Corps, connecting on its right. After disposing of my command as above directed, the position I occupied, as nearly as I can judge, was the left center.

About 11 a. m. I had sent out a regiment as skirmishers (the First Massachusetts Volunteers, Lieutenant-Colonel Baldwin commanding), and this regiment now covered my front.

At 4.08 p. m., by order of General Humphreys, I advanced my line 300 yards to the crest of a hill, and at the same time detailed 100 men from the Sixteenth Massachusetts Volunteers to occupy an old building, situated in an orchard on the left of my line. This detail perforated the house in several places, and materially aided in checking the advance of the enemy. My left first became engaged, and its position was held until the regiment on my left (the Collis Zouaves, of the First Division) gave way, when the enemy advanced in considerable force on my left flank, which compelled me to change my front; but no sooner was it accomplished than the enemy made his appearance on my right flank, pouring in a most destructive cross-fire.

Notwithstanding my apparent critical position, I could and would have maintained my position but for an order received direct from Major-General Birney, commanding the corps, to fall back to the crest of the hill in my rear. At that time I have no doubt that I could have charged on the rebels and driven them in confusion, for my line was still perfect and unbroken, and my troops in the proper spirit for the performance of such a task. In retiring, I suffered a severe loss in killed and wounded.

After I had reached the position designated by General Birney, the brigade was rallied by my assistant adjutant-general and aides, and moved forward, driving the enemy and capturing many prisoners. I continued to advance until I again occupied the field I had but a few moments previous vacated. Here my command remained until morning, the officers and men assisting in removing from the field as many of the wounded as the time and facilities would admit of.

I may be pardoned, perhaps, for referring in my report to the conspicuous courage and remarkable coolness of the brigadier-general commanding the division during this terrific struggle. His presence was felt by the officers and men, as the enthusiastic manner in which he was greeted will testify.

At daybreak on the morning of Friday, July 3, the enemy opened with his artillery, and kept up a continuous fire for an hour or more, with but little injury to my command.

At 6 a. m. I was ordered to the rear, where the balance of the corps was in bivouac. After replenishing my supply of ammunition, I was ordered to the front and left of the line, to support a division of the Fifth Corps, which was in the first line.

At 3.22 p. m. I was ordered to the center of the line, to support the Second Corps, which was engaged with the enemy.

As I lay in column of battalions, closed in mass, I suffered severely from the artillery fire of the enemy, losing several valuable officers and a number of men.

At dusk I was ordered to my former position, where I remained until 3.30 a. m. on Tuesday, July 7, at which hour my brigade moved from bivouac and marched to Emmitsburg, where we rested until 1.15 p. m., when we pushed on to Mechanicstown, going into bivouac about 1 mile from the town.

At 6 a. m. on Wednesday, July 8, marched to Frederick, going into camp outside the city at 10 p. m.

At 4 a. m. on Thursday, July 9, Major Hamlin, assistant adjutant-general, turned over to me the command of the division, Brigadier-General Humphreys having accepted the position of chief of staff to the major-general commanding the army.

In closing, I desire to call the attention of the general commanding the division to the gallant and meritorious conduct of Col. Robert McAllister, commanding Eleventh New Jersey Volunteers, twice wounded; Lieut. Col. Porter D. Tripp, commanding Eleventh Massachusetts Volunteers; Lieut. Col. Waldo Merriam, commanding Sixteenth Massachusetts Volunteers, wounded; Maj. Robert L. Bodine, commanding Twenty-sixth Pennsylvania Volunteers; Maj. Philip J. Kearny, Eleventh New Jersey Volunteers, seriously wounded (since dead); Major McDonald, Eleventh Massachusetts Volunteers, wounded; Captain Tomlinson, Twenty-sixth Pennsylvania Volunteers, acting lieutenant-colonel; Captain Goodfellow, Twenty-sixth Pennsylvania Volunteers, wounded; Adjt. John Schoonover, Eleventh New Jersey Volunteers, who was twice wounded, but remained in command of his regiment; and to the following officers of my staff, to whom my sincere thanks are due for valuable services rendered: Capt. Le Grand Benedict, assistant adjutant-general; Capt. George E. Henry, First Massachusetts Volunteers, acting aide-de-camp, and Lieut. John Oldershaw, Eleventh New Jersey Volunteers, acting assistant inspector-general.

Lieut. James Johnson, aide-de-camp and acting assistant quartermaster, and Lieut. James A. Cook, acting commissary of subsistence, are entitled to great credit for the promptness and efficiency displayed in the execution of the duties pertaining to their respective departments.

In justice to the surviving officers and men of the veteran brigade, who have on many hard-fought battle-fields distinguished themselves for gallantry and undaunted courage, I cannot close this report without expressing my admiration for their soldierly conduct on this occasion. At the same time I may be permitted to express my deep and heartfelt sympathy for those who now mourn the loss of husbands, fathers, brothers, and friends, who have sacrificed their lives on the altar of their country in upholding its honor and integrity.

I append herewith a tabular statement of the casualties up to and including the 8th ultimo:

Command.	Killed.		Wounded.		Missing.		Total.		
	Officers.	Enlisted men.	Officers.	Enlisted men.	Officers.	Enlisted men.	Officers.	Enlisted men.	Aggregate.
General staff..........................	.....	.....	2	.....	.....	.....	2	.....	2
1st Massachusetts	4	15	8	75	.....	21	9	111	120
11th Massachusetts	1	22	7	89	2	8	10	119	129
16th Massachusetts	3	12	4	49	.....	13	7	74	81
26th Pennsylvania	1	29	10	166	.....	7	11	202	213
11th New Jersey	3	14	9	115	.....	12	12	141	153
12th New Hampshire	1	13	5	62	.....	11	6	86	92
Total.............................	10	105	45	556	2	72	57	733	790

I have the honor to be, respectfully, your obedient servant,

JOS. B. CARR,
Brigadier-General.

Maj. CHARLES HAMLIN,
Asst. Adjt. Gen., Second Division, Third Corps.

—

HDQRS. FIRST BRIG., SECOND DIV., THIRD CORPS,
Camp near Beverly Ford, Va., August 13, 1863.

SIR: I have the honor to make the following report of the operations of my command from July 9 to 31, inclusive. My report of the campaign up to and including July 8 has already been rendered.

On Thursday, July 9, Major Hamlin, assistant adjutant-general, turned over to me the command of the division, Brigadier-General Humphreys having accepted the position of chief of staff to the major-general commanding the army.

The brigade moved at 5 a. m., and marched to Middletown, where rations were issued to the command.

At 10 a. m. marched to South Mountain, where I halted until 6 p. m., at which hour we marched across the mountain, going into bivouac at 7.30 p. m.

At 6.30 a. m. on Friday, July 10, I was relieved of the command of the division by Brigadier-General Prince, and resumed command of my brigade.   Marched to Antietam, and bivouacked at 9.30 p. m.

At 10 p. m. the brigade was again in motion, and, after marching about 5 miles, went into bivouac at 2 a. m.

On Saturday, July 11, at 6 a. m., advanced 2 miles to the front. At 4 p. m., again advanced 2 miles to the front, and bivouacked for the night.

On Sunday, July 12, at 3 p. m., moved about 1 mile, and went into bivouac.

At 5.25 a. m. on Tuesday, July 14, moved to the support of the Twelfth Corps, about three-quarters of a mile to the front, and at 3 p. m. marched 1 mile and bivouacked.

On Wednesday, July 15, left bivouac near Williamsport at 6.15 a. m., and marched to Sharpsburg, passing through the town at noon, and going into bivouac at 1 p. m.

On Thursday, July 16, left bivouac at 6 a.m., and marched by way of Brownsville to near Maryland Heights, encamping at 2 p. m.

At 4.30 p. m. on Friday, July 17, marched to Harper's Ferry, crossing the river on pontoons. Pushed on 5 miles farther, and went into bivouac at 8 p. m.

On Saturday, July 18, marched at 3 a. m. to Hillsborough, and halted at noon for the night.

On Sunday, July 19, marched to Woodgrove.

On Monday, July 20, left at 4.30 a. m., and marched to Upperville, at which place I was directed to be prepared at any moment to meet the enemy.

On Tuesday, July 21, marched to Piedmont, and bivouacked at 5.30 p. m.

On Thursday, July 23, in accordance with orders from Brigadier-General Prince, I broke camp at Piedmont at 4.30 a. m., marched to Manassas Gap, 9 miles distant, and halted for two hours. I was then ordered to the front, and at the same time notified that the enemy was advancing in force. Reaching the rear of the First Division, I was directed to form in column of battalions, closed in mass, to support the division in my front; also to send out one regiment to support the left of the line of skirmishers, and one regiment to support Winslow's battery. For these duties I detailed the First Massachusetts Volunteers, Lieutenant-Colonel Baldwin commanding, and the Twenty-sixth Pennsylvania Volunteers, Major Bodine commanding. During the course of the afternoon, I assumed several positions by direction of the brigadier-general commanding the division, but did not become engaged.

At 7 o'clock on the morning of Friday, July 24, I was ordered to move my command in the rear of the Third Brigade of this division, in the direction of Front Royal. When within a mile of that place, I formed line of battle on the right of the Third Brigade, throwing out skirmishers to the front, with two regiments to support them. This position I sustained for one hour without advancing. The enemy opened fire from one of his guns, but without doing any injury whatever. I then advanced over a lofty hill thickly studded with undergrowth, and through Front Royal, halting on the west side for one hour, when I took up the line of march in the direction of the Gap, reaching Markham at dusk, having marched about 20 miles.

At 4 a. m. on Saturday, July 25, I marched 3 miles to Piedmont, halting near that place until 12 m., at which hour, by direction of Brigadier-General Prince, I proceeded with my command 3 miles beyond Salem, going into bivouac on the Warrenton road at 5.30 p. m.

On Sunday, July 26, left camp at 5.25 a. m., and marched to and through the town of Warrenton, and formed camp 3 miles beyond.

During these operations but one casualty occurred in my command, viz, Private Thomas Richards, Company C, Eighty-fourth Pennsylvania Volunteers, wounded in leg by musket-ball.

I have the honor to remain, your most obedient servant,

JOS. B. CARR,
Brigadier-General.

Maj. CHARLES HAMLIN,
     Asst. Adjt. Gen., Second Division, Third Corps.

No. 161.

Report of Lieut. Col. Clark B. Baldwin, First Massachusetts In-fantry.

NEAR WARRENTON, VA.,
July 28, 1863.

CAPTAIN: I have the honor to make the following report of the operations of my command during the recent movements:

On June 11, marching orders were received, and we broke camp at 1 p. m. and moved at 2.30 p. m. Bivouacked at 8.30 p. m. at Hartwood Church, having marched 9 miles.

June 12.—Marched at 5.45 a. m., and halted at Morristown at 11.30 a. m. Rested one hour and a half, and moved forward to Beverly Ford, arriving at 10 p. m. Distance marched, 26½ miles.

Remained here performing picket duty until the evening of June 14, when we moved at 7.30 p. m. in the direction of Manassas. Marched all night, and arrived at Warrenton Junction at 7.45 a. m. Continued march to a point midway between Warrenton Junction and Catlett's Station, arriving at 9.45 a. m. Halted here until 12 m., and continued march to half a mile beyond Manassas Junction, and bivouacked at 12.30 a. m.

June 15.—Marched upward of 30 miles.

June 16.—Moved about 1 mile toward Centreville, and bivouacked.

June 17.—Moved at 9.30 a. m. Crossed Bull Run, and halted until 3 p. m., when we moved to Centreville, and went into bivouac half a mile outside of town.

June 18.—In bivouac until 7 p. m., when we moved to a position near the wagon park; distance, 1 mile.

June 19.—Moved at 2.30 p. m. to Gum Springs; distance, 10 miles. Immediately put on picket duty; time, 7.30 p. m. Relieved at 4 p. m. on the 20th, and went into bivouac with brigade.

June 21.—At 4 p. m. changed position to a piece of wood, acting as support to a picket line.

Remained here until the morning of the 25th, and moved at 7 a. m., arriving at Edwards Ferry at 5.30 p. m.; crossed on pontoon, and proceeded up tow-path of canal to mouth of Monocacy River, arriving at 12.45 p. m.; distance marched, 27 miles.

June 26.—At 9 a. m. moved toward Point of Rocks, arriving at 4 p. m., and bivouacked; distance marched, 10 miles.

June 27.—Moved at 7.45 o'clock, and bivouacked at Burkittsville at 5.30 p. m.

June 28.—Moved as rear guard of division at 10 a. m.; marched 6 miles to Middletown; halted half an hour, and continued march to Frederick; bivouacked 3 miles from Frederick City at 10 p. m.; distance marched, 17 miles.

June 29.—Marched at 5 a. m.; halted near Ladiesburg for half an hour, and continued march to Taneytown, arriving at 4 p. m., and bivouacked; distance marched, 20 miles.

June 30.—Regiment mustered for pay; moved at 3 p. m. 4 miles to Bridgeport, and went into bivouac for the night.

July 1.—Moved at 8.30 a. m. to Emmitsburg, and arrived at 2.30 p. m.; moved at 4.30 p. m., and went into bivouac at Gettysburg at 2.30 a. m.

July 2.—At 11 a. m. sent to the front as skirmishers. Considerable skirmishing along the lines during the day. Held our position until 4 p. m., when the enemy advanced in force, and a general engagement took place.   We retired, and formed line of battle in connection with the brigade, fighting until dark closed the contest; bivouacked on the battle-field at night.

July 3.—Skirmishing commenced at daylight; heavy fighting on right of line.

At 9 a. m. were moved to the front, as support to the right wing of the army.

At 10 a. m. changed to left wing of the army, and at 12.30 p. m. again moved to the center, where we remained until 7 p. m.; again changed position to the left, and went into bivouac for the night.

July 4.—In bivouac; no movement.

July 5.—Captain Stone, Company D, in charge of burying party.

July 6.—Remained in bivouac all day.

July 7.—Moved at 3 a. m.; marched 7 miles, and halted for breakfast; continued the march to Mechanicstown, a distance in all of 17 miles, and bivouacked at 5 p. m.

July 8.—Moved at 6.30 a. m.; marched 23 miles, and went into bivouac 3 miles beyond Frederick City at 8.30 p. m.

I have the honor to be, very respectfully, &c.,

C. B. BALDWIN,
Lieutenant-Colonel, Comdg. First Massachusetts.

Capt. LE GRAND BENEDICT,
Assistant Adjutant-General.

No. 162.

Report of Lieut. Col. Porter D. Tripp, Eleventh Massachusetts Infantry.

BIVOUAC NEAR WARRENTON, VA., *July* 27, 1863.

CAPTAIN: In obedience to instructions from brigade headquarters, I have the honor to report the following movements of this regiment during the late campaign of this army, up to and including the 8th instant :

On June 11, orders were received to march.   The regiment left camp about 3 p. m., and marched to Hartwood Church, where we remained all night.

Next morning proceeded toward Beverly Ford, where we arrived at 10 p. m. on the 12th ultimo.

Left Beverly Ford on the 14th ultimo, at about 8.30 p. m., and proceeded to Warrenton Junction, where we arrived at 8.30 a. m. on the 15th ultimo.

Left Warrenton Junction at 1 p. m. the same day, and marched to Manassas Junction, and from thence to Centreville Heights, where we arrived at 5 p. m. on the 17th ultimo.

We remained here until 1 p. m. on the 19th ultimo, when we took up the line of march toward Gum Springs, where we arrived the same night at 8.30 o'clock.   The regiment was immediately sent out on picket duty.

Was relieved from picket on the 20th ultimo at 4 p. m., and joined the rest of the brigade.

We remained at Gum Springs until the 25th ultimo, when we took up the line of march to Poolesville, Md., by way of Goose Creek and Edwards Ferry, where we arrived at 1 a. m.

On the 26th ultimo, marched to Point of Rocks, Md., where we remained until 8 a. m. on the 27th ultimo, when we proceeded to Jefferson, and from there to Burkittsville, where we halted for the night.

Left Burkitttsville next morning at 8 a. m., and marched to Middletown, and from there to Frederick, where we encamped 4 miles outside the town for the night.

Left Frederick next morning at 6 a. m., and marched to Taneytown, where we arrived at 6 p. m. on the 29th ultimo.

Left Taneytown at 3 p. m. on the 30th ultimo, and marched to Bridgeport, a distance of 4 miles, where we halted for the night.

Left Bridgeport at 7 a. m. on July 1, and marched through Emmitsburg to Gettysburg, Pa.,where we arrived at 2 a. m. on the 2d instant.

At 8 a. m. the same day orders were received to move to the front to support a line of skirmishers, in which position we remained until 3 p. m., when the regiment was ordered into line of battle to withstand a charge made by the enemy, led by General Barksdale, of Mississippi. The regiment was engaged with the enemy until 8 p. m. on the 2d instant, having made two distinct charges and helping to repulse the enemy from that point.

We were ordered to fall back to the edge of the woods, where we remained until 3 p. m. on the 3d instant, when we were moved at double-quick to the front. We lay in line of battle of brigades until 6 p. m., when we again fell back to the edge of the woods.

The loss in this regiment during the 2d and 3d instant was—

Officers and men.	Killed.	Wounded.	Missing.	Total.
Officers	1	7	2	10
Enlisted men	22	89	10	121
Total	23	96	12	131

We remained near Gettysburg until the morning of the 5th instant, when we marched back through Emmitsburg, and encamped for the night at Mechanicstown, a distance of 18 miles from Gettysburg.

Left Mechanicstown next morning, and marched through Frederick, Md., and encamped about 2 miles outside of the city for the night.

Left camp next morning, and marched through Fox's Gap, a mile beyond South Mountain, where we encamped for the night.

During this campaign the men suffered from excessive heat and long marches, both day and night, sometimes without any rest for forty-eight hours; yet they met the enemy with cheerfulness, and aided in driving him from the soil of Pennsylvania and Maryland.

Very respectfully, your obedient servant,

PORTER D. TRIPP,
Lieutenant-Colonel, Commanding Regiment.

Capt. LE GRAND BENEDICT,
Assistant Adjutant-General, First Brigade.

No. 163.

Report of Capt. Matthew Donovan, Sixteenth Massachusetts Infantry.

BIVOUAC IN THE FIELD, *July* 29, 1863.

CAPTAIN: In accordance with circular from brigade headquarters, dated July 27, 1863, asking for a report of the operations of the regiment from the date of leaving camp to July 8, inclusive, I have the honor to transmit the following:

Thursday, June 11, broke camp at 2 p. m.; marched to Hartwood Church; bivouacked for the night.

Friday, June 12, started at 6.30 a. m. and marched to Beverly Ford, on the Rappahannock; distance, 25 miles; bivouacked in woods, within 300 yards of the river.

Saturday, June 13, remained in bivouac all day; saw enemy's pickets across the river; no shots fired. Detail from First Brigade to throw up redoubt to-night; great delay caused by not getting intrenching tools until past 1 a. m.

Sunday, June 14, redoubts finished at 5.30 a. m.; the day passed quietly; received orders to be ready to start at sundown; got off at 8.30, and marched all night.

Monday, June 15, arrived at Warrenton Junction at 5 a. m.; bivouacked half a mile below Junction; slept until 12 m.; started at 1.30 p. m. for Manassas Junction, and arrived at 1 a. m. Tuesday, June 16; lay down and slept for the night.

At 7 a. m. packed up and marched 1½ miles; stacked arms, and remained all day and night.

Wednesday, June 17, received orders to start at 9.30 a. m.; marched about 3 miles toward Bull Run; halted until 3 p. m., in order to let the men bathe; off again, and marched to Centreville; bivouacked for the night.

Thursday, June 18, changed bivouac half a mile; remained all day and night.

Friday, June 19, received orders to start at 1 p. m.; marched to Gum Springs, arriving about dark; bivouacked for the night.

Saturday, June 20, remained in bivouac all day; all quiet.

Sunday, June 21, under arms all day; heard heavy firing in direction of Aldie; changed camp about 300 yards.

Monday, Tuesday, and Wednesday, June 22, 23, and 24, remained in bivouac; all quiet.

Thursday, June 25, received orders to pack up at 4 a. m.; started at 8.30 a. m.; marched to the mouth of Monocacy River (in Maryland) by way of Edwards Ferry, arriving at 1 a. m. of the 26th. On this march we did not have time to make coffee, day or night.

Friday, June 26, started at 9 a. m. and marched to Point of Rocks; bivouacked for the night.

Saturday, June 27, started at 8 a. m. for Jefferson, arriving at 1 p. m.; from there marched to Burkittsville, arriving at 5 p. m.; our regiment ordered on picket on Crampton's Gap, in the South Mountain; passed a quiet night.

Sunday, June 28, received orders to pack up and start for Middletown, arriving at 1 a. m.; remained one hour; started again for Frederick City, arriving at 7 p. m.; marched through the city (bands playing and colors flying), and bivouacked 3 miles outside the city.

Monday, June 29, started at 4.30 a. m.; marched to Taneytown, passing through the villages of Woodsborough and Middleburg, arriving about 5 p. m.; bivouacked for the night in woods in rear of the town.

Tuesday, June 30, the regiment was mustered for pay; started, and marched about 4 miles outside of Taneytown; halted, and bivouacked for the night.

Wednesday, July 1, started about 9 a. m.; marched to Emmitsburg and rested, expecting to stay all night, but got orders to start; marched toward Gettysburg; got on wrong road; about-faced, and marched toward Gettysburg, arriving some 3 miles from it at 1 a. m.; lay down and slept.

Thursday, July 2, up at daylight. At 8 a. m. were ordered into line of battle; lay down behind the stacks; skirmishing going on in front. At 4 p. m. we were ordered to advance in line of battle to an orchard; lay down under the crest of a hill. Soon after, the battle commenced in earnest. We were attacked in front and on the flank. Our men stood it bravely until overpowered by numbers; were forced to fall back a distance of 300 yards, when they again rallied, and drove the enemy back to their original lines. Our regiment lost, in killed, wounded, and missing, 81 officers and men.

Friday, July 3, at 6 a. m., cannonading commenced on our right. Our regiment, with the corps, was marched to a piece of woods, where it drew three days' rations, the first it had had for thirty-six hours. Lay in reserve until 3 p. m., when we were ordered to support a battery, at which time we had 1 officer wounded; firing ceased about 6 p. m.; we were ordered back to the woods; passed a quiet night.

Saturday, July 4, up at 2.30 a. m.; no firing in our front; a little skirmishing on our right; the day closed with a report that the enemy were skedaddling.

Sunday, July 5, up early; all quiet; received orders to be ready to start at 6 a. m.

Monday, July 6, remained in woods all day; again received orders to start at 3 o'clock next morning.

Tuesday, July 7, started at 3 a. m.; the roads were in very bad condition owing to late rains; halted half an hour to get breakfast near Monocacy River; off again, and marched through Emmitsburg; 11.30 o'clock, halted and had dinner; started again, and marched to Mechanicstown; bivouacked for the night.

Wednesday, July 8, started at 8 a. m.; marched to Frederick City, passing through several small villages on the way; heavy rain all forenoon; roads in bad condition; we marched through the city at sundown, and bivouacked for the night 1 mile outside.

Very respectfully, your obedient servant,

M. DONOVAN,
Captain, Comdg. Sixteenth Regiment Mass. Vols.

Capt. Le Grand Benedict,
Asst. Adjt. Gen., First Brig., Second Div., Third Corps.

No. 164.

Report of Col. Robert McAllister, Eleventh New Jersey Infantry.

Belvidere, N. J., *August* 3, 1863.

Captain: In compliance with circular from brigade headquarters, dated July 27, 1863, I hereby have the honor to report the operations of my command from June 11 to July 8, inclusive.

June 11.—Received orders at 12 m. to get ready for an immediate movement. Joined the brigade by order at 2.30 p. m. and marched until 9 p. m., when we halted and bivouacked near Hartwood Church.

June 12.—Resumed the march along the River road at 6.30 a. m. Halted at 9.30 p. m. at a point near Beverly Ford, on the Rappahannock. A very hard march, the heat and dust being almost intolerable and water scarce; yet the men kept up well.

June 13.—Under arms at daylight, and, agreeably to order from brigade headquarters, remained so half an hour. In the afternoon furnished a detail of 200 men to relieve a picket along the river.

June 14.—Again under arms at daylight, as on the 13th. Received orders in the afternoon to be in readiness to march at dark. Left at 9 p. m.; marched by way of Bealeton, on the Orange and Alexandria Railroad, and Warrenton Junction, and reached Cedar Run at 7.30 a. m. on the 15th.

June 15.—Resumed the march from Cedar Run at 2 p. m. and reached Manassas Junction at midnight, and bivouacked.

June 16.—Remained as on the 15th until late in the afternoon, when we were moved a mile.

June 17.—Resumed the march at 10 a. m.; crossed Bull Run, and halted until 3 p. m., when the command was moved to Centreville, arriving there early in the evening.

June 18.—Moved a mile in the afternoon to higher ground.

June 19.—Left Centreville at 3 p. m.; arrived at Gum Springs at dark, and bivouacked.

June 20, 21, 22, 23, *and* 24.—Remained at Gum Springs.

June 25.—Left Gum Springs at 10 a. m. and made rapid march to Edwards Ferry; crossed the Potomac, and proceeded along the Chesapeake and Ohio Canal to the Monocacy, where a remnant of the regiment arrived at 12.30 a. m. This march was so rapid and the road in such a bad condition that most of the men were compelled to stop at various points along the canal from complete exhaustion.

June 26.—Major Kearny was sent back early in the morning to bring up the men. Left early in the forenoon, most of the men having arrived, and marched to Point of Rocks, where we arrived late in the afternoon, and bivouacked on the heights half a mile from the town.

June 27.—The regiment was detailed to guard the division train, and reported, according to order, to Captain [Thomas P.] Johnston. The guard was distributed as follows: One man to each wagon, and the remainder of the regiment in squads at intervals along the train. Passed through Jefferson, and joined the remainder of the brigade at Burkittsville at dark.

June 28.—Resumed the march at 9 a. m. Passed through Middletown, and arrived at Frederick at 6 p. m. Marched to and bivouacked beyond the Monocacy.

June 29.—Left early this morning; marched to Taneytown, and bivouacked in the woods near by.

June 30.—Mustered the regiment during the forenoon. Left Taneytown early in the afternoon, and marched 3 miles on the Emmitsburg road, and bivouacked.

July 1.—Resumed the march at 7.30 a. m. Marched by way of Emmitsburg, and halted within 2 miles of Gettysburg, where we remained during the night.

July 2.—Morning dawned; considerable fog; breakfast over. Troops moving in different directions, apparently taking up their several positions. Received orders to move. We marched but a short distance when the brigade formed in column of regiments, my regiment in the rear. Cannonading now commenced on different parts of our lines, after which we received orders to deploy and form line of battle. The artillery fight now became general and very heavy; hard fighting on the extreme left of our lines; orders to move forward in line of battle, the third battalion the battalion of direction; my regiment on the left of our brigade.

The movement was executed handsomely. Before reaching the crest of the hill occupied by our line of pickets, on the summit of which stood a little farm house and garden, we were halted, with the right of my regiment in the orchard in front of the house, and ordered to lie down. In a short time a rebel battery secured our range, when I received orders to move by my left flank in front of the One hundred and twentieth New York Regiment, so as to give room for one of our batteries to take a position on the crest of the hill. After a severe cannonading on both sides, I was ordered back to my old position. In a few minutes I was ordered to change my front by throwing back my left. This done, we lay down awaiting the enemy. I ordered that when the enemy advanced on us we fire by rank, rear rank first, so as to be enabled to hold in check the enemy after the first fire. Captain Benedict, assistant adjutant-general, rode up and cautioned me to be careful and not fire on our own men, pointing to those around the house and garden, who seemed to remain as though no enemy were near them. It was but a few minutes until our pickets came rushing in, closely followed by the rebels, who took possession of the house and garden. I ordered "Fire!" at which time I fell, severely wounded by a Minie ball in my left leg and a piece of shell in my right foot, when I was carried to the rear.

In conclusion, permit me to say that during this day Major Kearny and Adjutant Schoonover displayed the same bold and dashing courage that distinguished them on the battle-field of Chancellorsville. They richly deserve promotion.

Up to the time I fell, all my officers and men present stood up nobly and did their duty. I fondly hope that they continued to do so to the end, though it is sad to think of the severe loss we sustained.

Respectfully, your obedient servant,

R. McALLISTER,
Colonel Eleventh New Jersey Volunteers.

Capt. LE GRAND BENEDICT,
Asst. Adjt. Gen., First Brig., Second Div., Third Corps.

No. 165.

Report of Lieut. John Schoonover, Eleventh New Jersey Infantry.

CAMP NEAR BEVERLY FORD, VA., *August* 7, 1863.

CAPTAIN: In continuation of the inclosed [preceding] report of Col. R. McAllister, I have the honor to submit the following:

A few minutes previous to the command "Fire!" spoken of in the accompanying report, Major Kearny, then standing near me on the left of the line, was struck by a Minie ball in the knee, and immediately carried to the rear.

At this moment Battery K, Fourth U. S. Artillery, then stationed a short distance to the left and front of the regiment, limbered their pieces and passed by our left to the rear, closely followed by a line of the enemy's infantry, upon which the regiment opened a rapid fire. I then passed rapidly to the right of the regiment, in order to inform the colonel of the absence of the major, and learned that he, too, had been wounded and taken to the rear. I immediately notified Captain Martin, the senior officer present, that he was in command of the regiment, and again passed to the left of the line, when an order was received from Brigadier-General Carr to slightly change the front by bringing the left to the rear. This being executed, the entire regiment opened an effective fire upon the advancing line of the enemy.

At this point, word was conveyed to me that both Captains Martin and Logan were wounded and being carried to the rear. A moment later, and Captain Ackerman fell dead by my side. The two former were killed before they reached a place of safety; and, in justice to the memory of these three officers, permit me to bear witness to their unexceptionable good conduct—ever to the front, distinguished for personal bravery, they leave behind them a spotless record.

By this time Captain Lloyd had also been wounded, and Captain Dunning being absent in assisting the colonel to the rear, I assumed command of the regiment. The fire of the enemy was at this time perfectly terrific; men were falling on every side. It seemed as if but a few minutes could elapse before the entire line would be shot down, yet the galling fire was returned with equal vigor. Slowly and stubbornly the regiment fell back, keeping up a continual fire upon the line of the enemy, which was still advancing, until more than half of its number had been killed and wounded.

Up to this time both officers and men nobly did their duty, but the ranks becoming so decimated and mingled with wounded men and the line in the rear, and having a short time previous been struck with a piece of shell in the breast, I found it impossible, under these circumstances, to longer keep the line together. At this time we neared the caissons, which were in line across the field to the left, when I was struck the second time with a buck-shot, and being nearly exhausted in my efforts to rally the men, and from the wound in my breast, I was counseled to go to the rear.

A portion of the regiment was rallied some distance to the rear by Captain Lloyd, and charged in line with the remainder of the brigade to a point near that occupied during the hottest of the action. Remaining there a short time, it marched some distance to the rear, and bivouacked.

Being able to ride, I joined the regiment on the morning of the 3d, and again took command, by request of Captain Sleeper, the senior officer present for duty. A number of officers and men also joined the regiment, having been collected near the stream farther to the rear.

Moving a short distance to the front, the regiment was halted until 3 p. m., when it was ordered out double-quick with the remainder of the brigade on the road toward Gettysburg. Proceeding nearly a mile, it was halted and formed in line of battle in rear of the batteries occupying the crest of the hill in front, the brigade being in column of regiments. The regiment remained in this position for nearly two hours, under a heavy fire of shot and shell, yet but one man was slightly wounded. During the time my horse was struck with a spherical case shot, from the effects of which he died the next day.

About 5 p. m. the regiment returned to its former position, where it remained during the night.

In conclusion, permit me to mention the general good conduct of both officers and men both upon the 2d and 3d. To mention some might do gross injustice to others, but I cannot pass by the untiring efforts of Lieutenant Buckley to rally the men. Captain Lloyd and Lieutenant Corey also deserve special mention for their coolness and bravery.

As an individual act of bravery, I desire to mention Corpl. Thomas Johnson, of Company I, whom, when two color-bearers had been shot down, I ordered to take the colors and advance 20 yards to the front, as the regiment was then wavering. He did so, and did not leave his position until ordered to the rear.

The services oɩ Lieut. James Baldwin on the 3d, as acting adjutant, were invaluable.

In the action of the 2d, the regiment sustained a very heavy loss. Out of 275 officers and men taken into the fight, 18 were killed, 130 wounded, and 6 missing, making a total of 154.

I am, sir, very respectfully, your obedient servant,

JOHN SCHOONOVER,
Adjutant Eleventh New Jersey Volunteers.

Capt. LE GRAND BENEDICT,
Asst. Adjt. Gen., First Brig., Second Div., Third Corps.

No. 166.

Report of Capt. William B. Dunning, Eleventh New Jersey Infantry.

CAMP NEAR BEVERLY FORD, VA., *August 7*, 1863.

CAPTAIN: I hereby have the honor to report the operations of the Eleventh New Jersey Volunteers from July 4 to 8, inclusive.

July 4, 5, and 6.—The regiment remained as on the 3d.

July 7.—Left this morning at daylight. Marched by way of Emmitsburg to Mechanicstown, and bivouacked.

July 8.—Resumed march at 6 a. m., and arrived at Frederick at 8 p. m., where we bivouacked,

I am, sir, most respectfully, your obedient servant,

WM. B. DUNNING,
Captain Eleventh New Jersey Volunteers.

Capt. LE GRAND BENEDICT,
Asst. Adjt. Gen., First Brig., Second Div., Third Corps.

No. 167.

Report of Maj. Robert L. Bodine, Twenty-sixth Pennsylvania Infantry.

CAMP NEAR WARRENTON, VA., *July* 28, 1863.

CAPTAIN: I have the honor to report, in compliance with circular of July 27, 1863, the operations of the regiment from the time it left Falmouth, Va., to and including July 8.

The regiment left Falmouth, Va., June 11, as a guard to the wagon train; marched to within 5 miles of Hartwood Church, distance 7 miles, and bivouacked for the night.

June 12.—Resumed the march, in connection with the wagon train, and arrived at Kelly's Ford at 10 p. m., after being relieved from the wagon train on the road 5 miles from Kelly's Ford; distance, 30 miles.

June 13.—Marched from Kelly's Ford to Beverly Ford; distance, 5 miles.

Remained in camp there until night of June 14, when we resumed the march, and arrived at Warrenton Junction at 1 p. m. of the 15th. Continued the march same day, and arrived at Manassas Junction 11 p. m., where we bivouacked for the night; distance, 30 miles.

Morning of 16th, resumed the march to Dangerfield, distance 1 mile, where we remained until next morning, June 17, when we marched to Centreville; distance, 5 miles.

June 18.—Marched 1 mile to northward of Centreville. Remained there until 1 p. m. of the 19th, when we resumed the march, and arrived at Gum Springs, distance 8 miles, where we remained in camp until June 25. Again took up the line of march to Noland's Ford, via Edwards Ferry and Poolesville; distance, 26 miles.

June 26.—Marched to Point of Rocks; distance, 7 miles.

June 27.—Marched to Burkittsville, via Jefferson; distance, 14 miles.

June 28.—Marched to 4 miles beyond Frederick City, via Middletown; distance, 18 miles.

June 29.—Marched to Taneytown, via Walkersville and Woodsborough, distance 18 miles, where we remained until 2 p. m. June 30. Again resumed the march to Bridgeport; distance, 4 miles.

July 1.—Marched, via Emmitsburg, to Gettysburg, distance 14 miles, where we arrived at 2 a. m. of July 2.

On the morning of July 2, my regiment was detailed to clear away the fences in front of the division, to facilitate the movements of our troops. It was soon after deployed to the right of the brigade, which position it held during the battle, in which I lost many valuable officers and enlisted men. We bivouacked on the battle-field during the night.

Next morning, 3d, again prepared for battle, but were not so much engaged or losses so heavy.

During the battle, the loss of the regiment was 1 officer and 34 men killed, 10 officers and 161 enlisted men wounded, and 7 enlisted men missing. Quite a number were very badly wounded, and in several cases amputation was necessary

July 4 *to* 7.—Remained on the battle-field.

July 7.—Again resumed the march, and arrived at Mechanicstown; distance, 20 miles.

July 8.—Marched to 2 miles beyond Frederick City; distance, 18 miles.

I cannot close this report without mentioning with pride the gallant conduct and bravery of my officers in the late battle of Gettysburg, and for the alacrity and willingness displayed in seconding their superiors in their efforts to make the contest a decisive one and do honor to our native State, the old Keystone. The men were also unusually anxious to meet the enemy, and seemed inspired with a feeling to do or die in the attempt to annihilate the invaders of their homes.

I remain, very respectfully,

ROBERT L. BODINE,
Major, Comdg. Twenty-sixth Pennsylvania Volunteers.

Capt. LE GRAND BENEDICT, *Assistant Adjutant-General.*

No. 168.

Report of Lieut. Col. Milton Opp, Eighty-fourth Pennsylvania Infantry.

BIVOUAC NEAR WARRENTON, VA., *July* 30, 1863.

SIR : In compliance with orders, I have the honor to make the following report of the operations of the Eighty-fourth Regiment Pennsylvania Volunteers, from June 11 to July 8 :

June 11.—Received marching orders at Stoneman's Switch at 9 a. m. to report to the commanding officer Third Brigade, Second Division, Third Corps. Reported, and were ordered to join the brigade on the march to Hartwood Church, Va., where we arrived at 8 p. m.; 8 miles.

June 12.—Marched at 6 a. m.; arrived at Rappahannock Station at 8 p. m.; 23 miles.

June 13.—Engaged in throwing up earthworks and demolishing railroad bridge.

June 14.—Performed picket duty on the bank of the river until 9 p. m., when we received orders to join the First Brigade, Second Division, Third Corps, and marched all night, arriving near Manassas Junction at 12 m. on the 15th; 28 miles.

June 16.—Moved at 1 p. m. 1 mile toward Bull Run, and bivouacked.

June 17.—Marched at 10 a. m., crossing Bull Run, and bivouacked near Centreville; 5 miles.

Jnne 18.—Moved camp 1 mile, near the wagon park. Companies F, G, and part of H were sent on picket, and, on being relieved, took the wrong road, and did not join us until the 23d, at Gum Springs, having marched to Leesburg, expecting to meet the regiment there.

June 19.—Marched to Gum Springs; 10 miles.

June 25.—Marched at 7 a. m. via Edwards Ferry, arriving at the mouth of the Monocacy at 12 p. m.; 25 miles.

June 26.—Marched at 9 a. m., arriving at Point of Rocks at 4 p. m.; 6 miles.

June 27.—Marched at 8 a. m., arriving at Burkittsville, Md.; 12 miles.

June 28.—Marched at 9 a. m. via Frederick City; 18 miles.

June 29.—Marched at 5 a. m., arriving at Taneytown, Md., at 4 p. m.; 18 miles.

June 30.—Was detailed to guard wagon train of the Second Division, Third Corps. Reported the regiment to Captain Johnston, assistant quartermaster Second Division, at the train at Taneytown, Md. Picketed the roads near the train.

July 1.—Moved with the train 4 miles on the road to Emmitsburg; then returned and marched all night with train to Westminster, Md., arriving at 7 a. m. on the 2d; 25 miles.

July 2 *to* 4.—Picketing roads near the wagon parks.

July 5.—Picketing roads and loading supply trains.

July 6.—Marched with train to Uniontown; 12 miles.

July 7.—Marched with train to Frederick City, Md.; 24 miles.

July 8.—Marched to Middletown, Md.; 8 miles.

Very respectfully, your obedient servant,

MILTON OPP,
Lieutenant-Colonel, Commanding Regiment.

Capt. LE GRAND BENEDICT,
Asst. Adjt. Gen., First Brig., Second Div., Third Corps.

No. 169.

Reports of Col. William R. Brewster, Seventy-third New York Infantry, commanding Second Brigade.

HEADQUARTERS EXCELSIOR (SECOND) BRIGADE,
August 15, 1863.

CAPTAIN: I have the honor to submit the following report of the operations of this brigade from the date of leaving Falmouth to July 8, when Major-General Humphreys left the division:

We left Falmouth on June 12, and marched to Hartwood Church.

June 13.—Marched to Rappahannock Station.

June 14.—At 2 a. m. I received orders to go with four regiments to Kelly's Ford and relieve a brigade from the Fifth Corps, then on picket at that point. On arriving at the ford, found the brigade which I was directed to relieve had left some hours previously. Remained on duty at Kelly's Ford until 7 p. m., when we rejoined the division at Rappahannock Station. Marched with it all night, arriving at Catlett's Station at 7 a. m. on the 15th, having in the previous twenty-nine hours marched 32 miles and performed fourteen hours' picket duty.

June 15.—Marched to Manassas Junction, and remained there until the 17th.

June 17.—Marched to Centreville, where we remained until the 19th.

June 19.—Marched to Gum Springs, remaining there until the 25th.

June 25.—Crossed the Potomac at Edwards Ferry, and marched to the mouth of the Monocacy River.

June 26.—Marched to Point of Rocks.

June 27.—Crossed the Catoctin Mountains. Passed through the town of Jefferson.

June 28.—Marched to near Walkersville, passing through Middletown and Frederick City.

June 29.—Marched to Taneytown, passing through Woodsborough and Middleburg.

June 30.—Marched about 6 miles beyond Taneytown, and bivouacked for the night.

July 1.—Marched to a point near Gettysburg, passing through Emmitsburg, reaching there about midnight.

At about 1 o'clock on the afternoon of the 2d, I received orders from the brigadier-general commanding the division to move the brigade to the front, and form line of battle in rear of the First Brigade (then going into position on the right of the First Division), and send one regiment to the crest of the hill, about 250 yards in advance of the First Brigade, with instructions that, should the enemy attempt to take it, to hold it at all hazards.

For this duty I detailed the Fourth Excelsior (Seventy-third New York Volunteers), commanded by Maj. M. W. Burns. The Second Excelsior (Seventy-first New York Volunteers), commanded by Col. H. L. Potter, and the Third Excelsior (Seventy-second New York Volunteers), commanded by Col. John S. Austin, were placed on the left of the First Brigade, and connected with the First Division. The Fifth Excelsior (Seventy-fourth New York Volunteers), Lieut. Col. Thomas Holt commanding, was placed on the right of the First Brigade, leaving only the First Excelsior (Seventieth New York Volunteers), commanded by Col. J. Egbert Farnum, and the One hundred and twentieth New York Volunteers, commanded by Lieut. Col. C. D. Westbrook, in support of the first line of battle of our division.

At about 4 o'clock we advanced our line of battle, and in our new position were exposed to a most terrible fire from the enemy's artillery on our left, which was most destructive, killing and wounding many men. At about 5.30 o'clock, the Fourth Excelsior, commanded by Maj. M. W. Burns, having been relieved from its first position on the crest of the hill, I was directed to send it to the support of General Graham's brigade, in the First Division. They advanced to this duty most gallantly.

Up to this time we had not been engaged at all, but now the troops on our left being obliged to fall back, the enemy advanced upon us in great force, pouring into us a most terrific fire of artillery and musketry, both upon our front and left flank. Our men returned it with great effect, and for some time held the enemy in check, but the troops on our left being, for want of support, forced still farther back, left us exposed to an enfilading fire, before which we were obliged to fall back, which was done in good order, but with terrible loss of both officers and men.

Seeing the enemy in possession of three of our guns, I made a charge at the head of about 150 men, from the Second, Third, Fourth, Fifth, and One hundred and twentieth Regiments, and succeeded in recapturing them, taking from one the colors of the Eighth Florida Regiment, and bringing in as prisoners the major of that regiment and some 30 of his men.

The colors were taken by Sergt. Thomas Hogan, Third Excelsior, who by his bravery attracted the personal attention of the general commanding the division.

Soon after sunset we were relieved by a brigade from the Second Corps, in the rear of which we reformed our line of battle, and bivouacked for the night.

On the morning of the 3d, we moved a little distance to the rear, to give the men rations and refill their cartridge-boxes. At about 3 p. m. we again moved to the front, in support of batteries. While here, we were exposed to a very severe artillery fire, and lost quite a number of men. At sunset, we returned to the position occupied in the morning, and bivouacked for the night.

On the 4th, 5th, and 6th, nothing was done beyond sending out parties to bury the dead.

On the morning of the 7th, we started in pursuit of the retreating enemy.

Our losses in the battle of Gettysburg were as follows:

Command.	Officers.		Enlisted men.			Total.
	Killed.	Wounded.	Killed.	Wounded.	Missing.	
Brigade staff		2				2
1st Excelsior		8	20	85	4	117
2d Excelsior	1	6	9	62	13	91
3d Excelsior		7	7	72	28	114
4th Excelsior	4	11	47	92	8	162
5th Excelsior		6	12	68	3	89
120th New York	7	10	23	144	19	203
Total	12	50	118	523	75	778

The strength of the brigade at the commencement of the action was 1,837 officers and men, out of which we lost 778, being nearly 45 per cent. of the entire number, showing the terrible fire to which we were exposed.

The conduct and bearing of both officers and men were so good under the fatigues of the long and tiresome marches, and so gallant, brave, and steady in action, that it is almost impossible to particularize individual acts. It is enough to say that every officer and man in the command seemed determined to sustain the reputation of the brigade, earned on many a hard-fought field, and how well they succeeded is best shown by the loss sustained.

The members of my staff, Adjt. Gen. J. P. Finkelmeier, Capt. George Le Fort, acting assistant inspector-general, and Lieuts. J. A. Smith and [Edward A.] Belger, were very active on the field, and behaved in the most gallant manner, conveying my orders under the hottest fire.

Major Finkelmeier and Captain Le Fort were both wounded, and obliged to leave the field before the action was over.

The medical department of the brigade was under the supervision of Surg. C. K. Irwin, and all the wounded men bear testimony to his kind consideration and care.

I am, captain, very respectfully, your obedient servant,

WM. R. BREWSTER,
Colonel, Commanding Brigade.

Capt. CARSWELL McCLELLAN,
Assistant Adjutant-General.

—

HDQRS. EXCELSIOR BRIG., SECOND DIV., THIRD A. C.,
August 21, 1863.

MAJOR : I respectfully beg leave to submit the following report of the operations of this brigade from July 9 to July 26 :

July 9.—Marched from Frederick to a point on the South Mountain, passing through Middletown.

July 10.—General Prince assumed command of the division, and we marched to a point near Antietam Creek, passing through Keedysville, and halted near General Meade's headquarters.

July 11.—Moved about 3 miles to the right, in support of the Fifth Army Corps. I was here relieved from command of the brigade by Brig. Gen. F. B. Spinola.

July 12.—Moved about 2 miles to the front, and remained until the morning of the 14th ultimo, when we relieved a division of the Twelfth Army Corps, ordered forward on a reconnaissance. About noon, having ascertained that the enemy had retreated, we moved forward about 3 miles, and bivouacked for the night.

July 15.—Marched to a point a short distance beyond Sharpsburg, passing through Fair Play.

July 16.—Marched to near Pleasant Valley.

July 17.—Crossed the Potomac and Shenandoah Rivers at Harper's Ferry, bivouacking for the night on the Leesburg road.

July 18.—Marched to Hillsborough.

July 19.—Marched to Woodgrove.

July 20.—Marched to Upperville, passing through Snickersville, where we bivouacked for the night, and remained until the 22d ultimo, when we moved to Piedmont.

The operations of the brigade on July 23, 24, and 25, including the action at Wapping Heights, are detailed in the following report of Col. J. Egbert Farnum, then commanding the brigade:

HDQRS. EXCELSIOR (SECOND) BRIG., SECOND DIV., THIRD ARMY CORPS,
July 27, 1863.

LIEUTENANT: I have the honor to submit the following report of the operations of my command during the days of July 23, 24, and 25:

Early on the morning of the 23d instant, being then in command of my regiment, First Excelsior (Seventieth New York Volunteers), the regiment and brigade left Piedmont, and marched with the other brigades comprising the Second Division on the road through the Manassas Gap toward Front Royal. On arriving at Linden Station, the One hundred and twentieth New York Volunteers was detached and sent upon picket on the road to the left, leading from the station. Arriving near Wapping Station, we were massed by divisions, and, taking the hills upon the right side of the road, advanced to the crossing at that station; then, crossing to the left range of hills, we were advanced close upon the line of skirmishers of the First Division, Third Corps, arriving and halting at about 4 p. m.

At about 5 p. m. we were informed by General Spinola, commanding the brigade, that he had received orders from General Prince to march the brigade through a defile up to the skirmish line, for the purpose of assaulting the enemy on a hill in our front. On the promulgation of this order, the brigade, marching left in front, proceeded to the designated position, and was there formed in line of battle. The order was given to fix bayonets and charge the line in front of us. My regiment, being on the left of the brigade, moved at a double-quick, in conjunction with the other four regiments, under a severe fire from the enemy, and, arriving on the crest of the hill, driving the enemy before us, we found the work but half done, the enemy being in strength on two hills in front of us, the farther being held by their artillery. The brigade charged on, returning the enemy's fire, taking prisoners, and carrying all before it.

At this time General Spinola fell, seriously wounded, and the command of the brigade devolved upon me by seniority. Having arrived at the crest of the second hill, I received orders from General Prince to reform the line of battle and hold the ground which we had charged and occupied. This being done, I threw out a strong line of pickets and scouts in front and on both flanks of my command, and, using stones and fence rails, threw up breastworks in front of our position.

Nothing of interest transpired during the night, and at early dawn I detached the First Excelsior (Seventieth New York Volunteers) and threw them forward to feel the enemy, and soon learned that he had evacuated all his positions in front of us during the night.

Having communicated these facts to General Prince, I received orders to bury the dead, which was done, but hastily, as we were soon ordered to march.

Leaving our position at about 7 a. m. on the 24th, we moved by the flank to within about a mile of Front Royal, where I formed line of battle on the left of the road, and, supporting the Third Brigade of the Second Division, which was the advanced line of battle, moved a short distance toward Front Royal, when we received orders to return. Marching by the flank, we reached Markham Station, and bivouacked for the night.

On the morning of July 25, taking up the line of march, we proceeded through Salem to a point within 7 miles of Warrenton, where we again bivouacked, and remained until we left for this camp.

During the 25th instant, the One hundred and twentieth Regiment rejoined the column, having been relieved from picket.

In an action where all sustained their reputation gained on other fields with so much gallantry, bravery, and devotion, I am constrained to speak of all alike. It is impossible to select any single officer or man who did less than his full duty; all were alike brave, true, and gallant soldiers.

I have the honor to append a list of casualties sustained by the brigade during the action of the 23d instant.

I have the honor to be, very respectfully, your obedient servant.

J. EGBERT FARNUM,
Colonel, Commanding Brigade.

Lieut. ALBERT ORDWAY,
Actg. Assistant Adjutant-General, Second Division, Third Corps.

[Inclosure.]

Command.	Killed.		Wounded.		Total.
	Officers.	Enlisted men.	Officers.	Enlisted men.	
Brigade staff..			1	......	1
70th New York.......................................	1	10	......	21	32
71st New York.......................................		2	......	13	15
72d New York.......................................			......	8	8
73d New York.......................................		1	......	7	8
74th New York.......................................	2	2	......	7	11
Total..	3	15	1	56	75

July 26.—Marched through Warrenton, halting 2½ miles beyond the town.

Having been absent from the brigade on sick leave from July 16 to August 10, I am unable to make a more complete report than the above.

I am, major. very respectfully, your obedient servant,

WM. R. BREWSTER,
Colonel, Commanding Brigade.

Maj. CHARLES HAMLIN,
Assistant Adjutant-General, Second Division, Third Corps.

No. 170.

Report of Maj. William H. Hugo, Seventieth New York Infantry.

HDQRS. FIRST REGIMENT, EXCELSIOR BRIGADE,
Camp near Rappahannock Station, Va., August 14, 1863.

MAJOR: In accordance with orders received yesterday, I have the honor herewith to forward the following report of the operations of this command since leaving Falmouth:

On June 11, received orders to be in readiness to move at a moment's notice.

About 5 p. m. of the same day, the wagon train moved, but the regiment with the rest of the brigade did not leave until the following morning, on account of a detail from the brigade being on picket. Commenced moving at 9 a. m., and marched to Hartwood Church, where we arrived at 5 p. m., and bivouacked for the night.

On the morning of the 13th, we took up our line of march at 4.30 a. m., and marched to Rappahannock Station, where we joined the division, and bivouacked for the night.

At 2 a. m. of the 14th, received orders to go on picket at Kelly's Ford, to which point we were marched, and where we remained until 7 p. m.. when we received orders to withdraw the pickets and rejoin our division at Rappahannock Station. After rejoining the division, continued to march during the night, arriving at Catlett's Station at 7 a. m. of the 15th, where we halted until 1 p. m., when we again resumed the march, and arrived at Manassas Junction at

11 p. m., where we bivouacked for the night, remaining in this position until the morning of the 17th.

At 9.30 a. m. of the 17th, we again resumed our march, and marched to Centreville, where we remained until the 19th.

On the afternoon of the 19th, marched to Gum Springs, where we remained for six days, performing in that space of time one tour of picket duty.

Left Gum Springs on the morning of the 25th, at 9.30 a. m.; crossed the Potomac into Maryland at Edwards Ferry about 2 p. m., and continued marching, following the tow-path of the Chesapeake and Ohio Canal, to the mouth of the Monocacy, where we bivouacked for the night.

On the 26th, marched to Point of Rocks, where we bivouacked for the night.

On the 27th, crossed Catoctin Mountains, and passed through Jefferson, bivouacking a short distance from Middletown.

On the 28th, we resumed our march, passing through Middletown and Frederick City, and bivouacking near Walkersville.

On the 29th, marched to Taneytown, having passed through Woodsborough, Ladiesburg, Middleburg, and Taneytown.

On the afternoon of the 30th, marched about 6 miles beyond Taneytown, where the regiment was detailed for picket duty.

On the morning of July 1, the pickets were withdrawn, and we resumed the march at 7.30 o'clock, arriving near Gettysburg at 12 m., having passed through Emmitsburg.

At 8 a. m. of the 2d, the regiment was formed in line of battle, and remained in this position until 1 p. m., when orders were received to advance, halting in rear of the First Brigade and acting as its support. We lay in this position under a heavy fire of artillery until 4 o'clock. At this time we engaged the enemy, and held our ground against a superior force until dark, when we were relieved by the Second Corps.

Our loss in this engagement was quite severe, losing in all 112—7 officers wounded, 21 men killed, 80 wounded, and 4 missing.

At daylight on the morning of the 3d, the regiment was formed in line of battle, supporting the Fifth Corps. We lay in this position until 3 p. m., when we were ordered to the right, to support a battery of the Second Corps. In supporting this battery, we were exposed to a heavy artillery fire, losing 3 men. At dark we were relieved and marched to the left, where we bivouacked for the night. No movement was made on the 4th, 5th, and 6th.

On the 5th and 6th, parties were sent out to bury the dead.

On the morning of the 7th, started in pursuit of the enemy, passing through Emmitsburg, and bivouacking near Mechanicstown.

On the 8th, marched to near Frederick City.

On the 9th, passed through Middletown, and bivouacked in the mountains.

On the 10th, resumed the march, and, crossing Antietam Creek, we bivouacked for the night at 7 o'clock, but receiving orders to move at 11 p. m., we again resumed the march, and continued marching until 3 a. m. on the following morning, when we halted at 6 a. m.

July 11, resumed the march, and, halting about 6 p. m., we bivouacked for the night.

On the morning of the 12th, we took our position in rear of the Twelfth Corps, where we remained for the night.

On the 13th, marched to near Williamsport, where we remained until the 15th.

On the 15th, we again resumed the march, and, passing through Fair Play and Sharpsburg, we halted for the night.

July 16, we marched about 16 miles, and bivouacked near Knoxville.

About 5 p. m. of the 17th, we again took up our line of march, and, crossing the Potomac and Shenandoah Rivers at Harper's Ferry, we bivouacked for the night about 5 miles from the river.

July 18, marched to Hillsborough, where we bivouacked.

July 19, resumed our march at 7 a. m., and marched to Wood Grove, when we received orders to go on picket.

July 20, the pickets were withdrawn, and we marched to Upperville, where we bivouacked for the night.

We lay in this position until the afternoon of the 22d, when we resumed our march, and marched to Piedmont.

At 4 a. m. of the 23d, we again took up our line of march, and came upon the enemy at Manassas Gap, when the brigade was ordered to charge, which it did in splendid style, driving the enemy before it.

In this engagement, which was of short duration, the regiment sustained a loss of 33—1 officer killed, Captain Price; 1 wounded, Major Mahen; 10 men killed, and 21 wounded.

After the enemy was driven from his position, the regiment was deployed as skirmishers for the purpose of finding his whereabouts. After advancing about 3 miles, and finding no enemy, the regiment returned to the brigade, when the regiment with the rest of the brigade advanced as far as Front Royal. Here, finding the enemy had gone, we were marched back, a distance of about 5 miles, and bivouacked for the night.

On the 25th, we resumed our march, passing through Salem, and bivouacking about 5 miles beyond the town.

On the 26th, marched 2 miles beyond Warrenton, where we bivouacked for the night.

On August 1, we left camp near Warrenton about 7 o'clock in the morning, and marched to our present position near Rappahannock Station the same day. Since then the regiment has been inactive, excepting that it has performed two tours of picket duty.

Colonel Farnum commanded the regiment from the time we left Falmouth until July 27, when he was detached on duty at New York. From that time until yesterday, when I assumed command, Captain Gruett commanded the regiment. This should excuse me from making as minute a report as otherwise I should have done.

I have the honor to be, very respectfully, your obedient servant,

WM. H. HUGO,
Major, Comdg. First Regiment.

Maj. J. P. Finkelmeier,
Assistant Adjutant-General, Excelsior Brigade.

No. 171.

Report of Col. Henry L. Potter, Seventy-first New York Infantry.

Hdqrs. Second Regiment, Excelsior Brigade,
Camp near Beverly Ford, Va., August 14, 1863.

Major: In compliance with orders, I would respectfully make the following report:

This regiment left camp near Falmouth, Va., June 12, and participated in all the various marches and movements with other regiments of the brigade.

The regiment was engaged at Gettysburg, Pa., July 2, where, out of 230 men and 13 officers, it lost—

Officers and men.	Killed.	Wounded.	Missing.	Total.
Commissioned officers	1	6	......	7
Enlisted men	11	62	10	83
Total	12	68	10	90

Taking a large number of prisoners, and recapturing one brass gun lost by Battery K, Fifth U. S. Artillery.

July 3.—This regiment also participated with the brigade in the engagement, with a loss of only 3 wounded.

From July 3, followed the various marches and movements until July 23, when it was again engaged at Wapping Heights, near Manassas Gap, where the loss was 2 enlisted men killed and 13 enlisted men wounded.

The conduct and bearing of the officers and men was generally so patient under the fatigues of the long and tiresome marches, and so brave and steady in action, that it is almost impossible to particularize individual acts of gallantry and good conduct.

Very respectfully, your obedient servant,

H. L. POTTER,
Colonel, Commanding Regiment.

Maj. J. P. FINKELMEIER,
  Assistant Adjutant-General, Excelsior Brigade.

No. 172.

Report of Col. John S. Austin, Seventy-second New York Infantry.

HDQRS. THIRD REGIMENT, EXCELSIOR BRIGADE,
  Camp near Beverly Ford, Va., August 15, 1863.

MAJOR: In compliance with circular from brigade headquarters, I have the honor to submit the following report of the part taken by this regiment during the recent movements from June 28 to July 26:

We left Middletown June 28, passing through Frederick to Walkersville, where we encamped for the night.

On the 29th, we marched through Woodsborough and Middleburg to Taneytown.

Left Taneytown on the morning of the 30th; marched through Bridgeport, and bivouacked for the night about 3 miles from the town.

July 1, we marched to Emmitsburg, and encamped about 2 p. m. Broke camp at 4 p. m., and marched to Gettysburg, arriving there at 2 a. m.

We were ordered to the front about 10 a. m. of the 2d, when our regiment was placed in reserve of the Second Brigade, Second Division.

At 2 p. m. we were ordered to advance across an open field in line of battle, the left of our regiment, which formed the extreme left of the brigade, resting on a cross-road, the line running parallel with the main road and in rear of the peach orchard. We remained in line of battle about two hours, under a most terrific fire of shot and shell, when we were pressed so hard on the left flank that we were obliged to fall back. This we did in as good order as the circumstances would permit.

At this time I was wounded in the arm and side, and a few minutes after had my horse killed. I was now obliged to give up the command to Lieutenant-Colonel Leonard, who fought the regiment after I left. He and the rest of the officers were indefatigable in their exertions to rally the men, who were still hard pressed and obliged to fall slowly back to the crest of the hill from which the brigade started in the morning, where they rallied, and, charging across the field, retook their guns and one battle-flag belonging to the Eighth Florida Regiment, together with a large number of prisoners, all of which they brought from the field.

It was now dark, and the remnants of the regiment were collected together, and bivouacked for the night in an orchard near the Gettysburg road.

The next morning the regiment was marched back to the rear, for the purpose of obtaining ammunition and rations for the men.

At 2 p. m. they were again moved to the front, to support a battery, where the regiment remained until 7 p. m., when it returned to the position that they occupied in the morning.

On the morning of the 5th, they were again moved forward, and took up a position in the second line of battle. In about two hours the regiment was marched back into a field and encamped.

On the morning of the 6th, it was found that the enemy had retreated, and we were at once ordered to march. We did not move over half a mile, and then returned to the same camp.

It would be doing an act of injustice to the brave men of the Third if I did not speak more at length in regard to their conduct on that memorable and ever-to-be-remembered July 2. It would also seem like an injustice to speak of one as having done better or performed his duty more nobly than another; still, I cannot pass by in silence the manner in which Lieutenant-Colonel Leonard and Major Abell performed their duties upon that occasion; also Captain Bailey and Lieut. William McConnell. Among the men it is hard to particularize, but I think that our color corporal, Edwin H. Tarry, deserves particular mention. He was ever to the front, and carried the flag through that storm of shot and shell with credit to the regiment and honor to himself.

Our loss was very severe. We took 22 officers and 283 men into the fight, and had 8 officers wounded, 1 of whom has since died, 7 men killed, 86 wounded, and 15 missing.*

On the 7th, the regiment marched to Mechanicstown, and encamped for the night.

Left camp on the morning of the 8th, at 6 a. m., and marched about 1 mile beyond Frederick, where it bivouacked for the night at 10 p. m.

On the 9th, it marched to Middletown, where it received rations for the first time in two days, and encamped for the night on the battle-field of South Mountain.

---

* But see revised statement, p. 178

Moved at 9 o'clock on the morning of the 10th, crossed the Antietam Creek, and halted on the old battle-field of Antietam. Moved again at 10 p. m., recrossed Antietam Creek, and marched until 2 o'clock in the morning.

Broke camp the 11th, at 6 a. m., and marched 2 miles. Remained in the same position until 4 p. m.; then moved across the Antietam Creek, and encamped for the night.

On the 12th, moved about 1 mile, and encamped in a piece of woods, and remained until the morning of the 14th; then again moved forward, and occupied the position that the enemy held the day before near Williamsport.

As the enemy had succeeded in crossing the Potomac, retraced line of march of the day before, passed through Sharpsburg, and encamped about 2 miles beyond the town.

On the 16th, moved to within about 2 miles of Harper's Ferry, and encamped at the foot of Maryland Heights.

The next day crossed the river, and encamped in Virginia.

On the 18th, 19th, and 20th, on the march, arriving at Upperville, where they remained for two days.

On the 22d, moved to Manassas Gap, and halted for the night at Piedmont Station, and on the morning of the 23d moved up the Gap to where our troops were skirmishing with the enemy. The enemy had taken up their position across the Gap, and all the efforts of the skirmishers to dislodge them proved unavailing. At this time the Excelsior Brigade, of which my regiment forms a part, was ordered to charge the heights and drive the enemy from their position.

With a yell that would have done credit to a band of demons, our boys sprang to their feet and rushed upon the foe. The first and second heights were carried in the face of a severe fire, when the enemy opened from the opposite hill with a four-gun battery, and the men, who were now completely exhausted, were ordered to hold the position, of which they had so gallantly taken possession.

The next morning at daylight it was discovered that the enemy had retreated. Moved forward to Front Royal, and remained about two hours, and then marched back through the Gap, and encamped for the night 6 miles beyond.

It would not be doing justice to the regiment for me to pass by this point without making some mention of the manner in which both officers and men performed their duty on that occasion; neither would it be proper for me to make any invidious distinction among men who have proved themselves soldiers in every sense of the word on many a hard-fought battle-field, for all did their duty nobly. Each seemed to vie with the other in his attempt to reach the enemy, thus making it a fight not only for victory but for personal honor. Owing to the uneven nature of the ground, our loss was comparatively small. Eight men were wounded, 1 of whom has since died from the effects of the wound.

On the 25th, marched through Salem, and bivouacked for the night 5 miles beyond.

The next day marched to Warrenton, encamping about 2 miles from the town, on the road to Sulphur Springs.

I have attempted in the foregoing brief and barren sketch to do justice to the brave officers and men who form the Third Excelsior, although I know I have but partially succeeded, and I cannot close without extending my heartfelt sympathy to the friends of those who have been called upon to mourn the loss of kind friends and brave soldiers.

The above is respectfully submitted.

I am, major, very respectfully, your obedient servant,
JOHN S. AUSTIN,
Colonel, Commanding Third Excelsior.

Maj. J. P. FINKELMEIER,
Assistant Adjutant-General, Excelsior (Second) Brigade.

No. 173.

Report of Capt. Abram L. Lockwood, One hundred and twentieth New York Infantry.

NEAR BEVERLY FORD, VA.,
August 14, 1863.

SIR: In compliance with circular from headquarters Army of the Potomac, of August 13, 1863, I respectfully submit the following report, begging leave to state, however, that the report is not as full and explicit as it ought to be, in consequence of my not having been in command of the regiment during the time for which the report is asked, and I am now but in temporary command:

On Sunday, June 28, our regiment, in company with the brigade (already foot-sore and weary from the incessant marches since leaving Falmouth), marched through Middletown and across the mountain *en route* for Pennsylvania, by way of Frederick, Taneytown, and Emmitsburg, arriving on the battle-field of Gettysburg about 2 o'clock on the morning of July 2. The march was a forced march, and both officers and men were, in consequence of their over-exertion, almost exhausted, but there was scarcely any straggling, and the regiment was marched on to the battle-field almost to a man.

On the afternoon of July 2, our brigade was ordered to advance to a position in the left center, to support the First Division of our corps, and in doing so we advanced across an open field, exposed to a terrific and murderous artillery fire from the enemy, which was kept up without cessation during the rest of the day. One officer and several privates were killed during this movement, besides several being wounded. The enemy at last broke the first line, and we advanced to meet him. The regiment soon became hotly engaged, and held its position without flinching until it was flanked. We retired slowly, fighting, across the field, when the brigade again rallied, and drove the enemy from the field at the point of the bayonet.

During the engagement both officers and men, without a single exception, displayed great bravery and coolness, and that the regiment did its full share of fighting, the list of the killed and wounded bears sufficient evidence.

Officers and men.	Killed.	Wounded.	Missing.	Total.
Commissioned officers	7	10		17
Enlisted men	24	143	19	186
Total	31	153	19	203

I will not take it upon myself to make special mention of individual instances of bravery, excepting in the case of our brave and gallant color-bearer, Corpl. William O'Brien, of Company B. His conduct in that engagement was so noticeable as to call forth praise from every officer and man in the regiment. We were ordered up to the front several times again, but the regiment sustained no further casualties.

Marched from Gettysburg on Tuesday, the 7th, to Williamsport, where we arrived Friday, July 10. We lay down until the rebels were found to have crossed the river, when we moved down, crossed the river at Harper's Ferry in pursuit, moving on and occupying the different gaps in the Blue Ridge until we came to Manassas Gap, where the celebrated charge of the brigade was made. Our regiment did not participate in that fight, having been sent to hold another position. Leaving there, we moved on to Warrenton by way of Salem, and from there into camp at this place.

Very respectfully,

A. L. LOCKWOOD,
Captain, Comdg. 120th Regiment New York Volunteers.

Maj. J. P. FINKELMEIER,
Assistant Adjutant-General.

No. 174.

Report of Col. George C. Burling, Sixth New Jersey Infantry, commanding Third Brigade.

HDQRS. THIRD BRIG., SECOND DIV., THIRD CORPS,
August 20, 1863.

MAJOR: I have the honor to make this as my report of the part taken by this brigade in the late marches and battles with the enemy:

The brigade left camp at Falmouth, Va., on Thursday, June 11, under command of Colonel Bowman, of the Eighty-fourth Regiment Pennsylvania Volunteers (that regiment being assigned to the brigade on the morning of June 11), and marched near Hartwood Church and bivouacked for the night.

The next morning the march was resumed. We reached Rappahannock Station near dark of that day, and picketed the river from Kelly's Ford, on our left, to a short distance above the railroad, connecting with the First Brigade of our division. We remained during Saturday and Sunday at this occupation.

Sunday afternoon, I received orders that the Eighty-fourth Pennsylvania Volunteers were detailed from the brigade, and for me to report to General Humphreys, division commander, for instructions, which order I obeyed.

In compliance with orders from General Humphreys, the brigade moved with the division that night toward Manassas Junction, reaching Catlett's Station about 7 o'clock Monday morning. Rested until nearly 2 o'clock, when the march was again resumed, reaching Manassas Junction about 12 o'clock that night.

Remained here until Wednesday morning, when we again started toward Centreville, arriving there that afternoon, remaining until

Friday, the 19th, and then started toward Gum Springs, arriving there near dark.

Remained in this place until Thursday, the 25th, and then marched to Edwards Ferry, crossing the river on pontoons, and continued our march to Monocacy Aqueduct, arriving about midnight.

The next morning the march was resumed to Point of Rocks. Bivouacked for the night, and resumed the march in the morning, passing through Jefferson about noon. Bivouacked near Middletown that night.

Started in the morning; crossed the Catoctin Mountain, passing through Frederick City, and bivouacked 7 miles out on the Liberty turnpike.

Marched the next morning at 5 o'clock through Woodsborough, Ladiesburg, and Bruceville to Taneytown, arriving near dark.

Marched the next day through Bridgeport, and bivouacked for the night.

July 1, we reached Emmitsburg, Md., at 12 m. I was ordered by Major Hamlin, assistant adjutant-general Second Division, Third Corps, to remain at this place with the brigade and Smith's battery, to guard the Hagerstown road. In conjunction with Colonel Sewell, of the Fifth New Jersey Volunteers, and Captain Smith, of the battery, I immediately made such disposition of my command as I deemed advisable to accomplish this object.

At 1.30 a. m., July 2, I received orders from General Meade to immediately rejoin the corps, near Gettysburg, Pa. In consequence of my command covering so much ground, and the night being so very dark, it was nearly 4 a. m. before I was able to march.

We joined the corps and division at 9 a. m., July 2. The brigade was massed in column of regiments, and remained in that position until nearly 12 m., when General Humphreys ordered us to our position as a reserve to the First and Second Brigades of our division. Shortly after, I received orders from General Humphreys to march to the left, and report to General Birney, commanding First Division, Third Corps. I did so, and was ordered by him to mass the brigade in a piece of woods in the rear of his division.

In a short time skirmishing commenced very heavily along his front. I was then ordered by General Birney out of the woods on an open field. Immediately on our unmasking ourselves, the enemy opened with a terrific artillery fire on our left flank, at a distance of not more than 1,000 yards. After remaining in this position for half an hour, upon the solicitation of several regimental commanders, whom I considered equally competent with myself, I ordered the brigade to fall back about 100 yards, where they would have the protection of a small rise in the ground, which was done in perfect order.

At this moment Captain Poland, of General Sickles' staff, rode up to me, and, in an excited manner, inquired by whose authority I moved the brigade. I answered, "By my own." He ordered me to take the brigade back again. I started with it, when an aide from General Birney ordered me to change direction to the left, and take a position behind a piece of woods, my front now being at right angles with my former front.

I now received orders from General Birney to detail two of my largest regiments to report to General Graham, in compliance with which I detailed the Second New Hampshire and Seventh New Jersey Volunteers. Shortly after this, I received orders from General Birney to detail the strongest regiment to report to General Humphreys for picket, in compliance with which I sent the Fifth New Jersey Volunteers, leaving me three small regiments.

I was now ordered by General Birney to form a line across a small wheat-field on my left, to connect two brigades of the First Division. Before I had executed this order, I received an order from General Birney to send the largest regiment to General Ward's support, on my left, and while I was attending to that, the Eighth New Jersey Volunteers was taken from me without my knowledge, leaving me with the One hundred and fifteenth Pennsylvania Volunteers, numbering 140 muskets. My command being now all taken from me and separated, no two regiments being together, and being under the command of the different brigade commanders to whom they had reported, I, with my staff, reported to General Humphreys for instructions, remaining with him for some time.

Seeing the colors and a portion of one regiment retiring, I immediately rode to them, and commenced collecting the brigade. Our whole line at this time being relieved, we lay on our arms until daylight of the 3d, and then joined the division. We were marched to the rear of the position occupied by us the day before, remaining there until some time after noon. We then moved to the right, to support batteries. We lay in this position for two hours, under a severe artillery fire, when night ended the battle. We now marched back to our former position, where we remained until the enemy retreated.

During the two days of fighting, both officers and men behaved with their usual gallantry. I thank Capt. T. W. Eayre, assistant adjutant-general; Capt. J. W. Crawford, acting commissary of subsistence; Lieut. Merritt Bruen, acting aide-de-camp, and Lieut. Henry R. Clark, ambulance officer, for their gallantry and promptness in conveying my orders. The last named was mortally wounded, and died on the field.

Appended is a tabular statement of the casualties, as follows:

Command.	Officers.			Enlisted men.				Aggregate.
	Killed.	Wounded.	Total.	Killed.	Wounded.	Missing.	Total.	
Brigade staff	1	......	1		......	......	......	1
5th New Jersey	1	5	6	11	60	16	87	93
6th New Jersey	......	3	3	1	29	8	38	41
7th New Jersey	1	10	11	14	76	13	103	114
8th New Jersey	......	7	7	7	31	2	40	47
115th Pennsylvania	......	......	......	3	18	3	24	24
2d New Hampshire	3	18	21	17	119	36	172	193
Total	6	43	49	53	333	78	464	513

Sunday, July 5, we received orders to be ready to move on short notice.

Monday morning we started after the fleeing enemy, but, after a very short march, returned to our starting point.

Tuesday we started at 3 a. m., and marched through Emmitsburg, and reached Mechanicstown at sunset. Bivouacked for the night.

Resumed the march at daylight, passing through Frederick, and bivouacked on the Middletown pike, 1 mile out, at 10 p. m. Started at 4 a. m., marched through Middletown, reaching New Baltimore about noon, where we halted until nearly dark; resuming the march again, halting about midnight in South Mountain Pass. Started again at 7 a. m., passing through Keedysville, and crossed Antietam Creek, and halted until 10 p. m. Resumed the march, recrossed the creek, and bivouacked for the night near Boolesville. Marched at 6 a. m. a short distance, when the Third Corps was massed in rear of one of the bridges crossing Antietam Creek, in reserve, starting again at 4 p. m., crossing the Antietam, marching about 3 miles to the right, and bivouacked for the night.

Sunday, 12th, received orders that the general commanding would attack the enemy. About noon we moved to the left, and massed in a woods about 1½ miles in the rear of Marsh Creek. Here we bivouacked for the night. Remained in this bivouac until Tuesday, the 14th. Started at 5 a. m. to occupy ground vacated by a division of the Twelfth Corps, which had advanced to reconnoiter the enemy's position; as they advanced, we followed within supporting distance. It being discovered that the enemy had crossed the Potomac, we bivouacked for the night.

The following morning we resumed the march at daylight, passing through Fair Play and Sharpsburg, crossing the Antietam over Burnside's bridge, marching about half a mile, and bivouacked for the night.

Marched at 6 a. m. the next morning (Thursday) to within 3 miles of Harper's Ferry, and remained until the next afternoon. Resumed the march at 4 o'clock, crossing the Potomac and Shenandoah at Harper's Ferry. Marched 1½ miles toward Hillsborough, and bivouacked for the night.

Started at 6 a. m., and reached Hillsborough about noon. Staid here all night, starting in the morning at 8 o'clock, and marched to within 5 miles of Snicker's Gap, bivouacking for the night ; started in the morning at 4 o'clock, and reached Upperville about 3 p. m.

Remained here guarding Ashby's Gap until noon of Wednesday, July 22, when we resumed the march, and reached Piedmont Station, on the Manassas Gap Railroad, about 1 p. m. At a late hour that night I was ordered to be ready to move the brigade with the division at 4 a. m., July 23, to support the First Division of this corps. We reached Linden Station, in Manassas Gap, near noon of the 23d. I was here ordered to detail a regiment to support a battery on the heights commanding Chester Gap road. The Seventh New Jersey Volunteers were detailed, in compliance with that order. I would here state that, at the time of our leaving Upperville, the Sixth New Jersey Volunteers were detailed to guard the wagon train, leaving me with four small regiments, numbering not more than 550 muskets. We advanced in column of division, closed in mass, changing our position from the right to the left side of the main road leading to Front Royal, and rising a high ridge which had been carried by the First Division. I was now ordered forward by General Prince to support the Second Brigade of our division, which had charged and was driving the enemy. The column was immediately put in motion, and deployed while advancing, and continued to advance in line of battle to a crest of a hill within easy supporting distance of the Second Brigade, where, by General Prince in person, we were ordered to halt. While in this position, the enemy opened a slight artillery fire, which wounded 2 men. We remained in this position all night, the men lying on their arms.

Early the next morning I was ordered to advance, leading the division column. The Second New Hampshire Volunteers were deployed as skirmishers on the right and left of the road; the One hundred and fifteenth Pennsylvania and Eighth New Jersey Volunteers supported the right, and the Fifth New Jersey the left of the skirmishers. In this order we passed the distance of 3 miles to Front Royal, the enemy falling back slowly before us. In approaching Front Royal, the line of skirmishers and supports passed over a steep mountain, densely wooded and with thick undergrowth. After a short stay at Front Royal, I was ordered by General Prince to withdraw my skirmishers and march to the rear by the flank, the object we came for being accomplished. At Markham Station we bivouacked for the night, and next day marched to within 7 miles of Warrenton.

It was extremely gratifying to me to observe the promptness which both officers and men evinced in overcoming the difficulties of the advance, the weather being extremely warm and the ground very uneven, and covered in many places with a thick undergrowth, almost impassable for man or beast.

I feel indebted to Capt. T. W. Eayre, assistant adjutant-general; Lieutenant [Lafayette] Culver, acting assistant inspector-general, and Lieutenant [William G.] Thompson, aide-de-camp, for their promptness in communicating my orders on the field.

Sunday, July 26, started at 5 a. m., and reached Warrenton at 11 a. m., where we went into camp.

I have the honor to be, very respectfully, your obedient servant,

GEO. C. BURLING,
Colonel Sixth New Jersey Volunteers, Comdg. Brigade.

Maj. CHARLES HAMLIN,
Assistant Adjutant-General, Second Div., Third Corps.

No. 175.

Report of Col. Edward L. Bailey, Second New Hampshire Infantry.

NEAR GETTYSBURG, PA., *July* 5, 1863.

COLONEL: I have the honor to submit the following report of the part taken by my regiment on the 2d instant in the battle at this place, commencing at the time it was detached from your command, it then being in position with your brigade in front of the Emmitsburg road:

At 3 p. m. I had the honor to receive your order to report to General Graham, and immediately moving by double-quick to the front, I had the honor to announce my presence to that general with 24 commissioned officers and 330 rifles. I was at once ordered to support Battery G, First New York Artillery, and one section of a battery unknown, all light 12-pounders, brass. In this position my left rested upon the right of the Sixty-third Pennsylvania, my right covered by a wood house situated upon the Emmitsburg road, line forming a right angle with that road. Two hundred yards in my front the Third Maine was skirmishing with the enemy.

At 4 o'clock, while experiencing a terrific fire of spherical case and canister from batteries in my front and on my right, 650 yards distant, I directed the rolls of my companies to be called, and found but

8 of the total number equipped absent. These had fallen out of the ranks from sunstroke and exhaustion while moving by double-quick to position.

At 4.30 p. m. the Third Maine was withdrawn from our front to our rear, and about this time a battery and a section of Rodman pieces were substituted for those we were supporting. These pieces were worked with great inefficiency, and at 5 o'clock it was observed that a brigade of the enemy was advancing on our right, in column of battalions massed, while two regiments were moving directly parallel with my front to the left, evidently with design to turn that flank.

I reported these facts to General Graham, and asked permission to charge, the enemy being close upon us—so near that the officer commanding the section of battery spiked his pieces, fearful that he should lose them. The general gave me directions to go forward, when I gave the order. My regiment started immediately, and advanced 150 yards at a run with a yell and such impetuosity as to cause the enemy to retire to a ravine 250 yards in our front, where they were covered from our fire, when I directed the fire of my battalion of the left oblique by the flank at about the same distance. My fire was so galling, assisted by that from the Third Maine, which had come up and taken part upon my left, as to cause them to break and seek shelter, when my attention was again called to my right, strengthened by the Sixty-third Pennsylvania forming at right angles with my front and parallel with the Emmitsburg road, upon which was advancing the brigade of the enemy, moving by battalion in mass, in line of battle. I immediately directed the fire of my battalion to the right oblique full upon it. Yet their line of fire, assisted by a terrible discharge of spherical case from their batteries, caused the Sixty-eighth Pennsylvania to retire, and at the same moment the Third Maine moved 200 yards to the rear, though in good order.

Finding myself thus unsupported, and the enemy steadily advancing, I ordered my regiment to fall back slowly, firing, which was fully executed. I moved to the rear 140 yards, and halted my line under the brow of the hill, halting also on the brow to give a volley to the enemy, then distant but 20 yards. The positions of the three regiments was that of *échelon* at about 20 paces, my regiment being the apex. The enemy continued advancing until they reached the brow of the hill, when their left swept toward the Sixty-third Pennsylvania in such overwhelming numbers as to cause it to give way; and fearing those regiments which had been observed marching toward my left might appear upon that flank, and knowing our efforts must prove futile against such fearful odds, I gave the order to retire, which was done quite rapidly, yet coolly, and without excitement as they went. I rejoined the brigade at about 6.30 p. m., fearfully diminished in numbers, yet firm and fearless still.

This battalion entered the fight with a firm determination to do or die, and the long list of fallen comrades, already submitted, will show how well it kept that resolution.

Where all did so well it would be invidious to make comparisons. Let it suffice to say that they did their part as becomes sons of the old Granite State. For our fallen braves, who have so gloriously perished fighting for their country, we drop a comrade's tear, while we extend our heartfelt sympathy to those dear ones far away who find the ties of kindred and friends thus rudely severed, and for those who must suffer untold agony and pain through long weeks of convalescence our earnest sympathy, yet leaving them to the watchful care of Him who will not prove unmindful of their necessities.

I have the honor to be, sir, your obedient servant,

ED. L. BAILEY,
Colonel Second New Hampshire Volunteers.

Col. GEORGE C. BURLING,
Comdg. Third Brig., Second Div., Third Corps.

No. 176.

Reports of Capt. Henry H. Woolsey and Col. William J. Sewell, Fifth New Jersey Infantry.

BIVOUAC NEAR UPPERVILLE, VA.,
July 21, 1863.

SIR: I have the honor to submit the following report of the part taken by the Fifth New Jersey Volunteers in the recent engagement at Gettysburg, Pa., July 2 and 3:

The regiment had been on picket on the night of the 1st instant about 1½ miles from Emmitsburg, Md., on the road leading from that place to Hagerstown, Md.

At 2 a. m. the pickets were called in, and the regiment joined the brigade, and at daybreak marched with the brigade toward Gettysburg, reaching the battle-field at about 10 a. m. From that time until 4 p. m. the regiment, in common with the rest of the brigade, changed its position several times, being from about 2 p. m. the most of the time under a heavy fire of artillery from the enemy's batteries, which had taken position to the left of the Emmitsburg road. The casualties in the regiment up to this time, however, were few.

At about 4 p. m. the regiment was ordered to relieve another regiment in support of Battery K (Captain Seeley), Fourth U. S. Artillery, which was in position near the Emmitsburg road, just south of the apple orchard. We took this position, moving by the right flank at the double-quick. In order to occupy the front assigned the regiment, it had to be deployed as skirmishers, thus forming rather a singular line for the protection of a battery of six guns.

At this point the rebel artillery fire was very severe and effective, one battery pouring an enfilading fire, principally of spherical case, immediately up the road. Very soon after we arrived on the road, another, or more probably more than one, rebel battery opened upon us from the woods to our left and front. Captain Seeley's battery then became engaged. A battery to our right soon after, and one to our left, facing south down the road, and which had been engaged before we arrived in the road, continued its fire. This artillery fire was kept up very rapidly for an hour or more, our regiment all the time losing men, the most of them, however, being but slightly wounded by the spherical case. During all this time there was no infantry firing on our part of the line.

At about 5 o'clock, however, the skirmishers in our front (the First U. S. Sharpshooters) were driven in, and immediately after a dense line of the enemy's infantry was seen advancing over a knoll about 600 yards distant to our left and front, and as this line advanced the infantry on both sides became engaged. The carnage at this time was fearful. The regiments to our left, however, were soon compelled to fall back, and our regiment, small as it was and deployed over so large a front, could offer but little resistance to the rebel line of battle. Seeley's battery, which we felt to be our especial care, was also compelled to fall back. The regiment was collected around the pieces of the battery, and it and the battery commenced firing in retreat. This was kept up until another line of ours was reached, near the position first occupied by our brigade in the morning, and about 100 yards from our position on the road.

During this retrograde movement we lost many men, and it was at this time that Colonel Sewell, our gallant leader, was seriously wounded by a musket-ball in the thigh. Captain Healy, acting major, was also wounded by shell in the hand and thigh. Before leaving the road, I had been slightly wounded in the head by a musket-ball, and had left the field. The regiment was now left under the command of Captain Godfrey, and, re-enforcements arriving from the Fifth Corps, was withdrawn from the field. That night the regiment bivouacked near the stream, in the rear of the battle-field.

On the morning of the 3d, I rejoined the regiment, and took command.

During the day we were under fire several times, but met with no casualties.

The loss on the 2d instant was very nearly 50 per cent. of the whole number engaged. A nominal list of the casualties is furnished below.*

We believe that our regiment assisted materially in gaining our glorious victory over the invading rebel army, and has added something to the reputation already won on so many hard-fought fields. Every officer and man was in his place and did his duty.   *   *   *

Recapitulation.

Officers and men.	Killed.	Wounded.	Missing.	Total.
Officers...	2	5	.....	7
Enlisted men...	11	60	16	87
Total...	13	65	16	94

I am, sir, very respectfully, your obedient servant,
H. H. WOOLSEY,
Captain Fifth New Jersey Volunteers, Comdg. Regiment.

Capt. THOMAS W. EAYRE,
Assistant Adjutant-General.

———

The undersigned adds the following corrections to the report of Captain Woolsey, who was mistaken as regards the duty which the regiment was intended to perform:

My orders were to report to General Graham, for the purpose of relieving the Sixty-third Pennsylvania, on picket. My right rested at a white house, my left extending to a large barn on the Emmitsburg

*Omitted.

road, thus covering the front of the Second Division; Seeley's battery a few paces in the rear of my center, and two brigades of the Second Division on the slope of the hill.

When the enemy's column of attack appeared in sight, I sent word to General Humphreys, and immediately afterward became engaged. Previous to this I had time to examine the ground, and was convinced that the only place to check the attack was on the road and crest of the hill which I held. My left became engaged first, and immediately after was entirely driven in by the giving way of some regiments of the First Division to my left and the enemy placing a battery where my left had rested. I had now a direct musketry fire and a battery of artillery on my flank, but still held the position, hoping for the advance of the troops in my rear. When obliged to fall back, I did so by rallying on my right, covering Seeley's battery, which was firing in retreat.

I found, on reaching the position occupied by the Second Division, General Humphreys changing front to rear on his right, so as to connect with the First Division, which had been driven back a considerable distance—so much so that the enemy was on the flank and rear of the Second Division thirty minutes after the attack commenced. I was wounded during this movement.

I am, sir, very respectfully, your obedient servant,
WILLIAM J. SEWELL,
Colonel Fifth New Jersey Volunteers.

No. 177.

Report of Lieut. Col. Stephen R. Gilkyson, Sixth New Jersey Infantry

CAMP NEAR WARRENTON, VA., *July 27, 1863.*

SIR: In compliance with orders from brigade headquarters, I have the honor to make the following report of the part taken by the Sixth Regiment New Jersey Volunteers in the late engagement at Gettysburg, Pa., July 2 and 3:

The regiment with the brigade arrived on the battle-field about 8 a. m. of the 2d instant, where we massed, and rested for about an hour, when we commenced to take position. After maneuvering for some time, the Sixth New Jersey Volunteers was detached from the brigade, and ordered to the support of General Ward's brigade, which was engaged with the enemy near the left of our line, partly in the woods, their left resting in an open field.

Advancing promptly through the woods, we came to a fence. Having no one to guide me, and not knowing the position the regiment was to occupy, I formed line, and opened fire on the enemy directly in our front. Soon ascertaining the position of our line, under a heavy fire from the enemy, I advanced the regiment about 200 yards across the open field, directly in front of the Fourth New York Battery, Captain Smith, taking position on the left of Ward's brigade. Here we secured a fine position, and opened fire with great effect, driving the enemy from our immediate front, remaining in this position for about two hours, being during this time actively engaged. Seeing the troops on my right retiring, I ordered my regiment to retire, which it did in good order, halting with the rest of the troops. I reported to General Ward, who informed me he had been relieved, ordering me to join my brigade, which we did about 7 p. m.

July 3.—The regiment with the brigade took position, massed in a woods in rear and near the left of our line, remaining in this position until about 2 p. m., when we were ordered farther to the right, to support some batteries, lying in mass for about two hours under a heavy shell fire, with the loss of 1 commissioned officer and 5 men wounded, when we returned to our old position.

Both officers and men behaved with their usual gallantry, fully sustaining their well-earned reputation.

My loss in the two days' engagement, in killed, wounded, and missing, was as follows, viz:

Officers and men.	Killed.	Wounded.	Missing.	Total.
Commissioned officers......	......	3	......	3
Enlisted men	1	30	7	38
Total	1	33	7	41

Very respectfully, your obedient servant,
                              S. R. GILKYSON,
      Lieutenant-Colonel, Comdg. Sixth New Jersey Volunteers.

Capt. T. W. EAYRE,
      Assistant Adjutant-General.

No. 178.

Report of Maj. Frederick Cooper, Seventh New Jersey Infantry.

IN THE FIELD, *July* 17, 1863.

SIR: I have the honor to report the following as the part performed by this regiment during the late engagement at Gettysburg, Pa., July 2 and 3:

About 4 o'clock in the afternoon of the 2d instant, Colonel Francine was ordered to report to Brigadier-General Graham, which was done, and soon after we were placed in position to support a battery. Soon after being posted, the enemy opened a heavy fire of shot and shell. Our position being greatly exposed, we suffered severely. We remained in this position until 5.30 p. m., when the enemy made a vigorous charge upon a battery on our left, which compelled the battery to retire. In falling back, the battery broke through our ranks, creating considerable confusion for a time, but through the exertions of the officers the line was reformed.

The enemy now being on our left flank, Colonel Francine threw the right of the regiment forward, and opened fire upon the enemy. After firing a few rounds, a charge was ordered, which was attempted, but the enemy's fire was so severe that we were compelled to fall back a short distance. At this juncture, Colonel Francine and Lieutenant-Colonel Price being wounded, I assumed command of the regiment, and, reforming the line, made an effort to hold our position until re-enforcements arrived.   Soon the enemy appeared upon the right flank, and, there being danger of being overwhelmed and captured, I ordered the regiment to fall back to the woods.   Our supports having arrived, I retired from the field and joined the brigade.

We remained in the woods all night, and on the morning of the 3d instant moved with the brigade to the front.   Nothing of note transpired until about 5 p. m., when we again moved with the brigade to the right, and were assigned to the support of two batteries.   For a short time we were subjected to a heavy artillery fire.   The enemy not essaying to attack us, we moved back to our former position.

The regiment behaved well during the whole engagement, both officers and men doing their whole duty.

I would especially mention Sergt. Charles A. Monks, Company C, for his bravery and gallant conduct on the field.

I regret to report the death of First Lieut. Charles F. Walker, Company B, a gallant and efficient officer, who was killed on the afternoon of the 3d instant.

My loss in killed is 16; wounded, 84; missing, 12; total, 112.*

Very respectfully, your obedient servant,

FREDERICK COOPER,
Major, Comdg. Seventh Regiment New Jersey Volunteers.

Capt. T. W. EAYRE,
Captain, and Assistant Adjutant-General.

No. 179.

Report of Brig. Gen. Washington L. Elliott, U. S. Army, commanding Third Division.

HDQRS. THIRD DIVISION, THIRD ARMY CORPS,
July 27, 1863.

CAPTAIN: In accordance with circular of this date from headquarters Third Army Corps, I have the honor to submit the following report of the operations of my division on July 23, 24, and 25:

The division is organized as follows: The First Brigade, Brig. Gen. W. H. Morris commanding: Sixth New York Artillery, One hundred and fifty-first New York Infantry, Tenth Vermont Infantry, Fourteenth New Jersey Infantry.   The Second Brigade, Col. J. W. Keifer, One hundred and tenth Ohio Infantry, commanding: One hundred and tenth and One hundred and twenty-second Ohio Infantry, One hundred and thirty-eighth Pennsylvania Infantry, and Sixth Maryland Infantry.   The Third Brigade, Col. B. F. Smith, One hundred and twenty-sixth Ohio Infantry, commanding: One hundred and twenty-sixth Ohio Infantry, One hundred and sixth New York Infantry, and Sixty-seventh and Eighty-seventh Pennsylvania Infantry.

On the 23d, the division marched from Piedmont to Linden, in Manassas Gap; the Tenth Vermont Infantry detached as guard for trains of corps.

About 5 p. m. the division advanced in order of battle to support the First and Second Divisions, and in the following order: The First Brigade on the left, Third Brigade on the right, and Second Brigade

---

*But see revised statement, p. 178.

in reserve. The One hundred and sixth New York Infantry, of the Third Brigade, was detached, by order of the major-general commanding, to report to Colonel De Trobriand, Fifty-fifth New York Infantry, the remainder of the Third Brigade to report to Brigadier-General Ward, commanding First Division. About dark the division bivouacked for the night.

On the 24th, the division was ordered to occupy the position vacated by the advance of the First Division.

About 12 o'clock the division was ordered to march and encamp near Piedmont. It reached there about sundown.

On the 25th, the division marched via Salem to camp near Warrenton, Va.

The only casualty I have to report is Private John Heffler, Company K, Sixth Maryland, severely wounded by the enemy on the 23d in right leg, rendering amputation necessary.

The division having been but recently organized, and the First Brigade composed of troops unaccustomed to marching, I think it due to the division to say that the severity of the march through mud and broken fields was cheerfully borne, and this, too, from necessity, upon a scanty ration. The entire division, officers and men, showed a desire to press forward to engage the enemy.

I am, captain, very respectfully, your obedient servant,

W. L. ELLIOTT,
Brigadier-General, U. S. Volunteers, Commanding.

Capt. W. F. A. TORBERT,
    A. D. C., and A. A. A. G., Headquarters Third Corps.

No. 180.

Report of Col. Benjamin F. Smith, One hundred and twenty-sixth Ohio Infantry, commanding Third Brigade.

HEADQUARTERS THIRD BRIGADE, THIRD DIVISION,
On the Rappahannock, near Fox's Ford, Va., August 15, 1863.

GENERAL: In compliance with circular from headquarters Army of the Potomac, dated August 12, 1863, I have the honor to make a report of the operations of my command from June 28 until its arrival in the vicinity of Warrenton.

The four regiments constituting this brigade were organized as the Third Brigade, Third Division, Third Army Corps, near Antietam Bridge, Md., on July 10. They were previously of the Eighth Army Corps, two of them, the Sixty-seventh and Eighty-seventh Pennsylvania Volunteers, of the Second Division (Milroy's), from Winchester; the other two of the First Division (Kelley's), from Martinsburg, W. Va., and on June 28 were at Maryland Heights. These regiments, with other Winchester and Martinsburg troops, all under Brig. Gen. W. L. Elliott, evacuated Maryland Heights, and went in twenty-six canal-boats by way of the Chesapeake and Ohio Canal to Washington, D. C., leaving on June 30 and arriving at Washington on July 4. Encamped at Tenallytown same day.

On July 6, marched to Washington depot, and went by railroad to Frederick, Md., arriving on the 7th.

Marching from thence, arrived near Antietam Bridge on the 10th, the date of the organization of this brigade.

Since, the Third Brigade has marched with the Third Corps to a point near Williamsport, Md.; thence, by way of Sharpsburg, Pleasant Valley, and Harper's Ferry, and along the eastern slope of the Blue Ridge Mountains, to Manassas Gap, arriving on the 23d ultimo, constituting a portion of the line of supports during the engagement at that time. It was not found necessary to bring these supports into action.

From Manassas Gap returned to Piedmont. Marched by way of Warrenton, arriving at the present camp on August 1.

I have the honor to be, very respectfully, your obedient servant,

B. F. SMITH,
Colonel One hundred and twenty-sixth Ohio Volunteers.

Brig. Gen. S. WILLIAMS,
    Assistant Adjutant-General, Hdqrs. Army of the Potomac.

No. 181.

Report of Capt. George E. Randolph, First Rhode Island Light Artillery, commanding Artillery Brigade, Third Army Corps.

HDQRS, ARTILLERY BRIGADE, THIRD ARMY CORPS,
September 2, 1863.

CAPTAIN: I have the honor to submit the following report of the artillery of the Third Army Corps, from June 28 to July 3:

On the morning of June 28, the batteries of the corps, with one exception, were encamped near Middletown, Md. Clark's battery was near Crampton's Pass, with one brigade of infantry.

Early in the day, in compliance with the order of Major-General Birney, commanding the corps, I marched to Frederick, where I encamped and fed about noon, and where I was joined by Clark's battery an hour or two later.

In the afternoon the corps marched to Woodville, and, on June 29, to Taneytown, encamping a mile north of the town.

On the afternoon of the 30th, the corps, including batteries, marched to Bridgeport, a place about 2 miles from Taneytown, on the road to Emmitsburg, and pushed on the next morning to the latter place.

In the afternoon of July 1, by command of Major-General Sickles, who had resumed command of the corps at Frederick, three batteries—Randolph's, E, First Rhode Island; Clark's, B, First New Jersey, accompanying the First Division, and Seeley's, K, Fourth U. S. Artillery, accompanying the Second Division—marched to Gettysburg, and encamped on the left of the town, near the Taneytown road.

Early on the morning of July 2, Randolph's and Clark's batteries were placed in position on the line held by General Birney's division, running from near the left of the Second Corps to the base of Signal or Round Top Mountain. The positions of both were low, unprotected, and commanded by the ridge along which runs the road from Emmitsburg to Gettysburg. Seeley's battery remained in the field where it had encamped, and, as there were no desirable positions on our part of the line, Smith's and Winslow's batteries, on their arrival from Emmitsburg, were parked near Seeley's until some better disposition could be made of them.

Between 1 and 2 p. m. Major-General Sickles notified me that he was about to change his line, throwing his right forward to the high ground, running his line from Round Top Mountain, on the left, to a peach orchard on the Emmitsburg road, and thence along the road toward Gettysburg to a second orchard. This new disposition seemed to me, notwithstanding the sharp angle in our line made necessary by the formation of the ground, to be a much more desirable one. I placed Smith's battery near the extreme left, between Round Top Mountain and the woods, on a rocky hill commanding a long valley running toward Emmitsburg. On the right of Smith's, after passing a belt of woods, was an opening, in which I placed Winslow's battery of light 12-pounders. This position was surrounded by woods, but, in my opinion, the line was materially strengthened by this battery of short-range guns. In the open field, with his left resting near the woods, I placed Captain Bigelow's (Massachusetts) battery, from the Artillery Reserve; on his right Clark's, and next, and in the peach orchard that stood in the angle formed by our lines, was Ames' battery, G, First New York, also from the Artillery Reserve. All these batteries fronted toward Emmitsburg, or in the direction from which the attack of the enemy was expected and afterward received. Randolph's battery was placed on the Emmitsburg road, fronting nearly perpendicular to those before mentioned; and, still farther to the right, and near the extreme left of the line held by the corps, was Seeley's.

With the exception of almost continual skirmishing between our sharpshooters and those of the enemy, the first movement of the latter toward attacking was, at about 2 p. m., to place a battery in position near the intersection of the Fairfield and Emmitsburg roads, near a barn, and easily visible from the peach orchard in the angle of our lines.

In obedience to the command of Major-General Sickles, as well as in accordance with my own conviction of the necessity of holding that point, I was examining the ground with a view of placing a battery in the orchard, when the enemy opened a smart artillery fire upon the troops massed in the open field. I directed Captain Clark to take the position before mentioned as held by his battery, and to silence, or at least reply to, the fire, while I placed Ames' battery of light 12-pounders in the orchard to assist him.

It soon became evident that the enemy was preparing for an attack at this point. He soon opened more batteries on the right of his first, and commenced a heavy fire from them upon our troops. Ames and Clark were soon so well at work that the advantage was not on the side of the enemy, and at last a well-directed fire from Smith's battery (10-pounder Parrotts) on the extreme left silenced them for a time.

The respite, however, was short, as at about 3 p. m. the enemy reopened fire, and, under cover of his artillery, began to push infantry against our position. The part of our line where Smith's battery was placed was assailed in the most furious and determined manner; and, notwithstanding the gallant conduct of our troops, after a long struggle it became evident that the line would break. The hill upon which the guns stood was very rough and rocky, rendering maneuvering with horses almost an impossibility. Four of Captain Smith's guns only had been at first placed in battery. These were served effectively till they could no longer be without danger to our own troops, who had advanced to the front of the battery. The remaining two were placed in position a few yards in rear, and pointed obliquely into the woods on the left, in front of Round Top Mountain, which were occupied by the advancing lines of the enemy. These guns continued their fire till their supports were compelled to retire, when they were with-drawn by Captain Smith, leaving three of the four that were in advance still on the hill and in possession of the enemy. Captain Smith says he supposed the hill would be immediately retaken by our troops, and that, as it was a place most difficult of access, it was wiser to leave them where they could be used against the enemy immediately we regained the hill. I regret the loss, but from my knowledge of the position and of the gallantry displayed by Captain Smith, I am convinced that it was one of those very unpleasant, but yet unavoidable, results that sometimes attend the efforts of the most meritorious officers.

The attack on the left of our line involved Winslow's battery. From the position of the battery and of the infantry supporting, it was deemed best for a time to fire solid shot into the woods over our troops, who were fighting in front under protection of a stone wall. This fire was very effective (as such use of solid shot always is when troops are engaged in woods, the moral effect being at least equal to the physical), and was continued till our troops in front fell back of his battery, when Captain Winslow used case shot, 1 and 1½ second fuse, ending with canister.

When the enemy had gained two sides of the woods, and the position was no longer tenable, Captain Winslow, by command of General Birney, retired handsomely by piece, losing heavily during the movement. The position of Captain Winslow's battery did not seem to be very good, owing to the nearness of the woods on all sides, but the result proved that the battery was able to do good service, and Captain Winslow deserves credit, not only for the good working of his battery, but for the handsome manner in which he withdrew under trying circumstances.

In the open field between the woods occupied for a time by Barnes' division, of the Fifth Corps, and the Emmitsburg road, were Bigelow's (Massachusetts), Clark's (New Jersey), and Ames' (New York) batteries.

Of Bigelow's, I can only say that they took the position I assigned them promptly under a heavy fire, and fought gallantly till compelled to retire. I have tried to obtain reports from the batteries of the reserve that reported to Major-General Sickles, but with no success, excepting in the case of Captain Ames, G, First New York.

Clark's battery, B, First New Jersey, was placed in position about 2 p. m. A column of the enemy had been discovered moving on the Fairfield road, toward the left of our line. Captain Clark opened with shell and shrapnel, making excellent shots, and diverting the column of the enemy to some road in rear of and covered by the ridge running perpendicular to the Emmitsburg road, near its intersection with the Fairfield.

An hour later the enemy's batteries opened from this ridge, and Clark replied, while Ames' battery was being placed in the peach orchard on his right. The combined fire of Smith's, Clark's, and Ames' batteries soon silenced those of the enemy. The artillery fire, however, was only preliminary.

Shortly after 3 p. m. the attack was made by the enemy's infantry. Beginning, as I have stated, on the left, near Smith's position, it extended to the right, and brought the whole line under a destructive fire of musketry. The attack on the peach orchard, where Ames' battery was placed, was hardly less furious than that on the left. Ames' battery maintained its position under a fire from front and right flank until it was relieved by Battery I, Fifth U. S. Artillery. Randolph's battery, E, First Rhode Island, was placed in position to counteract a cross-fire from the woods in front of the Emmitsburg road upon Ames' battery, and the troops in the peach orchard were immediately engaged with the enemy, composed of infantry and a battery of 12-pounders, in front and a little to the left of its position. The very effective fire of this battery of six light 12-pounders did great damage to our lines until it was silenced by the fire of Randolph's battery and a section of Ames' that had been turned upon it. Randolph's battery remained in this position, doing good service, but greatly exposed, as the returns attest, until the withdrawal of its support to strengthen the peach orchard and the subsequent repulse of our troops in that position made its withdrawal a matter not only of prudence but of necessity. Lieut. John K. Bucklyn, commanding, received a painful wound while endeavoring to take from the field a caisson, some of the horses of which had been killed.

All the batteries whose operations I have thus far described were supported gallantly and effectively by the First Division (Birney's), who held this very extended line, notwithstanding the overwhelming force thrown against it, from 3 p. m. until dark, fighting with the dogged determination that has made it famous.

Seeley's battery (K, Fourth U. S. Artillery), supported by the Second Division (Humphreys'), was placed near the left of our corps line about 3 p. m., and became immediately engaged with artillery and infantry in its direct front. After driving the batteries in its immediate front from the field, and having been two hours in position, it directed its fire upon the guns of the enemy farther to the left, that were firing upon the positions held by Ames', Clark's, and Randolph's batteries.

About 5.30 p. m. Lieutenant Seeley was badly wounded, and the command devolved upon Second Lieut. Robert James. At the same time, the enemy's infantry advanced under cover of the crest to very near the battery, and attacked it almost with impunity, and, as the supports had fallen back, the battery was withdrawn. A second position was taken and held till the next morning, when the battery was ordered to the rear.

I have chosen to report the action of each battery rather than the artillery of the corps as a whole, at the risk of being thought diffuse, because I consider that in no other way can I convey a distinct idea of the operations of my command. The batteries were widely separated, and each performed special duties that no other kind of narrative could describe.

At about 5 p. m. I rode along the line, and became aware that the batteries were becoming very much exhausted, and upon my representation of the fact to Major-General Sickles, he applied for batteries from the Artillery Reserve to relieve them; they arrived, however, too late for the purpose intended, but in time to be used by Major McGilvery in forming a second line.

I was especially fortunate in having the advice and assistance of Brigadier-General Hunt, chief of artillery, Army of the Potomac, who examined the ground with me, and who, at the commencement and during the action, was present to contribute by his valuable advice to the efficiency of our artillery.

I regret that I cannot more accurately locate the batteries. Having been absent from the army when our troops reoccupied the battle-field, I lost the opportunity of examining it after the battle, as well as of correcting the impressions received during an action and hearing many incidents that might be of interest, though not mentioned in battery reports.

A wound that I received in the shoulder early in the action prevented my being as active on the field as I desired, and although I was able from time to time to ride along the line and to keep informed of the progress of the battle in the various parts of the field where my batteries were stationed, I could not give the line the same personal attention I would had I been stronger.

The conduct of my command was admirable. They were all in exposed positions, as the loss will show. The battery commanders fully sustained the reputation they had gained by distinguished conduct in former battles, and to the old added the laurels of a new and most severely contested engagement.

It is proper that I acknowledge here the valuable aid rendered me by Lieut. P. S. Jastram, acting assistant adjutant-general of my brigade, whose duties were rendered more arduous by my own inability to keep the saddle, and who displayed the same energy, bravery, and good judgment that he had already given evidence of as a battery commander.

Although in this battle of July 2 each of my batteries was compelled to retire, I may be permitted to claim, in view of the grand results of the three days' fighting, that they contributed in no small degree to the success of our arms.

I append statement of losses in men* and *matériel.*

I have the honor to be, your obedient servant,

GEO. E. RANDOLPH,
Capt. First R. I. Art., and Chief of Art. Third A. C.

Capt. W. H. HILL,
Assistant Adjutant-General, Third Army Corps.

No. 182.

Report of Capt. A. Judson Clark, Battery B, First New Jersey Light Artillery.

NEAR BEVERLY FORD, VA.,
August 14, 1863.

CAPTAIN: I have the honor to submit the following report of the part taken by this battery in the engagement near Gettysburg, July 2:

Early on the morning of July 2, the battery was moved to the front, and placed in the second, near the left, of the line of batteries. About 9.30 a. m. the battery, by your orders, was moved to the front and left, and placed in line on the rise of ground midway between General Sickles' headquarters and the peach orchard, on the Emmitsburg road, where we remained until about 2 p. m. At this time the enemy's infantry was discovered passing in column across the Emmitsburg road to our left and front, and distant about 1,400 yards, and, by direction of General Sickles, I placed my battery in position, and opened fire upon their position, using shell and case shot, firing very slowly and apparently with good effect, as, after some 6 or 7 rounds, the columns had entirely disappeared, and no more were seen to pass that point.

* Embodied in revised statement, p. 178.

Nothing more transpired until about 3 p. m. (at this time the battery was in line at the foot of the next slope, near the peach orchard), when a rebel battery, which had just been placed in position near a house on the Emmitsburg road, about 1,400 yards to our front, opened fire on my position, and I was ordered by you to go back and attack the battery. This I did, using shell and case shot, and, after a pretty short fight, silenced the battery, but only for a short time, when they opened again, as did other batteries which they had brought into position on my right. From this time until night the fire from them was rapid and severe.

About 3.30 p. m. the enemy's infantry commenced moving down from our front and right in strong columns, under cover of a heavy artillery fire, and the fire soon became sharp and obstinate. I immediately opened on them with shell and case shot, but although the fire seemed very destructive, opening large gaps in their ranks, it only temporarily checked them, and they pressed steadily on. I continued firing case and shell, however, at the column, and, later in the fight, into the woods on my immediate front and left, in which the enemy were pushing our troops, that seeming to be at the time the main point of their attack.

About 6.30 p. m. another of the enemy's columns commenced moving across my front, and distant about 350 yards, when I began firing canister, doing great execution, throwing the column wholly into confusion, and causing it to seek shelter behind the slope of a hill just beyond them. By this time our infantry on both sides had fallen back, as had also several batteries, when, having no supports, I deemed it best to retire, which I did, to near the ground occupied the previous evening. In the battle of the following day the battery was not engaged.

I was obliged to leave one caisson and one caisson body on the field for the want of horses to bring them off, but subsequently recovered them.

My loss in men was as follows: One man killed, 16 men wounded, and 3 missing, 2 of whom are known to be prisoners. I had 17 horses killed, and 5 disabled so badly that I was obliged to abandon them.

Of the conduct of the officers and men, I can only say that it was in the highest degree commendable for courage and bravery.

I am, captain, your obedient servant,

A. JUDSON CLARK,
Captain First New Jersey Artillery, Comdg. Battery B.

Capt. GEO. E. RANDOLPH,
Chief of Artillery, Third Corps.

No. 183.

Report of Capt. George B. Winslow, Battery D, First New York Light Artillery.

CAMP NEAR WARRENTON, VA., *July* 28, 1863.

CAPTAIN: In compliance with instructions, I have the honor to submit the following report of the part taken by the battery under my command in the battle of Gettysburg:

On the afternoon of July 1, my battery was left with a brigade of the First Division at Emmitsburg.

At 3 o'clock on the morning of July 2, I received orders to march with the brigade and rejoin the corps at Gettysburg. When within about 3 miles of the latter place, the command halted for a brief rest, but, being informed by citizens that the enemy's skirmishers were only a mile distant, and advancing toward the road upon which we were marching, was immediately pushed on, reaching the corps about 11 a. m. My battery was put into position in the line of battle then being formed by the corps. An hour or two later the line was moved to the left and front. The position assigned my battery was near the left of the line, in a small wheat-field near the base of Round Top hill.

A battery of the enemy posted nearly in my front opened between 3 and 4 p. m. upon our lines. I could only see the smoke of their guns as it rose above the tree tops, but, by command of General Hunt, fired a few rounds of solid shot in that direction, probably with no effect, as it was evidently beyond the range of my guns. Soon after, the two lines of infantry became hotly engaged, but I was unable from my obscure position to observe the movements of the troops, and was compelled to estimate distances and regulate my fire by the reports of our own and the enemy's musketry.

By direction of Major-General Birney, I opened with solid shot, giving but sufficient elevation to clear our own troops in front, and firing in the direction of the heaviest musketry, lessening the range as our troops fell back and the enemy advanced. Our line of skirmishers fell back on their supports at the edge of the woods, little, if any, more than 400 yards from the front of my guns. This line was a weak one and soon fell back, but by using shell and case shot at about one degree elevation, and from 1 to 1½ second fuse, I kept the enemy from advancing from the cover of the woods. Having been just directed by General Birney, through an aide, to closely watch the movements and look for a route upon which I might withdraw in case it became necessary, I rode through the woods on my left, perhaps 200 yards in width, and found our line there formed perpendicular to my own, instead of parallel, as I had supposed, facing from me and closely pressed by the enemy. This line soon fell back irregularly, but slowly, passing in front of and masking my guns. A portion of Smith's battery, on my left, also withdrew by my rear.

The enemy's advance being within 25 yards of my left, and covered by woods and rocks, I ordered my left section limbered, with a view of moving it a short distance to the left and rear. Before this was accomplished, the enemy had advanced under cover of the woods upon my right, and was cutting down my men and horses. Having no supports in rear, and being exposed to a heavy fire of musketry in front and upon both flanks, I deemed it necessary to withdraw in order to save my guns, which was done by piece in succession from the left, continuing to fire until the right and last piece was limbered. Several horses were killed and disabled before moving 25 yards. In one instance it became necessary to use the limber of a caisson to secure the piece. By impressing 2 passing horses of Captain Smith's, not in use, the former was secured. Meeting Major-General Sickles and Captain Randolph immediately after leaving the field, I was ordered by them to move my battery to the rear, and refit as far as possible.

My battery was moved to the front next morning, but was not engaged in the action of that day.

On this, as on former occasions, my officers and men, with scarcely an exception, manifested a coolness and bravery highly commendable, the latter in more than one instance rendering valuable aid after being severely wounded. The casualties were 10 men wounded and 8 missing. Ten horses were killed and disabled.

All of my pieces could not have been brought off had my men been less brave.

I am, captain, very respectfully, your obedient servant,
GEORGE B. WINSLOW,
Capt., Comdg. Battery D, First New York Artillery.

Capt. A. J. CLARK,
Acting Chief of Artillery, Third Corps.

No. 184.

Report of Capt. James E. Smith, Fourth New York Battery.

CAMP NEAR SANDY HOOK, MD., *July 20, 1863.*

SIR: I have the honor to report the participation of the Fourth New York Battery, under my command, during the battle of Gettysburg, July 2.

In compliance with instructions received from you, I placed two sections of my battery on a hill (near the Devil's Cave) on the left of General Birney's line, leaving one section, together with caissons and horses, 150 yards in the rear. The Fourth Maine Regiment was detailed as support, forming line in rear under cover of a hill. On my left, extending half way to the Emmitsburg road, was a thick wood, in which I requested Lieutenant Leigh, aide-de-camp to General Ward, to place supports. He informed me that a brigade had already been placed there, but this must have been a mistake.

About 2.30 p. m. the enemy opened fire on my right and front from several guns, directing a portion of their fire upon my position. I was ordered by one of General Ward's aides to return their fire, which order I complied with. Twenty minutes later I discovered the enemy was endeavoring to get a section of light 12-pounder guns in position on my left and front, in order to enfilade this part of our line, but I succeeded in driving them off before they had an opportunity to open fire. Soon after, a battery of six light 12-pounders marched from the woods near the Emmitsburg road, and went in battery in the field in front, about 1,400 yards distant. A spirited duel immediately began between this battery and my own, lasting nearly twenty minutes, when Anderson's brigade, of Hood's division, Longstreet's corps (rebel), charged upon us. The rebel battery then left the field, and I directed my fire upon the infantry.

At this time I requested the officer in command of the Fourth Maine Regiment to place his regiment in the woods on my left, telling him I could take care of my front, but my request was not complied with. I used case shot upon the advancing column until it entered the woods, when I fired shell until they emerged from the woods on my left flank, in line of battle 300 yards distant; then I used canister with little effect, owing to numerous large rocks, which afforded excellent protection to their sharpshooters. I saw it would be impossible for me to hold my position without assistance, and therefore called upon my supports, who gallantly advanced up the hill and engaged the enemy. Fighting became so close that I ordered my men to cease firing, as many of the Fourth Maine had already advanced in front of the guns. I then went to the rear, and opened that section of guns, firing obliquely through the gully, doing good execution.

At this time the Sixth New Jersey Volunteers, Lieutenant-Colonel Gilkyson commanding, and Fortieth New York Regiment, Colonel Egan commanding, came to our support. These regiments marched down the gully, fighting like tigers, exposed to a terrific fire of musketry, and, when within 100 yards of the rebel line, the Fourth Maine, which still held the hill, were forced to retreat. Very soon afterward the Fortieth New York and Sixth New Jersey Regiments were compelled to follow. I then ordered my remaining guns to the rear.

When I left three guns on the hill (one having been sent to the rear disabled), I was under the impression we would be able to hold that position, but, if forced to retreat, I expected my supports would save the guns, which, however, they failed to do. I could have run my guns to the rear, but expecting to use them at any moment, and the position difficult of access, I thought best to leave them for awhile. Again, I feared if I removed them the infantry might mistake the movement for a retreat. In my opinion, had supports been placed in the woods, as I wished, the hill could not have been taken.

I conducted my command to a field near the Baltimore turnpike, three-quarters of a mile from Third Corps headquarters, and encamped for the night, reporting three guns for service next morning to Captain Clark, acting chief of artillery.

I regret to report the loss of 2 brave men, viz, Corpl. John A. Thompson and Private Isaiah Smith, and the wounding of 10 privates, many severely. Eleven horses were killed and disabled. Three 10-pounder Parrott guns and gun-carriages (supposed to have been taken from the field by the Twelfth Corps) were lost.

The non-commissioned officers and privates conducted themselves throughout the day with commendable bravery.

Total amount of ammunition expended, 240 rounds.

I trust no blame will be attached to me for the loss of my guns. I did that which in my judgment I thought best.

I am, captain, your most obedient servant,

J. E. SMITH,
Captain, Commanding Fourth New York Battery.

Capt. GEORGE E. RANDOLPH,
Chief of Artillery, Third Corps.

No. 185.

Report of Lieut. Benjamin Freeborn, Battery E, First Rhode Island Light Artillery.

NEAR WARRENTON, VA., *July* 28, 1863.

SIR: I have the honor to report the following as the part taken in the actions near Gettysburg by this command:

On the morning of July 2, the battery was in position in the second line of battle, under command of First Lieut. John K. Bucklyn, remaining there without firing until 3 p. m., when it was ordered to the front. We moved up and took a position near the Emmitsburg road, under a heavy artillery fire from the enemy. Commenced firing immediately, and succeeded in silencing several of the enemy's guns, but they soon opened from different points, and, owing to the peculiar formation of the line, we were at times exposed to a heavy cross-fire. The right section was detached from the rest of the battery and operated on the road near a small house. We were somewhat annoyed by sharpshooters, who were in a barn in front of the section, but dislodged them by a shell or two.

The enemy appeared to have massed their infantry on the left of the battery, and the fighting was severe there, so that our supports were either sent to that point or some other, as for twenty minutes before we left the battery was without any support, and nothing in front but a few sharpshooters. Some of them reported to me that the enemy was advancing in line in the ravine in front, probably with a view of charging on the battery. Nearly at the same time the artillery and infantry on our left fell back. It was deemed best to withdraw the battery, which was done, the enemy appearing within a few yards of us and delivering a heavy musketry fire, from which we suffered severely. We abandoned one caisson for want of horses, but regained it when our forces reoccupied the ground.

Lieutenant Bucklyn being wounded in coming off the field, the command devolved upon me, and the battery was ordered to the rear, and, being badly cut up, did not participate in any of the subsequent fighting.

The casualties were as follows: 2 officers wounded, 3 enlisted men killed, and 24 wounded; 17 horses killed and 23 disabled and abandoned.

Respectfully,

BENJ. FREEBORN,
Second Lieut. First Rhode Island Light Art., Comdg. Battery.

Lieut. P. S. JASTRAM,
Actg. Asst. Adjt. Gen., Art. Brig., Third Army Corps.

No. 186.

Report of Lieut. Robert James, Battery K, Fourth U. S. Artillery.

CAMP NEAR WARRENTON, VA.,
July 27, 1863.

SIR: In compliance with instructions from headquarters Artillery Brigade, Third Corps, I have the honor to submit the following report of the participation of Battery K, Fourth U. S. Artillery, in the battles of July 2 and 3:

About 3 p. m. on the afternoon of the 2d instant, the battery, under command of First Lieut. F. W. Seeley, Fourth U. S. Artillery, was ordered to a position on the crest of a small hill near the left center of our line, and immediately in front of the Second Brigade, Second Division, Third Corps. The enemy had a battery posted in our front, and distant about 800 yards, and were firing with good effect upon the infantry in our rear. We immediately opened fire with solid shot and spherical case, and, after a rapid and well-directed fire, lasting about fifteen minutes, succeeded in silencing this battery and causing it to retire.

About 5.30 p. m. the enemy placed in position to our left and front, and distant about 1,000 yards, some four batteries, and opened upon our line a most destructive fire. We immediately replied, but the enemy advancing their infantry in heavy columns, we turned our attention to them, firing as rapidly as possible shot, shell, and spherical case. The enemy having gained protection from our fire under cover of the slope of the hill in our front, we ceased firing, and prepared to receive them on its crest with canister. At this time it is with feelings of deep regret I have to report that Lieutenant Seeley was severely wounded, and had to be taken from the field, and I assumed command of the battery. The enemy advancing rapidly, and our infantry having fallen back, I had only time to fire a few rounds of canister, which, although creating great havoc in their ranks, did not check their advance, and, in order to save my guns, I was obliged to retire.

I then took a position about 400 yards to the right, and placed my guns in position for the purpose of enfilading their line. I had scarcely gotten my guns unlimbered when the enemy appeared on my right flank and in rear, deployed as skirmishers, and not more than some 30 yards distant, and, getting into the battery along with our own infantry, I could not fire, and it was with the utmost difficulty I succeeded in moving by the left flank and retiring to the rear, which I did in good order, losing, however, several of my men, who were taken prisoners, but most of whom fortunately succeeded in making their escape and returned to the battery. I then received orders from Major McGilvery, of General Hunt's staff, to take a position in an open field to the rear and left, and distant about 1,200 yards from our original position (not having a sufficient number of men to man my six guns, I sent a section of the battery to the rear, and went into this position with only four guns), where I remained during the night.

At daybreak on the morning of the 3d, the enemy opened upon the battery with sixteen guns from a position immediately in my front, and distant about 1,300 yards, and with their sharpshooters, who were posted on a small hill about 300 yards in our front and in the woods on our left. I replied, firing solid shot and spherical case, and, after expending nearly all of the ammunition in the limbers (my caissons having been ordered to the rear), and not having any supports, I deemed it advisable to retire. I then reported to the major-general commanding the corps, and, by your direction, the battery was held in reserve during the remainder of the day.

I have also to report that on the night of the 2d, with the assistance of the Sixth Maine Battery, and under the orders of Major McGilvery, I succeeded in bringing from the field seven guns (four 3-inch rifled and three light 12-pounders), which had been abandoned by our troops during the day. I brought the three light 12-pounders to the rear, and the next morning I returned them to the Ninth Massachusetts Battery, to which they belonged.

I had, for the want of time during the action of the 2d, to abandon four sets of harness, viz, one set wheel and three sets lead harness.

My loss in men was as follows: Killed, 2 enlisted men; wounded, 1 officer (Lieutenant Seeley) and 18 enlisted men; missing, 2 enlisted men. I had 9 horses killed and 19 disabled, 16 of which I have been compelled to destroy, owing to the nature of their severe wounds.

With regard to the conduct of officers and men, I can only say that they behaved in their usually brave and courageous manner.

My especial thanks are due to Second Lieut. E. S. Smith, Fourth New York Independent Battery, and to First Sergt. Gilbert H. Purdy and Sergt. Thomas Cusack, who each commanded a section, for the manner in which they performed their most arduous duties.

I am, sir, very respectfully, your obedient servant,

ROBERT JAMES,
Second Lieutenant Third U. S. Artillery, Commanding.

Capt. A. J. CLARK,
Acting Chief of Artillery, Third Corps.

No. 187.

Reports of Maj. Gen. George Sykes, U. S. Army, commanding Fifth Army Corps.

HEADQUARTERS FIFTH ARMY CORPS,
Camp near Warrenton, Va., July 31, 1863.

SIR: On the 28th ultimo, by the assignment of General Meade to the command of the Army of the Potomac, I became the senior general of this corps.

On June 29 and 30 and on July 1 and 2, I made long, rapid, and fatiguing marches, starting at Frederick, Md., and reaching the field of Gettysburg, via Liberty, Union Mills, Hanover, &c., about 8 a. m. on the latter date. My troops took position on the right of our line, but it being thought too extended, they were subsequently massed near the bridge over Rock Creek, on the Baltimore and Gettysburg pike, and within reach of the Twelfth Army Corps. While thus situated, I was directed to support the Third Corps, General Sickles commanding, with a brigade, should it be required.

At 3 p. m. General Meade sent for me, and while myself and other corps commanders were conversing with him, the enemy formed, opened the battle, and developed his attack on our left. I was at once ordered to throw my whole corps to that point and hold it at all hazards. This, of course, relieved my troops from any call from the commander of the Third Corps. *En route* to the position thus assigned the Fifth Corps, various staff officers from General Sickles met me, and, in the name of that officer, asked for assistance. I explained to them that it was impossible for me to give it; the key of the battle-field was intrusted to my keeping, and I could not and would not jeopardize it by a division of my forces.

A rocky ridge, commanding almost an entire view of the plateau held by our army, was on our extreme left. Between it and the position occupied by Birney's division, Third Corps, was a narrow gorge filled with immense bowlders and flanked on either side by dense woods. It afforded excellent cover and an excellent approach for the enemy, both of which he promptly made use of. The rocky ridge commanded and controlled this gorge. In examining it and the ground adjacent previous to posting my troops, I found a battery at its outer edge and without adequate support. I galloped to General Birney, whose troops were nearest, explained to him the necessity of protecting the guns, and suggested that he should close his division on the battery, and hold the edge of the woods on its right.   I promised to fill the gap he opened, which I did with Sweitzer's and Tilton's brigades, of my First Division, posting them myself.

In the meantime Vincent's brigade, of this division, had seized the rocky height, closely followed by Weed's brigade, Second Division. These troops were posted under the direction of General Warren, chief engineer of this army.   After closing the interval made by Birney with the brigades of General Barnes, I rode rapidly to the Taneytown pike to bring up the remaining troops of the corps, and on my return with them found the greater part of Weed's brigade moving away from the height where it had been stationed, and where its presence was vital.   I dispatched a staff officer to know of the general why he had vacated the ground assigned him.   His reply was, "By order of General Sickles."   I at once directed him to reoccupy it, which was done at the double-quick step.   Hardly had he reached it before the enemy came on in tremendous force.   Vincent's brigade and O'Rorke's regiment (Weed's brigade) were and had been sorely pressed.   Both those heroic commanders had fallen; but Weed again in position, Hazlett working his guns superbly, and the timely arrival of Ayres' brigades of regulars, who were at once ordered to attack, stemmed the tide, and rolled away the foe in our front.

At a later hour, by the withdrawal or retreat of the troops on his right—first, a division of the Third Corps, and next, Caldwell's command, of the Second Corps—a large body of the enemy gained his right and rear, and Ayres was compelled to fight his way, front and flank, to the heel of the gorge.   This he did steadily, in excellent order, and connected with his left brigade (Weed's) on the general line of battle.   But his loss was fearful; some of the regiments left 60 per cent. of their number on the ground.   As Ayres assumed this new position, General Crawford's command (my Third Division) was ordered to the front, and, entering the woods, became briskly engaged with the enemy.   This combat lasted till dusk, and resulted in General Crawford's gaining considerable ground, capturing many prisoners, and a flag of a Georgia regiment.

Night closed the fight.   The key of the battle-field was in our possession intact.   Vincent, Weed, and Hazlett, chiefs lamented throughout the corps and army, sealed with their lives the spot intrusted to their keeping, and on which so much depended.   The general line of battle on the left was shortened, strengthened, firm. Pickets were established, and the troops slept on their arms.   Sedgwick (Sixth Corps) had moved up to my aid.

On the 3d, Crawford held his ground in front, sustained by Bartlett's division, of Sedgwick's corps.   The troops remained as the day before.   Desultory firing from the pickets continued along our front. At 1 p. m. the enemy commenced a furious cannonade from more than one hundred guns, and occasionally a part of it was bestowed on the Fifth and Sixth Corps.   It was the prelude to his attack, which soon followed and raged to our right; but, beaten, baffled, and discomfited, he returned to the shelter of the forests west of the Emmitsburg and Gettysburg pike.   My artillery on the rocky ridge helped to shatter and disorganize his troops.

On the 4th, reconnaissances were made, but developed nothing save a line of skirmishers covering his troops, and artillery on the slope falling away from the turnpike to the west.

On the 5th, I began the march to Williamsport.

I respectfully call the attention of the major-general commanding to the services of the artillery of this corps, under its chief, Capt. A. P. Martin, and the subordinate battery commanders, as detailed in his report.

The regular batteries were the greatest sufferers. Hazlett's battery (D, Fifth U. S. Artillery) was especially distinguished, and Watson's battery (I, same regiment)—though unfortunately taken away by General Sickles without my consent or knowledge—after falling into the hands of the enemy, was recaptured by Lieutenant Peeples, of the battery, heading the Garibaldi Guard, in the most heroic and gallant manner. Lieutenant Peeples richly deserves promotion for his conduct, and I trust the Government will not withhold it.

I am happy to say the Fifth Corps sustained its reputation. An important duty was confided to it, which was faithfully and gallantly performed. Other brave men helped them in its execution, among whom the Sixth Corps was the most prominent.

I respectfully beg leave to call attention to the reports of division and brigade commanders, herewith inclosed.

The division commanders—Generals Barnes, Ayres, and Crawford—aided me in every particular with the utmost zeal and heartiness. I most urgently unite in their recommendations of the various gentlemen who distinguished themselves in and around the field of Gettysburg.

Colonel Rice, who succeeded to the command of the Third Brigade, First Division, on the fall of Colonel Vincent, deserves great credit for the management of his troops. His position on our extreme left was one of the most important held by the corps, and the unflinching tenacity with which he maintained it, and his subsequent forcible occupation of the ground possessed by the enemy, with Chamberlain's regiment (Twentieth Maine) and two regiments of Fisher's brigade, Third Division, are worthy of the highest praise.

The medical department, under Surg. J. J. Milhau and Asst. Surg. C. P. Russell, was organized in the most effective and satisfactory manner.

My personal staff and the chiefs of departments were zealous, indefatigable, and ready for any emergency. I name them in the order of rank, and respectfully recommend them to the notice of the Department of War: Lieut. Col. Fred. T. Locke, assistant adjutant-general; Lieut. Col. William H. Owen, chief quartermaster; Capt. D. L. Smith, acting chief commissary of subsistence; Surg. J. J. Milhau, U. S. Army, medical director; Asst. Surg. C. P. Russell, U. S. Army, medical inspector; Capt. John W. Williams, assistant adjutant-general and acting aide-de-camp; Capt. William Jay, aide-de-camp, and First Lieut. George T. Ingham, Eleventh U. S. Infantry, aide-de-camp.

The signal officers, Capt. W. H. Hill and Lieut. I. S. Lyon, performed their duties creditably.

General Weed and Colonel Vincent, officers of rare promise, gave their lives to their country. The former had been conspicuous during the war, won and adorned his promotion, and surrendered it and his life on the spot he was called upon to defend.

In this campaign of the Army of the Potomac, consequent upon Lee's second invasion of Maryland, troops never endured more, marched more in the same length of time, suffered more, deserved more, or fought better than they. Prompt response and obedience to all orders characterized them. Their record up to July 24, with its incalculable results, is a study, and has few parallels in the history of the rebellion.

Tabular and nominal lists have preceded this report.

I inclose the reports of division and other commanders, and with them a list of casualties in the corps.*

GEO. SYKES,
Major-General, Commanding Corps.

Brig. Gen. S. WILLIAMS,
Assistant Adjutant-General, Army of the Potomac.

—

HEADQUARTERS FIFTH ARMY CORPS,
Camp at Beverly Ford, Va., August 15, 1863.

GENERAL: The operations of this corps from June 28 to July 27, at which date it reached Warrenton, Va., embrace the following:

June 29.—Left Frederick; marched to and encamped in the vicinity of Liberty, Md.; 15 miles.

June 30.—Marched to Union Mills, via Johnsville, Union, and Frizellburg. Encamped on Big Pipe Creek, along the turnpike leading from Westminster to Gettysburg; 23 miles.

July 1.—Marched to Hanover, and relieved the cavalry there under General Kilpatrick. At 7 p. m. resumed the march, and at midnight bivouacked at Bonaughtown; 20 miles.

July 2.—Marched at 4 a. m. for Gettysburg, 6 miles; arrived early. Occupied the positions and performed the work explained in my report of that battle.

July 5.—Started *en route* for the Potomac. Reached the Antietam at Delaware Mills on the 10th, marching via Emmitsburg, Creagerstown, Utica, and Middletown, crossing the Catoctin and South Mountain ranges at High Knob and Fox's Gap; distance, 55 miles.

July 11, 12, 13, *and* 14.—Maneuvered in face of the enemy; constructed breastwork, rifle-pits, &c.; did picket duty; suffered and inflicted some loss; marched in pursuit of the enemy beyond Williamsport in the direction of Falling Waters; distance, about 10 miles.

July 15.—Marched to Burkittsville, 22 miles; thence on the 16th, 6 miles, to Petersville, Md.; thence on the 17th, 18th, 19th, 20th, 21st, and 22d, to Lovettsville, Wheatland, Purcellville, and Goose Creek, to Rectortown, Va.; 40 miles.

July 23.—Marched to Manassas Gap, 15 miles, and during the fight at that place formed in battle array, in support of the Third Corps, General French.

July 24.—Made a reconnaissance of the country to the right of General French, but the enemy having disappeared, at noon bivouacked in the Gap.

July 25.—Moved toward Warrenton via Farrowsville, Barbee's Cross-Roads, and Orleans, 15 miles; thence on the 26th and 27th, 14 miles, to and beyond Warrenton.

I am, sir, respectfully, your obedient servant,

GEO. SYKES,
Major-General, Commanding Corps.

Brig. Gen. S. WILLIAMS,
Assistant Adjutant-General, Army of the Potomac.

---

* Embodied in revised statement, p. 179.

HEADQUARTERS FIFTH ARMY CORPS,
July 5, 1863.

GENERAL: I have the honor to send herewith a sword and flag captured from the enemy. From the best information I can obtain, I believe the sword to have been taken from the body of the rebel General Barksdale on the field of battle. The flag was captured by Brigadier-General Kilpatrick in the fight at Hanover.

I am, general, very respectfully, your obedient servant,

GEO. SYKES,
Major-General, Commanding.

Brig. Gen. S. WILLIAMS,
Assistant Adjutant-General, Army of the Potomac.

—

HEADQUARTERS FIFTH ARMY CORPS,
Camp at Beverly Ford, Va., September 2, 1863.

GENERAL: In obedience to Paragraph III, Special Orders, No. 227, headquarters Army of the Potomac, I have the honor to report that no guns were captured from this command by the enemy during the recent operations in Pennsylvania and Maryland. One gun and two caissons, belonging to this army, were recaptured from the enemy by a portion of this command.

I am, general, very respectfully, your obedient servant,

GEO. SYKES,
Major-General, Commanding.

Brig. Gen. S. WILLIAMS,
Asst. Adjt. Gen., Hdqrs. Army of the Potomac.

—

HEADQUARTERS FIFTH ARMY CORPS,
Camp near Culpeper, Va., October 3, 1863.

GENERAL: In compliance with instructions from headquarters Army of the Potomac, I have the honor to make the following report:

Confederate dead buried:

First Division:		
	Officers	3
	Men	158
Second Division:		
	Officers	5
	Men	100
Third Division:		
	Men	138
		404

Small-arms captured:

First Division	2,550
Second Division	1,500
Third Division	9,301
	13,351

Napoleon gun (captured by Third Division)	1

Caissons captured by—
    First Division.. 4
    Third Division 2
                                                              _____
                                                                  6
                                                              =====
Limber (captured by Third Division)................................ 1
                                                              =====
Accouterments (captured by First Division).........sets.. 100
    Gun, caissons, and limber recaptured from the enemy.

I am, general, very respectfully, your obedient servant,
                                        GEO. SYKES,
                                Major-General, Commanding.
Brig. Gen. S. WILLIAMS,
    Assistant Adjutant-General, Army of the Potomac.

No. 188.

Report of Capt. James A. Bates, Chief Ambulance Officer.

HEADQUARTERS FIFTH CORPS,
                                August 27, 1863.

DOCTOR: I have the honor to report the part taken by the ambulances of the Fifth Corps during the fight at Gettysburg.

The corps went into action about 4 p. m. July 2, accompanied by the stretcher-bearers. The ambulances were brought in rear of the corps, and as near as was thought safe, to which place the wounded were carried by the stretcher-bearers, then transported by the ambulances to the hospital, a distance of about 1 mile from the scene of action.

As soon as it grew dark, the ambulances drove on to the battle-field, picking up the wounded. The ambulances kept constantly running from the hospital to the battle-field until 4 a. m. July 3, when it was found that all the wounded had been removed excepting about 6, who were beyond our pickets, in which case we were unable to get them.

I will here state that some of the attendants in charge of Lieutenant Clay, Second Division, went beyond the pickets to remove a wounded man. When in the act of removing him, they were fired on by the enemy's pickets.

The number of wounded transported by eighty-one ambulances from 4 p. m. July 2 to 4 a. m. July 3 was 1,300.

Great praise is due both officers and men for their promptness in removing the wounded.

The number of casualties in the ambulance corps was 1 man severely wounded in the arm.

About 10 a. m. July 3, orders were received from the medical director to remove the wounded 1 mile farther to the rear, as the enemy had commenced to shell the hospital. In consequence of having to remove the wounded a second time, the eighty-one ambulances transported 2,600 wounded men a distance of 1½ miles in forty-eight hours.

I will here state that the horses were in a very poor condition, having been constantly on the march for three weeks. While at Gettysburg, they had to live on half rations.

Orders were received by the chief of the First Division train to take his train to the battle-field and remove 100 wounded, which were still on the field. On reaching the battle-field, and after a thorough search, he found but 2 of the First Division. He found a number of the Third Corps, which he had put in his ambulances and transported to their corps hospital.

Yours, respectfully,

JAMES A. BATES,
Captain, and Chief Ambulance Officer, Fifth Corps.

Dr. J. J. MILHAU,
Medical Director, Fifth Corps.

No. 189.

Reports of Brig. Gen. James Barnes, U. S. Army, commanding First Division.

HEADQUARTERS FIRST DIVISION, FIFTH CORPS,
Aldie, Va., June 22, 1863.

COLONEL: I have the honor to submit the following report of the operations of this division while under the command of Brigadier-General Pleasonton, commanding the Cavalry Corps, on the 21st and 22d instant:

In conformity with instructions from Major-General Meade, commanding this corps, I reported for duty with the Cavalry Corps on the morning of the 21st, at 3 o'clock, and, receiving instructions from General Pleasonton, proceeded with the three brigades composing this division, under the command of Colonels Tilton, Sweitzer, and Vincent, of the First, Second, and Third Brigades, with the Third Massachusetts Battery (C), under the command of Lieutenant Walcott, to Middleburg.

At that point the Third Brigade, Colonel Vincent commanding, was detached to accompany the division of cavalry under Brigadier-General Gregg, to meet the enemy, strongly posted a short distance toward Upperville, and posted the First and Second Brigades, with the battery, at Middleburg.

For the operations of the Third Brigade, in conjunction with the division under General Gregg, I beg leave to submit the report of Colonel Vincent, which accompanies this report.

The First Brigade, Colonel Tilton, of the Twenty-second Massachusetts, commanding, was dispatched to the relief of the Third Brigade in the afternoon of the 21st, which had been continually engaged with the enemy during the day. This brigade followed the retiring enemy as far as Upperville, when they received orders to bivouac.

The Second Brigade, Colonel Sweitzer, of the Sixty-second Pennsylvania Volunteers, commanding, remained at Middleburg. Strong pickets were thrown out toward Hopewell, on the south, and toward the Snicker's Gap road, on the north, and Lieutenant Walcott, with his battery, took advantageous positions to prevent any successful attack which the enemy might contemplate during the absence of the remaining portion of the command in the direction of Ashby's Gap. The pickets of the enemy appeared on the Hopewell road, but made no attempt to approach to any point nearer than about 2 miles from the village.

In this position we remained until the following day, when, by direction of General Pleasonton, the command prepared to return to Aldie. The First and Third Brigades, returning, moved in good order, followed by the Second Brigade and the battery. The enemy, following carefully the force as it was withdrawn, endeavored to annoy us, but, under the direction of General Gregg, the command halted, and was drawn up to await further orders from General Pleasonton. These were soon received, and the First and Third Brigades resumed the march toward Aldie, while the Second Brigade with the battery were directed to remain to resist any attempt which the enemy might make to disturb the force as it was gradually withdrawn. With the exception of a few random shots, no important effort was made by them.

The two brigades returned in order to their camp at Aldie on the same evening, and, on the following morning, the Second Brigade resumed its former position in the division. Under orders from General Pleasonton, I reported the return of the division to Major-General Meade, commanding the Fifth Corps, the whole command having successfully accomplished the object which had been designated by General Pleasonton upon first reporting to him for orders.

It gives me pleasure to bear testimony to the zeal displayed by the command in their co-operation with the Cavalry Corps, and I mention with pleasure the names of the officers composing my staff in their prompt and ready discharge of the duties confided to them. Captain Mervine, my assistant adjutant-general; Major [William H.] Lamont and Lieutenant Ross, aides-de-camp; Captain [Percy B.] Spear, acting aide-de-camp, and Captain [George A.] Batchelder, ordnance officer, all discharged their duties in a manner highly creditable to them.

With great respect, I have the honor to be, your obedient servant,

JAMES BARNES,
Brigadier-General, Commanding Division.

Col. A. J. ALEXANDER,
Assistant Adjutant-General, Cavalry Corps.

———

HEADQUARTERS FIRST DIVISION, FIFTH CORPS,
Beverly Ford, Va., August 24, 1863.

COLONEL: I have the honor to submit the following report of the operations of the First Division of the Fifth Corps from June 28 to July 9, including the battle of Gettysburg and the movements of the command during the few days previous and subsequent thereto, in conformity with instructions from headquarters:

On June 28, after a succession of rapid marches from Virginia, the division encamped about 2 miles to the south of Frederick City, Md.

On the 29th, the command of the Army of the Potomac having devolved upon Major-General Meade, until then commanding the Fifth Corps, Major-General Sykes, who had succeeded to the command of the corps, directed an early movement forward. The First Division, under my command, moved accordingly through Frederick City toward the town of Liberty, and, passing beyond that place about 2 miles, bivouacked for the night.

On the 30th, at 4 a. m., the march was resumed and continued toward Union Mills, approaching the place with proper precautions, on account of a heavy body of cavalry of the enemy, some 8,000 or 10,000 in number, as reported, then occupying it. Upon reaching the town, we found that this cavalry force had left it some three or four hours before our arrival, and had gone in the direction of Hanover.

The division halted here for the night, and on the following morning, July 1, left at an early hour for Hanover, where it arrived at about 4 o'clock in the afternoon. Orders were here received to halt for the night, but scarcely had arms been stacked when news was received that an engagement had that day taken place between the enemy and a portion of the army at Gettysburg. Orders were received for an immediate resumption of the march toward Gettysburg, and, notwithstanding a long march had already been accomplished, the orders were received by the troops with the utmost enthusiasm. The division was soon on the road, and continued its march toward Gettysburg, halting after midnight about 2 miles from that place. Resuming its march, after a brief rest of two or three hours, the division reached Gettysburg at about 7 o'clock in the morning of July 2.

The Eighteenth Massachusetts, Colonel Hayes commanding, was immediately detached to support a battery upon the left of the road, and the remaining portion of the command was placed in position, by direction of General Sykes, on the right of the Second Division of the corps, south of and facing toward the village.

The Ninth Massachusetts, Colonel Guiney commanding, was here detailed from the Second Brigade as skirmishers, and deployed at some distance in front of the line.

The command here rested for further instructions. After the lapse of an hour or more, the division received orders to change its position, moving some distance to the rear and toward the left of this first line, but it remained in this new position for a short period only. Orders were again received to move still farther to the left, and, subsequently crossing the creek over a small bridge, we were held in reserve in an orchard on the left of the road, with instructions to wait there for further orders. Here the Eighteenth Massachusetts, detached as above stated early in the morning, rejoined the command, and was posted on the opposite side of the road. These various movements occupied the time until long after midday. The sound of the enemy's artillery still indicated a movement toward the left of the point where we were then halted.

Between 4 and 5 o'clock in the afternoon, orders were received from General Sykes to move toward the left and to the front. The column was immediately formed, and moved rapidly up by the Taneytown road to the ground assigned to the division. General Sykes and myself, preceding the advance of the column upon the ground upon which it was to take position, reconnoitered the field, and the position to be held by the command was determined upon by him.

Soon after, the head of the column entered upon the field. At the same time General Warren, of the staff of General Meade, came up, riding rapidly from the left, and, pointing out the position of the elevation known as the Round Top, not far off and toward the left, urged the importance of assistance in that direction. General Sykes yielded to his urgent request, and I immediately directed Colonel Vincent, commanding the Third Brigade, to proceed to that point with his brigade. Colonel Vincent moved with great promptness to the post assigned to him. The brigade consisted of the Sixteenth Michigan, the Forty-fourth New York, the Eighty-third Pennsylvania, and the Twentieth Maine Regiments.

The Second Brigade, commanded by Colonel Sweitzer, arrived next upon the ground. This brigade consisted of the Fourth Michigan, the Sixty-second Pennsylvania, the Ninth Massachusetts, and the Thirty-second Massachusetts. The Ninth Massachusetts, however, was absent, being upon the special duty for which it had been detailed in the morning. Upon receiving his instructions, Colonel Sweitzer placed his command promptly in position.

The First Brigade, under the command of Colonel Tilton, arrived next. This brigade was composed of the Eighteenth Massachusetts, the Twenty-second Massachusetts, the One hundred and eighteenth Pennsylvania, and the First Michigan Regiments. The position assigned to it was on the right of the ground occupied by the Second Brigade, and was immediately placed by Colonel Tilton in conformity with the instructions given to him.

The division thus in position constituted the right of the Fifth Corps, and its place in line was on the left of the ground assigned to the Third Corps. The line was on the edge of a thick wood, the ground to the front being cleared of timber, but interspersed with rocks and some straggling trees. As the two brigades entered the wood, they passed over a line of troops, understood to be a portion of a brigade of the Third Corps; they were lying down upon the ground.

Upon the right of our position an open space, apparently unprotected, extended to some distance. Upon calling the attention of General Sykes to it, he remarked, referring to the part of the Third Corps over which we had passed and then lying down in our rear, that those troops were to be removed. The remaining portion of the Third Corps was understood to be at some distance to the right, and much in advance of what seemed to be their natural and true position. This unguarded space was watched with great anxiety. There was little time, however, for deliberation. General Sykes, called by his duty to the left of the line, went toward that portion of his command. The attack of the enemy commenced almost immediately along my front. It was very severe, but was gallantly withstood.

After some time, during which the firing was very heavy, the enemy showed himself in great force upon our right flank. He had penetrated through the unguarded space there, and commenced pouring in a destructive fire from the advantageous position he had gained, and without changing my front there were no means of checking his advance toward my rear. Colonel Tilton, commanding the First Brigade, which was on the right, was immediately directed to change his front to the right, and the order was at once executed, deliberately, yet promptly, and in good order. Colonel Sweitzer, commanding the Second Brigade, on the left of the First, was immediately notified of this change upon his right, and directed to fall back in good order, and to take up a new position a short distance in his rear, for the purpose of co-operating in opposing this heavy attack upon the flank. This brigade, consisting at that time of only three regiments, numbering in all, officers and men, 1,010, was placed promptly and in good order as directed. The First Brigade numbered in all, officers and men, 654.

Affairs being in this position, General Caldwell, commanding a brigade of the Second Corps, came up in great haste, and stated to me that his brigade, then in the woods a short distance to the left, was driving the enemy in his front, and urgently requested assistance. I immediately directed Colonel Sweitzer to go to his relief. He moved his brigade forward in line, to the front and left, his men giving cheers as they advanced across an open field to the edge of the wood; but the progress of the enemy upon our flank still continued, and this brigade was compelled again to change its front to repel his advance, and soon found itself in close conflict with him. The Fourth Michigan and the Sixty-second Pennsylvania were in actual contact with him. Colonel Jeffords, commanding the Fourth Michigan, was thrust through with a bayonet while gallantly attempting to rescue his colors from the grasp of the enemy.

Finding himself unable to compete with numbers far superior to his own, and that the enemy was gaining ground to his rear, Colonel Sweitzer directed his command to retire slowly, but orderly, halting and firing as they retired, and took position on elevated ground a short distance to his rear, and succeeded in preventing the enemy from making any further progress in that direction.

In the meantime the movements of the First Brigade, under similar circumstances, corresponded with those of the Second. This brigade, small in numbers, fired, and retired in good order, and succeeded in reaching the ground on the opposite side of the open field toward the left, and there halted. The darkness put an end to the conflict, and the enemy was foiled in his effort to get in the rear of the command. The Ninth Massachusetts shortly afterward rejoined the Second Brigade, having been relieved from the duty upon which it had been detailed early in the morning. In this position the two brigades remained during the night.

On the following day, the First Brigade was directed to relieve the Third Brigade at Little Round Top, where it also had succeeded in maintaining the position assigned to it, as will appear in the sequel.

I cannot speak in terms too commendatory of the bearing of the officers and men of these two brigades during the progress of this conflict. Skillfully directed by the two brigade commanders, they obeyed with cool intrepidity every order issued to them, under the most trying circumstances, and long resisted superior numbers with firmness. Partly surrounded by the enemy, they succeeded in preventing the left of the line from being taken in reverse, resisting an attack not exceeded, I am sure, in violence in any contest hitherto occurring. The exposure of their flank, arising from whatever cause, placed them in a most dangerous position, and their heroic conduct alone saved the command at least, if not the entire left of the army, from disaster. The statement of the casualties of the contest is sufficient evidence of their gallant resistance, and it is alike due to those who have survived and to the memory of the gallant dead that this record should be made of their valor and devotion.

The Third Brigade, as above related, was detached from the division upon its arrival upon the ground, and was consequently removed from my immediate oversight. The record of its service, however, drawn principally from the report of its commander, belongs to this record of the service of the division.

Colonel Vincent, commanding the brigade, upon being detached, as above mentioned, proceeded promptly to the position assigned him. It was upon an elevated and rocky hill known as the Little Round Top. It was situated at some distance to our left, and near the ex-

treme left of the line of battle. Its defense was of the utmost importance. When the brigade was placed in position, the Twentieth Maine
occupied the left of the line, the Sixteenth Michigan the right, the
Eighty-third Pennsylvania and the Forty-fourth New York the center. The Third Division of the Fifth Corps was posted on the right
of the brigade. The enemy had concentrated a heavy force in front
of the line, and began a fierce attack immediately after the troops
were in position. Repeated charges were made upon the center of
the brigade, but the line was unbroken. A vigorous attack upon the
right caused a temporary wavering there, but the One hundred and
fortieth New York coming promptly to its support, it was re-established at once.

It was at this time that Colonel Vincent, commanding the brigade,
while rallying this part of his command, fell, mortally wounded. He
was a gallant officer, beloved and respected by his command and by
all who knew him. His death is a serious loss to the army and the
country.

Upon the removal of Colonel Vincent from the field, the command
of the brigade devolved upon Colonel Rice, of the Forty-fourth New
York Volunteers. The enemy, as stated, having in vain attempted
to break the right of the brigade, renewed his attack upon the center
and left. The Twentieth Maine, Colonel Chamberlain commanding,
was posted on the left. It consisted of 380 men and officers. While
the enemy in its front was making a fierce attack, a brigade was
observed in the rear of their lines moving by its right flank and
passing through a slight ravine on our left, with the evident purpose
of gaining a position on the left flank of this regiment.

Colonel Chamberlain at once threw back his left wing, and extended his right wing by intervals toward the left, in order to avoid
diminishing the extent of his front. The brigade of the enemy alluded to reaching a proper position, attacked him furiously on the
left flank, advancing within 10 paces and rapidly firing. They were
first checked and then repulsed by the left wing of the regiment,
thrown back for that purpose.

A second, third, and fourth time the enemy renewed their attempt
to break this line, and each time were they successfully repelled by
that handful of men. Four times that little interval of 10 paces was
the scene of a desperate conflict. The ground was strewed with
dead and wounded men of both sides, promiscuously mingled. Their
ammunition was exhausted; they replenished it from the cartridge-
boxes of the men lying around them, whether friends or foes, but
even this resource soon failed them; the enemy in greatly superior
numbers pressed hard; men and officers began to look to the rear for
safety, but the gallant commander of the regiment ordered the
bayonets to be fixed, and, at the command "Forward," that wearied
and worn body of men rushed onward with a shout. The enemy fell
back. Pressing on, and wheeling to the right in open intervals, the
left wing came again in line with the right wing, and then the whole
regiment, deployed at intervals of 5 paces, followed up the advantage they had gained. The enemy threw down their arms and surrendered in large numbers; the others fled rapidly from the contest;
368 prisoners, including 1 colonel, 1 lieutenant-colonel, and a dozen
other officers of lesser rank were sent to the rear; 50 of their dead
lay upon the field, and large numbers of their wounded; 30 of this
gallant regiment were killed, over 100 were wounded, but not one
was taken a prisoner, and none were missing.

It was now nearly dark. A portion of the enemy appeared to have occupied the summit of the rocky hill to the left. The men of this brave regiment, exhausted by their labors, had thrown themselves upon the ground, and many of them sunk at once in sleep. Colonel Rice, now in command of the brigade, directed Colonel Chamberlain to drive the enemy from this height. The order was at once given. Roused again to action, and advancing with fixed bayonets and without firing, lest the smallness of their numbers might be suspected, they rushed up the hill.

Twenty-five more prisoners, including some staff officers, were added to the number previously taken, with a loss to the regiment of 1 officer mortally wounded and 1 man taken prisoner by the enemy. It was ascertained that these troops occupying the hill had been sent from Hood's division, which was then massed a few hundred yards distant, and that their object was to reconnoiter the position as a preliminary to taking possession of the height.

In addition to the prisoners above mentioned as taken by this regiment, 300 stand of arms were also captured by them. It is due to this regiment and to its commander that their service should be thus recorded in some detail.

Upon receiving a re-enforcement of five regiments of the Third Division, under command of Colonel Fisher, Colonel Rice detached two of them to the aid of Colonel Chamberlain, in order to maintain the position he had gained, and he was thus enabled to hold it, and the enemy, having been repelled upon every point of his attack, and night coming on, withdrew from the conflict.

Colonel Rice directed the Forty-fourth New York and the Eighty-third Pennsylvania to move to the front and gather up the wounded, who, including those of the enemy who had been left upon the field, were carefully brought in. The total results of the service of this brigade are stated by Colonel Rice to be 500 prisoners captured, including 2 colonels and 15 other commissioned officers, and 1,000 stand of arms. The brigade numbered about 1,000 men.

The following day was principally occupied in burying the dead. The Third Brigade was relieved by the First Brigade, and held the position occupied by it.

It would be a grateful task to relate in detail the services of many who deserve a more particular mention, but the limits of this report will not permit. No one failed in his duty.

A tribute is due to the memory of Colonel Vincent, who fell, mortally wounded, early in the engagement. He lingered a few days after the engagement. His promotion as a brigadier-general was sent to him at once as an appreciation of his services by the Government, but it reached him too late for his own recognition. He expired soon after its receipt.

A special mention should also be made of Colonel Jeffords, of the Fourth Michigan Volunteers, who sealed his devotion to his country with his blood, while contending hand to hand with overpowering numbers, in endeavoring to rescue the colors of his regiment from the hands of the enemy.

To Colonels Tilton, Sweitzer, and Rice, the commanders of brigades, great credit is due for the successful and skillful management of their commands under the very trying circumstances in which they were placed. Colonel Chamberlain, of the Twentieth Maine Volunteers, whose service I have endeavored briefly to describe, deserves especial mention.

To the officers of my staff I am indebted for efficient and prompt attention to their arduous duties, namely: Captain [Catharinus B.] Mervine, assistant adjutant-general; Lieuts. [Charles H.] Ross and [T. Corwin] Case, aides; Captain [George M.] Barnard, assistant inspector-general of the division, and Dr. [Charles] Shippen, the medical director of the division.

The command remained in the same position the two following days.

Being disabled for further actual command of the division, the opportune arrival of General Griffin enabled me to relinquish it to him, and the division moved toward Middletown, where it arrived on July 8.

A tabular and a nominal return of casualties have been duly forwarded.* The total strength of the division upon entering the engagement was, in the three brigades, 2,664, and the aggregate of killed, wounded, and missing, 897.

Very respectfully, I have the honor to be, &c.,
JAMES BARNES,
Brigadier-General, U. S. Volunteers, Commanding.

Lieut. Col. FRED. T. LOCKE,
Assistant Adjutant-General, Fifth Corps.

No. 190.

Report of Brig. Gen. Charles Griffin, U. S. Army, commanding First Division.

HDQRS. FIRST DIVISION, FIFTH ARMY CORPS,
Near Beverly Ford, Va., August 14, 1863.

SIR: In compliance with circular from headquarters Army of the Potomac, dated August 12, 1863, I have the honor to report that I arrived at Gettysburg on July 3 last, and relieved General Barnes, in command of the division, on the 4th.

On the day following, the division took up its line of march toward the Potomac, arriving at Middletown on the 7th, and from thence proceeded by way of Fox's Gap to Jones' Cross-Roads, in which vicinity it was occupied in strengthening its position and in outpost duty until the 14th, when it marched to Williamsport.

From Williamsport the division proceeded to Berlin by way of Burkittsville; crossed the Potomac at that place on the 17th, and encamped for the night at Lovettsville, Va.

On the 18th, the march was resumed and continued without interruption to Manassas Gap, by the way of Purcellville and Piedmont.

Passing nearly through the Gap, it was deployed on the 23d in support of the Third Corps at the battle of Wapping Heights.

On the morning of the 24th, the division again took up its line of march to Warrenton, in the vicinity of which place it arrived, by the way of Barbee's Cross-Roads and Orleans, on the 27th ultimo.

Very respectfully, your obedient servant,
CHAS. GRIFFIN,
Brigadier-General, Commanding.

Lieut. Col. FRED. T. LOCKE,
Assistant Adjutant-General.

---

*But see revised statement, p. 179.

No. 191.

Report of Lieut. Joseph C. Ayer, Chief Ambulance Officer, First Division.

NEAR PURCELLVILLE, VA., *July* 19, 1863.

SIR: In accordance with orders, I have to report the operations of this ambulance corps during the battle of Gettysburg, Pa., and subsequent thereto to have been as follows, viz:

As soon as the division was placed in position, all my stretcher-men, under charge of their lieutenants and sergeants, were sent to the front, to follow in their respective regiments, leaving 3 sergeants and 1 lieutenant in charge of the train. Upon the receipt of orders, I conducted the train to a point about 200 yards in the rear of the Second and Third Brigades of this division, where the train was rapidly loaded with severely wounded. Owing to some misunderstanding in the location of the division hospital, the exact point where the wounded men were to be unloaded could not be ascertained, and the wounded remained in the ambulances about an hour, when a field hospital was established and the wounded unloaded. The ambulances then commenced regular trips to the battle-field, and were, in connection with the stretcher-men, who moved the wounded men from the field to the ambulances, continually at work during the night.

As soon as all the wounded of the division, as near as I could judge, were removed from the field, orders came to me to remove the wounded from the field hospital to one farther to the rear. Previous to so removing the wounded of this division, seventeen ambulances were ordered to report to the Second Division (Fifth Corps) hospital, where they loaded with wounded, whom they carried to the rear.

The whole of July 3 was consumed in removing the hospital. At sunset the horses were unharnessed for the first time for sixty hours.

At about 10 p. m. orders came to me to send up my whole train to the front, to remove from the field the remaining wounded of the division. Upon reaching the field, we succeeded, under the guidance of some regimental officers of this division, in finding one wounded man belonging to the One hundred and eighteenth Pennsylvania Volunteers, First Brigade, First Division, Fifth Corps; but there being a sufficient number of wounded belonging to the Third Corps, I loaded my trains with Third Corps wounded, whom I transported to their respective hospitals.

This train returned to camp near the hospital at sunrise on the 4th instant. It unhitched and fed, and then, having hitched up at 9 a. m. of that day, reported to the several corps and division hospitals of the army, and collected, as nearly as possible, all wounded men of this division, transporting them to the division hospital.

The officers and men under my command behaved unexceptionably, performing their arduous duties with care and alacrity, although deprived of their sleep for so long a period.

Upon July 5, the train received orders to move and follow the division toward Emmitsburg, Md., leaving two ambulances and 4 men at the division hospital, near Gettysburg, Pa. When not in use, the ambulances were kept in the front, near the division.

I estimate the total number of wounded of this division removed from the battle-field by this corps to have been 560; those of the Third Corps, 82 wounded. There might also be added to this the number of 430 wounded men transported from one hospital to the other when the hospital was changed; also 53 men transported for Second Division, Fifth Corps; also 32 wounded men collected from the several hospitals of the army and taken to division hospitals, making a total of 1,157 wounded men transported by this ambulance corps upon July 2, 3, and 4.

Very respectfully, your obedient servant,

JOS. C. AYER,
First Lieut., and Chief of Ambulance Corps.

Capt. J. BATES,
Chief of Ambulance Corps, Fifth Corps.

No. 192.

Report of Col. William S. Tilton, Twenty-second Massachusetts Infantry, commanding First Brigade.

HDQRS. FIRST BRIG., FIRST DIV., FIFTH ARMY CORPS,
Middletown, Md., July 9, 1863.

CAPTAIN: I have the honor to report the part taken by this brigade in the battles of the 2d and 3d instant.

At 4.30 p. m. on July 2, the brigade, under my command, advanced to the front, and was placed, by order of General Barnes, in order of battle in a piece of woods at the south of Mr. Rose's house. The Second Brigade was on our left, but there being no infantry upon our right, I made a crotchet by refusing the right wing of my right battalion (One hundred and eighteenth Pennsylvania Volunteers, Colonel Gwyn).

The line was like this:

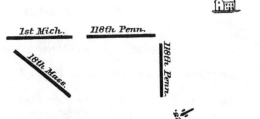

No sooner was the line formed than the foe attacked our front. The onslaught was terrible and my losses heavy—so much so that I was somewhat doubtful if our line could withstand it. This fact I communicated to the general commanding division, who ordered me to fall back in good order if unable to hold the position; but my men behaved nobly, and twice repulsed the assailants. My colonels wished to advance. Being anxious about my right, however, I reconnoitered in person, and discovered the enemy in large force coming from the direction of Rose's house, with the evident design of outflanking me. I immediately retired and took up a new position (in two lines), at the left and rear of a battery which had been posted about 300 yards to my right and rear. The battery soon commenced to retreat, firing, followed by the rebels, who were now again upon my right flank. To avoid this flank movement, I retired, firing, a short distance in the timber, and then moved across an open field, took up a new position upon the right of the Second Division, and reported to General Sykes. In this last movement I was greatly embarrassed by squads of men and parts of regiments, who, hurrying from the front, broke into and through my line. I think, however, that I saved my brigade from great disaster after it could no longer do any good in front, and succeeded in forming a new line, which was retained through the night.

All of my officers and men did their duty, their whole duty, and showed the greatest coolness and courage, and where all did so well it were invidious to mention names.

On the 3d, we relieved the Third Brigade, on duty, holding the rocky hill upon the extreme left.

On the 4th, I advanced the brigade to the edge of the woods in our front, and sent out a strong line of skirmishers to feel the enemy. The report of this reconnaissance has been made by order directly to Major-General Sykes.

My loss on the 2d instant was 12 killed, 80 wounded, and 17 missing; total, 109.

Owing to forced marches, we had remaining on the 2d only 474 men, and as part of these were not actually engaged, it will be seen that the percentage of loss is very great.

Very respectfully, your obedient servant,

WM. S. TILTON,
Colonel, Commanding First Brigade.

Capt. C. B. MERVINE,
Asst. Adjt. Gen., First Division, Fifth Corps.

No. 193.

Reports of Col. Jacob B. Sweitzer, Sixty-second Pennsylvania Infantry, commanding Second Brigade.

HDQRS. SECOND BRIGADE, FIRST DIVISION, FIFTH CORPS,
June 10, 1863.

GENERAL : I beg leave to report that on the receipt of your letter of instructions of 6 p. m., 8th instant, received at 8 p. m., I called on General D. McM. Gregg, submitted your note to him, and requested information as to how he desired me to co-operate with him.

The general explained to me the plan of his movements, and said he desired me to cross the river immediately after his forces had passed, and follow his column to a point beyond Mountain Run, which point would be indicated to me on my reaching it, and remain there until I should receive orders to withdraw. I then called his attention to so much of your note as directed me to occupy and hold the opposite side of the river after my connection with him had ceased, as I construed it. Finding he thought I should withdraw to this side of the river when I retired from the position assigned to me by him, on my return to these headquarters I addressed you a note asking further instructions on this point, and in reply received by daylight your note of 2.30 a. m. of the 9th instant, saying, *inter alia,* "When General Gregg shall notify you that he no longer needs your aid, you will reoccupy in *statu quo* this side of the ford."

My command was ready, and crossed the river in the rear of General Gregg's column, and followed it, keeping in sight all the way, to the point at which I was directed to halt, at, say, 10 o'clock. Colonel Abbott, with the First Michigan Volunteers, was in the rear of my column, and I directed him, as we passed out, to drop squads of men at the different cross-roads and other prominent points along the road, to keep open our communication.

The command of General Gregg passed on. I made my arrangements to receive the enemy from the direction of Germanna and Ely's Ford. After remaining in this position for some time, firing was heard in the direction of Rappahannock Station; in fact, while we were crossing the river, firing was heard in that direction. Then clouds of dust were seen approaching from the same direction; then down the road, at full speed, came the usual crowd of mounted contrabands, camp-followers, and stragglers, *et id genus omne* that should be in —— rather than with an army, shouting, "We are all cut to pieces; the rebels are coming, &c." We halted them until the road was choked up, and then, to get rid of them, allowed them to pass on.

Meanwhile the clouds of dust in the distance were approaching us, and then a large body of cavalry was seen coming over the crest of the hill in the direction of the dust. We were not certain whether they were our forces or those of the enemy. We endeavored to make them out with the aid of glasses. I could not distinguish, but supposed them to be ours; others thought they were the enemy. Meanwhile they were advancing by a road leading in our rear, and at the same time another cloud of dust was seen still farther to our rear, which seemed to indicate the passage of a large force, but who they were or which way they were going we could not make out. Under these circumstances, you can imagine that our situation was not quite as comfortable as it is on this side of the river; and we continued to watch with lively interest the current of events. Soon we saw the cavalry in the distance rally and make a stand; then reenforcements seemed to arrive; then they went back over the hill, the firing became more distant, and we did not see them again.

We afterward learned that General Gregg's cavalry had first met the enemy, composed of cavalry, artillery, and infantry, had engaged them, and, after a gallant contest, were compelled to retire some distance when we saw them; were then joined by Colonel Duffié's command, and then advanced and drove them.

At 2.30 p. m. I received a verbal communication to withdraw across the river; it was delivered by a sergeant of cavalry. I questioned him closely as to his name, regiment, and company, of which I took a memorandum, and knowing Colonel Duffié to be in the command of General Gregg, and the message agreeing with what had been previously agreed upon by General Gregg and myself, I concluded it was authentic, and acted upon it.

We started in at 3 p. m. and arrived shortly after 4 p. m. Nothing of interest occurred along the road. We have no casualties to report. Not a shot was fired by the command excepting at one of the picket posts.

Shortly after my arrival here, I received a note in writing from General Gregg, which came down on this side from Rappahannock Station, instructing me to "withdraw the infantry forces, if I had not already done so."

Both officers and men behaved in a manner to sustain the previous reputation of the division. I have especially to thank Colonel Abbott, of the First Michigan, for the valuable assistance rendered me by his regiment in guarding the road.

I am, sir, very respectfully, your obedient servant,

J. B. SWEITZER,
Colonel, Commanding Second Brigade.

Brig. Gen. JAMES BARNES,
Commanding First Division, Fifth Corps.

HEADQUARTERS SECOND BRIGADE,
Camp near Warrenton, Va., July 31, 1863.

GENERAL: In obedience to orders, I respectfully submit the following report of the operations of this brigade during the recent battle of Gettysburg:

After a hard march on the day previous, July 1, from Unionville, Md., by way of Hanover, the brigade bivouacked after 12 p. m., with the division in the woods by the roadside, 4 or 5 miles distant from the battle-field.

Next morning by daylight we were on the march again, the Second Brigade leading. Having arrived near what I supposed to be the right of our line, and near a farm-house and barn, the division was massed, the brigades occupying positions in the order of their numbers from right to left, General Sykes' division being on our left. Here a call was made for a regiment from this brigade for picket duty by General Barnes, and Colonel Guiney, with the Ninth Massachusetts, was directed to report to him for instructions, and did so.

Shortly after this, the division changed front to the left, at nearly a right angle with its former position, and formed in line of battalions in close column by division.

We had been in this position but a few moments before we were again moved a considerable distance to the left; then moved by the front across the creek, and massed in an orchard on the hill above the bridge on the Gettysburg turnpike. There we remained until late in the afternoon (the precise time I do not remember), and the command had a few hours' quiet and rest.

Meanwhile there had been very little firing along the line, and I came to the conclusion the day would pass without the division being called into action. But soon after cannonading was heard on the left, and we were moved quite a distance farther to the left, and diagonally to the front, skirting in our march the woods in rear of or in which our lines were formed. When we moved off from the orchard, the Third Brigade, being on the left of the division, moved first, the Second and First Brigades following in the inverted order.

The Second Brigade was placed in position in a wood fronting an open field, the woods bordering two sides of the field, the side in which we were and also that extending at right angles from our left toward the enemy, and in the last-mentioned wood the First Brigade was posted, connecting with our left. Having formed the three regiments of this brigade in line of battle (the Ninth Massachusetts being still absent on picket duty) in their regular order from right to left, and finding this formation threw the Thirty-second Massachusetts, which was on the left, into an exposed position beyond the woods in low, cleared ground, I directed Colonel Prescott to change his front to the rear, so as to give him the benefit of the elevated ground and the cover of the woods, which movement he executed.

We had not remained long in this position before an attack commenced by the enemy in front of the First Brigade and Thirty-second Massachusetts. As there was no appearance of the enemy in front of the line formed by the Sixty-second Pennsylvania and Fourth Michigan, I directed them to change front to the left, and form lines in rear of the Thirty-second Massachusetts, to strengthen that position. During the execution of this order, the attack continued; the firing was very severe, and we lost many brave officers and men. Here fell Major Lowry, second to none in all the attributes of a soldier and a gentleman.

When the attack commenced, word was sent by General Barnes that when we retired we should fall back under cover of the woods. This order was communicated to Colonel Prescott, whose regiment was then under the hottest fire. Understanding it to be a peremptory order to retire then, he replied, "I don't want to retire; I am not ready to retire; I can hold this place," and he made good his assertion. Being informed that he misunderstood the order, which was only intended to inform him how to retire when it became necessary, he was satisfied, and he and his command held their ground manfully.

Some time after that, word was sent that the First Brigade was retiring, and General Barnes sent me word to fall back also, which I did in perfect good order, the regiments retaining their alignments and halting and firing as they came back. Having arrived at the road leading along the rear of the wheat-field, the brigade was formed in line in the woods in rear of the road and parallel to it, the right resting at the corner of the woods toward the front. We had not remained here more than, say, fifteen minutes, when a general officer I had never seen before rode up to me, and said his command was driving the enemy in the woods in front of the wheat-field; that he needed the support of a brigade, and desired to know if I would give him mine.

I referred him to General Barnes, and said I would obey his directions with pleasure. He spoke to the general, who was not far off. General Barnes came and stated to me what had been said to him by General Caldwell (this I learned was the officer who had lately spoken to me), and asked me if I would take the brigade in. I told him I would if he wished me to do so. He said he did. The command was then called to attention. General Barnes got out in front of them, and made a few patriotic remarks, to which they responded with a cheer, and we started off across the wheat-field in a line parallel to the road, our right flank resting on the woods. We advanced to the stone fence beyond the wheat-field next to the woods, and took position behind it to support, as we supposed, our friends in the woods in front. The Fourth Michigan, being on the right of the brigade, extended beyond the stone fence, and was, consequently, most exposed.

We had scarcely got to this position before I noticed regiments retiring from the woods on our right, which I supposed were relieved by others who had taken their places, and would protect us in that direction. I observed also that there was considerable firing diagonally toward our rear from these woods, which I then thought were shots from our troops aimed over us at the enemy in the woods beyond and falling short. They were, however, much too frequent to be pleasant, and my color-bearer, Ed. Martin, remarked, "Colonel, I'll be —— if I don't think we are faced the wrong way; the rebs are up there in the woods behind us, on the right."

About this time, too, word was brought me from the Fourth Michigan and Sixty-second Pennsylvania that the enemy were getting into our rear in the woods on the right. I directed those regiments to change front, to face in that direction and meet them, which they did, the firing in the meanwhile being rapid and severe. I at the same time dispatched Lieutenant Seitz, aide-de-camp, to communicate to General Barnes our situation. He reached the point where he had last seen General Barnes. He was not there. Lieutenant Seitz found the enemy had reached that point, and he came near falling into their hands himself; his horse was killed, and he made his way back to me on foot; reported that General Barnes was not to be found; that the enemy was in the woods on our right as far back as where we had started from, and along the road in rear of the wheat-field.

Finding that we were surrounded—that our enemy was under cover, while we were in the open field exposed to their fire—I directed the command to fall back. This was done in order, the command halting and firing as it retired. The Fourth Michigan and Sixty-second Pennsylvania had become mixed up with the enemy, and many hand-to-hand conflicts occurred. Colonel Jeffords, the gallant commander of the Fourth Michigan, was thrust through with a bayonet in a contest over his colors, and Sergt. William McFairman, Company I, and Private William McCarter, Company A, Sixty-second Pennsylvania, receive honorable mention by Colonel Hull in his report for their conduct during this part of the engagement.

Finding, as we retired in the direction from which we advanced, that the fire of the enemy grew more severe on our right, I took a diagonal direction toward the corner of the wheat-field on our left and rear. We crossed the stone fence on this side of the field, and retired to the rear of the battery on the elevation beyond, where the command was halted.

We had lost heavily in our passage across the field. The Fourth Michigan and Sixty-second Pennsylvania had been surrounded, and a large proportion of those regiments were missing, either killed, wounded, or prisoners. What remained of the command formed in the rear of the battery, and we were shortly afterward joined by the Ninth Massachusetts, which had been absent all day on detached duty.

It is difficult to conceive of a more trying situation than that in which three regiments of this command had lately found themselves, and from which they had just effected their escape; in fact, I have since understood that one of General Barnes' aides remarked to him shortly after we had advanced, when it was discovered the enemy was behind us on the flank, that he might bid good-bye to the Second Brigade. I was also informed by General Barnes that, learning soon after we had advanced the situation on our right, he had dispatched an orderly to me with the information and a verbal order to withdraw, but the orderly never reached me.

Every officer and man in the command, so far as I am informed, did his whole duty. All stood their ground and fought unflinchingly until they were ordered by me to retire, and in falling back behaved with coolness and deliberation. We lost many of our best officers and men.

I subjoin a field report of the regiments engaged on the morning of July 2, and also a report of the same regiments on July 4. A nominal and tabular report of casualties in the command has already been forwarded.*

About dark on the evening of the 2d, the acting assistant adjutant-general of the First Brigade came to me and inquired for General Barnes; said he was directed by General Sykes to tell him to have the Second Brigade form on the right of the First in the position they then were. As General Barnes was not present, I received the order, and put the Second Brigade in the position indicated, where we remained until the evening of the 5th, when the division advanced toward Emmitsburg.

In conclusion, I desire to express my gratification at the conduct of my staff during the engagement—Captain [George] Monteith, acting assistant adjutant-general; Captain [Alvan C.] Lamson, acting assistant inspector-general; Captain [John S.] Burdett, acting commissary of subsistence, and Lieutenant [John A. M.] Seitz, acting aide-de-camp. They were prompt and fearless in the discharge of their duty. We were all fortunate enough to escape being hit, though a number of horses in the party were shot—two of the orderlies', the bugler's, Lieutenant Seitz's, and my own.

I am, sir, very respectfully, your obedient servant,

J. B. SWEITZER,
Colonel, Commanding Brigade.

Brig. Gen. CHARLES GRIFFIN, *Comdg. Division.*

[Inclosure.]

Report of commissioned officers and enlisted men present for duty in the Second Brigade, of the regiments engaged, before the action of July 2, and after the action of July 4.

Command.	Before the action, July 2.			After the action, July 4.		
	Officers.	Enlisted men.	Total.	Officers.	Enlisted men.	Total.
4th Michigan	26	316	342	14	125	139
62d Pennsylvania	26	400	426	14	217	231
32d Massachusetts	21	221	242	12	162	174
Total	73	937	1,010	40	504	544

Before action	1,010
After action	544
Loss	466

No. 194.

Report of Col. Strong Vincent, Eighty-third Pennsylvania Infantry, commanding Third Brigade.

HDQRS. THIRD BRIG., FIRST DIV., FIFTH CORPS,
Camp near Aldie, Va., June 22, 1863.

CAPTAIN: I have the honor to report that, in obedience to orders from the general commanding the division, I moved to Middleburg

---

* Embodied in revised statement, p. 179.

during the morning of Sunday, and at 7 a. m., under the direction of General Pleasonton, commanding the expedition, took the position on the left of the cavalry of General Gregg's column, on the Ashby Gap road. The dismounted men of the enemy were in position on the south side of this road, behind a series of stone walls running at right angles with it, the cavalry in the fields, and a battery of six guns placed near the road on the left. A belt of woods some 200 yards marked their position.

Under orders from General Pleasonton to advance at least one regiment of infantry, I directed Lieutenant-Colonel Welch, commanding the Sixteenth Michigan, to push his regiment forward and dislodge their carbineers. At the farther end of the woods his skirmishers opened fire briskly. Again General Pleasonton directed the infantry to advance in greater force, and I sent in the Forty-fourth New York, Colonel Rice commanding, and the Twentieth Maine, Lieutenant-Colonel [Freeman] Conner commanding (Lieutenant-Colonel Chamberlain and Major Gilmore being absent sick), with instructions to press the enemy hard and to pick off the gunners from his battery. At the same time I directed Captain Woodward, commanding Eighty-third Pennsylvania, to move rapidly through the woods to our left, keeping his force concealed, and, the instant he had passed the stone walls, to emerge and take the enemy in flank and rear.

The movement was entirely successful. Finding their position turned, the enemy fled in confusion, and the Sixteenth Michigan, under the lead of Lieutenant-Colonel Welch, advanced on the double-quick on the right, and gallantly compelled them to abandon one piece of their battery, a fine Blakely gun. Moving in conjunction with the cavalry, we drove them from this position to other stone walls immediately in the rear, dislodging them at each attack, until we pushed them across Crummer's Run.

Here they made a sharp resistance, and opened an artillery fire, from which we suffered. Our own artillery responded to them, and here, as throughout the day, abundantly evinced our superiority. Fording the stream, my skirmishers, in conjunction with those of the cavalry, soon flanked their stone-wall line again, and had them on the run. Thus the fight continued, with the same tactics on the part of the enemy, the same orders from General Pleasonton to dislodge them, and the same success in driving them for a distance of nearly 4 miles.

At Goose Creek they again took advantage of a stone wall commanding the defile and bridge through which we must pass, and opened a volley on the head of the column of cavalry just preparing to charge. Under directions from General Pleasonton to clear the position, I ordered the Eighty-third Pennsylvania to carry the bridge on the run, and the skirmishers of my entire line to ford the stream and turn the enemy's flank. The skirmishers of the Eighty-third Pennsylvania pushed into the stream, and the line of the Sixteenth Michigan, led by Captain Fuller, gallantly rushed over the bridge and up to the stone wall under a severe fire, dislodging the enemy and capturing a number of prisoners, officers and men, a list of which you will find appended.* The enemy fled in confusion, followed by our cavalry, who drove them repeatedly from one position to another from this point into and beyond Upperville.

---

* Omitted.

The charges of the cavalry, a sight I had never before witnessed, were truly inspiring, and the triumphant strains of the bands, as squadron after squadron hurled the enemy in his flight up the hills and toward the gap, gave us a feeling of regret that we, too, were not mounted and could not join in the chase. As fast as the tired condition of my men would permit, we proceeded to Upperville, and took position, under General Pleasonton's directions, in support of the artillery until 6 p. m., when we were relieved by Colonel Tilton, commanding First Brigade. General Pleasonton then left it to my choice whether I should return to Middleburg that night or encamp at a prudent distance in rear of Upperville. I determined upon the latter course, and at noon of Monday reported with my command to the general commanding at Middleburg.

I send herewith both a nominal and tabular list of casualties,[*] among which, I regret to say, you will find Captain Mott, of the Sixteenth Michigan, who was severely, if not fatally, wounded in the gallant charge of that regiment upon the battery.

I wish to express my thanks to the officers of my staff for their intelligent and energetic aid on the march and in the field, and commend them to the favorable notice of the general commanding.

In addition to the assistance of the acting assistant adjutant-general, Lieutenant Clark, my acting aides, Captains [Amos M.] Judson and [Prentiss M.] Fogler, Dr. [James P.] Burchfield, and Captain [William T. W.] Ball, commissary of subsistence, both non-combatants, tendered their services, and, with the others, behaved with great gallantry and coolness in carrying orders under fire.

To my regimental commanders I am indebted for the prompt execution of all orders, and for their skillful handling of their commands. Their bravery and judgment have long since been established.

I am, captain, your obedient servant,

STRONG VINCENT,
Colonel Eighty-third Pennsylvania, Comdg. Brigade.

Capt. C. B. Mervine,
Assistant Adjutant-General.

No. 195.

Reports of Col. James C. Rice, Forty-fourth New York Infantry, commanding regiment and Third Brigade.

HDQRS. FORTY-FOURTH NEW YORK VOLUNTEERS,
June 22, 1863.

LIEUTENANT: I respectfully report the following as the part taken by this command in the affair of June 21:

This regiment left camp on June 21, at 3 a. m., forming a portion of the Third Brigade. At Middleburg we took the White Plains road, following it nearly a mile; thence to the right across the fields, and by a circuitous and covered route into an oak wood, where we halted.

The regiment remained here about half an hour, when, in obedience to orders, it was moved forward and right-obliqued, with skirmishers

---

*Embodied in revised statement, p. 172.

thrown well to the front. After connecting on the right with the left of the Sixteenth Michigan Volunteers' skirmishers, the line was moved directly forward, our skirmishers being continually and sharply engaged with those of the enemy, who fell back as ours advanced. The regiment advanced rapidly in line of battle, with occasional halts to dress the line and allow the skirmishers to get a distance of about 2 miles farther to the front. The enemy appeared to have one battery of artillery, which fired occasionally, and fell back with our advance. When we reached a point about three-fourths of a mile this side of Goose Creek, this battery was posted upon the opposite bank, and opened upon us with shell and solid shot. The regiment went forward at double-quick under a very severe fire, and faltered not until it reached the stone wall on this side the creek. Skirmishers examined the creek, and, finding it not fordable, waited for orders upon the bank.

After the lapse of half an hour, we left this position by the right flank, and, marching into the road on our right, crossed the creek on a stone bridge, and formed line of battle again in the fields opposite, to support a battery in position on the brow of the hill.

Skirmishers were thrown to the front, and after a lapse of perhaps an hour the regiment again advanced. Continual skirmishing was kept up by the companies thrown out in advance. By successive advances and halts, we reached a point about 3 miles from Upperville, where we halted for an hour, at the expiration of which time we returned a distance of 1 mile, and bivouacked for the night.

At about 7 a. m. of the 22d, the regiment returned with the brigade to which it is attached to its original camp, near Aldie, reaching that place at about 4 p. m.

Herewith I transmit nominal report of casualties.*

I am, lieutenant, very respectfully, your obedient servant,

JAMES C. RICE,
Colonel, Comdg. Forty-fourth New York Volunteers.

JOHN M. CLARK,
Acting Assistant Adjutant-General.

———

HDQRS. THIRD BRIGADE, FIRST DIVISION, FIFTH CORPS,
July 31, 1863.

CAPTAIN: In compliance with orders from division headquarters, I have the honor to report the operations of this brigade during the battle near Gettysburg, on the 2d and 3d instant.

The brigade, under the command of the late Colonel Vincent, was detached from the division and ordered into position at about 4 p. m. of the 2d instant, on the extreme left of our line of battle. The Twentieth Maine occupied the extreme left of the brigade line, the Sixteenth Michigan the extreme right, connecting with the Third Division, under General Crawford, while the Eighty-third Pennsylvania and Forty-fourth New York occupied the center. The muskets taken into action by the brigade numbered about 1,000.

The ground occupied by the brigade in line of battle was nearly that of a quarter circle, composed mostly of high rocks and cliffs on the center, and becoming more wooded and less rugged as you approached to the left. The right was thrown forward somewhat to the

---

* Embodied in revised statement, p. 172.

front of the ledge of rocks, and was much more exposed than other parts of the line. A comparatively smooth ravine extended along the entire front, perhaps 50 yards from our line, while on the left and beyond a high and jagged mountain rises, called Round Top hill. That the disposition of the forces and the nature of the ground may the better be understood by the general commanding, I send with this report a diagram of the same.*

The brigade had scarcely formed line of battle and pushed forward its skirmishers when a division of the enemy's forces, under General Hood, made a desperate attack along the entire line of the brigade. He approached in three columns, with no skirmishers in advance. The object of the enemy was evident. If he could gain the vantage ground occupied by this brigade, the left flank of our line must give way, opening to him a vast field for successful operations in the rear of our entire army.

To effect this object the enemy made every effort. Massing two or three brigades of his force, he tried for an hour in vain to break the lines of the Forty-fourth New York and Eighty-third Pennsylvania, charging again and again within a few yards of these unflinching troops. At every charge he was repulsed with terrible slaughter. Despairing of success at this point, he made a desperate attack upon the extreme right of the brigade, forcing back a part of the Sixteenth Michigan. This regiment was broken, and, through some misunderstanding of orders, explained in the official report of the commanding officer, it was thrown into confusion; but being immediately supported by the One hundred and fortieth New York Volunteers, the line became again firm and unbroken.

It was at this point of time that Colonel Vincent, commanding the brigade, fell, mortally wounded. Of the character of this gallant and accomplished officer I will speak before I close this report.

The enemy again attacked the center with great vigor, and the extreme left with desperation. Passing one brigade of his forces by the right flank in three columns, he pushed through the ravine toward the left of our brigade, came immediately to a "front," and charged upon the Twentieth Maine. Now occurred the most critical time of the action. For above half an hour the struggle was desperate. At length the enemy pressed so strongly upon the left flank of Colonel Chamberlain's regiment that he wisely determined to change the order of battle, and commanded his left wing to fall back at right angles to his right. He then ordered a charge, and repulsed the enemy at every point.

On assuming the command of the brigade during this attack upon the center and left, I at once passed along the line, and notified the officers and men of my own regiment that I was about to take command of the brigade, and that they must hold their position to the last. I did this that no panic might arise. I then notified all the commanders of the regiments in person, and assured them of my determination to hold the line to the last. Colonel Chamberlain and other officers immediately informed me that their commands were out of ammunition. I had at this time neither an aide nor an orderly even to bear a message. (See P. S.) The enemy was still pressing heavily upon the line. I immediately pressed into service every officer and man in the rear not engaged in the action, whether known or unknown, and made them pledge their honor that they

---

* See p. 619.

would deliver in person every order that I should send by them. I sent four of them, one after another, with orders for ammunition. The ammunition came promptly, was distributed at once, and the fight went on.

The enemy was now attempting to take possession of Round Top hill, a commanding position overlooking our left. It was evident no time was to be lost, and I sent at once other officers, whom I pressed into my service, with messages to the general commanding the corps, asking for re-enforcements to support the brigade. The messages were promptly delivered, and five regiments were at once sent to my support from the Third Division, General Crawford, under command of Colonel Fisher.

Having, with the aid of this officer, properly disposed of three regiments of this force, I ordered Colonel Chamberlain, of the Twentieth Maine, to advance and take possession of the mountain. This order was promptly and gallantly executed by this brave and accomplished officer, who rapidly drove the enemy over the mountain, capturing many prisoners. Colonel Fisher at once ordered two regiments of his command to support Colonel Chamberlain, and the hill remained permanently in our possession.

The forces of the enemy being now repulsed on our left and front, I ordered a detachment from the Forty-fourth New York Volunteers and the Eighty-third Pennsylvania to push forward and secure all the fruits of this hard-earned victory.

It was now 8 o'clock in the evening, and before 9 o'clock we had entire possession of the enemy's ground, had gathered up and brought in all of our own wounded and those of the enemy, and had taken and sent to the rear over 500 prisoners, including 2 colonels and 15 commissioned officers, together with over 1,000 stand of arms belonging to the enemy.

The following morning the prisoners of the brigade buried all of our own dead and a large number of those of the enemy.

The fearful loss of the enemy during this struggle may be estimated from the fact that over 50 of his dead were counted in front of the Twentieth Maine Regiment, and his loss was nearly in that proportion along our entire line.

Although this brigade has been engaged in nearly all of the great battles of the Army of the Potomac, and has always greatly distinguished itself for gallant behavior, yet in none has it fought so desperately or achieved for itself such imperishable honors as in this severe conflict of the 2d instant.

A nominal and tabular list of the casualties of this brigade has already been forwarded to the major-general commanding,* but it is fitting again to mention the names of the brave and faithful officers of the command who fell in this desperate struggle. Of the Forty-fourth New York Volunteers, Capt. L. S. Larrabee and Lieutenants Dunham and Thomas; of the Twentieth Maine, Lieutenant Kendall, and of the Sixteenth Michigan, Lieutenants Browne, Jewett, and Borden were killed.

The brigade was relieved during the forenoon of the 3d instant by the First Brigade, and ordered to the center of the line, where it remained in reserve the balance of the day, exposed to a severe cannonading, but with no loss, from the security of its position.

The colonel commanding would commend to the favorable notice

---

* Embodied in revised statement, p. 179.

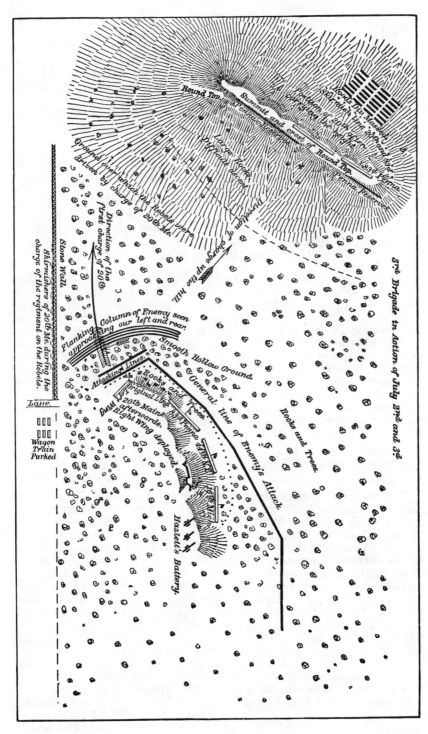

of the general commanding the following-named officers, for their
gallant conduct in battle on the 2d instant: Colonel Chamberlain and
Adjutant Chamberlain, of the Twentieth Maine; Lieutenant-Colonel
Conner and Major Knox, of the Forty-fourth New York Volunteers;
Captain Woodward and Adjutant Gifford, of the Eighty-third Penn-
sylvania, and Captain Elliott and Adjutant Jacklin, of the Sixteenth
Michigan.

Especially would I call the attention of the general commanding to
the distinguished services rendered by Colonel Chamberlain throughout the entire struggle.

To the loss sustained by this command in the death of Colonel Vincent I can refer in no more appropriate language than that used in
the general order announcing it to the brigade, a copy of which I
herewith annex.

I am, very respectfully, your obedient servant,
                                   JAMES C. RICE,
          Colonel Forty-fourth New York Vols., Comdg. Brigade.
Capt. C. B. MERVINE,
          Assistant Adjutant-General, First Division.

P. S.—In justice to the officers composing the staff, it gives me satisfaction to state, in explanation of my report, that at the time I took
command, Captain [Eugene A.] Nash, inspector-general of the brigade, was, in obedience to orders received from Colonel Vincent, at the
front watching the movements of the enemy, to report the same if
he should attempt a flank movement; that Captain [John M.] Clark,
assistant adjutant-general, in obedience to orders, was absent for ammunition, and that Captain [Amos M.] Judson, by orders, was absent
for re-enforcements. During the night these officers rendered me the
greatest service, and I desire to commend each of them to the most
favorable notice of the commanding general for their gallant conduct both under Colonel Vincent's command as well as my own.

[Inclosure.]

GENERAL ORDERS, } HDQRS. 3D BRIG., 1ST DIV., 5TH CORPS,
     No. 5.   }   *July 12, 1863.*

The colonel commanding hereby announces to the brigade the
death of Brig. Gen. Strong Vincent. He died near Gettysburg, Pa.,
July 7, 1863, from the effects of a wound received on the 2d instant,
and within sight of that field which his bravery had so greatly assisted
to win. A day hallowed with all the glory of success is thus sombered
by the sorrow of our loss. Wreaths of victory give way to chaplets
of mourning, hearts exultant to feelings of grief. A soldier, a scholar,
a friend, has fallen. For his country, struggling for its life, he will-
ingly gave his own. Grateful for his services, the State which
proudly claims him as her own will give him an honored grave and
a costly monument, but he ever will remain buried in our hearts, and
our love for his memory will outlast the stone which shall bear the
inscription of his bravery, his virtues, and his patriotism.

While we deplore his death, and remember with sorrow our loss,
let us emulate the example of his fidelity and patriotism, feeling that
he lives but in vain who lives not for his God and his country.

By command of Col. James C. Rice, commanding Third Brigade:
                                   GEO. B. HERENDEEN,
                              Acting Assistant Adjutant-General.

HEADQUARTERS THIRD BRIGADE,
August 14, 1863.

CAPTAIN: In reply to circular of the 12th instant, from head-quarters Army of the Potomac, I have the honor to submit the following report supplementary to that of the battle of Gettysburg:

June 28.—In camp near Frederick City.

June 29.—Left camp in the morning, and marched 2 miles beyond Liberty, in the direction of Johnsville. Camped at 7 a. m. [p. m.]

June 30.—Left camp at 4 a. m., arriving at Union Mills about 4 p. m., when we bivouacked for the night.

July 1.—Broke camp at 6 a. m., arriving at Hanover about 3 p. m. Left again at 5 [p. m.], and arrived within 3 miles of Gettysburg at 1 a. m. [July 2], when we bivouacked.

July 2.—Started at 4 a. m.; went about 2 miles, when we got into position; remained some 2 hours; then crossed the creek, and lay in position awaiting orders until about 4 p. m., when we were ordered dered to the front; immediately on arriving there became engaged; held that position, and bivouacked on the field that night. (See previous report.)

July 3.—Remained on the field of the previous day's fight until about 9 a. m., when we were relieved by the First Brigade and Ninth Massachusetts, of the Second Brigade, we taking their old position farther to the right.

July 4.—Same position of previous day until we were ordered to relieve General Bartlett's brigade, of the Second [Sixth?] Corps.

July 5.—Same position as previous day. Started about 5 p. m. in direction of Emmitsburg. Bivouacked on the road about 10 p. m.

July 6.—Started at 6 a. m., and arrived at 12 m. within 3 miles of Emmitsburg, when we camped.

July 7.—Left camp about 6 a. m., and arrived within 5 miles of Frederick City at 6 p. m., when we bivouacked.

July 8.—Broke camp early in the morning, and arrived at Middletown about 4 p. m.

July 9.—Left Middletown early in the morning, and arrived within 2 miles of Boonsborough about noon.

July 10.—Broke camp early in the morning, and arrived at Jones' Cross-Roads about 3 p. m. The Eighty-third Pennsylvania went on picket immediately.

July 11.—Changed direction of the line to the right early in the morning. In the afternoon advanced to Pleasant Valley.

July 12.—Changed front to the left, and advanced on the Hagerstown and Sharpsburg pike.

July 13.—Camped in front of pike; two companies of the Eighty-third Pennsylvania on picket.

July 14.—Advanced to within 1 mile of Williamsport.

July 15.—Left camp at 4 a. m., and arrived near Burkittsville at 5 p. m., where we bivouacked for the night.

July 16.—Left camp about 4 a. m., and arrived near Berlin 12 m., and went into camp.

July 17.—In same position until about 3 p. m., when we recrossed the Potomac and camped near Lovettsville.

July 18.—Broke camp at 4 a. m.; proceeded 7 miles in the direction of Purcellville; bivouacked at 12 m.

July 19.—Left camp at 8 a. m.; marched 4 miles to Purcellville.

July 20.—Broke camp early in the morning, and marched to near Upperville, on Goose Creek, arriving there at 2 p. m.

July 21.—Remained in same position.

July 22.—Broke camp in the afternoon, and went to Rectortown.

July 23.—Left camp early in the morning, and marched to Manassas Gap. Six companies were detached as skirmishers, and were on picket all night—four of the Eighty-third and two of the Forty-fourth New York Volunteers.

July 24.—In the morning advanced to the high hill in front of the position occupied the previous day. In the afternoon withdrew, and camped some 2 miles to the rear.

July 25.—Left early in the morning in the direction of Warrenton; at 4 p. m. bivouacked for the night.

July 26.—Broke camp early in the morning, and continued our march. When within 3 miles of Warrenton went into camp.

July 27.—Broke camp early next morning, and passed through Warrenton, camping about 3 miles from it.

Very respectfully, your obedient servant,

J. C. RICE,
Colonel, Commanding Third Brigade.

Capt. C. B. MERVINE,
Assistant Adjutant-General.

No. 196.

Report of Col. Joshua L. Chamberlain, Twentieth Maine Infantry.

FIELD NEAR EMMITSBURG, *July* 6, 1863.

SIR: In compliance with the request of the colonel commanding the brigade, I have the honor to submit a somewhat detailed report of the operations of the Twentieth Regiment Maine Volunteers in the battle of Gettysburg, on the 2d and 3d instant.

Having acted as the advance guard, made necessary by the proximity of the enemy's cavalry, on the march of the day before, my command on reaching Hanover, Pa., just before sunset on that day, were much worn, and lost no time in getting ready for an expected bivouac. Rations were scarcely issued, and the men about preparing supper, when rumors that the enemy had been encountered that day near Gettysburg absorbed every other interest, and very soon orders came to march forthwith to Gettysburg.

My men moved out with a promptitude and spirit extraordinary, the cheers and welcome they received on the road adding to their enthusiasm. After an hour or two of sleep by the roadside just before daybreak, we reached the heights southeasterly of Gettysburg at about 7 a. m., July 2.

Massed at first with the rest of the division on the right of the road, we were moved several times farther toward the left. Although expecting every moment to be put into action and held strictly in line of battle, yet the men were able to take some rest and make the most of their rations.

Somewhere near 4 p. m. a sharp cannonade, at some distance to our left and front, was the signal for a sudden and rapid movement of our whole division in the direction of this firing, which grew warmer as we approached. Passing an open field in the hollow ground in which some of our batteries were going into position, our brigade reached the skirt of a piece of woods, in the farther edge of which there was a heavy musketry fire, and when about to go forward into line we received from Colonel Vincent, commanding the brigade, orders to move to the left at the double-quick, when we took a farm road crossing Plum Run in order to gain a rugged mountain spur called Granite Spur, or Little Round Top.

The enemy's artillery got range of our column as we were climbing the spur, and the crashing of the shells among the rocks and the tree tops made us move lively along the crest. One or two shells burst in our ranks. Passing to the southern slope of Little Round Top, Colonel Vincent indicated to me the ground my regiment was to occupy, informing me that this was the extreme left of our general line, and that a desperate attack was expected in order to turn that position, concluding by telling me I was to "hold that ground at all hazards." This was the last word I heard from him.

In order to commence by making my right firm, I formed my regiment on the right into line, giving such direction to the line as should best secure the advantage of the rough, rocky, and stragglingly wooded ground.

The line faced generally toward a more conspicuous eminence southwest of ours, which is known as Sugar Loaf, or Round Top. Between this and my position intervened a smooth and thinly wooded hollow. My line formed, I immediately detached Company B, Captain Morrill commanding, to extend from my left flank across this hollow as a line of skirmishers, with directions to act as occasion might dictate, to prevent a surprise on my exposed flank and rear.

The artillery fire on our position had meanwhile been constant and heavy, but my formation was scarcely complete when the artillery was replaced by a vigorous infantry assault upon the center of our brigade to my right, but it very soon involved the right of my regiment and gradually extended along my entire front. The action was quite sharp and at close quarters.

In the midst of this, an officer from my center informed me that some important movement of the enemy was going on in his front, beyond that of the line with which we were engaged. Mounting a large rock, I was able to see a considerable body of the enemy moving by the flank in rear of their line engaged, and passing from the direction of the foot of Great Round Top through the valley toward the front of my left. The close engagement not allowing any change of front, I immediately stretched my regiment to the left, by taking intervals by the left flank, and at the same time "refusing" my left wing, so that it was nearly at right angles with my right, thus occupying about twice the extent of our ordinary front, some of the companies being brought into single rank when the nature of the ground gave sufficient strength or shelter. My officers and men understood my wishes so well that this movement was executed under fire, the right wing keeping up fire, without giving the enemy any occasion to seize or even to suspect their advantage. But we were not a moment too soon; the enemy's flanking column having gained their desired direction, burst upon my left, where they evidently had expected an unguarded flank, with great demonstration.

We opened a brisk fire at close range, which was so sudden and effective that they soon fell back among the rocks and low trees in the valley, only to burst forth again with a shout, and rapidly advanced, firing as they came. They pushed up to within a dozen yards of us before the terrible effectiveness of our fire compelled them to break and take shelter.

They renewed the assault on our whole front, and for an hour the fighting was severe. Squads of the enemy broke through our line in several places, and the fight was literally hand to hand. The edge of the fight rolled backward and forward like a wave. The dead and wounded were now in our front and then in our rear. Forced from our position, we desperately recovered it, and pushed the enemy down to the foot of the slope. The intervals of the struggle were seized to remove our wounded (and those of the enemy also), to gather ammunition from the cartridge-boxes of disabled friend or foe on the field, and even to secure better muskets than the Enfields, which we found did not stand service well. Rude shelters were thrown up of the loose rocks that covered the ground.

Captain Woodward, commanding the Eighty-third Pennsylvania Volunteers, on my right, gallantly maintaining his fight, judiciously and with hearty co-operation made his movements conform to my necessities, so that my right was at no time exposed to a flank attack.

The enemy seemed to have gathered all their energies for their final assault. We had gotten our thin line into as good a shape as possible, when a strong force emerged from the scrub wood in the valley, as well as I could judge, in two lines in *échelon* by the right, and, opening a heavy fire, the first line came on as if they meant to sweep everything before them. We opened on them as well as we could with our scanty ammunition snatched from the field.

It did not seem possible to withstand another shock like this now coming on. Our loss had been severe. One-half of my left wing had fallen, and a third of my regiment lay just behind us, dead or badly wounded. At this moment my anxiety was increased by a great roar of musketry in my rear, on the farther or northerly slope of Little Round Top, apparently on the flank of the regular brigade, which was in support of Hazlett's battery on the crest behind us. The bullets from this attack struck into my left rear, and I feared that the enemy might have nearly surrounded the Little Round Top, and only a desperate chance was left for us. My ammunition was soon exhausted. My men were firing their last shot and getting ready to "club" their muskets.

It was imperative to strike before we were struck by this overwhelming force in a hand-to-hand fight, which we could not probably have withstood or survived. At that crisis, I ordered the bayonet. The word was enough. It ran like fire along the line, from man to man, and rose into a shout, with which they sprang forward upon the enemy, now not 30 yards away. The effect was surprising; many of the enemy's first line threw down their arms and surrendered. An officer fired his pistol at my head with one hand, while he handed me his sword with the other. Holding fast by our right, and swinging forward our left, we made an extended "right wheel," before which the enemy's second line broke and fell back, fighting from tree to tree, many being captured, until we had swept the valley and cleared the front of nearly our entire brigade.

Meantime Captain Morrill with his skirmishers (sent out from my left flank), with some dozen or fifteen of the U. S. Sharpshooters who had put themselves under his direction, fell upon the enemy as they were breaking, and by his demonstrations, as well as his well-directed fire, added much to the effect of the charge.

Having thus cleared the valley and driven the enemy up the western slope of the Great Round Top, not wishing to press so far out as to hazard the ground I was to hold by leaving it exposed to a sudden rush of the enemy, I succeeded (although with some effort to stop my men, who declared they were "on the road to Richmond") in getting the regiment into good order and resuming our original position.

Four hundred prisoners, including two field and several line officers, were sent to the rear. These were mainly from the Fifteenth and Forty-seventh Alabama Regiments, with some of the Fourth and Fifth Texas. One hundred and fifty of the enemy were found killed and wounded in our front.

At dusk, Colonel Rice informed me of the fall of Colonel Vincent, which had devolved the command of the brigade on him, and that Colonel Fisher had come up with a brigade to our support. These troops were massed in our rear. It was the understanding, as Colonel Rice informed me, that Colonel Fisher's brigade was to advance and seize the western slope of Great Round Top, where the enemy had shortly before been driven. But, after considerable delay, this intention for some reason was not carried into execution.

We were apprehensive that if the enemy were allowed to strengthen himself in that position, he would have a great advantage in renewing the attack on us at daylight or before. Colonel Rice then directed me to make the movement to seize that crest.

It was now 9 p. m. Without waiting to get ammunition, but trusting in part to the very circumstance of not exposing our movement or our small front by firing, and with bayonets fixed, the little handful of 200 men pressed up the mountain side in very extended order, as the steep and jagged surface of the ground compelled. We heard squads of the enemy falling back before us, and, when near the crest, we met a scattering and uncertain fire, which caused us the great loss of the gallant Lieutenant Linscott, who fell, mortally wounded. In the silent advance in the darkness we laid hold of 25 prisoners, among them a staff officer of General [E. M.] Law, commanding the brigade immediately opposed to us during the fight. Reaching the crest, and reconnoitering the ground, I placed the men in a strong position among the rocks, and informed Colonel Rice, requesting also ammunition and some support to our right, which was very near the enemy, their movements and words even being now distinctly heard by us.

Some confusion soon after resulted from the attempt of some regiment of Colonel Fisher's brigade to come to our support. They had found a wood road up the mountain, which brought them on my right flank, and also in proximity to the enemy, massed a little below. Hearing their approach, and thinking a movement from that quarter could only be from the enemy, I made disposition to receive them as such. In the confusion which attended the attempt to form them in support of my right, the enemy opened a brisk fire, which disconcerted my efforts to form them and disheartened the supports themselves, so that I saw no more of them that night.

Feeling somewhat insecure in this isolated position, I sent in for the Eighty-third Pennsylvania, which came speedily, followed by the Forty-fourth New York, and, having seen these well posted, I sent a strong picket to the front, with instructions to report to me every half hour during the night, and allowed the rest of my men to sleep on their arms.

At some time about midnight, two regiments of Colonel Fisher's brigade came up the mountain beyond my left, and took position near the summit; but as the enemy did not threaten from that direction, I made no effort to connect with them.

We went into the fight with 386, all told—358 guns. Every pioneer and musician who could carry a musket went into the ranks. Even the sick and foot-sore, who could not keep up in the march, came up as soon as they could find their regiments, and took their places in line of battle, while it was battle, indeed. Some prisoners I had under guard, under sentence of court-martial, I was obliged to put into the fight, and they bore their part well, for which I shall recommend a commutation of their sentence.

The loss, so far as I can ascertain it, is 136—30 of whom were killed, and among the wounded are many mortally.

Captain Billings, Lieutenant Kendall, and Lieutenant Linscott are officers whose loss we deeply mourn—efficient soldiers, and pure and high-minded men.

In such an engagement there were many incidents of heroism and noble character which should have place even in an official report; but, under present circumstances, I am unable to do justice to them. I will say of that regiment that the resolution, courage, and heroic fortitude which enabled us to withstand so formidable an attack have happily led to so conspicuous a result that they may safely trust to history to record their merits.

About noon on the 3d of July, we were withdrawn, and formed on the right of the brigade, in the front edge of a piece of woods near the left center of our main line of battle, where we were held in readiness to support our troops, then receiving the severe attack of the afternoon of that day.

On the 4th, we made a reconnaissance to the front, to ascertain the movements of the enemy, but finding that they had retired, at least beyond Willoughby's Run, we returned to Little Round Top, where we buried our dead in the place where we had laid them during the fight, marking each grave by a head-board made of ammunition boxes, with each dead soldier's name cut upon it. We also buried 50 of the enemy's dead in front of our position of July 2. We then looked after our wounded, whom I had taken the responsibility of putting into the houses of citizens in the vicinity of Little Round Top, and, on the morning of the 5th, took up our march on the Emmitsburg road.

I have the honor to be, your obedient servant,

JOSHUA L. CHAMBERLAIN,
Colonel, Commanding Twentieth Maine Volunteers.

Lieut. GEORGE B. HERENDEEN,
A. A. A. G., Third Brig., First Div., Fifth Army Corps.

No. 197.

Report of Capt. Atherton W. Clark, Twentieth Maine Infantry.

CAMP NEAR BEVERLY FORD, VA.,
August 14, 1863.

LIEUTENANT: In compliance with circular of August 12, from headquarters Army of the Potomac, I have the honor to report that on the morning of the 5th ultimo this regiment moved forward on the battle-field of Gettysburg, and occupied the Carolina road during the day.

At night, marched 10 miles in the direction of Emmitsburg, and bivouacked at midnight near Marsh Creek.

Early on the morning of the 6th, marched 1 mile, and bivouacked.

Resumed march on the 7th through Creagerstown, and bivouacked 6 miles above Frederick City and 18 miles from bivouac of previous night.

On the 8th, moved in heavy rain 12 miles across the Catoctin Mountains, and encamped near Middletown in the afternoon.

On the morning of the 9th, the regiment crossed over South Mountain (a detachment of it assisting the train in its passage), and encamped near Boonsborough in the afternoon, 8 miles from Middletown.

The regiment moved early on the day following, and in the vicinity of the enemy, on the Sharpsburg pike, near Jones' Cross-Roads, was thrown forward to act as skirmishers. It was soon warmly engaged, and, after a severe and protracted skirmish, held the pike. The loss to the regiment was 2 killed and 6 wounded and missing.

On the 11th, the regiment moved along the pike and westward, through field and wood, 2 miles, and bivouacked.

On the morning of the 12th, advanced to the Williamsport road, and the next day crossed the Williamsport road and threw forward pickets.

On the 14th, marched to Williamsport, and the morning following returned, marching through Keedysville, over South Mountain, and encamped near Burkittsville, having marched 20 miles.

Moved forward on the 16th to vicinity of Berlin, where the regiment bivouacked until the afternoon of the 17th, when it crossed the Potomac, and marched 5 miles to Lovettsville.

On the 18th, 19th, and 20th, marched to Goose Creek, 30 miles from Lovettsville.

Resumed march on the 22d, and bivouacked near Rectortown, 10 miles distant from Goose Creek.

The regiment took part in the operations of the 23d and 24th, in Manassas Gap, returning on the 25th, and encamped near Orleans, after a march of 20 miles.

Resumed march in the morning, and on the 27th ultimo encamped 2 miles south of Warrenton.

Very respectfully, your obedient servant,

A. W. CLARK,
Captain, Commanding Twentieth Maine Volunteers.

Lieut. JOHN M. CLARK,
Acting Assistant Adjutant-General, Third Brigade.

No. 198.

Report of Lieut. Col. Norval E. Welch, Sixteenth Michigan Infantry.

NEAR EMMITSBURG, MD.,
July 6, 1863.

LIEUTENANT: In reply to circular of this date from brigade headquarters, as to the part this regiment sustained in the action of July 2 and 3, I have the honor to report:

The regiment, under my command, lay with the Third Brigade,

First Division, Fifth Corps, closed in mass, near and in rear of Gettysburg, to the left of the main road, during most of the day. The brigade was commanded by Col. Strong Vincent, Eighty-third Regiment Pennsylvania Volunteers.

About 4 p. m. we moved rapidly to the extreme left of our line of battle, and went into position on the left of the brigade, at that time circling the crest of a high rocky hill. After deploying two of my largest companies as skirmishers—Brady's Sharpshooters from the left, and Company A from the right—I was ordered at double-quick to the right of the brigade, and to take my position on the right of the Forty-fourth New York. Before this could be accomplished, we were under a heavy fire of the enemy's infantry. We succeeded, however, in securing our places after some loss.

We remained in this position nearly half an hour, when some one (supposed to be General Weed or Major-General Sykes) called from the extreme crest of the hill to fall back nearer the top, where a much less exposed line could be taken up. This order was not obeyed, except by single individuals. From some misconstruction of orders, and entirely unwarrantable assumption of authority, Lieutenant Kydd ordered the colors back. None left with them, however, but three of the color-guard. They followed the brigade colors to where Colonel Vincent, after being wounded, had been carried, where they remained all night, joining the regiment in the morning with 45 men, who had left the field during and after the fight. All the remainder of the regiment retained their position until relieved.

The two companies sent out as skirmishers numbered about 50. The number of muskets taken in line was about 150; the number killed and wounded 59—21 killed.* Several wounded have since died.

On the 3d, we took up a new line farther to the right, at the left of the brigade, and remained on our arms for twenty-four hours.

Captain Elliott and Adjutant Jacklin behaved with their usual gallantry. Captain Partridge, Lieutenants Borgman (wounded), Woodruff, Forsyth, Cameron (wounded, with arm amputated), Swart, Graham, Salter, and Captain Chandler, behaved nobly and handled their men with coolness and valor. Lieutenants Browne, Company E, Jewett, Company K, and Borden, Company F, died, bravely defending the flag they had sworn to support and that they loved in their hearts, and emulating the bravest. I had no truer or purer officers, and their loss cannot be replaced.

Very respectfully, your obedient servant,

N. E. WELCH,
Lieutenant-Colonel, Commanding Regiment.

Lieut. GEORGE B. HERENDEEN,
Acting Assistant Adjutant-General.

No. 199.

Report of Maj. Robert T. Elliott, Sixteenth Michigan Infantry.

CAMP NEAR BEVERLY FORD, VA.,
August 15, 1863.

LIEUTENANT: I have the honor to make the following report of the operations of this regiment, supplementary to the report of the

---

* But see revised statement, p. 179.

operations during the battle of Gettysburg, Pa., made by Lieut. Col. N. E. Welch, July 6:

July 7.—Broke camp near Emmitsburg, Md., and marched in the direction of Frederick, Md., halting for the night at ———.

July 8.—Marched over the Catoctin Mountains to Middletown, Md., and bivouacked for the night, and remained till July 9, when we marched to near Boonsborough, Md., and bivouacked for the night.

July 10.—Marched to near Jones' Cross-Roads, and a detail sent out to support skirmishers, in charge of Captain Elliott. Skirmishers became engaged with enemy's cavalry vedettes, in which Company A, of this regiment, had 1 man wounded. Bivouacked in rear of pickets until morning of July 11, when regiment moved to Jones' Cross-Roads, and occupied position in brigade in close column by division, and advanced 2 miles in the direction of Hagerstown, and bivouacked.

July 12.—Moved forward as yesterday, in close column by division, nearly a mile, when, a rain storm coming on, moved to the left, where the regiment bivouacked in an open field till the afternoon of July 13, when the regiment moved to the left in the direction of Williamsport, and a detail made for picket, which was sent out in charge of Lieutenant Eddy, Company G. Bivouacked for the night. During the night considerable skirmishing by the detail from this regiment.

On the morning of July 14, the enemy's skirmishers fell back, and quite a number of stragglers were picked up by our men. Regiment moved forward to Williamsport, remaining over night in bivouac.

July 15.—Took up the line of march, passing through Keedysville and over South Mountain, halting for the night near Burkittsville.

July 16.—Moved to near Berlin, Md., where we remained till the afternoon of July 17. We crossed the Potomac into Virginia, and bivouacked for the night near Lovettsville, Va., Captain (now Major) Elliott being in command of the regiment, Lieut. Col. N. E. Welch having left us on sick leave, to go to Michigan.

July 18.—Marched to and bivouacked near Wheatland.

July 19.—Marched to near Purcellville, and bivouacked for the night.

July 20.—Moved to near Union, and remained there in bivouac.

July 22.—In the forenoon we marched to Rectortown, and bivouacked for the night.

July 23.—Moved at daylight into Manassas Gap, going to near Wapping Heights, where, in conjunction with the brigade and division, acted as support of the Third Corps. Passing through Linden, bivouacked on Wapping Heights for the night.

July 24.—Formed in line of battle, and, with the other regiments of the brigade, were thrown forward as skirmishers toward Front Royal. Were recalled about 1 o'clock, and, after a rest, moved back to near Linden, and bivouacked.

July 25.—Marched at daylight, and, after a tedious march, bivouacked for the night near Orleans, the men having marched all day without rations.

July 26.—Moved forward toward Warrenton, passing through Orleans, and encamped 3 miles from Warrenton.

July 27.—Passed through Warrenton; moved 3 miles on the Fayetteville road, and went into permanent camp.

The commanding officer takes this occasion to make mention of the general good conduct of both officers and men. The line officers are deserving of all praise for the manner in which their companies were brought forward at times when the men were without food and many of them shoeless. His thanks are hereby tendered them for the invaluable services they have rendered him during the time he has been in command.

In conclusion, I have the honor to tender to the colonel commanding the brigade the assurance of the high esteem of the officers of this command, prompted not only by the knowledge of his former military service, but by the able manner he has handled the brigade.

Respectfully, your obedient servant,

ROBT. T. ELLIOTT,
Major, Commanding Sixteenth Michigan Volunteers.

Lieut. JOHN M. CLARK,
Actg. Asst. Adjt. Gen., Third Brig., First Div., Fifth A. C.

No. 200.

Reports of Lieut. Col. Freeman Conner, Forty-fourth New York Infantry.

HDQRS. FORTY-FOURTH NEW YORK VOLUNTEERS,
July 6, 1863.

LIEUTENANT: I have the honor to submit the following report of the action taken by this regiment in the engagement on July 2 :

About 4 p. m. our regiment, Col. J. C. Rice commanding, was placed in position on Round Top hill, with the Eighty-third Pennsylvania on our left and the Sixteenth Massachusetts on our right. Company B was immediately thrown out as skimishers. When they had advanced about 200 yards, they met the enemy advancing in three lines of battle.

Orders were immediately given by Capt. L. S. Larrabee, commanding the company, to fall back upon the battalion. It was while executing this order that that faithful and brave officer was shot through the body and instantly killed, being the first officer that this regiment ever had killed in battle.

The enemy continued to advance until the first line came within about 40 yards of our line. Upon their first appearance we opened a heavy fire upon them, which was continued until they were compelled to retreat. After they had disappeared in our immediate front, we turned our fire upon those who had advanced in the hollow to our right, and continued it until we were out of ammunition.

After we had been engaged about one hour, Colonel Vincent, commanding brigade, was wounded, and the command fell upon Col. J. C. Rice, and the command of the regiment upon myself.

We remained in our position until the next morning about 8 a. m., when we were relieved by Colonel Hayes, Eighteenth Massachusetts. We were then moved to the right about three-eighths of a mile, and formed in line of battle, the Sixteenth Michigan on our left and the Twentieth Maine on our right.

I regret to add that in addition to Captain Larrabee, whose death I have already noticed, the officers are called upon to mourn the loss of

First Lieut. Eugene L. Dunham, Company D, a brave and efficient officer, who was instantly killed during the heavy firing from the enemy in our front. Capt. William R. Bourne, Company K; Capt. Bennett Munger, Company C; Adjt. George B. Herendeen; First Lieut. Charles H. Zeilman, commanding Company F, and Second Lieut. Benjamin N. Thomas, Company K, were wounded, the latter, it is feared, mortally.

It affords me great pleasure to be able to state that both officers and men behaved with the greatest coolness and bravery, not a single case of cowardice having come to my ear.

Our casualties were:

Officers and men.	Killed.	Wounded.	Missing.	Total.
Commissioned officers	2	5	......	7
Enlisted men	24	73	7	104
Total*	26	78	7	111

Most respectfully, your obedient servant,
                      FREEMAN CONNER,
      Lieut. Col., Comdg. Forty-fourth New York Volunteers.

Lieut. GEORGE B. HERENDEEN,
      Acting Assistant Adjutant-General.

———

HDQRS. FORTY-FOURTH NEW YORK VOLUNTEERS,
                      August 14, 1863.

LIEUTENANT: I have the honor to make the following supplementary report of the operations of this command, from June 29 until its arrival at Warrenton, Va.:

On Friday, July 10, I was ordered to take my command, in company with the remainder of the Third Brigade, to Jones' Cross-Roads, Md., near Antietam Creek.

Pickets were established, for which my regiment furnished three companies.

The following morning at daylight skirmishing began, the enemy making his appearance in front in quite heavy force. Skirmishers were thrown out from my command with the others of the brigade, and the skirmishing was continued until I was relieved at 3 p. m. by a portion of the Second Corps, when I rejoined the brigade. Recrossed the Potomac River on Friday, July 17.

Reached Manassas Gap on Thursday, 23d instant, where we anticipated a fight, but were disappointed. Bivouacked near Warrenton, Va., July 29.

I am, very respectfully, your obedient servant,
                      FREEMAN CONNER,
      Lieutenant-Colonel, Comdg. Forty-fourth New York Vols.

Lieut. JOHN M. CLARK,
      Acting Assistant Adjutant-General.

* But see revised statement, p. 179.

No. 201.

Report of Capt. Orpheus S. Woodward, Eighty-third Pennsylvania Infantry.

NEAR EMMITSBURG, MD.,
July 6, 1863.

LIEUTENANT: In compliance with orders from headquarters Third Brigade, First Division, Fifth Corps, I have the honor to report the following as the operations of my command during the battle of the 2d, 3d, 4th, and 5th instant:

On the morning of the 2d instant, moved to the front. At about 2.30 p. m. was ordered into position on our extreme left, the Forty-fourth New York on my right, the Twentieth Maine on my left. At 3.15 p. m. the enemy advanced and engaged my skirmishers, pressing on in force, with bayonets fixed. They soon drove in my skirmishers and engaged my regiment, posted behind rocks and stones hastily thrown up for defense. The contest continued lively until nearly 6 p. m., when the enemy fell back. I instantly threw forward a strong line of skirmishers, who captured between 50 and 60 prisoners and 250 stand of arms.

My men and officers acted splendidly. Where all did so well, I cannot discriminate.

My loss amounted to 10 killed and 45 wounded.

At 1.30 a. m. on the 3d, moved to the support of the Twentieth Maine, which had succeeded in taking a high hill a little to the left of my former position. Remained here until 10 a. m., when, being relieved by a regiment of the Pennsylvania Reserves, rejoined my brigade, massed in the woods, just at the right of General Sykes' headquarters. Here I remained until 12 m., the 4th, when the brigade was thrown forward on a reconnaissance. We moved out, and occupied the position occupied by the enemy the previous day; threw forward skirmishers, but found no opposing force within 2 miles. I deem it but proper to state that but for the prompt and skillful disposition made by Colonel Vincent of the troops under his command (the Third Brigade), the enemy would have succeeded in turning our left. ·

I regret to state that Colonel Vincent was severely wounded. My command (his regiment) esteemed him highly as a gentleman, scholar, and soldier, and bitterly avenged his injury.

I am, very respectfully, your obedient servant,

O. S. WOODWARD,
Captain, Commanding Regiment.

Lieutenant HERENDEEN,
    Asst. Adjt. Gen., Third Brig., First Div., Fifth Corps.

———

No. 202.

Report of Maj. William H. Lamont, Eighty-third Pennsylvania Infantry.

HDQRS. EIGHTY-THIRD REGIMENT PENNSYLVANIA VOLS.,
August 14, 1863.

LIEUTENANT: In reply to circular of 13th instant, from headquarters Army of the Potomac, I have the honor to submit the following report, supplementary to that of the battle of Gettysburg :

June 28.—In camp near Frederick City.

June 29.—Left camp in the morning, and marched 2 miles beyond Liberty, in the direction of Johnsville; encamped at 7 p. m.

June 30.—Left camp at 4 a. m., arriving at Union Mills about 4 p. m., where we bivouacked for the night.

July 1.—Broke camp at 6 a. m., arriving at Hanover at about 3 p. m.; left again at 5 o'clock, and arrived within 3 miles of Gettysburg at 1 a. m., where we bivouacked.

July 2.—Started at 4 a. m.; went about 2 miles, when we got into position; remained some two hours, then crossed the creek and lay in position awaiting orders until about 4 p. m., when we were ordered to the front; immediately on arriving there became engaged; held that position, and bivouacked on the field that night.

July 3.—Remained on the field of the previous day's fight until about 9 a. m., when we were relieved by the First Brigade and Ninth Massachusetts, of Second Brigade, we taking their old position farther to the right.

July 4.—Same position as previous day until we were ordered to relieve General Bartlett's brigade, of the Second [Sixth] Corps.

July 5.—Same position as previous day; started about 5 p. m. in the direction of Emmitsburg; bivouacked on the road about 10 p. m.

July 6.—Started at 6 a. m., and arrived at 12 m. within some 3 miles of Emmitsburg, where we encamped.

July 7.—Left camp about 6 a. m., and arrived within 5 miles of Frederick City at 6 p. m., where we bivouacked.

July 8.—Broke camp early in the morning, and arrived at Middletown about 4 p. m.

July 9.—Left Middletown early in the morning, and arrived within 2 miles of Boonsborough about noon.

July 10.—Broke camp early in the morning, and arrived at Jones' Cross-Roads about 3 p. m.; went on picket immediately.

July 11.—Changed direction of line to the right early in the morning; in the afternoon advanced to Pleasant Valley.

July 12.—Changed front to the left, and advanced on to the Hagerstown and Sharpsburg pike.

July 13.—Encamped in front of pike; two companies on picket.

July 14.—Advanced to within 1 mile of Williamsport.

July 15.—Left camp at 4 a. m., and arrived near Burkittsville at 5 p. m., where we bivouacked for the night.

July 16.—Left camp about 4 a. m., and arrived near Berlin at 12 m.; went into camp.

July 17.—In same position until about 3 p. m., when we recrossed the Potomac, and encamped near Lovettsville.

July 18.—Broke camp at 4 a. m.; proceeded 7 miles in the direction of Purcellville; went into bivouac at 12 m.

July 19.—Left camp at 8 a. m.; marched 4 miles to Purcellville.

July 20.—Broke camp early in the morning, and marched to near Upperville, on Goose Creek, arriving there at 2 p. m.

July 21.—Remained in same position.

July 22.—Broke camp in the afternoon, and went to Rectortown.

July 23.—Left camp early in the morning, and marched to Manassas Gap; had four companies detached as skirmishers and on picket all night.

July 24.—In the morning advanced to the high hill in front of the position occupied the previous day; in the afternoon withdrew, and encamped some 2 miles in the rear.

July 25.—Left early in the morning in the direction of Warrenton; at 4 p. m. bivouacked for the night.

July 26.—Broke camp early in the morning, and continued our march; when within 3 miles of Warrenton went into camp.

July 27.—Broke camp early next morning, and passed through Warrenton, encamping about 3 miles from it.

Very respectfully, your obedient servant,

WM. H. LAMONT,
Major, Commanding.

Lieut. JOHN M. CLARK,
Acting Assistant Adjutant-General, Third Brigade.

No. 203.

Reports of Brig. Gen. Romeyn B. Ayres, U. S. Army, commanding Second Division.

HDQRS. SECOND DIVISION, FIFTH ARMY CORPS,
July 28, 1863.

COLONEL: I have the honor to submit a report of the operations of this division in the battle of Gettysburg, Pa.

The division was marched forward on the night of July 1 and 2 on the Gettysburg and Hanover road, and was formed in line of battle in rear of and facing that road, the First Division on its right. Later in the day it was marched to the left and center, and massed there. In the afternoon, the enemy's attack on the left of our position being developed, the division, preceded by the First Division, was marched to the support of our troops engaged, the Third Brigade being placed in position on the general line of battle upon a rocky hill (usually called Round Top hill) of great importance, facing the Emmitsburg and Gettysburg pike. This brigade was ordered to hold this hill, which duty it performed well and effectually.

The First and Second Brigades were placed on the general line, to the right of the Third, and, shortly after, these two brigades were ordered to advance and carry a point some 250 yards in advance, whence the enemy were annoying our line, that point offering facilities for his sharpshooters, &c., being wooded and rocky. This order was immediately put into execution, the brigades crossing the intermediate swampy ground rapidly, and forming on the left of a division of the Second Corps, the First Brigade in rear of and supporting the Second Brigade. Immediately the troops became actively engaged with the enemy in the woods, the line being now nearly at right angles to the line of the Third Brigade, the general line of battle.

After some time, perceiving the troops on my right moving to the rear of my regiments, I sought information for its cause. General Caldwell, commanding next me, informed me repeatedly that his troops were being relieved by fresh ones, they being out of ammunition, &c. I then determined to move forward and sweep through and occupy the woods in my front, and gave the preparatory orders therefor, when I found that all the troops on my right had gone, and a large force of the enemy was coming down on my rear from the right. I immediately ordered the two brigades to face about and move to the right and rear, and form on the general line of battle on the right of the Third Brigade. This order was at once executed. Some little delay occurred, owing to meeting other troops ordered up to our support as we arrived on the line. Subsequently these two brigades were massed in the woods, in rear of the Third.

When I withdrew the two brigades, the fight was virtually over, the enemy having failed to break the general line of battle. The division remained in this last position till we took up the line of march in pursuit of the enemy on the 5th instant, save that the First Brigade made a reconnaissance on the 4th.

The troops behaved with great gallantry on this occasion, and although, as the accompanying report of casualties* shows, the losses were terrible, no one thought of retiring till the order was given.

The brigade commanders—Col. H. Day, First Brigade, Col. S. Burbank, Second Brigade, and, after the fall of General Weed and Colonel O'Rorke, Colonel Garrard, Third Brigade—performed their duties with coolness and gallantry.

My staff performed their duties with intelligence and gallantry, and have my sincere thanks. I name them in the order of rank, viz: Capt. H. L. Chipman, Eleventh U. S. Infantry, acting assistant inspector-general; Capt. George Ryan, Seventh U. S. Infantry, acting assistant adjutant-general and chief of staff; First Lieut. William H. Powell, Fourth U. S. Infantry, acting aide-de-camp; First Lieut. J. A. Sayles, Fifth Vermont Infantry, aide-de-camp; Second Lieut. Louis McL. Hamilton, Third U. S. Infantry, aide-de-camp. Capt. A. L. Thomas, assistant quartermaster; Capt. E. Knowles, commissary of subsistence, volunteers; Asst. Surg. C. Wagner, U. S. Army, surgeon-in-chief; Lieut. W. W. Swan, Seventeenth U. S. Infantry, ordnance officer, and Second Lieut. George L. Choisy, Fourteenth U. S. Infantry, ambulance officer, also performed the duties of their several offices with great zeal and efficiency.

In the death of Brig. Gen. Stephen H. Weed, volunteers, and captain Fifth U. S. Artillery, the service lost a distinguished and gallant soldier. Col. P. H. O'Rorke, One hundred and fortieth New York Volunteers and first lieutenant U. S. Engineers, was a brave and valuable officer.

I inclose reports of brigade commanders. The list of casualties is now in your hands.*

Very respectfully, your obedient servant,

R. B. AYRES,
Brigadier-General, Commanding.

Col. Fred. T. Locke,
Acting Assistant Adjutant-General, Fifth Corps.

—

HEADQUARTERS SECOND DIVISION,
August 13, 1863.

COLONEL: Pursuant to the circular, headquarters Army of the Potomac, of August 12, 1863, I have the honor to make this supplemental report of the operations of this division in the recent campaign through Maryland and into Pennsylvania.

The 28th of June found the division camped near Frederick, Md. On the 29th of June, marched 14 miles, and bivouacked near Liberty, Md.

---

* Embodied in revised statement, pp. 179, 180.

The division left Liberty June 30; marched 23 miles.

July 1.—Left bivouac; marched 18 miles, and bivouacked 12 p. m. at ———.

On the morning of the 2d, left the bivouac of the 1st, and came into position as stated in my report of the 28th July.

For the operations of that day and the subsequent days, including the 4th of July, I respectfully refer to that report.

On the 5th of July, the division left its position in line of battle at Gettysburg, and, marching 6 miles, camped on Marsh Creek.

On the 7th of July, marched 20 miles.

July 8.—Marched 10 miles, camping near Middletown, Md.

July 9.—Marched 6 miles, camping near the base of South Mountain.

July 10.—Marched 8 miles, camping near Roxbury Mills, Antietam Creek.

July 11.—Advanced 2½ miles near Funkstown.

July 14.—Advanced 4 miles to Williamsport.

July 15.—Marched 20 miles, and bivouacked near Burkittsville, Md.

July 16.—Marched 6 miles, camping between Petersville and Berlin, Md.

July 17.—Crossed the Potomac, camping near Lovettsville, Va.

July 18.—Marching 6 miles, camped near Wheatland, Va.

July 19.—Marched 10 miles, camping near Purcellville, Va.

July 20.—Marched 12 miles, camping on Goose Creek.

July 22.—Marched 8 miles, camping near Rectortown, Va.

July 23.—Marched 15 miles, bivouacking in line of battle in Manassas Gap, supporting the Third Corps.

July 24.—Made a reconnaissance in conjunction with the other two divisions of the corps, moving forward in line of battle near the railroad in the Gap. It was discovered that the enemy had retreated; moved back about 2 miles and camped.

July 25.—Moved back, marching through Fairville toward Warrenton, camping near Orleans, Va.

July 26.—Marched 6 miles and camped.

July 27.—Marched 8 miles, through Warrenton, and went into camp near that place, making some 320 miles since the 1st of June.

Very respectfully, your obedient servant,

R. B. AYRES,
Brigadier-General, Commanding.

Col. FRED. T. LOCKE,
  Assistant Adjutant-General, Fifth Corps.

No. 204.

Report of Col. Hannibal Day, Sixth U. S. Infantry, commanding First Brigade.

HDQRS. FIRST BRIGADE, SECOND DIVISION, FIFTH CORPS,
  Camp near Warrenton, Va., July 28, 1863.

SIR: In forwarding the report of regimental commanders of operations of the several commands of my brigade near Gettysburg, Pa., although not called on myself for a report, I have the honor to say that among casualties not included in the reports of battalion commanders my acting assistant adjutant-general, Capt. S. Van Rensselaer, was wounded, as well as my orderly, private of Seventeenth Pennsylvania Cavalry; this on July 2. Nor can I refrain from commending the conduct of Captain Thatcher, of the Fourteenth U. S. Infantry, commanding skirmishers on the reconnaissance of July 4.

Very respectfully, your obedient servant,

H. DAY,
Colonel Sixth U. S. Infantry, Commanding Brigade.

ACTING ASSISTANT ADJUTANT-GENERAL,
Headquarters Second Division, Fifth Corps.

P. S.—My horse was killed in the affair of July 2.

[Indorsement.]

HEADQUARTERS SECOND DIVISION,
July 29, 1863.

Respectfully forwarded. So much delay has occurred in getting this paper that I will forward it as a substitute for the report of the brigade commander required by regulations and custom of service from time immemorial.

R. B. AYRES,
Brigadier-General, Commanding.

No. 205.

Report of Capt. Andrew Sheridan, Third U. S. Infantry.

CAMP NEAR WARRENTON, VA.,
July 28, 1863.

SIR: I have the honor to report that this regiment, under the command of Capt. Henry W. Freedley, moved with the division on June 13 from Banks' Ford, and marched to Hartwood Church, Va.; bivouacked near Catlett's Station on the 14th; marched to Manassas Junction on the 15th.

On the 17th, marched to and encamped near Gum Springs.

June 19.—Marched, and bivouacked near Aldie.

June 26.—Marched through Leesburg; crossed the Potomac at Edwards Ferry, and bivouacked 4 miles from the Ferry; left camp about 4 a. m. next day, and marched to camp near Frederick, Md.

June 29.—Bivouacked near Liberty, Md.

June 30.—Marched to camp near Union Mills, Md.

July 1.—Marched to camp near Hanover, Pa.; left at 6 p. m. same day, and marched in the direction of Gettysburg, and bivouacked on the road.

Marched next morning (July 2) near Gettysburg; formed in line of battle, and was engaged with the enemy until 8 p. m.; lost during the engagement of that day 8 killed, 60 wounded, and 2 missing in action.

Capt. Henry W. Freedley, commanding the regiment, was severely wounded; Lieuts. Daingerfield Parker and Stanley Mourton were wounded. After Captain Freedley was wounded, the command of the regiment devolved on Capt. Richard G. Lay. The regiment formed in line of battle, and remained so during July 3.

July 4.—The regiment advanced with the brigade and skirmished with the enemy, losing 1 man; returned from skirmishing and went on front line of picket, where Lieut. George B. Butler was so severely wounded that he lost his right arm. Remained there all night.

July 5.—Relieved from picket duty. At 5 p. m. marched about 5 miles on the Emmitsburg road and encamped. Remained in camp until July 7. Marched at 6 a. m., passing through Creagerstown and Utica, and encamped near Utica.

July 8.—Marched, and bivouacked near Middletown, Md.

July 9.—Marched over South Mountain, and encamped near Boonsborough, Md.

July 10.—Marched to and encamped near Antietam Creek.

July 11.—Left camp and marched about 1 mile; formed line of battle in close column by division, and remained so until about 5 p. m., when the regiment advanced about 1½ miles in line of battle, and bivouacked for the night.

July 12.—Advanced about 1½ miles in line of battle, and remained so all night.

July 13.—Remained in line of battle.

July 14.—Advanced and encamped near Williamsport.

These are the facts as far as I have any knowledge of them, not being present during the engagement.

During the engagements and marches the regiment lost 4 commissioned officers wounded, 8 enlisted men killed, 60 wounded, and 3 missing. *

The following officers were present at the engagement at Gettysburg: Capt. H. W. Freedley, commanding regiment (wounded); Capt. R. G. Lay, acting field officer; First Lieut. Daingerfield Parker, (wounded slightly); First Lieut. John Whitney, acting adjutant; First Lieuts. John H. Page, George B. Butler (severely wounded, arm amputated); Second Lieuts. Isaac A. Helm, George K. Pomeroy, August Kaiser, Stanley Mourton, and William Mitchell.

Very respectfully, your obedient servant,
                              ANDREW SHERIDAN,
          Captain Third U. S. Infantry, Commanding Regiment.

Captain WINTHROP,
          Actg. Asst. Adjt. Gen., First Brigade, Regular Infantry.

No. 206.

Report of Capt. Julius W. Adams, jr., Fourth U. S. Infantry.

HEADQUARTERS FOURTH U. S. INFANTRY,
                              July 17, 1863.

SIR: I have the honor to submit the following report of the operations of the Fourth U. S. Infantry in the engagement fought in and around Gettysburg, Pa., on July 2, 3, and 4:

The night of July 1 was passed on the Hanover and Gettysburg road, 5 miles east of the latter place.

On the morning of July 2, we broke camp at 4 o'clock, and marched 3 miles in a westerly direction. Halting, we there formed line of battle parallel to the road and about half a mile to the right of it. We remained in this position about one hour, when we recrossed the road, and, forming line of battle at right angles to it, moved in the

---

* But see revised statement, p. 179.

direction of Gettysburg. Leaving the city on our right, we halted at about 1 p. m. at about 2 miles from the position of our first line of battle. We lay on our arms here until 4 p. m.; then moving to the front down a road, we took up position in line of battle below the crest of a slight eminence lying between the two ranges of hills occupied, respectively, by our own and the enemy's forces.

We remained here about half an hour, when, in consequence of the troops on our right retiring and thus exposing us to a flank fire, we were ordered to fall back. Retiring across the open ground, we formed line of battle in the edge of the woods skirting the hills occupied by our forces, where we remained until 7 p. m., and then changed our position to one about 300 yards to the left, where we encamped for the night.

In this position we remained all of the 3d and until 10 a. m. on July 4, when we were ordered on a reconnaissance. Forming in line of battle, supporting a line of skirmishers, we advanced to a position about 1½ miles beyond our camp. The object of the reconnaissance being accomplished, we fell back to our original position. From this we moved at 3 p. m., and relieved the Third Division, Fifth Corps, on picket, throwing our picket line half a mile beyond the position previously occupied by them. Here we remained until 5 p. m. on July 5, when we took up our line of march for Emmitsburg, Md.

Our loss in the engagement of July 2 was 9 enlisted men killed, Second Lieut. George Williams and 27 enlisted men wounded. Our casualties on the 4th were, Second Lieut. Samuel T. Crowley and 2 enlisted men wounded.

The officers engaged were, Capt. J. W. Adams, jr., commanding regiment; Second Lieut. John Simons, adjutant; First Lieut. A. R. Benedict, commanding Company C; First Lieut. Thomas A. Martin, commanding Company H; First Lieut. Alexander Carolin, commanding Company F; First Lieut. William S. Collier, commanding Company K; First Lieut. Alexander E. Sheldon; First Lieut. Henry W. Patterson, regimental quartermaster, on temporary duty at brigade headquarters; Second Lieut. Samuel T. Crowley, wounded slightly July 4; Second Lieut. George Williams, severely wounded July 2, right leg amputated; Second Lieuts. John Miller, J. J. Scipio Hassler, George W. Dost, George Atcheson, Gerhard L. Luhn, and Capt. S. M. Sprole, unattached.

I have the honor to state that both the officers and enlisted men behaved with great gallantry during the engagement.

I am, sir, very respectfully, your obedient servant,

JULIUS W. ADAMS, JR.,
Captain Fourth U. S. Infantry, Commanding Regiment.

Capt. F. WINTHROP,
Actg. Asst. Adjt. Gen., First Brigade, Regular Infantry.

No. 207.

Report of Capt. Levi C. Bootes, Sixth U. S. Infantry.

CAMP NEAR BERLIN, FREDERICK COUNTY, MD.,
July 17, 1863.

SIR: I have the honor to report for the information of the colonel commanding the First Brigade, Second Division, Fifth Army Corps, the part taken by the Sixth U. S. Infantry in the operations around Gettysburg, Pa.

The regiment left its bivouac about 4.30 o'clock on the morning of the 2d, and marched to a wood in front of the enemy, where it lay in line of battle for a considerable time.

About 4.30 o'clock I received an order to march the regiment by the left flank to the front and near the pickets of the enemy, where a line of battle by the whole brigade was formed preparatory to advancing on the enemy. The position occupied by the regiment was the extreme left of the line of battle.

The order being soon thereafter given to march, we advanced in line through a small valley to the high ground a short distance in front, under a severe fire from the enemy's pickets and sharpshooters, posted on the hills above us, and protected by trees and rocky cliffs.

The casualties in the regiment were as follows: 4 killed; 1 commissioned officer (Second Lieut. T. Britton) and 39 enlisted men wounded.

The following officers were present, and behaved very well: Capt. J. McCleary, acting field officer; Capt. J. J. Upham, First Lieuts. D. D. Lynn and A. H. Freeman, and Second Lieuts. J. P. Schindel, G. Anderson, regimental adjutant, J. McKim, T. Britton, and J. W. Clous.

I am, sir, very respectfully, your obedient servant,

LEVI C. BOOTES,
Captain Sixth U. S. Infantry, Comdg. Regiment.

ACTING ASSISTANT ADJUTANT-GENERAL,
First Brigade, Second Division, Fifth Army Corps.

No. 208.

Report of Capt. Thomas S. Dunn, Twelfth U. S. Infantry.

HEADQUARTERS TWELFTH INFANTRY BATTALION,
Camp near Berlin, Md., July 16, 1863.

SIR: I have the honor to make the following report of the part taken by the battalion composed of Companies A, B, C, D, and G, of First Battalion, and Companies A, C, and D, Second Battalion, Twelfth U. S. Infantry, under my command, during the operations near Gettysburg, Pa., commencing July 2:

The First Brigade, Second Division, Fifth Army Corps, of which the battalion formed a part, was moved to the front about 5 p. m. on the 2d instant, and took position at the foot of a hill near our extreme left, and immediately in rear of a marsh dividing it from a wood held by the enemy. After remaining in this position under a slight fire of musketry for about fifteen minutes, the brigade advanced through the marsh to a hill immediately under the wood in front, there forming three lines, the Twelfth U. S. Infantry in rear. The men were ordered to lie down. In this position they were exposed to a severe fire from the enemy's sharpshooters, holding a hill to our left and slightly in our rear.

The battalion remained in this position until I received an order to move by the right flank a distance equal to my front. During the execution of this order, the troops on our right having fallen back in some disorder, the enemy rapidly advancing, I received from General Ayres, commanding division, the order to face by the rear rank and march to the position first occupied. The battalion marched to the rear in quick time under a galling fire, in good order, until I received an order to double-quick. This order was obeyed until the battalion reached a stone wall about midway in the valley. I then ordered the left wing to about-face and fire. They delivered their fire, and again joined the right wing, moving to the rear. The battalion was halted on the brow of the hill and faced to the front. The fire gradually slackened as night approached.

About 8 p. m. the regiment moved to the left into the wood in rear of Lieutenant Hazlett's battery. The regiment remained in this position during the 2d and 3d instant.

On the morning of the 4th, the battalion was ordered out with the brigade on a reconnaissance. Captain Winthrop, with his company (B) was sent skirmishing, under command of Captain Thatcher, Fourteenth U. S. Infantry. After moving to the front, across the marsh before mentioned, the regiment and Fourteenth U. S. Infantry were formed into one line, and supported the Third, Fourth, and Sixth U. S. Infantry. While lying down in a clover-field, the enemy opened with artillery upon the line in front, which then moved slowly to the rear through our line. When they were clearly off the field, we were ordered to rise and move to the rear, the object of the reconnaissance being accomplished.

During the whole of the operations our loss was 1 officer (Lieut. Silas A. Miller) and 7 men killed, 3 officers (Lieutenants Liscum, Alston, and Vanvalzah) and 67 men wounded, and 14 men missing; total, 4 officers and 88 men.*

The conduct of both officers and men throughout was entirely satisfactory—the officers giving confidence by their coolness, the men (especially when moving to the rear on the 2d instant under a very heavy fire) exhibiting a steadiness highly commendable.

I am, sir, very respectfully, your obedient servant,

THOMAS S. DUNN,
Captain Twelfth U. S. Infantry, Commanding Battalion.

Capt. F. WINTHROP,
  Actg. Asst. Adjt. Gen., First Brigade, Regular Infantry.

No. 209.

Report of Capt. W. Harvey Brown, Fourteenth U. S. Infantry.

CAMP NEAR ALDIE, VA., *June* 22, 1863.

CAPTAIN: I have the honor to report, in obedience to the instructions I received this morning from you, to take a sufficient force for the purpose of capturing a certain guerrilla party, which was supposed to frequent the house of Dr. Ewell in this vicinity, that I left the camp for that object at 1 a. m., with 100 men and 3 officers (Captain Ilges, Lieuts. P. Collins and Downey) and 30 cavalry, and 3 officers of the Seventeenth Pennsylvania Volunteers, and proceeded out the Aldie and Thoroughfare Gap road to a small church near the headwaters of Bull Run, or about 4 miles from this camp.

---

* But see revised statement, p. 179.

My object was to reach the point before daylight, but the difficulties I encountered in passing our picket line, in addition to the heavy roads, prevented me from accomplishing my purpose until broad daylight. The country being very open, I had but little choice in selecting a favorable position. I placed about half of my cavalry and a portion of the infantry in the rear of the church and at the head of a lane leading to Dr. Ewell's house, which place it was supposed the said party would pass. The balance of my force I stationed on the left of the above-mentioned lane and facing toward the house. But a short time had elapsed after I had made this disposition of my forces until I was informed by one of my men, whom I had placed in a tree, that there was a body of mounted men rapidly approaching. I permitted them to advance within pistol-shot, when we commenced to exchange firing, but almost immediately they fell back at full speed, and, in consequence of the rolling ground on our front, they were for a short time hidden from our view. To make a successful charge under the circumstances was impossible, although we pursued the enemy for about a mile, until they found refuge in the mountains beyond. Nothing was then left me but to return.

I regret to state that the efficiency of the cavalry did not in all respects answer my expectations. I was also much mortified to find that nearly one-half of the guns of the infantry were useless in consequence of defective ammunition, or for the reason that they had been damp before having been loaded, caused, no doubt, by the shower we had during the evening.

Casualties: 1 sergeant killed, Seventeenth Pennsylvania Volunteer Cavalry.

I am, very respectfully, your obedient servant,

W. HARVEY BROWN,
Captain Fourteenth U. S. Infantry, Commanding.

Capt. S. Van Rensselaer, *Assistant Adjutant-General.*

[Indorsements.]

HEADQUARTERS FIRST BRIGADE,
June 22, 1863.

Respectfully forwarded. Although the result of this expedition did not meet my expectations, still, with my present knowledge of facts, I think the commander did what in his judgment he deemed best under the circumstances.

R. B. AYRES,
Brigadier-General, Commanding.

HEADQUARTERS SECOND DIVISION, FIFTH CORPS,
Camp near Aldie, Va., June 23, 1863.

Respectfully forwarded. Captain Brown should have had the foresight to see that his infantry were efficient and their arms in firing condition before leaving camp, especially as the rain of the evening might have led him to expect the result he experienced.

GEO. SYKES,
Major-General, Commanding Division.

HEADQUARTERS FIFTH CORPS,
June 23, 1863.

Respectfully forwarded for the information of the commanding general. This expedition was sent out by my order on information given by a colored man, who stated Mosby had passed this place the morning previous, and had been overheard to tell Dr. Ewell that he would return at sunrise the next day. The result greatly disappointed my expectations, and a court of inquiry, called at the request of the officer commanding the cavalry detachment, will investigate the facts of the case.

GEO. G. MEADE,
Major-General.

No. 210.

Report of Maj. Grotius R. Giddings, Fourteenth U. S. Infantry.

CAMP NEAR BERLIN, MD.,
July 16, 1863.

SIR: In obedience to instructions, I have the honor to forward the following report of the part taken by the Fourteenth U. S. Infantry in the battle at Gettysburg:

The regiment moved from bivouac in the road at 4 a. m. on July 2, and marched forward to a small piece of woods, where it rested until 4 p. m., when it was ordered to the front as a support to the Second Brigade. In obedience to orders, we moved forward to the crest of a small hill, at a short distance in front of which the Second Brigade was engaged, where we were halted and ordered to lie down. While lying there, we suffered severely from the fire of the enemy in our front.

After lying in that position about twenty minutes, I received orders to face the regiment about and fall back, and while in the act of falling back we received a heavy fire of musketry from the rear and right flank, by which we suffered severely; but, falling back in good order, we faced about at the base of a hill in the rear. I soon after received orders to move to the left a short distance, where we bivouacked for the night.

The next day, July 3, we lay under a heavy artillery fire, with orders to hold ourselves in readiness to repel an expected attack on our left, but did not go into action.

At 7 a. m. on July 4, I received orders to hold my command in readiness to proceed upon a reconnaissance, as the brigade was ordered out for that purpose. Leaving camp about 7.30 a. m., we moved nearly a mile to the front, where we halted, skirmishers being ordered to advance and drive in the pickets of the enemy. They were soon engaged, when the Third, Fourth, and Sixth U. S. Infantry were ordered to advance as a support, leaving the Twelfth and Fourteenth U. S. Infantry as a reserve. Soon after, I received an order to advance the Fourteenth through a small piece of woods on the left, in order to ascertain whether the house was occupied by our forces or those of the enemy. Deploying a small line of skirmishers in front of the battalion, I moved forward to within about 50 yards of the house, and halted, Captain Ilges, in charge of the skirmishers, reporting quite a number of wounded, both our own and those of the enemy, inside the house, and also a large quantity of arms at the house. At that time a battery of two guns opened fire upon us with shell at easy range, when I received orders to fall back and join the brigade. Upon joining, we immediately moved back to camp, where we remained a short time, when we were ordered upon picket.

At 4 p. m. of July 5, we were ordered to withdraw the pickets and join the brigade on the march.

As to the behavior of both officers and men, there could not be too much praise given. It is enough to say that not one officer or private but did his whole duty.

Our casualties were:

Officers and men.	Killed.	Wounded.	Total.
July 2:			
Officers		2	2
Enlisted men	17	118	135
July 3:			
Enlisted men		1	1
July 4:			
Enlisted men		3	3
Total*	17	124	141

I have the honor to be, very respectfully, your obedient servant,
G. R. GIDDINGS,
Major, Commanding Fourteenth Regiment U. S. Infantry.

Capt. F. WINTHROP,
Actg. Asst. Adjt. Gen., First Brigade, Regular Infantry.

No. 211.

Report of Col. Sidney Burbank, Second U. S. Infantry, commanding Second Brigade.

HDQRS. SECOND BRIG., SECOND DIV., FIFTH A. C.,
July 21, 1863.

CAPTAIN: I have the honor to report that the brigade under my command, consisting of the Second, Seventh, Tenth, Eleventh, and Seventeenth Regiments U. S. Infantry, after a series of long and rapid marches, arrived in the vicinity of the enemy, near Gettysburg, Pa., on the morning of July 2.

The brigade was formed in line of battle, its left resting on the right of the Twelfth Army Corps. Skirmishers were deployed in front, and the line advanced slowly through a thick woods, behind which it had been deployed, The line halted on the edge of the woods, and remained in that position for an hour or more, the skirmishers feeling for the enemy in front. At the end of this time, I received orders to withdraw the brigade and to establish it in a new position somewhat to the rear. The movement was commenced, but instead of taking up a new position, the brigade continued its march to the left for some 2 miles, when it was halted.

There it remained until about 5 p. m., when, during a heavy cannonading, I received orders to advance, and the brigade took a route to the left. The rapidity of the firing increased, and I was soon met by a staff officer, directing me to move forward with the utmost dispatch. The command was, therefore, moved forward for some time at double-quick, but, fearing to exhaust the men, a little slower step was resumed. We were soon in the vicinity of the enemy, and I

---

* But see revised statement, p. 179.

was directed to deploy into line, the left resting on a battery then in position and its right extending back into the woods. As soon as deployed, the line was moved to the left, to occupy ground supposed to have been left by the Third Brigade; but this brigade was still occupying the ground, and I moved again to the right a short distance.

At this time the brigade occupied on the left the side of an extremely rough and rocky hill, the right extending into the woods and some heavy undergrowth. The whole line moved forward to the foot of the hill and out of the woods to the edge of a wide marsh, extending across its whole front, and soon after across this marsh at double-quick, and ascended to the crest of the hill on the opposite side, and moved forward to some shelter near a woods. At this time the left flank was much exposed to the enemy's sharpshooters, and the left company of the Seventeenth U. S. Infantry was thrown back to confront this fire and to a more secure position under a slight rise of ground.

During this time another army corps (the Second, I think) was advancing across our front and perpendicular to my line, to attack the enemy to the left. In a short time these troops fell back, and, as they did so, I ordered my line forward to a fence and stone wall on the edge of the woods, and near which we had been halting. A regiment of the Second Corps, however, halted after having reached my left, and persisted in holding that position, and did so until I was ordered to relieve it by changing my front to the left and occupy its place, this regiment passing to the rear through intervals in my line.

As soon as this position was obtained, a volley was fired, but there appearing to be no fire on our front, our firing ceased; but at this moment a heavy fire was opened on our right flank, and as I proceeded to make a disposition of the troops to meet this attack, I received orders to retire my brigade. The enemy was seen at this time moving through a wheat-field to our rear, and the brigade was withdrawn as rapidly and in as good order as the nature of the ground would permit. In doing so, however, the troops were exposed to a heavy fire on both flanks, and the loss of officers and men was very severe.

It had now become nearly dark, and the brigade was reformed in rear of the battery and near the ground of its first deployment. Although held in readiness, the brigade was not engaged again during the battle of Gettysburg.

The conduct of both officers and men in this severe contest was deserving of all praise, and was all I could wish. The reports of regimental commanders, with the lists of the casualties, are herewith transmitted.*

I beg leave to state that although the regiments named as composing the brigade preserve their organization, and are called regiments, yet they are greatly reduced in number, and the whole brigade went into action with less than 900 muskets.

Of 80 officers who went into this action, 40 were either killed or wounded, namely, 7 killed and 33 wounded, 1 mortally, since dead, and the proportion among the enlisted men was about the same.

Very respectfully, your obedient servant,

S. BURBANK,
Colonel Second U. S. Infantry, Commanding.

Capt. GEORGE RYAN,
Actg. Asst. Adjt. Gen., Second Div., Fifth Army Corps.

---

* Embodied in revised statement, p. 179.

No. 212.

Report of Maj. Arthur T. Lee, Second U. S. Infantry.

GENERAL HOSPITAL, FIFTH ARMY CORPS,
Near Gettysburg, Pa., July 4, 1863.

SIR: I have the honor to report for the information of the colonel commanding Second Brigade, Fifth Army Corps, the action of the Second Regiment U. S. Infantry in the battle of July 2.

About 3.30 a. m. the regiment marched from its place of bivouac, 5 miles from Gettysburg, advancing right in front by flank, and took position near Gettysburg, about 1½ miles southeast of the town. Twenty men from the regiment were thrown forward as skirmishers into a body of woods, beyond which and to the right could be seen the enemy's pickets.

After a skirmish of nearly two hours, during which there was considerable firing and some casualties, the line was marched by a flank movement to the left and rear some 2 miles, where the command rested until about 5 p. m., at which time I was ordered to march my regiment by the right flank in the direction of heavy cannonading on the left of our line of battle. We were advanced some distance, when the Second Brigade was brought into line, my regiment on the right, to advance down a steep hill and across a marsh about 50 yards wide, ankle-deep and miry, which I did at double-quick, under a severe fire of sharpshooters from the left, right, and front.

Passing the marsh, we reached a rocky and much-exposed elevation of ground, from which we drove, by our rapid advance, a body of sharpshooters through a belt of woods, which we entered. We were then ordered to halt, which we did, taking shelter behind a low stone wall. We could not then advance, as column after column of our infantry was moving across a rye-field in our front, the columns moving perpendicularly to our lines and engaging the enemy on our left. When these columns, one after one, had returned from the field, with the exception of one, which was retiring, my regiment was ordered to advance over the wall and wheel to the left through said field. After having made a half-wheel, we discovered the enemy moving rapidly to outflank us on our right, when the regiment was halted, and ordered to commence firing. The firing was carried on rapidly for some time, and sharply returned by the enemy.

A fresh column of the enemy at this time appearing upon our right, we were ordered to retire. The word was scarcely given when three lines of the enemy, elevated one above the other on the slope to our right, poured in a most destructive fire, almost decimating my regiment and cutting off the color-staff, causing the colors to fall into the hands of the color-bearer. We retired slowly to the shelter of the woods, recrossed the stone wall, rocky rising ground, and marsh in as good order as the ground would admit, under a most withering fire from sharpshooters on the left and a column of the enemy's infantry, which suddenly appeared upon our right and rear, enfilading our whole line, and a perfect storm of shot and shell. Reaching our line of battle on the crest of the hill, and finding myself unable longer to keep the field, from loss of blood, flowing from a wound which I received in the rye-field before we commenced retiring, by advice of a surgeon on the ground I retired, and the command of the regiment devolved upon Captain McKee.

During my participation in this action with the regiment, the men fully sustained their former reputation for gallantry and good conduct.

As I am unable in my present position to ascertain the casualties in the regiment, I respectfully refer you to the report of Captain McKee* for the information.

I desire to speak in the highest praise of the following officers, whose conduct came under my immediate observation, for coolness and earnest action during the engagement: Capt. S. A. McKee, acting field officer; First Lieut. and Adjt. A. W. Kroutinger; Second Lieuts. Francis E. Lacey, wounded (wounded also at Antietam, September 17, 1862), Thomas Byrne, D. W. Burke (wounded), Robert Davis, and James Butler.

To First Lieut. George H. McLoughlin, regimental quartermaster, who, I regret to learn, is wounded, I am deeply indebted, who, aside from his duties as acting aide to the colonel commanding the brigade, rendered me special service during the day. His companions have to deplore the loss of First Lieut. F. C. Goodrich, who fell in the heat of the battle.

I am, sir, very respectfully, your obedient servant,

A. T. LEE,
Major Second U. S. Infantry, Commanding Regiment.

Capt. J. W. Ames,
A. A. A. G., Second Brig., Second Div., Fifth A. C.

No. 213.

Report of Capt. David P. Hancock, Seventh U. S. Infantry.

Camp near Berlin, Md., *July* 17, 1863.

Sir: In compliance with circular, I have the honor to make the following report relative to the late operations of this regiment:

After leaving the Rappahannock and making the usual marches incident to following an advancing enemy, some of them being unusually severe, we arrived in front of the enemy on July 2, having been nineteen days, including all delays, on the march from Benson's Mills.

The regiment formed in line of battle on Rock Hill [Round Top] immediately in front of the enemy at about 5.30 p. m., and at once advanced against him down the hill and across an open field, and remained some minutes under cover of a stone fence inclosing a wood, being then under a slight fire. Shortly after, the part of the brigade the Seventh was in was ordered to cross the fence and wheel to the left, and form in a line perpendicular to the original direction and advance in the woods. This was immediately done, at the same time relieving a brigade already there. Our firing to the front then was slight, as no enemy was apparently visible in that direction. After remaining faced in this direction for a short time, the enemy became visible upon our right flank, and it was apparent he was endeavoring to flank us.

At this juncture we were ordered to retire slowly, which order was obeyed with great reluctance by the men. While retiring, the fire of the enemy became very destructive, and, after recrossing the stone

---

* Not found.

fence and over the open field, became frightful, we receiving there a fire from three different directions. After again reaching the hill, the men were halted and remained in that position, being no more engaged during the operations.

Although the loss during the engagement was frightful, being half of those engaged, I am happy to state that the regiment fell back in good order, and, with one exception, every man missing was finally accounted for as killed or wounded. No prisoners were taken from us. The loss was 1 officer (Lieutenant Miller) killed and 3 wounded; 10 enlisted men killed and 43 wounded;* 116 officers and men went into the engagement.

The names of the officers engaged are, Captain Martin, First Lieutenants Miller and Curtis, Second Lieutenants Cullen, Cole, Crawford, Woodruff, Comba, and Grossman. Lieutenants Woodruff, Comba, and Grossman were wounded.

As all the officers and men did their duty well, it is impossible for me to make individual distinctions in that regard, but I would respectfully remark upon the great coolness, gallantry, and intrepidity of Capt. J. P. Martin, acting field officer, and to his great efficiency in keeping order and preventing confusion in the regiment.

Since the day of the engagement to the present date, nothing of importance has occurred more than is ordinarily incident to a rapid march in the vicinity of the enemy.

I am, respectfully, your obedient servant,

D. P. HANCOCK,
Captain Seventh U. S. Infantry, Commanding Regiment.

Capt. J. W. AMES,
    A. A. A. G., Second Brig., Second Div., Fifth Corps.

No. 214.

Report of Capt. William Clinton, Tenth U. S. Infantry.

CAMP IN THE FIELD, *July* 12, 1863.

CAPTAIN: In compliance with circular from headquarters Second Brigade, Second Division, Fifth Corps, I have the honor to report that the Tenth Regiment U. S. Infantry, numbering 10 commissioned officers and 83 enlisted men, and forming part of the Second Brigade, Second Division, Fifth Corps, was engaged in the battle of Gettysburg, Pa., on July 2.

The regiment, after a long and fatiguing march, arrived in the vicinity of Gettysburg on the morning of the 2d instant. Upon reaching the right of our lines, a portion of the regiment had been detailed as skirmishers, and deployed in front of the brigade. The skirmishers kept up a brisk fire upon the enemy's pickets (who were driven in) until the brigade was ordered to the left. We moved at a rapid pace, part of the time at double-quick, until we arrived nearly opposite the center, where we halted and lay over until the afternoon, when we again proceeded to the left in rapid time and formed line of battle.

As soon as the line of battle was formed, we advanced upon the enemy, who was in considerable force about 300 or 400 yards in front

---

* But see revised statement, p. 179.

of us. His sharpshooters were posted to our left and front, upon a high point of ground, and protected by immense rocks. They did us considerable injury, as we were unable at the time to dislodge them. The enemy was driven from his position, which we held until he had been re-enforced and advanced against our right flank, which he turned. The enemy now opened a destructive fire upon our men, who were far inferior as to numbers. We then received orders to retire. The roar of musketry was so extensive that a great portion of our command did not hear the order to fall back until some minutes after it had been given. The enemy at this time was in front and on both our flanks. A portion of our corps coming to our assistance, drove the enemy in turn, and compelled him to retreat in great disorder. Our battery also opened upon him with grape and canister, slaughtering and driving him beyond his former position.

The conduct of both officers and men is worthy of all praise. They did their duty nobly, and as they vied with each other in the performance of their duty, I cannot mention specially any names without doing injustice to the balance.

I am grieved to report our loss as being very extensive. Of 10 officers and 83 enlisted men who were engaged with the enemy, 1 commissioned officer and 13 enlisted men were killed on the field, and 5 commissioned officers and 29 enlisted men wounded, with 3 missing in action. Three of the men who were wounded have since died, and a large number of the remainder are severely wounded. Inclosed is a list of casualties.*

I am, sir, very respectfully, your obedient servant,

WM. CLINTON,
Captain Tenth U. S. Infantry, Commanding Regiment.

Capt. J. W. AMES,
A. A. A. G., Second Brig., Second Div., Fifth Corps.

No. 215.

Report of Maj. De Lancey Floyd-Jones, Eleventh U. S. Infantry.

CAMP NEAR BERLIN, MD.,
July 16, 1863.

CAPTAIN: In obedience to the circular from brigade headquarters, I have the honor to furnish in brief a report of the operations of the Eleventh U. S. Infantry at the battle of Gettysburg, on the 2d instant.

In company with the other battalions of the brigade, we moved about 5 p. m. from our resting place, nearly opposite the center of the army, to near the Sugar Loaf or Round Top Mountain, a point near the left of the line.

Immediately upon reaching this, we were ordered to advance in line of battle, passing from the shelter of a wood across an open field, through which ran a heavy morass. We advanced in good order, although exposed to a flank fire from the enemy, and halted immediately in front of a piece of woods, where we lay some half hour or more. Our brigade then relieved some troops of the Second Corps, for which purpose we advanced into the woods, at the same time changing our direction by a wheel to the left.

---

*Embodied in revised statement, p. 179.

After firing a few rounds in the woods, it was discovered that the enemy was turning our right flank, and we were ordered to fall back, which was done in good order until we reached half way across the open field, when we became exposed to a cross-fire of the enemy, the effect of which was most deadly upon officers and men.

Our loss up to this time had been comparatively slight, but in a few minutes we lost nearly half of the regiment, and that, too, without inflicting the slightest damage upon the enemy. We finally reached the wood, when we were enabled to reform and face the enemy.

Our loss in this engagement was fearful. Out of 261 enlisted men and 25 officers, the regiment lost 106 enlisted men and 10 commissioned officers, among the latter some of our best officers. Capt. Thomas O. Barri was wounded early in the retreat, and while being kindly assisted to the rear by Lieut. Herbert Kenaston, Eleventh U. S. Infantry, both were struck down. The former lived long enough to die in the arms of his companions. In their loss the regiment mourns two gallant officers. The former had particularly endeared himself by his social and amiable qualities. Second Lieut. Henry Rochford, a promising young officer, fell about the same time, mortally wounded.

The following is a list of the officers who still survive their wounds: First Lieut. Matthew Elder and Second Lieut. A. J. Barber, legs amputated above the knee; Second Lieut. Lemuel Pettee, leg shattered above the ankle; Second Lieut. O. H. Nealy, wounded in neck; Capt. J. M. Goodhue, finger amputated; Capt. W. G. Edgerton, wounded by spent ball (for duty), and Second Lieut. A. A. Harbach, struck in thigh, not seriously.

Where all did so well it is difficult to particularize. I therefore give the names of those officers who participated, in addition to those already enumerated: Capts. George Gibson, C. S. Russell, and Caleb R. Layton; First Lieuts. E. A. Ellsworth, G. E. Head, I. B. Wright, James P. Pratt, Joseph M. Ritner, and F. A. Field, battalion adjutant, and Second Lieuts. E. S. Huntington, R. Robins, J. McIntosh, Wright Staples, and David Hazzard. Captain Gibson joined us from detached service in time to take part.

Respectfully,

DE L. FLOYD-JONES,
Major Eleventh U. S. Infantry, Comdg. Regiment.

ACTING ASSISTANT ADJUTANT-GENERAL,
Second Brigade, Second Division, Fifth Corps.

No. 216.

Report of Lieut. Col. J. Durell Greene, Seventeenth U. S. Infantry.

CAMP NEAR PURCELLVILLE, VA., *July* 19, 1863.

CAPTAIN: I have the honor to report that the Seventeenth U. S. Infantry, under my command, numbering 25 officers and 235 enlisted men, and forming a portion of the Second Brigade, Second Division, Fifth Army Corps, was engaged in the battle of Gettysburg, July 2.

The regiment formed the left of the brigade line, and went into action at 6 p. m. From the position in line, the nature of the ground passed over, and other circumstances, the regiment suffered severely from the fire of the enemy, as the list of casualties, recently forwarded, will show. The regiment was engaged in all about two hours, and retired with the brigade.

The regiment mourns as killed First Lieut. W. H. Chamberlin, and Second Lieut. E. S. Abbot, mortally wounded, young officers, but recently promoted from the ranks.

Both officers and men behaved with just credit under the trying circumstances in which they were placed. I particularly remarked Capt. E. H. Ludington, Company B, Second Battalion; First Lieut. A. Menzies, adjutant First Battalion, and Second Lieut. F. E. Stimpson, acting battalion quartermaster, as distinguished for coolness and gallantry.

I am, sir, very respectfully, your obedient servant,
                                       J. DURELL GREENE,
           Lieut. Col. Seventeenth U. S. Infantry, Commanding.

Capt. J. W. Ames,
    A. A. A. G., Second Brig., Second Div., Fifth Corps.

No. 217.

Report of Col. Kenner Garrard, One hundred and forty-sixth New York Infantry, commanding Third Brigade.

HDQRS. THIRD BRIG., SECOND DIV., FIFTH ARMY CORPS,
                Camp near Berlin, Md., July 16, 1863.

SIR: I have the honor to make the following report of the part taken by the Third Brigade in the late battle near Gettysburg:

On the 2d instant, after changing position several times in the early part of the morning, the brigade with the division remained idle, lying by their arms until about 4 p. m. At this time the brigade was moved rapidly forward (most of the time at the double-quick) nearly 1½ miles, when it came under the fire of the enemy's musketry.

At this point the leading regiment, under the direction of General Warren, chief engineer Army of the Potomac, was led to the left, up on what is known as Round Top ridge. Hazlett's battery ascended the ridge immediately in rear of this regiment (the One hundred and fortieth New York Volunteers, Col. P. H. O'Rorke commanding), and went into battery on the summit. The One hundred and fortieth was formed in line, and was immediately closely engaged with the enemy at short musket-range on the left slope of the ridge.

A portion of the First Division, Fifth Army Corps, was engaged to the left of the ridge, and this regiment and Hazlett's battery were brought up to assist the First Division in repelling a heavy assault of the enemy, with the evident design of gaining this ridge. Colonel O'Rorke was mortally wounded at the head of his regiment while leading it into action.

The other regiments—One hundred and forty-sixth New York Volunteers and the Ninety-first and One hundred and fifty-fifth Pennsylvania Volunteers—were led to the right and front some distance, and formed in line in a narrow valley to support a portion of the Third Corps and Watson's battery, then severely pressed by the enemy. Before becoming engaged, however, orders were received for these regiments to return at double-quick to Round Top ridge, and secure and hold that position. The Ninety-first was posted on the left of the battery, connecting with the One hundred and fortieth. The One hundred and forty-sixth and One hundred and fifty-fifth were posted on the right, extending from the battery on the summit, along the crest of the ridge, to the gorge on the right.

As soon as the regiments had their positions, men from each regiment were advanced down the slope to the front, in among the rocks, and, together with those in line on the crest, actively engaged the enemy during the rest of that day. At night this ridge, naturally strong, was strengthened by building a stone wall about half way down the slope, wherever the rocks offered no protection to the men.

The next day the brigade remained in the same position, and, though under the shells of the enemy and exposed to their sharp-shooters, it was not engaged to any extent.

When the brigade and Hazlett's battery seized this ridge, it was done under a heavy musketry fire, and was entirely unoccupied, excepting by a part of the First Division, on the extreme left, and I am gratified to report to the general commanding the division that the order to secure and hold this ridge was faithfully executed. At no time during July 2, 3, and 4, after its position was assigned it, did any regiment of the brigade leave its place, excepting at the time of the heavy assault a portion of some of the regiments advanced to the front down the slope of the ridge, in order to have a better fire at the enemy.

A few moments after General Weed, the brigade commander, had placed his command in position on this ridge, he was mortally wounded on the summit, near the battery. Lieutenant Hazlett, commanding the battery, while offering his assistance to General Weed, fell, mortally wounded.

I am pleased to report that all the regiments performed their duty well, and that during the two days' battle the officers and men conducted themselves in the most praiseworthy manner.

A report of the casualties has already been furnished.*

Very respectfully, your obedient servant,

K. GARRARD,
Col. One hundred and forty-sixth N. Y. Vols., Comdg. Brig.
Capt. GEORGE RYAN,
A. A. A. G., Second Division, Fifth Army Corps.

No. 218.

Reports of Brig. Gen. Samuel W. Crawford, U. S. Army, commanding Third Division.

HDQRS. PA. RESERVES, THIRD DIV., FIFTH CORPS,
July 10, 1863.

COLONEL: I have the honor to submit the following report of the operations of this division in the recent battle near Gettysburg, Pa.:

At daylight on the 2d instant, while resting my command near Mc-Sherrystown, having marched nearly all the previous night, I re-

---

* Embodied in revised statement, p. 180.

ceived an order from the major-general commanding the corps to march immediately toward Gettysburg. The column was put in motion at once, and by noon had arrived at the position occupied by the First and Second Divisions of the corps, near the Gettysburg and Hanover turnpike.

At 2 o'clock an order reached me to form my command at once, and proceed toward the left flank of our line, when my position would be indicated by a staff officer. The First Division of the corps, which I had been directed to follow, had taken a different road from that indicated to me. Under the guidance, however, of Captain Moore, an aide of the general commanding the army, who had come from the field for fresh troops, I pushed rapidly forward, and arrived in a short time upon the field, and reported to Major-General Sykes. I received orders at once to mass my troops upon the right of a road running through our line, near our left flank, and which, descending a rocky slope, crossed a low marshy ground in front to a wheat-field lying between two thick belts of woods beyond.

The position occupied by our troops on the left was naturally a strong one. A rocky ridge, wooded at the top, extended along the left of our position, ending in a high hill, called the Round Top, whose sides, covered with timber, terminated abruptly in the plain below, while the entire ridge sloped toward a small stream that traversed the marshy ground in front. Beyond this lay two thick masses of timber, separated by a large wheat-field, and skirting this timber a low stone wall ran from right to left.

, The movement indicated had not been completed when I received a subsequent order to cross the road to the slope of the rocky ridge opposite the woods, and to cover the troops then engaged in front, should it become necessary for them to fall back. In carrying out this order, I received instructions to detach one brigade of my command, to go to the left of Barnes' division, on the crest of the ridge. The Third Brigade, under Col. J. W. Fisher, was detailed, and moved at once. The firing in front was heavy and incessant. The enemy, concentrating his forces opposite the left of our line, was throwing them in heavy masses upon our troops, and was steadily advancing.

Our troops in front, after a determined resistance, unable to withstand the force of the enemy, fell back, and some finally gave way. The plain to my front was covered with fugitives from all divisions, who rushed through my lines and along the road to the rear. Fragments of regiments came back in disorder, and without their arms, and for a moment all seemed lost. The enemy's skirmishers had reached the foot of the rocky ridge; his columns were following rapidly.

My command was formed in two lines, the second massed on the first. The Sixth Regiment, Lieutenant-Colonel Ent, on the right, the First Regiment, Colonel Talley, on the left, and the Eleventh Regiment, of Fisher's brigade, under Colonel Jackson, in the center. The second line consisted of the First Rifles (Bucktails), Colonel Taylor, and the Second Regiment, Lieutenant-Colonel Woodward. Colonel McCandless, the brigade commander, commanded the whole.

Not a moment was to be lost. Uncovering our front, I ordered an immediate advance. The command advanced gallantly with loud cheers. Two well-directed volleys were delivered upon the advancing masses of the enemy, when the whole column charged at a run down the slope, driving the enemy back across the space beyond and across the stone wall, for the possession of which there was a short but determined struggle. The enemy retired to the wheat-field and the woods.

The second line was immediately deployed to the left, the First Rifles (Bucktails), under their gallant leader, Colonel Taylor, gaining the flank and dashing upon the enemy, who, endeavoring for a moment to make a stand, finally broke and fled in disorder across the field, leaving his dead and wounded in our hands. As night was approaching, and my flanks were unprotected, I directed Colonel Mc-Candless to hold the line of the stone wall and the woods on the right. Heavy lines of skirmishers were thrown out, and the ground firmly and permanently held.

I then rode to the left, toward Fisher's brigade. Upon ascending the crest of the ridge, I found, from the report of that officer, as well as from Colonel Rice, of Barnes' division, that the Round Top was still in possession of the enemy's skirmishers, who were firing upon our men.

It was important to hold this hill, as from its position it commanded that part of our line. I directed Colonel Fisher to occupy it at once. He immediately detached the Twelfth Regiment, under Colonel Hardin, the Fifth, under Lieutenant-Colonel Dare, and the Twentieth Maine Regiment, under Colonel Chamberlain, who advanced promptly, driving the enemy before them, capturing over 30 prisoners.

During the night the division commanded by Brigadier-General Bartlett, of the Sixth Corps, was moved up to my support. At 5 o'clock on the 3d, I received orders from General Sykes, commanding the corps, to advance that portion of my command which was holding the ground retaken on the left, and which still held the line of the stone wall in front, to enter the woods, and, if possible, drive out the enemy. It was supposed that the enemy had evacuated the position.

I proceeded at once to the spot, and directed the movement to be made. McCandless' brigade, with the Eleventh Regiment, under Colonel Jackson, were ordered to advance, throwing out skirmishers toward the right in the direction of a battery established by the enemy at noon, and which was plainly visible. I requested Brigadier-General Bartlett to move up one of his regiments to the stone wall from which I advanced, and also to throw a force toward my right, to protect that flank. The men of his command moved promptly into position, and rendered efficient service. The movement had hardly begun before this battery opened with grape and canister. The woods on the right were soon cleared; as soon as the skirmishers approached the battery, it ceased firing and fled.

The line was then formed, and, under the immediate direction of Colonel McCandless, dashed across the wheat-field and into the upper end of the woods. The enemy's skirmishers were driven back as he advanced, and the upper end of the woods was now cleared. The command then changed front to rear, and charged through the entire length of woods. One brigade of the enemy, commanded by Brigadier-General [George T.] Anderson and composed of Georgia troops, was encountered. It had taken position behind a stone wall running through the woods, and which they had made stronger by rails and logs. We fell upon their flank, completely routing them, taking over 200 prisoners, one stand of colors belonging to the Fifteenth Georgia, and many arms. The colors were taken by Sergt. John B.

Thompson, Company G, First Rifles.*   Another brigade, under General Robertson, and composed of Texas troops, which lay concealed beyond the woods and near the foot of the ridge, ran, as reported by the prisoners, without firing a shot.

The enemy's force at this point (his extreme right) consisted of the division of Major-General Hood, and was composed of three brigades, under the rebel Generals Anderson, [J. B.] Robertson, and [H. L.] Benning.   They very greatly outnumbered us, but the rapidity of the movement and the gallant dash of my men completely surprised and routed them.   They fell back nearly a mile to a second ridge, and intrenched themselves.   By this charge of McCandless' brigade and the Eleventh Regiment, Colonel Jackson, the whole of the ground lost the previous day was retaken, together with all of our wounded, who, mingled with those of the rebels, were lying uncared for.

The dead of both sides lay in lines in every direction, and the large number of our own men showed how fierce had been the struggle and how faithfully and how persistently they had contested for the field against the superior masses of the enemy.

The result of this movement was the recovery of all the ground lost by our troops, one 12-pounder Napoleon gun and three caissons, and upward of 7,000 stand of arms.   Large piles of these arms were found on brush heaps, ready to be burned.

Our wounded were at once cared for, and, under the able and prompt management of Surg. L. W. Read, surgeon-in-chief of this division, who came promptly upon the field, they were moved to hospitals in the rear, and carefully provided for.

On the 4th, the large number of arms were collected, under the immediate direction of Lieutenant Harding, the ordnance officer of the division, and the brigade, which had been on incessant duty for forty-eight hours, under an annoying picket fire for a great period of the time, was withdrawn to the rear.

My list in killed and wounded was 20 officers and 190 men, 3 only missing.

The nominal and tabular list † is inclosed.

Col. Charles Fred. Taylor, the gallant and brave leader of the Bucktail Regiment, fell while leading his regiment to the charge. No braver soldier and patriot has given his life to the cause.

The gallant men of this division fought upon their own soil—some of them at their very homes; and there was not an officer or private soldier who did not realize that the very contingency to meet which the division was formed had now arisen.   The result is evinced in the gallantry displayed by those who were fortunate enough to enter the field when our left was overpowered and the enemy was boldly advancing upon the key of our position.

Great credit is due to Col. William McCandless, commanding the First Brigade, for his management of his brigade and the prompt and faithful execution of the order given to him in the face of a galling fire on the 2d, and for the rapid and successful dash upon the enemy on the 3d, and I recommend him especially to the notice of the major-general commanding the corps.

To Colonel Fisher, commanding the Third Brigade, great credit is also due in early realizing the importance of the occupation of the

---

* A medal of honor awarded to Sergeant Thompson for this service.
† Embodied in revised statement, p. 180.

Round Top and in promptly and successfully occupying it. The enemy would undoubtedly have occupied it during the night.

The prompt and efficient support given to me by Brigadier-General Bartlett, commanding division, Sixth Corps, I desire here to acknowledge.

The officers of my staff accompanied me throughout the action. Captain [Louis] Livingston, my senior aide; Captain [Richard T.] Auchmuty, assistant adjutant-general; Major [James P.] Speer, inspector-general, and Lieutenant [Richard P.] Henderson, aide-de-camp, accompanied the command on the charge and were among the foremost.

Captain Livingston and Lieutenant Henderson are deserving of especial commendation for the prompt and fearless conveyance of orders intrusted to them on the 3d, under the immediate fire of the enemy's battery.

Lieutenant [William] Harding, the ordnance officer, managed his department with great credit, and promptly moved from the field a large proportion of the small-arms secured. His report has already been submitted.

Very respectfully, your obedient servant,

S. W. CRAWFORD,
Brigadier-General, Comdg. Third Division.

Lieut. Col. FRED. T. LOCKE,
Assistant Adjutant-General, Fifth Army Corps.

—

HEADQUARTERS PENNSYLVANIA RESERVES,
Near Gettysburg, Pa., July 4, 1863.

COLONEL: I have the honor to report the following list of arms captured on the 2d and 3d instant by my command:

First Brigade:

Enfield rifles	469
Springfield rifles	741
Smooth-bore, caliber .69	207
Austrian rifles, caliber .54	99
Remington rifles, caliber .54	15
Fowling pieces	2
French rifles	96
Springfield rifles, caliber .69	53
Springfield rifled muskets, caliber .58 (issued to Colonel Penrose, Fifteenth New Jersey Volunteers)	239
Stacked on battle-field	1,151

Third Brigade:

Pieces unassorted	600
Total	3,672

The assorted arms are mostly in good order. In addition, I have to report the capture of one Napoleon gun and three caissons.

The ammunition was used or destroyed on the field.

I have the honor to be, very respectfully, yours,

S. W. CRAWFORD,
Brigadier-General, Commanding Division.

Lieutenant-Colonel LOCKE,
Assistant Adjutant-General.

No. 219.

Report of Col. William McCandless, Second Pennsylvania Reserves, commanding First Brigade.

HDQRS. FIRST BRIGADE, PENNSYLVANIA RESERVES,
Near South Mountain, July 9, 1863.

SIR: I have the honor to forward the following report of the part taken by my command in the action of the 2d and 3d instant, near Gettysburg, Pa.:

After a week of continuous marching, the command arrived on the field about 1 p. m. of the 2d instant, and at 5 p. m. was assigned a position near the left, that being the point against which the enemy had massed a heavy force.

Our first position was naturally strong, being a rocky, wooded hillside, with good cover, sloping steeply down to a plain, which extended from the base about 700 yards to a stone wall. This plain was marshy and difficult to cross; over it, however, the enemy passed his infantry in a disordered mass, driving our forces back on my position.

I immediately formed my brigade, together with the Eleventh Regiment of the Third Brigade, in two lines, the first line being composed of the Sixth Regiment on the right, the First on the left, and the Eleventh in the center. The second line was massed on the first, and was composed of the First Rifles (Bucktails) and Second Regiment of Infantry. As soon as our front was uncovered, the brigade advanced in gallant style, the first line delivering one volley; then the whole brigade charged at a full run down the hillside and across the plain, driving the advancing masses of the enemy back upon the stone wall, for the possession of which there was a desperate struggle, we finally carrying it. . Prior to reaching the wall, however, my left flank being exposed to a galling fire, I deployed the second line, viz, the First Rifles and Second Regiment, to the left, forming a prolongation of my first line, along with which they steadily advanced. It was at this time, and when within a short distance of the wall, that the brave and lamented Col. Charles F. Taylor fell, while gallantly leading his regiment.

Being ordered not to advance beyond the stone wall, I formed a line along it, threw a strong line of skirmishers on my front, and flankers on my right and left. I remained in this position up to 6 p. m. of the 3d instant, the enemy occasionally shelling the position without effect.

On the evening of the 3d instant, I was ordered to advance and clear the woods on my front and left, to do which the command had to cross an open field about 800 yards wide. The enemy, noticing this movement, opened a battery directly in front. I pushed the Sixth Regiment through the woods on the right, and drove out the enemy's skirmishers, and annoyed the gunners, causing the battery to slacken its fire, and, as the remaining regiments of the brigade charged in line, and at a run across the open field, they compelled the enemy to retire. Having cleared the woods in front, and finding a line of the enemy in the woods on my left and at right angles therewith, I faced my command by the rear rank, and charged the enemy directly on the left flank, routing him, capturing nearly 200 prisoners (among whom was a lieutenant-colonel), also a stand of colors. The field was strewed with small-arms, 2,000 or 3,000 in number, the majority of which had been piled on brush heaps, ready to be burned.

The enemy took up a new position on a wooded ridge about half a mile in advance of our front, and were busy during the night chopping timber and fortifying.

About noon of the 4th instant, I was relieved by fresh troops, and moved back to my former position at the stone wall.

I cannot close this report without calling special attention to the gallantry displayed by both officers and men of this command who were fortunate enough to enter the field when our left was overpowered and the enemy was boldly advancing on the key of our position.

I am, sir, very respectfully, yours, &c.,

WM. McCANDLESS,
Colonel, Comdg. First Brigade, Pennsylvania Reserves.

Capt. R. T. AUCHMUTY,
    Assistant Adjutant-General.

No. 220.

Report of Col. Joseph W. Fisher, Fifth Pennsylvania Reserves, commanding Third Brigade.

HDQRS. THIRD BRIGADE, PENNSYLVANIA RESERVE CORPS,
    July 9, 1863.

SIR: I have the honor to report that at the recent battle of Gettysburg I marched my brigade to the left of General Sykes' corps, being the extreme left of the Army of the Potomac, and at once engaged the enemy, although very shortly afterward he retired, leaving large numbers of his killed and wounded on the field.

Soon after the close of the fight of the 2d, I discovered in my immediate front a hill called Round Top, from the summit of which the enemy was doing us great damage. I thought it highly important that we should at once occupy it. I accordingly took two regiments of my brigade, viz, the Fifth, Lieutenant-Colonel Dare, and the Twelfth, Colonel Hardin, and the Twentieth Maine, commanded by Colonel Chamberlain, and at 10 p. m. ascended the hill, which was occupied by a full brigade of the enemy. We went up steadily in line of battle, taking over 30 prisoners in our ascent.

In the morning I discovered that the hill was of immense importance to us, inasmuch as that if we had not taken it the enemy most undoubtedly would have done so, and in that event our left would have suffered very much, if, indeed, it could have held its position at all. I also discovered that our troops were not well posted for defense, so I changed my position, throwing the left flank of the two regiments which had not gone up the hill around so as to completely cover the ravine between the two hills, and at once threw up a stone wall across the entire ravine and up the hill, thus giving my men a sure protection against any advance which could possibly have been made by the enemy.

My officers and men behaved throughout with great coolness and bravery. Among others equally worthy of and deserving special mention, I beg leave to call your attention to the conduct of Colonel Hardin, of the Twelfth Regiment, who, still suffering from wounds received at Bull Run, went gallantly up the mountain, leading his regiment to where hot work was expected; Lieutenant-Colonel Dare, of the Fifth Regiment, who was also wounded at Fredericksburg, led his regiment up the hill, over rocks and ravines; Colonel Warner, of the Tenth Regiment, who is still so lame from wounds received at Antietam as to be unable to walk without support, went into the engagement against my wishes, and behaved with great coolness and courage; Lieutenant-Colonel Snodgrass, of the Ninth, evinced all the elements of a soldier in his calm and dignified demeanor, while all the subordinate field officers are deserving of special mention, especially Maj. James H. Larrimer, of the Fifth Regiment, who, suffering from acute rheumatism, refused to remain out of the battle, although, in my judgment, unfit for duty.

The members of my staff—Lieutenant [John L.] Wright, acting assistant adjutant-general; Captain [Hartley] Howard, brigade inspector; Lieutenants [Charles K.] Chamberlain and [William H. H.] Kerns, aides—all rendered me efficient support. Sergt. Thomas M. Fisher, acting as one of my orderlies, deserves special mention as exhibiting most remarkable coolness and bravery.

My brigade captured and turned in to the proper officer over 1,000 stand of arms, brought off over 200 wounded rebels, and buried 80 of their dead. Taking it all in all, I have no hesitation in saying that my brigade fulfilled their mission to Gettysburg.

[J. W. FISHER,
Colonel, Commanding Third Brigade.]

No. 221.

Reports of Capt. Augustus P. Martin, Third Massachusetts Battery, commanding Artillery Brigade, Fifth Army Corps.

HDQRS. ARTILLERY BRIGADE, FIFTH ARMY CORPS,
Camp near Warrenton, Va., July 31, 1863.

GENERAL: I have the honor to submit the following report of the operations of the Artillery Brigade, Fifth Corps, at the battle of Gettysburg, Pa.:

The artillery entered the field between 4 and 5 p. m. on the 2d instant, three batteries in rear of the First Division, viz: Battery D, Fifth U. S. Artillery, First Lieut. Charles E. Hazlett commanding; Battery C, Massachusetts Artillery, First Lieut. Aaron F. Walcott commanding, and Battery I, Fifth U. S. Artillery, First Lieut. M. F. Watson commanding. Two batteries in rear of the Second Division, viz: Battery L, First Ohio Artillery, Capt. Frank C. Gibbs commanding, and Battery C, First New York Artillery, Capt. Almont Barnes commanding.

On the 2d instant, about 4.30 p. m., Battery D, Fifth U. S. Artillery, was moved to the left of the First Division about three-quarters of a mile, and posted on an eminence known as Rock Hill [Round Top], forming a line nearly perpendicular to that of the First Division. Immediately upon taking up the position, the battery opened upon the enemy, who was engaging the First Division, completely enfilading the enemy's lines with marked effect. The battery kept up a continuous fire until dark.

On the 3d instant, the battery opened upon the enemy at intervals during the day, whenever he made his appearance in force.

The battery remained in position until the 5th instant, when it was withdrawn, and took up the line of march with the corps. First Lieut. B. F. Rittenhouse says:.

The battery had been engaged only about an hour, when First Lieut. Charles E. Hazlett (who commanded the battery) was shot in the head. He was carried to the rear, and died at 8 p. m. In his death the Government has lost one of its bravest and most able officers.

Second Lieuts. Charles H. Carroll and Samuel Peeples, Fifth U. S. Artillery, serving with Battery D, the latter having reported to this battery on the 3d instant, after the battery with which he was serving (Battery I, Fifth U. S. Artillery) was disabled, deserve especial mention for their services during the engagement; also First Lieut. B. F. Rittenhouse, upon whom the command of the battery devolved after the death of the lamented Hazlett, deserves credit for the manner in which the battery was served. The battery lost in killed, 1 officer and 6 men; in wounded, 6 men.

Battery C, Massachusetts Artillery, and I, Fifth U. S. Artillery, were left in rear of the line of battle of the First Division, with instructions to await orders. When positions had been selected and orders sent for the batteries to move to the front, they were not to be found. Subsequently Battery C, Massachusetts Artillery, was found in rear of the Third Corps. The officer commanding reported that he had been ordered there by an officer of General Sickles' staff, who had orders to take any batteries he could find, no matter where they belonged. Battery I, Fifth U. S. Artillery, was taken in the same way, thus depriving the Fifth Corps of its proper amount of artillery.

Battery C, Massachusetts Artillery, not having been relieved until about dark, was not put in position with the Fifth Corps. The battery lost 6 men slightly wounded, a list of which is inclosed ; also 2 horses killed and 4 wounded.

Battery I, Fifth U. S. Artillery, was placed in position by some unknown officer of the Third Corps. Second Lieutenant MacConnell, upon whom the command of the battery devolved when Lieutenant Watson was wounded, says:

The battery was without support of any kind. The enemy appeared shortly—say twenty minutes—after taking position, nearly in front, at a distance of about 350 yards, and the battery immediately opened on them with shell. As they approached nearer, the battery poured in canister, some twenty rounds, until men and horses were shot down or disabled to such an extent that the battery was abandoned.

It was, however, soon recaptured by the bravery and determination of Second Lieut. Samuel Peeples, Fifth U. S. Artillery, who, having procured the services of the Garibaldi Guards, took a musket and led the charge himself, driving the enemy from the guns, and retaking everything that was lost, and conveyed it safely to the rear.

Second Lieutenant MacConnell says:

First Lieut. M. F. Watson, commanding the battery, was wounded in the opening of the engagement, while in the faithful discharge of his duties. The conduct of officers and men throughout was unexceptionable.

He also says:

I would particularly notice the gallantry of Second Lieutenant Peeples and First Sergt. Lemuel Smith. The former I would most respectfully recommend for a brevet first lieutenancy, and the latter, in my opinion, is most deserving of promotion.

On the 3d instant, the battery was reported unserviceable, and General Sykes, commanding corps, directed Lieutenant MacConnell, with the approval of Brigadier-General Hunt, chief of artillery, Army of the Potomac, to go to Westminster, Md. It subsequently moved to Frederick City, Md., where Lieutenant MacConnell received orders from headquarters Army of the Potomac to report with the battery to Washington for re-equipment. The battery lost in killed, wounded, and missing, 1 officer and 21 men, a list of which is herewith inclosed; also 41 horses. The report of ammunition expended is not included in the report of the battery commandant.

Battery L, First Ohio Artillery, Capt. F. C. Gibbs, moved up to the field in rear of the Second Division. One section, commanded by First Lieutenant Guthrie, was posted on the slope of the hill known as Rock Hill [Round Top], to the right of Battery D, Fifth U. S. Artillery. Another section, under command of First Lieutenant Walworth, was posted at the base of the hill, commanding the ravine in front of Rock Hill [Round Top]. The remaining section was held in reserve. The two sections posted in front opened upon the enemy, when he advanced upon our lines, with spherical case and canister, doing good service in checking the advance of the enemy.

First Lieut. H. F. Guthrie and his section deserve special mention for the splendid manner in which the section was served.

On the 3d instant, the section in reserve was posted on the slope of the hill between Battery D, Fifth U. S. Artillery, and First Lieutenant Guthrie's section. This battery did not open upon the enemy on the 3d instant, they being out of range of light 12-pounder guns. The battery lost 2 men severely wounded; also 1 horse killed and 4 wounded.

Battery C, First New York Artillery, Capt. Almont Barnes, took up position on the right of Battery L, First Ohio Artillery, with instructions not to fire until orders reached him to do so, the First and Second Divisions being in line covering his front. The battery remained in position under fire until the fighting ceased, without firing a shot or losing anything in men, horses, or *matériel*.

At 3 a. m. on the 3d instant, in compliance with orders, Captain Barnes reported with Battery C, Massachusetts Artillery, and Battery C, First New York Artillery, to Brigadier-General Howe, commanding division in the Sixth Corps, and moved to the extreme left of the line, and there remained in position without being engaged until the close of the engagement.

Very respectfully, your obedient servant,

A. P. MARTIN,
Captain, Commanding Artillery Brigade, Fifth Corps.

Brigadier-General HUNT,
Chief of Artillery, Army of the Potomac.

———

———, ———, 1863.

Revised report of casualties in the Artillery Brigade, Fifth Corps, at the battle of Gettysburg, Pa., July 2 and 3: Killed, 9; wounded, 33, and missing, 2. Total, 44.*

A. P. MARTIN,
Captain, Commanding Artillery Brigade, Fifth Corps.

* But see revised statement, p. 180.

No. 222.

Report of Capt. Frank C. Gibbs, Battery L, First Ohio Light Artillery.

GETTYSBURG, PA.,
July 4, 1863.

DEAR SIR: I have the honor to report the following as the operations of Battery L, First Ohio Light Artillery, in the Gettysburg campaign:

While in position guarding Banks' Ford, on the Rappahannock, 7 miles above Fredericksburg, Va., supported by the Forty-fourth New York Infantry, I received orders to be ready to move at a moment's notice, and on the night of June 13 I started on the line of march with the Fifth Corps, Army of the Potomac, passing through Manassas Junction and crossing the Potomac River at Edwards Ferry on pontoons, and thence to Gettysburg. Marching nearly all night of July 1, we went into position about 8 a. m. on the morning of the 2d, to the right of the Baltimore pike, in a field of wheat, being thrown to the front of infantry support about 100 yards and in rear of our line of skirmishers some 60 yards. We remained under skirmish fire one hour, the infantry in our rear meeting with some casualties. From thence we took up our line of march, crossing the Baltimore pike, and going into park on the left of it.

About the middle of the afternoon an orderly came rapidly up, asking our battery to come to the assistance of the Fifth Corps. I started on the trot, and reported to General Sykes, who ordered the battery to cover the valley. The rocky nature of the ground compelled us to unhitch our horses and place our guns in position by hand; the left section, in charge of Lieut. H. F. Guthrie, on the left of a road leading from the valley, and on the right slope of Little Round Top (Weed's Hill); the center and right sections, in charge of Lieuts. James Gildea and William Walworth, on the right of said road. We had hardly placed our guns in position when the Fifth Corps was forced back by a terrific charge of Longstreet's corps, and came rushing through us, but began rallying on us as soon as they understood matters. Our front was hardly clear when the irregular, yelling line of the enemy put in his appearance, and we received him with double charges of canister, which were used so effectively as to compel him to retire. So rapidly were the guns worked that they became too hot to lay the hand on. But for the position of the battery, and the gallantry with which it was handled by the men, I have no doubt the enemy would have accomplished his purpose of breaking our lines at this point, and possibly changed the fortunes of the day.

On the 3d, we remained in the same position, occasionally working the battery.

A number were slightly wounded, and Asa Kline was severely wounded. The infantry suffered considerably while supporting us.

I have the honor to be, very respectfully,

F. C. GIBBS,
Captain, Comdg. Battery L, First Ohio Light Artillery.

Capt. A. P. MARTIN,
Commanding Artillery Brigade, Fifth Corps.

No. 223.

Reports of Maj. Gen. John Sedgwick, U. S. Army, commanding Sixth Army Corps.

HEADQUARTERS SIXTH ARMY CORPS,
Warrenton, Va., August 8, 1863.

GENERAL: I respectfully submit the following report of the operations of the Sixth Corps in the engagements near Gettysburg and since:

This command arrived on the field of Gettysburg on the afternoon of July 2, after a march of more than 30 miles.

Wheaton's and Eustis' brigades, of the Third Division, temporarily commanded by Brigadier-General Wheaton, and Bartlett's brigade, of Wright's division, went into action about 5 p. m. on the left center, between divisions of the Fifth Corps, and assisted in repulsing the assault of the enemy. Russell's and Torbert's brigades, of Wright's division, were held in reserve that night. Neill's brigade, of Howe's division, was sent to the right of the line, reporting to Major-General Slocum, and Grant's brigade, of the same division, was posted on the extreme left of the general line. Shaler's brigade, of Wheaton's division, was held in reserve near the left center. The artillery of the corps was placed under the orders of the chief of artillery of the Army of the Potomac.

On the next morning and subsequently the following changes were made in the positions stated above: Russell's brigade was sent to the extreme left of the line, General Wright taking command of the troops of this corps there stationed. Subsequently it was returned to the left center, and on the following day it was placed in position, relieving a brigade of the Fifth Corps. Torbert's brigade was sent to the center, reporting to Major-General Newton, and remained in position until the morning of the 5th. Eustis' brigade was sent to the right center, also reporting to Major-General Newton. Shaler's brigade was also ordered to the left, and then to the right, and subsequently returned to the left center, and held in reserve.

During these movements the troops were more or less exposed to the fire of the enemy's artillery, but, with the exception of the evening of July 2, they were at no time seriously engaged.

On July 5, Wright's division, supported by the rest of my command, was sent forward to determine the position of the enemy, who was discovered to be in retreat through Fairfield in the direction of Hagerstown. The rear of the column was shelled for a short time in the morning, and in the evening a brisk artillery fire was opened upon his wagon trains in the vicinity of Fairfield, while the infantry pursued the rear guard, which was posted to protect the passage of the trains; 250 prisoners were captured during the day.

On the following day the enemy continued his retreat through the mountain pass, with a strong rear guard well posted, with artillery in position.

During the night the corps marched to Emmitsburg, with the exception of Neill's brigade, which was detached and sent in pursuit of the retreating column. From Emmitsburg I marched by way of Hamburg to Middletown, and thence to Boonsborough, Md.

On July 11, the enemy was posted near Funkstown, Md., and the corps moved up and took position, after crossing Beaver Creek. The

Vermont Brigade (Grant's, of the Second Division) were deployed as skirmishers, covering a front of over 2 miles, and during the afternoon repulsed three successive attacks made in line of battle. The remarkable conduct of the brigade on this occasion deserves high praise.

On July 13, my command was placed in the general line of battle in the vicinity of Hagerstown, connecting with the Eleventh Corps on the right and the Fifth Corps on the left, and continued in this position, with occasional sharp skirmishing, until the enemy retired from the front and during the night recrossed the Potomac. He was closely followed to the river by Wright's division and the rest of the command.

On the day following the retreat of the enemy, I moved by way of Boonsborough and Middletown to Berlin, and crossed the river in rear of the army, and continued my march by way of Union, Rectortown, and Barbee's Cross-Roads to Manassas Gap, and thence by way of Barbee's Cross-Roads to Warrenton.

During the operations herein reported, the conduct of the troops was admirable. The marches were very severe, and the hardships undergone were greater than in any previous campaign.

The casualties of the corps were as follows.* A nominal list has been already forwarded.

Very respectfully,

JOHN SEDGWICK,
Major-General, Commanding Sixth Army Corps.

Brig. Gen. S. WILLIAMS,
Assistant Adjutant-General, Army of the Potomac.

—

HEADQUARTERS SIXTH ARMY CORPS,
September 12, 1863.

GENERAL: In compliance with Special Orders, No. 227, Paragraph III, Headquarters Army of the Potomac, August 24, 1863, I respectfully report that no guns were captured by or captured from my command during the recent operations in Maryland and Pennsylvania.

I am, general, very respectfully,

JOHN SEDGWICK,
Major-General, Commanding Sixth Corps.

Brig. Gen. S. WILLIAMS,
Assistant Adjutant-General, Army of the Potomac.

—

HEADQUARTERS SIXTH ARMY CORPS,
October 8, 1863.

GENERAL: I respectfully report that the number of Confederates buried by this command at Gettysburg was 4 officers and 91 enlisted men; total, 95.

I am, general, very respectfully,

JOHN SEDGWICK,
Major-General, Commanding Sixth Corps.

Brig. Gen. S. WILLIAMS,
Assistant Adjutant-General, Army of the Potomac.

---

* Embodied in revised statement, p. 182.

No. 224.

Reports of Brig. Gen. Horatio G. Wright, U. S. Army, commanding First Division.

HDQRS: FIRST DIV., SIXTH CORPS, ARMY OF THE POTOMAC,
Warrenton, Va., August 7, 1863.

COLONEL: I have the honor to submit, in pursuance of orders from corps headquarters, the following report of the operations of this division in connection with the battle of Gettysburg, on the 2d and 3d ultimo:

Just before dark on the evening of July 1, the corps being in camp near Manchester, orders were received to move to Taneytown, and the troops were immediately put in motion.

During the night, and some time after crossing the Baltimore and Gettysburg pike, other orders were received, changing the destination of the corps, and directing it to proceed by rapid marches to Gettysburg. The column, after some delay, was extricated from the narrow road on which it was then moving, and formed on the broad and excellent pike leading direct to Gettysburg. Without halting, except for a few moments each hour to breathe the men, and one halt of about half an hour to enable the men to make coffee, the corps was pushed on to Gettysburg, where it arrived about 4 p. m , after a march variously estimated at from 32 to 35 miles.

The corps here halted for about two hours, when orders came for it to move up with all dispatch, and support the Second, Third, and Fifth Corps, then actively engaged on the left center of the line. On our arrival, a portion of our line was falling back before the determined attack of the enemy's columns, and the Third Division and the Second Brigade, of my division, were promptly moved into position, while my First and Third Brigades were massed and held in reserve. This timely arrival of re-enforcements, with the determined resistance made by the troops already in position, and which had borne with such heroic valor and so severe loss the brunt of the battle, forced the enemy to retreat, and put an end to the contest of July 2.

During the night of the 2d, the brigades of this division held their positions as above noticed.

On the morning of the 3d, at an early hour, under instructions from Major-General Sedgwick, I posted Torbert's brigade near the center of the line, to fill up a gap on the left of the First Corps, when, leaving it attached temporarily to the command of Major-General Newton, I proceeded with Russell's brigade to the extreme left, and assumed the command of the troops at that point, consisting of the brigade just mentioned, the Vermont Brigade, of Howe's division, and two batteries of artillery.

About 5 p. m., orders having been received from Major-General Sedgwick to re-enforce the line on the right of the Fifth Corps against an apprehended attack at that point, I proceeded at once to the spot, but on reaching it the enemy had fallen back repulsed, and the brigade was held in reserve. The other brigades held mainly their positions of the morning through the entire day, neither being actively engaged, though constantly under fire.

On the morning of the 4th, Russell's brigade was posted to the left of the Fifth Corps, on the ascending slope of Round Top Mountain, where it remained during the day and night, the two other brigades holding their positions of the previous day.

On the morning of the 5th, orders having been received for a reconnaissance by the corps, my division, followed by the others, crossed the valley in our front, occupying the position held by the enemy the day before, and our artillery opened upon a body of the enemy on our right, which soon disappeared without replying, moving off to the rear in retreat. This was the last firing at Gettysburg on either side.

Although the division was not actively engaged at Gettysburg, and suffered but trifling loss, yet, as before remarked, the arrival of the corps of which it forms part was most opportune, and, in my opinion, had an important influence on the result of the contest.

Great credit is due to officers and men for the excellent spirit manifested by them on the fatiguing and extraordinary march accomplished in reaching the battle-field, and it is the more creditable as they had already performed a series of almost unprecedented marches, and were, to some extent, exhausted and required rest. I have made no attempt to detail the parts performed by each brigade, as they are embraced in the reports of the brigade commanders herewith, nor do I inclose a list of casualties, such list having been already furnished to corps headquarters.

Very respectfully, your obedient servant,

H. G. WRIGHT,
Brigadier-General, Commanding.

Lieut. Col. M. T. McMahon,
Assistant Adjutant-General, Hdqrs. Sixth Corps.

—

HEADQUARTERS FIRST DIVISION, SIXTH CORPS,
Warrenton, Va., August 21, 1863.

COLONEL: In pursuance of instructions from headquarters of the corps, to embrace in the report of the battle of Gettysburg all the operations of the troops from June 28 to the arrival of the army near Warrenton, I have the honor to present the following in addition to the report already submitted:

June 28.—At 4 a. m. the command broke camp near Edwards Ferry, and moved to Hyattstown, a distance of 18 miles.

June 29.—Marched at 4 a. m., via Monrovia, New Market, Ridgeville, and Mount Airy, to near New Windsor, a distance of 22 miles.

June 30.—Marched at 4 a. m. through Westminster; encamped about 2 miles from Manchester, a distance of 23 miles.

From the resumption of the march at about 9 p. m. on the night of July 1 until the 5th of that month, the operations of the division are detailed in the report of the battle of Gettysburg, already submitted.

July 5.—The entire corps moved to the front of the lines at Gettysburg to feel the enemy, and, on ascertaining that he was retreating, started in pursuit, overtaking his rear guard about 2 miles from Fairfield at about 5 p. m., and driving it into town after a sharp skirmish, in which we lost 1 killed and 2 wounded, and the enemy 2 killed and 2 officers and 4 privates taken prisoners.

July 6.—Moved through the town of Fairfield, and at 6 p. m. started for Emmitsburg, which place we reached a little before daylight; distance, about 8 miles.

July 7.—Started at 11.20 a. m., and halted at 10 p. m. in the mountains near Hamburg, in consequence of the severe storm and extreme darkness, which rendered farther progress impossible; distance, about 15 miles.

July 8.—Moved soon after daylight over the mountains to Middletown, reaching that place about noon, a distance of about 8 miles.

July 9.—Leaving Middletown at 5 a. m. and passing through South Mountain Gap, took position at Boonsborough, with the enemy reported at Funkstown, in our front; distance marched, about 8 miles.

July 10.—Moved about 3 miles toward Hagerstown, and took position beyond Beaver Creek and near the Antietam, where we remained through the next day.

July 12.—Moved with the division and Eustis' brigade, of the Third Division, about daybreak, with orders to take possession of Funkstown and carry the crossing of the Antietam Creek, and to take possession of the high grounds beyond. The order was executed, and the command was established in the position designated, the enemy falling back as we advanced. Some time after crossing, and after the rest of the corps had come up, our line was moved to the left, to connect with the Fifth Corps, the First and Twelfth taking position on the right, and occupying the ground we had left.

During the day, Capt. R. W. Furlong, commanding Company D, Sixth Maine Volunteers, with his company, broke through the enemy's skirmish line, and, without the loss of a man, captured an entire company of the enemy, consisting of a captain, a lieutenant, and 33 enlisted men, a feat which is described by General Russell, under whose direction it was accomplished, as "highly daring and gallant."

The movement to the left, above referred to, brought the division in front of the enemy's skirmishers, strongly posted on a ridge parallel to and commanding our position, while his line of battle, from 600 to 800 yards in rear, occupied an equally advantageous position, strengthened by long lines of intrenchments. The ridge held by his skirmishers being vital to us, an attack was made upon it by a strong skirmish force from the three brigades of the division, which carried it handsomely just before dark, and held it. Our casualties were, 4 officers and 4 men wounded.

During the evening, I received orders to make a reconnaissance of the enemy's position, with a view to develop his strength, in concert with commands from other corps, starting at 7 a. m.

At daylight of the 14th, I received intelligence from the picket line that the enemy had retreated during the night, and at once ordered the skirmishers forward, proceeding with them some 2 miles beyond the enemy's intrenchments, when I ordered the advance of the division, and proceeded with it to Williamsport, where it was found that the enemy's force had crossed the Potomac River some hours before, and that farther pursuit was impracticable, owing to the depth of the river, which was rapidly rising and then too deep for fording.

From Williamsport moved to Boonsborough on the 15th; to Berlin on the 16th; to Wheatland, crossing the Potomac, on the 19th; to Philomont on the 20th; to Little River pike on the 22d; to White Plains, via Rectortown, on the 23d, and to Warrenton, starting at 7 p. m. on the 24th, and arriving about 10 a. m. on July 25.

The reports of brigade commanders are herewith.

Very respectfully, your obedient servant,

H. G. WRIGHT,
Brigadier-General, Commanding.

Lieut. Col. M. T. McMahon,
Assistant Adjutant-General, Sixth Corps.

No. 225.

Reports of Brig. Gen. Alfred T. A. Torbert, U. S. Army, commanding First Brigade.

HDQRS. FIRST BRIG., FIRST DIV., SIXTH ARMY CORPS,
August 3, 1863.

SIR: I have the honor to report the following as the part taken by this brigade (First, Second, Third, and Fifteenth New Jersey Volunteers) at the battle of Gettysburg, Pa.:

On the night of July 1, about 10 o'clock, the brigade started from near Manchester, Md., for Gettysburg. The distance by the route we marched was about 35 miles, and we made it by 4 p. m. on the 2d, only stopping an hour, about 1 p. m. on the 2d, to make coffee. We rested near the battle-field about two hours, when we were ordered to the left of the line, where we arrived about dark, with only 25 men absent, and they came up by the morning. The brigade was held in this position in reserve till morning.

Early on the morning of the 3d, the brigade was detached from the corps, and put in position in front and about the center of the line. This position we held till the morning of the 5th.

In the meantime the brigade was not actively engaged, excepting on the picket line, where there were 11 enlisted men wounded, and during this time the brigade was under the orders of Major-General Newton, commanding First Corps.

Much credit is due to Lieutenant-Colonel Wiebecke, Second Regiment New Jersey Volunteers, in charge of the picket line, and also Lieutenant [Howard H.] Goldsmith, additional aide-de-camp (his assistant), for their good management of the same on July 3.

I am, very respectfully, your obedient servant,
A. T. A. TORBERT,
Brigadier-General of Volunteers.

Capt. HENRY R. DALTON,
Assistant Adjutant-General, Division Headquarters.

—

HDQRS. FIRST BRIGADE, FIRST DIVISION, SIXTH CORPS,
July 17, 1863.

Pursuant to circular from headquarters Army of the Potomac, inspector-general's office, of July 16, 1863, I have the honor to report as follows:

Strength of command.

Command.	Officers.	Enlisted men.	Total.
1st New Jersey	28	328	356
2d New Jersey	30	418	448
3d New Jersey	27	340	367
15th New Jersey	21	471	492
Total	106	1,557	1,663

Killed, wounded, and missing at and since the battle of Gettysburg.

Command.	Killed.	Wounded.	Date.	Remarks.
1st New Jersey	......	1	July 13, 1863	Skirmish near Funkstown, Md.
	......	6	July 3, 1863	Gettysburg, Pa.
2d New Jersey	......	2	July 11, 1863	Skirmish near Hagerstown, Md.
3d New Jersey	1	1	July 5, 1863	Skirmish near Fairfield, Pa.
	......	1	July 3, 1863	Gettysburg, Pa.
	......	1	July 12, 1863	Near Funkstown, Md.
15th New Jersey	......	3	July 3, 1863	Gettysburg, Pa. Since dead.
	......	2	July 12, 1863	Funkstown, Md.
Total	1	17		

HDQRS. FIRST BRIG., FIRST DIV., SIXTH ARMY CORPS,
August 13, 1863.

SIR: Agreeably to circular from headquarters Army of the Potomac, of August 13, I have the honor to report the following as the operations of this brigade—First, Second, Third, and Fifteenth Regiments New Jersey Volunteers—from June 28 to July 25:

June 28.—Marched from a point about half way between Edwards Ferry, on the Potomac, and Poolesville, Md., to Hyattstown; distance, about 18 miles.

June 29.—Marched from Hyattstown, Md., via New Market and Ridgeville, to near New Windsor, Md.; distance, about 22 miles.

June 30.—Marched from near New Windsor, via Westminster, to Manchester; distance, about 23 miles.

July 1.—Made a forced march from Manchester to Gettysburg, Pa.; distance, about 35 miles. Started at 10 p. m.; marched all night and the next day (July 2) until 4 p. m., only stopping about one hour at 1 p. m. to make coffee. Arrived on the battle-field with only 25 men absent. Rested near the center of the line for about two hours, when we were ordered to the left of the line, where we arrived about dark. The brigade was drawn up in two lines in reserve, in which position it was held until morning, the men sleeping on their arms.

July 3.—The absentees had joined their companies. Early in the morning the brigade was detached from the corps, and put in position in front and about the center of the line, and picketing strongly our own front, connecting on the right with the First Corps and on the left with the Fifth Corps. The brigade was not actively engaged on this day, excepting on the picket line, where there were 11 men wounded. A few men in the brigade were wounded by the explosion of shells.

July 4.—Held the same position as on the 3d. Much credit is due to Lieutenant-Colonel Wiebecke, Second Regiment, who was in charge of the picket line on the 3d, and also Lieutenant Goldsmith, additional aide-de-camp, who assisted him, for their very efficient management of the same. While the brigade was detached from the corps, I was under the orders of Maj. Gen. John Newton, commanding First Army Corps.

July 5.—Broke camp at 3 a. m.; joined my division and corps, taking the lead of the same. Started about 11 a. m. to follow the rear of the rebel army; marching in line of battle about 6 miles, covered by a heavy line of skirmishers, came up with their rear guard about 2 miles from Fairfield, and had a sharp skirmish. About 5 p. m. drove the enemy to Fairfield, and at night fell back about 1½ miles. Loss of the enemy, 2 killed, 2 officers and 4 privates prisoners. Our loss, 1 killed and 2 wounded.

July 6.—Started at 6 p. m. for Emmitsburg, as rear guard of the corps and trains; marched all night; arrived about daylight; distance, about 8 miles.

July 7.—Started at 6 a. m.; marched all day and until 10 p. m., stopping in the mountains near Hamburg in a severe rain storm; distance, about 15 miles.

July 8.—Marched at daylight over the mountain to Middletown; distance, about 8 miles.

July 9.—Started at 4 p. m.; marched to Boonsborough; distance, about 8 miles.

July 10.—Marched about 3 miles, and took position in two lines.

July 11.—Remained in same position.

July 12.—Marched about 6 miles; took position, first, about 2 miles from Hagerstown, on the Boonsborough and Hagerstown pike; about 2 p. m. changed position more to the left; 5 p. m. advanced picket line; drove in the enemy's pickets; lost 3 officers and 4 men wounded.

July 13.—Remained in same position.

July 14.—Advanced and marched to Williamsport, about 6 miles.

July 15.—Marched from Williamsport to Boonsborough; 16 miles.

July 16.—Marched from Boonsborough via Middletown and Petersville to Berlin; distance, about 20 miles.

July 17.—Remained in camp all day.

July 18.—Removed camp about 2 miles.

July 19.—Crossed the Potomac at Berlin on pontoon bridge; encamped near Wheatland, Va.; distance, 8 miles.

July 20.—Broke camp at 10 a. m., and marched via Purcellville to Aldie and Snickersville pike, and encamped near Philomont; distance, 14 miles.

July 21.—Remained in camp all day.

July 22.—Broke camp at 10 p. m., and marched via Union to the Little River turnpike; distance, 12 miles.

July 23.—Broke camp at 4 a. m.; marched via Rectortown to White Plains; distance, 12 miles.

July 24.—Broke camp at 6 p. m.; marched toward Warrenton; stopped about 12 o'clock at night near New Baltimore.

July 25.—Broke camp at 6 a. m., and marched to Warrenton via New Baltimore, distance 6½ miles, and took position on the Sulphur Springs road.

Too much praise cannot be given to officers and men for their patience and endurance on this long and tedious march of about 250 miles. There was far less straggling than was ever known in this brigade before.

I am, very respectfully, yours, &c.,

A. T. A. TORBERT,
Brigadier-General of Volunteers.

Capt. HENRY R. DALTON,
Assistant Adjutant-General, First Division.

No. 226.

*Reports of Brig. Gen. Joseph J. Bartlett, U. S. Army, commanding
Second Brigade, First Division, and Third Division.*

HDQRS. SECOND BRIGADE, FIRST DIVISION, SIXTH CORPS,
August 6, 1863.

SIR: I have the honor to report the part taken by this brigade in
the battle near Gettysburg, from the evening of July 2.

The brigade arrived on the field a little after 5 p. m., and was
formed in two lines, as a support to the forces under command of
Major-General Sykes, near the left of our line of battle.   When my
command arrived on the field, the troops in front were giving ground
to the rear.   The Third Brigade, Third Division, Sixth Corps,
formed on my left, and, before my formation was complete, moved
rapidly to the front and right, completely masking my troops, and
rendering an advance unnecessary.   Our loss was 2 privates wounded.

The troops rested in this position until the morning of July 3,
when I was ordered by Major-General Sedgwick to take command
of the Third Brigade, Third Division, with my own, and an advanced portion of the line assigned to me.

About 5 p. m. I was ordered by Major-General Sedgwick to co-
operate with Brigadier-General Crawford, commanding Pennsylvania Reserves, in a movement against the supposed position of General Hood's division.   The Reserves moved in a single line of battle,
the Third Brigade, Third Division, under command of Colonel Nevin,
Sixty-second New York Volunteers, forming a second line at an interval of 200 yards.   Skirmishing commenced soon after leaving our
original position, immediately followed by heavier firing.   The first
line was partly relieved by the second after being engaged about
twenty minutes.   At dusk the line was recalled, and occupied a position during the night a few hundred yards in advance of the original
one.

The loss in killed and wounded in my command was between 20
and 30 (a report has been furnished corps headquarters).   The
enemy's loss in killed and wounded I could not ascertain.   Prisoners
to the number of about 200 were taken by the joint command.

At 8 a. m., July 4, I was assigned to the command of the Third
Division, Sixth Corps, but was ordered to command the Second Brigade, First Division, as a support to Colonel Day, commanding a
brigade of regular troops, on a reconnaissance immediately in front
of my position.   The Second Brigade was not at any time during
this reconnaissance advanced more than 500 yards, and returned to
camp about 1 p. m. without loss.

I am, very respectfully, your obedient servant,

JOS. J. BARTLETT,
Brigadier-General, Commanding.

Captain DALTON,
Assistant Adjutant-General.

—

HDQRS. SECOND BRIGADE, FIRST DIVISION, SIXTH CORPS,
August 15, 1863.

SIR: I have the honor to submit the additional report of the movements of the Third Division, Sixth Corps, called for by circular from
headquarters Army of the Potomac, August 12, 1863.

On the morning of July 5, at 5 o'clock, the First and Second Brigades moved from their position, near the center, and reported to me, near headquarters Sixth Corps, the Third Brigade occupying a position in front of the line at that point.

The corps moved forward on the Fairfield road about 8 a. m., the Third Division bringing up the rear, and moved in the same formation to a point about 2 miles from Fairfield, where the enemy was found to occupy the road leading over the mountain.

The next morning, July 6, was very misty and dark, rendering it impossible to obtain correct information of the enemy's movements until after noon, when the corps moved to the foot of the mountain, a portion of it occupying the pass.

After dark, we moved on the road to Emmitsburg, and went into camp about 2 miles beyond the town at 1 o'clock the next morning.

July 7.—Marched at an early hour in the morning, and, after passing Catoctin Furnace, took a road to the right, leading over the Catoctin Mountain, encamping late in the evening at Hamburg, on the summit.

July 8.—Marched at 5 a. m., and arrived at Middletown about 9 a. m.

July 9.—Marched at 5 a. m., arriving at Boonsborough at 10 a. m.

July 10.—Marched at 6 a. m., in support of the Second Division, toward Funkstown. About 4 miles from Boonsborough, formed the division in two lines on the right of the pike. Skirmishing with cavalry and infantry was kept up until night, the enemy slowly retiring.

July 11.—Our position was unchanged, with the exception of throwing two brigades of my division forward, one for picket and the other to strengthen the line of the Second Division.

July 12.—About 10 a. m. passed through Funkstown, in rear of the First Division, Sixth Corps, and took up a position across the Antietam, in the center of the line occupied by the corps.

Late in the afternoon, I received orders to advance my skirmish line, in connection with the line of the First Division, and take, if possible, the crest occupied by the enemy's skirmishers. This movement on my front was but partially successful. Owing to the formation of the ground, the enemy's line of battle was much nearer their skirmish line in my front than in front of General Wright's division. My loss in this movement was 9 privates wounded, 2 mortally. During the night I threw up a line of defenses covering the front of the division.

On the morning of the 14th, information was sent me from my pickets that the enemy was not in sight. I immediately ordered an advance of my skirmishers, sent out a small scouting party, and sent information, as soon as it was found to be reliable, to corps headquarters. Soon after, I received orders to support General Wright, commanding First Division, in a reconnaissance in his front. Our advance was not interrupted by the enemy. We reached Williamsport about noon, and encamped.

On the 15th, marched to Boonsborough.

On the 16th, marched at 4 a. m., and encamped near Berlin.

The 17th and 18th were spent in camp, receiving clothing and stores.

On the morning of the 19th, moved at 7 o'clock, crossed the Potomac at Berlin, and encamped 6 miles from Lovettsville.

On the 20th, marched to the Aldie and Snickersville pike.

On the 21st, remained in camp.

On the 22d, marched to a point on the Little River pike about 4 miles from Upperville.

On the 23d, marched through Rectortown and Salem, and encamped late at night near Barbee's Cross-Roads.

On the 24th, marched at 4 a. m. for Markham Station, and returned by same route to Thumb River.

On the 25th, marched by way of Orleans to Warrenton.

I have the honor to be, very respectfully, your obedient servant,

JOS. J. BARTLETT,
Brigadier-General, Commanding.

Lieut. Col. M. T. McMahon, *Assistant Adjutant-General.*

No. 227.

Report of Col. Emory Upton, One hundred and twenty-first New York Infantry.

HDQRS. 121ST NEW YORK VOLUNTEERS, *August 6, 1863.*

SIR: I have the honor to make the following report of the participation of the Second Brigade while under my command in the operations around Gettysburg, Pa.:

The evening of July 1, I received orders from Brig. Gen. J. J. Bartlett to take command of the brigade.

It commenced its march from near Manchester, Md., toward Taneytown about 10 p. m. Arriving near Westminster, its destination was changed to Gettysburg, where it arrived about 3.30 p. m., having marched since the preceding evening 32 miles.

The brigade rested about three hours, when it was ordered to reenforce that part of our line which was engaged near Round Top Mountain. While on its march to that point, I was relieved from the command by General Bartlett.

I know nothing of the operations of the brigade that evening or the ensuing day, excepting so far as relates to my own regiment, which took position in line of battle to support a battery to the right of the summit of Round Top, the right of the regiment resting on the road leading out to the Emmitsburg pike.

One man was wounded by artillery on July 3. No other casualty occurred during the battle.

Respectfully submitted.

EMORY UPTON,
Colonel One hundred and twenty-first New York Vols.

Captain DALTON, *A. A. G., First Division, Sixth Corps.*

No. 228.

Reports of Brig. Gen. David A. Russell, U. S. Army, commanding Third Brigade.

HEADQUARTERS THIRD BRIGADE, *August 3, 1863.*

SIR: In obedience to circular from headquarters Army of the Potomac, of date August 1, 1863, I have the honor to submit the following report of the part taken by this brigade in the battle of Gettysburg:

This brigade reached Gettysburg on the evening of July 2.

On July 3, early in the morning, it was put in position on the extreme left of our line of battle, and there held until late in the afternoon, when it was brought up to aid in opposing an anticipated attack on the center of our line. This brigade was not, however, actually engaged on that day.

On the morning of July 4, this brigade relieved a portion of the Fifth Corps in the position held by a part of that corps, on the steep hill to the left of the center of our line. This position it retained until the morning of July 5, when, with the remainder of this corps, it was ordered in pursuit of the retreating enemy.

There were no casualties in this command during any of the engagements on July 2, 3, and 4.

Very respectfully,

D. A. RUSSELL,
Brigadier-General, Commanding Brigade.

Capt. HENRY R. DALTON,
Assistant Adjutant-General.

———

HEADQUARTERS THIRD BRIGADE,
August 20, 1863.

SIR: I have the honor to submit the following report, in obedience to circular of date August 12, 1863, from headquarters Army of the Potomac:

On June 28, this command broke camp near Edwards Ferry, Md., at 4 p. m. With the exception of much heavy marching and the share taken by it in the battle of Gettysburg, of which a report was forwarded from these headquarters on the 3d instant, nothing of moment occurred until Sunday, July 12, on the morning of which last-mentioned day we were encamped within about 2 miles of Funkstown, Md.

At 4.30 o'clock on the morning of July 12, we broke camp and marched out about half a mile beyond Funkstown, where we halted and formed line of battle. The Sixth Maine Volunteers was placed on the left of the road (its right resting on the road) leading from Funkstown to Williamsport; the Fifth Regiment Wisconsin Volunteers in the rear of the Sixth Maine; the One hundred and nineteenth Regiment Pennsylvania Volunteers on the right of the road, its left resting on the road, while the Forty-ninth Regiment Pennsylvania Volunteers was stationed by the general commanding the division about a third of a mile to the right of the road, to support a battery in position at that point. A strong line of skirmishers was thrown out in front of the Sixth Maine Volunteers, and the skirmish line was advanced a little during the morning, and some brisk skirmish firing ensued therein.

About 2 p. m. Capt. R. W. Furlong, commanding Company D, Sixth Maine Volunteers, with his company, in a highly daring and gallant manner, broke through the skirmish line, and, without losing a man, surrounded and captured 33 enlisted men, a captain, and a lieutenant—an entire company.

About 5 p. m. the entire command was moved about a mile to the left of the road and toward the river bank, on a line nearly parallel to that it had occupied during the day. At this point the enemy had a strong embankment, in front of which were rifle-pits and covers for sharpshooters. Here two companies of the Fifth Wisconsin Volunteers and Company B, of the Forty-ninth Pennsylvania Volunteers, were deployed as skirmishers, the right of the line connecting with the left of the First Brigade of this division, and the left of this line connecting with the right of the Second Division of this corps. There was much severe skirmishing at this point, and at about sunset the entire line, pushing the enemy's skirmishers before it, was advanced about half a mile to the crest of a hill most advantageously situated in regard to the enemy's position.

The list of casualties in the command in the skirmishes of this day was as follows: Fifth Wisconsin Volunteers, none; Sixth Regiment Maine Volunteers, none; Forty-ninth Pennsylvania Volunteers, 1 (First Lieut. Edward T. Swain, wounded in thigh); One hundred and nineteenth Pennsylvania Volunteers, none; total, 1. With the exception of 8 men of this command captured at White Plains (heretofore reported), there have been no casualties in the command other than have been reported since June 28.

Very respectfully,

D. A. RUSSELL,
Brigadier-General, Commanding Brigade.

Capt. HENRY R. DALTON,
Assistant Adjutant-General.

No. 229.

Report of Brig. Gen. Albion P. Howe, U. S. Army, commanding
Second Division.

HEADQUARTERS SECOND DIVISION, SIXTH CORPS,
Camp near Waterloo, Va., August 7, 1863.

SIR: In obedience to instructions, I have the honor to report the part the Second Division, Sixth Corps, took in the battle of Gettysburg.

The division left Manchester at 1 a. m. on July 2, and reached the field at Gettysburg at 5 p. m., 33 miles distant. The Third Brigade, under General Neill, was immediately placed in position to support artillery on one of the key-points of the line, and the remainder of the division was ordered to the support of the Fifth Corps. In this position it remained until the action of the day was over.

During the battle of July 2 and 3, the Third Brigade was ordered to take position on the extreme right flank of the army, and the portion of the division in support of the Fifth Corps was ordered, with two batteries, to take position on the extreme left, to hold the left flank of the army. This position the division held until the close of the action, and until the morning of July 5. The brigade under Brigadier-General Neill, on the right, he reports as being almost constantly engaged with the enemy's skirmishers and sharpshooters. The portion of the division on the left was not actively engaged, but held its position under the enfilading fire of the enemy's artillery during the engagement.

The dashing readiness with which the division went on to the field on the evening of the 2d, after its long and continuous march of the previous day and night, and the handsome manner in which it bore itself during the engagement, were worthy of its former reputation.

A list of the casualties of the division has been forwarded.*

I am, colonel, very respectfully, your obedient servant,

A. P. HOWE,
Brigadier-General, Commanding Division.

Lieut. Col. M. T. McMahon,
Assistant Adjutant-General, Sixth Corps.

No. 230.

Reports of Col. Lewis A. Grant, Fifth Vermont Infantry, commanding Second Brigade.

HEADQUARTERS FIRST VERMONT BRIGADE,
South side of the Rappahannock, Va., June 6, 1863.

SIR: The Vermont Brigade has again crossed the Rappahannock at the old point, about 1½ miles below Fredericksburg. It is the first brigade across, and, so far as my knowledge extends, it is the only one yet over.

We left camp yesterday soon after noon, and marched to the river, a distance of about 5 miles. The pontoons were on the ground, ready to be taken down the bank and thrown across the river. The rebels had constructed rifle-pits in front of and commanding the point where the bridges were to be placed. These rifle-pits were occupied by rebel infantry.

As soon as the artillery could be gotten into position, it opened a terrible fire upon the rifle-pits. It had but little effect, however, excepting to keep back re-enforcements that were coming to the assistance of those already in the rifle-pits. But very few of those in the rifle-pits were injured by the artillery fire. They managed to keep up a galling musketry fire upon the engineers that attempted to construct the bridges. It was determined to drive the rebels from the rifle-pits. The Fifth Vermont, Lieutenant-Colonel Lewis, and Twenty-sixth New Jersey, Lieutenant-Colonel Martindale, were ordered forward for that purpose. They rushed gallantly down the bank, and, with the assistance of the engineers, and under a galling fire from the rifle-pits, they launched the pontoon boats into the stream, jumped into them, rowed across, and landed upon the south bank. But a few companies of the Fifth had crossed when they sprang up the bank, and with shouts charged the rifle-pits, driving the enemy from them in great confusion, taking many of them prisoners.

The Twenty-sixth New Jersey came gallantly to the support of the Fifth, and did well, but it is believed the Fifth cleared the rifle-pits. The Third Vermont, Colonel Seaver; the Fourth Vermont, Colonel Stoughton; the Second Vermont, Colonel Walbridge, also crossed in boats, and gallantly supported the regiments already across. The rebels were driven across the plain into the woods. One bridge was soon completed, and the Sixth Vermont, Colonel Barney, also crossed. Our positions were taken and are still held.

It is impossible at this time to give particular instances of dashing

---

*Embodied in revised statement, p. 181.

gallantry, though there were many. It was quick work and splendidly executed.

The number of prisoners taken is not at this time known, but it is believed to be between 100 and 200. Captain Davenport sent in 2 officers and 34 enlisted men, who surrendered to him after dark, over Deep Creek, where Captain Davenport, of the Fifth, and Captain Boutin, of the Fourth, had been sent on picket.

The casualties in the Fifth Vermont are 7 wounded. No casualties in either of the other Vermont regiments.

I remain, general, very respectfully, your obedient servant,

L. A. GRANT,
Colonel, Commanding Brigade.

PETER T. WASHBURN, *Actg. Asst. Inspector-General.*

—

HEADQUARTERS FIRST VERMONT BRIGADE,
Camp near Rappahannock, Va., June 8, 1863.

SIR: On the 6th instant, I sent you from the thrice-tried battle-field of Fredericksburg an imperfect account of the gallant conduct of the Vermont troops in crossing the river and carrying the rifle-pits upon the other side. It was an exciting and brilliant affair, and no account can do ample justice to the brave officers and men engaged. Impetuous enthusiasm, when displayed in the face of the enemy, beggars description.

The two companies first in the works were the Rutland Company, Capt. B. R. Jennie, Fifth, and the Swanton Company, Capt. Friend H. Barney, Fifth. The first man in the rifle-pits was Private Henry Moren, Company G. After clearing the rifle-pits and sending the prisoners down the bank, these two companies advanced as skirmishers, and drove those who sought safety in flight across the plain into the woods. Other companies and regiments hurried over with all possible dispatch, but there were not boats enough to take them over as fast as desired. The returning boats brought back the prisoners. It was an amusing scene, our men crowding the boats, and with cheers rowing for the other side of the river, and at the same time boats returning with rebel prisoners.

On Saturday, the 6th instant, the Sixth Vermont was skirmishing nearly all day. They occupied a position from the river on the left by the Bernard house, around across the Bowling Green road to Deep Creek.

The Sixth lost in the skirmish of that day 4 killed and 13 wounded. Among the wounded was Lieutenant Raistrick. A list of the killed and wounded of the Sixth is herewith forwarded.* There were no casualties in the Second, Third, and Fourth Regiments. The loss of the Fifth and Sixth Regiments was 4 killed and 20 wounded. The loss of the Twenty-sixth New Jersey Regiment was 2 killed and 17 wounded, making a total loss of 43 in the brigade. The brigade was the only force upon the south side of the river for nearly twenty-four hours.

On the afternoon of the 6th, another brigade came over to our support, and on the morning of the 7th we were relieved from the skirmish line, but continued to hold the front line of battle until the evening of the 7th, when we were relieved by another division, and

---

* Embodied in revised statement, p. 193.

marched back to the north side of the river, having held the front in the face of the enemy about fifty hours. During a portion of the time, the enemy developed a very large force in our front.

Officers and men behaved as becomes Vermonters during the entire time.

I have the honor to be, very respectfully, your obedient servant,

L. A. GRANT,
Colonel, Commanding Brigade.

PETER T. WASHBURN,
Adjutant and Inspector-General.

—

HDQRS. SECOND BRIG., SECOND DIV., SIXTH CORPS,
August 3, 1863.

SIR: I have the honor to report the part taken by this brigade at the battle of Gettysburg.

The brigade arrived near the scene of action at about 5 p. m. July 2, having marched about 30 miles that day, and very soon moved out to the left center of our army, to take part, as was expected, in the struggle then going on.

The position of the brigade was once or twice changed, and soon after dark it moved still farther to the left, and took position on the extreme left of the army, and one regiment, the Fifth Vermont, was thrown out as pickets or skirmishers.

On the morning of the 3d, the brigade advanced a short distance, and took a position with its right resting on Round Top Mountain and its left on the Taneytown road, in which position it remained that day, taking no very active part in the battle, though exposed at times to solid shot and shell from the enemy's guns.

On July 4, the brigade held substantially the same position, and during the day the Fourth Vermont, then on picket, was ordered forward to feel the enemy's position. It advanced about 1½ miles, and had a slight skirmish with the enemy's pickets.

John F. Marshall, Fourth Vermont Volunteers, was severely wounded in the arm and knee, which was the only casualty in the brigade.

The officers and men all did their duty well. The cheerful and ready manner in which the regiments moved into position on the evening of the 2d, after the fatiguing march of that day, is worthy of especial mention.

I remain, very respectfully, your obedient servant,

L. A. GRANT,
Colonel, Commanding Brigade.

Maj. CHARLES MUNDEE, *Assistant Adjutant-General.*

———

No. 231.

Reports of Brig. Gen. Thomas H. Neill, U. S. Army, commanding Third Brigade and Light Division.

HDQRS. THIRD BRIG., SECOND DIV., SIXTH CORPS,
Camp near Berlin, Md., July 17, 1863.

SIR: I have the honor to state, for the information of the major-general commanding the Army of the Potomac, that on the night of the 5th instant I assumed command of Colonel McIntosh's brigade of cavalry, two pieces of light artillery accompanying it, Captain Martin's battery of rifled pieces, and my own brigade of infantry accompanying. I, in accordance with orders from headquarters Army of the Potomac, on the morning of the 6th pushed on from Fairfield to Waynesborough. The rear guard of the enemy only escaped capture by burning the bridge at the Antietam, 2½ miles from Waynesborough, on the Hagerstown road.

On the 7th, felt the enemy's pickets along the Antietam and Marsh Run, and found Ewell's corps in our front.

On the 8th, discovered a portion of Ewell's corps at Middleburg.

On the 9th, sent Colonel McIntosh, with the whole of his cavalry brigade and four pieces of artillery, to develop the strength of the enemy at the fords and bridges. Colonel McIntosh drew the fire of the enemy at the Antietam, and developed a force consisting of the three arms at Zeigler's Mills, near Chewsville, the pickets of the enemy being this side of the creek. Colonel McIntosh at once formed line of battle, dismounted his skirmishers, opened with his artillery, and drove them in full retreat across the Antietam, silencing their battery. He had 4 wounded, 1 mortally. This was between 3 and 4 miles from Hagerstown, on the north side.

The enemy did not appear this side of the Antietam after this, in our direction.

The cool and professional manner in which Colonel McIntosh handled his cavalry and posted his artillery has drawn upon him well-merited praise. In this as in every other duty which I called upon Colonel McIntosh to perform, his conduct and bearing impel me to suggest to the major-general commanding the Army of the Potomac that his rank should be increased so as to be proportionate to his gallant deeds and to his great ability.

In connection with the advice and orders of General W. F. Smith, two regiments of militia, supported by one old regiment of my own brigade, were sent down to Marsh Run, to feel an infantry picket of the enemy. When we arrived there, we found the picket had been withdrawn the night before, and we did not get the militia under fire.

On the 11th, marched to Leitersburg.

On the 12th, made a flank march along the Antietam, and rejoined the Sixth Corps, in line of battle west of Funkstown.

I may be permitted to state that all these events have lost their interest now by the more important developments which have since transpired, but, as the commander of the expedition which the major-general commanding saw fit to intrust to me, I have felt that it is but a simple act of justice to Colonel McIntosh to bear tribute to his gallantry and good judgment, and I believe he helped the enemy out of Hagerstown.

Since joining the Sixth Corps, my brigade has been either in line of battle or marching, which is my apology for not having sent this report before.

We have captured and picked up between 300 and 400 rebel prisoners or deserters. I sent them to Couch.

I am, general, very respectfully, your obedient servant,

THOS. H. NEILL,
Brigadier-General, U. S. Volunteers.

General S. WILLIAMS,
Assistant Adjutant-General, Army of the Potomac.

HDQRS. THIRD BRIG., SECOND DIV., SIXTH CORPS,
August 3, 1863.

SIR: I have the honor to report that immediately upon my arrival upon the battle-field of Gettysburg, 6 p. m., July 2, after a march of 30 miles, my brigade was detached by order of Major-General Meade to support a height crowned by a battery, which the major-general commanding the Army of the Potomac ordered to be held at all hazards. I took position accordingly, and found General Slocum in command, who subsequently ordered me to take position supporting the front line, then held by Generals Geary and Wadsworth.

At midnight was ordered to return to my original position, as directed by Major-General Meade, which was done.

On the morning of the 3d, Major-General Slocum ordered me to take position with two of my regiments on the extreme right of the whole army, and prevent the enemy from turning us. Upon taking position, I felt the enemy strong in sharpshooters, and put my whole brigade in position here, and stopped them from going any farther. Loss, 1 officer and 13 enlisted men killed and wounded.*

On the morning of the 4th, I advanced my skirmishers to drive away the sharpshooters, when I found the enemy gone.

On the morning of the 5th, rejoined my division, and marched with my division and corps, which drove the enemy out of Fairfield.

On the morning of the 6th, engaged the rear guard of the enemy, and drove them into the gap at Fairfield. In the afternoon they left. Followed them, and held the gap.

On this evening, was detached to command Light Division, consisting of my own brigade of infantry, Colonel McIntosh's brigade of cavalry, Lieutenant Martin's battery of rifled pieces, and two pieces of light artillery attached to Colonel McIntosh's brigade. The report of my operations with this command has already been sent direct to Major-General Meade

Very respectfully,

THOS. H. NEILL,
Brig. Gen., U. S. Volunteers, Comdg. Third Brigade.

Maj. CHARLES MUNDEE,
Assistant Adjutant-General.

No. 232.

Reports of Brig. Gen. Alexander Shaler, U. S. Army, command-
ing First Brigade, Third Division.

HDQRS. FIRST BRIG., THIRD DIV., SIXTH CORPS,
July 27, 1863.

CAPTAIN: I have the honor herewith to submit the following report of the movements and operations of this brigade during the battle of Gettysburg:

At 7 p. m. on the 2d instant, by direction of Brigadier-General Wheaton, commanding the division, this brigade was formed in line of battle on the left of the position held by the army, in rear of the Second Brigade.

---

*But see revised statement, p. 181.

At 8 a. m. of the 3d instant, under instructions from General Wheaton, I reported with my brigade to Brigadier-General Geary, commanding Second Division, Twelfth Corps, which held the right of the position the army occupied, and, by his direction, took a sheltered position in rear of a piece of woods, beyond which the action was then progressing. Accompanying this you will find a copy of a report made to General Geary of the operations of the brigade while under his command.

At 3.30 o'clock, by direction of General Wheaton, the brigade was moved, under a terrific fire of artillery, to report to General Newton. A subsequent order, however, from General Meade, directed me to remain in rear of the position of the Third Corps, reporting to Major-General Newton for instructions.

At 7 a. m. the brigade was moved, by direction of General Newton, about half a mile to the right, still in reserve, and remained in this position until 6 a. m. of the 4th instant, when the brigade rejoined the division, by an order received direct from General Meade.

The regiments composing the brigade, without exception, acquitted themselves in a highly commendable manner. I append a revised list of casualties.*

I am, captain, very respectfully, your obedient servant,
ALEXANDER SHALER,
Brigadier-General, Commanding Brigade.

Capt. A. J. Smith,
Actg. Asst. Adjt. Gen., Third Division, Sixth Corps.

—

Hdqrs. First Brigade, Third Division, Sixth Corps,
November 20, 1863.

Sir: My attention has been called to the report of the major-general commanding the army of the battle of Gettysburg, as published in the Washington Chronicle of the 13th instant, in which it is stated in substance that Wheaton's brigade, of the Third Division, was sent to the assistance of the Twelfth Corps.

In justice to the officers and men of my command, whose good services were acknowledged on the ground by General Geary, and as appears by the accompanying report, I beg to ask the major-general commanding the army, through the intermediate commanders, for a correction of the report in this particular.

The First Brigade, *and the First alone*, was directed, and did report to General Geary, commanding Second Division of the Twelfth Corps, on the morning of July 3, and went into action under my command by direction of General Geary.

I inclose a copy of my report to the assistant adjutant-general of the Second Division, Twelfth Corps, and also a copy of the report to the acting assistant adjutant-general of the Third Division, Sixth Corps, for the perusal of the major-general commanding.

I have the honor to be, very respectfully, yours,
ALEXANDER SHALER,
Brig. Gen., Comdg. First Brig., Third Div., Sixth Corps.

Capt. A. E. King,
Assistant Adjutant-General, Third Division.

---

*Embodied in revised statement, p. 181.

[Indorsements.]

HEADQUARTERS THIRD DIVISION, SIXTH CORPS,
November 21, 1863.
Respectfully forwarded, approved.

H. D. TERRY,
Brigadier-General, Commanding.

HEADQUARTERS SIXTH CORPS,
November 21, 1863.
Respectfully forwarded.

In my report of the operations at Gettysburg, it is stated that "Shaler's brigade was also ordered first to the left and then to the right, and subsequently returned to the left center and held in reserve;" and it appears also that Wheaton's brigade remained in the position in which it was placed on the evening of July 2, *i. e.*, on the left center.

The mistake in regard to the position of the two brigades may have originated in the report of the commanding officer of the Twelfth Corps.

JOHN SEDGWICK,
Major-General, Commanding Sixth Corps.

HEADQUARTERS ARMY OF THE POTOMAC,
November 23, 1863.
Respectfully forwarded, with the recommendation that the necessary correction in my report of the battle of Gettysburg, which was based upon that of the corps commanders, be made.

GEO. G. MEADE,
Major-General, Commanding.

[Inclosure.]

HDQRS. FIRST BRIG., THIRD DIV., SIXTH CORPS,
July 21, 1863.

MAJOR: I have the honor to hand you the following report of the movements and operations of the several regiments of this brigade while under command of Brigadier-General Geary, during the action of the morning of July 3:

At 9 a. m. the One hundred and twenty-second New York Volunteers, Col. Silas Titus commanding, was directed to relieve the One hundred and eleventh Pennsylvania Volunteers, then occupying a position in the front line.

Finding the breastworks had been hastily vacated by that regiment, they were immediately reoccupied by the One hundred and twenty-second, and held by them, under a severe fire of the enemy, until relieved by the Eighty-second Pennsylvania Volunteers at 11.30 a. m.

At 9.20 a. m. the Twenty-third Pennsylvania Volunteers, Lieut. Col. John F. Glenn commanding, was placed in position as support to, and 150 yards in rear of, the front line. After about three hours, five companies were, by direction of General Geary, reported to the lieutenant-colonel commanding a regiment of the Second Division, Twelfth Corps.

These companies, being deployed in rear of the works, were, under a galling fire of musketry, advanced into them. Owing to the heavy fire immediately opened by the enemy, the design of feeling them with skirmishers was found impracticable. Skirmishers were advanced, however, about 15 paces, but were shortly afterward withdrawn.

At 11 a. m. the Sixty-seventh New York Volunteers, Col. Nelson Cross commanding, marched into the woods and forward to the breastworks, from which the enemy were then fleeing. They succeeded in capturing about 20 prisoners.

At 11.15 o'clock the Sixty-fifth New York Volunteers, Col. Joseph E. Hamblin commanding, occupied a position as support to the Twenty-third Pennsylvania Volunteers, of this brigade.

At 11.30 a. m. the Eighty-second Pennsylvania Volunteers, Col. I. C. Bassett commanding, advanced to the front line, relieving the One hundred and twenty-second New York, and occupying the position until relieved by a portion of General Geary's command at about 3 p. m. At this hour the brigade was reformed under my command.

I annex a list of killed, wounded, and missing during the engagements.*

I am, very respectfully, your obedient servant,

ALEXANDER SHALER,
Brigadier-General, Commanding Brigade.

ASSISTANT ADJUTANT-GENERAL,
Second Division, Twelfth Corps.

No. 233.

Report of Col. Horatio Rogers, jr., Second Rhode Island Infantry, Second Brigade.

HEADQUARTERS SECOND RHODE ISLAND VOLUNTEERS,
Near Hagerstown, Md., July 10, 1863.

GENERAL: I have the honor to respectfully report that the regiment which I have the honor to command has been constantly moving since June 6.

The demonstration on the south side of the Rappahannock, below Fredericksburg, to keep the enemy's troops in that neighborhood, consumed little more than a week, as we recrossed to the north side of the river on the night of June 13.

We at once began our march northward, with the rest of the Sixth Corps, via Dumfries, Fairfax Court-House, Centreville, Dranesville, Edwards Ferry, Poolesville, New Market, and Manchester, halting here and there a day or two.

Passing through Maryland, we pushed into Pennsylvania, and arrived in the vicinity of Gettysburg on the afternoon of July 2, where we found a battle then going on. We were at once put into position on the extreme left, and lay on our arms all night on the field of battle.

The next day, July 3, was the hottest of the battle, and this was the severest engagement of the war. The brigade to which we are attached was constantly in posts of danger, but being used as a reserve, it was always sent to the points most pressed, and, though

---

* Embodied in revised statement, p. 181.

much exposed, was not directly engaged, but lay, seeing the fight progress, until our services were more actively needed, but we were not called on to fire a shot.

Never have I seen or heard of severer fighting. The field was bloody in the extreme. Our loss in this battle was 1 killed and 5 wounded. Killed: Private Charles Powers, Company C. Wounded: Corpl. John Leavitt, Company B, face; Private William McWilliams, Company E, hand; Private George Young, Company F, hand and arm; Private R. Barnett, Company H, knee and face; Private William Thomas, Company H, back.

Though the regiment has marched hundreds of miles in the last month, and performed much arduous duty, it is, I am happy to state, in excellent health and spirits.

I am, general, yours, very respectfully,
H. ROGERS, JR.,
Colonel Second Rhode Island Volunteers.

General E. C. MAURAN,
Adjutant-General of Rhode Island.

No. 234.

Report of Col. David J. Nevin, Sixty-second New York Infantry, commanding Third Brigade.

HDQRS. THIRD BRIG., THIRD DIV., SIXTH ARMY CORPS,
July 5, 1863.

SIR : I have the honor to make the following report of the operations of this brigade at the battle of Gettysburg, Pa.:

On the evening of July 1, I was placed temporarily in command of the four regiments present comprising it, viz: Sixty-second New York Volunteers, commanded by Lieut. Col. T. B. Hamilton ; Ninety-third Pennsylvania, Maj. John I. Nevin; Ninety-eighth Pennsylvania, Maj. J. B. Kohler, and One hundred and thirty-ninth Pennsylvania Volunteers, Col. F. H. Collier (the fifth regiment, One hundred and second Pennsylvania Volunteers, Col. J. W. Patterson, having been detailed to guard wagon train at Westminster, Md.).

At 9 p. m. of July 1, left bivouac near Manchester, Md., and, together with the other brigade of the division, marched toward Taneytown.

When a mile across the Gettysburg pike, were countermarched to the pike, and continued on in the direction of Gettysburg.

At 8 a. m. of July 2, passed through Littlestown, Pa., and halted at 2 p. m. within 2 miles of Cemetery Hill, having marched nearly 34 miles within seventeen hours.

At 4.30 p. m. we were hastily marched forward and to the left of Rocky Hill [Round Top], the extreme left of our line, to support the lines of the Second and Fifth Corps.

This brigade, having the advance, formed the first line of the Third Division, and had barely gotten into position when all the troops in front, excepting two regiments of the Pennsylvania Reserves, were driven back and up the hill, retreating irregularly through and past our line.

At that moment, three regiments (Sixty-second New York, Ninety-third and One hundred and thirty-ninth Pennsylvania Volunteers) were ordered to advance, supported on the left by the Ninety-eighth Pennsylvania Volunteers. They immediately closed up to the Pennsylvania Reserve regiments, and delivered two volleys into the ranks of the advancing rebels, and immediately after charged their column, breaking the same and driving them in disorder down the hill, recovering in the charge two light 12-pounder brass pieces which had been taken from the Fifth Corps. The brigade, after reaching the foot of Rocky Hill [Round Top], crossed a narrow swamp, and was halted at 100 yards beyond, the left resting at the foot of a small hill and the right in the works, connecting with the advance line of the —— Corps.

We remained in this position, supporting the two regiments of General Crawford's Pennsylvania Reserves, until 6 p. m. July 3.

On the 3d, at 10 a. m., the enemy made a reconnaissance in the front of the left of our line, but were repulsed.

At 2 p. m. the enemy shelled my whole line and the hill to our rear.

At 6 p. m. of July 3, orders were received to support a reconnaissance of General Crawford to the left. This was done, and, in addition to the support of two of my regiments, the Sixty-second New York and the One hundred and thirty-ninth Pennsylvania Volunteers, the latter commanded by Lieut. Col. W. H. Moody (Colonel Collier having been accidentally wounded early in the day), took an active part in the reconnaissance, the Sixty-second New York having advanced to the extreme left, and driving a regiment of rebels half a mile, capturing many prisoners, and the One hundred and thirty-ninth Pennsylvania advancing on the right of General Crawford's command, driving the rebel picket line back half a mile, and recapturing one brass Napoleon gun and three caissons, taken by the enemy from the Ninth Massachusetts Battery on the 2d.

At 9 a. m. on the morning of the 4th, orders were received to support a reconnaissance in force by General Sykes. During the rest of the day all remained quiet, and in the evening I was relieved of the command of the brigade by General F. Wheaton, who had temporarily commanded the Third Division.

The casualties in the brigade are as follows.*

In closing my report, I cannot withhold expression of my thanks to Capt. George Clendenin, jr., assistant adjutant-general, Third Brigade, for his valuable services; nor I can forget the assistance rendered me by Adjt. Samuel C. Thwait, Sixty-second New York Volunteers, acting aide-de-camp.

The extraordinary endurance evinced by my command, and their daring bravery at the turning point of the battle, deserve larger mention than the limit of the report will allow. Never did troops advance upon the enemies of their country with more cheerfulness and spirit.

Very respectfully, your obedient servant,
DAVID J. NEVIN,
Colonel Sixty-second New York Vols., Comdg. Brigade.

[Capt. GEORGE CLENDENIN, Jr.,
Assistant Adjutant-General.]

---

* Embodied in revised statement, p. 182.

No. 235.

Report of Maj. John B. Kohler, Ninety-eighth Pennsylvania Infantry.

HDQRS. NINETY-EIGHTH REGT. PENNSYLVANIA VOLS.,
August 1, 1863.

SIR: In accordance with circular of July 31, I have the honor to make the following statement:

On July 1, about 9 p. m., the regiment started from near Manchester, Md., where it had been resting since the previous evening, marched all night, and the following day arrived in the vicinity of the battle-field, to the left of Gettysburg, about 3 p. m., where soon after it formed in line of battle, supporting the part of the Second Corps which was engaged with the enemy. While getting into position, the regiment lost 1 officer and 9 men wounded by the enemy's sharpshooters.

During the whole of the 3d, the regiment was lying in the front line of battle, exposed to the enemy's fire, but protected by a stone wall. Here Lieutenant Manthe, of Company G, was wounded by one of the enemy's sharpshooters.

On the 4th, held the same position, nine companies going out on picket in the evening, the remaining one having been detailed to bury the dead.

On the 5th, the regiment again took up its line of march in the direction of Fairfield, and rested near Millersville.

On the 6th, passed through Fairfield and Emmitsburg, and on the 7th, through Spring Mills, Stocktonville, and Mechanicstown, resting near Hamburg, on the South Mountain.

On the 8th, passed through Lewistown, Franklinville, and Belleville, resting near Middletown.

On July 9, marched to Boonsborough, and July 10 to Funkstown, where heavy skirmishing was going on at the time, and formed in line of battle.

On the 11th, the regiment was again detailed for picket, relieving the Sixth Vermont, in command of Major Nelson.

On the morning of the 12th, passed through Funkstown, three companies having been previously detailed on the advance, under command of Lieutenant-Colonel Hamilton, Sixty-second New York Volunteers, and was engaged in throwing up earthworks during the night.

On the 13th, 4 officers and 200 men, under command of Lieutenant-Colonel Wetherill, Eighty-second Pennsylvania Volunteers, were ordered on picket again.

On the 14th, marched to Williamsport; on the 15th, to Boonsborough, and on the 16th to Berlin, where we remained until July 18.

I am, sir, respectfully, your obedient servant,

JOHN B. KOHLER,
Major, Comdg. Ninety-eighth Regiment Pennsylvania Vols.

[Capt. GEORGE CLENDENIN, Jr.,
Assistant Adjutant-General.]

No. 236.

Report of Col. John W. Patterson, One hundred and second Pennsylvania Infantry.

HDQRS. 102D REGIMENT PENNSYLVANIA VOLUNTEERS,
August 4, 1863.

SIR: In compliance with circular from brigade headquarters, dated August 3, 1863, I have the honor to forward the following report of the operations of my command from July 1 to 17, 1863, inclusive:

July 1, camp near Manchester.—Was ordered to report to division quartermaster, for the purpose of guarding supply train to Westminster. Arrived at the latter place on the morning of the 2d. Reported to General Buford, and received instructions to picket roads leading to Gettysburg, Emmitsburg, and Taneytown.

On the morning of the 5th, were relieved by cavalry, and moved to camp at wagon park.

July 6.—Moved my regiment to the north and west of the town. At midnight joined the corps trains, and, after a fatiguing march through mud and rain, arrived and bivouacked within 1 mile of Frederick City.

July 8.—At 12 m. of this date, resumed the march, passing through Frederick City, and at 7 p. m. reported myself and command to the general commanding the brigade, at Middletown.

July 9.—Left Middletown, arriving at Boonsborough about noon; went into line of battle, bivouacked for the night, and, on the morning of the 10th, moved forward to near Funkstown.

July 11.—Went on picket to the right of the Hagerstown road and near to Antietam Creek, relieving the Fifth Vermont Regiment, of the Second Division.

On the morning of the 13th, moved forward, and took up position about 4 miles east of Williamsport, hearing picket firing in our immediate front. Heavy rain until nearly dark.

At 1 a. m. of the 14th, relieved the Ninety-third Pennsylvania Volunteers, throwing up breastworks.

July 15.—Moved to Williamsport, and went into camp.

July 16.—Countermarched, and about noon reached Boonsborough.

July 17.—Company B, detached with ammunition train, reported to me for duty with regiment. Resumed the march, and in the evening arrived within 2 miles of Berlin, Md.

I am, sir, very respectfully, your obedient servant,

JOHN W. PATTERSON,
Colonel One hundred and second Regt. Pennsylvania Vols.

Capt. GEORGE CLENDENIN, Jr., *Assistant Adjutant-General.*

No. 237.

Report of Lieut. Col. William H. Moody, One hundred and thirty-ninth Pennsylvania Infantry.

HDQRS. 139TH PENNSYLVANIA VOLUNTEERS,
August 3, 1863.

SIR : I have the honor to report the operations of my command from July 1 to July 17, inclusive,

On the evening of July 1, we left our bivouac near Manchester,

Md. ; marched all night, and reached the battle-field of Gettysburg, Pa., about 3 o'clock on the afternoon of the 2d, having traversed a distance of 36 miles.

About 5 o'clock in the evening the regiment, together with the rest of the brigade, was ordered into action on our left, which was seriously threatened. General Sykes' regulars, unable to withstand the fierce onslaught of the enemy, broke through our line in confusion. We delivered two volleys, and then charged on the enemy, driving him back in disorder. We lay that night and during the day of the 3d in the second line of battle, supporting the Pennsylvania Reserves.

Early on the morning of the 3d, Col. F. H. Collier accidentally shot himself through the foot with a pistol-ball, and was compelled to leave his command.

In the evening of the same day, the regiment took a prominent part in advancing our left, driving the enemy and recapturing one brass piece and three caissons belonging to the Ninth Massachusetts Battery.

Our casualties in the battle of the 2d and the affair of the 3d (which have already been officially reported) were as follows : Three officers wounded, 1—Capt. Jeremiah M. Sample—mortally ; enlisted men, 17 wounded, two of whom have since died. Word of the death of Captain Sample has also been received.

During the 4th, we remained at the front, and, on the afternoon of the 5th, joined in the pursuit of the enemy ; came up with his rear guard near Fairfield. Remained in bivouac there until the evening of the 6th; then made a night march to Emmitsburg, Md.

On the 7th, crossed Catoctin Mountains.

On the 8th, marched to Middletown.

On the 9th, to Boonsborough.

On the 10th, lay in line of battle near Antietam battle-field.

On the 11th, the regiment was ordered on picket near Funkstown.

On the morning of the 12th, advanced my picket line on the south side of Antietam Creek as far as Funkstown, which was then evacuated by the enemy. Advanced through Funkstown, and went into line of battle a mile the other side, assisting during the night to erect breastworks. Remained there till the morning of the 14th, when it was ascertained that the enemy had left during the night and crossed the Potomac ; marched to Williamsport.

On the 15th, marched back to Boonsborough, and, on the 16th, to within a short distance of Berlin, where we bivouacked on the 17th.

Very respectfully, your obedient servant,

WM. H. MOODY,
Lieut. Col., Comdg. 139th Pennsylvania Vols.

Captain CLENDENIN, Jr., *Assistant Adjutant-General.*

No. 238.

Reports of Capt. William H. McCartney, First Massachusetts Battery, Artillery Brigade, Sixth Army Corps.

CAMP OF BATTERY A, MASSACHUSETTS ARTILLERY,
July 11, 1863.

SIR: I have the honor to report that on the 3d day of July, current, this command was ordered into position on the left of the cemetery near Gettysburg, by Major Osborn, chief of artillery Eleventh Corps, to relieve the First New Hampshire Battery, said to have been out of ammunition.

I have also the honor to report that I caused to be collected, from a piece of woods directly in rear of the ground which had been occupied by said First New Hampshire Battery, 48 rounds of 3-inch projectiles, perfect; 22 rounds having been found near the position which had been occupied by one limber.

I am, sir, with very much respect,

W. H. McCARTNEY,
Captain, Commanding.

Capt. A. E. KING,
Assistant Adjutant-General.

CAMP BATTERY A, MASSACHUSETTS ARTILLERY,
Near Sulphur Springs, Va., August 14, 1863.

SIR: I have the honor to submit the following as the operations of the battery from June 28, 1863, to the time of the arrival of this command at Warrenton:

On the morning of the 28th of June, being then near Edwards Ferry, the battery marched through Poolesville, Md., to near Franklinville. It continued moving in a northerly direction through Maryland each day until July 2.

At about 4 o'clock p. m. July 3, the command was ordered into position near the cemetery, on the left and rear of Gettysburg, but the enemy had been repulsed before the battery took position, and the battery was not engaged to any extent, four solid shot only having been fired.

In the afternoon of July 5, this battery marched toward Emmitsburg, and continued the march nearly every day until July 25, when it reached the immediate vicinity of Warrenton.

I have also the honor to submit that during the time above referred to nothing of importance occurred to weaken the men or *matériel* of this command, excepting the loss of horses by constant marches, which I am happy to say has been repaired since the date above last mentioned.

I am, sir, respectfully,

W. H. McCARTNEY,
Captain, Commanding.

Lieut. CRAWFORD ALLEN,
Acting Assistant Adjutant-General.

No. 239.

Report of Capt. Andrew Cowan, First New York Battery.

WARRENTON, VA.,
August 15, 1863.

SIR: I have the honor to submit the following report:

On the 28th of June, with the Artillery Brigade, Sixth Corps, I marched from Edwards Ferry, Md., to Hyattstown; thence, on the 29th, to Sam's Creek; on the 30th, to near Manchester.

Leaving camp near Manchester at 9 p. m. July 1, and marching constantly, I arrived near the battle-field of Gettysburg at 10 p. m. the 2d, having followed the leading brigade of the Third Division.

Early on the morning of the 3d, I received orders from you to report with my battery to General Newton, commanding the First Corps. Guided by an aide of that general, I reached the front about 10 a. m. General Newton being at the moment absent, I moved forward and reported to General Doubleday, who decided that no more batteries were then required, and directed me to park near by. I parked a short distance from the front, and General Newton having returned, I rode forward and pointed out my position, which was less than 100 yards distant. Here I remained till about noon, when the rebels suddenly opened a heavy artillery fire on our lines. The shells, passing over our line, struck with much accuracy in and about the spot where I was parked, and my horses were suffering, when I received orders from General Newton to move up my battery as quickly as possible.

I advanced at a brisk trot, and, leaving my caissons in rear, came into position with General Doubleday's division, and opened fire on the enemy's batteries in my front, firing slowly and with much accuracy. The enemy had excellent range of my position. I held this position for over an hour, and then received orders to move to the crest farther to my right, with General Webb's brigade, as the enemy was advancing. I moved up at a gallop, and came into position, several other batteries being on my right and left. The rebel skirmishers had just commenced firing, and their second line was advancing from the woods. The artillery fire was quite accurate and did much execution; still, the rebel line advanced in a most splendid manner. I commenced firing canister at 200 yards, and the effect was greater than I could have anticipated. My last charge (a double-header) literally swept the enemy from my front, being fired at less than 20 yards. The infantry in front of five of my pieces, and posted behind a slight defense of rails, some 10 yards distant, turned and broke, but were rallied, and drawn off to the right of my battery by General Webb in a most gallant manner. It was then I fired my last charge of canister, many of the rebels being over the defenses and within less than 10 yards of my pieces. They broke and fled in confusion. My battery was the only remaining one on this part of the hill.

The cannoneers being driven from ten pieces on my right, and the batteries on my left having retired, the enemy now advanced several smooth-bore batteries to within 1,300 yards, and opened on the part of the line which I occupied. I concentrated my fire on a single battery, and exploded four of its limbers in rapid succession, driving it from the field. Another 3-inch battery came up on my left, and also opened on them.

After about an hour, there was but one section of the enemy's batteries firing, and it soon limbered up. As it was retiring at a gallop, a shell from my right piece exploded one of its limbers.

My men performed their duty nobly. My loss was 4 privates killed instantly, and 1 soon after died of wounds; 4 enlisted men and 2 officers wounded.* As I have forwarded a report of their names, I deem it unnecessary to mention them here. I also lost 14 horses, and 8 wheels were disabled.

---

* But see revised statement, p. 182.

On the morning of the 5th, I was relieved by Battery G, First Rhode Island Artillery, and returned to camp, but immediately commenced to march in pursuit with the Sixth Corps. I placed one section in position near Millerstown, Pa., where we came up with the rebel rear.

On the night of the 6th, I marched from Millerstown, Pa., to Emmitsburg, Md.

On the 7th, marched in the direction of Middletown, but the mountain road, which we attempted to cross, being impassable, we were obliged to move in the road, and remained exposed to a drenching rain till morning.

On the 8th, crossed the South Mountain, and reached camp near Middletown at 4 p. m.

On the 9th, leaving Middletown at 12 m., marched to Boonsborough.

On the 10th, to Antietam Creek, where, by your orders, I came into battery on the left of the road. Remained in this position till 8 a. m. the 12th, when I received orders from you to report to General Wright. Was ordered into position by him on the right and left of the turnpike, about 2 miles from Hagerstown. Later the same day, by your orders, I took a position with the Third Division near the right center of our line. Remained here till July 14, when I marched to Williamsport.

On the 15th, marched to Boonsborough.

On the 16th, to near Berlin. Crossed the Potomac at 11 a. m. July 20, and marched out 8 miles on the Leesburg turnpike, and camped near Philomont.

On the 22d, marched to Goose Creek.

On the 23d, to the vicinity of Chester Gap.

On the 24th, to Manassas Gap, and thence to Orleans.

On the 25th, marched to Warrenton.

I am, sir, very respectfully, your obedient servant,

ANDREW COWAN,
Captain First Independent Battery, New York State Vols.

Col. C. H. Tompkins,
Commanding Artillery Brigade.

No. 240.

Report of Capt. William A. Harn, Third New York Battery.

——, —— —, 1863.

Sir: Started from Stafford Heights at daylight of the 14th June; halted at Stafford Court-House for a rest; started again about 10 p. m.

June 15.—Halted at Dumfries, and went into camp.

June 16.—On the road again about 2.30 a. m.; halted near Fairfax Station, Va.; very dusty traveling.

June 17.—In camp near Fairfax Station.

June 18.—Marched from camp near the station about 7 a. m.; passed through Fairfax, and went into camp about half a mile from the village.

June 19.—In camp near Fairfax; raining very hard.

June 20.—Still in camp; Lieutenant Harn received his commission as captain

June 21, 22, 23.—Still in camp near Fairfax.

June 24.—Left camp near Fairfax about 3 p. m.; arrived at camp near Centreville about 5 p. m.

June 25.—Shifted camp ; battery in camp on the heights of Centreville.

June 26.—Marched from Centreville to Dranesville.

June 27.—Marched from camp near Dranesville about 4 a. m.; crossed the Potomac at Edwards Ferry, and went into camp for the night near Poolesville, Md.

June 28.—On the march; about 4 a. m. passed through Barnesville and Hyattstown ; encamped in the field.

June 29.—On the road again at 4 a. m.; battery halted at New Market, bringing up the rear of the column ; reached camp at midnight.

June 30.—Marched again about 6 a. m. ; passed through Westminster, halted, and went into camp about 2 miles from Manchester.

July 1.—In camp near Manchester; started about 8 p. m. ; passed through Littlestown, Pa., about noon of the 2d of July.

July 2.—Encamped near the battle-field of Gettysburg, Pa.

July 3.—In camp, awaiting orders; battery hitched up. Battery ordered in front; went into position.

July 4.—Moved from position to the rear ; battery still hitched up, waiting orders.

July 5.—Marched about 6 a. m.; opened fire on the rear guard of the enemy about 8 a. m. with one section of the battery. Limbered up, and again took position, keeping within supporting distance of the skirmishers, until our advance was checked by the rear guard of the enemy, which was supported by artillery. The battery moved quickly to the front, and took up position on the heights overlooking the town of Fairfield, and opened fire on the enemy, driving him from his position. Battery remained in position all night.

July 6.—Marched at 4 p. m.; passed through Fairfield; battery in park outside the town. Started again about dusk; passed through Emmitsburg about midnight; went into camp.

July 7.—Started about 7 a. m. in the direction of Middletown; marched all day; took the wrong road; reversed limbers, and remained in the road all night.

July 8.—Started about daylight; proceeded over the mountain in the direction of Middletown; encamped about 1½ miles from the town.

July 9.—Marched about noon; passed through Middletown and Boonsborough; battery in position outside the town.

July 10.—Started about 5 a. m. in advance of the Vermont Brigade, supporting the cavalry and horse artillery of General Buford, driving the enemy in the direction of Funkstown, where we found him in strong position. Battery took up position, supporting the Vermont Brigade. Occasional firing during the day.

July 11.—Same position as the preceding day.

July 12.—Passed through Funkstown; went into position; limbered up, and went into camp about 7 p. m.

July 13.—Battery hitched up all day.

July 14.—Marched in the direction of Williamsport; encamped near the town.

July 15.—Marched through Hagerstown, Funkstown, and Boonsborough; encamped near the town.

July 16.—Marched about 4 a. m.; passed through Middletown; went into camp near Berlin about 5 p. m.

July 17.—In camp near Berlin; raining.
July 18.—Same as preceding day.
July 19.—Marched about 7 a. m.; crossed the Potomac at Berlin, Md.; passed through Lovettsville, Va.; went into camp about 5 p. m.
July 20.—Marched all day; went into camp at 7 p. m.
July 21.—Shifted camp.
July 22.—Marched from camp in the field about 10 a. m.; went into camp about 6 p. m., near Goose Creek.
July 23.—Started at daylight; arrived about 8 a. m. at Snickersville; left again about 10 a. m.; passed through Salem, and went into camp about 11 p. m.
July 24.—Left camp at 6 o'clock, and marched in the direction of Manassas Gap; battery halted for two hours or thereabouts; proceeded in the direction of Orleans; battery in camp about 8 p. m.
July 25.—Marched at 7 a. m.; passed through Orleans; went into camp about 1 mile from Warrenton at 5 p. m.

W. A. HARN,
Captain, Commanding Third New York Battery.

Col. C. H. TOMPKINS,
Commanding Artillery Brigade.

No. 241.

Report of Capt. Richard Waterman, Battery C, First Rhode Island Light Artillery.

NEAR NEW BALTIMORE, VA.,
August 16, 1863.

SIR: I have the honor to submit the following report of the operations of this battery since the 28th of June, 1863:

June 28.—Battery marched at 5 a. m. 18 miles, and camped near Hyattstown, Md.
June 29.—Command marched at 5 a. m. 25 miles; camped at dusk at Sam's Creek.
June 30.—Battery marched at 6 a. m. 15 miles. Section under command of Lieutenant Rich attached to General Torbert's brigade, to bring up the rear of the column. Camped at 11 p. m. near Manchester.
July 1.—Broke camp at 9 p. m.; marched during the night, and at 3 p. m. on the 2d instant, parked near Gettysburg, Pa.; marched 35 miles.
July 3.—Started for the front at 4.30 p. m., and remained within supporting distance till 6 p. m., when took position to left of Gettysburg, supported by a portion of Brigadier-General Webb's division. Remained in position during the night.
July 4.—Still in position.
July 5.—Relieved at 5 a. m., and joined corps. At 10 a. m. marched to within 2 miles of Fairfield, Pa., 6 miles, and camped.
July 6.—Battery marched at 3 p. m. 16 miles; camped near Emmitsburg at 3 a. m. on 7th instant.
July 7.—Marched at 7 a. m.; went 10 miles, and halted at 4 p. m. in road at foot of Cumberland [Catoctin] Mountains. Remained in road during the night.

July 8.—Started at daylight; arrived at top of Cumberland [Catoctin] Mountains at 6 p. m.; started down the mountains at nightfall; arrived at camp near Middletown, Md., at 4 a. m. on 9th instant.

July 9.—Four pieces moved at 3 a. m.; marched 8 miles; camped at Boonsborough, Md., at 5 p. m.

July 10.—Two pieces, under command of Lieutenant Rich, joined the battery at 9 a. m. Marched toward Funkstown, Md.; battery took position at 8.20. At 3.15, two pieces advanced and went into position, commanding woods in front.

July 11.—At 7 p. m. Lieutenant Rich's section advanced, and fired 4 rounds over Funkstown.

July 12.—Marched at 7 a. m. through Funkstown, and went into position one-half mile beyond the town. Moved farther to left at 5 p. m.

July 13.—Hitched up during the day.

July 14.—Marched at 10 a. m. 8 miles on Williamsport road; camped 3¼ miles from the town.

July 15.—Marched at 7 a. m. 20 miles, through Hagerstown and Funkstown; camped at Boonsborough at 4 p. m.

July 16.—Marched at 6 a. m. 12 miles; camped near Berlin, Md.

July 19.—Broke camp at 8 a. m.; marched through Berlin; crossed Potomac on pontoon bridge; camped at 3.30 p. m., having marched 11 miles.

July 20.—Marched at 10 a. m. 10 miles; camped at 7.30 p. m.

July 21.—Changed camp at 11 a. m.; marched 2 miles.

July 22.—Marched at 2 p. m. 7 miles; camped at Rector's Cross-Roads.

July 23.—Marched at 5.15 a. m. to Rectortown, Va.; arrived there at 7.30 a. m. Started again at 2 p. m.; camped at 10 p. m.; marched 10 miles.

July 24.—Marched at 5 a. m.; halted at 12 m.; watered, fed, and grazed horses. At 2 p. m. countermarched; went on road leading to Orleans; camped at dusk at Thumb Creek.

July 25.—Left camp at 7 a. m.; arrived at camp near Warrenton, Va., at 5 p. m.; marched 15 miles.

Very respectfully, your obedient servant,

RICH'D WATERMAN,
Captain First Rhode Island Artillery.

Lieut. CRAWFORD ALLEN, Jr.,
Acting Assistant Adjutant-General.

No. 242.

Report of Capt. George W. Adams, Battery G, First Rhode Island Light Artillery.

NEAR WARRENTON,
August 14, 1863.

June 28.—Left Edwards Ferry, Md., at 5 a. m.; passed through Poolesville and Barnesville; camped near New Market; 18 miles.

June 29.—Broke camp at 4.30 a. m.; passed through Monrovia, New Market, Ridgeville, and Mount Airy, and encamped at Sam's Creek; 25 miles.

June 30.—Broke camp at 3 a. m.; marched through Westminster, and encamped at night 2 miles from Manchester; 18 miles.

July 1.—Broke camp at 8 p. m.   After a march of 5 miles, entered the Westminster and Gettysburg turnpike, and continued the march rapidly throughout the night.

July 2.—Crossed the Maryland and Pennsylvania line at sunrise; passed through Littlestown; arrived at Gettysburg at 4 p. m.; 35 miles.

July 3.—Moved forward from position of last night toward the front and center; formed sections, and halted on the right of Hazlett's battery.   Remained in reserve during the day.   Toward night moved to the rear 1 mile, and encamped.

July 4.—Battery remained in camp all day.

July 5.—Battery moved to the front at 4 a. m., and relieved Cowan's New York Independent Battery.   Some hours after, advanced in line of battle; came up with the rear guard of the enemy near Fairfield; went into position; expended 162 rounds of ammunition, sustaining a fire of artillery without loss; bivouacked on the field; distance, 5 miles.

July 6.—Moved out of position at 3 p. m.; passed through Fairfield, and encamped at 11 p. m. near Emmitsburg; 11 miles.

July 7.—Broke camp at 6 a. m.; passed through Mechanicstown and Georgetown; took the road leading over the Catoctin Mountain, and bivouacked at the foot of the mountain.

July 8.—Crossed the mountain; entered the valley; moved toward Middletown over almost impassable roads, and bivouacked on the roadside near Middletown.

July 9.—Started at 6 a. m.; arrived at camp of Artillery Brigade, Sixth Corps, situated one-half mile from Middletown.

July 10.—Remained in camp all day.

July 11.—Left camp at 6 a. m.; passed through Middletown, South Mountain Gap, and Boonsborough, and encamped near Funkstown.

July 12.—Shortly after, were ordered into position on Antietam Creek.   Moved out of position at 2 p. m.; marched through Funkstown; crossed Antietam Creek, and went into position on the line of battle.

July 13.—In position all day.

July 14.—The enemy having fallen back, moved out of position; marched toward and encamped near Williamsport.

July 15.—Left Williamsport; passed through Hagerstown and Boonsborough, and encamped near the town.

July 16.—Left camp near Boonsborough; passed through South Mountain Gap and Middletown, and encamped near Berlin.

July 17.—In camp all day.

July 18.—In camp all day.

July 19.—Marched through Berlin; crossed the Potomac River; marched through Lovettsville, and encamped at Wheatland.

July 20.—Marched through Purcellville and Union, and encamped near Philomont.

July 21.—Passed through Union, and encamped near Millville.

July 22.—Marched through Millville, and encamped at Middleburg.

July 23.—Marched at sunrise on the road leading to Rectortown; halted at 12 m.; at 2 p. m. continued the march; passed through Salem, and encamped near Cobbler Mountain.

July 24.—Marched through Markham Station, and encamped 1 mile from Barbee's Cross-Roads.

July 25.—Broke camp; marched through Orleans, and encamped at Warrenton.

GEO. W. ADAMS,
Capt. First Rhode Island Light Artillery, Comdg. Co. G.

Col. C. H. TOMPKINS,
　　Commanding Artillery Brigade.

No 243.

Reports of Maj. Gen. Oliver O. Howard, U. S. Army, commanding Eleventh Army Corps, with congratulatory order.

HDQRS. ELEVENTH CORPS, ARMY OF THE POTOMAC,
July 1, 1863—5 p. m.

GENERAL: General Reynolds attacked the enemy as soon as he arrived, with one division, about 10.45 a. m. He moved to the front of the town, driving in the enemy's advance for about half a mile, when he met with a strong force of A. P. Hill's corps. I pushed on as fast as I could by a parallel road; placed my corps in position on his right. General Reynolds was killed at 11.15 a. m. I assumed command of the two corps, and sent word to Slocum and Sickles to move up. I have fought the enemy from that time till this. The First Corps fell back, when outflanked on its left, to a stronger position, when the Eleventh Corps was ordered back, also to a stronger position.

General Hancock arrived at 4 p. m., and communicated his instructions. I am still holding on at this time.

Slocum is near, but will not come up to assume command.

　　Respectfully,

O. O. HOWARD,
Major-General.

General MEADE.

HEADQUARTERS ELEVENTH CORPS,
July 1, 1863.

GENERAL: General Hancock's order, in writing, to assume command reached here at 7. At that time, General Slocum being present, having just arrived at this point, I turned over the command to him. This evening I have read an order stating that if General Slocum was present he would assume command. I believe I have handled these two corps to-day from a little past 11 until 4, when General H. assisted me in carrying out orders which I had already issued, as well as any of your corps commanders could have done.

Had we received re-enforcements a little sooner, the first position assumed by General Reynolds, and held by General Doubleday till my corps came up, might have been maintained; but the position was not a good one, because both flanks were exposed, and a heavy force approaching from the northern roads rendered it untenable, being already turned, so that I was forced to retire the command to the position now occupied, which I regard as a very strong one.

The above has mortified me and will disgrace me.   Please inform me frankly if you disapprove of my conduct to-day, that I may know what to do.

I am, general, very respectfully, your obedient servant,

O. O. HOWARD,
Major-General, Commanding.

Major-General MEADE,
Commanding Army of the Potomac.

—

HEADQUARTERS ELEVENTH CORPS,
July 1, 1863—10 p. m.

The loss in my corps is about 3,000 killed, wounded, and missing. In the two corps we have lost one piece of artillery.   This position is plenty good for a general battle unless you fear its being turned at a considerable distance from Gettysburg.

Respectfully,

O. O. HOWARD,
Major-General, Commanding.

Major-General. BUTTERFIELD,
Chief of Staff.

—

HEADQUARTERS ELEVENTH CORPS,
July 3, 1863—2.15 p. m.

SIR: The fire has been concentrated upon this point about an hour, with no great effect.

The batteries on our right do not reach us, and in the center invariably overshoot us.

Respectfully,

O. O. HOWARD,
Major-General, Commanding.

Major-General MEADE,
Commanding Army of the Potomac.

—

HDQRS. ELEVENTH CORPS, ARMY OF THE POTOMAC,
Gettysburg, Pa., July 4, 1863.

GENERAL: I have the honor to report that my command is supplied with two days' rations from to-morrow morning, and that two days' more are now on the road for this place.   This corps is entirely out of forage, but two days' [supply] will reach here to-night or early to-morrow.

Inclosed please find a sketch, showing the position of the corps; the First Division on the right, the Third Division in the center, and the Second Division on the left; my right extending 300 yards east of the Two Taverns road, connecting with the First Division of the First Corps, and my left connecting with the First Corps.   One brigade of the Second Division is occupying the town, the skirmishers connecting on the right and left with the First and Third Divisions, respectively.

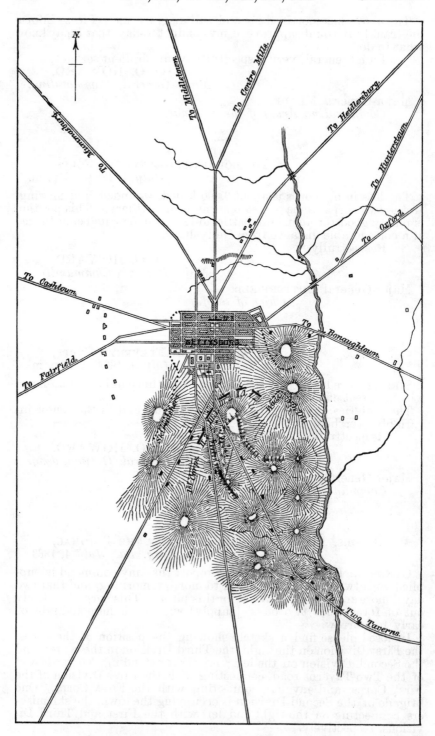

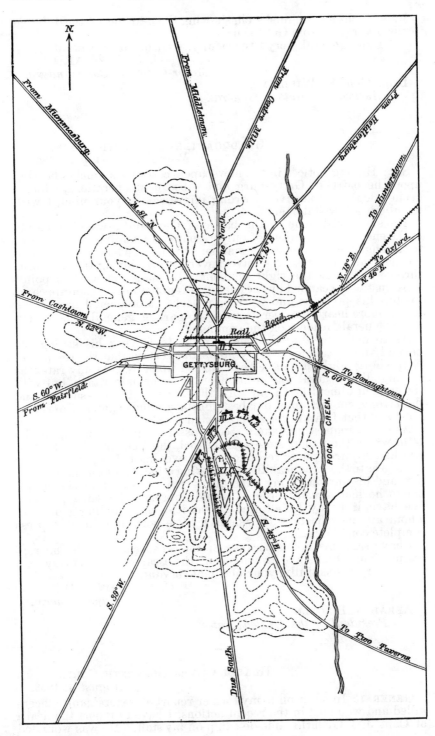

I also inclose a rough sketch, showing the bearings of the different roads diverging from Gettysburg.

I am, general, very respectfully, your obedient servant,

O. O. HOWARD,
Major-General, Commanding.

Brig. Gen. S. WILLIAMS,
Assistant Adjutant General.

HEADQUARTERS ELEVENTH CORPS,
Near Berlin, July 18, 1863.

SIR: Having noticed in the newspapers certain statements bearing upon the battle of Gettysburg and subsequent operations, which I deem calculated to convey a wrong impression to your mind, I wish to submit a few statements.

The successful issue of the battle of Gettysburg was due mainly to the energetic operations of our present commanding general prior to the engagement, and to the manner in which he handled his troops on the field. The reserves have never before during this war been thrown in at just the right moment. In many cases when points were just being carried by the enemy, a regiment or brigade appeared to stop his progress and hurl him back. Moreover, I have never seen a more hearty co-operation on the part of general officers than since General Meade took the command.

As to not attacking the enemy prior to leaving his stronghold beyond the Antietam, it is by no means certain that the repulse of Gettysburg might not have been turned upon us. At any rate, the commanding general was in favor of an immediate attack, but with the evident difficulties in our way, the uncertainty of a success, and the strong conviction of our best military minds against the risk, I must say that I think the general acted wisely.

As to my request to make a reconnaissance on the morning of the 14th, which the papers state was refused, the facts are, that the general had required me to reconnoiter the evening before, and give my opinion as to the practicability of making a lodgment on the enemy's left, and his answer to my subsequent request was that the movements he had already ordered would subserve the same purpose. We have, if I may be allowed to say it, a commanding general in whom all the officers with whom I have come in contact express complete confidence.

I have said this much because of the censure and of the misrepresentations which have grown out of the escape of Lee's army.

Very respectfully, your obedient servant,

O. O. HOWARD,
Major-General.

ABRAHAM LINCOLN,
President of the United States.

HEADQUARTERS ELEVENTH CORPS
August 4, 1863.

GENERAL: In addition to my former report of general staff officers killed and wounded in the recent actions, I have to report the death of Capt. J. J. Griffiths, aide-de-camp on my staff. He was wounded on the 5th of July, while on a reconnaissance with my body-guard, and died on the 10th of the same month.

I have the honor to be, very respectfully, your obedient servant,
O. O. HOWARD,
Major-General, Commanding.

Brig. Gen. S. WILLIAMS,
Assistant Adjutant-General, Army of the Potomac.

HEADQUARTERS ELEVENTH CORPS,
August 31, 1863.

GENERAL: On the evening of June 30, the First Corps, with the exception of one brigade and the supply train at Emmitsburg, was located in the vicinity of Marsh Run, on the direct road from Emmitsburg to Gettysburg, and nearly midway between those towns. The Eleventh Corps was at Emmitsburg.

Just at sunset I received a request from General Reynolds, commanding First Corps, to meet him at his headquarters. He then showed me the order from your headquarters placing him in command of the First, Eleventh, and Third Corps; also the circulars of the commanding general dated June 30, together with a confidential communication. The purport of these papers was that a general engagement was imminent, the issues involved immense, and all commanders urged to extraordinary exertions. General Reynolds and I consulted together, comparing notes and information, until a late hour. I then returned to Emmitsburg. A circular from your headquarters, of June 30, required corps commanders to hold their commands in readiness to move at a moment's notice.

At 3.30 a. m. July 1, orders were received from your headquarters to move the Eleventh Cor₁s to within supporting distance of the First Corps, which was to move to Gettysburg. I immediately sent an aide-de-camp to General Reynolds to receive his orders.

At 8 a. m. orders were received from him directing the corps to march to Gettysburg. The column was at once set in motion, my First Division, General Barlow commanding, following the First Corps by the direct route; my Third, General Schurz, and my Second, General Steinwehr, in the order named, taking the route by Horner's Mill. One battery accompanied the First Division; the remainder of the artillery (four batteries), under command of Major Osborn, accompanied the other two divisions. The distance by the direct route was between 10 and 11 miles, and by the other about 13. As soon as the corps was set in motion, I pushed on with my staff by the direct road, and when within 2 miles of Gettysburg received word from General Reynolds, pointing out the place where I was to encamp; but on approaching the town, heavy artillery firing was heard. For some little time I endeavored, by sending in different directions, to find General Reynolds, in order to report to him in person.

In the meantime I went to the top of a high building in Gettysburg, facing westward. I saw firing beyond Seminary Ridge and not far from the seminary. Toward the right, masses of cavalry were drawn up in order, to the east of the ridge and to the northeast of the town. A portion of the First Corps, of General Wadsworth's command, was between me and the seminary, taking position near the railroad. Another division of this corps was moving by the flank with considerable rapidity, along the ridge and in a northeasterly direction. I had studied the position a few moments, when a report reached me that General Reynolds was wounded. At first I hoped his wound might be slight, and that he would continue to command; but in a short time I was undeceived. His aide-de-camp, Major [William] Riddle, brought the sad tidings of his death. This was about 11.30 a. m. Prior to this the general had sent me orders to move up at double-quick, for he was severely engaged.

On hearing of the death of General Reynolds, I assumed command of the left wing, instructing General Schurz to take command of the Eleventh Corps. After an examination of the general features of the country, I came to the conclusion that the only tenable position for my limited force was the ridge to the southeast of Gettysburg, now so well known as Cemetery Ridge. The highest point at the cemetery commanded every eminence within easy range. The slopes toward the west and south were gradual, and could be completely swept by artillery. To the north, the ridge was broken by a ravine running transversely.

I at once established my headquarters near the cemetery, and on the highest point north of the Baltimore pike. Here General Schurz joined me before 12 m., when I instructed him to make the following dispositions of the Eleventh Corps. Learning from General Double-day, commanding the First Corps, that his right was hard pressed, and receiving continued assurance that his left was safe and push-ing the enemy back, I ordered the First and Third Divisions of the Eleventh Corps to seize and hold a prominent height on the right of the Cashtown road and on the prolongation of Seminary Ridge, each division to have a battery of artillery, the other three batteries, sup-ported by General Steinwehr's division (Second), to be put in position near me on Cemetery Hill.

About 12.30 [p. m.] General Buford sent me word that the enemy was massing between the York and Harrisburg roads, to the north of Gettysburg, some 3 or 4 miles from the town. Quite a large num-ber of prisoners had already been taken by the First Corps. They reported that we were engaging Hill's corps, or a portion of it, and that an aide of General Longstreet had arrived, stating that he would be up with one division in a short time. About this time the head of column of the Eleventh Corps entered and passed through the town, moving forward rapidly toward the position ordered.

The news of Ewell's advance from the direction of York was con-firmed by reports from General Schurz, General Buford, and Major [Charles H.] Howard, my aide-de-camp, who had been sent in that direction to reconnoiter. I therefore ordered General Schurz to halt his command, to prevent his right flank being turned, but to push forward a thick line of skirmishers, to seize the point first indicated, as a relief and support to the First Corps.

Meanwhile word was sent to General Sickles, commanding Third Corps, and General Slocum, commanding Twelfth, informing them of the situation of affairs, with a request that General Sickles for-ward my dispatch to General Meade. General Sickles was at that time, about 1 p. m., near Emmitsburg, and General Slocum reported to be near Two Taverns, distant between 4 and 5 miles from Gettys-burg.

At 2 p. m. a report of the state of things as then existing was sent to General Meade directly. About this time I left my chief of staff to execute orders, and went to the First Corps. I found General Doubleday about a quarter of a mile beyond the seminary. His

Third Division was drawn up to his front and left, facing toward the northwest, making a large angle with the ridge. The artillery of this division was engaging the enemy at this time. His First Division (Wadsworth's) was located a little to the right of the railroad, and his Second Division (Robinson's) on Wadsworth's right. The First Corps, in this position, made a right angle with the Eleventh Corps, the vertex being near the Mummasburg road. The cavalry of General Buford was located mainly upon the flanks. After inspecting the position of the First Corps, and examining the topography of that part of the field, I returned to my former position at the cemetery.

About this time (2.45 p. m.) the enemy showed himself in force in front of the Eleventh Corps. His batteries could be distinctly seen on a prominent slope between the Mummasburg and the Harrisburg roads.

From this point he opened fire upon the Eleventh Corps, and also more or less enfilading Robinson's division, of the First Corps. The batteries attached to the First and Third Divisions, Eleventh Corps, immediately replied, and with evident effect One battery of the enemy, a little more than a mile north from the cemetery, near the Harrisburg road, could be distinctly seen, and as I had a battery of 3-inch rifled guns, under Wiedrich, near my position, I directed him to fire, provided he could reach the enemy. He did so, but his shells for the most part fell short. Soon after, complaint came that they reached no farther than our own cavalry; however, I never heard that any of our own men were killed or wounded by this fire. The reason of this irregularity was the poor quality of the ammunition there used. Subsequently these guns did most excellent service.

I now sent again to General Slocum, stating that my right flank was attacked, and asking him if he was moving up, and stating that I was in danger of being turned and driven back. Before this, my aide-de-camp, Captain [Edward P.] Pearson, had been sent to General Sickles, requesting him to move up to Gettysburg as rapidly as possible. Owing to difficulty in finding General Sickles' headquarters, this message was not delivered until 3.30 p. m.

At 3.20 p. m. the enemy renewed his attack upon the First Corps, hotly pressing the First and Second Divisions. Earnest requests were made upon me for re-enforcements, and General Schurz, who was engaged with a force of the enemy much larger than his own, asked for a brigade to be placed *en échelon* on his right. I had then only two small brigades in reserve, and had already located three regiments from these in the edge of the town and to the north, and I felt sure that I must hold the point where I was as an ultimate resort. Therefore I at first replied that I could not spare any troops, but did afterward permit General Steinwehr to push out Colonel Coster's brigade beyond the town, to cover the retreat. General Buford was requested to support the center, near the right of the First Corps, as well as he could with his cavalry. A third battery was sent to the front, and put in position near the Third Division, Eleventh Corps.

At 3.45 [p. m.] Generals Doubleday and Wadsworth besought me for re-enforcements. I directed General Schurz, if he could spare one regiment or more, to send it to re-enforce General Wadsworth, and several times sent urgent requests to General Slocum to come to my assistance. To every application for re-enforcements, I replied, "H ld out, if possible, awhile longer, for I am expecting General

Slocum every moment." At this time General Doubleday's left was turned, and troops of the enemy appeared far outflanking him, and the enemy were also extending beyond my right flank.

About 4 p. m. I sent word to General Doubleday that, if he could not hold out longer, he must fall back, fighting, to Cemetery Hill and on the left of the Baltimore pike; also a request to General Buford to make a show of force opposite the enemy's right, which he immediately did. I now dispatched Major Howard, my aide-de-camp, to General Slocum, to inform him of the state of affairs, requesting him to send one of his divisions to the left, the other to the right, of Gettysburg, and that he would come in person to Cemetery Hill. He met the general on the Baltimore pike, about a mile from Gettysburg, who replied that he had already ordered a division to the right, and that he would send another to cover the left, as requested, but that he did not wish to come up in person to the front and take the responsibility of that fight. In justice to General Slocum, I desire to say that he afterward expressed the opinion that it was against the wish of the commanding general to bring on a general-engagement at that point.

At 4.10 p. m., finding that I could hold out no longer, and that the troops were already giving way, I sent a positive order to the commanders of the First and Eleventh Corps to fall back gradually, disputing every inch of ground, and to form near my position, the Eleventh Corps on the right and the First Corps on the left of the Baltimore pike. General Steinwehr's division, of the Eleventh Corps, and the batteries which he was supporting, were so disposed as to check the enemy attempting to come through the town, or to approach upon the right or left of Gettysburg. The movement ordered was executed, though with considerable confusion, on account of the First and Eleventh Corps coming together in the town.

At 4.30 p. m. the columns reached Cemetery Hill, the enemy pressing hard. He made a single attempt to turn our right, ascending the slope northeast of Gettysburg, but his line was instantly broken by Wiedrich's battery, in position on the heights.

General Hancock came to me about this time, and said General Meade had sent him on hearing the state of affairs; that he had given him his instructions while under the impression that he was my senior. We agreed at once that that was no time for talking, and that General Hancock should further arrange the troops, and place the batteries upon the left of the Baltimore pike, while I should take the right of the same. In a very short time we put the troops in position, as I had previously directed, excepting that General Wadsworth's division was sent to occupy a height to the right and rear of our position. In passing through the town we lost many prisoners, but the enemy, perceiving the strength of our position on the heights, made no further attempts to renew the engagement that evening.

About 7 p. m. Generals Slocum and Sickles arrived at the cemetery. A formal order was at the same time put into my hands, placing General Hancock in command of the left wing. But General Slocum being present, and senior, I turned the command over to him, and resumed the direct command of the Eleventh Corps; whereupon General Hancock repaired to the headquarters of General Meade.

The eventful day was over. The First and Eleventh Corps, numbering less than 18,000 men, nobly aided by Buford's division of cavalry, had engaged and held in check nearly double their numbers from 10 in the morning until 7 in the evening. They gave way, it is true, after hard fighting, yet they secured and held the remarkable position which, under the able generalship of the commander of this army, contributed to the grand results of July 2 and 3.

This day's battle cost us many valuable lives. Major-General Reynolds, a noble commander and long a personal friend, fell early in the action. Lieut. B. Wilkeson, a young officer of exceeding promise, was mortally wounded while in command of Battery G, Fourth U. S. Artillery. Brigadier-Generals Barlow and Paul were severely wounded. For mention of other distinguished officers killed or wounded, I would refer to reports of corps, division, and brigade commanders.

Major Osborn, commanding artillery of Eleventh Corps, reports that his artillery dismounted five of the enemy's guns, which were left on the field. He lost one of his own, which had been dismounted in the action.

I am conscious of an inability to do justice to the operations of the First Corps, never having received a single report from it. Doubtless the general commanding it gives directly and in full sufficient data to enable the commanding general to appreciate its noble behavior as well as its terrible sacrifices.

On the morning of July 2, about 3 a. m., the commanding general, who had previously arrived, met me at the cemetery gate, questioned me about the preceding day, and rode with me over the position then held by our troops. I expressed my opinion strongly in favor of the position. The general replied that he was glad to hear me speak thus, for it was too late to leave it. The Eleventh Corps was disposed with its center near the Baltimore pike—the First Division, General Ames, on the right; Third Division, General Schurz, in the center, and the Second Division, General Steinwehr, on the left. The batteries of the First and Eleventh Corps were united, being put in position with regard to the kind of gun. Colonel Wainwright, chief of artillery First Corps, took charge of all batteries to the right of the pike; Major Osborn, of the Eleventh, all batteries in the cemetery grounds to the left of the pike.

Very little occurred while the other corps were coming into position until about 4 p. m. Just before this, orders had been issued to the division commanders to make ready for battle, as the enemy were reported advancing on our left. Now the enemy opened from some dozen batteries to our right and front, bringing a concentrated fire upon our position. The batteries of Wainwright and Osborn replied with great spirit. Artillery projectiles often struck among the men, but in no case did a regiment break, though suffering considerably.

About 6.30 p. m. I sent word to General Meade that the enemy's batteries on our extreme right had been silenced or withdrawn. After the cannonading had ceased, and the enemy's infantry attack upon the left had been repulsed, another attack, said to be by Rodes' division, commenced between 7 and 8 p. m., beginning between Generals Slocum and Wadsworth, and extending along the front of Ames to the town of Gettysburg. A brigade of General Schurz's division was ordered to support General Ames. Another brigade of General Schurz pushed to the support of General Wadsworth, upon his right. Afterward General Greene, of the Twelfth Corps, came and thanked me for the good service done by this brigade. Lieutenant-Colonel [August] Otto, of General Schurz's staff, present with with it, was highly commended.

The attack was so sudden and violent that the infantry in front of Ames was giving way. In fact, at one moment the enemy had got within the batteries. A request for assistance had already gone to headquarters, so that promptly a brigade of the Second Corps, under Colonel Carroll, moved to Ames' right, deployed, and went into position just in time to check the enemy's advance. At Wiedrich's battery, General Ames, by extraordinary exertions, arrested a panic, and the men with sponge-staffs and bayonets forced the enemy back. At this time he received support from General Schurz. Effective assistance was also rendered at this time by a portion of General Steinwehr's command at points where the enemy was breaking through. This furious onset was met and withstood at every point, and lasted less than an hour.

At 9.30 p. m. the old position was resumed by the regiments of my corps, Colonel Carroll remaining between Ames and Wadsworth. Lest another attack should be made, Ames' position was further strengthened by the One hundred and sixth Pennsylvania Regiment, from the Second Corps. At the moment my left was weakened, as also at other times during the engagements, General Newton was ready with re-enforcements from the First Corps.

July 3, at 5 a. m., heavy infantry firing commenced on the right. It continued with more or less severity until after 10 a. m. Neither the artillery nor infantry of the Eleventh Corps were much engaged. Occasionally an attempt was made by the enemy to put batteries in position, and some shots were fired. He always received a prompt reply from our batteries, and failed to receive any advantage.

At about 1 p. m. a terrific cannonade opened upon us from the west, northwest, north, and northeast, hurling into the cemetery grounds missiles of every description. Shells burst in the air, in the ground to the right and left, killing horses, exploding caissons, overturning tombstones, and smashing fences. There was no place of safety. In one regiment 27 were killed and wounded by one shell, and yet the regiments of this corps did not move excepting when ordered.

At 2.30 p. m. we ceased our artillery fire. Soon after, the enemy's artillery also ceased, when a line of his infantry appeared, emerging from the woods upon Seminary Ridge, his left nearly opposite our front, and the line extending far to the left. Our batteries again opened fire, using shells at first. The gaps made by them seemed to have no effect in checking the onward progress of the enemy. Still his line advanced steadily, gaining ground gradually toward his right. When near our line of skirmishers, the batteries opened upon them with grape and canister from the hill. The infantry also commenced firing. The enemy's lines were broken, and the plain in our front was covered with fugitives running in every direction. Colonel Smith's brigade, of General Steinwehr's division, was pushed to the left and front, to the support of the First Corps, moving forward. At this time great numbers of prisoners were taken, in which this portion of the Second Division bore a part.

This was the last attack made by the enemy at the battle of Gettysburg. During the night he withdrew his entire force to and beyond Seminary Ridge.

Were I to accord praise to individuals, I would hardly know where to begin or where to end. I noticed Generals Schurz, Steinwehr, Schimmelfennig, and Ames; Colonels Orland Smith, Coster, Krzyzanowski, and von Gilsa, commanding brigades; also Major Osborn, commanding the artillery, and his battery commanders, and commend them for bravery, faithfulness, and efficiency in the discharge of duty.

I was highly gratified at the conduct and effectiveness of the artillery under Major Osborn. His report shows that he had three batteries at least sent to him from the Artillery Reserve besides his own. No officer could work harder or do better than he did during the batle.

I have mentioned General Barlow, who was so severely wounded the first day. General Schurz commends him highly for coolness and bravery on the field.

My inspector-general, acting chief of staff, my adjutant-general, my quartermaster, my chief commissary, and my aides, all were as brave and efficient as they could possibly be.

We all mourn the death of one specially beloved, Capt. J. J. Griffiths, aide-de-camp, who lived through the battle, but was mortally wounded during the reconnaissance of the Sunday following.

Every staff officer, in fact every officer and soldier who remained with his command, was almost constantly exposed to death or wounds during those three memorable days. My gratitude is so much due to them all that it seems almost invidious to particularize.

I wish to testify in this report to the hearty co-operation and generous support that I received from my associate corps commanders.

The grand results of the battle of Gettysburg are destined to bestow deserved and lasting honor upon the general commanding, and with him every true officer and brave man will claim a share; and yet no candid mind can review those scenes of horror, and doubt, and ultimate joy without feeling constrained to acknowledge the Divine hand which controlled and directed the storm.

Respectfully,

O. O. HOWARD,
Major-General.

Brig. Gen. S. Williams,
 Asst. Adjt. Gen., Hdqrs. Army of the Potomac.

—

HDQRS. ELEVENTH CORPS, ARMY OF THE POTOMAC,
September 9, 1863.

GENERAL: On the morning of June 28, my corps was located in the Middletown Valley, Md., two divisions near Middletown and one holding Boonsborough Gap.

About 2 p. m. an order was received to march to Frederick. Head of column left Middletown at 3 p. m., and arrived in camp north of Frederick, near Wormer's Mill, at 8 p. m. The entire corps, including train, was in camp by midnight.

At 11.30 p. m. the order came relieving General Hooker, and assigning General Meade to the command of the army; also the order of march for the following day. The First and Eleventh Corps were to march to Emmitsburg; the Eleventh to leave the turnpike to its left, marching by Creagerstown. The day was rainy, the roads heavy, and the march wearisome, yet the troops were in camp at Emmitsburg by 7 p. m., having made about 20 miles.

At 8.30 a. m. June 30, an order was received from headquarters to take position on the north side of Emmitsburg. The enemy was reported advancing on Gettysburg from Chambersburg. The First Corps, General Reynolds commanding, was moved to a position half way between Emmitsburg and Gettysburg, on Marsh Run. In case

of attack, the Eleventh Corps was directed to support the First
Corps. Subsequent orders, however, directed the First Corps to fall
back to Emmitsburg in case of attack. General Buford's division
of cavalry was already near Gettysburg. From this time until July
5 following, the ground is covered by my report of the battle of
Gettysburg.

At 4 a. m. July 5, the enemy were reported moving to the rear in
full retreat. Reconnaissances discovered the enemy's rear guard
about 2 miles to the west of Gettysburg. This was immediately reported to General Meade.

During the 4th and 5th, about 500 prisoners were taken by the
corps from the enemy's wounded and stragglers.

On the evening of the 5th, at 5.30 p. m., General Meade's order
to march to Middletown, by the way of Emmitsburg, Utica, and
High Knob, in two days, was received. The corps encamped near
Rocky [Rock] Creek that night. The Fifth and Eleventh Corps
were combined for the march, under my direction. The Fifth Corps
encamped upon the same creek. At this halt, an order was received
from your headquarters not to proceed with the march until further
orders.

The next day, July 6, the order for march was received, my corps
being ordered to Emmitsburg. At 7 p. m. the order was received to
execute the former order of march to Middletown.

The head of column left camp at 3.30 a. m. July 7, and about 8
p. m. the head of the column reached Middletown, Md. Owing to
the difficulty in crossing the mountains, and the fact that the artillery horses were nearly broken down by previous fatigue, only one
division (General Schurz's) succeeded in reaching Middletown; the
First and Second Divisions and artillery remained near High Knob.
The Fifth Corps encamped between Utica and High Knob.

The next day, July 8, the march was completed before 11 a. m.
The road over the mountain near High Knob was steep, narrow, and
very rocky, so that it was with the greatest difficulty that the artillery and trains were brought over. On this account the Fifth
Corps was conducted by another route, crossing the mountains a
little farther south.

At 1 p. m. an order was received to march at once to Boonsborough
Gap. The Third Division had executed the march at 5 p. m., when
General Buford, who was engaging the enemy, sent me word that
he was hard pressed, and asked for re-enforcements of infantry. The
Third Division (General Schurz's) was immediately sent forward
through the town of Boonsborough, while the First and Second Divisions and artillery were placed in position to the left of the pike,
on the western slope of the mountain, co-operating with the First
Corps, located on the right of the pike.

At 7 p. m. the Third Division took position on the Hagerstown
pike northwest of Boonsborough and 1 mile beyond. As soon as the
enemy saw our infantry approach, he retired toward Hagerstown.

During July 9, the First and Eleventh Corps remained in position,
excepting that the Sixth Corps, passing through the Gap, took position near Boonsborough, relieving my Third Division. During this
day every exertion was made to supply shoes and clothing that
were needed.

On the morning of July 10, the Sixth and First Corps were pushed
on to Beaver Creek and my corps to Boonsborough. I had hardly
arrived in camp when the order to report to General Sedgwick at

Beaver Creek was received. The corps renewed the march, and took position about 4.30 p. m. on the right of the Sixth Corps, near the Hagerstown and Smoketown road, 2½ miles from Funkstown. Occasional artillery firing was heard toward Funkstown.

July 11, the First, Eleventh, and Sixth Corps, under General Sedgwick, remained in position.

At 4 a. m. July 12, my First Division, under General Ames, marched to Hagerstown, to support Kilpatrick's cavalry. This force succeeded in entering Hagerstown, capturing some 100 prisoners.

At 11 a. m. the remainder of the corps marched to Funkstown; passed through the town; crossed the Antietam Creek, and took position on the right of the First Corps, about a mile south of Hagerstown.

At 7 p. m. the three corps, Sixth, First, and Eleventh, were marched to the left, in order to make connection with the rest of the army, already in position on the west bank of the Antietam. The Eleventh Corps still occupied the right of the line near Funkstown.

During the night, some covers for the artillery and rifle-pits were constructed. The general commanding called together his corps commanders during this evening, and counseled with them with regard to the enemy's position, strength, and intention, and asked their opinion with regard to making an attack upon the enemy, as affairs then stood. The decision was not to attack then, or until further information should be obtained.

July 13, one brigade was sent to Hagerstown as an outpost, and a support to the cavalry in case of necessity. I spent the day in personal reconnaissances, so as to obtain as accurate knowledge as possible of the enemy's works, a portion of which were in view from the church steeples in Hagerstown. I sent General Schimmelfennig with one regiment of infantry to reconnoiter the enemy's left. Before this regiment had passed Hagerstown, General Kilpatrick started to accomplish the same purpose, his cavalry being supported by a regiment of Pennsylvania militia, whereupon General Schimmelfennig joined the reconnaissance.

As soon as the cavalry skirmishers had approached the enemy's lines, he opened a brisk fire from infantry or dismounted cavalry. One or two pieces of artillery also fired at random from a battery near the Williamsport road. After this reconnaissance, and all the information I could collect, I was impressed with a belief that the enemy would retreat without giving us battle, and it was with a hope of being able to make a lodgment on the enemy's left that I then asked permission to make a reconnaissance at 3 a. m. of the next day (the 14th). Subsequently, the commanding general's order for several simultaneous reconnaissances at 7 a. m. reached me. I also received word, in answer to my request, that orders had already been sent out, which would probably effect the purpose I proposed.

On the morning of the 14th, a report was received from Hagerstown that the enemy had evacuated his position in that vicinity. At 11.20 a. m. orders were received from General Sedgwick to march to Williamsport, via Hagerstown. The enemy had completely crossed before my corps arrived. The inhabitants reported that he crossed on a bridge at Falling Waters, on flat-boats at Williamsport, and at a deep ford a little distance above that place; that many men and horses were drowned in fording the Potomac; that the bridge, boats, and all had been built at Williamsport and floated down to Falling Waters. The corps encamped near Leister's Mill, on Conococheague Creek, 1 mile from Williamsport.

At 1 a. m. July 15, the order of march for the next day to Berlin was given. The corps left camp at 4 a. m.; marched through Hagerstown, and thence to Middletown by the old Hagerstown road. It reached Middletown at 6 p. m. My train moved to Jefferson.

We took up the march at 5 a. m. of the 16th, and proceeded, via Jefferson, to Berlin. We went into camp near that place. Here orders were received and issued, directing the troops to replenish stores and prepare for an active campaign.

On the 17th, we remained in position.

On the 18th, orders having been received to follow the First Corps across the pontoon bridge at Berlin, observation was made as to the time when the First Corps should have crossed, when further orders were received to follow Buford's division of cavalry. My train and artillery began the crossing at 6 p. m., and encamped near Lovettsville, Va. The infantry began the march at 4 a. m. of the 19th, and the entire corps encamped about 4 p. m. near Warner's farm, on the Waterford and Hamilton road.

On the 20th, the corps marched under orders to Mountville, via Mount Gilead, making about 16 miles. During this march the enemy's guerrillas and bushwhackers annoyed us considerably, capturing a few stragglers.

During the 21st, the corps remained stationary, sending out scouting parties in different directions, one of which from General Schurz met a detachment of Mosby's guerrillas, and, after a little skirmish, recaptured those taken the day before.

On the 22d, a forage train, having started before its guard was ready, lost nine wagons, eight of which were retaken, but without the animals.

On the morning of the 23d, orders were received at 3.40 a. m. to march to New Baltimore. Head of column left camp within an hour from the receipt of the order. The weather was very warm and sultry. Head of column arrived at New Baltimore about 6 p. m.

On the 24th, the corps remained in camp, opening communication with the First Corps at Warrenton and receiving supplies from White Plains. Information received this day from general headquarters that but one division of the enemy was found at Front Royal; the rest of his force reported to have gone toward Culpeper and Gordonsville.

On the 25th, the march was made from New Baltimore to Warrenton Junction, in the vicinity of which the corps has been ever since, excepting Gordon's division (i. e., First Division of this corps), detached and sent to Alexandria for embarkation August 6.

General Gordon joined the corps at Berlin. Ten regiments, each about 500 strong, four of them being nine-months' troops, joined the corps as follows: Three at or near Funkstown with General Tyndale; the rest at Berlin or en route thither. One of these had but two days to serve, and left the corps near Hagerstown, viz, One hundred and sixty-ninth Pennsylvania.

During the entire campaign I received the most hearty co-operation from my division commanders, from the commander of the artillery, as also from every member of my staff.

I believe the corps successfully executed every order of the commanding general of the army. Sometimes the marches were long and tedious, but they were always performed with cheerfulness, and very little straggling can be laid to our charge.

I feel grateful to the officers and men of the corps for the part they have borne in this eventful campaign, and whatever misrepresentation or prejudice may have set against them, they nevertheless deserve the gratitude of their country.

I have the honor to be, respectfully,

O. O. HOWARD,
Major-General.

Brig. Gen. S. WILLIAMS,
Asst. Adjt. Gen., Army of the Potomac.

—

HEADQUARTERS ELEVENTH CORPS,
March 27, 1864.

GENERAL: Will you have the kindness to attach the inclosed copy of a letter written to Col. S. S. Carroll, commanding brigade, Second Corps, dated Warrenton Junction, Va., July 29, 1863, to my report of the battle of Gettysburg? Colonel Carroll never furnished me a report of the part taken by his command in that battle. I had presumed that he had done so to General Gibbon until I read General Gibbon's public letter complaining of my omissions. I will publish a card, with a view to setting the matter right.

Respectfully,

O. O. HOWARD,
Major-General.

Maj. Gen. GEORGE G. MEADE,
Commanding Army of the Potomac.

[Indorsement.]

HEADQUARTERS ARMY OF THE POTOMAC,
April 6, 1864.

Respectfully forwarded to the Adjutant-General, with the request that General Howard's wishes may be complied with.

GEO. G. MEADE,
Major-General, Commanding.

[Inclosure.]

HEADQUARTERS ELEVENTH CORPS,
Warrenton Junction, Va., July 29, 1863.

Col. S. S. CARROLL,
Commanding Brigade, Second Corps:

COLONEL: I wish to thank you for the prompt support you gave me on the evening of July 2, at Gettysburg, on the extreme right of General Ames' division. I was particularly weak at that point, having only a single thin line, through which the enemy were just breaking. You came up quickly, deployed, and moved into position after your old style. For this and for your subsequent patience in strengthening that position until the close of the attack on July 3, I tender you my hearty thanks.

Respectfully,

O. O. HOWARD,
Major-General.

—

HDQRS. ELEVENTH CORPS, ARMY OF THE POTOMAC,
Near Catlett's Station, Va., August 27, 1863.

GENERAL: In compliance with Paragraph III, Special Orders, No. 227, current series, from headquarters Army of the Potomac, I have the honor to report that one light 12-pounder gun was captured from this corps on July 1, at Gettysburg. No guns were captured by this corps.

I am, general, very respectfully, your obedient servant,

C. SCHURZ,
Major-General, Commanding.

Brig. Gen. S. WILLIAMS,
Assistant Adjutant-General.

GENERAL ORDERS, } HDQRS. 11TH CORPS, ARMY OF POTOMAC,
No. 18.   }   *Near Boonsborough, Md., July* 10, 1863.

The general again thanks his command for what has been done during the last month. You have now met the enemy, and feel conscious that you have done your duty.

On the 1st day of July, with the First Corps and Buford's division of cavalry, you held double your numbers in check from 12 m. until night, and thus opened the way for the victory that followed.

On the 2d, you held an important position during the cannonade, and repulsed the enemy when already within your batteries and breaking through your lines.

On the 3d, the same post was strongly held under the severest cannonade of the war. Our batteries, aided by our infantry, contributed a full share to the repulse of the enemy's last attempt to drive the army from its position.

The Eleventh Corps, as a corps, has done well—well in marching, well in fighting; the sacrifices it has made shall not be forgotten. In the retrospect, your general feels satisfied. Now, we must make one more effort. Let there be no wavering, no doubt. Our cause is right and our success sure.

O. O. HOWARD,
Major-General, Commanding.

No. 244.

*Report of Brig. Gen. Adelbert Ames, U. S. Army, commanding
Second Brigade and First Division.*

HEADQUARTERS SECOND BRIGADE, FIRST DIVISION,
Camp near Warrenton Junction, Va., July 28, 1863.

COLONEL: I have the honor to submit the following report of the action of the troops under my command at the battle of Gettysburg:

Early in the morning of July 1, my brigade left Emmitsburg, Md., and immediately upon its arrival at Gettysburg, Pa., it was pushed through the town and took a position near the pike leading toward Harrisburg. My brigade was ordered to a number of different positions, and finally it formed in rear of some woods, near a small stream some half a mile from town. From this position we were driven, the men of the First Brigade of this division running through lines of the regiments of my brigade (the Second), and thereby creating considerable confusion.

At this time General Barlow was wounded, and the command of the division devolved upon me. The whole division was falling back with little or no regularity, regimental organizations having become destroyed. An order was received from General Schurz, or one of his staff, to occupy the outskirts of the town, but soon after the order came to fall back through it. In this movement many of our men were taken prisoners. The hill in rear of the town was occupied after passing through the town, and in this position the division remained during the two following days, the 2d and 3d.

On the evening of the 2d, an attempt was made to carry the position we held, but the enemy was repulsed with loss. Colonel Carroll, with a brigade from the Second Corps, rendered timely assistance. The batteries behaved admirably.

I discharge a duty in calling attention to officers whose conduct is deserving the highest praise. Capt. J. M. Brown, my assistant adjutant-general, rendered most valuable services during the three days' fighting. With great coolness and energy he ably seconded my efforts in repelling the assault made by the enemy on the evening of the 2d.

Colonel Harris, of the Seventy-fifth Ohio Volunteers, took command of the Second Brigade soon after I assumed command of the division. With courage, he displayed ability in the discharge of his duties.

The adjutant of the One hundred and seventh Ohio Volunteers, Lieutenant Young, attracted my attention by his coolness and bravery.

I am, colonel, very respectfully, your obedient servant,

A. AMES,
Brigadier-General, Commanding Second Brigade.

Col. T. A. MEYSENBURG,
Assistant Adjutant-General, Eleventh Corps.

No. 245.

Report of Lieut. Col. Detleo von Einsiedel, Forty-first New York Infantry, First Brigade.

——, —— —, 1863.

SIR: I have the honor to submit the following report of the Regiment DeKalb, Forty-first New York Volunteer Infantry, in relation to the battle of July 1, 2, 3, and 4, near Gettysburg, Pa.:

The regiment, consisting of 14 commissioned officers, 187 file, and 17 musicians, under command of Lieut. Col. Detleo von Einsiedel, arrived, coming from Emmitsburg, at about 10 o'clock in the evening of July 1, at the cemetery near Gettysburg, and bivouacked on the field behind a square stone fence, about 1 mile from Gettysburg, to the right of the road leading from Baltimore to Gettysburg.

On July 2, at 4 a. m., six companies took position on the stone fence, with the front to Gettysburg. One company took position on the right of the square, and two companies were detached to the front as skirmishers.

At 2 p. m. the regiment was assembled; moved, by order of Col. Leopold von Gilsa, commanding First Brigade, to the front of the two batteries which were posted on a little hill, on the right of the Baltimore and Gettysburg road, near the cemetery. The regiment had instructions to support the One hundred and fifty-third Regiment Pennsylvania Volunteers in case of an attack from the front (Gettysburg). In this position the regiment remained under the heaviest cannonade until 5 p. m., when it received orders to take a position about half a mile north from the above position, with the same front as the right wing of the army; but the rebel infantry being about to push back a division of the Twelfth Corps posted in the woods on our right wing, and threatening to attack us in the rear, we received the order to move 1,000 steps backward and to keep the same front as before. The regiment was posted as follows: Five companies of the right wing connecting on the left with the right wing of the Seventh Regiment West Virginia Volunteers, which had connection with the Fourteenth Regiment Indiana Volunteers; four companies, under command of Capt. Henry Arens, of Company K, connecting on their left with the One hundred and fifty-third Regiment Pennsylvania Volunteers, Sixty-eighth and Fifty-fourth Regiments New York Volunteers. The five companies on the right wing had for their support the Thirty-third Regiment Massachusetts Volunteers.

An attack was made by the enemy at 6.30 p. m., but although the Seventh Regiment West Virginia Volunteers fell back a little in the first moment, this attack was repulsed with energy by our right wing without the assistance of the Thirty-third Regiment Massachusetts Volunteers. On the left wing, the enemy came so far as to break through the line, which was kept either by the Sixty-eighth Regiment New York Volunteers or Fifty-fourth Regiment New York Volunteers, and move on toward the batteries.

In this critical moment, Capt. Alfred Theinhardt, commanding Company I, Forty-first New York Volunteers, took two companies of the Forty-first New York Volunteers, which he placed with some men of other regiments from the left wing behind a stone wall, and he succeeded in holding the enemy in check until a regiment of the Second Corps arrived, which was sent from the cemetery to support him. During the night the regiment remained in the same position as before the attack, putting out pickets in the front.

On July 3, the five companies of the right wing remained in the same position, and skirmishers were sent out from the four companies of the left wing. The regiment stood between 12 m. and 1 p. m. under a very heavy fire of artillery without having considerable losses.

In the morning of July 4, the brigade marched to Gettysburg, and two hours afterward the regiment took the same position again as it had on the previous days, near the cemetery.

The loss of the regiment during July 1, 2, 3, and 4 is—

Officers and men.	Killed.	Wounded.	Missing.	Total.
Commissioned officers	1	8	......	9
Non-commissioned officers	3	10	1	14
Privates	11	40	2	53
Total	15	58	3	76

Respectfully submitted.

DETLEO von EINSIEDEL,
Lieutenant-Colonel, Commanding.

Col. Leopold von Gilsa,
Commanding First Brigade.

No. 246.

*Reports of Col. Andrew L. Harris, Seventy-fifth Ohio Infantry,
commanding regiment and Second Brigade.*

HEADQUARTERS SEVENTY-FIFTH OHIO VOLUNTEERS,
July 5, 1863.

SIR: In compliance with orders received at these headquarters, I
beg leave to submit the following condensed report of the part taken
by the Seventy-fifth Ohio Volunteer Infantry in the battle of July
1, 2, and 3:

Marched from Emmitsburg with about 160 officers and men on the
morning of July 1, leaving 100 enlisted men and 3 commissioned
officers to scout the country in the neighborhood of the Greencastle
road.

Arrived at Gettysburg at about 1 p. m., and was sent immediately
to the northwest part of the city and placed in line of battle ready to
meet the enemy on the right center of Second Brigade, First Division; was ordered forward in line of battle to receive the attack of
the enemy.   Advanced to the edge of the woods, when both flanks,
being unsupported and exposed to an enfilading fire, were compelled
to fall back with heavy loss in killed, wounded, and missing; rallied
again the few men left, and fell back to the hill, which we now occupy.   Here, by the return of a part of the scouting party before
mentioned, the number increased to 91 officers and men.

July 2 was spent in skirmishing with the enemy's sharpshooters
until about 4 p. m., when we were again ordered to prepare for action, and the Seventy-fifth was placed at the stone wall south of the
hill, with the Seventeenth Connecticut immediately on our left.   Just
before the attack was made, the Seventeenth was thrown to the extreme right of the line, and the space at the wall where they had been
was left unoccupied, excepting by a few of the Twenty-fifth Ohio Volunteers.   About dusk the enemy attacked the regiment in front and
on the flank and rear at nearly the same time, having come through
the space which had been vacated by the removal of the Seventeenth
Connecticut Volunteers.   From this attack but few escaped, and
those only in the darkness and smoke; the greater portion were no
doubt made prisoners.

But little transpired on the 3d, excepting a heavy artillery fire,
which we were exposed to during the day, and constant skirmishing
with the enemy's sharpshooters in the buildings on the outskirts of
the town, from which they fired with much effect, wounding quite a
number of the regiment during the day.

Hoping this imperfect report will be sufficient for the present, I remain, colonel, your obedient servant,

A. L. HARRIS,
Colonel, Comdg. Seventy-fifth Ohio Volunteers.

Colonel NOBLE,
Commanding Second Brigade, First Division.

—

JACKSONVILLE, FLA.,
April 7, 1864.

SIR: In compliance with your request, I lay before you the following facts in regard to the different positions and the part taken by

the Second Brigade, First Division, Eleventh Corps, in the battle of Gettysburg:

I assumed command of the brigade late in the afternoon of the 1st of July, and took my position, by order of General Ames, at a stone wall on the right, and nearly at right angles with the Baltimore road, throwing a heavy line of skirmishers into the edge of the town.

During the night a few random shots were fired; but early in the morning of the 2d the enemy attacked my skirmishers, firing from behind the fences and a brick-kiln on the right, and from the houses on the left. This continued until near sundown, when the positions of the different regiments of the brigade were changed to that desig nated in the diagram* yesterday.

In moving the Seventeenth Connecticut Volunteers to the extreme right and front of my line, their place at the wall was left vacant, thus endangering the left flank of the Seventy-fifth Ohio Volunteer Infantry and the right flank of the Twenty-fifth Ohio Volunteer Infantry. Before I could make any arrangements to remedy this breach in the line, the attack of the enemy on Cemetery Hill was made, and I was forced back by superiority of numbers, with heavy loss.

After the repulse of the enemy, I took up a position at the stone wall in the rear of and parallel with the one occupied the previous day, my left resting on the Baltimore road.

Before day on the morning of the 3d, I was ordered to move to the right along the wall until I joined the First Brigade, and to throw a strong line of skirmishers to the front, which was done. At daylight my skirmishers commenced a heavy fire upon the skirmishers of the enemy, which they replied to with vigor. This was kept up the entire day, in which my command suffered severely.

Early on the morning of the 4th, I was ordered by General Ames to throw my brigade forward into the town, which I did, finding but few of the enemy remaining, who were easily made prisoners. I may safely add that the Second Brigade was the first to enter the town of Gettysburg after the battle. While in the town, Colonel Noble arrived, and assumed command of the brigade.

I am, captain, very respectfully, your obedient servant,

A. L. HARRIS,
Colonel Seventy-fifth Ohio Volunteers.

Capt. J. M. BROWN,
Assistant Adjutant-General.

No. 247.

Report of Maj. Allen G. Brady, Seventeenth Connecticut Infantry.

GETTYSBURG, PA., *July* 4, 1863.

GENERAL: In compliance with instructions from headquarters, I have the honor to make the following report of the part taken by the Seventeenth Regiment Connecticut Volunteers in the engagement of the 1st, 2d, and 3d instant:

The regiment arrived in Gettysburg between 1 and 2 p. m. of the 1st instant, and was marched with the other regiments of the brigade through and to the lower end of the town, and there halted for a mo-

----

* Not found.

ment.   Four companies were immediately ordered out by Brigadier-General Ames, under command of Major Brady, to the right of the bridge at the lower end of the town, with instructions to throw out two companies as skirmishers, the other two to be held as a reserve, and to take and hold the brick house to the left and beyond the bridge.   Two companies were thrown out, and deployed as skirmishers as rapidly as possible to the right of the bridge, along the creek. The other two, held as reserve, were advanced in line, loading and firing as rapidly as possible, making at the same time a left wheel, so as to swing our right around the house, the reserve keeping near and conforming to the movements of the skirmishers.

When near the house, the enemy opened upon us with shot, shell, grape, and canister, which retarded our advance for a moment, until Major Brady dismounted, went in front of the line of skirmishers, and led them on until quite near the house.   The enemy, anticipating our movements, shelled the house, and set it on fire.   We, however, held our ground, and held the enemy's skirmishers in check.   Their loss up to this time was at least 5 to 1, most of the men in the four companies being excellent marksmen and having volunteered for this occasion.   They consisted of Companies A, B, F, and K, commanded, respectively, by Captains McQuhae, Hobbie, Allen, and McCarty.

We continued skirmishing briskly until Major Brady received orders from Brigadier-General Ames to draw in his skirmishers and return to town as rapidly as possible, and take command of his regiment.   The order was obeyed, and we fell back in good order, skirmishing with the enemy, who advanced as we retreated, and tried to cut us off and capture us before we got to the town, but we foiled them in this attempt by making a circuit and entering the town near the upper end, and soon joined the remainder of the regiment, which we found near the lower end of the town.

The loss in the four companies under Major Brady was 3 men killed, 1 captain and 1 lieutenant wounded, 1 sergeant and 3 men taken prisoners.

I would here state that I had great difficulty in drawing in Captain McCarty's company (K), as they were so earnestly engaged and making such sad havoc among the rebels.

The remainder of the regiment (six companies), under Lieutenant-Colonel Fowler, advanced with the other regiments of the brigade to the left and front of the town and directly in rear of the One hundred and seventh Ohio Volunteers, in close column by division; were ordered to the front; advanced and deployed at double-quick, and held their ground—notwithstanding the rush to the rear of troops directly in advance—until ordered by the brigade commander to fall back, which order was obeyed in good order, the men loading and firing as they fell back.

Lieutenant-Colonel Fowler was killed when the regiment advanced and deployed.   Captain Moore was killed about this time, and Captain French and Lieutenant Quinn were wounded, and many of the men were killed, wounded, and taken prisoners.

When the regiment reached the town, the four companies under Major Brady were still skirmishing with the enemy, and remained so until Brigadier-General Ames sent an aide with orders for Major Brady to return with his command and assume command of his regiment, he being the only field officer of the regiment present.   Upon arriving in the town, Major Brady assumed command of the regiment, and reported immediately to Brigadier-General Ames for instructions. The enemy were at this time advancing rapidly through the town. The regiment was immediately deployed in the streets, and fired several volleys into the ranks of the enemy, which thinned their ranks and retarded their advance. We kept the enemy from advancing through the town until ordered to clear the street of our men for the purpose of planting a battery. The battery not being placed in position as intended, and the regiment being in line on the sidewalk, the enemy took advantage of this, and, with a superior force, rushed though the main street, which compelled us to fall back, which we did reluctantly, but not without contesting the ground inch by inch.

As we retreated, we loaded, halted, and poured destructive volleys into their ranks, which cleared the main street of them several times, but we found the enemy too many for us. They poured in from every street in overwhelming numbers, which broke our ranks. Upon arriving near the battery on Cemetery Hill, the regiment was halted, and formed in line of battle fronting the town.

About this time Major-General Howard, who was in the thickest of the battle, regardless of danger, asked if he had troops brave enough to advance to a stone wall across a lot toward the town, and said he would lead them. We replied, "Yes, the Seventeenth Connecticut will," and advanced at once to the place indicated, remained a few moments, and again advanced across another lot still nearer the town and behind a rail fence at the upper end of the town, which position we held until late in the evening, exposed to a galling fire from the enemy's sharpshooters, when the whole regiment was ordered out on picket, and performed that duty until 2 o'clock of the 2d instant, when we were relieved, and took a position behind the rail fence and 150 paces farther to the right of the place we occupied before going out on picket.

We remained in this position, exposed to the enemy's batteries and sharpshooters, until 7 p. m., when we were ordered to the extreme right, behind a stone wall on each side of a lane, below the battery opposite the cemetery entrance. Two companies were advanced to the grain field near the woods, through which the enemy were rapidly advancing. We covered the wall on each side of the lane by compelling about 300 stragglers, who had no commander, to fall into our line. We had not more than time to form behind the wall before the enemy were discovered advancing rapidly upon us on our right and a full brigade obliquely toward our left. When within 150 paces of us, we poured a destructive fire upon them, which thinned their ranks and checked their advance. We fired several volleys by battalion, after which they charged upon us. We had a hand-to-hand conflict with them, firmly held our ground, and drove them back.

Soon after, some of the troops on our left giving way, the rebels succeeded in getting in our rear. We again drove them back and held our position. It was during this conflict that Major Brady was wounded by a fragment of shell, which hit him upon the right shoulder. After the enemy had been driven back, the firing ceased, excepting occasional shots from their sharpshooters.

We were relieved by the Fourth Ohio Volunteers, and were ordered to change front to the left behind a wall running at right angles with the one we had just occupied, and fronting the town, and where the enemy entered on our left. We remained at this wall all night and during the whole of the 3d instant, exposed to a cross-fire of the rebel batteries and their sharpshooters. With the latter our best marksmen exchanged shots, and succeeded in dislodging many of them.

When the regiment entered the engagement on the 1st instant, it numbered 17 officers and 369 enlisted men. We report at the present time 9 officers and 120 enlisted men. Capt. Wilson French and Lieutenant Bartram are the only officers known to have been taken prisoners. The former was wounded in the first day's engagement. We are not aware that either of them was paroled.

The regiment behaved gallantly. No troops in the world could behave better. Both officers and men are deserving of great credit for their coolness and bravery throughout the entire three days battle.

There are many deserving of especial mention for bravery on the field, but they are so numerous I will not undertake to give their names. The coolness and bravery displayed by the officers and men of Company D exceeded anything I ever saw.

I am, general, your most obedient servant,
A. G. BRADY,
Major, Comdg. Seventeenth Connecticut Vol. Infantry.

Brig. Gen. A. AMES, *Commanding Brigade.*

No. 248.

Report of Lieut. Israel White, Twenty-fifth Ohio Infantry.

GETTYSBURG, PA., *July* 4, 1863.

SIR: In compliance with orders received from brigade headquarters, July 4, I have the honor to report the part taken by this regiment upon July 1, 2, and 3.

Upon the first day of the engagement, the regiment was taken to the extreme right, as a support to a section of the Fourth Regular Battery [G, Fourth Artillery], where it remained until the section of battery was withdrawn. The regiment then took position in the woods on the left of the position occupied by the above-mentioned section of battery. Upon the approach of the enemy, the regiment was placed in position, fronting upon a small stream of water. The first division, consisting of Companies A and F, were deployed as skirmishers. Skirmishing commenced and continued until they were compelled to retire by the advance of the enemy's line. The regiment engaged the enemy, and maintained its position until compelled to retire before the superior force of the enemy.

On the evening of the 1st, the regiment was placed in line of battle on the heights in the rear of Gettysburg, where it remained, engaging the enemy's sharpshooters, until 2 p. m. of the 2d, when it was relieved, and took a position about 100 rods in the rear.

About 7 p. m. engaged the enemy's advance, and after an obstinate engagement, in which the enemy were repulsed, remained under arms until the morning of the 4th, when it was deployed as skirmishers, and advanced through the village; then retired to its former position.

Upon the 1st, the regiment was led into action by Lieut. Col. Jeremiah Williams, who is supposed to be a prisoner.

Upon the 2d, the regiment was commanded and led into action by Lieut. William Maloney, who was wounded.

Upon the 3d, the command devolved upon the present commanding officer.

Respectfully submitted.

ISRAEL WHITE,
Lieutenant, Commanding.

COLONEL COMMANDING SECOND BRIGADE.

No. 249.

Report of Capt. John M. Lutz, One hundred and seventh Ohio Infantry.

IN THE FIELD, NEAR GETTYSBURG, PA.,
July 4, 1863.

SIR: The following is the report of the part this regiment has taken in the action of July 1, 2, and 3:

The regiment arrived at Gettysburg, Pa., at about 1 p. m. July 1, and at about 2 p. m. marched through the town to the front, and engaged the enemy about half a mile north of the town.

The engagement lasted until about 4 p. m., during which time the regiment, being exposed to a heavy fire of artillery and musketry, suffered heavily in killed and wounded. The enemy appearing in heavy force, the regiment was ordered to the south end of the town, where it was posted behind a board fence, holding this position until 7 p. m. July 2, during which time heavy skirmishing was going on between the regiment and the enemy's sharpshooters.

At about 7 p. m. the enemy appeared in force. We fought them, retiring at the same time behind a stone wall and in front of a battery, at which the enemy made a desperate charge upon us, but without success. They were repulsed with great loss. It was at this point the regiment captured a stand of colors from the Eighth Louisiana Tigers. The engagement lasted about one hour and a half, after which the regiment retired for the night.

On July 3, the regiment was posted in front of the batteries, doing duty as skirmishers.

Very respectfully,

JOHN M. LUTZ,
Captain, Commanding 107th Ohio Volunteers.

Colonel NOBLE,
Commanding Second Brigade, First Division.

No. 250.

Report of Brig. Gen. Adolph von Steinwehr, U. S. Army, commanding Second Division.

HDQRS. SECOND DIVISION, ELEVENTH CORPS,
Near Bristoe Station, Va., August 30, 1863.

GENERAL: I have the honor to submit to you the following report of the part taken by this division in the battle of Gettysburg, on July 1, 2, and 3:

July 1, early in the morning, we marched from Emmitsburg to

Gettysburg. When about 5 miles from the latter place, I received your order to push on as fast as possible. General Reynolds had attacked the enemy, and had himself fallen. The First and Third Divisions, which were in advance of my command, were sent forward to support the First Corps.

At about 2 o'clock I arrived with my division near Gettysburg, and was ordered to occupy Cemetery Hill, where I found the reserve artillery of our corps in position. This hill is situated near the south end of Gettysburg, at the junction of the turnpikes leading to Baltimore and Emmitsburg. Toward the east and south, low ranges connect with it, while toward the north and west a belt of open fields from 1 to 2 miles in width extends along the whole length of these hills, forming a slightly depressed valley, beyond which the ground again rises into a series of broken elevations.

Cemetery Hill is the commanding point of the whole position, and its occupation by our troops had a decisive influence upon the further progress and the final result of the battle. When I arrived upon it, the First Corps and the First and Third Divisions of our corps were engaged with the enemy on the open fields below. I placed the First Brigade, Col. Charles R. Coster, on the northeast end of the hill, in support of Wiedrich's battery, which was then in position. The Second Brigade, Col. Orland Smith, took a position toward the northwest, supporting the reserve artillery of our corps. Colonel Coster threw forward one regiment as skirmishers in front of his position, and another one into a large stone church and the surrounding houses in town, in order to prevent the enemy's sharpshooters from annoying our artillery.

Shortly after this position had been taken, General Schurz sent an order for re-enforcements, and soon afterward another order to dispatch one brigade upon a reconnaissance upon the York road, whence Ewell's corps was expected to debouch. At this time, however, heavy columns of the enemy approached on the York road, which left no doubt that Ewell had arrived, and was upon the point of taking part in the conflict.

This arrival rendered the enemy's forces so strong that they outnumbered our troops very largely. The final issue of the engagement could no longer be doubtful, especially as the enemy had also the formation of the ground in his favor.

General Schurz at this crisis sent again for re-enforcements, and I ordered Colonel Coster to advance with his brigade through the town, to report to General Schurz. The Second Brigade I left on the hill, changing their position so as to support all the batteries upon the same, and fill with two regiments the place vacated by the First Brigade.

Colonel Coster met General Schurz in town, who ordered him to take a position north and east of Gettysburg, and to check the advance of the enemy, who were pressing for Gettysburg, and before whose overwhelming numbers the First and Third Divisions were forced to fall back. Colonel Coster had a severe engagement with the advancing enemy, but was, of course, not strong enough to restore the battle. He therefore ordered his men also to fall back, and again took up his position on Cemetery Hill, leaving one regiment to occupy the nearest brick houses of the town, which successfully prevented the farther advance of the enemy.

My division was now again in nearly the same position which it occupied at first. The other two divisions also took position on Cemetery Hill. Our position now was quite strong, the infantry being placed partly behind stone fences, and forming with our batteries a front fully able to resist an attack of even greatly superior forces. The occupation of this hill by our corps had great influence upon the further progress and the final result of the battle.

July 2.—The morning passed off quietly, while the other corps of our army arrived on the battle-field.

At about 4 p. m. the enemy's batteries opened a heavy fire upon our position, which lasted for two hours. This was particularly severe upon Cemetery Hill, as we were exposed here to a concentrated fire from nine batteries. Our artillery vigorously replied, and silenced several of the enemy's pieces. Our infantry was posted behind stone fences surrounding the hill, and suffered but little from the enemy's artillery.

My division formed the left wing of the corps, fronting north, excepting the Thirty-third Regiment Massachusetts Volunteers, who were detailed to support General Ames' brigade, on the right, fronting northeast.

At about 9 p. m. the Louisiana Brigade (Tigers) made a vigorous charge upon the First Brigade of my division, and Wiedrich's battery. Colonel Coster's brigade, and particularly the Twenty-seventh Regiment Pennsylvania Volunteers, Colonel Cantador, repulsed them.

Several rebels succeeded in reaching Wiedrich's battery, but were driven back by the cannoneers themselves.

During the night, the skirmishers of Colonel Smith's brigade were attacked several times, but succeeded in repelling the enemy every time.

July 3.—During this day the battle raged principally on the right and left wings of our army; my division, occupying, with slight changes, the same position as the day before, was not attacked.

At 2.30 o'clock the enemy again opened a terrific artillery fire upon our hill, which lasted until 4 p. m.

In regard to our loss, I would respectfully refer to the report previously forwarded. The First Brigade lost heavily; the Second Brigade had during the last two days over 300 men killed and wounded, principally of the Seventy-third Ohio Volunteers, by the enemy's sharpshooters, who fired from several buildings of the town at a great distance but with remarkable accuracy.

The division behaved gallantly, repelling every attack of the enemy, and standing unmoved under the heavy artillery fire of the last two battle days.

The commanders of my two brigades—Col. Orland Smith, Seventy-third Ohio Volunteers, and Col. Charles R. Coster, One hundred and thirty-fourth New York Volunteers—have assisted me very materially, both executing my orders with zeal, and exposing themselves freely. They have shown themselves able and gallant soldiers.

Of my staff I can also speak in terms of praise. Capt. F. W. Stowe, assistant adjutant-general of this division, was on the last day severely wounded in the head by a piece of shell.

Very respectfully, yours,

A. von STEINWEHR,
Brigadier-General, Commanding Division.

Maj. Gen. O. O. HOWARD,
Commanding Eleventh Corps.

No. 251.

*Report of Col. Orland Smith, Seventy-third Ohio Infantry, com-
manding Second Brigade.*

HDQRS. SECOND BRIG., SECOND DIV., ELEVENTH A. C.,
Near Catlett's Station, Va., August 5, 1863.

LIEUTENANT: I have the honor to report the operations of the
Second Brigade, Second Division, Eleventh Corps, from June 12 to
July 4, beginning with its departure from Brooke's Station and end-
ing with the battle of Gettysburg.

The brigade, consisting of the Seventy-third Ohio, Thirty-third
Massachusetts, Fifty-fifth Ohio, and One hundred and thirty-sixth
New York Volunteers, marched from its encampment at Brooke's
Station on Friday, June 12, at 1 p. m. Its marches and halts until
its arrival at Gettysburg were as follows:

Friday, June 12.—Brooke's Station to Hartwood Church, 13 miles.
Saturday, June 13.—From Hartwood Church to Weaverville, near
Catlett's.
Sunday, June 14.—Weaverville to Blackburn's Ford, 18 miles.
Monday, June 15.—Blackburn's Ford to Centreville, 5 miles, where
we tarried until Wednesday, June 17.
Wednesday, June 17.—Centreville to Goose Creek, 18 miles, where
the brigade took position on the north side of Goose Creek, picket-
ing that side, and sending scouting parties and patrols to Leesburg,
Hog Back Mountain, near Mount Gilead, and to Aldie. Remained
on Goose Creek till Wednesday, June 24; marched from Goose Creek
to Edwards Ferry, 7 miles.
Thursday, June 25.—Edwards Ferry to Jefferson, 22 miles.
Friday, June 26.—Jefferson to Middletown, 7 miles.
Saturday, June 27.—Middletown to Boonsborough Gap, 6 miles.
Sunday, June 28.—Boonsborough Gap to Frederick, 16 miles.
Monday, June 29.—Frederick to Emmitsburg, 22 miles. Tarried
here until Wednesday, July 1; Emmitsburg to Gettysburg, 9 miles.

The men marched fully equipped, with haversacks, knapsacks, &c.,
carrying three days' rations and 60 rounds of ammunition. The
previous comparative inactivity in camp caused some weariness
during the first few days, and before half the distance was accomplished the shoes began to fail, thus leaving many men to march
barefooted sometimes over very rough roads.

The march from Boonsborough Gap to Emmitsburg is worthy of
note. Starting at 4.40 p. m. on Sunday, 28th instant, we reached
Frederick, 16 miles distant, about midnight, having been somewhat
wearied, and impeded by the wagon trains which preceded us. Leaving Frederick at 4.30 a. m. on the 29th, we reached Emmitsburg at 5
p. m., having made 38 miles in twenty-four and one-half hours, with
scarcely an instance of straggling. At times the roads were in bad
order, being very heavy from the rains, rendering the marching very
painful to those whose shoes had given out. Every labor and hard-
ship was endured, however, with a cheerfulness which is worthy of
commendation.

On the march from Emmitsburg to Gettysburg, this brigade
brought up the rear of the entire corps; consequently it was the last
to arrive at the scene of action, which had been commenced earlier
in the day by the First Corps.

In compliance with orders from General Steinwehr, commanding the division, I immediately formed the brigade in line of battle by battalions in mass in rear of Cemetery Hill, and thus advanced through the cemetery to the front of the hill overlooking the town. It was soon evident our forces, consisting of the First Corps and First and Third Divisions, Eleventh Corps, were retreating before vastly superior numbers from the opposite side of the town. The moment seemed critical, and, under the directions of the general, dispositions were rapidly made to repel any assault upon the hill should the enemy see fit to advance so far. The movements and deployments were made with considerable rapidity, and positions were frequently made by changes, as will be indicated by the reports of the regimental commanders, which are herewith submitted.

The final disposition of the brigade was as follows: The base of the hill in front of the batteries of the corps was occupied by the Fifty-fifth and Seventy-third Ohio Volunteers and the One hundred and thirty-sixth New York Volunteers, the former being on the extreme right and reaching to the southwest corner of the town, the Seventy-third in the center, and the One hundred and thirty-sixth on the left, connecting with the Second Corps. The Thirty-third Massachusetts was placed on the northeasterly side of Cemetery Hill, and, as I learned from the report of Colonel Underwood, was put temporarily under the command of General Ames, of the First Division, this, however, being the first intimation to me of such a fact.

Our entire front was covered by a line of skirmishers thrown out toward the enemy's lines, the right resting near the town and the left connecting with a similar line of the Second Corps. These skirmishers were more or less engaged with those of the enemy during the whole period from the 1st to the night of July 3. This line was exposed not only to the fire of the enemy's front, but to a fire from the flanks and rear by the sharpshooters posted in the houses in the town. Indeed, the main line, though posted behind a stone wall, was constantly subjected to annoyances from the same source.

During the various contests which marked the three days' battle, the regiments were constantly exposed, not only to the fire in front, but to the shot and shell coming from the batteries placed opposite the Twelfth Corps, on the right. Moreover, some casualties were occasioned by the premature explosion of some of the shells from our own batteries. Though the situation was at times of the most trying character, never a man faltered, to my knowledge, or complained, but every man seemed inspired by a determination to hold his position, dead or alive.

On the night of the 2d, our line was threatened by a strong force of the enemy deployed in our front, while a vigorous attack was made upon the right wing of the corps. No attack was made on us, however, owing, as I have since been informed, to their failure to carry the hill on the right.

On Friday, the 3d, when the final terrific assault was made by the enemy, the direction of their march at first seemed to indicate that our brigade would be strongly attacked. A change of direction to the right, however, threw the whole force of the attack upon the Second Corps, our skirmishers being only partially engaged. Nevertheless, the firmness manifested, not only by the old troops, but by those who had never before been actively engaged, was remarkable.

With the reports of the respective regimental commanders will be found detailed lists of killed, wounded, &c., which foot up as follows:

Command.	Killed.		Wounded.		Missing.		Total.		
	Officers.	Enlisted men.	Officers.	Enlisted men.	Officers.	Enlisted men.	Officers.	Enlisted men.	Aggregate.
73d Ohio		32	3	101		7	3	140	143
55th Ohio		6	1	30	1	11	2	47	49
136th New York		17		88	1	2	1	107	108
33d Massachusetts		7		38				45	45
Total*		62	4	257	2	20	6	339	345

For specific accounts of the operations of each regiment, I respect-fully refer to the accompanying reports.

Where all vied with each other in the performance of their respect-ive duties, it is impossible to single out officers for special mention. I desire, however, to express my entire satisfaction at the conduct of the regimental commanders—Lieut. Col. R. Long, of the Seventy-third Ohio Volunteers; Col. C. B. Gambee, of the Fifty-fifth Ohio Volunteers; Col. A. B. Underwood, of the Thirty-third Massachu-setts Volunteers, and Col. James Wood, jr., of the One hundred and thirty-sixth New York Volunteers—all of whom, by their vigilance and watchfulness, contributed to lighten my own cares and respon-sibilities.

I cannot forbear mentioning with commendation the members of my staff—Capt. Benjamin F. Stone, jr., acting assistant adjutant-gen-eral; Capt. J. D. Maderia, acting assistant inspector-general; Capt. E. H. Pratt, and Lieut. H. E. Van Zandt, acting aides-de-camp, whose constant attention and ready response to all calls in seasons of the greatest danger entitle them to the greatest praise.

In closing, I venture to express the opinion that the arrival of this brigade upon Cemetery Hill at a critical moment, in good order and with full ranks, contributed much toward checking the enemy's advancing forces, and resulted in holding the hill, which, in my own opinion, was of the most vital importance, as was demonstrated by the subsequent actions.

Very respectfully, your obedient servant,

ORLAND SMITH,
Colonel, Commanding Second Brigade.

Lieut. R. E. BEECHER, Acting Assistant Adjutant-General.

No. 252.

Report of Col. James Wood, jr., One hundred and thirty-sixth New York Infantry.

IN THE FIELD, NEAR HAGERSTOWN, MD., July 12, 1863.

CAPTAIN: I have the honor to report that the regiment under my command, forming a part of the Second Brigade, Second Division, Eleventh Corps, Army of the Potomac, left Emmitsburg, Md., for Gettysburg, Pa., on Wednesday, July 1 instant, with the brigade and division of which it forms a part. When about half way be-

*But see revised statement, p. 183

tween Emmitsburg and Gettysburg, information was received that
the First Corps, under General Reynolds, had come in collision with
the enemy near the latter place, and that an engagement was then in
progress. The Eleventh Corps was ordered to hurry forward to re-
enforce the First.

On arriving near Gettysburg, the brigade was put in position on
Cemetery Hill, near to and south of the village of Gettysburg, for
the purpose of covering the retreat of the First Corps, it having
been compelled to fall back by the superior force of the enemy. The
position assigned to this regiment was on the left of the brigade, on
the road leading from Gettysburg to Taneytown, about 30 yards in
front of the artillery, placed in position in our rear, on the crest of
Cemetery Hill, and which artillery we were to support. The enemy's
line of battle being directly in our front, we were placed between the
fire of our own and the enemy's artillery. In the position assigned
us, the regiment was deployed in line of battle behind a stone wall or
fence, that fenced out the road from the adjoining field.

The enemy threw out a strong line of sharpshooters or skirmishers
directly in our front, and within musket range of our line. To meet
this, a similar line of sharpshooters or skirmishers was thrown out
upon our front toward the enemy. The sharpshooters were posted
at about 150 yards from those of the enemy. The enemy kept up an
almost continuous fire upon our skirmishers, and our line of sharpshooters was placed in the houses in the village of Gettysburg, from
which we were annoyed on our flanks.

Our position was near the center of the line of battle. This regiment was the extreme left of the Eleventh Corps, and connected
with the right of the Second Corps. This position substantially we
occupied during the three days' battle of Wednesday, Thursday, and
Friday, the 1st, 2d, and 3d instant, with the exception that on the
evening of the 2d we were ordered farther to the right, to assist in repelling an attack on our right wing, then in progress. The enemy
were repulsed without our assistance, and we were ordered back to
our former position. During the whole time we occupied this position, an almost continual conflict was kept up between the enemy's
sharpshooters and ours. Three or more companies of this regiment
were kept constantly detailed, and deployed as skirmishers, to take
care of and keep at proper distance the enemy's sharpshooters. The
regiment was also exposed to the terrific fire which the enemy brought
to bear upon the position in our rear on Cemetery Hill.

The loss of the regiment in killed, wounded, and missing was 108.

It is needless for me to say anything of the good conduct of the
officers and men of this regiment, as it was during the whole of the
battle under the immediate supervision and observation of the colonel commanding the brigade. I may be allowed, however, to remark that for new troops, for the first time under fire, the conduct
of both officers and men through the whole of this memorable contest is, in my judgment, deserving of the highest meed of praise, and
that the coolness and bravery exhibited could not have been excelled
even by veteran troops. I herewith inclose a list of casualties.*

I have the honor to be, very respectfully, your obedient servant,

JAMES WOOD, JR.,
Colonel, Commanding.

Capt. B. F. STONE, Jr., *Acting Assistant Adjutant-General.*

---

* Embodied in revised statement, p. 183.

No. 253.

Reports of Maj. Gen. Carl Schurz, U. S. Army, commanding Third Division.

HEADQUARTERS THIRD DIVISION, ELEVENTH CORPS,
August 20, 1863.

GENERAL: On the part taken by my command in the battle of Gettysburg, I have the honor to report as follows:

On July 1, at 7 a. m., the Third Division left its camp, near Saint Joseph's College, at Emmitsburg, with orders to march to Gettysburg by way of Horner's Mills.

About 10.30 o'clock, when my division had just passed the latter place, I received, through one of your aides, the order to hurry forward my command as fast as possible, as the First Corps was engaged with the enemy in the neighborhood of Gettysburg. Leaving the command of the division in General Schimmelfennig's hand, I hastened to the front, where I arrived about 11.30 o'clock, finding you upon an eminence east of the cemetery of Gettysburg, from which we overlooked the field of battle. You informed me that General Reynolds had just been killed; that you were in command of the whole, and that you had to turn over the Eleventh Corps to me.

I saw the First Corps engaged in a lively fight on the ridge northwest of Gettysburg. A dispatch from General Wadsworth informed us that he was advancing; that the forces before him were apparently not very strong, and that he thought, although he had no clear evidence of it, that the enemy was making a movement toward his right. The right of the First Corps seemed to extend across the Cashtown road and the railroad northeast of it. It was at the time difficult to see how far the ground was in our possession. Of the enemy we saw but little, and had no means of forming a just estimate of his strength. Either the enemy was before us in small force, and then we had to push him with all possible vigor, or he had the principal part of his army there, and then we had to establish ourselves in a position which would enable us to maintain ourselves until the arrival of re-enforcements. Either of these cases being possible, provision was to be made for both. Accordingly you ordered me to take the Third and First Divisions of the Eleventh Corps through the town, and to endeavor to gain possession of the eastern prolongation of the ridge then partly held by the First Corps, while you intended to establish the Second Division and the artillery, excepting the batteries attached to the First and Third Divisions, on Cemetery Hill and the eminence east of it as a reserve.

The Third Division arrived at — o'clock, at double-quick; the weather was sultry, and the troops, who had marched several hours without halting a single time, much out of breath. I ordered General Schimmelfennig, to whom I turned over the command of the Third Division, to advance briskly through the town, and to deploy on the right of the First Corps in two lines. This order was executed with promptness and spirit.

Shortly afterward the First Division, under General Barlow, arrived by the Emmitsburg road proper, advanced through the town, and was ordered by me to form on the right of the Third Division, its First Brigade to connect with the Third Division west of the road leading to Mummasburg, while I ordered the Second Brigade to be held *en échelon* behind the right of the First Brigade east of the

Mummasburg road.   Each division had one battery with it.   It was about 2 p. m. when the deployment of the two divisions was accomplished.   The Second Division arriving shortly after; the First remained with you in the position above indicated.

The engagement between the First Corps and the enemy had during that time continued briskly, the enemy being apparently driven to the crest of the ridge upon which the college building stands.

Hardly were the two divisions deployed a few hundred yards north of the town, when I received an order from you to remain in the position I then occupied, and to push my skirmishers forward as far as possible.   This was done, and our skirmishers, who became soon engaged, especially those of the Third Division, took a considerable number of prisoners.

While this was going on, two of the enemy's batteries, placed on a hillside opposite the Third Division, one above the other, opened upon us, flanking the First Corps.   Captain Dilger, whose battery was attached to the Third Division, replied promptly, dismounting in a short time four of the enemy's pieces, and driving away two regiments which were on a line with the enemy's artillery at the foot of the hill.

In the meantime the firing near my extreme left seemed to increase in volume, and, leaving the point I had selected for myself and staff, on the Mummasburg road, I rode over toward the left, in order to see what was going on.   The right of the First Corps seemed to be engaged in a very severe struggle.   The enemy was evidently pressing upon that point.   At the same time signs were apparent of an advance of the enemy upon my line, especially the right.   The enemy was evidently stronger than he had been at the commencement of the battle, and the probability was that re-enforcements were still arriving.   Feeling much anxiety about my right, which was liable to be turned if any of the enemy's forces were advancing by the Heidlersburg road, I dispatched one of my aides to you, with the request to have one brigade of the Second Division placed upon the north side of the town, near the railroad depot, as an *échelon* to the First Division.   My intention was to have that brigade in readiness to charge upon any force the enemy might move around my right.

After having taken the necessary observations on my extreme left, I returned to the Mummasburg road, where I discovered that General Barlow had moved forward his whole line, thus losing on his left the connection with the Third Division; moreover, the Second Brigade, of the First Division, had been taken out of its position *en échelon* behind the right of the First Brigade.   I immediately gave orders to re-establish the connection by advancing the right wing of the Third Division, and hurried off aide after aide to look after the brigade of the Second Division which I had requested you to send me for the protection of my right and rear, but it had not yet arrived.

Suddenly the enemy opened upon the First Division from two batteries placed near the Harrisburg road, completely enfilading General Barlow's line.   This fire, replied to by our batteries, produced but little effect upon our men.   Soon afterward, however, about 3 o'clock, before the forward movement of the First Division could be arrested by my orders, the enemy appeared in our front with heavy masses of infantry, his line extending far beyond our right.   It was now clear that the two small divisions under my command, numbering hardly over 6,000 effective men when going into battle, had a whole corps of the rebel army to contend against.

The simultaneous appearance of the enemy's battalions on so long a line led me to believe that they had been lying in position for some time behind the woods in our front, fully prepared for us, and that it was their intention, while entangling us in a fight where we were, to throw their left wing around our right, and thus to cut us off from the town. A movement to the rear became at once necessary, but before any orders to that effect could be transmitted, my whole line was engaged, and the Second Brigade, First Division, whose flank had been most exposed in consequence of the advance, fell back in considerable disorder. Unfortunately, General Barlow, who had been directing the movements of his troops with the most praiseworthy coolness and intrepidity, unmindful of the shower of bullets around, was severely wounded, and had to be carried off the battle-field. The command of the First Division devolved upon General Ames.

It was now of the highest importance to hold the Middletown and Mummasburg roads. Had the brigade of the Second Division been then at the appointed place, I would have ordered it to charge upon the flanking columns of the enemy, taking them in flank and rear; but that brigade not being there, all I could do was to endeavor to rally the Second Brigade, of the First Division, and to hold the ground west of those roads until the other brigades could be taken back. The enemy, however, pressing on with great vigor, that brigade could be rallied only in part, and the First Brigade, of the First Division, finding its right flank uncovered, was forced back also, not, however, without hotly contesting every inch of ground.

At that moment it was reported to me that the right wing of the First Corps had been pressed back, and one of Major-General Doubleday's aides brought me a request for a few regiments to be sent over to its assistance, which it was, under the circumstances, impossible for me to do. I received also a report from the Third Division, stating that it was flanked on the left. At the same time your order reached me to withdraw to the south side of the town, and to occupy the position on and near Cemetery Hill previously chosen by you.

While I was doing my utmost, assisted by the officers of my staff, to rally what was within my reach of the First Division, in order to check the enemy's advance upon my right and to hold the entrance of the town, the First Brigade, of the Second Division, under Colonel Coster, at last made its appearance. I led it out of the town, and ordered it to deploy on the right of the junction of the roads near the railroad depot, which the enemy was fast approaching. It was now too late for executing the offensive movement upon the enemy's left flank, which I had originally contemplated, and which might have been made to great advantage ten minutes before, but the brigade, assisted by a battery, succeeded, at all events, in checking the enemy long enough to permit the First Division to enter the town without being seriously molested on its retreat. The Third Division had meanwhile to sustain a furious attack. According to orders, it fell back toward the town in good order, contesting the ground step by step with the greatest firmness.

In this part of the action, which was almost a hand-to-hand struggle, officers and men showed the highest courage and determination. Our loss was extremely severe. The Second Brigade, Third Division, lost all its regimental commanders; several regiments nearly half their number in killed and wounded. Being flanked right and left, the situation of that division was most trying.

The retreat through the town, protected by part of our artillery, was effected as well as could be expected under such circumstances, the streets being filled with vehicles of every description and overrun with men of the First Corps. A considerable number of men, who became entangled in cross streets and alleys, were taken prisoners by the enemy, who entered the town immediately after us. General Schimmelfennig fell in this way into the hands of rebel skirmishers, but succeeded in hiding himself until, on July 4, we retook possession of Gettysburg.

It was after 5 o'clock when the Eleventh Corps occupied the position on Cemetery Hill; the Second Division behind the stone walls inclosing the cemetery on the west side; the Third Division immediately opposite the town, and the First Division on the right. The group of houses nearest the cemetery were occupied by our skirmishers. The enemy did not undertake to attack that position, and the corps remained in it undisturbed until the enemy resumed the attack on July 2.

I am, general, most respectfully, your obedient servant,

C. SCHURZ,
Major-General.

Maj. Gen. O. O. HOWARD,
Commanding Eleventh Corps.

HEADQUARTERS THIRD DIVISION, ELEVENTH CORPS,
August 20, 1863.

GENERAL : On the part taken by my division in the actions of July 2 and 3, I have the honor to submit the following report :

By the losses sustained in the battle of July 1, the Third Division was reduced to an effective force of about 1,500 men. A large number of officers were killed, wounded, or missing, many regiments being under the command of captains. General Schimmelfennig being still in his hiding place within the lines of the enemy, Colonel von Amsberg, of the Forty-fifth New York, commanded my First Brigade.

The position of the Third Division was behind the stone walls inclosing the cemetery on the northwest side, an orchard separating it from the first houses of the town. I had five regiments deployed in the first line, five in column in the second, connecting on my left with the Second Division, and on my right with the First. My skirmishers were from 300 to 500 yards in front, and a detachment in a group of houses near the cemetery.

The enemy made no attack in the forenoon of July 2. We observed his artillery moving on the ridges west, north, and east of Gettysburg, and taking position.

About 4 p. m. the enemy opened upon us from his batteries, the artillery on Cemetery Hill replying with great spirit. The fire continued for about two hours. Although the cannonade was fearful and many projectiles fell into our battalions, not a man belonging to the Third Division, unless wounded, left the ranks. After the cessation of the cannonade, the enemy made a heavy attack upon the left wing of the army, which resulted in a complete repulse.

Between 6 and 7 p. m. the enemy made a demonstration upon our right wing. As soon as the firing commenced, you ordered me to send one of my brigades to the support of General Ames, commanding the First Division. I took the First Brigade, Colonel von Amsberg commanding, out of its position, filling its place behind the stone wall with the reserve regiments of the Second Brigade. One of the five regiments of the First Brigade (Seventy-fourth Pennsylvania) was left with General Ames to strengthen his right wing. The remaining four were directed toward a strip of woods on the right of the First Division, in which the firing had become very heavy, and where, according to the reports of some staff officers of the First Corps, immediate aid was needed. Two regiments (the One hundred and fifty-seventh New York and the Sixty-first Ohio) were guided by one of these officers, while two others (the Eighty-second Illinois and Forty-fifth New York) were led by the chief of my staff, Lieutenant-Colonel Otto, of the Fifty-eighth New York. It had meanwhile become quite dark, the direction of the fight being indicated by nothing but the sound of the musketry. The regiments entered the woods with the greatest determination, and drove the enemy from our rifle-pits, of which at several points he had already gained possession.

It is my pleasant duty to mention as especially deserving, the names of Lieutenant-Colonel Otto, who superintended this operation with great judgment and courage, and of Lieutenant-Colonel Salomon, of the Eighty-second Illinois, who displayed the highest order of coolness and determination under very trying circumstances.

At 9 o'clock the enemy was repulsed at that point, and no further demonstration made. While this was going on, between 8 and 9 p. m., we suddenly heard a rapid musketry fire on the eminence immediately east of the cemetery, where Captain Wiedrich's battery stood. You ordered me to take two regiments across the road to the aid of that battery. This order was executed by two regiments of the Second Brigade, the One hundred and nineteenth and Fifty-eighth New York, headed by Colonel Krzyzanowski, commanding Second Brigade. I at once hastened with my whole staff toward the threatened point, driving back stragglers with our swords as we went. To my great surprise, we found a general *mêlée* in the battery itself, the enemy's infantry having already gotten possession of some of the guns. The cannoneers were defending themselves valiantly. Our infantry made a vigorous rush upon the intruders, and, after a short but very spirited hand-to-hand fight, succeeded in driving them down the hill.

I cannot refrain from speaking of the conduct of the officers and men on that occasion with the greatest satisfaction.

The regiments, thus scattered among other commands, were withdrawn during the night, and returned to their former positions.

In the action of July 3, no part of my command but my skirmishers was engaged. During the memorable cannonade of the afternoon, my men behaved with the same firmness which they had exhibited on the preceding day.

At daybreak on July 4, the Fifty-eighth New York, under command of Lieutenant-Colonel Otto, entered the town of Gettysburg, the enemy having retreated, and took over 280 prisoners, among whom were several commissioned officers.

At 8 a. m. Colonel Krzyzanowski, with the One hundred and nineteenth New York and the Twenty-sixth Wisconsin, made a reconnaissance toward the ridge opposite our right, and took 47 additional prisoners. He was called back without having found the enemy.

On the 5th, we marched to Emmitsburg.

A report exhibiting the heavy losses my division suffered in the three days' battle has already been submitted to you.* It bears ample testimony that my men in that battle fought with bravery, and never yielded without necessity.

I am, general, most respectfully, yours,

C. SCHURZ,
Major-General, Commanding Third Division.

Major-General HOWARD,
Commanding Eleventh Corps.

No. 254.

Report of Brig. Gen. Hector Tyndale, U. S. Army, commanding First Brigade.

HDQRS. FIRST BRIG., THIRD DIV., ELEVENTH ARMY CORPS,
Warrenton Junction, Va., July 29, 1863.

Pursuant to instructions from division headquarters, I have the honor to report that I assumed the command of this brigade on July 13, at Funkstown, Md.; that on July 14 the brigade took up the line of march for Williamsport, and arrived there on the afternoon of the same day.

The following day returned, and reached Middletown in the evening, where we encamped.

On the morning of July 16, resumed the march, and encamped near Berlin, on the Potomac River.

On the morning of July 19, crossed the Potomac, and encamped on Goose Creek, near Leesburg, Va.

The following day marched to and encamped at Mountville.

On July 23, left Mountville, marched to and encamped at New Baltimore; from thence the brigade marched to and arrived at Warrenton Junction on July 25.

I am, sir, very respectfully,

HECTOR TYNDALE,
Brigadier-General, Commanding.

Capt. F. TIEDEMANN,
Acting Assistant Adjutant-General.

No. 255.

Report of Col. Frederick Hecker, Eighty-second Illinois Infantry.

HDQRS. EIGHTY-SECOND REGT. ILLINOIS VOLUNTEERS,
August 21, 1863.

SIR: In compliance with the circular from headquarters First Brigade, August 20, 1863, requiring regimental reports of the battle of Gettysburg, inclusive of the operations from June 28 until the arrival of the Army of the Potomac at camp near Warrenton Junction, I have to report as follows:

At 3 p. m. on June 28, the regiment commenced its march from

---

* Embodied in revised statement, p. 183.

Middletown, Md., to Frederick, Md., a distance of 9 miles, arriving at the latter place about 7 p. m.; encamped southwest of the city.

At 6 a. m. on June 29, the regiment marched from Frederick to Emmitsburg, a distance of 22 miles, arriving at a field about 1 mile south of the latter place at 6.30 p. m., where we encamped during the night.

At 10 a. m. on June 30, the regiment was removed to within a few hundred yards of Emmitsburg.

At 12 m. the same day, the regiment received an order to detail 100 men to proceed immediately to Fairfield, Pa., a distance of 7 miles, for the purpose of ascertaining whether the enemy had occupied the above-named place. The above detail, under the command of Lieut. Col. Edward S. Salomon, reached Fairfield about 3 p. m. The citizens informed the colonel that, an hour previous to our reaching there, the enemy had occupied the above-named place, and evacuated the town, with a force of 2,000 infantry. After resting a half hour, the detail returned to Emmitsburg, joining the regiment at 8 p. m., where we encamped during the night.

My report of the battle of Gettysburg,* which was sent to headquarters in due time, forms the continuation of the course of events, and the following states all events from the day of the battle down to the arrival of the regiment near Warrenton Junction.

July 4.—We remained at Cemetery Hill, near Gettysburg.

July 5.—At 5.30 o'clock, we left the place of action to march to Emmitsburg, but on account of the horrible roads and darkness which prevailed, we encamped near a creek (name unknown) at the hour of 11.30 p. m.

July 6.—We started at 3.30 a. m., and reached Emmitsburg p. m.

July 7.—We started at 3.30 a. m. to Middletown, via Creagerstown and Utica Post-Office, a distance of 30 miles, and arrived there in a rain-storm at about 10 p. m.

July 8.—Cavalry fight near Boonsborough, in the South Mountain Gap. Our corps was sent to their assistance, the Third Division in advance. My regiment detailed to the defense of the town.

July 9.—At 11 a. m. we marched back through Boonsborough, and encamped one-half mile from said town, near the pike road.

July 10.—We marched again through Boonsborough, and arrived in the vicinity of Funkstown, and encamped during the day of July 11.

July 12, p. m.—We marched through Funkstown, formed line of battle, and took position near the breastworks in front of Hagerstown. We remained in this position until July 14, when a reconnaissance in a body of the Eleventh Corps was made through Hagerstown to within 3 miles of Williamsport. We encamped during the night.

July 15.—We started to go back at daybreak, via Funkstown and Marysville, to Middletown, say 25 miles.

July 16.—We left this town; marched, via Jefferson, to within 2 miles of Berlin. We encamped there until July 19, when we marched at 5 a. m., recrossing the Potomac at Berlin, passing through Lovettsville and Waterford, and encamped about 5 miles from the latter place.

July 20.—Marched to Goose Creek, and there encamped until July 23, when we marched our regiment, covering the artillery, via Mid-

---

*Not found.

dleburg and White Plains, to New Baltimore. Encamped until July 25, when we marched, passing near Warrenton, to Warrenton Junction.

Very respectfully, your most obedient servant,

F. HECKER,
Colonel, Commanding Eighty-second Illinois Volunteers.

Col. G. von Amsberg,
Commanding First Brigade.

No. 256.

Report of Lieut. Col. Adolphus Dobke, Forty-fifth New York Infantry.

WEAVERSVILLE, VA., *August* 21, 1863.

Sir : I have the honor to make the following report of the operations of the Forty-fifth Regiment New York Volunteers, from June 28 until its arrival at Warrenton Junction, including the battle at Gettysburg:

June 28.—Having rested one day at Middletown, the Forty-fifth Regiment resumed the march to Frederick City early in the morning; at 3 o'clock to Emmitsburg, 22 miles, where it rested on June 30.

Early in the morning of July 1, the regiment marched from Emmitsburg, without any rest, to Gettysburg, Pa., where it arrived at 11 a. m. The First Corps at this time being hotly engaged with and pressed by the enemy, the First Brigade, Third Division, Eleventh Corps, of which the Forty-fifth Regiment New York Volunteers is a part, was hurried to the battle-field in double-quick, to the right of the First Army Corps. Col. George von Amsberg at this moment was ordered to the command of the First Brigade, devolving the command of the Forty-fifth Regiment on Lieut. Col. Adolphus Dobke.

The Forty-fifth Regiment New York Volunteers, on the immediate right of the First Corps, threw out four companies as skirmishers at 11.30 a. m., but owing to the wide, open space which was left to be covered by this regiment, the whole regiment was deployed as skirmishers in the open field in the immediate line of battle; Dilger's battery, in the rear, and the Sixty-first Ohio, on the right, also deployed as skirmishers. The enemy opened at once on this line from his batteries on the summit and base of a hill on the road to York, and an incessant fire was pouring grape, canister, solid shot, and shell on our position.

At about 1.30 p. m. a long line of the enemy moved on the extreme right of the First Corps, passing the left of the Forty-fifth, and offering the flank to the Forty-fifth Regiment New York Volunteers. The left wing of our regiment at once gave fire at very short distance (50 or 100 yards) with such terrible effect that, in result with the combination of the fire from the extreme right of the First Corps, the whole of the enemy's line halted, gradually disappeared on the same spot where they stood, and the remainder, finding they could not retrace their steps, surrendered, partly to the First Corps and a great number to the Forty-fifth Regiment, which prisoners were at once sent to the rear, but in the heat of the battle no account could be taken. In the most raging fire and the most horrible scenes, when 8 comrades, one after another, were killed, and some shattered to pieces, not a single man flinched, but all were cheering, and fulfilled their duties nobly.

So we remained under fire until about 4 p. m., when the First Corps, on our left, gave way, and exposed our left flank, and at the same time heavy columns were moving on us in front and on the right, when the Forty-fifth Regiment was ordered to retreat. It rallied in line, and in splendid style retreated to the seminary, where it was ordered to halt and cover the retreat of the First and Eleventh Corps through Gettysburg. In a short time all sorts of missiles found their way through houses, fences, and gardens, and it was evident that to stay much longer would be certain destruction, so the regiment was ordered to follow the column which had passed, when, marching a few blocks, suddenly a few regiments of the First Corps were thrown in the way, and our regiment headed to the left to gain the other main streets.

When about the middle of the square, a sudden panic arose in a column on the street we were to gain throwing themselves in our column and into the houses. Not to become mixed up, the Forty-fifth Regiment turned again to the street just left, marched two squares down, and turned again to the left for the before-mentioned roads. About the middle of the block our column was received by the enemy's infantry fire, when the column headed into an alley leading to the direction we had to follow. Unfortunately this alley led into a spacious yard surrounded by large buildings, which only offered an entrance, but no way to pass out, excepting a very narrow doorway, to freedom and heaven; but the enemy's sharpshooters had already piled a barricade of dead Union soldiers in the street in front of this doorway. About 100 of the Forty-fifth Regiment extricated themselves from this trap, ran the gauntlet, and arrived safely at the graveyard. The remainder were taken prisoners, as meanwhile the whole town was surrounded and the enemy in possession of Gettysburg. Only one-third of the equipped men of the Forty-fifth Regiment assembled at the cemetery behind the stone fence, and two-thirds of the regiment were lost.

No demonstration was made by the enemy that night for the possession of Cemetery Hill, and we remained quiet for the night. Cartridges were distributed, as all had been used on July 1, and prepared for the conflict to come.

All remained quiet until 4 p. m. of July 2, when the enemy's batteries opened in a wide circle, concentrating their fire on Cemetery Hill, which place was under the most hellish cross-fire during this and all other subsequent engagements.

In the evening, at dark, a sudden attack was made on the Twelfth Corps, on our right, and the Forty-fifth Regiment ordered to support. For a mile through the complete darkness in the woods this regiment pushed up to the stone fence through an incessant shower of bullets, and shared well in the defense of this position. It is to be mentioned that while the regiment marched in the darkness through the woods, under guide of a staff officer, the march was considerably delayed by a number of general staff officers, each exerting himself to give his orders, and so, by movements, counter-movements, halts, &c., some time elapsed before the regiment found itself in the right place behind the fence. The firing lasted until midnight, and at 2.30 o'clock in the morning the Forty-fifth Regiment was ordered to return to its position on Cemetery Hill, in the center of the whole position.

In the forenoon of July 3, since 3.45 a. m., the right wing was the special object of attack, but in the afternoon, after 12 m., the left and center were attacked, the Forty-fifth Regiment not coming into immediate action with the rifles, excepting with the sharpshooters in town, but the most vehement artillery cross-fire had to be sustained from 12 m. to 4 p. m., and particularly from 2 to 4 p. m., the last attack by the enemy. Very little damage was done, however, to our ranks, and it proved only to be noisy.

The morning of July 4 showed us the great victory, and a summary of the loss of the Forty-fifth Regiment New York Volunteers proved as follows: Acting Second Lieut. Edward Milde; Sergts. E. May and J. Weitzel; Corpls. Rudolph Schwartz and E. Weissensel; Privates X. Feist, P. Schrüve, F. Roth, J. Ploughoft, August Schoch, and Charles Schade killed; Maj. Charles Koch and 34 enlisted men wounded, and 14 officers and 164 men missing. The loss of rifles and accouterments has to be compared with the loss of men, as those of the killed and wounded could not be transported, and those of the missing fell in the hands of the enemy. Particular mention of individuals for bravery is withheld, as every one did his duty with coolness.

Captain Gustavus Korn was untiring in all special duties, and Sergt. Charles Link, Company C, a fearless soldier, leading a squad to dislodge a party of sharpshooters in the town, who were very annoying, received a painful wound in the thigh in the attempt.

After the battle, the regiment remained on the battle-field on Cemetery Hill until 6 p. m. July 5, when it marched off toward Emmitsburg. At midnight the march was stopped, owing to the complete darkness and the horrible condition of the roads, which were nearly impassable from the heavy rain of the last two days.

At 4 p. m. on July 6, the regiment arrived at Emmitsburg.

On July 7, the heaviest march of the campaign was executed, marching 32 miles from Emmitsburg, and arrived at 10 p. m. at Middletown, a distance of 34 miles, through the open fields, taking a narrow pass road over the mountains in a circuit. Toward night the rain descended in torrents, amid which men and beasts sank down, tired to death, most of the soldiers without any shoes, barefooted, or shoes so ragged or torn that they did not deserve the name.

On July 8, the regiment marched over South Mountain Pass to Boonsborough, where it arrived on the battle-field in the afternoon in time to see the enemy retreating. From Boonsborough to Funkstown positions were changed several times, until July 12, when we crossed the Antietam Creek and took position east of Hagerstown in front of the enemy's works, remaining until the morning of the 14th, when a general forward movement was ordered, only to find the enemy's lines deserted. Following until within the vicinity of Williamsport, the regiment returned on July 15 to Middletown, and marched from there to Berlin, where it again crossed the Potomac into Dixie on July 19. From there the regiment marched, via Lovettsville, Waterford, Middleburg, White Plains, and New Baltimore, to Warrenton Junction, where it arrived without further accident on July 25.

Very respectfully,

A. DOBKE,
Lieut. Col., Comdg. Forty-fifth Regt. New York Volunteers.
Col. G. VON AMSBERG,
   Commanding First Brigade.

No. 257.

Report of Col. Horace Boughton, One hundred and forty-third New York Infantry.

HEADQUARTERS 143D NEW YORK VOLUNTEERS,
August 21, 1863.

CAPTAIN: In compliance with circular from brigade headquarters, dated August 20, 1863, I submit the following report of the operations of my regiment, from June 28 last until its arrival near Warrenton Junction, Va., July 25:

On June 28, my regiment was at White House Landing, Va., doing picket duty, and forming part of the First Brigade, Gordon's division, Seventh Army Corps, under command of Major-General Keyes. The regiment remained at White House Landing until the morning of July 8, when it marched with the balance of the division down the Peninsula, halting at night at Twelve-Mile Ordinary, having marched about 28 miles in a violent rain, through mud 6 inches deep.

At 5 o'clock the next morning, the march was resumed, and continued until about 1 p. m., when the regiment bivouacked about 2 miles beyond Williamsburg.

On the morning of the 10th, at 10 o'clock, I halted my regiment at Yorktown, and, under orders of Brigadier-General Gordon, embarked on board the steam transport Croton, which arrived at Washington, D. C., without a casualty, at 3 o'clock on the afternoon of the 11th.

At about 7 p. m. the regiment was on cars for Frederick City, Md., where it arrived at 8.30 o'clock on the next morning. Here I remained with my regiment, to obtain rations, transportation, and clothing, until the morning of the 13th, when, under orders from Colonel Schriver, inspector-general Army of the Potomac, I marched toward Funkstown, which place I reached about noon of July 14, and reported immediately to General Howard, and was assigned to the First Brigade, Third Division, Eleventh Army Corps. That p. m. my regiment marched with the Eleventh Corps to near Williamsport, and at 4 o'clock in the morning returned to Hagerstown, on the same road marched the day previous. From this last-named place the regiment kept to the left of Funkstown, halting at night near Middletown.

The march was resumed the next morning, and at 1 p. m. halted, and encamped within 2 miles of Berlin. Here I remained until the 19th, when I crossed the Potomac at Berlin, passed through the villages of Lovettsville, Waterford, and Middleburg, and on the afternoon of the 20th encamped at Mountville. Remained there two days.

On the 23d, marched as far as New Baltimore, and remained there until the 25th, when I marched my regiment to Warrenton Junction.

Owing to the deficiency in the number of ambulances, I was obliged to give men taken sick on the road passes to fall to the rear. One of these died on the road. One, I understand, was taken prisoner by the enemy. From Frederick City to Warrenton Junction, 6 men deserted.

Very respectfully,

HORACE BOUGHTON,
Colonel, Commanding.

Capt. J. C. HENSHAW, *Assistant Adjutant-General.*

No. 258.

Report of Lieut. Col. W. H. H. Bown, Sixty-first Ohio Infantry.

NEAR WARRENTON JUNCTION, VA.,
August 21, 1863.

GENERAL: I have the honor to submit to you, in accordance with orders this day received, a detailed report of the operations of the Sixty-first Regiment Ohio Volunteers, from June 28 to July 25 ultimo, the time of the arrival of the regiment at Warrenton Junction, Va., viz:

June 28.—Remained in camp, near Middletown, Md., until about 4 p. m., when we marched to Frederick City, Md.; weather rainy during the night.

June 29.—Marched from Frederick City to Emmitsburg; weather rainy.

June 30.—Remained in camp at Emmitsburg all day; weather rainy.

July 1.—Still in camp at Emmitsburg. At about 8 a. m. Lieutenant-Colonel Bown was sent to Mechanicstown with 4 commissioned officers and 100 enlisted men. At 9 a. m. the regiment marched from Emmitsburg, and arrived at Gettysburg, Pa., at about 1.30 p. m. The First Corps was already engaging the enemy when we arrived at the town. Having the honor to be the advance regiment of the Third Division, we were ordered on the double-quick through the town and into the open fields. As soon as we arrived on the field, were ordered to deploy as skirmishers. We were no sooner deployed than we engaged the enemy. After a severe skirmish of about half an hour, we drove them from the open field into the woods. We remained in this position nearly all the afternoon, covering a section of Captain Dilger's battery, which he had posted near the line of our skirmishers. Late in the afternoon, the enemy's massed column could be seen emerging from the woods in overwhelming numbers, and being so inferior in numbers compared to the enemy, we were ordered to fall back to the cemetery, upon the south of Gettysburg.

July 2.—Still in position behind the breastworks; very heavy skirmishing in our front. The expedition sent to Mechanicstown returned this morning at 8 o'clock; very heavy cannonading and skirmishing in our front all day.

At 1 p. m. 3 commissioned officers and 50 enlisted men were sent on picket, and 3 commissioned officers and 50 enlisted men were sent to support Captain Dilger's battery, leaving for duty about 90 enlisted men in the line of the regiment. In the evening, the Sixty-first Ohio and One hundred and fifty-seventh New York Volunteers, under command of Colonel McGroarty, were sent to support the Twelfth Corps. Owing to some mistake, we were ordered to our old position behind the breastworks, after having been severely repulsed by the enemy.

July 3.—Still in our old position.

July 4.—Still in our old position, with rain.

July 5.—Still in our old position behind the breastworks; marched at 6 p. m., and halted in the woods at 12 midnight.

July 6.—Marched to Emmitsburg, and encamped for the night.

July 7.—Marched from Emmitsburg to Middletown, Md.

July 8.—Marched to Boonsborough, Md.

July 9.—In camp at Boonsborough, Md.

July 10.—Marched to Funkstown, Md.
July 11.—In camp at Funkstown, Md.
July 12.—Marched to Hagerstown, Md.
July 13.—Still at Hagerstown, Md.
July 14.—Marched to Williamsport, Md.
July 15.—Marched to Middletown, Md.
July 16.—Marched to Berlin, Md.
July 17 *and* 18.—In camp at Berlin, Md.
July 19.—Marched this morning, crossing the Potomac River, to near Leesburg, Va.
July 20.—Marched to near Middleburg, Va.
July 21 *and* 22.—Still in camp near Middleburg, Va.
July 23.—Marched to New Baltimore, Va.
July 24.—Still in camp at New Baltimore, Va.
July 25.—Marched to Warrenton Junction, and encamped.
Yours, respectfully,

W. H. H. BOWN,
Lieut. Col., Comdg. Sixty-first Ohio Vol. Infantry.

Brig. Gen. HECTOR TYNDALE,
Commanding First Brigade, Third Division.

No. 259.

Report of Capt. Emil Koenig, Fifty-eighth New York Infantry, Second Brigade.

——, —— —, 1863.

SIR: I have the honor to submit the following report of the operations of the Fifty-eighth New York Volunteers during the period from June 12 until July 19:

On June 12, the Fifty-eighth Regiment New York Volunteers, then under command of Lieutenant-Colonel Otto, broke camp, and marched along with the rest of the brigade toward Hartwood Church, where it encamped for the night. After a very tedious march, we arrived at Centreville, in the vicinity of which we staid until the 17th, when we marched until near Goose Creek. Here we encamped until the 24th. This day we marched to Edwards Ferry, where we crossed the Potomac on the 25th, and marched to Jefferson, Md., where we arrived late in the evening.

Next morning we marched to Middletown, where we staid till noon on the 28th, when we were ordered to proceed to Frederick, Md.

Next morning we proceeded on our march to Emmitsburg, where the regiment staid until the morning of July 1.

As for myself, I was ordered in the night from June 30 to July 1 to take 100 men, and make a reconnaissance in the direction of Creagerstown, where, as it was said, some of the enemy's cavalry had been seen. After marching about 5 miles, according to orders received, and not finding anything extraordinary, I rested my command, when I received a dispatch ordering me to start back at once, as the corps had already marched to Gettysburg, Pa.

I arrived at the old camping place of the regiment about 9 a. m., where my command was joined by a squad of men of the regiment who had been on picket during the night. Rallying these men, with the greatest possible speed I started after the corps, which, however, I was unable to reach, as we had to march with the train, and

as the rain, falling down in torrents, caused the roads to be brought
into a very bad state. At the distance of about 4 miles from Gettysburg, I heard heavy cannonading in front, and hurried my men to
greater speed. The rain now ceased, and we arrived at Gettysburg
about 3.30 p. m.

I was not able to find where our corps was at that time, but arrived
on a hill on the left of Cemetery Hill, where our division had been
stationed a short while ago. It was then occupied by a battery of
the Second Corps, and a general of the same corps requested me to
remain there to support it, as no other troops were in that vicinity.
As I could not join the regiment then, I did as he requested me to do.
A little later, General Schurz arrived, and I reported to him. He
ordered me to remain in the same position temporarily. The division was retreating at the same time, and took position near Cemetery
Hill.

As nearly the whole number of our regiment had been on picket
duty and on the reconnaissance with me, and I had not been able to
find the brigade, it could take but little part in the fight of July 1,
but it had several wounded and 3 missing.

Late in the evening, I was ordered to proceed with my command to
the brigade, which was stationed behind a stone fence in front of
Cemetery Hill, in two lines, of which we formed part of the second.
As Lieutenant-Colonel Otto had been detached to act as chief of staff
of Major-General Schurz, I assumed command of the regiment, as
senior officer present. Nothing remarkable happened during the
night excepting that a patrol with some of our men, under command
of Lieutenant Ehrlich, Seventy-fifth Pennsylvania, went into town to
ascertain the condition of our wounded. On entering the town, they
were fired at by the enemy's pickets, of whom they killed and wounded
several, after which they retired into our lines without loss.

We remained in our position without any remarkable accident until
11 a. m. on the 2d, when we were ordered to detail some men to relieve the pickets in front of us. Two of our men were wounded while
relieving the pickets.

About 4 p. m. the rebels opened a murderous fire upon our division from three or four batteries in different positions, which was
briskly responded to by the batteries of Captain Wiedrich and Captain Dilger on the right and left of the division. In consideration of
the murderous fire which was kept up upon us without ceasing for
about three hours, our escape was truly miraculous, as we lost only
1 officer and 1 man killed and several wounded. During all this time
my men exhibited great courage and coolness.

About 8 p. m. our regiment was ordered ahead and to the left of the
brigade, behind a stone fence, where we were exposed to a severe
artillery fire, which, however, did us no damage. Suddenly we were
ordered to the right, where a column of the enemy, coming up under
cover of the darkness, had tried to storm Captain Wiedrich's battery,
but was repulsed before we arrived. As another attack was expected,
the regiment was ordered to stay there, and one company, under command of Lieutenant Schwartz, sent ahead as skirmishers to ascertain
whether the enemy was in front. He found nothing but dead and
wounded, and, after being relieved by the Forty-first New York, we
retired to our original position, where we rested during the night
without any disturbance.

On the morning of July 3, the firing commenced very early, ceasing at different intervals.

At 6 o'clock in the morning, we were ordered to the right of the road leading to Gettysburg. We were posted behind a stone fence to the left of Captain Wiedrich's battery. Lieutenant Schwartz, with one company, was sent to take possession of the next houses of the town to the left of the road. The enemy's sharpshooters kept up a brisk fire at these houses, and killed a girl who was living in one of them. Our men escaped uninjured, although they had possession of the house until the end of the battle, and the house was completely pierced by bomb-shells and rifle-balls. The fire of these sharpshooters was very annoying to us, as we could not show our heads above the fence without being fired at; however, they did us no damage.

We maintained our position until July 4, in the morning, when we were astonished not to hear any firing recommenced. Lieutenant Schwartz therefore sent a patrol of 10 men into the town, to ascertain whether the enemy had retreated. The citizens gave them signs, and showed them the houses which were occupied by the enemy. Our men entered them, and took most of the sharpshooters prisoners while asleep. Shortly afterward, Lieutenant Lauber, with 20 men of this regiment, was also sent into town, and these two squads took about 200 prisoners.

Later in the morning, the regiment was moved about 200 yards to the right again, where it staid until the 5th, in the evening, when it marched toward Emmitsburg. In this place we arrived on the 6th, about noon.

On the 7th, we started to Middletown, where we arrived about 10 o'clock that night.

On the 8th, in the afternoon, we were ordered to proceed to Boonsborough, to support General Kilpatrick's cavalry division, which was engaged with the enemy's cavalry. We arrived at sunset, when the enemy fell back.

On the 9th, we shifted camp, and marched toward Hagerstown, near which place we arrived and took position on the 11th, throwing up rifle-pits.

After remaining in this position until the 14th, we marched through Hagerstown until near Williamsport, and returned to Middletown the next day.

On the 15th, we marched through Jefferson to Berlin, Md., where we rested until the 19th. On this day we recrossed the Potomac, and ended our campaign in Maryland and Pennsylvania.

I can but express the greatest satisfaction with the behavior of the officers and men under my command. With very few exceptions they were equally devoted during the long and exhausting marches as well as during the tremendous fire of the battle. It gives me special pleasure to thank me in my endeavors to follow the order of my superiors.

Our loss was exceedingly small in proportion to the firing we had been exposed to. We have to mourn the loss of Adjt. Louis Deitrich, who was killed on July 2. Besides this, our loss consisted of 1 man killed, 14 wounded, and 3 missing.*

EMIL KOENIG,
Captain, Comdg. Fifty-eighth Regiment New York Vols.

Col. W. KRZYZANOWSKI,
Commanding Second Brig., Third Div., Eleventh Corps.

---

* But see revised statement, p. 183.

No. 260.

Report of Maj. Benjamin A. Willis, One hundred and nineteenth New York Infantry.

NEAR WARRENTON JUNCTION, VA.,
July 30, 1863.

GENERAL: I have the honor to submit, pursuant to request, the following report of the part taken by the One hundred and nineteenth New York Volunteers in the series of engagements fought at Gettysburg, on July 1, 2, and 3:

It may be proper for me to state at the outset that I was not in command of the regiment during the battle, and consequently cannot recite accurately the orders received by my regimental commander.

On July 1, about 5 a. m., we started on the road to Gettysburg; marched hastily over rough and muddy roads through a drenching rain, reaching there about 12 o'clock that day, a distance of 11 miles. At this time the First Corps had already been engaged for some time, and had commenced to retire. We continued the march through the town, and, according to your order, took position on the right of the road leading from Gettysburg to Chambersburg, in an orchard, where we for a short time halted, being subjected meanwhile to a severe cannonade of the enemy. Here one company (H) was ordered by you to deploy as skirmishers, which they did in handsome style, having instructions from you to prevent the enemy from advancing to a large barn and several adjacent buildings on our right. Your instructions were carried out to the letter.

The First Division of our corps had already advanced against the enemy, when, showing signs of being overwhelmed, we with the rest of the brigade were ordered forward to their support, taking position on their left, and having on our left the First Brigade, of the Third Division Here we withstood an enemy more than threefold our number, receiving volleys of musketry in swift succession, and suffering severely from a destructive fire of shot and shell. Our regiment did not yield, but stood firmly until the First Division, Second Corps, had fallen far back toward the town, and the First Brigade, of our division, on our left, had disappeared from the field.

At this juncture, with an enemy in front and on either flank, not only threatened with, but experiencing, a heavy enfilading fire, we retired in good order, and, I believe, were the last regiment to reach the foot of Washington street, where we again took a position to cover the town, and held the enemy in check until our trains of baggage-wagons and ambulances had withdrawn to the rear. This move-ment was a success, in part due to a section of Captain Dilger's renowned battery, planted upon an eminence near the square in the town of Gettysburg. You then ordered us to march to the opposite side of the town, which we accordingly did in most excellent order, taking a position along a stone wall by an orchard, on the edge of the town. In this position we remained until near nightfall, when we moved in a corn-field on the west side of the road from Emmitsburg to Gettysburg, between the cemetery and the town. Here we remained undisturbed during the night, sleeping on our arms; and here ends the first day's struggle.

Next day, July 2, continuous skirmishing was going on in our immediate front, and sharpshooters of the enemy, who during the night had couched themselves in houses and steeples of public buildings, harassed us constantly with their fire.

About 4 p. m. opened what is said to be the grandest cannonade of the war, which lasted for about five hours, chiefly directed to the position held by your brigade and the residue of the corps. My regiment endured it with a coolness and resolution most commendable.

Late in the evening (about 9 p. m.) the enemy made a most desperate charge upon a battery supported by the First Division of our corps. They rushed forward with incredible fierceness, driving back the First Division in disorder, and actually reached the guns (one of which our men had already spiked) and demanded a surrender, but the commander of the battery and his brave cannoneers did not yield. Then you, seeing the critical position of affairs, and well knowing how soon the enemy would possess himself of the battery and the commanding heights if not forced back, called upon our regiment and the Fifty-eighth New York Volunteers, also of your brigade, to fall in and advance against them. It is needless for me to say, general, for you led us in person, with what alacrity the regiment responded, and with what determination it moved forward, and with what courage it met the foe, and, in conjunction with the gallant Fifty-eighth, drove him back, saved the position, and thus secured the whole army from irreparable disaster. Here ends the second day's struggle.

During the night you ordered us to take position opposite the cemetery, in a field. Here the regiment remained during the whole of the day (July 3), maintaining its ground and receiving the attacks of the enemy with the greatest coolness and gallantry. As is well known, we were constantly perplexed as on the previous day, and that again from — a. m. until — p. m. the regiment was under the heaviest fire of the enemy's cannon, exhibiting the same coolness which had characterized it before. When night came, a heavy rain commenced, and firing ceased. We slept on our arms again, but had no encounter, it appearing that the enemy, defeated and disheartened, had fled away.

The next morning (July 4) about 8 a. m. you ordered us, with the Twenty-sixth Wisconsin Volunteers, on a reconnaissance, you commanding it in person. We advanced in an easterly direction toward York for the distance of about 2 miles, completely scouring the whole country, and taking many prisoners. You then, having accomplished your purpose, ordered us to return to the position we had left in the morning. This being done, we there remained until ordered forward with the rest of the corps in pursuit of the enemy toward Emmitsburg.

Our regiment had suffered very heavily in the loss of officers and enlisted men. Colonel Lockman fell, wounded, while gallantly standing at his post. Adjutant Dodge, Captain Volkhausen, and Lieutenant Trumpelman were all seriously wounded while nobly struggling against the enemy, the two former (Adjutant Dodge and Captain Volkhausen) having had their legs amputated, and the latter (Lieutenant Trumpelman), I regret to say, has since died from the effect of his wound. Lieut. M. Rasemann and Lieutenant Frost were, I am sad to say, killed. Both died the death of heroes. Lieutenant A. B. von Cloedt is a prisoner in the hands of the enemy.

Lieutenant-Colonel Lloyd, who assumed command of the regiment upon Colonel Lockman's receiving the wound, behaved with the utmost coolness. Of the other officers and soldiers, I can speak only in terms of the highest praise.

The loss of the regiment in killed, wounded, and missing amounts in the aggregate to the number of 144, including officers and privates.*

All of which is respectfully submitted.

I am, general, respectfully, yours,

BENJAMIN A. WILLIS,
Maj., Comdg. 119th Regt. New York Vols.

Col. W. KRZYZANOWSKI,
Comdg. Second Brigade, Third Division, Eleventh Corps.

No. 261.

Report of Lieut. Col. David Thomson, Eighty-second Ohio Infantry.

NEAR WARRENTON JUNCTION, VA., *August* 21, 1863.

SIR: In compliance with your order, I have the honor to submit the following report of the operations of this regiment at the battle of Gettysburg, and from that time to July 25, the date of our encampment near Warrenton Junction, Va.:

On July 1 last, this regiment, numbering 312 men present for duty, under the command of Col. James S. Robinson, and forming part of the Second Brigade, was assigned a position on the left of that brigade during the battle of that day, in the north of the town. By command of Colonel Robinson, the regiment fell back through Gettysburg with the remainder of the forces of the Third Division. Upon entering the town, Colonel Robinson was severely wounded, when I took command of the regiment. On arriving on the ground in front of the cemetery building, I was ordered to take a position near. I placed the regiment west of and near that building, where I remained during that day and until the evening of July 5, when we left Gettysburg, and marched with the Second Brigade until we arrived near Hagerstown, Md., on July 11, the regiment then numbering 220 present for duty.

During the battle, the regiment lost 4 officers killed, 2 mortally wounded (since died), 12 wounded, and 2 taken prisoners. Total loss of officers, 20. The loss in enlisted men was 13 killed, 10 mortally wounded, 61 wounded, and 77 missing. Total loss of enlisted men, 161.

The regiment remained near Hagerstown, Md., until July 14, when it was transferred to the First Brigade, under your command. Since then we have marched with the First Brigade from Hagerstown, Md., to Warrenton Junction, Va., where we arrived July 25, near 5 p. m. The strength of the regiment upon its arrival at the latter place was 224 present for duty.

I am, general, very respectfully, your obedient servant,

D. THOMSON,
Lieutenant-Colonel, Commanding Regiment.

Brigadier-General TYNDALE,
Comdg. First Brigade, Third Division, Eleventh Corps.

---

*But see revised statement, p. 183.

No. 262.

Report of Maj. August Ledig, Seventy-fifth Pennsylvania Infantry.

HDQRS. SEVENTY-FIFTH PENNSYLVANIA VOLUNTEERS,
July 28, 1863.

SIR: In compliance with an order received from division head-quarters to report the recent operations, I send you the following:

The regiment, with the corps, left camp near Brooke's Station June 12, on account of a threatening invasion of the enemy into Maryland and Pennsylvania. After different marches, we arrived at Emmitsburg, Md., June 29.

On the 30th, we rested.

July 1.—At 5 a. m. we left camp, and proceeded to Gettysburg. We arrived there at 1.30 a. m. We were immediately ordered to the north side of the town, where the regiment was placed as follows: On my left (the extreme left of the Second Brigade), the Eighty-second Ohio Volunteers; on my right, the One hundred and nine-teenth New York Regiment, in line of battle. Here we received a heavy fire from the enemy's 10-pounder rifled guns, which caused a loss in the regiment of 1 killed and 2 wounded.

About 2 o'clock, the whole brigade advanced nearly one-half mile, which was greatly interrupted by fences, which had to be taken down under a heavy fire of musketry from the enemy. When within 100 yards of them, in a wheat-field, we charged upon them and drove them back. We halted, and opened fire on the enemy. The Eighty-second Ohio, on my left, was flanked, and gave way. Col. F. Mahler's horse was shot, but he [the colonel] got up again, and went forward to direct the fire to the left flank, which was now unprotected, and the enemy threatening to cut off our retreat. He was already within 40 yards of our left and rear.

Colonel Mahler at this moment received a severe wound, and was disabled, so I took the command, and directed at once the fire left-oblique, and began to retreat behind a fence, which I could only pass by the flank, moving my left flank through first, so as to give the enemy battle on my left and front.

During this short period—say fifteen minutes—I lost 111 killed and wounded.

I began now to retreat about 200 yards into an orchard. The One hundred and nineteenth New York Regiment, on my right, suffered also heavily from the flank attack, and moved backward also in the garden. I received orders to fall back on the town. Here the Second Division arrived and went into the engagement. Shortly after this, a new line behind the town was ordered, and formed by my regiment in the best of order. I was ordered in a corn-field behind a stone wall, below the Evergreen Cemetery, the Eighty-second Ohio on my right, the First Brigade on my left.

On July 2 and 3, the regiment was not actively engaged. I lost here 3 men killed and wounded by the heavy bombardment.

On July 5, I was ordered to march to Emmitsburg; from there to South Mountain Pass.

On July 8, we passed through South Mountain Pass, and arrived at Boonsborough, where we were drawn up in line of battle.

Next morning, July 9, I was ordered to fall behind the town, in order to get a rest.

The Sixth Corps having relieved us at 10 a. m. July 10. I was ordered to march toward Hagerstown, and arrived at 5 o'clock within 3 miles of Hagerstown, where we took position on the right of the turnpike.

On July 11, we rested.

On July 12, we marched toward Hagerstown, within one-half mile of it, and, taking position, during the night rifle-pits were put up by my men.

On July 14, we marched toward Williamsport.

On July 15, marched back to Middletown.

On July 16, marched to Berlin. There we rested two days.

On July 19, early in the morning, left camp, and crossed the Potomac River, and marched to Hamilton, Va.

On July 20, marched to Mountville.

On July 21 and 22, rested.

On July 23, we marched to New Baltimore.

On July 24, two patrols of my regiment reconnoitered about 2 miles in front of our picket lines.

On July 25, we marched to Warrenton Junction and made camp. The men are greatly fatigued; hardly able for another campaign at present.

I remain, your most obedient servant,

AUGUST LEDIG,
Major, Commanding Regiment.

Col. W. KRZYZANOWSKI,
Commanding Second Brigade.

No. 263.

Report of Col. William H. Jacobs, Twenty-sixth Wisconsin Infantry.

WARRENTON JUNCTION, VA.,
July 28, 1863.

SIR: Pursuant to your order, I hereby respectfully submit a report of the part taken by my regiment in the late battle of Gettysburg, as stated to me by officers of the regiment, I myself having been absent on sick leave at the time.

About 2 p. m. on July 1, the regiment arrived with the rest of your command at the village of Gettysburg, and was ordered at once to the front. The position assigned it by you was the extreme right of the brigade. The regiment was furiously attacked by vastly superior numbers, but held its own until ordered by you to retreat, when a retreat in good order was effected.

The regiment suffered very severely in this engagement. The loss in officers is as follows: Lieutenant-Colonel Boebel, severely wounded; Major Baetz, wounded; Adjutant Wallber, taken prisoner; 4 line officers killed, 9 line officers wounded, and 1 line officer taken prisoner. The loss of enlisted men is an aggregate of 200 killed, wounded, and missing.*

At about 4 o'clock the regiment rallied on Cemetery Hill, and was ordered behind the stone fence.

---

*But see revised statement, p. 183.

During the artillery fire of July 2 and 3, the regiment suffered no loss.

The behavior of both officers and men was, so far as I can learn, exemplary. I can state nothing special for the praise of individuals.

Lieutenant-Colonel Boebel commanded the regiment during the engagement on July 1. After its arrival on Cemetery Hill, Captain Fuchs took command until July 4, when I arrived, and resumed command.

I remain, sir, your obedient servant,

W. H. JACOBS,
Colonel, Commanding Twenty-sixth Wisconsin Volunteers.

Col. W. KRZYZANOWSKI,
Commanding Second Brigade, Third Division.

No. 264.

Report of Maj. Thomas W. Osborn, First New York Light Artillery, commanding Artillery Brigade, Eleventh Army Corps.

HEADQUARTERS ARTILLERY, ELEVENTH CORPS,
July 29, 1863.

SIR: I have the honor to report, concerning the part borne by this command in the battle of Gettysburg on the 1st, 2d, and 3d instant, that on the morning of the 1st instant I moved from Emmitsburg toward Gettysburg with the artillery of the corps, consisting of five batteries, and marched in the following order: Captain Dilger in advance with the Third Division, Lieutenant Wheeler with the First Division and in the center, the three remaining batteries following closely in rear of the center division.

I herewith enumerate the batteries of the command: Battery G, Fourth U. S. Artillery, commanded by Lieut. B. Wilkeson, six light 12-pounders; Battery I, First Ohio Artillery, commanded by Capt. H. Dilger, six light 12-pounders; Battery K, First Ohio Artillery, commanded by Capt. L. Heckman, four light 12-pounders; Battery I, First New York Artillery, commanded by Capt. M. Wiedrich, six 3-inch, and Thirteenth New York Independent Battery, commanded by First Lieut. W. Wheeler, four 3-inch guns. Total, 26 guns.

After moving 5 or 6 miles, I received notice from Major-General Howard that the First Corps was already engaged with the enemy at Gettysburg, and that I should move the artillery to the front as rapidly as possible.

A little after 10 a. m. the first battery (Dilger's) reached the town, and was ordered by General Schurz to the front of and 300 yards beyond the town, where he took position, and at once became engaged with a rebel battery about 1,000 yards in its front. This battery was soon supported by another, when Captain Dilger was compelled to stand the fire from both until the arrival of Wheeler's battery half an hour later, when I ordered Lieutenant Wheeler to report to Captain Dilger. The result of this artillery duel was one piece of Wheeler's battery dismounted and five pieces of the enemy's, which they left upon the ground; besides, they lost comparatively heavier than we in horses and *matériel*.

During the short struggle both batteries changed position several times, and did so with excellent results and in the best possible manner, Captain Dilger using much judgment in the selection of his several positions. They did not leave their immediate locality until the corps was ordered by the commanding general to fall back to Cemetery Hill.

About 11 a. m. Lieutenant Wilkeson reached the field, and was ordered to report to General Barlow, commanding the First Division, which was engaged about three-fourths of a mile from the town and on the left of the York pike. The battery was assigned position by General Barlow, and when I reached the ground I found it unfortunately near the enemy's line of infantry, with which they were engaged, as well as two of his batteries, the concentrated fire of which no battery could withstand. Almost at the first fire, Lieutenant Wilkeson was mortally wounded, and carried from the field by 4 of his men. The command of the battery now devolved upon Lieutenant Bancroft. By changing position several times, the battery maintained its relative position until the division fell back to the town, when it retired to Cemetery Hill. During this engagement the battery was separated into sections or half batteries, and its struggle to maintain itself was very severe and persistent.

Captain Heckman was not ordered in until the corps had begun to fall back. He was then put into position, with a view of holding the enemy in check until the corps had time to retire through the town to the hill beyond, and though he worked his battery to the best of his ability, the enemy crowded upon it, and was within his battery before he attempted to retire. He was compelled to leave one gun in the hands of the enemy. I think no censure can be attached to this battery for the loss of the gun. The battery was so severely disabled otherwise that I was compelled to send it to the rear, thus losing the benefit of it during the fight of the second and third days.

Captain Wiedrich was assigned, on his arrival upon the field, to a position on the hill immediately in front of the cemetery entrance and overlooking the town. He was engaged several times during the day with the enemy's artillery at long range. He maintained the same position during the three days' fighting, but on this p. m. Colonel Wainwright, chief of artillery First Corps, took command of his battery, with the artillery on that side of the Baltimore pike. The artillery of the corps ceased firing for the day, when the corps fell back to Cemetery Hill.

I would remark here that during the p. m. of the 1st and the a. m. of the 2d, I furnished Colonel Wainwright, chief of artillery First Corps, with ammunition from the Eleventh Corps train, the train of the First Corps not being within reach. This of necessity caused considerable annoyance later in the engagement, on account of the difficulty in procuring a supply of ammunition sufficient to cover the great expenditure we were compelled to make through the engagement.

On the morning of the 2d, I applied to General Hunt, chief of artillery Army of the Potomac, for a greater amount of artillery than we then had, as our position was finely adapted to its use, and I did not consider that we had sufficient to assist our small infantry force in holding the position if the enemy should attack us in heavy force. The following batteries were ordered to report to me: Battery H, First U. S. Artillery, Lieutenant Eakin, six light 12-pounders; Fifth New York Independent Battery, Captain Taft, six 20-pounder Parrotts; Battery C, First West Virginia Artillery, Captain Hill, four 10-pounder Parrotts; Battery H, First Ohio Artillery, Captain Huntington, six 3-inch rifles; Second Maine Battery, Captain Hall, four 3-inch rifles; First New Hampshire Battery, Captain [Edgell] six 3-inch rifles. Total, 32.

Heckman's battery having been sent to the rear and one gun of Wheeler's battery dismounted, gave us on the morning of the 2d a total of fifty-two guns.

In the morning, before General Slocum had occupied his position, and while he was doing so, I placed three batteries on the right of the Baltimore road, commanding the ravine between the two prominent hills on our right; yet, as General Slocum withstood every assault on his lines without assistance, later in the day I withdrew these batteries to the hill. As soon as the enemy developed the position he would probably occupy with his batteries, I placed mine in position commanding them. By the assignment on the hill, Dilger had the right, resting next the Baltimore road and parallel with the Emmitsburg road; on *his left, and in order, were Bancroft, Eakin, Wheeler, Hill, and Hall, commanding the enemy's batteries to the right of the town; and across the Baltimore road I placed Taft in rear of and perpendicular to Bancroft; also Huntington in rear of and perpendicular to Wheeler, but farther in the rear of Wheeler than Taft was of Bancroft, so that Taft's battery would not obstruct his line of fire.

By this assignment of artillery, I commanded with a reputable number of guns every point on which the enemy could place artillery commanding Cemetery Hill. I also occupied every point of the hill available for artillery, and during the engagement every gun, at different times, was used with good effect, and the fire of no one gun interfered with the fire of another. A sharp curve in the side of the hill also afforded good and convenient protection for the caissons. Most of the day the firing of the enemy's artillery was irregular, they scarcely opening more than one battery at a time, and when they did so we readily silenced them.

On our entire front the enemy held a fine crest for the protection of artillery, at a distance of 1,000 to 1,400 yards from us; but at the time the heavy attack was made on the extreme left of our line, the firing was very severe, and especially upon the hill. They engaged the greater portion of our whole line, and from both the right and left of the town much of the fire was concentrated on our position, but we soon gained a decided advantage over them, and long before the infantry struggle on the left was decided, we had silenced most of their guns.

In this artillery fire, Lieutenant Eakin was wounded in the hip, and carried from the field.

Between 7 and 8 o'clock in the evening, a rebel brigade charged from the town upon the hill and upon Captain Wiedrich's battery. The charge was very impetuous, and the infantry at first gave way, and the battery was held for a moment by the enemy, when the cannoneers rallied with the infantry, and, seizing upon any weapons they could reach, threw themselves upon the enemy, and assisted to drive them back. All was done that could be, both before and after the repulse of the enemy, by the use of canister upon their ranks.

Colonel Wainwright speaks in highly complimentary terms of both officers and men for their gallant conduct on this occasion. Although the command was much exhausted by the two days' work, most of the night was passed in replenishing the batteries with ammunition and making repairs.

On the morning of the 3d, we were in position the same as on the 2d, but little was done during the a. m. by our corps. Occasionally a rebel battery would open upon the cemetery, evidently with a view to obtain the exact elevation and time to make their fire effective in the p. m.'s work on our position. At each attempt we silenced them, with but little loss to ourselves.

About 2 p. m. they opened along our whole front with an unbroken line of artillery, and also heavily on our right flank, apparently using every description of missiles and field artillery. The crest which the enemy occupied varied from 1,000 to 1,900 yards distance, and afforded an excellent protection. I judge that the guns of not less than one-half mile of this front were concentrated on our position, besides several batteries on our right, which enfiladed our position, excepting Captains Taft's and Huntington's batteries.

Our artillery endured this fire with surprising coolness and determination. No battery even showed a disposition to retire, and several times during the cannonading we silenced several of their batteries, but at a moment's cessation on our part they would reopen upon us. The fire was extremely galling, and by comparing the rapidity with which the shells fell among and passed by our guns with the rapidity with which our guns replied, the number of guns playing on the hill was very much greater than the number in position there; probably double.

Our guns were worked with great coolness, energy, and judgment, but as no satisfactory results were obtained, I ordered all our guns to cease firing, and the men to lie down to await developments. At the same time the artillery of our entire front ceased firing, and a few moments later the infantry of the enemy broke over the crest from where their artillery had been playing, and made their grand charge across the plain upon our lines. The left of the charging column rested on a line perpendicular to our front, then stretching away to the right beyond our view, thus offering an excellent front for our artillery fire. We used, according to distance, all descriptions of projectiles. The whole force of our artillery was brought to bear upon this column, and the havoc produced upon their ranks was truly surprising.

The enemy's advance was most splendid, and for a considerable distance the only hinderance offered it was by the artillery, which broke their lines fearfully, as every moment showed that their advance under this concentrated artillery fire was most difficult; and though they made desperate efforts to advance in good order, were unable to do so, and I am convinced that the fire from the hill was one of the main auxiliaries in breaking the force of this grand charge. But while the enemy was advancing, and after having been repulsed, I insisted that the artillery fire should be turned intensely upon the infantry, and no notice whatever was to be taken of their artillery.

I am not able to speak of any one or more batteries as deserving especial notice over another. Every battery did its whole duty; the officers proved themselves brave and efficient, and the men on the battle-field were most willing, brave, and gallant; in fact, the only fault I could mention was too great willingness to use ammunition at small squads of men and on unimportant objects, yet this was not carried to excess.

The artillery of the reserve proved all that could be expected or even asked of it; without their assistance I do not conceive how I could have maintained the position we held. I feel most thankful for their assistance, and the very willing and cordial manner in which it was rendered.

I would also speak of Lieut. George W. Freeman, acting assistant adjutant-general of the command, for the great assistance he was to me and to the whole command during the engagement.

I am unable to give any definite estimate of the amount of ammunition expended during the engagement. After we had exhausted the supply with the batteries, I replenished from our train. Colonel Wainwright, on the p. m. of the 1st, also replenished from our train, and, after this source was exhausted, I drew from the reserve train of the army.

The casualties of this command are as follows.*

Our loss in pieces and horses is as follows:

	Horses killed.
Battery G, Fourth U. S. Artillery	31
Battery I, First Ohio Artillery (one piece disabled)	28
Battery K, First Ohio Artillery (one piece lost)	9
Battery I, First New York Artillery (one piece dismounted)	18
Thirteenth New York Independent Battery (one piece dismounted)	12
Total	98

I am, respectfully, your obedient servant,

T. W. OSBORN,
Major, Commanding Artillery, Eleventh Corps.

General HENRY J. HUNT,
Chief of Artillery, Army of the Potomac.

No. 265.

Report of Capt. Michael Wiedrich, Battery I, First New York Light Artillery.

——, —— —, 1863.

SIR: I have the honor to report to you the part my battery has taken in the battle of Gettysburg, July 1, 2, and 3.

On arriving on the 1st instant near the cemetery at Gettysburg, I was ordered by you to take position on a hill on the north side of the Baltimore-turnpike, and near the cemetery and east of the city.

During the afternoon, we had some skirmishing with a rebel battery which was posted near the road leading from Gettysburg to York.

When, about 5 p. m., our infantry, which had advanced through the town, was repulsed, I changed the direction of my pieces in the direction from where the enemy was advancing, and opened with shells on their columns with good effect; and after our infantry was driven out of the town, and the enemy made his appearance in our front, I received him with canister, which checked his progress, and gave our troops time to rally in rear of the battery, to advance on the enemy again, and to drive him back into town, when the fire was kept up until late in the evening.

Thursday, July 2, from early in the morning until about 3 p. m., we exchanged some shots with two rebel batteries planted directly in front of mine, at which time the battle became general, when my

---

* Embodied in revised statement, p. 183.

battery was exposed to the fire of two of the enemy's batteries, the one before mentioned and one in our left flank on the west side of the city, but did not sustain much damage from either of them. Only one shell struck one of my pieces and dismounted the same.

About 8 p. m. the enemy charged on the battery with a brigade of infantry, which succeeded in turning our infantry, and got into the intrenchments of my battery. After they were repulsed by our forces, I opened on them again with canister with good effect.

Friday, we had several artillery duels during the forenoon, but of short duration, as we silenced their batteries after a few rounds as often as they brought them against us, until about 1 p. m., when the battle became general, and the enemy brought all his guns to bear on our lines. My battery was exposed again to the same cross-fire as the day before, but without sustaining any loss whatever from those guns. All the loss we sustained was from their sharpshooters, who were secreted in the houses of the town, and who molested us continually for two days.

During the three days' fighting we held the position first taken. Our losses are 3 men killed, 2 severely and 9 slightly wounded.[*] Among the latter are Lieutenants Sahm and Stock.

I am happy to say that all the officers and men behaved well, and with a determination not to be excelled.

Very respectfully, your obedient servant,

M. WIEDRICH,
Captain, Comdg. Battery I, First New York Artillery.

Major OSBORN, *Chief of Artillery, Eleventh Corps.*

No. 266.

Report of Lieut. William Wheeler, Thirteenth New York Battery.

WARRENTON JUNCTION, VA., *July* 29, 1863.

SIR: I have the honor herewith to transmit a detailed report of the part taken by the Thirteenth New York Battery in the battle of July 1, 2, and 3, at Gettysburg, Pa.

On July 1, I marched from Emmitsburg with the Second Division (General Steinwehr), but, when within about 5 miles of Gettysburg, I was ordered to move forward at double-quick, which I did, proceeding at a rapid trot, and losing a large amount of forage from the roughness of the road.

Upon arriving at Gettysburg, I took position, by your order, on the right of the town, but soon received orders to move through the town to the front, and to support Captain Dilger's battery. In passing through the town, the rear body of two of my caissons broke down. One of these was subsequently recovered, but the other was too badly shattered to be repaired. I took up my position on Captain Dilger's right, and as soon as my guns had got the range of the hostile battery, they responded to it with good effect. Under their cover, Captain Dilger moved several hundred yards forward into a wheat-field. As soon as he commenced firing, I limbered up and followed, again taking position on his right. A very heavy fire was opened on us here both in front and upon the right flank, but we continued to hold the position.

---

*But see revised statement, p. 183.

The enemy then massed his infantry and threw them upon the troops on our right, who fell back after some severe fighting. I changed the direction of my right section, and fired into the advancing column of the enemy with canister, but did not succeed in checking them. I did not leave this position until the enemy was almost in rear of my battery. I then moved back to a point on the road near the town, and held this until the enemy were again nearly behind me, and the infantry supports had withdrawn.

While moving across the field to this point, a shot struck the axle of one of my pieces and broke it, dismounting the piece. I slung the piece under the limber with the prolonge, and carried it for some distance until the prolonge broke, when I was obliged to abandon the gun, but recovered it on the 5th, and it is now in serviceable condition. I then moved through the town, and was assigned by you a position on Cemetery Hill, being on the left wing of the batteries of the corps.

On the morning of July 2, my battery threw a few shells at the rebel train, &c., without eliciting a response.

At about 2 p. m. the rebel batteries opened along our front and on our right flank. My battery replied to them with good effect, and the guns directly in my front were several times silenced and compelled to change their position.

At about 5.30 p. m. my ammunition became exhausted (as I had lost 200 rounds in the caissons that broke down), and you sent another battery to relieve me. I took my battery to the Artillery Reserve train, and filled up with percussion and canister, which was the only 3-inch ammunition on hand.

During the morning of July 3, I lay in reserve behind Cemetery Hill. During the heavy cannonade from 1 to 3 p. m., I lost some horses, but fortunately no men.

At about 4 p. m. I received an order from you to go to assist the Second Corps, upon which a very heavy attack was being made. I immediately reported to General Hancock, who showed me my position. Upon coming into battery, I found the enemy not more than 400 yards off, marching in heavy column by a flank to attack Pettit's battery, which was on my right and somewhat in advance of me. This gave me a fine opportunity to enfilade their column with canister, which threw them into great disorder, and brought them to a halt three times. The charge was finally repulsed, and most of the enemy taken prisoners. I then returned to the corps at Cemetery Hill.

My loss consisted of 4 men severely wounded, 6 slightly wounded, and 3 missing;* 12 horses killed.

My men behaved with courage and spirit, and are anxious for another opportunity to try their 3-inch guns.

I beg leave to mention by name Orderly Sergt. Henry Miller and Corporals [Edward] Trafford, [John] O'Connor, and [John A.] Rusk, as distinguished for coolness and skill.

Eight hundred and fifty rounds of ammunition were expended.

The above is respectfully submitted.

WM. WHEELER,
First Lieutenant, Comdg. Thirteenth New York Battery.

Major Osborn,
Chief of Artillery, Eleventh Corps.

---

* But see revised statement p. 183.

No. 267.

Report of Capt. Hubert Dilger, Battery I, First Ohio Light Artillery.

JULY 29, 1863.

MAJOR: In regard to the part my battery took in the engagement July 1, 2, and 3, near Gettysburg, Pa., I have the honor to report:

The battery arrived at Gettysburg at about 10 a. m. July 1, attached to the division of Maj. Gen. C. Schurz, commanded by Brig. Gen. A. Schimmelfennig, who ordered me to take a position between the Taneytown and Baltimore road, wherever I might find it necessary, to which order I complied by putting one section, Lieutenant [Clark] Scripture commanding, on the highest point of the field. A four-gun battery of the enemy immediately opened fire at about 1,400 yards on this section, and compelled me very soon to bring my whole battery into action. During this heavy artillery duel, the enemy had been re-enforced to eight pieces, of which two advanced [to within] 800 or 1,000 yards, but I finally succeeded in silencing them, with a loss of five carriages, which they had to leave on the ground, after several efforts to bring them to the rear with new horses.

Short time afterward, a rifled battery commenced to play on me, and you brought, at my request, Lieutenant Wheeler's battery to my support, and gave me the honor of taking charge of both batteries. I instantly advanced Lieutenant Weidman's section about 600 yards on our right, on the Baltimore and Harrisburg road, and returned from there the other four pieces of my battery on the left, under protection of Lieutenant Wheeler's fire, about 400 yards.

In advancing, a ditch (5 feet wide and 4 feet deep, crossing the field in our front) had to be filled up, so as to form at least a passage for a column by pieces, which was executed under a very heavy fire. Lieutenant Wheeler followed as soon as my pieces were in position, and we remained here until the enemy's infantry commenced to mass on our right flank 100 yards, supported by about four batteries, which concentrated their fire on us, one of them enfilading our line completely, causing great damage to men and horses, and disabling one piece of mine and one of Wheeler's battery.

Our final retreat was executed in the same manner as the advance, and our infantry falling back toward the town, which could only be reached on one road, I sent all the pieces back excepting one section of each battery, commanding with them the entrance of the town as long as possible. The two rifled guns had to retire first, because I would not expose them too much at this short range, at which they commenced to become useless.

Our infantry having reached the town, I left my position, and was relieved on the Market road by two pieces of Battery G, Fourth U. S. Artillery.

The main road was completely blockaded by artillery, infantry, and ambulances, and I took the first road to the left, marched around the town, and rejoined my command on Cemetery Hill, having lost on this day 14 men, 24 horses, and 1 piece disabled.

During the whole engagement, three of my caissons were always employed to carry ammunition, and as slowly as I directed the fire, we were twice nearly out of ammunition.

In regard to the ammunition, I must say that I was completely dissatisfied with the results observed of the fuses for 12-pounder shells and spherical case, on the explosion of which, by the most careful preparation, you cannot depend. The shell fuses, again, were remarkably less reliable than those for spherical case. The fuses for 3-inch ammunition caused a great many explosions in our right before the mouth of the guns, and it becomes very dangerous for another battery to advance in the fire of his batteries, which kind of advancing of smooth-bore batteries is of very great importance on the battlefield, and should be done without danger. I would, therefore, most respectfully recommend the use of percussion shells only.

The other three days, major, I had the honor to stay under your immediate command, and cannot report any fact of special importance, excepting the loss of 2 men and 4 horses more.

The behavior of officers and men of my battery was excellent. Also, I am very much obliged to Lieutenant Wheeler for his kind and gallant assistance on the first day.

I have the honor, major, to sign, your obedient,

H. DILGER,
Captain, Commanding Battery I, First Ohio Artillery.

Maj. T. W. Osborn,
Chief of Artillery, Eleventh Corps

No. 268.

Report of Capt. Lewis Heckman, Battery K, First Ohio Light Artillery.

HDQRS. BATTERY K, FIRST OHIO ARTILLERY,
July 28, 1863.

MAJOR: I have the honor of making the following report of the operations of my battery in the late battle of Gettysburg:

On July 1, in obedience to your order, I placed my battery in position on the east side of the town. The enemy was already in range when my battery went into position. I unlimbered, and commenced firing as soon as possible, as the enemy were close to me and advancing. My battery was engaged thirty minutes. During that time I expended 113 rounds of ammunition, mostly canister.

I lost 2 men killed and 10 wounded, and 1 commissioned officer wounded severely.* I lost 9 horses that died from the wounds received.

The enemy in the meantime were advancing, and had gotten very close. The order was given to limber up, but too late to save my whole battery. I fell back through the town, leaving two pieces in the hands of the enemy.

My battery was not engaged again during the battle, but by your order went to the rear.

The above I respectfully submit.

LEWIS HECKMAN,
Captain Battery K, First Ohio Artillery.

[Maj. THOMAS W. OSBORN,
Chief of Artillery, Eleventh Corps.]

---

* But see revised statement, p. 183.

No. 269.

Report of Lieut. Eugene A. Bancroft, Battery G, Fourth U. S. Artillery.

NEAR WARRENTON JUNCTION, VA.,
July 28, 1863.

SIR : I have the honor to report the services of this battery since the 1st instant.

The battery, under the command of First Lieut. Bayard Wilkeson, Fourth U. S. Artillery, left camp, near Emmitsburg, Md., at 9 a. m. July 1, and marched to Gettysburg, Pa. When about 2 miles from the latter place, the order to trot was received, and, moving rapidly forward, the battery reached the town at 11 a. m.; passed directly through the village, and, turning to the right, in rear of our lines of batteries, moved about 1 mile through some fields, and immediately engaged the enemy. Leaving the left section, under Second Lieut. C. F. Merkle, on the south side of the York road, near the poor-house, the right and center sections took position on the north side of the road, and some distance eastward of the poor-house.

At this point, Lieutenant Wilkeson was struck in the right leg by a shot from the enemy's artillery, and mortally wounded. After engaging two of the rebel batteries for about half an hour, these two sections retired a short distance, and a few minutes thereafter three of the pieces went into action on the left of their first position, to resist the advance of a line of the enemy's infantry, firing spherical case and canister, until, our infantry giving way in great disorder, the want of support compelled me to withdraw the guns. On entering the road leading into the village, I was joined by the left section, under Lieutenant Merkle, and assumed command of the whole. Halting to fill the ammunition chests of the gun limbers, the battery then retired slowly through Gettysburg, and took position in the cemetery, on the south side of the village, at 5 p. m., whence I fired a few shell and solid shot at the enemy, but without eliciting any reply.

The casualties during the day were as follows, viz: Lieutenant Wilkeson, mortally wounded ; Private [Charles F.] Hofer, killed; Corporal [John] Monroe and Privates [Ira C.] Bumpus, [William] Clark, Taffender, and [Edwin S.] Libby, severely wounded; Bugler [Charles A.] Lockwood, Corporal [Adolphus C.] Hardy, Privates [William] Curtis and [Frank E.] Jordan, missing; 12 horses killed.

On the 2d instant, the battery was ordered to take position in a field in the rear of the cemetery, facing the Baltimore road, where it remained until 4.30 p. m., when it went into action at the cemetery, the right and center sections engaging a rebel battery stationed on a hill east of the cemetery, and the left section the enemy's batteries in front, to the north. The battery continued firing until 7 p. m., when the right and center sections were relieved, and, after filling the ammunition chests, retook the position occupied in the first part of the day, and were held in readiness to assist our infantry in holding the woods on the right.

The casualties this day were as follows: Privates [Charles C.] Converse, [Charles A.] Green, and [Philip] Kistner, slightly wounded; 8 horses killed.

On the 3d, in the morning, the left section rejoined the battery from the cemetery, where it had remained through the night.

At about 2 p. m., four guns being ordered into action, the right and center sections again took position in the cemetery, and engaged the enemy's batteries and infantry until their final repulse at about 5 p. m.

The casualties this day were Private [Patrick] Hartney severely, and Sergeant [William] Leroy and Private [Alfred] Johnson slightly, wounded; 4 horses killed and 7 wounded.

Number of rounds of ammunition expended during three days:

Solid shot	616
Shells	158
Spherical case	588
Canister	18
Total	1,380

The non-commissioned officers and men of the battery who came under my immediate observation behaved themselves with great coolness and gallantry. Exposed for hours to the hottest fire of the war, there was no faltering, and every man did his duty, each contributing his quota to the grand result.

Lieutenant Merkle was detached with his section on the first day by order of Major Osborn. His report of the part taken by him in that day's action is annexed herewith.

I have to report that Lieutenant Merkle fully sustained his previous reputation for coolness and bravery in the action of the 2d and 3d.

I am, sir, very respectfully, your obedient servant,

E. A. BANCROFT,
First Lieut. Fourth U. S. Artillery, Comdg. Battery G.

Lieut. W. H. MICKLE,
A. A. A. G., Artillery 11th Corps, Army of the Potomac.

No. 270.

Report of Lieut. Christopher F. Merkle, Battery G, Fourth U. S. Artillery.

NEAR WARRENTON JUNCTION, VA.,
July 28, 1863.

SIR: I have the honor to forward to your headquarters a report of the battle of Gettysburg, Pa.

I was assigned to a position by First Lieut. Bayard Wilkeson with my section about 1 mile or three-quarters northwest of the poor-house. I engaged one battery of the enemy for a few moments with solid shot, and then directed my attention to the rebel infantry as they were advancing in mass upon us. I used shell and spherical case shot at first, and, as the line of the enemy came closer, and I ran out of shot, shell, and case shot, I used canister; the enemy was then within canister range. At the same time, our infantry fell back rapidly, and left me almost without support. I then limbered to the rear, and retired toward the town. The enemy came rather close at the time, so I fired two double rounds of canister, with prolonge fixed, at their line at the end of the town; then limbered up and retired.

When I arrived upon this side of the town, I was ordered by Major Osborn to take up a position with my section on the right of Captain

Wiedrich, and about 100 yards north of the graveyard, on a small range of hills. At the same time he ordered me to get another gun from Lieutenant Bancroft and place it in the road or pike. I remained in that position until dark, when I was relieved.

I reported for orders to Major Osborn, and he ordered me to bring the left half battery in rear of the graveyard, and wait for further orders. I remained there all that night, and received orders next morning to join Lieutenant Bancroft.

The men in my section behaved well and bravely, especially Sergeants Leroy and Monroe.

The casualties during the day were Sergeant Monroe, Privates Bumpus, Clark, and Taffender, severely wounded, and Private Curtis missing; 5 horses killed.

Ammunition expended:

	Rounds.
Solid shot	24
Case shot	24
Shells	8
Canister	14
Total	70

I am, sir, very respectfully, your obedient servant,

C. F. MERKLE,
Second Lieutenant Fourth U. S. Artillery.

First Lieut. W. H. MICKLE,
A. A. A. G., Artillery 11*th Corps, Army of the Potomac.*

No. 271.

Reports of Maj. Gen. Henry W. Slocum, U. S. Army, commanding Twelfth Army Corps.

HDQRS. TWELFTH CORPS, ARMY OF THE POTOMAC,
August 23, 1863.

GENERAL: I have the honor of submitting the following report of the operations of the Twelfth Corps, and such other troops as were placed under my command, between June 28 and July 26:

The Twelfth Corps was at Knoxville, Md., on the morning of June 28, from which place it marched at 6 a. m., and arrived near Frederick City at 2 p. m. of the same day.

The march was resumed at 7 a. m. on the following day, and although nearly the entire army was obliged to move through the city in its march northward, and great delay was necessarily caused by the obstruction of the roads by baggage-wagons, &c., still the corps marched 23 miles, performing most of it during a heavy rain-storm.

On the 30th, the march was resumed at 5 a. m., and the corps encamped for the night about 1 mile beyond Littlestown, Pa., on the road leading from that place to Hanover.

On the morning of July 1, the corps was moved to Two Taverns, and remained at that place until information was received that the First and Eleventh Corps were engaged at Gettysburg, when the march was at once resumed, and, agreeably to suggestion from General Howard, the First Division was put in position on the right of our line, near Rock Creek. The Second Division was moved forward as rapidly as possible, and placed, pursuant to orders from General Hancock, on the extreme left of the line.

The corps remained in this position until the following morning, when, by direction of the commanding general, the Second Division was moved to the right of our center, and placed in the woods east of the turnpike, between Rock Creek and the crest of the hill held by our troops under Brigadier-General Wadsworth.

The Fifth Corps arrived at 5 a. m. on July 2, and, by direction of the commanding general, was placed in line on the right of the Twelfth Corps.

At about 8 a. m. this corps (the Fifth) and the First Division of the Twelfth Corps were moved to the left and across Rock Creek, the First Division taking position on the right of the Second, with its right resting on the creek. (See map annexed.)

As soon as the corps was established on its new line, a strong force was detailed for the construction of breastworks and abatis, which subsequently proved of great value, as they enabled us at a critical moment to detach portions of the command to other points of the line. The Fifth Corps was massed between the extreme right and left of the line occupied by the army, and held in readiness to move to the support of any part of the line. About half an hour before the attack on our left, this corps (the Fifth) was moved by order of the commanding general to the support of that part of the line. This attack was made by the enemy in strong force, and with great spirit and determination. Had it been successful, the result would have been terribly disastrous to our army and to the country. The arrival of the Fifth Corps at the point of attack at so critical a moment afforded it an opportunity of doing service for the country the value of which can never be overestimated. Of the manner in which this opportunity was improved, I need not speak. The long list of its killed and wounded attests more clearly than language can the valor of its officers and men.

As soon as the attack on our left commenced, the First Division and two brigades of the Second Division, Twelfth Corps, were ordered to that part of the line. The First Division moved at once, and arrived in time to assist in repelling the assault. The two brigades of the Second Division, under Brigadier-General Geary, by some unfortunate and unaccountable mistake, did not follow the First Division, but took the road leading to Two Taverns, crossing Rock Creek. Immediately after the First Division and the two brigades of the Second Division had moved from their intrenchments, the enemy attacked the remaining brigade of the corps left to hold the line. This brigade was under command of Brigadier-General Greene, and the attack commenced before he had succeeded in extending his command so as to occupy the part of the line previously occupied by the troops sent to the support of our left. Although General Greene handled his command with great skill, and although his men fought with gallantry never surpassed by any troops under my command, the enemy succeeded in gaining possession of a portion of our intrenchments.

After a severe engagement of nearly three hours' duration, General Greene remained in possession of the left of our line of works, while the right, which had previously been held by the First Division, was in possession of the enemy. During this engagement, General Greene was re-enforced by three regiments from the First Corps and three from the Eleventh Corps, all of which did good service. Immediately after the repulse of the enemy on the left, the First Division was

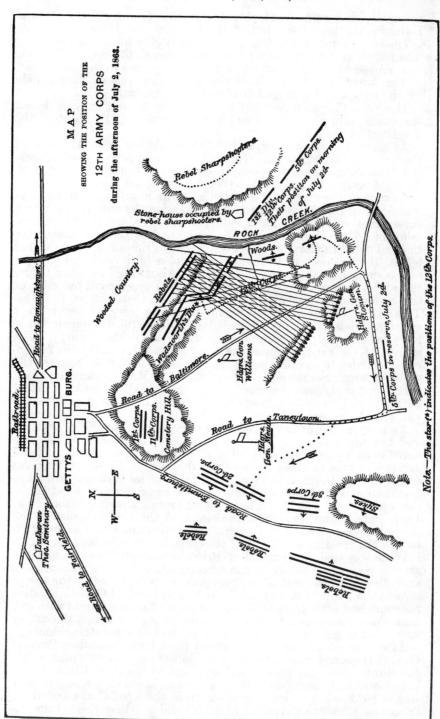

MAP

SHOWING THE POSITION OF THE

12TH ARMY CORPS

during the afternoon of July 2, 1863.

Note.—The star (*) indicates the positions of the 12th Corps.

ordered to return to its position on the right, and General Geary, with the two other brigades of the Second Division, was ordered back to his original position.   It was nearly midnight before this movement was fully completed.

Orders were at once issued for an attack at daybreak, for the purpose of regaining that portion of the line which had been lost.   The artillery of the Twelfth Corps, consisting of Battery F, Fourth U. S. Artillery;. Battery K, Fifth U. S. Artillery; Battery M, First New York, and Knap's Pennsylvania battery, was placed in position during the night by Lieutenant-Colonel Best, and opened the battle at 4 a. m. on the following morning, and during the entire engagement all these batteries rendered most valuable aid to our cause.

The enemy had been re-enforced during the night, and were fully prepared to resist our attack.   The force opposed to us, it is said, belonged to the corps under General Ewell, formerly under General Jackson, and they certainly fought with a determination and valor which has ever characterized the troops of this well-known corps. We were re-enforced during the engagement by Shaler's brigade, of the Sixth Corps, and by two regiments from General Wadsworth's division, of the First Corps, and also by Neill's brigade, of the Sixth Corps, which was moved across Rock Creek, and placed in position to protect our extreme right.   All these troops did excellent service.

The engagement continued until 10.30 a. m., and resulted in our regaining possession of our entire line of intrenchments and driving the enemy back of the position originally held by him ; in the capture of over 500 prisoners in addition to the large number of wounded left on the field, besides several thousand stand of arms and three stand of colors.   Our own loss in killed and wounded was comparatively light, as most of our troops were protected by breastworks.

The portion of the field occupied by the enemy presented abundant evidence of the bravery and determination with which the conflict was waged.   The field of battle at this point was not as extended as that on the left of our line, nor was the force engaged as heavy as that brought into action on that part of the line.   Yet General Geary states that over 900 of the enemy's dead were buried by our own troops and a large number left unburied, marching orders having been received before the work was completed.

Soon after the repulse of the enemy at this point, he opened from his entire line the severest artillery fire that I have ever witnessed. The losses of the Twelfth Corps from this fire were, however, light, and when the fire ceased, and was followed by an assault from his infantry on the left of the line, the entire command was in readiness to move to the support of our troops at that point.   The First Division was moved, and reached the scene of conflict in time to have rendered assistance if required.   They were not, however, called into action, the enemy being driven from the field by the troops already in position.

On the following morning, July 4, I moved forward with one brigade (General Ruger's), and found the enemy had retired from our immediate front.

The next day the Twelfth Corps marched to Littlestown.

On July 7, the march was resumed at 4 a. m., and although many of the men were destitute of shoes, and all greatly fatigued by the labor and anxiety of a severely contested battle, as well as by the heavy marches which had preceded it, still, a march of 29 miles was made this day.

On the following day the command passed through Frederick, and halted for the night near Jefferson.

On the 9th, we crossed South Mountain at Crampton's Pass, and encamped near Rohrersville.

On the 10th, we marched to Bakersville, and on the 11th to Fair Play.

The 12th and 13th were spent in endeavoring to ascertain the position of the enemy in our front, which we found great difficulty in accomplishing. Marsh Run extended along the position held by the enemy in our front, and at this time it was passable only at the bridges, the heavy rains having raised the water much beyond its usual depth, and caused it to overrun the marsh land in our front.

During the night of the 13th, the enemy recrossed the Potomac.

On the 15th, I marched the command to Sandy Hook, near Harper's Ferry, with orders to procure clothing and other supplies as soon as possible, and hold it in readiness to cross the river.

Three days were spent in procuring supplies, and on the 19th the corps crossed the river, and encamped for the night near Hillsborough.

On the following day the command marched to Snickersville, and remained there, guarding the pass in the Blue Ridge, until the 23d, when it was moved to Ashby's Gap, at which point it arrived at 2 p. m., and made preparations to encamp for the night; but at 4 p. m. I received orders to move forward at once to Markham Station, near Manassas Gap, and the march was immediately resumed, the troops arriving near the station late at night.

At 3 a. m. on the 24th, marched through Markham to Linden. At 12 m. on the same day returned, via Markham, and encamped at Piedmont.

On the 25th, marched to Thoroughfare Gap, and on the 26th to Warrenton Junction.

The enemy commenced the movement toward Pennsylvania early in the month of June. My command left its camp near Aquia Creek on the 13th of the same month. From that day until its arrival at Warrenton Junction, on July 26, it was constantly engaged in services of the most fatiguing nature. Marches of from 25 to 30 miles per day were frequently performed. We were constantly in the presence of the enemy, and even while remaining in camp for a day or two, nothing like rest or relaxation from care and anxiety was known.

The complete ration allowed the soldier was not issued to him a single day during the entire campaign. It cannot be surprising that, under these circumstances, officers as well as men were greatly exhausted on our arrival at Warrenton.

The conduct of the entire command during this campaign was such as entitles it to the gratitude of the country, and justifies me in the indulgence of a deep and heartfelt pride in my connection with it. At Gettysburg, when we were brought into conflict with the entire force of the enemy, although every one felt convinced that we were greatly his inferior in point of numbers, yet all seemed to realize the vast responsibility thrown upon our army and the fearful consequence which must result from our defeat, and every one was nerved to the task, and entered upon the duties devolving upon him with a spirit worthy of the highest praise. Their confidence in the final result of this important battle was greatly increased by the fact, which soon became apparent to all, that in this battle, at least, all our forces were to be used; that a large portion of the army were not to remain idle while the enemy's masses were being hurled against another portion.

My own corps during this conflict was moved from one point of the line to another, and all of those thus moved had the satisfaction of knowing that, where the battle was waged by the enemy with the greatest fury, there our troops were concentrated, ready and eager to meet them.

My staff officers discharged their duties during the campaign to my entire satisfaction. Supplies were furnished by all the different departments as liberally and with as little delay as could have been an ticipated under the circumstances.

I am, general, very respectfully, your obedient servant,
H. W. SLOCUM,
Major-General of Volunteers, Commanding.

Brig. Gen. S. WILLIAMS,
Assistant Adjutant-General, Army of the Potomac.

HDQRS. TWELFTH CORPS, ARMY OF THE POTOMAC,
July 4, 1863.

GENERAL: I have the honor to forward herewith two flags captured by the Sixtieth New York Volunteers, of the Third Brigade, Second Division, in the action of July 2. One was borne by the "Stonewall Brigade," and is represented as the brigade flag. The other was the battle-flag of a Virginia regiment.

Very respectfully, your obedient servant,
H. W. SLOCUM,
Major-General of Volunteers, Commanding.

Brig. Gen. S. WILLIAMS,
Assistant Adjutant-General.

ADDENDA.

HDQRS. TWELFTH CORPS, ARMY OF THE CUMBERLAND,
Tullahoma, Tenn., December 30, 1863.

Maj. Gen. GEORGE G. MEADE,
Commanding Army of the Potomac:

GENERAL: I inclose herewith the report of General T. H. Ruger of operations of the First Division, Twelfth Corps, at the battle of Gettysburg, together with the reports of his brigade and regimental commanders. General Ruger, with a large portion of his division, was ordered to New York City soon after the battle, and immediately after his return from New York the corps was ordered to this department. The reports of General Williams and myself were delayed with the hope of receiving General Ruger's report in time to forward it with them.

I deeply regret the necessity which compelled me to send my report and that of General Williams unaccompanied by any report of the operations of the First Division, for although an account of the operations of this division was given in the report of General Williams, who commanded the corps during the battle, I think the absence of Ruger's report may account for some of the errors contained in your report as to the operations of the Twelfth Corps.

I inclose a letter from General Williams, calling my attention to these errors, to which I respectfully invite your attention, and if anything can be done at this late day to correct these errors, I trust you will do it. Your report is the official history of that important battle, and to this report reference will always be made by our Government, our people, and the historian, as the most reliable and accurate account of the services performed by each corps, division, and brigade of your army. If you have inadvertently given to one division the credit of having performed some meritorious service which was in reality performed by another division, you do an injustice to brave men and defraud them of well-earned laurels. It is an injustice which even time cannot correct. That errors of this nature exist in your official report is an indisputable fact.

You give great credit to Lockwood's brigade for services on the evening of July 2, but state that this brigade was a portion of the First Corps, while it never at any time belonged to that corps, but was a portion of the Twelfth Corps, and was accompanied in its operations on the evening of July 2 by General Williams in person. A portion of this brigade (the One hundred and fiftieth New York) is still in General Williams' division.

I copy the following statement from your report:

During the heavy assault on our left, portions of the Twelfth Corps were sent as re-enforcements. During their absence, the line on the extreme right was held by a very much reduced force. This was taken advantage of by the enemy, who, during the absence of General Geary's division, of the Twelfth Corps, advanced and occupied part of the line. On the morning of the 3d, General Geary, having returned during the night, attacked at early dawn the enemy, and succeeded in driving him back and reoccupying his former position. A spirited contest was maintained all the morning along this part of the line. General Geary, re-enforced by Wheaton's brigade, of the Sixth Corps, maintained his position, and inflicted severe losses on the enemy.

From this statement it would appear that Geary's division marched to the support of your left; that Williams' division did not; that his (Williams') division, or a portion of it, was guarding the intrenchments when the enemy gained possession; that General Geary returned, and with his division drove the enemy back; that the engagement on the following morning was fought by Geary's division, assisted by Wheaton's brigade. This I know is the inference drawn from your history of those operations by every person unacquainted with the truth. Yet the facts in the case are very nearly the reverse of the above in every particular, and directly in contradiction to the facts as set forth in the report of General Geary, as well as that of General Williams. Geary's division did not march even in the direction of your left. Two of his brigades, under his immediate command, left the intrenchments under orders to move to the support of your left, but through some unfortunate mistake he took the road leading to Two Taverns. Williams' entire division did move to the support of your left, and it was one of his brigades (Lockwood's), under his immediate command, which you commend, but very singularly accredit to the First Corps.

Greene's brigade, of the Second Division, remained in the intrenchments, and the failure of the enemy to gain entire possession of our works was due entirely to the skill of General Greene and the heroic valor of his troops. His brigade suffered severely, but maintained its position, and held the enemy in check until the return of Williams' division. The "spirited contest maintained by General Geary, re-enforced by Wheaton's brigade," was a contest for regaining the portion of our intrenchments held by the enemy, and was conducted under the immediate command of General Williams, and was participated in by the entire Twelfth Corps, re-enforced not by Wheaton's but by Shaler's brigade.

Although the command of the Twelfth Corps was given temporarily to General Williams by your order, and although you directed him to meet at the council with other corps commanders, you fail to mention his name in your entire report, and in no place allude to his having any such command, or to the fact that more than one corps was at any time placed under my command, although at no time after you assumed command of the army until the close of this battle was I in command of less than two corps. I have now in my possession your written orders, dated July 2, directing me to assume command of the Sixth Corps, and, with that corps and the two then under my command (the Fifth and Twelfth), to move forward and at once attack the enemy.

I allude to this fact for the purpose of refreshing your memory on a subject which you had apparently entirely forgotten when you penned your report, for you have not failed to notice the fact of General Schurz and others having held, even for a few hours, commands above that previously held by them. I sincerely trust that you will endeavor to correct as far as possible the errors above mentioned, and that the correction may be recorded at the War Department.

I am, general, very respectfully, your obedient servant,

H. W. SLOCUM,
Major-General of Volunteers, Commanding.

[Inclosure.]

HEADQUARTERS FIRST DIVISION, TWELFTH CORPS,
Tullahoma, Tenn., December 26, 1863.

Maj. Gen. H. W. SLOCUM,
Commanding Twelfth Army Corps:

GENERAL: In forwarding the report of Brigadier-General Ruger, commanding First Division, Twelfth Army Corps, at the battle of Gettysburg, delayed to this late day for reasons stated in the letter accompanying the report, I embrace the occasion to call your attention to certain errors and omissions in Major-General Meade's official report of that battle, which I think do much injustice to some portions of this corps. These, briefly stated, are:

1. In crediting Lockwood's brigade to the First Corps.

2. In omitting all notice of the gallant defense by Greene's brigade of the left flank of our intrenched line on the evening of July 2, after the other troops of the corps had marched out to the support of the left.

3. In wholly ignoring the operations of the First Division.

4. In repudiating most of the material statements of my report as temporary commander of this corps.

1. As to Lockwood's brigade, the following is the notice taken of it in General Meade's report:

In the meantime, perceiving great exertions on the part of the enemy, the Sixth Corps (Major-General Sedgwick) and part of the First Corps (to the command of which I had assigned Major-General Newton), particularly Lockwood's Maryland brigade, together with detachments from the Second Corps, were all brought up, &c.

I cannot be mistaken in asserting that Lockwood's brigade was at no time during this battle a part of the First Corps, or under the command of General Newton. It was a part of the Twelfth Corps, and was brought up under my immediate command, with the First Division of same corps, to the support of the left. This brigade, composed then of the One hundred and fiftieth New York and First Maryland Potomac Home [Brigade] Regiment, coming from Balti-more, or its vicinity, reported to me as temporary commander of the corps early on the morning of July 2, while the skirmishers of the First Division, still on the south side of Rock Creek, were engaged with the enemy. General Lockwood being senior to General Ruger, then commanding First Division, and a stranger to the division, I directed him to take his orders directly from me as an unassigned brigade during the pending operations. When the First Division and Lockwood's brigade were ordered to support the left on the after-noon of the same day, I went in command of the supporting column, leaving the Second Division to cover our entire intrenched line.

On reaching the crest of Cemetery Ridge, Major (now, I believe, Lieutenant-Colonel) McGilvery, of Maine artillery, in command of one or more reserve batteries, reported to me that he was threatened by the enemy, and was without infantry supports, and that the enemy but a few moments before had drawn off into the woods in his front several pieces of artillery. I ordered General Lockwood to move into the woods indicated, which was promptly done, and our artil-lery, abandoned by the enemy, was almost immediately recaptured. The First Division at the same time was ordered into the woods on the left of Lockwood's brigade, and both advanced for some dis-tance and until halted, pursuant to superior orders, meeting very little resistance at any point from the retiring enemy. Though we passed large masses of our disorganized men, we saw not one line or body of our troops in position. The enemy seemed to have a clear field in that part of our line, and were helping themselves to our artillery until interrupted by the approach of re-enforcements from the Twelfth and Sixth Corps, advancing at about the same time. These facts having been fully reported, I am at a loss to comprehend (when all other corps sending supports to the left are especially named) why the Twelfth Corps should be not only not named, but deprived of the small credit of Lockwood's Maryland brigade for the benefit of the First Corps.

2. In omitting any mention of the gallant defense made by Gen-eral Greene's brigade on the left flank of the intrenched line of the Twelfth Corps on the evening of July 2.

General Meade's report thus speaks of the manner in which the enemy got possession of our line of breastworks :

> During the heavy assault upon our extreme left, portions of the Twelfth Corps were sent as re-enforcements. During their absence, the line of the extreme right was held by a much reduced force, and was taken advantage of by the enemy, who, during the absence of Geary's division, of the Twelfth Corps, advanced and occu-pied a part of the line.

It was the absence of the whole of the First Division and of Lock-wood's brigade (supporting the left) and of two brigades of the Second (Geary's) Division (marching toward Littlestown by mis-take) that the enemy took advantage of, not only to occupy our line on the right and center, but also to attack with great vigor Greene's brigade, of the Second Division (the only portion of the corps left behind), on the extreme left of our intrenched line. General Meade omits all mention of this gallant contest, which lasted fully three hours, and resulted in our retaining this important part of our line of defenses, and enabling us to resist for hours, with comparatively little loss, his heavier attacks on the following day, and finally to expel him wholly from our line.

General Meade speaks of another attack in a different part of the field at about the same hour, as follows:

On the extreme left another assault was, however, made about 8 p. m. on the Eleventh Corps from the left of the town, which was repulsed with the assistance of the Second and First Corps.

The similarity of time and circumstances leads me to think that there is a mistake in locality of this attack. It is quite certain that Greene was attacked and was re-enforced by the First and Eleventh Corps about the same hour that the report says that the attack on the Eleventh Corps was repulsed by aid of troops from the First and Second Corps. Be that as it may, the defense made by General Greene was eminently worthy of notice and commendation.

3. In wholly ignoring the operations of the First Division, Twelfth Corps.

The active participation of the Twelfth Corps in the battle of Gettysburg was, first, the marching of the First Division and Lockwood's brigade to the support of the left on Thursday afternoon, July 2; secondly, the defense of the left flank of the intrenched line on the evening of the same day; and, thirdly, the long contest on Friday morning, July 3, to recover possession of our line of breastworks. I have spoken of both operations of Thursday. Of those of Friday morning, General Meade thus speaks in his report:

On the morning of the 3d, General Geary, having returned during the night, was attacked at early dawn by the enemy, but succeeded in driving him back and occupying his former position. A spirited contest was maintained all the morning along this part of the line. General Geary, re-enforced by Wheaton's [a mistake for Shaler's] brigade, Sixth Corps, maintained his position, and inflicting very severe losses on the enemy. With this exception, the lines remained undisturbed, &c.

This is certainly neither a full nor a fair statement of a conflict which was waged almost without cessation for fully seven hours, and in which all the infantry and artillery of the corps were engaged. The idea conveyed by General Meade's report is a simple defense by one division of the corps. The engagement really began on our side by a heavy cannonading from guns placed in position after midnight. The plan of attack, arranged the night before, to dislodge the enemy from our breastworks, was for Geary's division to follow the cessation of artillery firing by an attack along the intrenchments which he held on our left, while the First Division was placed in preparation to assault over the marshy grounds on the extreme right, or attack the enemy's flank should he attempt to move beyond the breastworks. The enemy, on the other hand, had brought up strong re-enforcements, with the design of carrying the position of our intrenched line, which he failed to drive Greene from on the previous night, and which would have placed him in the rear of our army, and given him possession of our main line of communication—the Baltimore pike. Both parties started at daylight with plans of attack, each with the expectation of expelling the other.

Not only, as General Meade's report says, did Geary's division (or, more correctly, the two absent brigades of it) return during the night, but so also did the whole of the First Division and Lockwood's brigade, and the whole corps (not Geary's division alone), artillery and infantry, succeeded in driving the enemy back and occupying its former position. It is a noticeable fact, too, that the portion of the corps not mentioned by General Meade lost more in killed and wounded in this contest, from its exposed line of attack, and, I think, captured more prisoners, than did the division which gets the entire credit in General Meade's report. The commendation given to Geary's division was justly merited, but the same praise might safely have been extended so as to have embraced the conduct of the whole corps, without doing injustice or giving offense to any portion of it. The entire omission of the First Division is so marked, and the report of the contest on Friday morning so meager, and so at variance with official statements of the superior officers of the corps, that I am at a loss to conceive from what source General Meade derived his information. Not, I know, from my report as temporary commander of the corps, and not, I think, from yours as commander of the troops of the right wing.

4. The fourth item of omissions stated at the commencement of this communication is sufficiently shown in the comments already made.

General Meade either has not seen my report, or he has intentionally repudiated all its material statements as to the operations of the Twelfth Corps at Gettysburg. No commanding general can verify by personal knowledge all the occurrences in his own command in a great battle; but so confident am I of the truth of every material statement of my report in this instance, that I could confidently submit its correctness to a decision on proofs in any respectable court of justice.

There is another omission which, in connection with those I have named, has a significant bearing.

General Meade carefully names all general officers temporarily in command of corps. Major-General Schurz, in command of Eleventh Corps for six hours, from 10.30 a. m. of July 1 (when General Howard assumed command of the field) to 4 p. m. of same day (when General Howard was relieved by the arrival of General Hancock), is properly reported as such. So are Major-General Birney, Third Corps, and Brigadier-General Gibbon, Second Corps (Major-General Hancock commanding left center), named as temporarily commanding corps on different days.

I was in command of the Twelfth Corps part of July 1 and all of July 2 and 3, and on the evening of the 2d (Thursday) attended a council of corps commanders on a summons conveyed to me by a staff officer of General Meade. I may be pardoned, therefore, for expressing some surprise that my name alone of all those who temporarily commanded corps in this great battle is suppressed in General Meade's report. I know General Meade to be a high-toned gentleman, and I believe him to be a commander of superior merit and of honest judgment, and I confess to have read that part of his official report relating to the Twelfth Corps with a mixed feeling of astonishment and regret.

I submit these comments to you as the commander of the Twelfth Corps, not in the expectation that any adequate remedy can now be applied after the official report of the commanding general has become an historical record, but because I deem a statement of the facts and grievances an act of justice to the corps with which I have been long connected (and which I commanded on the occasion referred to), and especially to the gallant division which I have had the honor to command for nearly two years.

I have the honor to be, general, very respectfully, your obedient servant,

A. S. WILLIAMS,
Brig. Gen. of Vols., Comdg. First Div., Twelfth Army Corps.

HDQRS. ARMY OF THE POTOMAC, *February* 25, 1864.
Major-General SLOCUM,
  Comdg. Twelfth Corps, Tullahoma, Tenn.:

GENERAL: Your letter of the 30th of December last* was received at these headquarters during my temporary absence from the army, which, owing to sickness, was prolonged till recently. This will be excuse for the delay in acknowledging it.

I very much regret that any injustice should have been done in my official report of the battle of Gettysburg to any part of the Twelfth Corps or any officer in it. I do assure you most sincerely that nothing was further from my intentions, and that what has occurred was the result of accident and not of design, the occurrence of which I will endeavor to explain. To do this, I will take up each of your points *seriatim:*

1. Crediting Lockwood's brigade to the First Corps.

This I acknowledge a palpable error, which I am utterly unable to account for, unless it is that Major-General Newton, in his report of the operations of the First Corps, makes marked mention of the arrival and services of Lockwood's brigade—and this being in my mind at the time of writing, induced the error.

2. The omission to mention the services of Greene's brigade on the afternoon of the 2d July.

I am not prepared to admit this as an error. My report, as is fully stated at the close, only pretends to be a general statement of the battle. It was impossible for me to recapitulate and do justice to each brigade and division in detail, and hence I refer to the sub-reports. I am willing to admit that, if my attention had been called to the services of Greene's brigade in the pointed manner it now is, I would have given it credit for this special service. I wrote my report very hurriedly, having been delayed by the failure of corps commanders to send in their reports. The great number of these sub-reports rendered it out of the question for me to read and study all of them. I therefore confined myself exclusively to the reports of corps commanders, and I think in this I was misled by considering you the commander of the Twelfth Corps, not knowing that you had considered yourself by my orders relieved from that command and that General Williams commanded it throughout the battle. This brings me to—

3. The omission to mention General Williams as corps commander.

This I very much regret, particularly on account of the good opinion I have always entertained for that officer, and the personal regard from long acquaintance which rendered him the last man in the army I would intentionally wrong. But, to tell you the truth, I was not aware, or at least it did not occur to me at the time of writing my report, that he was in command, and this arose possibly from the fact that I did not expect or design him to be so. I remember perfectly well that the Fifth Corps, early on the morning of the 2d, was placed under your command. I also remember that before the Sixth Corps had actually arrived, I proposed on its arrival to make an attack with your corps, the Fifth, and Sixth; but inasmuch as both these corps were removed to another part of the field early in the afternoon, and never returned, I presumed you would understand your command over them was only temporary, and ceased with their removal. I remember perfectly well General Williams being present at the con-

* See p. 763.

sultation held on the night of the 2d, but I do not remember having sent for him individually, though I of course sent for corps commanders, and I also remember being puzzled to account for his presence, and refraining from courtesy to him from asking any explanation, this arising, as I said before, from the impression on my mind that you were in command of your own corps on the removal of the Fifth and Sixth. I cannot say anything more beyond the fact that General Williams' commanding the corps was not impressed on my mind either on the field or when reading your report; hence the failure to read his report and the omission to mention his name.

4. The failure to make special mention of the First Division on the afternoon of the 2d and on the 3d.

This is again an omission which I am not prepared to acknowledge, either as an error or an act of injustice. There is no corps in the army which would not have equal cause of complaint, as it was out of my power, as I stated before, to make mention of the special services of each division, brigade, and regiment. I do not agree with you that the inference can be drawn from my report that Geary's division alone went to the left on the 2d, and alone repulsed the enemy on the 3d, though I am willing to admit that marked prominence is given to the part that division took on the 3d, and that I was under the impression the main attack of that day was on Geary. Moreover, if you remember, at the time, from a report made to me by General Wadsworth, I was led to believe General Geary was unnecessarily expending ammunition, and notified you of this. Afterward, I was satisfied of the reverse, and, perhaps, the fear of doing injustice, this impression having existed, induced me to dwell more on Geary than I should otherwise have done. But I remember your dispatch in the night of the 2d stated that part of Geary's vacated rifle-pits were occupied by the enemy, and you asked for authority for Geary to attack with artillery and infantry at daylight, which I gave you.

5. The error in the case of Shaler was due to General Sedgwick's report, which he acknowledged as soon as my report appeared in print.

I have now, general, endeavored to explain the errors and omissions charged, or, rather, to show how they occurred. As you say, it will be difficult to repair them. I will, however, immediately forward to the General-in-Chief the sub-reports of General Ruger, and accompany it with a letter, a copy of which is herewith inclosed,* and which I trust will meet with your approval.

Respectfully, yours,

GEO. G. MEADE,
Major-General, Commanding Army of the Potomac.

No. 272.

Reports of Brig. Gen. Alpheus S. Williams, U. S. Army, commanding First Division of, and Twelfth Army Corps.

HEADQUARTERS FIRST DIVISION, TWELFTH CORPS,
Kelly's Ford, Va., August 22, 1863.

COLONEL: In compliance with circular order, Army of the Potomac, August 20, I have the honor to submit the following report

------

* See Meade to Halleck, February 25, 1864, p. 120.

of the movements of this division from June 28 to its arrival at War-renton Junction on July 26 last, excepting July 1, 2, and 3, when the division was under the command of Brigadier-General Ruger:

On June 28, the division marched from Knoxville, Md., to Frederick City.

On June 29, through Frederick to Taneytown, Md., and, on the 30th, from Taneytown to Littlestown, Pa. On approaching Littles-town, report was sent me that the enemy's cavalry, with artillery, were approaching that place, and were probably followed by infantry. Firing was heard at some distance beyond the town. The division was hastened through, and took post to the north of it. It was soon ascertained that our cavalry were driving the enemy's, and by order of Major-General Slocum, commanding the corps, the division encamped for the night.

July 1.—The division marched to Two Taverns, on the Gettysburg pike, where information was received of the engagement of the First and Eleventh Corps with the enemy beyond Gettysburg. The division moved rapidly up the pike, and when near Rock Creek was directed by a cross-road toward the Hanover road, to occupy an eminence a mile or so east of Gettysburg. The hill was found in possession of the enemy, and the division, when about to assault the position, was ordered to withdraw, as our forces had retired behind the town, which had fallen into the hands of the enemy.

Major-General Slocum having turned over the temporary command of the corps to me, Brigadier-General Ruger assumed command of the division.

For operations of the division on July 2 and 3, I respectfully refer to the official report of that officer.

July 5.—The division was engaged in burying the dead and collecting arms in front of our positions. One brigade was sent on a reconnaissance toward the Bonaughtown road, and returned through Gettysburg.

Brig. Gen. H. H. Lockwood's brigade, which reported on the 2d and 3d instant—consisting of the First Maryland Potomac Home Brigade, Colonel Maulsby; First Maryland Eastern Shore Regiment, Colonel Wallace, and One hundred and fiftieth New York Volunteers, Colonel Ketcham—was attached by orders to the division.

July 6.—Marched 3 miles toward Bruceville, and were halted for further orders, and finally encamped for the night.

July 7.—Resumed march at daylight, and encamped about dusk at Monocacy, near Frederick City, after a march of 30 miles.

July 8.—Moved through Frederick, via Middletown and Burkitts-ville, to Crampton's Gap, and encamped for the night, one brigade occupying the summit of the pass, and relieving a regiment of the Third Corps.

July 9.—Advanced to Rohrersville.

July 10.—Marched to Bakersville, through Keedysville.

July 11.—Marched to Fair Play; thence to Jones' Cross-Roads, taking up a position in two lines on the left of the Second Corps.

July 12.—Corrected our line somewhat, and began the construction of breastworks. The enemy appeared in strong force in our front, especially in the vicinity of Saint James' College.

July 13.—Remained in same position, strengthening defenses.

July 14.—The division was ordered to make a reconnaissance along the Williamsport road, in connection with a division of the Second Corps. Marched out at 6 a. m. and sent forward a regiment from each brigade as skirmishers. Found the enemy's works deserted, and advanced the skirmishers, followed by the brigades, excepting Lockwood's, down the peninsula toward Falling Waters, until information was received from the commanding officer of cavalry that the enemy had wholly crossed, when the brigades were halted. Our skirmishers had a sharp engagement with the enemy's rear guard, and sent in between 200 and 300 prisoners, a special report of which has been forwarded. At 4 o'clock recalled the skirmishers, and fell back and encamped in the vicinity of Williamsport.

July 15.—The division marched, via Sharpsburg, to within 3 miles of Maryland Heights, and encamped on the hiᵣh grounds in Pleasant Valley, near Sandy Hook.

July 17 and 18.—Remained in camp.

July 19.—The division crossed the Potomac and Shenandoah Rivers at Harper's Ferry, and moved up Loudoun Valley, encamping toward evening near Hillsborough.

July 20.—Marched to Snickersville, and remained in camp there the 21st and 22d. Being somewhat annoyed by guerrilla parties, patrols were sent out, and suspected houses were searched.

July 23.—The division marched, via Upperville, and encamped after dark near Somerset Mills.

July 24.—We advanced to Markham, and, after a halt of several hours, countermarched in the direction of White Plains, and encamped about 10 p. m. in the vicinity of that place.

July 25.—The division marched through Thoroughfare Gap to Hay Market, and on the 26th to Warrenton Junction, via Greenwich, where it remained in camp four days.

On the 31st, it marched to the present camp, via Elkton.

It gives me pleasure to state that during these long marches, exposures, watchings, and battlings, officers and men have conducted themselves with patience, fortitude, and courage.

The reports of brigade and regimental commanders being in the hands of Brigadier-General Ruger, now absent on detached duty, I am not able to forward them with this report, but will do so as soon as received.

These reports, with that of General Ruger and mine, as temporarily in command of the corps (sent herewith), will furnish for the period herein embraced the list of casualties * and the particular participation of the division in the operations around Gettysburg.

I have the honor to be, colonel, very respectfully, your obedient servant,

A. S. WILLIAMS,
Brigadier-General U. S. Volunteers, Commanding Division.

Lieut. Col H. C. Rodgers,
    Assistant Adjutant-General.

—

HEADQUARTERS FIRST DIVISION, TWELFTH CORPS,
    Kelly's Ford, Va., August 22, 1863.

COLONEL : The temporary command of the Twelfth Army Corps having devolved upon me from July 1 to 4, inclusive, I have the honor, in obedience to order, to submit the following report of the

---

* Embodied in revised statement, p. 184.

part taken by it in the recent operations in the vicinity of Gettysburg:

On the morning of July 1, the corps left Littlestown, moving on the Baltimore pike toward Gettysburg. While halting near Two Taverns, information was received that the First and Eleventh Corps were engaged with the enemy beyond Gettysburg, and that Major-General Reynolds was mortally wounded. The corps was immediately put in rapid march toward the scene of action, and Major-General Slocum proceeded at once to the front, to assume command. In this temporary transfer of commands, Brig. Gen. T. H. Ruger took command of the First Division, and Colonel Colgrove, Twenty-seventh Indiana Volunteers, of the Third (Ruger's) Brigade, First Division. Before reaching Rock Creek, the First Division was directed to the right, following a cross-road to the Hanover road, for the purpose of seizing upon a commanding position easterly of the town of Gettysburg. The position was found to be in possession of the enemy. Preparations were, however, at once made to carry it, and a brigade was advancing up the hill to the assault when information was received that our troops had fallen back and that the enemy occupied the town. To preserve our communications, the division took a position nearer the Baltimore pike, and bivouacked for the night.

The Second Division (Geary's), under the direct orders of Major-General Slocum, crossed Rock Creek, and took up a position for the night on the left of the First Corps. My headquarters were with the First Division.

Early on the morning of July 2, Brig. Gen. H. H. Lockwood reported to me with a brigade of two regiments, First Maryland Home Brigade, Colonel Maulsby, and One hundred and fiftieth New York, Colonel Ketcham. Our skirmishers were smartly engaged with the enemy toward the Bonaughtown road. The Fifth Corps arrived, and took position on our right.

At 8 a. m. orders were received to unite the two divisions of the corps, and occupy a new line on the right of Wadsworth's division, of the First Corps, north of Rock Creek. This new line was along the crest of a rocky and wooded ridge of moderate elevation, running in irregular shape in a southeasterly direction from Gettysburg to Rock Creek. Wadsworth's division, First Corps, occupied the portion nearest the town, or Cemetery Hill. The Second (Geary's) Division, and First (Colonel McDougall's) Brigade, of First (Ruger's) Division, Twelfth Corps, held the rest of the ridge to Rock Creek, and the Third (Colonel Colgrove's) Brigade, First Division, and Lockwood's brigade continued the line along the creek almost at right angles to the ridge, 600 to 700 yards to the Baltimore pike. This strong natural position was at once strengthened by construction of log breastworks along the entire crest of the ridge. A thick stone fence parallel to the ridge, less than 50 yards behind it, furnished an excellent cover for this second line.

During the afternoon, three pieces (10-pounder Parrott's) of Knap's Independent Pennsylvania Battery, under Lieutenant Geary, and one section (12-pounder Napoleons), K, Fifth U. S. Artillery, under Second Lieut. William E. Van Reed, were placed in position in an open space on the left of the corps, and succeeded in about thirty minutes in blowing up a caisson of the enemy and dislodging a battery of eight guns on an eminence in front of our position. The artillery lost in killed and wounded in this operation 8 men.

Between 5 and 6 p. m. orders were received from Major-General

Slocum to detach the First Division (Ruger's) and Lockwood's brigade to support the left wing of the army, then heavily attacked. Geary's division was at the same time ordered to cover and defend the intrenched line of the whole corps. I marched with the supporting detachment with all possible dispatch, under a severe artillery fire, following as nearly as possible the direction of the heavy firing.

When near the position occupied originally by the Second Corps, as I was informed, Major McGilvery, of the Maine artillery (attached to the Artillery Reserve), reported to me that his battery was without support, and threatened by the enemy's infantry in the woods in front, to which it had just retired, carrying several pieces of our guns. I ordered General Lockwood, whose brigade was in advance, to deploy his line and occupy the woods, which he did in gallant style, pushing a considerable distance to the front, and recapturing three pieces of artillery abandoned by the enemy in his retreat. Ruger, with the First Division, in the meantime occupied the woods on the left of Lockwood, and pushed forward in two lines, the enemy retiring with but little resistance.

It was now quite dark. I therefore ordered both commands to halt for further instructions, and soon after, in compliance with orders from Major-General Slocum, directed them to return to their original position in the breastworks. Soon after Ruger's and Lockwood's commands had moved out in support, General Geary, by direct orders from Major-General Slocum, was directed to follow with two brigades, leaving Greene's brigade, cf his division, to hold the breastworks. By some mistake, Geary took the road toward Littlestown, and did not join the supporting party. He took up a position on the south side of Rock Creek, from which he was recalled during the night.

General Greene, in attempting to extend his brigade to occupy the entire line of breastworks, after the withdrawal of the rest of the corps, found that the enemy had already seized upon and occupied in strong force the right of the line, from which he attacked Greene's brigade with great vigor. Fortunately, this brigade occupied a portion of the breastworks, which, turning at almost right angles to the line on the right, ascended a broken and rocky slope toward our left, and presented a steep wall of rock toward the enemy. A narrow space between the angle of the breastworks and the open field toward the Baltimore pike was densely wooded and full of large rocks and bowlders. General Greene seized with skill and judgment the advantages of this position, and held it with his small brigade against overwhelming numbers with signal gallantry and determination. At length, after three hours' night conflict, having been re-enforced by detachments from the First and Eleventh Corps, and subsequently by Kane's brigade returning to its position, General Greene succeeded in repulsing the enemy from his immediate front. This gallant officer merits especial mention for the faithful and able manner in which he conducted this defense, and protected, under difficult circumstances, a most important part of our line.

The First Division (Ruger's) and Lockwood's brigade reached the open fields behind our breastworks on their return from the left about the time the attacks on Greene were discontinued. General Ruger pushed his skirmishers into the woods, and found the whole of his original intrenched line, as well as the stone fence, held in force by the enemy. Apprehensive of the mishaps and confusion of a night attack upon such concealed positions, he withdrew his regiments, and placed them in two lines, under cover, on the open fields between the breastworks and the Baltimore pike.

Having been called to the headquarters of the army on returning from the left, I did not learn this state of affairs until nearly 12 o'clock at night, when I reported them to Major-General Slocum, and received his orders to drive the enemy from our intrenchments at daylight.

I made such arrangements for a heavy artillery fire, with infantry feints upon the right, followed by a strong assault by Geary's division from Greene's position on the left, as I judged would speedily dislodge the enemy. The artillery opened with a tremendous fire at daylight, at from 600 to 800 yards range, which was continued by arrangement for fifteen minutes. On the discontinuance of the fire, the enemy, without waiting our assault, themselves attacked Geary's division with great fury, and with evident confidence of carrying our position and getting possession of the Baltimore pike, a movement of vast consequence had it been successful. It was plain they had brought up strong re-enforcements at night for this purpose. Prisoners report that their force consisted of two strong divisions of Ewell's corps. Geary's division received the attack with marked steadiness and valor. The combat continued for seven hours in almost unremitting fury. During its continuance, Lockwood's brigade—strengthened during the morning by the arrival of the First Maryland Eastern Shore Regiment—was ordered to re-enforce Geary's division, and afterward General Shaler's brigade, of the Sixth Corps, came to its support, and rendered important aid.

In the meantime, Ruger pushed a strong line of skirmishers from his position on the right into the woods and against the stone wall and breastworks on that flank, occupied in strength by the enemy. A broad marsh intervening between his line and the breastworks, presented a serious obstacle to a direct attack, and the stone wall, the natural rocky defenses, and the open, deep, marshy ground on the extremity of the breastworks near the creek, prevented any hopeful attempt to turn this flank of the enemy's position.

At length, after seven hours' continuous combat, the enemy attempted to push beyond the intrenchments on our right, and was in turn repulsed and followed sharply beyond the defenses by regiments of the First Division posted in the woods to observe his movements.

An advance from Geary's division at the same time effectually and finally expelled them from our breastworks, which were at once occupied by our troops in their entire length. Several hundred prisoners were taken in the final charge, and the numerous dead left on the field presented fearful proof of the stubbornness and numbers of the enemy, as well as the coolness and enduring valor of our own troops. At the same time the comparative smallness of our own losses give gratifying evidence of the skill and judgment with which this long and fierce engagement was conducted on the part of our officers.

In the afternoon of the same day, during the severe attack on our left, one brigade of the First Division and Lockwood's brigade were detached to support the center, but the enemy was repulsed without their assistance.

The enemy kept up strong pickets, and made a considerable front to us during the night of July 3, but on the morning of the 4th were reported as withdrawing. Our line was at once advanced, and occupied the line of Rock Creek without opposition. Subsequently a brigade of the First Division, under the personal direction of Major-General Slocum, made a reconnaissance several miles to the east of Gettysburg, returning through the town.

July 4 was occupied in burying the dead and in collecting arms. This duty was not completed before we received marching orders. The reports of these duties are therefore imperfect. Over 2,000 arms were collected, and more than 600 of the enemy's dead were buried in front of our positions. Estimates of the number left on the ground are mere conjectures, and furnish no valuable or reliable information.

Our own casualties are reported at 1,088, as follows.*

Officers and men, almost without exception, behaved with coolness, steadiness, and valor, and throughout this great battle upheld with signal fidelity the proud reputation of the corps.

I desire to bring to the notice of the major-general commanding the faithful and gallant conduct of my staff officers, who remained with me while in discharge of my temporary duties as corps commander: Capt. S. E. Pittman, assistant adjutant-general; Maj. P. B. Buckingham, Twentieth Connecticut Volunteers, acting assistant inspector-general; Capt. M. P. Whitney, Fifth Connecticut Volunteers, provost-marshal of division; Lieut. E. W. Pattison, Second Massachusetts Volunteers, assistant commissary of musters, and Lieut. George Robinson, One hundred and twenty-third New York Volunteers, aide-de-camp.

I forward herewith the reports of division, brigade, and subordinate commanders, excepting the reports of Brigadier-General Ruger, First Division, absent on detached service, which have not been received.

I annex also a small sketch,† which, without any pretensions to accuracy of details, will represent the relative position of the corps as taken up on the morning of July 2, and reoccupied again after the severe conflict on the morning of July 3.

I have the honor to be, colonel, very respectfully, your obedient servant,

A. S. WILLIAMS,
Brigadier-General of Volunteers.

Lieut. Col. H. C. RODGERS,
    Assistant Adjutant-General.

—

HDQRS. TWELFTH CORPS, ARMY OF THE POTOMAC,
September 12, 1863.

GENERAL: In reply to circular of September 11, headquarters Army of the Potomac, I have the honor to report that no guns were lost or captured during the recent campaign by this command.

Very respectfully, your obedient servant

A. S. WILLIAMS,
Brigadier-General, Commanding Corps.

Brig. Gen. S. WILLIAMS,
    Assistant Adjutant-General.

---

*Embodied in revised statement, pp. 184, 185.
†See map accompanying General Slocum's report, p. 760.

ADDENDA.

HEADQUARTERS FIRST DIVISION, TWELFTH CORPS,
Kelly's Ford, Va., August 8, 1863.

Brigadier-General GEARY,
Commanding Second Division, Twelfth Corps:

GENERAL: In your report of the operations of the Second Division near Gettysburg, you speak of me as commanding First Division. As I am preparing a report as temporarily commanding the corps from July 1 to 4, inclusive, it will be necessary for you to correct your report in that particular. I suppose the paragraph I allude to was inserted by you through a supposition that I was to report as division commander.

There is another point of your report, not very material, in which you are in error. The artillery was not ordered to report to you. Its position was fixed by Lieutenant Muhlenberg and myself, and it opened fire on the morning of the 3d under my personal command. I remained with it for some time to notice the effect. It is a matter of very little consequence, however, excepting as a matter of pure fact, which, in official reports, becomes sometimes incidentally important.

To speak of me as commanding a division, when I am reporting as commanding a corps, would have a very strange aspect in future history, if there should be any. But for this mistake I should not return the report for correction.

I am, general, very respectfully, your obedient servant,

A. S. WILLIAMS,
Brigadier-General of Volunteers.

No. 273.

Report of Brig. Gen. Thomas H. Ruger, U. S. Army, commanding First Division.

HEADQUARTERS FIRST DIVISION, TWELFTH CORPS,
Tullahoma, Tenn., December 5, 1863.

SIR: I have the honor to submit the following report of the part taken by the First Division, Twelfth Corps, Army of the Potomac, in the battle of Gettysburg:

The Twelfth Corps arrived at the village of Two Taverns, Pa., on the turnpike from Littlestown to Gettysburg, on July 1. The First and Eleventh Corps having engaged the enemy beyond Gettysburg, the corps moved forward to their support. The First Division, leaving the turnpike and bearing to the right at a point about 2 miles from Gettysburg, gained a position threatening the left flank of the enemy, who had compelled the First and Eleventh Corps to retire toward Gettysburg. The appearance of the division in this position at the time it occurred was apparently a timely diversion in favor of our forces, as the farther advance of the enemy ceased.

About sunset, the division, in accordance with orders, took up a position about three-quarters of a mile in rear of the position previously occupied, and so remained during the night of the 1st.

At daylight of July 2, shots were exchanged between our pickets and those of the enemy, with some slight loss on our side.

About this time the advance of the Fifth Army Corps arrived, and took position on the right of the division.

Up to this time the division was under the command of its commander proper—Brig. Gen. A. S. Williams. I now received orders from General Williams to take command of the division, General Williams having been placed in command of the corps. I turned over the command of my brigade, the Third, to Col. Silas Colgrove, Twenty-seventh Indiana Volunteers, senior colonel, and assumed command of the division.

About 9 a. m. I received orders from General Williams, commanding corps, to move the division by the Baltimore turnpike toward Gettysburg, and place it in position next on the right of the Second Division of the corps, distant about 1½ miles by the road indicated. I immediately moved the division as ordered, and placed it in position as indicated by General Williams, commanding corps, present on the ground, on the right of the Second Division of the corps and in line of battle, two lines formation, the First Brigade immediately on the right of the Second Division, the Third Brigade on the right of the First Brigade.

The line of the First Brigade was in prolongation of the right portion of the line of the Second Division, and along the crest of a rocky, wooded ridge, called Culp's Hill, about 700 yards from, on the right of, and nearly parallel with, the turnpike, the right reaching nearly to Rocky Run [Rock Creek], a creek which approached the position from the left and front. The line of the Third Brigade made an angle with that of the First Brigade, inclining to the rear and following the general directions of the creek, and was cut by a marshy ravine or swale, some 50 yards in width, which put in to Rocky Run [Rock Creek] from the rear, leaving space enough on left of swale from the right of the First Brigade line for one regiment front.

Breastworks were immediately constructed of logs, rocks, and earth along the whole line, and at the gap in the line caused by swale, so as to give cross-fire in front of gap. In rear of breastworks of First Brigade, and about 75 yards therefrom, and nearly parallel therewith, was a stone wall, behind which the second line of the First Brigade was placed. In front of the line of the Third Brigade Rocky Run [Rock Creek] was from 4 to 6 feet deep, with muddy bottom, caused by a dam near the turnpike. The whole position was covered with rocks. The ground in front of the First Brigade descended to Rocky Run [Rock Creek], and in front of the Third Brigade, on the opposite side of the creek, ascended therefrom, and was covered with rocks, and wooded.

The following rough sketch shows generally position of troops and main topographical features of ground. (See map annexed.)

The division remained in this position until about 6 p. m., the enemy not having appeared in force in its immediate front. At this time I received orders from Brigadier-General Williams, commanding corps, to move with the division to the assistance of the left of the general line, then hotly engaged with the enemy, reporting my arrival to the corps commander of the forces engaged. The division was moved in the direction ordered, being exposed on part of the line of march to a heavy artillery fire. Having approached the point of heavy fire of musketry, which had become feeble, I formed the division in line of masses preparatory to moving forward.

At this time I received orders from Brigadier-General Williams to move the division back to the position recently left as quickly as pos-

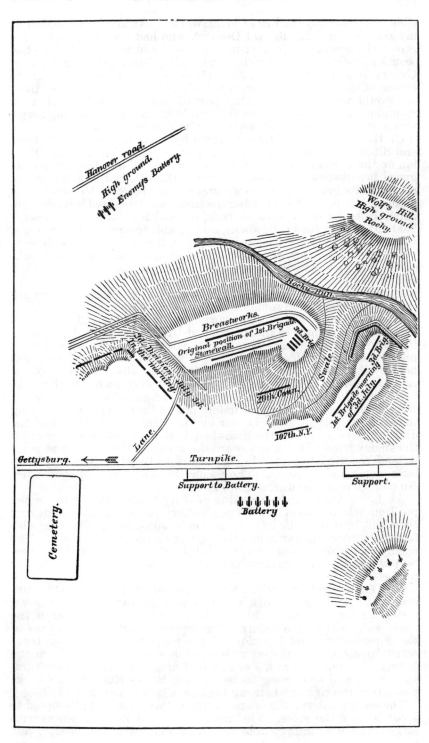

sible, and reoccupy the line of breastworks. At about the same time my aide-de-camp, Lieutenant Dechert, who had been sent forward to report the coming of the division, returned and reported that he had seen Major-General Sedgwick, commanding Sixth Corps, and Major-General Sykes, commanding Fifth Corps, who informed him that the attack of the enemy had been repulsed, and the services of the division would not be needed on that part of the field. The division, on receipt of order therefor from General Williams, commanding corps, was moved as rapidly as possible for its former position.

On the march back, I was informed by a staff officer of Major-General Slocum, commanding right of main line, that the Second Division of the corps, which, with the exception of one brigade left to guard breastworks, had been ordered to the left, had been ordered to return to its line of breastworks, and was supposed to be then in possession of them. After crossing the turnpike, I directed brigade commanders to throw forward skirmishers and ascertain if the enemy held any part of the breastworks, and, if not, to occupy them at once. It was ascertained that the breastworks on the right of the swale were unoccupied, and they were taken possession of, but the breastworks on the left of swale, being the whole original position of the First and of part of the Third Brigade, were found to be occupied by the enemy in force. Seventeen men were captured from the skirmish line by the enemy and some captures made by them.

The occupancy of the breastworks by the enemy, and absence of firing from the right of line of Second Division, rendered it evident that the Second Division was not in possession of its whole line of breastworks, a considerable portion of which I soon ascertained was held by the enemy, and also that the Second Division had not returned. I deemed it unwise to attack the enemy, owing to the darkness, difficult character of the ground, and want of knowledge of the force of the enemy, and immediately placed the division in line along the crest of a slight ridge bordering the swale, with the left of the division advanced from the line, the position best adapted to prevent the enemy from advancing toward the turnpike if he should attempt it, and reported the situation of affairs to Brigadier-General Williams, commanding corps. The Second Division came up soon after. No change occurred during the night.

At 4.30 o'clock on the morning of July 3, fire was opened on the position held by the enemy from a battery placed in position during the night in rear of the left of the then position of the division; also from a battery still farther to the right, on a commanding hill. The enemy soon after moved forward his infantry, and attacked that portion of the line of breastworks of the Second Division still in our possession.

The Twentieth Connecticut Volunteers, supported by the One hundred and seventh New York Volunteers, First Division, was thrown forward from the left of the division into the woods in rear of the stone wall held by the enemy. The general relation of the lines of the First and Second Divisions of the corps was a two-sided, truncated triangle, the apex at which point was the battery from the enemy, the ends toward the enemy inclining to the right and left, respectively, and too strong to be carried, Rocky Run [Rock Creek] protecting the right and strong breastworks occupying the left.

The enemy entered the space between the lines, and attempted to force one of the sides. The ground, covered in most places with large rocks, was unfavorable for rapid movements of troops, and exposed to a cross-fire from the batteries in our rear. No considerable development of line by the enemy that would have been of advantage to him could be made by him in front of lines of either division without exposure of a portion of his line to an enfilading fire of musketry from the other divisions. The batteries fired over the line of the division, which was unavoidable, but the loss from this was small.

This state of things continued until about 10 a. m., the enemy maintaining the attack with great constancy, throwing forward fresh troops from time to time, suffering severely, but gaining no advantage, while our loss was comparatively slight. At this time I received orders to try the enemy on the right of the line of breastworks, to the left of the swale, with two regiments, and, if practicable, to force him out. I sent orders by a staff officer to Colonel Colgrove, commanding Third Brigade, to advance skirmishers against the enemy at that point, and, if not found in too great force, to advance two regiments, and dislodge him from the breastworks. From mistake of the staff officer, or misunderstanding on the part of Colonel Colgrove, it was attempted to carry the position without first ascertaining the force of the enemy. The regiments selected—the Second Massachusetts Volunteers and Twenty-seventh Indiana Volunteers, of Third Brigade—moved forward gallantly, crossed the swale in line under a severe fire, gained the woods on the opposite side, forced the enemy back part way up the slope to breastworks, but could not dislodge him, owing to the natural obstacles to the advance and heavy fire of the enemy from his well-protected position. The regiments were withdrawn. The enemy attempted to follow, but was quickly driven back by the two regiments, who turned and opened fire, assisted by their supports.

About 100 prisoners were captured from the enemy at this time, who was followed by skirmishers.

The One hundred and twenty-third New York Volunteers, First Brigade, which had meantime been advanced from the left of the division, gained the stone wall; the enemy fell back over the breastworks, which were occupied by that regiment and the skirmishers. The line of the division from center to left was at once advanced, and the breastworks reoccupied, the enemy retiring from under fire. The enemy's sharpshooters kept up an annoying fire from cover in front of the line during the remainder of the day, but no more fighting took place.

At about 2 p. m., in accordance with orders, one brigade (the First) was sent to the support of the left center of main line, its place being temporarily supplied by regiments from Third Brigade. The attack of the enemy was repulsed without the services of the brigade being required, and it returned to its place.

At about 5 p. m. two regiments of Third Brigade—the Thirteenth New Jersey Volunteers, Colonel Carman, and One hundred and seventh New York Volunteers, Colonel Crane—were sent to act as supports to cavalry force of Brigadier-General Gregg on the right of the army, and remained until about 9 a. m. of the next day.

On the morning of July 4, it was ascertained that the enemy had withdrawn during the night from our immediate front. A reconnaissance, under the direction of Major-General Slocum, was made by the Third Brigade, and Forty-sixth Pennsylvania Volunteers and Fifth Connecticut Volunteers, of the First Brigade, under my command, around the right of the army, the line of march being along the turnpike about 2 miles, thence by a cross-road to the Hanover road, and by the Hanover road to Gettysburg. The enemy had wholly withdrawn from the front of the right of the army. General Williams at this time resumed command of the division, and I of the Third Brigade.

The services of the division in defeating, in conjunction with the Second Division of the corps, the attack by a superior force of the enemy on July 3, on that portion of the general line held by them, were of the first importance. If the enemy had succeeded, and thereby gained possession of the turnpike and a position in rear of Cemetery Hill, the army would have been in great peril.

There were present with me, of my staff, First Lieut. Robert P. Dechert, acting assistant adjutant-general and aide-de-camp; First Lieut. William M. Snow, acting assistant inspector-general, and Second Lieut. James E. Crane, aide-de-camp, who performed their duty faithfully.

The following is a statement of force carried into action* and of casualties.†

Of the brave dead is Lieutenant-Colonel Mudge, Second Massachusetts Volunteers, a gallant officer, who was killed while in command of his regiment, in the charge on the right on the forenoon of July 3.

Accompanying are the reports of brigade commanders, to which I respectfully refer for details of the parts taken by their respective brigades.

Very respectfully, your obedient servant,

THOS. H. RUGER,
Brig. Gen. of Vols., Comdg. First Div., Twelfth Corps.

Capt. S. E. Pittman,
Assistant Adjutant-General.

No. 274.

Report of Col. Archibald L. McDougall, One hundred and twenty-third New York Infantry, commanding First Brigade.

HDQRS. FIRST BRIG., FIRST DIV., TWELFTH ARMY CORPS,
Catlett's Station, Va., July 26, 1863.

CAPTAIN: I have the honor to report that after a march from near Stafford Court-House, Va., commencing on June 13, this brigade arrived on June 30 at Littlestown, Pa., when we first came in proximity to the enemy. On our appearance, he immediately withdrew, and we remained near Littlestown, on the Hanover road, until the 1st instant, when we resumed our march toward Gettysburg.

Arriving near this place toward evening, we formed a line of battle about 1½ miles from the town, in rear of the Third Brigade of this division, and about half a mile to the right of the pike on which we had been marching. Remaining in this position but a short time, about dusk we were withdrawn, and placed upon the right of said pike, and there we lay upon our arms until morning.

---

* Of the First Brigade, 1,830, and of the Third Brigade, 1,571.
† Embodied in revised statement, p. 184.

July 2.—General Williams, commanding the division, having been placed in command of the corps, General Ruger, commanding the Third Brigade, assumed command of the division.

Early in the morning we were again moved to the front upon the right, when we formed a line of battle, threw out skirmishers, and held this position until about 11 a. m., when we were withdrawn, and marched by the way of Littlestown and Gettysburg turnpike across Rock Creek, and formed in the woods about half a mile to the right of Cemetery Hill, in two lines of battle, on the right of the Second Division of this corps, under command of General Geary; our rear line behind a stone wall, our front line parallel to the stone wall and about 40 paces in advance, when we immediately built breastworks to protect the front line.

The brigade, after having established its breastworks in front, with the stone wall in rear, had a very strong position, and was able to resist almost any assault that could have been made in front.

Late in the afternoon, I received orders to march in the rear of the Third Brigade, and we proceeded about 1½ miles to the left of the general line, where our forces had been having a desperate engagement with the enemy, and which continued until our arrival, and we commenced forming a line of battle by way of relieving and re-enforcing our exhausted and wearied troops, which had been maintaining the fight on this part of the line.

The enemy at this moment withdrew, and we remained in line until dusk, when the general commanding the division ordered me to return in the same order to our intrenchments. Before arriving at our former position, anticipating that the enemy might be occupying our works, before entering the woods south of the works, pursuant to orders from the general commanding, the brigade was placed in double line of battle, and one company from the One hundred and twenty-third New York Volunteers and one from the Fifth Connecticut were forwarded into the woods as skirmishers, with instructions to approach cautiously the intrenchments and ascertain whether they were occupied or not.

It was soon ascertained by the skirmishers that the enemy had not only obtained possession of our works, and were occupying them in force, but had advanced into the woods south of them. On our men retiring, they were fired upon by the enemy from the woods south of the works and immediately in front of our line. This firing temporarily produced some confusion upon the right of the rear line, occupied by the One hundred and forty-fifth New York Volunteers, under the command of Col. E. L. Price, who, for the time, apparently lost command of his men. By the steadiness of the line in front and left of the rear line, the efficient action of the various members of my staff, strongly aided by the general commanding, present at the time, the men soon resumed their position, and order was restored.

The One hundred and twenty-third New York Volunteers, which was one of the regiments in the front line, lost 1 man killed—but whether it was from the fire of the enemy or from a responding fire improperly commenced by some of our men in the rear line cannot be determined—when this brigade, under the orders of the general commanding the division, was moved a short distance to the rear, where they were, in a measure, concealed by a rise of ground in front, and remained upon their arms until morning.

Skirmishers advanced during the night. Lieut. Marcus Beadle, Company I, One hundred and twenty-third New York Volunteers, in command of the company of skirmishers sent from that regiment, was, while reconnoitering near the intrenchments, taken prisoner, as also were 5 men of the company of the Fifth Connecticut Volunteers.

July 3.—An attack was made in the morning upon the enemy in our intrenchments both by infantry and artillery. The Twentieth Connecticut Volunteers were advanced into the woods in front of our troops, where the enemy had posted himself, and to which point was evidently advancing more forces. Lieutenant-Colonel Wooster, who was in command of this regiment, had a difficult and responsible duty to perform. He was not only required to keep the enemy in check, but encountered great difficulty, while resisting the enemy, in protecting himself against the fire of our own artillery, aimed partly over his command at the enemy in and near our intrenchments. His greatest embarrassment was, the farther he pushed the enemy the more directly he was placed under the fire of our own guns. Some of his men became severely wounded by our artillery fire.

For several hours this regiment occupied a most important position in these woods south of our line of intrenchments in preventing the enemy getting around the right of General Geary's forces in the intrenchments on our left, and holding the enemy back so that our artillery could have free play upon his columns without destroying our own troops.

About 2 p. m. this regiment was relieved by the One hundred and twenty-third New York Volunteers, which soon reported to me that, not finding any enemy, they had entered and then held the breastworks, which information was immediately communicated by me to the general commanding the division, when I received orders to move the other regiments of my brigade into the intrenchments, which was immediately done.

During the cannonading in the forenoon from the battery placed upon a hill in our rear, the fire of which was directed over the regiments of this brigade at the enemy in our intrenchments in our front, Col. E. L. Price, One hundred and forty-fifth, sent a messenger to me, informing me that this battery was firing very low and near his command. The messenger was asked by me if any of the troops had been hurt, to which the messenger replied that they had not, so far as he knew or had heard. Recollecting the near approach to a panic to which Colonel Price's command had reached the evening before, without any sufficient cause, and at this time not hearing any complaint from other regiments of the brigade equally exposed, I made the cautionary remark, in reply, that Colonel Price should not get frightened before he was hurt, or words to that effect. Afterward I was informed by officers in command of other regiments that men in their regiments had been wounded, and by the fire of this battery, when I immediately dispatched Capt. E. J. Rice, my acting assistant adjutant-general, to the commanding general and the officer commanding the battery, with information of the fact, requesting of this latter officer that proper and adequate care should be used to avoid the infliction of further injury. Whether from want of proper heed to this remonstrance on the part of the persons in charge of the battery, or whether from imperfect fuse or defective shells, most probably the latter, other men in different regiments were afterward wounded and some killed, when further remonstrance was made, and the command was ordered some distance to the rear, near the creek at the base of the hill, and while here a shell under my own eye fell unexploded into this creek in the rear of my men. No further injury, however, I believe, occurred from this source. Col. E. L. Price, One hundred and forty-fifth New York Volunteers, in his report, says :

I dispatched Sergt. Maj. M. J. Shanly to inform the colonel commanding the brigade that several of my men had been wounded by the fire of our own artillery. On the delivery of this message, the said Sergeant-Major Shanly was instructed by the commanding officer of the brigade to tell Colonel Price not to fret. Shortly after the arrival of this message, 3 more of my command were wounded, including a commissioned officer.

No such message was communicated to me by Colonel Price through Sergeant-Major Shanly or any other person, but, on the contrary, the messenger from Colonel Price, with the only communication to me from him on this subject, distinctly told me, in reply to a question asked by me, that none of the troops had been hurt, as far as he knew or had heard, as before stated.   Colonel Price's report is forwarded with this correction in statement of facts.

After the arrival of the several regiments of the brigade in the intrenchments, a heavy cannonading was commenced upon our left, and as the line of the breastworks occupied by this brigade was perpendicular to the position of the general line on the left attacked, my command for several hours was under the range of the artillery of the enemy, covering us with an enfilading fire, shells and solid shot passing through and crushing the tops of trees over our heads and falling within and on both sides of our works.   The command bore this dangerous fire with commendable coolness.

Pursuant to orders from division headquarters, between 4 and 5 p. m., having been relieved in the occupancy of the breastworks by regiments from the Third Brigade, I proceeded with my command to the rear of the left center, near the headquarters of the commander-in-chief, when I was halted in column by an officer from the headquarters of the army, who had met me on the march and conducted me to this position.   While at a halt, I received orders from the major-general commanding the corps to remain here until further orders, and, after remaining in this position about three-quarters of an hour, the enemy having been repulsed completely along our whole line, I was ordered, by order from corps headquarters, to return to my breastworks.   In returning, I was ordered to place a portion of my command in rear of the Third Brigade, in doing which, while passing through a ravine, Capt. Norman F. Weer, of the One hundred and twenty-third New York Volunteers, a brave and most valuable officer, was wounded in the knee by a musket-shot from one of the enemy's sharpshooters, and has since died.   Several men in this regiment were also wounded.

On this day, while behind the breastworks engaged with the enemy's sharpshooters, Capt. Henry Fenton, Company G, Third Maryland Volunteers, an excellent and gallant officer, was killed by a musket-ball through the head, entering his forehead.

While in the breastworks this afternoon, my command was subjected to a very annoying fire from concealed sharpshooters in the woods in front.

In the early part of the evening, the regiments of the Third Brigade were removed from my breastworks, and the regiments of my brigade resumed their former position.

During the forepart of the night, a fire was elicited from my front line by some firing from the enemy in front, which, however, was of short duration and without injury to our side.

July 4.—The One hundred and twenty-third New York Volunteers, Fifth Connecticut, and Forty-sixth Pennsylvania Volunteers were detached from my brigade and placed under the command of Colonel Colgrove, of the Twenty-seventh Indiana Volunteers, and, in connection with other regiments of the Third Brigade of this division, with a battery attached, made a reconnaissance in front of the right of our line, around and through the town of Gettysburg, when they returned to the intrenchments.

During this day, the enemy having retired the night before, my command was engaged in gathering arms left on the field by the enemy and taking care of the wounded and burying the dead of both friend and foe.

July 5.—The burying of the rebel dead was still continued in front of our line until all were buried. A very large number of the enemy's dead and wounded were found in the woods in rear, within and in front of our intrenchments. Many were killed by our artillery fire, but the large majority by musketry.

About 10.30 a. m. the brigade, in connection with the corps, commenced march, and proceeded by way of Littlestown, Pa., Frederick City, Md., and Crampton's Gap to near Fair Play, Md.

July 11.—Formed line of battle.

July 12.—In connection with the other brigades of the division, we advanced our line of battle upon the left of the Williamsport and Hagerstown pike about a mile, and remained in this position for awhile, when we fell back about 400 yards, and commenced building breastworks.

July 13.—We remained behind our breastworks, having a line of pickets in front.

July 14.—The brigade was moved to the front; formed a line of battle on the left of the pike; threw out the Third Maryland Regiment as skirmishers, who soon reported that the enemy had evacuated their position in front the night before, when we commenced our march in column down the pike toward Williamsport, and, after advancing about 2 miles, turned to the left toward Falling Waters, and, after proceeding about 2 miles farther, were halted, when our skirmishers, who had preceded us, brought in 6 commissioned officers and 235 enlisted men as prisoners, being a portion of the rear guard of the enemy. It was ascertained at this time that the enemy had crossed the river, and for the time had eluded our pursuit.

During July 2 and 3, Brig. Gen. A. S. Williams being in command of the corps, I was under the immediate command of Brig. Gen. Thomas H. Ruger, commanding the division, and most, if not all, the movements detailed by me during these two days were under his immediate eye and constant advisement, and I cannot let this opportunity pass without acknowledging my obligation to him for the aid and support I derived during those trying days from his superior experience, as well as for the confidence and encouragement inspired by the kind and generous manner in which he maintained the command.

It is also my duty to acknowledge the brave and gallant manner with which Lieutenant-Colonel Wooster, commanding the Twentieth Connecticut Volunteers, as well as the officers and men under his command, while in action on the 3d instant, aided in the recovery of our intrenchments. For several hours, without flinching, they maintained a steady contest with the enemy, enduring part of the time an afflictive and discouraging, though accidental, fire of our own batteries.

Much credit is also due to the gallant and prompt manner with which Capt. A. H. Tanner, in command of the One hundred and twenty-third Regiment New York Volunteers, relieved the Twentieth Connecticut Volunteers, and took and held possession of the breastworks until the arrival of the other regiments of the brigade.

I cannot omit to acknowledge the cordial co-operation of Colonel Sudsburg, of the Third Maryland Volunteers; Colonel Packer, of the Fifth Connecticut Volunteers, and Colonel Selfridge, of the Forty-sixth Pennsylvania Volunteers (though my juniors in rank, yet my seniors in military experience), in all the arduous duties to which this brigade was subjected, not only during the battle at Gettysburg, but both before and during the march afterward and the operations near Williamsport.

But higher, and above all, appear conspicuous the courage, endurance, constancy, and fidelity of the men of the six regiments composing the brigade, without an exception; unawed by danger, unsubdued by privation, fatigue, and hardships, no duty could be or was required of them but was promptly and faithfully performed.

While my command was not brought into as severe action as others, I deem it safe to assume, if not assert, it performed and was subjected, in connection with other troops of the corps, to more varied movement than any other troops on the field.

On July 1, it was placed in position upon the extreme right of the general line.

On the morning of the 2d, it was placed in another position, still on the right. We were that forenoon moved 1½ miles to the right center, where we built breastworks.

In the afternoon of that day we were marched to the extreme left of the line, to return and find our former position occupied by the enemy.

In the morning of the 3d, the corps had a protracted and fearfully severe contest with the enemy in retaking our lost position. This being done, my brigade was moved to the left center to re-enforce troops, and for a while was under the most terrible and desperate attack of the battle.

While action in battle did not follow all of these movements, troops from the Twelfth Corps seemed to be everywhere present along that whole line of battle of 6 miles in extent, wherever troops were or might be needed, and always in time, ready for any dire emergency.

I append a list of casualties to my report,* and, in conclusion, cannot omit to mention the efficient aid rendered me during the battle by the various members of my staff. Lieutenant [Darwin S.] Gilger, aide-de-camp, was severely wounded during the terrible artillery fire of the afternoon of the 3d. Capt. William Cogswell, assistant inspector-general, rendered me valuable aid, and Capt. E. J. Rice, acting assistant adjutant-general, distinguished himself by marked fearlessness, and by being ever present where his services were required, and prompt in their discharge.

Very respectfully, your most obedient servant,

A. L. McDOUGALL,
Colonel 123d New York Vols., Comdg. First Brig.

Capt. S. E. PITTMAN,
Asst. Adjt. Gen., First Division, Twelfth Army Corps.

---

* Embodied in revised statement, p. 184.

HEADQUARTERS 123D NEW YORK VOLUNTEERS,
August 13, 1863.

LIEUTENANT: I have the honor to report, in compliance with your request of August 13, the number of men carried into the engagement at Gettysburg, Pa., July 1, 2, and 3, of each regiment belonging to the First Brigade, First Division, Twelfth Corps, as follows:

Twentieth Connecticut Volunteers (July 1)	321
Twentieth Connecticut Volunteers (July 2)	317
Twentieth Connecticut Volunteers (July 3)	310
Third Maryland Volunteers (July 1)	290
Third Maryland Volunteers (July 2)	...
Third Maryland Volunteers (July 3)	...
Forty-sixth Pennsylvania Volunteers	262
One hundred and forty-fifth New York Volunteers	245
Fifth Connecticut Volunteers	221
One hundred and twenty-third New York Volunteers	495

Very respectfully, your obedient servant,

A. L. McDOUGALL,
Colonel 123d *New York Vols., Comdg. First Brig.*

Lieut. ROBERT P. DECHERT,
Actg. Asst. Adjt. Gen., Third Brig., First Div.

No. 275.

Reports of Col. Warren W. Packer, Fifth Connecticut Infantry.

CAMP NEAR SNICKERSVILLE, VA.,
July 21, 1863.

COLONEL: In reply to orders from brigade headquarters, July 19, 1863, I have the honor to report concerning the movements of this regiment since leaving Stafford Court-House, Va., and up to the time of its arrival at camp near Snickersville, Va.

We left Stafford Court-House June 13, and, marching by way of Dumfries, Fairfax Court-House, and Dranesville, stopping for one day at Fairfax Court-House, arrived at Leesburg upon the 18th. Here the regiment was detailed for provost duty in the city, remaining one week.

Resuming the march, we crossed the Potomac at Edwards Ferry June 26. We then moved by way of Point of Rocks and Jefferson to Frederick, Md., reaching the latter place June 28. From thence we moved the following day toward the Pennsylvania line, marching by way of Walkersville, Woodsborough, and Ladiesburg, to Littlestown. At about the distance of 1 mile from the latter place, this regiment was thrown out as picket upon the left of the turnpike, distant from it about 1 mile, remaining but three hours, when we rejoined the brigade.

The following morning, July 1, marched from thence to within 1 mile of Gettysburg, Pa. We then filed to the right, and, after marching nearly 1 mile, formed line of battle; were then ordered to support a section of Battery M, First New York Artillery. Upon being relieved of this duty, we were thrown forward as skirmishers.

On the morning of the 2d, we rejoined the brigade, which moved forward, taking a new position, which we proceeded to fortify by throwing up breastworks,

On the evening of the 2d, we moved to the left about 2 miles, remaining but a short time. Upon attempting to return to the breastworks, we found them occupied by the enemy, in consequence of which, after detailing Company E as skirmishers, they losing 5 men taken prisoners, we remained in the field until the morning of the 3d, occupying the same position until 12 m., when the regiment moved a short distance to the rear, taking position in a ravine, for the purpose of watching the movements of the enemy upon our right flank.

Left this position at 5 p. m., moving to the rear by the Bonaughtown road about 2 miles, in support of General Gregg's cavalry.

Remained here until 7 a. m. July 4, when we resumed our old position in the breastworks previously constructed (in so doing marched completely around our right flank; also in front of our line of battle, being the first regiment of infantry to pass through the town of Gettysburg), holding the same until 11 a. m. the following day, July 5, when, it having been ascertained that the enemy were retreating toward the river, we left the latter position and retraced our march, arriving at Frederick, Md., July 8, passing directly through the city, and, by way of Middletown, Burkittsville, and Crampton's Gap, arrived at Fair Play on the morning of July 11, when we were thrown forward as skirmishers, and were relieved by details from different regiments at 6 p. m. of the same day.

July 12.—Remained in line until 11 a. m., when we moved forward to the extreme front of the ground skirmished over the previous day. Later in the day we moved to the rear for better position, and commenced erecting breastworks, continuing them until finished, July 13.

July 14.—Moved forward to within 1½ miles of Falling Waters, when, it being ascertained that the enemy had escaped across the river, we moved 2 miles to the rear, remaining over night.

The following day, July 15, marched in the direction of Maryland Heights, by way of Fair Play, Antietam, and Sharpsburg, arriving at night near Maryland Heights.

July 16.—Resumed the march, and, crossing the Heights, arrived at camp, near Sandy Hook, at 10 a. m. of same day. Here we remained, obtaining supplies, &c., until the 19th, when we crossed the Potomac at Harper's Ferry, and marched to camp, near Snickersville, Va., arriving at nightfall July 20, where we now remain.

I am, with respect, your obedient servant,

WARREN W. PACKER,
Colonel Fifth Connecticut Volunteers.

Col. A. L. McDougall,
Comdg. First Brigade, First Division, Twelfth Corps.

KELLY'S FORD, VA.,
August 16, 1863.

SIR: I have the honor to submit the following official report of the operations of this regiment during the recent campaign, from June 13 to August 2, inclusive:

On June 13, orders were received to move at sunrise, at which time line of march was taken up in direction of Hope Landing, on Aquia Creek, where we arrived at 4 p. m. An hour later, orders were received to march immediately, and, retracing our march from Stafford

Court-House, we continued the same all night, reaching a place called Dumfries at 12 m. the following day.

Here we remained until 3 a. m. June 15, when we resumed our march, crossing the Occoquan, and arriving at Fairfax Court-House, Va., at 10 p. m. This march was peculiarly exhausting to the men, as the weather was intensely warm and the distance nearly 30 miles.

Remaining here until the morning of June 17, we again broke camp at 3 a. m., marching in the direction of Leesburg, encamping at night near the cross-roads.

In the morning resumed the march at 7 o'clock, reaching Leesburg at 6 p. m., and had but just encamped when orders were received detailing my command as provost guard. Accordingly, we moved into town, and were quartered in previously unoccupied buildings.

We remained in Leesburg until Friday, June 26, performing guard and other duties necessary to the maintenance of order. Upon this day, the remainder of our corps having left the vicinity, my command was ordered to hold the town until the Fifth Corps should move up and relieve us. Upon the arrival of the latter, we took up our line of march, crossing the Potomac at Edwards Ferry, encamping near the Monocacy River.

The following morning, 27th, we rejoined the brigade, and moved toward Knoxville, Md., arriving there at 9 p. m.

The following day we resumed the march in the direction of the city of Frederick, encamping there for the night.

Upon the 29th, we reached Woodsborough, where we remained until morning, when we moved toward Littlestown, Pa.

At 10 a. m., hearing that the enemy were in our front prepared for action, the regiment was ordered out to protect a road upon the left, but saw no enemy.

At 2 p. m. we rejoined the brigade, and went into camp near Littlestown, Pa.

Upon the morning of July 1, we moved forward as far as Two Taverns, where we arrived at 11 a. m., and could distinctly hear the sounds of the engagement then progressing in front.

At 12 m. we advanced to the vicinity of Gettysburg, and immediately took up position upon the extreme right, this regiment being ordered to support Battery M, First New York Artillery.

At 6 p. m. we took up a new position, when my command was thrown forward as skirmishers 1½ miles in advance of the brigade, and remained in this position all night, or until 4 a. m. on the morning of the 2d. During this time saw no enemy. We then received orders to rejoin the brigade, and, upon so doing, the whole moved forward to a new position upon the right, and commenced throwing up breastworks. Brisk skirmishing was in progress all the morning both upon the left and center.

About noon, the artillery opened along the entire line, the fighting being very severe.

At 4 p. m. our division was ordered to the extreme left, in assuming which position we passed through a heavy fire of artillery. Arriving at the designated point, the danger being over, we were ordered back to our position in the breastworks. Having arrived near them at 9 a. m., we learned that they were occupied by the enemy in force. The commanding general immediately threw forward skirmishers to ascertain the situation of affairs, Captain Chinery and 13 men from his company (E) composing a part of the same. Their instructions were not to fire upon or otherwise alarm the enemy, but merely to ascertain and report their strength and position. In endeavoring to carry out these instructions, 5 enlisted men of my command were taken prisoners. Others coming in reported our works occupied by the enemy in heavy force.

At about 10 p. m., as we were preparing to move back to the crest of the hill in our rear, we received a volley from the enemy's skirmishers. No damage was done, however. Having reached the crest of the hill, we passed the night in that position.

At 4 a. m. July 3, the battle opened upon our side by twenty pieces of artillery sweeping the woods in which the enemy was concealed, our regiment being at the same time in reserve.

At 10 a. m. we were ordered to move back about half a mile, for the purpose of watching the movements of the enemy upon our right. Having taken our position, skirmishers were thrown forward, but were troubled by no one excepting the enemy's sharpshooters. Here we remained until 6 p. m., when we were ordered to report with the Thirteenth New Jersey as support for General Gregg's cavalry, who were protecting the extreme right of our army. We moved off about 2 miles, and stopped for the night.

Our loss this day (July 3) was 3 men wounded by fragments of shell.

At 7 a. m. July 4, we moved around, passing over the ground previously occupied by Ewell's corps of the rebel army, into Gettysburg, rejoining the brigade at 10 a. m., and remaining in this position all night.

The following day we marched back to Littlestown, and remained all night.

On July 6, marched at 7 a. m., but were halted after going about 3 miles, as the fighting was renewed at the front.

On July 7, marched toward Frederick City, encamping within 5 miles of the town.

On July 8, we moved at 5 a. m., passing through Frederick City, and Middletown, halting for the night at Burkittsville, near Crampton's Gap.

Leaving Burkittsville on the 9th, passing over the mountain through Crampton's Gap, we encamped at 11 a. m. in Pleasant Valley.

Broke camp at 4 a. m. the morning of the 10th; passed through Keedysville, and soon after crossing Antietam Creek, were drawn up in line of battle; but it having been ascertained that there was no enemy in front, we went into camp.

Upon the 11th, we left camp at 7 a. m., and, soon after advancing through Fair Play, found the enemy's pickets. My command was then thrown forward as skirmishers, and as such were briskly engaged all day. At sundown we rejoined the rest of the brigade.

At about 10 o'clock upon the 12th, we moved to the front about 1 mile from line of battle, and commenced building breastworks, working all night. It was expected that we should receive orders to advance upon the morning of the 13th, but no such orders being received, we continued work upon the breastworks, finishing them at nightfall.

At 4 a. m. 14th, we advanced, or rather broke camp, and at 7 o'clock were fairly in motion, without opposition, in the direction of Williamsport, the skirmishers, however, taking many prisoners.

At 2 p. m. we halted, all the rebels being driven across the Potomac.

At 3 p. m. we left Falling Waters, and marched for Williamsport, where we encamped.

The following day we again marched, encamping at night in Pleasant Valley.

Continued our march the ensuing day toward Sandy Hook; crossed the mountain, and encamped upon the ground occupied by the regiment upon their first arrival in Maryland, August 1, 1861. Here we remained until Sunday, July 19, when we crossed the Potomac into Virginia for the fourth time, and encamped in Loudoun Valley.

Upon the following day we reached Snickersville, and remained until the 23d.

Upon the 23d, we again took up line of march for Paris, where we arrived at 4 p. m., when we were ordered to move to Markham Station, where we arrived at 12 midnight. This was the severest march of the campaign.

Upon the 24th, we left Markham Station for Manassas Gap, where we remained until 2 p. m., when we again took up the march for White Plains, where we arrived at 1 a. m., having marched thus far into the night.

The following morning we moved at 8 a. m., halting at 10 o'clock and resuming the march at 12 m., passing through Thoroughfare Gap, and encamping at Hay Market.

Upon the 26th, acting as guard to the train, passed through Greenwich about noon, arriving at Warrenton Junction at 5 p. m., where we found the brigade encamped. We remained here until July 30, when we moved at 6 a. m., and arrived at Kelly's Ford at 4 p. m., and encamped upon the river bank.

August 1, we moved at 3 a. m., crossing the Rappahannock upon pontoons, and were immediately deployed as skirmishers, and thrown out 2 miles to the front, where we remained until 9 p. m. August 2, when we recrossed the river, and are now encamped 1 mile from the ford, awaiting orders.

In conclusion, allow me to say that both officers and men conducted themselves in a manner which won the cordial approval of their superior officers in every instance; and although our list of casualties is comparatively small by the side of those of other regiments, yet, in respect to a disposition to do, and the record of arduous duties well performed, I claim for my command a place second to none.

I cannot conclude this report without calling your especial attention to the conduct and good deeds of the esteemed chaplain of this regiment, Rev. M. C. Welch, who, totally regardless of self or personal safety, was invariably found in the front whenever the regiment or any portion of it occupied a position of danger or responsibility, encouraging the men by his presence, doing all in his power to relieve the wounded; once taken prisoner, but making his escape, and reporting himself immediately for the duties of his position. All this has greatly attached the regiment to Mr. Welch, and we hope for a continuance of his connection with us during our term of service.

A report of casualties has been forwarded to the adjutant-general, so that it is thought unnecessary to append it to this report.

Very respectfully, your obedient servant,

WARREN W. PACKER,
Colonel, Commanding Fifth Connecticut Volunteers.

His Excellency WILLIAM A. BUCKINGHAM,
Governor of the State of Connecticut.

No. 276.

Report of Lieut. Col. William B. Wooster, Twentieth Connecticut
Infantry.

CAMP NEAR WARRENTON JUNCTION, VA.,
July 26, 1863.

COLONEL: I have the honor to submit that, under your orders, the
Twentieth Regiment Connecticut Volunteers, on the morning of July
1, moved from Littlestown, Pa., to Two Taverns.

At 1 p. m. we moved forward to a point near Gettysburg, Pa., and
were placed in line of battle, being supported by other forces of the
First Brigade, the First Division of the Twelfth Army Corps holding
the right of the battle line.

At evening we were withdrawn from our position, and with the
division rested near the Gettysburg road for the night.

At daybreak on the morning of the 2d instant, we were moved to a
position in line of battle on the right, holding the front line, supported
by other forces of the brigade. Company B was deployed as skirmishers, and well advanced from the main line.

Between 10 and 11 a. m. we were withdrawn, and with the division
moved to the Gettysburg road, and thence advanced near to Cemetery
Hill, and were placed in position as a support to the Second Division
of the Twelfth Army Corps, thus remaining until about 4 p. m.,
when the attack of the enemy became so determined on our left center
that we were moved to the support of our forces (the Second and
Third Corps) there engaged. Here we were placed in position, but
before becoming engaged the enemy were repulsed, and we endeavored to return to the position on the right that we had last occupied,
but it was found that during our absence the enemy had advanced
on the right, and gained the breastworks in front and the stone wall,
where we had previously been placed as a reserve, and the hills and
woods on each side of the wall. Owing to the darkness of the night
and the strength of the enemy in position, the First Division was
unable to regain its original position.

This night my regiment lay on its arms in a corn-field, near the
woods in line of battle, ready to move at an instant's notice. Company G was advanced as skirmishers to a line near the woods, and
so remained during the night, at intervals engaging the enemy's skirmishers. At daylight our artillery commenced shelling the woods,
breast-works, and locality of the wall formerly held by us, then occupied by the rebels.

A little after 5 a. m. my regiment advanced under orders into the
edge of the woods. From this position a heavy force of skirmishers
proceeded but a few rods to the brow of the hill before they engaged the enemy. From this time for over five hours parts of my
regiment were unceasingly engaged with the enemy, the advanced
line being frequently relieved from my main line. The enemy were
endeavoring to advance through the woods, so as to turn the right
flank of the Second Division, and were met and successfully resisted
by my regiment. In this position I was enabled to repeatedly communicate to the colonel commanding the brigade and the general
commanding the division the movements of the enemy in our immediate front, thereby enabling our artillery to more accurately obtain
the range of the enemy and to greatly increase the effectiveness of
our shells. At times it became necessary to advance my left wing
to successfully repulse the advancing column of the enemy, and again

to retire my whole command to save it from being destroyed by our own artillery.

We continued thus advancing and fighting until about 10.30 a. m., when, the rebels having been driven by our fire and shells from the stone wall and breastworks in our front, my regiment steadily advanced in line, and occupied both the wall and breastworks under a continuous fire from sharpshooters in tree-tops, whom we had been unable thus far to silence. Immediately on gaining the breastworks, my regiment was relieved by the One hundred and twenty-third Regiment New York Volunteers. We proceeded forthwith to the ammunition train, replenished, and, under orders, returned to the support of the One hundred and twenty-third Regiment New York Volunteers, then in the breastworks, where we remained under a most terrific shelling from rebel batteries until nearly 5 p. m. The regiment with the remainder of the First Brigade was then moved across the Gettysburg road to support the center in an attack then being made with great determination on the part of the enemy. Before we were placed in position the enemy were repulsed, and my regiment once more returned to our breastworks, and remained in line during the night of the 3d and all day and night of the 4th instant.

On the 4th, a detail was furnished as a burial party, and also another detail to collect arms and accouterments left by the enemy on the field between the breastworks and the wall and in our immediate front.

On the 5th, the burial party still continued its services, commanded by Capt. W. W. Smith, of my regiment, until 1 p. m., when all the dead in the immediate front of the First Division were buried.

On the afternoon of the 5th instant, we moved from the battle-ground and marched to Littlestown, Pa. I lost of enlisted men 5 killed and 23 wounded.

Our position on that day was one calculated to put to the severest test the courage of both officers and men. For nearly six hours in the morning my regiment was constantly engaged with the enemy, and did most effective service in driving them from the position they then held, thereby regaining our breastworks.

With the exception of one officer—no longer belonging to my regiment—and some half dozen men, whom I have reason to believe became more seriously indisposed the nearer they approached danger, all in my command conducted themselves with true courage and devotion to duty; and while some of my officers, from the position in which they were placed, fought more valiantly than others, yet, where all did so well their duty, it might give rise to unjust inferences to particularize. Each officer and man then with me seemed intent only on doing his whole duty, cheerfully and promptly executing every order.

With the movements of the Twelfth Corps in its many weary marches and advances upon the enemy, the laborious construction of breastworks at Williamsport, and the unceasing vigilance necessarily imposed, from the battle-field at Gettysburg until our arrival at this camp, my regiment bore its part well, rendering no special services worthy of note here.*

I have the honor to be, your very obedient servant,

WM. B. WOOSTER,
Lieut. Col. 20th Regt. Connecticut Vols., Comdg. Regt.

A. L. McDougall,
Col. 123d Regt. N. Y. Vols., Comdg. 1st Brig., 1st Div.

_____

* Nominal list of casualties, here omitted, embodied in revised statement, p. 184.

No. 277.

Report of Col. Joseph M. Sudsburg, Third Maryland Infantry.

CAMP NEAR KELLY'S FORD, VA.,
August 14, 1863.

SIR: In compliance with circular of August 12, 1863, I have the honor to report that my regiment was engaged, July 2, at Gettysburg on the extreme right of the line, but in the evening we were ordered to the left, where we remained about one hour, when we returned to occupy our former position, but found the enemy had taken possession.

On Friday morning, the 3d, we were held in reserve. At noon we advanced and took our former position. At 2 p. m. we were ordered to the center, where we remained until 4 p. m., when orders were received to move again to the right, when we were drawn up in line of battle behind breastworks, and one company was thrown out as skirmishers.

Our casualties this day were 1 commissioned officer killed and 7 enlisted men wounded.

On Saturday, the 4th, a detachment was sent out in front to collect arms and accouterments and to bury the dead of the enemy.

On Sunday, the 5th, received orders to march. We went to Littlestown, Pa., where we encamped; distance, 8 miles.

On the 6th, marched about 2 miles in the direction of Taneytown, where we encamped.

On the 7th, marched at 6 a. m. and encamped near Frederick, Md.; distance, 27 miles.

On the 8th, marched to Burkittsville; distance, 17 miles.

On the 9th, marched through Crampton's Gap and encamped near Rohrersville, Md.; distance, 10 miles.

On the 10th, marched to Bakersville; distance, 6 miles.

On the 11th, marched to Jones' Cross-Roads; distance, 6 miles.

On the 12th, advanced 1 mile; fell back half way, and were engaged in the erection of breastworks.

On the 13th, still at work.

On the 14th, we were thrown out as skirmishers. We were in close pursuit of the enemy to Falling Waters, and succeeded in capturing 280 prisoners. We then marched to within 1 mile of Williamsport, and encamped.

On the 15th, marched 17 miles, and encamped.

On the 16th, marched to Sandy Hook, distance 7 miles, where we remained until the 19th, when we crossed the Potomac and Shenandoah Rivers, and marched to Woodsborough; distance, 15 miles.

On the 20th, marched to Snickersville, distance 18 miles, where we remained until the 23d, when we marched past Chester and Ashby's Gaps, and encamped near Linden Station; distance, 20 miles.

On the 24th, marched to White Plains; distance, 20 miles.

On the 25th, marched to Hay Market; distance, 14 miles.

On the 26th, marched to Warrenton Junction, distance 12 miles, where we remained until the 31st, when we moved to Kelly's Ford, Va., distance 16 miles, where we are encamped at this time.

I am, sir, &c.,

J. M. SUDSBURG,
Colonel, Commanding Regiment.

Lieut. J. H. KNIPE,
Acting Assistant Adjutant-General, First Brigade.

No. 278.

Report of Lieut. Col. Gilbert P. Robinson, Third Maryland Infantry.

CAMP NEAR SNICKERSVILLE, VA., July 21, 1863.

SIR: I have the honor to make the following report of the Third Regiment Maryland Volunteer Infantry:

On Saturday, June 13, received orders to march. Broke camp at Kane's Landing, Va., and marched to near Hope Landing. Then countermarched to Dumfries. Arrived at said place on the 14th ultimo at 10 a. m.; distance, 30 miles.

On the 15th, marched at 3 a. m.; crossed the Occoquan River at noon, and encamped at Fairfax Court-House at 9 p. m.; distance, 25 miles.

On the 17th, marched at 3 a. m., and encamped at 1 p. m. near Spring Vale, Va.; distance, 9 miles.

On the 18th, marched at 4 a. m.; crossed Broad Run and Goose Creek, and encamped at 5 p. m. near Leesburg, Va.; distance, 16 miles.

On the 26th, marched at 8 a. m.; crossed the Potomac at Edwards Ferry on pontoons; passed through Poolesville, Md., and encamped near Monocacy River; distance, 30 miles.

On the 27th, marched at 9 a. m. in the direction of Harper's Ferry, and encamped at Petersville, Md., at 9 p. m.; distance, 14 miles.

On the 28th, marched at 5 a. m., and encamped at Frederick City, Md., at 2 p. m.; distance, 14 miles.

On the 29th, marched at daylight, and encamped at Ladiesburg, Md., at 9 p. m.; distance, 22 miles.

On the 30th, marched at daylight; crossed the Pennsylvania line, and encamped at Littlestown about 2 p. m.; distance, 14 miles.

July 1, marched at 5 a. m. in the direction of Gettysburg, and were detailed as guard to the division ordnance train.

On the 2d, were relieved, and joined the brigade. We were in the reserve. The balance of the corps was engaged building breastworks. There was heavy fighting all day, extending from right to left.

In the evening were ordered to the assistance of the left wing, when the enemy fell back. We were then ordered to return to our former position, but on arriving there found the enemy there, and, after exchanging a few shots, fell back. We were then ordered to lie down for the night.

July 3, at daylight, our artillery opened fire on our lost breastworks. We were held in reserve, but under fire, all day.

At 3 p. m. we advanced and relieved the Second Division, where we kept up a continual fire with the enemy's sharpshooters. Our loss was 1 commissioned officer killed and 5 enlisted men wounded.

On the 4th, the enemy had evacuated. We sent out a detachment to gather arms and equipments.

On the 5th, resumed the line of march; passed through Littlestown about dark, and encamped; distance marched, 8 miles.

On the 6th, marched at 4 a. m. to 5 miles south of Littlestown, and encamped.

On the 7th, marched at daylight; passed through Taneytown and Ladiesburg, and encamped 3 miles north of Frederick City, Md.; distance marched, 27 miles.

On the 8th, marched at 5 a. m.; passed through Frederick, Middletown, and Burkittsville, and encamped 1 mile east from Cramp ton's Gap.

On the 9th, marched at 7 a. m.; took the Boonsborough road, and encamped at Rohrersville; distance marched, 5 miles.

On the 10th, marched at daylight, and encamped near Fair Play; distance, 10 miles.

On the 11th, marched at 4 a. m.; passed through Fair Play; formed line of battle 3 miles from town, and marched 5 miles in the direction of Hagerstown, where we encamped.

On the 12th, advanced our line of battle 1 mile; at 5 p. m. fell back to a high ridge; formed a new line, and commenced to build breast-works.

On the 13th, we held the breastworks.

On the 14th, ordered to march. At 5 a. m. relieved by the Third Corps. Our corps advanced and formed line; our regiment was thrown out as skirmishers. We advanced 4 miles in the direction of the river. We took 6 commissioned officers and 235 enlisted men prisoners.

On the 15th, marched at daylight; passed through Fair Play and Sharpsburg, and encamped 3 miles from Harper's Ferry; distance, 22 miles.

On the 16th, marched at 4 a. m.; crossed Maryland Heights, and encamped in Pleasant Valley, above Sandy Hook, distance, 5 miles, where we remained until the 19th instant, when we broke up camp at 6 p. m.; crossed the Potomac and Shenandoah Rivers; went up Loudoun Valley, and encamped near Hillsborough; distance, 9 miles.

On the 20th, were detailed as wagon-train guard. Marched at 8 a. m., and encamped near Snicker's Gap, where we are at present; distance, 10 miles.

GILBERT P. ROBINSON,
Lieut. Col., Comdg. Third Regt. Maryland Vols.

Capt. E. J. RICE, *Acting Assistant Adjutant-General.*

No. 279.

Report of Lieut. Col. James C. Rogers, One hundred and twenty-third New York Infantry.

PLEASANT VALLEY, MD., *July* 18, 1863.

SIR: In compliance with circular from brigade headquarters, dated July 18, 1863, I have the honor to submit the following report of the marches and duties performed by this regiment for the last six weeks:

At 6 a. m. June 13, the regiment left camp, near Stafford Court-House, Va., and marched to within a mile of Brooke's Station, where a camp was laid out: Then an order came to move at 6 p. m., and before sunset we marched back toward Stafford Court-House. Continued the march all night, and arrived at Dumfries at 9 a. m.

On the 15th, left Dumfries, and, after a march of 25 miles through heat and dust, arrived at Fairfax Court-House at 9 p. m.

At 4 a. m. of Wednesday, June 17, started from camp, and, after a march of about 10 miles, encamped about 2 miles southeast of Dranesville.

The next day, June 18, marched 20 miles, and encamped at Leesburg.   Here we remained for a week, the regiment in the meantime going on picket for three days.

At 4 p. m. June 26, started from camp; crossed the Potomac at Edwards Ferry; passed through Poolesville, and bivouacked near the bank of the Monocacy, after a march of about 20 miles.

The next day, 27th, crossed the Monocacy, and passed through Point of Rocks; encamped within a mile of Knoxville, Md.

June 28, moved at 6 a. m., and, passing through Jefferson, reached Frederick a little after noon.   Here it was announced that General Hooker was relieved and General Meade placed in command of the Army of the Potomac.

Monday, June 29, left camp, passed through Frederick, and, marching about 18 miles, encamped near Middleburg.

June 30, passed through Middleburg and Taneytown, and halted for the night a mile outside of Littlestown, on the Hanover road. While approaching Littlestown, our cavalry was attacked and the infantry ordered to be hurried forward.   We accordingly marched through the town at a double-quick, but the rebels had flown.

The next morning marched to Two Taverns, and thence toward Gettysburg, where a battle was then raging; formed line near Rock Creek.   Lay on our arms that night.

Next morning we were ordered in position on the hill near Rock Creek.   Afterward were moved toward the town, into the woods to the right of Cemetery Hill.   Here the regiment, being in the front line of the brigade, built a strong breastwork along its front.

About 4 p. m., in connection with the rest of the brigade, marched to the left of the line, and took position behind the Third Corps.

About dark it was ordered back to its old ground.   On approaching the woods in which the works were located, Company I was sent out as skirmishers, who soon reported the rebels in the works.   First Lieut. Marcus Beadle was taken prisoner at this time.   The regiment was then moved a little farther back, and a number of shots were fired from the woods into its ranks, killing 1 man.   It lay on its arms until morning, when a battery was planted in its rear to shell the woods in front.   One man was killed and 1 wounded by the bursting of the shells of this battery in our ranks.   The regiment lay in this position as a reserve until about 2 p. m., when, the enemy having been driven from the breastworks, it moved forward and occupied them.

About 4 p. m. it was ordered to march out to the left.   After marching some distance, and before coming in a line, the order was countermanded, and the regiment returned to the breastworks, where it lay until morning, when, in connection with two other regiments and a battery, it made a reconnaissance to the north and east of the town as far as the railroad.   Found the enemy had fallen back.   Returned through the town to the works again.

I regret to state that Captain Weer, a brave and accomplished officer, was severely wounded on Friday by a rebel sharpshooter.

The casualties in the regiment were as follows:

Officers and men.	Killed.	Wounded.	Missing.	Total.
Officers	......	1	1	2
Enlisted men	3	8	......	11
Total*	3	9	1	13

*But see revised statement, p. 184.

July 5.—Left our old position, and, marching 10 miles, encamped near Littlestown.

July 6.—Moved only 2 or 3 miles.

July 7.—Marched about 30 miles, and encamped about 4 miles north of Frederick.

July 8.—Passed through Frederick; crossed the Catoctin Range; passed through Middletown, and at night encamped near Burkittsville.

July 9.—Passed through Crampton's Gap, and encamped near Rohrersville.

July 10.—Marched 10 miles, and encamped near Bakersville.

July 11.—Encamped just beyond Fair Play. Came up with the enemy at this place.

Next day, moved forward about a mile behind the skirmishers, but before dark moved back on to a rocky ridge behind a marsh, and commenced throwing up breastworks. Worked all night and most of next day in adding traverses, in accordance with orders from brigade headquarters.

At 5 a. m. of the 14th, moved to the front; the enemy had left; marched to within a short distance of Falling Waters; lay near there for the night.

The next morning at 4 a. m. marched back, and, passing through Fair Play, Bakersville, and Sharpsburg, halted for the night on the west side of Maryland Heights.

July 16.—Crossed the Heights, and encamped in Pleasant Valley, near Sandy Hook, our present location.

All, both officers and men, have borne the arduous duties of the campaign cheerfully and well.

To Captain Tanner, of Company C, upon whom the command has fallen whenever I have been absent or on other duty, especial credit is due for promptness and ability in performing whatever duty was assigned him.

All of which is respectfully submitted.

JAMES C. ROGERS,
Lieutenant-Colonel, Commanding.

Capt. E. J. RICE,
Acting Assistant Adjutant-General.

No. 280.

Report of Col. E. Livingston Price, One hundred and Forty-fifth New York Infantry.

IN THE FIELD, CAMP NEAR SNICKERSVILLE, VA.,
July 23, 1863.

CAPTAIN: In compliance with orders, I have the honor to submit the following report of the services rendered by my command during the operations of this army, from July 1 to 15:

On the morning of July 1, my command moved from Littlestown, Pa., and halted about 2 miles from Gettysburg, where it was drawn up in line of battle on the right of the Gettysburg pike. Heavy cannonading being heard in the direction of Gettysburg, we were ordered to advance with the brigade to within supporting distance of the Eleventh Corps, but afterward, by orders received from General Williams, we retired to an open space beyond the woods, where we encamped for the night.

About 4 o'clock on the morning of the 2d instant, I received orders to be in readiness to move farther to the front, in order to take up a new line.

At 6 o'clock I accordingly moved my command to the front by the way of the Gettysburg turnpike, and, after maneuvering a short time, I was ordered to form my regiment in the second line of battle, parallel with and behind a stone wall, some 125 feet in rear of the first line. The Third Maryland Volunteers formed on the left and the Fifth Connecticut Volunteers on the right of my command. I would state that the position occupied by my command was some 200 or 300 yards northeast of the Gettysburg pike, on the crest of a hill covered with heavy timber. The ground was of a rough and rocky nature, and affording good means of defense.

About 12 m. I received orders to detach a company of my command as skirmishers. I accordingly detailed Company K, Captain George W. Reid commanding, and said company was afterward deployed in front of the first line along the line of Rock Creek. My command remained in the position before described until 6.30 p. m. (repairing the stone wall in the meantime, the regiments in the first line building breastworks), at which time I received orders to follow in rear of the Forty-sixth Pennsylvania Volunteers toward the left of the general line. My command (excepting Company K, which remained as before stated) then proceeded toward the left a distance of some 2 miles, being exposed to a fire of the enemy's artillery, but without injury to my command. I was then ordered to form my regiment on the left of the Fifth Connecticut Volunteers, in rear of the Fifth Army Corps. Scarcely, however, had my command formed, ere I received an order to return to my former position on the right and follow in the rear of the Fifth Connecticut Volunteers. Upon approaching the former position on the right, it was ascertained that during the absence of our forces the enemy had attacked our skirmishers on Rock Creek, who, after a slight resistance, were driven back, the enemy taking possession of the breastworks built by the regiments in the first line, and the stone wall behind which my command, with other regiments of the same line, had previously formed.

I was then ordered to form my command in an open field about an eighth of a mile in rear of my former position, on the right of the Third Maryland Volunteers, and parallel to my former line behind the stone wall. About this time I received an order to detail a company of skirmishers to report to Capt. E. J. Rice, acting assistant adjutant-general, First Brigade. I accordingly detailed Company C, Capt. S. T. Allen commanding, as skirmishers.

During the formation of the line as above described, a volley was fired directly in front of my command (probably by the enemy's skirmishers), wounding 2 of my men and causing some confusion; order was, however, quickly restored. It was now 10.30 o'clock. In this position my men rested on their arms during the night; nothing unusual occurred.

About 4 o'clock on the morning of the 3d, some twelve guns belonging to artillery, posted some 500 paces in rear of my regiment, opened upon the woods in front of my command, and the skirmishers became briskly engaged. This state of affairs continued about thirty minutes, when the artillery fire partially ceased and the infantry in front of my line became hotly engaged. Company C was engaged with the enemy, and lost 1 private killed and 2 wounded, when it was recalled, and rejoined my command. The artillery occasionally opened upon the woods in my front, the shells of which barely cleared, the men of my command, who at that time were lying down. Subsequently several of my men were wounded by the fire of our artillery, and, deeming it advisable and proper to report the facts to my commanding officer, I dispatched Sergt. Maj. M. J. Shanly to inform the colonel commanding the brigade that several of my men had been wounded by the fire of our own artillery.

On the delivery of this message, the said Sergeant-Major Shanly was instructed by the commanding officer of the brigade to tell Colonel Price "not to fret." Shortly after the arrival of this message, 3 more of my command were wounded, including a commissioned officer.

In company with Colonel Selfridge, Forty-sixth Pennsylvania Volunteers, I proceeded to the battery which had injured my command, where I met Major-General Slocum, whom I informed of the injury done by said battery, when my command was withdrawn a short distance, and no further injury inflicted upon it.

My command was afterward moved forward to occupy the position of the day before, the enemy having been driven beyond the stone wall and breastworks before alluded to. My command remained in this position, under a severe fire from the enemy's artillery, until 4.30 o'clock, when it was moved to the support of the center, but had hardly reached there before receiving orders to return to my former position on the right. My regiment was afterward thrown forward into the first line, behind the breastworks, where it engaged the enemy's sharpshooters until darkness put an end to further operations.

I was relieved by the One hundred and twenty-third Regiment New York Volunteers, Captain Tanner commanding, about 8 p. m., and retired to my former position behind the stone wall, where my command rested on their arms during the night.

Nothing unusual occurred during the night save the alarm in the first line which caused it to fire.

On the morning of the 4th, I was again thrown into the front line behind the breastworks, but nothing of importance occurred, the enemy having evacuated his position in our front during the night, leaving his dead upon the field; also many of his wounded. My command was again relieved about 12 o'clock, and again took up a position in the second line, behind the said stone wall; but this time my command was deprived of its former position by the posting of the One hundred and twenty-third New York Volunteers in my former position, and placing me in a small open field to the left of my original position. At this time the weather had changed, and the rain was falling in torrents, wetting my men thoroughly, and depriving them of rest and sleep during the following night.

Thus for four days and three nights were the men of my command subjected to the severest hardships, besides trials and dangers of almost every description; yet throughout all I cannot but speak in the highest terms of both the officers and men of my command. All behaved with a nobleness of spirit well worthy of record; each and every one seemed aware of the great issues involved, and the importance of the struggle in which they were engaged.

On the morning of July 5, my command moved at 10.30 o'clock, marching through Littlestown, and encamping just outside that place.

On the morning of the 6th, we again started, continuing the march, passing through the towns of Frederick and Burkittsville, and on Saturday, the 11th instant, [encamped] near Fair Play, Md., about 5 miles from Williamsport, where we were employed during the three days of our stay at this place in throwing up breastworks.

On Sunday, the 14th instant, finding the enemy had fallen back, we followed with the main body of the army, halting near Williamsport.

On the following morning we took up our line of march, and halted near Harper's Ferry, W. Va.

On the 16th, we moved again a short distance, and encamped at Pleasant Valley, Md., where my command was allowed to rest, and requisitions were made to furnish it with arms, ammunition, and clothing, for which, after such a severe campaign, my command stood greatly in need.

I cannot but mention the valuable services rendered me during the engagement at Gettysburg by Sergt. Maj. M. J. Shanly, who acted as adjutant, the adjutant of my regiment being absent during the battle.

In conclusion, I cannot omit speaking of the nobleness with which my command endured the privations, hardships, and trials of these fifteen days. It marched over 150 miles, engaged the enemy for two or three days at Gettysburg, built breastworks and abatis, was deprived continually of both rest and sleep, performed forced marches of nearly 30 miles per day through mud and rain, sometimes with inadequate rations, and many of my men without shoes or sufficient clothing. When I remember all this; when I consider the trials of these four days and nights before Gettysburg; the great fortitude and courage exhibited by the officers and men of my command; that not a man faltered; that not a single case of disobedience of orders occurred, I am constrained to believe that additional and greater honors await it on future fields of victory.

I have the honor to be, captain, very respectfully, your most obedient servant,

ED. LIVINGSTON PRICE,
Colonel 145th New York Volunteers.

Capt. E. J. Rice,
    A. A. A. G., First Brig., First Div., Twelfth A. C.

No. 281.

Report of Col. James L. Selfridge, Forty-sixth Pennsylvania Infantry.

Camp near Sandy Hook, Md.,
July 18, 1863.

Sir: I have the honor to submit the following report of my command from the 13th ultimo to the present date:

On the 13th ultimo, I proceeded with my command from the camp near Stafford Court-House, Va., to a point designated by you near Brooke's Station, where, after several hours' halt and active preparations for a permanent camp ground, I received orders to report with my command at Stafford Court-House without delay, to the commandant of the corps train, as guard to the same.

On the evening of the same date, guarding the train, my command proceeded on the march, and reached Fairfax, Va., via Dumfries and Occoquan City, on the 14th of the same month. At this point I was relieved of further charge as guard to the train, and reported to you.

After a halt until the 17th, I proceeded from this point with the brigade, under your command, to Leesburg, Va., arriving at the latter place on the 18th ultimo. Encamped at that point until the 20th, when, in accordance with your orders, I relieved the Twentieth Regiment Connecticut Volunteers, then on picket duty within 3 miles of said town, remaining there on picket duty until the 24th, when I was relieved by a regiment of your brigade, and immediately reported to you. Encamped with the brigade at the town of Leesburg until the 26th, when, under your command, commenced march, and proceeded to a point in the vicinity of Gettysburg, Pa., arriving there on the evening of the 1st instant, and encamping for the night.

On the 2d instant, marched to a position nearer the town and south of it, and to the right of the Gettysburg and Littlestown pike, and, by your orders, commenced making breastworks in great haste, which were completed in the afternoon of the same day, and I immediately guarded the same.

On the same evening, under your command, I was called from the breastworks, and proceeded with other regiments of your brigade to a point near the left of the main line. After a short halt and several hours' absence from the breastworks, I retraced my steps with the intention of reoccupying my late position in the breastworks.

When I approached the breastworks, found the enemy in possession of the same, and, in accordance with your orders, I took up a position in an open field on protecting ground near the breastworks, where I remained until the morning of the 3d, with the men concealed as much as possible from the bullets of the sharpshooters.

At daybreak our artillery opened fire on the enemy, and several batteries in our rear, from an eminence, were obliged to throw their shot and shell immediately over my command, and from the premature explosions of our shells, and others from our batteries unexploded, falling in the midst of my command, I regret very much to record the following casualties.*

During the day my command was much annoyed by sharpshooters, but I suffered no loss of life or injury in my command from the same.

In the evening of the same (3d instant), I took possession of my breastworks, and guarded the same until the 5th instant, when, together with the remainder of your command, I took up line of march, via Littlestown, Pa., Frederick City, Md., Crampton's Gap, Williamsport, Sharpsburg, and Maryland Heights, to this camp, arriving on the 16th instant.

Very respectfully, your obedient servant,

JAS. L. SELFRIDGE,
Colonel, Commanding Regiment.

Col. A. L. McDOUGALL,
Comdg. First Brig., First Div., Twelfth Army Corps.

---

* Nominal list, here omitted, embodied in revised statement, p. 184.

No. 282.

Report of Brig. Gen. Henry H. Lockwood, U. S. Army, commanding Second Brigade.

HDQRS. SECOND BRIG., FIRST DIV., TWELFTH CORPS,
July 16, 1863.

CAPTAIN: I have the honor to render the following report of the operations of this command during the late battle near Gettysburg:

After a long and painful march from Baltimore, via Frederick City, two regiments of this command, namely, the First Regiment Potomac Home Brigade, Maryland Volunteers, Col. William P. Maulsby, and the One hundred and fiftieth New York Volunteers, Col. J. H. Ketcham, arrived, and reported to the First Division, Twelfth Army Corps, at 8 a. m. July 2. They were posted at various places until about 5 p. m. of that day, when, having received an order to support the left wing of the army, then heavily engaged, they were marched to and deployed near a battery, then firing on the enemy. The First Regiment Potomac Home Brigade, Maryland Volunteers, Col. William P. Maulsby, formed the first line, and the One hundred and fiftieth New York Volunteers, Colonel Ketcham, the second line. Thus formed, these regiments, under my charge, advanced about 1 mile, a portion in double-quick, amid the most terrific firing of shells and musketry, to and beyond the extreme front, driving the enemy before them and entirely clearing the field. A battery which had fallen into the hands of the enemy was retaken, and on our return drawn off the field by hand by a detachment of the One hundred and fiftieth New York.

On a portion of the ground over which we drove the enemy, was found a number of dead and wounded. The latter were cared for by Dr. Willard, assistant surgeon, First Regiment Potomac Home Brigade, Maryland Volunteers, who, having with difficulty procured ambulances, removed them to the hospitals. This occupied him nearly the whole night. The command withdrew from the field by special order after full darkness set in.

I cannot too much commend the cool and steady courage of both officers and men on this trying occasion, which is the more remarkable as it was the first time they had been under fire.

I am specially indebted to Colonel Maulsby, not only for his daring and intrepidity, but for many suggestions, which were the more valuable in consequence of his knowledge of the ground upon which we were operating.

Early on the morning of the 3d, these regiments supported a battery placed to shell the woods in front of the rifle-pits on our right. At about 6 a. m. I received orders to deploy a regiment and engage the enemy within these woods. Colonel Maulsby's regiment (First Potomac Home Brigade, Maryland Volunteers) was selected for this purpose. Under my command, the wood was entered, and the enemy engaged and driven back behind a stone wall, which was nearly parallel with the turnpike. While preparing to charge and drive him from this cover, information reached me that another regiment was taking him on his right, and that our fire would damage that movement. Having already lost in killed and wounded some 80 men, and our ammunition being short, I withdrew the regiment, and returned to the turnpike.

I cannot too strongly commend the courage and good conduct of every officer and man engaged in this fearful enterprise.

Soon after our return, the One hundred and fiftieth New York was detailed for duty in the rifle-pits, and successively the other regiments of the command (now increased by the arrival of the First Eastern Shore [Regiment], Maryland Volunteers, Colonel Wallace) were assigned to the same duty. Finding Brigadier-General Greene already on duty at this position, I declined taking command, though his senior, and served under him there. The detailed operations of the regiments here are made in the accompanying regimental reports. I believe that every man did his duty.

Toward the close of the day, I was ordered to cover the center, and, on my arrival near the cemetery, was directed to hold myself in readiness to re-enforce any point requiring aid. Here we remained inactive until near evening, when we were ordered to occupy the breastworks on the right, near the position we had held on the previous day.

It only remains for me to notice the conduct of the troops. Considering that these regiments, as such, had never before been under fire, I claim for them praise for the coolness and firmness exhibited by them. Beyond a too rapid fire and a too hasty and inconsiderate advance, I have nothing to find fault with.

I beg leave to notice favorably my personal staff, to whom I am indebted for very efficient service, and both of whom had their horses killed by shot and shell on the 3d.

I am, very respectfully, your obedient servant,
               HENRY H. LOCKWOOD,
                         Brigadier-General.

Capt. S. E. PITTMAN,
     Asst. Adjt. Gen., First Division, Twelfth Army Corps.

No. 283.

Reports of Col. William P. Maulsby, First Potomac Home Brigade, Maryland Infantry.

HDQRS. FIRST REGIMENT P. H. B., MARYLAND VOLS.,
                              July 4, 1863.

CAPTAIN: I have the honor, in obedience to orders, to submit the following report:

This regiment and the One hundred and fiftieth New York Volunteers, Colonel Ketcham, part of the brigade of Brig. Gen. H. H. Lockwood, marched together from the city of Baltimore, through Frederick City, to Gettysburg, where they arrived on the morning of the 2d instant. They were immediately posted on the right, and formed in line of battle, under the orders of Major-General Slocum.

During the day they were twice advanced, but without meeting the enemy until about 5 p. m., when, under the command of Brigadier-General Lockwood, they were led up to the support of the left wing, then heavily engaged with the enemy. On their arrival on the field of battle, they were instantly deployed in line, this regiment forming the first and the One hundred and fiftieth New York the second and supporting line of battle, and ordered to advance and engage the enemy. The advance was made at double-quick for about 1 mile to and beyond the extreme front, driving the enemy before us and entirely clearing the field. A battery which had fallen into the hands of the enemy was retaken, and drawn off the field by hand by some of the One hundred and fiftieth New York.

This regiment was especially occupied in bringing in and caring for the wounded of our own army, all of whom, it is believed, were properly attended to.

It is due to Assistant Surgeon Willard, of this regiment, to state that he remained on the field with these unfortunates during almost the whole night, and until he had succeeded, with difficulty, in procuring ambulances and in having them removed to the hospitals.

About midnight the command returned from the field, and about 4 a. m. the 3d instant this regiment was ordered to attack a position of the enemy on the right, behind a stone wall, running through and covered by a dense woods. The attack was made with energy under a severe musketry fire, and the stone wall nearly reached, and bayonets were fixed for a charge over it, when a brigade of National troops was perceived approaching for the purpose of flanking the enemy's position, and this regiment was compelled to cease firing, lest it should destroy its own friends. At this moment numbers of the enemy were distinctly seen fleeing from behind the stone wall to the rear. The number of lamented dead and suffering wounded attests the severity of this engagement, and subsequent ascertainment left no room to doubt that the enemy had paid a fearful penalty.

About 9 o'clock of the same morning, this regiment was ordered to advance to and hold the front of the rifle-pits on the right, which it did until the enemy's fire wholly ceased, about 12 m.

During this period a portion of my command occupied the rifle-pits at intervals, and other portions the plain surface at the top of the embankment, behind which the troops were sheltered, and poured upon the enemy a direct and deliberately aimed fire, pending which a white flag was raised by the enemy, and the firing, by my order, ceased. It was not again resumed on the right. At the time when this flag was raised, many other regiments were pouring upon the enemy a terrible fire, and it would be most unjust for any one to claim that the raising of the flag was due to the fire of any particular one or number of those engaged. The heaps and mounds of dead and wounded enemies which were found on the position occupied by them might well satisfy the ambition for bloody deeds of each man of every regiment engaged, however craving such ambition might be.

During the final effort of the enemy on the left on the afternoon of the 3d instant, this regiment was ordered, with the remainder of the brigade, to the support of the troops engaged, but while on the march the order was countermanded, the enemy having been fully and finally repulsed.

In the engagement at the stone wall early on the morning of the 3d, were killed First Lieut. James T. Smith, of Company C, and First Lieut. John L. Willman, of Company D, and in that at the rifle-pits on the same day was killed First Lieut. Charles E. Eader, of Company I. Of each of these officers I can truly say, for I know, that no braver man ever took arms to vindicate his country's honor and uphold its glory, or was animated by purer or simpler patriotism. Their faith was unmixed with complications or side issues of any kind. For their flag, the emblem of the grand constitutional Republic, they died. They lived with hearts full of love for it.

The following is a list of casualties :

Officers and men.	Killed.	Wounded.	Missing.	Total.
Commissioned officers	3	3	......	6
Enlisted men	21	69	1	91
Total*	24	72	1	97

The gallantry of our lost brethren in arms, enlisted and commissioned, has embalmed their memories in the affections of their surviving comrades, while the sufferings of the wounded elicit their profoundest sympathies.

The advances of this command on the afternoon of the 2d and the morning of the 3d were led by Brigadier-General Lockwood in person, whose unqualified exposure of his own person has impressed this command with a sense of the gallantry of their brigade commander which will ever prompt them confidently to follow where he may lead.

I have the honor to be, very respectfully, your obedient servant,

WM. P. MAULSBY,
Colonel, Commanding.

Capt. William M. Boone,
Assistant Adjutant-General.

—

HDQRS. FIRST MARYLAND REGIMENT, P. H. B.,
Camp near Rohrersville, Md., July —, 1863.

GENERAL: In compliance with your suggestion that I would explain to Brig. Gen. G. S. Greene the exact circumstances under which my regiment was withdrawn from the front of the rifle-pits on the night after the surrender of a part and the withdrawal of the rest of the rebel forces on the 3d instant, near Gettysburg, I did so to-day, and he requested that I would reduce it to writing, and submit it to you, with a request that you would transmit it to him.

My command, about 11 o'clock the preceding night, had returned from service on the left, and, without rations and very little rest, had been, early in the morning of the 3d, ordered into action at a position held by the rebels behind a stone wall on the right, some distance below the rifle-pits. Shortly after the termination of that action, it was ordered to the front of the rifle-pits, which position it held until after the withdrawal of the rebel forces, about three hours. Under its fire at the rebel position in rear of the rifle-pits the white flag was raised by the enemy, and firing ceased by my order, which was reported by me to you, and a gentleman was present, participating in the remarks made, whom I afterward learned to be Brigadier-General Greene.

I then requested your permission to withdraw my command for rest, as the action had terminated, and you were aware of its exhausted condition, which you gave, but remarked that it would be well to communicate with Brigadier-General Greene, who, for the first time, I was informed, was in command at that point. A young officer, representing himself to be an aide to General Greene, and

* But see revised statement, p. 184.

whom I have since been unable to recognize, suggested or requested that I would withdraw my command and rest it without waiting for further orders, and that I would ask the regimental commanders on my right and left to extend their ranks so as to fill the vacated space; which was done, and my regiment returned to the point from which you had ordered it.

In a short time afterward, Brigadier-General Williams, commanding First Division, ordered me to take my command to the position on the right, near the stream, which it had occupied the preceding day, and, in reply to my suggestion that I might wait until you and the other regiments constituting the brigade came up, General Williams said that I had better go without any delay, and that you and the two regiments would follow.

Not appreciating the importance of this communication, apart from the fact of General Greene's request that I would make it, I have made it simply in obedience to his expressed wish. In speaking uncertainly whether it was a suggestion or a request by the aide of General Greene before mentioned, I mean to say that I did not notice the precise expressions used, but that the meaning and intent of the aide, as clearly understood by me, was to convey the authority of General Greene to me to do what was so manifestly proper and necessary to be done.

I have the honor to be, very respectfully, your obedient servant,

WM. P. MAULSBY,
Colonel, Commanding.

Brig. Gen. H. H. LOCKWOOD.
Comdg. Second Brig. First Div., Twelfth Corps.

No. 284.

Report of Col. James Wallace, First Eastern Shore Maryland Infantry.

NEAR GETTYSBURG, PA.,
July 4, 1863.

GENERAL: I have the honor to report that, in obedience to your order, I put my command in motion at 6.30 a. m. on yesterday, and reached the field of battle a short time before 8 o'clock, where we were immediately formed into line of battle, and prepared to relieve another regiment then engaged in the fight.

At 8 o'clock the order was given to advance, and the regiment went forward with a shout to relieve their exhausted comrades, who had been fighting for seven hours. They had to advance up a considerable slope, and when reaching the open level space immediately in rear of the breastworks we became exposed to a terrible fire of musketry. Owing to some misunderstanding as to the point of the works designed to be supported, four companies, under Lieutenant-Colonel Comegys, passed to the left, and five, under my own immediate supervision, moved directly to the front. Upon reaching the brow of the hill, the five companies halted for an instant upon the discovery of the enemy attempting to rush upon our works, and then delivered a very effective volley over the heads of the men occupying the position we were ordered to relieve. The officer in command of the men in the breastworks, supposing we were firing into his command, requested that the fire should cease. That volley, however, with the fire from the regiment in the works, effectually checked all farther advance of the enemy. The men immediately moved forward, and relieved the regiment in the advance, opened their fire, and kept it up until they had expended their ammunition, when they were in turn relieved by the One hundred and fiftieth New York Regiment. In crossing the open space between the hill and the breastworks, we lost 1 man only, though the fire upon us was severe. As soon as we reached the breastworks, the enemy opened upon the five companies above referred to from the flank and from a point not fully protected by our works. There we met with nearly all the casualties which we suffered during the fight; but I am happy to state that our loss has been small for the length of time we were engaged and the severity of the fire received. Five were killed, 22 wounded, and 7 missing.*

The conduct of my men was very satisfactory. All did their duty, and, considering that this was the first time they were under fire, their behavior was very steady. Where all did their duty so well it is impossible to discriminate. We remained upon the field until 8 p. m., when, in obedience to orders, we took up another position, and bivouacked for the night. Thus ended the participation of my command in the glorious achievements of yesterday.

From the prisoners taken we have been credibly informed that the enemy we fought was the First Maryland (rebel) Regiment [Battalion].

I have the honor to be, very respectfully,
JAS. WALLACE,
Colonel First Regt. Eastern Shore Maryland Vols.

Brig. Gen. H. H. LOCKWOOD,
Comdg. Second Brig., First Div., Twelfth Army Corps.

No. 285.

Reports of Col. John H. Ketcham, One hundred and fiftieth New York Infantry.

IN CAMP NEAR GETTYSBURG, PA.,
July 4, 1863.

CAPTAIN: In compliance with orders, I have the honor to make the following report of the movements of the One hundred and fiftieth New York Volunteer Infantry during the recent battle near Gettysburg:

This regiment arrived here about 8 a. m. July 2, and was held in reserve on the right until about 6 p. m., when it was ordered with the First Maryland Potomac Home Brigade Volunteers, Colonel Maulsby, to proceed at once and re-enforce General Sedgwick on the extreme left. Upon reaching the battle-ground, these two regiments were ordered forthwith to the front in double-quick time amid the most terrific firing of shell and musketry. They continued to advance until after they had crossed the line of battle of the enemy, the rebels meanwhile retreating, when the firing ceased. The One hundred and fiftieth Regiment New York Volunteers brought off three pieces of artillery which had been abandoned to the enemy. This regiment then, about 9 p. m., returned to the right, and re-

---

* But see revised statement, p. 184.

mained under arms all night, in consequence of heavy skirmishing on the right.

About 4 a. m. we were ordered to support Best's battery, on the left of the Gettysburg road, where we remained nearly two hours.

About 6 a. m. this regiment was ordered into the rifle-pits on the right, under command of General Geary, where it remained about two and a half hours, when it was relieved. In about an hour it was again ordered into action, where it remained about the same time as before.

The average number of rounds of ammunition expended by each man was 150, and from the large number of dead bodies lying upon the ground, as seen the following morning, it is evident the shots did good execution. A detail from my regiment was made to collect and bury the rebel dead.

The enemy kept up a continuous, direct, and terrible firing of musketry during the whole time engaged. My men rallied to the front in double-quick time, cheering loudly, and they fought earnestly and bravely. Not a man faltered or displayed the least cowardice. This regiment was never before under fire, and for the coolness and courage displayed on this occasion the men are entitled to the highest praise.

After this last engagement it was ordered to a position on the left as a reserve, where it remained until about 6 p. m., when it was ordered into camp.

About 7 a. m. the following morning it was ordered into rifle-pits on the right, where it remained about two hours; then relieved.

I am, captain, very respectfully, your obedient servant,

J. H. KETCHAM,
Colonel One hundred and fiftieth Regiment New York Vols.
Capt. WILLIAM M. BOONE,
Asst. Adjt. Gen., General Lockwood's Brigade.

—

KELLY'S FORD, VA., *August* 13, 1863.

SIR: In compliance with the terms of the circular just received by me, I have the honor to report as follows:

Enlisted men present in the engagement at Gettysburg, Pa.: July 1 (regiment did not reach Gettysburg until the morning of the 2d), —; July 2, 579; July 3, 579.

I am, sir, very respectfully, your obedient servant,

J. H. KETCHAM,
Colonel One hundred and fiftieth New York Volunteers.
Lieut. ROBERT P. DECHERT, *A. A. A. G., Third Brigade.*

No. 286.

Reports of Col. Silas Colgrove, Twenty-seventh Indiana Infantry, commanding regiment and Third Brigade.

NEAR KELLY'S FORD, VA., *August* 7, 1863.

SIR: I have the honor of submitting the following report of the part taken by the Twenty-seventh Regiment Indiana Volunteers on July 1, during the first day's fighting at the battle of Gettysburg, Pa.:

The Twenty-seventh Regiment Indiana Volunteers, with the balance of the troops composing the Third Brigade, marched on the morning of the 1st, from Littlestown, Pa., on the pike toward Gettysburg, by way of Two Taverns, and when within about 2 miles of Gettysburg the brigade filed to the right, leaving the pike, and proceeded about 1½ miles, apparently with the intention of flanking the enemy's left, the Twenty-seventh Indiana having the advance.

After arriving in front of the enemy's left, the brigade was halted in a piece of woods, and, in obedience to orders from General Ruger, commanding the brigade, I threw out Company G, deployed as skirmishers to the front and right, who soon reported the hill in our front to be held by the enemy's mounted skirmishers. I immediately communicated this fact to the brigade commander, and received orders to advance my regiment and take possession of the hill occupied by the enemy, which order was immediately obeyed. I advanced my regiment in line, keeping my skirmishers well to the front. By the time the regiment had reached a ravine or small creek, thickly skirted with undergrowth, at the foot of the hill, my skirmishers had nearly reached the crest of the hill occupied by the enemy, who had retired as my skirmishers advanced.

At this point, I received orders to halt and fall back to my original position in the woods, which order was obeyed. The regiment, with the balance of the brigade, was subsequently moved back by the same route it had advanced about 1 mile, and, after throwing out a strong line of pickets, bivouacked for the night.

Early on the morning of July 2, I was ordered to advance my regiment to the front, in the direction of the position occupied by the brigade on the evening of the 1st. I immediately deployed Company F as skirmishers, and advanced. I had not proceeded more than half a mile beyond our picket line when my skirmishers became engaged with those of the enemy. The enemy's skirmishers occupied a piece of woods in my front, and a stone house and a large barn on my right. They also endeavored to gain a house and barn immediately on my left. This movement of theirs I anticipated, and threw a part of my skirmishers forward, and took possession of the house and barn on my left and front. The balance of my line of skirmishers occupied open ground and without protection, while the enemy's line was entirely covered by woods and buildings. In this position sharp firing was kept up for something like an hour, at which time I received notice from General Ruger that the brigade had been ordered to fall back, with orders to hold my position until further orders. Subsequently I received orders to fall back, which was done by moving my regiment in line, keeping the skirmishers deployed in the rear. I rejoined the brigade on the ground upon which we had bivouacked the night previous.

At this point I was ordered to take command of the Third Brigade in place of General Ruger, who had been placed in command of the division. The subsequent part taken by the Twenty-seventh Regiment will be reported by Lieutenant-Colonel Fesler, who commanded the regiment during the 2d, 3d, and 4th.

In the skirmishing of the morning of the 2d, Company F had 1 man killed and 4 wounded.

Respectfully, your obedient servant,

S. COLGROVE,
Colonel.

Lieut. Robert P. Dechert,
A. A. A. G., Third Brig., First Div., Twelfth Corps.

NEAR KELLY'S FORD, VA., *August* 8, 1863.

SIR: I have the honor of submitting the following report of the part taken in the action at Gettysburg, Pa., on July 2 and 3, by the Third Brigade:

On the morning of July 2, I was informed by Lieutenant Dechert, acting assistant adjutant-general of the brigade, that the command of the division had devolved upon you, and that I was ordered to take the command of the brigade. I immediately took command of the brigade, and, in obedience to orders received from you, I moved it back to the Gettysburg pike, at the point where we had left the same on the day previous, leaving my line of skirmishers engaged with the enemy, and the Twenty-seventh Indiana as a rear guard. Subsequently, according to instructions, I withdrew the line of skirmishers and the Twenty-seventh Indiana.

The brigade was then, together with the balance of the division, moved to the front on the hill, forming a part of the line of battle, and then to the right into a piece of woods; and then again to the right, and formed in line on the right of the First Brigade, the One hundred and seventh New York forming the left of the line; the Thirteenth New Jersey formed in double column closed in mass in rear of the One hundred and seventh New York. Immediately on the right of the Thirteenth New Jersey was a small meadow of very low ground, which was considered untenable, and on its right was a small piece of timber, into which I placed the balance of the brigade in the following order: Second Massachusetts, Third Wisconsin, and the Twenty-seventh Indiana on the extreme right of the line. The three last-named regiments occupied three sides of an irregular square.

I ordered the One hundred and seventh New York to construct breastworks, their line fronting southeast and forming an angle of about 45 degrees to that of the line occupied by the First Brigade, and completely enfilading the open ground or meadow not covered by our line; the Second Massachusetts fronting to the northeast at nearly the same angle, and also enfilading the open space; the Third Wisconsin fronting to the east, and the Twenty-seventh Indiana to the south. The ground occupied by the two latter regiments was protected in the front by a small creek (Rocky Run) [Rock Creek], some 60 to 80 feet in width and from 6 to 8 feet deep, rendering the position of these two regiments not assailable from the east or south. Breastworks of rails, timber, and stone were speedily thrown up, covering the whole line.

In obedience to orders received from you, I subsequently changed the disposition of the regiments. I placed the Third Wisconsin on the left, on that portion of the line occupied by the One hundred and seventh New York; the Thirteenth New Jersey in the position occupied by the Third Wisconsin, and the One hundred and seventh New York in the rear of the three right regiments as a reserve.

Shortly before sundown, I received information through one of your aides that the extreme left of our line was hard pressed, with orders to immediately proceed with the brigade to the left, to the support of that part of the line. I immediately put the brigade in motion, and proceeded, I should judge, to the left about 1½ miles, where the battle appeared to be raging the fiercest. By the time I had gained the point indicated, it had become quite dark. I immediately formed the brigade in line of battle, under your direction, and threw out skirmishers to the front.

By this time the firing had entirely ceased, and, after remaining in this position from forty minutes to one hour, I received orders to march the brigade back, and occupy the position we had left. The brigade was immediately put in motion. We arrived on the open ground within a few hundred yards of our old position about 10 p. m., as near as I can judge. The night being quite dark and our line of breastworks being covered by the timber, it was impossible to tell whether they were occupied or not.

In obedience to instructions from you, I threw forward one company of skirmishers from the Second Massachusetts. In or near the breastworks they captured one of the enemy. With this exception, we found the works on the right of our line unoccupied. We immediately took possession of them. The skirmishers were ordered to cross the open space between the right and left of our line, and reconnoiter the woods and line of works on that side. They shortly returned with 23 prisoners, and reported that the enemy held our works on the left in large force. It was also ascertained from the prisoners that [John M.] Jones' and [George H.] Steuart's brigades occupied our works. It was deemed unsafe to undertake to recover them at that time, owing to the darkness of the night; consequently the brigade was held in position in the works on the right during the night.

I wish to state here that great credit is due the officers and men of Company F, Second Massachusetts, as skirmishers. They advanced into the woods, where it was impossible to tell friend from foe, and before they scarcely knew it were in the midst of a brigade of the enemy, from whom they captured 23 prisoners and brought them in, with a loss of only 2 captured on their side.

Early on the morning of the 3d, before it was fairly light, the battle commenced on our left, on that portion of the line held by the Second Division, and almost simultaneously the enemy's sharpshooters, from the breastworks and large ledges of rocks on our left, opened fire upon us.

I immediately deployed sharpshooters from the Third Wisconsin and Second Massachusetts in front of our breastworks, covered by a small belt of timber, and returned their fire briskly for about two hours. About this time the firing on our left, which had been very heavy, was fast receding, and loud cheering was heard along our lines. It was evident to me that General Geary had dislodged the enemy, and had retaken the breastworks occupied by him the day before. At this time I discovered the First Brigade, which was on my right, advance in line to the woods, forming a line at nearly right angles with my line.

At this juncture, Lieutenant Snow, of your staff, came up and said, "The general directs that you advance your line immediately." The position of the First Brigade was such that it was impossible for me to advance more than two regiments in line. Between the enemy and our line lay the open meadow, about 100 yards in width, The enemy were entirely sheltered by the breastworks and ledges of rock. It was impossible to send forward skirmishers. The enemy's advantages were such that a line of skirmishers would be cut down before they could fairly gain the open ground that intervened. The only possible chance I had to advance was to carry his position by storming it.

I selected the Second Massachusetts and Twenty-seventh Indiana for the work, and ordered the Second Massachusetts to charge the works in front of their position; the Twenty-seventh, as soon as they should gain the open ground, to oblique to the right and carry the position held in the ledges of rocks.   At the command, "Forward, double-quick!" our breastworks were cleared, and both regiments, with deafening cheers, sprang forward.   They had scarcely gained the open ground when they were met with one of the most terrible fires I have ever witnessed.

Up to this time the enemy had remained entirely concealed.   It had been impossible to tell anything about his strength in our immediate front, but it was now clearly ascertained that he had massed a heavy force at that point.   It seemed that the two regiments were devoted to destruction.   Undaunted, on they charged, officers leading and cheering their men.   The Second Massachusetts succeeded in clearing the open ground to the left of the breastworks.   The Twenty-seventh Indiana, having obliqued to the right, had nearly double the distance to traverse to gain the position of the enemy, but on it went; at every volley of the enemy, gaps were being cut through its ranks.   It became evident to me that scarcely a man could live to gain the position of the enemy.   I ordered the regiment to fall back behind the breastworks, which it did.   The Second Massachusetts was also overpowered by numbers, and had to fall back.

The Twenty-seventh had scarcely gained the breastworks when the rebels in turn charged, with the intention of carrying our works.   As soon as they had fairly gained the open ground, I ordered fire to be opened upon them, the Third Wisconsin, Twenty-seventh Indiana, and part of the Thirteenth New Jersey firing from the breastworks; the Second Massachusetts, from the new position on the left, had an enfilading fire upon them.   At the first fire they were completely checked, and at the second they broke in confusion and fled, leaving their dead and wounded upon the field.   I threw forward skirmishers from the Third Wisconsin, and ascertained that they had abandoned the breastworks.   Colonel Hawley was ordered to advance his regiment (Third Wisconsin) and take possession of the works, which he did, and held them during the day.   During the whole day my entire line was exposed to the enemy's sharpshooters, and quite a number in all the regiments were killed and wounded by them.

In the charge, the Second Massachusetts lost about 130 killed and wounded.   Among the killed was its commander, Lieutenant-Colonel Mudge, who fell while gallantly leading his men in the charge; a most gallant and brave officer, his gallant conduct will be cherished by his brother officers and men.   The Twenty-seventh lost 112 in killed and wounded.   Among the latter were 8 commissioned officers.   The loss of these two regiments was much the heaviest, being the only two regiments engaged in the charge.   Aside from this, the losses are about equal.

I take pleasure in bearing willing testimony to the good conduct and bravery not only of the officers, but also of the soldiers, of this command during the time I had the honor of commanding the brigade. Exposed as they were to extreme peril; doomed as they were during the latter part of the day on the 3d to remain inactive under one of the most terrific artillery fires the world has ever witnessed; shell, shot, and missiles bursting over them, around them, and among them for hours, and at the same time sustaining the fire of the enemy's sharpshooters, I scarcely witnessed a single instance upon the part of any soldier or officer of flinching from duty.   The highest compliment that I can possibly pay them is to say that the reputation which they had won upon so many hard-contested fields during the war— at Winchester, Cedar Mountain, Antietam, and Chancellorsville— was fully sustained.

The casualties* of the different regiments of this brigade having heretofore been reported in detail, supersede the necessity of making the same in this report. For a more detailed report of the part taken by each regiment during the three days' fighting, I respectfully refer you to the accompanying reports of the commandants of the several regiments composing this command.

Very respectfully, your obedient servant,

S. COLGROVE,
Colonel, Commanding Brigade.

General T. H. RUGER,
Comdg. First Div., Twelfth Corps, Army of the Potomac.

No. 287.

Report of Lieut. Col. John R. Fesler, Twenty-seventh Indiana Infantry.

KELLY'S FORD, VA., *August* 8, 1863.

SIR: I have the honor to submit the following report of the part taken by the Twenty-seventh Indiana Volunteers at the battle of Gettysburg, Pa., July 2, 3, and 4:

When the command of the regiment was turned over to me, it was occupying a position on a hill and to the right of Gettysburg, in front of where the Third Brigade bivouacked on the night of the 1st instant, with skirmishers out in front of the regiment.

I received orders from you, through Maj. T. F. Colgrove, about 8 a. m., to march the regiment to a position occupied by the remainder of the brigade, which I did, and by your orders took my position on the right of the brigade and in rear of a cliff of rocks, but that not giving shelter to the two left companies, I had breastworks of stone erected to shelter them from the fire of the enemy's sharpshooters.

About 6 p. m. I received orders from you to move the regiment to the left of the line, which had been hotly engaged during the afternoon. Arrived there about dark, and, by your order, formed the regiment in line of battle on the right of the brigade, and had skirmishers deployed in front. After remaining there for about twenty minutes, was ordered by you to call my skirmishers in and move back to my former position. Just before arriving at the ground I had formerly occupied (or within 200 yards of there), I then, in accordance with your orders, sent one company forward as skirmishers, to ascertain if the position was unoccupied. The way being clear, I moved the regiment forward and occupied the ground, and remained there unmolested until between 5 and 6 o'clock on the morning of the 3d, and then received orders from you to occupy the breastworks erected by the Third Wisconsin on the night of the 2d.

On arriving there, the enemy's sharpshooters immediately opened fire on the regiment from the breastworks built by the Third Brigade on the 2d. I was then ordered by you to charge their works. I immediately moved the regiment forward, but, on arriving within about 100 yards of their position, their fire was so deadly that I was compelled to fall back to the works I had previously occupied, which was done in good order. Remained there until about 8 a. m. on the

---

*Embodied in revised statement, p. 184. The number of officers and men carried into action by this brigade was as follows: Second Massachusetts, 320; Third Wisconsin, 246; Twenty-seventh Indiana, 339; One hundred and seventh New York, 319, and Thirteenth New Jersey, 347, making a total of 1,571.

morning of the 4th; kept up occasional firing on the 3d until about 4 p. m.; then, in accordance with your orders, made a reconnaissance to the right of Gettysburg. Found no enemy, and returned to position I left in the morning.

In the charge on the enemy on the 3d, loss in killed, 15; loss in wounded, including 7 commissioned officers, 83. Loss in killed in works, 3 enlisted men; loss in wounded, 10, including 1 commissioned officer. Total loss : Killed, 18; wounded, 93 ; total, 111.*

Respectfully, your obedient servant,

JOHN R. FESLER,
Lieutenant-Colonel Twenty-seventh Indiana Volunteers.

Col. S. Colgrove,
Comdg. *Third Brigade, First Division, Twelfth Corps.*

No. 288.

Report of Lieut. Col. Charles F. Morse, Second Massachusetts Infantry.

———, —— —, 1863.

Sir: I have the honor to make the following report:

The Second Massachusetts Regiment, under command of Lieutenant-Colonel Mudge, rejoined the Third Brigade after the battle of Beverly Ford, at Fairfax Court-House, Va., June 16, and marched with the brigade, by the way of Leesburg, Poolesville, Knoxville, and Frederick, to Littlestown, Pa., where it arrived June 30.

July 1.—The regiment, in connection with the other troops of the Twelfth Corps, marched about 4 miles on the Gettysburg turnpike to Two Taverns. Here the sound of cannonading first reached us.

In the afternoon we were again moved forward 2 or 3 miles, and to the right of Gettysburg. Here we first took up position in a woods. Company F, First Lieutenant Carroll commanding, was sent out and deployed as skirmishers. They advanced through the woods into an open meadow, and to within about 300 yards of the crest of a hill which was occupied by the enemy's cavalry. The line was here halted by order of the general commanding the Third Brigade, and remained in this position for about half an hour, when the brigade was moved to a new position some distance to the rear. Here the regiment was put in reserve of the first line, and formed in double column at half distance. The men lay on their arms throughout the night. •

July 2.—At daylight our position was slightly changed. Company B, Lieutenant George commanding, was sent forward, and skirmished for about half an hour with the enemy.

Early in the morning the regiment, in connection with the other regiments of the brigade, moved forward on the Gettysburg turnpike about half a mile, and took up position on the right of it. The regiment was placed in reserve.

About 6 p. m. we left our position to go to the support of the left wing, which had been heavily engaged during the afternoon. We had hardly reached this place when we were ordered to return to the right. The regiment moved back by the left flank. It was ordered to occupy the breastworks on the left of the Third Wisconsin Regiment. In order to do this it was necessary to cross an interval of

---

*But see revised statement, p. 184.

open ground about 100 yards wide, over which the breastworks did not extend. Before moving farther forward, as it was then night, a few skirmishers were thrown out. A prisoner was captured almost at once. A company (F) of skirmishers was sent out, and they took 23 prisoners, one of them a captain. The regiment now crossed the open ground behind the skirmishers, and began to occupy the breastworks. At this time I was in command of the skirmishers. I found that we were very near a force of the enemy, as talking could be plainly heard and a line indistinctly seen. Two men were sent to inquire who they were. They answered, "Twenty-third Virginia." One of these men was taken prisoner; the other escaped. The regiment now moved back across the open ground, and formed in line at right angles with the line of breastworks. Our skirmishers afterward took 3 more prisoners. We had 3 men of Company K wounded. During the night breastworks were constructed along our new line.

At daylight, July 3, our skirmishers, Company E, Captain Robeson, became engaged. Firing was kept up until 5.30 o'clock, when the regiment was ordered to charge the woods in front of us. Colonel Mudge gave the order, "Forward!" The men jumped over the breastworks with a cheer, and went forward on the double-quick. The fire while crossing the open ground was terrible, but the woods were reached and the regiment began firing, steadily advancing, and driving the enemy before it.

I now took command of the regiment, Colonel Mudge having been killed. I found on going to the right that the regiment that had advanced with us had never reached the woods, and that we had nothing on our right flank, and that the enemy were throwing a force in our rear. I ordered the regiment at once back far enough to uncover the right flank, which left the enemy in a very exposed position. They fell back rapidly, but lost heavily in so doing. I remained in my new position, inflicting a heavy loss upon the enemy, until my ammunition was nearly exhausted, when I sent to Colonel Colgrove, commanding Third Brigade, for further instructions. He ordered me to bring the regiment back to the rear of its former position. This was done, with a loss during the movement of 1 man killed and 1 officer and about 6 men wounded.

My loss in this action was 2 officers killed, 2 severely wounded, who have since died, and 6 other officers badly wounded, 21 men killed, 102 wounded, and 3 missing—probably prisoners, as they have not since been heard of.*

The regiment after this was not actually engaged, although it occupied the breastworks on the left of the First Brigade during the following afternoon and night.

The officers and men of the regiment did their duty bravely and faithfully throughout the action. There was not a single instance of cowardice or skulking, and there were a great many of individual gallantry.

The color-sergeant and 2 other color-bearers were killed while carrying the regimental flag, and 2 were severely wounded.

I am, very truly, your obedient servant,

C. F. MORSE,
Lieutenant-Colonel Second Massachusetts Regiment.

Lieut. ROBERT P. DECHERT,
Acting Assistant Adjutant-General.

---

* But see revised statement, p. 184.

NEAR KELLY'S FORD, VA., *August* 13, 1863.

SIR: I have the honor to report, in pursuance of orders, that there were 294 enlisted men taken into action by this regiment July 3.

Very respectfully, your obedient servant,

WM. COGSWELL,
Colonel Second Massachusetts Infantry.

Lieut. Col. H. C. RODGERS,
Assistant Adjutant-General, Twelfth Corps.

No. 289.

Report of Lieut. Col. John Grimes, Thirteenth New Jersey Infantry.

————, ———— —, 1863.

SIR : I have the honor to make the following report of the part taken by the Thirteenth New Jersey Volunteers in the battle of Gettysburg, July 1, 2, and 3 :

Having passed through and encamped near Littlestown, Pa., in the afternoon of June 30, on the morning of July 1 we counter-marched, again passing through Littlestown, and took the turnpike leading to Gettysburg, Pa.   After marching to within about 3 miles of Gettysburg, we took a road leading to the right, which we fol-lowed about 1½ miles, when the rest of the brigade deployed in a piece of woods, and our regiment was held as a reserve.   Remaining in this position for about an hour, our regiment countermarched about a mile, and took a position supporting Battery M, First New York Artillery, during the night.

July 2.—Moved out on the turnpike again, and in the direction of Gettysburg, to within 1 mile of that place, when we took a wood road leading to the right, on which we marched about half a mile, when we formed in double column and rested from 10 a. m. until 6 p. m., when we moved with our brigade to the extreme left, where we re-mained but a short time, when we were ordered to our old position, where we arrived at midnight, and, after changing position several times, we assisted in building breastworks, which formed the ex-treme right of our line, resting on Rock Creek, and which position flanked to some extent the enemy, who for the time occupied a por-tion of our works.

At 4 a. m. July 3, firing commenced by the enemy, and our regi-ment was immediately under arms, and was soon engaged with the enemy's sharpshooters, and fighting the enemy as they fell back from the position they had held.

We remained thus under fire for fourteen hours, when, at 6 p. m., we moved from the position on the extreme right farther up the line to a position formerly occupied by the First Brigade, where we re-mained until 7.30 p. m., firing occasionally, when we moved out of the breastworks, and, with the One hundred and seventh New York Volunteers and the Fifth Connecticut Volunteers, the whole under command of Colonel Carman, moved in the direction of Lit-tlestown.   Marched 2 miles, then took a road leading to the left, and marched 2 miles to a large cavalry camp, where we bivouacked in a meadow at 11 p. m., and remained during the night.

The foregoing report is taken from the diary of Captain Beardsley, and approved by Captain Harris, said officers being with the regiment during the time. Colonel Carman at present being absent, sick, and as I was at that time absent from my regiment, occasioned by a wound received at Chancellorsville, from which I had not recovered, I am unable to give a more correct and minute report.*

I have the honor to be, very respectfully, your obedient servant,

JOHN GRIMES,
Lieut. Col., Comdg. Thirteenth New Jersey Volunteers.

Col. S. COLGROVE,
Comdg. Third Brig., First Div., Twelfth Corps.

No. 290.

Reports of Col. Nirom M. Crane, One hundred and seventh New York Infantry.

HEADQUARTERS 107TH NEW YORK VOLUNTEERS,
August 6, 1863.

SIR: Pursuant to orders, I have the honor to submit the following report of the part taken in the battle of Gettysburg by my regiment on July 1, 2, and 3:

On the 1st ultimo, about the hour of 4 p. m., we arrived near the field where the First and Eleventh Corps were engaged, after a severe march. The brigade took position on the extreme right of the line of battle, about 1 mile from the turnpike. In pursuance to orders from General Ruger, I formed my regiment in double column about 150 yards in rear and in support of the Twenty-seventh Indiana. By order, I afterward deployed. I threw out Company E, Captain Bachman, as flankers, on the right, about 150 paces, to cover the right flank of my regiment.

After advancing in the proper order about 500 or 600 yards in the woods, and no enemy being discovered (I suppose), was ordered to move to the rear, and then by the left in front about half a mile toward the turnpike, where my regiment was placed in rear, in support of Captain Best's Fourth Regular Battery, placed on a slight eminence commanding an open field and woods in front. I then sent forward Company B, Lieutenant Swain commanding, as picket, and the regiment lay in line of battle all night.

About daybreak of the 2d ultimo, I moved with the brigade about 1 mile to the front on the pike, and took position, by your order, on the extreme right of the First Brigade, the Twenty-seventh Indiana, Second Massachusetts, and Third Wisconsin being across a small swale farther on my right, the Thirteenth New Jersey being about 75 paces to my rear and in support. Here we were ordered to build breastworks, or rifle-pits, forming a line in connection with the Second Division, Twelfth Corps.

About 7 p. m., the works being finished, I was ordered by you to move with the rest of the brigade to the pike. We moved thence and to the left and rear of the battle-field to the support of the left wing of the army, where a desperate fight was raging. While crossing to the left, we were subjected to some danger from the shots and shells of the enemy's artillery, but no damage was done to my regiment.

---

*The number of enlisted men present at the battle of Gettysburg, Pa., July 1, 2, and 3, was 322.

On our arrival on the left, I received orders to form my regiment in double column, in support of the Second Massachusetts. I only remained in this position a short time, when we were ordered back to the old position of the day; the enemy having been driven back from this point, there was no need of our assistance. I received orders from General Ruger to take position in rear and in support of the Second Massachusetts, who were to take the position I had occupied in the afternoon in the rifle-pits.

On our arrival near the wood (about 10 p. m. and quite dark), the Second Massachusetts leading, Lieutenant-Colonel Mudge sent forward a small squad of skirmishers to reconnoiter the ground, having been informed the enemy were or had been in the breastworks. Very soon after his skirmishers had advanced into the woods they captured and brought out about 20 prisoners, and reported the enemy in the woods in some considerable force.

The state of affairs was reported to you, and, after halting a few moments, I received orders to advance. The Second Massachusetts passed into the rifle-pits, and my regiment, by the flank, about 50 paces to their left and rear, into the woods. I halted when the battalion was about three-quarters its length into the bushes, and proceeded on foot forward alone to see the situation of the ground, &c. I had proceeded about 20 rods when I found myself very near a regiment of the enemy, who were in line some distance to the left, and in or near the breastworks. Not being discovered by them, I hastily retired, and meeting the acting major of the Second Massachusetts, he informed me that his regiment was retiring. I at once moved my battalion out of the woods across the swale, and reported the fact to you. I formed the regiment in double column, facing the woods, and let them lie down. Soon I received orders from General Ruger to report to him, and was ordered by him to move my command to the rear of the First Brigade, form in double column, hold that position, and await further orders.

I did so, and remained until about daybreak July 3, when I received orders to report with the regiment near the wall, where I found General Ruger, and by his orders placed my regiment in the road to the left and in front of Captain Best's battery, Fourth U. S. Artillery. The artillery soon commenced shelling the woods, and the Second Division became engaged on our left with the enemy in the woods. The First Maryland Regiment advanced just on my left to the woods in front, and very soon became engaged. They remained perhaps twenty minutes, when they fell back in some disorder, when General Ruger ordered me forward a short distance to a crest of the ground, with orders to hold that position as long as possible. In this position we lay down, the musket-balls occasionally passing over and around the regiment, but only one man was wounded in the leg, which I since learn had to be amputated.

While here, the regiment was in considerable danger from premature bursting of the shells from our own batteries, which were firing over us, being some distance to the right and rear.

I remained in this position until afternoon, when I received orders to advance into the wood and take position in rear and support of the Third Wisconsin, Colonel Hawley, who were occupying the breastworks I had occupied the afternoon of the 2d. I at once obeyed the order, and lay in this position some time, while the shot and shell from the enemy's artillery were passing over and around us rather lively, but doing no damage to my command.

About 4 p. m. I was ordered to the breastworks, to relieve the Forty-sixth Pennsylvania, which I did. While taking that position, the enemy's sharpshooters annoyed us considerably, but without injury. While in this position, I had only 1 man wounded, and he was shot in the arm.

Near 6 p. m. I received orders from you to report to Colonel Carman, Thirteenth New Jersey, for the purpose of proceeding about 3 or 4 miles to the rear with my regiment, the Thirteenth New Jersey, and Fifth Connecticut, to act as a sustaining force to General Gregg, who was hard pressed by the enemy's cavalry.

On our arrival near the scene of action, it was about dark, and the fighting had ceased ; were ordered into camp until morning, expecting to renew the attack at an early hour. In the morning it was ascertained the enemy had disappeared.

This finishes the part which my regiment took in the battle of Gettysburg, it being the first action in which the regiment had been engaged since I assumed command, June 23. I am highly pleased with the conduct of the officers and men ; prompt and ready to obey orders ; willing to do any duty assigned them without murmuring.

I am, colonel, your obedient servant,

N. M. CRANE,
Colonel, Commanding.

Col. S. COLGROVE,
Twenty-seventh Indiana Volunteers.

NEAR KELLY'S FORD, VA.,
August 13, 1863.

SIR: The following is the number of men of this regiment in line at Gettysburg, Pa., July 1, 2, and 3:

Officers ann men.	July 1.	July 2.	July 3.
Officers	26	26	26
Enlisted men	293	293	293
Total	319	319	319

Very respectfully, your obedient servant,

N. M. CRANE,
Colonel, Commanding.

Lieut. ROBERT P. DECHERT,
Acting Assistant Adjutant-General.

No. 291.

Report of Lieut. Col. Martin Flood, Third Wisconsin Infantry.

CAMP NEAR FAIRFAX COURT-HOUSE, VA.,
June 16, 1863.

CAPTAIN: I have the honor respectfully to report that pursuant to orders from Brigadier-General Ruger, commanding brigade, I marched with the detachment of this division from Stafford Court-House, Va., to the Spotted Tavern on the night of the 6th instant. Arrived there at 1 a. m., and reported to Brig. Gen. A. Ames.

On the 7th instant, by his order, I marched thence at 10 a. m. to Bealeton Station, arriving at 6 p. m.

Marched thence on the 8th instant to near Beverly Ford, on the Rappahannock River.

On the 9th instant, at daybreak, moved by his order across the river and down the road toward Culpeper. Approaching the front, where our cavalry was engaged with that of the enemy, I formed line of battle by his order, and threw forward a company from the Third Wisconsin Regiment and one from the Second Massachusetts as skirmishers. Soon after, by his order, I moved the Third Wisconsin Regiment farther to the right, to cover the interval between General Buford, on the right, and Colonel Devin, on our left, leaving, however, the skirmishers already thrown out and two companies of the Second Massachusetts, under command of Major Hubbard, of the Third Wisconsin Regiment, and the remainder of the Second Massachusetts, immediately under command of General Ames.

The enemy pressing heavily on the left, I was then ordered by General Ames to report to Colonel Devin, commanding cavalry on our left. I left one company of the Third Wisconsin and one from the Second Massachusetts (then with me), under command of Captain Stevenson, Third Wisconsin Volunteers, and proceeded with the remainder of the Third Wisconsin to Colonel Devin. By him I was ordered to move forward of his line of cavalry, and to drive out a force of dismounted cavalry, who were posted in the woods and pouring a deadly fire upon his line. I did so, throwing forward a heavy line of skirmishers, and, advancing cautiously, my skirmishers were soon warmly engaged, and, after a sharp skirmish of about an hour, in which 1 of my men was killed and 12 were wounded, drove the enemy from his cover, leaving a number of his dead and wounded on the field.

Meanwhile the force left under command of Captain Stevenson was sent, by order of General Ames, to General Buford, on the right. By him they were ordered to dislodge a force of dismounted cavalry of the enemy, who were advantageously posted behind a stone wall in such position that they had repulsed several charges of our cavalry. By a circuitous movement they gained the same side of the wall with the enemy, moved immediately upon them under cover of a little rise of ground, and opened a deadly enfilading fire upon them. After replying impetuously for some minutes, the rebel force, several hundred strong, fled in confusion, leaving a number of dead and wounded on the field greater than that of the force which had thus driven them. Ten prisoners were also captured. I was then ordered to advance by Colonel Devin, and during the remainder of the day supported a battery near, on our left.

At about 5 p. m. my command was assembled, and was ordered to retire. Recrossed the river at 6 p. m.; bivouacked near the ford, and on the following morning returned, by order of General Ames, to the camp near Bealeton Station.

On the morning of the 13th instant, I was ordered by General Ames to report to Brigadier-General Russell, commanding detachment which had co-operated with General Gregg's cavalry.

On the 14th instant, marched, by his order, to near Brentsville, and encamped.

On the 15th, marched, by his order, to Fairfax Station, and on the 16th instant marched to Fairfax Court-House, Va., reporting to Brigadier-General Ruger, commanding brigade.

I cannot speak too highly of the good conduct of the men of this detachment, both upon the march, in which there was no straggling, and in action, where there was no flinching. The officers without exception behaved nobly during the expedition.

I beg leave to make honorable mention of the name of David Agnew, private Company H, Third Wisconsin Volunteers. While skirmishing in front of Colonel Devin's cavalry, he advanced beyond our line, saved the life of a comrade, and captured a rebel who was in the act of firing.

I deem it but just also to make honorable mention of John H. Burghardt, Second Massachusetts, who was in charge of the ordnance train of the detachment, for the prompt and faithful manner in which he performed all his duties.

I have the honor to be, sir, very respectfully, your obedient servant,

MARTIN FLOOD,
Lieutenant-Colonel Third Wisconsin Volunteers.

Capt. S. E. Pittman,
  Asst. Adjt. Gen., First Division, Twelfth Corps.

No. 292.

Report of Col. William Hawley, Third Wisconsin Infantry.

Camp near Kelly's Ford, Va., August 4, 1863.

Colonel: I have the honor, very respectfully, to forward the following report of the part taken by my command, the Third Regiment Wisconsin Volunteers, in the battle at Gettysburg, Pa., July 2 and 3:

On July 1, my command, included in the Third Brigade, First Division, Twelfth Corps, marched from Littlestown to near Gettysburg, and took supporting position on the right of and to the rear of our general line of battle.

On the morning of the 2d, by your order, sir, I took the position at daylight in line of battle which you assigned me, and threw out a company of skirmishers, who kept up a desultory fire with the skirmishers of the enemy for about two hours, when, by your command, my regiment, with the rest of your command, was withdrawn from that position and marched to the front. The brigade under your command being assigned to the right of our line, I took position, by your order, along the east bank of Rock Creek between the Twenty-seventh Indiana and Second Massachusetts Regiments, and proceeded to throw up breastworks of earth and rails, and to throw down such stone walls and fences in my front as might afford cover to the enemy. My position thus strengthened, I rested behind my works until 6 p. m., when, by your order, I marched with the brigade to the left of our line, then the scene of action, and there took the assigned position in line of battle.

Darkness coming on, I received orders from you, sir, to move out as we had marched in, and, following the regiment on my right flank, was marched back to the position which I had spent the day in fortifying, and there rested under arms. It then being ascertained that the enemy had advanced over our breastworks and occupied a rocky, wooded hill on my left, thus enfilading my position and severing our line, by your order I took position perpendicular to my former line, so as to face the enemy's advance in this position, and there lay under arms for the remainder of the night.

At daybreak on the morning of the 3d, I was aroused by a volley from the enemy. By a slight movement of my regiment forward and to the right, I placed it in position, well covered by bushes, rocks, and a hastily erected breastwork of rails, and, by your order, threw forward two companies as skirmishers, instructing them to keep well covered by the rocks and trees, which afforded them shelter from the very accurate fire of the enemy's sharpshooters, who were posted on our right and front.

Relieving these companies from time to time, I kept up a constant fire until about 11 a. m., when, a part of the rebels on my front having surrendered, I was ordered by you, sir, to advance. I moved forward by my left flank, so as to avoid an enfilading fire, advanced into the woods, found the enemy retreating, and pushed forward and reoccupied the breastworks erected on our line the day previous.

Here I remained during the day and succeeding night, my men being engaged in a desultory fire with the enemy's skirmishers and sharpshooters.

Owing to the advantage of position which my command was so fortunate as to occupy during the engagement, the loss sustained was comparatively slight—2 men killed and 1 commissioned officer and 8 men wounded, of which the official lists have heretofore been forwarded. The number of officers and enlisted men engaged in the battle was 21 officers and 239 enlisted men.

I have the honor, sir, to be, very respectfully, your obedient servant,

WILLIAM HAWLEY,
Col., Comdg. Third Regiment Wisconsin Volunteers.

Col. S. COLGROVE,
Comdg. Third Brig., First Div., Twelfth Army Corps.

No. 293.

Report of Brig. Gen. John W. Geary, U. S. Army, commanding Second Division.

HDQRS. SECOND DIVISION, TWELFTH ARMY CORPS,
Near Catlett's Station, Va., July 29, 1863.

COLONEL: I have the honor to submit the following report of the military operations of this division from June 28 until the 26th instant, including the engagement with the enemy near Gettysburg, Pa., on the 2d and 3d instant:

On June 28, agreeably to orders, my command broke camp at 6.30 a. m., near Knoxville, Md., which place it had reached the evening previous, and marched through Petersville and Jefferson to within a mile of Frederick, where it encamped at 2 p. m., having been impeded by the trains of various commands.

At 4 o'clock on the following morning the march was resumed, and at 6 the camp of the Eleventh Corps was reached. We were here detained four hours, until that command was on the road and to allow the Artillery Reserve to pass. Passing through Ceresville, Walkersville, and Woodsborough, we crossed Big Pipe Creek, and encamped at 7 p. m., having marched 21 miles.

At 5 o'clock on the morning of the 30th, the division again moved, and marched through Taneytown and Littlestown, encamping near the latter place at noon. A half hour before reaching this place our cavalry had there a skirmish with that of the rebels. The command was hastened forward and dispositions at once made to receive the enemy, who, however, retired in the direction of Hanover.

On July 1, we moved from camp at 5 a. m., and reached Two Taverns at 11 a. m., where we halted to await further orders. The distance marched from the 28th to this time was 52 miles.

At Two Taverns I received orders to forward the command in the direction of Gettysburg, on the turnpike leading from Baltimore to that place, and, accordingly, at about 2 p. m. advanced rapidly on the road to the town. I received instructions from you while on the march to leave one brigade with a section of artillery in reserve, and with the balance of my command to report to Major-General Howard, whom I should have found at a point some mile and a half east of the town, where an engagement with the right wing of the enemy's forces was then in progress; but not finding General Howard, I reported to Major-General Hancock, commanding Second Corps, who informed me that the right could maintain itself, and the immediate need of a division on the left was imperative. By his direction, upon this threatening emergency, I took up a position on the extreme left of the line of battle, as the enemy was reported to be attempting to flank it, and cavalry were already skirmishing in front of that position.

At 5 p. m. this movement was consummated, and my line extended at that time from about half a mile west of the Baltimore turnpike to the left of the First Army Corps, to a range of hills south and west of the town, which I occupied with two regiments of the First Brigade. These hills I regarded as of the utmost importance, since their possession by the enemy would give him an opportunity of enfilading our entire left wing and center with a fire which could not fail to dislodge us from our position. This line was held by the First and Third Brigades.

The Second Brigade, with two pieces of Battery K, Fifth U. S. Artillery, pursuant to orders from Major-General Slocum, was detached during the march to take position in reserve on the immediate left of the turnpike, about 2 miles from Gettysburg. No attack was made upon me at either point, the speedy formation of the line on the left frustrating the enemy's design, which would, if successful, have proved disastrous to the entire position. The command rested on their arms during the night.

At 5 a. m. on the 2d, having been relieved by the Third Army Corps, in obedience to orders from Major-General Slocum, the division was placed on the right of the center of the main line of battle, east of the turnpike. General Williams' division, commanded by Brigadier-General Ruger, joined ours, forming the extreme right, and extending toward the Bonaughtown turnpike and at right angles to it. Here I had formed a double line of battle, fronting Rock Creek, and about 400 yards from it, along a rocky, thickly wooded ridge which sloped eastwardly to the creek. The Third Brigade (Greene's) occupied our extreme left, joining the right of the First Corps on a steep, rocky mount, which was a continuation of Cemetery Hill. Our line was nearly at a right angle with that of the First

Corps. The Second Brigade (Kane's) extended from the right of Greene's brigade at an angle of about 45 degrees forward, conforming its line to the crest of the ridge. The First Brigade (Candy's) was formed in rear of the Third in line of battalions, in double column, as a support to the other two brigades.

Breastworks were immediately thrown up along our entire line, unusual facilities being afforded by the wood and rock and nature of the soil. Skirmishers were thrown out to the creek, where they encountered the enemy's pickets. I ordered the Twenty-eighth Pennsylvania Volunteers forward as a support to the skirmishers of the Third Brigade. They deployed in a heavy line in rear of the advance skirmishers, and remained until withdrawn in the evening.

At 4 p. m. the enemy opened with a fierce attack on the left and center of the army, and subjected our men to severe artillery fire. Finding that a battery of the enemy posted on a hill across Rock Creek was enfilading the lines of the First and Eleventh Corps, I ordered a section of Knap's (Pennsylvania) battery and one of Battery K, Fifth U. S. Artillery, to take position on the eminence at the left of Greene's brigade and to silence the enemy's battery. This they did after a hot artillery duel of about thirty minutes. The guns of these two sections were admirably served in the midst of a deadly fire from a battery which raked at short range the point they occupied. Occasional picket firing was kept up until 6 p. m.

By a staff officer of Major-General Slocum, at 7 p. m. I received orders to move the division by the right flank, and follow the First Division, leaving one brigade to occupy the line of works of the entire corps. The First Division had gone nearly half an hour previously. Leaving Greene's brigade in the intrenchments, I rapidly moved the First and Second Brigades to the right, across Rock Creek, and, having reached the turnpike across Rock Creek Bridge, halted and reported my position, through an aide, to corps headquarters.

When ordered thus to leave my intrenchments, I received no specific instructions as to the object of the move, the direction to be taken, or the point to be reached, beyond the order to move by the right flank and to follow the First Division. The First Division having gone out of sight or hearing, I directed the head of my column by the course of some of the men of that division who appeared to be following it. While moving in this direction, the enemy's artillery fire crossed our route, causing a few casualties among my troops.

At 7.30 o'clock I received an order to hold the position down to the creek at all hazards. I therefore formed my line, with my right resting on the turnpike, near the bridge, and my left on Rock Creek.

In the meantime General Greene had commenced to extend his brigade, as ordered, along the line of intrenchments, and had barely occupied General Kane's original position when a vigorous attack was made upon his front and right by the enemy, who quickly occupied the intrenchments left by the First Division. To meet this attack on his flank, the One hundred and thirty-seventh New York Volunteers, which held the right of Greene's brigade, changed front, forming at a right angle to the rifle-pits, thus covering the right of the entire brigade. At this time the California Regiment, Colonel Smith, of Cutler's brigade, Wadsworth's division, First Corps,* reported as reenforcements. General Greene placed this regiment on the right of the One hundred and thirty-seventh. It soon fell back and was with-

---

* The regiment mentioned belonged to Webb's brigade, of Gibbon's division, Second Corps.

drawn by its colonel, who stated that he was ordered so to do by his general. This withdrawal placed the right of Greene's brigade in a critical position.

Greene's brigade now behaved with the most unflinching gallantry, sustaining their desperate position during an incessant attack of two and a half hours from vastly superior numbers. During this time the noble brigade repelled four separate and furious charges on their entire line without losing a foot of ground. The heaps of rebel dead and wounded in front of their lines afterward attested their desperate determination.

As soon as the attack commenced, Generals Wadsworth and Howard were petitioned by General Greene for support, to which they promptly responded—the Sixth Wisconsin, Colonel Dawes, Fourteenth Brooklyn, Colonel Fowler, and One hundred and forty-seventh New York Volunteers, Major Banta* (in all, 355 men), being sent from Wadsworth's division, and the Eighty-second Illinois, Lieutenant-Colonel Salomon, Forty-fifth New York Volunteers, Colonel Amsberg, and the Sixty-first Ohio, Colonel McGroarty (in all, about 400 men) from the Eleventh Corps. These regiments rendered good service, relieving temporarily regiments of Greene's brigade whose ammunition was exhausted, and by whom they were again in turn relieved.

The enemy, meeting with so determined a resistance, discontinued their attack at about 10 p. m., and remained in occupancy of the ridge formerly held by the First Division, General Greene still holding all his original position, with the One hundred and thirty-seventh New York Volunteers placed in line perpendicularly to the rest of the brigade, its left resting on the intrenchments and its right near a stone wall, which extended parallel to Generals Ruger's and Kane's intrenchments and about 200 yards in rear of them. This stone wall was occupied by a force of the enemy as a protection against attack from the direction of the turnpike.

At 9 p. m. I ordered Kane's brigade to return to its original position and Candy's to follow it. On entering the woods, and when within 200 yards of the breastworks, Kane's brigade was met by a sharp fire, which, in the midst of the surrounding darkness, was at first supposed to be from General Greene's troops. Without replying, the brigade was withdrawn to the turnpike, taken in past the rear of Greene's brigade and past Greene's right, when it was again met with a volley, thus proving that the enemy still occupied the ground to Greene's right; a fact of which in the dark night there remained some doubt.

It being injudicious to attack the enemy in the night in their new position, I formed the Second Brigade in double line perpendicular to the Third Brigade and joining its right, thus relieving the One hundred and thirty-seventh New York Volunteers, which had so long and so well held that position. Between this new line of the Second Brigade and that of the enemy in their front was a shallow ravine. The whole ground was very rough and rocky, affording some shelter on both sides for infantry. I devoted the rest of the night, after consultation with Major-General Slocum and Brigadier-General Williams, to such an arrangement of my troops as, by a vigorous attack at daylight, to drive the enemy from the ground they had gained.

At 1 a. m. on the 3d, the First Brigade, which had been held in readiness on the turnpike, was placed in position on the right of Kane's brigade, in extension of Kane's line, its right resting on an

---

* Reference is probably to Major Harney.

orchard near the turnpike. Immediately in front of the First Brigade was a narrow lane running from the turnpike to the stone wall previously mentioned. Along this lane Candy's brigade was placed in double line of battle, and screened from the enemy's observation by the woods. All these dispositions were made with the utmost silence and secrecy and within a few rods of the enemy's lines.

By your order, Lieut. E. D. Muhlenberg, chief of artillery of the corps, reported with fourteen pieces of artillery. These were posted on a hill west of the turnpike and about 500 yards in rear of the intrenchments gained by the enemy, and I trained them so as to command the enemy's position without injury to our own troops. To Knap's (Pennsylvania) battery, which was in position on the hill near corps headquarters, I gave similar directions regarding their line of fire. At my request, General Williams, commanding corps, readily sent to my support Lockwood's brigade, composed of the First Eastern Shore Maryland Regiment, Colonel Wallace, and the One hundred and fiftieth New York, Colonel Ketcham. This brigade I placed in position to support the artillery.

Everything being thus in readiness, at 3.30 a. m. (early dawn) a simultaneous attack was made by artillery and the infantry of the Second and Third Brigades. This attack was most furious, but was stubbornly met. Our artillery fire continued, by previous arrangement, for ten minutes. This tremendous assault at first staggered the enemy, by whom it was seemingly unexpected; but, rallying as my troops charged at the close of the artillery fire, Johnson's division of Ewell's corps, followed by Rodes', and that supported by Early's, each division massed in three lines, advanced, charging heavily upon our front and right, and yelling in their peculiar style. They were met at every point by the unswerving lines and deadly fire of my Second and Third Brigades, our men cheering loudly and yielding not an inch of ground. Line after line of the enemy broke under this steady fire, but the pressing masses from behind rushed forward to take their places.

During this contest, Greene's brigade was protected by his breastworks, while Kane's fought without shelter, excepting such as might be afforded by inequalities of the ground. After a lapse of twenty minutes, I directed the artillery fire again to open, having myself sighted the pieces so as to bear directly upon the masses of the enemy in the woods. This artillery fire lasted about fifteen minutes. A part of it being directed to the valley of Rock Creek, where the enemy's left rested, prevented them from flanking the troops of the First Division, which were engaging the enemy in front. This flank movement the enemy made repeated attempts to effect, but they were driven back by well-directed shells from our artillery. Meanwhile the musketry fire continued with unabated fierceness.

At 5 a. m. the One hundred and forty-seventh Pennsylvania Volunteers, of Candy's brigade, was ordered to charge and carry the stone wall occupied by the enemy. This they did in handsome style, their firing causing heavy loss to the enemy, who then abandoned the entire line of the stone wall. At this time the Fifth Ohio, on Candy's left, was exposed to a severe enfilading fire from the enemy, but they held their position, punishing the enemy severely.

At 5.45 a. m. the Sixty-sixth Ohio was ordered to advance outside of Greene's intrenchments and perpendicular to them, in order to harass the enemy by a raking fire. This they accomplished with great gallantry, driving the enemy and holding the ground until recalled by an order at 11 a. m. Although exposed without shelter to the enemy's fire from front and flank, so eager was their attack that a few of their men advanced too far, and fell by our own artillery fire.

At 6 a. m. the Twenty-eighth Pennsylvania, and Fifth, Seventh, and Twenty-ninth Ohio, of Candy's brigade, were ordered into the intrenchments, to relieve some of Greene's regiments which were out of ammunition, and went in with loud cheering, keeping up the continuous fire while the relieved regiments passed to the rear between the files.

At 7.30 o'clock Lockwood's brigade, of the First Division, 1,700 strong, reported to me as a support, and was rested in line in the woods about 25 yards in rear of Greene's breastworks. This brigade, composed almost entirely of untried troops, was engaged for a short time as a relief to other regiments, and rendered efficient service.

About 8 a. m. the enemy redoubled their efforts, and, massing all the force against us that the ground would admit, pressed forward with an evident determination to carry the position at all hazards. Our entire line was hotly engaged, and, fearing that the overwhelming force might prove too much for us, General Slocum was solicited for re-enforcements, and General Alexander Shaler's (First) brigade, Third Division, Sixth Corps, reported at 8.45 o'clock, and was posted as a reserve. Ten minutes before the arrival of this brigade, the Fourteenth Brooklyn and One hundred and forty-seventh New York Volunteers (both together about 150 strong) reported again from General Wadsworth's division, and were sent in to re-enforce Kane's brigade, on the right. They were shortly afterward relieved by Candy's and Lockwood's troops. Instructions having been given me not to actively engage Shaler's brigade, unless unavoidable, only a portion of it was employed briefly. Those engaged displayed the accustomed gallantry which has enrolled Shaler's brigade among the best veterans of the army.

At 9 a. m. the One hundred and twenty-second New York (Col. Silas Titus), of this brigade, relieved the One hundred and eleventh Pennsylvania, of Kane's, which had been engaged in the front line all the morning, and whose ammunition was failing. The Eighty-second Pennsylvania (Col. Isaac C. Bassett), Shaler's brigade, relieved the One hundred and twenty-second New York after our occupancy of the breastworks.

At 9.20 o'clock the Twenty-third Pennsylvania (Col. John F. Glenn), of the same, was placed in support of the front line, about 150 yards to the rear, and subsequently five companies of it were deployed by my order in rear of the works, and advanced into them. Toward the close of the engagement, a portion of them was pushed out a few spaces as skirmishers, but the impracticability of feeling the enemy with skirmishers was demonstrated by their increased fire, and they were withdrawn. The Sixty-fifth (Col. Joseph E. Hamblin) and Sixty-seventh New York (Col. N. Cross) and Eighty-second Pennsylvania were placed well to the front, after the enemy had been driven back, to resist any renewed demonstration of hostility on the part of the enemy, while several already overworked regiments of my division were allowed a much needed respite for their energies, which had been so many hours stretched to their utmost tension. They were not, however, called upon for further active operations.

About 2 o'clock the brigade was ordered to rejoin its corps. While subject to my orders it behaved with admirable coolness, and manifested to an eminent degree the possession of the greatest attributes of the soldier, both during the brief period (as per orders) they were actively engaged and while under heavy fire as they awaited the moment they might be called upon.

Their casualties numbered in the aggregate 45, 11 enlisted men being killed.

Their brave and efficient commander, Brig. Gen. Alexander Shaler, is entitled to the warmest eulogies for his readiness to participate in any measure to provide for the emergencies besetting us.

Our troops, cheered by the arrival of supports, soon repulsed the fierce attack made upon them. The enemy wavered, but kept their ground by pushing forward fresh troops in heavy columns.

At 10.25 o'clock two brigades of Johnson's division, having formed in column by regiments, charged upon our line on the right. They met the determined men of Kane's little brigade, which, though only 650 strong, poured into them so continuous a fire that when within 70 paces their columns wavered and soon broke to the rear. The First Maryland Battalion (rebel) was in the advance, and their dead lay mingled with our own. This was the last charge. As they fell back, our troops rushed forward with wild cheers of victory, driving the rebels in confusion over the intrenchments, the ground being covered with their dead and wounded. Large numbers of them crawled under our breastworks and begged to be taken as prisoners. Among these were many of the celebrated Stonewall Brigade, who, when ordered for the last time to charge upon Greene's breastworks, advanced until met by our terrible fire, and then, throwing down their arms, rushed in with white flags, handkerchiefs, and even pieces of paper, in preference to meeting again that fire which was certain destruction. As they threw themselves forward and crouched under our line of fire, they begged our men to spare them, and they were permitted to come into our lines. The commanding officer of a regiment raised the white flag, when Major [B. W.] Leigh, assistant adjutant-general of Johnson's division, rode forward to order it down, and fell, pierced by a dozen balls, his body remaining in our possession.

This final charge, made at 10.30 a. m., which was so eminently successful to us, resulted in the rout of the enemy, terminating the attempt to turn our position and gain the Baltimore turnpike, which Ewell, it is represented by the rebel officers taken prisoners, had sworn to accomplish or to lose every man he had. With great gallantry our troops sustained for seven hours and a half a battle fraught with persistent and obstinate effort and unremitting fire of an intensity seldom prolonged beyond a limited period, and where desperation or dash is necessary to carry a point.

To make distinctions among the regiments of my division would be unjust where all fought with such unanimity of courage and vigor. For the particular efforts of each I have the honor to refer you to the reports of the commanding officers, which I forward with this.

The regiments of the brigades relieved each other alternately during the progress of the battle, those of the First [Brigade] being originally kept in reserve as support, and for that purpose being frequently called upon, and each time rallying to the front with enthusiasm. I cannot pass a better eulogium upon the conduct of them all than to say they manifested the same unflinching gallantry which has distinguished them upon many battle-fields, and which has rightly won these veterans laurels of which they are justly proud and jealous.

I also feel called upon and proud to mention that not an instance of straggling from the front was witnessed from the beginning to the end of the conflict, and every man who left his post did so upon authority.

The terrific cannonading from the batteries of the rebels massed upon the left center subjected my lines from the rear from 1 p. m. to 3.15 p. m. to a galling fire, as the missiles thickly swept over and into the position occupied by us, causing a number of casualties. I disposed my men under the best cover their duties and the ground could afford.

From the moment of the retiring of the enemy in our front, active sharpshooting was kept up by them along our entire line until dark. Detachments of skirmishers were sent out, and ably managed by Lieutenant-Colonel Redington, of the Sixtieth New York Volunteers. The Twenty-eighth Pennsylvania Volunteers was early pushed forward, and maintained lively skirmishing with the rebel skirmishers, causing them considerable annoyance, as they carried out their instructions to pick out their adversaries and fire deliberately.

Several night attacks were made upon our position, evidently in the vain hope of taking us by surprise.

At 9.30 p. m., when about to be relieved in the intrenchments by Greene's brigade, Candy's brigade was opened upon by the enemy with heavy fire, which was silenced by a timely and well-directed resistance.

At 10.30 p. m. the enemy were discovered advancing in force up the slope, but were met by a heavy fire, which they returned, but they were compelled to retire after an active fight of from twelve to fifteen minutes.

The day was a most disastrous one to Ewell's corps, and equally, if not more so, to the whole rebel army, in consideration of the importance which the turning of our flank would be to them, and which alone could compensate them for the repulses they had received upon other parts of the line in their well-conceived designs upon the key-points to the position of our army. They were not only defeated, but terribly punished.

I estimate upon personal observation—in which I am supported by statements from intelligent prisoners in our hands—their killed in front of our lines at nearly or quite 1,200, of which we succeeded in burying 900, and wounded in the ratio of at least four to one killed, the greater portion of whom were carried off during the night by the enemy.

We took over 500 prisoners, independent of those who were wounded, 600 of the latter from Rodes' division alone falling into the hands of our army. About 5,000 small-arms were left upon the field by the enemy, 2,000 of which were turned over to the division ordnance officer, and the balance secured by adjacent commands and carried away as trophies by citizens; also, three colors, viz: The brigade colors of the Stonewall Brigade, taken by the Sixtieth New York Volunteers ; a battle-flag of a Virginia regiment, taken by the same, and the battle-flag of the Fourteenth Virginia Infantry, taken by the Seventh Ohio Volunteers.

The battle-field remained in our possession, and the following day, July 4, was devoted to burying the dead of both sides and collecting the arms.

The efficiency of our intrenchments was clearly demonstrated from an early period in the action. Not only did they impede the advance of the overwhelmingly superior numbers of the enemy, but our men were afforded by them a shelter which rendered our casualties surprisingly incompatible with so terrible and prolonged an engagement.

On the 5th, the Seventh Ohio Volunteers were pushed forward on a reconnaissance, pursuant to instructions from corps headquarters, and advanced to Seminary Ridge and 2 miles from our position. Discovering the enemy had retired, they were ordered back, and at 1 p. m., in obedience to orders, the line of march from Gettysburg was taken up.

In closing this report, I desire to express in as public a manner as possible my sense of obligation to Generals Greene and Kane and Colonel Candy, commanding the several brigades of the division; to each of these officers the service and their country owe especial thanks for the patriotic self-sacrifice with which they devoted their entire energies to the success of the contest. Hand in hand they co-operated with me for the general good, and by their cheerful promptitude and alacrity in massing together the troops of their respective commands wherever the attack of the enemy seemed most to require a united effort to oppose him, they contributed in a marked degree to the success which ultimately crowned the engagement.

To Col. G. A. Cobham, jr., I also take pleasure in officially tendering an expression of my high appreciation of his untiring energy in commanding the Second Brigade throughout the entire campaign until General Kane assumed command on the morning of the 2d instant. Colonel Cobham, with his superior advocacy of discipline and his soldierly qualifications, has, during the several months he commanded the brigade, contributed greatly to the sustenance of its most excellent reputation as a high-toned organization.

I desire also to acknowledge the fraternal and courteous conduct of Brigadier-General Williams, commanding Twelfth Corps, in forwarding re-enforcements to my lines when heavily pressed by the furious assault of the enemy's columns. On several occasions during the battle, perceiving the attack of the enemy to be mainly concentrated upon my command, he freely tendered the use of fresh regiments to assist me in repulsing the attack.

The conduct of the whole command, both officers and men, was such as to afford me the highest gratification. It was with feelings of pleasure and pride that I witnessed many deeds of bravery and that higher grade of true courage—self-denial under trying difficulties and hardships—throughout the entire command. Deprived of shelter and exposed to continuous rains and dampness, their only bed the hard rock of the hill they had vowed to defend; stinted for some days in their supplies, and deprived of rest day and night by the incessant attack of the fresh troops of the enemy, each man seemed to vie with his comrade in exhibiting his superior quality of bravery, which distinguishes the true soldier from the mere creature of military discipline.

It is due to the officers of my staff that mention should be made of their valuable assistance to me during the engagement as well as throughout the entire campaign. The nature of their duties since the commencement of our operations had required of them the most unceasing vigilance and activity, and it gives me pleasure to testify to their unflagging zeal and devotion throughout the engagements of the 1st, 2d, and 3d instant. From the peculiar nature of their duties, their untiring diligence and activity subjected them to severe drafts upon their physical endurance and to exposure to danger, and I am happy to bear my testimony to the fact that I found them always not only ready and willing, but most desirous, to contribute all their energies to the success of the contest.

Those serving throughout the movements were : Capt. Thomas H. Elliott, assistant adjutant-general; Capt. Reuben H. Wilbur, aide-de-camp; Lieut. Llewellyn R. Davis, aide-de-camp; Capt. Henry H. Wilson, aide-de-camp; Capt. William T. Forbes, acting assistant inspector-general; Capt. Moses Veale, assistant commissary of musters.

I also beg to mention the eminent degree of energy and efficiency manifested in their respective departments during the campaign by Surg. John E. Herbst, surgeon-in-chief; Capt. Gilbert M. Elliott, ordnance officer; Capt. G. L. Parker, assistant quartermaster, and Capt. James Gillette, commissary of subsistence. The duties of Surgeon Herbst and Capt. G. M. Elliott upon the field at Gettysburg called them frequently under my observation, and I feel gratified in commending them as accomplishing their responsible tasks in a masterly and energetic manner.

The following is a list of the regiments, with their commanding officers, engaged in the battle of Gettysburg:

First Brigade, Col. Charles Candy.--Twenty-eighth Pennsylvania Volunteers, Capt. John Flynn; One hundred and forty-seventh Pennsylvania Volunteers, Lieut. Col. Ario Pardee, jr.; Fifth Ohio Volunteers, Col. John H. Patrick; Seventh Ohio Volunteers, Col. William R. Creighton; Twenty-ninth Ohio Volunteers, Capt. Wilbur F. Stevens; Sixty-sixth Ohio Volunteers, Lieut. Col. Eugene Powell.

Second Brigade, Brig. Gen. Thomas L. Kane.—Twenty-ninth Pennsylvania Volunteers, Col. William Rickards, jr.; One hundred and ninth Pennsylvania Volunteers, Capt. Frederick L. Gimber; One hundred and eleventh Pennsylvania Volunteers, Col. G. A. Cobham, jr.

Third Brigade, Brig. Gen. George S. Greene.—Sixtieth New York Volunteers, Col. Abel Godard; Seventy-eighth New York Volunteers, Lieut. Col. H. von Hammerstein; One hundred and Second New York Volunteers, Col. James C. Lane; One hundred and thirty-seventh New York Volunteers, Col. David Ireland; One hundred and forty-ninth New York Volunteers, Col. H. A. Barnum.

The following is a statement of the number of officers and men taken into the engagement:

Organizations.	Officers.	Enlisted men.	Total.
First Brigade	98	1,700	1,798
Second Brigade	48	652	700
Third Brigade	74	1,350	1,424
Total	220	3,702	3,922

The entire numbers of casualties in the division during the operations in front of Gettysburg are herewith appended.*

The command expended in the fight on July 3, and in subsequent skirmishing, 277,000 rounds of ammunition.

---

*Embodied in revised statement, p. 185.

At 1 o'clock on the afternoon of the 5th, pursuant to orders from corps headquarters, my command left its position near Gettysburg, marched to Littlestown, and encamped at 5.30 p. m. We remained at this place until 4 o'clock on the morning of the 7th, when the line of march was resumed, and, passing through Taneytown, Middleburg, and Woodsborough, accomplishing a march of 29 miles, we encamped near Walkersville at 5.45 p. m.

On the 8th, we started at 5 a. m., and, marching through Frederick and over the Catoctin Range, halted for the night a half mile beyond Jefferson.

At 5 a. m. on the following day, left camp, and proceeded through Crampton's Pass and Burkittsville to Rohrersville, where we encamped at 11 a. m.

At 5 a. m. on the 10th, left Rohrersville, passed through Keedysville, and reached Bakersville at 11 a. m. Cavalry pickets of the enemy retired upon our advance. We here formed in line of battle, with the First Division on the left and Second Corps on the right. Some light breastworks were thrown up and heavy pickets advanced.

We bivouacked for the night in that position, and on the morning of the 11th advanced to Fair Play, formed line of battle, pursuant to orders from corps headquarters, and advanced skirmishers. Cavalry pickets of the enemy could be seen in our front. We remained in line all night.

Early on July 12, advanced line of pickets to a more elevated ridge, resulting in some slight skirmishing, the rebel skirmishers falling back.

During the night changed our position to the right, withdrawing our left to a ridge, forming a perfect line, joining the left of the First Division.

On the 13th, we covered our entire front with extensive breastworks, with numerous traverses, and with flanks well protected. Picket firing at intervals all day.

At 5 p. m. our pickets were ordered to advance until they met those of the enemy. They encountered them under cover of belts of woods about a quarter of a mile in our front, and lively skirmishing ensued, with, however, no casualties on our side. At dusk the original picket line was resumed.

On the 14th, remained in intrenchments under arms, to support the First Division, which advanced to the front. Discovering from this movement that no opposition was immediately in front of us, I ordered our skirmishers (the Twenty-eighth Pennsylvania and Seventh Ohio Regiments) to reconnoiter toward Downsville. They discovered the enemy's works at that place deserted, and returned with several prisoners.

On the 15th, pursuant to orders, the division marched at 6 a. m., and encamped within 4 miles of Harper's Ferry at 4 p. m., and, resuming the march early on the following morning, encamped in Pleasant Valley shortly after 7 a. m.

The command had marched since leaving Gettysburg up to this point 101 miles, during which time they suffered much from the excessive heat of the weather.

Remaining on the 17th and 18th in camp at Pleasant Valley, enabled the troops to receive much-needed supplies of clothing and to recruit their energies.

On the 19th, at 5 a. m., marched through Harper's Ferry, crossing the Potomac and Shenandoah Rivers on pontoon bridges, and passed up Piney Run Valley to near Hillsborough.

On the 20th, started at 6 a. m., and marched through Woodgrove to Snickersville, where we remained during the 21st and 22d, in conjunction with the First Division, to guard against any attempt of the enemy to force Snicker's Gap.

On the 23d, marched at 5 a. m. to Paris. The Second Brigade (Colonel Cobham) was ordered into Ashby's Gap, to guard it, relieving a brigade of the Second Corps.

At 4 p. m. the entire command was ordered to resume the march, and, taking the mountain road, passed through Scuffletown to near Markham Station, where we encountered the trains of the Second Corps. The day's march was 23 miles.

At 3 a. m. on the 24th, marched through Markham to Linden, which was reached at 8 a. m. Had marched 30 miles in the preceding twenty-seven hours. The command remained under arms until noon, when the march was resumed. We repassed Markham, and encamped at Piedmont, after a day's march of 22 miles.

On the 25th, marched at 4 a. m. through Rectortown and White Plains to Thoroughfare Gap, 16 miles. ·The roads were found in very bad condition and the weather was oppressively warm.

On the 26th, marched at daylight by way of Greenwich and Catlett's Station to near Warrenton Junction, 22 miles, and encamped. We remained at this point until the 31st, refitting the command.

Since leaving Pleasant Valley we marched 103 miles, making a total of 204 miles from Gettysburg.

I have the honor, to be, colonel, very respectfully, your obedient servant,

JNO. W. GEARY,
Brig. Gen. U. S. Volunteers, Comdg. Division.

Lieut. Col. H. C. RODGERS,
Assistant Adjutant-General, Twelfth Army Corps.

No. 294.

Reports of Col. Charles Candy, Sixty-sixth Ohio Infantry, commanding First Brigade.

HDQRS. FIRST BRIG., SECOND DIV., TWELFTH CORPS,
Camp at Littlestown, Pa., July 6, 1863.

CAPTAIN: In compliance to circular dated headquarters Second Division, Twelfth Army Corps, near Littlestown, Pa., July 6, 1863, calling for an official report of the part taken by the several brigades of the division in the recent operations, I have the honor to submit the following report of the part taken by the First Brigade:

June 28.—Left camp near Knoxville, Md., at 5 a. m.; marched to near Frederick City, Md., distance 14 miles, and arrived in camp about 3 p. m. Sunday.

June 29.—Left camp at 4.30 a. m.; marched to near Bruceville, Md., distance 22 miles, and arrived in camp at 7 p. m. same day.

June 30.—Left camp at 6.30 a. m.; marched to near Littlestown, Pa. On the arrival of this division (Second) at Littlestown, this brigade was ordered to take a position in the woods on the right of the town (Littlestown), in the direction of Hanover, and on the right of the road, and hold it at all hazards. The cavalry skirmishing with the enemy in the front, I immediately moved with the brigade to the point designated, formed in column by two battalion front, threw forward skirmishers, and picketed to my front and right. Remained over night.

On the morning of July 1, received orders to join the division, and proceeded with the other brigades in the direction of Two Taverns. Arrived at the Two Taverns; remained there for an hour or two, and marched in the direction of Gettysburg, Pa. Arrived in the vicinity of the latter place, and ordered to form line in the rear of the Third Brigade, and then double column on the center. Moved to the front and left of the hills surrounding Gettysburg, and halted for the night, the command bivouacking. Near about dark was ordered to throw forward two regiments to the left, and occupy a high range of hills overlooking the surrounding country, and watch for any attempted advance of the enemy on the left of the army. This order was executed, and the Fifth Ohio and One hundred and forty-seventh Pennsylvania Volunteers occupied the above position during the night of July 1.

On the morning of the 2d, the brigade was ordered to the front and to take position with the rest of the Second Division on the left of the First Division, Twelfth Corps, and right of the First Corps. The brigade took position on the right of the Third Brigade, Second Division, Twelfth Army Corps.

After taking position, it was ordered to form line in rear of the Third Brigade, and double column on the center. A regiment of this brigade, the Twenty-eighth Pennsylvania Volunteers, was ordered to the front as a support to the skirmishers of the Third Brigade, under the command of Lieut. Col. O. J. Crane, Seventh Ohio Volunteers, he having been assigned to this duty.

The brigade remained in this position until about 7 p. m. the 2d instant, when the brigade was ordered to the right, for the purpose of supporting a corps, supposed to be General Hancock's. Arrived on the east bank of Rock Creek, and halted, with instructions to picket well the banks (east) of the creek and hold the position.

Remained in position until about 12 p. m.; ordered up to the former position on the right of the First Corps, and for the purpose of supporting the Third Brigade, Second Division, Twelfth Army Corps, which had been engaged, and to retake the intrenchments lately occupied by the First Division, Twelfth Army Corps, but then occupied by the enemy. Received instructions from General Geary, commanding Second Division, to form a line in rear of the right of the Third Brigade, and a line also perpendicular to the pike leading to Gettysburg and to the enemy in the First Division intrenchments. This was promptly executed.

Remained in the latter position until 3.45 a. m. [July 3], when the enemy were opened upon by a battery placed for the purpose of shelling them.

After several rounds, the One hundred and forty-seventh Pennsylvania Volunteers were ordered forward, and occupied a stone fence in front of the enemy, and by their fire caused considerable casualties and havoc among them (the enemy). The remainder of the brigade, consisting of the Fifth, Seventh, and Sixty-sixth Ohio and Twenty-eighth Pennsylvania Volunteers, was posted in rear of the Third Brigade for its support. The Fifth Ohio Volunteers, being on the extreme right of my line, were exposed to a harassing and heavy enfilading fire from the enemy. They returned it promptly, and held their position for seven hours, causing great execution and punishing the enemy severely. The remainder of the regiments were engaged in relieving the regiments of the Second and Third Brigades in the trenches.

The Sixty-sixth Ohio Volunteers were ordered to advance outside of the intrenchments and perpendicular to them, and harass the enemy by an enfilading fire in front of the intrenchments. This order was promptly and gallantly executed. This regiment was considerably annoyed by the enemy's sharpshooters, but they held their ground until recalled about 11 a. m., causing considerable execution among the enemy.

The officers and men of the regiments composing this brigade sustained their usual gallantry and bravery in front of the enemy. Subjected to repeated charges on their works, they held their ground under a galling fire for over seven hours, cheerfully obeying every order with promptness and punctuality.

About 9.30 p. m., when about to be relieved by the Third Brigade, the enemy opened a heavy fire, which was silenced in a few moments. The remainder of the night passed off quietly, excepting occasional shots from sharpshooters.

On the morning of the 4th, at daybreak, it was found that the enemy had left our front, leaving their dead and quite a number of their wounded in our possession, also in the neighborhood of 1,500 stand of arms, mostly Enfield rifles. The Seventh Ohio Volunteers captured a State flag of Virginia belonging to the Fourteenth Regiment from that State, which was duly forwarded to your headquarters, as per existing orders.

During the day of the 4th, our men were engaged in burying our own dead, [the number of] which, I am happy to say, is small, considering the number left by the enemy. Owing to the scarcity of tools, few of the enemy's dead were buried until the morning of the 5th, when the pioneer corps of this brigade, assisted by a detail of over 100 men, buried quite a number. Marching orders for this point having been received July 5, the details were compelled to leave quite a number unburied.

Accompanying this report you will receive detailed reports from regimental commanders.

I cannot close this report without mentioning the members of my staff for their gallantry and bravery in conveying messages and orders to the trenches under the heavy fire to which the troops were exposed, viz, First Lieut. A. H. W. Creigh, One hundred and forty-seventh Pennsylvania Volunteers, acting assistant adjutant-general; Capt. W. M. Gwynne, Sixty-sixth Ohio Volunteers, acting assistant inspector-general; Lieut. C. W. Kellogg, Twenty-ninth Ohio Volunteers, and Lieut. J. W. Hitt, Sixty-sixth Ohio Volunteers, aides-de-camp.

I have the honor to be, captain, very respectfully, your obedient servant,

CHAS. CANDY,
Colonel Sixty-sixth Ohio Volunteers, Comdg. Brigade.

Capt. Thomas H. Elliott,
Asst. Adjt. Gen., Second Div., Twelfth Army Corps.

——, —— —, 1863.

Sir : In compliance with circular from headquarters Army of the Potomac, dated August 12, 1863, I have the honor to continue the above report of the part taken by the brigade in the recent operations, to include July 26, the date of its arrival at Warrenton Junction, Va.

The above includes all operations to July 5.

July 5.—About 1 p. m. received marching orders. Left Gettysburg, and marched to Littlestown, Pa., distance 10 miles, and arrived in camp about 6 p. m. Sunday.

July 6.—Remained in camp at Littlestown, Pa.

July 7.—Left camp at 4.30 a. m. and marched to Walkersville, Md., distance 27 miles, and arrived in camp about 7 p. m. Tuesday.

July 8.—Left camp at 5 a. m. and marched to Frederick City. Arrived at 10 a. m.; halted for three hours, and moved on to Jefferson, Md.; distance that day, 17 miles. Arrived in camp at 5.30 p. m.

July 9.—Left camp at 5 a. m. and marched to near Rohrersville, Md.; distance, 7 miles. Arrived in camp about 11 a. m.

July 10.—Left camp at 4.30 a. m. and marched to Bakersville, Md.; distance, 7 miles. Arrived in camp at 11 a. m. and took up position in line.

July 11.—Left camp at 7 a. m. and marched to Fair Play, Md., distance 5 miles, and took position. By direction of General Geary, commanding division, threw forward the One hundred and forty-seventh Pennsylvania Volunteers, supported by the Twenty-ninth Ohio, to skirmish and picket the rising ground beyond Marsh Creek; succeeded in establishing a line of pickets, which was done without any molestation of note. Everything quiet during the night in front of the pickets above mentioned.

July 12.—Brigade moved forward and occupied the woods on the west side of Marsh Creek; remained over night.

July 13.—Moved position about three-fourths of a mile northeast, and took up position on the left of the First Division, Twelfth Corps, and threw up breastworks.

July 14.—Remained in camp.

July 15.—Left position, and took up line of march; marched to west side of Maryland Heights, and encamped. Marched 12 miles, and arrived in camp about 4 p. m.

July 16.—Left camp at 5 a. m. and marched to Sandy Hook, Md.; distance, 5 miles. Arrived in camp about 9 a. m.

July 17 and 18.—At Sandy Hook.

July 19.—Left camp at 5 a. m. and marched to Hillsborough, Va., crossing the Potomac and Shenandoah Rivers at Harper's Ferry. Arrived in camp about 4 p. m.; distance, 13 miles.

July 20.—Left camp at 6 a. m. and marched to Snickersville, Va. Arrived at 6 p. m.; distance, 13 miles.

July 21 and 22.—At Snickersville.

July 23.—Left camp at 5 a. m. and marched to Paris; halted for two hours; continued march to near Markham, and arrived at 8.30 p. m.; distance from Snickersville, 23 miles.

July 24.—Left camp at 4 a. m. and marched to Linden (summit of Manassas Gap); halted for three hours, and returned to near Piedmont. Arrived about 8 p. m.; distance, 18 miles.

July 25.—Left camp at 4 a. m. and marched to near Thoroughfare Gap. Arrived at 5 p. m.; distance, 14 miles.

July 26.—Left camp at 5 a. m. and marched to near Warrenton Junction. Arrived about 9 p. m.; distance, 23 miles.

I have the honor to be, captain, very respectfully, your obedient servant,

CHAS. CANDY,
Colonel Sixty-sixth Ohio Volunteers, Comdg. Brigade.

Capt. Thomas H. Elliott,
Asst. Adjt. Gen., Second Div., Twelfth Army Co·~ns.

No. 295.

Report of Col. John H. Patrick, Fifth Ohio Infantry.

Gettysburg Battl⁻-field,
July 4, 1863.

Lieutenant: In pursuance to orders from brigade headquarters, I have the honor to make the following report of the part taken by the Fifth Ohio Volunteers in the action near Gettysburg:

We commenced operations by an order to proceed to the extreme left of our line, and occupied a hill covered with trees. The One hundred and forty-seventh Pennsylvania Volunteers was also placed under my command, to extend and increase the front of our position. We deployed as skirmishers in our front across an open valley to a light strip of woods, and in front of that timber facing an open field, for the purpose of guarding against a flank movement of the enemy.

We remained there until the following morning, when we received orders at 5 o'clock to return to the brigade. We advanced to the right of our line; halted, formed double column closed *en masse,* stacked arms, and remained until evening, when we were ordered to a position on our right flank, for the purpose of holding the enemy in check, for they had advanced on our right. We remained there about two hours, when we were ordered to return and take position.

The men rested on their arms until daylight, when we were replaced, by an order from Col. Charles Candy, commanding brigade, farther forward, in order that we might have a better view of the enemy and be well protected from his fire. The first firing commenced about 3.50 a. m., and continued until 11 a. m. without intermission.

As the fight progressed and the forces took position, it became obvious to me that a line of skirmishers should be thrown forward on our flank and behind a stone wall, which would enable us to give the enemy a cross-fire. I immediately ordered Company F, of our regiment, in command of Lieutenant Brinkman (a brave and gallant officer, who fell during the action), to advance with his company as skirmishers, having the stone wall for a protection. I instructed him to fret the enemy as much as possible, for the purpose of drawing him from his intrenchments.

The result was most satisfactory, the skirmishers annoying the enemy so much that they were compelled to make a charge on our skirmishers, and either capture or drive them, neither of which was accomplished. As soon as they were fully uncovered, they received volley after volley, until they were forced to retire. The same effort was made a second time, and with the same result.

To the above strategy I attribute a large share of our success, for the rebels were driven back with terrific slaughter after the second repulse, and retreated from the breastworks. Very soon after this last repulse, we occupied the intrenchments. During the rest of that day and the night following, they annoyed us considerably with their sharpshooters. Some of them had air-rifles, and we could not discover their whereabouts. At night the flashes of the regular rifles can be seen, but there is no warning from the air-rifle. The enemy retreated from our front some time in the forepart of the night.

Respectfully submitted.

J. H. PATRICK,
Colonel Fifth Ohio.

Lieut. A. H. W. CREIGH,
A. A. A. G., First Brig., Second Div., Twelfth Corps.

No. 296.

Report of Col. William R. Creighton, Seventh Ohio Infantry.

HDQRS. SEVENTH REGT. OHIO VOLUNTEER INFANTRY,
July 6, 1863.

SIR: I have the honor to submit the following report of the part taken by the Seventh Regiment Ohio Volunteer Infantry in the engagement of July 2 and 3, near Gettysburg, Pa.:

On Thursday morning, July 2, we were encamped on the left side of the Gettysburg and Littlestown pike. At 6 a. m. we received marching orders, and at 6.30 moved out in line, changing our position to the right of the turnpike, forming our line of battle in the woods bordering on the hill at the right of the road. In obedience to your order, I sent forward Company H, under command of Capt. Samuel McLelland, to picket our front. They were posted along the stream which runs through the hollow at our left, and remained there until 6 p. m., when they rejoined my regiment. At this time the "fall in" was sounded, and my regiment, in company with the remainder of the brigade, moved by the right flank to the right and rear of the position which we had held during the former part of the day.

I formed my regiment in the open field in the rear of a stone wall at the left of and near the turnpike. At this place I allowed my men to sleep, having their arms and accouterments in perfect readiness to fall in at any moment. My regiment had not during any part of the day been exposed to the fire of musketry, but for some time in the afternoon we were exposed to quite a heavy fire of artillery, although not suffering any serious loss from it.

At 11.30 p. m. July 2, I was ordered to form my command. It was then moved under your directions out on to the pike, and advancing toward Gettysburg, but turned from the pike to our right at the same place which we had in the morning when first advancing. My line was formed in the hollow, at the right and rear of General Greene's brigade. At this place we received a volley of musketry from the enemy's guns, wounding 1 man from Company I. In a few moments we were ordered to move by the right flank back to the open field, forming our line in the rear of a stone wall which runs parallel with the road leading to the pike. In a few moments, by order of General Geary, I moved my command over the wall into the road, throwing out to the front 20 men, under charge of Sergeant [Isaac] Stratton, to act as skirmishers.   At this place Sergeant Stratton received a severe if not a mortal wound.

Soon after daylight on the morning of the 3d, in compliance with your order, I drew in my skirmishers, and in a few moments moved my regiment by the left flank back near the position which we had occupied the morning previous.   When in the edge of the woods, I formed my command in line of battle, and, in compliance with orders, I advanced forward double-quick, and relieved the Sixtieth New York Volunteers.

My regiment remained at the intrenchments until near 8 o'clock, when it was relieved by the Sixtieth New York Volunteers.   When relieved, I formed my regiment in the hollow at the rear of the breast-works, remaining until 9.30 a. m., when I was again ordered forward to relieve a regiment.   I was not again relieved until 9.30 p. m., having been under fire of musketry most of the day.

When relieved, I again formed my line in the hollow, and remained there until 1.30 a. m. on the morning of July 4, when my command was again ordered forward to the intrenchments, which position I held until the brigade moved out on the pike, preparatory to our return to Littlestown.

About 11 a. m. July 3, I observed a white flag thrown out from the rocks in front of our intrenchments.   I immediately ordered my men to cease firing, when 78 of the enemy advanced and surrendered, including 3 captains, 2 first lieutenants, and 2 second lieutenants. At the time the white flag was raised, a mounted rebel officer (Major Leigh, assistant adjutant-general to General Ewell [Edward Johnson]), was seen to come forward and endeavor to stop the surrender, when he was fired upon by my men and instantly killed.

Early in the morning of July 4, Corpl. John Pollock, Company H, of my regiment, advanced over the intrenchments, and captured the rebel flag belonging to the Fourteenth Virginia Regiment, which, in compliance with orders received, was delivered to your head-quarters.

I went into action with 265 enlisted men and came out with 247, losing 1 killed and 17 wounded,

In conclusion, I feel it my duty to mention the officers and men under my command, but when each and every one advanced forward to the contest without any exception whatever, I will merely say that every officer and man performed his duty manfully, every order being obeyed promptly.

Very respectfully, your obedient servant,

W. R. CREIGHTON,
Colonel Seventh Ohio.

Lieut. A. H. W. CREIGH,
A. A. A. G., First Brig., Second Div., Twelfth Corps.

No. 297.

Report of Capt. Wilbur F. Stevens, Twenty-ninth Ohio Infantry.

IN THE RIFLE-PITS, NEAR GETTYSBURG, PA.,
July 4, 1863.

SIR : In compliance with circular from headquarters First Brigade, Second Division, Twelfth Corps, I have the honor to forward the following report of the part taken by this regiment (Twenty-ninth Ohio Volunteer Infantry) in the action of July 2 and 3, near Gettysburg, Pa.:

On the morning of the 2d, at 5.30 a. m., we were ordered from our camp, in the wheat-field on the left of the road approaching Gettysburg, to the road, down which we moved with balance of the brigade to rear of the front of our line; from there we moved to the right of our line.

Shortly after, about 8 a. m., we moved to the left in the hollow in rear of the intrenchments occupied by our troops, where we formed in close column of divisions, doubled on the center, as a support to those of our forces in the intrenchments to our front, and remained there during the day until about 7.30 p. m., when we moved with the rest of our brigade to the right and rear to near the road leading to the pike. We then formed line of battle, and threw out pickets to our front, remaining there until about 2 o'clock on the morning of July 3, when we with our brigade were ordered back to our position in rear of the intrenchments on the right of our line, as a support to General Greene's brigade (Third Brigade, Second Division, Twelfth Corps), then in the intrenchments.

The firing commenced about 3.45 o'clock on the morning of the 3d instant. We remained as a support to the troops in our front until about 5.45 o'clock, and about fifteen minutes before receiving the order to move forward to the intrenchments, I was struck in the neck with a spent ball, causing very severe pain and giddiness, from which cause I turned the command of the regiment over to Capt. E. Hayes, of this regiment, having received permission of Col. Charles Candy, commanding brigade, to go to the rear. I returned to the regiment (it being then in the intrenchments) about 12 m. of the 3d instant, but not feeling able to resume command, Captain Hayes kept command until about 4.30 p. m. of the same day. Captain Hayes' report while he was in command is herewith inclosed.

I resumed command at 4.30 p. m. There was no heavy firing during the balance of the afternoon or evening until just as we were being relieved, when the enemy opened a heavy fire on our right, and moved forward with the intention of storming our position. My command immediately resumed their places in the intrenchments with the One hundred and thirty-seventh Regiment New York Volunteers, who had come forward to relieve us (time, 10 p. m.). We remained until the enemy were forced back, when I brought my command back to the rear in the hollow for rest and rations, as the men had had nothing to eat since the morning of July 2.

We remained here until 1 a. m. on the morning of July 4, when we were again ordered forward to relieve the One hundred and thirty-seventh New York Volunteers, then in the intrenchments, where we remained until the morning of July 5.

I would refer you to Captain Hayes' report for instances of bravery and good conduct, as he had command during the hardest of the action.

Both officers and men did their duty well.

I am, sir, very respectfully, your obedient servant,

WILBUR F. STEVENS,
Capt., Comdg. Twenty-ninth Regt. Ohio Vol. Infantry.

Lieut. A. H. W. CREIGH,
A. A. A. G., First Brig., Second Div., Twelfth Corps.

No. 298.

Report of Capt. Edward Hayes, Twenty-ninth Ohio Infantry.

IN THE RIFLE-PITS, NEAR GETTYSBURG, PA.,
July 4, 1863.

SIR: I have the honor to report the part taken by the Twenty-ninth Ohio Infantry during the brief space of time it was under my command in the action at Gettysburg, on July 3.

Captain Stevens turned over the command to me at 5.30 a. m. Shortly after this time I received from Colonel Candy, through Captain Gwynne, an order to move the regiment forward to the rifle-pits and relieve the One hundred and thirty-seventh New York Volunteers, Col. D. Ireland, then engaged.

As I did not know the exact position our regiment was to occupy, I did not feel justified in taking the regiment into action without first looking at the ground. I therefore crossed the ridge in front of our position, saw Colonel Ireland, and found and ascertained the position we were to occupy. Returned to my command, and, having briefly explained the work expected of us, gave the necessary orders.

The regiment moved over the ridge at a run without firing a shot until fairly in the trenches, when it opened a heavy fire upon the enemy, under cover of which Colonel Ireland was able to withdraw his regiment with but small loss. Shortly after entering the rifle-pits, Lieut. George Hayward received a ball in the neck, killing him instantly.

The regiment entered the pits at 5.45 a. m., and was under a heavy fire for two hours and ten minutes, being relieved by the Twenty-eighth Pennsylvania Volunteers, under command of Capt. John Flynn, who came forward in their usual gallant style. Under cover of their fire, I withdrew my command, and, assisted by Adjt. James B. Storer, formed again in the hollow in rear of our line of battle. This interval of rest was employed by the men in cleaning arms, &c.

At about 9.30 a. m. I received from Col. Charles Candy an order to get into line, ready, if necessary, to repel the enemy, who were pressing the troops near the meadow on the right of our position. They were, however, repelled at this point without our assistance. Shortly after this time, Captain Horton, adjutant-general of the Third Brigade, came to me with a request that I would take my regiment forward and relieve the troops in the pits in front of us, as they were being hard pressed and were getting short of ammunition. Ordinarily I should not have felt justified in moving without an order from the commander of our own brigade, but the men in front were falling back by twos and threes, and there did not seem to be any time to lose. Besides, I had been informed by Lieutenant Hitt, of Colonel Candy's staff, that we would soon be ordered forward. The regiment responded to the order in the most splendid manner, cheering as they charged; but, rapid as was the movement, it was not effected without severe loss. Lieut. John G. Marsh fell, mortally wounded, and just two-thirds of the loss sustained by the regiment in the whole action occurred while crossing the ridge at this time.

The regiment went into action the second time at 9.55 a. m. The firing was heavy on both sides until about 11 a. m., when the enemy withdrew from our front, some 5 of their men showing a flag of truce and coming in as prisoners.

Excepting an occasional shot from the enemy's sharpshooters, there was very little fighting from this time until 1 p. m., when the enemy again showed themselves in some force, and the fight was pretty general until nearly 3 p. m., when it again slackened. At 4.30 p. m. I turned the command over to Captain Stevens.

You request me to mention any instance of bravery and good conduct that came under my notice. It is hardly possible to do so where all were alike brave. I was frequently along the line during the action, and I know that every man did his duty. Every order was promptly obeyed, and I cannot close my report without mentioning Captains Schoonover, Wright, Baldwin, and Lieutenants Hulbert, Dice, Wilson, Woodbury, Storer, Russell, Grant, Crane, Fulkerson, and Nash. They all did well, and obeyed every order promptly that was given. Lieut. and Adjt. James B. Storer rendered me important assistance in maneuvering the regiment.

In Lieutenants Hayward and Marsh the regiment loses two valuable officers. Prompt, cool, brave, and efficient, their loss will long be regretted by the officers and men with whom they were associated.

For an account of the other casualties in the regiment, I respectfully refer you to the accompanying official list.*

I am, sir, very respectfully, your obedient servant,

EDWARD HAYES,
Captain, Comdg. Twenty-ninth Ohio Volunteer Infantry.

Lieut. A. H. W. CREIGH,
A. A. A. G., First Brig., Second. Div., Twelfth Corps.

No. 299.

Report of Lieut. Col. Eugene Powell, Sixty-sixth Ohio Infantry.

BATTLE-FIELD, *Gettysburg, Pa., July* 4, 1863.

SIR: In compliance with circular dated headquarters First Brigade, Second Division, Twelfth Army Corps, of this date, I have the honor to submit the following report of the part taken by the Sixty-sixth Regiment Ohio Volunteer Infantry in the engagement on the 3d instant:

Early on the morning of July 3, under orders from Col. Charles Candy, commanding First Brigade, Second Division, Twelfth Army Corps, I crossed with my regiment to the intrenchments in front of the First Corps, for the purpose of giving the enemy an enfilading fire. With my left resting on the intrenchments and the right down the hill, we poured in a murderous fire on the enemy's flank. After a short time I found that the enemy had posted sharpshooters at the foot of the hill, behind a fence, who were annoying us very much. I ordered my regiment to take up a sheltered position behind trees and stones, and direct their fire on the sharpshooters, whom we soon dislodged. I then received orders to recross the intrenchments and relieve the One hundred and fiftieth New York Regiment, where we remained until relieved at 9 p. m.

The officers and men all behaved well while under fire, and sustained the reputation won on former fields.

It also becomes my painful duty of reporting to you that Maj. J. G. Palmer fell, mortally wounded, while cheering on the men in our advance across the intrenchments.

----

* Embodied in revised statement. p. 185.

The regiment lost 3 commissioned officers wounded, 14 enlisted men wounded, and 1 killed.

I have the honor to be, colonel, very respectfully, your obedient servant.

E. POWELL,
Lieut. Col. Sixty-sixth Regt. Ohio Vols., Comdg. Regt.

Lieut. A. H. W. CREIGH,
A. A. A. G., First Brig., Second Div., Twelfth Corps.

No. 300.

Report of Capt. John Flynn, Twenty-eighth Pennsylvania Infantry.

GETTYSBURG, PA., *July* 4, 1863.

LIEUTENANT: I have the honor to submit the following report of the part taken by the Twenty-eighth Regiment Pennsylvania Volunteers in the action of July 2 and 3, near Gettysburg, Pa.:

Agreeably to orders received from brigade headquarters, on the morning of the 2d, the regiment was thrown to the front along the stream near the right of the line of battle, and remained in that position during the day, supporting the line of skirmishers of General Greene's brigade. Some skirmishing with the enemy, in which 3 men were lost to the command.

Retired at dark with the brigade, and formed line about 1 mile in the rear.

Remained in that position until 12.30 a. m. July 3, when the regiment moved forward to retake the position left the morning before. Took position in the breastworks, relieving the Twenty-ninth Ohio Volunteers. Were under heavy fire while there, and lost during the engagement 3 killed and 22 wounded and missing.

Were relieved, and rested in rear of the brigade until nearly 4 p. m., when we were again ordered into the breastworks, and remained there until 10 p. m.

Again relieved, and again ordered at 2 a. m. to relieve the Sixtieth and Seventy-eighth New York Volunteers, still remaining there.

I take pleasure in stating that officers and men, without exceptions, exhibited the greatest coolness and bravery, and I would consider it injustice to the command did I attempt to single out individual cases of bravery, as all performed well their part.

I remain, very respectfully, your obedient servant,

JOHN FLYNN,
Capt., Comdg. Twenty-eighth Regt. Pennsylvania Vols.

Lieut. A. H. W. CREIGH,
A. A. A. G., First Brig., Second Div., Twelfth Corps.

No. 301.

Report of Lieut. Col. Ario Pardee, jr., One hundred and forty-seventh Pennsylvania Infantry.

NEAR GETTYSBURG, PA., *July* 4, 1863.

SIR: In compliance with circular of this day, I have the honor to submit the following report of the part taken by the One hundred and Forty-seventh Regiment Pennsylvania Volunteers in the actions of July 2 and 3:

My regiment was relieved from picket duty early on the morning of the 2d, and marched with the brigade to the position on the right of the line occupied by the First Army Corps. In this position we remained until evening, when we marched with the brigade to a position near and east of the turnpike leading from Gettysburg to Baltimore.

On the morning of the 3d, we marched to a point near the line of the previous day and toward the right of the line of the brigade, having on our right the Seventh Regiment Ohio Volunteers and on our left the Fifth Regiment Ohio Volunteers. Soon after the line was formed, I was ordered by General Geary, commanding division, to move forward with my regiment to a point which commanded the right of the line of intrenchments, and from which a view could be had of the movements of the enemy. My regiment, soon after reaching its assigned position, became engaged with the skirmishers of the enemy, who were soon driven from their position. Skirmishers were sent to the front and right flank, into the woods, from which they greatly harassed the enemy.

At about 8 a. m. an attempt was made by the enemy to turn the right of the line of the intrenchments. They boldly advanced to within about 100 yards without discovering my regiment. I then ordered the regiment to fire, and broke their line. They reformed again as a body and advanced. Their advance was checked by the heavy fire they received, when they broke and ran. I would have charged them, but had no support, and would not have been able to have held their position against the column in their rear.

I have the honor to report that I held the position assigned me until late in the afternoon, when I was ordered to report to General Wadsworth, of the First Corps.

My loss has been, I am happy to say, slight, when my exposed position is taken into consideration. The casualties are, 1 commissioned officer (Lieut. William H. Tourison, Company E) killed, 4 enlisted men killed, and 16 wounded. A list of the casualties has already been furnished you.

I am, sir, very respectfully,

ARIO PARDEE, JR.,
Lieut. Col. 147th Regt. Pennsylvania Vols., Comdg.
Lieut. A. H. W. CREIGH, *Actg. Asst. Adjt. Gen.*

No. 302.

Report of Brig. Gen. Thomas L. Kane, U. S. Army, commanding Second Brigade.

HDQRS. SECOND BRIG., SECOND DIV., TWELFTH CORPS,
Near Littlestown, Pa., July 6, 1863.

CAPTAIN: I respectfully inclose two of the special reports ordered of the commanders of regiments of my brigade. The report of the One hundred and eleventh Regiment Pennsylvania Volunteers has not yet been received.

I assumed command at 6 a. m. on the morning of the 2d instant, communication with the army having been cut off so completely by

Stuart's cavalry that I succeeded with great difficulty in making my way through their lines in citizen's dress.

I have to express my thanks to Colonel Cobham, One hundred and eleventh Pennsylvania Volunteers, who commanded the brigade in my absence, for the high state of efficiency in which I found it. I have recommended this most deserving officer for promotion.

The brigade was ordered forward into line with the rest of the division soon after my arrival, and before sundown threw up a substantial breastwork, as directed, upon the excellent position assigned them.

At twilight we were removed to the batteries on the turnpike, and shortly after ordered to return to our former position. On entering the wood, within 200 paces of our breastwork, we were met by a sharp fire, which we supposed to come from the First Brigade, misled by the darkness. The men were, therefore, ordered not to reply, but withdrawn to the turnpike and marched in by another road. We moved directly to the position of the Third Brigade (where the noble veteran Greene, by his resistance against overwhelming odds, it should be remembered, saved the army), and, making our way past Greene's right, were again fired upon, thus discovering that the enemy had entire possession of our works. Their front was then opposite Greene's right flank, he holding them there. There was nothing to be done but to connect with Greene, fold down to the right along the best ground offering, and strengthen the right flank as much as possible.

The attack in force upon us commenced at 3.30 a. m., July 3. The Confederate Major-General Johnson's division led, followed by Rodes'. The statement by our prisoners is that they advanced in three lines, but they appeared to us only as closed in mass. We ceased firing occasionally for a minute or two, to induce the enemy to come out of advantageous positions, when they paid for their temerity; but with this exception kept up a fire of unintermitting strength for seven hours, until about 10.30 o'clock, when the enemy made their last determined effort by charging in column of regiments. Their advance was Steuart's brigade, of Johnson's division. The First Maryland Battalion (Confederate States) left most of their dead in line with our own. It cannot be denied that they behaved courageously. Our own loss was but 23 killed and 73 wounded. Twenty men have been missing since we were fired on in the woods on Thursday night.

After this repulse the enemy fell back, and, although they kept up a desultory fire for some time after, it was plain, as the result proved, that the battle was over.

By the accompanying report of Lieut. W. H. White,* Company G, Twenty-ninth Pennsylvania Volunteers, you will see that the number of Enfield rifles left by the enemy, on an area of about two acres in front of our second position, was 1,803. The reports of burying parties will probably show that not less than 500 men were left dead there. The whole number of men of my brigade who were in this action was 652. They justified their reputation as marksmen.

I have not the name of a single straggler or recreant reported to me. Every officer and man of my command did his duty, and I must on this account refuse myself the privilege of naming particularly any of the numerous examples of heroism which I witnessed.

---

* Omitted.

I should acknowledge the valuable services of Lieuts. Thomas J. Leiper and J. Spencer Smith, of my staff. In the absence of Capt. J. P. Green, assistant adjutant-general, Lieutenant Leiper served as acting assistant adjutant-general with unvarying ability.

The few of our killed were unhappily among our best men. Second Lieut. Edward J. Harvey, Company K, Twenty-ninth Pennsylvania Volunteers, was a man of fine mind and elevated character; Lieutenant McKeever, Company A, Twenty-ninth Pennsylvania Volunteers, an ardent patriot and faithful officer; Sergeant-Major [Charles H.] Letford, Twenty-ninth Pennsylvania Volunteers, a youth of the fairest promise; Color-Sergt. John E. Greenwood, One hundred and ninth, Sergts. E. F. Allen, One hundred and eleventh, and Anthony E. Thomas, Edward N. Sommerkamp, and Jacob Lower, Twenty-ninth; Corporal [William] Louder, Twenty-ninth, and Privates [John] Sheemer, [Orlando S.] Campbell, [Charles] Miller, [John M.] Richardson, One hundred and eleventh; [Casper H.] Warner, [Thomas] Acton, [Robert] Hews, [Robert] Lockhart, [John] Applegate, [John] Watson, [Emanuel] McLaughlin, [James] Morrow, Twenty-ninth, and [Thomas C.] Ochs and [De Lany S.] Veale, One hundred and ninth, were all patriotic and brave men, whose loss is seriously to be deplored. Young Veale, often noticed for his singularly handsome and bright countenance, was adjutant's clerk of his regiment, but insisted on going into action with his rifle.

Very respectfully, your obedient servant,

THOMAS L. KANE,
Brigadier-General U. S. Volunteers.

Capt. Thomas H. Elliott,
Assistant Adjutant-General.

No. 303.

Report of Col. George A. Cobham, jr., One hundred and eleventh Pennsylvania Infantry, commanding Second Brigade.

Hdqrs. Second Brig., Second Div., Twelfth Corps,
Near Ellis' Ford, Va., August 15, 1863.

Captain: In compliance with circular order from headquarters Army of the Potomac, August 12, 1863, I have the honor to submit the following report of the movements of this brigade from June 28 to July 26:

At 4 o'clock on the morning of June 29, the brigade broke camp about 1 mile from Frederick City, Md., marching through Frederick, Walkersville, Woodsborough, Pipeville, and Bruceville, and encamped for the night, having marched 20 miles.

On the 30th, marched to Littlestown, Pa., 15 miles.

July 1, marched by the Baltimore turnpike to Two Taverns, and from there to within about 2 miles from Gettysburg, when the brigade was placed in position, by direction of Brigadier-General Geary, commanding division, on the crest of a hill overlooking part of the battle-field, and in support of a battery stationed on the hill. Here the troops lay on their arms during the night.

About 6 o'clock on the morning of July 2, Brigadier-General Kane arrived on the field in an ambulance of the Second Army Corps, and assumed command of the brigade. I then took command of my own regiment, the One hundred and eleventh Pennsylvania Volunteers, but in a few minutes General Kane sent me an order by one of his aides (Lieutenant Leiper) to resume the command of the brigade. I reported to the general, when he repeated the order to me. I accordingly turned over the command of my regiment to Lieutenant-Colonel Walker, and resumed the command, General Kane being too much prostrated to continue it. However, he gallantly remained on the field, although too feeble to resume the arduous duties of his post.

Orders were then received to move forward into line with the rest of the division. An excellent position was chosen for us by General Geary, connecting on the left with the Third Brigade, on a heavy wooded hill, where we threw up a breastwork of logs, stone, and earth, running at right angles to those of the Third Brigade. The position was a strong one, and admirably located to command the approaches by Rock Creek.

Here we remained till evening, when we were ordered to the support of the Third Corps; but before marching a mile this order was countermanded, and I was directed to return to our former position. On the head of the column entering the woods, they were fired upon from behind a stone wall in the rear of our breastworks, which the enemy had taken possession of during our absence. Not being certain whether the fire came from the enemy or our own division (it being dark), I withdrew the brigade to the pike, and marched farther up the road, and, entering the woods in the rear of the Third Brigade, took a position in line nearly at a right angle with our breastworks, sheltered in a great part of the line by a ledge of rocks, and connecting on the left with the Third Brigade, thus partially enfilading the enemy's position. The One hundred and forty-seventh Pennsylvania Volunteers, of the First Brigade, which arrived soon after, took position on our right, which position they resolutely held during the heavy attack next morning.

At 3 o'clock next morning, July 3, the enemy's skirmishers commenced firing on us, and by 4 o'clock the firing had become general along the whole line on both sides. The regiments of the brigade relieved one another, one at a time, long enough to replenish their supply of ammunition and wipe out their rifles. The firing was kept up briskly on both sides with but little intermission till about 10 a. m., when a desperate charge was made on our lines. The enemy advanced in column closed in mass, determined to make one last desperate effort to drive us back at the point of the bayonet. They were, however, driven back with heavy loss, and retired in confusion, retiring beyond the line of breastworks. The brigade was now relieved for a short time by a brigade of the Sixth Army Corps.

About 2 p. m. the brigade again took possession of the breastworks, relieving the other brigade (Shaler's). Occasional firing was kept up during the night, and by daylight the enemy withdrew from the front of our lines.

The Twenty-ninth, One hundred and ninth, and One hundred and eleventh Regiments Pennsylvania Volunteers are deserving of much praise for their courage and good conduct during the severe fire to which they were exposed. Colonel Rickards, Twenty-ninth Pennsylvania Volunteers, Lieutenant-Colonel Walker, One hundred and eleventh Pennsylvania Volunteers, and Captain Gimber, One hundred and ninth, who commanded the regiment, also deserve special mention for their gallant conduct on this occasion.

Our loss was 23 killed, 66 wounded, and 9 missing.

On the 4th, the brigade remained on the battle-field; burial parties were sent out with every available pick and shovel to bury the dead. Our own, as well as a large number of the enemy, were buried, but a very large number of the rebel dead were left unburied on the field.

On the 5th, left the battle-field, and marched to Littlestown, 10 miles.

July 7.—Left camp, and, marching through Bruceville, Pipeville, Woodsborough, and Walkersville, encamped for the night; distance, 26 miles.

July 8.—Started at 4.30 a. m.; marched through Frederick and Jefferson; distance, 18 miles.

July 9.—Broke camp at 5 a. m.; marched to Burkittsville; crossed the Blue Ridge at Crampton's Gap; encamped at Rohrersville; distance, 9 miles.

July 10.—Started at 5 a. m.; marched through Keedysville, and took up position in line on the right of the First Brigade, near the edge of a piece of woods.

July 11.—Advanced about 3½ miles; took position on the left of the line of battle; threw out skirmishers in front and on the left flank.

July 12.—Changed position about 1 mile to the right.

July 13.—About 1 a. m. again changed position half a mile to the right, on a rise of ground near Saint James' College and Marsh Run. Here an excellent and substantial breastwork of rails and earth was constructed under the personal direction and supervision of the general commanding the division.

July 14.—The brigade remained in the intrenchments ready to support the troops that advanced on the enemy's position at 5 a. m. of this day.

July 15.—Left intrenchments about 7 a. m.; marched through Sharpsburg and past Antietam Iron Works, and encamped near the foot of Maryland Heights, having marched 17 miles.

July 16.—Left camp at 5 a. m. and marched by way of Harper's Ferry to Pleasant Valley, where we encamped, and remained until the 19th, to obtain necessary clothing and equipage for the troops; distance, 9 miles.

July 19.—Broke camp at 4 a. m.; crossed the Potomac and Shenandoah at Harper's Ferry, and marched up Loudoun Valley to near Hillsborough, Va.; distance, 15 miles.

July 20.—Left at 4.30 a. m.; marched through Woodgrove, and Slabtown, and encamped near Snicker's Gap, remaining until the 23d; distance, about 10 miles.

July 23.—Broke camp at 5 a. m., marching through Snickersville to Upperville and Paris, relieving a brigade of the Second Army Corps stationed in Ashby's Gap; left at 3.30 p. m., and, marching through Milltown and Forestville, encamped for the night near Manassas Gap; distance marched, 23 miles.

July 24.—Marched through Manassas Gap to near Front Royal, and returned and encamped for the night near Piedmont; distance, 18 miles.

July 25.—Left camp at 5.30 a. m. and marched through White Plains to near Thoroughfare Gap, and encamped for the night; distance, 16 miles.

July 26.—Marched at 5 a. m. through Thoroughfare Gap, Hay

Market, Greenwich, and Catlett's Station, and encamped near War-renton Junction; distance, 22 miles.

The distance marched from June 28 to July 26 was 250½ miles.

Very respectfully, your obedient servant,

GEO. A. COBHAM, JR.,
Colonel, Commanding Second Brigade.

Capt. THOMAS H. ELLIOTT,
A. A. G., Second Division, Twelfth Army Corps.

No. 304.

Report of Col. William Rickards, jr., Twenty-ninth Pennsylvania Infantry.

ON THE FIELD, NEAR GETTYSBURG, PA.,
July 4, 1863.

GENERAL: For the information of the general commanding, I respectfully submit the following report of the part taken by my regiment in the action of July 1, 2, and 3:

On the afternoon of July 1, we arrived within 3 miles of Gettysburg, having left Littlestown at 7 a. m. Formed line of battle on the left of the pike and lay on our arms all night.

On the 2d, at 9 a. m., moved to a hill about three-quarters of a mile in advance, and from thence we advanced and crossed the pike, and took position in the woods at the head of a ravine, which spreads into a wide plateau on Rock Creek. We commenced to fortify our position, and had nearly finished, when we were, at 7 p. m., ordered by General Geary to leave our breastworks and move rapidly to the rear, with, as I suppose, the intention of re-enforcing some point on the left of our lines. Having forded the creek and moved about 1½ miles to the rear on the pike, we were halted, and ordered to return to our former position.

We moved back on the pike, turned to the right, the Twenty-ninth Pennsylvania Volunteers in advance, and as we were about to enter the woods in which our breastworks were, it being dark, we were fired on by a heavy force from behind a stone wall, at a distance of 25 paces, killing Lieutenant Harvey, Company K, and 3 men, and wounding 10 men.

Believing we had been fired on by the men of the Third Brigade in mistake, I gave the order for my men not to fire, and, gathering up our dead and wounded, about-faced the regiment, and marched back about 100 yards; halted the regiment, and then rode back to the wall, and called to those behind it, telling them who I was, and was answered by a heavy discharge of musketry. I returned to my regiment, and found an order directing me to march my regiment to the pike, where I found the other two regiments of the brigade. The brigade then moved to the left of our old position, and entered the woods in rear of General Greene's brigade, and moved near our position, when we learned to a certainty that the firing on us came from the enemy.

Being ordered by General Kane to send out a company of skirmishers, I sent Company B, Captain Johnson, to ascertain the position of the enemy. The captain and 5 men were captured, having, as I learned from those who returned, passed through the enemy's lines and been surrounded. The enemy then fired on us from the breastworks on our right, having taken possession of them in our absence. We then formed line of battle at right angles with our breastworks, and lay on our arms all night, with occasional firing from the enemy, wounding 1 man of Company K.

At 3 a. m. of the 3d, having observed objects moving in front, Colonel Cobham, Lieutenant-Colonel Zulick, and I met in rear of the center of the brigade to consult, when they opened fire on us, extending entirely across our front, showing them to be in strong force. The fire was returned with spirit by our brigade, and the enemy soon ceased firing, having retreated a short distance behind the crest of the hill. We were then ordered to move back about 50 paces, behind a ledge of rocks.

At 3.30 a. m. the enemy again opened on us from behind trees and rocks and the breastworks on our front, and the fight became general. My regiment, having fired their 60 rounds of ammunition, was relieved by the One hundred and eleventh Pennsylvania Volunteers, and moved to the field to replenish. After an absence of forty-five minutes, I returned, relieved the One hundred and eleventh Pennsylvania Volunteers, and continued the fight.

About 10.30 a. m. the enemy advanced to charge us, Steuart's brigade leading. Our men stood to their ground well, firing with great rapidity and execution. When within 70 paces, their column began to waver, and soon after broke and ran from reach of our fire, leaving a large number of their dead and wounded on the field. The fight was, however, still continued from behind the rocks and trees by the enemy, and our last supply of ammunition having been expended, we were relieved by the First Maryland, Colonel Maulsby, at 11 a. m.

The fight had been kept up for seven and three-quarter hours without cessation, during which time the Twenty-ninth Pennsylvania Volunteers was absent forty-five minutes to replenish their ammunition.

My men and officers behaved with great spirit and bravery.

The loss of the Twenty-ninth is, as far as known, 70, viz: Captain Johnson, Company B, and 10 men, prisoners; Lieutenant Harvey, Company K, and Lieutenant McKeever, Company A; Sergt. Maj. Charles H. Letford (son of the adjutant), 3 sergeants, 1 corporal, and 8 privates killed, and 45 enlisted men wounded.*

We returned to our breastworks at 3 o'clock in the afternoon, and occupied our old position, with considerable annoyance from the sharpshooters.

At 9.30 p. m. the enemy advanced on our lines in force, but they were received with such a heavy fire from our lines that they soon retired.

At daybreak on the 4th, a company of the Twenty-ninth was sent out as skirmishers, who soon ascertained that the enemy had left this side of Rock Creek.

By order of General Kane, I sent a company to assist in carrying off the arms left on the field by the enemy.

I heartily commend the officers and men of my command for their steadiness and bravery. I sincerely deplore the loss of many brave officers and men of my command.

---

*But see revised statement, p. 184.

The reports of the company officers will be sent in as soon as received.

I am, sir, with great respect, your very obedient servant,
WM. RICKARDS, JR.,
Colonel, Comdg. Twenty-ninth Pennsylvania Vols.

Brig. Gen. THOMAS L. KANE,
Comdg. Second Brig., Second Div., Twelfth Army Corps.

No. 305.

*Report of Capt. Frederick L. Gimber, One hundred and ninth
Pennsylvania Infantry.*

NEAR GETTYSBURG, PA.,
July 4, 1863.

SIR: I have the honor to submit the following report in reference
to the part taken by my regiment during the late engagement near
Gettysburg, Pa., on July 2 and 3 instant:

On the morning of the 2d, the regiment assisted in erecting breastworks in the woods 1 mile from Gettysburg, Pa., and took position
behind them, remaining there until evening, then changing our position with the brigade to a field along the Gettysburg pike half a mile
distant, being subjected to an artillery fire from the enemy.   Arriving here, we were immediately ordered back to our breastworks, and,
upon entering the woods, were suddenly fired upon, causing some
surprise and temporary confusion.   The fire was supposed to come
from our own troops, the darkness causing the mistake.   The regiment was quickly reformed, withdrawn, and taken by another route
near the position we previously occupied, viz, the breastworks.
Finding that during our brief absence the enemy had moved to the
right, occupying the breastworks, we moved our position to the open
ground between the stone fence and breastworks, our right resting
near the former.   We remained in this position all night, exchanging occasional shots with the enemy, our front being protected by a
line of skirmishers.

Toward morning we retired some 25 paces behind rocks, being an
admirable protection from the enemy's fire and at the same time a
very advantageous position to do execution.

At 4 o'clock on the morning of the 3d, the firing commenced im
mediately in our front, we occupying the right of the brigade.   From
occasional shots the firing soon became regular, being handsomely
replied to by us.   A constant fire of musketry was kept up.   We
assisted in successfully repelling a charge of the enemy, causing terrible slaughter, throwing them into confusion, and putting them to
flight.

At 10.30 a. m. we were relieved by a regiment of the First Division,
Sixth Corps, having been in action six consecutive hours.   We
merely retired to the rear some 300 yards.

We remained here until 2.30 p. m., when we were ordered again
to the woods to hold the fortifications—those that the enemy held in
the morning—our original position.   While here we were exposed to
an artillery fire with occasional musketry in our front, which lasted
at intervals during the night, ceasing as the morning dawned.

Both officers and men did their duty. Our conduct we prefer others to speak and judge of rather than ourselves.

Our loss was small, owing to our strong defensive position. Enlisted men killed, 3; wounded, 6, and missing, 10; total, 19.* Of those missing some have turned up, reducing the loss fully one-third.

Twice during the engagement our color-bearers were shot down, killing 1 instantly and wounding the other.

We took into action 142 enlisted men and 1 staff and 6 line officers, including myself; total, 149.

Very respectfully, your obedient servant,

FREDERICK L. GIMBER,
Capt., Comdg. One hundred and ninth Pennsylvania Vols.

Lieut. THOMAS J. LEIPER,
Acting Assistant Adjutant-General.

No. 306.

Report of Lieut. Col. Thomas M. Walker, One hundred and eleventh Pennsylvania Infantry.

LITTLESTOWN, PA., *July 6, 1863.*

SIR: I have the honor to report the part taken by the One hundred and eleventh Regiment Pennsylvania Volunteers in the action of July 3, on the heights before Gettysburg.

The regiment in connection with the brigade was moved into line of battle on the right of the Baltimore pike during the forenoon of the 2d instant, the One hundred and ninth Pennsylvania Volunteers on our left, and connections with the First Division on the right. We at once began building a rifle-pit of logs and stone, which was finished in about three hours.

We were undisturbed behind this, and remained until a little before dark, when we were ordered to move to the rear and abandon our works. After marching about a mile to the rear, we were again conducted up the Baltimore pike to occupy our old position. The Twenty-ninth Pennsylvania Volunteers, that preceded us, having been fired on from the position we were to occupy, we halted, and then moved with caution, endeavoring to get back to the trenches.

At about 11 o'clock, having got into the rear of General Greene's brigade, which still occupied their rifle-pits, I was ordered to place my men in the trenches, and proceeded to do so, under the supposition that there was no enemy in our vicinity. Two companies on the left, which were marching in front, had been placed in position, when we received a volley from the hill, not over 6 rods from our flank and rear. I immediately placed the remaining companies in line perpendicular to the works and facing the direction of the fire we had received, sent out scouts, and ascertained positively that the hill and works on the right were occupied by the rebels, and reported to Colonel Cobham. I was ordered again by Colonel Cobham to place my men in the rifle-pits, but, protesting that my regiment would then rest so as to be enfiladed by the line of the enemy, he permitted me to retain the position I had selected.

We remained in this position watching the enemy until 3 a. m.,

---

* But see revised statement, p. 184.

when it was determined the line should be changed a very little to the rear, so as to get the advantage of a wing of General Greene's trenches. I was endeavoring to move my regiment, a man at a time, with the utmost caution, when our watchful enemy detected a move, and, supposing we were about to retire, opened fire upon us. My men returned the fire, silencing theirs, and then moved to the position assigned them, awaiting daylight for the work to begin.

Picket firing began with the first streak of light, and about 3.45 o'clock the line of the enemy advanced with a yell. We opened fire briskly, quickly compelling them to take the shelter of the rocks and of our own trenches that were in their possession.

We continued fighting in this way until 5.55 o'clock, when we were relieved by the Twenty-ninth Regiment Pennsylvania Volunteers, for the purpose of renewing our ammunition. After filling our boxes and wiping our guns, we returned to the same position, and continued the fight until we had again exhausted our ammunition, and were in turn relieved by the Twenty-ninth Pennsylvania Volunteers. Soon after this, about 1 o'clock, the enemy retired, giving up the contest.

In this fight, about half of my regiment was in open line, fighting a desperate enemy behind the very rifle-pits they had built for their own protection. I am proud to say they fought feeling they were Pennsylvanians in Pennsylvania. We expended 160 rounds to the man.

I wish to mention as deserving praise for great bravery and coolness, Captains Woeltge, Thomas, and Warner; also that Sergeants [Henry] Dieffenbach, [George] Selkregg, [Andrew W.] Tracy, [Andrew J.] Bemis, [John L.] Wells, and [Mills F.] Allison, and Privates John Hughes and Orrin Sweet deserve mention.

We lost in this contest 5 men killed and 16 wounded, lists of which have been forwarded.

Most respectfully, your obedient servant,

THOS. M. WALKER,
Lieutenant-Colonel, Comdg. 111th Pennsylvania Volunteers.

Lieut. THOMAS J. LEIPER,
Acting Assistant Adjutant-General.

No. 307.

Reports of Brig. Gen. George S. Greene, U. S. Army, commanding Third Brigade.

HDQRS. THIRD BRIG., SECOND DIV., TWELFTH CORPS,
Camp near Fair Play, Md., July 12, 1863.

CAPTAIN: I have the honor to report to the general commanding the operations of the Third Brigade, Second Division, Twelfth Army Corps, under my command, on July 1, 2, and 3, at the battle of Gettysburg.

Arriving from Littlestown on the field of battle, we were posted with the division on the left, on the right of the division, about half a mile to the right of Sugar Loaf Mountain, in front of the Taneytown road. There were no incidents to note on this day.

On the 2d, we took position at about 6 a. m. on the right of the First Corps, on the crest of the steep and rocky hill, being thrown back nearly at right angles with the line of the First Corps, Rock Creek running past our front at the distance of 200 to 400 yards. Our position and the front were covered with a heavy growth of timber, free from undergrowth, with large ledges of rock projecting above the surface. These rocks and trees offered good cover for marksmen. The surface was very steep on our left, diminishing to a gentle slope on our right. The Second Brigade was on our right, thrown forward at a right angle to conform to the crest of the hill. On the right of this brigade was the First (Williams') Division, his right resting on an impassable mill-pond on Rock Creek. As soon as we were in position, we began to intrench ourselves and throw up breastworks of the covering height, of logs, cord-wood, stones, and earth. The same was done by the troops on my right.

By 12 o'clock we had a good cover for the men. The value of this defense was shown in our subsequent operations by our small loss compared with that of the enemy during the continuous attacks by a vastly superior force. Our skirmishers were thrown out immediately on taking position, and moved toward the creek in our front, when they came to the enemy's pickets.

We remained in this position, with occasional firing of the pickets, until 6.30 p. m., when the First (Williams') Division and the First and Second Brigades of the Second Division were ordered from my right, leaving the intrenchments of Kane's brigade and Williams' division unoccupied on the withdrawal of the troops.

I received orders to occupy the whole of the intrenchments previously occupied by the Twelfth Army Corps with my brigade. This movement was commenced, and the One hundred and thirty-seventh Regiment, on my right, was moved into the position occupied by Kane's (Second) brigade. Before any further movements could be made, we were attacked on the whole of our front by a large force a few minutes before 7 p. m. The enemy made four distinct charges between 7 and 9.30 p. m., which were effectually resisted.

About 8 p. m. the enemy appeared on our right flank, in the intrenchments (which were thrown back perpendicularly to Kane's line, occupied by Colonel Ireland with the One hundred and thirty-seventh Regiment New York Volunteers) from which Williams' division had been withdrawn, and attacked the right flank of the One hundred and thirty-seventh Regiment New York Volunteers. Colonel Ireland withdrew his right, throwing back his line perpendicular to the intrenchments in which he had been in position, and presenting his front to the enemy in their new position.

At this time the California Regiment, Colonel Smith, reported to assist me. He was ordered into position on the right of Ireland's regiment. They soon fell back and were withdrawn—the commanding officer saying that he had received orders from his commanding general to retire—leaving our right in a very critical position. As soon as the attack commenced, I sent to General Wadsworth, commanding the division of the First Corps on our left, and to General Howard, commanding the Eleventh Corps, posted on the left of the First Corps, for assistance, to which they promptly responded, by sending to my support the Sixth Wisconsin, Colonel Dawes; Fourteenth Brooklyn, Colonel Fowler; One hundred and forty-seventh New York, Major Banta* (in all about 355 men), from the First Corps, and the Eighty-second Illinois, Lieutenant-Colonel Salomon; Forty-fifth New York, Colonel Amsberg; Sixty-first Ohio, Colonel Mc-Groarty (in all about 400 men), from the Eleventh Corps. These

---

* Reference is probably to Major Harney.

regiments rendered good service, being sent into the trenches to relieve our regiments as their ammunition was exhausted and their muskets required cleaning. At the close of this night attack, we occupied all the trenches of the Third Brigade. Colonel Ireland had withdrawn his regiment from Kane's trenches, and formed a line with his left in our intrenchments, and in continuation of our line toward a stone wall, which was parallel to Kane's line and about 200 yards in its rear, behind which we found the enemy posted.

About 10 o'clock I was informed that General Kane, with his brigade, was returning to his position, and immediately sent a staff officer to advise him that the enemy were in his intrenchments, and to bring him round by the rear to my right. He had, however, already been fired on by the enemy on our right. General Kane soon arrived, and gallantly assisted us by placing his small, but very reliable, command on my right, securing that flank.

The First Brigade returned to our support at 1.30 a. m. on the 3d, and took position in support of our right. At 4 a. m. our artillery, which had been posted to attack the enemy in the intrenchments of Kane's brigade and Williams' division, opened, and the attack was general on our line, and continued until 10.30 a. m., when the enemy retired, their pickets remaining in our front until the night of the 4th, when they retired. The enemy were early in the day driven from our intrenchments on our right, which were occupied by Kane's brigade and Williams' division.

At 7.30 a. m. General Lockwood, with his brigade—First Maryland Home Brigade, Colonel Maulsby; First Eastern Shore, of Maryland, Colonel Wallace; One hundred and fiftieth New York, Colonel Ketcham, about 1,700 men—came to our support from Williams' division and rendered efficient service. The First Maryland Home Brigade and the One hundred and fiftieth New York were distinguished for their good conduct.

Colonel Creighton, of the First Brigade, with his regiment (Seventh Ohio), arrived to my immediate support at 6 a. m., and was at once sent into the trenches. The Twenty-ninth Ohio, Captain Hayes, of the First Brigade, arrived soon after, followed by the Fifth Ohio, Colonel Patrick, and Sixty-sixth Ohio, Lieutenant-Colonel Powell.

The troops from the First and Eleventh Corps were returned to their commands as soon as their place was supplied by Lockwood's and Candy's brigades, having rendered good service and efficient aid. The regiments in the intrenchments were relieved from thirty to ninety minutes by others with fresh ammunition and clean arms, going forward at a double-quick and with a cheer, the regiments relieved falling back through their files when they arrived in the trenches, so that the fire was kept up constantly and efficiently over our whole line, and the men were always comparatively fresh and their arms in good order, the regiments relieved going to work with alacrity to clean their arms as soon as in rear.

Our own regiments engaged were New York Volunteers, viz: Sixtieth, Col. Abel Godard; One hundred and second, Col. J. C. Lane (who was severely wounded on the night of the 2d instant while gallantly discharging his duty, and obliged to resign the command to Capt. L. R. Stegman); Seventy-eighth, Lieutenant-Colonel Hammerstein; One hundred and thirty-seventh, Col. David Ireland, and One hundred and forty-ninth, Col. H. A. Barnum. Colonel Barnum, who is still suffering from a severe wound received at Malvern Hill, with great resolution kept the field during the action, and part of the time in active command of his regiment. During most of the time the regiment was gallantly commanded by Lieutenant-Colonel Randall, who was severely wounded in the morning of the 3d.

The officers and men behaved admirably during the whole of the contest. Colonel Ireland was attacked on his flank and rear. He changed his position and maintained his ground with skill and gallantry, his regiment suffering very severely. Where all so well did their duty it is difficult to specially commend any individual, but all have my hearty commendations for their gallant conduct and for the good service rendered their country.

To my own staff—Capt. C. P. Horton, assistant adjutant-general; Capt. A. B. Shipman, who, though suffering from disease, was able to be on the field part of the time, and to my aides, Lieut. C. T. Greene, Sixtieth New York Volunteers, and Lieut. J. J. Cantine, One hundred and thirty-seventh New York Volunteers—my thanks are due for their gallantry and great activity during this contest as at all other times.

Our own force engaged at different times was—

My brigade 1,350
Sent from First Corps 355
Sent from Eleventh Corps 400
Part of Colonel Candy's brigade 1,000

Total 3,105

Not more than 1,300 men were in the lines at any one time.

The loss of the enemy greatly exceeds ours. We found of their dead in front of our lines 391, and there were across the creek a number of dead, estimated at 150, making a total of killed, 541. Of the 2,000 muskets picked up on our position and in front, 1,700 must have belonged to the enemy, showing clearly a loss of killed and wounded, in addition to those who may have carried their arms off the field, estimated at 500. My brigade took 130 prisoners, showing clearly a loss to the enemy of nearly 2,400 men in our front. The loss of the enemy in officers was heavy. Maj. B. W. Leigh, General Johnson's adjutant-general, was killed in our front, and papers indicating the troops engaged in our front found on him and forwarded to headquarters. The enemy's force was vastly superior to ours, and is reported to be Johnson's division, of Ewell's corps, which attacked us on the night of the 2d instant, and the same division re-enforced by Rodes' division on the 3d.

Officers and men.	Killed.	Wounded.	Missing.	Total.
Commissioned officers	6	10	1	17
Enlisted men	56	203	31	290
Total*	62	213	32	307

Herewith are presented the regimental reports of Colonel Ireland, One hundred and thirty-seventh New York; Colonel Barnum, One hundred and forty-ninth New York; Colonel Godard, Sixtieth New York; Lieutenant-Colonel Hammerstein, Seventy-eighth New York,

---

* But see revised statement, p. 185.

and Capt. L. R. Stegman, One hundred and second New York, officers who commanded the several regiments at the close of the action.

Very respectfully, your obedient servant,

GEO. S. GREENE,
Brig. Gen., Comdg. Third Brig., Second Div., Twelfth Corps.

Capt. THOMAS H. ELLIOTT,
Asst. Adjt. Gen., Second Division, Twelfth Army Corps.

—

HDQRS. THIRD BRIG., SECOND DIV., TWELFTH CORPS,
Near Ellis' Ford, Va., August 15, 1863.

SIR: In addition to the above, I have the honor to report to the commanding general, in conformity with circular from headquarters Army of the Potomac, dated August 12, 1863, requiring reports of the operations from June 28 until we arrived in the vicinity of Warrenton, that the Sixtieth, Seventy-eighth, One hundred and second, One hundred and thirty-seventh, and One hundred and forty-ninth Regiments New York Volunteers, composing my brigade, marched with the Second Division, as follows:

June 28.—Marched from Knoxville to Frederick, Md.; 11 miles.

June 29.—Marched to Big Pipe Creek; 21 miles.

June 30.—Marched to Littlestown, Pa.; 12 miles.

July 1.—Marched to Two Taverns, Pa.; 8 miles; thence to the left of the battle-field near Gettysburg; 5 miles.

July 2.—Marched to the right of the line of battle; 1½ miles.

July 5.—Marched to Littlestown, Pa.; 13 miles.

July 7.—Marched to Walkersville and through Frederick, Md.; 29 miles.

July 8.—Marched to Jefferson, Md.; 15 miles.

July 9.—Marched to Rohrersville, Md.; 11 miles.

July 10.—Marched to near Bakersville, Md.; 7 miles.

July 11.—Marched to Fair Play; 6 miles.

July 13.—Changed position to the right, to the left of the First Division of the Twelfth Corps, this brigade being the right of the Second Division; threw up intrenchments, covering our front and in continuation of the intrenchments in the other brigades of the division, and in position with the intrenchments of the First Division, on our right.

July 14.—Brigade remained in line of battle behind intrenchments, and worked on intrenchments while the troops on our right advanced to the front.

July 15, 5 *a. m.*—Marched toward Pleasant Valley, through Sharpsburg and Antietam Furnace. Bivouacked near Harper's Ferry, on northwest of Maryland Heights; 16 miles.

July 16.—Marched to Pleasant Valley; 3 miles.

July 17 *and* 18.—Remained in camp. Received supplies of clothing and provisions.

July 19.—Crossed the Potomac to Harper's Ferry on pontoon bridge, and the Shenandoah, and marched up Loudoun Valley; 9 miles.

July 20.—Marched to Snickersville; 11 miles.

July 21 *and* 22.—Remained in camp at Snickersville.

July 23.—Marched to Ashby's Gap, and thence to near Markham Station; 23 miles.

July 24.—Marched to Linden Station; thence to Markham and to Piedmont; 22 miles.

July 25.—Marched to Thoroughfare Gap; 16 miles.

July 26.—Marched to Warrenton Junction; 22 miles.

July 27 *to* 30.—Encamped at Warrenton Junction.

July 31.—Marched to Ellis' Ford, on the Rappahannock River; 26 miles.

The Sixtieth, Seventy-eighth, One hundred and second, and One hundred and forty-ninth New York Volunteers took position at Ellis' Ford, and the One hundred and thirty-seventh Regiment New York Volunteers took position at Kemper's Ford.

Most respectfully, your obedient servant,

GEO. S. GREENE,
Brig. Gen., Comdg. Third Brig., Second Div., Twelfth Corps.

Capt. THOMAS H. ELLIOTT,
Assistant Adjutant-General.

No. 308.

Report of Col. Abel Godard, Sixtieth New York Infantry.

NEAR GETTYSBURG, PA.,
July 4, 1863.

CAPTAIN: Herewith I have the honor to report that the situation and condition of the Sixtieth Regiment New York Volunteers, under my command at the battle of Gettysburg, Pa., July 2 and 3, were as follows, to wit:

On July 2, at or about 6 a. m., the regiment with the brigade assumed position in line of battle, connecting with the right of the First Army Corps, where my command threw up intrenchments, by order of General Greene, in person commanding Third Brigade. The men of the regiment worked with a will until about 9 a. m., by that time completing the intrenchments, which commanded on the left and center of the regiment the brow of a precipitous hill, and on the right extending to low ground. This line of intrenchments was about 1 mile from the enemy's front, as I estimated the distance. Our works connected on the right with those of the One hundred and second New York Volunteers, of our brigade.

From 9 a. m. to 4 p. m., or thereabouts, my men lay quietly behind our line of arms in the rear of our works. In the meanwhile General Greene passed frequently, inspecting the works.

At about 4 p. m. General Geary, commanding our division, espying the enemy in line, apparently a brigade, in force on my left, placed in position four guns, one in my line, whose firing scattered the enemy from our view. During the half hour's firing of the gun in our line, the gunners, being wounded, were replaced by men from my regiment who were acquainted with artillery practice.

The gun was removed before 5 p. m., and the line of the regiment was quiet until about 7 p. m., when the enemy's infantry advanced in force, our skirmishers falling back within our line, and we opened a fire upon the enemy's line, which continued along our whole line at close range, with, as was afterward discovered, terrible effect for about two hours, when, the firing of the enemy being nearly silenced,

I ordered an advance of a portion of our regiment, who eagerly leaped the works and surrounded about 50 of the enemy, among whom were 2 officers, and took at the time two flags, one a brigade color and the other a regimental banner. At the receipt of these flags, a quiet enthusiasm pervaded the men and officers of the regiment.

After the opening of the infantry fire, an order was received from General Greene that I must hold the works under all circumstances. I sent frequently for ammunition, which was promptly furnished, the right being out of ammunition but one time, when, by my order, bayonets were fixed, and thus remained until their boxes were replenished.

All the commands were received by the men coolly, and instantly obeyed, more especially the orders "commence firing" and "cease firing." During this time 9 men were killed and 16 wounded.

There was occasional firing by our regimental line until the break of day, July 3, when, with the exception of a reply to rebel sharpshooters, the firing ceased. We could then see large numbers of the enemy's dead within less than 50 feet of our line.

My men numbered 255 and 16 line officers, 1 adjutant, 1 field officer (Lieutenant-Colonel Redington on July 2 being brigade officer of the day, but after the picket and skirmishers came in did not report to me during the engagement, only being at the rear of the regiment late in the morning of the 3d).

The light firing above mentioned continued until a repeated advance of the enemy's infantry at about 4 a. m. July 3, when heavy firing opened on both sides, and continued until 9.30 a. m., the enemy being steadily held in check, at which time they retired, leaving only sharpshooters, who kept up interval firing until about 2 p. m., when my men being much exhausted, the Sixtieth were relieved for one hour, retiring from and returning to the intrenchments under a sharp fire of sharpshooters.

During the morning we sustained a loss of 2 men killed and 19 wounded, in addition to 2 lieutenants, one slightly, the other severely, wounded.

Our men resumed their places behind the works about one hour after being first relieved, and then remained until 2 a. m. July 4, meanwhile there being no firing.

Too much praise cannot be awarded the regiment for its coolness and perfect obedience to orders. Officers and men are alike entitled to a proud reputation for efficient service in defending the hill on which they were situated, it being a most commanding position on the left of the Twelfth Corps.

The colors above named captured by the regiment have been forwarded to brigade headquarters, thence to be sent to the proper department. The proper record of capture is inscribed upon them.

A full and complete list of killed, wounded, and missing has already been forwarded to brigade headquarters.*

This supplementary report is most respectfully submitted.

ABEL GODARD,
Colonel, Commanding Sixtieth New York Volunteers.

Capt. C. P. HORTON,
A. A. G., Third Brig., Second Div., Twelfth Army Corps.

---

* Embodied in revised statement, p. 185.

No. 309.

Report of Lieut. Col. John C. O. Redington, Sixtieth New York Infantry.

CAMP NEAR LITTLESTOWN, PA.,
July 6, 1863.

CAPTAIN: I have the honor to report the action of the brigade skirmishers at Gettysburg on July 2.

We relieved about 8 a. m. two companies of the Seventh Indiana, of the First Corps, my force consisting of 7 officers and 170 men, with which I covered the entire front of the Second Division. We advanced beyond the brook, and held our line until the advance of the line of battle of the enemy, about 7 p. m. During the day scouts were sent out in front of the line of skirmishers, and information obtained.

About 4 p. m. the enemy planted a battery on a hill opposite the left of our line. I sent forward about 25 sharpshooters, who opened a brisk fire on the cannoneers. A fire from Knap's battery was also opened upon it. Under both fires the position was soon evacuated. The enemy four times advanced their skirmishers (once or twice in a double line), but our skirmishers drove them back.

At about 7 p. m. they began the advance with their line of battle. I immediately withdrew my line to this side of the brook, and threw forward every man of my reserve. We held this point with the briskest fire we could concentrate. Their line of battle was seen to lie down in the grass. We fell back as slowly as possible, the men under my command behaving in a truly splendid manner. Many had never drilled in skirmish tactics. I desired to hold a line about 100 yards this side of the brook and sweep them as they crossed the brook. I sent back to the commander of the Twenty-eighth Pennsylvania, which had been sent out as a reserve, asking him to move up to that line. He returned answer that he had been ordered to return to the intrenchments. I therefore fell back slowly with my 170 men, contesting every inch of ground, the enemy close on to our heels and firing occasional volleys at us. The darkness was so great in this part of the woods that we could not see the enemy, and we fired at the flashes of their guns. They were so close to us that we took 12 prisoners. When within 50 yards of the works, I ordered the line to fall back into the earthworks.

It was a half hour by the watch from the time that the enemy's line of battle started when my line of skirmishers entered our works. I regret to have to report that a portion of the line in the trenches commenced firing before our skirmishers had come in, killing and wounding several.

Our loss from the enemy's fire was very small, so perfect was our concealment.

I desire to mention for his conspicuously gallant conduct the name of Private Peter Fifer, of Company B, One hundred and second New York.

Respectfully, your obedient servant,
JOHN C. O. REDINGTON,
Lieut. Col. Sixtieth New York Vols., Field Officer of the Day.

Capt. C. P. HORTON,
     A. A. G., Third Brig., Second Div., Twelfth Corps.

No. 310.

Report of Lieut. Col. Herbert von Hammerstein, Seventy-eighth New York Infantry.

LITTLESTOWN, PA., *July* 6, 1863.

CAPTAIN: I have the honor to report the part which my regiment took in the engagement on July 2, 3, and 4.

On the morning of the 2d, about 6 o'clock, my regiment took position on the left of the brigade, in line of battle, having the Sixtieth New York Volunteers on its right and the First Army Corps on its left. It covered part of the crest of a steep hill. A breastwork of trees and dirt was soon thrown up, and the day passed till about 4 o'clock without any incident. At about that time a battery of the enemy, numbering eight pieces, opened on a battery on our left, the shots passing our line without doing injury, when Battery K, Fifth U. S. Artillery, with two 10-pounder Parrott and two Napoleon guns, was at 4.30 o'clock ordered up to occupy the position which my regiment occupied and silence the rebel guns. I fell back a few yards to the rear of the battery, and remained there during the artillery contest.

The firing of this battery was masterly; at 5.30 o'clock every gun of the enemy was silenced, the battery losing several of their gunners and drivers. My men volunteered to supply their places, and, besides, assisted during the whole engagement in carrying ammunition from the caissons to the guns. We only lost 1 man killed and 1 wounded at that place.

At about 6 o'clock the battery was withdrawn, and, after reoccupying my old position, I received orders from Brigadier-General Greene to relieve the Twenty-eighth Pennsylvania Volunteers as skirmishers with my regiment. I at once marched the regiment down to the center of our brigade, crossed the breastworks, and deployed my skirmishers, not being able to see the Twenty-eighth Pennsylvania Volunteers, and having no time to look for them, as the enemy was already pressing all the skirmishers back. Our skirmishers came in soon, and, after giving and receiving some severe volleys of musketry, we fell back across the breastworks. The whole line behind the works was then occupied by our brigade, no interval existing. General Greene ordered me to fall in, with my regiment in front of me, which I did. I joined the One hundred and second New York, and we, with the rest of the brigade, succeeded in repulsing a most furious attack of the enemy, beginning at 6.40 o'clock and ending at 9.30 o'clock, when the enemy fell back, and we fired our last round of ammunition.

The rest of the night we remained behind the breastworks under arms, only annoyed by sharpshooters.

Filling our boxes with ammunition, at 3.30 a. m. I received orders to occupy a place between the One hundred and second and Sixtieth Regiments, which was done immediately, and ten minutes afterward the attack began with the same energy which the rebels displayed on the evening before. Our men succeeded in repulsing them totally, with the same coolness and determination, before 6 a. m.

At 7.40 o'clock my regiment was relieved by the One hundred and fiftieth New York Volunteers, to rest and clean their guns.

At 9 a. m. we reoccupied our old place, remaining there until 1 p. m., only annoyed by sharpshooters.

At 1 o'clock we were relieved again.

From 9 p. m. till 1 a. m. we were at the breastworks again. After that we remained somewhat in the rear of the breastworks, the enemy having entirely abandoned his lines in our front.

The official list of killed, wounded, and missing has been forwarded already to your headquarters.* Among the wounded is Major Randall, who was shot while gallantly discharging his duties. The main loss endured was while the regiment was skirmishing.

Having commanded this regiment the first time in action (its strength being not more than 200), I am fully satisfied with the conduct of officers and men; they fought with cool determination, like good soldiers and brave men.

Adjutant Postley was conspicuous for the coolness and zeal with which he kept the regiment supplied with ammunition under a very hot fire.

In submitting this report, I have the honor to be, captain, very respectfully, your obedient servant,

H. HAMMERSTEIN,
Lieutenant-Colonel, Commanding.

Capt. C. P. HORTON,
  Assistant Adjutant-General.

No. 311.

Report of Capt. Lewis R. Stegman, One hundred and second New York Infantry.

NEAR LITTLESTOWN, PA., *July 6, 1863.*

CAPTAIN: I have the honor to submit the following report of operations of the One hundred and second Regiment New York Volunteers in the battle of Gettysburg, Pa., July 1, 2, and 3:

July 1, this regiment marched with the brigade from Two Taverns to a position on the extreme left of our army, then engaged with the enemy's skirmishers; were advanced, and the position occupied until shortly after daylight the next morning, July 2.

The division being moved to the right of the army, the One hundred and second New York was formed in line upon the side of a precipitous hill; the One hundred and forty-ninth New York upon the right, and the Sixtieth New York upon the left. Skirmishers and pickets from the First Corps occupied our front, but were relieved by detail. The men were ordered to build breastworks, and did so with the best material at hand—cord-wood and rock—making, however, a strong line. The Sixtieth and One hundred and forty-ninth New York Regiments extended their lines to connect with ours, thus forming a long and continuous breastwork. Artillery firing took place from our immediate rear upon the enemy, drawing a fire in reply, but doing no serious damage. This occurred about 4 p. m., and continued for about an hour, perhaps more.

Shortly after 6 p. m. the regiment was moved by the right flank to the intrenchments occupied by the One hundred and forty-ninth New York, the men forming in single file, with intervening spaces of a foot or more. The men had scarcely taken this position when some sharp musketry firing took place, proving an advance of the enemy,

---

*Embodied in revised statement, p. 185.

and causing our pickets to retire. The Seventy-eighth New York was dispatched through our lines to their relief, bravely led by Lieutenant-Colonel Hammerstein. The blaze of fire which lighted up the darkness of the valley below us; the desperate charging yell and halloa of the rebel troops, convinced us of an immediate engagement. The men were cheered by their officers, continued to be on the alert, and to allow our pickets to pass.

The Seventy-eighth soon fell back in good order before the heavy columns of the foe, forming on the rear of our right wing, where they remained during the battle, relieving our men and in turn being relieved, fighting desperately and bravely. The pickets having crossed the breastworks, the whistling of the balls announced the advance of the enemy to close quarters. It was answered by volley after volley of the most destructive musketry from our regiment, being unceasing for two hours.

About 8 p. m. the right wing was re-enforced by the Sixth Wisconsin Regiment, Wadsworth's division, First Army Corps. About 8.30 p. m. the left was re-enforced by the Forty-fifth New York, Eleventh Corps, which occupied the position until the firing ceased. The One hundred and second New York never left its position, nor did one man flinch from his full duty. The firing ceased along the line about 9.30 p. m. During the night, about 1 a. m. and again at 2 a. m., volleys were delivered by both sides.

At 3.30 a. m. the engagement recommenced with renewed intensity, this regiment holding the breastworks until nearly 9 a. m., in the face of a fearfully destructive fire, when they were relieved by the One hundred and fiftieth New York Volunteers. In about twenty minutes the regiment relieved the One hundred and fiftieth New York. About an hour thereafter the regiment was again relieved by the One hundred and fiftieth New York. They had scarcely formed near brigade headquarters when the First Maryland Regiment retired from the trenches without orders, and the One hundred and second New York was ordered to the position left vacant. Under a heavy fire from sharpshooters, they occupied this position until 2 p. m., when they were relieved by the Sixtieth New York Volunteers.

About 4 p. m. this regiment was ordered to report to Brigadier-General Wadsworth, First Corps, by whom they were placed in reserve to his left wing, but in position to be used at any point in the line.

This position was occupied until the brigade vacated its position July 5.

Too much credit cannot be given to the officers and men of the regiment for their unflinching courage and devotion; when their ammunition was expended, with determined spirits they awaited the enemy's onset with fixed bayonets. True and trusty, they have added renewed luster to the bright name already borne, so hardly won on many a desperately contested field.

Ever conspicuous in the battle, cheering on the men by his presence and voice, Colonel Lane was wounded about 9 p. m. Sorrowfully I record the fact of the loss of two brave officers—Capt. John Mead, Company K, and Adjt. J. Virgil Upham, while gallantly cheering the men in their labors.

Where every officer acted conspicuously, bravely, and courageously, I can scarcely find one action more creditable than any other in any one. All acted most nobly and heroically.

Our loss in killed, wounded, and missing amounted to but 32,* ᵤₑ breastworks forming a splendid protection.

I am, sir, with great respect, your most obedient servant,

L. R. STEGMAN,
Captain, Comdg. One hundred and second New York Vols.

Capt. C. P. HORTON,

　　A. A. G., Third Brig., Second Div., Twelfth Army Corps.

No. 312.

Report of Col. David Ireland, One hundred and thirty-seventh New York Infantry.

IN THE FIELD, AT LITTLESTOWN, PA.,
July 6, 1863.

CAPTAIN: I have the honor to submit the following report of the part taken in the late engagement by the One hundred and thirty-seventh Regiment New York Volunteers:

On the afternoon of July 1, we marched from the village of Two Taverns to near the town of Gettysburg, when we took a road to the left, and on arriving at the left of our lines we formed column of division, and deployed a company as skirmishers. In this manner we advanced about half a mile to the brow of a hill, and there remained for the night.

Early on the morning of Thursday, July 2, we marched from the position on the left to a position on the right of the road to Gettysburg and parallel to it. In this position we constructed a line of breastworks covering the front of the regiment. The breastworks were completed about noon. We marched in them and remained there until about 6 p. m., when I received orders to send out a company of skirmishers. Company H, Capt. C. F. Baragar, was detailed. At the same time we were ordered to change our position to the line of works constructed by General Kane's brigade, to occupy which we had to form line one man deep. In this position the right of our regiment was entirely unprotected.

About 7 p. m. our skirmishers were driven in by the enemy, who were advancing in force, and, as near as I could see, in three lines.

We remained in this position fighting the enemy until about 7.30 o'clock, when the enemy advanced on our right flank. At this time I ordered Company A, the right-flank company, to form at right angles with the breastworks, and check the advance of the enemy, and they did for some time, but, being sorely pressed, they fell back a short distance to a better position, and there remained until Lieutenant Cantine, of General Greene's staff, brought up a regiment of the First Corps. I placed them in the position occupied by Company A, but they remained there but a short time. They fell back to the line of works constructed by the Third Brigade. At this time we were being fired on heavily from three sides—from the front of the works, from the right, and from a stone wall in our rear. Here we lost severely in killed and wounded.

At this time I ordered the regiment back to the line of works of the Third Brigade, and formed line on the prolongation of the works,

---

*But see revised statement, p. 185.

and there held the enemy in check until relieved by the Fourteenth New York Volunteers, Colonel Fowler commanding, and the Second Brigade, Second Division, General Kane commanding.

While in this position, and previous to being relieved, Captain Gregg, in command of a small squad of men, charged with the bayonet the enemy that were harassing us most, and fell, mortally wounded, leading and cheering on his men.

When relieved by the Fourteenth New York, we formed line in their rear, and in that position remained during the night.

At 3 a. m. of Friday, July 3, we relieved the One hundred and forty-seventh New York Volunteers in the breastworks, and at 4 a. m. the enemy advanced with a yell and opened on us. Their fire was returned, and kept up unceasingly until 5.45 o'clock, when we were relieved in splendid style by the Twenty-ninth Ohio Volunteers, commanded by Captain Hayes.

We relieved them at 7 a. m., and were relieved again at 9.30 a. m. We relieved the Twenty-ninth Ohio again about 10.15 a. m. We were there but a short time when the fire slackened, and we retired a short distance, when the men rested and cleaned their arms.

We relieved the Fifth Ohio Volunteers, Colonel Patrick commanding, at 9 p. m., and were relieved by him at 1 a. m. on Saturday, July 4. We were not under fire again during the engagement.

During the heavy musketry firing on the morning of Friday, July 3, a squad of 52 rebels surrendered to Capt. Silas Pierson, who sent them to the rear. From them we learned that we had been engaged with the Stonewall Division, of Ewell's corps.

Throughout the whole of the engagement the officers and men of this regiment did their duty, and did it well—more especially those officers that are killed. Captain Gregg fell, nobly leading on his men. I had thanked Captain Williams for his coolness and courage but a short time before he fell, and Lieutenant Van Emburgh, acting adjutant, was everywhere conspicuous for his bravery, and fell, cheering the men. He was a good and brave officer. His loss will be much regretted. Lieutenant Hallett fell, doing his duty. From our heavy loss in killed and wounded, some idea may be formed of the severity of the fire we were under. We had killed, wounded, and missing as follows: Killed, 38, and wounded, 86.*

Very respectfully, your obedient servant,

DAVID IRELAND,
Colonel, Commanding 137th New York Volunteers.

Capt. C. P. HORTON,
Assistant Adjutant-General, Third Brigade.

No. 313.

Report of Col. Henry A. Barnum, One hundred and forty-ninth New York Infantry.

CAMP NEAR LITTLESTOWN, PA., *July 6, 1863.*

CAPTAIN: I have the honor to submit the following report of the operations of my command at the battle of Gettysburg, on July 1, 2, and 3:

On the 1st instant, the regiment broke camp with the corps at Lit-

---

* But see revised statement, p. 185.

tlestown, and marched to Two Taverns, where we arrived at about 12 m., and the command rested until 3.30 p. m., when we were hastened forward in support of the First and Eleventh Corps, which had engaged the enemy at Gettysburg. We were posted in double columns with the balance of the division near what was afterward the left of our general line of battle. A strong line of skirmishers at about 6 p. m. was thrown well to the front, and remained in position until about 4 a. m. of the 2d instant, when, with the division, we were marched across the fields, and placed in line of battle along the crest of a wooded hill of slight elevation, at the right of the First Division, First Corps, and near the right of our general line of battle. A strong line of skirmishers was thrown well to the front.

My command was second from the right of our brigade. A substantial breastwork of stones, logs, rails, and earth was hastily constructed, and the regiment rested in its rear until about 6.45 p. m., when the enemy drove in our skirmishers and attacked us in large force. The enemy made repeated and desperate charges upon our position, but was as often repulsed with great slaughter to him until our ammunition gave out, when we held the position with the bayonet and such limited firing as could be made with the ammunition of the killed and wounded.

At about 8 p. m. the enemy gained a hill on the right flank of our position. Seeing the regiment on my right give way, I attempted to change the front of the three right companies to resist him. The order was understood by the line officers for the regiment to fall back, which it proceeded to do in good order, but was brought to the right-about before getting 3 rods away, and again put in the trenches. This movement was executed under a most galling fire and when wholly exposed, as the ground a short distance to the rear of the works was elevated so as to give full range to the enemy's musketry.

At about 9.30 p. m. the enemy, repulsed in his every effort, withdrew. The regiment was relieved at about 10 p. m., but remained immediately in rear of the trenches during the night.

At about 4 a. m. of the 3d, the regiment was again put into the trenches, and had barely settled into position when the enemy again furiously attacked us. His charges were most impetuous and his fire terrific. Twice was our flag shot down, and a rebel first sergeant, in a brave attempt to capture it, fell within 2 feet of the prostrate banner, pierced with five balls. Its record of the bloody contest is eighty-one balls through its field and stripes and seven in its staff. Each time it fell, the color-sergeant, William C. Lilly, spliced the staff, and again placed it upon the works, and received a slight wound in doing so. The regiment was relieved at 6.30 o'clock, but went into the works three other times before the fight closed, which was about 1 p. m.

With a single exception among the officers, and but very few among the men, all performed their duty to my entire satisfaction, and far exceeded what might have been reasonably expected of a regiment in its second engagement. The exceptions I have noted, and the delinquents will be properly disciplined. When so many did so well, it would be invidious to make special mention of some in the rank and line who were particularly brave and meritorious. I should disappoint my entire command, however, if I did not call especial attention to the consummate skill and unsurpassed coolness and bravery of Lieut. Col. Charles B. Randall, who was dangerously wounded in the left breast and arm while cheering the men to their work. Through illness of myself, he was in command of the regiment after the fight closed on the 2d instant, and during the whole of the fight of the 3d until wounded, which was near the close of the contest. I was present during a part of the time the regiment was engaged on the 3d, but was unable to assume command.

Appended is a list of our casualties,* which are so small, in view of the long exposure and heavy fire under which the command was placed, only because of the excellent management of its officers, the substantial character of our works, and the advantage of our position.

I am, captain, very respectfully, your obedient servant,

H. A. BARNUM,
Colonel, Comdg. 149th New York Vols.

Capt. C. P. HORTON,
Assistant Adjutant-General.

No. 314.

Report of Lieut. Edward D. Muhlenberg, Fourth U. S. Artillery, commanding Artillery Brigade, Twelfth Army Corps.

HDQRS. ARTILLERY BRIGADE, TWELFTH CORPS,
Near Kelly's Ford, Va., August —, 1863.

GENERAL: I have the honor to submit the following movements and operations of the artillery arm of the Twelfth Corps, from the date of its departure from camp at Aquia to its arrival in its present position:

The brigade—F, Fourth U. S. Artillery; K, Fifth U. S. Artillery; Knap's Independent Pennsylvania, and M, First New York—broke camp on June 13. Marched, via Stafford Court-House, Dumfries, and Occoquan City, to Fairfax Court-House, Va. Left the latter place, and occupied Leesburg on the 17th, the batteries. to be prepared for any emergency, taking positions near the fortifications situated on the west, northeast, and southeast approaches to said place.

On the 26th, the corps was again in motion. Two batteries (F, Fourth U. S. Artillery, and M, First New York), with First Division, and two (K, Fifth U. S. Artillery and Knap's Independent Pennsylvania), with Second Division, crossed the Potomac at Edwards Ferry; marched, via Rockville, Jefferson, Frederick, and Brentsville, Md., to Littlestown, Pa., entering the latter place on the 30th.

On July 1, the brigade, moving along the Baltimore pike to a point 5 miles southeast of Gettysburg, called Two Taverns, took position there to counteract any movement of the enemy from the Hanover side.

About noon of the same day, the two batteries attached to it moved with the First Division away from the pike in a northeasterly direction toward the Hanover road, and, approaching Gettysburg from the east, took position on tolerably favorable ground about 1½ miles from it; the two batteries moving with the Second Division along the Baltimore pike encamped about the same distance from the town.

On the morning of the 2d, the batteries operating with First Divis-

---

* Embodied in revised statement, p. 185.

ion moved with it over to the Baltimore pike. The infantry, going into the heavy woods on the northeast side of same and forming junction with the Second Division, completed the right wing of the army. The density of the growth of timber, the irregularity and extremely broken character of the ground, studded with immense bowlders, prevented the artillery from taking position in the line proper of the corps. It was, therefore, held in reserve and readiness to answer all calls which might be made upon it by the future movements of the opposing forces. The enemy seriously annoying the left of the line of the Twelfth, a vacant space eligible for a battery was found about 200 yards on the right of the First Corps. At 3.30 p. m. one gun (10-pounder Parrott), and at 5 p. m. two more of the same caliber, Knap's Independent Pennsylvania, the three under charge of Lieutenant Geary, were placed in position, and were joined by one section of 12-pounder Napoleons (K, Fifth U. S. Artillery), under charge of Second Lieut. William E. Van Reed. The moment their presence was observed, the enemy opened with eight guns; continued an incessant fire for some thirty minutes; then, having a caisson exploded, ceased.

The conduct of both the officers above mentioned, as well as of their commands, is creditable in the highest degree. The remarkable coolness exhibited under a very galling fire, and the bravery displayed in sustaining all the parts assigned to them, deserve notice.

In this engagement, or artillery duel, Lieutenant Geary had 1 killed and 2 wounded; Lieutenant Van Reed, 2 mortally and 3 severely wounded.

The rebel artillery having ceased firing, no infantry making its appearance, and the corps having been ordered to the left of the army, to support it, if necessary, these guns were withdrawn from the above position, and Knap's Independent Pennsylvania Battery, Lieut. Charles A. Atwell commanding, was placed on a knob situated southwest of the pike 100 yards from it, and known on that day as Slocum's Hill; Battery M, First New York Artillery, Lieutenant Winegar commanding, on a second elevation, a quarter of a mile distant, and nearly due east from the first mentioned, both overlooking and commanding the ground just vacated by the corps. These two batteries retained these positions during the whole engagement and did excellent service. Battery F, Fourth U. S. Artillery, and Battery K, Fifth U. S. Artillery, remained in park at base of the Slocum's Hill, ready for a move to the left, if called upon.

After the return of the corps from the left, it found the greater portion of its intrenchments already in possession of the enemy, supposed to be a portion of General Ewell's corps, variously estimated from 5,000 to 8,000 strong.

On the morning of the 3d, at 1 a. m., Batteries F, Fourth U. S. Artillery, and K, Fifth U. S. Artillery, were placed in position parallel to and on the southwest side of the Baltimore pike, almost directly opposite the center of the line formed by the Twelfth, and controlling the approach of the enemy along the ravine formed by the stream known as Rock Creek.

At 4.30 a. m. the two rifle batteries (ten guns) and the two light 12-pounder batteries (ten guns) opened, and fired for fifteen minutes without intermission at a range of from 600 to 800 yards; ceased firing, and allowed infantry to take part. Commenced at 5.30 a. m., and continued firing at intervals until 10 a. m., at which hour the enemy had retreated and the infantry of the corps had regained their works. The artillery was of essential service, and did excellent execution at this part of the field, and no doubt contributed greatly in preventing the enemy from establishing himself in so desirable a position, whence he could either have held the pike or have moved his force along the southeast slope and occupied a sufficiency of Cemetery Hill to annoy, if not to entirely control, the position held by the army. The marks on the trees and immense bowlders contiguous to the line of intrenchments prove conclusively that the practice of the artillery was excellent and splendidly accurate.

Batteries F, Fourth U. S. Artillery, and K, Fifth U. S. Artillery, remaining in the position just mentioned, were exposed to a most terrific fire during the afternoon of the 3d, the enemy opening with all his artillery upon the left and center of the army. The direction of their lines of fire was such that almost every projectile passing over Cemetery Hill found its bed within the battery line of these two batteries. The commands stood nobly under this unexpected and incessant hail, and displayed by their actions the attributes of true soldiers. I take the greatest pleasure in presenting to your favorable notice Lieut. D. H. Kinzie, commanding Battery K, Fifth U. S. Artillery, and his second lieutenant, William Egan, as well as Lieut. S. T. Rugg, of my own command, Battery F, Fourth U. S. Artillery.

The batteries, observing the same order of march as before, moved with the corps on the 5th, via Littlestown, Pa., Frederick, Burkittsville (one section in position at Crampton's Gap on the 8th, under Second Lieut. S. T. Rugg), Rohrersville, Bakersville, and Fair Play, Md., and took position on the 12th on the left of the new line of battle, 1 mile from Jones' Cross-Roads, on the west side of the Hagerstown and Sharpsburg pike. Remained here until the 14th. Made a reconnaissance with the First Division batteries toward Falling Waters, and found the enemy had recrossed the Potomac.

Broke camp on the 15th. Recrossed the Potomac at Harper's Ferry on the 19th. Marched, via Snickersville, Paris, Manassas Gap, Rectortown, White Plains, Thoroughfare Gap, Hay Market, Catlett's Station, and Warrenton Junction, to our present position, on the south side of the Rappahannock River, which we reached on the 30th ultimo.

A list of casualties is herewith annexed.*

I have the honor to remain, your most obedient servant,

EDWARD D. MUHLENBERG,

First Lieut. 4th U. S. Arty., Comdg. Arty. Brig., 12th Corps.

Brig. Gen. HENRY J. HUNT,

Chief of Artillery, Army of the Potomac.

No. 315.

Reports of Brig. Gen. Robert O. Tyler, U. S. Army, commanding Artillery Reserve, Army of the Potomac.

HEADQUARTERS ARTILLERY RESERVE,
Camp near Warrenton Junction, Va., August 30, 1863.

GENERAL: I have the honor to submit herewith a report of the operations of the Artillery Reserve, from June 28 to July 4. I also inclose the reports of brigade, battery, and other commanders.

June 28.—The reserve remained in camp near Frederick City. At

---

*Embodied in revised statement, p. 185.

night Captain Robertson's brigade of horse artillery, temporarily attached, was ordered to join the command of Major-General Pleasonton.

June 29.—Marched from Frederick City to about 1 mile beyond Bruceville.

June 30.—Marched to Taneytown, and encamped a short distance beyond the village, on the Emmitsburg turnpike.

On the evening of July 1, I was ordered to proceed to Gettysburg with about eight batteries and report to Major-General Hancock. I detailed the brigades of Captains Ransom and Fitzhugh, and, leaving about sundown, reported with them to General Gibbon, in the absence of General Hancock, at about 10.30 p. m.

The same day, Lieutenant Sheldon, with his battery (B, First New York Artillery), was ordered to report to the chief of artillery of the Second Corps. I encamped that night on the Taneytown road, near the cross-road leading to Two Taverns.

July 2.—In the morning I moved from camp with my brigades, and placed them in park behind the line of battle of the Third Corps, about 1½ miles from Gettysburg. The remainder of the reserve batteries, having been ordered to join me, left Taneytown at early dawn, under command of Major McGilvery, and reported to me with the ammunition train about 10.30 a. m. They were held in reserve on a cross-road between the main road and the Baltimore turnpike. Much to my regret, the two batteries of 4½-inch guns (B and M, First Connecticut Artillery) were ordered to Westminster, to remain with the supply train. I am satisfied that the action of Gettysburg would have demonstrated their extreme mobility and usefulness as field guns, in addition to their already proved excellence as guns of position.

Early in the day I stationed Captains Fitzhugh (K, First New York Artillery) and Rigby (A, First Maryland Artillery) and Lieutenant Parsons (A, First New Jersey Artillery) along the Baltimore turnpike, at points designated by Generals Meade and Hunt.

At 3.30 p. m., pursuant to instructions received, I ordered Major McGilvery with two batteries (Fifteenth New York Battery and C and F, Pennsylvania artillery) of his brigade to report to Major-General Sickles. Afterward, as the action went on, I sent forward, as they were called for, the remaining batteries of that brigade, and, in addition, those commanded by Captains Sterling (Second Connecticut Battery) and Ames (G, First New York Artillery), making in all six batteries of thirty-four guns.

These batteries were placed in position so as to fire upon the masses of the enemy moving up on our left flank, which made the general artillery line make a large angle to the infantry line of battle, and exposed it to a very galling enfilading fire of the enemy's artillery, in addition to the continual annoyance of their sharpshooters. These batteries, under Major McGilvery, held their places, doing terrible execution upon the successive columns attacking our left until about 6 p. m., when, our infantry falling back, they were compelled to retire, though contesting the ground gallantly under great disadvantages.

Upon the crest of the hill, Major McGilvery formed a new line with the guns which he could collect, being re-enforced by Lieutenant Dow with his battery (Sixth Maine), and the farther advance of the enemy was checked by the fire of artillery almost unaided by infantry.

The reserve batteries lost very heavily on this occasion in horses and men, so that several guns were necessarily left upon the field, but, after dark, parties were sent out and all but one gun, belonging to Captain Thompson's battery (C and F, Pennsylvania), were returned to the command to which they belonged. The gun in question was left behind much nearer the new position than many others which were regained, and it is not improbable that it was brought in by troops of some of the corps. I would respectfully call attention to Major McGilvery's report of this part of the action.

When the action became general, I ordered Captain Ransom's Regular Brigade (C, Fourth U. S. Artillery; C, Fifth U. S. Artillery; F and K, Third U. S. Artillery; H, First U. S. Artillery) to form line of battle on the crest of the hill near General Meade's headquarters. Soon two batteries—Lieutenant Turnbull's (F and K, Third U. S. Artillery) and Captain Ransom's (C, Fifth U. S. Artillery)— were ordered forward to General Humphreys, and occupied a much exposed position near the right center when the enemy's advance was made. Lieutenant Turnbull (F and K, Third U. S. Artillery) was compelled to retire, with the loss of 1 officer and 8 men killed, 14 men wounded, and 45 horses killed. Four guns were left on the field, but were afterward brought off by infantry. No report has yet been received from Captain Ransom's (C, Fifth U. S. Artillery) or Captain Sterling's (Second Connecticut) batteries.

Lieutenant Eakin (H, First U. S. Artillery) was ordered to Cemetery Hill, where he was wounded soon after his guns went into battery. Lieutenant Thomas, with his battery (C, Fourth U. S. Artillery), held the crest of the hill, and did excellent service in repelling the attack on our center. Captain Huntington's brigade (H, First Ohio Artillery; F and G, First Pennsylvania Artillery; A, First New Hampshire Artillery; C, First West Virginia) and Captain Taft's battery (Fifth New York) of 20-pounders were ordered to report to Major-General Howard, commanding the Eleventh Corps, and by him placed in position in the vicinity of the cemetery, where they engaged the enemy's batteries opposite, firing upon bodies of troops as they appeared in force until daylight was ended by the darkness.

During the charge upon our right center, two of the guns belonging to Captain Ricketts' battery (F and G, First Pennsylvania Artillery), of this brigade, were captured, and one of them spiked, but the enemy was held in check by the cannoneers with pistols, handspikes, &c., and afterward driven back by a brigade of the Second Corps, and the guns recaptured.

Lieutenant Gillett, First Connecticut Artillery, ordnance officer of this command, was engaged the entire night in issuing ammunition to the batteries of the several corps, as well as those of the Artillery Reserve. Seventy wagons were unloaded, which were sent to the rear on the morning of the 3d.

At daylight on July 3, Captain Rigby's battery (A, First Maryland Artillery) opened fire, by direction of Major-General Slocum, upon the troops across Rock Creek moving on our right. The ammunition train and some of the reserve batteries, which had been refitted during the night, were moved up near the Taneytown road, together with the Horse Artillery Brigade of Captain Robertson, who had been ordered to report temporarily to me. On riding along the lines, I found all the reserve batteries (twelve in number), which had been ordered to the different corps on the day previous, in position. The infantry had constructed a slight breastwork of such materials as the ground afforded along the entire crest of the hill, and some shelter had been thrown up for the artillery. The enemy had brought out a large number of guns, and held them in position in sight on the opposite side of the Emmitsburg road.

Everything was moderately quiet until about 12 o'clock, when, as I was returning with Captain Robertson from reconnoitering a position for artillery opposite our left, the enemy opened a terrific fire of artillery, which, passing over the crest of the hill, concentrated behind the lines where the reserve was lying.

Several officers and men were wounded and animals killed both in the batteries and the ammunition train. My own horse was killed at this time, just as I reached the park.

Orders were given to move the whole to the rear, out of range, the cannonading being kept up for more than two hours. There being signs of an intention to attack on the part of the enemy, all the reserve batteries and one battery of horse artillery were ordered into position.

Captain Fitzhugh (K, First New York Artillery) and Lieutenant Parsons (A, First New Jersey Artillery) came up very opportunely to the support of the troops of Brigadier-General Webb, of the Second Corps, at a time when artillery was much needed, and with their steady and well-directed fire rendered great assistance.

After 3 p. m. the enemy moved up immense bodies of troops, and made a series of attacks upon our center, but, despite the vigor and gallantry with which they were led and handled, they could not withstand the heavy fire of artillery to which they were subjected, combined with the brave and obstinate defense of the infantry, and were hurled back from our position with immense loss.

The company of the Thirty-second Massachusetts (Company C, Capt. J. C. Fuller commanding) and the battalion of the Fourth New Jersey, guarding my train, were formed in line, and assisted in driving back stragglers during the afternoon's engagement.

I wish to explain here that the dispositions of my batteries were generally made upon orders of General Hunt, chief of artillery, though sometimes by orders direct from the commanding general or requisitions of corps commanders.

Most of the batteries remained in position until July 5, when they were withdrawn for the march on that day.

Appended and marked A will be found a tabular statement of losses and expenditures during the battle.

I believe it almost unnecessary to speak of the value of the services rendered by the Artillery Reserve during the last two days of this action and the great share it had in the glorious result. The one hundred and eight guns which were on the field were all in position, their fire being concentrated and felt wherever the battle was hottest. The skill and gallantry with which they were handled is amply attested by the dead of the enemy, slain by shell and canister, lying in their front, and the fierce fire under which they did their work is proved by the heavy loss of horses and the long record of men and officers killed and wounded.

From the ammunition train, as already stated, seventy wagon-loads were issued on the night of the 2d to the batteries of the army, and, as shown by the report of my ordnance officer, 10,090 rounds were issued to batteries outside of the reserve during the battle. The necessity and usefulness of the organization, I believe, is beyond a question.

I would respectfully call the attention of the commanding general to the defects of a system which fails to give field officers for the necessary subdivisions of so large a body of artillery. There should be at least a field officer with a proper staff to each four batteries in action, and the supervision of a commander of superior rank is equally necessary in camp or on the march.

There was no exception to the gallantry, coolness, and steadiness of the officers and men of my command, and I would call attention to the many special instances of distinguished good conduct mentioned in accompanying reports.

I feel it due to bring to the notice of the commanding general the intrepid conduct and excellent judgment displayed by Maj. F. Mc-Gilvery, First Maine Artillery, under whose immediate command fell many of the reserve batteries engaged on our left center, as well as to the tenacity and bravery of Capt. P. Hart, Fifteenth New York Battery; Capt. N. Irish, Battery F, Pennsylvania Artillery, and Lieutenant Baldwin, Fifth U. S. Artillery, who, though painfully wounded, remained on the field and fought with their batteries during the whole action; also, of Captain Ransom, Third U. S. Artillery, who was severely wounded by a sharpshooter while gallantly reconnoitering a position for his guns. Lieutenant Milton, upon whom the command of his battery devolved after every other officer belonging to it had been either killed or wounded, displayed remarkable coolness and resolution.

I wish to make special mention of gallantry coming under my notice on the part of Private William Sheridan, First Connecticut Artillery, who was the only one of several orderlies who remained with me under the terrific cannonading of the 3d. He immediately gave me his horse when mine was killed, and brought off from the field my entire arms and horse equipments, carrying them on foot for nearly a mile under a fire the concentration of which few who experienced it will fail to remember.

I desire to especially express my obligations to the officers of my staff. The gallantry and activity of Lieutenant [Gustav von] Blucher, the only aide-de-camp with me, were specially conspicuous. The work of bringing up and the care of the ammunition train devolved upon Lieutenant-Colonel [William E.] Morford, quartermaster, and Lieutenant [S. A.] Wood, acting assistant quartermaster, the former of whom, with Lieutenant [Lowell A.] Chamberlin, my commissary of musters, afforded me much valuable assistance on the field. Lieutenant Gillett, my ordnance officer, worked day and night after the action commenced, issuing ammunition to the corps as well as to the reserve, and to his labor and excellent system much of the efficiency of the artillery on the 3d is due. I am greatly indebted to my assistant adjutant-general, Capt. C. H. Whittelsey, for his gallant and untiring labors during the whole action and the cheerfulness and energy with which he executed every duty that he was called upon to perform.

My thanks are also due Captain Robertson, who did excellent service in withdrawing the reserve batteries during the confusion attending the heavy cannonading of the 3d, and upon whom devolved the command of the batteries during a temporary indisposition that succeeded the fall from my horse.

I am, general, very respectfully, your obedient servant,

R. O. TYLER,
Brigadier-General of Volunteers, Commanding.

Brig. Gen. S. WILLIAMS,
Assistant Adjutant-General, Army of the Potomac.

A.

HEADQUARTERS ARTILLERY RESERVE,
Near Gettysburg, Pa., July 4, 1863—2 p. m.

GENERAL: I have the honor to state that I have lost from my command as follows:

Officers wounded * 14
Privates killed, wounded, and missing* 216
Rounds of ammunition expended, about............................... 11, 653
Rounds of ammunition on hand....................................... 3, 900

I am, general, very respectfully, your obedient servant,
R. O. TYLER,
Brigadier-General of Volunteers.

General S. WILLIAMS,
Assistant Adjutant-General, Army of the Potomac.

—

HEADQUARTERS ARTILLERY RESERVE,
Culpeper Court-House, Va., October 3, 1863.

GENERAL: I have the honor to inclose herewith a statement of the operations of the Artillery Reserve, from the date of the battle of Gettysburg until the command reached Warrenton Junction, which I had previously omitted. I also forward a copy of a report of First Lieut. G. V. Weir, commanding Battery C, Fifth U. S. Artillery, for the action of Gettysburg. This report is but just received, a circumstance which has prevented the services of the battery from being suitably mentioned in my own report.

I would respectfully call attention in it to the names of non-commissioned officers and soldiers whose meritorious conduct is specially noticed.

I am, general, very respectfully, your obedient servant,
R. O. TYLER,
Brigadier-General, Commanding.

Brig. Gen. S. WILLIAMS,
Assistant Adjutant-General, Army of the Potomac.

[Inclosure.]

HEADQUARTERS ARTILLERY RESERVE,
Camp near Culpeper Court-House, Va., October 3, 1863.

GENERAL: I have the honor to submit the following statement of the operations of the Artillery Reserve, from the battle of Gettysburg until August 1, when this command reached Warrenton Junction :

July 4.—The batteries remained in the position held during the battle, with few exceptions.

July 5.—They were drawn in, and marched about 3 p. m., proceeding to Littlestown, Pa., where they went into camp about 10 p. m.

July 6.—The reserve remained at Littlestown.

July 7.—The batteries left Littlestown, Pa., at 5 a. m., and encamped near Woodsborough, Md., at 8.30 p. m.

July 8.—This command left camp at 11 a. m., and encamped near Frederick City, Md., at 3 p. m.

July 9.—The batteries left Frederick City at 12 m.; marched through South Mountain Gap, and encamped in rear of Boonsborough, Md., at 10.20 p. m.

_____

* But see revised statement, p. 187.

July 10.—They changed camp to the west side of Boonsborough, on the Hagerstown turnpike.

July 11.—The reserve left camp at 6 a. m. and proceeded on the turnpike to the vicinity of Benevola, where it encamped.

July 12.—The batteries of Captains Ames (G, First New York Artillery) and Ricketts (F and G, First Pennsylvania Artillery) were transferred to the Second Army Corps.

July 13.—The command left Benevola at 5 a. m. and proceeded across Antietam Creek to Jones' Four Corners, where I left two brigades, composed of eight batteries, under command of Major Reynolds. I then returned, by order of Major-General Meade, with the remaining batteries to camp, near Benevola.

July 14.—The batteries remained in camp.

July 15.—The batteries left at Jones' Four Corners having returned at 4 a. m., I left camp at 5 a. m. and marched to Berlin, by way of South Mountain Gap and Middletown.

July 16.—Battery C, Fifth U. S. Artillery, under command of Second Lieut. H. H. Baldwin, was detached, and ordered to New York City.

July 17.—The reserve remained in camp.

July 18.—I crossed the Potomac with my command upon the pontoon bridge, and proceeded to the vicinity of Wheatland, Va., arriving at 3 p. m.

July 19.—The batteries left Wheatland at 7.30 a. m. and encamped near Purcellville, Va., at 2 p. m.

July 20.—I resumed the march at 9.30 a. m. and proceeded to Union, Va., arriving at 6 p. m.

July 21 *and* 22.—The reserve remained in camp.

July 23.—The batteries left camp at 11.30 a. m. and parked on Delany's farm, near Rock Creek, at 5 p. m.

July 24.—The command resumed the march at 7 a. m. and reached White Plains, Va., at 4 p. m. The batteries left camp at 6.30 p. m. and proceeded to Warrenton, Va., by way of New Baltimore, arriving at 3 a. m. July 25.

July 25 *to* 31.—The reserve remained in camp.

August 1.—I left Warrenton with my command at 6 a. m. and encamped near Warrenton Junction, Va., at 11.30 a. m.

Very respectfully, your obedient servant,

R. O. TYLER,
Brigadier-General of Volunteers, Comdg. Artillery Reserve.

Brig. Gen. S. WILLIAMS,
Assistant Adjutant-General, Army of the Potomac.

HEADQUARTERS ARTILLERY RESERVE,
July 10, 1863.

GENERAL: I have the honor to forward you herewith a report of the casualties in batteries in the Artillery Reserve during the engagement of July 2 and 3, near Gettysburg, Pa.

I am, general, very respectfully, your obedient servant,

R. O. TYLER,
Brigadier-General of Volunteers.

Brig. Gen. S. WILLIAMS,
Assistant Adjutant-General, Army of the Potomac.

[Inclosure.]

Report of Casualties in batteries of the Artillery Reserve, in the battle of July 2 and 3, 1863, near Gettysburg, Pa.

Batteries.	Killed.		Wounded.		Missing.		Remarks.
	Officers.	Enlisted men.	Officers.	Enlisted men.	Officers.	Enlisted men.	
C, 5th U. S. Artillery		2	2	12			Captain Ransom and Lieutenant Baldwin wounded.
F and K, 3d U. S. Artillery	1	8		14		1	Lieutenant Livingston killed.
H, 1st U. S. Artillery		1	1	7		1	Lieutenant Eakin wounded.
C, 4th U. S. Artillery		1	1	16			Lieutenant McGilvray wounded.
C and F, Pennsylvania Artillery.		1	5	18		4	Captains Thompson and Irish and Lieutenants Hazlett, Stephenson, and Miller wounded.
E, 1st Massachusetts		4	1	16			Lieutenant Scott wounded.
15th New York Independent		3	2	11			Captain Hart and Lieutenant Knox wounded.
9th Massachusetts	1	7	2	16		2	Lieutenant Erickson killed, and Captain Bigelow and Lieutenant Whitaker wounded.
5th New York Independent		1		2			
2d Connecticut				3		2	
H, 1st Ohio Artillery		2		5			
C, 1st West Virginia Artillery		2		2			
A, 1st New Hampshire Artillery				3			
F and G, 1st Pennsylvania Artillery		6	1	13		3	Lieutenant Spence wounded.
K, 1st New York Artillery				7			
A, 1st Maryland Artillery							
G, 1st New York Artillery				7			
A, 1st New Jersey Artillery		2		7			
6th Maine Battery				13			
Total	2	40	15	172		13	

No. 316.

Report of Lieut. Cornelius Gillett, First Connecticut Heavy Artillery, Ordnance Officer, Artillery Reserve.

CAMP NEAR WARRENTON JUNCTION, VA., *August* 23, 1863.

CAPTAIN: I have the honor to report that, pursuant to orders from these headquarters, I proceeded with the ammunition train of the Artillery Reserve on July 2 from Taneytown to the position then held by our army near Gettysburg, Pa., which place we reached soon after midday. The train was parked in a field to the right of the road, and I immediately commenced supplying ammunition to the batteries both of this command and, by General Hunt's direction, to those of other corps.

On the evening of the 2d, I received orders to move to a field to the right and rear of the position I then occupied, which I did, and was kept busy the entire night sending out wagons and issuing to batteries.

On the morning of July 3, I was directed to move the train back to the position occupied by it on the 2d. After taking our old position, the wagons which had been unloaded were ordered to the rear, and I sent about seventy teams, which were taken by Captain [Simon P.] Suydam, assistant quartermaster, to Westminster.

About 2 p. m. the enemy commenced a heavy artillery fire upon that portion of our line behind which the train was parked. Several shells passed over the train, and three or four fell among the teams, only one exploding. A mule in one of the teams was struck by a solid shot and killed, and many of the animals became so unmanageable that there was danger of a stampede. As soon as the batteries and trains which were moving to the rear had passed, I was directed to move to a field about 1,000 yards to the rear, and behind a small piece of woods, where I remained until the 5th, when the command moved back to Littlestown, Pa.

The amount of issues during our stay at Gettysburg is as follows:

	Rounds.
From wagons sent to Major McGilvery and by him supplied to batteries:	
10-pounder	480
Light 12-pounder	758
3-inch	2,792
	4,030
Sent to report to Brigadier-General Hunt, chief of artillery, Army of the Potomac:	
Light 12-pounder	360
To batteries, most of which was packed in caissons before leaving the park:	
3-inch	3,705
Light 12-pounder	2,144
10-pounder	1,305
20-pounder	320
	7,474
To supply train of Second Corps	2,825
To chief of artillery, Third Corps	3,000
To supply train of Eleventh Corps	1,500
	7,325
Total issued at Gettysburg	19,189

I had remaining on hand 4,694 rounds, nearly all of which, though not in the best possible condition, could have been used to advantage had occasion required. In my opinion, the practice of sending wagons loaded with ammunition to batteries in action often causes a loss of *matériel*, a number of cases having been reported to me in which, after unloading the wagon and sending it to the rear, the battery has changed its position, leaving the ammunition on the ground.

I am, sir, very respectfully, your obedient servant,

C. GILLETT,
Second Lieutenant, and Ordnance Officer, Artillery Reserve.

Capt. C. H. WHITTELSEY, *A. A. G., Artillery Reserve.*

No. 317.

Report of Lieut. Gulian V. Weir, Battery C, Fifth U. S. Artillery, First Regular Brigade.

CAMP OF BATTERY C, FIFTH U. S. ARTILLERY,
September 20, 1863.

SIR: I have the honor to report the part Battery C, Fifth U. S. Artillery, took during the engagements of July 2 and 3, at the battle of Gettysburg.

July 2.—Left camp near Taneytown, Md., and marched to within a mile and a half of Gettysburg, Pa., and went into park. After remaining here until the afternoon, moved to the front, by order of General Tyler.

About 4 o'clock was ordered by Major-General Hancock to take up a position about 500 yards to the right and front, with orders to watch my front, as our troops were falling back on the left at the time. I was ordered by General Gibbon to open fire to the left with solid shot at 4 degrees elevation. In a short time the enemy showed themselves in front, and, in their advance toward the battery, met with no opposition whatever from our infantry, who were posted on my right and front. I opened with solid shot and spherical case, and as they continued to advance, I opened with canister. Soon it was reported to me that we were out of canister. The enemy being within a few rods of us, I immediately limbered up, and was about to retire when a regiment of infantry took position on my left and rear, and opened fire. I immediately came into battery again, hoping that our infantry would drive the enemy back, as their force seemed to be small and much scattered. The enemy were too close. I endeavored to get my guns off the field; succeeded in getting off but three, as some of the drivers and horses were disabled while in the act of limbering up.

My horse was shot at this time, and, as I was rising from the ground I was struck with a spent ball, and everything seemed to be very much confused. I hastened off with the remaining guns. After the enemy had been driven back by the infantry, the other guns were brought off.

July 3.—Replenished ammunition. Remained in park until 1.30 o'clock near General Tyler's headquarters, about 500 yards in rear of our lines, when the enemy opened fire along the whole line, and it became so hot that we fell back out of range. Lieutenant Baldwin was wounded by a piece of shell at this time.

In a short time I was ordered to report to General Newton. On taking the battery up and reporting to him, I was told that he did not want light 12-pounders, and was ordered to return. I had moved but a few hundred yards when I was halted and ordered to the front, about the center of the line, which at the time was being hard pressed. I was conducted to General Webb's position, and came into battery under a heavy musketry fire. I opened at once with canister. In a few minutes our infantry charged, and the enemy were driven back. I was relieved about 6.30 o'clock, and returned to the Artillery Reserve camp.

Of the officers and men I cannot speak too highly. I would especially mention the names of Sergts. Henry Menard, [Ephraim N. R.] Ohl, [William E.] Lines, and [Daniel A.] Whitesell; the latter lost his leg. Private John Trevor is worthy of the highest praise.

List of casualties.*

Ammunition expended: 50 rounds of solid shot, 160 rounds of spherical case, and 70 rounds of canister; total, 280 rounds. One caisson lost.

Capt. D. R. Ransom commanded the brigade, and was with Lieutenant Turnbull's battery at the time he was wounded.

Very respectfully, your obedient servant,

G. V. WEIR,
First Lieutenant Fifth Artillery, Commanding Battery.

Capt. C. H. WHITTELSEY, *A. A. G., Artillery Reserve.*

---

*Embodied in revised statement, p. 187.

No. 318.

Report of Lieut. Col. Freeman McGilvery, First Maine Light Artillery, commanding First Volunteer Brigade.

—————, ————— —, 1863.

GENERAL: I have the honor to respectfully report the part taken by the First Volunteer Brigade, Artillery Reserve, and other batteries under my command, in the battle near Gettysburg, Pa., July 2 and 3.

My brigade—Battery F and C, consolidated Pennsylvania artillery, Captain Thompson; Ninth and Fifth Massachusetts Batteries, Captains Bigelow and Phillips; Fifteenth New York Independent Battery, Captain Hart—being in park at a central position near our line of battle, at about 3.30 p. m. on July 2, I received an order from yourself to report to General Sickles with one light 12-pounder and one rifled battery.

The Fifth Massachusetts Battery, Captain Phillips, and Ninth Massachusetts Battery, Captain Bigelow, were marched immediately to a position occupied by General Sickles, near a belt of oak woods, considerably in front of the prolongation of the natural line of defenses of our army, on the left center, in which General Sickles' command was then engaged with the enemy. By General Sickles' order, I made an examination of the grounds, and placed the two Massachusetts batteries in a position that commanded most of the open country between the woods held by our troops on the left center and high ground occupied by the enemy on their right. A New Jersey battery immediately on the right of the two Massachusetts batteries was receiving the most of the fire of two or more rebel batteries. Hart's Fifteenth New York Independent Battery reporting at that time, I placed it in position in a peach orchard on the right and a little in front of the New Jersey battery.

The four batteries already mentioned presented a front nearly at right angles with the position occupied by our troops, facing toward our left, the fire of which I concentrated on single rebel batteries, and five or more were driven in succession from their positions. Captain Thompson's battery (F and C, consolidated Pennsylvania artillery), of my brigade, took position on the right of the Fifteenth New York Battery, two sections of which battery fronted and fired in the direction of those heretofore mentioned, and the right section fronted to the right, and opened fire on a section or more of rebel artillery posted in the woods, at canister range, immediately on the right of the batteries under my command, the enfilade fire of which was inflicting serious damage through the whole line of my command.

At about 5 o'clock a heavy column of rebel infantry made its appearance in a grain-field about 850 yards in front, moving at quick time toward the woods on our left, where the infantry fighting was then going on. A well-directed fire from all the batteries was brought to bear upon them, which destroyed the order of their march and drove many back into the woods on their right, though the main portion of the column succeeded in reaching the point for which they started, and sheltered themselves from the artillery fire.

In a few minutes another and larger column appeared at about 750 yards, presenting a slight left flank to our position. I immediately trained the entire line of our guns upon them, and opened with various kinds of ammunition. The column continued to move on at double-quick until its head reached a barn and farm-house immediately in front of my left battery, about 450 yards distant, when it came to a halt. I gave them canister and solid shot with such good effect that I am sure that several hundred were put *hors de combat* in a short space of time. The column was broken—part fled in the direction from whence it came; part pushed on into the woods on our left; the remainder endeavored to shelter themselves in masses around the house and barn.

After the battle, I visited the position where this column in its confusion massed up around the house and barn heretofore mentioned, and found 120 odd dead, belonging to three South Carolina regiments. This mortality was no doubt from the effect of the artillery fire. The asperities of the ground in front of my batteries were such as to enable the enemy's sharpshooters in large numbers to cover themselves within very short range.

At about a quarter to 6 o'clock the enemy's infantry gained possession of the woods immediately on the left of my line of batteries, and our infantry fell back both on our right and left, when great disorder ensued on both flanks of the line of batteries. At this period of the action, all of the batteries were exposed to a warm infantry fire from both flanks and front, whereupon I ordered them to retire 250 yards and renew their fire. The New Jersey battery mentioned, being out of ammunition, retired to the rear. The Fifteenth New York Battery also retired from the field. Captains Bigelow and Phillips, who were under my observation about all the time, evinced great coolness and skill in retiring their batteries. Captain Phillips, Lieutenant Scott, and 4 men hauled one of his pieces off by hand, every horse in the limbers having been shot down, at which work Lieutenant Scott received a serious wound in the face, and it is a mystery to me that they were not all hit by the enemy's fire, as they were surrounded and fired upon from almost every direction. Captain Bigelow retired by prolonge, firing canister, which, with Captains Phillips and Thompson firing on his right in their new position, effectually checked the enemy in his advance for a short time. Captain Thompson, having all his horses belonging to one of the limbers of one of his pieces killed while retiring, was compelled to leave the piece, which fell into the hands of the enemy.

The crisis of the engagement had now arrived. I gave Captain Bigelow orders to hold his position as long as possible at all hazards, in order to give me time to form a new line of artillery, and justice demands that I should state Captain Bigelow did hold his position and execute his firing with a deliberation and destructive effect upon the enemy in a manner such as only a brave and skillful officer could, until—one officer killed and the others wounded, and more than half his men either killed or wounded, and his horses all shot down at the limbers—he was forced to leave four guns and retire. Two guns under command of Lieutenant Milton were taken safely to the rear.

In the meantime I formed a new line of artillery about 400 yards to the rear, close under the woods, and covering the opening which led into the Gettysburg and Taneytown road, of the following batteries and parts of batteries: Battery I, Fifth Regular, and a volunteer battery which I have never been able to learn the name of; three guns of the Fifth Masschusetts and two of Captain Thompson's Pennsylvania battery, and commenced firing on the enemy's line of infantry and artillery, which had formed in the open field only about 700 or 800 yards in our front. A brook, running through low bushes parallel to our front, midway between ours and the enemy's lines, was occupied by rebel sharpshooters. As soon as the Sixth Maine Battery reported, which was just before sundown, I ordered canister to be used on the low bushes in front, which compelled them to retire. About this time Pettit's New York battery reported, and changed position on the right of the Sixth Maine.

At this time the enemy's artillery fire was very heavy and rapid. The unknown volunteer battery, heretofore mentioned, left the field; the guns of Battery I, Fifth Regulars, were abandoned; Captain Thompson's guns, being out of ammunition, were sent to the rear; Pettit's First New York Battery [B] remained only a few minutes, and left while I was directing the fire of the Sixth Maine and a section of the Fifth Massachusetts, Captain Phillips. Lieutenant Dow, with the Sixth Maine and one section of the Fifth Massachusetts, Captain Phillips, remained in position, and kept up a well-directed fire upon the enemy's lines until they had ceased firing, which was about 8 o'clock. I then placed Captain Seeley's regular battery, Lieutenant James, in position near Lieutenant Dow's battery, with instructions to watch the enemy closely and fire upon any advancing column, or reply to any artillery that might be opened upon us. Here ended the engagement of July 2.

At 8 p. m. a detail was made from the Sixth Maine and Seeley's battery to go to the front and haul off the guns of Battery I, First [Fifth] Regulars. I instructed Lieutenant Dow to procure an infantry detail, and haul off the four guns of the Ninth Massachusetts, all of which was accomplished. The guns of the two batteries, numbering eight, were brought safely to the rear, and arrangements immediately made to secure their safe transportation in the event of any contingency that might necessitate a retreat or other movement.

During the engagement my horse was hit four times in the fore-shoulder and breast by musketry, once on the fore-leg by shell, and once on the hip by spent solid shot, of which wounds he soon after died.

During the night I ascertained the whereabouts of all my batteries, and early on the morning of July 3 brought them into line on the low ground on our left center, fronting the woods and elevated position occupied by the enemy along the Gettysburg and Emmitsburg road, a point at which it was plain to be seen they were massing artillery in great force.

The line of batteries under my command, commencing on the left, which rested on an oak wood, occupied by our infantry, were, in numbers and kind of guns, as follows: Ames' battery, six light 12-pounders; Dow's Sixth Maine Battery, four light 12-pounders; a New Jersey battery, six 3-inch guns; one section New York [Pennsylvania] Artillery, Lieutenant Rock [Captain Rank], two 3-inch guns; First [Second] Connecticut, four James rifled and two howitzers; Hart's Fifteenth New York Independent Battery, four light 12-pounders; Phillips' Fifth Massachusetts, six 3-inch rifled guns; Thompson's battery, F and C, consolidated Pennsylvania Artillery, five 3-inch rifled guns; total, thirty-nine guns. In front of these guns I had a slight earthwork thrown up, which proved sufficient to resist all the projectiles which struck it, and the commanders of batteries were repeatedly ordered that, in the event of the enemy opening a cannonading upon our lines, to cover their men as much as possible, and not return the fire until ordered.

At about 12.30 o'clock the enemy opened a terrific fire upon our lines with at least one hundred and forty guns. This fire was very rapid and inaccurate, most of the projectiles passing from 20 to 100 feet over our lines.   About one-half hour after the commencement, some general commanding the infantry line ordered three of the batteries to return the fire.   After the discharge of a few rounds, I ordered the fire to cease and the men to be covered.   After the enemy had fired about one hour and a half, and expended at least 10,000 rounds of ammunition, with but comparatively little damage to our immediate line, a slow, well-directed fire from all the guns under my command was concentrated upon single batteries of the enemy of those best in view, and several badly broken up and successively driven from their position to the rear.

At about 3 p. m. a line of battle of about 3,000 or 4,000 men appeared, advancing directly upon our front, which was completely broken up and scattered by our fire before coming within musket range of our lines.   Immediately after, appeared three extended lines of battle, of at least 35,000 men, advancing upon our center.   These three lines of battle presented an oblique front to the guns under my command, and by training the whole line of guns obliquely to the right, we had a raking fire through all three of these lines.   The execution of the fire must have been terrible, as it was over a level plain, and the effect was plain to be seen.   In a few minutes, instead of a well-ordered line of battle, there were broken and confused masses, and fugitives fleeing in every direction.   This ended the operations of the batteries under my command at the battle of Gettysburg.

In conclusion, I feel it a duty to state that the officers and men of the batteries in my brigade behaved in the most gallant manner. On July 2, where the battle raged most furiously, part of the Fifth and Ninth Massachusetts, and C and F, consolidated Pennsylvania Artillery, contested every inch of ground, and remained on the field to the very last.   The Sixth Maine Battery came into action in very opportune time, and rendered very valuable service.   Captain Irish, of Battery F, Pennsylvania Artillery, acting volunteer aide to me, was hit on the thigh in the early part of the engagement by solid shot, but would not leave the field to have his wound dressed until ordered by me to do so, and, notwithstanding a serious contusion which he was suffering under, reported to me on the morning of July 3, and remained with me during the day, ready to discharge any duty.   Captains Phillips' and Bigelow's conduct was gallant in the extreme.*

F. McGILVERY,
Lieutenant-Colonel, Commanding Brigade.

General R. O. TYLER, *Comdg. Artillery Reserve.*

No. 319.

Report of Capt. Charles A. Phillips, Battery E, Massachusetts Light Artillery.

HDQRS. BATTERY E, MASSACHUSETTS ARTILLERY,
July 6, 1863.

MAJOR: I have the honor to forward a report of the battery during the action of July 2 and 3.

---

* The number taken into action by this brigade was as follows: E, Massachusetts Artillery, 4 officers and 100 men; Ninth Massachusetts, 4 officers and 100 men; Fifteenth New York, 2 officers and 68 men; and C and F, Pennsylvania Artillery, 5 officers and 100 men; making a total of 15 officers and 368 men.

On the morning of the 2d, I marched from Taneytown toward Gettysburg, and came into park near the battle-field.

At 4 o'clock I was ordered into action, and took position on the right of Captain Bigelow and left of Captain Hart. The enemy soon opened a heavy artillery fire on our front and right, one battery on my right, which I could not see, giving us a very hot enfilading fire.

Toward 5 o'clock the enemy succeeded in forcing back our lines on our right and left, and the battery was subjected to a heavy musketry fire on both flanks. Accordingly, upon receiving the order from you, I limbered to the rear and retired. The horses on the left piece were shot before limbering, and we were obliged to bring the piece off by hand, leaving the limber. This was, however, brought off on the 4th.

Lieut. Henry D. Scott was shot in the face and severely wounded while bringing off this piece.

After retiring about 1,000 yards, I came into battery by the side of the Sixth Maine Battery, Lieutenant Dow commanding, and remained until my ammunition was expended, when I marched to the rear and went into park for the night.

At daylight on the 3d, I was ordered to the front, and took position to the right and rear of the position of the day before, on the right of Captain Hart and left of Captain Thompson. Under your directions, the guns were protected by a slight parapet, which proved of very great service.

About 1 o'clock the enemy opened a heavy fire from a long line of batteries, which was kept up for an hour, but beyond the noise which was made no great harm was done. Having received orders from General Hunt and from you not to reply to their batteries, I remained silent for the first half hour, when General Hancock ordered us to open. We then opened fire on the enemy's batteries, but in the thick smoke probably did very little damage. By your orders, we soon ceased firing. Soon after, a charge was made by General Longstreet's corps, and from my position I was enabled to pour a heavy enfilading fire into the rebel infantry. After the repulse of this charge, another was made by a Florida brigade within range of my guns. During the charge of General Longstreet, the rebels advanced a battery of 12-pounders on our left, whereupon the batteries of the First Brigade were ordered to concentrate their fire on it, which was done with such good effect that the rebel cannoneers were driven from their posts almost immediately, and left their guns on the field. I remained in this position until Saturday forenoon.

I beg leave to express entire satisfaction with my officers and men.

During the two days I fired 690 rounds; lost 1 officer, wounded; 4 men killed and 16 wounded, and 40 horses killed and a number disabled.

A number of small implements were lost during the falling back of the first day, but the only losses of *matériel* which interfere with the efficiency of the battery are 1 wheel harness for 1 horse, 4 sets of lead harness, and 2 wheels.

I am, very respectfully, your obedient servant,

CHAS. A. PHILLIPS,
Captain Battery E, Massachusetts Artillery.

Major McGILVERY,
Comdg. First Volunteer Brigade, Artillery Reserve.

No. 320.

Report of Lieut. Richard S. Milton, Ninth Massachusetts Battery.

CAMP NEAR BERLIN, MD., *July* 17, 1863.

SIR: I have the honor to submit to you the following report of the part taken by this command in the action at Gettysburg, Pa., July 2, 3, and 4:

Left Taneytown the morning of the 2d. Arrived at Gettysburg at 10 a. m. Went into park on the left of the Taneytown road with the rest of the reserve. Remained in park until 4 p. m., when ordered by Lieutenant-Colonel McGilvery to move to the left, to the support of General Sickles' corps. Went in battery in line with batteries of the Third Corps, on extreme left of the line, our left being within 50 yards of a dense woods; opened fire upon the enemy's batteries, about 1,600 yards in front of us, under cover of some buildings and a grove of woods.

After an hour's slow firing, the batteries fell back, and the enemy advanced in two lines of battle directly across our front, the Third Corps having fallen back, leaving us without support. At this time, having covered the withdrawal of the batteries upon our right, and receiving orders to retire, prolonges were fixed, and, firing at skirmishers on our left and the approaching line of battle on our right, we retired 300 yards, until we reached a position near which two stone walls met at an obtuse angle. This position, without infantry support and under an enfilading artillery fire, we were ordered to hold at all hazards. The rebel line of battle could not be checked, although its center was badly broken by our canister fire. Its flanks closing in on either side of us, obtained a cross-fire, which silenced the four pieces on my right, and prevented their withdrawal from loss of officers, men, and horses.

Having succeeded in retiring my section, I found myself in command of the battery. Under orders from Lieutenant-Colonel McGilvery, to whom I then reported, I withdrew a mile and a half to the rear and went into park, it being then 9 p. m. Our four guns were recovered the same day.

During the action, 1 commissioned officer, 1 sergeant, and 6 men were killed; 2 commissioned officers, 6 non-commissioned officers, and 9 men were wounded, and 2 taken prisoners; 45 horses were killed and 15 wounded.

The next morning drew ammunition, and, by your command, went into park near position of first day; remained there until 12 o'clock, when the enemy commenced vigorously shelling our line. The troops in our immediate vicinity having fallen back, and receiving no orders, I did the same, with the loss of 1 man wounded and 5 horses killed; retired to near reserve headquarters. Was ordered by Lieutenant [Lowell A.] Chamberlin to report to Major Robertson; by him ordered to report to Lieutenant-Colonel Warner, of General Hunt's staff, and, with two pieces of Battery K, Third U. S. Artillery, under command of Lieutenant Turnbull, was placed in position on right center, on left of Cemetery Hill, under immediate command of General Baxter, First Corps. Fired 15 rounds at skirmishers in a barn about 600 yards to our front. Was under fire of two Whitworth guns, planted by the enemy about 2 miles distant, the rest of the day, but sustained no loss.

Remained in same position until about 10 a. m. of the 5th; was then ordered to report to Lieutenant-Colonel McGilvery, then on the right of the Baltimore pike, about 2 miles to the rear.

I have the honor to remain, your obedient servant,

R. S. MILTON,
Lieutenant, Comdg. Ninth Massachusetts Vol. Battery.

Captain WHITTELSEY, *A. A. G., Artillery Reserve.*

No. 321.

Report of Capt. Patrick Hart, Fifteenth New York Battery.

NEAR WARRENTON JUNCTION, VA., *August* 2, 1863.

CAPTAIN: I have the honor to report, in compliance with the circular of July 17, the proceedings of the Fifteenth Independent New York Light Battery.

On the 2d instant [ultimo], I was ordered by Major McGilvery to go to the front with him, to take a position in the line of battle. I proceeded to the left and center, when we met General Sickles, with whom the major consulted. I halted my battery, and received orders to go with the major to reconnoiter the enemy. The major, General Tyler's aide, and I proceeded to the front, when the major pointed out the position I was to occupy. According to Major McGilvery's orders, I formed my battery into line, and was proceeding to take position when I met General Hunt, chief of artillery, who ordered me to take a position on the left of the peach orchard. I immediately obeyed the general's orders, and came into battery as directed. I then directed the fire of my battery on one of the enemy's batteries, which was doing heavy execution on our line of battle. This battery was to my right and front, and distant about 900 yards. I used solid shot and shell with such effect that the enemy was compelled to withdraw their battery. They then brought a battery still farther to my right. They poured a tremendous cross-fire into me, killing 3 of my men and wounding 5, also killing 13 horses.

At this time my attention was drawn to a heavy column of infantry advancing on our line. I directed my fire with shrapnel on this column to good effect. I then changed to canister, repulsing the attack made on my battery. At this time the batteries on my right were abandoned, with the exception of Captain Ames', which retired in good order to the rear.

After the first repulse of the enemy, they reformed and advanced on me a second time, and were repulsed. At this very moment I saw a very heavy column of the enemy advancing on the left of the barn and through a wheat-field, distant about 400 yards. I directed the fire of the left piece of my battery with canister upon this column, which did excellent execution, the enemy breaking in confusion. At this time the enemy were advancing in heavy force on me. I fired my last round of canister at this column before I retired. Previous to this I had sent to the rear for two of my caissons. There came word to me that they were not where I left them. I sent another messenger to bring them up. When they were convenient to me, they were again ordered to the rear. The only projectiles I had left were a few solid shot. I then limbered to the rear, and retired about 1 mile. When I got to the rear it was after dark. I then repaired damages, drew a supply of ammunition, and reported to General Tyler. I was ready for action again at 4 a. m. of the 3d.

I think it my duty to mention the brave and gallant conduct of General Tyler's aide, and also that of Lieutenant Knox, of my battery.

Early on the morning of the 3d, I received orders by Major McGilvery's orderly to proceed to the front, which order I immediately obeyed. When I reached the front, not being able to find Major McGilvery, I reported to Captain Thompson. He told me to come into position anywhere on his left, so as to leave room for Captain Phillips. I took position accordingly. A short time after, General Hunt, passing along the line, told me to hold my position and not to return the enemy's fire unless I saw his infantry advancing; then to open fire to the best advantage. This order was afterward repeated to me by Major McGilvery, which I obeyed, until ordered by General Hancock to open on the enemy's batteries. I obeyed this order, but after firing a few rounds Major McGilvery ordered me to cease firing. After the enemy opened with all of his batteries, I was ordered by Major McGilvery to return their fire, which I did.

At this time Second Lieut. E. M. Knox and I were wounded; Lieutenant Knox severely and myself slightly. First Lieut. A. R. McMahon being at the rear in arrest, and I having no officer to place in charge of the right section, I placed —— —— in charge of it, and Sergt. William Sheehy in charge of the left. The conduct of the latter during that terrific day's fight is deserving of the highest praise.

While firing at the enemy's batteries I used solid shot and shell, but when his infantry commenced to advance, I fired shell and shrapnel until the right of his first column came within about 500 yards of me, when I opened with canister, which took good effect. His second line appeared to be coming direct for my battery. I turned all my guns on this line, every piece loaded with two canisters. I continued this dreadful fire on this line until there was not a man of them to be seen.

At this time the enemy opened a battery on his right, in front of a barn, his projectiles killing many of my horses. I directed my fire on this battery and on his caissons, which were partly covered by the barn. I candidly believe it was I who caused his caissons to explode and set the barn on fire. Immediately afterward he brought a section to bear on me. I brought all the guns of my battery to bear on this section. The first gun that I fired exploded one of his limbers. Corporal Hammond with the next shot dismounted, I believe, one of his guns. Sergt. William Sheehy, I believe, followed with equal success. There was not a gun fired or a man to be seen at this section afterward, until, late in the evening, they sent down horses and took away one limber. My battery remained in position until near noon on the 4th, when I was ordered to the rear.

I think it my duty to mention here the gallant conduct of my sergeants and to recommend them. Their names are as follows: Sergts. William Sheehy, Alexander L. Robinson, Edmund Sheehy, James Sheehy, Thomas Fitzgerald (was severely wounded nobly doing his duty), John McGowan, and Corpl. Josiah B. Hammond. The corporals and men of my battery acted nobly during those two days' hard fighting. The noble and gallant conduct of Lieutenant Knox deserves the highest honor that could be conferred on him.

P. HART,
Captain, Commanding Battery.

Capt. C. H. WHITTELSEY,
   Assistant Adjutant-General.

No. 322.

Report of Lieut. Andrew R. McMahon, Fifteenth New York Battery.

NEAR BERLIN, MD., *July* 17, 1863.

CAPTAIN: I have the honor to report, in compliance with the circular of this day, the proceedings of my battery, commanded by Captain Hart, during the engagement at Gettysburg, Pa., July 2 and 3.

On the 2d instant, we were ordered to take up our position, which we did, in a peach orchard on the left and center at 4.30 p. m. We opened fire upon a rebel battery which had taken up position about 1,100 yards directly in front of us, being partly protected by a house on their right. While we were engaged, the rebel infantry were advanced, in order to carry our position. This was about 5.30 p. m. We immediately changed the direction of our fire, and brought it to bear upon the approaching columns with good effect, but this was not sufficient to stay their advance. When within the proper range, we commenced firing canister, and did not cease firing until the infantry which were supporting us were driven back and the battery on our right had limbered up and retired from the fight. We were then ordered to retire, which we did at 6.30 p. m.

Our loss during this day's fight was 3 men killed, 5 wounded, and 13 horses killed.

We encamped for the night about 2 miles from the field of battle. On the 3d instant, we were ordered to proceed to the front at 12 m., and took up our position on the left of the cemetery, and prepared for action. At 3 p. m. the rebels commenced a heavy firing upon the whole of our line. We did not return any answer (according to orders) until about 4 p. m., when, by General Hancock's orders, we commenced firing.

At about 5 p. m. the rebel infantry advanced in two lines of battle. The first line, moving by a flank march to the right, advanced on the cemetery; the second line, forming in rear of the first, advanced in a direct line for my battery. We immediately commenced shelling them very effectively. They advanced steadily to within 300 yards. We then commenced firing double-shotted canister into them, which had the immediate effect of staying their attack and throwing them into disorder. They then became an easy prey to our infantry, who charged on their right flank. We immediately ceased firing, and were ordered to remain in position until further orders, which we did until the morning of the 4th.

Our loss on the 3d was 1 man killed, 2 commissioned officers and 4 men wounded, and 12 horses killed and wounded.

Very respectfully, your obedient servant.
ANDREW R. McMAHON,
First Lieutenant, Commanding Battery.

Capt. C. H. WHITTELSEY, *Assistant Adjutant-General.*

———

No. 323.

Report of Capt. James Thompson, Batteries C and F, Pennsylvania Light Artillery.

CAMP NEAR GETTYSBURG, PA., *July* 4, 1863.

CAPTAIN: I would most respectfully report that at about 5 p. m. on the 2d instant, in accordance with orders received from Major

McGilvery, commanding First Brigade, Artillery Reserve, I proceeded with my battery to the front, and took a position which he assigned me, occupying the angle where the right of our line was thrown back, and facing southward, about 2 miles from the town.

I placed two guns in battery facing west, and four guns facing to the south, and was engaged with the enemy's infantry and artillery for about one hour, when the enemy advanced and drove back our infantry supports, capturing one of the two guns facing west, but our infantry, rallying, recaptured it, when I limbered them up and retired about 300 yards, as our infantry was again falling back, and brought them into action again with the four guns that were in action facing to the south, and fired a few rounds, when we were driven back, having the horses in one of the gun's limbers killed, and also in one of the caisson's limbers, the enemy again capturing a gun and one caisson. I had the gun horses disengaged, and the piece moved off some distance by hand, and as the enemy was gaining ground rapidly on us, the infantry that were assisting us left, and we were compelled to leave it, having 1 man killed, 8 wounded, and 4 missing, supposed to have been taken prisoners. We then retired, and afterward fired a short time from a position about 1,200 yards in rear. I was then permitted to retire the battery and replace the disabled horses, &c., and was ordered into park until morning.

Casualties as follows.* Had also 1 horse shot under me, and 18 more killed and wounded.

At about 5 a. m. July 3, was placed in position in line with Battery K, Fourth U. S. Artillery, on our right, and Captain Hart's Fifteenth New York Independent Battery on our left, at which place we were hotly engaged with the enemy frequently during the day, with the following casualties.†

I have also most cheerfully to report very highly as to the conduct of my officers, non-commissioned officers, and men; and of the enlisted men would make special mention of Sergt. Thomas Brown, and also of Private C. R. Carlisle, who, when the 4 lead horses of one of the guns were killed, 1 wheel horse badly wounded, and drivers also wounded, assisted me to disengage the traces of the dead leaders, under a heavy musketry fire (in action of the 2d instant), and he mounted the wheel horses, and took the gun off the field, thereby saving it, and I recommend that a medal be granted him for his conduct on this occasion and subsequent good conduct on the 3d instant.

Most respectfully submitted.

J. THOMPSON,
Capt. Comdg. Batteries C and F, Pennsylvania Artillery.

Capt. C. H. WHITTELSEY, *Assistant Adjutant-General.*

No. 324.

Report of Capt. Franklin A. Pratt, Battery M, First Connecticut Artillery, Second Volunteer Brigade.

CAMP NEAR BERLIN, MD., *July 17, 1863.*

CAPTAIN: I have the honor to report that during the late movements my battery was with the Artillery Reserve until July 2, when

---

*Nominal list, here omitted, shows 1 man killed, 1 officer and 8 men wounded, and 1 man missing.
†Nominal list, here omitted, shows 4 officers and 10 men wounded.

it was ordered from Taneytown to Westminster, where it remained until the 6th instant, when, by orders from General Tyler, it started to join the Artillery Reserve at Taneytown, but when part way there it was ordered back to Westminster, and went into position there, an attack from the enemy's cavalry being anticipated. The enemy not appearing, was ordered after dark to proceed to Frederick; moved to Uniontown, and encamped.

July 7, moved on as far as Liberty.

July 8, joined Artillery Reserve near Frederick; continued with it to Jones' Cross-Roads, at which place remained until the 15th instant, when rejoined Artillery Reserve at Boonsborough, and moved with it to this place.

I have had no difficulty in moving my guns over the worst roads we have passed, but have worn down my caisson teams and met some delays with the caissons, which I respectfully submit should be furnished with 8 horses to a carriage.

Very respectfully, your obedient servant,

F. A. PRATT,
Captain First Regt. Conn. Arty., Comdg. Siege Batty. M.

Capt. C. H. WHITTELSEY,
Assistant Adjutant-General, Artillery Reserve.

No. 325.

Report of Capt. Elijah D. Taft, Fifth New York Battery.

CAMP OF ARTILLERY RESERVE, ARMY OF THE POTOMAC,
July 19, 1863.

SIR: I have the honor to report that the battery commanded by me (Fifth New York Independent) marched from Taneytown, Md., on the morning of the 2d instant, to near Gettysburg, Pa., where it halted in park about 10.30 a. m., and at 3.30 p. m. marched from park to the cemetery, where we arrived at 4 p. m., and reported to Major-General Howard. At 5 p. m. took position in the cemetery, and engaged a battery on the north of the cemetery with four guns, and one west with two guns, also firing at the enemy's infantry to the west, at times with good effect, firing until too dark to be effective, remaining in the same position during the night.

On the 3d instant, the enemy opened fire about 8 a. m. I returned it at intervals until about 10 a. m. The enemy opened fire again about 1.30 p. m., which was returned by my battery. Soon after, one of my guns burst at the muzzle, and at 3 p. m. that portion of the battery firing northward ceased firing, as the enemy had ceased in that direction, and at 4 p. m. those three guns relieved the section firing westward, and remained firing on the enemy's artillery and infantry until the close of the engagement, about 6 p. m.

Remained in the same position until 10 a. m. of the 5th instant, when, by orders of General Tyler, I again joined the reserve at the Artillery Reserve camp, 2 miles from Gettysburg.

I also have to report the following casualties during the late engagement at Gettysburg, Pa.: Private John C. Begg, Fifth New York Independent Battery, mortally wounded by the accidental explosion of a caisson limber July 2, while approaching the battlefield, from which he died July 7, near Gettysburg, Pa.; Private Anton Thalheimer, wounded in the bowels by a bullet at 9 a. m. on the 3d instant, died at 12 o'clock on the same night; Sergt. Henry Dillon, slightly wounded in the neck by a bullet about 10 a. m. of the 3d instant; Private Adolph Wittenberg, severely wounded by a bullet through the leg about 2 p. m. of the 3d instant. One caisson body broken by a shot from the enemy, since replaced by spare parts taken from the field. One 20-pounder Parrott gun exploded.

Destroyed and lost in action 1 spare pole, 1 shovel (long handle), 1 tar-bucket, 5 sponges and staves, 4 handspikes, 1 pickax, 1 leather water-bucket, I gunner's haversack, and 1 tarpaulin; and during the engagement I expended the following ammunition: 80 Schenkl percussion shell, 63 Schenkl combination shrapnel, 32 Parrott time-fuse shell, 382 Parrott time-fuse shrapnel, and 557 cartridges.

All of which is respectfully submitted.

I have the honor to be, your obedient servant,

E. D. TAFT,
Captain Fifth New York Independent Battery.

Capt. C. H. WHITTELSEY,
Assistant Adjutant-General, Artillery Reserve.

No. 326.

Report of Capt. Frederick M. Edgell, First New Hampshire Battery, Third Volunteer Brigade.

LIGHT BATTERY A, FIRST N. H. ARTILLERY,
Camp Artillery Reserve, July 6, 1863.

SIR: I have the honor to submit the following account of the operations of the First New Hampshire Battery during the recent action near Gettysburg, Pa.:

The battery arrived on the field from Taneytown on July 2, at 10 a. m., and at 4 p. m., by order of Major Osborn, chief of artillery, Eleventh Corps, went into position on Cemetery Hill, immediately on the left of the cemetery, relieving a battery, the name of which I did not ascertain. At that time the fire of the enemy's artillery was directed upon the hill from positions in our front and to the left. After getting the range, I commenced throwing percussion and time shell at their batteries, engaging but one at a time; the first one, situated on the Chambersburg road and opposite the seminary, I succeeded in silencing for the time. The firing was necessarily slow, on account of the distance (2,000 yards and over), and later in the afternoon gradually ceased, only an occasional shot being fired. Up to this time I had expended 105 rounds of ammunition, and had one horse killed and one wheel smashed.

An attack being now apprehended on the right, I was directed by Major Osborn to move to a position in a corn-field near the Baltimore turnpike, with instructions to cover the possible retreat of our troops from the woods on the right. Our troops, however, maintained their position, and my battery was not employed. The men were kept at the guns during the night, as the firing of musketry was sharp and continuous. As the morning of the 3d began to dawn, the firing became more rapid, and did not cease until about 11 a. m.

At about 1.30 p. m. the enemy opened a rapid artillery fire on our center and left. Their batteries, in a semicircle about this point, swept the hill with a terrible cross-fire. The battery was now much exposed to the plunging shots of the enemy, which fell continually among my pieces, but fortunately without doing much damage.

At 2.30 p. m. I was ordered to take up my old position on Cemetery Hill, relieving Captain Huntington's Ohio battery. I commenced again to throw shell at the enemy's batteries, and also at some bodies of troops, apparently picket reserves, which caused them to break and retreat to the woods. The firing of the enemy's artillery was now very inaccurate, most of the shots being too high, and by the direction of General Meade the firing was discontinued by the batteries on the hill, and the men ordered to lie down.

Soon after, at about 4 p. m., a grand attack was made by the enemy on our left, and I commenced a rapid fire of case shot on his advancing lines. I fired obliquely from my position upon the left of the attacking column with destructive effect, as that wing was broken and fled across the field to the woods. I next saw what appeared to be the remainder of the attacking force come into our lines prisoners. There was no firing by my battery after this.

I expended this day 248 rounds of shell and case shot, making 353 total expended. The Hotchkiss time shell and Schenkl percussion worked well, but the Schenkl combination case seldom exploded. From what experience I have had with this fuse, I think it is not reliable.

The casualties in my battery were 3 men wounded (only 1 seriously). I also lost 3 horses killed, and a wheel and axle broken. The latter were replaced during the night of the 4th from the field.

I am happy to state that the officers and men of the New Hampshire battery behaved nobly. Although for forty-eight hours under fire, and a part of that time exposed to a terrific cannonade, not a man left his post or wavered, and, by their steadiness and precision of fire on the afternoon of the 3d, I believe contributed much toward repulsing the enemy's attack. For confirmation of this, I would respectfully refer to Major Osborn, chief of artillery, Eleventh Corps, under whose direction my battery was placed during the action of the 2d and 3d.

I am, sir, very respectfully, your obedient servant,
F. M. EDGELL,
Captain First New Hampshire Battery.

Capt. C. H. WHITTELSEY,
Assistant Adjutant-General, Artillery Reserve.

No. 327.

Report of Lieut. George W. Norton, Battery H, First Ohio Light Artillery.

BERLIN, MD., *July* 17, 1863.

CAPTAIN : I have the honor to submit the following report of the part taken by Battery H, First Ohio Artillery, attached to Third Volunteer Brigade, in the late battle near Gettysburg :

The battery was put in position on Cemetery Hill on the 2d instant, about 4 p. m., under direction of Major Osborn, chief of artillery, Eleventh Corps, and opened fire on a rebel battery situated on the right of the town, and continued firing at intervals all the afternoon.

Toward evening, a battery was opened on us from a wheat-field at about 1,800 yards, which we silenced after a sharp duel of about twenty minutes' duration. Considerable annoyance was experienced from the enemy's sharpshooters, but only 2 men were hit.

On the 3d instant, the battery fired at intervals during the day at batteries in various positions on the left and front.

The men were much exhausted by heat and fatigue, and after the close of the battle of Friday the battery was relieved and went to the rear, where it remained until the next morning, when it was sent up again to relieve one of the batteries of the First Corps, by request of Colonel Wainwright, chief of artillery, and occupied gun-covers near the cemetery until the afternoon of the 5th instant, when it rejoined the reserve, and proceeded that night to Littlestown.

Our loss was 2 killed and 5 wounded, 8 horses killed or rendered useless, and 1 gun-carriage disabled. We expended during the two days' fight 360 shell and 407 shrapnel; total, 767 rounds. Our loss, considering the position, exposed as we were to heavy enfilading and cross fire, was very small, and, judging from the appearance of the ground occupied by the batteries which we silenced, our ammunition in that instance was expended to good advantage.

All of which is respectfully submitted.

G. W. NORTON,
First Lieut., Comdg. Co. H, First Regt. Ohio Light Arty.

Capt. C. H. WHITTELSEY,
Asst. Adjt. Gen., Artillery Reserve.

No. 328.

Report of Capt. R. Bruce Ricketts, Batteries F and G, First Pennsylvania Light Artillery.

HDQRS. BATTERIES F AND G, FIRST PA. ARTILLERY,
August 30, 1863.

CAPTAIN: In compliance with your communication of the 29th instant, I have the honor to submit the following report of the part taken by my battery in the battle of July 2 and 3, at Gettysburg:

On July 2, my battery moved from Taneytown to Gettysburg with Captain Huntington's brigade, to which it was attached, arriving on the field about noon.

At 4 p. m. I was ordered by Captain Huntington to report to Col. C. S. Wainwright, First New York Artillery, who placed me in position on Cemetery Hill, to the right of the turnpike leading into Gettysburg. During the afternoon, I was engaged with the batteries on the enemy's left, and in shelling a column of the enemy that charged into the woods on my right, which was occupied by the Twelfth Army Corps.

At about 8 p. m. a heavy column of the enemy charged on my battery, and succeeded in capturing and spiking my left piece. The cannoneers fought them hand to hand with handspikes, rammers, and pistols, and succeeded in checking them for a moment, when a part of the Second Army Corps charged in and drove them back. During the charge I expended every round of canister in the battery, and then fired case shot without the fuses. The enemy suffered severely.

During the battle of July 3, I was engaged with the batteries on the enemy's left and center.

During the battle of the 2d and 3d, I expended 1,200 rounds of ammunition.

The casualties were as follows: Killed, 6; wounded, 14; missing, 3. Horses killed, 20.

First Lieut. C. B. Brockway, Battery F, First Pennsylvania Artillery, First Lieut. Beldin Spence, Battery G, First Pennsylvania Artillery, and First Sergt. Francis H. Snider, fought their sections with the greatest gallantry.

I am, captain, very respectfully, your obedient servant,

R. BRUCE RICKETTS,
Capt. First Pa. Artillery, Comdg. Batteries F and G.

Capt. C. H. WHITTELSEY,
Asst. Adjt. Gen., Artillery Reserve.

No. 329.

Report of Capt. Wallace Hill, Battery C, First West Virginia Light Artillery.

BERLIN HEIGHTS, MD.,
July 17, 1863.

SIR: In compliance with your order of the present date, requiring a detailed report of the action my battery took in the late battle of Gettysburg, I have the honor to tender the following:

On Thursday, July 2, about 4.30 p. m., the Third Brigade was ordered to the front. Arrived there, my battery was immediately ordered into position on Cemetery Hill, where it remained until the afternoon of the 5th instant.

Shortly after engaging the enemy, I had the misfortune to lose Stephen J. Braddock, one of my cannoneers, and on Friday afternoon Charles Lacey, a driver, fell, mortally wounded. Both were excellent soldiers, and fell at their posts. James Loufman and John Hill were slightly wounded, but have fully recovered. My loss in horses was 5. I expended 1,120 rounds of ammunition.

Finally, I think I have just cause to feel proud of the part my men sustained during the entire terrible engagement.

All of which is most respectfully submitted.

Your obedient servant,

WALLACE HILL,
Capt., Comdg. Battery C, First W. Va. Vol. Arty.

Capt. C. H. WHITTELSEY,
Assistant Adjutant-General.

No. 330.

Report of Capt. Robert H. Fitzhugh, First New York Light Artillery, commanding Fourth Volunteer Brigade.

HDQRS. FOURTH VOL. BRIG., ARTILLERY RESERVE,
——, —— —, 1863.

CAPTAIN: I have the honor to submit the following report of the part taken by the batteries under my command at the battle of Gettysburg, July 1 to 5:

Arriving on the field from Taneytown about 8 a. m. July 2, I was ordered by Brig. Gen. R. O. Tyler, commanding Artillery Reserve, to take two batteries (K, First New York Artillery, and A, First New Jersey Artillery, First Lieut. A. N. Parsons commanding) and go into position on the Baltimore turnpike, near General Slocum's line.

From this time until July 5, the other batteries of the Fourth Brigade were detached from my command, G, First New York Artillery, and the Sixth Maine Battery, First Lieut. E. B. Dow commanding, being under command of Lieut. Col. F. McGilvery, and Battery A, First Maryland Artillery, Capt. J. H. Rigby, being sent to the Twelfth Corps.

The two batteries left with me—A, First New Jersey Artillery, First Lieut. A. N. Parsons commanding, and K, First New York Artillery—remained unengaged until 1 p. m. of Friday, July 3, when, by order of General Hunt, I put them in position near the stone fence in front of General Webb's division of the Second Corps, Battery A, First New Jersey Artillery, on the left of K, First New York Artillery.

At this time the enemy were making a strong effort to break the Second Corps line, their infantry having charged up to the stone fence near a small wooded knoll about 75 yards on my right, while their artillery fire swept the ground occupied by the two batteries. Just then there were no other batteries at that point, and there seemed to be a good deal of confusion. The rebel artillery fire, from near a house and barn about 1,000 yards on my left and front, was especially severe, but soon materially slackened, and became very wild under a fire of percussion and time shell from Battery K. In the meantime, Lieutenant Parsons poured about 40 rounds of shrapnel into the flank of the rebel infantry charging the Second Corps, and in about half or three-quarters of an hour the enemy abandoned the attack on that point altogether.

After a pause of about an hour, the rebel infantry began forming on the right of the house and barn before spoken of, while from the same quarter their artillery opened upon us a brisk but poorly directed and inefficient fire, to which, by direction of General Hunt, I made no reply, but awaited the attack of their infantry, who soon charged over the open field toward some broken ground about 500 yards on my left, as they did so giving the two batteries an opportunity to pour in an enfilading fire, which they did with great effect, for the enemy did not reach the point, but broke and gave way in all directions when about the middle of the field.

After this, we remained in position on the same ground until about 10 a. m. July 5, when I was ordered to rejoin the Artillery Reserve.

Of the conduct of officers and men, both of Battery A, First New Jersey Artillery, Lieut. A. N. Parsons commanding, and of K, First New York Artillery, with the Eleventh New York Battery attached, I cannot speak too highly. Coming into position at a critical point of the rebel charge on our center, and under a galling fire, the guns were worked with great deliberation and a most decided effect.

Casualties in Battery K, First New York Artillery, and Eleventh New York Independent Battery attached : Wounded, 7. Losses in *matériel*, &c.: Horses, 5. Ammunition expended: Percussion shell, 57; shrapnel, 15, and time shell, 17. Total, 89.

Casualties in Battery A, First New Jersey Artillery : Killed, 2;

wounded, 7. Losses in *matériel*, &c.: Horses, 5. Ammunition expended: Shrapnel, 120; shell, 80. Total, 200.
Very respectfully, your obedient servant,

R. H. FITZHUGH,
*Captain Battery K, First New York Artillery,
Comdg. Fourth Volunteer Brigade, Artillery Reserve.*

Capt. C. H. WHITTELSEY,
Assistant Adjutant-General, Artillery Reserve.

No. 331.

Report of Lieut. Edwin B. Dow, Sixth Maine Battery.

CAMP NEAR BERLIN, MD., *July* 17, 1863.

CAPTAIN: I have the honor to report the action taken by the Sixth Maine Battery, under my command, at the battle of July 2 and 3, near Gettysburg, Pa.

I received orders from General Tyler, through Lieutenant Blucher, to report to General Sickles' (Third) corps, on the left center, about (p. m. 2d instant. I immediately marched my command to the front, meeting an ambulance with General Sickles in it, badly wounded.

I had not gone far when Major McGilvery ordered me into position in rear of the first line, remarking that he had charge of the artillery of the Third Corps. On going into position, my battery was under a heavy fire from two batteries of the enemy, situated some 1,000 yards in my front. I replied to them with solid shot and shell until the enemy's line of skirmishers and sharpshooters came out of the woods to the left front of my position and poured a continual stream of bullets at us. I soon discovered a battle line of the enemy coming through the wood about 600 yards distant, evidently with a design to drive through and take possession of the road to Taneytown, directly in my rear. I immediately opened upon them with spherical case and canister, and, assisted by a section of Captain Phillips' (Fifth Massachusetts) battery, drove them back into the woods. Their artillery, to which we paid no attention, had gotten our exact range, and gave us a warm greeting.

We continued to shell the woods after their infantry retired, and upon visiting the spot the same night, about 9 o'clock, found many rebels dead and wounded. It was evidently their intention, after capturing the Ninth Massachusetts Battery and Company I, Fifth Regulars, to have charged right through our lines to the Taneytown road, isolating our left wing and dividing our army; but owing to the prompt and skillful action of Maj. Freeman McGilvery, in forming this second line as soon as he found the first line lost, their plan was foiled, for they no doubt thought the woods in our rear were filled with infantry in support of the batteries, when the fact is we had no support at all. At this crisis, my orders from Major McGilvery were to hold my position at all hazards until he could re-enforce the position and relieve me. It was about 7 o'clock when the enemy retired, and I was in action altogether about one hour and a half.

At 7.30 p. m. I was relieved by Major McGilvery, who placed Seeley's battery, under command of Lieutenant James, in my position, and I retired into the edge of the woods. Lieutenant Rogers, of this battery, in reconnoitering found the enemy had retired from the field in haste, and had not taken the captured guns with them, nor even spiked them.   He immediately reported the fact to me, and as many men as I could spare were sent under his charge to bring them off the field.   With the aid of the Garibaldi Guard, of New York, he brought off, under a fire from the enemy's sharpshooters, four 3-inch rifled guns and two limbers belonging to Company I, Fifth Regulars, which we immediately limbered on our caissons and ran to the rear.

I was then ordered by Major McGilvery to go to the front and see if any other public property was on the field, which order I obeyed, and discovered four light 12-pounder guns and a limber of the Ninth Massachusetts Battery.   The remnant of the One hundred and fiftieth New York Regiment, although tired and weary, took hold of the guns and ran them up to Lieutenant James' position, where I turned them over to Lieutenant James, not having force sufficient to bring them off the field.   Lieutenant James brought the guns off, and, I understood, turned them over to the Ninth Massachusetts Battery.

By order of Major McGilvery, I reported to Generals Tyler and Hunt what we had done.   General Hunt ordered me to go to the rear near the reserve train with the guns.   I did so, and next morning had the satisfaction of returning the guns of Company I, Fifth Regulars, to their commanding officer.

I am happy to state that in this action, although under the most severe artillery and sharpshooters' fire, I had only 8 men wounded, not one killed.   Ammunition expended, 244 rounds.

After repairing damages and getting a new supply of ammunition, I reported to Major McGilvery on the morning of the 3d, and was ordered into position between the Second Connecticut Battery and Ames' (First New York) battery, supported by a brigade of the Second Corps.   I built earthworks in front of my guns.

Nothing of importance occurred until about 11 o'clock, when, at a signal of one gun, the whole rebel line opened a most terrific fire upon our position.   Case shot and shell filled the air.   The men were ordered to cease firing and take refuge behind their earthworks.   This fire lasted without much abatement about one hour and a half, when we discovered the enemy advancing under cover of the artillery.   A light 12-pounder battery of four guns ran some 400 or 500 yards in front of the enemy's line, so as to enfilade the batteries on our right. We opened with solid shot and shell upon this battery, and succeeded in dismounting one gun, disabling the second, and compelled the battery to leave the field minus one caisson and several horses.

I deem it due to Major McGilvery to say that he was ever present, riding up and down the line in the thickest of the fire, encouraging the men by his words and dashing example, his horse receiving eight wounds, of which he has since died, the gallant major himself receiving only a few scratches.

The enemy fired mostly case shot and shell at our position, nearly all of which passed over our line of artillery and supports and exploded in the woods behind, covering the road with their fragments. Our loss this day was only 5 men wounded and 5 horses killed.

Owing to an injunction from General Hunt not to reply to the enemy's fire, but save our ammunition, we expended only 139 rounds. In the two days' action we did not lose a gun or carriage, but reported for duty again as soon as our stock of ammunition was replenished. I was ably seconded by Lieutenant Rogers, to whom we owe much of our success,

Where all did well it is useless to specify any certain individual among the non-commissioned officers and privates.

I have the honor to be, captain, most respectfully, your obedient servant,

EDWIN B. DOW,
First Lieutenant, Commanding Sixth Maine Battery.

Capt. C. H. WHITTELSEY,
Assistant Adjutant-General, Artillery Reserve.

No. 332.

Report of Capt. James H. Rigby, Battery A, Maryland Light Artillery.

BERLIN, MD., *July* 17, 1863.

SIR: I have the honor to report the following as the part taken by my battery in the recent fight at Gettysburg:

On the morning of July 2, I was ordered to place my battery in position on a hill about 1 mile south of Gettysburg and 500 yards west of the Baltimore turnpike. The Twelfth Corps, under the command of Major-General Slocum, occupied the woods in front. I opened fire at about 2 o'clock on a battery of the enemy, distant about 2,500 yards; but, finding the distance too great, I ceased firing for that day.

At daylight on the morning of the 3d, I commenced shelling the woods in my front, and continued firing slowly for about three hours.

I remained in this position until Sunday afternoon, July 5. During the whole time I only fired 211 rounds—41 rounds of Schenkl percussion shell and 170 Hotchkiss shell. I have been informed by Major-General Slocum that the battery did terrible execution.

On Sunday afternoon I was ordered to report to the headquarters Artillery Reserve.

I am happy to state that I had no casualties whatever.

I am, sir, most respectfully, your obedient servant,

JAMES H. RIGBY,
Captain, Commanding Battery A, Maryland Artillery.

Captain WHITTELSEY,
Assistant Adjutant-General, Artillery Reserve.

No. 333.

Report of Lieut. Augustin N. Parsons, Battery A, New Jersey Light Artillery.

BATTERY A, FIRST NEW JERSEY ARTILLERY, ART. RES.,
July 17, 1863.

GENERAL: I have the honor to report that on the 3d instant, about 3 p. m., I received orders from General Hunt to move the battery to the front as quickly as possible. I at once obeyed the order, and soon had the battery in position about one-fourth of a mile south of Gettysburg Cemetery and near the Second Division, Second Corps, Captain Fitzhugh's battery following immediately after me and taking position on my right. At this time the enemy's infantry were advancing very rapidly. I at once opened fire upon them with case shot, and fired about 120 rounds with good effect. As soon as they fell back, I opened fire upon one of the enemy's batteries (which by this time had gotten an exact range of my position) with shell, and used 80 rounds, when I received orders from General Hunt to cease firing. My shell were telling upon the enemy's battery, and I believe that I could have completely silenced it in five minutes more.

During the action I lost 2 men killed and 7 wounded. I also lost 3 horses killed and 2 wounded, which have since died.

I am, sir, very respectfully, your most obedient servant,

A. N. PARSONS,
First Lieutenant, Commanding Battery.

General TYLER,
Commanding Artillery Reserve, Army of the Potomac.

No. 334.

Report of Capt. Nelson Ames, Battery G, First New York Light Artillery.

CAMP AT ELKTON, VA., *September 7, 1863.*

SIR: I have the honor to submit the following report of the operations of Company G, First New York Light Artillery, in the battle of Gettysburg, Pa., on July 2 and 3:

At 11 o'clock on the morning of the 2d, I received orders from headquarters Artillery Reserve to report with my battery to Major-General Sickles, commanding Third Army Corps. Having reported, I was ordered to move forward and shelter the battery behind the piece of woods on the Emmitsburg road, near the stone barn. I remained there until 3 p. m., when Captain Randolph, chief of artillery Third Army Corps, ordered me to move forward about 800 yards, take position in a thick peach orchard, and engage the enemy's batteries at a distance of 850 yards. I immediately moved forward, and, while crossing a cleared field, the enemy opened fire from one of their batteries. They got an excellent range of my battery, nearly all of their shot striking in my battery, but fortunately they did no other damage than killing 2 horses.

Before gaining the position assigned me, I was obliged to halt in plain sight of the enemy, to clear away two fences which the supporting infantry had failed to throw down as they had been ordered to do. As soon as I could come into battery, I opened upon the battery in my front with spherical case and shell, and, after firing about thirty minutes, the enemy's fire greatly slackened, and in a few moments more it nearly ceased; but before I had time to congratulate myself or men upon our success with this battery, a four-gun battery of light 12-pounders opened upon my right from a grove 500 yards distant, and at the same time a new battery opened on my front. I immediately ordered Lieutenant McClellan, commanding the right section, to turn his two pieces upon the flank battery, while Lieutenants Hazelton and Goff kept up their fire upon the battery in front, and for a short time I had as sharp an artillery fight as I ever witnessed. I was soon pleased to see one piece of the flank battery dismounted, and the cannoneers of another either killed or wounded, when the other two pieces were taken from the field. I then turned my whole attention upon the batteries in front, but was obliged to fire very slowly, as my ammunition was getting exhausted, having but a few rounds of spherical case left, with a small supply of solid shot and canister.

About this time the rebel infantry advanced in line of battle across the wheat-field to my left and front. Lieutenant Hazelton opened upon them with spherical case—he having collected all there was in the battery—with great success as long as that kind of ammunition lasted. He then ceased firing, and ordered his cannoneers to shelter themselves until the enemy advanced within canister range, when he purposed to drive them back with the unwelcome messenger—grape and canister—Lieutenants McClellan and Goff meanwhile keeping up a steady, slow fire with solid shot upon the batteries in front. After having been engaged for two and a half hours, at 5.30 p. m. I was relieved by Battery I, Fifth U. S. Artillery.

My loss during the two and a half hours' fighting was 7 men wounded, 1 mortally and 2 seriously; also a loss of 11 horses killed.

Moving to the rear upon being relieved, I parked the battery near the ammunition train of the Artillery Reserve.

At daylight on the morning of the 3d, I refilled with ammunition and reported to reserve headquarters, and received orders to move forward near the Frederick and Gettysburg pike, and there await further orders. I remained there until about 10 a. m., when the cannonading from the rebel lines commenced. I then received orders from Captain Whittelsey to move to the rear and take shelter behind a piece of woods. I remained sheltered until about 12 m., when I received your orders to move to the front as soon as possible, and take position wherever I could find room, as the enemy's lines were being advanced, under cover of their artillery fire, to charge upon our lines. I took position on the left, near the mountain, and opened fire with spherical case upon the advancing lines as they crossed the fields. These lines falling back, I ceased firing, for my ammunition was again getting low, although the enemy's batteries continued to throw shell into my battery, killing 3 horses and wounding 1 man. I held this position until 3 p. m. of July 4, when I was ordered to withdraw.

My loss in the two days' fighting consisted of 8 men wounded, 14 horses killed, and a very light loss and breakage of *matériel*. The loss in *matériel* was one wheel slightly shattered, one pole broken, and some small parts of carriages shot away.

My lieutenants and men, one and all, performed their duties with that alacrity and promptness that shows them possessed of the qualities that make the patriot soldier.

I am, sir, yours, respectfully,

N. AMES,
Capt. First N. Y. Light Arty., Comdg. Company G.

Capt. C. H. Whittelsey,
A. A. G., Artillery Reserve, Army of the Potomac.

No. 335.

Report of Maj. Charles Ewing, Fourth New Jersey Infantry, Train Guard.

Near Warrenton Junction, Va.,
August 23, 1863.

Captain: In obedience to orders received from headquarters Artillery Reserve, I have the honor to report that on July 2, while in charge of the ammunition train of the Artillery Reserve, my regiment arrived at the scene of action at Gettysburg, Pa.

The part taken by the regiment was insignificant, being that of guarding the train, until about noon on the 3d instant, at the time of the enemy's terrific attack upon the left center, at which time the fugitives from the field began to rush toward the rear upon the road upon which I was stationed. I immediately deployed across the road and into the woods on my right flank with fixed bayonets, where I stopped and reorganized between 400 and 500 men, whom I turned over to General Patrick. As soon as the panic subsided, I resumed my former duty with the ammunition train, which was not again interrupted during the battle.

All of which is respectfully submitted.

I am, captain, very respectfully, your obedient servant,

CHAS. EWING,
Major, Commanding Fourth New Jersey Volunteers.

Capt. C. H. Whittelsey,
A. A. G., Artillery Reserve, Army of the Potomac.

No. 336.

Reports of Maj. Gen. Alfred Pleasonton, U. S. Army, commanding Cavalry Corps. *

Headquarters Cavalry Corps, *June 5, 1863.*

General: I have the honor to inform you, for the information of the commanding general, that on the 3d instant the enemy crossed some squadrons of cavalry and two pieces of artillery, with which they attacked our pickets, consisting of one platoon of the First Massachusetts Cavalry, under Lieutenant Gleason. The skirmish took place near Fayetteville; the enemy crossed at Sulphur Springs. Lieutenant Gleason charged them gallantly, repulsing them with loss, and causing them to retire across the river before the force sent to support the pickets could reach the scene of action. The enemy left 4 men dead on the field.

Our casualties were Lieutenant Gleason, severely wounded by a saber-cut on the head. The gallantry of Lieutenant Gleason is highly commended by the commanding officer of the brigade to which his regiment is attached. The enemy left 3 horses in our possession.

I am, general, very respectfully, your obedient servant,

A. PLEASONTON,
Brigadier-General, Commanding.

Brig. Gen. S. Williams, *Assistant Adjutant-General.*

—

Headquarters Cavalry Corps,
Beverly Ford, June 9, 1863—6 a. m.

Enemy has opened with artillery, and shows some force of cavalry. Had a sharp skirmish. Colonel Davis, commanding Second Brigade, First Division, led his column across, and is badly wounded.

A. PLEASONTON,
Brigadier-General.

Major-General Hooker.

----

* See also his dispatches in Part III.

HEADQUARTERS CAVALRY CORPS,
June 9, 1863—11 a. m.
(Received 12.45 p. m.)

GENERAL: All the enemy's force are engaged with me. I am holding them until Gregg can come up. Gregg's guns are being heard in the enemy's rear.

A. PLEASONTON,
Brigadier-General, Commanding.

General S. WILLIAMS,
Asst. Adjt. Gen., Army of the Potomac.

—

HEADQUARTERS CAVALRY CORPS,
Near Beverly Ford, Va., June 9, 1863—12.30 p. m.
(Received 3.20 p. m.)

General Gregg has joined me, and I will now attack the enemy vigorously with my whole force. Prisoners report that Stuart has 30,000 cavalry here. Both Lees, Jones, and Hampton are with him. We have had a sharp fight, and have lost heavily, as we had the whole force in front of one-half of my command. Colonel Davis, Eighth New York, and Captain Canfield, Second [U. S.] Cavalry, are killed; Major Morris, Sixth Pennsylvania Cavalry, a prisoner, with a number of others. We have about 100 in hospital, wounded; Major Beveridge, Eighth Illinois, among the number. Buford and Ames have driven their whole force out of their strongest position. It would be well to send a good force of the Fifth Corps toward Brandy Station, if it can be spared.

A. PLEASONTON,
Brigadier-General, Commanding.

Major-General HOOKER,
Headquarters Army of the Potomac.

—

CAVALRY HDQRS., NEAR RAPPAHANNOCK STATION, VA.,
June 9, 1863—8 p. m.
(Received 10.45 p. m.)

GENERAL: A short time after my last dispatch to you, General Gregg, with his infantry and cavalry, joined me about 2 miles from the river, to which point I had driven the enemy. He reported that he had encountered a much superior number of the enemy's cavalry, and had a severe fight; also that a train of cars had been run up to Brandy Station filled with infantry, who opened on his men. I also received information from letters and official reports captured in the enemy's camp, as well as from prisoners, that the enemy had upward of 12,000 cavalry (which was double my own force of cavalry) and twenty-five pieces of artillery. I also learned from contrabands and prisoners that a large force of infantry had been sent for from Culpeper as well as Longstreet's command at Ellis' Ford. And having crippled the enemy by desperate fighting so that he could not follow me, I returned with my command to the north side of the Rappahannock. Gregg's command crossed at Rappahannock Bridge.

To-morrow morning Stuart was to have started on a raid into Maryland, so captured papers state. You may rest satisfied he will not attempt it.

Buford's cavalry had a long and desperate encounter, hand to hand, with the enemy, in which he drove handsomely before him very superior forces. Over 200 prisoners were captured and one battle-flag.

The troops are in splendid spirits, and are entitled to the highest praise for their distinguished conduct.

A. PLEASONTON,
Brigadier-General.

Major-General HOOKER,
 Commanding Army of the Potomac.

—

HDQRS. CAVALRY CORPS, ARMY OF THE POTOMAC,
June 10, 1863—5.30 a. m.

We had splendid fighting yesterday, and I think it will prevent Stuart making his raid, which he was to have commenced this morning. Toward night, they opened 20-pounder Parrott guns at a long distance, showing they were re-enforced. They did not attempt to follow us with any vigor. My old division and the regulars have covered themselves with glory. We captured Stuart's camp, with his orders, letters, &c. He was to move to Maryland with 12,000 cavalry and twenty-five guns, and he was camped at the ford we crossed, a perfect hornet's nest, but we drove them over 2 miles before Gregg came up, and, when I found out he had had as hard a time as ourselves, and no fresh troops to call on, I returned to the north bank of the Rappahannock. The enemy lost very heavily.

Buford's loss is 250 wounded. Killed not yet known. At least a dozen officers among the latter. I don't know Gregg's loss yet.* Gregg lost two guns before he joined me, but they were lost with honor; all his people were engaged, and his battery was without support. The battery men fought their pieces until cut down at their side. One gun in the same battery burst—Sixth New York. We blew up a caisson for the enemy, and killed a number.

Tell the general I will send in a report to-day, as soon as I can collect the facts.

A. PLEASONTON,
Brigadier-General.

Brig. Gen. R. INGALLS,
 Chief Quartermaster, Army of the Potomac.

—

HEADQUARTERS CAVALRY CORPS,
Warrenton Junction, Va., June 11, 1863.

GENERAL : I have the honor to inclose a list of casualties of this command, and the infantry under Brigadier-Generals Russell and Ames, in the late engagement near Brandy Station and Beverly Ford. This list does not include the casualties of the Second Cavalry Division, which has been on picket, and has not been able to complete it. Their loss is not greater than 25. I also inclose the strength of the command at the battle, and as it was this morning on review. My detailed report, with those of subordinate commanders, will be forwarded as soon as it can be prepared. I cannot, however, refrain from saying at this time that the Cavalry Corps, by its brilliant con-

---

*See revised statement, pp. 168–170.

duct in the combat day before yesterday, has my highest commendation.

I am, general, very respectfully, your obedient servant,

A. PLEASONTON,
Brigadier-General, Commanding.

P. S.—This will be handed you by Captain Custer, aide-de-camp, who will take down the standard captured and report the prisoners taken.

[Inclosure No. 1.]

List of Casualties in Brigadier-General Pleasonton's command, on the south side of the Rappahannock River, June 9, 1863.

Command.	Officers.				Enlisted men.				Aggregate.
	Killed.	Wounded.	Missing.	Total.	Killed.	Wounded.	Missing.	Total.	
CAVALRY RESERVE.									
General staff			1	1					1
1st U. S. Cavalry					1	1		2	2
2d U. S. Cavalry	1	4	3	8	10	25	23	58	66
5th U. S. Cavalry		2		2	6	15	15	36	38
6th U. S. Cavalry	1	1	2	4	7	25	30	62	66
6th Pennsylvania Cavalry	1	2	3	6	2	18	120	140	146
Company E, 4th U. S. Artillery									
Total Cavalry Reserve	3	9	9	21	26	84	188	298	319
FIRST BRIGADE, FIRST DIVISION.									
8th New York Cavalry	3	2		5	9	29	7	45	50
8th Illinois Cavalry		4		4	1	42	3	46	50
3d Indiana Cavalry		1		1	1	22		23	24
Companies B and L, 2d U. S. Artillery						3		3	3
Total First Brigade	3	7		10	11	96	10	117	127
SECOND BRIGADE, FIRST DIVISION.									
9th New York Cavalry		2		2		13	1	14	16
6th New York Cavalry		1		1		3		3	4
3d West Virginia Cavalry						3		3	3
17th Pennsylvania Cavalry		2		2					2
Total Second Brigade		5		5		19	1	20	25
Total right wing	6	21	9	36	37	199	199	435	471
INFANTRY.									
2d Massachusetts					1	3		4	4
124th New York		1		1	2	11	2	15	16
86th New York					3	23		26	26
33d Massachusetts						3		3	3
3d Wisconsin					1	14		15	15
Total infantry		1		1	7	54	2	63	64
Graham's battery, 1st U. S. Artillery						2		2	2
Total artillery and infantry, right wing	6	22	9	37	44	255	201	500	375
THIRD CAVALRY DIVISION.									
Division staff			1	1					1
First Brigade		6		6		32	98	130	136
Second Brigade	1	4	3	8	18	24	162	204	212
Martin's battery						9	12	21	21
Total Third Division	1	10	4	15	18	65	272	355	370
Grand total right and left wings*	7	32	13	52	62	320	473	855	907

A. PLEASONTON,
Brigadier-General, Commanding Cavalry Corps.

JUNE 12, 1863.

---

*The Second Division not accounted for. But see revised statement, pp. 168-170.

[Inclosure No. 2.]

Statement showing strength of Brigadier-General Pleasonton's command in en-gagement near Beverly Ford, Rappahannock River, June 9, 1863.

BRIGADIER-GENERAL BUFORD'S COMMAND, RIGHT WING.

Reserve Brigade (regulars and Sixth Pennsylvania Cavalry)	1,857
First Cavalry Division..	2,061
Brigadier-General Ames' detachment of infantry	1,500
	5,418

BRIGADIER-GENERAL GREGG'S COMMAND, LEFT WING.

Second Cavalry Division...	1,893
Third Cavalry Division..	2,170
Brigadier-General Russell's detachment of infantry	1,500
	5,563
Total effective force...	10,981
Total effective strength of cavalry.......................................	7,981
Total effective strength of infantry.....................................	3,000
Total effective strength of cavalry and infantry	10,981

CAVALRY AND ARTILLERY.

Present on review at Warrenton Junction, June 11.......................	4,973
Absent on scout and picket...	1,680
Total effective strength of cavalry, June 11........................	6,653

A. J. ALEXANDER,
Assistant Adjutant-General.

—

HEADQUARTERS CAVALRY CORPS,
Aldie, [June] 17, 1863—5 p. m.

I arrived at 4.30, and found a brigade of Fitzhugh Lee just into Aldie. I attacked at once, and, by a charge, have taken 50 prisoners, whom I am sending in. There is no infantry this side of the Blue Ridge; this is certain.

A. PLEASONTON.
Brigadier-General.

General WILLIAMS,
Assistant Adjutant-General.

P. S.—Fight still going on.

—

HEADQUARTERS CAVALRY CORPS,
Aldie, June 17, 1863—6.30 p. m.
(Received 1 a. m., 18th.)

GENERAL: I have driven Fitzhugh Lee's cavalry from this place, and they are going off in the direction of Snicker's Gap; 9 commissioned officers and 54 privates have been captured in a charge, and their killed and wounded is very large. They also lost heavily in horses and arms. They opened four guns. I had only Gregg's division up at the time, and Kilpatrick's brigade did the fighting. I have a regiment in this (Thoroughfare) Gap, and as it has not yet reported, I am satisfied there are no troops in that vicinity. We have marched 22 miles to-day, and gone through a pretty sharp fight. You shall know to-morrow certainly as to the valley beyond. The fact of Fitzhugh Lee's cavalry being here does not speak well for Stuart's raid.

Please send me your orders by my aide-de-camp.

Very respectfully,

A. PLEASONTON,
Brigadier-General.

Major-General HOOKER.
Commanding Army of the Potomac.

P. S.—Kilpatrick has done remarkably well. Our loss small.

—

HEADQUARTERS CAVALRY CORPS,
June 18, 1863—5 a. m.

GENERAL: The fight yesterday evening was more severe for us than I first supposed, from the dash and ease with which our troops drove the enemy from a strong position. The following-named officers were killed and wounded: Colonel Douty, First Maine, killed; Colonel Di Cesnola, Fourth New York, killed, wounded, or prisoner; Major Stanhope, Sixth Ohio, Major Higginson and Captain Sargent, First Massachusetts, and Lieutenants Homan and Raymond, Second New York, wounded; Captain Summat, First Maine, and Lieutenants Whittaker and Martenson, Second New York, killed. About 30 enlisted men were killed, and 120 wounded.* Among the prisoners taken was a company of sharpshooters, which accompany each brigade of their cavalry. These men are thrown out as skirmishers, to pick off our officers and skirmishers. They were dismounted for this purpose when charged upon and captured.

The enemy left a number of dead on the field, and some of the prisoners report Stuart present, directing the operations. They fired several heavy pieces of artillery. Colonel Duffié, with his regiment, reached Middleburg last night, and reported the enemy in his front, and also that a regiment had gotten up on his rear in Thoroughfare Gap. This was reported about 11 o'clock last evening. I send, this morning early, one of Buford's brigades to Thoroughfare Gap, to ascertain all the facts, and assist Duffié, if it is needed. I am also sending a brigade, with a couple of guns, to Snicker's Gap, to scout the valley, and send parties toward Winchester, Harper's Ferry, and Sperryville.

From all the information I can gather, there is no force of consequence of the enemy's infantry this side of the Blue Ridge. The raid into Pennsylvania was made by [John S.] Mosby, [Albert G.] Jenkins, and [E. V.] White. Jenkins was in command. This information comes from the prisoners taken yesterday. The prisoners state they had a hard march yesterday, and have just arrived at Aldie. I judge, therefore, they came from the vicinity of Winchester. I shall hold this position until I obtain further information of the enemy's movements. I would state that a good many of the young and small horses, which have been sent for cavalry use, gave out yesterday, and I shall have many more dismounted men in a short time, from the hard service required of the horses and their unfitness

---

* But see revised statement, p. 171.

to stand it. Please call the general's attention to this. Nine officers and 74 privates were taken in all yesterday. One major, Fifth Virginia, was taken.

I am, very respectfully, your obedient servant,

A. PLEASONTON,
Brigadier-General.

Brigadier-General WILLIAMS, *Assistant Adjutant-General.*

—

HEADQUARTERS CAVALRY CORPS,
June 18, 1863—6 p. m.
(Received June 19, 12.45 a. m.)

GENERAL: I sent this morning a brigade on a reconnaissance toward Philomont, where the enemy showed some force. They have succeeded in driving the enemy from Philomont, and have sent parties toward Snicker's Gap and Union, driving the enemy (cavalry) in small parties before them. Some prisoners have been captured who state Fitz. Lee's cavalry was at Middleburg this morning.

As soon as the parties out return, this brigade will fall back on this point. No infantry, nor any indications of it, has been seen in this direction.

A second brigade has arrived at Middleburg, with part of its force in the town. A considerable force is there, and some skirmishing took place at the town. Some prisoners have also been taken on this side. I have directed this reconnaissance to be pushed to Upperville and Ashby's Gap, if it can be done. The falling back from Middleburg may only be to draw our troops on to their infantry.

A third force is covering Throughfare Gap, which is reported clear of any of the enemy's forces.

I have learned from some scouts just in that Hampton's cavalry is in the vicinity of Stafford Court-House, and is moving up toward the Occoquan. No rebel infantry has crossed to this side of the Rappahannock.

Some negroes report that they heard Lee's forces were returning toward Culpeper. Should this prove to be the case, it seems to me this entire movement of Lee's has been with the object of getting off re-enforcements from his army to Vicksburg.

I sent an extract from a Richmond paper to you this morning, which intimated that Vicksburg was the point to which all their energies were directed.

If the general will send Meade's corps to hold this Gap, or even a division of his command, I will push my entire command through, and compel the enemy to show his hand if he has any in this part of the country. Please have the detachment of cavalry at the mouth of the Monocacy sent to me as soon as practicable, by way of Leesburg. I need them very much.

Yesterday—I omitted to mention before—we captured one standard, and compelled the enemy to abandon a caisson.

I inclose a list of ordnance captured. The Austrian rifles were taken from the mounted sharpshooters of Fitzhugh Lee's brigade.

As soon as I hear further from the front, I will send the information. The country here is rough, and the turnpike cripples up our horses when they are unshod.

I am about to propose that General Ingalls will let me have a corps of farriers with these headquarters, under a quartermaster, to keep

all horses shod as soon as they need it. The present arrangements are inadequate for this. I trust the general will approve the plan.
I am, general, very respectfully, your obedient servant,
A. PLEASONTON,
Brigadier-General, Commanding.

Brig. Gen. S. WILLIAMS,
Assistant Adjutant-General.

[Inclosure.]

HEADQUARTERS OF THE CAVALRY BRIGADE,
June 18, 1863.

GENERAL: I have the honor to report to you the following ordnance stores picked up on the battle-field:
Carbines, 42; sabers, 67; Austrian rifles, 13; saber-blades, without scabbards, 25.
Very respectfully, your obedient servant,
C. ROSS SMITH,
Lieutenant-Colonel, Chief of Ordnance, Cavalry Corps.

—

HEADQUARTERS CAVALRY CORPS,
June 19, 1863—10.20 a. m.

GENERAL: Your dispatch of 8 p. m. of last evening is just received. The reconnaissance of yesterday on the Philomont road was extended to Snicker's Gap. No infantry was met with, but the Gap was occupied by a force of cavalry, with some artillery. This brigade fell back at night to within a few miles of this point, having ascertained from parties sent out that no force of the enemy were at Union, Bloomfield, or Philomont, excepting the cavalry which was driven out by our force. Constant skirmishing was going on all day.

The brigade that went to Middleburg met a heavy force of cavalry at that point, and succeeded in driving out the enemy from the town, but gradually the brigade fell back toward night to within 2 miles of this place, skirmishing all the way.

Early this morning, I directed three brigades under Gregg to move on Middleburg, drive out the enemy, and send a force on to Upperville and Ashby's Gap. One brigade moved by way of Union, to turn Middleburg and take the rebels in the rear. A sharp cannonading has been going on, but from the sound our troops are advancing.

From my operations here, I am satisfied it is not the intention of the enemy to cross from the Shenandoah Valley into this one to give us battle. They have all the gaps leading through the Blue Ridge well guarded; to force them will require infantry.

I have Thoroughfare Gap and New Baltimore well picketed, and to-day's reconnaissance will determine as to Upperville and Ashby's Gap. Chester Gap is well guarded by the rebels; this information comes from scouts. The rebel troops yesterday fell back toward Ashby's and also Snicker's Gaps.

The infantry prisoners taken belong to the mounted force. Some 10 or 15 were taken yesterday.

This command has been fighting constantly for three days, and I cannot give you our exact loss; yesterday it was small.

I have heard nothing from Duffié. Some of his men are in, and they say Duffié gave the order for his men to scatter and get back the best way they could. Buford's people brought in some 20 of them yesterday, and, as my troops are on both sides of the mountains in strong force, we ought to get them all back.

I cannot understand Duffié's conduct, and must await further advices. Can the Eighth Pennsylvania Cavalry be spared?

I shall report again as soon as I hear from the troops engaged.

Very respectfully,

A. PLEASONTON,
Brigadier-General, Commanding.

Major-General BUTTERFIELD,
 Chief of Staff.

P. S.—I send you a box of cartridges of rebel manufacture. They are better put up than ours.

—

HEADQUARTERS CAVALRY CORPS,
Aldie, June 19, 1863—3 p. m.

GENERAL: I have the honor to report for the information of the commanding general that General Gregg, with two brigades of his own and one of General Buford's division, advanced on the Middleburg road this morning, and has, up to this time, driven the enemy steadily before him in the direction of Upperville, with sharp fighting and considerable loss to the enemy. He has sent in about 50 prisoners so far, one lieutenant-colonel and a number of officers of less rank, all from North Carolina, who say that the brigade in front of Gregg is [B. H.] Robertson's, composed of North Carolina troops, supported by two other brigades, all under command of General Stuart.

From similar sources, I learn that Fitz. Lee's brigade, which I engaged here day before yesterday, went on that night to Warrenton.

Colonel Devin, who went through Thoroughfare Gap with his brigade, reports that—

Colonel De Forest went to within 3 miles of Warrenton yesterday. I did not see him. but his men report that they learned that there were 2,000 cavalry (enemy's) there. De Forest returned to Fairfax Court-House last night.

The return of Colonel De Forest exposes my left flank, as I understood that General Stahel was to have a force at Warrenton, and in consequence advanced my left farther than I should otherwise have done.

I inclose a pass taken from an infantry soldier of Longstreet's command, just captured, who states that [R. B.] Garnett's brigade was between Amissville and Little Washington yesterday, and the fact of his being required to return by 10 to-day shows those troops are moving this way.

A copy of the dispatch of the 17th (the original of which was taken on Major Stirling), has just been received by Lieutenant Spangler.

Very respectfully, your obedient servant,

A. PLEASONTON,
Brigadier-General, Commanding.

Brig. Gen. S. WILLIAMS,
 Assistant Adjutant-General, Army of the Potomac.

HEADQUARTERS CAVALRY CORPS,
Aldie, Va., June 20, 1863—12.30 p. m.   (Received 5 p. m.)

GENERAL: I am just in from General Gregg's battle-field of yesterday. He had a very hard fight, and lost 5 officers killed and 1 wounded, besides some 75 men killed and wounded,* but drove the enemy most gallantly from a very strong and difficult position, leaving Colonel Wilcox, of the Seventh Virginia Cavalry,† and some 16 men dead upon the field, taking also the prisoners reported yesterday. Our cavalry is really fighting infantry behind stone walls. This is the reason of our heavy losses. One of the rebel infantry soldiers captured had 200 cartridges in his haversack.

As the Second Corps is going to Thoroughfare Gap, I shall move up the brigade at that point to Middleburg, leaving a regiment to picket for the Second Corps at the Gap and New Baltimore.

A rebel infantry soldier, brought in to General Gregg this morning, states that the infantry force which was on this side of the Blue Ridge, and was of Longstreet's corps, passed through Ashby's Gap yesterday into the Shenandoah Valley, and that only Stuart's force is this side of the Blue Ridge. General Gregg and I both believe this to be the case, from all the information we can obtain. I would, therefore, respectfully request that the general commanding permit me to take my whole corps to-morrow morning, and throw it at once upon Stuart's whole force, and cripple it up. At the same time, to do this effectually, I should like to have a couple of large brigades or a division of infantry, to move out at, say, 3 o'clock to-morrow morning, so that they can get in position without being seen by the enemy, and engage the dismounted sharpshooters with Stuart while the cavalry attacks and puts to flight their horses. I believe that this, properly managed, can be done, and it would seriously impair the enemy's force for offensive operations. Should the general commanding consent to this, let me have immediate notice, that the necessary orders may be given to-night, so that the plan may not fail by delay in time.

For the last three days the cavalry have been constantly fighting, and have behaved splendidly, and are in the highest spirits and confidence.

Very respectfully, your obedient servant,
                          A. PLEASONTON,
                   Brigadier-General, Commanding.
Brig. Gen. S. WILLIAMS,
   Assistant Adjutant-General, Army of the Potomac.

—

HEADQUARTERS CAVALRY CORPS,
Camp near Upperville, Va., June 21, 1863—5.30 p. m.

GENERAL: I moved with my command this morning to Middleburg, and had the assistance of General Barnes' division in the operations of this day. I left two of General Barnes' brigades at Middleburg, to hold the town, and with my corps and Colonel Vincent's brigade attacked the cavalry force of the rebels under Stuart, and steadily drove him all day, inflicting a heavy loss at every step. I drove him through Upperville into Ashby's Gap, and assured myself that the enemy had no infantry force in Loudoun Valley.

---

* But see revised statement, p. 193.
† An error. Colonel Dulany commanded the Seventh Virginia Cavalry.

We took two pieces of artillery (one being a Blakely gun) and three caissons, besides blowing up one; also upward of 60 prisoners, and more are coming in. A lieutenant-colonel, major, and 5 other officers, besides a wounded colonel and a large number of wounded rebels, left in the town of Upperville. They left their dead and wounded upon the field. Of the former I saw upward of 20. We also took a large number of carbines, pistols, and sabers. In fact, it was a most disastrous day to the rebel cavalry.

Our loss has been very small both in men and horses. I never saw the troops behave better or under more difficult circumstances. Very many charges were made, and the saber used freely, but always with great advantage to us.

Ewell's corps went toward Winchester last Wednesday; Longstreet on Friday, and another corps (A. P. Hill's, I think) is to move with Longstreet into Maryland. Such is the information given by the negroes here. I have not been able to send to the top of the Blue Ridge. Stuart has the Gap covered with heavy Blakelys and 10-pounder Parrotts.

I shall return to-morrow to Aldie. My command has been fighting almost constantly for four days, and must have a day or two to rest and shoe up and get things in order.

Very respectfully,

A. PLEASONTON,
Brigadier-General.

Brig. Gen. S. WILLIAMS,
Assistant Adjutant-General.

—

HEADQUARTERS CAVALRY CORPS,
Aldie, June 22, 1863—10 a. m.

GENERAL: I have just returned. The enemy have not followed us. I leave a brigade to hold Middleburg, and have one on the Snicker's Gap road, picketing as far as Philomont.

Two deserters from the Ninth Georgia Regiment of infantry came in this morning, and state they deserted day before yesterday while their regiment was crossing the Shenandoah River. They belong to Longstreet's corps. They state that General Lee is at Winchester, and that Longstreet's troops were on their way to that place; that A. P. Hill's corps was on the road up from Culpeper, on the other side of the mountains, but had not yet joined. Pickett's division was holding Snicker's Gap. The rebel forces in the Shenandoah Valley were a good deal scattered; the greater part had crossed the river. Infantry and artillery held all the gaps, and no one is allowed to come or go from this side of the mountains.

Longstreet's wagon train passed through Ashby's Gap on Saturday. The people at Upperville told me that about four hundred wagons of wounded were carried through Ashby's Gap yesterday during the fight. This is probably exaggerated, but at least 50 dead of the enemy were left on the field; what they took off can be conjectured. Our loss will run in killed, wounded, and missing to 175.* In my report of yesterday I omitted to mention that the enemy left a gun-carriage of a 10-pounder Parrott on the field. It is thought they threw the gun into Goose Creek. Their loss in artillery horses

---

* But see revised statement, p. 172.

yesterday was considerable. In one caisson 5 out of 6 were killed. We have captured upward of 100 prisoners, including several officers of rank, and yesterday's fight cost the rebels 2 colonels.

I had five brigades engaged, and the enemy had fully as many men as we had. Colonel Vincent's brigade was kept busy by their dismounted infantry.

I especially commend Brigadier-Generals Gregg and Kilpatrick for their gallant zeal and efficiency throughout the day. I desire to inform the general commanding that the losses my command has sustained in officers require me to ask for the promotion of good commanders. It is necessary to have a good commander for the regular brigade of cavalry, and I earnestly recommend Capt. Wesley Merritt to be made a brigadier-general for that purpose. He has all the qualifications for it, and has distinguished himself by his gallantry and daring. Give me good commanders and I will give you good results.

General Buford operated independently yesterday on the right to turn the enemy, but their force was too great. He drove them handsomely, and took a number of prisoners, among whom were 2 lieutenant-colonels. He sent a party to the top of the Blue Ridge, that saw a rebel infantry camp about 2 miles long on the Shenandoah, just below Ashby's Gap. The atmosphere was so hazy they could not make out anything more beyond.

Being satisfied I had accomplished all that the expedition designed, I returned to this place.

I am, general, very respectfully,

A. PLEASONTON,
Brigadier-General, Commanding.

Brig. Gen. S. WILLIAMS,
Assistant Adjutant-General.

—

LEESBURG, VA., *June* 26, 1863.

I shall send Buford's division to the mouth of the Monocacy, to cross at that point, and proceed thence to Middletown. His train I will send with the other trains, to cross at Edwards Ferry and get supplies. From present appearances, my command will not be able to cross to-night.

A. PLEASONTON,
Major-General.

General BUTTERFIELD,
Major-General.

—

HEADQUARTERS CAVALRY CORPS, *August* 31, 1863.

GENERAL: I have the honor to submit the following report of the operations of the Cavalry Corps in the late campaign, including the battle of Gettysburg, with accompanying reports of subordinate commanders:

On June 28, the army being in the vicinity of Frederick City, Md., the Cavalry Corps was placed as follows: The First Division (Buford's) was posted near Middletown, covering the left, and watching the enemy in the direction of Hagerstown. The Second Division (Gregg's) was stationed at different points from Frederick City to Ridgeville, on the Baltimore turnpike, covering the right of the army. The Third Division (Kilpatrick's) was at Frederick City, and was assigned to the corps on that day.

Orders having been issued for the advance of the army toward Pennsylvania, on June 29, Buford's division moved as follows, to cover and protect the left flank of the line of march: The Reserve Brigade was detached under Brigadier-General Merritt, and moved to Mechanicstown and afterward to Emmitsburg. The First and Second Brigades passed through Boonsborough, Cavetown, and Monterey Springs, and encamped near Fairfield, within a short distance of a considerable force of the enemy's infantry. '

On June 30, these two brigades moved toward Gettysburg; met two regiments of rebel infantry, with some artillery, and after some skirmishing, not wishing to use artillery, they turned off, and reached Gettysburg in the afternoon, just in time to meet the enemy entering the town, and to drive him back before he secured a position. The enemy withdrew in the direction of Cashtown, leaving his pickets about 4½ miles from Gettysburg.

By daylight on July 1, General Buford had obtained positive information of the enemy's position and movements, and made his dispositions to hold him in check until the First Corps, under Major-General Reynolds, could arrive upon the field.

Between 8 and 9 o'clock in the morning, the rebels advanced with superior numbers on Buford's position, but for more than two hours were gallantly checked in every attempt that was made, when the troops of the First and Eleventh Corps began to arrive and to relieve the cavalry from their perilous position. This division continued in the fight throughout the day, displaying great obstinacy in holding all their positions, and splendid courage and skill in their treatment of the rebels.

On July 2, Buford's division held a position on our left at Gettysburg until relieved by the Third Corps, when it was directed to take post at Westminster, to assist in guarding the army trains at that point.

On June 29, Gregg's division moved by the right flank of the army on Westminster, covering the country toward York and Carlisle by reconnaissances and patrols. Kilpatrick's division advanced from Frederick City, on June 29, direct to the front on Hanover by way of Littlestown.

On the morning of the 30th, they were attacked by Stuart's cavalry in full force. After a gallant fight, the enemy was repulsed, losing one battle-flag, and retreated in the direction of Carlisle.

On July 1, they were pursued as far as Berlin, by the way of Abbottstown, a detachment under Lieutenant-Colonel Alexander, chief of staff, proceeding as far as Rosstown.

Kilpatrick's division on July 2 moved toward Gettysburg from the direction of Heidlersburg, to prevent the enemy from concentrating his forces by that road, and to protect our right flank from being turned. Late in the afternoon, this division met the rebel cavalry near Hunterstown, and, after a spirited affair for two hours, the enemy was driven from his position. The division was then ordered to Two Taverns, which it reached at daylight.

It being now apparent that the rebel army intended making a vigorous attack on the left of the position held by our army on the heights of Gettysburg, General Kilpatrick was directed to move to the right of the enemy's line, connect with Merritt's brigade, ordered up from Emmitsburg, and attack the enemy in flank and rear, as

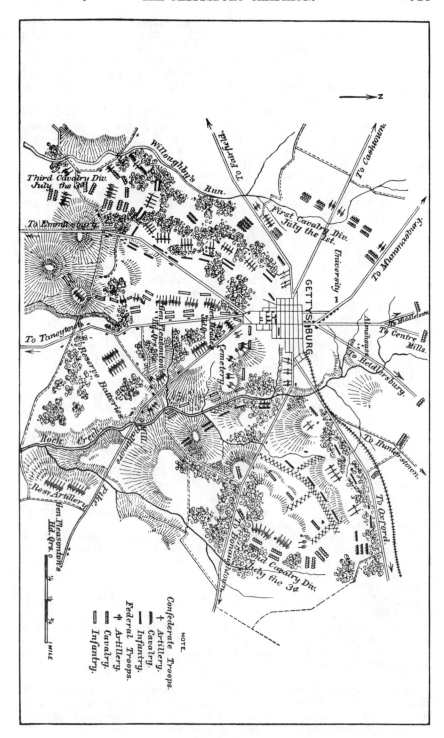

well as prevent our own flank from being turned, Custer's brigade, of this division, remaining on our right flank, in connection with General Gregg. General Kilpatrick did valuable service with the First Brigade, under General Farnsworth, in charging the enemy's infantry, and, with the assistance of Merritt's brigade and the good execution of their united batteries, caused him to detach largely from his main attack on the left of our line.

It was in one of these brilliant engagements that the noble and gallant Farnsworth fell, heroically leading a charge of his brigade against the rebel infantry. Gifted in a high degree with a quick perception and a correct judgment, and remarkable for his daring and coolness, his comprehensive grasp of the situation on the field of battle and the rapidity of his actions had already distinguished General Farnsworth among his comrades in arms. In his death was closed a career that must have won the highest honors of his profession.

On June 30, immediately after the fight of Kilpatrick at Hanover, the enemy hastily withdrew his forces from York and Carlisle and began to concentrate on Gettysburg. As soon as this was known, Gregg's division was directed to leave one brigade (Huey's) to cover the depot at Westminster, and move with the other two brigades toward Gettysburg, to take up a position on the right of our line of battle, and prevent the enemy from turning the flank and gaining the rear. This position was established about noon of July 2, and was at the intersection of the Gettysburg and Hanover turnpike with the road which ran in rear of our line of battle. The enemy attacked this point late in the evening with two regiments deployed, but were compelled to retire.

On July 3, Custer's brigade, of Kilpatrick's division, having occupied the position of Gregg's division of the day before, the latter was posted three-quarters of a mile nearer the Baltimore and Gettysburg turnpike.

About noon the enemy threw a heavy force of cavalry against this position, with the intention of gaining our rear. This attack was met and handsomely defeated by General Gregg, who reports several fine charges made by the First Michigan Cavalry, of Custer's brigade, and the First New Jersey and Third Pennsylvania Cavalry, of his own division. The enemy withdrew from his position with heavy loss, and evacuated his lines that night. Custer's brigade then proceeded to join its division on our left.

The grand attack of General Lee's army on July 3, on the left of our line at Gettysburg, having been successfully repulsed and defeated, orders were given for the cavalry to gain his rear and line of communication, and harass and annoy him as much as possible in his retreat.

Buford's division started from Westminster, passed through Frederick City, where it was joined by Merritt's brigade from Gettysburg, and proceeded to the vicinity of Williamsport on July 6, where the enemy's pickets were driven in to within a half mile of his trains, at the town. A small train and some 40 mules were captured, but the enemy was in too strong force to permit further damage at this point.

From July 7 to 15, this division had a succession of combats with the enemy, the particulars of which are fully given in General Buford's report. These actions were always in our favor, and showed a decided superiority on the part of our troops.

Kilpatrick's division passed through Emmitsburg on July 4, without halting, was joined by Huey's brigade, of Gregg's division, and moved on toward Monterey. After a series of fierce engagements with the enemy's cavalry, in which this command was always successful and distinguished, a very large train was captured and destroyed, and 1,360 prisoners, 1 battle-flag, and a large number of animals taken.

On July 6, while Buford attacked at Williamsport, Kilpatrick's division attacked the enemy at Hagerstown. The particulars of this engagement are given in General Kilpatrick's report.

Until July 14, this division was posted on the right of the army. It was constantly engaged with the enemy, as was Buford's division, on the left, and Huey's brigade, of Gregg's division, in the center.

In the pursuit of the enemy from Gettysburg, Gregg's division acted in detachments. Huey's brigade, as above mentioned, moved with Kilpatrick. Colonel Gregg's brigade, of Gregg's division, followed up the enemy by the way of Cashtown, came up with him near Greenwood, and found the road filled with broken-down wagons, abandoned limbers, and caissons filled with ammunition. A large number of prisoners were captured and sent into Gettysburg. The pursuit was continued to Marion and Chambersburg. From thence this brigade rejoined its division at Boonsborough. McIntosh's brigade, of Gregg's division, was placed at Emmitsburg, to prevent any raids on our rear by the enemy's cavalry. It then formed part of General Neill's command, to follow up the enemy on the Fairfield road, after which duty this brigade joined its division at Boonsborough.

On July 14, General Gregg, with McIntosh's and Gregg's brigades, of his division, crossed the Potomac at Harper's Ferry, and quickly drove a force of the enemy's cavalry back upon Charlestown. The entire rebel army having effected a crossing of the Potomac on that day, Gregg was re-enforced by Huey's brigade, and directed to gain the flank and rear of the rebels, and harass them as much as possible. He marched to Shepherdstown, found the roads to Martinsburg and Winchester strongly picketed, and Huey's brigade not having joined him, he waited until the 16th, when the enemy attacked him in force. A spirited contest was maintained until some time after dark, when the enemy withdrew. A large quantity of bacon and flour was captured by our troops at Shepherdstown. General Gregg speaks of the high soldierly qualities exhibited by his officers and men on that occasion.

On July 14, both Buford's and Kilpatrick's divisions pursued the rebels to Falling Waters, capturing many prisoners; a good deal of abandoned property also fell into our hands. The enemy's rear guard made an obstinate resistance near Falling Waters, but was dispersed by General Kilpatrick, who took from them, among other trophies, three infantry battle-flags.

On July 15, Buford's and Kilpatrick's divisions moved to Berlin to obtain supplies. Here the campaign of Gettysburg properly ended. The pursuit of the rebel army through Loudoun Valley to the Rappahannock River was made by the cavalry in detachments, of whose movements the reports of the division and brigade commanders give full details.

In reviewing the conduct of the cavalry corps in this campaign, it becomes a proud gratification to call the attention of the major-general commanding to the devoted spirit and resolution that animated the officers and men throughout all the difficulties, privations, trials, and dangers they had constantly to meet, and which they overcame so gloriously.   Not a single mishap occurred to mar the recollection of their noble and brilliant deeds.

A report of this kind can only mention the names of those in position and for distinguished service, but I cordially indorse all the recommendations of the subordinate commanders.   Brigadier-Generals Buford, Gregg, and Kilpatrick have proved themselves distinguished as division commanders, and I tender to them my warmest thanks for the intelligence and harmony with which they have invariably and skillfully executed every design transmitted from these headquarters. Brigadier-Generals Merritt and Custer, brigade commanders, have increased the confidence entertained in their ability and gallantry to lead troops on the field of battle.   Colonel Devin, Sixth New York Cavalry; Colonel Gamble, Eighth Illinois; Colonel Gregg, Sixteenth Pennsylvania; Colonel McIntosh, Third Pennsylvania; Colonel Huey, Eighth Pennsylvania Cavalry, in command of brigades, are entitled to mention for their meritorious and gallant conduct throughout the campaign.

The following-named officers of the staff were conspicuous for the zeal, intelligence, and daring with which they discharged their arduous and dangerous service, not unfrequently having to pass through the enemy's forces to reach our own: Lieut. Col. A. J. Alexander, assistant adjutant-general and chief of staff ; Col. G. A. H. Blake, First U. S. Cavalry, commissary of musters ; Lieut. Col. A. S. Austin, commissary of subsistence; Lieut. Col. C. Ross Smith, Sixth Pennsylvania Cavalry, ordnance officer; Lieut. Col. W. H. Crocker, inspector-general; Surg. G. L. Pancoast, medical director; Capt. John Green, Second U. S. Cavalry, assistant inspector-general; Capt. F. C. Newhall, Sixth Pennsylvania Cavalry, assistant inspector-general; Capt. V. E. von Koerber, acting topographical engineer; First Lieut. J. W. Spangler, Sixth U. S. Cavalry, acting assistant quartermaster; Asst. Surg. G. M. McGill, medical department; First Lieut. W. M. Taylor, Eighth Illinois Cavalry, ambulance officer ; First Lieut. Clifford Thomson, First New York Cavalry, aide-de-camp ; First Lieut. L. Walker, Fifth U. S. Cavalry, aide-de-camp ; First Lieut. G. W. Yates, Fourth Michigan Infantry, aide-de-camp; Capt. G. A. Crocker, Sixth New York Cavalry, acting aide-de-camp; First Lieut. C. B. McClellan, Sixth U. S. Cavalry, acting aide-de-camp; First Lieut. James F. Wade, Sixth U.S.Cavalry, acting aide-de-camp; First Lieut.G.H.Thompson, First Rhode Island Cavalry, acting aide-de-camp; Second Lieut. E. B. Parsons, Eighth New York Cavalry, acting aide-de-camp; First Lieut. J. G. Birney, Seventh Michigan Cavalry, acting aide-de-camp; First Lieut. D. W. Littlefield, Seventh Michigan Cavalry, acting aide-de-camp.

A report of casualties of the Cavalry Corps during the campaign in Pennsylvania, Maryland, and Virginia, from June 28 to July 31, is inclosed.   Capts. J. M. Robertson and Tidball, Second U. S. Artillery, commanding the First and Second Brigades of Horse Artillery, respectively, rendered the most valuable service in their respective positions.

I am, general, very respectfully, your obedient servant,

A. PLEASONTON,
Major-General, Commanding.

Brig. Gen. S. WILLIAMS,
Assistant Adjutant-General, Army of the Potomac.

[Inclosure No. 1.]

Consolidated report of Casualties of the Cavalry Corps at the battle of Gettysburg.

Command.	Killed.		Wounded.		Missing.		Total.	
	Officers.	Enlisted men.	Officers.	Enlisted men.	Officers.	Enlisted men.	Officers.	Enlisted men.
FIRST DIVISION.								
Reserve Brigade............................		24	3	60	7	333	10	417
First Brigade................................	1	15	8	86	......	29	9	130
Second Brigade............................		3	1	18	1	25	2	46
Total................................	1	42	12	164	8	387	21	593
SECOND DIVISION.								
First Brigade		2	6	14	......	20	6	36
Second Brigade*............................		2	......	9	......	83	......	94
Third Brigade		3	......	6	1	5	1	14
Total................................	......	7	6	29	1	108	7	144
THIRD DIVISION.								
First Brigade..............................	6	33	10	116	18	479	34	628
Second Brigade............................	3	35	18	169	9	247	30	451
Total................................	9	68	28	285	27	726	64	1,079
Grand total†......	10	117	46	478	36	1,221	92	1,816

A. J. ALEXANDER,
Chief of Staff, and Assistant Adjutant-General.
JULY 14, 1863.

[Inclosure No. 2.]

Recapitulation of the Casualties in the Cavalry Corps during the engagements from June 28 to July 31, 1863.

Command.	Killed.		Wounded.		Missing.		Total.	
	Officers.	Enlisted men.	Officers.	Enlisted men.	Officers.	Enlisted men.	Officers.	Enlisted men.
First Division Cavalry	1	63	19	212	8	398	28	673
Second Division Cavalry......................	......	11	14	100	......	118	14	229
Third Division Cavalry.	15	114	38	341	18	542	71	997
First Brigade, Horse Artillery................	2	9	1	38	......	......	3	47
Second Brigade, Horse Artillery..............	......	1	......	2	......	......	......	3
Total Cavalry Corps	18	198	72	693	26	1,058	116	1,949

HEADQUARTERS CAVALRY CORPS,
September 21, 1863.

GENERAL: I have the honor to report, in compliance with Paragraph III, of Special Orders, No. 227, current series, from head-

* A mistake ; brigade not engaged.
† But see revised statement, pp. 185, 186,

quarters Army of the Potomac, that there were no guns captured by the enemy from the Cavalry Corps during the Pennsylvania and Maryland campaigns.

The accompanying tabular statement of the guns captured by the divisions of my command during the same campaigns is respectfully forwarded.

Very respectfully, your obedient servant,

A. PLEASONTON,
Major-General, Commanding Corps.

Brig. Gen. S. WILLIAMS,
  Assistant Adjutant-General, Army of the Potomac.

[Inclosure.]

Report of guns captured by the Cavalry Corps, Army of the Potomac, during the Pennsylvania and Maryland Campaigns.

Command.	Caliber.	Locality.	Date.	Number.
First Division........................	10-pounder Parrott ..	Falling Waters, Md...	July 14, 1863	1
Second Division *.....................	......do	....do	July 14, 1863	2
Third Division				....
Total	....	....	....	3

A. PLEASONTON,
Major-General, Commanding Corps.

C. C. SUYDAM,
  Assistant Adjutant-General.

HEADQUARTERS CAVALRY CORPS,
  Culpeper Court-House, Va., September 21, 1863.

No. 337.

Reports of Brig. Gen. John Buford, U. S. Army, commanding First Division.

HEADQUARTERS FIRST DIVISION, CAVALRY CORPS,
  Aldie, Va., June 24, 1863.

SIR: I have the honor to report that at 12 o'clock on the night of the 20th instant, the brigadier-general commanding the corps gave me instructions to move my whole division at 2 a. m. on the 21st to Middleburg. The night was extremely dark. Nearly the whole of the division was on duty, very much divided, and without rations or forage. To concentrate and draw supplies which had arrived during the night, and to move at so short a notice, proved to be impracticable. The command, however, got off shortly after daylight, without supplies, and reached Middleburg in season for the day's operations. The Reserve Brigade, which had been sent to General Gregg the day before, joined me at Middleburg.

From Middleburg I started to turn the enemy's left flank. On reaching Goose Creek, I took the command up the right bank of the creek, over a most difficult country, and came up to the enemy on his extreme left, in a position where I could not turn him. I then

---

*Sic. But see Kilpatrick's report, p. 990, where the Third Division claims the captures.

marched back to the ford, drove the enemy's pickets off, crossed, and started up the creek, intending to recross at Millville. The enemy threw a considerable force (three regiments) in my front to dispute my advance. He was driven steadily before us for some time, until I thought I was getting too far off from the force in front of General Gregg. The Reserve Brigade was then sent across at Millville. Shortly after it had reached the opposite bank, it became apparent that I had not succeeded in gaining the enemy's flank, and to recall the Reserve Brigade would delay me too long; so I sent word to Major Starr to march to General Gregg, while I took Colonel Gamble's and Colonel Devin's brigades, and pushed for Upperville. My advance was disputed pretty warmly by the enemy, but he made no stand save with his skirmishers. These were severely punished.

When within a mile of Upperville, I saw a large force in front of General Gregg, who appeared to be outnumbered. I resolved to go to his aid. The column struck a brisk trot, but ran afoul of so many obstructions in the shape of ditches and stone fences, that it did not make fast progress, and got out of shape. While in this position, I discovered a train of wagons and a few troops to my right marching at a trot, apparently making for Ashby's Gap. I turned the head of my column toward them, and very soon became engaged with a superior force. The enemy brought four 12-pounder guns into position, and made some excellent practice on the head of my regiments as they came up. The gunners were driven from the guns, which would have fallen into our hands but for two impassable stone fences. The enemy then came up in magnificent style from the direction of Snickersville, and for a time threatened me with overwhelming numbers. He was compelled, however, to retire before the terrific carbine fire which the brave Eighth Illinois and Third Indiana poured into him. As he withdrew, my rear troops came up, formed, and pressed him back to the mountains. He was driven over the mountains into the valley.

I am happy to say that my loss is much smaller than I had reason to suppose. A list of casualties is appended. It is small in comparison with that of the enemy.

Toward night I came back, and encamped on the ground which had been so hotly contested. The enemy's dead were buried and his wounded provided for. At this place alone, Colonel Gamble's command buried 18 of the enemy.

After the Reserve Brigade was sent to General Gregg, I had but a section of Graham's battery, under Lieutenant [Theophilus B. von] Michalowski. He worked his guns with skill and judgment, throwing his shot in the right place, and on one occasion dispersed a column in front of General Gregg.

I transmit the reports of the subordinate commanders. I saw most of the engagement from the start to the end. I cannot conceive how men could have done better. My staff, Captains [Myles W.] Keogh, [Theodore C.] Bacon, Lieutenants [William] Dean, [John] Mix, and P. Penn Gaskill, were most efficient in bringing up troops and delivering messages.

I am, very respectfully, your obedient servant,

JNO. BUFORD,
Brigadier-General of Volunteers, Commanding.

Lieut. Col. A. J. ALEXANDER,
Chief of Staff, and Asst. Adjt. Gen., Cavalry Corps.

[Inclosure.]

Casualties in the First Division, Cavalry Corps, in engagement near Upperville, Va., June 21, 1863.

Command.	Officers.				Enlisted men.				Aggregate.
	Killed.	Wounded.	Missing.	Total.	Killed.	Wounded.	Missing.	Total.	
FIRST BRIGADE.									
8th New York Cavalry									
8th Illinois Cavalry					2	17		19	19
3d Indiana Cavalry						4	1	5	5
12th Illinois Cavalry		1		1	2	13	4	19	20
Total in First Brigade		1		1	4	34	5	43	44
SECOND BRIGADE.									
9th New York Cavalry									
3d West Virginia Cavalry									
17th Pennsylvania Cavalry		1		1		7		7	8
6th New York Cavalry									
Total in Second Brigade		1		1		7		7	8
RESERVE BRIGADE.									
1st U. S. Cavalry		2		2	1	11	39	51	53
2d U. S. Cavalry									
5th U. S. Cavalry						1		1	1
6th U. S. Cavalry		1		1		5	3	8	9
6th Pennsylvania Cavalry									
Total in Reserve Brigade		3		3	2	16	42	60	63
Total in First Division		5		5	6	57	47	110	115

JUNE 30, 1863—5.30 a. m.

The enemy has increased his forces considerably. His strong position is just behind Cashtown. My party toward Mummasburg met a superior force, strongly posted. Another party that went up the road due north, 3 miles out, met a strong picket; had a skirmish, and captured a prisoner of Rodes' division. Another party that went toward Littlestown heard that Gregg or Kilpatrick had a fight with Stuart, and drove him to Hanover.

I am, very respectfully, your obedient servant,

JNO. BUFORD,
Brigadier-General of Volunteers.

General REYNOLDS.

—

JUNE 30, 1863—12.20 p. m.

My extreme left reports a large force coming from toward Fairfield, in a direction to strike the Emmitsburg road this side of Marsh Creek.

Reliable.

Respectfully,

JNO. BUFORD,
Brigadier-General of Volunteers.

General PLEASONTON.

HEADQUARTERS FIRST CAVALRY DIVISION,
Gettysburg, June 30, 1863.

I entered this place to-day at 11 a. m. Found everybody in a terrible state of excitement on account of the enemy's advance upon this place. He had approached to within half a mile of the town when the head of my column entered. His force was terribly exaggerated by reasonable and truthful but inexperienced men. On pushing him back toward Cashtown, I learned from reliable men that [R. H.] Anderson's division was marching from Chambersburg by Mummasburg, Hunterstown, Abbottstown, on toward York. I have sent parties to the two first-named places, toward Cashtown, and a strong force toward Littlestown. Colonel Gamble has just sent me word that Lee signed a pass for a citizen this morning at Chambersburg. I can't do much just now. My men and horses are fagged out. I have not been able to get any grain yet. It is all in the country, and the people talk instead of working. Facilities for shoeing are nothing. Early's people seized every shoe and nail they could find.

I am, very respectfully, your obedient servant,
JNO. BUFORD,
Brigadier-General of Volunteers.

General PLEASONTON.

[P. S.]—The troops that are coming here were the same I found early this morning at Millersburg or Fairfield. General Reynolds has been advised of all that I know.

[Indorsement.]

This information contradicts Kilpatrick's, of Lee being in *Berlin.**
A. PLEASONTON,
Major-General, Commanding.

—

GETTYSBURG, *June* 30, 1863—10.30 p. m.

The Reserve Brigade, under General Merritt, is at Mechanicstown with my trains. General Pleasonton wrote he would inform me when he relieved it. To-day I received instructions saying it would picket toward Hagerstown and south. I am satisfied that A. P. Hill's corps is massed just back of Cashtown, about 9 miles from this place. Pender's division of this (Hill's) corps came up to-day— of which I advised you, saying, "The enemy in my front is increased." The enemy's pickets (infantry and artillery) are within 4 miles of this place, on the Cashtown road. My parties have returned that went north, northwest, and northeast, after crossing the road from Cashtown to Oxford in several places. They heard nothing of any force having passed over it lately. The road, however, is terribly infested with prowling cavalry parties. Near Heidlersburg to-day, one of my parties captured a courier of Lee's. Nothing was found on him. He says Ewell's corps is crossing the mountains from Carlisle, Rodes' division being at Petersburg in advance. Longstreet, from all I can learn, is still behind Hill. I have many rumors and reports of the enemy advancing upon me from toward York. I have to pay attention to some of them, which causes me to overwork my horses and men. I can get no forage nor rations; am out

---

*See Kilpatrick (as reported by Alexander), and his own report, p. 987.

of both.   The people give and sell the men something to eat, but I can't stand that way of subsisting; it causes dreadful straggling. Should I have to fall back, advise me by what route.

Respectfully,

JNO. BUFORD.

Major-General REYNOLDS.

—

GETTYSBURG, *June* 30—10.40 p. m.

I have the honor to state the following facts: A. P. Hill's corps, composed of Anderson, Heth, and Pender, is massed back of Cashtown, 9 miles from this place.   His pickets, composed of infantry and artillery, are in sight of mine.   There is a road from Cashtown running through Mummasburg and Hunterstown on to York pike at Oxford, which is terribly infested with roving detachments of cavalry.   Rumor says Ewell is coming over the mountains from Carlisle.   One of his escort was captured to-day near Heidlersburg. He says Rodes, commanding a division of Ewell's, has already crossed the mountains from Carlisle.   When will the reserve be relieved, and where are my wagons?   I have no need of them, as I can find no forage.   I have kept General Reynolds informed of all that has transpired.   The inclosed * is in reply to last dispatch.

I am, very respectfully, your obedient servant,

JNO. BUFORD,
Brigadier-General of Volunteers.

General PLEASONTON.

[Indorsement.]

Respectfully forwarded.   A report from General Buford and one from General Kilpatrick. †   Kilpatrick has done very well.

A. PLEASONTON,
Major-General, Commanding.

—

HEADQUARTERS FIRST CAVALRY DIVISION,
Gettysburg, July 1, 1863—10.10 a. m.

The enemy's force (A. P. Hill's) are advancing on me at this point, and driving my pickets and skirmishers very rapidly.   There is also a large force at Heidlersburg that is driving my pickets at that point from that direction.   General Reynolds is advancing, and is within 3 miles of this point with his leading division.   I am positive that the whole of A. P. Hill's force is advancing.

JNO. BUFORD,
Brigadier-General, Commanding.

General MEADE,
Commanding Army of the Potomac.

—

HEADQUARTERS FIRST CAVALRY DIVISION,
July 1, 1863—3.20 p. m.

I am satisfied that Longstreet and Hill have made a junction.   A tremendous battle has been raging since 9.30 a. m., with varying success.   At the present moment the battle is raging on the road to Cashtown, and within short cannon-range of this town.   The enemy's

---

* Not identified.   † Of same date, made by Alexander, p. 987.

line is a semicircle on the height, from north to west.   General Reynolds was killed early this morning.   In my opinion, there seems to
be no directing person.

JNO. BUFORD,
Brigadier-General of Volunteers.

General PLEASONTON.

P. S.—We need help now.

—

HAGERSTOWN AND SHARPSBURG PIKE,
Midway between the two places, July 7, [1863.]
(Received 11.45 p. m.)

GENERAL: I attempted to take Williamsport yesterday, but found
too large a force of infantry and artillery.   After a long fight, I withdrew to this place.   Heavy forces were coming into Williamsport
all night.   There are a good many wagons at Williamsport.   There
is no bridge there.   Troops and wagons are being ferried across in
two flat-boats very slowly.   I can do nothing with the enemy sav\
observe him.   There is nothing at Sharpsburg.

I am, very respectfully, your obedient servant,

JNO. BUFORD,
Brigadier-General of Volunteers, Comdg. First Division.

Major-General FRENCH.

—

HEADQUARTERS FIRST DIVISION,
Boonsborough, July 8, 1863.

I have had a very rough day of it.   Early this morning the enemy
advanced upon me in a pretty strong force (cavalry, infantry, and
artillery).   During the first part of the day they pressed me severely,
and came near the town.   Toward night, I turned the tables upon
them, and drove them across the Antietam, toward Hagerstown and
Williamsport.   You never saw the division behave better.   My loss
is not heavy.   The artillery fire was very hot.   All of my fighting
had to be on foot.   The river is 5 feet higher than before, and rising.
I have drawn in close to this place, to sleep.   My train has been interfered with by the Eleventh Corps.   I hope it may arrive in the
night.   There are no rebs this side of Antietam; none on the old
battle-ground, and none at Sharpsburg.   Plenty of them, however,
can be found between Greencastle and Williamsport and between
Hagerstown and Williamsport.   Hurrah for Vicksburg.

Very respectfully, your obedient servant,

JNO. BUFORD,
Brigadier-General of Volunteers, Commanding.

Colonel ALEXANDER,
Chief of Staff, Cavalry Corps.

(Received by General Pleasonton "during the night," and forwarded to army headquarters July 9, 1863.)

—

HEADQUARTERS FIRST DIVISION,
Three-fourths of a mile east of Funkstown, July 10, 1863.

GENERAL: I have been fighting Fitzhugh Lee's, Hampton's, and
Jones' brigades, have driven them back upon Longstreet's whole

corps, which occupies the crest beyond the Antietam. My information is that the whole of Lee's army is in the vicinity of Hagerstown, Jones' Cross-Roads, and extending toward Williamsport. His line will be along the Antietam. He has a large force in front of a bridge a mile below Funkstown. I don't care about going any farther just now. I will cease firing, and try to watch their movements. Staff officers have been all over this section, examining ground and measuring distances.

Respectfully,

JNO. BUFORD,
Brigadier-General of Volunteers.

—

HEADQUARTERS FIRST CAVALRY DIVISION,
August 27, 1863.

COLONEL: I have the honor to make the following report of the operations of the First Cavalry Division, from its crossing the Potomac at Edwards Ferry, on June 27, to its crossing of the Rappahannock on August 1:

After passing the Potomac on the upper pontoon bridge, the division marched over almost impassable roads, crossing the Monocacy near its mouth by a wretched ford, and bivouacked on the east side of the mountains, 3 miles from Jefferson, being halted there by the whole train of General Stahel's division blockading the road through the mountains.

June 28, the division moved through Jefferson, and went into camp near Middletown, for the purpose of shoeing and refitting.

June 29, the Reserve Brigade was detached and moved to Mechanicstown. The First and Second Brigades moved through Boonsborough, Cavetown, and Monterey Springs, and encamped near Fairfield, within a short distance of a considerable force of the enemy's infantry. The inhabitants knew of my arrival and the position of the enemy's camp, yet not one of them gave me a particle of information, nor even mentioned the fact of the enemy's presence. The whole community seemed stampeded, and afraid to speak or to act, often offering as excuses for not showing some little enterprise, "The rebels will destroy our houses if we tell anything." Had any one given me timely information, and acted as guide that night, I could have surprised and captured or destroyed this force, which proved next day to be two Mississippi regiments of infantry and two guns.

June 30, the two brigades moved out very early to go to Gettysburg, via Fairfield. At the latter place my advance ran upon the force referred to. I determined to feel it and drive it, if possible, but, after a little skirmishing, found that artillery would have to be necessarily used. Resolved not to disturb them, for fear cannonading from that quarter might disarrange the plans of the general commanding. Fairfield was 4 or 5 miles west of the route assigned me, and I did not wish to bring on an engagement so far from the road I was expected to be following. I immediately turned my column toward Emmitsburg without serious molestation, and was soon on my proper road and moving on Gettysburg, where I had reason to suppose I should find some of General Stahel's [Kilpatrick's] cavalry. We entered Gettysburg in the afternoon, just in time to meet the enemy entering the town, and in good season to drive him back before his getting a foothold. He withdrew toward Cashtown, leaving his pickets about 4½ miles from Gettysburg.

The night of the 30th was a busy night for the division. No reliable information of value could be obtained from the inhabitants, and but for the untiring exertions of many different scouting parties, information of the enemy's whereabouts and movements could not have been gained in time to prevent him from getting the town before our army could get up.

By daylight on July 1, I had gained positive information of the enemy's position and movements, and my arrangements were made for entertaining him until General Reynolds could reach the scene.

On July 1, between 8 and 9 a. m., reports came in from the First Brigade (Colonel Gamble's) that the enemy was coming down from toward Cashtown in force. Colonel Gamble made an admirable line of battle, and moved off proudly to meet him. The two lines soon became hotly engaged, we having the advantage of position, he of numbers. The First Brigade held its own for more than two hours, and had to be literally dragged back a few hundred yards to a position more secure and better sheltered. Tidball's battery, commanded by Lieutenant Calef, Second U. S. Artillery, fought on this occasion as is seldom witnessed. At one time the enemy had a concentric fire upon this battery from twelve guns, all at short range. Calef held his own gloriously, worked his guns deliberately with great judgment and skill, and with wonderful effect upon the enemy. The First Brigade maintained this unequal contest until the leading division of General Reynolds' corps came up to its assistance, and then most reluctantly did it give up the front. A portion of the Third Indiana found horse-holders, borrowed muskets, and fought with the Wisconsin regiment that came to relieve them. While this left of my line was engaged, Devin's brigade, on the right, had its hands full. The enemy advanced upon Devin by four roads, and on each was checked and held until the leading division of the Eleventh Corps came to his relief.

After the fall of General Reynolds, whose advance troops partially drove back the enemy and made heavy captures of prisoners, the enemy brought up fresh troops, and engaged General Doubleday's command, which fought bravely, but was greatly outnumbered and forced to fall back. Seeing our troops retiring, and their need of assistance, I immediately rushed Gamble's brigade to Doubleday's left, and dismounted it in time to render great assistance to our infantry, and to check and break the enemy's line. My troops at this place had partial shelter behind a low stone fence, and were in short carbine range. Their fire was perfectly terrific, causing the enemy to break and rally on their second line, which made no farther advance toward my position.

Shortly after this, I placed my command on our extreme left, to watch and fight the enemy should he make another attack, and went to Cemetery Hill for observation. While there, General Hancock arrived, and in a few moments he made superb disposition to resist any attack that might be made.

My division bivouacked that night on the left of our position, with pickets extending almost to Fairfield.

The zeal, bravery, and good behavior of the officers and men on the night of June 30, and during July 1, was commendable in the extreme. A heavy task was before us; we were equal to it, and shall all remember with pride that at Gettysburg we did our country much service.

July 2, the division became engaged with the enemy's sharpshooters on our left, and held its own until relieved by General Sickles' corps, after which it moved to Taneytown, and bivouacked for the night.

The next day, July 3, it moved to Westminster, to guard the trains of the army at that point.

July 4, the division marched toward Frederick, *en route* to Williamsport.

July 5, reached Frederick, drew supplies, and remained all night.

July 6, the whole division (the Reserve Brigade having joined the night before) marched at 4 a. m. toward Williamsport, to destroy the enemy's trains, which were reported to be crossing the Potomac into Virginia.

At about 5 p. m., when near Saint James' College, the enemy's pickets were discovered, driven in, and preparations made to capture the town. The enemy was driven handsomely to within half a mile of his trains, at the town, when he came out strong enough to prevent our farther progress. General Merritt's brigade, with Graham's battery, was on the right, Colonel Gamble's (First) brigade on the left, and Colonel Devin's (Second) brigade on the left rear as reserves. The enemy made an attack upon Gamble, who had posted his men under shelter, and who held his fire until the rebel line came within short carbine range, when he opened upon it, doing terrible execution, and driving it back into its stronghold. This was repeated with similar success. In Merritt's front the enemy made no direct attack, but were so obstinate that General Merritt could not dislodge them without too much sacrifice. The enemy, however, attempted to turn our right with a brigade of infantry. This attempt was most admirably foiled by General Merritt.

While our hottest contest was in progress, General Kilpatrick's guns were heard in the direction of Hagerstown, and as they grew nearer, I sent word to him to connect with my right for mutual support. The connection was made, but was of no consequence to either of us. Just before dark, Kilpatrick's troops gave way, passing to my rear by the right, and were closely followed by the enemy.

It now being dark, outnumbered, and the First and Reserve Brigades being out of ammunition, Devin was ordered to relieve Gamble and a portion of Merritt's troops. This being done, I ordered the command to fall back, Devin to hold his ground until the entire road to the Antietam was clear. Devin handsomely carried out his instructions, and the division bivouacked on the road to Boonsborough.

The expedition had for its object the destruction of the enemy's trains, supposed to be at Williamsport. This, I regret to say, was not accomplished. The enemy was too strong for me, but he was severely punished for his obstinacy. His casualties were more than quadruple mine.

Colonel Chapman, with his regiment, dashed off to the road leading from Falling Waters to Williamsport, and destroyed a small train of grain, and returned with about 40 mules and their harness.

At Williamsport, Captain Graham fought his battery with marked ability, and to the admiration of all witnesses. The officers and men behaved with their usual courage, displaying great unwillingness to fall back, and requiring repeated orders before they did so.

July 7, the division moved to Boonsborough, the Reserve Brigade camping well in advance on the Hagerstown road, after having a successful cavalry brush with the enemy's advance, of which I have as yet received no report.

July 8, the enemy attacked at 5 a. m., and the fighting lasted until about 5 p. m. He was driven back about 4 miles, when the division then bivouacked for the night.

July 9, attacked the enemy at 4 p. m. and drove him handsomely about 2 miles.

July 10, attacked the enemy at 8 a. m. and drove him through Funkstown to his intrenchmeñts beyond Antietam, when he came out with a heavy force of infantry and artillery and gave battle. The division held the crest on our side of the town like veterans until its ammunition was exhausted. Howe's division, of the Sixth Corps, was in easy supporting distance, but had no orders to aid me. At 3 p. m. I could no longer reply with carbines, for want of cartridges, and consequently ordered the division to fall back. A brigade of the Sixth Corps then began to advance, but did not occupy the position that I held when I left the field.

There was splendid fighting on the part of the division on the 7th, 8th, 9th, and 10th. There was no faltering or hesitation. Each man went to work determined to carry anything in reason. For the particulars I refer you to the reports of the brigade commanders.

July 11, the First and Second Brigades moved in the afternoon to the vicinity of Bakersville. The Reserve Brigade was detached.

July 12 and 13, remained at Bakersville, and pushed pickets to within 800 yards of the enemy's intrenchments at Downsville.

July 14, at 7 a. m., the division was ordered to advance, and at 7.30 o'clock it was discovered that the enemy had evacuated during the night. The few remaining scouts were run into the rear guard of Lee's army, which was soon seen in front of Kilpatrick, who had advanced from the north. Kilpatrick was engaged. I sent word to him that I would put my whole force in on the enemy's rear and flank, and get possession of the road and bridge in their rear. The division succeeded in getting the road, and attacked the enemy in flank and rear, doing him great damage, and scattering him in confusion through the woods and ravines. Our spoils on this occasion were one 10-pounder Parrott gun, one caisson, over 500 prisoners, and about 300 muskets. General Merritt came up in time to take the advance before the enemy had entirely crossed, and made many captures. The enemy's bridge was protected by over a dozen guns in position and sharpshooters on the Virginia side. As our troops neared the bridge, the enemy cut the Maryland side loose, and the bridge swung to the Virginia side.

July 15, the division moved to Berlin.

July 16, moved camp to Petersville.

July 17, remained at Petersville.

July 18, crossed during the afternoon, and encamped near Purcellville.

July 19, marched through Philomont, and encamped on Goose Creek, near Rector's Cross-Roads.

July 20, marched to Rectortown. Detached General Merritt with his brigade to hold Manassas Gap, Gamble to hold Chester Gap, and Devin, with all the train, moved to Salem.

July 21, Merritt in Manassas, Gamble near Chester Gap, finding it already in possession of a superior force of the enemy. General Merritt and Colonel Gamble each had a fight and made captures, for particulars of which see their reports.

July 22, wagon train sent to Warrenton in charge of Sixth New York Cavalry. Devin moved toward Barbee's Cross-Roads.

July 23, whole division concentrated at Barbee's Cross-Roads, and remained until the 26th, when the division took position at Warrenton and Fayetteville, picketing the Rappahannock River from Sulphur Springs to Kelly's Ford.

During the whole campaign, from June 27 to July 31, there has been no shirking or hesitation, no tiring on the part of a single man so far as I have seen; the brigade commanders report none.

To General Merritt and Colonels Gamble and Devin, brigade commanders, I give my heartfelt thanks for their zeal and hearty support. Neither of them ever doubted the feasibility of an order, but on its reception obeyed its dictates to the letter.

My staff—Captains [Charles E.] Norris, Keogh, [Craig W.] Wadsworth, and Bacon, and Lieutenants Mix, P. Penn Gaskill, Dean, [Albert P.] Morrow, [Malcomb H.] Wing, and [George M.] Gilchrist—were always on hand, and gave me much valuable information from where the fire was hottest, and were of immense assistance in conveying orders on the field of battle, and seeing that they were obeyed. During the campaign they were all under heavy fire on different occasions, and for coolness and gallantry cannot be excelled in this army.

Lieutenant [Aaron B.] Jerome, signal corps, was ever on the alert, and through his intrepidity and fine glasses on more than one occasion kept me advised of the enemy's movements when no other means were available. Surgeon Hard, Eighth Illinois Cavalry, surgeon-in-chief to the division, deserve great credit for his zealous and untiring attention and labors with the sick and wounded. Through his exertions their sufferings have been greatly alleviated, their wants supplied, and many lives saved. Many wounded soldiers are indebted to him for his timely aid on the battle-field, who, but for his energy, would have shared the fate of many poor fellows who had less attentive surgeons.

I transmit with this the reports of the brigade commanders.

The First Brigade captured 854 head of beef-cattle and 602 sheep at Chester Gap, which were turned over to the subsistence department at Markham, July 24.

I am, very respectfully, your obedient servant,

JNO. BUFORD,
Brigadier-General of Volunteers, Commanding.

Lieut. Col. C. ROSS SMITH,
Chief of Staff, Cavalry Corps.

[Inclosure.]

Recapitulation of Casualties in the various engagements of July, 1863, in the First Cavalry Division.

Command.	Officers.				Enlisted men.				Aggregate.	Remarks.
	Killed.	Wounded.	Missing.	Total.	Killed.	Wounded.	Missing.	Total.		
First Brigade	1	6	....	7	12	64	28	104	111	At Gettysburg, Pa., July 1 and 2.
Second Brigade	....	....	....	....	3	4	13	20	20	Do.
Reserve Brigade	....	7	5	12	20	50	271	341	353	At Gettysburg, Pa., July 3.
Total*	1	13	5	19	35	118	312	465	484	

* But see revised statement, p. 185.

Recapitulation of Casualties, &c.--Continued.

Command.	Officers.				Enlisted men.				Aggregate.	Remarks.
	Killed.	Wounded.	Missing.	Total.	Killed.	Wounded.	Missing.	Total.		
First Brigade		2	....	2	3	7	1	11	13	At Williamsport, Md., July 6.
Second Brigade			1	1	....	....	3	3	4	Do.
Reserve Brigade			1	1	6	11	37	54	55	Do.
Total			2	2	4	9	18	41	68	72	
First Brigade		2	1	3	5	14	2	21	24	At Boonsborough and Funkstown, July 8, 9, and 10.
Second Brigade		1	....	1	3	13	18	34	35	Do.
Reserve Brigade				....	4	24	10	38	38	Do.
Total		3	1	4	12	51	30	93	97	
First Brigade		1	....	1	....	4	....	4	5	Falling Waters, July 14.
Second Brigade					2	....		2	2	Do.
Reserve Brigade										
Total		1	....	1	....	6	....	6	7	
First Brigade				....	1	8	16	25	25	At Chester Gap, Va., July 21 and 22.
Second Brigade										
Reserve Brigade				....	9	12	8	29	29	At Manassas Gap, Va., July 21.
Total				....	10	20	24	54	54	
Total in division	1	19	8	28	66	213	407	686	714	

JNO. BUFORD,
Brigadier-General of Volunteers.

HEADQUARTERS FIRST CAVALRY DIVISION,
August 20 .863.

—

RAPPAHANNOCK, August 1, 1863.

I sent a brigade to cross this morning at Beverly Ford ; the river is swimming, and I could not cross. The engineers give me no co-operation. I can cross in boats and drive away the rebels, after which, if the engineers are instructed to lay a bridge, I can cross and hold the opposite bank. If I am to advance, I would like to see some disposition shown to aid me. Everything seems to be awaiting orders.

JNO. BUFORD,
Brigadier-General.

Major-General MEADE.

[Indorsement.]

——, —— —, 1863.

DEAR WARREN : I suppose the bridge at Rappahanock Station will be thrown over as soon as the enemy is cleared away.

A. A. H. [HUMPHREYS.]

—

RAPPAHANNOCK STATION, August 1, 1863.

Have been driving Jones' and Hampton's brigades of cavalry all day. Have arrived within 1½ miles of Culpeper. Have found A. P. Hill's corps, and have to come back. I can't fight so many. There is no one else at Culpeper.

JNO. BUFORD,
Brigadier-General of Volunteers.

Major-General MEADE,
Headquarters Army of the Potomac.

HEADQUARTERS FIRST CAVALRY DIVISION,
August 2, 1863.

I have the honor to report that at 3 a. m. yesterday my division was massed at Rappahannock Station for the purpose of crossing the river at that point. Through mismanagement of some kind, I was not able to cross over the division before 11 a. m. Shortly after crossing, I became engaged with Hampton's and Jones' brigades, commanded in person by Stuart. He evidently did not intend to allow me to gain any information of Lee's whereabouts, and made a most obstinate resistance. By keeping my men well in hand, I managed to drive him back to within 1½ miles of Culpeper, where I met a heavy force of infantry belonging to A. P. Hill's corps. I then ordered everybody to fall back, and was followed and pressed by at least 5,000 infantry and three batteries as far as Brandy Station. The fighting was very handsomely executed; there were several charges, and sabers were used with success.

My casualties will exceed 100;* the enemy's loss exceeds mine. As Stuart was driven, he carried with him every citizen and negro. The prisoners say Lee's main army is toward Gordonsville. All of Hill's corps is at Culpeper. The infantry prisoners belong to Pender's division. Pender is dead. Stuart has not been relieved from the cavalry. Merritt fought beautifully yesterday. Nearly everybody did well.

I am, respectfully, your obedient servant,

JNO. BUFORD,
Brigadier-General of Volunteers, Commanding.

Col. A. J. ALEXANDER,
Chief of Staff, Cavalry Corps.

No. 338.

Reports of Col. William Gamble, Eighth Illinois Cavalry, commanding First Brigade.

HDQRS. FIRST CAVALRY BRIGADE,
June 22, 1863.

CAPTAIN : I have the honor to report the part taken by this brigade in the cavalry fight of yesterday.

The brigade—composed of the Eighth New York, Eighth Illinois, three squadrons Third Indiana, and two squadrons Twelfth Illinois Cavalry, with one section of the First U. S. Artillery, under Lieutenant Michalowski, in all about 1,600 strong—left Aldie at 5 a. m.; marched to Middleburg; from thence west across a ford at Goose Creek. The rebel skirmishers occupying the opposite bank under cover of a stone wall at the ford, one squadron of the Third Indiana Cavalry was dismounted, and, with the advance guard deployed, drove the rebels from the opposite bank, when the column crossed, and advanced south on the Upperville road. Encountered the enemy 1 mile from the ford, on the right of the road; deployed the column in line of battle, and a few well-directed shells into the enemy's column dispersed him rapidly in retreat through the woods southward. One mile farther, found the enemy behind stone walls, near a house;

---

* See p. 194.

a few more shells drove them again toward Upperville. Two miles farther, the enemy's skirmishers, supported by artillery, were found strongly posted. I deployed the column in line; advanced and drove the enemy from two strong positions behind stone walls, his guns continually throwing shells at us.

We continued the march, and found the enemy strongly posted west of Upperville, at the base of the mountain. The Eighth Illinois, Third Indiana, and Twelfth Illinois Cavalry, about 900 strong, leading the column, came on rapidly at a gallop; formed in line; charged up to the enemy's five guns amid a shower of shells, shrapnel, and case shot; drove the rebel gunners from their pieces, when the enemy's cavalry, seven regiments strong, emerged from the woods, and a hand-to-hand conflict ensued, the enemy outnumbering us three to one. We retired a short distance behind a stone wall, and maintained our position, repulsing the repeated charges of the enemy by well-directed carbine and pistol firing.

The enemy then, on account of his superior numbers, attempted to turn both flanks, when a squadron of the Eighth Illinois and one of the Third Indiana Cavalry were deployed to cover the flanks, and, after a sharp conflict, repulsed the enemy, after which the section of artillery arrived, supported by the Eighth New York Cavalry, and shelled the enemy from his position. The enemy then retreated toward Ashby's Gap, pursued for 2 miles by the First and Second Cavalry Brigades, which at sunset returned, and encamped on the battle-field, buried the dead, and took care of the wounded. Eighteen dead bodies of the enemy were buried, and over 30 of their wounded were found, in addition to what they carried away, besides prisoners, the exact number of which the provost-marshal of the division will report.

Our loss is as follows:

Command.	Killed.	Wounded.	Missing.	Total.
8th Illinois Cavalry	2	17	.....	19
3d Indiana Cavalry	......	4	1	5
12th Illinois Cavalry (Captain Brown wounded)	2	14	4	20
Total	4	35	5	44

Horses killed—Third Indiana Cavalry, 18; Eighth Illinois Cavalry, 17. Total, 35 horses of enlisted men; 1 horse of Colonel Gamble; 36 horses in all killed.

All of which is respectfully submitted.

WM. GAMBLE,
Colonel, Commanding First Cavalry Brigade.

Capt. T. C. Bacon,
Assistant Adjutant-General, First Cavalry Division.

———

HDQRS. First Cavalry Brigade, First Division,
Camp near Catlett's, Va., August 24, 1863.

CAPTAIN: I have the honor to submit the following report of the part taken by this brigade in the several engagements with the enemy, from June 28 to July 31 last, in accordance with orders from division headquarters:

NEAR GETTYSBURG, PA., JULY 1.

About 8 o'clock on the morning of the 1st instant, while in camp at the seminary building, the officer commanding the squadron on picket *in front gave me notice that the enemy, consisting of infantry and artillery, in column, were approaching his pickets from the direction of Cashtown, with deployed skirmishers in strong force, about 3 miles distant. This information was immediately communicated to the general commanding the division, who ordered my command to be in immediate readiness to fight the enemy. My brigade—consisting of the Eighth New York, Eighth Illinois, three squadrons of the Third Indiana, and two squadrons of the Twelfth Illinois Cavalry, about 1,600 strong, with Tidball's battery, Second U. S. Artillery—was placed in line of battle about 1 mile in front of the seminary, the right resting on the railroad track and the left near the Middletown or Fairfax [Fairfield] road, the Cashtown road being a little to the right of the center, at right angles with the line. Three squadrons, part dismounted, were ordered to the front, and deployed as skirmishers to support the squadron on picket, now being driven back by the enemy's artillery and skirmishers. Our battery of six 3-inch rifled guns was placed in battery, one section on each side of the Cashtown road, covering the approaches of the enemy, and the other section on the right of the left regiment, to cover that flank. The enemy cautiously approached in column on the road, with three extended lines on each flank, and his and our line of skirmishers became engaged, and our artillery opened on the enemy's advancing column, doing good execution. The enemy moved forward; two batteries opened on us, and a sharp engagement of artillery took place. In a short time we were, by overpowering numbers, compelled to fall back about 200 yards to the next ridge, and there make a stand.

In the meantime our skirmishers, fighting under cover of trees and fences, were sharply engaged, did good execution, and retarded the progress of the enemy as much as could possibly be expected, when it is known they were opposed by three divisions of Hill's corps. After checking and retarding the advance of the enemy several hours, and falling back only about 200 yards from the first line of battle, our infantry advance of the First Corps arrived, and relieved the cavalry brigade in its unequal contest with the enemy.

In the afternoon, the enemy, being strongly re-enforced, extended his flanks, and advanced on our left in three strong lines, to turn that flank. The general commanding division ordered my brigade forward at a trot, and deployed in line on the ridge of woods, with the seminary on our right. Half of the Eighth New York, Third Indiana, and Twelfth Illinois were dismounted and placed behind a portion of a stone wall and under cover of trees.

The enemy being close upon us, we opened a sharp and rapid carbine fire, which killed and wounded so many of the first line of the enemy that it fell back upon the second line. Our men kept up the fire until the enemy in overwhelming numbers approached so near that, in order to save my men and horses from capture, they were ordered to mount and fall back rapidly to the next ridge, on the left of the town, where our artillery was posted. The stand which we made against the enemy prevented our left flank from being turned, and saved a division of our infantry.

My brigade fought well under disadvantageous circumstances against a largely superior force. Every officer and soldier did his duty. The list of casualties is large, but could not be less, considering the position we occupied. Major Lemon, Third Indiana, was mortally wounded, since dead; Lieutenant Conroe, Twelfth Illinois Cavalry, killed; Captain Fisher and Lieutenant Voss, same regiment, wounded; Captain Follett, Eighth New York, severely wounded; Captain Martin, Third Indiana, wounded; Captain Morris, Eighth Illinois Cavalry, serving on my staff, was wounded, and one of my orderlies killed. Tidball's horse battery, under Lieutenant Calef, attached to my brigade, was worked faithfully, did good execution, and fully sustained its former high reputation. This brigade had the honor to commence the fight in the morning and close it in the evening.

NEAR WILLIAMSPORT, MD., JULY 6.

This brigade was ordered to engage the enemy on the left of the Boonsborough road, near Williamsport, the Reserve Brigade being on the right of the road. The Third Indiana Cavalry was ordered to capture and destroy a train of seven wagons of the enemy on our left, on the Downsville road, which was successfully accomplished, making prisoners of the drivers and those in charge of the train. The brigade was then placed in line of battle, and three-fourths of it dismounted to drive in the enemy's skirmishers; and Tidball's battery of four guns, placed in position, supported by the balance of the mounted men, opened on the enemy, many times our superior in numbers, and did excellent execution; the dismounted men in the meantime, keeping up a sharp carbine fire, drove in the rebel pickets on their reserve. The dismounted men were under the immediate command of the gallant and lamented Major Medill, Eighth Illinois Cavalry, who fell, mortally wounded.

We held our position until dark, and were then relieved by Colonel Devin's brigade, and ordered to fall back to Jones' Cross-Roads, in the direction of Boonsborough, which we reached about midnight, the delay being caused by Kilpatrick's division having been driven back in confusion from the direction of Hagerstown, completely blockading the road in our rear, making it impassable for several hours.

NEAR BOONSBOROUGH, MD., JULY 8.

The enemy was reported advancing on the Hagerstown road. General Buford ordered my brigade to take position on the crest of the ridge on the right of the road to Hagerstown, about 1½ miles from Boonsborough, my dismounted men thrown out to the front and in the strip of woods on the right of the road; the battery in position in the center of the line, supported by the mounted men. The rebels moved forward to drive in our skirmishers, supported by their battery, but after a sharp contest were unable to drive me from my position on the right. The enemy, however, gradually worked round on the left, driving in the skirmishers of Kilpatrick's division; placed a section of artillery so as to bring a cross-fire on my brigade, when I was ordered to fall back on Boonsborough. Afterward Kilpatrick's division was relieved on the left and placed on the right, but being unable to dislodge the enemy from the woods I formerly occupied, my brigade was again ordered forward; the battery placed in position under a heavy fire; three-fourths of the brigade dismounted and ordered to drive the enemy out of the woods in front, which was accomplished rapidly under a heavy fire of shell and musketry, General Buford in person leading the advance line of skirmishers; drove the enemy 3 miles, and across Beaver Creek, on the Williamsport or Funkstown road. General Kilpatrick, with two squadrons of his command, galloped down the road within a short distance of the enemy; halted, looked at each other, and retired, when the dismounted men of my brigade came up and drove the enemy across Beaver Creek.

NEAR FUNKSTOWN, MD., JULY 10.

The brigade having driven the rebels along the Hagerstown road from Beaver Creek to within 3 miles of Funkstown on the 9th instant, we advanced again on the 10th instant with dismounted skirmishers and artillery, supported by the balance of the mounted men. The division advanced in line of battle, Reserve Brigade on the right, First Brigade in the center and on both sides of the road, and the Second Brigade on the left. Drove the enemy rapidly, under a heavy fire of artillery and musketry, into Funkstown, on a large reserve of the enemy. We occupied the heights above Funkstown, with Tidball's battery, under Lieutenant Calef, which did good execution, and our skirmish line was advanced to the suburbs of the town. The enemy tried hard with a much superior force to dislodge us from our position, but so long as our ammunition lasted he was unable to do so. Our infantry finally arrived to within half a mile in our rear, and although we were hard pressed by the enemy, and nearly all our ammunition expended, the infantry pitched their shelter-tents, and commenced cooking and eating, in spite of repeated and urgent requests to the commanding officer of the infantry to occupy our excellent position and relieve us. When our ammunition was expended, we were ordered by General Buford to fall back. The rebels then occupied our position, and our infantry afterward had to retake it, with the unnecessary loss of several killed and wounded.

NEAR FALLING WATERS, MD., JULY 14.

On the morning of the 14th instant, the brigade was ordered to march on the enemy in the direction of Downsville from our camp, near Bakersville. We proceeded in that direction, found the enemy's earthworks at Downsville abandoned, and were informed that the enemy had retreated toward Falling Waters and Williamsport, to cross the Potomac during the night. The brigade marched rapidly toward Falling Waters, and when near there observed a division of the enemy intrenched on a hill, covering the approaches to the ford. While the brigade was moving round to flank and attack the enemy in rear, to cut them off from the ford and capture them all, in connection with the other two brigades of the First Cavalry Division, which we could easily have accomplished, I saw two small squadrons of General Kilpatrick's division gallop up the hill to the right of the rebel infantry, in line of battle behind their earthworks, and, as any competent cavalry officer of experience could foretell the result, these two squadrons were instantly scattered and destroyed by the fire of a rebel brigade, and not a single dead enemy could be found when the ground there was examined a few hours afterward. This having alarmed the enemy, he fell back toward the ford before we could get round to his rear. We, however, with our dismounted men, attacked him in flank on rough ground, and had a sharp carbine engagement, taking about 511 prisoners, 61 of whom, together with 300 stand of arms, were turned over to an officer of Kilpatrick's division by mistake; also a 3-inch Parrott gun, captured from the enemy by the Eighth New York Cavalry, which was afterward sent by General Kilpatrick to the camp of this brigade, where it properly belonged.

NEAR CHESTER GAP, VA., JULY 21 AND 22.

In obedience to orders, this brigade marched from near Rectortown, Va., to Chester Gap (about 20 miles), arriving in that vicinity at 3.30 p. m., July 21. About a mile from the Gap our advance line of skirmishers encountered the enemy's pickets. I dismounted six squadrons, and drove the enemy's pickets to the crest of the Gap on their reserve, which was found to consist of Pickett's division of infantry, one regiment of Jones' cavalry, and a battery of six guns, occupying the Gap, on the crest of the mountain. Upon obtaining this information, and not having a sufficient force to drive the enemy from the Gap, having no support nearer than 20 miles, we fell back 1½ miles from the Gap, and took position so as to cover the two roads leading from the Gap, one toward Barbee's Cross-Roads, the other to Little Washington and Sperryville; placed the guns in battery, and a strong line of pickets in front and flanks.

We captured to-day 23 prisoners, 84 horses, 12 mules, 654 beef-cattle, 602 sheep, all purchased and on the way to be delivered to the rebel army at the Gap, in charge of a commissary agent and his son, who were also captured.

July 22, at 8 a. m., my pickets reported the enemy advancing in column with skirmishers on the road from the Gap toward Sperryville. When the head of the enemy's column came within easy range, we opened fire on it with artillery and the carbines of the dismounted men so effectually that his column, with his wagon train, halted and fell back out of our range, his advance guard and skirmishers being still engaged with ours, and continued firing, we holding our position, and preventing the head of Longstreet's corps from moving forward from the Gap from 8 a. m. till 6 p. m., when the enemy brought five regiments of infantry around out of sight in the woods, and, approaching my left flank, drove in our skirmishers, and only by overwhelming numbers compelled me to fall back slowly toward Barbee's Cross-Roads, keeping my vedettes and pickets watching the enemy.

I think it proper to state that our battery, under Lieutenant Heaton, Second U. S. Artillery, had the very worst kind of ammunition, and consequently could do but comparatively little execution. About one shell in twelve would explode, and then it would be prematurely, over the heads of our own men.

A tabular recapitulation of killed, wounded, and missing is herewith appended, the usual list of casualties by name having previously been forwarded, according to orders.

All of which is respectfully submitted.

WM. GAMBLE,
Col., Comdg. First Brigade, First Cavalry Division.

Capt. T. C. BACON,
Assistant Adjutant-General, First Cavalry Division

[Inclosure.]

Number of killed, wounded, and missing of First Cavalry Brigade, from June 28 to July 31, 1863.

Locality.	Date.	Killed.	Wounded.	Missing.
Gettysburg, Pa*	July 1, 1863	16	80	29
Williamsport, Md	July 6, 1863	3	.....	1
Boonsborough, Md	July 8, 1863	2	14	1
Funkstown, Md	July 10, 1863	3	3	1
Falling Waters, Md	July 14, 1863	......	5	......
Chester Gap, Va	July 21, 22, 1863	1	8	16
Total		25	110	48

WM. GAMBLE,
Colonel, Commanding First Cavalry Brigade.

HEADQUARTERS FIRST CAVALRY BRIGADE,
August 24, 1863.

No. 339.

Report of Col. Thomas C. Devin, Sixth New York Cavalry, commanding Second Brigade.

HDQRS. SECOND BRIGADE, FIRST CAVALRY DIVISION,
August 6, 1863.

CAPTAIN: I have the honor to submit the following report of the operations of this brigade, since crossing the Potomac at Edwards Ferry to take part in the Maryland campaign:

Arriving at Poolesville, Md., June 27, the brigade marched with the division to Jefferson, where it encamped for the night, reaching Middletown on the morning of the 28th.

On the 29th, marched by way of Cavetown and Monterey across South Mountain to Fountain Dale, near Millerstown.

On the 30th, marched by Emmitsburg to Gettysburg, Pa., and encamped. Scouting parties were immediately sent out to observe the a proaches from Carlisle, Harrisburg, and York. The country toward the above points was thoroughly scoured, and a number of prisoners were taken, from whom important intelligence was elicited and forwarded to headquarters.

BATTLE OF GETTYSBURG, PA.

On the morning of July 1, the pickets of the First Brigade, on the road to Cashtown, were driven in by a heavy force advancing from that direction, and the Second Brigade was ordered to prepare for action, and form on the crest of the hill on the right of the First Brigade. I immediately formed as ordered, with my right resting on the road to Mummasburg, and deployed a squadron of the Sixth New York to the front and left as skirmishers, dismounted, and connecting with those of the First Brigade, at the same time connecting by skirmishers and vedettes with my pickets on the three roads on the right leading toward Carlisle, thus establishing a continuous line from the

* But see revised statement, p. 185.

York road, on the extreme right, to the left of the First Brigade, on the Cashtown road. The infantry not having arrived, and the enemy's artillery fire increasing, I was ordered to retire gradually, as they succeeded in getting the range of my position. This I effected in successive formations in line to the rear by regiment, in the face of the enemy, the troops behaving well, and forming with perfect coolness and order.

About this time, my skirmishers on the right were forced back by the advance of the enemy's line of battle, coming from the direction of Heidlersburg. Knowing the importance of holding that point until the infantry could arrive and be placed in position, I immediately placed the Ninth New York in support, and, dismounting the rest of my available force, succeeded in holding the rebel line in check for two hours, until relieved by the arrival of the Eleventh Corps, when I was ordered to mass my command on the right of the York road and hold that approach. While in that position—immediately in front of the town, the command faced to the front and my pickets on the York road advanced three-quarters of a mile—a heavy fire of shells was opened on us from one of our own batteries on Cemetery Hill, immediately in my rear. The fire becoming very hot and persistent, and many of the shells bursting among us, I was led to suppose for a moment that the enemy had succeeded in gaining that position, and I immediately removed my command into the town, the column being shelled the whole distance. After I had retired, the battery turned its attention to my pickets on the road, and shelled them out. I was then ordered to the Emmitsburg road, where the brigade was formed in line, in rear of the batteries of the division, with its right flank resting on the town.

The enemy, having gained the York road, entered the town immediately after my pickets retired, and, passing through with their sharpshooters, attacked the flank of the brigade, killing and wounding several men and horses. I immediately dismounted one squadron of the Ninth New York, who, with their carbines, drove them some distance into the town, punishing them severely. The brigade was then ordered to the extreme left, where it bivouacked for the night.

The next morning, July 2, while I was engaged reconnoitering in rear of the enemy's right, our sharpshooters became engaged with a division of the enemy advancing to feel our lines in front of my position. I immediately dismounted and deployed two squadrons in support of Berdan's Sharpshooters (who were engaged in my front), and formed the brigade into line on the left of the First, with one section of Tidball's battery in position. The enemy not pressing his advance, and the Third Corps coming into position, we were ordered to march to Taneytown, where we bivouacked, and marched the next morning, July 3, to Westminster.

The brigade was here ordered to refit and shoe their horses, but on the following day (Sunday) we were ordered to march with the division to Frederick. Bivouacked outside of the town that night, and the next day we were ordered with the division to advance by Boonsborough to Williamsport.

BATTLE OF WILLIAMSPORT, MD.

On arriving near Williamsport, I found our batteries engaging the enemy, supported by parts of the First and Reserve Brigades, a part of which were also dismounted and engaged with the enemy's infantry. I was ordered to mass my brigade in the woods in the rear of the position and await instructions.

At 7 p. m. I was ordered to relieve the First Brigade, then engaged on the left front, and at dark to retire my command again to the wood, which I was to hold until daylight, to enable the other brigades to retire on a suitable position near the cross-roads. Retiring as ordered, I withdrew my skirmishers to a line 500 yards in advance of my position, and connecting with the woods at the same distance on each flank, completely covering the road. I had previously strongly picketed the roads in rear toward Sharpsburg on the left and Hagerstown on the right. Lieutenant Blunt, of the Sixth New York, whom I had sent to the right to reconnoiter, ascertained the presence of a strong force of infantry and artillery in close proximity to my right flank. The enemy's skirmishers also commenced to feel their way on my left.

About midnight, the enemy advanced on my front, and engaged the skirmishers. He was repulsed, and soon after retired. Our loss was Captain Van Buren, Sixth New York, 2 sergeants, and 1 private missing.

Just at daybreak, I made a demonstration on the enemy's front by charging down with a squadron of the Sixth New York, driving in his skirmishers and pickets on the reserve, and throwing them in confusion, under cover of which movement I withdrew the main body 1 mile to the rear, and took up a position in front of the road running from Hagerstown to Sharpsburg. I then withdrew my skirmishers from the front and the pickets from the roads, and retired slowly, the enemy following very cautiously, and halting when my rear guard faced about. After retiring about 2½ miles, I was ordered to halt, rest men and horses, strongly picket the roads to the rear, and, if possible, hold the position until the division of General Kilpatrick and the two brigades of General Buford's division had crossed Antietam Creek.

About 11 a. m. the enemy appeared in force in our rear with infantry and artillery. I immediately ordered up the Ninth New York (Colonel Sackett) to hold him in check, and sent an orderly to notify General Buford. As soon as I ascertained that the rear of General Buford's column was crossing Antietam Bridge, I ordered Colonel Sackett (who by this time was hotly engaged) to fall back on the brigade. I then took up the line of march, and followed the division, the enemy becoming bolder, and closely pressing my rear, under Colonel Sackett, who fell back, fighting, his men behaving splendidly, making a stand at every favorable point, and often repulsing and punishing the enemy's sharpshooters. On arriving near the creek, I dismounted two squadrons of the Seventeenth Pennsylvania, and posted them on the hill commanding the bridge, intending to give the enemy a warm reception. He was, however, too cautious to approach the creek, which we crossed unmolested, and joined the division, having suffered a loss of 8 killed and wounded while retiring, all of the Ninth New York. That night the brigade encamped at Boonsborough.

BATTLE OF BOONSBOROUGH, MD.

The next morning, July 8, the enemy advanced in force down the Hagerstown turnpike. The alarm being sounded, I formed the brigade in line of battle along the crest in my front, and at nearly a right angle with the line of the First and Reserve Brigades, connecting with the left of the latter and covering the approach from Williamsport. I also deployed two squadrons to the front as skirmishers, connecting with those on the right, and ordered Major Beardsley, Sixth New York, to advance to the hill on the left of the Williamsport road. The enemy having gained possession of and established a battery on the heights on the right, completely commanding the Williamsport road, Major Beardsley was unable to reach the hill, but was forced to retire into the woods under a hot fire. He, however, retained the latter position for two hours without loss.

In the meantime my skirmishers had been more or less engaged, but about 2 p. m., the enemy being re-enforced, a determined and vigorous attack was made on my position. I was forced to dismount the whole of the Seventeenth Pennsylvania and Sixth New York, which held the enemy with varying success, sometimes being forced back and again regaining their lost ground. I was obliged to relieve those engaged with others as their ammunition became expended, so that by 5.30 p. m. my whole command had been engaged, and I had not a dozen cartridges left. I was, therefore, obliged to retire the brigade, after notifying General Kilpatrick of my action. One regiment of his command had been put in on my front about 3.30 p. m., but could not have held the position for ten minutes had I withdrawn sooner, as proved by the fact that as soon as my brigade was withdrawn the enemy carried the position nearly up to the turnpike, and was only held in check by the batteries posted near the road. Our men behaved splendidly, holding and even driving the enemy with their pistols after their carbine ammunition was expended.

About 6 p. m. I was ordered to advance to the extreme front and right, and support the First Brigade, then rapidly driving the enemy up the turnpike. I advanced as ordered, forming in the fields in rear of the First Brigade, under the fire of the enemy's battery, and closing up in support until ordered at dark to retire, when the brigade returned, and bivouacked between Boonsborough and the Gap.

BATTLE OF BEAVER CREEK, MD.

On the following morning, July 9, the brigade again advanced with the division to a point 2½ miles in front of Boonsborough, where it was halted and massed in the fields.

About 5.30 p. m. the division was ordered to advance, and, crossing Beaver Creek, to carry the crest, if practicable, and feel the enemy's position. The Second Brigade being on the left, I deployed a squadron as skirmishers, mounted, to sweep the left to the bend of Antietam Creek previous to the general advance; directed Lieutenant [Albert O.] Vincent to place his section of battery in position on the crest in front of my center; dismounted two squadrons as skirmishers, connecting with the left of the First Brigade, and advanced with the division line. After a short but sharp skirmish, the crest was carried in a most gallant manner by the skirmishers alone, and in a space of time remarkably short, considering the position. The squadron on the extreme left running into an extensive cavalry camp and dispersing the force, I immediately followed with the brigade and section of battery, and the enemy was driven for nearly 2 miles, until darkness rendered farther pursuit useless. The brigade bivouacked on the field.

BATTLE OF FUNKSTOWN, MD.

Early the next morning, July 10, the brigade moved forward on the left of the division, and soon became engaged with the enemy's skirmishers, who, after a sharp action, were driven along the south bank of Antietam Creek and across the bridges on the left of Funkstown. Ascertaining that the latter place was held by Longstreet's corps, the brigade was halted, and remained in position, holding the approaches across the two bridges on the left until about 2 p. m., when, the Sixth Corps having arrived, the brigade was ordered to retire behind Beaver Creek, where it bivouacked for the night.

The following day the First and Second Brigades marched by Boonsborough to Bakersville, where they remained until the morning of July 14. During this time the country in front of the Second Brigade was thoroughly examined, and the position of the enemy on the left definitely ascertained.

FALLING WATERS, MD.

On the morning above mentioned [July 14], the two brigades were ordered to advance and feel the enemy's position, the Second Brigade sweeping the country between the Potomac and the road to Falling Waters. On approaching the enemy's works near Downsville, they were found to be evacuated. The brigade rapidly advanced on the left of the First, and soon engaged the skirmishers of the enemy's rear guard, capturing a large number of prisoners and driving the skirmishers ahead of them to Falling Waters. On approaching the crest of the hill at the ford, they were opened upon by the enemy's batteries, posted upon the opposite bank. A regiment was then dismounted, and deployed through the woods on the right of the ford, which the main force had by this time succeeded in crossing, leaving a rear guard to engage our advance. The country in the neighborhood of the ford having been thoroughly scoured, the command returned to Bakersville, and bivouacked for the night.

On the next day, July 15, marched by Sharpsburg to Berlin, and went into camp.

Throughout the whole of these sharp and rapidly succeeding engagements, the men have behaved like veterans—as most of them now are—not a single instance of misbehavior having been brought to my notice. The officers were also prompt, brave, and efficient in the execution of their duties.

The brigade staff—Captain [Harrison] White and Lieutenants [J. Henry] Mahnken, [Raymond L.] Wright, and [James] Cating—have rendered invaluable service in conducting reconnaissances, ascertaining the position of the enemy's lines, and transmitting orders on the battle-field, and to them, as much as to myself, is owing whatever success has attended the operations and dispositions of the brigade.

When all have done so nobly it is hard to discriminate, but if any one named deserves to be mentioned above that of others for cool and daring bravery and valuable services rendered on many occasions, it is that of Second Lieut. John W. Blunt, Troop M, Sixth New York Cavalry.

Majors Anderson and Reinhold, Seventeenth Pennsylvania Cavalry; Captains Hanley, Corrigan, and Bentley, Ninth New York Cavalry, and Pierce and Heermance (wounded at Boonsborough), Sixth New York Cavalry, were also distinguished for bravery and efficient service.

Corporal [John W.] Shumaker, Third West Virginia (taken prisoner scouting without the enemy's lines at Gettysburg); Sergeants [Silas N.] Pierce and [Lorenzo D.] Coal, Sixth New York Cavalry; Regimental Commissary Sergt. S. M. Whicher, Corpls. Alpheus

Hodges and John Samuelson, Ninth New York Cavalry, and Sergeant [Samuel] Snyder, jr., Seventeenth Pennsylvania Cavalry, were also distinguished for many acts of personal bravery. Assistant Surgeon Morton, Third West Virginia, and surgeon-in-chief of Second Brigade, is entitled to special mention for active service on the field, and unremitting and efficient discharge of duty in his care of the wounded.

Very respectfully, your obedient servant,

THOS. C. DEVIN,
Colonel, Commanding Second Brigade.

Capt. T. C. BACON, *A. A. G., First Cavalry Division.*

No. 340.

Reports of Brig. Gen. Wesley Merritt, U. S. Army, commanding Reserve Brigade.

HEADQUARTERS CAVALRY RESERVE BRIGADE,
Near Petersville, Md., July 18, 1863.

CAPTAIN: I have the honor to submit a report of the operations of the Cavalry Reserve Brigade during the battle of the army around Gettysburg.

On the 29th ultimo, we marched, by order, through Frederick City, and encamped near Mechanicstown, Md. At this point the brigade was engaged for two days picketing, scouting, and patrolling the roads through the mountains. Detachments visited Hagerstown, Cavetown, and other important points, keeping headquarters informed as to the movements of the enemy in those localities.

On the 2d instant, we marched to Emmitsburg, where Lieutenant Thompson was killed or captured, attempting to communicate with corps headquarters.

On the 3d instant, in compliance with orders received from corps headquarters, I marched with the brigade about 12 m. to attack the enemy's right and rear, and annoy him, while the battle was progressing on the right. I marched on the Gettysburg road about 4 miles, where my advance and skirmishers were engaged. Here the brigade drove the enemy more than a mile, routing him from strong places, stone fences, and barricades. This fight lasted about four hours (some time after the cannonading had ceased on the right), and was finally brought to a close by a heavy rain.

In the meantime, Major Starr, of the Sixth U. S. Cavalry, was detached with his regiment toward Fairfield or Millerstown; engaged a superior force of the enemy, not without success. His regiment lost heavily in officers and men, and I regret to say that the major himself—than whom there is no more gallant soldier in the service—was seriously wounded, losing an arm. The reports of this regiment, since detached, I have not been able to get. They will very materially increase the list of casualties.

On the 4th and 5th, we marched to Lewistown, from near Gettysburg, to Frederick City, where the brigade joined the division, from which it had been temporarily detached.

On the 6th instant we were engaged with the rest of the division fighting the enemy near Williamsport. Here the extreme right, under Kilpatrick, being driven back, the brigade, after the fight was over, withdrew.

On the 7th and 8th, the brigade again met the enemy near Boonsborough, and fought him with advantage several hours each day.

On the 9th, he was again engaged and driven several miles, when, on the 10th, we fought him near Funkstown, and with the best success all the way through. During these combats, which were mostly on foot (the enemy's infantry being engaged), there were some dashing, telling charges made, mounted. I mention particularly one made by the Sixth U. S. Cavalry, followed up by the First U. S. Cavalry, on the Boonsborough and Hagerstown road. In both of these the enemy was severely punished, and captures were made in hand-to-hand conflicts. Battery K, First U. S. Artillery (Captain Graham), did excellent service during all this season. It was directed with skill by its accomplished, soldierly commander. It was disabled by the breaking and springing of the axles during the firing, but all the guns were brought away, and the battery is now in good repair.

In the affair of the 14th, at Falling Waters, the brigade made captures and took part as set forth in reports of regimental commanders.

The list of casualties is remarkably small for so much hard fighting. The men of the brigade, from long and constant practice, are becoming perfect in the art of foot-fighting and skirmishing, and obeyed all orders (save the one to retire) with an alacrity and vim which shows a determination and courage that cannot be conquered by double their number. They drove infantry from strong positions, and always worsted the enemy's cavalry wherever found. It is next to impossible to furnish any elaborate account of events which occurred, as these did, through several days of exteme activity in the field. Part of the time the brigade was without wagons or packs, and for five days during the time from the 1st we were without a regular issue of rations or forage. The rations, I think, should be commuted to the command.

The regimental commanders and officers, without exception, to my knowledge, displayed a zeal and valor which shows them eminently fitted for the command of the brave soldiers in the brigade.

My staff did everything that finished officers could do. The lines were necessarily long, and they were continually called on to ride in exposed places along the entire front. Lieutenant McQuesten, acting assistant adjutant-general, is particularly deserving of praise for his untiring exertions in transmitting orders and expediting their execution ; so, also, Lieutenants [Edward] Myers and [Eugene P.] Bertrand. I cannot close this report without specially thanking Capt. C. E. Norris, Second U. S. Cavalry, who was acting on my staff, for his valuable services during the entire time embraced in this report. Sergeant [Charles] Polk and Corporal [James A.] Pearson, Second U. S. Cavalry, performed important service.

I inclose list of casualties* and reports of regimental commanders.

Very respectfully, your obedient servant,

W. MERRITT,
Brig. Gen. of Volunteers, Commanding Reserve Brigade.

Capt. M. W. KEOGH,
A. A. A. G., First Division, Cavalry Corps.

P. S.—Since writing the above, I have been able to get reports from the Sixth U. S. Cavalry, as also list of casualties,* which I inclose. They are necessarily more or less informal.

---

* Embodied in revised statement, p. 185.

MANASSAS GAP, VA.,
July 21, 1863—9 p. m.

CAPTAIN: We have had two small fights to-day with the enemy at the west end of the Gap. The first, in which the First Cavalry was engaged, in attempting to penetrate to Front Royal; the second, in which the First, Second, and Fifth were engaged, for the same object. I found the enemy in force at the west end of the Gap. I can learn nothing further as regards Lee's army more than what I have already reported. The only prisoners taken are all from the Seventeenth Virginia Infantry, and number about 20, including 4 commissioned officers. The regiment is about 600 strong, which of itself in this country is enough to hold my entire brigade in check, as I cannot use my artillery to advantage. The wounds inflicted on the men of my brigade are very severe, and the arms captured from the enemy are the Springfield rifle. Longstreet is reported at Front Royal, and, it is said, has sent out a force this way and toward Chester Gap. I at first thought they had only one regiment in my front, but am now convinced that Hoover's brigade of Corse's division* is this side of Front Royal. The fact that we have captured prisoners from only one regiment is attributable to this regiment being on picket to-day. I will feel them again to-morrow.

Very respectfully, &c.,

W. MERRITT,
Brigadier-General of Volunteers, Commanding.

Captain KEOGH,
Acting Assistant Adjutant-General.

—

HEADQUARTERS CAVALRY RESERVE BRIGADE,
Rappahannock Station, Va., July 31, 1863.

CAPTAIN: I submit report of the operations of the brigade, including the time embraced by list of casualties inclosed herewith.†

On the 20th, the brigade was detached from the division at Rectortown, with orders to march to and occupy Manassas Gap.

On the 21st, the Gap was taken possession of and the summit held while the First U. S. Cavalry was ordered to penetrate as far as practicable toward Front Royal. The enemy was soon engaged, and in superior numbers. The Fifth and Second U. S. Cavalry reenforced the First, and a severe skirmish took place, in which 5 commissioned officers and 21 enlisted men of the enemy's infantry were captured.

On the 22d, there was more or less skirmishing all day, but the enemy made no efforts to drive us from the position held, save by turning our flanks. The artillery was used to hold them in check.

Early on the morning of the 23d, the brigade was relieved by General Ward's division, Third Army Corps, and marched to Markham, by orders from corps headquarters; thence, by order from same source, along the ridge of the Blue Mountains to near Chester Gap, for the purpose of observation, &c. Here about 50 prisoners were captured near Chester Gap, after a small skirmish, by part of the First U. S. Cavalry.

---

* Corse was commanding a brigade of Pickett's division. "Hoover's" brigade cannot be identified.

† Embodied in revised statement, p. 194.

On the 25th, the brigade rejoined the division and marched to Orleans.

Very respectfully, your obedient servant,

W. MERRITT,
Brig. Gen. of Volunteers, Comdg. Reserve Brigade.

Capt. M. W. KEOGH,
A. D. C., and A. A. A. G., First Div., Cavalry Corps.

No. 341.

Report of Capt. Julius W. Mason, Fifth U. S. Cavalry.

HEADQUARTERS FIFTH U. S. CAVALRY,
June 23, 1863.

SIR: In compliance with circular, I have the honor to report that the Fifth U. S. Cavalry Regiment moved with the brigade from camp, near Middleburg, Va., on the morning of June 21. During the first hours of the march, the regiment was in advance of the brigade, but having moved on a road that was not the proper route, or it being deemed expedient to go in another direction, the regiment countermarched, and, retracing its route, struck the column of the balance of the brigade moving on another road. I here received an order from the major commanding not to follow him in advance of the brigade, but take place in rear of the First U. S. Cavalry. This brought my regiment nearly in rear of the brigade. In this order the regiment moved forward in column of fours until it arrived at Upperville, at about 4.30 p. m. Here the regiment was formed in close column of squadrons, and moved forward at a brisk trot. At this point, the Sixth and First U. S. Cavalry, with the exception of one squadron, which was immediately in my front, charged. I here lost 1 man killed by a bullet.

I then broke my column by fours, to enable me to get through a stone fence bordering the road, and, on entering the road, met General Pleasonton, who ordered me to form in front of a skirt of woods on the left of the road. I did so promptly at the gallop, and moved forward at the trot, to participate in the fighting then going on. I had moved but a short distance when I received a peremptory order from General Pleasonton, through an aide, to halt my command until I received orders from him to move. I remained halted until Captain Merritt, of the Second U. S. Cavalry, coming up, informed me that he had orders from General Pleasonton to move forward with his regiment and the Fifth.

I accordingly moved at a trot, and my movements were afterward directed by the acting assistant adjutant-general of the brigade, the Second U. S. Cavalry moving to the left and the Fifth moving to the front, when, being in close column of squadrons, the regiment, together with the Sixth U. S. Cavalry, were dismounted, and thrown forward as skirmishers.

After being dismounted about an hour, and having compelled the enemy to retire, the regiment was recalled and mounted, and again took the advance of the brigade, moving forward in column of squadrons in the direction of Ashby's Gap. Advanced to the outside line of skirmishers of Colonel Gregg; then moved to the rear and right. Was at this time subjected to a lively shelling from the enemy's artillery, by which the Fifth U. S. Cavalry lost 2 horses. Went into camp near Upperville at sundown.

Very respectfully, your obedient servant,

J. W. MASON,
Captain Fifth U. S. Cavalry, Commanding Regiment.

JAMES F. McQUESTEN,
Actg. Asst. Adjt. Gen., Reserve Cavalry Brigade.

No. 342.

Report of Capt. George C. Cram, Sixth U. S. Cavalry.

CAMP NEAR ALDIE, VA., *June 23, 1863.*

SIR: I have the honor to transmit the following report of the part taken by the Sixth U. S. Cavalry in the operations of June 21:

The regiment marched before breakfast from its position on picket near Aldie, in the brigade column, and, crossing Goose Creek, was employed at different portions of the day, with the rest of the brigade, as a supporting reserve until reaching the slopes on the hither side of Upperville, when, forming squadron and advancing for some time at a trot, it was suddenly called on to defeat an effort of the enemy on our left flank, the volunteer cavalry at this time being engaged with the enemy in front of us. Instantly breaking from its formation in column of squadrons, and passing through a narrow gap in a stone wall, and reforming on the other side, as well as the time allowed it and the circumstances and ground would permit, moved immediately forward, and, on the command being given, charged up to the enemy, under a harassing artillery fire and over a long stretch of heavy and marshy ground, intersected by a most difficult ditch and terminating in a hill of plowed ground, beyond which, on the firm ground in the edge of the woods, the enemy in large force awaited it. The charge was unsuccessful, the most of the horses being so blown that it was impossible to bring or keep them for such a distance at a charging pace.

On the regiment rallying and reforming on the nucleus of the second squadron, commanded by Captain Claflin, on more favorable ground, the enemy being within easy reach and everything favorable for a successful charge, for which it was then preparing, the regiment was then ordered to dismount and fight on foot, and was used dismounted, under the cover of stone walls, to protect our left flank, the enemy retiring at the same time into the woods on our front.

On being relieved from this position, and the engagement having terminated, it moved in column of squadrons, with the rest of the brigade, through the woods and toward the entrance of Ashby's Gap, till it succeeded in attracting the fire of the enemy's artillery, when it was withdrawn, and went into bivouac on the hither side of the town of Upperville.

The regiment marched out 12 commissioned officers and 242 enlisted men strong.

Its casualties were Second Lieut. Henry McQuiston, severely wounded. Privates John Might, of Company E, slightly wounded; C. F. H. Reomer, of Company A, mortally; Jacob Couts, of Company G, slightly; [Michael] Slattery, Company F, slightly; [Michael Kurnan, Company A, slightly. Privates [Joshua W.] Dubois, Company

E, Thomas McKeffrey, Company F, and Nelson H. Turner, Company B, missing.

In closing this report, out of justice to my regiment, I would respectfully call the attention of my superiors to the dispiriting circumstances attending the unsuccessful charge, before described. The men were exhausted and worn out by the recent imposition of incessant picket duty in their position near Middleburg. They were taken from behind stone walls which they had been guarding all night and the day before, mounted on horses as famished as themselves, and immediately marched with the column, and at the end of a fatiguing day were required to charge over ground almost impracticable in its nature and 750 paces in extent, as proved by the measurement of experienced officers on the morning of the 22d.

I am, sir, very respectfully, your obedient servant,

G. C. CRAM,
Captain Sixth U. S. Cavalry, Comdg. Regiment.

Lieut. JAMES F. McQUESTEN,
Actg. Asst. Adjt. Gen., Regular Cavalry Reserve Brigade.

No. 343.

Report of Lieut. Nicholas Nolan, Sixth U. S. Cavalry.

HDQRS. RESERVE CAVALRY BRIGADE, *July* 27, 1863.

SIR: I have the honor to report that on the 3d instant the Sixth U. S. Cavalry was ordered to proceed in the direction of Fairfield, Pa., for the purpose of intercepting a train of wagons of the enemy, supposed to be in that vicinity. On the arrival of the regiment at Millerstown, the First Squadron, commanded by Captain Cram, was sent in the direction of Fairfield. When about 2 miles from the regiment, I saw the enemy's cavalry charge in the direction of Millerstown. I immediately notified the squadron commander of the fact. He then moved the squadron on the enemy's right, and charged them, when he (Captain Cram) was captured. I, being the only officer then left with the squadron, took command. I found I was entirely cut off from the regiment, and had the enemy on both flanks and rear of me. After the regiment was repulsed from Millerstown, I immediately commenced retreating, disputing every inch of ground with the enemy. Finding the enemy in force, I gradually fell back in the direction of Mechanicstown, where I found the regiment, and also ascertained that the commanding officer was wounded and in the hands of the enemy; Lieutenant Balder killed; Lieutenants Paulding, Wood, Chaffee, and Bould, and Drs. Forwood and Notson missing, and supposed to be in the hands of the enemy; also 290 enlisted men and 292 horses killed, wounded, and missing. I, being the senior officer, assumed command of the regiment, which I found in command of Lieut. L. Henry Carpenter. I then received orders to join the brigade. On my arrival at the brigade, I turned over the command of the regiment to Captain Claflin.

On the 7th instant, the regiment was ordered to make a reconnaissance in the direction of Funkstown, under command of Captain Claflin. On arriving in the vicinity of the town, we drove in the enemy's pickets; immediately afterward made dispositions of the regiment to resist the enemy, who was in force. The captain commanding proceeded to the front to reconnoiter, and when about 150 yards in front of the regiment (and with the advance guard) was wounded in the shoulder by one of the enemy's sharpshooters. I, being the senior officer with the regiment, again assumed command. I immediately proceeded to the front, where my advance guard was posted, when I saw the enemy's cavalry preparing to charge my command. I then made preparations to meet them, but, being over-powered by superior numbers, was forced to fall back; inflicting, however, great damage to the enemy in a running fight of 4½ miles, my command losing 59 men in killed, wounded, and missing; 10 of the above men were brought in dead by the First U. S. Cavalry same afternoon.

In closing my report, I would respectfully call the attention of the general commanding to the following-named officers of the regiment Second Lieut. T. C. Tupper and Lieut. L. Henry Carpenter, for their gallantry in rallying the regiment, and for their general bravery throughout the whole affair. I have also to call the attention of the general commanding to the following non-commissioned officers and privates of the regiment: Chief Bugler [Jacob K.] Schuck, who fought his way through the enemy's lines, and rendered great assist-ance during the engagements of the 3d and 7th instant; Sergeant [John] McCaffery, Company A, who during the fight at Funkstown shot the enemy's standard-bearer, made a gallant effort to capture the flag, but, being overpowered, was unable to accomplish the act; Ser-geant [Martin] Schwenk, Company B, who cut his way through the enemy's lines at Millerstown, Pa., when sent by me to communi-cate with the regiment, but was unable to accomplish his mission; I also saw him extricate an officer from the hands of the enemy; Sergeant [Michael C.] Gorman, Company I, who extricated an officer from the hands of the enemy, and during the whole engagement acted with the most reckless gallantry; and Private [Patrick] Kelly, of Company H (this man at Fairfield made a desperate effort to cap-ture one of the enemy's standards, at which place he was near losing his life, and rendered great service throughout both engagements).

The above non-commissioned officers and one private formed the rear guard of the regiment during the fight of the 7th instant, and maintained the honor of the regiment.

I am, sir, very respectfully, your obedient servant,

NICHOLAS NOLAN,
Second Lieut. Sixth U. S. Cavalry, Comdg. Regiment.

First Lieut. JAMES F. MCQUESTEN,
Second U. S. Cavalry, A. A. A. G., Res. Cav. Brigade.

No. 344.

Reports of Brig. Gen. David McM. Gregg, U. S. Army, com-manding Second Division.

HDQRS. SECOND AND THIRD CAVALRY DIVISIONS,
June 12, 1863.

COLONEL: I have the honor to submit the following report of the operations of the Second and Third Cavalry Divisions* in the en-gagement of the 9th instant:

Agreeably to my instructions from Brigadier-General Pleasonton,

---

*The Second and Third Divisions here referred to became the Second Division, under orders, June 11, 1863.

commanding corps, on the afternoon of the 8th instant I moved the Second and Third Divisions from their camp near Warrenton Junction to the vicinity of Kelly's Ford. At this point I found Brig. Gen. D. A. Russell, with 1,500 infantry and a battery of horse artillery. This force, which was designed to take part in the operations of the ensuing day, having been reported to me by Brigadier-General Russell, I at once made every preparation for crossing at daylight on the following morning. The Second Division, Col. A. N. Duffié commanding, was ordered to be at the ford at 3.30 a. m. and to cross in advance, in order that it might move at once upon Stevensburg. A late start from camp and an unexpected difficulty in following the direct road to the ford on the part of this division delayed the crossing of my advance until between 5 and 6 o'clock. The enemy offering but slight opposition, in a very short time the entire command was on the south bank of the river.

In compliance with my instructions to establish the left of my line at Stevensburg, I directed Colonel Duffié to move with the Second Division to that place; General Russell with his infantry to proceed directly from Kelly's Ford to Brandy Station. With the Third Division I started to Brandy Station, taking a road west of that occupied by the infantry (about 5 miles). While crossing the Rappahannock, the artillery firing on the right was evidence that General Buford was already engaged with the enemy. Couriers from General Pleasonton, commanding corps, gave me the same information, as also that he had met the entire cavalry force of the enemy. I pushed on rapidly, and, after marching about 5 miles, overtook the rear of Colonel Duffié's division, and there had a dispatch from him that his advance was at Stevensburg. Turning to the right from this point, I pushed on for Brandy Station and toward the firing in front. Another dispatch from General Pleasonton, informing me of the severity of the fight on the right and of the largely superior force of the enemy, determined me to direct Duffié's division also upon Brandy Station. Colonel Duffié having sent me a dispatch that his advance had reached Stevensburg without encountering the enemy, I sent forward an order to push to Brandy Station, but at a point about 3½ miles from the station I came upon the rear brigade of the Second Division, and, in order to get the whole force at once to Brandy Station, I again sent to Colonel Duffié to follow with his division on the same road that the Third Division was following. I would thus have my entire command in hand. When the head of the Third Division arrived near Brandy Station, it was discovered that the enemy were there in great force.

The country about Brandy Station is open, and on the south side extensive level fields, particularly suitable for a cavalry engagement. Coming thus upon the enemy, and having at hand only the Third Division (total strength 2,400), I either had to decline the fight in the face of the enemy or throw upon him at once the entire division. Not doubting but that the Second Division was near, and delay not being admissible, I directed the commanders of my advance brigade to charge the enemy, formed in columns about Brandy House. The whole brigade charged with drawn sabers, fell upon the masses of the enemy, and, after a brief but severe contest, drove them back, killing and wounding many and taking a large number of prisoners. Other columns of the enemy coming up, charged this brigade before it could reform, and it was driven back. Seeing this, I ordered the First Brigade to charge the enemy upon the right. This brigade came forward gallantly through the open fields, dashed upon the enemy, drove him away, and occupied the hill. Now that my entire division was engaged, the fight was everywhere most fierce. Fresh columns of the enemy arriving upon the ground received the vigorous charges of my regiments, and, under the heavy blows of our sabers, were in every instance driven back. Martin's battery of horse artillery, divided between the two brigades, poured load after load of canister upon the rebel regiments. Assailed on all sides, the men stood to the guns nobly. Thus for an hour and a half was the contest continued, not in skirmishing, but in determined charges. The contest was too unequal to be longer continued. The Second Division had not come up; there was no support at hand, and the enemy's numbers were three times my own. I ordered the withdrawal of my brigades. In good order they left the field, the enemy not choosing to follow.

Retiring about 1 mile south of the station, I again formed my brigades, and discovered the Second Division some distance in the rear. Hearing that General Russell had gotten up to General Buford's left with his infantry, I moved my command in the direction of Rappahannock Bridge, and soon united with General Buford's left. On the hills near Brandy Station the enemy had artillery posted, the fire of which they directed upon my line in this new position. A few guns well served were sufficient to prevent any advance in that direction. When engaged with the enemy at Brandy Station, cars loaded with infantry were brought there from Culpeper. Before they could quite get to the station, I sent a party to obstruct the rails. Finding a switch above the station, they reversed it, and thus prevented the cars from running into my command.

The field having been well contested and the enemy being reenforced with infantry, which could be thrown in any force upon us from Culpeper, I received orders from Brigadier-General Pleasonton to recross my command at Rappahannock Ford. The Second Brigade, Second Division, covered my crossing. I got my command entirely over without being molested by the enemy. When the last man had crossed, the enemy displayed a regiment in front of the ford. I directed a regiment of the Second Brigade, Second Division, to recross and offer them fight. This they declined, and the regiment quietly returned to this side.

In this engagement the loss of the Third Division was very severe. Three field officers (3 regimental commanders) were wounded and missing, 2 line officers killed, and 15 wounded; 18 enlisted men killed, 65 wounded, and 272 missing.* Of these last many were killed and wounded. The division captured from the enemy 8 commissioned officers and 107 enlisted men and 2 colors (these taken by the First Maine and First Maryland). The field on which we fought bore evidence of the severe loss of the enemy.

The Third Division behaved nobly, and where every officer and man did his duty it is difficult to particularize. I would, however, mention Col. P. Wyndham, First New Jersey Cavalry, commanding Second Brigade, and Col. J. Kilpatrick, Second New York, commanding First Brigade, who gallantly led their brigades to the charge, and throughout the entire engagement handled them with consummate skill. Colonel Wyndham, although wounded, remained on the field, and covered with a portion of his command the withdrawal of the division. Capt. J. W. Martin, commanding Sixth New York Bat-

---

*But see revised statement, p. 170.

tery of Horse Artillery, did most excellent service. His sections were charged by the enemy's regiments on all sides. Two of his pieces disabled and one serviceable fell into the hands of the enemy, but not until 21 of his men were cut down, fighting stubbornly, and nearly all of the horses killed.

Although the loss of these pieces is to be regretted, still, the magnificent defense of them establishes in the highest degree the soldierly character of the officers and men of the battery. The serviceable gun was spiked before the enemy got it.

All the regiments of the Third Division were engaged, viz: First Brigade, Col. J. Kilpatrick commanding—Tenth New York Cavalry, Lieut. Col. William Irvine commanding; Second New York Cavalry, Lieut. Col. H. E. Davies, jr., commanding; First Maine Cavalry, Col. C. S. Douty commanding. Second Brigade, Col. P. Wyndham commanding—First New Jersey, Lieutenant-Colonel Brodrick commanding; First Pennsylvania, Col. J. P. Taylor commanding; First Maryland, Lieut. Col. J. M. Deems commanding.

Colonel Duffié reports that his division met a regiment of the enemy at Stevensburg; that his advance engaged and defeated it, capturing 1 officer and 57 men, and that his advance was thus engaged at the time he received my order to follow the Third Division, and hence was unavoidably delayed in coming to my support. Colonel Duffié reports the good conduct of his troops when engaged during the day.

The loss in the Second Division was: Enlisted men killed, 4; wounded, 12; missing, 13.

I cannot close this report without favorably mentioning my division staff officers. Surgeon Phillips; Major Gaston, First Pennsylvania Cavalry; Capt. H. C. Weir, assistant adjutant-general; Capt. J. W. Kester, First New Jersey Cavalry; Capt. E. A. Tobes, acting commissary of subsistence; Lieuts. W. Phillips and T. J. Gregg, Sixth Pennsylvania Cavalry, employed in transmitting my orders, proved their efficiency in the highest degree.

Major Gaston and Captain Tobes were captured, but the former escaped his captors.

Lieutenant [Clifford] Thomson, aide-de-camp to General Pleasonton, who accompanied me, having tendered his services on my staff, performed the duties of an aide, and in a most excellent manner.

Accompanying this is a list of casualties in the two divisions.*

Very respectfully, your obedient servant,

D. McM. GREGG,
Brigadier-General, Commanding.

Lieut. Col. A. J. ALEXANDER,
Assistant Adjutant-General, Cavalry Corps.

HEADQUARTERS SECOND DIVISION, CAVALRY CORPS,
September 19, 1863.

CAPTAIN: I have the honor to submit the following report of the operations of the Second Division, Cavalry Corps, in the engagements at Aldie, Middleburg, and Upperville:

On June 17, the division left Manassas Junction for Aldie, being the advance division of the Cavalry Corps. Major-General Pleasonton, commanding, accompanied it, and at a point about 9 miles from

* See p. 169.

Aldie directed me to send forward one brigade through Aldie and thence toward Front Royal, and later to join the division at Noland's Ferry. The Second Brigade, Brigadier-General Kilpatrick commanding, moved forward rapidly to execute this order. Arrived within less than 1 mile of Aldie, the advance guard of this brigade encountered the advance of a column of the enemy's cavalry. A reconnaissance to the front ascertained the presence of the enemy in force. General Kilpatrick at once made his dispositions and attacked the enemy. The First and Third Brigades arriving about this time, were placed in position to support the Second Brigade in its attack. Moving to the front, I found the Second Brigade hotly engaged with a superior force. The necessity for re-enforcements being apparent, the First Maine Regiment was ordered to report to General Kilpatrick. This regiment moved to the front, charged the enemy at the critical moment, and, in connection with the regiments of the Second Brigade, which had been charging the enemy and resisting his charges, drove the enemy from the field, inflicting upon him severe loss in killed, wounded, and prisoners. This action was very severe. The enemy, strongly posted and in superior force to Kilpatrick's brigade, seemed determined to repossess himself of the town, but the gallant charges of the Second New York, First Massachusetts, Sixth Ohio, Fourth New York, and First Maine, and the well-directed fire of Randol's battery, were more than enough to make him fail in this, and compel his flight to the hills beyond.

In this action the brave and generous Col. C. S. Douty, First Maine Cavalry, fell, at the head of his regiment.

On the 18th instant, agreeably to orders from Brigadier-General Pleasonton, commanding Cavalry Corps, I sent forward the Third Brigade, Col. J. I. Gregg commanding, to make a reconnaissance toward Middleburg and Upperville, and, if possible, take possession of the former place. After a sharp skirmish with the enemy's cavalry, Middleburg was taken possession of, and on the same evening, agreeably to orders, Colonel Gregg fell back to a point midway between Middleburg and Aldie.

On the morning of the 19th, the brigade was again advanced to Middleburg, which, during the night, had been reoccupied by the enemy. A gallant charge of the Fourth Pennsylvania Cavalry cleared the town. The enemy (Robertson's brigade) took a strong position on the wooded heights about a mile beyond the town, on the road leading to Upperville. At this time I arrived upon the field, and found the enemy's line well extended along a commanding crest, his center resting upon the turnpike. So extended was this line that almost the whole of Colonel Gregg's brigade was deployed as skirmishers against the enemy. The enemy's artillery was posted in such positions as to have a raking fire of canister upon our skirmishers, and his skirmishers, concealed in wheat-fields and woods, made any advance of our line apparently impracticable.

Determined to drive the enemy from his position, I directed Colonel Gregg to disregard the menaces on his flanks, and to direct all his available force upon his center. An increased force of dismounted skirmishers was placed to the right and left of the turnpike, and regiments held in readiness to charge upon the road. An advance was ordered, the fields cleared, and a brigade of rebel cavalry discovered, which was gallantly charged. The enemy made a strong resistance, but at last yielded and abandoned his position, leaving his dead and wounded upon the field. A large number of prisoners was taken.

In this action all the regiments of the Third Brigade were engaged, and all acquitted themselves well.

On the morning of the 21st, the major-general commanding the corps having determined to attack the enemy, I was directed to make a feint in front of the enemy on the turnpike, while the First Division, moving to the right, would attack on the flank. The Second Brigade, Brigadier-General Kilpatrick commanding, being in advance, moved a line of skirmishers against the enemy. This advance drew the fire of his artillery, which was replied to by Fuller's light battery. Our skirmishers became engaged, and after an hour an advance was ordered. The advance of the Second Brigade was so rapid that the enemy was compelled to abandon a gun and caisson which had been disabled. Taking up position after position, with his battery of six pieces the enemy stubbornly contested our advance. The heights at Goose Creek were particularly favorable to his resistance, but the advance of the skirmishers of Vincent's brigade of infantry to the edge of the creek, and a gallant charge of the Second and Fourth New York Regiments of cavalry across the bridge, compelled him to abandon this strong position.

From Goose Creek to Upperville the retreat of the enemy was rapid. At Upperville the enemy had massed his cavalry, his artillery having been placed in position at Ashby's Gap. Arrived at Upperville, the advance regiments of the Second Brigade charged the enemy, but were momentarily repulsed. The Regular Brigade, of the First Division, which had reported to me near Goose Creek, acting under the direct orders of the major-general commanding, was now brought to the front and left of the Second Brigade of my division. The attack by charges now became general and very determined. The First Division was engaged on our right; the two brigades (Regular and Second Brigades, Second Division) drove the enemy back into the town and to the left of it. Our artillery was placed in position, and the Second Brigade hurried forward to charge through the town. The charge was made, and an abandoned gun found in the street.

The enemy again made a stand at the west end, and here expended their remaining strength in charges, at first successful, but finally changed to a pell-mell retreat toward the Gap. The force in our front united with the fugitives in front of Buford, and, under cover of their guns on the mountain, made a disorderly escape through the Gap. The Regular Brigade and Third Brigade, Second Division, engaged in pursuit of the enemy on the left, and by their rapid advance added to the confusion in the enemy's retreating columns.

In these engagements—at Aldie, Middleburg, and Upperville—the brigades of this division displayed the very greatest gallantry. The battle of Brandy Station had demonstrated to the men their superior strength, and in these subsequent operations they felt they had but to encounter the enemy to defeat him.

Too much credit cannot be given to Brig. Gen. J. Kilpatrick and Col. J. I. Gregg, commanding, respectively, the Second and Third Brigades of this division, for the able manner in which they performed their duties as brigade commanders. The accompanying reports of these officers will furnish the detailed accounts of the operations of the respective regiments of their brigades. My several staff officers performed their duties most efficiently; especially may this be said of Surg. W. W. L. Phillips, chief surgeon of this division.

Nominal lists of the killed, wounded, and missing in these engagements have heretofore been forwarded.   Accompanying is a numerical list.

During these operations of the Second and Third Brigades, the First Brigade was on detached service at Thoroughfare Gap.

The total number of prisoners captured from the enemy was 250, including many commissioned officers.

I am, captain, very respectfully, your obedient servant,

D. McM. GREGG,

Brigadier-General of Volunteers, Comdg. Second Division.

Capt. C. C. SUYDAM,
   Assistant Adjutant-General, Cavalry Corps.

[Inclosure.]

List of Casualties in Second Division, Cavalry Corps, June 21, 1863.

Command.	Killed.		Wounded.		Missing.	
	Officers.	Enlisted men.	Officers.	Enlisted men.	Officers.	Enlisted men.
SECOND BRIGADE.*						
1st Massachusetts Cavalry			1	17	1	8
4th New York Cavalry			1	3		7
6th Ohio Cavalry		1		13		
2d New York Cavalry		1	1	4		
THIRD BRIGADE.						
4th Pennsylvania Cavalry			1	3		2
1st Maine Cavalry			1	6		2
Battery C, Third U. S. Artillery		1				
Total		4	6	43	1	19

D. McM. GREGG,
Brigadier-General of Volunteers, Commanding Second Division.

——

HEADQUARTERS SECOND DIVISION, CAVALRY CORPS,
            Shepherdstown, Va., July 15, 1863—3 p. m.

This morning had a skirmish with the enemy's cavalry near Charlestown. The enemy used artillery. Have taken 100 prisoners, including sick. On the roads to Winchester and Martinsburg, strong pickets; on that to Winchester, infantry. Have directed Colonel Huey to come here. The enemy moving to Winchester. This place was occupied by cavalry.

D. McM. GREGG,

Brig. Gen. of Vols., Commanding Second Division.

Col. A. J. ALEXANDER,
   A. A. G., Cavalry Corps, Hdqrs. Army of the Potomac.

——

HEADQUARTERS SECOND DIVISION, CAVALRY CORPS,
         Harper's Ferry, Va., July 17, 1863—7.30 a. m.

COLONEL: Was engaged with the enemy yesterday from noon until after dark; a sharp fight; the enemy attacked, but did not succeed.

* First Brigade not engaged.

My loss in killed and wounded about 70, including 7 officers. Huey did not get up until late last night. My two brigades are entirely out of ammunition and rations. The enemy's cavalry moved toward Leetown. What orders?

D. McM. GREGG,
Brigadier-General of Volunteers.

Lieut. Col. A. J. ALEXANDER,
A. A. G., Cavalry Corps, Hdqrs. Army of the Potomac.

HEADQUARTERS SECOND DIVISION, CAVALRY CORPS,
July 25, 1863.

COLONEL: The First and Third Brigades, of the Second Division, Cavalry Corps, arrived on the battle-field at Gettysburg, July 2, about noon, the Second Brigade having been sent to Westminster.

In compliance with orders from Major-General Pleasonton, commanding the corps, I placed these brigades on the extreme right of our line of battle, and at the point of intersection of the Gettysburg and Hanover turnpike with the road which ran in rear of the right of our line of battle. A line of pickets was established in front, connecting with the right of the infantry line and extending well to the right of the turnpike. An attempt made to dislodge some of the enemy's sharpshooters posted in front of the center of my line caused the enemy to throw out two regiments deployed. This force advanced against my line, but was soon compelled to withdraw under the admonition of a half dozen well-directed shells and a telling carbine fire from behind a line of stone fence.

On the morning of July 3, I was again ordered to take a position on the right of our line, and make a demonstration against the enemy. The First and Third Brigades were again posted on the right of the infantry, but about three-fourths of a mile nearer the Baltimore and Gettysburg turnpike. This position was taken because I learned that the First [Second] Brigade, of the Third Division, was occupying my position of the day before. A regiment was dismounted and put in the woods as skirmishers, but the enemy was not found in any considerable force.

At 12 m. I received a copy of a dispatch from the commander of the Eleventh Army Corps to the major-general commanding the Army of the Potomac, that large columns of the enemy's cavalry were moving toward the right of our line. At the same time I received an order from Major-General Pleasonton, through an aide-de-camp, to send the First [Second] Brigade, of the Third Division, to join General Kilpatrick on the left. The First Brigade of my division was sent to relieve the brigade of the Third Division. This change having been made, a strong line of skirmishers displayed by the enemy was evidence that the enemy's cavalry had gained our right, and were about to attack, with the view of gaining the rear of our line of battle. The importance of successfully resisting an attack at this point, which, if succeeded in by the enemy, would have been productive of the most serious consequences, determined me to retain the brigade of the Third Division until the enemy were driven back. General Custer, commanding the brigade, fully satisfied of the intended attack, was well pleased to remain with his brigade. The First New Jersey Cavalry was posted as mounted skirmishers to the right and front in a wood, the Third Pennsylvania Cavalry deployed as dismounted skirmishers to the left and front in open fields, and the First Maryland on the Hanover turnpike, in position to protect the right of my line.

The very superior force of dismounted skirmishers of the enemy advanced on our left and front required the line to be re-enforced by one of General Custer's regiments. At this time the skirmishing became very brisk on both sides, and an artillery fire was begun by the enemy and ourselves. During the skirmish of the dismounted men, the enemy brought upon the field a column for a charge. The charge of this column was met by the Seventh Michigan Cavalry, of the First [Second] Brigade, Third Division, but not successfully. The advantage gained in this charge was soon wrested from the enemy by the gallant charge of the First Michigan, of the same brigade. This regiment drove the enemy back to his starting point. Other charges were made by the enemy's columns, but in every instance were they driven back. Defeated at every point, the enemy withdrew to his left, and on passing the wood in which the First New Jersey Cavalry was posted, that regiment gallantly and successfully charged the flank of his column. Heavy skirmishing was still maintained by the Third Pennsylvania Cavalry with the enemy, and was continued until nightfall. During the engagement, a portion of this regiment made a very handsome and successful charge upon one of the enemy's regiments. The enemy retired his column behind his artillery, and at dark withdrew from his former position. At this time I was at liberty to relieve the First [Second] Brigade of the Third Division, which was directed to join its division.

Our own and the enemy's loss during this engagement was severe. Our loss: Officers, 1 killed, 17 wounded, and 1 missing; enlisted men, 33 killed, 140 wounded, and 103 missing.*

On the morning of the 4th, I advanced to the enemy's position, but found him gone. Following toward Hunterstown, I found many of his wounded abandoned. From these we learned that the enemy had been severely punished and his loss heavy. One general officer was severely wounded

Brigadier-General Custer, commanding First [Second] Brigade, Third Division, very ably assisted me in the duties of my command. Col. J. B. McIntosh, commanding First Brigade of my division, handled his brigade with great skill, and deserves particular mention for his gallantry and untiring energy throughout the day. The Third Brigade, Second Division, Col. J. Irvin Gregg commanding, was held in reserve upon the field. The batteries commanded by Capt. A. M. Randol and Lieut. A. C. M. Pennington, jr., rendered most effective service. The fire of the artillery during this engagement was the most accurate that I have ever seen.

It gives me great pleasure to bring to the notice of the major-general commanding the efficiency and gallantry exhibited by my entire staff on this occasion.

A list of casualties of this engagement has heretofore been forwarded, and will again be found in a consolidated list.†

I am, very respectfully, your obedient servant,

D. McM. GREGG,
Brig. Gen. of Volunteers, Comdg. Second Division.

Lieut. Col. A. J. ALEXANDER, *A. A. G., Cavalry Corps.*

---

* But this includes the losses in Gregg's division, July 2, and those of Custer's brigade, July 3. See Addenda to this report.
† Embodied in revised statement, p. 186.

ADDENDA.

Return of Casualties in the Union Cavalry engaged on the right flank at Gettysburg, Pa., July 2–3, 1863.

[Compiled from nominal list of casualties, returns, &c.]

Command.	Killed.		Wounded.		Captured or missing.		Total.
	Officers.	Enlisted men.	Officers.	Enlisted men.	Officers.	Enlisted men.	
JULY 2.							
McIntosh's brigade:							
1st Pennsylvania						1	1
3d Pennsylvania				1			1
Gregg's brigade:							
1st Maine				3			3
10th New York		2		4	1	2	9
16th Pennsylvania		2		4			6
Total Gregg's division, July 2		4		12	1	3	20
JULY 3.							
McIntosh's brigade:							
1st Maryland				2		1	3
1st New Jersey			2	7			9
1st Pennsylvania						1	1
3d Pennsylvania			5	9		6	20
Gregg's brigade:							
1st Maine		1		1			2
Total Gregg's division, July 3		1	7	19		8	35
Custer's brigade, July 3	1	28	11	112		67	219
Total on right flank, July 3	1	29	18	131		75	254
Total Gregg's division, July 2 and 3		5	7	31	1	11	55

HEADQUARTERS SECOND DIVISION, CAVALRY CORPS,
August 22, 1863.

CAPTAIN: A report heretofore made and forwarded to corps headquarters gave the part taken by the Second Division in the battle of Gettysburg.

In compliance with circular, headquarters Army of the Potomac, dated August 20, 1863, the following is submitted as an account of the operations subsequent to the battle and to the date of July 24:

The peculiar service required of the cavalry in the operations of the army subsequent to July 4, necessitated the constant detaching of brigades for special service. This was particularly the case in the Second Division. A report of the operations of the division will necessarily be made up of the reports of the commanders of its brigades detached.

The Second Brigade, Col. P. Huey, Eighth Pennsylvania Cavalry, commanding, was detached at Hanover Junction on July 1, and did not rejoin until the 9th; was again detached and placed in advance of the Twelfth Corps on the 11th, and again rejoined the division at Shepherdstown on the 16th. The report of the operations of this brigade is appended, marked A.*

*See Report No. 352, p. 970.

The First Brigade was detached at Gettysburg on July 4, and rejoined the division at Boonsborough on the 12th; was again detached at Harper's Ferry on the 19th, and rejoined at Warrenton Junction on the 28th. The report of the operations of this brigade while detached is appended, marked B.*

The Third Brigade, Col. John I. Gregg, Sixteenth Pennsylvania Cavalry, commanding, was detached and sent in pursuit of the enemy on July 5, and rejoined the division on July 11, at Boonsborough, Md. The report of the operations of this brigade is appended, marked C.†

The three brigades of the division having been thus detached, division headquarters were on the 9th transferred to Boonsborough from Gettysburg.

On the 14th, agreeably to instructions from the major-general commanding Cavalry Corps, I moved with the First and Third Brigades of the division to Harper's Ferry, and at that point crossed the Potomac. On the road leading from Harper's Ferry to Charlestown, a force of the enemy's cavalry was met and quickly driven back upon Charlestown. This movement, with two brigades to the west side of the Potomac, had for its object interference with the enemy's line of communication between Winchester and the river. Every preparation was made for carrying out fully the plan of sweeping the road between Winchester and Martinsburg, when a telegram from the major-general commanding Cavalry Corps informed me that the entire rebel army had effected a crossing, and also that the Second Brigade of my division had been ordered to me.

With the view of getting in rear of and on the flank of the rebels, on the 15th I marched with the First and Third Brigades to Shepherdstown.

Finding the roads leading from that town to Winchester and Martinsburg both strongly picketed with infantry and cavalry, I halted to await the arrival of the Second Brigade, so that I might have sufficient force to advance upon either of these roads.

On the 16th, the Second Brigade not having arrived, and from reconnaissances having ascertained that with the force with me I could not successfully advance, I determined to withdraw toward Harper's Ferry, and from thence operate on another route.

At about noon, a few shots heard on the road leading to Winchester announced an attack on our pickets. Repairing to the front, I learned that an advance guard of the enemy's column had attacked our pickets. Seeing this advance party dismount to remove the fences and make preparations for an attack by the columns in rear, I at once placed the Third Brigade (Colonel Gregg's) in position to meet it.

As was expected, the enemy attacked in large force, and brought to the assistance of their dismounted cavalry the fire of six pieces of artillery.

Soon the engagement became very spirited. The Fourth and Sixteenth Pennsylvania and First Maine Regiments were principally engaged in my front; the Tenth New York on the right, covering the road leading to Martinsburg. The enemy threatening to attack at the same time on the Martinsburg road, the First Brigade was placed on the south side of the town to hold the roads leading to Harper's Ferry and Charlestown, and also in position to be brought

---

*See Report No. 348, p. 967. †See Report No. 355, p. 974.

to the aid of the Third Brigade or to check any advance of the enemy on the Martinsburg road. Seeing that the force attacking on the Winchester road was largely superior to and was pressing Gregg's brigade, I ordered the First Pennsylvania, of McIntosh's brigade, to its support. One section of Captain Randol's light battery (E, First U. S. Artillery) during the engagement was employed with Gregg's brigade.

During the whole afternoon and until some time after dark the fight was maintained. The enemy was determined to get possession of Shepherdstown, at which were hospitals and also stores of provisions. Attacks with dismounted skirmishers, charges with his cavalry mounted, and incessant fire of his artillery would not accomplish his object. Having discovered that the enemy had gained the roads leading to Harper's Ferry, and the river in rear of Shepherdstown being unfordable, and attacked thus by so largely a superior force, we dare not yield our position, and it was held heroically. A line of skirmishers thrown out by Colonel McIntosh in his front effectually checked the advance of the enemy on our left.

At about dark, Colonel Huey, Eighth Pennsylvania Cavalry, arrived with the Second Brigade. His report that he had been attacked on the march from Harper's Ferry determined me to withdraw to that point. The wounded having been collected in the hospital in Shepherdstown, transportation was procured for such as could be removed. Those who could not bear transportation were left in charge of a medical officer. At about 9 p. m. it was discovered that the enemy was withdrawing.

The rear of my command left Shepherdstown at daylight on the 17th. The command reached Harper's Ferry, the enemy not appearing on the march. At Shepherdstown my command captured a large quantity of bacon and flour.

Our loss in this engagement was 4 officers wounded, 8 enlisted men killed and 68 wounded, and 1 officer and 10 enlisted men missing.*

Col. J. I. Gregg, commanding the Third Brigade, displayed the highest soldierly qualities in this action of his brigade. In the midst of his men, his coolness and bravery inspired them with confidence in their ability to hold their position. Colonel Gregg mentions Colonel Smith and Major Boothby, First Maine; Major Young, Fourth Pennsylvania Cavalry, and Captains Fisher and Swan, Sixteenth Pennsylvania Cavalry, as especially worthy of mention for distinguished conduct.

Agreeably to orders from the major-general commanding Cavalry Corps, on the 19th I moved with the Second and Third Brigades from Harper's Ferry, passing through Leesburg.

On the 21st, I arrived at Manassas Junction.

On the 22d, moved to Bristoe Station; on the 24th, to Warrenton Junction, at which place the First Brigade joined, it having been detached at Harper's Ferry.

Lists of casualties have been heretofore forwarded.

I am, very respectfully, your obedient servant,

D. McM. GREGG,
Brigadier-General of Volunteers, Comdg. Second Division.

Capt. A. J. COHEN,
Assistant Adjutant-General, Cavalry Corps.

---

*But see revised statement, p. 193.

No. 345.

Reports of Col. Alfred N. Duffié, First Rhode Island Cavalry, commanding Second Division and regiment.

HDQRS. SECOND CAVALRY DIVISION, CAVALRY CORPS,
June 12, 1863.

CAPTAIN: In compliance with yours of this date, I have the honor to report that on the 8th instant I received orders from the general commanding the Second and Third Cavalry Divisions to move with my (Second) cavalry division in the afternoon of the same day to Morrisville, proceeding by the Elk Run road. This place was reached by my command at 7 o'clock in the evening, where I encamped.

At 12.15 a. m. I received a verbal order from a staff officer from headquarters of the Second and Third Cavalry Divisions, to move my command to Kelly's Ford, and to report in person to the general commanding. After my communication with the general, my orders were to cross the ford at once, leaving my wagon train and pack-mules at Mount Holly Church.

After the crossing of the ford by my whole command, I established my line of battle on the Stevensburg road, near the ford, the First Rhode Island and Sixth Ohio Cavalry on the right, the First Massachusetts on the left, a section of my battery in the center, the Third Pennsylvania Cavalry forming the reserve and supporting the balance of the artillery, taking care to protect well my flanks. I moved in this order on the road leading to Stevensburg and crossing Mountain Run. At this place I sent one battalion of the Sixth Ohio to proceed immediately and as rapidly as possible to Stevensburg. This battalion entered the place without meeting the enemy.

At 8.30 a. m. I was informed by a dispatch from Major Stanhope, commanding the battalion, that he was in Stevensburg, and that the enemy was in sight, skirmishing toward the town. I sent orders to him to hold the place at all hazards, and, in case of his being pushed too hard, to retreat slowly. A few minutes afterward a dispatch from him informed me that he could not hold the place, as the enemy were approaching in force.

One and a half miles from Stevensburg I met the battalion retreating, its skirmishers closely engaged with the enemy. I immediately threw forward the skirmishers of the First Massachusetts, First Rhode Island, and Sixth Ohio Cavalry, who immediately became engaged with the enemy, who were strongly posted and partly concealed in the woods. Pushing steadily forward, the enemy were quickly dislodged from the dense woods into open fields, where the First Rhode Island Cavalry was ordered to charge on the right, the First Massachusetts on the left, and one squadron of the Sixth Ohio Cavalry on the road, in order to cut off the retreat of the enemy on his flank and check him in his front. By this movement I succeeded in cutting into two parts the Fourth Virginia Cavalry, commanded by Colonel [Williams C.] Wickham, who escaped with half of his command through the woods on my right. In this charge I captured 1 officer and 57 men.

My command was then reformed, and I moved forward and took position on an elevation at one end of the town, which commanded the road to Culpeper, and also that leading to Brandy Station, on which, about half a mile from Stevensburg, the enemy reformed his line of battle. I succeeded, by the admirable manner in which Lieutenants Pennington and Clarke managed their guns, in forcing them to abandon this line. The First Massachusetts Cavalry were then thrown forward for the purpose of charging, when I received orders from the general commanding Second and Third Divisions, by a staff officer, to return and join the Third Division, on the road to Brandy Station.

I then withdrew my command, leaving the Third Pennsylvania Cavalry, commanded by Col. J. Irvin Gregg, and one section of my battery to form the rear guard, and retired on the same road by which I had advanced, the enemy following my movements with two regiments of cavalry and one piece of artillery.

On approaching the road leading from the Stevensburg road to Brandy Station, I found one squadron of the Tenth New York Cavalry, moved up with pack-mules, fleeing in the greatest disorder toward the Stevensburg road. Upon inquiring the cause, I was informed that the flank had been charged by a party of the enemy, and been thrown into the greatest confusion. This detained me for a half hour.

I then moved forward by that road (capturing several of the enemy) to join General Gregg, who ordered me upon arriving to halt my command and relieve the batteries of the First and Third Cavalry Divisions, and cover the retreat of the Cavalry Corps.

All the cavalry having left the ground at this point, I moved on the road leading to Beverly Ford the evening following, with two regiments and one gun, at a proper distance. Upon my arrival near Beverly Ford, General Pleasonton directed me to move with one brigade to support General Buford, and send the Second Brigade on the road leading to Rappahannock Ford, to cover the crossing of the Third Division. My command crossed Beverly Ford at about 5 p. m., and was then ordered to join General Gregg at Rappahannock Station, which I did.

The regiments which were engaged are as follows: The First Massachusetts, First Rhode Island, Sixth Ohio, and Third Pennsylvania Cavalry, and Battery M (Pennington's), Second U. S. Artillery. The force engaged from this division numbered 1,600 cavalry and one battery of artillery, six guns.

I have the honor to be, very respectfully, your obedient servant,

A. N. DUFFIÉ,
Colonel, Comdg. Second Cavalry Division.

Capt. A. J. Cohen,
   Assistant Adjutant-General.

HEADQUARTERS FIRST RHODE ISLAND CAVALRY,
Near Centreville, Va., June 18, 1863.

Sir: I have the honor to report that on the morning of the 17th instant I received from the headquarters of the Second Brigade, Second Cavalry Division, the following order:

Col. A. N. Duffié,
   First Rhode Island Cavalry:

   You will proceed with your regiment from Manassas Junction, by way of Thoroughfare Gap, to Middleburg. On your arrival at that place, you will at once communicate with the headquarters of the Second Cavalry Brigade, and camp for the night. From Middleburg you will proceed to Union; thence by way of Snickersville to Percyville [Purcellville]; from Percyville [Purcellville] to Wheatland; then passing through Waterford to Noland's Ferry, where you will join your brigade.

In accordance with this order, I left camp on the morning of the 17th instant, and proceeded with my regiment (275 strong) to Thoroughfare Gap. At this place my skirmishers met and engaged the enemy, which proved to be Lee's brigade of cavalry approaching the Gap. The enemy being much stronger than my command, I was obliged to make a demonstration on my left flank in order to pass my column unseen. At this demonstration the enemy retired, and I was enabled to pass my column on to the Middleburg road safely. Nevertheless they followed in my rear, but at a considerable distance, causing me no uneasiness. It was then 9.30 a. m., and at 11 o'clock their skirmishers disappeared, and I proceeded unmolested toward Middleburg, using a negro for a guide.

Arriving near Middleburg at 4 p. m., I again engaged the enemy, capturing his first picket in the road, and ordered Captain Allen, commanding the advanced squadron, to charge through the town. By this movement the rear guard of General Stuart was cut off, and then a sharp cavalry fight ensued between his rear and my advance guard. This engagement lasted half an hour, when the enemy was compelled to retreat in the greatest disorder and confusion, scattering in all directions. Having received information that Stuart, with 2,000 cavalry and four pieces of artillery, had left town but half an hour before my arrival, and was proceeding to Aldie, I directed that the different roads leading into the town be barricaded and strongly picketed, and gave instructions to the officer commanding the outposts to hold the town at all hazards, hoping that after effecting communication with General Kilpatrick, whom I supposed to be at Aldie, I should receive re-enforcements. Captain Allen was selected to carry a dispatch to General Kilpatrick, and was directed to avoid as much as possible all main roads. The town was held by my command from 4.30 to 7 p. m., the skirmishers having been constantly engaged during that time.

At 7 o'clock I ascertained that the enemy was approaching in force from Aldie, Union, and Upperville. Determined to hold the position if possible, I dismounted one-half of my regiment, placing them behind stone walls and the barricades. The enemy surrounded the town and stormed the barricades, but were gallantly repulsed by my men with great slaughter. They did not, however, desist, but, confident of success, again attacked, and made three successive charges. I was compelled to retire on the road by which I came, that being the only one open to retreat. With all that was left of my command, I crossed Little River northeast of Middleburg, and bivouacked for the night, establishing strong pickets on the river.

In this engagement I lost Major Farrington, Captains Rogers, Wyman, and Chase, Lieutenant Brown, and 27 men killed, wounded, and missing.

At 10 p. m., having heard nothing from my dispatch sent to General Kilpatrick, I sent 20 men, under an officer, with a second dispatch. I have heard nothing from either party, and believe that both have been captured.

At 3.30 o'clock the next morning, 18th instant, I was informed by scouts whom I had previously sent out that the roads in every direction were full of cavalry, and that the Aldie road was commanded by a brigade, with four pieces of artillery. Under these circumstances I abandoned the project of going to Union, but determined not to surrender in any event. I directed the head of my column on the road to Aldie, when an engagement commenced at once, the enemy opening on both flanks with heavy volleys, yelling to us to surrender. I at once ordered Captain Bixby, the officer commanding the advance, to charge any force in his front, and follow the Aldie road to the point where it connects with the road to White Plains. This order was executed most admirably. Captain Bixby's horse was shot and he himself wounded. My command was in a most hazardous position, the enemy being in front, rear, and on both flanks, and we were intermixed with them for more than an hour, until we struck the road leading to Hopewell Gap.

I must openly praise the gallant conduct of the brave officers and men who were fighting side by side with overwhelming numbers of the enemy, with the most determined valor, preferring rather to die than to surrender.

I returned here exhausted at 1.30 p. m. to-day with the gallant *débris* of my much-loved regiment—4 officers and 27 men. My colors did not fall into the hands of the enemy, but were destroyed when they could not be saved. The color-bearer was mortally wounded.

I shall praise no one more than another, but I desire to call your attention to the gallant conduct of all the officers and men of the First Rhode Island Cavalry.

The following is our loss in killed, wounded, and missing: Lieut. Col. J. L. Thompson, Maj. P. M. Farrington, Asst. Surg. A. A. Mann, Adjt. E. B. Parker, Capts. John Rogers, Joshua Vose, Frank Allen, E. E. Chase, J. J. Gould, Arnold Wyman, G. N. Bliss, and A. H. Bixby, First Lieuts. Lathrop B. Shurtleff, C. G. A. Peterson, W. P. Prentiss, Barnard Ellis, and H. B. Barker, Second Lieuts. J. A. Chedel, jr., Simeon A. Brown, and J. M. Fales—20 officers and 248 enlisted men.

With much respect, your obedient servant,

A. N. DUFFIÉ,
Colonel, Commanding First Rhode Island Cavalry.

The ADJUTANT-GENERAL,
Army of the Potomac.

No. 346.

Report of Capt. Frank Allen, First Rhode Island Cavalry.

ALEXANDRIA, VA., *June* 22, 1863.

SIR: I have the honor to report that about 5 p. m. on the evening of the 17th instant I was sent from Middleburg, where the regiment was then engaged with the enemy, to carry a dispatch to General Kilpatrick at Aldie, accompanied by 2 men. I first attempted to proceed by the main road, but was halted and fired upon by a body of the enemy, who said they were the Fourth Virginia Cavalry. I then returned toward Middleburg, and, leaving the road, attempted to make my way across the country. I found the fields and woods in every direction full of bodies of the enemy. By exercising the greatest care, I succeeded in making my way through them to Little River.

Here I encountered 5 of the enemy, and forced them to give me passage. Following the river down, I struck the main road about 1 mile from Aldie, and, by inquiry, learned that our pickets were on that road.

I reached Aldie, and delivered my dispatch to General Kilpatrick at 9 p. m. General Kilpatrick informed me that his brigade was so worn out that he could not send any re-enforcements to Middleburg, but that he would report the situation of our regiment to General Gregg. Returning, he said that General Gregg had gone to state the facts to General Pleasonton, and directed me to remain at Aldie until he heard from General Pleasonton. I remained, but received no further orders.

Respectfully submitted.

FRANK ALLEN,
Captain First Rhode Island Cavalry.

Col. A. N. DUFFIÉ.

No. 347.

Report of Col. Percy Wyndham, First New Jersey Cavalry, commanding Second Brigade, Third Division. *

HDQRS. SECOND BRIG., THIRD DIV., CAVALRY CORPS,
June 10, 1863.

CAPTAIN: I have the honor to make the following report of the part my command took in the action of yesterday:

After crossing the river and coming up with Colonel Duffié, I turned to the right, and, in obedience to orders from the general commanding, pushed on rapidly to Brandy Station. On arriving at that place I found the enemy strongly posted in the rear and on the right of the station, with batteries planted on the heights near the Barbour house. I immediately formed my command in line of battle, and had the section of artillery attached to it placed in position, and opened on their battery in front of the Barbour house. Observing the enemy breaking away on the left, I ordered a portion of the First Maryland Cavalry, led by Major Russell, to charge on the station, which they did in fine style, capturing a number of the enemy, and bringing away an ambulance and 4 horses captured by our advance guard. I next ordered the section of artillery to advance, as they had completely silenced the battery they had been firing upon, and at the same time ordered the First New Jersey to charge on a battery stationed in rear of the Barbour house, and the First Pennsylvania Reserve Cavalry and the balance of the First Maryland to charge the heights on which the house stands. The whole command moved gallantly forward and nobly accomplished the work assigned them.

The First Maryland, which consisted of little more than a squadron, led by Lieutenant-Colonel Deems, charged first, but were met by fully a regiment of the enemy, posted behind the buildings and drawn up in the garden and orchard, and, after a brief and spirited fight, were compelled to fall back. The First Pennsylvania, coming up, charged next. Colonel Taylor, leading part of the regiment, struck the enemy in front, while Lieutenant-Colonel Gardner, with the balance, dashed on his flank next to the house. Attacked at both points, he was forced back, cut off from the house, his rear gained, and driven from his cover into the open plain below, where he was again met by the First Maryland Cavalry, which had rallied. Thus assailed on both sides, his force was completely scattered, a large number being killed, wounded, or captured.

----

* Afterward First Brigade, Second Division.

The charge of the First New Jersey in rear of the house I led in person, aided by Lieutenant-Colonel Brodrick. At the first onset the enemy were driven from their guns, the support coming up was met, and in a few minutes also driven back. Re-enforced, it returned and was again repulsed.

My command being now much scattered by the charges it had made, Colonel Duffié not coming up to my support as I expected, and seeing the enemy, strongly re-enforced, advancing from several points, I was compelled to withdraw. This was done by the greater part of the command forming on the Brandy Station road, while I collected the balance at the station, and, forming them into a rear guard, remained until the field was cleared.

The enemy charged upon my lines twice, but were repulsed each time by my carbineers with heavy loss. While engaged here, I received a bullet in the leg. After joining the balance of my command, I reported to the general commanding, and received orders to move to the right. Forming my command near —— Church, I remained until about 4 o'clock in the afternoon, when, becoming very much exhausted from the loss of blood, I turned over the command to Col. J. P. Taylor, of the First Pennsylvania Reserve Cavalry, and left the field. He reports that shortly afterward he received orders to report to General Buford, and assisted in covering the withdrawal of his command across the river.

In closing my report, it affords me no small degree of pleasure to be able to say that all my command that followed me on the field behaved nobly, standing unmoved under the enemy's artillery fire, and, when ordered to charge, dashing forward with a spirit and determination that swept all before them.

I cannot speak too highly of the manner in which the field officers of my command, without exception, acted, gallantly and efficiently performing every duty assigned them; and of the line officers I can say the same.

Major Janeway, who was doing duty as field officer of the day, and Capt. H. S. Thomas, assistant inspector-general; Lieut. William P. Lloyd, acting assistant adjutant-general; Lieut. S. Greenlee (wounded), and Lieutenant [Edwin H.] Parry, acting aides-de-camp, of my staff, all rendered invaluable services by the prompt and efficient manner in which they had my orders executed, and the assistance they afforded in rallying and reforming the different portions of the command.

As a brief summary, I may add that six distinct regimental charges were made, besides a number of smaller ones. We took one battle-flag, captured 128 of the enemy, among whom were General Stuart's adjutant-general, and several other officers whose rank was not learned.

The section of artillery attached to my command was well handled and did good execution. One piece burst while firing, and was left; the other was brought off.

My loss is 1 officer killed and 14 wounded or missing; 14 men killed and 120 wounded or missing.* A list of the casualties accounted for by name will accompany this report.

[P. WYNDHAM,
Colonel, Commanding.]

The above report was furnished by Colonel Wyndham's assistant

---

* But see revised statement, p. 169.

adjutant-general, and prepared under the direction of the colonel before he left for Washington, to which I can certify as correct.

I am, very respectfully, your obedient servant,

J. P. TAYLOR,
Commanding.

Capt. H. C. WEIR,
Asst. Adjt. Gen., Third Division, Cavalry Corps.

No. 348.

Report of Col. John B. McIntosh, Third Pennsylvania Cavalry, commanding First Brigade, Second Division.

HDQRS. FIRST BRIG., SECOND DIV., CAVALRY CORPS,
Near Warrenton, Va., August 20, 1863.

CAPTAIN: In compliance with orders received, I have the honor to submit the following report of the movements of the First Brigade of this division since the battle of Gettysburg, July 3, 1863:

Late in the afternoon of July 4, I received orders from the division general to report with my brigade to Major-General Pleasonton for orders. In accordance with his orders, I placed my brigade on the extreme left of the army, to picket the different roads and to observe the movements of the enemy in that direction.

July 5, I received orders from Major-General Pleasonton to move my command at once to Emmitsburg, as some of the enemy's cavalry had gone in that direction, with further instructions that, should the enemy attempt to gain the rear of the army, I must follow them up to prevent it.

In obedience to those orders, I moved my command at once to Emmitsburg, and found that the enemy's cavalry, under General Stuart, had gone through there in the morning, moving toward Frederick. I also ascertained that after proceeding on the road to Frederick as far as Graceham, they turned toward Hagerstown.

Hearing during the day that the enemy was on the road leading from Emmitsburg to Waynesborough, I proceeded with my command in that direction, and soon met the enemy's picket, which I drove in, capturing a dispatch showing the position of both Generals Longstreet's and Ewell's corps, which I immediately forwarded to Major-General Meade, and a copy of it to Major-General Pleasonton. I then found that, in order to reach the enemy, it became necessary for me to advance in a deep mountain gorge, where it would be impossible to use either cavalry or artillery to advantage in attacking. This, in connection with the knowledge that a large force of infantry was in my immediate front, caused me to withdraw my command in front of Emmitsburg, which [fact] I communicated to the major-general commanding the corps.

In answer to my dispatch, I received orders to move my brigade in front of Emmitsburg, and feel the enemy on the different roads to Fairfield, Jake's Mountain, and Hagerstown, to ascertain his position, and also to find out if he was on the retreat. I proceeded to carry out these instructions, and had been engaged with the enemy about an hour when I received orders from Major-General Pleasonton to move my command to the Sixth Corps, in front of Fairfield, and report to General Neill for service in following up the enemy from that point, which I promptly complied with.

On the morning of the 7th, I moved with my brigade, in advance of General Neill's column, by the mountain road toward Waynesborough, picking up a number of the enemy's stragglers. I reached Waynesborough about 2 p. m. of that day, only two hours behind the rebel army, who, on my approach, burned the bridges over the Antietam.

I remained with my brigade near Waynesborough, picketing well out toward the enemy, until the morning of the 10th instant, when I received orders from Major-General Smith, who had assumed command, to move with my brigade through Smithsburg and Cavetown, to ascertain if any enemy was in that locality. Finding none, I retraced my steps toward Leitersburg, and 3 miles to the west of it, and about a mile from Antietam Creek, met the enemy's cavalry, which I drove across that stream, and which I found strongly guarded with cavalry, infantry, and artillery. Having determined the object upon which I was sent, I withdrew my command to Waynesborough.

July 12, I received orders from General Neill, who at this time was detached from General Smith's command, to move in conjunction with his brigade toward Funkstown. I was here met by an aide from Major-General Pleasonton, with orders to move to Boonsborough and report to General Gregg, which I did the same day.

My brigade continued with the division until the 19th, when, in obedience to orders, I moved to Purcellville, in rear of the Twelfth Corps, arriving there July 20, when I was ordered to report to Major-General Pleasonton for orders. My orders were to proceed to Hillsborough, to draw my supplies from Harper's Ferry, and to scout the country on the opposite side of the Shenandoah toward Charlestown. These orders were obeyed, and valuable information sent to corps headquarters.

At 3 a. m. July 23, I received orders to move my command at once to Snickersville, relieve a regiment of the Third Division at Snicker's Gap, and also a regiment of the same division at Ashby's Gap.

I remained at Snickersville until July 26, when I withdrew from the Gaps, and moved through Upperville and Middleburg to Warrenton, and reported to Major-General Pleasonton on the evening of July 27.

On July 28, I again reported to General Gregg at Warrenton Junction.

I am, captain, very respectfully,

J. B. McINTOSH,
Colonel, Commmanding First Cavalry Brigade.

Capt. H. C. WEIR,
Assistant Adjutant-General.

No. 349.

Report of Maj. Hugh H. Janeway, First New Jersey Cavalry.

HDQRS. FIRST NEW JERSEY CAVALRY,
August 31, 1863.

COLONEL: I have the honor to report that the First New Jersey Cavalry took no part in the engagements at Aldie, Middleburg, and

Upperville. When, however, on the 22d of June the forces retired from Upperville toward Aldie, the regiment was ordered to cover the rear on the north of the pike, which it did until the enemy retired toward Middleburg, and the First Brigade was relieved by that of Col. J. I. Gregg.

Our loss, though continually exposed to a heavy fire from sharpshooters and artillery, was but 1 man killed—Louis Vandergrift, of Company D.

I have the honor to be, colonel, very respectfully, your obedient servant,

HUGH H. JANEWAY,
Major, Comdg. First New Jersey Cavalry.

Col. J. B. McIntosh,
Comdg. First Brig., Second Div., Cav. Corps.

No. 350.

Report of Col. John P. Taylor, First Pennsylvania Cavalry.

HDQRS. FIRST PENNSYLVANIA RESERVE CAVALRY,
August 31, 1863.

Captain: In obedience to circular from division headquarters, through brigade headquarters, concerning the battles of Aldie, Middleburg, and Upperville, I have the honor to report that during the first day's fight at Aldie, June 18, my regiment was drawn up in reserve, but not engaged.

On the day following (19th), went on a reconnaissance to Hay Market.

On the 21st, acted as reserve at Middleburg.

On the 22d, my regiment was the principal regiment covering the retreat from Upperville to Aldie. The enemy, following up, engaged my regiment at Goose Creek, and skirmished and fought from that point to Aldie.

During the day, Second Lieut. Amos M. Herrick, Company E, was wounded and taken prisoner. Three horses were lost in action.

I am, very respectfully, your obedient servant,

J. P. TAYLOR,
Colonel, Commanding Regiment.

Capt. A. Wright,
A. A. A. G., First Brig., Second Div., Cav. Corps.

No. 351.

Report of Maj. Oliver O. G. Robinson, Third Pennsylvania Cavalry.

HEADQUARTERS THIRD PENNSYLVANIA CAVALRY,
September 1, 1863.

Captain: In accordance with orders received this day, I have the honor to transmit the following report, viz:

On June 17, the regiment moved from Manassas Junction, and, acting as rear guard of the train, reached Aldie, Va., about 7 p. m.

On June 18, the regiment was ordered back to picket the road in rear of wagon train. Remained there until 5 p. m., when the regiment rejoined the brigade and encamped.

On the evening of June 19, about 8 p. m., moved with the brigade to Hay Market, reaching that place and encamping about 1 a. m., and the next day picketed the roads leading to Thoroughfare Gap.

Remained on picket until the morning of the 21st, when the regiment and brigade moved back to Aldie, and, continuing on the mountain road, passing Middleburg and Upperville, relieved General Buford's cavalry. Regiment went on picket toward Ashby's Gap.

On the morning of June 22, the pickets were drawn in. The skirmish line having been formed, two squadrons (eight companies) of our regiment were thrown out in support, the remaining squadron (four companies) being placed in support of the battery.

The regiment covered the retiring skirmishers during the entire day, passing through Upperville and Middleburg, until about 6 p. m., when the regiment was relieved, and went into camp near Aldie, Va.

I have the honor to be, very respectfully, your obedient servant,

O. O. G. ROBINSON,
Major, Commanding.

Captain WRIGHT,
    A. A. A. G., First Brig., Second Div., Cav. Corps.

No. 352.

Report of Col. Pennock Huey, Eighth Pennsylvania Cavalry, commanding Second Brigade.

HDQRS. SECOND BRIG., SECOND DIV., CAVALRY CORPS,
                                        August 6, 1863.

CAPTAIN: I have the honor to report the movements of this command from the time of separating from the Second Cavalry Division at Hanover Junction, Pa., June 30.

After leaving Hanover Junction, in pursuance of orders from division headquarters, we arrived at Manchester at 11 p. m., when all the roads were immediately taken up by my pickets, and held until the afternoon of July 3, when I received orders to move my command to Emmitsburg, for the purpose of taking possession of and holding that place. I moved on as far as Westminster, where my command bivouacked, to receive rations and forage.

Early on the morning of July 4, I moved forward, arriving at Emmitsburg at 12 m., when I met the command of General Merritt advancing on the same place from the direction of Gettysburg.

At 1 p. m. July 4, I received orders to report with my command to General Kilpatrick, who was in pursuit of General Ewell's (late Jackson's) command, which was reported as being in the mountains in the vicinity of Monterey. After moving a short distance from the town, we came in contact with the rebel pickets, who were handsomely driven by the Sixth Ohio Regiment, of my command. The evening was very dark and rainy, affording a fine opportunity for bushwhackers, who succeeded in killing 1 commissioned officer and 4 enlisted men in General Kilpatrick's command.

At 3 a. m. July 5, the wagon train was reached at and near Monterey, and 150 wagons captured, together with 1,500 prisoners, besides a large number of horses, mules, and contrabands. We moved on to Smithsburg, where we encamped, this brigade taking the east and rear of the village, picketing the roads and approaches in that direction.

Very soon the enemy made his appearance, driving in my pickets, when a regiment was sent to their support. A sharp skirmish ensued. The enemy, putting his artillery in position, opened on us and the town. Lieutenant Fuller, Company C, Third U. S. Light Artillery, returning his fire with spirit and effect, soon drove him from the field, after which we moved on to Boonsborough.

At 1 a. m. on the morning of the 6th instant, we moved to Hagerstown, where we met the enemy in force, this brigade taking the left, and fought against greatly superior force for about three hours, when we were obliged to fall back in the direction of Williamsport, taking a position to hold the enemy in check and cover General Kilpatrick's rear, which we did, under a severe fire of shot and shell, until dark, when we followed General Kilpatrick into camp at Boonsborough.

Since leaving Emmitsburg my command has lost, in killed, wounded, and missing, 1 commissioned officer and 144 enlisted men, and been obliged to abandon 197 horses.

On the afternoon of the 7th, the enemy made an attack on our front at Boonsborough. All our cavalry and artillery were brought into action, repulsing him, and driving him handsomely a distance of 3 miles.

On the morning of July 10, my brigade was ordered to Antietam, via Keedysville, to guard the crossing of the infantry near Booth's Mills. Here I received orders to move my command on the Williamsport road to Jones' Cross-Roads, where we met the enemy, and, after a severe skirmish, drove him about 1 mile. Our loss was 4 enlisted men killed and 6 wounded. Night coming on, we were compelled to go into camp, after picketing the front.

On the morning of the 11th, I was ordered to make a reconnaissance on the Williamsport road. We had not moved far when we came upon the enemy's infantry in force. Finding they had the advantage in position, we opened upon them with artillery, driving them from it, and our dismounted men, pushing forward, captured 5 in a house and killed 3. We were then ordered to cease the pursuit, and hold the ground we had taken, which we did until dark, when we were relieved by infantry, and retired half a mile to camp for the night.

On the following morning, July 12, being ordered to renew the skirmish, we advanced our artillery to the skirmish line, and the dismounted skirmishers drove the enemy into his breastworks along the whole line, excepting a few who took refuge in Saint James' College. We now held a position about 150 yards from the first line of the enemy's breastworks, which they were busily engaged in extending. Orders now came for us to retire, and we went into camp at Jones' Cross-Roads.

On the morning of July 14, I was again ordered out to feel the enemy. We marched to Williamsport, but found no enemy; thence to Falling Waters, where we bivouacked, not having been engaged during the day.

On the morning of the 16th [15th], we were ordered to Harper's Ferry, where we arrived on the 18th [16th], via Boonsborough, where we rested on the night of the 17th [15th].

Resting my command for a short time, was ordered to join General Gregg at Shepherdstown. On the march to the last-named place, my advance was charged by a squadron of the enemy's cavalry, but they were repulsed, and scattered in all directions. Reached Shepherdstown, and reported at 7 p. m. July 18 [16].

During all this time the officers and enlisted men of my command were all that could be desired, exhibiting a willingness and determination on all occasions where duty required.

I am, general, very respectfully, your obedient servant,

PENNOCK HUEY,
Colonel Eighth Pennsylvania Cavalry, Comdg. Brigade.

Capt. H. C. Weir, *Assistant Adjutant-General.*

No. 353.

Report of Lieut. Col. William Stedman, Sixth Ohio Cavalry.

Warrenton, Va.,
September 5, 1863.

Sir: I have the honor to report, in reply to your order of August 30, requiring a report of the battles of Aldie, Middleburg, and Upperville, that on June 17, when near Aldie, I received an order from General Kilpatrick to take my regiment beyond the town, and support the Second New York Cavalry, who were then skirmishing with the enemy on the road to Middleburg.

I placed my regiment in line of battle on the right of the road, with the left resting on the road. On the hill ahead was a strawstack, behind which the enemy were hid. I ordered a charge in line, and, passing the stack, captured all the enemy there, and I found in the next ravine a ditch varying from 3 to 7 feet in depth and from 6 to 8 feet in width, and in which I found nearly 40 of the enemy, all of whom I captured, making in all over 50 prisoners, who were turned over to the provost-marshal, with their horses, arms, and equipments.

In the engagement we lost 3 men killed and 11 wounded, including Major Stanhope, who has since died of his wounds. We also lost 10 horses.

The enemy opened on us from the hill beyond with grape and canister; but we held the position until dark, when we were ordered to retire.

At Middleburg, on June 19, we were ordered to support the battery, and took position on the hill to the right of it, one squadron being thrown out to a high hill on the right, to guard against a flank movement. We were then thrown out as skirmishers on the extreme right of Kilpatrick's line. We cleared the woods, losing 2 men wounded, 1 of whom has since died of his wound; 1 horse was also killed.

We were then ordered back again to support the battery, and at night went on picket in the woods where the principal fighting had been done, where we remained until the morning of the 21st.

From Middleburg to Upperville, on the 21st, we were on the right of the pike and the extreme right of General Kilpatrick's line, on the east side of Goose Creek, losing here 1 man killed and 2 wounded. From Goose Creek to Upperville, our left rested on the pike. When near Upperville, one squadron, under Captain Cryer, charged upon the enemy on the pike, breaking their columns, but losing 7 men wounded, 4 of whom the enemy captured; 4 horses were also lost. The remaining squadrons of the regiment charged upon the left flank of the enemy, who had dismounted and ranged themselves behind a stone fence. We drove them from this position, with a loss on our part of 1 man killed and 2 officers and 4 men wounded.

Beyond Upperville, one squadron, led by Captain Northway, charged along the pike, routing the enemy. In this charge we lost 7 men wounded, 5 of whom were captured. Captain Northway was himself wounded, but escaped. We pressed on until the enemy were driven into the Gap, when we fell back near Upperville, and encamped for the night in support of a battery on the right of the road.

The behavior of both officers and men was brave in the extreme, and where all did so nobly it is hard to signalize single deeds of daring and bravery.

Very respectfully, your obedient servant,

WM. STEDMAN,
Lieutenant-Colonel, Commanding Sixth Ohio Cavalry.

Capt. H. C. WEIR, *Assistant Adjutant-General.*

No. 354.

Reports of Capt. William A. Corrie, Eighth Pennsylvania Cavalry.

KING GEORGE COUNTY, VA.,
June 13, 1863.

SIR: I have the honor to report that, in pursuance to orders, scouting parties were sent out on roads leading to the Potomac, as well as Rappahannock, for upward of 18 miles below our picket lines, and have reported all quiet in that section, and no signs of the enemy on this side of the river. The points reconnoitered were Port Conway, Leedstown, Shiloh, Office Hall, Edge Hill, Mattapula Creek, &c. From a deserter from the Forty-seventh Virginia, who has just come from Westmoreland, we learn that there is no enemy in that section. He has been sent to general headquarters provost-marshal. I have ordered a party this morning to proceed to Brazoes Mines, and will report to you if anything occurs.

Yours, respectfully,

W. A. CORRIE,
Captain, Commanding.

M. T. McMAHON,
Assistant Adjutant-General and Chief of Staff.

[Inclosure.]

CAPTAIN: You will immediately after dark withdraw all of your pickets, and with your entire force report to Major-General Hancock, commanding Second Corps, at his headquarters near Falmouth.

Please return receipt for this order by bearer.

By command, &c.

Captain CORRIE, *Commanding Cavalry Pickets.*

NEAR THOROUGHFARE GAP, VA.,
June 23, 1863.

COLONEL: I have the honor to report that, in obedience to instructions from General Hancock, a squadron commanded by Captain McCallum was sent from Gainesville on the afternoon of the 21st, with orders to go as far as New Baltimore, on the Warrenton turnpike. At the same time a squadron, under command of Captain Wilson, was dispatched from Thoroughfare Gap by the road skirting the base of the mountain, with orders to form a junction with Captain McCallum, and proceed with him to New Baltimore. Near the junction of the roads, Captain McCallum met the advance guard of the enemy advancing down the Warrenton road toward Gainesville, and charged them, driving them back upon their main column. The rebels then charged him, compelling him to retreat to within a mile and a half of Gainesville. Captain McCallum reports that his men fought gallantly. Our loss was 23 captured, mostly occasioned by their horses being worn out.

Captain McCallum's force when he started from Gainesville was 45 men. Captain Wilson exchanged shots with the enemy.

Very respectfully, your obedient servant,

W. A. CORRIE,
Captain, Commanding Eighth Pennsylvania Cavalry.

Lieutenant-Colonel MORGAN,
Chief of Staff.

[Indorsement.]

HEADQUARTERS SECOND CORPS,
June 23, 1863.

Respectfully forwarded.

The force sent down toward New Baltimore from Gainesville was as large as could be mustered for that purpose. A somewhat larger force was ordered, but General French thought it necessary to divert a part toward Sudley Springs.

WINF'D S. HANCOCK,
Major-General, Commanding Corps.

No. 355.

Reports of Col. J. Irvin Gregg, Sixteenth Pennsylvania Cavalry, commanding Second and Third Brigades.

CAMP, SECOND BRIGADE, SECOND DIVISION,
Bealeton, Va., June 10, 1863.

SIR: I have the honor to make the following report of the action of my command on the 9th instant:

On the morning of June 9 my brigade,* composed of the Third, Fourth, and Sixteenth Pennsylvania Cavalry, moved from Fayetteville about daylight, and arrived at Kelly's Ford, on the Rappahannock, about 9 a. m. After halting for a few minutes, the command, with Pennington's battery of artillery, moved out on the Stevensburg road, following the First Brigade, under the immediate command of Colonel Duffié, commanding the division.

---

* This (Second) became, in the reorganization of June 11, the Third Brigade.

Within 2 miles of the ford (Kelly's), the advance skirmishers of the enemy were encountered, and they were pushed rapidly to Stevensburg. At this point Colonel Duffié received orders to halt and return to the main body, under General D. McM. Gregg, which had moved toward Brandy Station on a road branching from the main Stevensburg road about 1 mile south of Kelly's Ford. My brigade, with one section of the battery, was left at Stevensburg, with instructions to hold the place, and I remained about one hour; but seeing no enemy, and hearing heavy and continuous firing on my right and front, I withdrew from the position, and moved in the direction of the firing.

I arrived on the battle-field of Brandy Station about 4 p. m. and after the battle was over. My command covered the falling back of the army, which was accomplished without molestation.

Very respectfully, your obedient servant,

J. IRVIN GREGG,
Colonel Sixteenth Pennsylvania Cavalry, Comdg. Brigade.

Capt. H. C. WEIR,
    Assistant Adjutant-General.

HDQRS. THIRD BRIG., SECOND DIV., CAVALRY CORPS,
                                September —, 1863.

GENERAL: I have the honor to report that, on the morning of June 16 [17], the Third Brigade, Second Division, Cavalry Corps, consisting of the First Maine, Tenth New York, and Fourth and Sixteenth Pennsylvania Cavalry, marched from Union Mills, and arrived at Aldie about 4 p. m., and were drawn up in line of battle near that village, the Second Brigade, under General Kilpatrick, being engaged with the enemy beyond the Gap. About 6 p. m. I sent the First Maine Cavalry, under command of Colonel Douty (who was killed while gallantly leading his regiment into action), to re-enforce General Kilpatrick.

On the morning of June 17 [18], I was ordered with my brigade to make a reconnaissance toward Middleburg and Hopewell, and, if possible, get possession of the former place, which I accomplished, after a sharp skirmish, about 3 p. m. I held possession of the town until 6 o'clock, when I received an order directing me to return to Aldie, which order was countermanded, and I bivouacked midway between the two places.

On the morning of the 18th [19th], drove the enemy from Middleburg, the Fourth Pennsylvania Cavalry charging through the town and following the enemy nearly a mile beyond, where he was strongly posted on the crest of a hill in the woods and behind stone fences. The enemy continued to deploy to the right and left, and compelled me to do the same, so that by 8 a. m. one-half of my force was upon the skirmish line, viz, the Fourth Pennsylvania, Tenth New York, and a portion of the Sixteenth Pennsylvania, the lines close together, and the enemy throwing canister among my skirmishers.

About this time, Brigadier-General Gregg arrived upon the field, and directed me to drive the enemy from his position. Dismounting the Sixteenth Pennsylvania, I moved them forward into a woods already occupied by a portion of the Fourth Pennsylvania, and brought up the First Maine to support them. After carefully reconnoitering the position of the enemy, I ordered the Sixteenth and a part of the Fourth Pennsylvania to deploy and charge at the double-quick across the open space intervening between me and the enemy, bringing the First Maine up to their support. The hill on the left of the wood was carried in gallant style, the First Maine pushing through and several hundred yards beyond the woods, where an entire brigade of cavalry was drawn up ready to charge. The enemy still held possession of the woods and stone walls on the right of the road, and I feared for a moment we would be repulsed; but at this juncture the Tenth New York, under Major Avery, charging gallantly up the road in column, and the First Maine, Sixteenth and Fourth Pennsylvania Cavalry pushing through the woods, the entire position was carried.

I have to regret the loss of several valuable officers, viz, First Lieuts. George S. Kimball, E. H. Taylor, and Mark Neville, First Maine Cavalry, and Second Lieuts. H. H. Boyd and E. S. Hawes, Tenth New York Cavalry, killed.

My brigade was not actually engaged in the battle of Upperville on June 20 [21], excepting the First Maine Cavalry and Fourth Pennsylvania, which were sent to the support of General Kilpatrick late in the afternoon. They charged the enemy repeatedly, driving him from the town and capturing one piece of artillery.

The officers and men displayed the utmost gallantry, and are deserving of the highest praise. Captain Brown and Lieutenant Ellis, First Maine Cavalry, deserve especial notice for capturing more prisoners than they had men in their command.

Inclosed I send a list of casualties.

I am, sir, very respectfully, your obedient servant,

J. IRVIN GREGG,
Colonel, Commanding Brigade.

General D. McM. GREGG,
Comdg. Second Division, Cavalry Corps.

[Inclosure.]

List of Casualties in the Third Brigade, Second Division, Cavalry Corps.

Command	Killed		Wounded		Missing		Total	
	Officers.	Enlisted men.	Officers.	Enlisted men.	Officers.	Enlisted men.	Officers.	Enlisted men.
1st Maine Cavalry	5	11	4	41	.....	10	9	62
10th New York Cavalry	2	1	1	7	.....	18	3	26
16th Pennsylvania		1	1	9		.....	1	10
4th Pennsylvania		2		9		5		16
Total	7	15	6	66	.....	33	13	114

HDQRS. THIRD BRIG., SECOND DIV., CAVALRY CORPS,
Amissville, Va., August 5, 1863.

SIR: I have the honor to report the following as the part taken by this command in the battle of Gettysburg:

My command arrived and took up position on the pike leading from Gettysburg to Hanover, about 2 miles distant from Gettysburg and in close proximity to General Ewell's corps, about 11 a. m. on

July 2. At this time there were two regiments of infantry a short distance in my front, deployed as skirmishers. These regiments were withdrawn about 3 p. m., and, by order of General Gregg, I threw forward the Tenth New York Cavalry, under command of Major Avery, and deployed skirmishers to occupy the ground vacated.

During the afternoon, my vedettes were considerably annoyed by the enemy's sharpshooters from the hill and woods immediately in my front, and at 6 o'clock I ordered 50 dismounted men to clear the hill and find out what was beyond, but they were driven back by a much superior force, and followed until the enemy were checked and driven back by Col. J. B. McIntosh's command.

On the morning of July 3, by order of General Gregg, my command took up position on the road leading from Gettysburg to Baltimore, not far distant from the position occupied by General Slocum's corps, but was subsequently moved, and took up a position near the one occupied on July 2.

My command did not participate in the cavalry fight of July 3, excepting one section of Captain Randol's battery, under command of Lieutenant Chester, which was hotly engaged, and was obliged to retire about 200 yards on account of a portion of General Custer's command giving way. The Fourth Pennsylvania Cavalry, having been sent to report to General Pleasonton, was not with me during July 3, but joined me in the evening of that day, when my command was ordered to move to the front and take up a position on the left, in order to meet a threatened attack from that direction. While remaining in that position, the enemy got my range, and wounded several men in the Tenth New York Cavalry by bursting shells.

On July 4, 5, and 6, my command was engaged in pursuing the enemy as far as Marion, on the pike leading from Chambersburg to Greencastle, Franklin County. During the pursuit, a large number of prisoners were captured, and the enemy obliged to abandon a number of limbers and caissons filled with ammunition, which were left in condition for immediate use.

The casualties are as follows: Killed, 4; wounded, 5.*

I have the honor to be, very respectfully, your obedient servant,

J. IRVIN GREGG,
Colonel Sixteenth Pennsylvania Cavalry, Comdg. Brigade.

Capt. H. C. WEIR,
  Asst. Adjt. Gen., Second Division, Cavalry Corps.

HDQRS. THIRD BRIG., SECOND DIV., CAVALRY CORPS,
August 17, 1863.

SIR: I have the honor to report that this command was engaged from the date of the battle of Gettysburg until it arrived at Warrenton Junction, Va., as follows:

On July 4, made a reconnaissance to Hunterstown, and drove in the enemy's pickets at that place.

On July 5 and 6, in pursuit of the enemy. Came up with him and engaged him near Greenwood. Lost 1 man killed on the evening of the 5th.

Continued the pursuit on the 6th to Marion, finding the road filled with broken-down wagons, abandoned limbers and caissons filled

———
* But see revised statement, p. 186.

with ammunition ready for instant use. Captured and sent into Gettysburg a large number of prisoners.

On July 7, 8, and 9, were on the march from Chambersburg, Pa., to Middletown, Md.

July 11, marched to Boonsborough.

July 12 and 13, in camp.

July 14, marched to Harper's Ferry.

On the morning of July 15, this brigade moved on the Charlestown road as far as Halltown, halted, and the First Maine Cavalry was thrown forward to make a reconnaissance to Charlestown. Proceeding half a mile, they encountered and drove in the enemy's vedettes on their position in a skirt of woods in front of Charlestown. The First Maine lost in the skirmish 1 man wounded. Leaving the Thirteenth Pennsylvania Cavalry and a detachment of Scott's Nine Hundred on picket at Halltown, the brigade moved on the Shepherdstown road, encountering and capturing a number of the enemy's stragglers, and, on arriving at that place, two squadrons of the Sixteenth Pennsylvania Cavalry, under command of Major Fry, charged through the town.

The Sixteenth lost 1 man wounded.

On July 16, at 1 p. m., the enemy attacked in force and drove in my vedettes and reserve, consisting of two squadrons of the Tenth New York Cavalry. Fortunately, however, the First Maine Cavalry had been ordered out a short time before on that road after forage, and checked the enemy's advance about 1 mile in front of my position.

Finding that the enemy was outflanking and slowly driving back Colonel Smith's command, I sent two squadrons of the Fourth Pennsylvania Cavalry, under command of Major Young, about 3 p. m., to re-enforce him.

The enemy still continuing to extend his skirmish line and to throw forward fresh troops, at 4 p. m. I sent one squadron of the Sixteenth Pennsylvania Cavalry to support the left of the line.

At 5 p. m. moved up the balance of the Sixteenth Pennsylvania Cavalry and all of the Fourth Pennsylvania Cavalry excepting one small squadron, left in reserve to support the battery, and my entire force became engaged ; and from this time until dark the fight raged without cessation, the enemy making repeated and desperate charges, endeavoring to break my center.

About 6.30 p. m. three squadrons of the First Pennsylvania Cavalry, under command of Colonel Taylor, reported to me, and were posted about 100 yards in rear of my center, in reserve. The Tenth New York Cavalry was posted on the right, on the Martinsburg road, on which the enemy made several demonstrations during the engagement, but were gallantly repulsed.

Captain Randol's battery (E, First U. S. Artillery), only one section of which, under command of Lieutenant [Ernst L.] Kinney, was engaged, did excellent service in shelling the woods in front of my line and in checking the enemy's advance.

Too much credit cannot be awarded to the officers and men of this command for the gallantry displayed in resisting for eight hours and finally repulsing the attack of a force outnumbering it at least three to one, supported by eight pieces of artillery.

When all engaged acquitted themselves so creditably, it is extremely difficult to discriminate, but I desire specially to mention Lieutenant-Colonel Smith and Major Boothby, First Maine Cavalry;

Major Young, Fourth Pennsylvania Cavalry, and Captains Fisher and Swan, Sixteenth Pennsylvania Cavalry.

I am indebted to Capt. H. M. Hughes and Lieut. J. B. Maitland, Fourth Pennsylvania Cavalry; Lieut. A. N. Martin, Sixteenth Pennsylvania Cavalry, and Lieut. F. M. Cutler, First Maine Cavalry, for valuable assistance in carrying orders to various parts of the field.

On July 17, marched to Harper's Ferry.

July 19 to 24, on the march to Warrenton Junction.

I am, sir, very respectfully, your obedient servant,

J. IRVIN GREGG,
Colonel, Comdg. Third Brig., Second Div., Cavalry Corps.

Brig. Gen. D. McM. GREGG,
Comdg. Second Division, Cavalry Corps.

ADDENDA.

CAMP NEAR SULPHUR SPRINGS, VA.,
August 13, 1863.

COLONEL: I have the honor to report that on July 15 and 16, while the brigade was fighting at Shepherdstown, my command, consisting of the Thirteenth Pennsylvania Cavalry and Scott's Nine Hundred, was ordered to hold Halltown, Va., on the Charlestown road, and do picket duty thereabouts. This order was strictly obeyed, the enemy offering no molestation. The command remained on picket duty three days, after which the command joined the brigade, and has not been separated from it up to the present date. The command did three days' picket duty at Rappahannock Station; also three days' picket duty at Jefferson, Va.

M. KERWIN,
Major, Comdg. 13th Penn. Cav. and Scott's Nine Hundred.

Col. JOHN I. GREGG,
Commanding Brigade.

No. 356.

Reports of Col. Charles H. Smith, First Maine Cavalry.

HEADQUARTERS FIRST MAINE CAVALRY,
August 31, 1863.

LIEUTENANT: I have the honor to submit the following report of the part sustained by this regiment in the action at Aldie on June 17 last:

After the brigade had drawn near to the town, Col. C. S. Douty, commanding, was ordered forward with his regiment to report to Brigadier-General Gregg, commanding division. Having reported, the colonel was ordered to proceed with his command to a position to the left of the town, but before arriving there was ordered to return in haste. The regiment returned at the trot, left in front, and ascended the hill on the right of the town near the battery just in time to meet and resist the impetuous charge of the enemy upon our exhausted forces. A portion of the regiment, led by Colonel Douty, charged, turned the enemy, and drove him from the hill and his stronghold among the stone walls. The regiment gained the position, secured our wounded, collected the trophies of the field, and were burying the dead when relieved just before dark. The casualties were as follows: Killed, 6; wounded, 19; missing, 5.

I am, very respectfully, your obedient servant,

C. H. SMITH,
Colonel First Maine Cavalry.

Lieut. JOHN B. MAITLAND,
A. A. A. G. Second Brig., Second Div., Cavalry Corps.

—

HEADQUARTERS FIRST MAINE CAVALRY,
August 14, 1863.

LIEUTENANT: In compliance with orders from headquarters Second Brigade (Col. J. Irvin Gregg), I have the honor to report the part taken by my regiment in the operations of July 15.

On the morning of July 15, when the column had reached Halltown, the colonel commanding the brigade ordered me to go forward with my regiment on the Charlestown pike, and directed that I should go into Charlestown or until I found the enemy in force. Having advanced nearly a mile, we surprised the pickets of the enemy, and drove them until we were met by a regular line of dismounted skirmishers; then the engagement became general. I deployed six companies, kept two companies on the pike to charge the center of the enemy from time to time after his flanks were sufficiently forced back, and kept but three small companies in reserve and to guard our flanks and rear. Thus, by a bold front and two hours' severe skirmishing, we drove a very much larger number over a mile and from several good positions, when ordered to retire and join the column. The enemy opened upon us with two pieces of artillery. The officers and men of my regiment behaved with the utmost gallantry.

All of which is respectfully submitted.

I am, lieutenant, very respectfully, your obedient servant,

C. H. SMITH,
Colonel First Maine Cavalry.

Lieut. JOHN B. MAITLAND,
A. A. A. G., Second Brig., Second Div., Cavalry Corps.

—

HEADQUARTERS FIRST MAINE CAVALRY,
August 14, 1863.

LIEUTENANT: In accordance with orders from Colonel Gregg, commanding Second Brigade, I have the honor to report the part taken by my regiment in the action at Shepherdstown, July 16.

On July 16, about 12 m., I was ordered by the colonel commanding brigade to proceed from Shepherdstown with my regiment out about 4 miles on the Winchester pike for forage. Having advanced about a mile, I met a courier from the picket (a squadron of the Tenth New York Cavalry), who reported that the picket had been attacked, and were hotly pursued by the enemy. Looking forward, I observed that about half a mile ahead the pike crossed a ridge covered by a belt of timber, and, being desirous of obtaining that position, I ordered the gallop, and the regiment dashed forward. As we drew near the timber, we met the squadron on picket completely overwhelmed by a superior foe, making every effort to cover its led horses and wounded men. The advance of the enemy reached the crest of the ridge first, but, in spite of their steady firing, two companies from my regiment, commanded respectively by Lieutenants Coleman and Cole, when ordered to take the summit of the hill, charged with such impetuosity as to drive back the enemy, killing 1 and wounding 3. The enemy thus received a serious check, the position was gained, and the regiment was immediately disposed for still further defense. In that position we opposed the rapidly increasing number of the enemy for more than an hour, strengthening our line from time to time until the regiment was nearly all deployed and engaged in the front.

Here it was that Major Boothby and Lieutenant Hunton were wounded, while engaged urging the men to still more gallant resistance.

Subsequently the enemy massed in such numbers on our left flank as to make longer resistance impossible, and our line of skirmishers was driven back about 200 yards to a favorable position. Supported by a portion of the Fourth Pennsylvania Cavalry, the regiment defended this position against every effort of the enemy to rout it, even driving the gunners from a howitzer that the enemy had the rashness to bring within carbine range, until relieved by the Sixteenth Pennsylvania Cavalry, when it retired from the front and took position as support. But a short time afterward, however, the enemy opened with several pieces of artillery, and simultaneously advanced with such overwhelming numbers as to peril the thin line of skirmishers of the Sixteenth. Observing this, I at once ordered four companies to the front just in season to render timely assistance, and shortly after the rest of the regiment became actively engaged again, and thus shared the fortunes of the rest of the day until withdrawn from the field at midnight.

I am, lieutenant, very respectfully, your obedient servant,

C. H. SMITH,
Colonel First Maine Cavalry.

Lieut. JOHN B. MAITLAND,
   A. A. A. G., Second Brig., Second Div., Cavalry Corps.

No. 357.

Report of Maj. M. Henry Avery, Tenth New York Cavalry.

NEAR JEFFERSON, VA.,
August 13, 1863.

SIR: I have the honor to submit the following report of the part taken by my regiment in the operations of the Third Brigade, Second Cavalry Division, subsequent to the battle of Gettysburg and up to the arrival of the same at Warrenton, Va.:

On the morning of July 5, I left bivouac, about 1½ miles east of Gettysburg, passing through the village on the Chambersburg pike. The Tenth New York on that day having the right of the brigade, nearly the whole of the regiment was disposed as flankers, for the purpose of thoroughly scouring the country and arresting the numerous stragglers of the enemy, who, singly and in squads, were endeavoring to make their way into the mountains. Owing to the wholesale capture of prisoners, and the necessity of the column following as rapidly as possible the rear of the enemy, I am unable to make any accurate estimate of the number taken. Each detachment under my command, on accumulating as large a number as could be safely guarded, proceeded to Gettysburg, and turned them over to the provost-marshal. Encamped that night at Graefenburg Springs.

Next day marched, via New Franklin, to Chambersburg; encamped at that point.

July 7, commenced march for Middletown, passing through Quincy, Fayetteville, and Waynesborough, arriving there July 10.

July 11, marched to Boonsborough, rejoining the division at that point.

July 13, marched to Harper's Ferry.

July 15, the Second Cavalry Division marched on a reconnaissance to Shepherdstown, the Third Brigade having the advance. A few pickets and a small supporting force of the enemy were encountered at this point, and easily captured or dispersed by our advance. This regiment on that day, being the third in column, took no part in the engagement. Encamped that night at Shepherdstown.

Next morning two squadrons, consisting of Companies H and L, under command of Captains Peck and Vanderbilt, and Companies C and G, under command of Lieutenants Sceva and McKevitt, the battalion being under command of Maj. A. D. Waters, were placed on picket on the Winchester pike, one squadron, under Captain Peirce, on the Dam No. 4 road, and the remaining three squadrons, under my command, were ordered to picket the Martinsburg road.

No force of the enemy was visible until about 2 p. m., when the vedettes from the battalion on the Winchester road were rapidly driven in by the advance guard of a heavy force, since ascertained to be under the command of General Stuart. Major Waters at this time, feeling seriously indisposed, retired, leaving Captain Peck in command. Lieutenant Sceva's squadron, being at the outer post, succeeded in momentarily checking the charge of the enemy, and then retired on the reserve without losing a prisoner, although the attack had been fierce, impetuous, and by an overwhelming force. At this reserve, Captain Peck succeeded in temporarily repulsing their advance, with a loss of 7 men missing and wounded, 3 of which latter have since died in hospital, and Lieut. John T. McKevitt, of Company G, a brave and gallant officer, severely wounded through the lung.

The enemy having brought forward a strong re-enforcement, Captain Peck was compelled to retire until re-enforced by the First Maine, when the enemy was held in check until the remainder of the brigade came up. Soon after, Captain Peck was withdrawn and sent to strengthen the line picketed by my command, and which, by the nature of the attack, had become a line of skirmishers, covering the extreme right of the division.

During the remainder of the engagement this regiment remained comparatively idle and without any loss on our part, annoying the opposing skirmishers of the enemy and driving back any force which appeared. On the cessation of the firing, my line remained the same as at the commencement of the attack, and was held as a line of pickets until midnight, when we were withdrawn, and marched for Harper's Ferry, arriving there soon after daylight.

July 19, marched for Warrenton, via Leesburg, encamping, respectively, at Goose Creek, Manassas, Broad Run, Warrenton Junction, and Bealeton, until July 29. During the period from the 22d ultimo to that date we were engaged in picketing the line of the Orange and Alexandria Railroad.

July 29, marched for Amissville, encamping that night about 2 miles from Warrenton.

Annexed please find a report of the casualties in this regiment during the period covered by this report.*

I have the honor to remain, very respectfully, your obedient servant,

M. HENRY AVERY,
Major, Commanding Tenth New York Cavalry.

Lieut. JOHN B. MAITLAND,
  Acting Assistant Adjutant-General.

No. 358.

Reports of Lieut. Col. William E. Doster, Fourth Pennsylvania Cavalry.

HEADQUARTERS FOURTH PENNSYLVANIA CAVALRY,
September 3, 1863.

SIR: I have the honor to report that, on the morning of June 21, I received orders from Colonel Gregg to mount my regiment, which was encamped in the woods about 1 mile from Middleburg, on the Upperville road, and to move out in column of squadrons on the left of the Tenth New York and one battalion of the First Maine, on the right of the road leading to Upperville, which I accordingly did, moving at intervals from the protection of one knoll to another until we had advanced perhaps 1 mile, when my pioneer corps took possession of a small rifled gun which had been abandoned by the enemy in his flight.

After proceeding about 1 mile farther, I was ordered to cross the road and proceed parallel to it. This I did, at the same time deploying one company, dismounted, as skirmishers on my front, and afterward adding one squadron on my left. In this manner we reached a point within one-half mile of the town, occasional shots being exchanged between our skirmishers and those of the enemy. Here I was ordered to form my regiment as a support to and on the left of, I think, some regular regiments. Before the order to advance was given, I was ordered to the support of Tidball's battery, then on the rising ground on the right of the road, in full view of the town and of the enemy.

After remaining here a short time, I was ordered forward to the support of the battalion of the First Maine, which had been ordered to charge and drive the enemy from and beyond the town. I immediately ordered my regiment forward at a gallop, and, after passing through and beyond the town some hundreds of yards, came up with the First Maine, which was formed on the road, apparently awaiting a charge by the enemy. In a few minutes the enemy came dashing down the road, when I ordered my first two squadrons to advance carbines, to be ready to receive them. The First Maine,

---

* Embodied in revised statement, p. 193.

after firing a few shots, scattered to the right and left. The fire of my regiment being too hot for him, the enemy wheeled, and I ordered a charge, which was obeyed most promptly and gallantly by both officers and men. The enemy were driven from the field, leaving a number killed, many wounded, and several prisoners in our hands. I then deployed two squadrons in the field on the right of the road as skirmishers, falling back some distance in the field with the principal part of my command. The enemy again charged, my men at the same time wheeling, so as to throw a flank fire into him as he passed along the road. About 20 of my men then dashed into the road in his rear, and, after a desperate hand-to-hand conflict, utterly routed and discomfited him, thus preventing his escape, and causing the capture of the entire party, variously estimated at from 20 to 50 men. The division coming up at this time, it was impossible to give the exact number.

I now received orders to rally my men and fall back beyond Upperville, where I encamped for the night.

During the actions of the day the regiment sustained a loss of 1 killed, 3 severely wounded, 1 slightly wounded, and 2 taken prisoners.

I am, sir, very respectfully, your obedient servant,

W. E. DOSTER,
Lieutenant-Colonel Fourth Pennsylvania Cavalry.

Lieut. JOHN B. MAITLAND,
Actg. Asst. Adjt. Gen., Second Cavalry Brigade.

—

SULPHUR SPRINGS, VA.,
August 13, 1863.

SIR: I have the honor to report that, immediately after the battle of Gettysburg and the pursuit of Lee as far as Marion (described in my last report*), this regiment accompanied the brigade to Middletown and Boonsborough, Md., without any event of note occurring until July 14, when the regiment recrossed the Potomac at Harper's Ferry, and encamped on Bolivar Heights.

On the 15th, we marched with the brigade as far as Shepherdstown. About 4 p. m. was ordered by Colonel Gregg to advance 4 miles out the Winchester road to Wolper's Cross-Roads, and report my arrival. About 1 mile from Shepherdstown my advance guard encountered and drove before them a party of 10 rebels, which was increased to about 40 by the time I reached the cross-roads. They fled into the woods beyond the cross-roads and renewed the attack, but were again dispersed.

I learned from a prisoner whom we captured that about 500 rebel cavalry, belonging to [A. G.] Jenkins, was encamped at Leetown, in front; that a rebel cavalry force was on my left near Charlestown, and that a portion of Ewell's corps, whose drums were heard distinctly, was near Martinsburg and about 3 miles to my right, and sent the information to the colonel commanding brigade. I threw out pickets on all the roads, and held them without further molestation until 11 p. m., when I was ordered back with three squadrons to Shepherdstown, the balance being relieved next morning.

At about 1 p. m. of the 16th, I was ordered to move my regiment

---

* Not found. But see Gregg's report, p. 977.

on the right of the Winchester road and Randol's battery, and instructed to support the battery while watching and holding the enemy in check on the right of the line. I successively advanced three squadrons—Captains Peale and Duncan and Lieutenant Andrews—to the right of the line, which became warmly engaged about 5 p. m., and so remained until the close of the day.

Meanwhile two squadrons, Captains Peale's and Dart's, had been sent under Major Young to the support of the First Maine, and held their ground on the right of the road until orders were given to retire. Captain Robison remained as support of the battery.

For gallant and meritorious conduct, First Sergt. John Harper, Company B, deserves special mention.

In this action 7 were wounded and 6 missing.

I fell back with the brigade to Harper's Ferry the same evening, and thence moved to Bristoe Station and Warrenton without meeting with anything unusual, excepting rest, rations, and forage.

I am, very respectfully, your obedient servant,

W. E. DOSTER,
Lieutenant-Colonel, Commanding.

Lieutenant MAITLAND,
Acting Assistant Adjutant-General.

No. 359.

Reports of Brig. Gen. Judson Kilpatrick, U. S. Army, commanding First Brigade of, and Third Division.

HDQRS. FIRST BRIG., THIRD DIV., CAVALRY CORPS,
June 10, 1863.

CAPTAIN: I have the honor to submit the following report of the part taken by my brigade* in the cavalry action of yesterday:

After receiving orders from General Gregg to move to the right of Colonel Wyndham and engage the enemy, I formed line of battle in *échelons* of regiments, with a section of artillery on the right of the second regiment, and moved rapidly forward, pushing my whole line of skirmishers up to and beyond the railroad crossing. At this moment the enemy, with a large and superior force, drove our forces from the hill on my left, so gallantly taken by Colonel Wyndham.

I ordered Colonel Irvine, of the Tenth New York, who was on the left of my line, to charge and drive the rebels from the hill and hold it. Colonel Irvine had scarcely advanced 100 yards when my whole line was threatened by a superior force of the enemy. I ordered a section of artillery to commence firing, and advanced Colonel Davies, of the Harris Light Cavalry, with one battalion, to charge the enemy in flank. Before, however, Colonel Irvine or Colonel Davies had passed the railroad crossing with any considerable portion of their commands, the enemy, in two heavy columns, struck their advance and threw them into confusion. I sent orders to these two officers to withdraw and rally their commands, and with the First Maine (Colonel Douty) swept to the right and charged the enemy in flank.

---

*Consisting then of the First Maine, Second and Tenth New York, and Orton's (District of Columbia) cavalry company. On June 14, Kilpatrick was assigned to command of the Second Brigade of the reorganized Second Division, and on June 28 to command of the new Third Division, formerly Stahel's.

They outnumbered us three to one, but could not withstand the heavy saber blows of the sturdy men of Maine, who rode through them and over them, gained the hill, captured a battle-flag and many prisoners, among them the rebel General Stuart's adjutant-general. From this moment the fight was one series of charges, every regiment of the brigade charging, rallying, and again charging until ordered to retire. Each regiment left the field with its organization preserved and in good order.

We captured one stand of colors, upward of 100 prisoners, and a battery of four guns, two by Colonel Douty and two by Colonel Davies. The guns could not be brought off, but all the horses were killed.

The following is a list of casualties in my brigade:

Harris Light Cavalry—1 lieutenant and 14 enlisted men wounded, and 33 enlisted men missing.

The First Maine Cavalry—3 enlisted men wounded, 14 missing, and 7 prisoners.

The Tenth New York Cavalry—3 commissioned officers wounded and missing, 2 wounded and present; 8 enlisted men wounded, and 44 missing. Total, commissioned officers, 6 wounded; enlisted men, 32 wounded and 98 missing.

I regret the loss of Lieutenant-Colonel Irvine, of the Tenth New York Cavalry, who since the fight has been missing. He led his regiment most gallantly in the last charge, and was seen to fall, over-powered by numbers.

I take great pleasure in bringing to your notice Captains McIrvin and [Frederick W.] Armstrong; Dr. [Charles E.] Hackley, brigade surgeon; Lieutenant [Lewellyn G.] Estes, aide-de-camp; Lieutenant and Quartermaster [Butler] Coles, and Lieutenant and Commissary [Timothy] Hedges, all of whom are deserving of the greatest praise. I cannot single out individual cases of gallantry. Each regiment rivaled the other in deeds of daring.

For the first time we have fought as a brigade. We tried to do our duty like brave men. I am proud of my brigade, and only hope that in this its first effort it has won the good opinion of our general.

Respectfully submitted.

J. KILPATRICK,
Colonel, Commanding Brigade.

Capt. H. C. WEIR,
Assistant Adjutant-General.

HEADQUARTERS THIRD CAVALRY DIVISION,
Hanover, June 30, 1863.

GENERAL: Five minutes after your dispatch saying that Stuart was making for Littlestown, my rear guard was attacked in Hanover, driven in, and a vigorous charge was made upon the rear and flanks of my command; at the same time the enemy opened with artillery from the hills at the right of the town. Brigadier-General Farnsworth quickly threw his brigade into position, and, by quick and vigorous charges, checked their attacks and drove the enemy out of town. The enemy soon showed himself in force on the left of the town, and foolishly put himself in my rear. After a fight of about two hours, in which the whole command at different times was engaged, I made a vigorous attack upon their center, forced them back upon the road to Littlestown, and finally succeeded in breaking their center.   One portion retreated toward York; the other passed to the right, toward Gettysburg.   As the enemy was reported to be advancing from the direction of Berlin, I made no further attempts to intercept Stuart's command.   I have taken one battle-flag, a lieutenant-colonel, 1 captain, and 45 privates, and upward of 15 of the enemy have been killed.   My loss is trifling.   I have gone into camp at Hanover.   My command will be in readiness to move again at daylight to-morrow morning.   We have plenty of forage, the men are in good spirits, and we don't fear Stuart's whole cavalry.

Very respectfully,

J. KILPATRICK,
Brigadier-General of Volunteers.

Major-General PLEASONTON,
Commanding Cavalry Corps.

P. S.—The enemy was under the command of Stuart, who had with him three brigades—Lee's, Hampton's, and Robertson's.

———

HDQRS. THIRD CAV. DIV., PLEASONTON'S CORPS,
Hanover, June 30, 1863.

GENERAL: I have the honor to report that after an encounter with General Stuart's force, I have succeeded in cutting his column in two. One portion, estimated at about 4,000, with from five to seven pieces of artillery, is now encamped in the woods on the left (east) side of the road from Hanover to Baltimore; the other is also in the woods on the right (west) side of the road from Hanover to Littlestown.   I am not informed as to its strength.   I have sent out scouts to ascertain the exact position of the first division, and intend, if possible, to attack their camp at daybreak; otherwise I expect to be attacked by them.

A strong column of the enemy's forces left York at daybreak this morning, to march to this place, from which circumstance and other information I conclude that they are concentrating at Gettysburg. They have with them 15 wagons; also about 113 mules.   They spoke in their camp to-day of burning these wagons, as they could not carry them out with them.   I shall attack them if I can by any means find proper roads.   My information is reliable.

Very respectfully,

J. KILPATRICK,
Brigadier-General of Volunteers.

Major-General PLEASONTON.

[P. S.]—The enemy (Stuart's command) is moving toward York, cutting his way through the fields.   I think there is a considerable force at Berlin.   I am now midway between Abbottstown and Hanover.   I cannot well advance farther and keep communications open with Littlestown.   Scouting parties will be sent out in the direction of York, Dover, and Carlisle.   Stuart is moving toward York.

———

HEADQUARTERS, *Littlestown, June* 30, 1863—6 p. m.

[Major-General PLEASONTON:]

GENERAL: A messenger has just come in from Kilpatrick, asking for re-enforcements.   I sent him every cavalryman that I could get hold of.   I also informed him of the infantry at this place.   I think there is no doubt but there is a heavy infantry force at Berlin and Gettysburg. Kilpatrick has information that Lee's headquarters are at Berlin. The enemy struck the rear of his column just as it entered Hanover, creating some confusion in one regiment. A charge was, however, immediately made, which resulted in the repulse of the enemy and the capture of about 50 prisoners, one lieutenant-colonel among them. As soon as my horse rests a little, I will come to headquarters.

Very respectfully, your obedient servant,

A. J. ALEXANDER,
Assistant Adjutant-General.

[Indorsement.]

Respectfully forwarded. General Lee's being in *Berlin is impor-tant.**

A. PLEASONTON,
Major-General, Commanding.

—

HEADQUARTERS THIRD DIVISION, CAVALRY CORPS,
Smithsburg, Md., July 5, 1863.
(Received 1.45 p. m.)

GENERAL : Yesterday, at 12 m., I attacked the right flank of the enemy at different points, and found him in force at each point. I passed through Emmitsburg, and ordered one brigade to pass through the mountain. [W. E.] Jones' brigade of cavalry drove back my people, and I was attacked at the same time on my right flank. Knowing that the train of wagons was passing, I gave battle, forced my way through the pass, drove back the rebel cavalry and artillery, captured one entire regiment, colonel, lieutenant-colonel, most of the officers, and one battle-flag. General Custer here had a hard fight. The enemy's cavalry and infantry made every effort to drive me back, but we passed on, reached the train, barricaded the road in our rear, and the entire train from the mountains to Ridgeville was in my possession. I have destroyed the wagons of Ewell's entire corps, and over 1,500 prisoners have been taken. I have sent them to Frederick City. I now hold a strong position; my lines of retreat are certain. The enemy is in sight, tired and worn out; he shall not have one moment's rest. The pontoons between Williamsport and Sharpsburg are destroyed. General Early was cut off last night from his people, and my men are chasing both himself and staff over the country. He is wounded.

Very respectfully,

J. KILPATRICK,
Brigadier-General of Volunteers.

Major-General PLEASONTON.

—

HEADQUARTERS THIRD CAVALRY DIVISION,
Hagerstown, Md., July 12, 1863.

GENERAL: I have the honor to report that, in obedience to orders from headquarters Cavalry Corps, I have driven the enemy through and out of Hagerstown, capturing a large number of prisoners, with but slight loss. General Ames' division of infantry is now in the

---

* See indorsement on Buford's report of same date, p. 923.

town, and we are picketing the roads in the direction of Williamsport heavily with infantry and cavalry.

I made a demonstration in front of the town, in the direction of the enemy on the road to Williamsport, but was unable to force him back a single step, and drew the fire of 20-pounder rifled guns. Citizens informed me that Ewell and Longstreet marched through the place yesterday, in the direction of Sharpsburg and Williamsport, and that the enemy now occupy a position a mile and a half from town. Their line is in the form of a horseshoe, with its concavity toward Williamsport; one branch of the shoe is in rear of Hagerstown, the other toward Sharpsburg.

Very respectfully,

J. KILPATRICK,
Brigadier-General of Volunteers.

Major-General PLEASONTON,
Chief of Cavalry.

ADDENDA.

HEADQUARTERS ARMY OF THE POTOMAC,
August 9, 1863.

GENERAL: My attention has been called to what purports to be an official dispatch of General R. E. Lee,* commanding Confederate Army, to General S. Cooper, Adjutant and Inspector General, denying the accuracy of my telegram to you of July 14, announcing the result of the cavalry affair at Falling Waters. I have delayed taking any notice of General Lee's report until the return of Brigadier-General Kilpatrick (absent on leave), who commanded the cavalry engaged on the occasion referred to, and on whose report from the field my telegram was based.

I now inclose the official report of Brigadier-General Kilpatrick, made after his attention had been called to General Lee's report. You will see that he reiterates and confirms all that my dispatch averred, and proves most conclusively that General Lee has been deceived by his subordinates, or he would never, in the face of the facts now alleged, have made the assertions his report contains.

It appears that I was in error in stating that the body of General Pettigrew was left in our hands, although I would not communicate that fact until an officer from the field reported to me he had seen the body. It is now ascertained from the Richmond papers that General Pettigrew, though mortally wounded in the affair, was taken to Winchester, where he subsequently died.

The three battle-flags captured on this occasion and sent to Washington belonged to the Fortieth, Forty-seventh, and Fifty-fifth Virginia Regiments (infantry). General Lee will surely acknowledge these were not left in the hands of "stragglers asleep in barns."

In conclusion, I desire, if it meets with your approval, that this communication, together with General Kilpatrick's report, may be published, that justice may be done to all parties concerned, and the truth of history vindicated.

Respectfully, yours,

GEO. G. MEADE,
Major-General, Commanding.

Major-General HALLECK,
General-in-Chief.

---

* Copy, taken from General Lee's letter-book, attached.

[Inclosure.]

HEADQUARTERS THIRD DIVISION, CAVALRY CORPS,
Warrenton Junction, Va., August 7, 1863.

COLONEL: In compliance with letter just received from headquarters Cavalry Corps, Army of the Potomac, directing me to give the facts connected with my fight at Falling Waters, I have the honor to state that at 3 o'clock on the morning of the 14th ultimo I learned that the enemy's pickets were retiring in my front. Having been previously ordered to attack at 7 a. m., I was ready to move at once.

At daylight I had reached the crest of the hills occupied by the enemy an hour before, and at a few moments before 6 o'clock General Custer drove the rear guard of the enemy into the river at Williamsport. Learning from citizens that a portion of the enemy had retreated in the direction of Falling Waters, I at once moved rapidly for that point, and came up with the rear guard of the enemy at 7.30 a. m., at a point 2 miles distant from Falling Waters. We pressed on, driving them before us, capturing many prisoners and one gun. When within a mile and a half of Falling Waters, the enemy was found in large force, drawn up in line of battle, on the crest of a hill commanding the road on which I was advancing. His left was protected by earthworks, and his right extended to the woods far on my left. The enemy was, when first seen, in two lines of battle, with arms stacked. Within less than 1,000 yards of this large force, a second piece of artillery with its support (consisting of infantry) was captured while attempting to get into position. The gun was taken to the rear.

A portion of the Sixth Michigan Cavalry, seeing only that portion of the enemy behind the earthworks, charged. This charge, led by Major Weber, was the most gallant ever made. At a trot he passed up the hill, received the fire from the whole line, and the next moment rode through and over the earthworks; passed to the right, sabering rebels along the entire line, and returned with a loss of 30 killed, wounded, and missing, including the gallant Major [P. A.] Weber killed.

I directed General Custer to send forward one regiment as skirmishers. They were repulsed before support could be sent them, and driven back, closely followed by the rebels, until checked by the First Michigan and a squadron of the Eighth New York. The Second Brigade, having come up, was quickly thrown into position, and, after a fight of two hours and a half, we routed the enemy at all points, and drove him toward the river. When within a short distance of the bridge, General Buford's command came up and took the advance.

We lost 29 killed, 36 wounded, and 40 missing. We found upon the field 125 dead rebels, and brought away upward of 50 wounded. A large number of the enemy's wounded was left upon the field, in charge of their own surgeons. We captured 2 guns, 3 battle-flags, and upward of 1,500 prisoners.

To General Custer and his brigade, Lieutenant Pennington and his battery, and one squadron of the Eighth New York Cavalry, of General Buford's command, all praise is due.

Very respectfully, your obedient servant,

J. KILPATRICK,
Brigadier-General of Volunteers, Commanding Division.

Col. A. J. ALEXANDER, *Chief of Staff, Cavalry Corps.*

HEADQUARTERS ARMY OF NORTHERN VIRGINIA,
July 21, 1863.

GENERAL: I have seen in the Northern papers what purported to be an official dispatch of General Meade, stating that he had captured a brigade of infantry, two pieces of artillery, two caissons, and a large number of small-arms, as this army retired to the south bank of the Potomac, on the 13th and 14th instant.

This dispatch has been copied into the Richmond papers, and as its official character may cause it to be believed, I desire to state that it is incorrect. The enemy did not capture any organized body of men on that occasion, but only stragglers and such as were left asleep on the road, exhausted by the fatigue and exposure of one of the most inclement nights I have ever known at this season of the year. It rained without cessation, rendering the road by which our troops marched to the bridge at Falling Waters very difficult to pass, and causing so much delay that the last of the troops did not cross the river at the bridge until 1 p. m. on the 14th. While the column was thus detained on the road, a number of men, worn down with fatigue, lay down in barns and by the roadside, and though officers were sent back to arouse them as the troops moved on, the darkness and rain prevented them from finding all, and many were in this way left behind.

The two guns were left in the road. The horses that drew them became exhausted and the officers went forward to procure others. When they returned, the rear of the column had passed the guns so far that it was deemed unsafe to send back for them, and they were thus lost.

No arms, cannon, or prisoners were taken by the enemy in battle, but only such as were left behind under the circumstances I have described. The number of stragglers thus lost I am unable to state with accuracy, but it is greatly exaggerated in the dispatch referred to.

I am, with great respect, your obedient servant,

R. E. LEE,
General.

General S. COOPER,
Adjutant and Inspector General, Richmond, Va.

—

HEADQUARTERS THIRD DIVISION, CAVALRY CORPS,
August 10, 1863.

CAPTAIN: I have the honor to submit the following report of the part taken by the Third Division in the Maryland and Pennsylvania campaign :

On June 29, in compliance with orders from headquarters Cavalry Corps, I assumed command of the Third Division, till then known as Stahel's division.

The actual strength of the division was 3,500, although it numbered on paper upward of 4,000 men for duty.

On the morning of June 29, the First Brigade (General Farnsworth), consisting of the Fifth New York, Eighteenth Pennsylvania, First Vermont, First West Virginia Cavalry, and Elder's battery, U. S. Horse Artillery, left Frederick City, and marched to Littlestown, Pa.

The Second Brigade (General Custer), consisting of the First, Fifth,

Sixth, and Seventh Michigan Cavalry, and Pennington's battery, U. S. Horse Artillery, reached the same place at 10 p. m. the same day.

At daylight on the morning of the 30th, the division marched to find the enemy. We reached Hanover at 10 a. m., and, while passing through the town (the Second Brigade in advance), the First Brigade (General Farnsworth) was attacked in flank and rear by the Confederate cavalry under Stuart. Some confusion ensued. The attack was determined and fierce. The main and side streets swarmed with rebel cavalry. The Eighteenth Pennsylvania was routed, but the gallant Farnsworth had passed from front to rear ere the shout of the rebel charge had ceased to ring through the quiet street, faced the Fifth New York about, countermarched the other regiments, and with a rush and blow struck the rebel hosts in full charge. For a moment, and a moment only, victory hung uncertain. For the first time our troops had met the foe in close contact; but they were on their own free soil; fair hands, regardless of the dangerous strife, waved them on, and bright, tearful eyes looked pleadingly out from every window. The brave Farnsworth made one great effort, and the day was won. The foe turned and fled. He had for the first and last time polluted with his presence the loyal town of Hanover.

General Custer's brigade had now returned, and to save the town I moved first to its left and afterward to its right. The main streets were barricaded and held by our troops and the citizens, who gallantly volunteered to defend their homes. After an artillery duel of an hour, in which Pennington and Elder both participated, the enemy gave way, and we formed a junction with the main army, from which we had been separated for several hours.

In this engagement we lost—officers, 2 killed, 6 wounded, and 5 missing; enlisted men, 17 killed, 35 wounded, and 118 missing, making an aggregate of 197 killed, wounded, and missing. Owing to the nature of the attack, our loss was greater than that of the rebels. We killed upward of 20, took 50 prisoners, and captured one battle-flag.

The First Brigade (General Farnsworth), and especially the Fifth New York Cavalry, was greatly distinguished in this engagement.

July 1, the division marched to Berlin, via Abbottstown, to intercept Stuart, but failed. A detachment under Lieut. Col. A. J. Alexander pursued Stuart to Rossville.

July 2, received orders to move as quickly as possible toward Gettysburg. I proceeded rapidly across the country in the direction of the firing. Reached the battle-field at 2 p. m. Received orders from headquarters Cavalry Corps, through Brigadier-General Gregg, to move over to the road leading from Gettysburg to Abbottstown, and see that the enemy did not turn our flank. Was attacked by Stuart, Hampton, and Lee at sundown near Hunterstown. After a spirited affair of two hours, the enemy was driven from this point with great loss, and we encamped for the night.

The Second Brigade (General Custer) fought most handsomely. It lost, in killed, wounded, and missing, 32. The conduct of the Sixth Michigan Cavalry and Pennington's battery is deserving of the highest praise.

At 11 p. m. I received orders to move to Two Taverns, which point we reached at daylight.

At 8 a. m., received orders from headquarters Cavalry Corps to move to the left of our line and attack the enemy's right and rear with my whole command and the Regular Brigade. By some mistake, General Custer's brigade was ordered to report to General Gregg, and he did not join me during the day.

At 1 p. m. General Farnsworth had reached the rear and right of the enemy's position and become engaged with his skirmishers.

At 3 p. m. General Merritt came in on General Farnsworth's left, and the enemy was driven over 1 mile.

At 5.30 p. m. I ordered an attack with both brigades. The Regulars, dismounted, were pushed in on the left, and Brigadier-General Farnsworth moved down with two regiments—the First West Virginia and Eighteenth Pennsylvania—closely followed by the First Vermont and Fifth New York, through a piece of woods, and drove the enemy from one position to another until a heavy stone wall was reached, behind which the rebel infantry was gathered in great numbers. Our cavalry broke, rallied, and broke again before that formidable barrier, but the First Vermont and First West Virginia, led by the gallant Farnsworth, cleared the fence, sabered the rebels in the rear, rushed on over a second line of infantry, and were only stopped by another fence and a third line of infantry and artillery. The artillery, under Elder and Graham, all this time was doing good execution.

Previous to this attack, the enemy had made a most fierce and determined attack on the left of our main line of battle, with the view to turn it. We hope we assisted in preventing this. I am of the opinion that, had our infantry on my right advanced at once when relieved from the enemy's attack in their front, the enemy could not have recovered from the confusion into which Generals Farnsworth and Merritt had thrown them, but would have been rushed back, one division on another, until, instead of a defeat, a total rout would have ensued.

The firing had now ceased, and the great battle was over. At dusk we encamped on the field so dearly won.

In these various attacks throughout the day, both by Generals Farnsworth and Custer, who were engaged on the right, the enemy was known to have sustained great loss.

We lost 4 officers killed, 13 wounded, and 4 missing; 34 enlisted men killed, 138 wounded, and 117 missing, making an aggregate of 319 killed, wounded, and missing. In this battle the division lost many brave and gallant officers. Among the list will be found the name of Farnsworth; short but most glorious was his career—a general on June 29, on the 30th he baptized his star in blood, and on July 3, for the honor of his young brigade and the glory of his corps, he gave his life. At the head of his men, at the very muzzles of the enemy's guns, he fell, with many mortal wounds. We can say of him, in the language of another, "Good soldier, faithful friend, great heart, hail and farewell."

On the morning of the 4th, I received orders from headquarters Cavalry Corps to move with my division to Emmitsburg, where I would find Colonel Huey's brigade, of Brigadier-General Gregg's division; that Lee's army had evacuated Gettysburg at 3 o'clock that morning; that a heavy train of wagons was moving on the road to Hagerstown; that I was expected to take with me my entire division and the brigade referred to, destroy this train, and operate on the enemy's rear and flanks.

We reached Emmitsburg at 3 p. m. Colonel Huey's brigade joined the division at this place. Without halting, passed out on the road to Monterey, intending to cross the mountain at that point. Stuart's cavalry was at Miller's. We forced him off the road and passed on. The top of the mountain had nearly been gained when the enemy opened on the advance with artillery and infantry. At the same time the rear, under Colonel Huey, was attacked by Stuart's cavalry. On my left was a deep ravine, on my right a steep, rugged mountain, and a road too narrow to reverse even a gun. To add to this unpleasant position, it was raining in torrents.

Never under such perilous circumstances did a command behave better; not a word was spoken; there was no confusion. From a farmer's boy I learned the nature of the road and country on the mountain, made my disposition, and ordered a charge. In a moment the heights were gained and many prisoners taken. Now the rumble of the enemy's train could be heard rolling down the mountain. The enemy was in position half a mile farther on, at the intersection of the road from Gettysburg to Hagerstown and the road upon which I was moving. The enemy's infantry and artillery were approaching rapidly on the Gettysburg road, and he had already opened on my position with two guns. No time was to be lost if I wished to reach the train and save my command. Pennington, always ready, always willing, quickly came into position, and returned the enemy's fire. General Custer's brigade was ordered to move forward, clear the road, and attack the train. The attack was successful.

In the meantime the First Vermont Cavalry (Lieutenant-Colonel Preston) had been sent along the mountain over a wood road to Smithsburg, and thence to Hagerstown, to intercept the train. A strong force of dismounted men and two guns of Pennington's battery were now sent on the road in the direction of Gettysburg, to barricade the road and hold the enemy in check until the column had passed. Many fierce but unsuccessful attacks were made on this position during the night.

At daylight the whole command had safely passed, and Ewell's large train was entirely destroyed, save eight forges, thirty wagons, and a few ambulances loaded with wounded rebel officers (sent with prisoners to Frederick City).

At 9 a. m. on the 5th, the command reached Smithsburg with 1,360 prisoners, one battle-flag, and a large number of horses and mules, several hundred of the enemy's wounded being left upon the field.

We lost 5 killed, including 1 commissioned officer, 10 wounded, and 28 missing, making an aggregate of 43 killed, wounded, and missing.

Stuart, having failed the previous day in forcing my rear guard, passed through Emmitsburg to Mechanicstown, intending to cross the mountain and intercept my command. I learned of his approach in time to receive him. On three hills commanding the two mountain roads upon which he must approach, I placed my artillery. Colonel Huey's brigade, with Fuller's artillery, occupied the first hill, forming my front line of battle ; Colonel Richmond's brigade, with Elder's battery, in the rear and right of this line, occupied the second hill ; and General Custer's brigade, with Pennington's battery, in rear and some distance to the left, occupied the third hill.

At 5 p. m. the rebel columns were seen debouching from the wooded mountain passes. At 5.30 p. m. Fuller's battery opened ; a few moments later Elder's followed. Under this artillery fire, Stuart essayed in vain to take up a position. In less than one hour he was in full retreat down the mountain side toward Wrightsville. I did not pursue.   To save my prisoners, animals, and wagons, I returned to Boonsborough, which place we reached at 10 p. m.

On the evening of the 5th, having succeeded in turning over my prisoners and captured property to General French, and learning that Stuart was at Hagerstown, barricading the roads and intrench-ing his position to protect the large train near that place and at Williamsport, I marched early the following morning to attack him. While on the march, I was informed that Brigadier-General Buford was at Boonsborough, and about to march on Williamsport.   I rode back, and informed General Buford of my intentions, at the same time placing my command at his disposal.   It was then decided that my division should attack Stuart, while General Buford's command attacked Williamsport.   I moved on Hagerstown, and fell suddenly on Stuart, who, expecting me from the direction of Gettysburg, was surprised, routed, and driven toward Greencastle and Gettysburg. One of the pursuing parties having returned and brought in prison-ers belonging to Hood's division of infantry, who informed me that their whole division was marching for Hagerstown, and but a few miles distant, I left one brigade under Colonel Richmond to hold the enemy in check, and marched rapidly with the two remaining bri-gades for Williamsport, to assist General Buford, hoping that the command united would be able to destroy the train at Williamsport before the enemy's infantry could come up.   General Custer's bri-gade moved down the pike, drove in the rebel pickets, and soon be-came hotly engaged with the enemy on General Buford's right, within less than 1 mile of Williamsport.   General Custer had finally pushed his regiments one after another to the front, and was about to advance, with every prospect of success, when I received a dispatch from Colonel Richmond, saying that the enemy had attacked him with infantry, cavalry, and artillery.   Word came at the same time that a column of infantry was moving on my right flank.   It was now 6 p. m.   A few moments later General Buford sent a staff officer to say that he was about to retire; that he feared the enemy would move down on the Sharpsburg pike and intercept our retreat.   My command was in a most perilous position, attacked in front, rear, and flank, and no prospect of a safe retreat till night.   Slowly the regiments of each brigade fell back, taking up one position after another, repulsing each attack until night set in, and we formed a junction with General Buford, both commands going into camp near Jones' Cross-Roads.

I cannot pass over this engagement without mentioning a few among the many individual cases of gallantry that came under my own observation: Captains Snyder, Dahlgren, and Chauncy, the first killed, the last two wounded, leading a daring charge through the streets of Hagerstown.   The officers of my regular staff—Major Taggart, Captains Estes, Armstrong, and McMasters, Lieutenants Whittaker and Blunt, and Dr. Capehart—all did their duty in this engagement, as they have in all others, like brave and gallant gen-tlemen.   Colonel Richmond, commanding First Brigade, and Lieu-tenants Elder, Pennington, and Hamilton, of the artillery, deserve the greatest praise.   I am greatly indebted to the officers and men of the Harris Light Cavalry for the safe and successful retreat of the command.

The enemy's loss, as we afterward learned, was great.   We lost: Officers, 4 killed, 4 wounded, and 8 missing; enlisted men, 11 killed, 48 wounded, and 100 missing.

We failed in destroying the large trains parked at Williamsport, but forced the enemy to burn a large train northwest of Hagerstown.

On the morning of July 7, we marched to Boonsborough, and encamped.

On the morning of July 9, the enemy attacked General Buford's command near Funkstown, and was reported to be advancing in force. The division was at once moved out on the Hagerstown pike, and placed in position in rear of General Buford.

At 12 m. General Custer relieved General Merritt's brigade, giving me the right center.

At 1.30 p. m. Colonel Richmond relieved Colonel Devin, of General Buford's division. I then had the center and left, General Buford holding the right with one brigade. All day we fought the enemy, mounted and dismounted.

Late in the evening, General Buford dismounted his brigade on the right, and, with one regiment of General Custer's brigade, forced the enemy to give way. I signaled an advance to my whole column. Colonel Huey had the left, Colonel Richmond the center, and General Custer the right.

The movements commenced at sundown. The enemy gave way at all points, and was pursued until too dark to follow farther.

We lost in this affair: Officers, 1 killed and 9 wounded; enlisted men, 5 killed, 15 wounded, and 21 missing. The enemy's loss is unknown.

On the 11th, the division was ordered to move to the right of Major-General Sedgwick's corps, which had the extreme right of our line of battle.

On the 12th, I was ordered to advance with one brigade of infantry (Brigadier-General Ames') on Hagerstown, drive the enemy out, and occupy the town, which order was obeyed with slight loss. The enemy suffered greatly. We captured 100 prisoners.

On the 13th, the enemy made a slight attack on my position, but were repulsed. Five hundred militia (the Philadelphia Blues) assisted in this repulse.*

Respectfully submitted.

J. KILPATRICK,
Brig. Gen. of Volunteers, Comdg. Third Division.

Capt. A. J. COHEN,
Assistant Adjutant-General, Cavalry Corps.

No. 360.

Report of Lieut. Col. Henry E. Davies, jr., Second New York Cavalry, First Brigade.†

RAPPAHANNOCK STATION, VA., *June* 10, 1863.

LIEUTENANT: I herewith forward a report of the part taken by my regiment in the cavalry action at Brandy Station, Va., June 9.

Arriving upon the field, by order of Colonel Kilpatrick formed

---

* Portion of report here omitted relates to fight at Falling Waters, and is a duplicate of account given under date of August 7. See p. 990.

† After reorganization of June 11, the regiment was in Second Brigade, Second Division.

column of squadrons, and charged upon a regiment of the enemy, drawn up on the north side of the railroad. On reaching the railroad, by reason of an order improperly given, as is alleged, the head of the column was turned to the left, and proceeded some distance down the railroad, where it crossed, and charged another body of the enemy. Having crossed the railroad myself, and charged directly on the enemy, I am unable to give a detailed report of the execution that was done. After the first charge, the command was broken up into detachments, which attacked the enemy in different directions. Captain Hasty, with his squadron, retook two of our guns that had been taken by the enemy, but, in consequence of the horses being all killed, was unable to bring them off the field, and was obliged to abandon them.

When the order was given for retiring, I collected and withdrew the regiment in perfect order, covering the retreat by Captain Mitchell's squadron and skirmishers under the command of Major Cooke, who held the enemy completely in check.

I add a list of wounded and missing. The wounded, reported as such, have been brought in and sent to hospital. The missing are either killed or wounded and prisoners in the hands of the enemy.

I desire to mention, for gallant conduct on the field, Major Cooke, Captains Mitchell, Downing, and Hasty, and Second Lieut. Robert Stuart, who, with 6 men only, charged into a regiment of the enemy. There are other officers, doubtless, entitled to distinguished mention, but owing to the separation of the command that I have mentioned, I cannot report from my own knowledge what was done.

The number of wounded brought in is 1 commissioned officer (First Lieutenant Poughkeepsie) and 14 enlisted men. The number of missing is 33 enlisted men. The number of prisoners taken by my command I cannot state, as all, when taken, were sent to the rear, and turned over to division headquarters. No colors were taken by my regiment.

Respectfully submitted.

H. E. DAVIES, Jr.,
Lieutenant-Colonel, Commanding Regiment.

First Lieut. P. O. JONES,
Regimental Adjutant, and Actg. Asst. Adjt. Gen.

No. 361.

Reports of Brig. Gen. George A. Custer, U. S. Army, commanding Second Brigade of, and Third Division.

HEADQUARTERS SECOND BRIGADE, THIRD DIVISION,
September 9, 1863.

I have the honor to submit the following report of the engagements in which my command participated during the Pennsylvania and Maryland campaigns. Owing to the frequency with which this brigade encountered the enemy, my report assumes the form of a diary:

FIRST MICHIGAN CAVALRY.

On June 30, the regiment was ordered to support Battery M, Second U. S. Artillery, at Hanover, Pa. No loss was sustained by the regiment here, as it was not actively engaged.

On July 2, at the battle of Hunterstown, one squadron, under command of Captain Duggan, was detailed to hold the road leading into the town from the right front of it. One platoon was deployed as skirmishers on the left of the road leading into town from the rear. This platoon was actively engaged and did good service. The regiment sustained no loss upon this day.

On July 3, engagement 2 or 3 miles to the right of the Two Taverns, in which this regiment charged in close column upon Hampton's brigade, using the saber only, and driving the enemy from the field, with a loss to this regiment of 6 officers and 80 men.

On July 4, the regiment moved with the division toward Monterey Gap. At Fountain Dale, was sent upon a road leading from the right of the town to Fairfield Gap, where the enemy was found occupying it. A charge was made by one squadron, under command of Lieutenant-Colonel Stagg, with success and against superior numbers. The enemy were driven out and the Gap held until the entire column and train had passed.

Here the regiment sustained a heavy loss. Colonel Stagg, in leading the charge, had his horse killed, and was himself seriously injured by the falling of the same. Here Capt. William R. Elliott was mortally wounded, and Lieut. James S. McElhenny killed; 17 men also lost. At Monterey Pass, the regiment lost 2 officers and 6 men.

On July 5 and 6, at Smithsburg, the regiment supported Battery M, Second U. S. Artillery, sustaining no loss.

At Boonsborough on July 8 the regiment was often under fire, but met with no loss.

On July 12, this regiment had the advance to Hagerstown. Five companies were deployed as skirmishers before the town. One squadron, by order of Brigadier-General Kilpatrick, charged into the town, capturing several prisoners, one man only of the squadron being injured

On July 13, the regiment was on outpost duty, and engaged with the enemy most of the day. Loss, 3 men severely wounded.

On the 14th, this regiment was engaged in the action at Falling Waters, and had the honor of capturing 2 battle-flags and so much of the Forty-seventh Regiment Virginia Infantry as was upon the field, being 5 officers and 56 men. Captain Snyder, of this regiment, was mortally wounded while gallantly leading a squadron of the Eighteenth Pennsylvania Cavalry in the streets of Hagerstown, July 6. Since the engagement at Falling Waters this regiment has been under the command of Maj. M. Brewer, and has participated in the following engagements: At Newby's Cross-Roads, Va., July 24; lost, in killed, wounded, and missing, 7 men. A portion of the regiment was engaged in a skirmish at Barbee's Cross-Roads on July 25.

FIFTH MICHIGAN CAVALRY.

June 30.—Was engaged in severe skirmishing with the enemy near Hanover, Pa.

July 3.—At 10 a. m. moved out, and met the enemy on the right, at Gettysburg. The regiment was dismounted to fight on foot on the left of the brigade. Major Ferry was killed. Participated in the several charges made on that day.

July 4.—Participated in the engagement at Monterey Pass, where part of a large train and many prisoners were captured.

July 5.—Was in the engagement at Smithsburg.

July 6.—In engagements at Hagerstown and Williamsport.

July 8.—Moved out on the pike toward Funkstown; deployed as skirmishers on the right, on foot.   Colonel Alger was wounded here. Charged and drove the enemy in force from a piece of woods, which was afterward hotly shelled by the enemy while we held possession. Subsequently the enemy fell rapidly back while the regiment pursued them closely until dark.

July 10 *and* 11.—Picketed in front of Funkstown.

July 12.—Was in the charge at Hagerstown.   Lieutenant-Colonel Gould wounded.   Five squadrons of this regiment dismounted on the left of the city, and drove a superior force from its position.

July 14.—Led the advance toward Williamsport, and charged into the town, meeting no considerable force, and driving the enemy's rear guard across the river, capturing a number of prisoners.

July 17.—After sharp skirmishing with the enemy, drove them from Snicker's Gap, and occupied the same, capturing several prisoners.

July 20.—Occupied Ashby's Gap after slight skirmishing.

July 24.—Had the advance to Newby's Cross-Roads; were at the extreme front during the engagement there, and acted as rear guard when our forces engaged were ordered to fall back.

SIXTH MICHIGAN CAVALRY.

June 30.—This regiment, with the Fifth Michigan Cavalry, occupied Littlestown, Pa.   Company A was sent on a reconnaissance to Westminster.   The remainder of the regiment proceeded to Hanover. Here we met the enemy's skirmishers; drove them to their guns, which we found supported by a heavy force of cavalry.   A sharp engagement followed, in which we were outnumbered by the enemy six to one.   Our loss was some 15 or 20 captured.   The enemy lost several wounded and captured.   Later in the day, Company A, of this regiment, had an engagement with a considerable force of the enemy.

July 2.—This regiment, being in the advance, encountered the enemy's cavalry at Hunterstown.   Here Company A, Capt. H. E. Thompson, charged a brigade of cavalry.   Though suffering great loss, he checked the enemy, so as to enable our battery to be placed in position.   The other squadrons of the regiment drove the enemy back, when the guns of the battery caused them precipitately to surrender the field.

July 3.—Were in engagement at Gettysburg.

July 4.—Were deployed as skirmishers on either side of the road in the attack on Monterey Pass.   Loss, slight.

July 5.—The regiment was employed in supporting a battery in the engagement at Smithsburg.

July 6.—Were ordered to the front at Hagerstown.   On arriving there, General Custer, having driven the enemy, ordered us back.

Same day, were engaged with the enemy at Williamsport, losing 1 officer killed and 3 men wounded.   The First and Sixth Michigan Cavalry were the last to return from the field, protecting our guns and holding the enemy in check while the remainder of the command fell back toward Boonsborough.

July 8.—Met the rebel General Stuart and his forces at the left of the Hagerstown road, near Boonsborough, repulsing and routing his forces, and driving them until night closed the pursuit.

July 11.—Regiment on picket duty before Hagerstown.   During the entire day was engaged skirmishing with the enemy's sharpshooters. Loss, 2 wounded. The enemy was seen to carry several of his dead and wounded from the field.

July 12.—Participated in the capture of Hagerstown.

July 14.—Was in the engagement at Falling Waters. Two companies—B and F, commanded by Major Weber—charged the enemy, who were in position behind earthworks on the crest of a hill. Major Weber and Lieutenant Bolza, with many valuable men, were killed.

July 20.—The regiment participated in the capture of Ashby's Gap; also encountered the enemy strongly intrenched on the opposite side of the Shenandoah, near Berry's Ford. Loss, 3 wounded.

July 24.—Eng ged in reconnaissance from Amissville to Newby's Cross-Roads. Loss, slight.

SEVENTH MICHIGAN CAVALRY.

June 30.—Engaged at Hanover, Pa.

July 2.—The regiment, excepting one squadron, was advanced as dismounted skirmishers in the engagement at Hunterstown.

July 3.—Charged the advance line of the enemy's skirmishers at Gettysburg. Held the field until the advance of the First Michigan Cavalry.

July 4.—Was engaged at Monterey Pass.

July 5.—The regiment supported Battery M, Second U. S. Artillery, at Smithsburg.

July 6.—Participated in the engagement at Hagerstown. Same day at Williamsport.

July 8.—Deployed as skirmishers at Boonsborough.

July 12.—Being temporarily attached to the First Brigade, with it entered Hagerstown under a sharp fire from the enemy, and in the afternoon was advanced to the extreme right of the town, to support the infantry.

July 14.—Was engaged on the right at Falling Waters, capturing from the enemy a 10-pounder Parrott gun, 400 prisoners, the battle-flag of the Fifty-fifth Virginia Infantry, and the colonel of the above-named regiment, with several other officers

BATTERY M, SECOND U. S. ARTILLERY.

June 29.—The battery was assigned to the Second Brigade, Third Division, Cavalry Corps, commanded by Brig. Gen. G. A. Custer.

June 30.—While between Hanover and Abbottstown, Pa., a limber-chest of one caisson exploded, mortally wounding 1 man, killed 2 horses and wounded 2. At Hanover met a battery of the enemy, which was withdrawn after twenty minutes' firing.

July 1.—Was engaged with the enemy at Hunterstown, silencing his battery, and having 4 horses killed, 3 wounded, and 1 wheel disabled.

July 3.—Took up a position on the right of the line at Gettysburg, and was engaged with Stuart's cavalry; battery engaged all day.

July 4.—Was in an engagement at Monterey Pass, where a large portion of Ewell's train and a large number of prisoners were captured.

July 5.—Battery placed in position at Smithsburg, but not used.

July 6.—Marched to Hagerstown; thence to Williamsport, where the battery was engaged. Sergeant Frain was here wounded in the head, and 3 privates were also wounded.

July 8.—Engaged the enemy near Boonsborough.

July 12.—Marched to Hagerstown, and shelled brigade of the enemy's cavalry, our force taking possession of the town.

July 14.—Marched to Falling Waters, via Williamsport, shelling the enemy at the latter place, he being on the opposite side of the river. At Falling Waters the battery was employed throughout the day.

July 24.—Was engaged with the enemy at Battle Mountain, near Newby's Cross-Roads, Lieutenants Clarke, Woodruff, and Hamilton in this, as in every other engagement, performing their duties with skill and judgment.

The non-commissioned officers—Sergeants Morris, [Nicholas] Hasenzahl, and [Michael] Frain, and Corporals [Charles K.] Galligher, [William] Dowdes, [William M.] Baker, and [Robert] Burke—directed their pieces with coolness and precision, doing their duty handsomely in every engagement.

Respectfully submitted.

G. A. CUSTER,
Brigadier-General, Commanding.

Captain ESTES,
   A. A. G., Third Div., Cav. Corps, Army of the Potomac.

—

HEADQUARTERS THIRD DIVISION, CAVALRY CORPS,
Purcellville, Va., July 18, 1863.

Yesterday I sent the Fifth Michigan Cavalry to occupy Snicker's Gap. I received a note from the commanding officer of the regiment last night, informing me that after a brisk fight he had taken possession of the Gap, with a loss of 2 wounded. We captured about 12 of the enemy, belonging to Jones' brigade. All is quiet to-day, with the exception of some little bushwhacking. Mosby is reported at Aldie. We drove White's battalion out of this country yesterday. He captured and paroled 2 of my men. The rebels were collecting all the horses in the county, and were unaware of our presence until we came upon them. I will relieve Colonel De Forest as soon as Colonel Richmond returns from Frederick, Md. I am shoeing as rapidly as possible, and hope soon to be ready for service.

Very respectfully, yours, &c.,

G. A. CUSTER,
Brigadier-General, Commanding.

General PLEASONTON,
   Commanding Cavalry Corps.

P. S.—I have sent scouts to Chester Gap and Front Royal.

—

HEADQUARTERS THIRD DIVISION, CAVALRY CORPS,
Amissville, Va., July 23, 1863—8.30 p. m.

The regiment I sent in the direction of Gaines' Cross-Roads encountered the skirmishers of the enemy (infantry) about 1½ miles from this place, and drove them to within 1 mile of the cross-roads, where they [found the] enemy in force, and in such position as prevented our farther advance. We sustained a loss of 6 or 7 wounded. The regiment now holds its advanced position, which is within 1 mile of

Gaines' Cross-Roads. Since dark, a contraband has come in from Newby's Cross-Roads with very reliable information. He reports the enemy moving hurriedly by Newby's Cross-Roads on the Culpeper road. They have been moving in a continuous column all day, and the rebel soldiers told him their troops would be passing all night. Their column consists of infantry and artillery; no cavalry, and but few wagons. The negro says it is Hill's corps. The enemy seemed to be dreading an attack from our forces, and are making a forced march. Several of the enemy inquired of the contraband if that was the right road to Culpeper and the distance to that point. I do not expect to obtain any more information to-night. I will endeavor to annoy the enemy to-morrow morning as much as it is in my power to do.

I shall keep you informed of what transpires in this vicinity.

Very respectfully,

G. A. CUSTER,
Brigadier-General, Commanding.

Major-General PLEASONTON,
Commanding Cavalry Corps.

HEADQUARTERS THIRD DIVISION, CAVALRY CORPS,
Amissville, Va., July 24, 1863—2 p. m.

I have just returned with my command from the vicinity of Newby's Cross-Roads. I started this morning about daylight with five regiments and two batteries, leaving one regiment on the road to Gaines' Cross-Roads. I have had a very severe engagement, with a loss not exceeding 15 men. I met with no resistance until the head of my column had arrived within one mile and a half of Newby's Cross-Roads, when I took 2 men belonging to Longstreet, who reported that Longstreet's corps was on the road at the cross-roads. I pushed forward with but three regiments and one battery (Pennington's), sending the other battery and two regiments of cavalry back to re-enforce the regiment stationed on the road to Gaines' Cross-Roads, as I had received a note from the commanding officer of the regiment informing me that three regiments of cavalry, one battery, and a considerable force of infantry were in position on his front. When within 1 mile of Newby's Cross-Roads, my advance guard met the enemy's skirmishers (infantry), and drove them back on the main body, strongly posted on a ridge. From a prisoner taken on the ground, I learned that a citizen of this place had gone early this morning to the enemy and informed him that the Yankees had a force of 20,000 at Amissville, and were marching to attack Longstreet's column. This story I now know to have been credited by Longstreet, and he made his dispositions accordingly. I opened upon them with my battery, to which they replied with infantry and artillery, they showing no cavalry. As soon as I ascertained that I could advance no farther, and that an overwhelming force was advancing upon me, I prepared to retire on Amissville. I withdrew one regiment and four guns, leaving two regiments and two guns in advance. Before a position could be obtained for my retiring guns, the enemy burst upon us with a heavy column of infantry, and succeeded in getting between the two advanced regiments with the two guns and the remainder of my command, thus completely cutting off the two regiments and two guns. No road was left to escape by. I placed my four guns in position, supported with but one regiment. With these I managed to check the enemy's advance in the direction of Amissville, but their attention was now directed against the rear guard, now completely cut off and surrounded by infantry and artillery on three sides.

By a circuitous route I managed to convey a message to them, and succeeded in cutting a road through a dense woods, to enable the artillery to retire. The enemy had a line of battle formed for miles on my left. This line kept advancing, and, I having no force to check him, time was everything. Taking advantage of a temporary check in our immediate front, I succeeded in uniting my command, and withdrew deliberately and in excellent order to Amissville, with a loss not exceeding 15. There is not a doubt but that an entire corps was in line of battle and advancing upon me. We have a prisoner from Hill's corps, who was taken in the fight, who states that a part of his corps was there also. Longstreet was convinced that 20,000 men were attacking him. Within one mile and a half of Newby's Cross-Roads we captured a servant of Jeb Stuart's medical director. He is very intelligent and communicative. He ran away from the rebels at 9 p. m. last evening. He saw General Stuart and staff at that time at Gaines' Cross-Roads, where he had just arrived with his column. He heard General Stuart give Fitz. Lee orders to take his brigade and occupy Amissville. (One of my regiments met his advance, and drove it to within one mile and a half of Gaines' Cross-Roads.) Upon arriving at Gaines' Cross-Roads, General Stuart remarked that he would rest awhile. The contraband states that Stuart's force has been marching every night for one week, with not over an hour's rest each night. Stuart proposed pushing on to Culpeper last night. I learned to-day that a force of cavalry had been seen marching in that direction. The horses and men are completely worn out and have nothing to eat. The enemy had fears of being cut off from Culpeper. The regiment which I have between here and Gaines' Cross-Roads have seen a continuous line of troops pass since yesterday; also an immense train of wagons. The latter were moving on a more distant road, probably the Sperryville road. This agrees also with the statement of the contraband. Ewell's corps is also reported by a prisoner to be passing. I am convinced that the rebel army is moving to Culpeper as rapidly as it can march. About one corps and most of Stuart's cavalry have already passed; the other corps are still in rear.

A family has just applied to me for a pass to go to Warrenton, intending to go from there to Washington. They left Culpeper yesterday, and report no rebel troops of any consequence at that point, and met none yesterday on the road. This shows that the rebel army has not reached that point yet.

My horses are greatly in need of forage. My supplies are exhausted. I will send for my train to join me loaded as soon as possible.

I think our position to-day the most critical I was ever in.

Very respectfully, &c.,

G. A. CUSTER,
Brigadier-General, Commanding.

Major-General PLEASONTON.

[P. S.]—I sent you two dispatches last night, but my messengers have not reported yet.

HEADQUARTERS SECOND BRIGADE, THIRD DIVISION,
CAVALRY CORPS, ARMY OF THE POTOMAC,
August 28, 1863.

CAPTAIN: In obedience to instructions, I submit the following report of the operations of this division while under my command:

On the morning of July 15, I assumed command of the division, which was then lying near Falling Waters. At the same time I received orders to march my command and encamp near Berlin, Md.

July 17, crossed the Potomac into Virginia, and encamped near Purcellville. The Fifth Michigan, under Major Trowbridge, was sent forward to occupy Snicker's Gap. The enemy were found in considerable force, but, after a brisk skirmish, were driven through and beyond the Gap, with a loss of 12 prisoners and several wounded. Our loss was 2 slightly wounded.

On July 19 [20], the First and Sixth Michigan Cavalry, under Colonel Town, of the former, occupied Ashby's Gap, after a slight skirmish with the enemy.

On the morning of July 24, I moved from my camp at Amissville, Va., with the First, Fifth, and Sixth Michigan Cavalry and Battery M, Second U. S. Artillery. I proceeded in the direction of Newby's Cross-Roads, at which point I expected to encounter the enemy's column.

My advance guard came upon the skirmishers of the enemy when within a half mile of the road leading from Gaines' Cross-Roads to Culpeper, at a point called Battle Mountain. The force in my front proved to be the corps of A. P. Hill. I attacked with both cavalry and artillery, compelling the enemy to halt his column and form line of battle. Having done this much, and knowing the overwhelming force the enemy was bringing to bear against me, I prepared to withdraw my command. An unlooked-for delay occurring in relieving my skirmishers, the enemy succeeded in pushing two brigades of infantry to my left and rear. By this movement the Fifth and Sixth Michigan Cavalry (Colonel Gray), and two guns of Battery M, under command of Lieutenant Woodruff, were entirely cut off, but, by a display of great courage by both officers and men, Colonel Gray succeeded in extricating his command from this perilous position with but slight loss. Great credit is due to Colonel Gray, commanding Second Brigade, and Lieutenant Woodruff, commanding one section of Battery M, Second U. S. Artillery, for their gallant conduct on this occasion.

I returned to my camp near Amissville, my command having suffered a loss of 30 in killed, wounded, and missing, while that of the enemy was known to be much greater.

On July 30, the Third Division was relieved by the Second Division, Brigadier-General Gregg commanding.

On the 31st, I marched with my command to Warrenton Junction, where the division encamped.

On August 4, I was relieved from the command of the division by the return of Brigadier-General Kilpatrick from leave of absence.

Respectfully submitted.

G. A. CUSTER,
Brigadier-General, Commanding.

Captain ESTES,
Assistant Adjutant-General, Third Div., Cav. Corps.

No. 362.

Report of Col. Nathaniel P. Richmond, First West Virginia Cavalry, commanding First Brigade, Third Division.

CAMP NEAR HARTWOOD CHURCH, VA., *September* 5, 1863.

SIR : In accordance with instructions this day received from division headquarters, I have the honor to make the following report of the part taken by the First Brigade, of this division, in the various actions in which this division was engaged, from June 28 to July 9, at which latter date I was relieved from command of the brigade and ordered upon detached duty :

The First Brigade, Third Division, Cavalry Corps—composed of the following regiments: First West Virginia, Col. N. P. Richmond ; First Vermont, Lieutenant-Colonel Preston; Eighteenth Pennsylvania, Lieutenant-Colonel Brinton ; Fifth New York, Major Hammond; and Battery E, Fourth U. S. Artillery, Lieutenant Elder, commanded by Brigadier-General Farnsworth, U. S. Volunteers— marched from camp near Frederick, Md., on the morning of June 29, and encamped for the night near Littlestown, Pa.

On the morning of June 30, the brigade moved in the direction of Hanover, where the advance of the column arrived about noon of the same day without encountering the enemy, who, from reports of the citizens, was supposed to be quite near our line of march and upon our right flank.

As the Eighteenth Pennsylvania, which was in rear of the brigade, was entering the town, the enemy's cavalry made a dash upon it, opening at the same time with their artillery, which was posted in a wood about half a mile from the town. Owing to the suddenness of the attack, the regiment was thrown into some confusion, and forced back upon the main column, throwing that also into confusion, and for a few moments the enemy evidently had a decided advantage, but at this point General Farnsworth, with great coolness, reformed the command, and charged, driving the enemy out of the town and into the woods in rear of their battery. After some skirmishing, the enemy withdrew, leaving us in possession of the town, near which we encamped until the day following.

The brigade lost in this action : Commissioned officers, 2 killed, 2 wounded, and 3 missing ; enlisted men, 8 killed, 60 wounded, and 86 missing.

This brigade was not engaged with the enemy during the two days following—July 1 and 2—but in the afternoon of July 3, having passed in rear of our forces, then engaged with the enemy near Gettysburg, Pa., General Farnsworth was ordered to charge the enemy's right, which he at once did, making one of the most desperate, and at the same time most successful, charges it has ever been my lot to witness, and during which that gallant officer (General Farnsworth) was killed while in the thickest of the fight. In the death of Brigadier-General Farnsworth this brigade suffered an almost irreparable loss, as a more gallant officer or perfect gentleman cannot, in my opinion, be found.

The brigade lost in this action : Commissioned officers, 3 killed, 4 wounded, and 2 missing; enlisted men, 17 killed, 26 wounded, and 55 missing.

As senior officer of the brigade, I was assigned to command of the same by General Kilpatrick on the morning of July 4, and was ordered to move at once with my command, following the Second Brigade, commanded by Brigadier-General Custer, in the direction of Emmitsburg, Md., passing which place we entered a mountain pass, during the passage of which the brigade of General Custer had quite a spirited skirmish with the enemy, this brigade not being engaged until it reached the summit, after passing which we charged upon a long wagon train of the enemy, capturing nearly the entire train, together with a large number of prisoners.

The brigade lost in this action 1 commissioned officer killed, and enlisted men, 1 killed, 1 wounded, and 6 missing.

On July 5, I marched my command to Smithsburg, when we were attacked by the enemy during the afternoon of the same day, my command not being engaged, with the exception of Elder's battery, which fired a few rounds with good effect. The enemy soon retired, and, in accordance with orders received, I marched my command to near Boonsborough, where I halted, and encamped for the night.

On the morning of July 6, I was ordered by General Kilpatrick to take the advance with my brigade, and move on Hagerstown. When near that place, I ordered two squadrons of the Eighteenth Pennsylvania and one of the First West Virginia to charge into and through the town, which they did in a most gallant manner, driving the enemy, in superior force, through and out of the town with heavy loss to them (the enemy), capturing at the same time the colonel of the Tenth Virginia (rebel) Cavalry. The enemy, receiving heavy re-enforcements, rallied and drove our men back through the town, and were in turn forced to fall back. About this time a battery of the enemy, posted on an eminence about half a mile in rear of the town, opened fire upon us, doing, however, no damage. Lieutenant Elder's battery immediately went into position, and fired several rounds at this battery, one of which blew up a caisson or limber-chest of the enemy. For two or three hours we contested the possession of the place most desperately, but were at last compelled, by the vastly superior force of the enemy, to fall back, which we did in good order for a distance of about 2 miles, fighting over every foot of the ground, retiring two regiments and two guns, and holding the enemy in check with two regiments and two guns until those retiring again took position.

After fighting in this manner for an hour or more, the enemy pressed my command so closely as to throw it into considerable confusion, and one of the guns must have been lost but for the fierce determination with which Lieutenant Elder and his men fought this piece, assisted by a few gallant officers and men of the several regiments who rallied in support of the piece. Four different times did the enemy charge this piece, which was placed upon the pike, and as often were they repulsed with heavy slaughter, Lieutenant Elder pouring his canister into their ranks with most deadly effect. So close was the conflict, that No. 1 of the piece, turning his sponge-staff, knocked one of the enemy from his horse.

Too much credit cannot be given to Lieutenant Elder for the splendid manner in which he fought this piece; and the men of his battery are also deserving of special mention for their bravery and good conduct under fire, and their superior discipline both in camp and upon the march.

The enemy, meeting so warm a reception at every fresh attack upon us, finally drew off the most of his force, and I retired with my command in tolerable order in the direction of Boonsborough, marching about 5 miles, and halting for the night.

The brigade lost in this action 2 commissioned officers killed, 3 wounded, and 7 missing; 12 enlisted men killed, 41 wounded, and 201 missing. The majority of casualties in this engagement were occasioned by the fire of the enemy's infantry, who, posted in almost every house, poured in a most destructive volley upon our men as they charged through the streets.

On July 7, I returned with my brigade to Boonsborough, and went into camp near that place until the next day, when the enemy attacked us in heavy force. Soon after the attack, I received an order to move out the pike and take a position about the center of our line of defense, with which order I proceeded at once to comply.

Upon arriving at the point indicated, I found the enemy in strong force in my immediate front, under cover of a thick piece of woods and large rocks. I immediately deployed one regiment (Eighteenth Pennsylvania) dismounted as skirmishers, and advanced them at double-quick upon the enemy's position, and at the same time ordered one section of Elder's battery to take position and shell the woods, which they did most effectively. About this time one gun of Pennington's battery (M, Second U. S. Artillery), commanded by Lieutenant Clarke, came up and went into position, and by my orders also opened fire upon the woods, from which the enemy soon began a precipitate retreat. I then ordered the First Vermont to charge down the pike, which they at once did, and, taking the gun commanded by Lieutenant Clarke, the Fifth New York and First West Virginia started on the left of the pike in pursuit of the fleeing enemy, who made such excellent time that it was impossible for me again to engage him; so, withdrawing my command, I returned to camp.

The brigade lost in this action 2 enlisted men killed, 5 wounded, and 2 missing.

A full statement of the losses sustained by the several regiments of this brigade in the various actions heretofore mentioned is herewith annexed, marked A.

On the morning of July 9, Col. O. De Forest, Fifth New York Cavalry, having reported for duty, I was relieved from command of the brigade, and ordered with my regiment to Frederick, Md., on provost duty.

It is impossible that I should be able at this late date to make a very full report of the movements of the brigade, especially as there are no regimental reports before me from which to refresh my recollection as to the exact part taken by the several regiments composing the command.

The officers and men, with some few exceptions, behaved themselves in the various engagements in the most praiseworthy manner, and I consider it my duty to make special mention of Lieutenant-Colonel Preston, First Vermont; Lieutenant-Colonel Brinton, Eighteenth Pennsylvania; Major Hammond, Fifth New York, and Major Capehart, First West Virginia, all of whom displayed in the most decided manner that gallantry and coolness so requisite in an officer. Lieutenant Elder has been referred to elsewhere in this report.

All of which is most respectfully submitted.

I have the honor to be, very respectfully, your obedient servant,

N. P. RICHMOND,
Col. First West Virginia Vol. Cav., Formerly Comdg.
First Brig., Third Div., Cav. Corps, Army of the Potomac.

Lieut. L. G. Estes, *A. A. G., Third Div. Cav. Corps.*

A.

Report of Casualties in the First Brigade, Third Division, Cavalry Corps, from June 29 to July 9, 1863.

Commands and places of action.	Date.	Officers.			Enlisted men.		
		Killed.	Wounded.	Missing.	Killed.	Wounded.	Missing.
5th New York Cavalry, Major Hammond commanding:							
Hanover, Pa.	June 30	2	1	...	2	24	13
Gettysburg, Pa.	July 3	...	...	...	1	1	6
Monterey, Pa.	July 4	...	...	...	...	...	4
Hagerstown, Md.	July 6	...	...	4	...	6	75
Boonsborough, Md	July 8	...	...	...	...	1	1
18th Pennsylvania Cavalry, Lieutenant-Colonel Brinton commanding:							
Hanover, Pa.	June 30	..	...	2	4	30	50
Gettysburg, Pa.	July 3	...	...	...	1	5	8
Hagerstown, Md	July 6	1	..	2	7	19	69
Smithsburg, Md.	July 5	.	...	...	...	5	...
1st Vermont Cavalry, Col. E. B. Sawyer commanding:							
Hanover, Pa.	June 30	...	..	...	...	...	8
Gettysburg, Pa	July 3	..	1	1	13	18	35
Hagerstown, Md	July 5	1	1	1	...	...	11
Hagerstown, Md	July 6	...	1	..	4	13	48
Boonsborough, Md	July 8	.	...	...	2	4	1
1st West Virginia Cavalry, Colonel Richmond commanding:							
Gettysburg, Pa.	July 3	2	3	1	2	5	5
Monterey, Pa.	July 4	1	...	...	1	1	1
Hagerstown, Md	July 6	1	2	1	...	1	9
Hanover, Pa.	June 30	...	1	.	2	6	15
Battery E, Fourth U. S. Artillery, Lieutenant Elder commanding:							
Gettysburg, Pa.	July 3	...	...	...	...	4	...
Hagerstown, Md.	July 6	...	...	...	1	2	...
Total		8	10	12	40	141	363

No. 363.

Report of Maj. John Hammond, Fifth New York Cavalry.

————, ——— —, 1863.

BATTLE OF HANOVER, PA., JUNE 30.

On the morning of June 30, this command left Littlestown, Pa., and took up the line of march, being fourth in column, the First Vermont, First West Virginia, and Elder's battery being in advance and the Eighteenth Pennsylvania Cavalry in rear. About noon, we entered the town of Hanover, and halted in the main street. While resting, an attack was made upon the ambulances and stragglers in rear of the Eighteenth Pennsylvania, driving them in upon the regiment, and completely breaking up the column, which ran in confusion up the street upon the rear of my regiment, which had faced about, and was trying to clear the streets of the fugitives preparatory to making a charge upon the advancing column of the enemy. They finally succeeded; and, without waiting for orders, immediately charged upon the enemy, driving them to the outside of town, where we found a large force drawn up in the road as a reserve and received from them a severe fire, causing the men to halt for a moment. General Farnsworth arriving at this time from the front, the men were reformed, and made another charge, driving the rebels in confusion along the road and through the fields. Private [Thomas] Burke, of Company A, captured a battle-flag from the enemy in this charge, and subsequently turned it over to General Kilpatrick.* The enemy, finding himself repulsed, opened upon the town with artillery. Skirmishers were immediately sent forward, and a reserve force placed at the outer edge of town. On returning to the other side, where the rest of the brigade were drawn up in line, I was ordered to act as a support to Elder's battery. Finding that our position endangered the town, we moved around to the eastern side, when, the Second Brigade having returned, I was ordered by General Kilpatrick to flank the enemy's position, and capture the battery, if possible, and to order an advance of the skirmishers on the right, which was done. The enemy, finding what our intentions were, retreated, and we immediately started in pursuit, but failed to come up with him. We were then ordered back, and went into bivouac outside the town. I regret to state that, in the first charge, Adjutant Gall was killed and Major White severely wounded. The officers and men behaved nobly.

Our loss was 2 officers killed, 2 enlisted men killed, 25 wounded, and 10 missing.

BATTLE OF GETTYSBURG, PA., JULY 3.

At about 7 o'clock on the morning of July 3, the command was ordered to move, and marched toward the left of our line of battle. On arriving upon the field, we were ordered into position as supports for Elder's battery. Soon after taking position in the edge of some timber, the enemy obtained the range so exactly as to throw their shells into our midst, doing considerable damage. General Farnsworth then ordered me to get under cover of a ridge a little more to the left, which was done. Shortly after, I was ordered to divide my command into two sections, and send Major Bacon with one on the right, while I took the other on the left, of the Eighteenth Pennsylvania, and, in connection with them, make a charge upon one of the enemy's guns, which was very troublesome. We moved forward some distance, when the enemy removed the piece, and we were ordered back, and took up a position in rear of our battery, and stood to horse during the remainder of the fight. At night we withdrew a short distance to the rear, and did picket duty upon the field.

BATTLE OF SMITHSBURG, MD., JULY 5.

As the command was in line awaiting the order to march, the artillery of the enemy opened to the right of the town, when I was ordered with Elder's battery to take position in rear of the town. I posted the regiment in a corn-field on the left of the battery, and for a short time was exposed to the enemy's shells, which did no damage, however. After a time I was ordered to take position upon a high ridge to the left about half a mile, and the first squadron, under Captain McGuine, was sent forward to reconnoiter, as there were evidences of a flank movement by the enemy; but at dusk the reconnaissance, being completed, reported the enemy retreating. We then took up our line of march, and arrived at Boonsborough at 12 p. m., where we went into bivouac.

BATTLE OF HAGERSTOWN, MD., JULY 6.

At 8 a. m. orders were received for the command to march, and we moved on toward Hagerstown. Arrived within a mile and a half of

---

* A medal of honor awarded to Sergeant Burke for this service.

the town, and took position in rear of Elder's battery. A few rebel cavalry only being reported in town, we were again ordered on. Our advance having been repulsed by a force of concealed sharpshooters in the town, and the enemy's artillery opening to our right, skirmishers were thrown out in that direction. I was ordered to dismount my carbineers and send them forward into town as a check upon the sharpshooters, and to take position with the rest of my command near the seminary, in support of the battery. After awhile the enemy's sharpshooters became annoying to the artillerists, and a change of position was ordered, the First Vermont, First West Virginia, and Fifth New York alternately supporting the battery during the change of position toward the left of the town. The enemy closely followed and kept up a sharp cannonade, which did no damage beyond wounding and killing a few horses. The enemy being in superior numbers, we were ordered to fall back, and I was ordered to bring up the rear with my regiment. Finally a stand was made about 2 miles from town, on the Williamsport road. One gun was placed in the road, with the First Vermont on the right and my regiment on the left in an open field. I was ordered to throw out one squadron as skirmishers, which was done under a severe fire of the enemy, who followed us closely. They swarmed in the woods on both flanks, and poured in their fire, which was so severe as to throw my men into some confusion. Hearing that the enemy were coming down a small by-road in our rear, I detached Lieutenant Dimmick with a small command to drive them back. In a few minutes they were driven back with loss, the lieutenant being severely wounded. I then sent Captain Penfield with more men to hold the way at all hazards, since which time I have not seen him. He and several others had their horses killed under them, and were probably captured. After being subjected to a very severe fire in an exposed position, and aiding in repelling several charges of the enemy, I received orders to fall back, which I did, though not without loss. The pursuit of the enemy being checked, we retired with the rest of the command, and went into bivouac. Next day reached Boonsborough, and encamped.

Our loss was 5 officers and about 100 enlisted men wounded and missing. Of the number killed, nothing definite is known.

BATTLE OF BOONSBOROUGH, MD., JULY 8.

The enemy having advanced from Hagerstown and made an attack upon our forces, I received orders to move down to the field and support Captain Elder's battery. I put the column in motion, and moved over the hill, and took position on a ridge outside the town, on the left of the pike leading to Hagerstown. The battery opened upon the skirmishers of the enemy, and our skirmishers being ordered forward, drove those of the enemy. They, being re-enforced, in turn drove ours nearly back to the guns. I was ordered to send forward my carbineers to re-enforce them, which was done, and the enemy was gradually forced to retire. By sundown the enemy was in full retreat, and I was ordered to return to the camp I had left in the morning. Although the enemy's shells fell fast about us during the fight, I am happy to state we met with no loss in men and but few losses in horses.

Very respectfully submitted.

JOHN HAMMOND,
Major, Commanding.

No. 364.

Reports of Maj. William B. Darlington, Eighteenth Pennsylvania Cavalry.

STAFFORD COURT-HOUSE, VA.,
August 9, 1863.

SIR: I have the honor to submit the following report of the battles in which this regiment has been engaged since June 29 :

On June 30, while passing through the town of Hanover, Pa., it was attacked by a brigade of rebel cavalry under General Stuart. Several squadrons had formed, when some ambulances, which were in the rear, were driven by the frightened drivers through our ranks, creating so much confusion that we were compelled to retreat through the town, when we reformed. We were not afterward engaged during the day. This is the only engagement in which the regiment has been broken. Lieut. T. P. Shields, with some 25 men, received the enemy's charge on our flank bravely, but was overpowered and captured.

Casualties, 4 killed, 27 wounded, 50 missing; total, 81.

On the evening of July 2, in the skirmish at Hunterstown, Pa., the regiment was again under fire. It was assigned to the support of the battery. We lost only 1 man wounded.

On July 3, were moved to the left of the line of the Union army at Gettysburg. The regiment was employed in skirmishing during most of the day.

At about 5 p. m., it was recalled, formed, and ordered to charge, which it did with energy, and remained under fire until recalled.

Casualties, 1 killed, 5 wounded, 16 missing; total, 22.

On the night of July 4, in connection with the rest of the division, it captured the train of General Ewell's (Confederate) corps.

Casualties, 1 man missing.

On July 5, at Smithsburg, the regiment was deployed as skirmishers, and remained in position till recalled.

Casualties, 3 men missing.

On July 6, was in the engagement at Hagerstown. The First and Third Battalions charged through the town; drove three times their number back to the enemy's batteries on the hill, when they were ordered back. They retired in good order. In this charge they captured several prisoners, among them a rebel colonel. Subsequently, when the division retired, the regiment was assigned to the support of a battery, and, though hard pressed, held its position, and brought off all the guns.

Casualties, 8 killed, 18 wounded, 65 missing; total, 91.

On July 8, when Stuart attacked the First and Third Cavalry Divisions, our regiment was deployed as skirmishers, and subsequently supported a battery. We suffered no loss.

On July 12, we again entered Hagerstown, and on it and the following day skirmished at long range. No casualties.

At the battle of July 14, at Falling Waters, but not engaged.

On July 24, the regiment present at Amissville, but not under fire.

I am, very respectfully, your obedient servant,

W. B. DARLINGTON,
Major, Commanding Eighteenth Pennsylvania Cavalry.

Capt. L. SIEBERT, Assistant Adjutant-General.

STAFFORD COURT-HOUSE, VA.,
August 9, 1863.

SIR: I have the honor to report that, on the night of July 2 and 3, the regiment moved from Hunterstown to the rear center of the Union army at Gettysburg.

Early in the forenoon of July 3, we were moved to the left in line of battle. During the afternoon the regiment was deployed as skirmishers. At or about 5 p. m. it was recalled, formed in column of squadrons, and ordered to charge a chosen and naturally strong position of the enemy in the woods and to the left of Round Top Mountain. The charge was made with energy, and, although checked by a strong force of rebel infantry, posted behind a stone wall, yet the squadrons were not broken, but remained under a heavy fire until recalled.

Casualties, 1 killed, 5 wounded, 16 missing; total, 22.

I am, very respectfully, your obedient servant,

W. B. DARLINGTON,
Major, Comdg. Eighteenth Pennsylvania Cavalry.

Capt. L. SIEBERT,
Assistant Adjutant-General.

No. 365.

Reports of Lieut. Col. Addison W. Preston, First Vermont Cavalry.

HARTWOOD CHURCH, VA.,
August 7, 1863.

SIR: I have the honor to make the following report of the part taken by the First Vermont Cavalry in the engagement at Hanover, Pa., June 30:

Our column having been attacked in the rear, I was ordered by Brigadier-General Farnsworth to send a squadron to aid in repelling the attack. This was promptly obeyed by sending Major Bennett, with Companies M and D, who assisted in repelling the enemy by a vigorous charge, capturing about 20 prisoners. I was afterward ordered to support Elder's battery, which was done with the First and Second Battalions. The Third Battalion, under Major Bennett, by order of the brigade commander, held an important position on the left of the town. This battalion during the day was warmly engaged, and succeeded in repelling several attacks of the enemy.

Our loss in this engagement was 1 wounded and 16 missing.

Very respectfully, your obedient servant,

A. W. PRESTON,
Lieutenant-Colonel, Comdg. First Vermont Cavalry.

Capt. L. SIEBERT,
Assistant Adjutant-General.

HARTWOOD CHURCH, VA.,
August 7, 1863.

SIR: I have the honor to report that in the engagement at Hunterstown, July 2, this regiment was deployed as skirmishers on the right of the Second Brigade and to the front and right of Elder's battery. It was here subjected to a severe fire from the enemy's guns. I remained in this position until the division retired. In this engagement I have no loss to report.

Very respectfully, your obedient servant,

A. W. PRESTON,
Lieutenant-Colonel, Comdg. First Vermont Cavalry.

Capt. L. SIEBERT,
    Assistant Adjutant-General.

—

HARTWOOD CHURCH, VA., *August 7*, 1863.

SIR : I have the honor to report the part borne by the First Vermont Cavalry in the engagement at Gettysburg, July 3.

In approaching the enemy's position on their extreme right, this regiment had the advance, Companies A, D, E, and I, dismounted, and were deployed as skirmishers. They soon succeeded in driving the enemy behind their breastworks and from behind some buildings on our extreme left.

Heavy skirmishing was kept up along this line through the entire day, the left of the line being supported by one squadron mounted (Companies L and F), which suffered considerably from the enemy's sharpshooters. Company M, of the Third Battalion, under Captain Woodward, was sent to reconnoiter the enemy's position on our right. This detachment, connected with our infantry in that direction, discovered the enemy's position.

At 5 p. m., in the charge made by General Farnsworth, the Second Battalion of this regiment, under Major Wells, formed the right, and was led by Brigadier-General Farnsworth in person. This charge was made over severe obstacles, but succeeded in breaking the enemy's lines. Many of our dead, together with the body of General Farnsworth, were found in the rear of the position held by the enemy's second line. I was immediately ordered by Brigadier-General Kilpatrick to support this charge with the balance of my regiment, which I did with the First Battalion, under Captain Parsons, and a part of the Third Battalion, under Captain Grover. In charging over the wall and hill carried by the first column, I encountered a very large force of the enemy, which had been sent in from their left to re-establish their line and cut off the retreat of the first column. The contest for the possession of this hill was most desperate. Being temporarily checked in a direct attack, I obliqued my force to the right, and succeeded in gaining the top of the hill by a flank movement. The opposing forces were now completely intermingled, and the contest became a hand-to-hand one, in which our sabers were effectually used. The enemy, being completely cut up, surrendered in squads, and were sent to the rear. Had I had two companies of carbineers at my command, I think I could have held this position and removed my wounded, but, being exposed to the fire of the enemy's batteries and sharpshooters, I was obliged to fall back.

Both officers and men deserve the warmest praise for the coolness, courage, and heroism which they displayed in this engagement. Individual instances of bravery were too numerous to mention. Where all did so well it would be difficult to say who did best. All have my heartfelt gratitude.

Our loss on this occasion was 12 killed, 20 wounded (2 of whom have since died), and 35 missing.

In this charge, Captain Parsons, Company L, Captain Cushman, Company E, and Lieutenant Cheeney, Company C, were severely wounded.

Very respectfully, your obedient servant,

A. W. PRESTON,
Lieutenant-Colonel, Commanding First Vermont Cavalry.

Capt. L. SIEBERT,
Assistant Adjutant-General.

—

HARTWOOD CHURCH, VA.,
August 7, 1863.

SIR: I have the honor to report that, having been ordered by General Kilpatrick at 12 o'clock on the morning of July 5, at Monterey, Md., to proceed with my command to Smithsburg and destroy such of the enemy's trains as could be found in the vicinity, I moved rapidly to the point directed, arriving there at 3 a. m. Not finding anything here, I moved to Leitersburg, 5 miles distant, where I intercepted and captured 100 prisoners, comprising cavalry and infantry, and one drove of cattle and many wagons. A large train of the enemy having passed two hours previous, I reported the same to the general commanding, and pressed on as far as Hagerstown, 6 miles. Not succeeding in overtaking them, and having marched our horses thirty-six hours with scarcely any food or rest, I went into camp near Hagerstown, throwing out strong pickets. Learning that the rebel General Jenkins was approaching on the Greencastle road, I reported the same to the general commanding at Smithsburg, and received orders to join him at Boonsborough, which I did the same night. I lost many horses, worn out by fatigue and want of food.

Very respectfully, your obedient servant,

A. W. PRESTON,
Lieutenant-Colonel, Commanding First Vermont Cavalry.

Capt. L. SIEBERT,
Assistant Adjutant-General.

—

HARTWOOD CHURCH, VA.,
August 7, 1863.

SIR: I have the honor to report that in the engagement at Hagerstown, July 6, the First Vermont Cavalry was disposed as follows:

The First Battalion, under Captain Scofield, were deployed as skirmishers on the extreme right of the town, and succeeded in driving the enemy from a strong position behind a house, and occupied it. Companies A and D, under Captain Cummings and Lieutenant Edwards, were sent into the town, and succeeded in holding a position there until ordered in the afternoon to retire. In so doing, 16 of my men were cut off, but were secreted by the Union citizens until our troops reoccupied the place on the 12th instant. The Second Battalion and one squadron of the Third Battalion remained in line in rear of the town. When our forces retired from Hagerstown in the afternoon, I was ordered by Colonel Richmond, commanding brigade, to act as rear guard, and I disposed my command accordingly. We were severely pressed in front and on the right flank by the enemy, and twice we were nearly surrounded.

When the charge was made upon Elder's battery, about 2 miles from Hagerstown, I sent the First Battalion to assist the Fifth New York in support of the battery, while I repulsed a flank attack with the balance of my command. Captain Beeman, with the Third Squadron, whom I ordered to hold a strong position, being cut off, was ordered to surrender. He coolly replied, "I don't see it," and escaped by leaping a fence upon his extreme right flank.

I again endeavored to hold another position near the toll-gate, on the Williamsport road. Captain Grover, with Company K, made a vigorous charge upon the enemy's column in the road, and repulsed them temporarily, but the enemy's sharpshooters told too severely upon him, and he was obliged to fall back. Captain Woodward, Company M, fell here, and many other brave men. About half a mile to the rear of this position I rallied my men again, and, giving three cheers, succeeded in turning back the enemy. At this point we were so intermingled with the enemy that we suffered equally from our own as well as rebel batteries.

About half a mile from this position, I came upon Brigadier-General Kilpatrick at dark with the balance of our division, and marched to Jones' Cross-Roads.

Officers and men on this occasion behaved well, and charged desperately, though greatly outnumbered.

Our loss in this engagement will be, as near as can be ascertained, 5 killed, 16 wounded, and 55 missing.

Very respectfully, your obedient servant,

A. W. PRESTON,
Lieutenant-Colonel, Commanding First Vermont Cavalry.

Capt. L. SIEBERT,
Assistant Adjutant-General.

—

HARTWOOD CHURCH, VA.,
August 7, 1863.

SIR: I have the honor to report that in the engagement at Boonsborough July 8, the First Vermont Cavalry was held in reserve until 3 o'clock in the afternoon, when I was ordered to send one squadron of carbineers to the extreme right of our lines, which I obeyed by sending the Sixth Squadron, under Captain Cummings, who succeeded in gaining position very near one of the enemy's batteries, and annoyed them severely. I was again ordered to send another squadron of carbineers to the front. I immediately sent forward Companies E and I, under Captain Scofield, who took position in front, near the Hagerstown road, and aided in pressing the enemy back at night. A battalion being now ordered to the front, I sent Major Bennett, with Companies L, F, K, and M, to report to the brigade commander. This force took a position in the front and on the right of the road leading to Hagerstown, and suffered severely from the enemy's batteries. The Second (and remaining) Battalion, now numbering but 55 men, was ordered to the front, and, under Major Wells, was ordered to charge the enemy, in a strong position on the Hagerstown road, at a point where there was a bridge. The charge was spiritedly made and sabers freely used, as the heads of my men will attest; but, not being in sufficient numbers, our men were obliged to come back, but not without inflicting serious injury upon the enemy. I was now ordered to draw in my various detachments, and to go into camp in my old position, which I accordingly obeyed.

The loss in this action is 2 killed, 8 wounded, and 5 missing.

Very respectfully, your obedient servant,

A. W. PRESTON,
Lieutenant-Colonel, Commanding First Vermont Cavalry.

Capt. L. SIEBERT,
Assistant Adjutant-General.

No. 366.

Report of Col. Edward B. Sawyer, First Vermont Cavalry.

GROVETON, VA.,
October 24, 1863.

SIR: I have the honor of submitting to you the following report of the part taken by this regiment in the Maryland and Virginia campaign, from July 10 to 25:

I rejoined the regiment at Boonsborough on July 10, having been separated from it since the 22d ultimo by painful but unavoidable necessity. In this interim the regiment had passed through an arduous but brilliant campaign. I found it much reduced in officers and men, but its spirit as good as ever. The enemy, though beaten at Gettysburg, was in our immediate front in strong force, and another great and decisive battle was daily expected. We were ordered to advance on the afternoon of the 10th, and night marches and skirmishing and picketing constituted our duties. We had advanced and occupied Hagerstown on the 12th.

On the afternoon of July 13, I was ordered to report with my regiment to General Kilpatrick at his headquarters. I found it to be his intention to make a reconnaissance to the left of the enemy's line of works above the town with my regiment and some Pennsylvania militia. Leaving the town, the infantry took the advance. Just at the outskirts of the town, a strong line of the enemy's pickets was encountered in front of their earthworks. I was ordered to send forward a squadron as skirmishers, which I did, supporting them with my whole command. My skirmishers took the advance, and my whole command passed the infantry, who were covered by a strong fence.

Captain Cummings commanded the skirmishers, and he and Lieutenant Grant led them up in gallant style. A very spirited skirmish ensued, our boys, now assisted by the infantry skirmishers, steadily driving the enemy. Here General Kilpatrick ordered me to send a squadron—"only a squadron"—to charge. The enemy's line of skirmishers was deployed on the right and left of the road, which had a very strong and high fence on each side. Captain Scofield and Lieutenant Newton, with Companies L and F, led the charge. I ordered them to charge up the road, passing the enemy's skirmish line, and to capture some of the enemy if possible. By this time the enemy had retreated to near their earthworks and to the cover of the woods, and their fire, raking the road, was sharp and galling. Led by Captain Scofield and Lieutenant Newton, the boys absolutely "pitched in" to this charge. It had become apparent as they advanced that some force was in their front on the road covered by the woods. The squadron never faltered. The enemy now opened a heavy fire from their batteries, but the boys went gallantly on until they had nearly reached the woods, when they received a terrific volley from a force of about 300 infantry or dismounted cavalry, under cover of the woods and fence, which compelled them to return; not, however, until they had accomplished their object, so far as to capture 2 of the enemy, whom they brought back as they retired.

Skirmishing continued until the enemy were driven inside their works and silenced, when we were ordered back to Hagerstown.

In the charge Captain Scofield was wounded and taken prisoner; and Lieutenant Newton's horse was hit in the shoulder by a musket-ball, which passed up and through the saddle, giving the lieutenant a very narrow escape with his life. My loss in killed, wounded, and missing was 13 men and 1 officer.

This affair, though not as considerable as many the regiment had before and has since passed through, was one which tested the spirit and mettle of the men and officers severely and gave me good earnest for the future. Adjutant Gates did efficient service in promptly communicating my orders, and Majors Wells and Bennett showed coolness under a severe fire while forming their battalions to cover them from the enemy's batteries. Lieutenant-Colonel Preston, having been absent when the regiment moved, did not go with us; but, returning to camp and finding we had gone, followed, and arrived in season to render me important assistance.

Next morning we followed the enemy to Williamsport, and were in reserve at the thrilling affair at Falling Waters.

On the 15th, we returned to Boonsborough, and next day marched to Harper's Ferry, via Berlin, and on the 17th crossed the Shenandoah. Passing down the south bank of the Potomac, we arrived at Purcellville on the 18th. Next day marched to Ashby's Gap.

On the 20th, the Gap was occupied by our forces, and we returned to Upperville.

On the 21st, we marched to Snickersville, and on the 22d occupied the Gap, and held it until the night of the 23d, and returned to Upperville.

On the 24th, marched from Upperville and crossed the Rappahannock, and bivouacked near Amissville.

On the 25th, joined the brigade at that place, and was immediately placed in command, of the First Brigade, of Kilpatrick's division, which was already formed upon our arrival to the front. I here turned the command over to Lieutenant-Colonel Preston, and excused it from duty that day in consideration of its recent great fatigues, and proceeded with the remainder of the brigade to Gaines' Cross-Roads. I did not again return to my regiment until August 22. I have, however, had command of it as brigade commander meantime, yet its particular affairs in this interim are more properly reported to you by its then immediate commander. I shall make its operations from August 22 to September 12 the subject of a separate report.

Very respectfully, your obedient servant,

EDWARD B. SAWYER,
Colonel, Commanding.

PETER T. WASHBURN,
Adjutant and Inspector General, State of Vermont.

No. 367.

Report of Maj. Charles E. Capehart, First West Virginia Cavalry.

HEADQUARTERS FIRST WEST VIRGINIA CAVALRY,
Near Hartwood Church, Va., August 17, 1863.

SIR : In compliance with an order emanating from brigade headquarters, I have the honor to submit the following as the report of
the First West Virginia Cavalry, from the beginning to the end of
the late campaign in Maryland and Pennsylvania :

On June 24, in compliance with an order from division headquarters, this regiment (under command of Col. N. P. Richmond), together
with the First Vermont and Fifth New York Cavalry, which formed
the Third Brigade, Third Division, Twenty-second Army Corps, Department of Washington, left their camp at Fairfax Court-House,
Va., and moved to Edwards Ferry; thence to Poolesville, Crampton's
Gap, and Frederick City, Md., where the division was reorganized.
Major-General Stahel was relieved of the command of the division
and Brig. Gen. J. Kilpatrick assigned in his stead.   Col. O. De Forest
was relieved of the command of the brigade and Brigadier-General
Farnsworth assigned to command it.

On June 29, we moved from near Frederick, and on the 30th met
and repulsed the enemy at Hanover, Pa.   The First West Virginia
was in the advance of the brigade, and had passed through the town,
when the Eighteenth Pennsylvania (which was now attached to the
brigade), which was at the time marching in the rear, was attacked
by both cavalry and artillery.

This regiment, First West Virginia, by order formed in line of
battle, and charged back through the town, driving the enemy's cavalry back to their artillery and to the cover of the woods.   Lieut. M.
Carroll, Company F, was severely wounded; Sergeant [George] Collins, Company L, and Sergeant [Garrett C.] Selby, Company F, were
killed, and 4 others badly wounded, and 1 officer (Lieutenant Wheeler,
Company E) and 17 men taken prisoners.

On July 1, we marched to Abbottstown; thence to Berlin and a
point 10 miles beyond, and moved back on the night of the same day,
not finding any of the enemy.

July 2, we marched from Abbottstown to Oxford; thence to Hunterstown, and picketed the front of the enemy's left wing.

On the morning of the 3d, we moved up to a point immediately in
the rear of the center of the Army of the Potomac, then near Gettysburg.

At 10 a. m. our brigade (then First Brigade, Third Division) was
ordered to move to the extreme right wing of the enemy, and, if
possible, hold in check any movement they might make at that
point.

At 3 p. m. we found them in position with infantry, cavalry, and
artillery.   General Kilpatrick ordered General Farnsworth to make
ready to charge them.   Everything was in readiness in a moment.
The First West Virginia was ordered to the front, and ordered to
charge upon them.   Col. N. P. Richmond led the regiment, with
Maj. Charles E. Capehart and Acting Majors Farabee and Carman,
which made one of the most desperate charges during the present
rebellion.

I cannot fail to refer you to the defensive position the enemy had
availed themselves of, which is one that above all others is the worst
for a cavalry charge—that is, behind stone fences so high as to pre-

clude the possibility of gaining the opposite side without dismounting and throwing them down. The whole ground over which we charged was very adverse in every particular, being broken and uneven and covered with rock. Neither can I fail to bring to your notice that this regiment here charged upon infantry, and still did not falter in any of its movements until it had scaled two stone fences and had penetrated some distance the enemy's lines, which had kept up a continual fire of musketry. The entire regiment was entirely surrounded, when they received an order to return. The First Texas Regiment having occupied the ground over which we advanced, and as that was by far the best way to return, an order was given by Col. N. P. Richmond for the officers and men to cut their way through, which they did, and brought with them quite a number of prisoners. Any one not cognizant of the *minutiæ* of this charge upon infantry, under cover of heavy timber and stone fences, will fail to form a just conception of its magnitude.

The casualties of the regiment were 5 killed and 4 wounded.

Apparently our mission there had been filled, for we withdrew some 3 miles from where the engagement had taken place, and bivouacked in the open field.

On the morning of July 4, Col. N. P. Richmond was placed in command of the brigade, *vice* General Farnsworth, who had been killed in the engagement of the previous day. Maj. Charles E. Capehart took command of the regiment, and assigned Captains Farabee and Carman as acting majors.

At 10 o'clock we moved down the enemy's left to Emmitsburg; thence up through a mountain gap to Monterey Springs, where quite a body of the enemy were found guarding a wagon train. The Second Brigade (General Custer) had been deployed as skirmishers, and had engaged them (the enemy) for an hour, when Major Capehart received an order to report with his regiment to General Kilpatrick, then at Monterey house. On his doing so, General Kilpatrick ordered him to report with his regiment to General Custer, who was at that time engaged with the enemy a half mile in advance. On his reporting to General Custer, he (Major Capehart) was ordered to charge upon the wagon train, and, if possible, take it. Major Capehart immediately informed his officers and men of the duty which devolved upon them. The charge was ordered, and, with a whoop and yell, the regiment dashed down upon the train. The night was one of inky darkness; nothing was discernible a half dozen paces ahead. As the advance came up to the train, they received a heavy volley of musketry, which at once showed the exact position of the enemy. Onward they dashed, and a hand-to-hand conflict ensued. The scene was wild and desolating. The road lay down a mountain side, wild and rugged. On either side of the road was a heavy growth of underbrush, which the enemy had taken as a fit place to conceal themselves and fire from upon us. The road was interspersed with wagons and ambulances for a distance of 8 miles, and the whole train was taken—300 wagons, 15 ambulances, together with all the horses and mules attached. The number of prisoners taken was 1,300, including 200 commissioned officers. The casualties of this regiment were 2 killed and 2 wounded.

The only assistance Major Capehart had was 40 men of the First Ohio Cavalry, under command of Captain Jones. With but two exceptions, the officers and men acquitted themselves as true and brave soldiers.

July 5, we moved to Smithsburg, and, while resting there, the enemy appeared with artillery. This regiment was ordered to guard a mountain pass, and in the evening was called in, and joined the command, and marched to Boonsborough.

July 6, we marched from Boonsborough to Hagerstown, where a part of the regiment—one squadron—was ordered to charge the town. After this was executed, two squadrons were ordered to the right of the town as skirmishers, but held their position but a little time, as the enemy advanced in superior numbers.

In the engagement we lost 2 killed, 4 wounded, and 14 missing. The superior numbers of the enemy caused us to fall back on the Williamsport road. Here this regiment brought up the rear, and supported Battery E, Fourth Regular Artillery. The enemy charged this battery four different times, and were repulsed as often. Finally their superiority of numbers caused us to withdraw, via Antietam Creek, to Boonsborough, arriving there on the morning of the 7th.

On the 8th, the enemy advanced from Hagerstown, and we became engaged with them, and fought until evening. This regiment supported Battery E, Fourth Regular Artillery.

July 9, Colonel N. P. Richmond was relieved of the command of the brigade, and the regiment, by order, went to Frederick City, Md., for the purpose of doing provost duty and arresting all stragglers, and to form a stragglers' camp. The regiment remained here until July 16, when we left and moved to Berlin; thence to Purcellville, Va., where we joined the brigade.

On the 19th, we moved to Upperville.

On the 22d, to Piedmont.

On the 23d, to Amissville, arriving there in the evening. This regiment was ordered on picket at Gaines' Cross-Roads. Immediately after leaving, we met the enemy, and drove them to within half a mile of the cross-roads, where we met them in force. Major Capehart ordered the regiment to charge, which it did, but we were repulsed by infantry and cavalry. Here we had 2 of our men wounded. Our picket line was finally established within three-quarters of a mile of the cross-roads, where we remained until the evening of the 24th, when we were relieved.

We then moved back, and went into camp at Amissville. Remained there until the 30th, when we moved to Warrenton Junction, and on the evening of the 31st the regiment was ordered on duty to Stafford Court-House, Va.

All of which is respectfully submitted.

CHARLES E. CAPEHART,
Major, Comdg. First West Virginia Cavalry.

Capt. L. SIEBERT, *A. A. G., First Brig., Third Div.*

No. 368.

Report of Capt. James M. Robertson, Second U. S. Artillery, commanding First Brigade, Horse Artillery.

HEADQUARTERS FIRST BRIGADE, HORSE ARTILLERY,
August 22, 1863.

SIR: I have the honor to submit the following report of the operations of the First Brigade, Horse Artillery, since June 28:

On June 28, I reported with my brigade—consisting of Lieutenant

Pennington's battery (M, Second U. S. Artillery), Elder's battery (E, Fourth U. S. Artillery), Heaton's battery (B and L, Second U. S. Artillery), and Captain Martin's (Sixth Independent New York) battery of horse artillery—to General Pleasonton, commanding Cavalry Corps. In obedience to instructions from General Pleasonton, two batteries (Pennington's and Elder's) were detailed, and left camp at daylight on the 29th, to report for duty with the Third Division, Cavalry Corps. These two batteries have been on duty with this division since that time, and make their reports through its commanding officer.

At 8 a. m. I was ready to move with the remaining two batteries (Heaton's and Martin's), but owing to the road being blocked with troops and wagons, I was unable to move until 4 p. m. After marching about 2 miles, was joined by Captain Daniels, commanding Ninth Michigan Battery, who reported to me, and was assigned to my brigade by order of the general commanding Cavalry Corps.

Continuing the march, I arrived at Middleburg, Md., at 2 a. m. the 30th, when I fed, and rested my command until 9 a. m., and then marched to Taneytown, arriving at 4.30 p. m., and remained encamped at the latter place until 11.30 p. m. July 1, when I marched, and arrived near the battle-ground of Gettysburg at 5.30 a. m. on the 2d, and reported to the general commanding the Cavalry Corps, and by his direction held my batteries in reserve near the battle-ground until nearly dark, when, by his direction, I moved back about 2 miles on the Baltimore pike, and encamped for the night.

On the morning of the 3d, I again moved to the front, and occupied the same ground as the day previous, and, by direction of General Pleasonton, I reported to Brigadier-General Tyler, to assist him with the Reserve Artillery. While out with General Tyler examining our lines, with a view of selecting points for artillery, the enemy opened fire with all his batteries, and we returned to our commands. Finding that the reserve occupied a very exposed position, it was ordered to fall back to where it could get cover from the fire of the enemy. While executing this move, General Tyler's horse was shot and killed under him. From the extreme heat and over-exertion, General Tyler received a sunstroke, which prostrated him for the time, and he turned over the command of the entire reserve to me.

Soon after this (about 12 m.), there being an urgent demand for rifled artillery, and having no other at my disposal, I sent forward the battery of horse artillery (Ninth Michigan) commanded by Capt. J. J. Daniels, who reported to General Newton, and was placed in position by him, where he remained, doing good execution, until the close of the battle.

Captain Daniels' loss in this engagement was 1 man killed, 4 wounded, and 23 horses killed. Captain Daniels bivouacked for the night on the field where he had fought. Captain Daniels in his report of this engagement (a copy of which report I herewith inclose) does not particularize any officers or soldiers of his battery, but speaks of all in terms of the highest praise for their coolness and steadiness under fire. Captain Daniels and the officers and men under his command deserve all the more credit, as this was the first time his battery had ever been engaged.

General Tyler having recovered so as to resume his duties, about dark I moved back on the Baltimore pike with my two remaining batteries to the camp occupied by me the night previous, and was joined by Captain Daniels on the 4th.

I remained here until 10 o'clock on the 5th, when I marched, and arrived at Creagerstown at 10 o'clock the same evening.

Marched from Creagerstown at 9 a. m. the 7th, and arrived at Middletown, via Frederick City, at 10 p. m.

On the 9th, I moved forward to Boonsborough, where two more of my batteries were detached—Captain Martin's (Sixth Independent New York) battery to General Gregg, Second Division, Cavalry Corps, and Lieutenant Heaton's battery (B and L, Second U. S. Artillery) to General Buford, First Division, Cavalry Corps. These two batteries have been on duty with these divisions since that time, and make their reports to these headquarters. Having but one battery remaining with me, by direction of General Pleasonton I reported to General Tyler to assist him with the Artillery Reserve should it be called into action, and remained with it until our arrival at Berlin on July 15, without anything happening worthy of note.

On the 16th, Lieutenant Williston, commanding Battery D, Second U. S. Artillery, and Lieutenant King, commanding Battery A, Fourth U. S. Artillery, each with four light 12-pounder guns, were assigned to my brigade, and ordered to be equipped as horse artillery. Horses were procured at Berlin on July 19, but equipments could not be obtained at that place.

With the three batteries, Williston's, King's and Daniels', I marched from Berlin at 6 p. m. July 19, and arrived and encamped near Warrenton, Va., on the 25th, without anything transpiring worthy of note.

On the 30th, the last of the equipments were received for the two light 12-pounder batteries, and on the 31st they were completed and ready for active field service.

Great credit is due to First Lieut. J. H. Bell, of the Sixth New York Cavalry (the only officer on my staff), for the efficient manner in which he has performed the duties of acting assistant adjutant-general, assistant commissary of subsistence, and acting assistant quartermaster, not only in procuring horses and supplies of all kinds for the batteries which were held in reserve, but also for procuring and forwarding horses and other supplies to those on duty with the different cavalry divisions.

Very respectfully, your obedient servant,

J. M. ROBERTSON,
Captain Second U. S. Artillery, Commanding Brigade.

Capt. A. J. COHEN,
Assistant Adjutant-General, Cavalry Corps.

No. 369.

Report of Capt. Jabez J. Daniels, Ninth Michigan Battery.

CAMP NEAR GETTYSBURG, PA., *July 5, 1863.*

SIR: I would respectfully submit the following report:

I received orders from Captain Robertson, commanding this brigade, at 12 m. on the 3d instant, to report with my battery to Major-General Newton, commanding First Army Corps, then engaged in the battle of Gettysburg. After reporting to General Newton, received orders from him to take a position on the hill and west of the town, and engage the enemy's batteries. I proceeded at once and took position as directed, and opened fire at 12.30 p. m. I succeeded in silencing one of the enemy's batteries at 2 p. m. Another battery was then brought into the open field at a range of 700 yards. This battery was disabled before they could do me any damage. The enemy then formed a division of infantry, and charged desperately upon my battery, but were promptly repulsed and driven back from the field with great slaughter by our infantry and artillery. The enemy made a second attempt to form, but were broken and forced to retire.

I ceased firing at 5.30 p. m., by order of General Doubleday, after five hours' engagement.

I remained on the field until 7 a. m. the 4th instant, at which time I was relieved by Captain Clark, commanding a New Jersey battery, and permitted to retire from the field. I expended 322 rounds. The ammunition used was Hotchkiss shot and shell and canister.

My loss during the engagement was Private John W. Barber killed; Corpl. C. Hass, Privates T. P. Smith, Harvey Collins, and J. M. C. Forbes, all slightly wounded. I also lost 23 horses killed, and received slight damage to two ammunition chests.

The officers and men behaved well, evincing great coolness and bravery.

I am, sir, your most obedient servant,

J. J. DANIELS,
Capt., Comdg. Ninth Michigan Battery, Horse Artillery.

J. H. BELL,
Acting Assistant Adjutant-General.

No. 370.

Report of Capt. Joseph W. Martin, Sixth New York Battery.

NEAR FAIRFAX COURT-HOUSE, VA., *June* 20, 1863.

LIEUTENANT: I beg leave to submit herewith the report of the part taken by my battery (the Sixth Independent New York) in the late movements of the Cavalry Corps of this army.

In accordance with orders, dated headquarters First Brigade, Horse Artillery, June 6, I reported with my battery to Col. Thomas C. Devin, commanding First Cavalry Division, at Brooke's Station, and marched with Col. B. F. Davis' brigade, of that division, to Hartwood Church, arriving there at 3.15 o'clock on the evening of the 7th instant.

At 6.30 o'clock the march was resumed, and at 4 p. m. I arrived at Warrenton Junction, and, in accordance with orders from headquarters Cavalry Corps, reported for duty to Brig. Gen. D. McM. Gregg, commanding Third Cavalry Division.

On the 8th instant, at 1.30 p. m., I marched in rear of Colonel Kilpatrick's brigade to Kelly's Ford, and went into park at 8.30 p. m.

At 3.30 a. m. 9th instant, the battery was harnessed, and at 6 a. m. commenced crossing the ford, under the following assignment of pieces: The right section, without caissons, commanded by First Lieut. M. P. Clark, in advance, following the lead regiment of Colonel Wyndham's brigade; the left section, under command of Second Lieut. J. Wade Wilson (also without caissons), in front of the rear regiment of Colonel Kilpatrick's brigade, and the two guns of the center section, with the column of caissons, marching between the two brigades.

The march from the ford to Brandy Station was pursued without extraordinary incident until we reached a point a few hundred yards distant from the station, when a shot from the advance section and an order from General Gregg to form at once in position was sufficient notice that we had come upon the foe. The enemy had a battery in position on an eminence close to a house which was occupied by their commanding general as headquarters, and from this battery poured a heavy fire on the section under Lieutenant Clark. They made no reply to the section under my own immediate command, and did not withstand the combined fire of the two sections more than a quarter of an hour. The distance from the advanced section to the enemy's battery was about 800 yards, and from the center section about 1,000 yards.

While the guns were engaged, an aide-de-camp from Colonel Wyndham, commanding the advance, reached me with an order to report to him immediately with the two guns I was commanding. I told the officer that I had been posted in the position I occupied by General Gregg's orders, was firing under his immediate directions, and I should consequently remain there until I received other orders from him or his superior in authority.

A few minutes after this, an order from General Gregg reached me to cease firing, and report with the two guns to Colonel Wyndham without delay. I did this as soon as I could, urged to a greater rapidity in the execution of the movement by the fact of receiving three separate messages from Colonel Wyndham to "hurry up." The aide who brought me the order to report to Colonel Wyndham told me that I would receive my support from him, but seeing none of our troops on the advanced position, which Lieutenant Clark already occupied with one piece (the remaining one of his section being temporarily disabled), I sent two separate messages for my support, and in reply received word that they were already on the way and would be at the position before my guns were.

During the entire time, however, that I occupied this position I saw no supporting force, and had I not been so hotly pressed by the enemy I should have taken the responsibility of withdrawing my guns to where their safety would have been insured, nor would I have ever allowed the guns to be so much exposed had I for a moment supposed that they would be sent there unsupported. I understand that the support was ordered, but it is certain that it never took the position assigned it. Immediately on arriving at the position where Lieutenant Clark was engaged with his remaining piece, I formed the section on his right, and immediately commenced firing at the house which I before mentioned as having been occupied by General Stuart as his headquarters, and which was completely surrounded by a dense mass of the enemy's cavalry. Almost simultaneously the enemy commenced their attack by repeated charges on the guns, but it was not until they had been twice repulsed that their efforts were successful, and I am confident that even then they would have been discomfited had their final charge not been made almost simultaneously front and rear. It took but one round of canister shot from each piece to repulse their charges, and could I have reversed my.

pieces in sufficient time on their last effort to have given them a round before they were in the battery, they should never have taken the guns—there, at least. Once in the battery, it became a hand-to-hand fight with pistol and saber between the enemy and my cannoneers and drivers, and never did men act with more coolness and bravery, and show more of a stern purpose to do their duty unflinchingly, and, above all, to save their guns; and while the loss of them is a matter of great regret to me, it is a consolation and a great satisfaction to know that I can point with pride to the fact that of that little band who defended the battery not one of them flinched for a moment from his duty.

Of the 36 men that I took into the engagement, but 6 came out safely, and of these 30, 21 are either killed, wounded, or missing, and scarcely one of them but will carry the honorable mark of the saber or bullet to his grave.

The three guns lost were so disabled by bursting, wedging, and spiking that their possession was of no benefit to the enemy for the remainder of the engagement, and the ammunition (fuse shell and case shot) which they took with the guns was rendered useless by the destruction of the fuses belonging to them. All this was accomplished in less time than it takes to write it, but it was complete and effectual.

Finding that it was futile to do more than had been done, I made my way to where I hoped to find the general commanding the division, my object being, if possible, to secure sufficient force to recapture the guns (and I believe, from the character of the enemy's fighting, that it could have been done with little loss), and to assist in their recapture I intended to take up three of the caisson limbers to bring off the guns with (the horses belonging to the guns having all been either killed or wounded) if the effort was successful, and, if it was attended with no success, I felt assured that I could fall back with the limbers as safely as could the assisting force. After fifteen minutes' unsuccessful search, I returned and found that our forces were falling back on the road leading to Berry's Hill, and I accordingly moved my caissons and the remaining portions of the two sections to that point, and left them under the charge of Lieutenant Clark, while I went to the headquarters of the corps to report my disaster to Captain Robertson, corps chief of artillery.

The operations of the left section were conducted solely by its chief, Lieutenant Wilson, and from all sides I hear nothing but high encomiums on his excellent management of his command and of the gallantry of himself and his men. The reports of his operations and of those of Lieutenant Clark* from the time he took the advance until I joined him on the field, are herewith inclosed.

At 3 p. m., in accordance with orders from the general commanding the division, I crossed the Rappahannock at the station ford, and remained in camp until 7 a. m. on the 10th, when I marched with the division to Warrenton Junction, remaining, under the order of the general commanding the division, until the 13th instant, when I reported to your headquarters for duty with the brigade.

I have the honor to report the following casualties: 8 wounded and 13 missing. None known to be killed.

Amount of ammunition expended : 122 rounds Schenkl percussion shell, 126 rounds Hotchkiss case shot, and 15 rounds Hotchkiss can-

---

* Clark's report not found.

ister. The working of the ammunition used was excellent. The only fault to be found was in the paper fuses used with the case shot, and their inaccuracy, it seems, cannot be remedied. The percussion shell was in this case, as I have always found it, true to its reputation. I want no better projectile in my chests. The loss in *matériel*, I regret to say, is great, and consists, in part, as follows: Three 3-inch rifled guns, carriages, and equipments complete, 3 sets double lead harness, 2 sets double wheel harness, 24 lead traces, 15 wheel traces, 16 sets horse equipments, and 20 artillery horses.

I beg leave to tender my sincere thanks to the general commanding the Third Cavalry Division for the uniform kindness and forbearance with which he treated myself and my command during the short time I was acting under his orders; and to Captain Weir and his entire staff, and to Lieutenant Thomson, aide-de-camp to the general commanding Cavalry Corps, who accompanied the left wing of the advance, I am also sincerely grateful.

Of the conduct of my chiefs of sections—Lieutenants Clark and Wilson and First Sergeant [James E.] Tileston (acting)—I am deservedly proud. They are well fitted to command men of the caliber and stamina such as those who fought so nobly and so heroically at Brandy Station on the memorable June 9.

I am, sir, very respectfully, your obedient servant,

J. W. MARTIN,
Captain, Comdg. Sixth Independent New York Batteiy.

First Lieut. J. H. BELL,
Acting Assistant Adjutant-General.

No. 371.

Report of Lieut. J. Wade Wilson, Sixth New York Battery.

CAMP NEAR FAIRFAX COURT-HOUSE, VA., *June* 21, 1863.

CAPTAIN: In obedience to your order, I assumed command of the left section of the Sixth Independent New York Battery at Warrenton Junction, Va., on June 8, and continued the march thence toward Kelly's Ford, within a mile of which we bivouacked for the night.

On the morning of the 9th, pursuant to orders from General Gregg, through Captain Martin, I detached the two caissons, with corporals, and with the two pieces reported to Colonel Kilpatrick, commanding the First Brigade of General Gregg's division of cavalry, and was placed as support to the rear guard of the column, marching in front of the rear regiment of the First Brigade. The march was continued without interruption and with great rapidity up the road on the south side of the Rappahannock.

At about 10.30 a. m. rapid cannonading was heard at the front, and almost immediately thereafter an order was received to pass the two pieces from the rear to the front of the First Brigade. Leaving the main road to the left by obliquing to the right, I sought a position on the slope of the ridge which stretched from the former residence of Colonel Thorne, deceased (now the headquarters of the rebel General Stuart), toward the Rappahannock, and bending to the rear.

At this time the fight for the possession of the house was very spirited. To reach the position sought, I was compelled to cross a morass, several immense ditches, and a fence, all of which was accomplished without accident, and the section went into action and opened a vigorous fire with Schenkl percussion on a column of rebel cavalry pushing rapidly from the right toward Thorne's house, on my left and front. The firing was rapid and effective, producing much confusion in the enemy's column. Perceiving this, and pursuant to an order from Colonel Kilpatrick, I limbered to the front, and advanced upon the moving column some 150 yards, and again went into action, effectively delaying and disconcerting the enemy's concentration on their own center, near the Thorne house.

Again, pursuant to orders from Colonel Kilpatrick, I limbered to the front, and sought a position on the crest of the hill behind which the enemy was rapidly massing to force back the advance of Colonel Kilpatrick upon the house. Before reaching the crest, however, a halt was ordered by Colonel Kilpatrick, and soon after a retreat from that position, which was executed without panic and in admirable order. The enemy, perceiving the retreat, charged furiously up the hill and through the section 50 yards in rear of the pieces, charging desperately on the cavalry, some hundreds of yards in the advance of the pieces in retreat. The capture of the section seems to have been thought accomplished by the enemy, and the rebel line wheeled into column and pushed rapidly by the flanks, with the intent to turn the right of the First Brigade, leaving, as they supposed, a sufficient force to secure the guns.

At this time was displayed the heroism of the section, and valor of which any command and country may be justly proud. In reversing, one of the gun limbers was nearly capsized, one wheel being in the air and the axle nearly vertical. Perceiving this, I ordered the cannoneers to dismount and restore to its position the limber. We were surrounded by a squad of rebel cavalry, firing with carbine and pistol. The order was scarcely needed, for the cannoneers had seen the peril of their gun, and, anticipating the order, had dismounted to restore it, and, with revolvers in hand, they defended the gun as if determined to share its destiny and make its fate their own. The bearer of a rebel battle-flag was shot by Private [Sylvanus] Currant, who would have recovered it but for the great difficulty of approaching the colors with a lame and skittish horse, upon which he was at the time mounted. The flag was taken by the First Maine Cavalry. The column of rebel cavalry was rapidly moving toward our right, or rather left, as we were in retreat, and the section moved in the same direction in parallel line in column of pieces, stopping now and then to throw a few shell in the column, and again seeking safety in retreat, until we reached the woods, when the pursuit ceased. Not knowing the whereabouts or fate of the remaining two sections of the battery, I reported to General Gregg, who ordered a continuance of the retreat until we reached a large open field, where I was ordered to report to Colonel Taylor (then, by the wound of Colonel Wyndham, in command of the Second Brigade), with whom I again returned to the front, crossing the Rappahannock road and passing to the right of the position occupied in the morning; then, obliquing to the left and rear, I went into battery and action on a line of cavalry and artillery behind a ridge which masked them partially from view. My ammunition becoming exhausted, I was relieved by Battery M, Second U. S. Artillery, and recrossed the river at Rappahannock Station. I then went into battery near a fort, to command the road leading to the ford. Some rebel cavalry appearing, I opened fire, and by a few well-directed shots, caused them to retire into the woods.

The section was in action at eight different times during the day, and the accuracy of the fire secured the commendation of the generals commanding both brigades and divisions of cavalry, while the conduct of the men was in the highest degree creditable to their valor and skill as soldiers and artillerists.

I am, captain, very respectfully, your obedient servant,

J. WADE WILSON,
Second Lieut., Comdg. Section, Sixth Ind. N. Y. Battery.

Capt. J. W. MARTIN,
Comdg. Sixth Independent New York Battery.

No. 372.

Report of Capt. John C. Tidball, Second U. S. Artillery, commanding Second Brigade, Horse Artillery.

CAMP NEAR WARRENTON, VA., *August* 4, 1863.

SIR: I have the honor to submit herewith the reports of Lieutenant Calef, commanding Horse Battery A, Second U. S. Artillery, and Lieutenant Fuller, commanding Horse Battery C, Third U. S. Artillery, detailing in as concise form as possible the operations of their respective batteries in the recent movements of the Army of the Potomac, which resulted so successfully in the expulsion of the Confederate army from Pennsylvania and Maryland.

In submitting these reports, it is unnecessary for me to add anything to show the important part acted by these batteries in conjunction with the cavalry with which they were serving in these operations. Never in the Army of the Potomac has such arduous service been required of batteries, and in every instance in marching and in fighting they proved themselves equal to all requirements, and received the well-earned commendation of those with whom they served.

As the operations of the cavalry are mostly on the exterior of the army and out of view of the greater part of it, but an imperfect knowledge exists of the importance and arduousness of its service. So also of the batteries of horse artillery serving with the cavalry; batteries and sections, constantly detached and frequently engaged with the enemy, with that uncertainty of position, force, and other circumstances which always attend reconnaissances and skirmishing, necessarily call to the fullest extent for the intelligence and all other resources of the officers commanding, and it is with pride and satisfaction that I request the special attention of the major-general commanding to the recent services of Second Lieutenants Calef and Roder, of Horse Battery A, Second U. S. Artillery, and of First Lieutenants Fuller, Meinell, and Kelly, and Second Lieutenant Lancaster, of Horse Battery C, Third U. S. Artillery. Horse Battery K, First U. S. Artillery (Graham's), and E, First U. S. Artillery (Randol's), the other two of the Second Brigade, Horse Artillery, are still detached with the First and Second Cavalry Divisions, and the reports of their operations will doubtless be made through the commanding officers of those divisions.

Very respectfully, your obedient servant,

J. C. TIDBALL,
Capt. 2d U. S. Artillery, Comdg. 2d Brig., Horse Artillery.

Lieut. Col. A. J. ALEXANDER,
Asst. Adjt. Gen., Cavalry Corps, Army of the Potomac.

No. 373.

Report of Capt. William M. Graham, Battery K, First U. S. Artillery.

CAMP, RESERVE CAVALRY BRIGADE,
June 23, 1863.

LIEUTENANT: I have the honor to submit the following report of the operations of Horse Battery K, First U. S. Artillery, in the engagement of the 21st instant:

One section was detached from the command, under Lieutenant Michalowski, and ordered to report to Colonel Gamble, at Middleburg. The four remaining pieces marched with the brigade to the heights beyond the stone bridge, and opened upon the enemy's cavalry upon the plain below, driving them from their position. The battery then advanced with the brigade, and took position to the left of the pike above Upperville, where it opened upon the enemy's cavalry in the wood, to which they had been driven by the charge of the brigade, forcing them to retire to the heights beyond.

I am, very respectfully, your obedient servant,

WM. M. GRAHAM,
Captain First U. S. Artillery, Comdg. Horse Battery K.

First Lieut. JAMES F. McQUESTEN,
Adjt. Second Cavalry, A. A. A. G., Cavalry Reserve Brigade.

No. 374.

Report of Lieut. John H. Calef, Battery A, Second U. S. Artillery.

CAMP NEAR WARRENTON, VA.,
July 27, 1863.

SIR: I have the honor to make the following report of the operations of Light Company A, Second U. S. Artillery, since it joined the cavalry command of General Buford on June 14:

June 14.—Battery arrived at Warrenton Junction with Second Brigade, Horse Artillery, Captain Tidball, which relieved First Brigead, Captain Robertson. Same day joined the cavalry command of General Buford.

June 15.—Command marched from Warrenton Junction to Bristoe Station, and bivouacked at 12 p. m.

June 16.—Marched from Bristoe Station to Bull Run, and bivouacked for the night near old battle-field. Battery assigned to Colonel Gamble's brigade, Buford's division.

June 17.—Marched from Bull Run to Aldie, Va.; very fatiguing march.

June 18.—Battery on a reconnaissance in the direction of Philomont, Va. Our cavalry skirmishers met those of enemy near bridge over Goose Creek, and drove them through Philomont. Right section, under Lieutenant Roder, and left section, under First Sergeant [Joseph] Newman, crossed the bridge. Other section posted on a hill on south side of creek, to enfilade road leading to bridge from north side. Object, to cover retreat in case our troops were obliged to fall back. Object of expedition accomplished, we retired to camp near Aldie.

June 19.—Lieutenant Roder on picket with a section, posted on an elevation commanding roads leading to Aldie from the north.

June 20.—Remained in same camp. Lieutenant Roder relieved at dusk by First Sergeant Newman.

June 21.—Whole cavalry and artillery force in motion at 4 a. m. in direction of Middleburg, Va. My battery relieved Lieutenant Fuller's from positions on right and left of town, on north side. About 9 a. m. our cavalry and artillery engaged the enemy sharply, and drove them in the direction of Upperville. My battery was ordered from its position to the front about 1 p. m., and joined the main body of our force near Upperville. Enemy made a stand on edge of town. Lieutenant Roder's section was thrown in the extreme advance, posted on right of road, and opened on enemy's cavalry on left of road while they were charging ours. The enemy was soon checked, and driven back into edge of woods. Here they reformed, and charged with great force on our cavalry, which, not being in sufficient force to resist them, fell back. At this time the other two sections were ordered into position on left of road. As soon as the enemy saw them coming out of the wood skirting the road, they were heard plainly to cry, "Charge that battery!" They were then going by a flank off to our left. About half a dozen shots were fired at them, checking them effectually. I then changed front forward on my left piece, to be in readiness for them in case they gained our left flank, but the main body of our cavalry arriving about this time, the enemy was driven through the town in the direction of the Gap. They were again charged and driven on the north side of the town, but darkness put an end to further operations for the day, and we bivouacked for the night near the town.

June 22.—Command retired to old camp near Aldie. Enemy followed up close and harassed our rear guard. Battery got into position again toward evening, but as soon as the alarm was over we retired to camp. Ordered to be ready to turn out at a moment's warning.

June 23.—Remained in same camp, without anything of interest occurring, till June 26.

June 26.—Command marched from Aldie to Leesburg, where we bivouacked for the night; long and severe march.

June 27.—Marched from Leesburg to Edwards Ferry, where we crossed the Potomac into Maryland. Also crossed the Monocacy near Aqueduct Bridge, fording the river. Bivouacked near Petersville, Md.

June 28.—Marched from Petersville through Jefferson to Middletown, and bivouacked for the night near town.

June 29.—Marched from Middletown through Boonsborough, Cavetown, and Smithsburg, and encamped for the night near Millerstown; very long and fatiguing march; horses very much used up.

June 30.—Marched through Emmitsburg, Md., to Gettysburg, Pa., and went into position just outside of town. Hill's corps of the enemy reported to be about 3 miles from town. Strong cavalry pickets thrown out about a mile and a half. Our position on Carlisle road.

July 1.—Enemy reported to be advancing in heavy columns on Carlisle pike, and preparations were immediately made to receive them. This was about 8 a. m. Colonel Gamble, commanding the brigade of cavalry to which my battery was attached, requested me to select my own position. I accordingly selected a position about 600 yards in front of the one held during the night. As soon as the pioneer party had leveled the intervening fences, as well as the one in front of my position, I moved forward and took up the advanced position. No sooner was this accomplished than General Buford sent for me, and told me he wished one section on the left of the road and one still farther to the left. I accordingly placed First Sergeant Newman, commanding left section, on immediate left of road, and Sergeant Pergel, commanding center section, still farther to the left. No sooner was the latter placed in position than I heard the enemy's skirmishers open upon our pickets, who were retiring.

Lieutenant Roder now fired the first gun (which opened the sanguinary battle of Gettysburg) on the head of a column of rebel cavalry advancing on the right of the road. Two of the enemy's batteries, one on each side of the road, now opened on my guns near the road. The number of guns in each battery, as near as I could judge, was four; so that they outnumbered mine just two to one. The enemy's infantry advanced rapidly, and the musketry and artillery fire soon became extremely warm. We, however, held our position until the arrival of the First Corps. At this juncture, General Buford ordered me to withdraw my guns in each section by piece, which was accordingly executed in good order. Sergeant Newman having four horses killed and disabled at his left piece, I immediately sent back for a limber from one of the caissons, but before it could be gotten up, Sergeant Newman, by strenuous exertions, drew off the piece with one team. The enemy's infantry was so close that it was impossible to take off all the harness; two sets out of the four were, however, afterward recovered by Sergeant Newman.

Riding over to Sergeant Pergel's section, I found that the enemy had advanced out of the woods in his front, and were making rapidly for his guns. He had already opened on them, and, by well-directed shots, had succeeded in checking them for the time. Having but a small cavalry support, and the woods occupied by the enemy extending up within 200 yards of the right of the section, I thought it unadvisable to wait till they arrived within canister range, and therefore withdrew the section, and took it, with the remainder of the battery, which had by this time withdrawn, to a point indicated by Colonel Gamble, and awaited orders. While there, I had the ammunition chests replenished, which was no sooner accomplished than General Buford sent for a piece to enfilade a ditch occupied by the enemy. Lieutenant Roder took his right piece to the spot, and opened with canister, which had the effect of driving the enemy in great confusion. As he was bringing the piece into battery, the enemy, seeing it, rushed forward and exclaimed, "There is a piece—let's take it!" As soon as the piece was unlimbered, Corporal [Robert S.] Watrous, chief of piece, in bringing up a round of canister, was shot in the leg by a Minie bullet, and dropped. Private [Thomas] Slattery, with commendable presence of mind, took the round from his hands, and carried it to the piece. The effect of that round probably saved the piece.

Captain Hall's (Rhode Island) [Maine] battery, belonging to the First Corps, occupied the first position on the right of the road held by Lieutenant Roder's section after the latter had withdrawn. In about half an hour this battery was disabled, and, leaving two pieces on the field, withdrew. The left and center sections of my battery were then ordered up again by General Wadsworth to reoccupy the ground just abandoned by Captain Hall, which was done under a heavy fire of musketry. As soon as the first gun was fired from my battery, three four-gun rebel batteries opened from the front and right of my position.

In this spot I had most men wounded, and by musketry. After occupying the ground about fifteen minutes, the rebel battery on my right and front moved off still more to the right, under cover of the woods, and took up a position so as to nearly enfilade my guns. I held this position as long as possible, but, the enemy having a cross-fire with several batteries, I was forced to withdraw. I then took up a position nearly on a line with my former one, but better covered by a corner of woods from the batteries in front, and remained in that position until relieved by a battery of the First Corps; then took up a position in a wheat-field about 500 yards to the rear and left of former position. Here I opened on a heavy column of rebel infantry advancing down the Carlisle pike. Remained in this position until toward evening, when we moved to the left about a mile, and bivouacked for the night.

In this engagement, which was a very severe one, the battery lost 12 men badly wounded and 13 horses killed.

All behaved nobly. I took notice particularly of the coolness and intrepidity of the chiefs of sections during the hottest of the firing. Lieutenant Roder behaved very handsomely, showing himself equal to every emergency. Being short of officers, First Sergeant Newman and Sergeant Pergel each commanded a section. Of the other non-commissioned officers, Sergeants [Michael] Quinn, [James] Callanan, [Charles] Crittenden, [John] Brothers, [Malachi] Killern, and Watrous deserve mention, the latter losing a leg. The battery did well, and I was highly gratified by the compliments paid it by General Buford, commanding division, and Colonel Gamble, commanding brigade to which the battery was attached.

On the evening of the 1st we had, as before stated, removed well to the left of our line.

On the morning of the 2d, the attack commenced directly in front of where my battery was parked. Dispositions were made to receive the enemy, who were driving our skirmishers rapidly. For want of men, I could serve but five guns. Notwithstanding the severe work of the 1st, every one showed himself ready for a continuation on the morning of the 2d. We had hardly got into position when an order came from General Buford for me to follow with my battery the First Brigade, of his division, and march with it to Taneytown, Md., for supplies and forage. Reached Taneytown about 4 p. m., and went into camp.

July 3.—Marched from Taneytown to Westminster, Md., where we obtained one day's forage.

July 4.—Marched from Westminster to Union Bridge.

July 5.—Marched from Union Bridge to Frederick. Obtained forage, and encamped near the city.

July 6.—Marched from Frederick to Williamsport, which we reached about 5 p. m., and skirmished with the enemy until dark. Enemy's skirmishers advanced on Lieutenant Roder's section, which had been detached for the purpose of shelling the enemy's sharpshooters, who had possession of the buildings near our position. The enemy was repulsed by the timely use of canister, which also rallied our line of skirmishers, so that we were enabled to hold our position for the remainder of the day. At dusk, we fell back to Jones' Cross-Roads, and bivouacked for the night.

July 7.—Marched to Boonsborough, and took up a position just outside of town.   The enemy shelled the rear of our column.   Remained in position all night.

July 8.—Report came about 8 a. m. that the enemy was advancing in force on the Boonsborough and Hagerstown pike.   Battery moved to the front with the brigade, and took up a position on right of road, and soon opened with good effect on a column of the enemy advancing down the pike.   As soon as two guns had been fired, the enemy opened with their batteries.   In this position some good firing was done at a rebel battery posted near a barn on left side of pike; obliged it to take up a new position.   We remained in this position about three hours, when, in consequence of the enemy working round on our left to gain possession of the Williamsport pike, we were ordered to fall back to the right of the town.   Scarcely had this been done when Colonel Gamble was ordered to reoccupy the ground he had left.

The enemy's batteries had in the meantime, under good cover, worked up very close to our position.   The enemy's sharpshooters had also gained possession of a stone barn, from which it was necessary to dislodge them before we could advance.   Lieutenant Roder was detached with one piece for this purpose.   Scarcely had he fired the first shot, when a rebel battery opened on him about 1,000 yards in front.   Their first shot severely wounded 1 man and killed 1 horse. I placed the remainder of the battery in position as soon as possible, and opened.   The enemy having obtained accurate range of my position, the fire was extremely warm.   By well-directed shots, however, they were driven, and as our skirmishers advanced, I took up a more advanced position with my battery, and opened again, but being nearly out of ammunition, only a few rounds were fired at their retreating cavalry.   It being nearly dark, we were ordered to withdraw to our old camp.

July 9.—The enemy were again driven.   I took up three successive positions, and opened with my battery.   The last position was held during the night with horses in harness.

July 10.—Our skirmishers advanced about daylight.   Battery opened on enemy's skirmishers, who were in a strong line, with good effect. As our skirmishers advanced, I took up a second position, and shortly after a third, with one section.   No sooner had I opened with this section, than eight guns of the enemy opened from the ridge beyond, about 1,000 yards, and a very short distance from Funkstown, Md. As soon as I discovered their force, I sent back for the other section immediately—also word to General Buford—and for the moment withdrew my guns under cover.   Here I had 1 horse killed.

About five minutes after, our skirmishers advanced and the enemy's batteries withdrew to a position on the right of Funkstown, from which they attempted to prevent, by a warm fire of artillery, our farther advance up the pike.   As soon as my other section came up, I occupied the next ridge beyond, just abandoned by the enemy.   Here I remained about four hours engaged with the enemy's batteries. Their sharpshooters had gained possession of all the buildings and outhouses on the edge of town, and succeeded in opening a warm fire on our skirmishers and my cannoneers.   After awhile, our carbineers getting out of ammunition and the infantry not coming up to occupy our position, we were obliged to withdraw.   We returned, and bivouacked near to where we were in position the night before.   In this engagement, notwithstanding the fire was very hot, I had only 1 man wounded and 1 horse killed.

July 11.—Marched from Boonsborough to Bakersville, and went into position.

July 12.—In same camp. Stampeded by the return of a reconnoitering party from Colonel Devin's brigade; quickly got ready to move to the front, but later in the day unharnessed when the cause of the alarm was discovered.

July 13.—In the same position. Again alarmed by the sound of firing as if between pickets on our right and front; battery got ready for action, expecting an immediate attack; proved to be infantry firing off their muskets to clean them; consequently unharnessed.

July 14.—Advanced in the direction of Falling Waters, and found the enemy had recrossed the Potomac. A portion of their rear guard was captured by Kilpatrick.

July 15.—Command marched from Bakersville to Berlin, Md., where my battery was relieved from General Buford's command, to refit and recruit.

Respectfully submitted.

JOHN H. CALEF,
Second Lieut. Second U. S. Artillery, Comdg. Battery.

Capt. J. C. TIDBALL,
    Second U. S. Artillery, Comdg. Second Brig., Horse Art.

No. 375.

Report of Lieut. William D. Fuller, Battery C, Third U. S. Artillery.

WARRENTON, VA.,
July 28, 1863.

CAPTAIN: I have the honor to make the following report of the movements of Horse Battery C, Third U. S. Artillery:

I assumed command of the battery on June 6, at Falmouth, Va.

On June 7, I reported to General Russell at Hartwood Church, and marched from that point on the 8th with his command to Kelly's Ford, on the Rappahannock River, where we encamped.

Early the next morning the battery crossed the river there, and marched as far as Brandy Station, the right section in advance, under Lieutenant Meinell, firing on the enemy. Later in the day the battery recrossed the river at Rappahannock Station, and was put in position to cover the ford. Three guns were sent up to Beverly Ford, but were sent back the same night. The whole battery was under fire at Brandy Station. The battery reached Bealeton Station on the 11th, and on the 13th reported to General Gregg, at Catlett's Station, from which place it marched to Union Mills, near Fairfax Station.

On June 17, it marched with General Pleasonton's cavalry to Aldie, and went into position in front of the town that night.

On the morning of the 18th, Lieutenant Lancaster moved with his section toward Middleburg, and was engaged.

The whole battery marched to Middleburg on the 19th, taking position beyond the town, and engaging with the enemy's skirmishers.

On the morning of June 21, the right section, Lieutenant Meinell, advanced beyond the woods in front of the town, and was engaged with a Confederate battery. General Pleasonton having sent for another section, I ordered the whole battery forward, and came into action on the right of Lieutenant Meinell. After a hot cannonading of a little over half an hour, the limber case of one of the enemy's guns was blown up by a percussion shell from this battery, when they moved off hastily, leaving behind one gun and its limber, the horses of which had been disabled by the explosion of the ammunition chest. The battery immediately advanced, taking up new positions, and engaging the enemy in his next position, from which he had again opened fire. The enemy was driven from this position as before, leaving 1 man dead on the ground, horribly mangled, and traces of blood where they had carried off their wounded, to testify to the accuracy of our fire.

The battery was also engaged at Goose Creek, Upperville, and near the entrance to Ashby's Gap. At the latter place it remained in position until after dark, in advance of all but our pickets, when it was withdrawn to Upperville for the night, and returned next day to Aldie. On this occasion our loss was 1 man killed by a round shot, and 3 wounded by the accidental explosion of an ammunition chest.

We captured from the battery which engaged us one iron rifled gun (Blakely's patent), limber, and caisson. The gun was turned over by the battery to the quartermaster at Fairfax Station for transportation to Washington, D. C., as a trophy. This gun threw a projectile weighing 16 or 17 pounds with great force and precision. It was stamped with the date 1862, and was made in Liverpool, England. It is superior to our 3-inch ordnance gun in every respect.

On June 26, we marched to Leesburg, and on the 27th crossed the Potomac at Edwards Ferry. The same night marched on, reaching Frederick City, Md., about noon on the 28th. The same day the battery was ordered to move with the cavalry to meet Stuart's cavalry, then moving toward Washington. The battery marched to Ritchieville, remained all night on the road in position until the next night (29th), when we marched all night, reaching Westminster early in the morning of the 30th. After a few hours' rest, the battery marched to Manchester, and encamped.

On the succeeding morning, July 1, we marched for York, Pa. On arriving within a few miles of that town, we were ordered back to Manchester.

On the night of July 3, the battery marched for Emmitsburg, Md., arriving there on July 4, and immediately received orders to join Kilpatrick's division of cavalry. This division was accompanied by two fresh batteries, and was itself composed of cavalry with fresh horses. At 6 p. m. left Emmitsburg.

July 4, crossed the mountains a little to the north of Emmitsburg, reaching the Monterey house, on the summit of the mountains, at midnight and in a drenching rain-storm. The cavalry passed down the mountain, capturing prisoners and destroying wagons without much resistance from the enemy.

The division and batteries pushed on to Smithsburg, or Cavetown, on the other side of the mountains, reaching that place at about noon on the 5th. This battery took position on a hill to the north of the town. The enemy had closely followed us all night, capturing our stragglers, but did not appear in force until after 4 o'clock in the afternoon, when a column of Confederate cavalry came out in sight to the north of Smithsburg. I fired three case shot at them with effect, as they rapidly withdrew, and immediately opened fire from six guns at the distance of about a mile. A spirited action ensued for about an hour, when the enemy ceased firing, and left the field, followed by our fire as long as they were in sight. Two of their guns were smoothbores, and their shells all burst short of us. The rifle shells were, as usual, of superior caliber and quality to our 3-inch ammunition. Shortly after the firing ceased, the whole command marched for Boonsborough, arriving there just before daybreak on the 6th.

Kilpatrick's division marched on the morning of the 6th for Williamsport and Hagerstown, but I could send but one section with him. My ammunition was nearly expended—the percussion shells entirely— and men and horses were worn out, while Kilpatrick had a fresh division of cavalry and two batteries lately equipped. In my opinion the safety of my guns would have been compromised by exposing them in the crippled condition of the battery. The best horses were collected, and one section fitted out by borrowing ammunition, and, under command of Lieutenant Meinell, marched to Williamsport, where he was severely engaged. He rejoined the battery, which had been left at Boonsborough, on the morning of the 7th, having had 4 horses killed.

I will add that out of Colonel Huey's brigade of cavalry, with which we had served, only 200 men could be mounted to accompany Lieutenant Meinell's section, so severe had been our previous service.

On July 8, the battery was again engaged with the enemy at Boonsborough.

On July 10, the battery marched to Keedysville with Colonel Huey's brigade of cavalry. Crossed the Antietam, and proceeded up the river, reconnoitering the enemy's position at Jones' Cross-Roads. Engaged the enemy at that point, driving back their skirmishers.

On July 11, again engaged the enemy just beyond Jones' Cross-Roads, firing canister at skirmishers, placing a section out on the skirmish line.

Advanced on the 12th, and took position just in front and to the east of Saint James' College.

Marched to Williamsport on the 13th and to near Falling Waters.

On July 15, marched to Hagerstown and to Boonsborough.

On the 16th, marched to Harper's Ferry, and crossed the Potomac, marching to Shepherdstown. On the march to the latter place, Lieutenant Kelly, in the advance with two guns, was charged by a squadron of Confederate cavalry, who drove our own cavalry back on top of his guns, but they shortly rallied and drove off the enemy. The same night the entire command returned to Harper's Ferry.

On the 17th, received orders to report to Cavalry Corps headquarters, and accordingly marched from Harper's Ferry to Berlin, Md., on the 18th.

On the 19th, crossed the Potomac, and marched to Wheatland, Va.

On the 20th, marched to Philomont.

On the 21st, marched to Uniontown.

On the 22d, marched to Upperville.

On the 23d, marched to Piedmont Station.

On the 24th, marched to Manassas Gap.

On the 25th, marched to Salem.

On the 26th, marched to Warrenton.

The services of this battery have been fatiguing in the extreme. The chiefs of sections have been on all occasions in positions demanding decision and judgment, and often receiving contradictory and perplexing orders from cavalry officers of inferior rank.   First Lieut. H. C. Meinell, First Lieut. J. R. Kelly, and Second Lieut. James Lancaster, commanding the sections of this battery, have in most of the engagements fought their sections necessarily as independent commands, and with the skill and gallantry they have always displayed throughout the war.   I beg to call your attention to the efficient services in action of First Sergt. Daniel Munger and Sergeants [William H.] Miller and [George A.] Niforth, all cool and valuable men in battle.

I am, captain, very respectfully,

WILLIAM D. FULLER,
First Lieutenant Third U. S. Artillery, Comdg. Battery.

Capt. J. C. TIDBALL,
Commanding Second Brigade, Horse Artillery.

No. 376.

Report of Col. James B. Swain, Eleventh New York Cavalry, of skirmish near Fairfax Court-House, Va.

CAMP RELIEF, SCOTT'S NINE HUNDRED,
June 27, 1863.

SIR: At 3 o'clock yesterday afternoon I received an order to detail a squadron of this command to proceed to Centreville without delay, there to ascertain the position of affairs, &c.

I beg leave respectfully to report, in connection with the foregoing order, that I detailed Major Remington, with Companies B and C, of this regiment, to execute the foregoing order; that about 4.30 o'clock Major Remington left this camp, proceeding in the direction indicated by his orders.

About 8.30 a. m. of this day, Major Remington, having proceeded as far as Fairfax Court-House, encountered the pickets of the Sixth Virginia Cavalry.   Major Remington charged upon the enemy with drawn sabers, and succeeded in capturing about one-half of the enemy.   Before, however, he could succeed in rallying his small force, the rebels recovered their presence of mind, and Companies B and C were forced to cut their way through, abandoning prisoners and all.   Major·Remington's horse was shot in the breast in two places, and at least one-third of his command is killed, wounded, or missing.   The last seen of Lieutenant Dagwell, of Company C, he was charging the rebels with the second platoon, composed of Company C; he had about a dozen men with him.

Captain Campbell, of Company B, was last seen when charging the rebels; he had shot and killed 1 rebel officer.   Lieutenant Hazelton, of Company B, was twice fired at and missed; he was leading his detachment when last seen.

Sergeant Morris, of Company B, was not wounded, although he shot the officer who assaulted Major Remington.

Sergeant Beebe is known to be wounded in the ankle, and is probably a prisoner.

Major Remington returned to camp with 18 men; he took with him about 100 men.   He went out supposing that he was to go and recover and return Government property, in charge of a guard.   He found himself and his handful of men precipitated upon a regiment of rebel cavalry. Whatever valor, coolness, and determination could perform was accomplished by Major Remington and his command. I am agreeably surprised to see even the remnant he brings into camp.

Respectfully,

JAMES B. SWAIN,
Colonel.

Maj. J. P. SHERBURNE,
Assistant Adjutant-General.

No. 377.

Report of Col. Henry L. Abbot, First Connecticut Heavy Artillery, of affair on the Little River turnpike, Va.

NEAR FORT RICHARDSON, VA.,
June 29, 1863.

CAPTAIN: I have the honor to report that the enemy have been reconnoitering on the Little River turnpike, just in front of our pickets, both last night and to-day. On the first occasion, 3 men put to flight a whole company of the One hundred and seventy-eighth New York, although the only demonstration they made was to retreat on being challenged by the pickets. On the second, 2 armed men shot a civilian and drove 2 others into our lines in sight of our pickets.

Fort Worth is too high to command this road by night by artillery fire, and my infantry is too bad to be trusted to protect even a section of the light battery there, where there is no retreat for it, from cavalry.

I have ridden over the position this morning, and would respectfully suggest that the Twenty-fifth Maine regiment, now near my right, be placed where this company now is, to hold the road, and cover a section of my battery (Hazard's) to-night.

After due examination, I have decided, unless more force is available, to put the whole battery in position in the rifle-pits between Forts Worth and Ward, covered by three companies of the One hundred and seventy-eighth New York, with orders to hold the Leesburg turnpike, and await further developments in case of an attack to-night.

I cannot hold the Little River turnpike without more infantry. If the rebels pass Fort Worth on it, they ought to be stopped by the forces near Alexandria; if they then turn up on the Seminary plateau, the light battery is ready to prevent their attacking our line in rear in that vicinity, and the convalescent camp men ought to hold their own camp. Their raid will thus do little good to them.

If I try to block the Little River pike, I fear I shall lose my guns to no purpose.

I am, captain, very respectfully, your obedient servant,

HENRY L. ABBOT,
Colonel First Connecticut Artillery, Commanding.

Capt. THOMAS THOMPSON,
Assistant Adjutant-General.

No. 378.

Report of Col. Charles R. Lowell, jr., Second Massachusetts Cavalry, of reconnaissance, July 11–14.

LANGLEY, *July* 14, 1863—1 p. m.

CAPTAIN: I have the honor to report that, in obedience to your instructions of July 10, I reported to Colonel Wyndham, and received from him a copy of your instructions to him, and an order to take all his available men in camp at Alexandria. I started early on the 11th, with 304 men of the Second Massachusetts Cavalry and 60 men from Colonel Wyndham's command, and reached Aldie at 6 p. m., having seen or heard of no troops excepting Mosby's scouts. I had intended, in accordance with your instructions, to send 100 men by way of Thoroughfare Gap to cover my left, and to push on with the rest of my command to Middleburg that evening, but hearing from various sources at Aldie that a portion of Jones' Maryland [Virginia] Brigade was at Middleburg, I determined not to divide my party, and camped for the night 1 mile out on the Snicker's Gap road. Did not hear of any troops or any movements in the direction of Thoroughfare Gap.

On the 12th, moved forward through Middleburg and Upperville, hearing of no troops but two companies of [B. H.] Robertson's brigade (North Carolina cavalry) at Ashby's Gap, and some of the Sixth and Twelfth Virginia and a portion of Jones' brigade at Snicker's Gap.

Reached Paris at noon; found three platoons of cavalry formed in the village, which my advance guard drove out and chased up the Gap; near the summit they were fired upon by dismounted men from behind stone walls and in the brush, and fell back. Sent two companies to turn the Gap by the left. The enemy immediately left, and my advance guard followed them to the Shenandoah and for 3 miles up the bank toward Chester Gap. The day was so hazy that I could see nothing of camps or trains in the Shenandoah Valley. The river at Berry's Ford is entirely too deep for fording, and, from what I could learn from inhabitants, will scarcely run out for ten days.

The party at Ashby's Gap seems to have been a portion of Robertson's brigade, under Captain [Lewis A.] Johnson, with dismounted men from various regiments and some of Mosby's scouts. Left Ashby's Gap about 4 p. m., and passed through Union to Philomont, where I camped.

As the 13th was still cloudy and hazy, I thought it useless to make another effort to see into the valley, and accordingly marched through Mount Gilead to Leesburg, and thence to Dranesville, where I camped last night.

I omitted to mention that on the west bank of the Shenandoah, at Ashby's Gap, the enemy have a picket of 20 or 25 men and a small depot of commissary stores, probably for use of detachment at Gap; also a small skiff. They fired at my advance guard for some time, but did no damage.

My loss is 2 killed; 1 severely wounded, cannot live; 4 slightly wounded; 1 lieutenant and 3 privates captured. I am also sorry to report 4 stragglers still missing, and 1 deserter. I lost several horses, but captured enough to replace them.

We have brought in 1 lieutenant from the Sixth Virginia Cavalry,

6 privates from North Carolina cavalry regiments, 1 man acknowledged to belong to Mosby's gang, and 2 citizens who were in company with the party at the Gap; also, from Leesburg, Captain [A. M.] Chichester, of the rebel Engineer Corps, now aide-de-camp to General Rodes, commanding D. H. Hill's division, with an orderly from headquarters body-guard; also, at Dranesville, Alfred Leigh, private Sixth Virginia Cavalry, said to be a notorious bushwhacker.

From Chain Bridge I shall send Colonel Wyndham's detachment to Alexandria, and shall return with my companies to Brightwood, where I left my tents and sick horses, and where I shall await further orders.

I am convinced there is no force of rebels on this side of the Blue Ridge north and west of Thoroughfare Gap.

Your obedient servant,

C. R. LOWELL, JR.,
Colonel Second Massachusetts Cavalry.

Capt. C. H. POTTER,
Assistant Adjutant-General.

APPENDIX.

Embracing documents received too late for insertion in proper sequence.

Recommendation of Maj. Gen. George G. Meade, U. S. Army, commanding Army of the Potomac, for the promotion of Col. Strong Vincent, Eighty-third Pennsylvania Infantry.

HEADQUARTERS ARMY OF THE POTOMAC,
July 3, 1863.

Maj. Gen. H. W. HALLECK,
Washington:

I would respectfully request that Col. Strong Vincent, Eighty-third Pennsylvania Regiment, be made a brigadier-general of volunteers for gallant conduct on the field yesterday. He is mortally wounded, and it would gratify his friends, as well as myself. It was my intention to have recommended him with others, should he live. Among the general officers wounded to-day I omitted to mention in previous dispatch Major-General Butterfield, not seriously, and Major-General Doubleday.

GEO. G. MEADE,
Major-General.

Report of Col. Wheelock G. Veazey, Sixteenth Vermont Infantry.

HEADQUARTERS SIXTEENTH VERMONT VOLUNTEERS,
Camp at Berlin, Md., July 17, 1863.

CAPTAIN : I have the honor to report the following as the part taken by the Sixteenth Regiment Vermont Volunteers in the battle of Gettysburg, fought July 1, 2, and 3, 1863:

The regiment arrived on the field near the close of the action of the first day, but was not engaged.

On the morning of the second day the regiment was moved to the rear of Cemetery Hill, and remained there in column, closed in mass (except Company B, Captain Armes, which was moved forward to the skirmish line at 4.30 p. m.), until about 5 p. m., when it was moved to the left about 100 rods, and forward to the crest of the hill, and there deployed in support of the batteries engaged. In this movement the regiment was under a severe fire, and several men were killed and wounded. Later still it was moved farther to the left and forward, and when the battle closed it occupied the front line of battle. Soon after dark I was detailed as general field officer of the day, and the whole regiment was detailed for picket duty.

On the morning of the third day, at a quarter before 4 o'clock, the enemy engaged the left of the picket line, and at 4 a. m. opened with their artillery, which was replied to by a battery on the elevated ground in our rear, firing over our heads. This fire continued but a short time. At about 2 p. m. the enemy again opened with their artillery severely. They are reported to have had over one hundred pieces in our front. This continued for about two hours. At about 4 p. m. the enemy advanced a line of battle against my picket line with great vigor. The pickets stood firm and opened fire upon them. The Fourteenth Vermont was moved down to the right of my reserves, which consisted of six companies. Two of the other four companies were on the picket line before they rallied on the reserves, and two (B and G) were in support of a battery. The Thirteenth Vermont moved forward to the right of the Fourteenth and a little to the rear of their line, and the three regiments opened a rapid and destructive fire upon the right of the line of the enemy (Pickett's division), which soon diverged to their left, and thereby left their right flank exposed.

Pursuant to an order to me, the Sixteenth Regiment passed back and along by the rear of the Fourteenth and moved to the left of the Thirteenth, and, joining on to the left of that regiment, changed front forward, corresponding to a like movement of the Thirteenth, and the two regiments charged into the flank of the enemy and very soon crushed the force in our new front. Very many prisoners were taken in this charge. This line of the enemy had scarcely been destroyed before another line advanced farther to the left and obliquely to my rear. I immediately received an order to march back and get into position to oppose this new line. I moved about 15 rods by marching by the left flank and filing to the left, so as to gain upon the enemy and bring my front facing obliquely to his left flank. When this position was gained I received permission to charge. The result of this charge was a very large number of prisoners, and, in the two movements, three stand of colors, the colors being stripped from one standard. The two brought in were the Second Florida and the Eighth Virginia. The former had inscribed upon it "Williamsburg" and "Seven Pines." No further demonstrations were made by infantry in our front, but my regiment suffered severely from artillery after we had destroyed their infantry lines.

I could not speak too highly in praise of the conduct of both officers and men. I know of no instance of a man leaving the ranks until disabled.

I regret to mention as one of the killed Lieutenant Lawton, Company F. He was a young man of great fidelity and bravery, to whom I was much attached. He fell mortally wounded near the close of the battle.

A list of the killed and wounded is hereto attached.*
Respectfully submitted.

W. G. VEAZEY,
Colonel, Comdg. Sixteenth Regiment Vermont Vols.

Capt. W. H. HILL,
Assistant Adjutant-General.

---

*See revised statement, p. 174.

Report of Brig. Gen. Adelbert Ames, U. S. Army.

HEADQUARTERS INFANTRY,
Bealeton Station, June 10, 1863.

SIR· I have the honor to submit the following report of the part taken by the troops under my command in the action of the 9th [at Beverly Ford] :

Two-thirds of the infantry crossed the ford after the cavalry, and moved up the road and through the woods to the front and center of our line.   The edge of the woods we occupied soon after the enemy's cavalry advanced upon us ; afterward attacks were made by his dismounted cavalry, but in each instance he was repulsed, with considerable loss.

At 11 a. m. our entire line advanced.   In the afternoon all of my available force moved toward a ridge of hills on our right.   By this movement a very superior force of the enemy's infantry and cavalry was discovered.

A section of the artillery crossed the river with the infantry, and was engaged first on the left, afterward on the right.   The remaining two sections crossed later in the day, as did the infantry left on this side, moved to the extreme front, and engaged the enemy.   My command was withdrawn unmolested.

My forces were as follows:

The Eighty-sixth New York Volunteers, Major Lansing; One hundred and twenty-fourth New York Volunteers, Lieutenant-Colonel Cummins, commanded by Colonel Ellis, of the Third Corps; the Thirty-third Massachusetts Volunteers, Colonel Underwood, of the Eleventh Corps; Second Massachusetts Volunteers, Major Mudge; Third Wisconsin, Major Hubbard, commanded by Lieutenant-Colonel Flood, of the Twelfth Corps, and Graham's battery of Horse Artillery.

The entire command was engaged more or less the entire day, and always with success.   The conduct of all was admirable.   I forward the reports of regimental commanders.

I am, sir, most respectfully, your obedient servant,

A. AMES,
Brigadier-General of Volunteers, Commanding.

Lieut. Col. A. J. ALEXANDER,
Assistant Adjutant-General.

Report of Maj. Charles R. Mudge, Second Massachusetts Infantry.

BIVOUAC NEAR BEALETON STATION,
June 10, 1863.

SIR: I have the honor to report the part taken by my regiment in the late expedition, as follows:

In accordance with orders received, my regiment, consisting of 291 enlisted men and 21 officers, formed line with the Third Wisconsin Regiment, and the detachment under Lieutenant-Colonel Flood, Third Wisconsin, left Stafford Court-House, Va., at about 6 p. m., the 6th instant.   We arrived at Spotted Tavern at 2.10 a. m. the 7th instant, and leaving there at 10 a. m. the same day, arrived near Bealeton Station about 6 p. m. the same instant.   Three men were sent back from the tavern with the extra ambulance, being unable to march.   Three more from the station for same reason.

On the 8th instant we marched to Beverly Ford, and crossed the next morning at 6 o'clock. Threw out four companies as skirmishers, who were misled by the next detachment, and when on their way to join the regiment, were taken by General Pleasonton and placed in different positions on the right. While there, one company, in connection with one of the Third Wisconsin, took 16 prisoners of the Second North Carolina Cavalry, which regiment they dislodged from behind a stone wall. I threw out two more companies to take their place, afterward one more to fill a gap caused by the moving of the cavalry with whom I connected on the left. Then sent two companies to support a section of artillery on my left, which left me with only the color company as reserve.

The men, whenever engaged, behaved well and inflicted severe loss upon the enemy. When he advanced, the three companies last detailed rejoined me, and I was sent to the support of Colonel Underwood, Thirty-third Massachusetts. When the line was drawn back I was sent to the support of General Buford, by order of General Pleasonton, where I remained until ordered to take the Twelfth Corps detachment across the river, near which we camped that night, and this morning came to this place with 20 officers and 279 enlisted men.

Our loss in the engagement was 1 killed, 3 wounded, and 2 missing.

I have the honor to be, very respectfully, your obedient servant,
C. R. MUDGE,
Major, Commanding Second Massachusetts Infantry.

Brigadier-General AMES,
Commanding Infantry Detachment.

Report of Brig. Gen. Alfred Pleasonton, U. S. Army, commanding Cavalry Corps, Army of the Potomac.

HDQRS. CAVALRY CORPS, ARMY OF THE POTOMAC,
June 15, 1863.

GENERAL: I have the honor to submit the following report of the operations of the expedition placed under my orders by your instructions of the 7th instant:

On the 8th, two commands were formed as follows: The First Cavalry Division, the Reserve Brigade, and Brigadier-General Ames' command of infantry constituted one command, under the orders of Brig. Gen. J. Buford, to cross the river at Beverly Ford.

The other command, under the orders of Brig. Gen. D. McM. Gregg, was to cross the Rappahannock at Kelly's Ford, and was composed of the Second and Third Cavalry Divisions and the infantry command of Brig. Gen. D. A. Russell.

I myself moved with Buford's command until the junction of the two forces near Brandy Station, when I directed the movement of the whole.

The orders to each command were to cross the river at daylight on the 9th instant and push rapidly for Brandy Station. Buford's command, at half past 4 o'clock in the morning, crossed Beverly Ford in splendid style, attacked the enemy at once, before he had time to form, and would have captured his guns but for the untimely loss of the brave and accomplished Col. B. F. Davis, of the Eighth New York Cavalry, who, while commanding a brigade, charged at the head of his column into the midst of the enemy, and was shot through the head.

In less than an hour I succeeded in forming my entire line, covering the ford, and advanced on the enemy. His force was so superior to mine, at least three to one at every point, that I determined to hold him until I could hear from Gregg. After very heavy skirmishing and artillery firing for several hours, the distant boom of Gregg's guns was heard coming up on the left and rear of the enemy. I immediately ordered the whole line to advance, and the enemy gave way rapidly. The camp of the Stuart Horse Artillery, with important papers, was captured, and Gregg's force seized Stuart's headquarters with all its documents. A junction was then formed with Gregg, and orders were issued to press the enemy at all points. This was done until it was discovered infantry was being brought up in the cars to Brandy Station very rapidly, as was also a heavy column on foot from Culpeper. We had also captured infantry soldiers. These facts determined me to withdraw to the north side of the Rappahannock. Orders were accordingly given for Gregg to retire by the ford at Rappahannock Bridge, while Buford should return by the way of Beverly Ford. Before, however, this movement commenced a grand attack was made by our right, and the finest fighting of the war took place. Regiments of our cavalry would charge whole brigades of the enemy, would rally and charge again, never yielding, and always crushing the mass opposed to them. The enemy's cavalry would retreat, and their officers were seen to saber and shoot their men to keep them up to the fight. I rapidly re-enforced this point, and General Buford withdrew his command in beautiful style to this side, the enemy not daring to follow, but showing his chagrin and mortification by an angry and sharp cannonading.

The Third Division, under the immediate orders of General Gregg, inflicted a severe loss on the enemy near Brandy Station, and would have achieved more had Colonel Duffié, commanding the Second Division, brought up his command to his assistance in the time he should have done. This delay caused the loss of two guns of the Sixth New York Battery, as Gregg had his whole force engaged with superior masses and the section could not be properly supported; but this mishap only reflected higher honor on Lieutenant Martin, who fought his guns to the last, had 21 men of his small party killed and wounded, with 32 horses, and then rendered his guns useless by spiking one and ramming a shot the wrong way into the other; but 30 rounds were left to these guns when taken, and all the fuses were destroyed by the gunners. For this noble defense of their guns, I request this battery may be permitted to place the name of Beverly Ford on their guidon. I also ask this honor to be accorded to the regiments of the Third Division, the First Division, and the Reserve Brigade of Cavalry.

Three colors and 279 prisoners, including a number of officers, were captured in this battle.

I have the honor to recommend Brigadier-Generals Buford and Gregg for promotion for the gallantry and ability with which they fought their respective commands. The recommendations of these officers are also fully indorsed.

The following officers came especially under my notice : Colonel Devin, Sixth New York, commanding First Division ; Captain Harrison, Sixth Cavalry, commanding regiment ; Captain Merritt, Second Cavalry, commanding regiment ; Captain Lord, First Cavalry, commanding regiment; Major McClure, Third Indiana, commanding regiment; Captain Farnsworth, Eighth Illinois, commanding regiment; Captain Forsyth, Eighth Illinois; Captain Waite, Eighth Illinois.

Captains Dahlgren and Cadwalader, aides-de-camp of Major-General Hooker, were frequently under the hottest fire, and were untiring in their generous assistance in conveying my orders.

Captain Dahlgren was among the first to cross the river and charged with the first troops; he afterward charged with the Sixth Pennsylvania Cavalry when that regiment won the admiration of the entire command, and his horse was shot four times. His dashing bravery and cool intelligence are only equaled by his varied accomplishments

First Lieutenant Custer, Fifth Cavalry, aide-de-camp, charged with Colonel Davis, in the taking of Beverly Ford, and was conspicuous for gallantry throughout the fight.

First Lieutenant Thomson, First New York Cavalry, aide-de-camp, is mentioned most favorably by General Gregg, with whose column he served.

Lieutenant-Colonel Alexander, chief of staff and adjutant-general, rendered valuable and important service in obtaining information of the enemy's movements and communicating with General Gregg.

Capt. J. M. Robertson, Second Artillery, commanding Brigade of Horse Artillery, while serving on my staff, had two horses shot under him; his services in placing batteries and serving the artillery were distinguished, as were those of Captain Elder, Captain Graham, Lieutenants Vincent and Williams, of the horse batteries.

Lieutenant-Colonel Smith, of the Sixth Pennsylvania; Captain Newhall, of the Sixth Pennsylvania; Captain Green, Second Cavalry; Major Crocker, Sixth New York Cavalry; First Lieutenant Walker, Fifth Cavalry; First Lieutenant Yates, Fourth Michigan Infantry; First Lieutenant Thompson,* Sixth Pennsylvania Cavalry, and Captain Drummond, Fifth Cavalry, acted as aides-de-camp and in other capacities on the field, and were frequently under hot fire, and rendered valuable assistance.

Surgeon Pancoast, medical director, and Assistant Surgeon McGill, formed efficient and ample arrangements for the wounded, and by their operations facilitated the return of the troops.

Captain von Koerber, topographical engineer, took an accurate sketch of the entire field during the engagement.

To Brigadier-Generals Russell and Ames, with their respective commands, I am under many obligations for the effective co-operation they gave at all times. The marked manner in which General Ames held and managed his troops under a galling fire of the enemy for several hours, is entitled to higher commendation than I can bestow.

A sketch of the battle-field,† with the reports of regimental and brigade commanders and a nominal list of casualties,‡ are herewith transmitted.

I am, very respectfully, your obedient servant,

[A. PLEASONTON,
Brigadier-General, Commanding.]

Brig. Gen. S. WILLIAMS,
    Asst. Adjt. Gen., Army of the Potomac.

---

* Probably Lieut. George H. Thompson, First Rhode Island Cavalry.
† Not found.
‡ See p. 168.

Report of Maj. William S. McClure, Third Indiana Cavalry, commanding First Brigade, First Division, and regiment.

HEADQUARTERS THIRD INDIANA CAVALRY,
Camp near Catlett's Station, Va., June 12, 1863.

LIEUTENANT: I have the honor to submit the following report of the operations of this command, and also of the First Brigade of the First Cavalry Division, of which I assumed command after the fall of Col. B. F. Davis:

At 4.30 a. m. the brigade marched from the camp of the night, distance from the river one-half mile, under command of Col. B. F. Davis, the Eighth New York Cavalry in advance, supported by the Eighth Illinois Cavalry, and my command, composed of one battalion Third Indiana Cavalry, one squadron Third [West] Virginia Cavalry, and one battalion of the Ninth New York Cavalry. Before reaching the ford, two squadrons of the Sixth New York Cavalry were detached and sent forward to surprise and capture any of the enemy's pickets at the ford: these, dashing over, secured the ford after a sharp engagement. Closely following came the brigade.

Advancing rapidly, we soon gained a large body of timber, where the Eighth New York Cavalry, squadrons of which were deployed as skirmishers, met a large force of the enemy, and, wavering, finally fell back before them.

It was at this critical juncture, and while trying to rally his men, that the lamented Col. B. F. Davis fell mortally wounded. Captain Clark, commanding Eighth Illinois Cavalry, immediately charged the enemy, while my command was formed on the right of the road to protect and support the charging column. Here Captain Clark was wounded, and the command devolved upon Captain Forsyth, who also was shortly after wounded.

Under these most unfavorable circumstances, and while considerable confusion prevailed, I received orders to assume command of the brigade. By order of General Buford, I moved my command to the left, he occupying the right, and checked a large body of the enemy advancing in column of squadrons. With some difficulty, I succeeded, about 6.30 a. m, in forming my command in close column of squadrons on the left of the road and in the timber. Immediately the Eighth Illinois Cavalry was detached by order of General Pleasonton, and I saw nothing more of them during the day. Colonel Devin coming up, ordered me to retain command.

By 7 a. m. the enemy was reported advancing two heavy lines of skirmishers, supported by about two regiments. I immediately ordered Major Lemmon, now in command of Third Indiana Cavalry, to deploy to the left one squadron, and Captain Hanley, of the Ninth New York, to move his squadron to the extreme left to watch the movements of the enemy. Another squadron, under Major Patton, Third Indiana Cavalry, was dismounted and sent out as skirmishers. At 8.30, the enemy still continuing to advance slowly, Col. Devin ordered one section of Robertson's battery up. Finding no suitable position, they gave us very little aid. The enemy still continuing to advance, and inclining to my left and rear, I ordered Major Pope, of the Eighth New York, to deploy one squadron of his regiment so as to connect Captain Hanley on the left with Majors Patton and Lemon. To this line I gave two more squadrons for support. For a time the advance of the enemy was checked, but by 9.30 he began to advance rapidly, driving my skirmishers up to the guns, which, without orders, the officer in command sent to the rear. While the guns were retiring and the enemy advancing, Maj. W. B. Martin, Ninth New York, charged with the remaining squadron of his battalion, forcing the enemy to fall back and taking some prisoners. He himself was wounded and retired from the field, leaving Captain Ayres in command.

Immediately I caused our lines to be advanced. The enemy fell back rapidly, and by noon we were in complete possession of the whole timber, and the lines were advancing in the open field beyond, supported by the whole command moving in columns of fours. The rear of the enemy was charged by Lieut. L. C. Wilson, in command of Company F, of the Third Indiana Cavalry, who captured a few prisoners.

Discovering that the enemy was massing a large force in advance and a little to the right, I halted the columns until a section of artillery joined us. Again advancing until the road by which General Gregg joined us was reached, the guns were placed in position and the command formed in line and column of squadrons to support the guns and skirmishers. In this position we remained until about 3 p. m. under the fire of three of the enemy's guns, when, General Gregg having come up, we were ordered to the rear to protect the recrossing of General Buford. Soon, and before General Buford recrossed, I was ordered to this side. Lieutenant-Colonel Clendenin, of the Eighth Illinois Cavalry, being present, I immediately turned the command over to him, to whom the regimental reports were made; in consequence, I can furnish no list of casualties in the command, nor can I mention instances of bravery and ability which came under my immediate notice without, perhaps, injustice to others equally deserving; yet I would not omit to mention Captain Foote and Lieutenant Cutler, of the Eighth New York, who fell mortally wounded just before we gained possession of the timber. At the same time Adjt. Gem. S. Taylor, Third Indiana Cavalry, and Lieutenant Herrick, of the Ninth New York, were slightly wounded.

Very respectfully, your obedient servant,

W. S. McCLURE,
Major, Comdg. 3d Indiana Cavalry and Detachments of 9th N. Y. and 3d [W.] Va. Cav.

Lieut. J. H. MAHNKEN,
Acting Assistant Adjutant-General.

Reports of Col. Alfred N. Duffié, First Rhode Island Cavalry, commanding Second Division.

HEADQUARTERS SECOND CAVALRY DIVISION,
June 4, 1863.

CAPTAIN : I have the honor to report that at 5 p. m. yesterday, I received a dispatch from the commanding officer of the First Massachusetts Cavalry (Lieutenant-Colonel Curtis), on picket near Fayetteville, stating that a force of the enemy, 250 strong, were crossing the ford at Sulphur Springs. The enemy subsequently attacked his picket of 33 men, under the command of Lieutenant Gleason, who, after a brisk skirmish, fell back, according to instructions, on the road leading to the reserve (near Fayetteville).

On the receipt of this dispatch I sent the Third Pennsylvania Cavalry, under command of Lieutenant-Colonel Jones, to make a reconnaissance toward Warrenton, and from there to move by the road leading to Waterloo, leaving at the junction of this road with the road leading to Jefferson, where the river crosses the road, one squadron, and with the balance of his command to proceed on this last road and take possession of the ford at Sulphur Springs, in order to intercept the recrossing of the enemy.

At 5.30 p. m. I received another dispatch from Lieutenant-Colonel Curtis, informing me that after having observed the movements of the enemy, he ascertained that their force consisted of six squadrons, with two pieces of artillery. I transmitted this information to you at the time received. At the same time, with two regiments and one section of the battery in my command, I proceeded in person on the road leading to Warrenton by way of Germantown and Liberty.

When 3 miles from Warrenton I received a dispatch from Major Higginson, who was holding the ford at Sulphur Springs, that the enemy's whole force had recrossed. From information received from persons living near Sulphur Springs, I learned that the enemy had taken no prisoners or horses across the ford.

The enemy, in his retreat, left on the ground of the skirmish 4 of his killed. We captured 6 prisoners, who were recaptured by the enemy. Three of their horses were left in our hands.

I have to mention to the general commanding the gallant conduct of Lieutenant Gleason, First Massachusetts Cavalry, who charged the enemy twice, receiving in the skirmish a severe saber cut on the top of his head.

The only force engaged with the enemy was the platoon mentioned, who, by their gallantry, obliged the enemy to recross at once.

Our casualties are as follows: Wounded, 1 commissioned officer (Lieutenant Gleason).

The loss the enemy sustained, as nearly as can be ascertained: Killed, 4. Captured, 3 horses.

My pickets below Sulphur Springs were not disturbed. After having re-established my picket line, I returned to camp with my command.

I have the honor to be, very respectfully, your obedient servant,

A. N. DUFFIÉ,
Colonel, Commanding Division.

Capt. T. C. BACON,
    Asst. Adjt. Gen., Hdqrs. Cavalry Forces.

—

[JUNE —, 1863.]

SIR : I have the honor to report that on the 6th instant, at 3 a. m., I started with my command and a battery of artillery on the road to Sulphur Springs to make a demonstration on Culpeper Court-House. The ford was crossed without trouble. During my crossing one squadron of the Fourth New York was crossing at Freeman's Ford; another near Waterloo, to make a reconnaissance on my flank. The squadron which crossed at Freeman's Ford made a reconnaissance to Springfield, where I did not find any opposition. The other squadron made a reconnaissance to Amissville, where they found a small party of the enemy, capturing 1 of them. During this time I, with my command, proceeded on the road leading to Jefferson, waiting at this place during ten minutes for the two squadrons on my right and left to make their junction with me; then I proceeded from Jefferson to Rixeyville, sending a small party to capture the enemy's pickets, having been informed that the enemy were picketing Aestham River. I succeeded in capturing 2 of them. Crossing all the fords with opposition, I arrived at Muddy Run with my command. I formed a line of battle, concealing my own forces as much as possible. During this time the First Massachusetts Cavalry was sent to make a demonstration on Culpeper in order to oblige the enemy to come out. This regiment went to within 4 miles of the town without meeting any force of the enemy. As it was late in the evening and my horses tired, I was obliged to return to camp, dividing my forces in four columns, one to cross at Freeman's Ford, one at Fox's Ford, one at Thompson's Ford, and the other at Sulphur Springs, where four pieces of artillery were left to protect my recrossing in case of a retreat. The enemy did not follow.

During this reconnaissance I have received the following information: There is no enemy at all between Sulphur Springs and Aestham River, which was ascertained by my reconnaissance. The enemy is picketing Aestham River. His pickets do not allow any citizens to cross, motive for which I could not ascertain. There were two brigades of cavalry at Culpeper, commanded by Fitzhugh and W. H. F. Lee. Their regiments are very weak. There is also at Culpeper two companies of infantry, and the general idea is that the troops are expected to move in the Shenandoah Valley. The brigade of Fitzhugh Lee is composed as follows: First, Second, Third, and Fifth Virginia Cavalry. Jones' brigade is in the Valley at Harrisonburg, the Sixth, Seventh, Eleventh, and Twelfth Virginia Cavalry, with 400 infantry.

Captures: 2 prisoners, 4 horses.

No loss in the division.

Very respectfully,

A. N. DUFFIÉ,
Colonel, Commanding Second Cavalry Division.

Capt. A. J. COHEN,
Asst. Adjt. Gen., Second Cavalry Division.

Report of Col. John B. McIntosh, Third Pennsylvania Cavalry, commanding First Brigade, Second Division.

HDQRS. FIRST BRIGADE, SECOND CAVALRY DIVISION,
Near Amissville, August 4, 1863.

CAPTAIN: I have the honor to report that, in obedience to orders from Brigadier-General Gregg, I moved with my brigade at 1 p. m., July 3, 1863, to relieve Brigadier-General Custer's brigade, which was at that time posted about 4 miles from Gettysburg and near the road leading from Hanover to the former place.

Hearing that the enemy were advancing from three directions, I immediately placed the First New Jersey Cavalry, under command of Major Beaumont, well to the right of the road leading to Gettysburg and facing a belt of woods on a ridge overlooking the town, when they became immediately engaged. Finding the enemy coming down in a pretty strong force from the woods above alluded to,

I ordered up the section of artillery under command of Lieutenant Chester, of the First U. S. Artillery, attached to my brigade, who opened upon them. I then immediately sent word to the general that a larger force would be required than my brigade. In consequence, General Custer's brigade was detained, and I was enabled to strengthen my line of skirmishers who were then hotly engaged. I placed the Third Pennsylvania Cavalry, with the exception of Captain Treichel's squadron, in a woods to our right, and had that part of the regiment mostly dismounted and deployed as skirmishers, where they did good service in holding in check the enemy's skirmishers, who were advancing upon our line from that direction. Captain Treichel's squadron was mostly dismounted and placed in the front line of skirmishers to strengthen that part of the line. The enemy, finding their skirmishers hotly pressed, advanced a regiment of cavalry for the purpose of driving back our line. That movement was immediately responded to by a regiment of General Custer's brigade, the Seventh Michigan, advancing to meet their charge.

I regret to state that in the encounter the enemy succeeded in their charge, and compelled the Seventh Michigan Regiment to fall back. I was at that time busily employed with the dismounted skirmishers, holding them up to their line, but when our cavalry was driven back, I immediately ordered Captain Treichel to call in and mount his squadron at once, which was soon done, although some few were cut off. This squadron then charged upon the head of the enemy's column. It was gallantly led by Captain Treichel and Captain Newhall, my acting assistant adjutant-general. Every officer of the squadron was wounded, and I would particularly call attention to their gallant conduct. Their names have already been handed in.

The First Maryland Regiment was placed in reserve during the early part of the action, but was removed to a point on the extreme right, which was reported threatened, by order of the general. The whole of my brigade was employed, and all behaved very handsomely.

I take this opportunity to mention the valuable services of my staff, Captains Newhall, Thomas, and Lieutenant Ward, who were at all times very actively engaged. Captain Newhall, my acting assistant adjutant-general, was severely wounded in the charge with Captain Treichel's squadron.

A list of the killed and wounded has already been furnished.*

I am, very respectfully,

JOHN B. McINTOSH,
Colonel, Commanding First Brigade.

Capt. H. C. WEIR,
Assistant Adjutant-General.

Reports of Col. Horace B. Sargent, First Massachusetts Cavalry.

HEADQUARTERS FIRST MASSACHUSETTS CAVALRY,
Near Warrenton, Va., September 5, 1863.

CAPTAIN: In accordance with order from brigade headquarters, I have the honor to submit the following report of the part taken by this regiment in the battles of Aldie, Middleburg, and Upperville:

The regiment, Lieutenant-Colonel Curtis commanding, then in

* See p. 958.

the brigade commanded by General Kilpatrick, was ordered to advance up the Snicker's Gap road and drive the enemy from the heights on our right. The first squadron, Captain Sargent commanding, deployed as skirmishers, advanced up the hill, driving the enemy a short distance, when they were charged upon by a squadron of the enemy's cavalry. This was met by that portion of the squadron acting as a reserve for the skirmishers by a counter charge. The enemy was driven 1½ miles, when a large body of the enemy's cavalry appeared in their rear. The remaining squadrons not coming up promptly and occupying the ground gained by the first squadron, it was entirely cut off from the main body, and the heights again held by the enemy.

At this time the second squadron, Captain Tewksbury commanding, arrived, and charging, with Lieutenant-Colonel Curtis and Major Chamberlain, then not on duty, drove the enemy a short distance. The latter soon rallied, however, and coming back in overwhelming numbers the squadron fell back through a ravine to a hill beyond occupied by the third squadron, under command of Captain Adams. The fourth squadron, Lieutenant Davis commanding, then charged up the road, but was immediately cut off and the larger portion killed, wounded, or captured.

At this time the third squadron advanced a short distance, but being met by a most severe flank fire from the enemy, who then occupied the road and the field beyond, the stone walls being lined by their sharpshooters, this squadron with the second was obliged to fall back at short distances with frequent loss. At this moment the Fourth New York Cavalry, being ordered to our support, came up, but immediately turned and fell back in confusion, thus causing a complete rout. Major Higginson, Captain Sargent, and Lieutenant Fillebrown, who accompanied the first squadron, were severely wounded, and Lieutenants Davis, Duchesney, Higginson, and Carey, of the fourth squadron, were taken prisoners; the latter is supposed to have been killed.

The loss of the regiment in the above engagement was as follows: Killed, 26 enlisted men; wounded, 3 officers and 52 enlisted men; missing, 4 officers and 84 enlisted men.

Very great gallantry was shown by officers and men.

In the battle of Middleburg the regiment acted as a reserve and was not actively engaged. During the battle of Upperville the regiment was engaged in supporting the Third U. S. Battery.* It met with no loss.

The above report has been compiled from the reports of the only officers now with the regiment, all of which reports are submitted with the exception of the report of Major Chamberlain, which he has with him on detatched service, but which confirms the report submitted.

An order has been sent to Lieutenant-Colonel Curtis and Major Higginson for their reports.

Very respectfully, your obedient servant,

> HORACE B. SARGENT,
> *Colonel First Massachusetts Cavalry*

Capt. A. WRIGHT,
    Actg. Asst. Adjt. Gen., First Cavalry Brigade.

---

* Battery C, Third U. S. Artillery.

Report of Maj. Myron H. Beaumont, First New Jersey Cavalry.

HDQRS. FIRST REGIMENT NEW JERSEY CAVALRY,
Near Warrenton Junction, Va., June 11, 1863.

GOVERNOR: I have the honor to report that, in obedience to orders, we broke camp at this place on the afternoon of the 8th instant, and marched with our division, under General Gregg, to near Kelly's Ford, where we bivouacked.

At 3.30 a. m. of the 9th, we were under arms. At 5.30 o'clock we heard the guns which announced the fact that General Buford had opened the fight on the right. Soon after we crossed the river by fording it, having had to wait since 3.30 o'clock for Colonel Duffié (commanding Second Division) to come up. Our division then marched southward and then took the main road to Brandy Station, in order to attack the enemy in the rear while he was engaged with General Buford. The Second Brigade, consisting of the First New Jersey Cavalry, First Maryland, and First Pennsylvania, under command of Colonel Wyndham, was in the advance and marched in the order above indicated. We advanced with great caution, and nearly all the enemy's vedettes were captured by Capt. P. Jones Yorke, who led the advance guard with much judgment. On approaching Brandy Station, the enemy (cavalry and artillery) was discovered in considerable force occupying an elevation on the west of the railroad, about a half mile distant. On the top of the hill was a large house, in which I have since learned Major-General Stuart had his headquarters during the battle.

Our artillery having been planted, began shelling, which was replied to by a battery of the enemy, which did us no injury whatever. The hill being a very commanding position, we were ordered to take and hold it. The brigade then charged in the following order, in column of battalions: First New Jersey Cavalry, First Maryland, and First Pennsylvania. The First New Jersey was in the advance, under Lieut. Col. V. Brodrick, who led the charge. The enemy had withdrawn behind the crest of the hill, and it was not until we were within a hundred yards of the top that they advanced to meet us. They were armed, principally, with pistols and carbines, our men using generally the saber. Then began the most spirited and hardest fought cavalry fight ever known in this country. For several hours the conflict was carried on, until, the enemy having received large re-enforcements and now outnumbering us two to one, being totally without support, we were obliged to retire to another position, which we held until ordered to fall back.

This regiment in this battle nobly sustained the reputation it had already won, and there are no terms too high to use in speaking of the dash and gallantry displayed by the officers and men.

It would be invidious to particularize any officer where all without exception sustained their parts so well. Colonel Wyndham was wounded. Lieutenant-Colonel Brodrick, Major Shelmire, and Captain Sawyer were wounded and taken prisoners. First Lieutenant Brooks was wounded by a saber cut in the left arm. Second Lieut. H. Crocker was taken prisoner. Lieutenant-Colonel Brodrick, Captains Lucas and Maulsbury, and Adjutant Kitchen had their horses killed while in the thickest of the fight.

I inclose a list of casualties, which is necessarily somewhat incomplete. I trust that the number of missing may be lessened.*

---

*Nominal list (omitted) shows 5 killed, 14 wounded, and 33 missing.

We went into the fight about 250 strong.

From the encomiums passed by all on the conduct of this regiment, New Jersey has reason to be proud of her sons, who on this, as on all occasions where it has been necessary, have upheld the honor, dignity, and patriotism of the State, and the enviable reputation of their sires.

I have the honor to be, governor, very respectfully, your obedient servant,

M. H. BEAUMONT,
Major, Commanding.

His Excellency JOEL PARKER,
Governor of New Jersey.

Report of Maj. Hugh H. Janeway, First New Jersey Cavalry.

HEADQUARTERS FIRST NEW JERSEY CAVALRY,
Rappahannock Station, June 10, 1863.

GOVERNOR: I have the honor to report that the regiment has been engaged in another very severe cavalry fight. On the 8th instant, the division broke camp at Warrenton Junction and marched to Kelly's Ford, where we bivouacked for the night. The next day (the 9th instant), at 5 a. m., we crossed the river and moved on Brandy Station. As is usual in times of danger, we were in the advance. Meanwhile, General Buford was fighting hard opposite Rappahannock Station. The object of our movement was to turn the right flank of the rebels. Colonel Wyndham was in command of the Second Brigade, composed of the First New Jersey, First Indiana, and First Pennsylvania Cavalry, and the command of our regiment devolved upon Lieutenant-Colonel Brodrick. Captain Yorke, of Company I, had the advance guard, composed of Companies C and I. He moved his men so carefully that he captured every vedette on the road, so that the first intimation the enemy had of our being in their rear was by seeing the head of our column debouch from the woods.

Colonel Wyndham moved his troops with such celerity that we were upon them almost before they were aware of our vicinity. The fight lasted four hours, and was a continual succession of the most brilliant charges ever made. Every officer behaved with the utmost bravery and coolness, and it is impossible for men to behave better than did ours. They proved themselves well worthy of the State from which they come. More cannot be said in their praise.

Lieutenant-Colonel Brodrick and Major Shelmire were both wounded and taken while leading one of the numerous charges. Accounts of the nature of their capture are so conflicting that I defer sending any statement regarding it till I learn something definite; but that they both behaved with the greatest daring and gallantry, there can be no question.

Captain Sawyer, Company K, and Lieutenant Crocker, Company H, are also prisoners, but not thought to be wounded. Captain Lucas, Company F, Captain Maulsbury, and Adjutant Kitchen, while in the thickest of the fray, had their horses shot under them; that of Adjutant Kitchen fell dead, carrying him along with it. His escape seems almost miraculous. When the order was given to retire, our regiment covered the rear. I am told that General Gregg expressed the greatest satisfaction at the conduct of the regiment. Toward the close of the engagement, Colonel Wyndham received a bullet wound in the calf of the leg, but we are thankful to know that it will not prove dangerous. He kept the field for some time after being hit, but was finally obliged to give up. He goes to Washington to-day. We hope he will soon return, as he can ill be spared from his command. He also paid the regiment the highest compliments for its steady and dashing charges. The fight was hand to hand throughout.

We had in the engagement 4 field officers, 14 line officers, and 281 enlisted men.

Our loss in killed, wounded, and missing is at present 3 field officers, 2 line officers, and 52 enlisted men. This of itself speaks volumes for the bravery of the regiment. The *morale* of the regiment has been greatly benefited by yesterday's work, and I am confident that the men will fight better now than ever. Major Beaumont will probably be soon relieved from his present command to assume that of the regiment, and will be able to collect fuller accounts of the capture and wounds of the missing officers than I am able now to do.

I have the honor to be, governor, very respectfully, your obedient servant,

HUGH H. JANEWAY,
Major, Commanding First New Jersey Cavalry.

His Excellency JOEL PARKER,
Governor of the State of New Jersey.

Report of Lieut. Col. John L. Thompson, First Rhode Island Cavalry.

HEADQUARTERS FIRST RHODE ISLAND CAVALRY,
Warrenton, Va., September 5, 1863.

SIR: I have the honor to make the following report of the part taken by the First Regiment Rhode Island Cavalry in the battles of Aldie and Middleburg in June, 1863:

On the morning of June 17, 1863, this regiment, of about 275 men, Colonel Duffié commanding, moved from Manassas Junction, with orders from General Kilpatrick (in whose brigade it was then serving) to proceed through Thoroughfare Gap to Middleburg, and communicate with him by messengers at Aldie, at which place he could be found with his brigade, remaining at Middleburg the night of the 17th, to proceed through Snickersville and Purcellville and rejoin the brigade at Nolan's Ferry.

We left the brigade a short distance from Manassas Junction, taking the road to Thoroughfare Gap, the brigade moving directly to Aldie.

At Thoroughfare Gap a force of the enemy's cavalry was encountered, estimated at 300, and driven toward Salem. The regiment then turned to the right and passed through Hopewell to Middleburg.

Soon after leaving Hopewell a scout of the enemy was captured, from whom we learned that General Stuart was passing through Middleburg with a large force of cavalry, afterward discovered to be Fitzhugh Lee's brigade going toward Aldie.

On approaching Middleburg a few scouts or pickets were discovered watching us and keeping directly in our front, and there the inhabitants confirmed the story of the scout about the movements of the enemy's cavalry.

We charged into Middleburg, but found nothing except the tracks of the cavalry on the road leading to Aldie. Pickets where thrown out in every direction, and a position taken in a wood about half a mile from the town toward Hopewell Gap. The pickets were attacked on each road about the same time by the brigade returning from Aldie, and by another brigade (Robertson's) coming from Upperville.

The pickets held their ground manfully, but were overpowered and retired with some loss. After driving in the pickets the enemy (Robertson's brigade in advance) charged down the road toward our position, but were handsomely repulsed by the carbineers, dismounted, in the woods and behind the stone walls. Only one-third of the regiment was armed with carbines.

Three successive charges were repulsed by the dismounted men, when the enemy dismounted a large number of men and nearly surrounded the woods in which our position had been taken. We then retired under cover of the night toward Little River. Some of our men, mistaking the enemy's columns for our own, were captured in this engagement, but we lost none killed or wounded. The enemy's loss in this night attack can only be ascertained from themselves, and they admit from 25 to 150. Major Farrington, with other officers and a few men who had been dismounted, lay concealed near Middleburg during the night and all the next day, arriving safely at Aldie on the 19th.

We lay all night on the banks of Little River in a very secluded spot, intending in the morning to find our way over the mountains to Aldie.

On the morning of the 18th, coming out of our hiding place, we discovered the enemy completely surrounding us. We forced a way, however, toward the mountains, but with severe loss, and retreated as rapidly as possible. We suffered very severely in our retreat, only 84 reaching the lines of our army.

Of those who escaped some found their way on foot over the mountains, but most followed Colonel Duffié through Hopewell Gap.

There were many instances of coolness and courage on the part of officers and men, some of which have been handsomely acknowledged.

This regiment took no part in any of the other engagements at Middleburg or Upperville.

Our loss in the affair was:

Officers and men.	Killed.	Wounded.	Missing and prisoners.	Total.
Commissioned officers	1	3	6	10
Enlisted men	4	7	193	204
Total	5	10	199	214

Very respectfully, your obedient servant,

J. L. THOMPSON,
Lieutenant-Colonel, Commanding Regiment.

Capt. A. WRIGHT,
  A. A. A. G., 1st Brig., 2d Div., Cavalry Corps.

Report of Col. Pennock Huey, Eighth Pennsylvania Cavalry, commanding Second Brigade, Second Division.

HDQRS. SECOND BRIG., SECOND DIV., CAVALRY CORPS,
July 27, 1863.

GENERAL: I have the honor to report that a patrol, consisting of 1 sergeant and 4 men, of a squadron of the Second New York Cavalry, on outpost duty near Cedar Run, was attacked by guerrillas at about 1 o'clock to-day, near the house of a Mr. Richard Colvin, about 5 miles from these headquarters, on the road leading to Brentsville. As soon as information of the attack reached the reserve, they were promptly turned out and repaired to the scene of action, and an orderly sent to these headquarters to report the fact, whereupon another squadron was immediately sent out to support the one already there.

Subsequently, parties were sent out to patrol the country as far as Harrow or Harrison's Ford (on the Occoquan), Brentsville, and Elkton. The patrols have just returned, and have failed in securing any of these guerrillas or eliciting any definite information in regard to their whereabouts. Every possible effort has been made to discover these men. Houses were searched, and all citizens and negroes minutely interrogated, but no information obtained.

A young girl, at the house of Mr. Colvin, stated that yesterday 3 citizens and 4 soldiers (South Carolina troops) passed there at about 5 p. m. They said they were going across the river, and that for several days past small squads of Confederates passed there.

The impression prevails among the officers who were sent out that the rendezvous of these guerrillas is some point in the vicinity of Brentsville.

Casualties are as follows, viz: Private Cole, Company F, Second New York Cavalry, captured (horse found wounded); Private Dennis, Company F, Second New York Cavalry, captured (horse found wounded).

Respectfully submitted.

PENNOCK HUEY,
Colonel, Commanding Second Cavalry Brigade.

Brigadier-General GREGG,
Commanding Second Cavalry Division.

Report of Col. Charles H. Smith, First Maine Cavalry.

HEADQUARTERS FIRST MAINE CAVALRY,
At Amissville, Va., August 5, 1863.

Report of the part taken in the action of Gettysburg, Pa., by the First Maine Cavalry, on the 3d day of July, 1863:

Most of the day, Friday, 3d July, I supported Randol's battery. Toward night I was ordered to report to Brigadier-General Gregg, on the extreme right, where the most of his division was hotly engaged, and was assigned to a position on the right of his forces, to meet the expected attack of a column of the enemy seen to pass around in that direction. Subsequently was recalled from the right of the division by Colonel Gregg, commanding brigade, and posted on the left.   Threw out a line of skirmishers to meet the enemy's, advancing in that direction.   After a few shots being fired, the enemy retired, and my regiment rejoined the brigade.

I am, lieutenant, very respectfully, your obedient servant,

C. H. SMITH,
Colonel First Maine Cavalry.

Lieut. JOHN B. MAITLAND,
    A. A. A. G., 3d Brig., 2d Div., Cavalry Corps.

Report of Maj. M. Henry Avery, Tenth New York Cavalry.

HEADQUARTERS TENTH NEW YORK CAVALRY,
On Picket, August 3, 1863.

SIR: I would respectfully report that the detachment, under command of Lieutenant Sceva, has returned, having encountered a reconnoitering party of the enemy, about 20 strong, three-quarters of a mile this side of Little Washington, who fired on his advance guard, but were immediately charged by Lieutenant Sceva, and pursued about 1½ miles beyond W. [Little Washington], toward Sperryville, when, having captured 3 of their number, and his horses being very much jaded, he halted, threw out pickets, and fell back to Little Washington, remaining there about an hour, when he returned. Lieutenant Sceva also took a prisoner this side of Little W[ashington], who represents himself as being a conscript, making his way inside of our lines.

The non-commissioned officer in command of the picket placed by Lieutenant Sceva beyond the town reports seeing a detachment about 20 strong going from the direction of Flint Hill toward Sperryville. I shall send an officer and 20 men a few miles beyond Gaines' Cross-Roads, toward evening, for the purpose of bringing in the Government wagons and mules reported to be there, and also to procure information.   The prisoners report Fitz. Lee in command of his own and Jenkins' brigade, and that a rumor was current among their men that they were to attack us to-morrow or next day.   From their statements it appears that their picket line was advanced in this direction yesterday, as the Seventeenth Virginia, to which the prisoners belong, did not relieve any pickets, but made new posts near Little Washington.   I have made no new departure of my line.

I am, very respectfully, your obedient servant,

M. HENRY AVERY,
Major Commanding.

Lieut. JOHN B. MAITLAND,
    Acting Assistant Adjutant-General.

Report of Lieut. Col. William E. Doster, Fourth Pennsylvania Cavalry.

HDQRS. FOURTH REGIMENT PENNSYLVANIA CAVALRY,
August 4, 1863.

SIR: In accordance with orders received, I have the honor to report the following as the position of my regiment, and the part taken by it in the battle of Gettysburg:

At noon of the 2d of July, I was ordered to report with my regiment to Major-General Pleasonton, and was stationed in rear of a battery in the center of our line by a captain on General Pleasonton's staff.

On reporting to General Pleasonton in person, I was ordered to return to General Gregg, there being sufficient cavalry at that point, which was done.

About 9 p. m. I received orders to report again with my regiment to General Pleasonton, who ordered me to picket the whole of the left of our line to the east of his own headquarters and in advance of our infantry pickets.

Remained here until 2 p. m. of the 3d, when the enemy being reported advancing on the Littlestown road in our rear, I was ordered by General Pleasonton to advance toward the right and hold them in check. Found the enemy on the extreme right and reported to Colonel Gregg, who was engaged with his brigade, and remained there until ordered to camp.

On the 4th, advanced under Colonel Gregg on the right.

On the 5th, was ordered into Gettysburg by the York road. On the route took possession of five hospitals and about 300 wounded rebels. Advanced same evening to Stevens' Furnace under Colonel Gregg, where 1 man of this regiment was killed by the rebel rear guard.

On the 6th, was ordered to advance toward Greencastle. Captured 100 rebels, 8 horses, destroyed about twenty caissons and gun carriages, and a large quantity of ammunition and wagons. The movement was so rapid that out of 250 horses with which I left Gettysburg, only 60 had been able to keep up at Marion, near where I fell in with the rebel rear guard, under General Fitzhugh Lee, and accordingly was ordered to fall back, rejoin the brigade, and march to Chambersburg.

I am, respectfully, your obedient servant,

W. E. DOSTER,
Lieutenant-Colonel, Commanding.

Lieutenant MAITLAND,
Actg. Asst. Adjt. Gen., Third Cavalry Brigade.

ALTERNATE DESIGNATIONS

OF

ORGANIZATIONS MENTIONED IN THIS VOLUME.*

Abbott's (Henry L.) Infantry. See *Massachusetts Troops, 20th Regiment.*
Abbott's (Ira C.) Infantry. See *Michigan Troops, 1st Regiment.*
Adams' (George W.) Artillery. See *Rhode Island Troops, 1st Regiment, Battery G.*
Adams' (Julius W., jr.) Infantry. See *Union Troops, Regulars, 4th Regiment.*
Alger's (Russell A.) Cavalry. See *Michigan Troops, 5th Regiment.*
Allen's (David, jr.) Infantry. See *Massachusetts Troops, 12th Regiment.*
Allen's (Daniel B.) Infantry. See *New York Troops, 154th Regiment.*
Allen's (Frank) Cavalry. See *Rhode Island Troops, 1st Regiment.*
Allen's (Harrison) Infantry. See *Pennsylvania Troops, 151st Regiment.*
Allen's (Thomas S.) Infantry. See *Wisconsin Troops, 5th Regiment.*
Ames' (Nelson) Artillery. See *New York Troops, 1st Regiment, Battery G.*
Amsberg's (George von) Infantry. See *New York Troops, 45th Regiment.*
Arnold's (William A.) Artillery. See *Rhode Island Troops, 1st Regiment, Battery A.*
Atwell's (Charles A.) Artillery. See *Pennsylvania Troops, Battery E.*
Austin's (John S.) Infantry. See *New York Troops, 72d Regiment.*
Avery's (M. Henry) Cavalry. See *New York Troops, 10th Regiment.*
Bailey's (Edward L.) Infantry. See *New Hampshire Troops, 2d Regiment.*
Baily's (William P.) Infantry. See *Delawa e Troops, 2d Regiment.*
Baldwin's (Clark B.) Infantry. See *Massachusetts Troops, 1st Regiment.*
Baldwin's (Homer H.) Artillery. See *Union Troops, Regulars, 5th Regiment, Battery C.*
Bancroft's (Eugene A.) Artillery. See *Union Troops, Regulars, 4th Regiment, Battery G.*
Barnes' (Almont) Artillery. See *New York Troops, 1st Regiment, Battery C.*
Barney's (Elisha L.) Infantry. See *Vermont Troops, 6th Regiment.*
Barnum's (Henry A.) Infantry. See *New York Troops, 149th Regiment.*
Bassett's (Isaac C.) Infantry. See *Pennsylvania Troops, 82d Regiment.*
Batchelder's (N. Walter) Infantry. See *Massachusetts Troops, 13th Regiment.*
Bates' (James L.) Infantry. See *Massachusetts Troops, 12th Regiment.*
Baxter's (De Witt C.) Infantry. See *Pennsylvania Troops, 72d Regiment.*
Beardsley's (John D.) Infantry. See *Maine Troops, 10th Regiment.*
Beardsley's (William E.) Cavalry. See *New York Troops, 6th Regiment.*
Beaumont's (Myron H.) Cavalry. See *New Jersey Troops, 1st Regiment.*
Bentley's (Richard C.) Infantry. See *New York Troops, 63d Regiment.*
Berdan's (Hiram) Sharpshooters. See *Union Troops, Volunteers, 1st Regiment.*
Best's (Clermont L.) Artillery. See *Union Troops, Regulars, 4th Regiment, Battery F.*
Beveridge's (John L.) Cavalry. See *Illinois Troops, 8th Regiment.*
Bicknell's (Emerson L.) Sharpshooters. See *Massachusetts Troops, 1st Company.*
Biddle's (Alexander) Infantry. See *Pennsylvania Troops, 121st Regiment.*
Biddle's (Chapman) Infantry. See *Pennsylvania Troops, 121st Regiment.*

Biddle's (George H.) **Infantry.** See *New York Troops, 95th Regiment.*
Bidwell's (Daniel D.) **Infantry.** See *New York Troops, 49th Regiment.*
Bierer's (Jacob J.) **Infantry.** See *Pennsylvania Troops, 11th Regiment.*
Bigelow's (John) **Artillery.** See *Massachusetts Troops, 9th Battery.*
Bingham's (Daniel G.) **Infantry.** See *New York Troops, 64th Regiment.*
Blunt's (Asa P.) **Infantry.** See *Vermont Troops, 12th Regiment.*
Bodine's (Robert L.) **Infantry.** See *Pennsylvania Troops, 26th Regiment.*
Boebel's (Hans) **Infantry.** See *Wisconsin Troops, 26th Regiment.*
Bootes' (Levi C.) **Infantry.** See *Union Troops, Regulars, 6th Regiment.*
Both's (Ernst) **Infantry.** See *New York Troops, 54th Regiment.*
Boughton's (Horace) **Infantry.** See *New York Troops, 143d Regiment.*
Bourry's (Gotthilf) **Infantry.** See *New York Troops, 68th Regiment.*
Bowen's (Edward R.) **Infantry.** See *Pennsylvania Troops, 114th Regiment.*
Bown's (W. H. H.) **Infantry.** See *Ohio Troops, 61st Regiment.*
Boynton's (Joseph J.) **Infantry.** See *Vermont Troops, 13th Regiment.*
Bradley's (Leman W.) **Infantry.** See *New York Troops, 64th Regiment.*
Brady's (Allen G.) **Infantry.** See *Connecticut Troops, 17th Regiment.*
Brady's Sharpshooters. See *Michigan Troops.*
Breck's (George) **Artillery.** See *New York Troops, 1st Regiment, Battery L.*
Brinton's (William P.) **Cavalry.** See *Pennsylvania Troops, 18th Regiment.*
Broady's (K. Oscar) **Infantry.** See *New York Troops, 61st Regiment.*
Brodrick's (Virgil) **Cavalry.** See *New Jersey Troops, 1st Regiment.*
Brooker's (Albert F.) **Heavy Artillery.** See *Connecticut Troops, 1st Regiment, Battery B.*
Brooklyn 14th, Infantry. See *New York Troops, 84th Regiment.*
Brown's (Hiram L.) **Infantry.** See *Pennsylvania Troops, 145th Regiment.*
Brown's (Philip P., jr.) **Infantry.** See *New York Troops, 157th Regiment.*
Brown's (T. Frederick) **Artillery.** See *Rhode Island Troops, 1st Regiment, Battery B.*
Brown's (W. Harvey) **Infantry.** See *Union Troops, Regulars, 14th Regiment.*
Bucklyn's (John K.) **Artillery.** See *Rhode Island Troops, 1st Regiment, Battery E.*
Bucktails, Infantry. See *Pennsylvania Troops, 13th Reserves.*
Bull's (James M.) **Infantry.** See *New York Troops, 126th Regiment.*
Burke's (Denis F.) **Infantry.** See *New York Troops, 88th Regiment.*
Burling's (George C.) **Infantry.** See *New Jersey Troops, 6th Regiment.*
Burnham's (Hiram) **Infantry.** See *Maine Troops, 6th Regiment.*
Burns' (Michael W.) **Infantry.** See *New York Troops, 73d Regiment.*
Butler's (John H.) **Artillery.** See *Union Troops, Regulars, 2d Regiment, Battery G.*
Byrnes' (Richard) **Infantry.** See *Massachusetts Troops, 28th Regiment.*
Cain's (John H.) **Infantry.** See *Pennsylvania Troops, 155th Regiment.*
Calef's (John H.) **Artillery.** See *Union Troops, Regulars, 2d Regiment, Battery A.*
California Regiment, Infantry. See *Pennsylvania Troops, 71st Regiment.*
Campbell's (Edward L.) **Infantry.*** See *New Jersey Troops, 3d Regiment.*
Cantador's (Lorenz) **Infantry.** See *Pennsylvania Troops, 27th Regiment.*
Capehart's (Charles E.) **Cavalry.** See *West Virginia Troops, 1st Regiment.*
Carman's (Ezra A.) **Infantry.** See *New Jersey Troops, 13th Regiment.*
Carpenter's (Leonard W.) **Infantry.** See *Ohio Troops, 4th Regiment.*
Carpenter's (Louis H.) **Cavalry.** See *Union Troops, Regulars, 6th Regiment.*
Carroll's (Edward) **Infantry.** See *Pennsylvania Troops, 95th Regiment.*
Cassin's (Walter L.) **Engineers.** See *New York Troops, 15th Regiment.*
Cavada's (Frederick F.) **Infantry.** See *Pennsylvania Troops, 114th Regiment.*
Chamberlain's (Joshua L.) **Infantry.** See *Maine Troops, 20th Regiment.*
Chapman's (Alford B.) **Infantry.** See *New York Troops, 57th Regiment.*
Chapman's (George H.) **Cavalry.** See *Indiana Troops, 3d Regiment;* also *Illinois Troops, 12th Regiment.**

---

*Temporarily commanding.

Chester's (James) **Artillery.** See *Union Troops, Regulars, 1st Regiment, Batteries E and G.*

Christman's (Charles H.) **Infantry.** See *Delaware Troops, 2d Regiment.*

Claflin's (Ira W.) **Cavalry.** See *Union Troops, Regulars, 6th Regiment.*

Clark's (A. Judson) **Artillery.** See *New Jersey Troops, 2d Battery.*

Clark's (Atherton W.) **Infantry.** See *Maine Troops, 20th Regiment.*

Clarke's (Robert) **Artillery.** See *Union Troops, Regulars, 2d Regiment, Battery M.*

Clinton's (William) **Infantry.** See *Union Troops, Regulars, 10th Regiment.*

Coates' (Henry C.) **Infantry.** See *Minnesota Troops, 1st Regiment.*

Cobham's (George A., jr.) **Infantry.** See *Pennsylvania Troops, 111th Regiment.*

Coburn's (James H.) **Infantry.** See *Connecticut Troops, 27th Regiment.*

Cogswell's (William) **Infantry.**' See *Massachusetts Troops, 2d Regiment.*

Colgrove's (Silas) **Infantry.** See *Indiana Troops, 27th Regiment.*

Collier's (Frederick H.) **Infantry.** See *Pennsylvania Troops, 139th Regiment.*

Collis' (Charles H. T.) **Zouaves, Infantry.** See *Pennsylvania Troops, 114th Regiment.*

Colvill's (William, jr.) **Infantry.** See *Minnesota Troops, 1st Regiment.*

Conger's (Seymour B.) **Cavalry.** See *West Virginia Troops, 3d Regiment.*

Conner's (Freeman) **Infantry.** See *New York Troops, 44th Regiment;* also *Maine Troops, 20th Regiment.**

Connor's (Selden) **Infantry.** See *Maine Troops, 7th Regiment.*

Cook's (John E.) **Infantry.** See *New York Troops, 76th Regiment.*

Coons' (John) **Infantry.** See *Indiana Troops, 14th Regiment.*

Cooper's (Frederick) **Infantry.** See *New Jersey Troops, 7th Regiment.*

Cooper's (James H.) **Artillery.** See *Pennsylvania Troops, 1st Regiment, Battery B.*

Corrie's (William A.) **Cavalry.** See *Pennsylvania Troops, 8th Regiment.*

Coulter's (Richard) **Infantry.** See *Pennsylvania Troops, 11th Regiment.*

Cowan's (Andrew) **Artillery.** See *New York Troops, 1st Battery.*

Craft's (William S.) **Cavalry.** See *Pennsylvania Troops, 1st Regiment;* also *New Jersey Troops, 1st Regiment.**

Craig's (Calvin A.) **Infantry.** See *Pennsylvania Troops, 105th Regiment.*

Cram's (George C.) **Cavalry.** See *Union Troops, Regulars, 6th Regiment.*

Crandell's (Levin) **Infantry.** See *New York Troops, 125th Regiment.*

Crane's (Nirom M.) **Infantry.** See *New York Troops, 107th Regiment.*

Creighton's (William R.) **Infantry.** See *Ohio Troops, 7th Regiment.*

Crocker's (John S.) **Infantry.** See *New York Troops, 93d Regiment.*

Cross' (Nelson) **Infantry.** See *New York Troops, 67th Regiment.*

Cross' (Richard E.) **Infantry.** See *New Hampshire Troops, 5th Regiment.*

Cummins' (Francis M.) **Infantry.** See *New York Troops, 124th Regiment.*

Cummins' (Robert P.) **Infantry.** See *Pennsylvania Troops, 142d Regiment.*

Cunningham's (Henry W.) **Infantry.** See *Maine Troops, 19th Regiment.*

Curry's (William L.) **Infantry.** See *Pennsylvania Troops, 106th Regiment.*

Curtis' (Greely S.) **Cavalry.** See *Massachusetts Troops, 1st Regiment.*

Curtis' (Sylvanus W.) **Infantry.** See *Michigan Troops, 7th Regiment.*

Cushing's (Alonzo H.) **Artillery.** See *Union Troops, Regulars, 4th Regiment, Battery A.*

Dana's (Edmund L.) **Infantry.** See *Pennsylvania Troops, 143d Regiment.*

Daniels' (Jabez J.) **Artillery.** See *Michigan Troops, 9th Battery.*

Danks' (John A.) **Infantry.** See *Pennsylvania Troops, 63d Regiment.*

Dare's (George) **Infantry.** See *Pennsylvania Troops, 5th Reserves.*

Darlington's (William B.) **Cavalry.** See *Pennsylvania Troops, 18th Regiment.*

Darrow's (John) **Infantry.** See *New York Troops, 82d Regiment.*

Davies' (Henry E., jr.) **Cavalry.** See *New York Troops, 2d Regiment.*

Davis' (Milton S.) **Infantry.** See *Pennsylvania Troops, 68th Regiment.*

Davis' (William) **Infantry.** See *Pennsylvania Troops, 69th Regiment.*

Dawes' (Rufus R.) **Infantry.** See *Wisconsin Troops, 6th Regiment.*

---

* Temporarily commanding.

Deems' (James M.) **Cavalry.** See *Maryland Troops, Union,* 1st *Regiment.*
De Kalb Infantry. See *New York Troops,* 41st *Regiment.*
Dent's (John T.) **Infantry.** See *Delaware Troops,* 1st *Regiment.*
Devereux's (Arthur F.) **Infantry.** See *Massachusetts Troops,* 19th *Regiment.*
Dilger's (Hubert) **Artillery.** See *Ohio Troops,* 1st *Regiment, Battery 1.*
Dobke's (Adolphus) **Infantry.** See *New York Troops,* 45th *Regiment.*
Donovan's (Matthew) **Infantry.** See *Massachusetts Troops,* 16th *Regiment.*
Doster's (William E.) **Cavalry.** See *Pennsylvania Troops,* 4th *Regiment.*
Douty's (Calvin S.) **Cavalry.** See *Maine Troops,* 1st *Regiment.*
Dow's (Edwin B.) **Artillery.** See *Maine Troops,* 6th *Battery.*
Duffié's (Alfred N.) **Cavalry.** See *Rhode Island Troops,* 1st *Regiment.*
Dunn's (Thomas S.) **Infantry.** See *Union Troops, Regulars,* 12th *Regiment.*
Dunne's (John P.) **Infantry.** See *Pennsylvania Troops,* 115th *Regiment.*
Dunning's (William B.) **Infantry.** See *New Jersey Troops,* 11th *Regiment.*
Duvall's (Robert E.) **Cavalry.** See *Purnell Legion, Cavalry, post.*
Dwight's (Walton) **Infantry.** See *Pennsylvania Troops,* 149th *Regiment.*
Eakin's (Chandler P.) **Artillery** See *Union Troops, Regulars,* 1st *Regiment, Battery H.*
Eastern Shore, 1st, Infantry. See *Maryland Troops, Union.*
Edgell's (Frederick M.) **Artillery.** See *New Hampshire Troops,* 1st *Battery.*
Edwards' (Albert M.) **Infantry.** See *Michigan Troops,* 24th *Regiment.*
Edwards' (Clark S.) **Infantry.** See *Maine Troops,* 5th *Regiment.*
Edwards' (Oliver) **Infantry.** See *Massachusetts Troops,* 37th *Regiment.*
Egan's (Thomas W.) **Infantry.** See *New York Troops,* 40th *Regiment.*
Einsiedel's (Detleo von) **Infantry.** See *New York Troops,* 41st *Regiment.*
Elder's (Samuel S.) **Artillery.** See *Union Troops, Regulars,* 4th *Regiment, Battery E.*
Elliott's (Robert T.) **Infantry.** See *Michigan Troops,* 16th *Regiment.*
Ellis' (A. Van Horne) **Infantry.** See *New York Troops,* 124th *Regiment.*
Ellis' (Theodore G.) **Infantry.** See *Connecticut Troops,* 14th *Regiment.*
Ellmaker's (Peter C.) **Infantry.** See *Pennsylvania Troops,* 119th *Regiment.*
Ent's (Wellington H.) **Infantry.** See *Pennsylvania Troops,* 6th *Reserves.*
Ernst's (Louis) **Infantry.** See *New York Troops,* 140th *Regiment.*
Ewing's (Charles) **Infantry.** See *New Jersey Troops,* 4th *Regiment.*
Excelsior, 1st Regiment, Infantry. See *New York Troops,* 70th *Regiment.*
Excelsior, 2d Regiment, Infantry. See *New York Troops,* 71st *Regiment.*
Excelsior, 3d Regiment, Infantry. See *New York Troops,* 72d *Regiment.*
Excelsior, 4th Regiment, Infantry. See *New York Troops,* 73d *Regiment.*
Excelsior, 5th Regiment, Infantry. See *New York Troops,* 74th *Regiment.*
Fairchild's (Lucius) **Infantry.** See *Wisconsin Troops,* 2d *Regiment.*
Farnham's (Augustus B.) **Infantry.** See *Maine Troops,* 16th *Regiment.*
Farnum's (J. Egbert) **Infantry.** See *New York Troops,* 70th *Regiment.*
Fesler's (John R.) **Infantry.** See *Indiana Troops,* 27th *Regiment.*
Finnicum's (Mark) **Infantry.** See *Wisconsin Troops,* 7th *Regiment.*
Fitzhugh's (Robert H.) **Artillery.** See *New York Troops,* 1st *Regiment, Battery K.*
Flood's (Martin) **Infantry.** See *Wisconsin Troops,* 3d *Regiment.*
Floyd-Jones' (De Lancey) **Infantry.** See *Union Troops, Regulars,* 11th *Regiment.*
Flynn's (John) **Infantry.** See *Pennsylvania Troops,* 28th *Regiment.*
Foerster's (Hermann) **Infantry.** See *New York Troops,* 8th *Regiment.*
Foust's (Benezet F.) **Infantry.** See *Pennsylvania Troops,* 88th *Regiment.*
Fowler's (Douglas) **Infantry.** See *Connecticut Troops,* 17th *Regiment.*
Fowler's (Edward B.) **Infantry.** See *New York Troops,* 84th *Regiment.*
Fox's (George B.) **Infantry.** See *Ohio Troops,* 75th *Regiment.*
Francine's (Louis R.) **Infantry.** See *New Jersey Troops,* 7th *Regiment.*
Fraser's (John) **Infantry.** See *Pennsylvania Troops,* 140th *Regiment.*
Freeborn's (Benjamin) **Artillery.** See *Rhode Island Troops,* 1st *Regiment, Battery E.*
Freedley's (Henry W.) **Infantry.** See *Union Troops, Regulars,* 3d *Regiment.*

French's (Winsor B.) **Infantry.** See *New York Troops, 77th Regiment.*
Freudenberg's (Charles G.) **Infantry.** See *New York Troops, 52d Regiment.*
Frueauff's (John F.) **Infantry.** See *Pennsylvania Troops, 153d Regiment.*
Fry's (William H.) **Cavalry.*** See *William H. Fry.*
Fuchs' (John W.) **Infantry.** See *Wisconsin Troops, 26th Regiment.*
Fuger's (Frederick) **Artillery.** See *Union Troops, Regulars, 4th Regiment, Battery A.*
Fuller's (Josiah C.) **Infantry.** See *Massachusetts Troops, 32d Regiment.*
Fuller's (William D.) **Artillery.** See *Union Troops, Regulars, 3d Regiment, Battery C.*
Gambee's (Charles B.) **Infantry.** See *Ohio Troops, 55th Regiment.*
Garibaldi Guard, Infantry. See *New York Troops, 39th Regiment.*
Garrard's (Kenner) **Infantry.** See *New York Troops, 146th Regiment.*
Gates' (Theodore B.) **Infantry.** See *New York Troops, 80th Regiment.*
Geary's (Edward R.) **Artillery.** See *Pennsylvania Troops, Battery E.*
Gibbs' (Frank C.) **Artillery.** See *Ohio Troops, 1st Regiment, Battery L.*
Giddings' (Grotius R.) **Infantry.** See *Union Troops, Regulars, 14th Regiment.*
Gifford's (Henry J.) **Infantry.** See *New York Troops, 33d Regiment.*
Gilkyson's (Stephen R.) **Infantry.** See *New Jersey Troops, 6th Regiment.*
Gimber's (Frederick L.) **Infantry.** See *Pennsylvania Troops, 109th Regiment.*
Gleason's (D. H. L.) **Cavalry.** See *Massachusetts Troops, 1st Regiment.*
Glenn's (James) **Infantry.** See *Pennsylvania Troops, 149th Regiment.*
Glenn's (John F.) **Infantry.** See *Pennsylvania Troops, 23d Regiment.*
Godard's (Abel) **Infantry.** See *New York Troops, 60th Regiment.*
Godfrey's (Thomas C.) **Infantry.** See *New Jersey Troops, 5th Regiment.*
Graham's (William M.) **Artillery.** See *Union Troops, Regulars, 1st Regiment, Battery K.*
Gray's (George) **Cavalry.** See *Michigan Troops, 6th Regiment.*
Greene's (J. Durell) **Infantry.** See *Union Troops, Regulars, 17th Regiment.*
Grimes' (John) **Infantry.** See *New Jersey Troops, 13th Regiment.*
Grover's (Andrew J.) **Infantry.** See *New York Troops, 76th Regiment.*
Grover's (Ira G.) **Infantry.** See *Indiana Troops, 7th Regiment.*
Guiney's (Patrick R.) **Infantry.** See *Massachusetts Troops, 9th Regiment.*
Gwyn's (James) **Infantry.** See *Pennsylvania Troops, 118th Regiment.*
Haines' (Benjamin F.) **Infantry.** See *Pennsylvania Troops, 11th Regiment.*
Hall's (James A.) **Artillery.** See *Maine Troops, 2d Battery.*
Hamblin's (Joseph E.) **Infantry.** See *New York Troops, 65th Regiment.*
Hamilton's (Theodore B.) **Infantry.** See *New York Troops, 62d Regiment.*
Hammell's (John S.) **Infantry.** See *New York Troops, 66th Regiment.*
Hammerstein's (Herbert von) **Infantry.** See *New York Troops, 78th Regiment.*
Hammond's (John) **Cavalry.** See *New York Troops, 5th Regiment.*
Hancock's (David P.) **Infantry.** See *Union Troops, Regulars, 7th Regiment.*
Hapgood's (Charles E.) **Infantry.** See *New Hampshire Troops, 5th Regiment.*
Hardin's (Martin D.) **Infantry.** See *Pennsylvania Troops, 12th Reserves.*
Harhaus' (Otto) **Cavalry.** See *New York Troops, 2d Regiment.*
Harlow's (Franklin P.) **Infantry.** See *Massachusetts Troops, 7th Regiment.*
Harn's (William A.) **Artillery.** See *New York Troops, 3d Battery.*
Harney's (George) **Infantry.** See *New York Troops, 147th Regiment.*
Harris' (Andrew L.) **Infantry.** See *Ohio Troops, 75th Regiment.*
Harris' (Edward P.) **Infantry.** See *Delaware Troops, 1st Regiment.*
Harris Light Cavalry. See *New York Troops, 2d Regiment.*
Hart's (Patrick) **Artillery.** See *New York Troops, 15th Battery.*
Hartshorne's (William R.) **Infantry.** See *Pennsylvania Troops, 13th Reserves.*
Hartung's (Adolph von) **Infantry.** See *Pennsylvania Troops, 74th Regiment.*
Haseltine's (James H.) **Cavalry.** See *Pennsylvania Troops, 6th Regiment.*
Haskell's (Harry L.) **Infantry.** See *New York Troops, 125th Regiment.*

---

*Improvised.

Hastings' (Matthew) **Artillery.** See *Keystone Artillery, post.*

Hawley's (William) **Infantry.** See *Wisconsin Troops, 3d Regiment.*

Hayes' (Edward) **Infantry.** See *Ohio Troops, 29th Regiment.*

Hayes' (Joseph) **Infantry.** See *Massachusetts Troops, 18th Regiment.*

Hazard's (Jeffrey) **Artillery.** See *Rhode Island Troops, 1st Regiment, Battery H.*

Hazlett's (Charles E.) **Artillery.** See *Union Troops, Regulars, 5th Regiment, Battery D.*

Heath's (Francis E.) **Infantry.** See *Maine Troops, 19th Regiment.*

Heaton's (Edward) **Artillery.** See *Union Troops, Regulars, 2d Regiment, Batteries B and L.*

Hecker's (Frederick) **Infantry.** See *Illinois Troops, 82d Regiment.*

Heckman's (Lewis) **Artillery.** See *Ohio Troops, 1st Regiment, Battery K.*

Henry's (William, jr.) **Infantry.** See *New Jersey Troops, 1st Regiment.*

Hesser's (Theodore) **Infantry.** See *Pennsylvania Troops, 72d Regiment.*

Higgins' (Benjamin L.) **Infantry.** See *New York Troops, 86th Regiment.*

Hildebrandt's (Hugo) **Infantry.** See *New York Troops, 39th Regiment.*

Hill's (John T.) **Infantry.** See *New Jersey Troops, 12th Regiment.*

Hill's (Wallace) **Artillery.** See *West Virginia Troops, Battery C.*

Hizar's (Thomas B.) **Infantry.** See *Delaware Troops, 1st Regiment.*

Hofmann's (J. William) **Infantry.** See *Pennsylvania Troops, 56th Regiment.*

Holt's (Thomas) **Infantry.** See *New York Troops, 74th Regiment.*

Hopper's (George F.) **Infantry.** See *New York Troops, 10th Regiment.*

Hubbard's (Edwin L.) **Infantry.** See *Wisconsin Troops, 3d Regiment.*

Hugo's (William H.) **Infantry.** See *New York Troops, 70th Regiment.*

Huidekoper's (Henry S.) **Infantry.** See *Pennsylvania Troops, 150th Regiment.*

Hulings' (Thomas M.) **Infantry.** See *Pennsylvania Troops, 49th Regiment.*

Full's (James C.) **Infantry.** See *Pennsylvania Troops, 62d Regiment.*

Huntington's (James F.) **Artillery.** See *Ohio Troops, 1st Regiment, Battery H.*

Huston's (James) **Infantry.** See *New York Troops, 82d Regiment.*

Ireland's (David) **Infantry.** See *New York Troops, 137th Regiment.*

Irvin's (John) **Infantry.** See *Pennsylvania Troops, 149th Regiment.*

Irvine's (William) **Cavalry.** See *New York Troops, 10th Regiment.*

Jackson's (Allan H.) **Infantry.** See *New York Troops, 134th Regiment.*

Jackson's (Samuel M.) **Infantry.** See *Pennsylvania Troops, 11th Reserves.*

Jacobs' (William H.) **Infantry.** See *Wisconsin Troops, 26th Regiment.*

James' (Robert) **Artillery.*** See *Union Troops, Regulars, 4th Regiment, Battery K.*

Janeway's (Hugh H.) **Cavalry.** See *New Jersey Troops, 1st Regiment.*

Jeffords' (Harrison H.) **Infantry.** See *Michigan Troops, 4th Regiment.*

Jenkins' (David T.) **Infantry.** See *New York Troops, 146th Regiment.*

Johnson's (Riley) **Cavalry.** See *New York Troops, 6th Regiment.*

Jones' (David M.) **Infantry.** See *Pennsylvania Troops, 110th Regiment.*

Jones' (Edward S.) **Cavalry.** See *Pennsylvania Troops, 3d Regiment.*

Jones' (George W.) **Infantry.** See *Pennsylvania Troops, 150th Regiment.*

Jones' (Noah) **Cavalry.** See *Ohio Troops, 1st Regiment.*

Joslin's (George C.) **Infantry.** See *Massachusetts Troops, 15th Regiment.*

Kelley's (Daniel F.) **Infantry.** See *Pennsylvania Troops, 73d Regiment.*

Kellogg's (Josiah H.) **Cavalry.** See *Pennsylvania Troops, 17th Regiment.*

Ketcham's (John H.) **Infantry.** See *New York Troops, 150th Regiment.*

Keystone Artillery. See *Pennsylvania Troops.*

King's (Rufus, jr.) **Artillery.** See *Union Troops, Regulars, 4th Regiment, Battery A.*

Kinzie's (David H.) **Artillery.** See *Union Troops, Regulars, 5th Regiment, Battery K.*

Kirby's (Edmund) **Artillery.** See *Union Troops, Regulars, 1st Regiment, Battery I.*

Knap's (Joseph M.) **Artillery.** See *Pennsylvania Troops, Battery E.*

Koenig's (Emil) **Infantry.** See *New York Troops, 58th Regiment.*

---

* Temporarily commanding.

Kohler's (John B.) **Infantry.** See *Pennsylvania Troops,* 98*th Regiment.*
Kovacs' (Stephen) **Infantry.** See *New York Troops,* 54*th Regiment.*
Krauseneck's (Henry) **Infantry.** See *Pennsylvania Troops,* 74*th Regiment.*
Lakeman's (Moses B.) **Infantry.** See *Maine Troops,* 3*d Regiment.*
Lamont's (William H.) **Infantry.** See *Pennsylvania Troops,* 83*d Regiment.*
Lane's (James C.) **Infantry.** See *New York Troops,* 102*d Regiment.*
Langley's (John F.) **Infantry.** See *New Hampshire Troops,* 12*th Regiment.*
Langston's (John G.) **Infantry.** See *New Jersey Troops,* 8*th Regiment.*
Lansing's (Jacob H.) **Infantry.** See *New York Troops,* 86*th Regiment.*
Lay's (Richard G.) **Infantry.** See *Union Troops, Regulars,* 3*d Regiment.*
Leavitt's (Archibald D.) **Infantry.** See *Maine Troops,* 16*th Regiment.*
Ledig's (August) **Infantry.** See *Pennsylvania Troops,* 75*th Regiment.*
Lee's (Arthur T.) **Infantry.** See *Union Troops, Regulars,* 2*d Regiment.*
Lefferts' (Marshall) **Infantry.** See *New York Troops,* 7*th Regiment, Militia.*
Leonard's (John) **Infantry.** See *New York Troops,* 72*d Regiment.*
Leonard's (Samuel H.) **Infantry.** See *Massachusetts Troops,* 13*th Regiment.*
Lessig's (William H.) **Infantry.** See *Pennsylvania Troops,* 96*th Regiment.*
Lewis' (John R.) **Infantry.** See *Vermont Troops,* 5*th Regiment.*
Libby's (Edwin) **Infantry.** See *Maine Troops,* 4*th Regiment.*
Lloyd's (Edward F.) **Infantry.** See *New York Troops,* 119*th Regiment.*
Lloyd's (William H.) **Infantry.** See *New Jersey Troops,* 11*th Regiment.*
Lockman's (John T.) **Infantry.** See *New York Troops,* 119*th Regiment.*
Lockwood's (Abram L.) **Infantry.** See *New York Troops,* 120*th Regiment.*
Lockwood's (Jonathan H.) **Infantry.** See *West Virginia Troops,* 7*th Regiment.*
Long's (Richard) **Infantry.** See *Ohio Troops,* 73*d Regiment.*
Lord's (Richard S. C.) **Cavalry.** See *Union Troops, Regulars,* 1*st Regiment.*
Lowell's (Charles R., jr.) **Cavalry.** See *Massachusetts Troops,* 2*d Regiment.*
Lumbard's (George W.) **Infantry.** See *Michigan Troops,* 4*th Regiment.*
Lusk's (Isaac M.) **Infantry.** See *New York Troops,* 111*th Regiment.*
Lutz's (John M.) **Infantry.** See *Ohio Troops,* 107*th Regiment.*
Lyle's (Peter) **Infantry.** See *Pennsylvania Troops,* 90*th Regiment.*
McAllister's (Robert) **Infantry.** See *New Jersey Troops,* 11*th Regimen..*
McCalmont's (Alfred B.) **Infantry.** See *Pennsylvania Troops,* 142*d Regiment.*
McCartney's (William H.) **Artillery.** See *Massachusetts Troops,* 1*st Battery (A).*
MacConnell's (Charles C.) **Artillery.** See *Union Troops, Regulars,* 5*th Regiment, Battery I.*
McCrea's (Tully) **Artillery.** See *Union Troops, Regulars,* 1*st Regiment, Battery I.*
MacDougall's (Clinton D.) **Infantry.** See *New York Troops,* 111*th Regiment.*
McFadden's (William) **Infantry.** See *New York Troops,* 59*th Regiment.*
McFarland's (George F.) **Infantry.** See *Pennsylvania Troops,* 151*st Regiment.*
McFarlane's (Robert) **Infantry.** See *Pennsylvania Troops,* 148*th Regiment.*
McGroarty's (Stephen J.) **Infantry.** See *Ohio Troops,* 61*st Regiment.*
McKee's (Samuel A.) **Infantry.** See *Union Troops, Regulars,* 2*d Regiment.*
McKeen's (H. Boyd) **Infantry.** See *Pennsylvania Troops,* 81*st Regiment.*
McMahon's (Andrew R.) **Artillery.** See *New York Troops,* 15*th Battery.*
McMichael's (Richards) **Infantry.** See *Pennsylvania Troops,* 53*d Regiment.*
MacThomson's (James) **Infantry.** See *Pennsylvania Troops,* 107*th Regiment.*
Macy's (George N.) **Infantry.** See *Massachusetts Troops,* 20*th Regiment.*
Madill's (Henry J.) **Infantry.** See *Pennsylvania Troops,* 141*st Regiment.*
Mahler's (Francis) **Infantry.** See *Pennsylvania Troops,* 75*th Regiment.*
Mallon's (James E.) **Infantry.** See *New York Troops,* 42*d Regiment.*
Maloney's (William) **Infantry.** See *Ohio Troops,* 25*th Regiment.*
Mann's (Daniel P.) **Cavalry.** See *Oneida Cavalry, post.*
Mann's (William D.) **Cavalry.** See *Michigan Troops,* 7*th Regiment.*
Manning's (Nathaniel J.) **Infantry.** See *Ohio Troops,* 25*th Regiment.*

Mansfield's (John) **Infantry.** See *Wisconsin Troops*, 2d *Regiment*.

Markell's (William L.) **Cavalry.** See *New York Troops*, 8th *Regiment*.

Martin's (Joseph W.) **Artillery.** See *New York Troops*, 6th *Battery*.

Martin's (Leonard) **Artillery.** See *Union Troops, Regulars*, 5th *Regiment, Battery F.*

Martin's (Luther) **Infantry.** See *New Jersey Troops*, 11th *Regiment*.

Martindale's (Edward) **Infantry.** See *New Jersey Troops*, 26th *Regiment*.

Mason's (Julius W.) **Cavalry.** See *Union Troops, Regulars*, 5th *Regiment*.

Mason's (Philip D.) **Artillery.** See *Union Troops, Regulars*, 1st *Regiment, Battery H.*

Maulsby's (William P.) **Infantry.** See *Maryland Troops, Union*, 1st *Regiment, P. H. B.*

Maxwell's (William R.) **Infantry.** See *New Jersey Troops*, 4th *Regiment*.

Mendell's (George H.) **Engineers.** See *Union Troops, Regulars*.

Merkle's (Christopher F.) **Artillery.** See *Union Troops, Regulars*, 4th *Regiment, Battery G.*

Merriam's (Waldo) **Infantry.** See *Massachusetts Troops*, 16th *Regiment*.

Merrill's (Charles B.) **Infantry.** See *Maine Troops*, 17th *Regiment*.

Merwin's (Henry C.) **Infantry.** See *Connecticut Troops*, 27th *Regiment*.

Messick's (Nathan S.) **Infantry.** See *Minnesota Troops*, 1st *Regiment*.

Meyer's (Seraphim) **Infantry.** See *Ohio Troops*, 107th *Regiment*.

Michalowski's (Theophilus B. von) **Artillery.** See *Union Troops, Regulars*, 1st *Regiment, Battery K.*

Miller's (Francis C.) **Infantry.** See *New York Troops*, 147th *Regiment*.

Milton's (Richard S.) **Artillery.** See *Massachusetts Troops*, 9th *Battery*.

Mitzel's (Alexander von) **Infantry.** See *Pennsylvania Troops*, 74th *Regiment*.

Moesch's (Joseph A.) **Infantry.** See *New York Troops*, 83d *Regiment*.

Moffett's (Samuel A.) **Infantry.** See *New York Troops*, 94th *Regiment*.

Moody's (William H.) **Infantry.** See *Pennsylvania Troops*, 139th *Regiment*.

Moore's (John W.) **Infantry.** See *Pennsylvania Troops*, 99th *Regiment*.

Moroney's (Richard) **Infantry.** See *New York Troops*, 69th *Regiment*.

Morris' (Orlando H.) **Infantry.** See *New York Troops*, 66th *Regiment*.

Morrow's (Henry A.) **Infantry.** See *Michigan Troops*, 24th *Regiment*.

Morse's (Charles F.) **Infantry.** See *Massachusetts Troops*, 2d *Regiment*.

Mudge's (Charles R.) **Infantry.** See *Massachusetts Troops*, 2d *Regiment*.

Muhlenberg's (Edward D.) **Artillery.** See *Union Troops, Regulars*, 4th *Regiment, Battery F.*

Mulholland's (St. Clair A.) **Infantry.** See *Pennsylvania Troops*, 116th *Regiment*.

Munson's (William D.) **Infantry.** See *Vermont Troops*, 13th *Regiment*.

Musser's (John D.) **Infantry.** See *Pennsylvania Troops*, 143d *Regiment*.

Nelson's (Alanson H.) **Infantry.** See *Pennsylvania Troops*, 57th *Regiment*.

Nelson's (Peter) **Infantry.** See *New York Troops*, 66th *Regiment*.

Nelson's (Thomas) **Infantry.** See *Vermont Troops*, 6th *Regiment*.

Nevin's (David J.) **Infantry.** See *New York Troops*, 62d *Regiment*.

Nevin's (John I.) **Infantry.** See *Pennsylvania Troops*, 93d *Regiment*.

New York 2d Militia, Infantry. See *New York Troops*, 82d *Regiment*.

New York 9th Militia, Infantry. See *New York Troops*, 83d *Regiment*.

New York 14th Militia, Infantry. See *New York Troops*, 84th *Regiment*.

New York 20th Militia, Infantry. See *New York Troops*, 80th *Regiment*.

Nichols' (William T.) **Infantry.** See *Vermont Troops*, 14th *Regiment*.

Nolan's (Nicholas) **Cavalry.** See *Union Troops, Regulars*, 6th *Regiment*.

Northrup's (Charles) **Infantry.** See *New York Troops*, 97th *Regiment*.

Norton's (George W.) **Artillery.** See *Ohio Troops*, 1st *Regiment, Battery H.*

O'Kane's (Dennis) **Infantry.** See *Pennsylvania Troops*, 69th *Regiment*.

Oliver's (Moses W.) **Infantry.** See *Pennsylvania Troops*, 145th *Regiment*.

Oneida Cavalry. See *New York Troops*.

Opp's (Milton) **Infantry.** See *Pennsylvania Troops*, 84th *Regiment*.

O'Rorke's (Patrick H.) **Infantry.** See *New York Troops*, 140*th Regiment.*
Orton's (William H.) **Cavalry.** See *District of Columbia Troops.*
Otis' (George H.) **Infantry.** See *Wisconsin Troops*, 2*d Regiment.*
Otto's (August) **Infantry.** See *New York Troops*, 58*th Regiment.*
Overmyer's (John B.) **Infantry.** See *Pennsylvania Troops*, 11*th Regiment.*
Owens' (Walter L.) **Infantry.** See *Pennsylvania Troops*, 151*st Regiment.*
Packer's (Warren W.) **Infantry.** See *Connecticut Troops*, 5*th Regiment.*
Pardee's (Ario, jr.) **Infantry.** See *Pennsylvania Troops*, 147*th Regiment.*
Parsons' (Augustin N.) **Artillery.** See *New Jersey Troops*, 1*st Battery.*
Parsons' (Joseph B.) **Infantry.** See *Massachusetts Troops*, 10*th Regiment.*
Patrick's (John H.) **Infantry.** See *Ohio Troops*, 5*th Regiment.*
Patterson's (Edmund Y.) **Infantry.** See *Pennsylvania Troops*, 88*th Regiment.*
Patterson's (John W.) **Infantry.** See *Pennsylvania Troops*, 102*d Regiment.*
Pennington's (A. C. M., jr.) **Artillery.** See *Union Troops, Regulars*, 2*d Regiment, Battery M.*
Pennsylvania 1st Rifles, **Infantry.** See *Pennsylvania Troops*, 13*th Reserves.*
Penrose's (William H.) **Infantry.** See *New Jersey Troops*, 15*th Regiment.*
Perrin's (Walter S.) **Artillery.** See *Rhode Island Troops*, 1*st Regiment, Battery B.*
Pettes' (William H.) **Engineers.** See *New York Troops*, 50*th Regiment.*
Pettit's (Rufus D.) **Artillery.** See *New York Troops*, 1*st Regiment, Battery B.*
Philadelphia Blues, **Infantry.** See *Pennsylvania Troops*, 33*d Regiment, Militia.*
Phillips' (Charles A.) **Artillery.** See *Massachusetts Troops*, 5*th Battery (E).*
Pierce's (Byron R.) **Infantry.** See *Michigan Troops*, 3*d Regiment.*
Pierce's (Edwin S.) **Infantry.** See *Michigan Troops*, 3*d Regiment.*
Pierce's (Francis E.) **Infantry.** See *New York Troops*, 108*th Regiment.*
Plumer's (William) **Sharpshooters.** See *Massachusetts Troops*, 1*st Company.*
Potomac Home Brigade (1st), **Infantry.** See *Maryland Troops, Union.*
Potter's (Henry L.) **Infantry.** See *New York Troops*, 71*st Regiment.*
Powell's (Eugene) **Infantry.** See *Ohio Troops*, 66*th Regiment.*
Pratt's (Franklin A.) **Heavy Artillery.** See *Connecticut Troops*, 1*st Regiment, Battery M.*
Prescott's (George L.) **Infantry.** See *Massachusetts Troops*, 32*d Regiment.*
Preston's (Addison W.) **Cavalry.** See *Vermont Troops*, 1*st Regiment.*
Prey's (Gilbert G.) **Infantry.** See *New York Troops*, 104*th Regiment.*
Price's (E. Livingston) **Infantry.** See *New York Troops*, 145*th Regiment.*
Price's (R. Butler) **Cavalry.** See *Pennsylvania Troops*, 2*d Regiment.*
Proctor's (Redfield) **Infantry.** See *Vermont Troops*, 15*th Regiment.*
Pruyn's (Augustus) **Cavalry.** See *Michigan Troops*, 5*th Regiment.*
Pulford's (John) **Infantry.** See *Maryland Troops, Union.*
Purnell Legion, **Cavalry.** See *Maryland Troops, Union.*
Pye's (Edward) **Infantry.** See *New York Troops*, 95*th Regiment.*
Ramsey's (John) **Infantry.** See *New Jersey Troops*, 8*th Regiment.*
Randall's (Charles B.) **Infantry.** See *New York Troops*, 149*th Regiment.*
Randall's (Francis V.) **Infantry.** See *Vermont Troops*, 13*th Regiment.*
Randol's (Alanson M.) **Artillery.** See *Union Troops, Regulars*, 1*st Regiment, Batteries E and G.*
Randolph's (George E.) **Artillery.** See *Rhode Island Troops*, 1*st Regiment, Battery E.*
Rank's (William D.) **Heavy Artillery.** See *Pennsylvania Troops*, 3*d Regiment, Battery H.*
Ransom's (Dunbar R.) **Artillery.*** See *Union Troops, Regulars*, 5*th Regiment, Battery C.*
Read's (Edwin W. H.) **Infantry.** See *Union Troops, Regulars*, 8*th Regiment.*
Revere's (Paul J.) **Infantry.** See *Massachusetts Troops*, 20*th Regiment.*
Reynolds' (Gilbert H.) **Artillery.** See *New York Troops*, 1*st Regiment, Battery L.*

---

* Temporarily commanding.

Reynolds' (John W.) **Infantry.** See *Pennsylvania Troops*, 145th Regiment.

Rice's (James C.) **Infantry.** See *New York Troops*, 44th Regiment.

Richmond's (Nathaniel P.) **Cavalry.** See *West Virginia Troops*, 1st Regiment.

Rickards' (William, jr.) **Infantry.** See *Pennsylvania Troops*, 29th Regiment.

Ricketts' (R. Bruce) **Artillery.** See *Pennsylvania Troops, 1st Regiment, Batteries F and G.*

Rider's (Henry W.) **Infantry.** See *New York Troops*, 12th Regiment.

Rigby's (James H.) **Artillery.** See *Maryland Troops, Union, Battery A.*

Rittenhouse's (Benjamin F.) **Artillery.** See *Union Troops, Regulars, 5th Regiment, Battery D.*

Roath's (Emanuel D.) **Infantry.** See *Pennsylvania Troops*, 107th Regiment.

Roberts' (Richard P.) **Infantry.** See *Pennsylvania Troops*, 140th Regiment.

Robertson's (James M.) **Artillery.** See *Union Troops, Regulars, 2d Regiment, Batteries B and L.*

Robinson's (Gilbert P.) **Infantry.** See *Maryland Troops, Union, 3d Regiment.*

Robinson's (James S.) **Infantry.** See *Ohio Troops, 82d Regiment.*

Robinson's (Oliver O. G.) **Cavalry.** See *Pennsylvania Troops, 3d Regiment.*

Robinson's (William W.) **Infantry.** See *Wisconsin Troops, 7th Regiment.*

Robison's (John K.) **Cavalry.** See *Pennsylvania Troops, 16th Regiment.*

Rodenbough's (Theophilus F.) **Cavalry.** See *Union Troops, Regulars, 2d Regiment.*

Rogers' (Horatio, jr.) **Infantry.** See *Rhode Island Troops, 2d Regiment.*

Rogers' (Isaac) **Infantry.** See *Pennsylvania Troops*, 110th Regiment.

Rogers' (James C.) **Infantry.** See *New York Troops*, 123d Regiment.

Rogers' (Robert E.) **Artillery.** See *New York Troops, 1st Regiment, Battery B.*

Rolfe's (Frank A.) **Heavy Artillery.** See *Massachusetts Troops, 1st Regiment.*

Root's (Adrian R.) **Infantry.** See *New York Troops*, 94th Regiment.

Rorty's (James McKay) **Artillery.*** See *New York Troops, 1st Regiment, Battery B.*

Rugg's (Sylvanus T.) **Artillery.** See *Union Troops, Regulars, 4th Regiment, Battery F.*

Sackett's (William) **Cavalry.** See *New York Troops*, 9th Regiment.

Salomon's (Edward S.) **Infantry.** See *Illinois Troops, 82d Regiment.*

Sargent's (Horace B.) **Cavalry.** See *Massachusetts Troops, 1st Regiment.*

Sawyer's (Charles F.) **Infantry.** See *Maine Troops, 4th Regiment.*

Sawyer's (Edward B.) **Cavalry.** See *Vermont Troops, 1st Regiment.*

Sawyer's (Franklin) **Infantry.** See *Ohio Troops, 8th Regiment.*

Scherrer's (William) **Infantry.** See *New York Troops*, 52d Regiment.

Schleiter's (Gustav) **Infantry.** See *Pennsylvania Troops*, 74th Regiment.

Schoonover's (John) **Infantry.** See *New Jersey Troops*, 11th Regiment.

Scott's Nine Hundred, Cavalry. See *New York Troops*, 11th Regiment.

Seaver's (Thomas O.) **Infantry.** See *Vermont Troops, 3d Regiment.*

Seeley's (Aaron P.) **Infantry.** See *New York Troops*, 111th Regiment.

Seeley's (Francis W.) **Artillery.** See *Union Troops, Regulars, 4th Regiment, Battery K.*

Selfridge's (James L.) **Infantry.** See *Pennsylvania Troops*, 46th Regiment.

Sellers' (Alfred J.) **Infantry.** See *Pennsylvania Troops*, 90th Regiment.

Sewell's (William J.) **Infantry.** See *New Jersey Troops*, 5th Regiment.

Sharra's (Abram) **Cavalry.** See *Indiana Troops, 1st Regiment.*

Sheldon's (Albert S.) **Artillery.** See *New York Troops, 1st Regiment, Battery B.*

Sheridan's (Andrew) **Infantry.** See *Union Troops, Regulars, 3d Regiment.*

Sherrill's (Eliakim) **Infantry.** See *New York Troops*, 126th Regiment.

Sherwin's (Thomas, jr.) **Infantry.** See *Massachusetts Troops, 22d Regiment.*

Sides' (Peter) **Infantry.** See *Pennsylvania Troops*, 57th Regiment.

Sims' (Robert) **Artillery.** See *New Jersey Troops, 2d Battery.*

Sinex's (Joseph H.) **Infantry.** See *Pennsylvania Troops*, 91st Regiment.

Sleeper's (Samuel T.) **Infantry.** See *New Jersey Troops*, 11th Regiment.

---

* Temporarily commanding.

Smith's (Charles H.) **Cavalry.**   See *Maine Troops, 1st Regiment.*
Smith's (George F.) **Infantry.**   See *Pennsylvania Troops, 61st Regiment.*
Smith's (James E.) **Artillery.**   See *New York Troops, 4th Battery.*
Smith's (James J.) **Infantry.**   See *New York Troops, 69th Regiment.*
Smith's (Richard Penn) **Infantry.**   See *Pennsylvania Troops, 71st Regiment.*
Smith's (William) **Infantry.**   See *Delaware Troops, 1st Regiment.*
Snodgrass' (James McK.) **Infantry.**   See *Pennsylvania Troops, 9th Reserves.*
Stanford's (Samuel N.) **Cavalry.**   See *Ohio Troops, 1st Regiment.*
Starr's (James) **Cavalry.**   See *Pennsylvania Troops, 6th Regiment.*
Starr's (Samuel H.) **Cavalry.**   See *Union Troops, Regulars, 6th Regiment.*
Stedman's (William) **Cavalry.**   See *Ohio Troops, 6th Regiment.*
Steele's (Amos E., jr) **Infantry.**   See *Michigan Troops, 7th Regiment.*
Stegman's (Lewis R.) **Infantry.**   See *New York Troops, 102d Regiment.*
Sterling's (John W.) **Artillery.**   See *Connecticut Troops, 2d Battery.*
Stevens' (Greenleaf T.) **Artillery.**   See *Maine Troops, 5th Battery.*
Stevens' (Wilbur F.) **Infantry.**   See *Ohio Troops, 29th Regiment.*
Stewart's (James) **Artillery.**   See *Union Troops, Regulars, 4th Regiment, Battery B.*
Stoughton's (Charles B.) **Infantry.**   See *Vermont Troops, 4th Regiment.*
Stoughton's (Homer R.) **Sharpshooters.**   See *Union Troops, Volunteers, 2d Regiment.*
Stroh's (Amos) **Infantry.**   See *Pennsylvania Troops, 81st Regiment.*
Sudsburg's (Joseph M.) **Infantry.**   See *Maryland Troops, Union, 3d Regiment.*
Swain's (James B.) **Cavalry.**   See *New York Troops, 11th Regiment.*
Taft's (Elijah) **Artillery.**   See *New York Troops, 5th Battery.*
Talley's (William C.) **Infantry.**   See *Pennsylvania Troops, 1st Reserves.*
Tammany Regiment, Infantry.   See *New York Troops, 42d Regiment.*
Tanner's (Adolphus H.) **Infantry.**   See *New York Troops, 123d Regiment.*
Tappen's (John R.) **Infantry.**   See *New York Troops, 120th Regiment.*
Taylor's (Charles F.) **Infantry.**   See *Pennsylvania Troops, 13th Reserves.*
Taylor's (Constantine) **Cavalry.**   See *Maine Troops, 1st Regiment.*
Taylor's (John P.) **Cavalry.**   See *Pennsylvania Troops, 1st Regiment.*
Taylor's (William C. L.) **Infantry.**   See *Indiana Troops, 20th Regiment.*
Thoman's (Max A.) **Infantry.**   See *New York Troops, 59th Regiment.*
Thomas' (Evan) **Artillery.**   See *Union Troops, Regulars, 4th Regiment, Battery C.*
Thompson's (James) **Artillery.**   See *Pennsylvania Troops, Batteries C and F.*
Thompson's (John L.) **Cavalry.**   See *Rhode Island Troops, 1st Regiment.*
Thompson's (William) **Cavalry.**   See *Pennsylvania Troops, 17th Regiment.*
Thomson's (David) **Infantry.**   See *Ohio Troops, 82d Regiment.*
Throop's (William A.) **Infantry.**   See *Michigan Troops, 1st Regiment.*
Tidball's (John C.) **Artillery.**   See *Union Troops, Regulars, 2d Regiment, Battery A.*
Tilden's (Charles W.) **Infantry.**   See *Maine Troops, 16th Regiment.*
Tippin's (Andrew H.) **Infantry.**   See *Pennsylvania Troops, 68th Regiment.*
Titus' (Silas) **Infantry.**   See *New York Troops, 122d Regiment.*
Touhy's (Thomas) **Infantry.**   See *New York Troops, 63d Regiment.*
Town's (Charles H.) **Cavalry.**   See *Michigan Troops, 1st Regiment.*
Trepp's (Casper) **Sharpshooters.**   See *Union Troops, Volunteers, 1st Regiment.*
Tripp's (Porter D.) **Infantry.**   See *Massachusetts Troops, 11th Regiment.*
Trowbridge's (Luther S.) **Cavalry.**   See *Michigan Troops, 5th Regiment.*
Turnbull's (John G.) **Artillery.**   See *Union Troops, Regulars, 3d Regiment, Batteries F and K.*
Underwood's (Adin B.) **Infantry.**   See *Massachusetts Troops, 33d Regiment.*
Upton's (Emory) **Infantry.**   See *New York Troops, 121st Regiment.*
Van Reed's (William E.) **Artillery.**   See *Union Troops, Regulars, 5th Regiment, Battery K.*
Veazey's (Wheelock G.) **Infantry.**   See *Vermont Troops, 16th Regiment.*

Vincent's (Albert O.) **Artillery.** See *Union Troops, Regulars, 2d Regiment, Batteries B and L.*

Walbridge's (James H.) **Infantry.** See *Vermont Troops, 2d Regiment.*

Walcott's (Aaron F.) **Artillery.** See *Massachusetts Troops, 3d Battery (C).*

Walker's (Elijah) **Infantry.** See *Maine Troops, 4th Regiment.*

Walker's (Thomas M.) **Infantry.** See *Pennsylvania Troops, 111th Regiment.*

Wallace's (James) **Infantry.** See *Maryland Troops, Union, 1st Regiment, E. S.*

Ward's (George H.) **Infantry.** See *Massachusetts Troops, 15th Regiment.*

Warner's (Adoniram J.) **Infantry.** See *Pennsylvania Troops, 10th Reserves.*

Waterman's (Richard) **Artillery.** See *Rhode Island Troops, 1st Regiment, Battery C.*

Watson's (Malbone F.) **Artillery.** See *Union Troops, Regulars, 5th Regiment, Battery I.*

Weir's (Gulian V.) **Artillery.** See *Union Troops, Regulars, 5th Regiment, Battery C.*

Welch's (Norval E.) **Infantry.** See *Michigan Troops, 16th Regiment.*

Westbrook's (Cornelius D.) **Infantry.** See *New York Troops, 120th Regiment.*

Wheeler's (John) **Infantry.** See *Indiana Troops, 20th Regiment.*

Wheeler's (William) **Artillery.** See *New York Troops, 13th Battery.*

Wheelock's (Charles) **Infantry.** See *New York Troops, 97th Regiment.*

White's (Elijah V.) **Cavalry.** See *Virginia Troops, Confederate, 35th Battalion.*

White's (Israel) **Infantry.** See *Ohio Troops, 25th Regiment.*

Whiteside's (Henry) **Infantry.** See *Pennsylvania Troops, 88th Regiment.*

Whittier's (Edward N.) **Artillery.** See *Maine Troops, 5th Battery.*

Wickersham's (Charles J.) **Cavalry.** See *Pennsylvania Troops, 8th Regiment.*

Wickham's (Williams C.) **Cavalry.** See *Virginia Troops, Confederate, 4th Regiment.*

Widdis' (Cornelius C.) **Infantry.** See *Pennsylvania Troops, 150th Regiment.*

Wiebecke's (Charles) **Infantry.** See *New Jersey Troops, 2d Regiment.*

Wiedrich's (Michael) **Artillery.** See *New York Troops, 1st Regiment, Battery I.*

Wilber's (Benjamin W.) **Artillery.** See *New York Troops, 1st Regiment, Battery L.*

Wilkeson's (Bayard) **Artillery.** See *Union Troops, Regulars, 4th Regiment, Battery G.*

Williams' (Jeremiah) **Infantry.** See *Ohio Troops, 25th Regiment.*

Williams' (Samuel J.) **Infantry.** See *Indiana Troops, 19th Regiment.*

Willis' (Benjamin A.) **Infantry.** See *New York Troops, 119th Regiment.*

Williston's (Edward B.) **Artillery.** See *Union Troops, Regulars, 2d Regiment, Battery D.*

Wilson's (John) **Infantry.** See *New York Troops, 43d Regiment.*

Wilson's (J. Wade) **Artillery.** See *New York Troops, 6th Battery.*

Winegar's (Charles E.) **Artillery.** See *New York Troops, 1st Regiment, Battery M.*

Winslow's (George B.) **Artillery.** See *New York Troops, 1st Regiment, Battery D.*

Wister's (Langhorne) **Infantry.** See *Pennsylvania Troops, 150th Regiment.*

Wood's (James, jr.) **Infantry.** See *New York Troops, 136th Regiment.*

Woodruff's (George A.) **Artillery.** See *Union Troops, Regulars, 1st Regiment, Battery I.*

Woodward's (George A.) **Infantry.** See *Pennsylvania Troops, 2d Reserves.*

Woodward's (Orpheus S.) **Infantry.** See *Pennsylvania Troops, 83d Regiment.*

Woolsey's (Henry H.) **Infantry.** See *New Jersey Troops, 5th Regiment.*

Wooster's (William B.) **Infantry.** See *Connecticut Troops, 20th Regiment.*

INDEX.

Brigades, Divisions, Corps, Armies, and improvised organizations are "Mentioned" under name of commanding officer; State and other organizations under their official designation. (See Alternate Designations, pp. 1061–1072.)

Reports of

Duffié, Alfred N.	Halleck, Henry W.	Smith, Charles H.
Gregg, David McM.	Pleasonton, Alfred.	Stedman, William.

See also *Hooker to Halleck*, p. 50. Also Part II.

---

* A mistake in the original report as to the number of the regiment. The 16th Alabama did not belong to the Army of Northern Virginia.

(1073)

---

* No circumstantial reports on file.

Page.

Page.

* No circumstantial reports on file.

Page.

---

* No circumstantial reports on file.

Page.

---

* No circumstantial reports on file.

1092

INDEX.

*No circumstantial reports on file.

1094

INDEX.

*No circumstantial reports on file.

*No circumstantial reports on file.

1098

INDEX.

Bartlett, Joseph J.	Gamble, William.	Merritt, Wesley.
Biddle, Alexander.	Harn, William A.	Moody, William H.
Buford, John.	Hays, Alexander.	Neill, Thomas H.
Calef, John H.	Hecker, Frederick.	Russell, David A.
Dana, Edmund L.	Irvin, John.	Sedgwick, John.
Daniels, Nahum.	Kilpatrick, Judson.	Sudsburg, Joseph M.
Devin, Thomas C.	Kohler, John B.	Swain, Julius M.
Farnham, Augustus B.	McKeen, H. Boyd.	Wright, Horatio G.

---

*No circumstantial reports on file.

1100 INDEX.

1102 INDEX.

Page

* No circumstantial reports on file.

Page.

1114

1116 INDEX.

Page.

* No circumstantial reports on file.

Page.

*No circumstantial reports on file.

* No circumstantial reports on file.

*Sometimes called 14th Massachusetts.

---

* No circumstantial reports on file.   † Attached to 16th Michigan Infantry.

* No circumstantial reports on file.

*No circumstantial reports on file.

---

* No circumstantial reports on file.

Page.

Ohio Troops. Mentioned—Continued.

Infantry—*Regiments:* **4th,** 158, 176, 456, 457, 459–461, 463, 718; **5th,** 165, 184, 828, 829, 833, 836, 839, 840, 846, 857, 867; **7th,** 165, 184, 829, 831–834, 836, 837, 840, 841, 846, 857; **8th,** 158, 176, 372, 457, 45ᵈ, 461–463; **25th,** 164, 182, 715, 716, 719, 720; **29th,** 165, 184. 829, 833. 838, 841-845, 857, 867; **55th,** 164, 183, 723–725; **61st,** 164, 183, 731, 734, 738, 739, 827, 856; **66th,** 165, 184, 828, 833, 836, 837, 844, 845, 857; **73d,** 164, 183, 722–725; **75th,** 164. 182, 715, 716; **82d,** 164, 183, 744, 745; **107th,** 164, 182, 717, 720; **110th, 122d, 126th,** 492, 579.

Ohl, Ephraim **N. R.** Mentioned 880
O'Kane, Dennis. Mentioned 158, 191, 375, 418, 431
Old Antietam Forge, near Leitersburg, **Md.** Skirmish at, July 10, 1863. See Part II.
Oldershaw, John. Mentioned 535, 544
Oliphant, David. Mentioned 219
Oliver, Moses **W.**
    Mentioned 157, 414
    Report of Gettysburg Campaign, June 3–Aug. 1, 1863 415
O'Neil, Bernard **S.** Mentioned 389
Opequon Creek, near Winchester, **Va.** Skirmish at, June 13, 1863. See Part II.
Opp, Milton.
    Mentioned 160
    Report of Gettysburg Campaign, June 3–Aug. 1, 1863 557
Ordway, Albert. Mentioned 540
           For correspondence as A. A. A. G., see *Henry Prince.*
O'Reilly, James **K.** Mentioned 462
Organization, Strength, etc.
    Confederate Troops. See Part II.
    Union Troops 151–168, 613, 906
O'Rorke, Patrick **H.** Mentioned 162, 189, 635, 651
Osborn, Thomas **W.**
    Mentioned 112,
        153, 165, 183, 230, 232, 233, 238, 241, 242, 689, 701, 705–707, 757, 758, 892, 893
    Report of Gettysburg Campaign, June 3–Aug. 1, 1863 747
Osborne, J. **D.** Mentioned 24, 26
Otis, George **H.** Mentioned 155
Ottey, Hamill **W.** Mentioned 188, 403
Otto, August. Mentioned 164, 705, 731, 739, 740
Overmyer, John **B.** Mentioned 156
Owen, William **H.** Mentioned 594
Owens, Walter **L.** Mentioned 156, 318, 321, 328
Oyster Point, Pa. Skirmish near, June 28–29, 1863. See Part II.
Packer, Warren **W.**
    Mentioned 165, 787
    Reports of Gettysburg Campaign, June 3–Aug⸱ 1, 1863 .... 788, 789
Page, John **H.** Mentioned 638
Paine, Sumner. Mentioned 188
Palmer, Henry **I.** Mentioned 189
Palmer, Innis **N.** Assumes command of 18th Army Corps 3
Palmer, Joshua **G.** Mentioned 191, 844
Pancoast, George **L.** Mentioned 918, 1046
Pardee, Ario, jr.
    Mentioned 165, 833
    Report of Gettysburg Campaign, June 3–Aug. 1, 1863 845

Page.

* Consolidated.

*No circumstantial reports on file.

*No circumstantial reports on file.

Page.

* No circumstantial reports on file.

---

* No circumstantial reports on file.

Page.

---

*Consolidated.

Buford, John.	Graham, William M.	Rice, James C.
Calef, John H.	Gregg, David McM.	Robinson, Oliver O. G.
Cram, George C.	Gregg, J. Irvin.	Stedman, William.
Doster, William E.	Mason, Julius W.	Taylor, John P.
Fuller, William E.	Pleasonton, Alfred.	Vincent, Strong.
Gamble, William.		

Page.

West Virginia. Department of.
Constituted, June 24, 1863... 2
Kelley, Benjamin F., assumes command of............................ 2
West Virginia Troops. Mentioned.
Artillery, Light—*Batteries:* **C,** 168, 187, 233, 238, 749, 873, 878, 895.
Cavalry—*Regiments:* **1st,** 167, 186, 991, 993, 1005–1008, 1010, 1018–1020 ; **3d,** 166, 168, 172, 185, 905, 922, 1047.
Infantry—*Regiments:* **7th,** 158, 176, 457, 459, 463, 464, 714.
West Virginia and Southeastern Virginia. Operations in. See *report of Halleck*, p. 14.
Wetherill, John M. Mentioned.. 686
Wheaton, Frank. Mentioned.117, 120, 153, 163, 181, 182, 663, 680–682, 684, 685, 764, 767
Wheeler, Charles M. Mentioned.. 189
Wheeler, John. Mentioned.................................... 159, 188, 484, 494
Wheeler, Newbery W. Mentioned 1018
Wheeler, Thomas. Mentioned... 191
Wheeler, William.
Mentioned.. 165, 229, 233, 747, 749, 754, 755
Rep rt of Gettysburg Campaign, June 3–Aug. 1, 1863 752
Wheelock, Charles.
Mentioned.................................... 156, 255, 290, 292, 293, 307, 308
Report of Gettysburg Campaign, June 3–Aug. 1, 1863 309
Whicher, S. M. Mentioned... 942
Whitaker, A. H. Mentioned 240, 878
Whitcomb, Ebenezer. Mentioned.............................. 191, 494, 510
White, Amos H. Mentioned.. 1009
White, Ansel L. Mentioned.. 421
White, Elijah V. Mentioned 50, 907, 1001
White, Harrison. Mentioned.. 942
White, Israel.
Mentioned.. 164
Report of Gettysburg Campaign, June 3–Aug. 1, 1863 719
White, W. H. Mentioned.. 847
Whitehouse, Stephen C. Mentioned 188
White House, Va. Expeditions from, July 1–7, 1863. See *South Anna River and Bottom's Bridge, Va., Expeditions to. July* 1–7, 1863.
White Post, Va. Skirmish at, June 13, 1863. See Part II.
Whitesell, Daniel A. Mentioned..................................... 501, 880
Whiteside, Henry. Mentioned 156
Whiting, Charles J. Mentioned 168, 169
Whiting, H. Rees. Mentioned..................................... 269, 271
Whiting, William H. C. Assignment to command............................ 2
Whitney, J. J. Mentioned.. 401
Whitney, John. Mentioned 638
Whitney, M. P. Mentioned 776
Whittaker, Daniel. Mentioned..................................... 171, 907, 995
Whittier, Edward N.
Mentioned.. 157
Report of Gettysburg Campaign, June 3–Aug. 1, 1863 360
Whittlesey, Charles H. Mentioned.................................. 875, 901
Wickersham, Charles J. Mentioned 399
Wickham, Williams C. Mentioned..................................... 961
Widdis, Cornelius C. Mentioned................................ 156, 250, 347
Wiebecke, Charles. Mentioned.............................. 162, 668, 669